Hannah M. Cotton

Roman Rule and Jewish Life

Studia Judaica

Forschungen zur Wissenschaft des Judentums

Begründet von
Ernst Ludwig Ehrlich

Herausgegeben von
Günter Stemberger, Charlotte Fonrobert,
Elisabeth Hollender, Alexander Samely
und Irene Zwiep

Band 89

Hannah M. Cotton

Roman Rule and Jewish Life

Collected Papers

Edited by
Ofer Pogorelsky

DE GRUYTER

ISBN 978-3-11-151853-4
e-ISBN (PDF) 978-3-11-077043-8
e-ISBN (EPUB) 978-3-11-077060-5
ISSN 0585-5306

Library of Congress Control Number: 2021946975

Bibliographic Information published by the Deutsche Nationalbibliothek
The Deutsche Nationalbibliothek lists this publication in the Deutsche Nationalbibliografie; Detailed bibliographic data are available in the Internet at http://dnb.dnb.de.

This volume is text- and page-identical with the hardback published in 2022.

Typesetting: Dörlemann Satz, Lemförde

www.degruyter.com

לזכר אימי, לנה, לבית נאה
In memory of my mother, Lena, née Naeh

Preface

The collection of articles in this volume does not include all the articles that I have written, nor is it centered around one or two themes. I have chosen most of my favourite pieces, though this was not the sole criterion for selection. Most, but not all, of the pieces included, are devoted to legal and administrative issues, both private and public, which emerge from a close reading of literary and documentary texts. Despite the title of the book, some of the articles have nothing specifically to do with Jews – nor do the issues treated in them concern only Jews.

I began my career as an historian by exploring the administrative and legal problems in the Roman Empire that are revealed in literary texts such as Cicero's speeches and letters, and the earliest articles in this collection reflect this. Later I began to use the other primary sources at our disposal, in particular inscriptions and above all papyri. Reading of papyri not only brings one down from the Olympian heights of grand literary history and monumental public epigraphy: it reveals the texture of life itself as lived by ordinary people all over the Roman Empire.

My first experience with the decipherment and interpretation of non-literary texts took place while working together with Joseph Geiger on the Greek and Latin part of Yigael Yadin's 'Nachlass' from Masada: ostraca in Latin and Greek and a few, but exciting, fragmentary papyri – all published in *Masada II*. It was uplifting to come across a fragment from Virgil's Aeneid IV: *[An]na [s]or[o]r, o quae me sus-p[ensam insomnia terrent]*, or to become aware of the daily life of a Roman soldier through reading a salary bill with its list of deductions, which was left behind in the camps at the foot of Masada.

The appearance of the Dead Sea Scrolls encouraged both Bedouin and archaeologists to explore the Dead Sea area and the wadis leading to it in search of more such survivals. Once again, when in the 1990s it was decided to make a combined effort to publish all the known documents from the Dead Sea which had accumulated but remained unpublished for so long, I was fortunate to be granted the opportunity to publish that portion of the discovered documents which was written in Greek.

The Babatha Archive was discovered, intact, by Yigael Yadin's mission in the Cave of Letters in Naḥal Ḥever: the papyri were labelled *P.Yadin*. The Salome Archive, once believed (wrongly, as we know now) to come from Naḥal Ṣe'elim, comes from Naḥal Ḥever as well. It was published by the late Ada Yardeni and myself, in a volume dedicated to our mothers. Our intense collaboration, two women working on the remains of the lives of women who lived long ago, made us close friends until Ada's death in 2018. Working together in a bilingual context had great advantages. It so happened that when the illiterate Greek of the scribes

https://doi.org/10.1515/9783110770438-201

made no sense to the experts, my native knowledge of the Semitic languages turned out to be an asset. From time to time I had to guess what the writers meant to express in what they believed to be written in Greek. *DJD* XXVII, no. 64, a deed of gift in Greek, is a salient example: without having Ada Yardeni's edition of an Aramaic deed of gift (*P.Yadin* 7) before me, it would have been quite difficult to understand its content.

I have derived great pleasure from my long acquaintance with Babatha, daughter of Shimeon and with Salome Komaise, daughter of Levi. Were it not for their numerous legal contracts and endless disputes my life would certainly have been much duller. However, I have left it to others to compose books and invest in reading and studying the vast bibliography which has accumulated over the years both on the relevance of these documents to the subjects I have addressed, and to other issues which I have not touched.

But although the documents from the Judean Desert have generated an enormous amount of literature, some of it taking issue with my interpretations, the articles in this collection reflect my views and the state of knowledge when they were published. I have deliberately not tried to bring them up to date, nor to revise them in light of subsequent publications.

Nonetheless, my views on some of the themes in the articles published here have developed and somewhat changed since their first appearance in print. These new views have been presented in lectures which I gave in several academic conferences from 2017 onwards which have not yet appeared in print. These changes were stimulated by my growing understanding of the importance in Jewish law and tradition of oral acts such as that of betrothal – an understanding that is reflected in the article 'The Conception of Jesus' in this volume. I would like to give a summary of these views here.

For a long time I assumed that the use of the Greek language in Jewish legal contracts reflected the flexibility of an age where Rabbinic authority was weaker and was an adjustment to conditions of life then: bringing a case before a Greek-speaking court of law, whether that of the governor or a polis, would have made it more likely that the verdict would be carried out. From time to time, the unidiomatic Greek in some of the contracts makes the attempt look quite pathetic, as for example in the literal translation into Greek of מתנת ע(ו)לם as δόσις αἰωνίου: not being aware of the idiomatic expression δόσις εἰς ἀεὶ, they translated literally the Semitic term.

What I had failed to recognize was that some legal acts required then, as they do now, the use of a specific language. Thus, although the languages of the Jewish diaspora were and still are reflected in many contracts, they were (and still are) completely excluded from many others. To be binding, so far as traditional Jews are concerned, such legal acts did not need to be written, they needed to be *said*, and this could only be done in a language appropriately empowered to do so: these are legal speech acts, as one would call them nowadays. As such, they do not always leave a record. Consequently, the historian, beholden to texts, can mistakenly overlook them.

The Greek marriage contracts, as they have been labelled, which mention the sanction of the *Nomos Hellenikos* (or the variant 'according to the laws' κατὰ τοὺς νόμους), did not establish the legal status of the marriage. The change of legal status from unmarried to married follows the oral act of betrothal (קידושין). The *ketubba* (literally a 'written document') given to the bride at the wedding ceremony is the equivalent of the Greek marriage contract, and it specifies property arrangements and obligations. Neither the Greek marriage contract nor the *ketubba* established the personal status of marriage.

The divine and immaculate conception of Jesus by a virgin in the New Testament takes the 'two-stage marriage' for granted: Miriam was betrothed to Joseph, but not yet married to him: 'he did not *know* her yet' (see the discussion of this in the paper 'The Conception of Jesus,' below). As is made clear in *P.Polit.Iud.* 4, the cancellation of a betrothal would call for a divorce: μετ' οὐ π̣[ολὺν χ]ρ̣ό̣νον ὁ Λυσί̣μ̣α̣χ̣ο̣ς συνήρμοκεν ἄγ̣ε̣υ̣ λόγου ἑ̣τ̣έ̣ρωι ἀ̣νδ̣ρὶ τὴν Νε̣ίκαιαν̣ πρὶν ἢ λαβεῖν παρ' ἐμοῦ τ̣ὸ̣ εἰθ̣ισμένον τοῦ ἀποσ̣τ̣ασίου τὸ β̣υβλ̣ίο̣ν (cf. Deut. 24:1 for the term); 'Not long afterwards, Lysimachos without justification joined Nikaia to another man before having received from me the customary bill of divorce.'

Thus the Greek marriage contract presumed an oral betrothal, and it contained mainly provisions concerning property. It is quite likely that it was written in Greek to provide for the option of bringing it before a Greek-speaking court of law.

All that *agraphos gamos* 'unwritten marriage' can mean when people refer to the Greek *P.Hever* 65 (= *P.Yadin* 37) is the period before the dowry was given, and once it was given it needed to be recorded in a document; there was no reason to write a contract so long as the dowry had not been paid. In Egyptian marriage papyri we even find the expression *engraphos gamos*, i. e. written, recorded marriage, which implies that the dowry has been paid. The phrase 'continue life together as before' (ll. 5–6) does not attest to our modern sexual relations out of wedlock, as some have tried to make it mean. All it does is acknowledge a delayed payment of the dowry. Once the marriage had come to an end by divorce or death and the financial provisions specified in the Greek marriage contract had been fulfilled, the document was, so to speak, cancelled, as is implied by the diagonally crossing pen strokes (*DJD* XXVII, no. 69).

The act of divorce, like the act of betrothal, is a legal speech act pronounced by the husband; the latter repeats three time the word מגורשת (literally 'divorced'), that is to say: 'you are herewith divorced by me.' Only now is the deed of divorce, in which conditions and terms are specified, handed to the divorced woman. Once received, the deed is torn up: all that matters is that the words have been said – and witnessed. No wonder then that *no deed of divorce has survived from antiquity* – with the exception *of P.Mur* 19, written 'in the 6th year on Masada,' and discovered in a cave in Wadi Murabba'at (not far from Jerusalem). The divorced wife left Masada (more likely escaped from there) in possession of the means to prove in the future that she was free to marry another (see 'The Conception of Jesus').

Another instance in which I mistakenly found a pre-Rabbinic flexibility in Jewish marriage rules was in the attempt by myself together with E. Qimron to turn *DJD* XXVII, no. 13 – rightly described in its first publication as "a waiver of claims" (by a woman) – into an indirect record of a divorce given by a Jewish woman to her husband. The document should be read as a dialogue, as it had been by the late Ada Yardeni: thus, the crucial phrase די הווי לך מני גט שיבוקין ותירוכין ('you have from me a deed of divorce') comes from the husband's mouth, as it does to this very day. Other documents written by the same scribe follow this idiosyncratic dialogue form (echoing speech), as Hillel Newman has pointed out. Moreover, the claim (namely, of a divorce given by a woman) contradicts the underlying assumption in the story of the divine Conception of Jesus in the Gospels of Matthew and Luke. We may recall that this story proves the constitutive force of the betrothal in post-biblical Jewish society and clearly confirms the existence of a two-stage union: namely, betrothal followed by marriage. At the same time it proves that the act of divorce comes from the husband: having discovered Mary's pregnancy Joseph was about to divorce her when he was stopped by the divinity. The NT had no axe to grind– that was not the point of the story.

Finally, the law of succession. Since there exists *no* deed of gift for male heirs, I assumed that daughters were altogether debarred from intestate inheritance. In her book, *The Relationship between Roman and Local Law in the Babatha and Salome Komaise Archives* (2007), Jacobine G. Oudshoorn argues correctly that the law of succession in the documents from the Judaean Desert denies intestate inheritance to married daughters but not to unmarried ones. It was the change from unmarried to marriage *to an outsider* that called for a deed of gift to a daughter (ibid. pp. 244–45): "the law of succession of the time would not deny a daughter her right to inherit her father's estate, as long as she was unmarried or married to the next of kin."

Thus the articles in this volume should be read with these new considerations in mind. They do not undo the arguments I have made in them, but they do put them in a different light.

I used to believe that having published my views in print (once) was enough. Moreover, I anticipated writing more and adding more, so any collection appeared to me to be premature. It took me a long time to come to terms with the realisation that I will not produce many more articles, and that having them published together in a single volume is a gift to myself – when shared with others. With this realisation, the time was ripe to accept the generous offer made by Günter Stemberger to include them in the Studia Judaica series.

It is both customary and necessary in publications such as this to thank (and absolve from responsibility for mistakes) all those who have provided help, intellectual and technical, in research, in formulation of ideas, and in publication. I have never shied away from asking for help when I needed it, and as my full list of publications shows, a great deal of my research has been conducted and published in collaboration with others. Very many have helped me: teachers, colleagues, and students – too many to mention all, but I should like to single out some of them.

First, since I am *not* a trained papyrologist, I often resorted to picking the brains of well-known and patient papyrologists, in Oxford, Cologne and Heidelberg, who overlooked my ignorance and tolerated being exploited. I am most grateful to Roger Bagnall, James Cowey, Robert Daniel, Dieter Hagedorn, Peter Parsons and John Rea for their patience and generosity. They saved me from many errors.

Several devoted student assistants helped me to assemble printed texts and old files and convert them to a format that could be edited: I would like to thank Ori Shapir, Vladimir (Vova) Zuckerman, Nir Stern, and Doron Shomrony for having made this collection possible. Only then could these raw data be put into a uniform style, creating consistency and cross-references where none existed before. My Greek teacher, who has become a lifelong friend, Professor Ra'anana Meridor, went through many of these articles before they were submitted to press, and even afterwards, finding mistakes even in the offprints! Ofer Pogorelsky, my editor has inserted them all.

Not being a native speaker of English, I turned frequently to my friend of very many years, David Wasserstein, to give them the *manus ultima*. He did so at the speed of light which saved me the guilt of feeling I have imposed on him.

I have deliberately left my editor, Ofer Pogorelsky, to the end: I would never have been in the position to write a preface to this work without him. As I grew older, I had more or less put aside the idea of publishing this selection of my articles. Ofer came at the right time: his initiative, devotion, and painstaking, conscientious and intelligent editing brought the project to a happy end: it has made it possible for me to repay Günter Stemberger for his endless patience and trust in me.

Editor's Note

A quick glance at Hannah Cotton's list of publications (below, pp. xxv–xxxii) is enough to make one realize that the thirty-four articles collected in this volume are only part of her immense scholarly work. In her four decades of research at the Hebrew University of Jerusalem, Cotton has made invaluable contributions both to Roman history at large and to Roman provincial history, primarily that of Judaea and Arabia. Her scholarly interests led her through all the major fields of ancient studies, resulting in a rich variety of published works. A word of explanation is thus in order as to the selected content and structure of this volume.

The volume is divided into four sections, and the order of the articles in each section follows their publication date. Section A, "Government, Power, and Jurisdiction," is composed of studies that deal with the workings of the Roman government, analyzing its formal and judicial aspects, as well as its informal characteristics, which may be defined as political etiquette. Some of these studies stem directly from Cotton's doctoral thesis and thus represent her early scholarly pursuits.

The remaining three sections revolve around what became Cotton's main field of research, the Judaean Desert Documents. Her acclaimed publication of the Greek documents from Naḥal Ḥever (*P.Hever*) along with many influential studies has rightly earned her recognition as a leading authority on the subject. In the words of a senior scholar in the field, "Professor Cotton contributed more than any other single scholar to the study of the Greek documents from the Judaean Desert."[1]

Each of these three sections deals with key aspects of the Judaean Desert Documents. Section B, "Documents, Languages, and Law," includes studies which have a broad papyrological significance or address issues that are relevant to the entire body of documents. Section C, "Land, Army, and Administration," deals with historical geography and with the administrative history of Judaea and Arabia, as well as the Roman military presence in and around these areas. Section D, "Law, Custom, and Provincial Life," examines various legal aspects in the Judaean Desert Documents against the backdrop of Roman law on the one hand, and Jewish law on the other.

The distinction in content between section A and sections B-D reflects Cotton's academic trajectory. Her doctoral thesis, submitted in 1977 at the University of Oxford, dealt with Roman letters of recommendation, focusing on the writings

1 Ranon Katzoff, *On Jews in the Roman World: Collected Studies* (Tübingen: Mohr Siebeck, 2019), 10, n. 22.

https://doi.org/10.1515/9783110770438-202

of Cicero and Pliny the Younger as primary sources. Non-literary texts, recorded on inscriptions and papyri, featured only as an addendum in her thesis. These were later augmented and published as a monograph on documentary letters of recommendation (1981). This monograph indicates, in retrospect, the way Cotton's career was about to turn.

In 1985 Cotton was invited, together with Joseph Geiger, to publish the Latin and Greek documents from Masada. With the Greek documents written by Jews and the Latin documents produced by the Roman army, the Masada material "shifted between these two conflicting worlds."[2] It seems almost natural, therefore, that Cotton's next papyrological project was the publication of the Greek documents, written by Jews, from Naḥal Ḥever. The final publication of these documents was carried out in collaboration with Ada Yardeni, who edited the Semitic part of the collection. It is the Naḥal Ḥever documents, together with two other corpora of Greek and Semitic documents from the Judaean Desert – the Yadin Papyri from the 'Cave of Letters' (*P.Yadin*) and the documents from Wadi Murabba'at (*P.Mur*) – that form the basis of the studies in sections B-D of this volume.

The articles have been kept in their original form. The bibliographical references have all been edited to appear in a unified style; this has occasionally led to some minor changes of phrasing. In cases of cross-references (that is, references to articles which appear also in this volume), the corresponding pages in the volume are indicated in square brackets. A complete bibliography of all works cited is provided at the end.

The one major update made throughout the volume has to do with references to forthcoming publications. This relates both to scholarly works and to documents or epigraphical finds that were not yet formally published when cited. An effort has been made to update all these references to their published form. This accounts for the seemingly odd situation of having references which postdate the article in which they are cited. However, not all 'forthcomings' eventually came forth, and in those rare cases where it was safe to assume that future publication is not expected, the reference has been omitted.

Cotton's frequent reference to forthcoming works by her colleagues shows her profound commitment to drawing on every possible piece of evidence or scholarly opinion to strengthen her arguments. But it is also a sign of her personality, in demonstrating one of Cotton's most outstanding abilities, defined by a close friend and colleague as "a genius for creating networks of friends."[3]

2 Hannah M. Cotton and Joseph Geiger, *Masada II: The Latin and Greek Documents* (Jerusalem: IES, 1989), vii.

3 Miriam Griffin, "The Prince and his Tutor: Candour and Affection," *SCI* 33 (2014): 67 [Special Issue in Honour of Hannah M. Cotton].

Acknowledgments are due to people and institutions that assisted in the preparation of this volume. Alice Meroz of De Gruyter provided sound support throughout the various stages of preparation, and Antonia Mittelbach was responsible for the professional typesetting. The original publishers of the articles, indicated in the 'article note' of every paper, gave their kind permission to include them in this collection. Roi Sabar created the map at the end of the volume. Ari Paltiel was helpful and supportive in crucial stages of the work process.

Contents

Preface —— VII

Editor's Note —— XIII

Abbreviations —— XXI

List of Publications —— XXV

A Government, Power, and Jurisdiction

Cicero, ad Familiares XIII, 26 and 28: Evidence for *revocatio* or *reiectio Romae/ Romam*? —— 3

Military Tribunates and the Exercise of Patronage —— 23

The Concept of Indulgentia under Trajan —— 35

The Role of Cicero's Letters of Recommendation: *Iustitia* versus *Gratia*? —— 61

Cassius Dio, Mommsen and the Quinquefascales —— 79

The Evolution of the So-Called Provincial Law, or: Cicero's Letters of Recommendation and Private International Law in the Roman World —— 99

B Documents, Languages, and Law

Subscriptions and Signatures in the Papyri from the Judaean Desert: The χειροχρήστης —— 115

The Languages of the Legal and Administrative Documents from the Judaean Desert —— 127

'Diplomatics' or External Aspects of the Legal Documents from the Judaean Desert: Prolegomena —— 147

Survival, Adaptation and Extinction: Nabataean and Jewish Aramaic versus Greek in the Legal Documents from the Cave of Letters in Naḥal Ḥever —— 161

The Bar Kokhba Revolt and the Documents from the Judaean Desert: Nabataean Participation in the Revolt (*P. Yadin* 52) —— 173

Language Gaps in Roman Palestine and the Roman Near East — 195

Private International Law or Conflict of Laws: Reflections on Roman Provincial Jurisdiction — 213

Continuity of Nabataean Law in the Petra Papyri: A Methodological Exercise — 237

Change and Continuity in Late Legal Papyri from Palaestina Tertia: *Nomos Hellênikos* and *Ethos Rômaikon* — 257

C Land, Army, and Administration

Babatha's 'Patria': Maḥoza, Maḥoz 'Eaglatain and Ẓo'ar — 275

Courtyard(s) in Ein-Gedi: P.Yadin 11, 19 and 20 of the Babatha Archive — 285

Land Tenure in the Documents from the Nabataean Kingdom and the Roman Province of Arabia — 293

Ἡ νέα ἐπαρχεία Ἀραβία: The New Province of Arabia in the Papyri from the Judaean Desert — 309

Some Aspects of the Roman Administration of Judaea/Syria-Palaestina — 317

The Legio VI Ferrata — 337

Ein Gedi between the Two Revolts — 347

The Roman Census in the Papyri from the Judaean Desert and the Egyptian κατ' οἰκίαν ἀπογραφή — 363

The Administrative Background to the New Settlement Recently Discovered near Giv'at Shaul, Ramallah-Shu'afat Road — 379

The Impact of the Roman Army in the Province of Judaea/Syria Palaestina — 387

D Law, Custom, and Provincial Life

The Guardianship of Jesus Son of Babatha: Roman and Local Law in the Province of Arabia — 403

The Guardian (ἐπίτροπος) of a Woman in the Documents from the Judaean Desert — 431

The Law of Succession in the Documents from the Judaean Desert Again — 443

The Rabbis and the Documents — 453

The Impact of the Documentary Papyri from the Judaean Desert on the Study of Jewish History from 70 to 135 CE — 467

Jewish Jurisdiction under Roman Rule: Prolegomena — 485

Women and Law in the Documents from the Judaean Desert — 501

Eleuthera and *Brat Horin*: Another Look at Babatha's Ketubba, *P.Yadin 10* — 525

'The Conception of Jesus' — 533

Map of Judaea and Arabia — 547

Bibliography — 549

General Index — 585

Index of Sources — 595

Abbreviations

ACOR	The American Center of Research
AE	L'Année Épigraphique
AIESEE	Association internationale d'études du Sud-Est européen
AJA	American Journal of Archaeology
AJPhil.	American Journal of Philology
Amic.	Cicero, *De amicitia*
APA	American Philological Association
Arch. Pap.	Archiv für Papyrusforschung
Att.	Cicero, *Epistulae ad Atticum*
BASP	Bulletin of the American Society of Papyrologists
BE	Bulletin épigraphique, pub. in *Revue des études grecques*
Ber. Sächs. Ges. Wiss.	Berichte über die Verhandlungen der sächsischen Gesellschaft der Wissenschaften zu Leipzig (1848)
BGall.	Caesar, *Bellum Gallicum*
BGU	Berliner Griechische Urkunden
BICS	Bulletin of the Institute of Classical Studies
BMC	H. Mattingly, *Coins of the Roman Empire in the British Museum* (1923–1950)
BSAC	Bulletin de la Société d'archéologie copte
Bull. Com. Arch.	Bullettino della Commissione archeologica comunale di Roma
CGL	Corpus Glossariorum Latinorum
ChLA	Chartae Latinae antiquiores
CIIP	Corpus Inscriptionum Iudaeae/Palaestinae
CIJ	Jean-Baptiste Frey (ed.), *Corpus Inscriptionum Judaicarum*, 2 Vols. (Citta del Vaticano: Pontificio Istituto di archeologia cristiana, 1936–1952)
CIL	Corpus Inscriptionum Latinarum
CIS	Corpus Inscriptionum Semiticarum
CJ	Codex Justinianus
CNRS	Centre National de la Recherche Scientifique
Cod. Theod.	Codex Theodosianus
Corn.	Asconius, *Commentary on Cicero, Pro Cornelio de maiestate*
CPhil.	Classical Philology
CPJ	Victor A. Tcherikover, Alexander Fuks, and Menahem Stern (eds.), *Corpus Papyrorum Judaicarum*, 3 Vols. (Cambridge, Mass.: Harvard University Press, 1957–1964)
CR	Classical Review
CR Acad. Inscr.	Comptes rendus de l'Académie des Inscriptions et Belles-lettres
Dig.	Digesta
Diz. Epigr.	E. de Ruggiero, *Dizionario epigrafico di antichità romana*
DJD	Discoveries in the Judaean Desert
Fam.	Cicero, *Epistulae ad familiars*
FIRA	S. Riccobono, *Fontes Iuris Romani AnteIustiniani*, 2nd Ed. (1941)
GRBS	Greek, Roman and Byzantine Studies
Harv. Stud.	Harvard Studies in Classical Philology

https://doi.org/10.1515/9783110770438-203

Harv. Theol. Rev.	Harvard Theological Review
HUCA	Hebrew Union College Annual
IAA	Israel Antiquities Authority
IC	M. Guarducci, *Inscriptiones Creticae* (1935–1950)
ICUR	Inscriptiones Christianae Urbis Romae
IEJ	Israel Exploration Journal
IES	Israel Exploration Society
IGLS	Inscriptions grecques et latines de la Syrie
IGRom.	Inscriptiones Graecae ad res Romanas pertinentes
ILAlg.	Inscriptions latines de l'Algérie 1, ed. S. Gsell (1922); 2, ed. H.-G. Pflaum (1957)
ILTG	P. Wuilleumier, *Inscriptions latines des trois Gaules* (1963)
ILS	H. Dessau, *Inscriptiones Latinae Selectae* (1892–1916)
INJ	Israel Numismatic Journal
INR	Israel Numismatic Research
Inst.	Quintilian, *Institutio oratoria*
Inst. Just.	Institutiones Justiniani
Inv. rhet.	Cicero, *De inventione rhetorica*
IRT	Joyce M. Reynolds and John B. Ward-Perkins, *The Inscriptions of Roman Tripolitania* (1952)
JAOS	Journal of the American Oriental Society
JEA	Journal of Egyptian Archaeology
JHS	Journal of Hellenic Studies
JJP	Journal of Juristic Papyrology
JJS	Journal of Jewish Studies
JNES	Journal of Near Eastern Studies
JÖAI	Jahreshefte des Österreichischen Archäologischen Institutes
JQR	Jewish Quarterly Review
JRA	Journal of Roman Archaeology
JRS	Journal of Roman Studies
JSQ	Jewish Studies Quarterly
JSS	Journal of Semitic Studies
LBW	Philippe Le Bas and William Henry Waddington, *Voyage archéologique en Grèce et en Asie Mineure*. Paris 1847–1877. III, Part 5, *Inscriptions grecques et latines recueillies en Grèce et en Asie Mineure* (1870–1876); III, Part 6, ed. W.H. Waddington, *Inscriptions grecques et latines de la Syrie* (1870)
LSJ	Liddell, Scott, Jones, *Greek-English Lexicon*
MAMA	Monumenta Asiae Minoris Antiquae
MÉFRA	Mélanges d'archéologie et d'histoire de l'École française de Rome
MH	Museum Helveticum
Mitteis, Chr.	L. Mitteis and U. Wilcken, *Grundzüge und Chrestomathie der Papyruskunde* (1912)
NH	Pliny the Elder, *Naturalis historia*
OCT	Oxford Classical Texts
Off.	Cicero, *De officiis*
OGIS	W. Dittenberger, *Orientis Graeci inscriptiones selectae* (1903–1905)

PCPS	Proceedings of the Cambridge Philological Society
PEQ	Palestine Exploration Quarterly
PG	J.P. Migne, *Patrologiae Cursus, series Graeca*
PIR	Prosopographia Imperii Romani
PL	J.P. Migne, *Patrologiae Cursus, series Latina*
Planc.	Cicero, *Pro Plancio*
PPUAES IIIA	Syria. Publications of the Princeton University Archaeological Expeditions to Syria in 1904–1905 and 1909. Division III, Greek and Latin Inscriptions in Syria, Section A, Southern Syria. 1907–1921
Prov. cons.	Cicero, *De provinciis consularibus*
PSI	Papiri Greci e Latini, Pubblicazioni della Società italiana per la ricerca dei papiri greci e latini in Egitto
QFr.	Cicero, *Epistulae ad Quintum fratrem*
RB	Revue Biblique
RE	A. Pauly, G. Wissowa, and W. Kroll, *Real-Encyclopädie d. klassischen Altertumswissenschaft*
Rep.	Cicero, *De republica*
RES	Répertoire d'épigraphie sémitique
RHDFÉ	Revue historique de droit français et étranger
RIB	Roman Inscriptions of Britain
RIDA	Revue Internationale des Droits de l'Antiquité
SB	F. Preisigke and others, *Sammelbuch griechischen Urkunden aus Ägypten*
SCI	Scripta Classica Israelica
SEG	Supplementum Epigraphicum Graecum
Stud.Pal.	*Studien zur Palaeographie und Papyruskunde*, ed. C. Wessely. Leipzig 1901–1924
Sull.	Cicero, *Pro Sulla*
Syll.	W. Dittenberger, ed. *Sylloge Inscriptionum Graecarum* (3rd edition; 1915–1924)
TAPA	Transactions of the American Philological Association
TLL	Thesaurus Linguae Latinae
Vat.	Cicero, *In Vatinium*
Verr.	Cicero, *In Verrem*
W.Chr.	L. Mitteis and U. Wilcken, *Grundzüge und Chrestomathie der Papyruskunde*, I Bd. Historischer Teil, II Hälfte Chrestomathie. Leipzig-Berlin 1912
ZDPV	Zeitschrift des Deutschen Palästina-Vereins
ZPE	Zeitschrift für Papyrologie und Epigraphik
ZSS	Zeitschrift der Savigny-Stiftung für Rechtsgeschichte: Romanistische Abteilung
ZVglRWiss	Zeitschrift für Vergleichende Rechtswissenschaft

List of Publications

Books

L. Ullmann – H.M. Cotton, *M. Tullius Cicero: Pro M. Marcello Oratio: Introduction and Commentary*. Jerusalem: The Hebrew University, 1972 (Latin and Hebrew).

H.M. Cotton, *Letters of Recommendation: Cicero-Fronto*. University of Oxford Doctoral Thesis, 1977.

H.M. Cotton, *Documentary Letters of Recommendation in Latin from the Roman Empire*. Beiträge zur klassischen Philologie 132. Königstein: Hain, 1981.

H.M. Cotton – J. Geiger, *Masada II: The Latin and Greek Documents*. Jerusalem: IES, 1989.

H.M. Cotton – A. Yardeni, *Aramaic, Hebrew and Greek Documentary Texts from Naḥal Ḥever and other Sites*. Discoveries in the Judaean Desert XXVII. Oxford: Clarendon Press, 1997.

Edited Books

A.K. Bowman – H.M. Cotton – M. Goodman – S. Price (eds.), *Representations of Empire: Rome and the Mediterranean World*. Proceedings of the British Academy 114. Oxford: Oxford University Press, 2002.

H.M. Cotton – G.M. Rogers (eds.), Fergus Millar, *Rome, the Greek World, and the East*. Chapel Hill: University of North Carolina Press, 2002–2006.
Vol. 1: The Roman Republic and the Augustan Revolution.
Vol. 2: Government, Society, and Culture in the Roman Empire.
Vol. 3: The Greek World, the Jews, and the East.

H.M. Cotton – R.G. Hoyland – J.J. Price – D.J. Wasserstein (eds.), *From Hellenism to Islam: Cultural and Linguistic Change in the Roman Near East*. Cambridge: Cambridge University Press, 2009.

J. Geiger – H.M. Cotton – G. Stiebel (eds.), *Israel's Land: Papers Presented to Israel Shatzman on his Jubilee*. Ra'anana: The Open University of Israel, 2009 (Hebrew and English).

H.M. Cotton – L. Di Segni – W. Eck – B. Isaac – A. Kushnir-Stein – H. Misgav – J.J. Price – I. Roll – A. Yardeni, *Corpus Inscriptionum Iudaeae/Palestinae, Vol. I: Jerusalem. Part 1: 1–704*. Berlin: De Gruyter, 2010.

W. Ameling – H.M. Cotton – W. Eck – B. Isaac – A. Kushnir-Stein – H. Misgave – J.J. Price – A. Yardeni, *Corpus Inscriptionum Iudaeae/Palestinae, Vol. II: Caesarea and the Middle Coast: 1121–2160*. Berlin: De Gruyter, 2011.

H.M. Cotton – L. Di Segni – W. Eck – B. Isaac – A. Kushnir-Stein – H. Misgav – J.J. Price – A. Yardeni, *Corpus Inscriptionum Iudaeae/Palestinae, Vol. I: Jerusalem. Part 2: 705–1120*. Berlin: De Gruyter, 2012.

W. Ameling – H.M. Cotton – W. Eck – B. Isaac – A. Kushnir-Stein – H. Misgav – J.J. Price – A. Yardeni, *Corpus Inscriptionum Iudaeae/Palaestinae, Vol. III: South Coast 2161–2648*. Berlin: De Gruyter, 2014.

Note: First compiled by Avner Ecker and published in *SCI* 33 (2014): ix–xv [Special Issue in Honour of Hannah M. Cotton]. Updated by the editor.

https://doi.org/10.1515/9783110770438-204

W. Ameling – H.M. Cotton – W. Eck – A. Ecker – B. Isaac – A. Kushnir-Stein – H. Misgav – J.J. Price – P. Weiß – A.Yardeni, *Corpus Inscriptionum Iudaeae/Palaestinae, Vol. IV: Iudaea/ Idumaea. Part 1: 2649–3324; Part 2: 3325–3978*. Berlin: De Gruyter, 2018.
Sh. Aḥituv – H.M. Cotton – M. Morgenstern, *Eretz Israel: Archaeological, Historical and Geographical Studies, Volume 34, Ada Yardeni Volume*. Jerusalem: IES, 2021.

Articles

"Cicero, ad Familiares 13, 26 and 28: Evidence for *revocatio* or *reiectio Romae/Romam*?" *JRS* 69 (1979): 39–50.
"Military Tribunates and the Exercise of Patronage." *Chiron* 2 (1981): 229–38.
"Review of: Miriam T. Griffin, Nero: The End of a Dynasty." *SCI* 7 (1983/84): 134–37.
"Greek and Latin Epistolary Formulae: Some Light on Cicero's Letter Writing." *AJPhil.* 106 (1984): 409–25.
"The Concept of 'Indulgentia' under Trajan." *Chiron* 14 (1984): 245–66.
"Mirificum genus commendationis: Cicero and the Latin Letter of Recommendation." *AJPhil.* 106 (1985): 328–34.
(with A. Yakobson), "Caligula's Recusatio Imperii." *Historia* 34 (1985): 497–503.
"The Role of Cicero's Letters of Recommendation: Iustitia versus Gratia?" *Hermes* 114 (1986): 443–60.
"A Note on the Organization of Tax-Farming in Asia Minor (Cicero, Fam. XIII, 65)." *Latomus* 45 (1986): 367–73.
"The Date of the Fall of Masada: The Evidence of the Masada Papyri." *ZPE* 78 (1989): 157–62.
(with J. Geiger), "Wine for Herod." *Cathedra* 53 (1989): 3–12 (Hebrew).
(with D. Gera), "A Dedicatory Inscription to the Governor of Syria(?) from Dor." *Qadmoniot* 85–86 (1989): 42 (Hebrew).
"Documents of the Tenth Legion Fretensis Discovered at Masada." *Qadmoniot* 89–90 (1990): 54–58 (Hebrew).
(with J.J. Price), "Who Conquered Masada in 66 CE, and Who Lived There until the Fortress Fell?" *Zion* 55 (1990): 449–54 (Hebrew).
"Fragments of a Declaration of Landed Property from the Province of Arabia." *ZPE* 85 (1991): 263–67.
"Imperium sine fine – Review of: B. Isaac, The Limits of Empire: The Roman Army in the East." *Cathedra* 60 (1991): 99–105 (Hebrew).
(with D. Gera), "A Dedication from Dor to a Governor of Syria." *IEJ* 41 (1991): 258–66. Reprinted in *Excavations at Dor: Final Report, Volume I B*, Qedem Reports 2, edited by E. Stern et al., 497–500. Jerusalem: The Insitute of Archaeology of the Hebrew University, 1995.
"Another Fragment of the Declaration of Landed Property from the Province of Arabia." *ZPE* 99 (1993): 115–21.
"The Guardianship of Jesus Son of Babatha: Roman and Local Law in the Province of Arabia." *JRS* 83 (1993): 94–108.
"A Cancelled Marriage Contract from the Judaean Desert (Ẋev/Se Gr. 2)." *JRS* 84 (1994): 64–86.
"Rent or Tax Receipt from Maoza." *ZPE* 100 (1994): 547–57.
"Loan with Hypothec: Another Papyrus from the Cave of Letters?" *ZPE* 101 (1994): 53–59.

(with J.C. Greenfield), "Babatha's Property and the Law of Succession in the Babatha Archive." *ZPE* 104 (1994): 211–24. Reprinted in *'Al Kanfei Yonah: Collected Studies of Jonas C. Greenfield on Semitic Philology*, edited by S.M. Paul, M.E. Stone, and A. Pinnick, 540–53. Leiden: Brill, 2001.
(with D. Gera), "Greek Inscriptions from Dor." In *Excavations at Dor: Final Report, Volume I B*, Qedem Reports 2, edited by E. Stern et al., 501–503. Jerusalem: The Insitute of Archaeology of the Hebrew University, 1995.
"Subscriptions and Signatures in the Papyri from the Judaean Desert: The χειροχρηστής." *JJP* 25 (1995): 29–40.
"The Archive of Salome Komaise, Daughter of Levi: Another Archive from the Cave of Letters." *ZPE* 105 (1995): 171–208.
(with W.E.H. Cockle – F. Millar), "The Papyrology of the Roman Near East: A Survey." *JRS* 85 (1995): 214–35.
(with J. Geiger), "A Greek Inscribed Ring from Masada." *IEJ* 45 (1995): 52–54.
(with J. Geiger – E. Netzer), "A Greek Ostracon from Masada." *IEJ* 45 (1995): 274–77.
(with J.C. Greenfield), "Babatha's 'Patria': Maḥoza, Maḥoz 'Eglatain and Ẓo'ar." *ZPE* 107 (1995): 126–32.
"Courtyard(s) in Ein-Gedi: P.Yadin 11, 19 and 20 of the Babatha Archive." *ZPE* 112 (1996): 197–201.
"Deeds of Gift from the Archives of the Judaean Desert and the Law of Succesion." *Eretz Israel* 25 (1996): 410–15 (Hebrew).
(with O. Lernau – Y. Goren), "Fish Sauces from Herodian Masada." *JRA* 9 (1996): 223–38.
(with O. Lernau – Y. Goren), "Fish Sauces from Herodian Masada." *Archeofauna* 5 (1996): 35–41.
(with J. Geiger), "The Economic Importance of Herod's Masada: the Evidence of the Jar Inscriptions." In *Judaea and the Greco-Roman World in the Time of Herod in the Light of Archaeological Evidence*, edited by G. Foerster and K. Fittschen, 163–70. Göttingen: Vandenhoeck & Ruprecht, 1996.
(with W. Weiser), "'Gebt dem Kaiser, was des Kaisers ist ...': Die Geldwährungen der Griechen, Juden, Nabatäer und Römer in syrisch-nabatäischen Raum unter besonderer Berücksichtigung des Kurses von Sela'/Melaina und Lepton nach der Annexion des Königreiches der Nabatäer durch Rom." *ZPE* 114 (1996): 237–87.
(with W. Eck), "Ein Ehrenbogen für Septimius Severus und seine Familie in Jerusalem." In *Donum Amicitiae. Studies in Ancient History Publisher on Occasion of the 75th Anniversary of Foundation of the Department of Ancient History of the Jagiellonian University*, Electrum 1, edited by E. Dąbrowa, 11–20. Krakow: Jagiellonian University Press, 1997.
"Deeds of Gift and the Law of Succession in Archives from the Judaean Desert." In *Akten des 21. Internationalen Papyrologenkongresses, Berlin, 13–19.8.1995*, edited by B. Kramer, W. Luppe, H. Maehler, and G. Poethke, Vol. I, 179–88. Stuttgart – Leipzig: Teubner, 1997.
"Ἡ νέα ἐπαρχεία Ἀραβία. The New Province of Arabia in the Papyri from the Judaean Desert." *ZPE* 116 (1997): 204–208.
"The Guardian (ἐπίτροπος) of a Woman in the Documents from the Judaean Desert." *ZPE* 118 (1997): 267–73.
"Land Tenure in the Documents from the Nabataean Kingdom and the Roman Province of Arabia." *ZPE* 119 (1997): 255–65.
(with W. Eck), "Ein Staatsmonopol und seine Folgen: Plinius, Naturalis Historia 12,123 und der Preis für Balsam." *Rheinisches Museum für Philologie* 140 (1997): 153–61. Reprinted in W. Eck, *Judäa – Syria Palästina*, 204–11. Tübingen: Mohr Siebeck, 2014.

(with J. Geiger), "Herod and Masada: The Written Finds." In *The Story of Masada: Discoveries from the Excavations*, edited by G. Hurvitz, 77–84. Provo, Utah: BYU Studies, 1997.
(with J. Geiger), "The Roman Army and Masada: The Written Finds." In *The Story of Masada: Discoveries from the Excavations*, edited by G. Hurvitz, 131–38. Provo, Utah: BYU Studies, 1997.
"The Law of Succession in the Documents from the Judaean Desert Again." *SCI* 17 (1998): 115–23.
"The Rabbis and the Documents." In *Jews in a Greco-Roman World*, edited by M. Goodman, 167–79. Oxford: Oxford University Press, 1998.
(with E. Qimron), "Ḫev/Se ar 13 of 134 or 135 C.E.: A Wife's Renunciation of Claims." *JJS* 49 (1998): 108–18.
"The Languages of the Legal and Administrative Documents from the Judaean Desert." *ZPE* 125 (1999): 219–31.
"The Impact of the Documentary Papyri from the Judaean Desert on the Study of Jewish History from 70 to 135 CE." In *Jüdische Geschichte in hellenistisch-römischer Zeit: Wege der Forschung – von alten zu neuen Schürer*, edited by A. Oppenheimer, 221–36. München: Oldenbourg, 1999.
"Die Papyrusdokumente aus der judäischen Wüste und ihr Beitrag zur Erforschung der jüdischen Geschichte des 1. und 2. Jh.s n. Chr." *ZDPV* 115 (1999): 228–47.
"Some Aspects of the Roman Administration of Judaea/Syria-Palaestina." In *Lokale Autonomie und römische Ordnungsmacht in den kaiserzeitlichen Provinzen vom 1. bis 3. Jahrhundert*, edited by W. Eck, 75–91. München: Oldenbourg, 1999.
(with W. Eck), "Ein Statthalter von Syria Palaestina unter Marc Aurel und Lucius Verus in einer Bauinschrift aus Jericho." *ZPE* 127 (1999): 211–15. Reprinted in W. Eck, *Judäa – Syria Palästina*, 92–97. Tübingen: Mohr Siebeck, 2014.
(with L. Di Segni – W. Eck – B. Isaac), "Corpus Inscriptionum Judaeae/Palaestinae." *ZPE* 127 (1999): 307–308.
"4QAccount gr." In *Qumran Cave 4, Volume XXVI: Cryptic Texts and Miscellanea, Part 1*, Discoveries in the Judaean Desert XXXVI, edited S.J. Pfann et al., 294–95. Oxford: Clarendon Press, 2000.
Contributions in *Miscellaneous Texts from the Judaean Desert*, Discoveries in the Judaean Desert XXXVIII, edited by J.H. Charlsworth et al., 93–100 (Ketef Jericho: "Jericho papText Mentioning the Emperor Hadrian gr"; "Jericho papDeed? gr"; "Jericho papFiscal Acknowledgement gr"), 171–72 (Naḥal Ḥever: "8Ḥev papUnidentified Text gr"), 203–206 (Naḥal Mishmar: "1Mish papList of Names and Account gr"), 215–30 (Naḥal Ṣe'elim: "34Ṣe'elim: Introduction"; "34Ṣe papCensus List from Judaea or Arabia gr"; "34Ṣe papAccount gr"). Oxford: Clarendon Press, 2000.
Contributions in *Encyclopedia of the Dead Sea Scrolls*, edited by L.H. Schiffman and J.C. VanderKam, 212–15 ("Documentary texts"), 324–26 ("Greek"), 359–61 ("Ḥever, Naḥal: Written Material"), 474–75 ("Latin"), 860–61 ("Ṣeʾelim, Naḥal: Written Material"), 984–87 ("Women: The Texts"). New York: Oxford University Press, 2000.
"Cassius Dio, Mommsen and the quinquefascales." *Chiron* 30 (2000): 217–34.
"Marriage Contracts from the Judaean Desert." *Materia Giudaica* 6 (2000): 2–6.
"Recht und Wirtschaft. Zur Stellung der jüdischen Frau nach den Papyri aus der judäischen Wüste." *Zeitschrift für Neues Testament* 3, no. 6 (2000): 23–30.
"The Legio VI Ferrata." In *Les legions de Rome sous le haut-empire: actes du congres de Lyon (17–19 septembre 1998)*, edited by Y. Le Bohec, Vol. I, 351–57. Lyon: Centre d'etudes romaines et gallo-romaines, 2000.

(with W. Eck), "Governors and Their Personnel on Latin Inscriptions from Caesarea Maritima." *Proceedings of the Israel Academy of Sciences and Humanities* 7 (2001): 215–40.

"Documentary Texts from the Judaean Desert: A Matter of Nomenclature." *SCI* 20 (2001): 113–19.

"Ein Gedi between the Two Revolts." *SCI* 20 (2001): 139–54.

"L'impatto dei papiri documentari del deserto di Giudea sullo studio della storia ebraica dal 70 al 135/6 e.v." In *Gli ebrei nell'impero romano*, edited by Ariel Lewin, 217–31. Florence: Giuntina, 2001.

(with J.J. Price), "A Bilingual Tombstone from Zo'ar (Arabia) (Hecht Museum, Haifa, inv. no. H-3029, Naveh's list no. 18)." *ZPE* 134 (2001): 277–83.

(with J.J. Price), "Bilingual Funerary Monument from Zoar in the Hecht Museum Collection – The Greek Inscription." *Michmanim* 15 (2001): 10–12 (Hebrew).

"Greek Letters." In *The Documents from the Bar Kokhba Period in the Cave of Letters: Hebrew, Jewish Aramaic and Nabataean Aramaic Papyri*, Judean Desert Studies III, edited by Y. Yadin, J.C. Greenfield, A. Yardeni, and B.A. Levine, 349–66. Jerusalem: IES, 2002.

"Jewish Jurisdiction under Roman Rule: Prolegomena." In *Zwischen den Reichen: Neues Testament und römische Herrschaft. Vorträge auf der ersten Konferenz der European Association for Biblical Studies*, edited by M. Labahn and J. Zangenberg, 13–28. Tübingen: Francke Verlag, 2002.

"Women and Law in the Documents from the Judaean Desert." In *Le rôle et le statut de la femme en Égypte hellénistique, romaine et byzantine: actes du colloque international, Bruxelles-Leuven 27–29 novembre 1997*, edited by H. Melaerts and L. Mooren, 123–47. Leuven: Peeters, 2002.

(with W. Eck), "A New Inscription from Caesarea Maritima and the Local Elite of Caesarea Maritima." In *What Athens Has to Do with Jerusalem. Essays on Classical, Jewish, and Early Christian Art and Archaeology in Honor of Gideon Foerster*, edited by L.V. Rutgers, 375–91. Leuven: Peeters, 2002.

(with W. Eck), "P.Murabba'at 114 und die Anwesenheit römischer Truppen in den Höhlen des Wadi Murabba'at nach dem Bar Kochba Aufstand." *ZPE* 138 (2002): 173–83.

(with A. Yakobson), "Arcanum Imperii: The Powers of Augustus." In *Philosophy and Power in the Graeco-Roman World: Essays in Honour of Miriam Griffin*, edited by G. Clark and T. Rajak, 193–209. Oxford: Oxford University Press, 2002.

(with W. Weiser), "Neues zum tyrischen Silbergeld herodianischer und römischer Zeit." *ZPE* 139 (2002): 235–50.

"The Roman Fasti of Judaea/Syria Palaestina." In *Memorial for Menachem Stern*, 55–69. Jerusalem: Israel Academy of Sciences and Humanities, 2002 (Hebrew).

(with W. Eck – B. Isaac), "A Newly Discovered Governor of Judaea in a Military Diploma from 90 C.E." *Israel Museum Studies in Archaeology* 2 (2003): 17–31.

"The Bar Kokhba Revolt and the Documents from the Judaean Desert: Nabataean Participation in the Revolt (P.Yadin 52)." In *The Bar Kokhba War Reconsidered*, edited by P. Schäfer, 133–52. Tübingen: Mohr Siebeck, 2003.

"'Diplomatics' or External Aspects of the Legal Documents from the Judaean Desert: Prolegomena." In *Rabbinic Law in its Roman and Near Eastern Context*, edited by C. Hezser, 49–61. Tübingen: Mohr Siebeck, 2003.

"The Roman Census in the Papyri from the Judaean Desert and the Egyptian κατ' οἰκίαν ἀπογραφή." In *Semitic Papyrology in Context: A Climate of Creativity*, edited by L.H. Schiffman, 105–22. Leiden – Boston: Brill, 2003.

"Survival, Adaptation and Extinction: Nabataean and Jewish Aramaic versus Greek in the Legal Documents from the Cave of Letters in Naḥal Ḥever." In *Sprache und Kultur in der kaiserzeitlichen Provinz Arabia: Althistorische Beiträge zur Erforschung von Akkulturationsphänomenen im römischen Nahen Osten*, edited by L. Schumacher and O. Stoll, 1–11. St. Katharinen: Scripta Mercaturae Verlag, 2003.

(with W. Eck), "Eine Provinz entsteht: Alte und neue lateinische Inschriften in Iudaea unter Vespasian." In *The Roman Near East and Armenia*, Electrum 7, edited by E. Dąbrowa, 25–37. Krakow: Jagiellonian University Press, 2003.

(with E. Larson), "4Q460/4Q350 and Tampering with Qumran texts in Antiquity?" In *Emanuel: Studies in Hebrew Bible, Septuagint and Dead Sea Scrolls in Honor of Emanuel Tov*, edited by S.M. Paul, R.A. Kraft, L.H. Schiffman, and W.W. Fields, 113–25. Leiden: Brill, 2003.

(with W. Eck), "Lateinische Inschriften aus der Ustinov Collection in Oslo und ein Opistograph mit der damnatio memoriae des Kaisers Probus." In *Orbis Antiquus: Studia in Honorem Ioannis Pisonis*, edited by L. Ruscu, C. Ciongradi, R. Ardevan, C. Roman, and C. Găzdac, 48–57. Cluj-Napoca: Nereamia Napocae Press, 2004.

"Language Gaps in Roman Palestine and the Roman Near East." In *Medien im antiken Palästina: Materielle Kommunikation und Medialität als Thema der Palästinaarchäologie*, edited by C. Frevel, 151–69. Tübingen: Mohr Siebeck, 2005.

"Sprache und Kultur in der keiserzeitlischen Provinz Arabia." In *Prozesse des Wandels in historischen Spannungsfeldern Nordostafrikas/Westasiens – Akten zum 2. Symposium des SFB 295, Mainz, 15.10–17.10.2001*, edited by W. Bisang, T. Bierschenk, D. Kreikenbom, and U. Verhoeven, Vol. 2, 257–59. Würzburg: Ergon-Verlag, 2005.

(with W. Eck), "Josephus' Roman Audience? Josephus and the Roman Elites." In *Flavius Josephus and Flavian Rome*, edited by J. Edmondson, S. Mason, and J. Rives, 37–52. Oxford: Oxford University Press, 2005.

(with W. Eck), "Roman Officials in Judaea and Arabia and Civil Jurisdiction." In *Law in the Documents of the Judaean Desert*, edited by R. Katzoff and D. Schaps, 23–44. Leiden – Boston: Brill, 2005. Reprinted in W. Eck, *Judäa – Syria Palästina*, 186–203. Tübingen: Mohr Siebeck, 2014.

"The Yadin Papyri (P.Yadin): 1961–2004." In *In Memory of Yigael Yadin (1917–1984), Lectures Presented at the Symposium on the Twentieth Anniversary of his Death*, 36–44. Jerusalem: IES, 2006 (Hebrew).

"Ein Gedi between the Two Revolts: A Study based on the Documents from the Judaean Desert." In *Ein Gedi – A Very Large Village of Jews*, edited by Y. Hirschfeld, 21–27. Haifa: Hecht Museum, 2006 (English and Hebrew).

(with W. Eck), "Governors and their Personell in Roman Inscriptions from Caesarea Maritima." *Cathedra* 122 (2006): 31–52 (Hebrew).

"Private International Law or Conflict of Laws: Reflections on Roman Provincial Jurisdiction." In *Herrschen und Verwalten. Der Alltag der römischen Administration in der Hohen Kaizerzeit*, edited by R. Haensch and J. Heinrichs, 234–55. Köln: Böhlau, 2007.

"The Impact of the Roman Army in the Province of Judaea/Syria Palaestina." In *The Impact of the Roman Army (200 B.C. – A.D. 476): Economic, Social, Political, Religious and Cultural Aspects*, edited by L. De Blois and E. Lo Cascio, 393–407. Leiden – Boston: Brill, 2007.

"Naphtali Lewis 1911–2005: Obituary." *SCI* 26 (2007): 255–58.

(with J.J. Price), "Corpus Inscriptionum Iudaeae/Palestinae: A Multilingual Corpus of Inscriptions." In *Acta XII congressus internationalis epigraphiae Graecae et Latinae:*

provinciae imperii Romani inscriptionibus descriptae: Barcelona, 3–8 Septembris 2002, edited by M.M. i Olivé, G. Baratta, and A.G. Almagro, 327–32. Barcelona: Institut d'Estudis Catalans, 2007.

"The Administrative Background to the New Settlement Recently Discovered near Giv'at Shaul, Ramallah-Shu'afat Road." In *New Studies in the Archaeology of Jerusalem and its Region, Volume I*, edited by J. Patrich and D. Amit, *12–*18. Jerusalem: IAA, 2007.

(with M. Wörrle), "Seleukos IV to Heliodoros: A New Dossier of Royal Correspondence from Israel." *ZPE* 159 (2007): 191–205.

"In Lieu of an Article: Reflexions on Hadrian, Antiochus Epiphanes and the Jews." In *A Roman Miscellany: Essays in Honour of Anthony R. Birley on His Seventieth Birthday*, edited by H.M. Schellenberg, V.E. Hirschmann, and A. Krieckhaus, 19–23. Gdańsk: Foundation for the Development of Gdańsk University, 2008.

"Continuity of Nabataean Law in the Petra Papyri: A Methodological Exercise." In *From Hellenism to Islam: Cultural and Linguistic Change in the Roman Near East*, edited by H.M. Cotton, R.G. Hoyland, J.J. Price, and D.J. Wasserstein, 154–74. Cambridge: Cambridge University Press, 2009.

"L'impatto dell'esercito romano sulla provincia della Giudea." In *Divus Vespasianus – Il bimillenario dei Flavi*, edited by F. Coarelli, 28–33. Roma: Electa, 2009.

(with W. Eck), "An Imperial Arch in the Colonia Aelia Capitolina: A Fragment of a Latin Inscription in the Islamic Museum of the Haram ash-Sharif." In *Israel's Land: Papers Presented to Israel Shatzman on his Jubilee*, edited by J. Geiger, H.M. Cotton, and G. Stiebel, 97–118. Ra'anana: The Open University of Israel, 2009.

(with W. Eck), "Inscriptions from the Financial Procurator's Praetorium in Caesarea." In *Man Near a Roman Arch: Studies Presented to Prof. Yoram Tsafrir*, edited by L. Di Segni, Y. Hirshfeld, J. Patrich, and R. Talgam, 98–114. Jerusalem: IES, 2009.

(with B. Legras), "Presentazione del libro di Silvia Bussi, Le élites locali nella provincia d'Egitto di prima età imperiale." In *Roma e l'eredità ellenistica. Atti del convegno internazionale. Milano,Università statale, 14–16 gennaio 2009*, edited by S. Bussi and D. Foraboschi, 177–82. Pisa – Roma: Fabrizio Serra editore, 2010.

(with W. Eck), "The Impact of the Bar Kokhba Revolt on Rome: Another Military Diploma from AD 160 from Syria Palaestina." *Michmanim* 23 (2011): 7–22 (Hebrew).

(with A. Ecker), "The Date of the Founding of Aelia Capitolna." In H. Gitler, "Roman Coinages of Palestine." In *The Oxford Handbook of Greek and Roman Coinage*, edited by W.E. Metcalf, 492–95. Oxford: Oxford University Press, 2012.

"Change and Continuity in Late Legal Papyri from Palaestina Tertia: Nomos Hellênikos and Ethos Rômaikon." In *Jews, Christians and the Roman Empire: The Poetics of Power in Late Antiquity*, edited by N.B. Dohrmann and A.Y. Reed, 209–21. Philadelphia: University of Pennsylvania Press, 2013.

"The Evolution of the So-Called Provincial Law, or: Cicero's Letters of Recommendation and Private International Law in the Roman World." In *Integration in Rome and in the Roman World: Proceedings of the Tenth Workshop of the International Network Impact of Empire (Lille, June 23–25, 2011)*, edited by G. de Kleijn and S. Benoist, 43–56. Leiden – Boston: Brill, 2013.

(with G. Gambash – H. Gitler), "Iudaea Recepta." *INR* 8 (2013): 89–104.

(with G. Gambash – H. Gitler), "IUDAEA RECEPTA." In *New Studies in the Archaeology of Jerusalem and its Region, Volume VIII*, edited by G. Stiebel, O. Peleg-Barkat, D. Ben-Ami, and Y. Gadot, 37–49. Jerusalem: IAA, 2014 (Hebrew).

(with R. Avner – R. Greenwald – A. Ecker), "A New-Old Monumental Inscription from Jerusalem Honoring Hadrian." In *New Studies in the Archaeology of Jerusalem and its Region, Volume VIII*, edited by G. Stiebel, O. Peleg-Barkat, D. Ben-Ami, and Y. Gadot, 96–101. Jerusalem: IAA, 2014 (Hebrew).

(with A. Ecker – D. Gera), "Preliminary Report on the Finding of a Another Copy of the Decree of Seleucus IV at Maresha (Heliodoros/Olympiodoros Inscritption)." In *New Studies in the Archaeology of Jerusalem and its Region, Volume VIII*, edited by G. Stiebel, O. Peleg-Barkat, D. Ben-Ami, and Y. Gadot, 153–58. Jerusalem: IAA, 2014 (Hebrew).

(with W. Eck), "The Greek Inscriptions from the Shrine." In *Caesarea Maritima, Volume I: Herod's Circus and Related Buildings. Part 2: The Finds*, IAA Reports 57, edited by Y. Porath, 197–202. Jerusalem: IAA, 2015.

"Appendix: On the Rediscovery of P.Nessana 77." In R.G. Hoyland, "The Earliest Attestation of the *Dhimma* of God and His Messenger and the Rediscovery of P.Nessana 77 (60s AH/680 CE)." In *Islamic Cultures, Islamic Contexts: Essays in Honor of Professor Patricia Crone*, edited by A.Q. Ahmed, B. Sadeghi, R.G. Hoyland, and A. Silverstein, 64–67. Leiden: Brill, 2015.

(with A. Ecker – D. Gera), "Juxtaposing Literary and Documentary Evidence: A New Copy of The So-called Heliodoros Stele and the Corpus Inscriptionum Iudaeae/Palaestinae (CIIP)." *BICS* 60 (2017): 1–15.

"*Eleuthera* and *Brat Horin*: Another Look at Babatha's Ketubba, *P.Yadin* 10." *JJS* 68 (2017): 225–33.

(with A. Ecker – S. Ganor – D.J. Wasserstein), "A Dedication of a Naos to Skorpon's Ourania in Ascalon (Ashkelon)." *Kernos* 31 (2018): 111–18.

(with W. Eck), "A Latin Inscription from Building G in the Western Wall Plaza (CIIP I 2, 727)." In *New Studies in the Archaeology of Jerusalem and its Region, Volume XII*, edited by J. Uziel, Y. Gadot, Y. Zelniger, O. Peleg-Barkat, and O. Gutfeld, *43–*46. Jerusalem: IAA, 2018.

"The Conception of Jesus." In *To the Madbar and Back Again: Studies in the Languages, Archaeology, and Cultures of Arabia Dedicated to Michael C.A. Macdonald*, edited by L. Nehmé and A. Al-Jallad, 581–98. Leiden: Brill, 2018.

"Two Marital Financial Agreements from the Judean Desert." In *The Words of Japheth: An Analogy of Writings by Greek Intellectuals in Ancient Palestine*, edited by D. Dueck, D. Gera, and N. Shoval-Dudai, 19–23. Jerusalem: Yad Ben-Zvi Press, 2018 (Hebrew).

(with A. Ecker), "The Legio X Fretensis Welcomes the Emperor: A Latin Inscription on a Monument Erected for Hadrian in 129/130 CE." *Israel Museum Studies in Archaeology* 9 (2018–2019): 59–67.

(with A. Ecker), "Reflections on the Foundation of Aelia Capitolina." In *The Past as Present: Essays on Roman History in Honour of Guido Clemente*, edited by G.A. Cecconi, R. Lizzi Testa, and A. Marcone, 681–95. Turnhout: Brepols, 2019.

"Fergus Millar 1935–2019: Obituary." *SCI* 39 (2020): 204–206.

"Ada Yardeni: Memorial." In *Eretz Israel: Archaeological, Historical and Geographical Studies, Volume 34, Ada Yardeni Volume*, edited by Sh. Aḥituv, H.M. Cotton, and M. Morgenstern, xv-xvii. Jerusalem: IES, 2021 (English & Hebrew).

A Government, Power, and Jurisdiction

Cicero, ad Familiares XIII, 26 and 28: Evidence for *revocatio* or *reiectio Romae/Romam*?

I

The two letters of recommendation, *ad Familiares* XIII, 26 and 28, were addressed in 46 BC to Ser. Sulpicius Rufus, the foremost jurist of the day, and at the time the governor of Achaea. They were written on behalf of Cicero's former quaestor, L. Mescinius Rufus,[1] in anticipation of legal difficulties in the succession of the latter to the inheritance left to him in Achaea by his cousin(?) M. Mindius.[2]

Cicero's request, "*ut ... eos* (i. e. Mescinius' opponents) ... *Romam reieceris*," backed, as he informed his correspondent, by a letter (*litterae quasi commendaticiae*) from the consul in Rome (*Fam.* XIII, 26, 3) has received the most contradictory and mutually exclusive interpretations. Whereas some see in it a perfect example of an appeal launched before trial,[3] others firmly deny this,[4] or reject the very existence of this form of appeal.[5] In its stead a little-used right of Roman

1 Mescinius served as Cicero's quaestor in Cilicia in 51–50 BC until succeeded by C. Coelius Caldus; cf. T. Robert S. Broughton, *The Magistrates of the Roman Republic*, Vol. II (New York: American Philological Association, 1952), 242, 250. Opinions vary about Cicero's relations with Mescinius at the time; cf. L.A. Thompson, "Cicero's Succession-Problem in Cilicia," *AJPhil.* 86 (1965): 375–86, esp. 381 f.; *contra* Anthony J. Marshall, "The Lex Pompeia de Provinciis (52 BC) and Cicero's Imperium in 51–50 BC: Constitutional Aspects," in *Aufstieg und Niedergang der römischen Welt*, Vol. I.1 (Berlin: De Gruyter, 1972), 917 and nn. *Fam.* V, 19 (49 BC) and 21 (46 BC) as well as the letters under discussion suggest a renewed or newly developed intimacy; cf. W.K.A. Drumann and P. Groebe, eds., *Geschichte Roms in seinem Übergange von der republikanischen Verfassung* (Hildesheim: G. Olms, 1964), 96.

2 For *frater* as cousin cf. Robert Yelverton Tyrrell and Louis Claude Purser, eds., *The Correspondance of M. Tullius Cicero*, Vol. IV (Dublin: Hodges, Figgis & Co., 1918), 505–6, n. 2: '*frater patruelis*'; cf. D.R. Shackleton Bailey, ed., *Cicero: Epistulae Ad Familiares*, Vol. I (Cambridge: Cambridge University Press, 1977), 466 on *Fam.* V, 20 (no. 128) – brother, half brother or cousin. For Mindius see *Fam.* V, 20, 3, and cf. Claude Nicolet, *L'ordre équestre à l'époque républicaine (312–43 Av. J.-C.)*, Vol. I (Paris: E. De Boccard, 1966), 258–9; Vol. II (1974), no. 233.

3 A.H.M. Jones, "Imperial and Senatorial Jurisdiction in the Early Principate," in *Studies in Roman Government and Law* (Oxford: Blackwell, 1960), 76–7.

4 Cf. Max Kaser, *Das römische Zivilprozessrecht* (München: Beck, 1966), 181, n. 10: "eine Vorentscheidung in der Sache selbst, gegen die appelliert würde, ist hier nicht vorausgesetzt."

5 Cf. Peter Garnsey, "The Lex Iulia and Appeal under the Empire," *JRS* 56 (1966): 167–8; 180 f.

Article note: First published in *JRS* 69 (1979): 39–50, with the following note: I should like to thank M.W. Frederiksen, P.A. Brunt and I. Shatzman for criticism which has improved this article. F. Millar has helped and encouraged me at every stage of the research which led to it.

https://doi.org/10.1515/9783110770438-001

citizens in the provinces to request a remittal of their case to Rome is invoked.[6] The alleged appeal or right is variously designated *revocatio Romae,*[7] *revocatio Romam,*[8] *reiectio Romae*[9] or most recently, *reiectio Romam.*[10]

Further disagreement among scholars as to what the consul's letter could have contained creates even greater difficulties. For, whereas it is generally conceded that it would normally have rested with the governor, who was competent to try the case,[11] whether or not to grant the request to transfer it to the courts in Rome,[12] there are those who consider the consul's letter to have altered the situation completely. In other words, the letter represents a curtailment of the governor's freedom of action. According to Mommsen this letter contains "in höflichen Formen einen Befehl der Regierung."[13] A.H.M. Jones believed that it contained a promise on the consul's part to grant *auxilium* upon an appeal from Mescinius.[14] Against these views it has been asserted that though the governor was permitted to send to Rome cases in which Roman citizens were involved, nevertheless, since this was a free decision on his part, it did not limit his competence.[15] And in a stronger vein: "no legal right to the change of court was possessed by the parties

---

6 Garnsey (above, n. 5), 182–3; cf. Peter Garnsey, "The Criminal Jurisdiction of Governors," *JRS* 58 (1968): 56–7, and Peter Garnsey, *Social Status and Legal Privilege in the Roman Empire* (Oxford: Clarendon Press, 1970), 263–4.

7 Jones, "Imperial and Senatorial Jurisdiction in the Early Principate," 75.

8 A.H.J. Greenidge, *The Legal Procedure of Cicero's Time* (Oxford: Clarendon Press, 1901), 292, who, however, does not regard it as a right but as "an outcome of customary law."

9 Jones, "Imperial and Senatorial Jurisdiction in the Early Principate," 76: "*revocatio* or *reiectio Romae.*"

10 Garnsey, "The Criminal Jurisdiction of Governors," 56; Garnsey, *Social Status and Legal Privilege in the Roman Empire*, 76; 263–4.

11 Cf. *Dig.* 1, 16, 7, 2 (Ulpian). As Mommsen points out (*Römisches Strafrecht* (Leipzig: Duncker & Humblot, 1899), 233), the fact that *praetor* was a generic term for provincial governors indicates that civil jurisdiction always belonged to them. For the evidence on the use of *praetor* as a generic term cf. Theodor Mommsen, *Römisches Staatsrecht*, Vol. II (Graz: Akademische Druck- u. Verlagsanstalt, 1952), 240, n. 5.

12 Mommsen, *Römisches Staatsrecht*, Vol. II, 267–8 and n. 1 on 268.; Vol. III, 748 and n. 5; 1214 and nn. 3 and 4; Moriz Wlassak, *Römische Processgesetze*, Vol. II (Leipzig: Duncker & Humblot, 1891), 256; Moriz Wlassak, *Der Judikationsbefehl der römischen Prozesse* (Wien: In Kommission bei A. Holder, 1921), 95–6 – to cite only those who mention the two letters explicitly.

13 *Römisches Staatsrecht*, Vol. III, 1214, n. 2. But it should be pointed out that Mommsen considers this an abuse.

14 Jones, "Imperial and Senatorial Jurisdiction in the Early Principate," 76–7.

15 Wlassak, *Römische Processgesetze*, Vol. II, 256.

and *no compulsion could be placed on the governor.*"[16] Moreover, the consul's letter is the very proof that this was so.[17]

II

In the face of such basic disagreement a re-examination of the entire case seems to be called for. An attempt is made here to free the discussion from the legalistic terms which have dominated it, and to re-consider the question in the light of the conventions which governed letters of recommendation.

In many respects Cicero's letters of recommendation are the best primary evidence we have for determining the minutiae of provincial government under the Republic, the day-to-day working of provincial administration and jurisdiction as well as certain prevailing attitudes and conventions of conduct. The value of these letters has long been recognized; but, as far as I am aware, no serious attempt has been made to use the evidence they provide for a re-evaluation of general theories about Roman provincial government.[18] Instead it has become common practice to pluck certain phrases arbitrarily out of their context. In our particular case Cicero's request "*ut eos Romam reieceris*" and his qualifying phrase "*non quae te aliquid iuberent*" have been used as counters in larger games: the problem of appeal in the late Republic and early Principate; the consul's *imperium* vis-à-vis that of the proconsul; the control exercised by the central government over provincial governors; the legal position of Roman citizens in the provinces, etc.[19] As a result the mood and import of these phrases, dependent as they are on the context in which they appear, has been falsified and distorted.

An analysis of *Fam.* XIII, 26 as a letter of recommendation obeying certain rules which govern the genre will precede the detailed examination of the theories outlined above which were offered as interpretations of certain crucial phrases in the letter. In view of their inadequacies, mainly the result of having ignored the context in which the phrases occur, a new interpretation, which takes into

---

16 Greenidge, *The Legal Procedure of Cicero's Time*, 292.
17 Garnsey, "The Criminal Jurisdiction of Governors," 57.
18 Most of those addressed to provincial governors can be found in Book XIII of *Ad Familiares* (cf. Ludwig Gurlitt, "De M. Tulli Ciceronis Epistulis Earumque Pristina Collectione" (University of Göttingen Thesis, 1879), 14 f., for a plausible hypothesis that this collection was made in Cicero's own lifetime). But there are others elsewhere among Cicero's letters. Nicolet, *L'ordre équestre à l'époque républicaine*, Vol. I, 680, n. 5 comments on the absence of a special study and expresses the hope of providing one.
19 See below, p. 10 f.

account the over-all character and bearing of letters of recommendation, will be put forward.

The actual request in the first of the two letters is preceded by an elaborate and lengthy preamble:

> *L. Mescinius ea mecum necessitudine coniunctus est, quod mihi quaestor fuit; sed hanc causam, quam ego, ut a maioribus accepi, semper gravem duxi, fecit virtute et humanitate sua iustiorem. Itaque eo sic utor ut nec familiarius ullo nec libentius. Is quamquam confidere videbatur te sua causa quae honeste posses libenter esse facturum, magnum esse tamen speravit apud te meas quoque litteras pondus habituras. Id cum ipse ita iudicabat tum pro familiari consuetudine saepe ex me audierat quam suavis esset inter nos et quanta coniunctio.*

The themes of this preamble are familiar from other letters of recommendation:[20] the excellent character of the recommended person;[21] his close ties with Cicero (whose quaestor he had been) sanctified and solemnized by tradition, which makes it the latter's duty and pleasure to come to his aid;[22] and finally, Cicero's known intimacy with Sulpicius, a pledge, under Roman notions of the duties entailed by friendship, that the request would not go unheeded.[23] Nevertheless, as will be shown below, the passage just quoted goes beyond the rules laid down by the *decorum* of writing in this genre.[24] This fact alone alerts us to the possibil-

---

20 For a brief survey of both the form of letters of recommendation and their recurring themes cf. Friedrich Lossmann, *Cicero und Caesar im Jahre 54: Studien zur Theorie und Praxis der römischen Freundschaft* (Wiesbaden: F. Steiner, 1962), 11–24. Some useful comments can be found in Wilhelm Kroll, *Die Kultur der ciceronischen Zeit* (Leipzig: Dieterich, 1933), 60 f. and Otto Plasberg, *Cicero in seinen Werken und Briefen* (Leipzig: Dieterich, 1926), 27 f.

21 For other examples cf. *Fam.* XIII, 3; 10, 3; 13; 14, 1; 15, 1; 16, 2; 21, 1; 25; 30, 1. There are many others.

22 For the relationship between provincial quaestors and governors cf. L.A. Thompson, "The Relationship between Provincial Quaestors and Their Commanders-in-Chief," *Historia* 11 (1962): 339–55.

23 See Fritz Schultz, *Principles of Roman Law* (Oxford: Clarendon Press, 1936), 233–4; and cf. *Fam.* XIII, 70: "*Quia non est obscura tua in me benevolentia sic fiat ut multi per me tibi velint commendari*"; *Fam.* XIII, 71: "*Multos tibi commendem necesse est quoniam omnibus nota nostra necessitudo est tuaque erga me benevolentia.*" As a matter of fact, the recommender would be guilty of *neglegentia* towards the recommended person if the request was not complied with; cf. *Fam.* XIII, 1, 5; 19, 3.

24 The *decorum* observed in letters of recommendation deserves a special study. For some comments see Ludwig Gurlitt, "Die Briefe Ciceros an M. Brutus," *Philologus Supplement* 4 (1884): 593 f.; Lossmann, *Cicero und Caesar im Jahre 54*, 11–24. Cf. in general A.B. Miller, "Roman Etiquette of the Late Republic as Revealed by the Correspondence of Cicero" (University of Pennsylvania Thesis, 1914); Edwin S. Ramage, *Urbanitas: Ancient Sophistication and Refinement* (Norman, Oklahoma: University of Oklahoma Press, 1973).

ity that the request which follows might have been quite unprecedented and had no basis in law, customary or otherwise. This is not to say, however, that Cicero's request should necessarily be described as an attempt to override the law,[25] nor that it should be branded as an abuse of the prevailing system of provincial jurisdiction.[26]

The introduction of the request itself seems at first to come with the phrase *peto igitur*, but this turns out to be a false scent. No specific request is enunciated; instead a lengthy, rambling sentence concludes with a vague and general appeal for aid: *eius negotia ... explices et expedias*. This is hardly a cause for surprise. A specific request is rarely if ever made in letters of recommendation, where a deliberate vagueness and lack of specification are the rule.[27] Often the recommender may not have a specific request in mind and may intend no more than a general recommendation.[28] However, it seems that it was one of the unwritten rules of the system not to spell out to the recipient the ways and means in which the latter's benevolence should express itself: the choice of methods and measures is left entirely to the recipient's discretion. Consequently, the very vagueness sustained by the use of conventional set-phrases and hackneyed expressions could be used by the recipient to reconcile the request with his own interests or to refuse without damaging his friendship with the recommender. It will be suggested below that in the present case Cicero had one specific request in mind. Moreover, in this instance he was not going to leave it to the governor's initiative and discretion to choose the measures to be used, but was going to outline the course of action to be taken. Cicero's predicament made it of paramount importance not to broach the subject without adequate preparation. He had to use all the tact, ingenuity and resourcefulness he could muster in order not to commit too vulgar a breach of the rules of *decorum*. The task facing him was of a most delicate nature, if Sulpicius' dignity

---

25 So John Maurice Kelly in a chapter entitled "Improper Influences in Roman Litigation," in *Roman Litigation* (Oxford: Clarendon Press, 1966), 69–84.

26 We may ask, indeed, whether hard and fast rules regarding the legal status of Roman citizens in the provinces could have crystallized by this time into a system. It seems to me that everything we know suggests the contrary, but this is not the place to argue for this view.

27 E.g. *Fam.* XIII, 13: "*Cui quibuscumque rebus commodaveris*"; 18, 2: "*qibuscumque officiis in Epiroticis reliquisque rebus Atticum obstrinxeris*"; 22, 2: "*T. Manlium quam maxime, quibuscumque rebus honeste ac pro tua dignitate poteris, iuveris atque ornaver*"; 27, 3: "*quiquid habent negoti, des operam, quod commodo tuo fiat, ut te obtinente Achaiam conficiant*"; cf. also 23, 2; 31, 1; 32, 2; 35, 2; 63, 2; 66, 2; 67, 2; 79.

28 As seems to be the case in *Fam.* XIII, 17 (M. Curius); 20 (Ascalpo); 22 (T. Manlius); 23 (L. Cossinius Anchialus); 25 (Hagesaretus of Larissa); 28a (The Lacedaemonii), to mention only those sent to Ser. Sulpicius Rufus.

and emotions were to be spared.[29] Hence he was taking his time, carefully preparing the ground, slowly progressing from the more general to the more specific.

In the sentence which follows this stage seems to have been reached. But on one interpretation, as we shall see, Cicero was again throwing us off the scent (*Fam.* XIII, 26, 2):

> *Sic enim praescripsimus iis, quibus ea negotia mandavimus, ut omnibus rebus, quae in aliquam controversiam vocarentur, te arbitro et, quod commodo tuo fieri posset, te disceptatore uterentur.*

In view of what follows one wonders whether there is any need to point to a real distinction between *arbiter* and *disceptator*.[30] Admittedly, the insertion of the clause *quod commodo tuo fieri posset* seems to suggest that some distinction is intended. However, even if the latter term denotes formal arbitration in a *controversia*,[31] the very next sentence shows that Sulpicius' formal arbitration was not going to be used: in the case of a *controversia* he was asked to refer the matter to Rome. Indeed, if one of the terms is interpreted as referring to formal arbitration, then it must be admitted that Cicero is clearly contradicting himself (or rather dissembling), requesting first that Sulpicius would arbitrate in the case of a controversy and then (see below) recanting by saying that in such a case the matter should go to Rome.

Of course one might object that only if the opponents proved to be '*difficiliores*' should they be sent to Rome. Does '*difficiliores*' mean in this case 'refusing to accept Sulpicius' arbitration'? Hardly so. '*Difficiliores*' is followed by its own exegesis: "*ut rem sine controversia confici nolint.*" If it came to litigation, the case should go to Rome.

The alternative of formal arbitration is therefore ruled out (if it was suggested, it was not meant to be taken seriously) but it may still be possible to construe the

29 To spare the governor's *existimatio* a saving clause is often inserted, e. g.: "*quoad tibi aequum et rectum videbitur,*" *Fam.* XIII, 14, 2; "*quibuscumque rebus honeste ac pro tua dignitate poteris, iuveris atque ornaveris,*" 22, 2; "*commendo tibi hominem, sic ut tua fides et meus pudor postulat … quae aequa postulabit ut libente te impetret,*" 58; "*servabis, ut tua fides et dignitas postulat, edictum et institutum tuum,*" 59; cf. also *Fam.* XIII, 61; 63; 67; 69, 2; 70; 72, 2; 73, 2. An elaborate expansion of the saving clause to justify the custom of recommendation is found in Fronto, *Epistulae Ad Amicos* I, 1 (M.P.J. Van den Hout, ed., *M. Cornelii Frontonis Epistulae* (Leiden: Brill, 1954), 164). On the importance of a man's *existimatio* cf. Zvi Yavetz, "Existimatio, Fama, and the Ides of March," *Harv. Stud.* 78 (1974): 35–65, esp. 41–2 on the governor's *existimatio*.

30 So Tyrrell and Purser, *The Correspondance of M. Tullius Cicero*, 505–6, n. 2.

31 As is implied in Shackleton Bailey's commentary ad loc., *Cicero: Epistulae Ad Familiares*, Vol. II, 447 (no. 202).

sentence quoted above as implying informal personal arbitration by virtue of the '*auctoritas*' and '*consilium*' vested in Sulpicius and referred to before in the same breath as his official powers, the '*ius*' and '*potestas*.'[32] However, if this is the case we must postulate a distinction between the usage of *controversia* in this section and its usage in the following one: only in the latter case is it used as a technical term to denote litigation and court proceedings.

There is not enough evidence to decide between the two alternatives offered above. It may be suggested, however, that the first is the true one: although the literal meaning of Cicero's words is formal arbitration, he had no intention that it should take place. For, in the first place, it is hardly conceivable that two different meanings of *controversia* could appear in such close proximity, and in the same context. Secondly, it is more than probable that Cicero was sending up a smoke-screen of politeness in order not to offend Sulpicius. However, whichever way the case is decided, the conclusion does not affect the main argument.

For, on both interpretations, with '*Illud praeterea*' we have reached the crux of the letter, where specific measures are proposed. Cicero is treading warily, as the staccato rhythm of the sentence clearly demonstrates. Caution was due, presumably, to make up for the fact that he wished Sulpicius to surrender a case which the latter was competent to judge himself; but perhaps for other reasons as well, not least those dictated by the *decorum* of writing letters of recommendation:

> *Illud praeterea, si non alienum tua dignitate putabis esse, feceris mihi pergratum, si qui difficiliores erunt, ut rem sine controversia confici nolint, si eos, quoniam cum senatore res est, Romam reieceris.*

Who were the potential litigants? Some assume that they were provincials.[33] Yet, if one juxtaposes here the letter sent subsequently, it becomes extremely probable

32 "*Peto igitur ... ut eius negotia, quae sunt in Achaia ex eo quod heres est M. Mindio, fratri suo ... explices et expedias cum iure et potestate, quam habes, tum etiam auctoritate et consilio tuo*" (*Fam.* XIII, 26, 2). For other instances of the juxtaposition of official powers and personal qualities see *Fam.* XIII, 42: "*vehementer opus est nobis et voluntatem et auctoritatem et imperium tuum accedere*"; 6, 4: "*omne genus liberalitatis, quod et ab humanitate et potestate tua proficisci poterit.*"

33 So Mommsen, *Römisches Staatsrecht*, Vol. III, 748 and n. 5; 1214, n. 3; Garnsey, *Social Status and Legal Privilege in the Roman Empire*, 195, and n. 3; 217, n. 1; 236, n. 6; M.I. Henderson, "Potestas Regia," *JRS* 57 (1957): 83; Shackleton Bailey, *Cicero: Epistulae Ad Familiares*, Vol. II, 448. Since these provincial claimants could not have been heirs, Mommsen *et al.* must have assumed that they had claims on the estate. For such a case cf. *QFr.* I, 2, 10–11: the city of Apollonis was instructed by Q. Cicero not to let the praetor designate, L. Flavius, come into the inheritance left to him in Asia by L. Octavius Naso, before the demands on it were met. But I doubt if this is the case here; see text above.

that the potential litigant was Mindius' widow, who had appropriated most of the inheritance (*Fam.* XIII, 28, 2):

> *deinde, cum fere consistat hereditas in iis rebus, quas avertit Oppia, quae uxor Mindi fuit, adiuves ineasque rationem quem ad modum ea mulier Romam perducatur. Quod si putarit illa fore, ut opinio nostra est, negotium conficiemus.*

The close verbal resemblance between the measures proffered here and those suggested for dealing with her (she could be threatened with being sent to Rome) suggests that "*si qui difficiliores*" hints at this woman without explicitly naming her.

The measure itself, "*ut ... eos ... Romam reieceris,*" is better dealt with in conjunction with what follows immediately after:

> *Quod quo minore dubitatione facere possis, litteras ad te a M. Lepido consule, non quae te aliquid iuberent (neque enim id tuae dignitatis esse arbitramur), sed quodam modo quasi commendaticias sumpsimus.*

The legal and constitutional background to this request poses difficult problems which must be discussed before a new interpretation is offered.

III

A.H.M. Jones took the measure requested here to be:[34]

> a clue to the true nature of *Romae revocatio*. In asking for it a provincial litigant announced his intention of appealing from the proconsul to the consul at Rome, whose *imperium* extended to all provinces and was *maius* in relation to that of their proconsuls; for as Cicero remarks, '*omnes in consulis iure et imperio debent esse provinciae.*' A reasonable proconsul would no doubt usually allow the litigant to go to Rome and make his appeal, but as it was not physically possible for him to make the actual appeal except after a long delay, a stubborn proconsul would ignore his request and proceed with the trial. A litigant could only make sure of securing a *revocatio Romae* by approaching the consul beforehand, as Mescinius did through Cicero's agency, and getting from him a letter in which he informed the proconsul that he would give his *auxilium* if an appeal were made to him, and ordered him in that case to remit the case to Rome.

Jones' reconstruction is based on several preconceptions: (1) that this is a case of an appeal; (2) that an appeal could be launched before the judicial proceedings have started; (3) that there was an appeal from the proconsul to the consul in Rome.

34 Jones, "Imperial and Senatorial Jurisdiction in the Early Principate," 76–7.

Garnsey, on the other hand, does not consider this a case of appeal. To him it is a special case of the *reiectio iudicii*, under which he subsumes not only cases of a rejection of a limited number of *iudices* and *recuperatores*, which was permitted under civil procedure and in *quaestiones*, but even a rejection of the form of trial laid down by the magistrate, and his *reiectio Romam* falls into this category.[35]

Lintott criticized Garnsey's model on two fronts. It is his view that an appeal was possible at any stage, at least theoretically, and therefore he maintains that Garnsey "goes too far in limiting *provocatio* to appeals after sentence." Secondly he asserts that "although rejection of a limited number of *iudices* or *recuperatores* was permitted under civil procedure and in *quaestiones*, whether permanent or *ad hoc*, in the Republic as a right, rejection of the form of trial laid down by a magistrate in any respect, including his provisions for the selection of judges, seems to have needed backing from the tribunes, if it was to be effective."[36]

We know of only one other attempt in the late Republic to transfer a civil suit from the provinces to Rome. P. Scandilius, a Roman knight, challenged Q. Apronius to a *sponsio*: "*ni te* (i. e. Verrem) *Apronius socium in decumis esse dicat*," and asked Verres for a *iudex* or *recuperatores*. On realizing that Verres was going to impose on him *recuperatores* from his own biased *cohors*, rather than from *conventus* of *negotiatores*, Scandilius demanded ("*postulat*") from the governor: "*ut Roman rem reicias*." Verres refused: "*negas te Romam reiecturum*."[37]

These two instances, usually quoted together, constitute, it seems, the only evidence for the so-called right of Roman citizens in the provinces to ask for a remittal of their case to Rome, or to put it differently, for a choice between two Roman courts, that of the provincial governor and that of the praetor in Rome.[38]

---

35 Garnsey, "The Lex Iulia and Appeal under the Empire," 122–3; Garnsey, "The Criminal Jurisdiction of Governors," 56–7; Garnsey, *Social Status and Legal Privilege in the Roman Empire*, 263–4.

36 Andrew W. Lintott, "Provocatio. From the Struggle of the Orders to the Principate," in *Aufstieg und Niedergang der römischen Welt*, Vol. I.2 (Berlin: De Gruyter, 1972), 264–5, and cf. 239, n. 68.

37 *Verr.* II, 3, 135–140. On the procedure '*sponsione provocare*' see now John Crook, "Sponsione Provocare: Its Place in Roman Litigation," *JRS* 66 (1976): 132–38; once the *sponsio* offered outside the court is accepted, normal legal proceedings take place in court.

38 It is an entirely different matter to speak, as Wlassak and Mommsen do (above, n. 12), of the right of the governor to surrender a case to Rome. It should be noted, though, that in *Römisches Strafrecht*, 234, Mommsen states that "es mag auch der beklagte Römer unter Umständen die gleiche Befugnis (i. e. to demand a trial in Rome) gehabt haben." No evidence, however, is brought in support of this statement. Wlassak regards the two cases of '*reicere Romam*' as one of the proofs that the praetor's jurisdiction extended to the provinces (*Der Judikationsbefehl der römischen Prozesse*, 85 f.).

However, choice of courts was, as Garnsey seems to admit, a special privilege individually bestowed and not part and parcel of the possession of Roman citizenship.[39] The fact that it was also granted to *peregrini*[40] suggests that there was no necessary connection between citizenship and choice of court; the latter called for a special grant, and even then it was liable to certain restrictions. Asclepiades and the *socii* could use their privilege only to seek redress for debts incurred during their absence from Rome. Seleucus and his kin had recourse to choice of courts only *qua* defendants; the privilege did not constitute any derogation of the principle *actor sequitur forum rei.*[41]

Another doubt supervenes: is the assumption that the two cases, namely that of Scandilius and that of Mescinius, are identical at all well grounded? It should be recalled that the request to send the matter to Rome took place at different stages in these two instances. Scandilius' request came after the *sponsio* had been made and the parties had failed to agree on the judges. Verres, according to Scandilius, rejected any *iudex* from the province: "*ex provincia Sicilia tota statuas* (i. e. Verres) *idoneum iudicem aut recuperatorem nullum posse reperiri*,"[42] and Scandilius refused to accept the *recuperatores* proposed by Verres. It was, therefore, during the *reiectio* stage, the challenge of the judges, that Scandilius asked that the case be sent to Rome; not as an 'alternative *forum*' but as the only one, since none that was not *iniquum* was available in the province. He was not exercising

39 Garnsey, "The Criminal Jurisdiction of Governors," 57, concurring with Giuseppe Ignazio Luzzatto, *Epigrafia giuridica greca e romana* (Milano: A. Giuffrè, 1942), 292f., 317f.; Leopold Wenger, "Neue Diskussionen zum Problem 'Reichsrecht und Volksrecht,'" in *Mélanges Fernand de Visscher*, ed. Lucien Caes, Vol. II (Bruxelles: Office international de librairie, 1949), 542f. for the controversy. Francesco De Martino, *Storia della costituzione romana*, Vol. II (Napoli: E. Jovene, 1973), 385, Léon Gallet, "Essai sur le sénatus-consulte 'de Asclepiade Sociisque,'" *RHDFÉ* 16 (1937): 287, and Vincenzo Arangio-Ruiz, "Sul problema della doppia cittadinanza nella Repubblica e nell'impero romano," in *Scritti giuridici in onore di Francesco Carnelutti* (Padova: CEDAM, 1950), 68, maintain that Roman citizens in the provinces always enjoyed a choice between local courts and Roman courts.

40 Asclepiades of Clazomenae, Polystratus of Carystus, Meniscus of Miletus and their families received this privilege in 78 BC; see *S.C. de Asclepiade Sociisque* in Robert K. Sherk, *Roman Documents from the Greek East* (Baltimore: Johns Hopkins Press, 1969), 127, no. 22, ll. 17–20.

41 Fernand De Visscher, "Le statut juridique des nouveaux citoyens romains et l'inscription de Rhosos," *L'Antiquité Classique* 14 (1945): 44: "dans la mesure où il s'agirait d'obtenir réparation des torts qu'ils auraient subis par suite de leur absence." A similar view is expressed by Anthony J. Marshall, "Friends of the Roman People," *AJPhil.* 89 (1968): 39–55, who claims against Gallet, "Essai sur le sénatus-consulte 'de Asclepiade Sociisque'" that the legal privilege of choice of court was not part and parcel of the status of *amicus populi Romani*, Marshall, "Friends of the Roman People," 50–1.

42 *Verr.* II, 3, 138.

his right as a Roman citizen to have his case tried in Rome, but his right to have a just *iudex*. It is on this score that Cicero took Verres to task, and not for denying a Roman citizen his 'natural' right.

In Mescinius' case we are at an earlier stage: the matter should be taken to Rome only if legal proceedings could not be avoided.[43] Only here can we speak of a request for a change of venue proper. And, as was hinted before, Cicero's manner and tone do not suggest that he was vindicating Mescinius' right to be tried in Rome.

Nor does a survey of linguistic usage at the time (or even later) lend any support to the notion of *reiectio Romam* as an established legal right: the precise phrase occurs nowhere in either legal or non-legal sources.[44] In the two known instances from the late Republic a concrete phrase is used: "*Romam reicias*" and "*Romam reieceris.*"[45] There is no attestation of an 'action noun' to describe the idea of '*reicere ad/in aliquem locum.*' We have here yet another instance of the fundamental importance of the distinction, established by Daube, between the use of 'action verbs' and the crystallization of the concept in the form of the corresponding noun.[46] The noun *reiectio* is applied to "one sector of the verb," to use Daube's words, that of '*reicere aliquem*' or '*aliquid,*' which conveys an entirely different idea. To make the *reiectio*-procedure include not only a challenge of a limited number of *iudices* but also a change of venue is an illegitimate extension of the term which distorts not only the legal situation (as Lintott rightly observed),[47] but linguistic usage as well.

Moreover, "the power to launch a *reiectio Romam*" indicates "a yet further evolution of the theory" and "is secondary compared with the act itself."[48] Two instances of a request to remit a case to Rome, which are not even identical, do not permit us to postulate the existence of the institution, let alone the right, of *reiectio Romam*.

---

43 Even in the subsequent letter, *Fam.* XIII, 28, where a *cautio* is mentioned, we are still before the *litis contestatio* stage. See Kaser, *Das römische Zivilprozessrecht*, 209, and below p. 17.

44 The noun *reiectio* is not attested at all in the *Vocabularium Iurisprudentiae Romanae*; its occurrences in Cicero's speeches (*Verr.* I, 1, 10; 16; *Verr.* II, 2, 41; *Planc.* 36; *Sull.* 92; *Vat.* 28) and letters (*Att.* I, 16, 3) invariably refer to the challenging of *iudices* or *recuperatores*, never to a transfer of the case from one court to another.

45 Cf. also the concrete verbal expression used to convey the idea of remitting a case to a local court: "*ad leges suas reicere,*" *Verr.* II, 2, 59; 60; 90.

46 David Daube, *Roman Law: Linguistic, Social and Philosophical Aspects* (Edinburgh: Edinburgh University Press, 1969), chapter 1 *passim*, esp. 37.

47 See n. 36 above.

48 Daube, *Roman Law: Linguistic, Social and Philosophical Aspects*, 21 and 56.

If we cannot accept Garnsey's *reiectio Romam* as the key to the interpretation of Cicero's request on Mescinius' behalf, can we admit the original doctrine which he challenged, namely Jones' *revocatio Romae* as a case of appeal?

Unlike Garnsey's *reiectio Romam*, Jones' *revocatio Romae* is attested once in our sources. The Fragmentum Atestinum declares that it is not the purpose of the present law to allow a *Romae revocatio* of cases already instituted before the local magistrates, even when the sum of money involved exceeded the latter's competence.[49] However, as Kaser points out, the *revocatio Romae* does not presuppose a judgement given by a local magistrate, and therefore does not imply as appeal.[50] Moreover, as we learn from the Lex Rubria, the remittal of a case to Rome by means of *vadimonium Romam faciendum* is carried out through a judgement (*decretum*) of a local magistrate who had the power to enforce it if the party concerned failed to enter into it.[51] In other words, *revocatio Romae*, if used here at all as a technical term (which may be doubted) was a procedural measure reflecting the division of powers between the central court in Rome and municipal courts in Italy, and was made probably in the interests of convenience of cases which went beyond the competence of the local magistrates.[52] In any case, nowhere does the *revocatio Romae* procedure appear to be consequent upon an appeal launched by the litigant against the local magistrate's decision.

Finally, *revocatio Romae* in the sense in which it is used in the Fragmentum Atestinum and implied in the Lex Rubria is not pertinent in the case of provincial governors whose full competence in the sphere of civil jurisdiction has never been questioned.[53]

But although *Fam.* XIII, 26, 3 cannot serve as Jones' "clue to the true nature of *revocatio Romae*," it may still be argued that it represents the right procedure for lodging an appeal against a provincial governor. On this view Mescinius secured in advance a promise of *auxilium* from the consul, which made a remittal of the

---

49 Salvatore Riccobono, ed., *Fontes Iuris Romani AnteIustiniani*, Vol. I (Florence: Barbèra, 1941), 177, ll. 17–23: "*eius rei pequn[iaeve] quo magis privato Romae revocation sit ... ex h(ac) l(ege) n(ihilum) r(ogatur).*"

50 Kaser, *Das römische Zivilprozessrecht*, 128, n. 43.

51 Riccobono, *Fontes Iuris Romani AnteIustiniani*, Vol. I, 174, ll. 23 f. If not actually a portion of the Lex Rubria, the fragment from Ateste is at least closely related to it. So M.W. Frederiksen, "The Lex Rubria: Reconsiderations," *JRS* 54 (1964): 129–34. F.J. Bruna, *Lex Rubria: Caesars Regelung für die richterlichen Kompetenzen der Munizipalmagistrate in Gallia Cisalpina* (Leiden: Brill, 1972), 308–25, puts the fragment earlier, but admits that it is part of the same legislation. See Mommsen, *Römisches Staatsrecht*, Vol. III, 817–18.

52 Frederiksen, "The Lex Rubria: Reconsiderations," 132–3.

53 Giovanni Pugliese, *Il processo civile romano*, Vol. II (Milano: Giuffre, 1963), 156–7, and above n. 11.

case to Rome compulsory. An appeal to the consul in matters concerning civil jurisdiction was theoretically possible: our almost complete lack of evidence for consular intervention in civil jurisdiction in the Late Republic does not of itself prove that Mescinius was legally debarred from doing so.[54] It might be suggested, therefore, that the consul could impose his authority by virtue of his right of *intercessio*.[55] The two passages which seem to exclude *intercessio* in the provinces might represent no more than "a practical exemption of the provincial governor from this check."[56] But, if the consul's *litterae quasi commendaticiae* represented an *intercessio*, then Cicero's protest "*non quae te aliquid iuberent*" puts its author in the worst light possible: he is patently insincere and Sulpicius will realize this as soon as he reads the consul's letter. Thus Jones' attempt to detect behind our letter an *appellatio-auxilium* mechanism is incompatible with what is actually said about the nature of the consul's letter.

Garnsey, on the other hand, sees an entirely different causal connection between the request for remittal to Rome and the consul's letter; to him the latter is the ultimate proof that the governor was under no compulsion to transfer the case to Rome, that is, that his hands were not tied by an appeal: "The request was backed by *commendaticiae litterae* from the consul, a manoeuvre which was surely superfluous if the governor was allowed no discretion in the matter."[57]

A letter of recommendation (*litterae commendaticiae*), as can be inferred from the present context, had no official status and, therefore, did not purport to achieve its aim by command but by request. A comparison of the present usage of the term with that occurring in an earlier letter addressed to Cicero's former colleague in the consulate, C. Antonius Hibrida, then (end of December, 62 BC) governor of Macedonia, confirms this impression and yields more information about the connotation of the term:[58]

---

54 Cf. *Valerius Maximus* VII, 7, 6 (77 BC) for consular interference with a praetor's decision. Mommsen (*Römisches Staatsrecht*, Vol. II, 101) allows the consuls an *intercessio* against the praetor, by virtue of their *maior potestas*, although he denies that the consuls possessed civil jurisdiction after 366 BC. But cf. Greenidge, *The Legal Procedure of Cicero's Time*, 28–9.

55 But since the result of the *intercessio* was only purely cassatory (cf. Greenidge, 517–18; Kaser, *Das römische Zivilprozessrecht*, 125–6), it is hard to see how it could have helped Mescinius to transfer his case to Rome.

56 *Verr.* II, 2, 30; *QFr.* I, 1, 22; Greenidge, *The Legal Procedure of Cicero's Time*, 289.

57 Garnsey, "The Criminal Jurisdiction of Governors," 57.

58 *Fam.* V, 5, 1. On the background see Erich S. Gruen, "The Trial of C. Antonius," *Latomus* 32 (1973): 301–10.

> *Etsi statueram nullas ad te litteras mittere nisi commendaticias (non quo eas intellegerem satis apud te valere, sed ne iis, qui me rogarent, aliquid de nostra coniunctione imminutum esse ostenderem), tamen, cum T. Pomponius, homo omnium meorum in te studiorum et officiorum maxime conscius, tui cupidus, nostri amantissimus, ad te proficisceretur, aliquid mihi scribendum putavi, praesertim cum aliter ipsi Pomponio satis facere non possum.*

Cicero wrote letters of recommendation to Antonius not because he believed in their effectiveness, but in order to conjure up the atmosphere that the exchange of such letters evokes: a close relationship between two friends who are ready to do each other a good turn.

But it may be argued that the consul's letter was '*quasi commendaticiae*' and that Cicero's qualifying phrase "*non quae te aliquid iuberent*" still shows that "a consul could issue commands to a proconsul by letter,"[59] or "might actually have done so in the case of a governor of less exalted status."[60] Indeed Cicero's qualifying phrase has been used to prove that the consul held an *imperium* that was *maius* than that of the proconsul. Even those who contest the consul's superiority and dismiss the whole notion of *imperium maius* as a piece of antiquarianism and as 'trivial theorizing' seem to admit that the only natural implication of Cicero's phrase is that an order could have been issued from Rome. Thus, M.I. Henderson suggests that "this hypothetical instruction need not have come from the consul *iure suo*, rather than from the Senate, whose instructions it was his normal duty to transmit."[61] This is more or less a recasting of Mommsen's "ein Befehl der Regierung."[62]

Fortunately we do not have to take sides in the larger issue, namely, the implication which Cicero's phrase has for the question of the control exercised by the Roman government on provincial governors.[63] Whichever way the matter is decided there does not seem to be good reason why we should doubt Cicero's sincerity when he denies that the consul's letter is an order. On the other hand,

---

59 A.H.M. Jones, "The Imperium of Augustus," *JRS* 41 (1951): 113, n. 7. Similarly Victor Ehrenberg, who in "Imperium Maius in the Roman Republic," *AJPhil.* 74 (1953): 116, n. 8, describes the consul's letter as the "*imperium maius*" of the consul taking "the form of an advice rather than a command."

60 Shackleton Bailey, *Cicero: Epistulae Ad Familiares*, Vol. II, 448 (no. 292).

61 Henderson, "Potestas Regia," 83 f.

62 "Die Regierung" clearly refers to the Senate. See *Römisches Staatsrecht*, Vol. III, 1211 f. for the Senate's supervisory role in the provinces. Moreover the post-Sullan consuls, according to Mommsen, lost all influence over the provinces (*Römisches Staatsrecht*, Vol. II, 94 f.; Mommsen, *Römische Geschichte*, Vol. II (Leipzig: Weidmannsche Buchhandlung, 1855), 354 f.).

63 Cf., however, Hugh Last, "Imperium Maius: A Note," *JRS* 37 (1947): 157–64, for a balanced view.

because it was a letter from the consul and not from a *privatus* it would be hard to account for it simply as one of the unofficial interventions in provincial affairs (including jurisdiction) which fill the pages of Book XIII of the *Ad Familiares*, powerful though these may often have been.[64] It is this semi-official nature of the consul's letter that distinguishes it from other letters of recommendation and which is, as we shall see, one of the clues to its meaning.

Serious gaps in essential background information make the interpretation of the two letters, *Fam*. XIII, 26 and 28, difficult. Did Cicero really desire that the legal proceedings should be conducted in Rome? If he did, what were his reasons for insisting on it? Was his reluctance to leave litigation in Sulpicius' hands due to a personal distrust of Sulpicius the man, or was there a fundamental disadvantage in its being left in the province? In other words, was the provincial governor less competent to provide legal remedies than the praetor in Rome, in spite of all that we know to the contrary?

A different set of problems is provided by *Fam*. XIII, 28: might there have been a plurality of claims and not, as we have tacitly assumed so far, only one counter-claimant?

Cicero opens the letter with an enthusiastic expression of gratitude to Sulpicius for all that the governor had promised and done for Mescinius through the latter's procurators. He then puts forward two requests which are hard to reconcile with the enthusiastic *actio gratiarum*, or with those made in *Fam*. XIII, 26. Firstly, Cicero asks that if 'security' has to be given to guarantee that the action would not be repeated by the *dominus* ("*amplius eo nomine non peti*"), then he, Cicero, should be made responsible ("*cures, ut satis detur fide mea*"). He clearly envisages here that legal proceedings might be conducted in the province by the procurators acting in Mescinius' name.[65] But in contradistinction to *Fam*. XIII, 26, 2–3, this time he raises no objections; he is not even disappointed with this turn of events, as one might have expected. But if he has reconciled himself to litigation in the province, he still seems not to have entirely given up his previous plan, to judge by his next request (*Fam*. XIII, 28, 2):

> *deinde, cum fere consistat hereditas in iis rebus, quas avertit Oppia, quae uxor Mindi fuit, adiuves ineasque rationem quem ad modum ea mulier Romam perducatur.*

64 See, for example, *Fam*. XIII, 41; 42; 56, where Cn. Pompeius Magnus' influence is brought to bear, and *Fam*. XIII, 50, where Cicero reminds the governor, M. Acilius, of the latter's obligation to him: the governor was indebted to Cicero for defending him twice successfully in capital trials, *Fam*. VII, 30, 3.

65 See Francesco Guizzi, "In tema di origini della 'cautio de rato,'" *Labeo* 7 (1961): 334–5; Franco Casavola, *Actio Petitio Persecutio* (Napoli: Jovene, 1965), 94 f.

The two requests, notwithstanding the way in which they are put by Cicero, are alternative rather than complementary ways of action.

These problems must be stated, even though they cannot be solved. We simply do not possess all the necessary facts, and, therefore, cannot hope to grasp all the issues involved in the case. The elusive evidence contained in the letters accords well with the genre to which they belong; much is left unsaid or taken for granted.[66] Therefore, no further attempt will be made here to smooth over seemingly self-contradictory statements and irreconcilable pieces of evidence. But it may be stated once more that it is highly probable that it is precisely the question of bringing Mindius' widow (and other parties?) to Rome which is foreshadowed in *Fam.* XIII, 26, 3 by the phrase: "*si qui difficiliores erunt.*" Thus we may now proceed to offer a new interpretation of Cicero's request "*ut eos* (i.e. "*si qui difficiliores erunt*") *Romam reieceris*" and of the purpose of the consul's letter.

IV

The consul's letter was of a semi-official nature. To construe it, as both Mommsen and Jones do,[67] as a decree aiming to force Sulpicius' hand against his wishes, or regardless of his wishes, is a gross misapprehension of what is actually said and implied about its purpose. Instead, there is room for quite a different interpretation, namely that the consul's letter *aimed to free Sulpicius' hand* to force the recalcitrant opponents to go to Rome, to dispel any doubts he might have had about doing so (*Fam.* XIII, 26, 3): "*Quod quo minore dubitatione facere possis, litteras ad te a M. Lepido consule ... sumpsimus.*" Cicero suspected that the governor's scruples might stand in his way, and the consul's letter was designed to mollify them. 'The most eminent living jurist' might well have entertained some doubt about the plaintiff's attempt to force the defendant to leave his (or her) *forum* and face a legal action in Rome. It may be suggested that it was precisely because Mescinius

66 For reasons of *decorum* (see p. 7 above), or because the letter of recommendation does not constitute the only source of information available to the recipient. Here presumably, Mescinius' procurators will supply the governor with information (*Fam.* XIII, 26, 2; 28, 1). Elsewhere we hear of an oral recommendation which preceded the written one (e.g.: *Fam.* VI, 8, 3; XIII, 3; 6, 1; 7, 1; 9, 1; 55, 1–2; 72, 1; 75, 1). It is sometimes attested that the letter was delivered by the recommended person's own hand (e.g.: *Fam.* XIII, 6a; VII, 30, 3; VI, 8, 3); we may safely assume that having been given a proper introduction, the recommended himself will go into further details. See *Dig.* 41, 1, 65 pr. for the implication that a letter of recommendation becomes the legal property of the interested party.

67 Above, pp. 3, 10.

did not possess a right to demand a remittal of the case to Rome,[68] that both Cicero and the consul chose a "diffident and delicate approach," to use Henderson's words.[69] Far from standing up for a so-called right possessed by his protégé, or by the régime, to demand a remittal to Rome, Cicero, as the whole drift of the letter shows, is at pains to deal with the difficulties arising from the absence of legal means to force the opponents to go to Rome; and, above all, to make it possible for Sulpicius to comply with Cicero's request without compromising his own dignity and integrity.[70] It is, therefore, at this crucial juncture, i. e. before specifying his request, that Cicero inserts the saving clause, familiar from other interventions in litigation: "*Illud praeterea, si non alienum tua dignitate putabis esse, feceris mihi pergratum.*"

The consul's letter, on this interpretation, commits its writer to supporting Sulpicius' action. It also gives a semi-official sanction to Cicero's request. However, its semi-official nature, which is of crucial importance, is a double-edged weapon: its import and meaning might be misconstrued by Sulpicius, as they were by modern scholars, as an attempt to coerce him, perhaps by virtue of "some vague and traditional control of the consul over the proconsuls."[71] To forestall such suspicions, Cicero hastens to add: "*non quae te aliquid iuberent (neque enim id tuae dignitatis esse arbitramur), sed quodam modo quasi commendaticias* ...";

---

68 In Cyprus and Sicily, it was forbidden to 'evoke' provincials from their *forum*. See *Att.* V, 21, 6, where the prefect Q. Volusius is sent to Cyprus to administer justice to Roman citizens: "*nam evocari ex insula Cyprios non licet*"; *Verr.* II, 3, 38: "*Iam vero illud non solum contra legem Hieronicam nec solum contra consuetudinem superiorum, sed etiam contra omnia iura Siculorum quae habent a senatu populoque Romano, ne quis extra suum forum vadimonium promittere cogatur.*" We cannot take it for granted that the same judicial order prevailed in Achaea, nor that provincials and Roman citizens were treated alike, but these two possibilities cannot be dismissed out of hand. The request to the governor of Asia to force Alabanda and Mylasa to send *ecdici* to Rome (*Fam.* XIII, 56, 1) does not prove that a different rule held there; both were free cities (see Pliny the Elder, *Naturalis Historia* V, 108) and therefore outside the provincial governor's authority. Legal proceedings in which free cities were involved were presumably to be conducted in Rome. On judicial rights of free cities see Rainer Bernhardt, "Imperium und Eleutheria: Die römische Politik gegenüber den freien Städten des griechischen Ostens" (University of Hamburg Thesis, 1971), 98 f.

69 Henderson, "Potestas Regia," 83.

70 In other words, the consul's letter was intended to take care of Sulpicius' concern for his *existimatio*, on which see above, n. 29. The list of saving clauses quoted and referred to there makes it abundantly clear that the governor's reputation rested entirely on his *iustitia*, *fides*, *aequitas* and preservation of what is *ius*, *honestum* and *rectum*. Cf. also Cicero's exhortation to his brother Quintus when the latter was governor of Asia: "*Qua re sint haec fundamenta dignitatis tuae: tua primum integritas et continentia*" (*QFr.* I, 1, 18), and a little further: "*qua re sit summa in ius dicendo severitas, dum modo ea ne varietur gratia sed conservetur aequabilis*" (*Ibid.*, 20).

71 So Ronald Syme, *The Roman Revolution* (Oxford: Clarendon Press, 1939), 330.

lest Sulpicius take offence, Cicero explains to which category the consul's letter belongs: "*quasi commendaticias*," namely a letter between friends.

It is legitimate to inquire at this point whether a procedure existed which Sulpicius could follow if he were to comply with the request and send the defendant to Rome. The evidence is inconclusive, but it does suggest that the governor could have demanded that the defendant give a guarantee (*vadimonium*) to appear before the praetor in Rome. This is suggested by a document from the very province with which we are dealing, namely from Achaea. However, unlike our case, it concerns a matter of criminal jurisdiction involving a non-citizen. Timotheus, found to be less guilty than the other two insurgents in Dyme, who have been put to death by the governor, is ordered by the latter (in 115 BC) to proceed (or be taken) to Rome. The governor has made him swear (ὁρκίσας) to appear before the peregrine praetor by a certain date, and not to return home until ... (here the text breaks off).[72]

The procedure existed then, but did it apply also in civil cases, when the party concerned was a Roman citizen, as Mescinius' opponents probably were, and to a defendant as well? We simply do not know, but Cicero's tone, as suggested above, does imply that it was irregular, and, if the present interpretation is followed, the consul's letter was intended to anticipate any reluctance on Sulpicius' part to act irregularly.

The consul's letter may have served an additional purpose, namely of intimidating Mescinius' opponents. And if it is right to suggest high social status for the potential opponents – i. e. if "*difficiliores*" in *Fam.* XIII, 26, 3 is a reference to Mindius' widow, Oppia – the governor might have found the consul's support quite useful.[73]

---

72 Sherk, *Roman Documents from the Greek East*, no. 43 (= *Syll.* 684), ll. 23–7: Τιμόθεον δὲ Νικία τὸμ μετὰ τοῦ Σώσου | [γεγονό]τα νομογράφον, ἐπεὶ ἔλασσον ἐφαίνετο ἠδικηκώς, ἐ||[κέλευσα] προάγειν εἰς Ῥώμην ὁρκίσας, ἐφ' [ὧ]ι τῆι νουμηνίαι τοῦ ἐν||[άτου μηνὸ]ς ἔστα[ι] ἐκεῖ καὶ ἐμφανίσας τ[ῶι ἐ]πὶ τῶν ξένων στρατη||[γῶι τὸ δόξ]αν, [μὴ π]ρότερον ἐπά[ν]εισ[ιν εἰ]ς οἶκον, ἐὰ[ν μ]ὴ ΑΥ[-] For the date see Broughton, *The Magistrates of the Roman Republic*, Vol. II, 644. Naphtali Lewis and Meyer Reinhold, eds., *Roman Civilization: Selected Readings*, Vol. I (New York: Columbia University Press, 1951), no. 127, translate προάγειν as 'to proceed'; taken as transitive, it is the equivalent of *perducatur* in *Fam*. XIII, 28, 2.

73 M. Mindius was a knight (above, n. 2). His wife could have belonged to a senatorial family; cf. Nicolet, *L'ordre équestre à l'époque républicaine*, Vol. I, 258. *Fam*. XIII, 72 provides us with impressive evidence for the influence that a woman of high social standing could have brought to bear on the governor. Caerellia, Cicero's friend, seems to have procured the passage of a *senatus consultum* in favour of the heirs to the property of the *negotiator* C. Vennonius in Asia. Little doubt is left about its purpose: "*Equidem existimo habere te magnam facultatem ... ex eo s. c., quod in heredes C. Vennoni factum est Caerelliae commodandi*" (*Fam*. XIII, 72, 2). It may be noted in pass-

Confirmation of this conjecture can be found in the subsequent letter, *Fam.* XIII, 28, 2, where Cicero suggests that if Oppia is induced to believe that she could be taken to Rome, then the matter could be settled, probably out of court ("*sine controversia*"), as Cicero desired in the first place:

> *ineasque rationem quem ad modum ea mulier Romam perducatur. Quod si putarit illa fore, ut opinio nostra est, negotium conficiemus.*

The modified request lends itself to two interpretations. Perhaps Cicero despaired of bringing about a remittal to Rome. From Cicero's protestations of gratitude (*Fam.* XIII, 28, 1) it appears that Sulpicius politely insisted on offering his good services, and thus, one can assume, had graciously turned down Cicero's request. This may be the reason for the absence of any reference to the consul's letter in *Fam.* XIII, 28. However, Cicero was still at pains to bring about a quick solution, and this, he believed, depended on the woman believing that she *could* be sent to Rome. For this, too, the governor's co-operation was needed;[74] he might not have wished to use his wide discretionary powers irregularly, but the *vadimonium* procedure did exist, and people could envisage being sent to Rome by the governor. Sulpicius, as Cicero implies, need do no more than pretend to be contemplating sending the woman to Rome; this will be sufficient to conclude the matter: "*negotium conficiemus.*" Or, according to the second interpretation, Cicero had *never* really intended to drag the woman to Rome, but merely to use the possibility as a threat which would induce her to settle out of court. The words "*Quod si putarit illa fore ... negotium conficiemus*" support the latter reading. In the light of these two interpretations the purpose of the consul's letter in *Fam.* XIII, 26, 3 can be seen as follows: either it was meant to lead directly to Sulpicius' sending the woman to Rome, or, it could increase the pressure on Oppia to settle out of court. There is a third possibility, albeit less likely, that by 'pulling rank' the letter might have hoodwinked the woman, who may not have known her rights,[75] into believing that she had no choice but to go to Rome. However, on all readings of the situation, the consul's letter in *Fam.* XIII, 26, 3 should be seen as part of the stratagem which Cicero had to enter into in the absence of regular legal devices.

---

ing that the *senatus consultum*, like the consul's letter, was not intended to force the governor's hand, but rather to stimulate action where a governor might otherwise have been reluctant to use his powers, even those in his discretion.

74 Cf. Cicero's emphasis on the freedom enjoyed by the provincial magistrates as compared with those in Rome, *QFr.* I, 1, 22.

75 See above, pp. 12 and 18 f. and nn. 41 and 68.

To conclude, it is suggested that these letters do not demonstrate that Roman citizens, even senators,[76] possessed a legal right to demand a remittal of their case from the provinces to Rome. Instead what we see is how Cicero and Mescinius simply resorted to the use of influence and semi-official pressure to secure their objective. The consul's letter was designed to ensure the success of the trick as well as to make sure of Sulpicius' co-operation, which was indispensable for it. As for the woman, she might well have walked into the trap, just as some modern scholars were to do.

76 The "*quoniam cum senator res est*" (*Fam.* XIII, 26, 3) appeals to Sulpicius' feeling of solidarity but it does not imply a right possessed by Mescinius to demand a remittal to Rome.

Military Tribunates and the Exercise of Patronage

Pliny's correspondence with imperial legates often proves a rich source of information which the author did not intend to convey – perhaps even tried to suppress.[1] Thus his requests for military tribunates for his protégés[2] constitute, together with one later document,[3] the only evidence we have for the right of imperial legates to grant this post directly and without reference to the emperor.[4] Otherwise our sources seem to be united in the belief that commissions to the equestrian military posts, namely the prefecture of a cohort, the military tribunate

1 See Ronald Syme, "Pliny and the Dacian Wars," *Latomus* 23 (1964): 750 = *Danubian Papers* (Bucharest: AIESEE, 1971), 245, who comments on the omission, deliberate according to him, of all military details in all of Pliny's letters to consular legates.

2 *Ep.* III, 8; IV, 4; VII, 22. *Ep.* II, 13 is often taken as a request for this post; cf. Theodor Mommsen, *Römisches Staatsrecht*, Vol. II (Graz: Akademische Druck- u. Verlagsanstalt, 1952), 266, n. 3. Syme gives along with the tribunate the alternative of a post on the governor's staff; cf. "Pliny's Less Successful Friends," *Historia* 9 (1960): 365 = *Roman Papers*, Vol. II (Oxford: Oxford University Press, 1979), 480. See below, p. 32. *Ep.* III, 2 might also be a request for this post, but it is fraught with problems. The addressee, Vibius Maximus, should perhaps not be identified with his homonym, the Prefect of Egypt in 103–107, cf. Arthur Stein, *Die Präfekten von Ägypten in der römischen Kaiserzeit* (Bern: Francke, 1950), 49 f.; there were at least three Vibii Maximi at the time, cf. Peter White, "Vibius Maximus, the Friend of Statius," *Historia* 22 (1973): 295–301. Moreover, Syme, who does make the identification, alerts us to the fact that *Ep.* III, 2 belongs before 103, hence when Vibius Maximus held a different post, "C. Vibius Maximus, Prefect of Egypt," *Historia* 6 (1957): 483 = *Roman Papers*, Vol. I, 356.

3 *CIL* XIII 3162, col. ii; cf. Hans-Georg Pflaum, *Le marbre de Thorigny* (Paris: H. Champion, 1948), 26–7. See below, p. 25 f.

4 Cf. Mommsen, *Römisches Staatsrecht*, Vol. II, 256–6; Fergus Millar, *The Emperor in the Roman World* (London: Duckworth, 1977), 284 f.

Article note: First published in *Chiron* 11 (1981): 229–238, with the following note: I am grateful to F. Millar and N. Horsfall for a critical reading of an earlier draft of this paper.

https://doi.org/10.1515/9783110770438-002

and the prefecture of an *ala* – as well as commissions to the centurionate[5] – were all in the gift of the emperor.[6]

We happen to possess two pieces of literary evidence, contemporary with Pliny's, whose message is diametrically opposed to his. The first is Statius' famous address to Abascantus, Domitian's freedman and *ab epistulis*:[7] *Silvae* V, 1. Enumerating the man's various responsibilities (*numerosior cura*), he mentions inter alia (94–98):

Praeterea, fidos dominus si dividat enses,
pandere quis centum valeat frenare, maniplos
inter missus eques, quis praecepisse cohorti,
quem deceat clari praestantior ordo tribuni,
quisnam frenigerae signum dare dignior alae.

It has long been recognized that the equestrian *militia* are enumerated here in an ascending order following upon the centurionate.[8] It was the *ab epistulis*' task to

5 Cf. Eric Birley, "Promotions and Transfers in the Roman Army, II: The Centurionate," *Carnuntum Jahrbuch*, 1963/64, 21. However, it seems that the Prefect of Egypt could commission auxiliary decurions: cf. *P.Mich.* III 164 (= Robert O. Fink, *Roman Military Records on Papyrus* (Cleveland: APA, 1971), no. 20), AD 213–244, with Henry Arthur Sanders, "Papyrus 1804 in the Michigan Collection," in *Classical Studies in Honor of John C. Rolfe*, ed. George Depue Hadzsits (Philadelphia: University of Pennsylvania Press, 1931), 265, esp. 281 and James Franklin Gilliam, "The Appointment of Auxiliary Centurions (P.Mich. 164)," *TAPA* 88 (1957): 155; *BGU* 696, col. i, ll. 20 f. (= Fink, *Roman Military Records on Papyrus*, no. 64), AD 156 with James Franklin Gilliam, "Paganus in BGU 696," *AJPhil.* 73 (1952): 75–6. *AE* 1917/18, nos. 74–5 are dedications to the legate of Numidia in AD 211–12, M. Aurelius Cominius Cassianus (*PIR* (2nd ed.) C 1265), and to his wife by his former *cornicularius* made a *decurio* by him: *C. Iulius Rogatianus decur ... ex corniculario eius provectus ab eo.*

6 Mommsen, *Römisches Staatsrecht*, Vol. II, 851. For a full discussion of the evidence see Millar, *The Emperor in the Roman World*, 284 f.

7 *CIL* VI 8598–9; *PIR* (2nd ed.) F 194.

8 Mommsen, *Römisches Staatsrecht*, Vol. II, 851, n. 3, followed by Alfred von Domaszewski, *Die Rangordnung des römischen Herres* (Köln: Böhlau, 1967), 47 f. and Pflaum, *Le marbre de Thorigny*, 26–7, identifies the *quis centum valeat frenare maniplos / inter missus eques* as the officer of the legionary cavalry, also called *tribunus militum* or *legionis*, who, as one may infer from the ascending order in Statius, occupied the lowest grade of the *militia equestris*. Hence Domaszewski, *Die Rangordnung des römischen Herres*, 47 f. (esp. 48, n. 1) makes the further identification of this commander with the *tribunus semestris* (on whom see below p. 31 f.). However, the only epigraphic proof for the post of *tribunus militum* standing beneath that of the *praefectus cohortis* is *ILS* 9471 discussed by Anton von Premerstein, "Die Offizierslaufbahn eines kleinasiatischen Ritters," *JÖAI* 13 (1910): 200 f., who, while accepting Mommsen's and Domaszewski's four-stage equestrian *militia* starting with the cavalry officer, restricts it to the period between Domitian and Trajan. However, it has been suggested recently by David Breeze, "The Organization of the

inform (*pandere*)[9] the man concerned – or perhaps, as will be suggested below, his commander-in-chief – of his commission, after the emperor had made the various appointments ("*fidos diminus si dividat enses*").[10]

Florus uses similar terms in *Vergilius, Poeta an Orator* III, 5:[11] "*Nempe si mihi maximus imperator vitem,*[12] *id est centum homines regendos tradidisset, non mediocris honos habitus mihi videtur; cedo si praefecturam, si tribunatum: nempe idem honos, nisi quod merces amplior.*"

Neither Statius nor Florus could have stated in less ambiguous terms the fact that all appointments emanated from the emperor. However, Pliny's evidence that imperial legates exercised complete freedom in this sphere is likewise beyond suspicion. His appeals to them to bestow military tribunates upon his protégés show that he entertained no doubt as to his addressees' ability to comply with his wish, did they so desire; no other obstacles were foreseen. Nor would a man like Pliny be found guilty of such gross indiscretion as to solicit a post knowing that the man solicited was not free to grant it.

The only way to reconcile these contradictory – and contemporary[13] – pieces of evidence seems to be to accept Mommsen's solution, namely that imperial

---

Legion: The First Cohort and The Equites Legionis," *JRS* 59 (1969): 50–55, that the absence of epigraphic evidence for the post of a commander of the legionary cavalry may not be accidental, especially in view of the fact that we do possess such evidence for non-commissioned officers of the cavalry: this post may not have existed at all. Millar's neat proposal, *The Emperor in the Roman World*, 286, n. 49, to identify Statius' *eques* as *centurio ex equite Romano* (on whom cf. Hans Zwicky, "Zur Verwendung des Militärs in der Verwaltung des römischen Kaiserzeit" (University of Zurich Thesis, 1944), 90 ff.) seems much more attractive.

9 For *pandere* = to inform, make known, followed by an indirect interrogative clause cf. Statius, *Thebais* I, 671 f.: *tu pande, quis Argos / advenias.*

10 Eric Birley understands the indirect object of *pandere* to be the emperor; his interpretation turns the *ab epistulis* into an "Adjutant General" and "Military Secretary": "The Equestrian Officers of the Roman Army," in *Roman Britain and the Roman Army: Collected Papers* (Kendal: T. Wilson, 1953), 142, 151; cf. also by the same author: "Promotions and Transfers in the Roman Army, II: The Centurionate," 21–2. But surely the emperor is personally responsible for the appointments; he is the one who distributes 'loyal swards.' The *ab epistulis* merely makes it known which job went to whom. This interpretation given long ago by Otto Hirschfeld, *Die kaiserlichen Verwaltungsbeamten bis auf Diocletian* (Berlin: Weidmann, 1905), 322, n. 2, seems to have been dormant for a long time. Pflaum, *Le marbre de Thorigny*, 26–7, however, accepts it. The issue is of considerable importance for the present discussion, as will be seen shortly.

11 Henrica Malcovati, ed., *L. Annaei Flori Quae Extant* (Rome: Libreria dello Stato, 1938), ad loc. = Carolus Halm, ed., *Flori Epitomae de Tito Livio* (Lipsiae: Teubner, 1854), 108.

12 For the 'rod' as the symbol of the centurionate cf. Juvenal, *Sat.* XIV, 193: *vitem posce libello* with Mayor's comment ad loc. in *Thirteen Satires of Juvenal* (London: Macmillan, 1872–1878).

13 Those letters of Pliny which come under discussion here, namely II, 13 (cf. above, n. 2); III, 8; IV, 4; and VII, 22, belong to the years 100/101 (cf. below, n. 45); 101 (cf. Ronald Syme, *Tacitus*, Vol.

legates were entitled to dispose of a limited number of military tribunates.[14] A clue to the exact way in which this was done is perhaps to be found in the later document mentioned above.[15] In a letter to his friend and protégé, the Viducassian T. Sennius Sollemnis, the governor of Lower Britain at the time (ca. 220), T. Claudius Paulinus,[16] writes:[17] "*semestris autem epistulam,*[18] *ubi propediem vacare coepi[t], mittam.*" From this text Mommsen concludes that a certain number of commissions (*epistulae*), taking the form of 'letters-patent' or 'blank forms' were issued (perhaps by the *ab epistulis*) to the legate, who would insert the names of his nominees later on.[19] In this way these commissions too would be regarded as emanating ultimately from the emperor.[20] Conversely, one may suggest, that without losing his grip on the 'power of patronage,' the emperor was graciously sharing it with his legates, who, in their turn – as Pliny's correspondence makes quite clear – shared it with their friends. Thus the continuous and inexorable growth of the imperial power was counter-balanced by the simultaneous emergence of a system of patronage going in the other direction – a not unfamiliar feature of political systems "where all decisions were made at the centre."[21] Del-

II (Oxford: Clarendon Press, 1958), 647, app. 14, no. 27); 103 (cf. below, n. 43); and 107 (cf. below, n. 51) respectively. Book IV of the *Silvae* was published in AD 95; cf. Friedrich Vollmer, ed., *P. Papinii Statii Silvarum Libri* (Leipzig: Teubner, 1898), 10 f. Book V might have been published posthumously, cf. D.W.T.C. Vessey, "Varia Statiana," *Classical Bulletin* 46 (1970): 51; however, there is no evidence that Statius outlived Domitian. *Vergilius, Poeta an Orator's* dramatic date is AD 102–3, and it shows traces of immediate publication: cf. Paul Jal, ed., *Florus, Æuvres*, Collection Budé (Paris: Les Belles Lettres, 1967), 101 f.

14 Mommsen, *Römisches Staatsrecht*, Vol. II, 266.

15 Above, n. 3.

16 Cf. *CIL* VII 1044 (*RIB* 1280, High Rochester) from 1 Jan.-Dec. 220; cf. Anthony R. Birley, "The Roman Governors of Britain," *Epigraphische Studien* 4 (1967): 88, no. 48.

17 *CIL* XIII 3162, col. ii, ll. 13–15.

18 For *semestris epistulam* = *semestris tribunatus epistulam* cf. Pliny, *Ep.* IV, 4: "*Hunc rogo semestri tribunatu splendidiorem et sibi et avunculo suo facias*" (below, p. 31 f.) and Juvenal VII, 88: "*ille et militiae multis largitur honorem / semestris, vatum digitos circumligat auro.*"

19 Mommsen, *Römisches Staatsrecht*, Vol. II, 266: "Vermutlich stellte der Kaiser den einzelnen Statthaltern nach Maßgabe ihres Ranges eine Anzahl solcher von ihm vollzogener Offizierspatente zu beliebiger Ausfüllung zu," followed by Pflaum, *Le marbre de Thorigny*, 26–7.

20 Mommsen, *Römisches Staatsrecht*, 266: "und sind dem Rechte nach auch diese Ernennungen als kaiserliche zu betrachten."

21 Millar, *The Emperor in the Roman World*, 286. See also the apt comment of Peter A. Brunt in "Review: Peter Garnsey, Social Status and Legal Privilege in the Roman Empire. Oxford: The Clarendon Press, 1970," *JRS* 62 (1972): 169: "A monarch may seek to depress all his subjects to the same level: the Roman Emperors upheld a hierarchical order." For modern examples of similar political systems see e.g. the anthropological studies of John K. Campbell, *Honour, Family and Patronage: A Study of Institutions and Moral Values in a Greek Mountain Community* (Oxford:

egation of power was thus painlessly achieved, not by means of an impersonal set of rules,[22] but by personal influence exercised by well-placed persons close to the emperor, who obtained for their protégés the favours (*beneficia*), which it was the emperor's exclusive prerogative to grant. The case of military tribunates was, therefore, unique only in so far as it seems that here the exercise of patronage was not merely encouraged from above,[23] but made technically possible with the aid of letters-patent.

Pliny's correspondence with imperial legates gives us the rare opportunity to discover how and under what terms this 'power of patronage' was shared with friends; secondly, as will be seen below, it adds some technical detail to the actual working of the system, and in turn may be used in support of Mommsen's hypothesis; finally, Pliny's requests for military tribunates for his protégés are highly reminiscent of a late Republican practice well documented in Cicero's correspondence with Caesar and his own brother, Quintus, in Gaul: they sometimes echo the vary terminology used in that context. The continuity in language, style and social assumptions has interesting implications if Mommsen's hypothesis is accepted. It may suggest that the extra-legal, unofficial Republican practice of sharing one's 'power of patronage' with friends had gone through a process of formalization under the Empire. In other words, once the emperor had become the sole recognized source of patronage, the Republican practice crystallized into an official and formal prerogative bestowed by the emperor on his legates and taking the form of letters-patent.[24]

We may begin with the last-mentioned point. It fell to the commanders of the Roman army in Republican times to nominate military tribunes in excess of the twenty-four *tribuni militum a populo*, or *comitiati*, elected in the *comitia tributa* and assigned to the first four legions. Those personally chosen by the command-

---

Clarendon Press, 1964), 259 f. and of J.A. Pitt-Rivers, *The People of the Sierra* (London: Weidenfeld and Nicolson, 1954), 155 f.

22 For the frame of reference see Max Weber, "The Types of Legitimate Domination," in *Economy and Society* (Berkeley: University of California Press, 1978), 212 f.

23 Cf. below, p. 29 and n. 32 there.

24 Another illustration of the process may be seen from a comparison of a late Republican and an Imperial grant of citizenship. Cicero, *Fam.* XIII, 36 (46 BC) and the 'Tabula Banasitana' (text in William Seston and Maurice Euzennat, "Un dossier de la chancellerie romaine, la Tabula Banasitana: Étude de diplomatique," *CR Acad. Inscr.* 115 (1971): 470–2) are extremely similar in both terminology and procedure: the Republican document mentions the intercession of Cicero (*rogatu meo*) and the Imperial document mentions *favor, testimonia* and *suffragatio* of the procurator who supported the request for citizenship; Caesar's *beneficium* has its counterpart in the *indulgentia principalis*, but the latter has acquired by now almost a technical sense and a legal status, for the emperor alone could grant citizenship.

ers were known by the obscure title of *Rufuli*.[25] The bestowal of the military tribunate would be regarded by the beneficiary as a *beneficium*, as Cicero's words in the recommendation of his former tribune, Q. Fufidius, seem to suggest: "*fuit in Cilicia mecum tribunus militum, quo in munere ita se tractavit, ut accepisse ab eo beneficium viderer, non dedisse*" (*Fam*. XIII, 12, 1).

Cicero, no doubt, was personally acquainted with Q. Fufidius, who hailed from his own home town[26] and belonged to the municipal aristocracy.[27] However, personal acquaintance was by no means an indispensable condition: on occasion a governor in command of legions might bestow a military tribunate on a complete stranger, being induced to do so by the intervention of a third party. Furthermore, like Caesar he might betray complete indifference as to the identity of the candidate, and seek simply to satisfy the latter's patron.[28] Nor, it would seem, did the patron himself care much for the military tribunate: his foremost concern was to obtain the governor's goodwill for his protégé. Thus Cicero did not press for any particular post in his recommendation of the young jurisconsult, C. Trebatius Testa, to Iulius Caesar in Gaul in 54 BC (*Fam*. VII, 5, 3): "*Huic ego neque tribunatum neque praefecturam neque ullius beneficii certum nomen peto, benevolentiam tuam et liberalitatem peto neque impedio quo minus, si tibi ita placuerit, etiam hisce eum ornes gloriolae insignibus*." As it happened, Caesar offered Trebatius a military tribunate which the latter looked down upon (*Fam*. VII, 8, 1): "*Sed ex tuis litteris cognovi praeproperam quandam festinationem tuam et simul sum admiratus cur tribunatus commoda, dempto praesertim labore militiae, contempseris*."[29] Somewhat earlier Cicero requested and obtained a military tribunate for M.

25 Cf. Mommsen, *Römisches Staatsrecht*, Vol. II, 577–9; Jaakko Suolahti, *The Junior Officers of the Roman Army in the Republican Period* (Helsinki: Suomalainen Tiedeakatemia, 1955), 36 f.

26 See his warm recommendation of the three legates from Arpinum: "*non dubito quin scias non solum cuius municipii sim, sed etiam quam diligenter soleam meos municipes Arpinates tueri*" (*Fam*. XIII, 11, 1).

27 As suggested by his equestrian status as well as by his presence among the three legates sent by Arpinum to collect the municipality's revenues in Cisalpine Gaul: *Fam*. XIII, 11, 1. See further, Claude Nicolet, *L'ordre équestre à l'époque républicaine (312–43 Av. J.-C.)*, Vol. II (Paris: E. De Boccard, 1974), no. 153.

28 Cf. Cicero, *Fam*. VII, 5, 2, cited on p. 29.

29 Paul Sonnet ("Gaius Trebatius Testa" (University of Giessen Thesis, 1932), 54 f. = *RE*, Vol. VI A.2, 2259) maintains that Caesar never offered Trebatius a tribunate, but only the financial benefits that went with the post, understating *commoda* as the salary of a tribune. *Commoda*, however, may also mean 'advantages' in this context (cf. D.R. Shackleton Bailey's translation of the passage in *Cicero's Letters to His Friends*, Vol. I (Harmondsworth: Penguin Books, 1978), 90), in other words the advantage of holding the tribunate as a sinecure *dempo labore militiae*. This could be viewed as the prototype of the "*imaginariae militiae genus, quod vocatur super numerum, quo absentes et titulo tenus fungerentur*" instituted by Claudius (Suetonius, *Claud*. 25), namely a

Curtius from Caesar (*QFr.* III, 1, 10): "*De tribunatu quod scribis (scil. Quintus), ego vero nominatim petivi Curtio et mihi ipse Caesar nominatim Curtio paratum esse rescripsit meamque in rogando verecundiam obiurgavit.*" In fact on this occasion Caesar invited Cicero to put more requests of this kind before him (*Fam.* VII, 5, 2): "*M. Curti fulium,*[30] *quem mihi commendas, vel regem Galliae faciam, vel hunc Leptae delega, si vis. Tu ad me alium mitte quem ornem.*" The last phrase sets the familiar 'petition and request' pattern into which fell such a large proportion of the emperor's contacts with his subjects.[31] Moreover, it heralds the new regime's unconcealed – even advertised – readiness to grant favours to individuals (and communities) for the sake of the intercessor – a key role in the life of the Empire.[32]

Caesar did indeed turn Cicero into a lodestone for petitions by shedding on him the 'power of patronage.' No wonder that applicants for military tribunates became insistent and pestered Cicero, as the latter informs his brother (*QFr.* III, 1, 10): "*Si cui praeterea petiero ... facile patiar mihi negari, quoniam illi qui mihi molesti sunt sibi negari <a> me non facile patiuntur.*"

The bitter remark of the consul of that year (54 BC), L. Domitius Ahenobarbus, is exceptionally apposite in this context: "*se ne tribunum militum quidem facere*" (*QFr.* II, 14, 3). He was conscious of the weak hold he had on the 'power of patronage' and would have felt himself derided, had Cicero requested a tribunate from him ("*nam Domitius se derideri putasset, si esset a me rogatus,*" *QFr.* II, 14, 3). Caesar's monopoly over the sources of patronage galled his rivals, who felt the loss to their prestige keenly.

One can hardly avoid the impression that as early as the Late Republic, military tribunates, even if not used merely as sinecures,[33] derived their importance from the fact that their bestowal was triggered by the exercise of personal influence on the one hand and demonstrated the donor's 'power of patronage' on the other.

---

titulary tribunate which may not have compelled its bearer to leave his home town; cf. Millar, *The Emperor in the Roman World*, 284.

30 Shackleton Bailey's emendation of the meaningless "*M. itfiuium*" to "*M. Curti Filium*" (cf. *Cicero: Epistulae Ad Familiares*, Vol. I (Cambridge: Cambridge University Press, 1977), 329–30, no. 26) is extremely attractive, especially in view of *QFr.* II, 14, 3, and III, 1, 10, cited in the text.

31 Cf. Millar, *The Emperor in the Roman World*, 6 f.

32 Octavian in a letter of 30 BC to the people of Rohsus invites them to put forth requests which he will grant them on account of their citizen Seleucus (Robert K. Sherk, *Roman Documents from the Greek East* (Baltimore: Johns Hopkins Press, 1969), 298, no. 58, iv, ll. 91–93): οἳ γὰρ τοιοῦτοι ἄνδρες καὶ τὴν πρὸς τὰς [πατρίδας] εὐνοίαν προθυμοτέραν ποιοῦσιν· ὡς οὖν ἔμου πάντα δύνατα ποιήσοντος ὑμεῖν ἥδει[ον διὰ Σέλ]ευκον, θαρροῦντες περὶ ὧν ἂν βούλησθε πρός με ἀποστέλλετε.

33 Cf. above, n. 29.

Pliny's *Ep.* III, 8 is perhaps the best illustration of the persistence of the same emphasis and the same attitudes under the Empire. In it we discover the future biographer of the Caesars, C. Suetonius Tranquillus, still a young protégé of Pilny,[34] declining to take up the military tribunate Pliny had obtained for him from the governor of Britain, L. Neratius Marcellus,[35] and proposing to transfer it to his relative, Caesennius Silvanus: "*petis ut tribunatum, quem a Neratio Marcello clarissimo viro impetravi tibi, in Caesennium Silvanum propinquum tuum transferam.*" However, no one loses as a result of Suetonius' change of mind; on the contrary, it looks as if everybody stands to gain by it, as Pliny politely suggests (or archly hints?):[36] "*Praeterea intellego mihi quoque gloriae fore, si ex hoc tuo facto non fuerit ignotum amicos meos non gerere tantum tribunatus posse verum etiam dare.*" By now no less than five people have become involved in the allocation of this one single tribunate: the Emperor, the governor of Britain, Pliny, Suetonius and Caesennius; the economy with which the benefits from the 'power of patronage' could be distributed stands in need of no further comment.

This letter may also give us a clue as to the concrete way in which the system of requesting, obtaining and granting military tribunates operated. The crucial passage comes towards the end of the letter: "*Neque enim adhuc nomen in numeros relatum est, ideoque liberum est nobis Silvanum in locum tuum subdere.*" The expression "*nomen in numeros referri,*" once known only from legal sources relating to military affairs, is now documented in military records on papyrus. Thus we learn from the former that a soldier could make a military will only

34 Born about AD 70 (cf. Syme, *Tacitus*, Vol. II, 778, app. 76), Suetonius was now (AD 101) in his early thirties. For the age of military tribunes see Birley, "The Equestrian Officers of the Roman Army," 135 f.

35 By January 19, 103 he was governor of Britain: cf. *CIL* XVI 48 (= *ILS* 1032). However, he was not at the beginning of his tenure; cf. Syme, *Tacitus*, Vol. II, 647, app. 14, no. 27; Ronald Syme, "The Jurist Neratius Priscus," *Hermes* 85 (1957): 491 = *Roman Papers*, Vol. I, 349. We have now a reference to *]m Marcellum* described as *clarissimum* and *consularem* in the 'Vindolanda Tablets'; cf. Alan K. Bowman and J. David Thomas, "The Vindolanda Writing Tablets and Their Significance: An Interim Report," *Historia* 24 (1975): 463 ff. and Alan K. Bowman, "Roman Military Records from Vindolanda," *Britannia* 5 (1974): 360–73.

36 I would not put it beyond him to be actually hinting to Suetonius to advertise what had happened: after all it is but another feather in Pliny's own cap. Cf. his argument in the recommendation of T. (Priferinus Paetus) Rosianus Geminus, his ex-quaestor, to the Emperor Trajan (*Ep.* X, 26, 3): "*teque, domine, rogo, gaudere me exornata quaestoris mei dignitate, id est per illum mea, quam maturissime velis.*" An observation made about the fourth century Empire applies no less to the early second century: "The strongest evidence of the existence of ... close relations (with prominent officials of the administration) was ability to obtain favours for third parties," Wolf Liebeschuetz, "Did the Pelagian Movement Have Social Aims?," *Historia* 12 (1963): 230.

from the day "*ex quo in numeros relatus est*";[37] the best commentary on this is an instruction of the Prefect of Egypt, C. Minucius Italus,[38] to the prefect of the *cohors* III (or II) *Ituraeorum* (AD 103):[39] "*tirones sexs probatos a me in coh· cui praes· in numeros referri iube ex xi kalendas marias.*" As the context suggests, *numeri* has the meaning of 'lists' or 'rolls' and the phrase as a whole means 'to be entered on the rolls.'[40] Since Suetonius' name had not yet been on the rolls, no technical difficulty arose as a result of his sudden withdrawal from the tribunate.

The exact location of the 'rolls' or 'lists' (*numeri*) in the case of appointments made by imperial legates is not clear.[41] We may be right in assuming that the names of people who received their appointment directly from the emperor were kept on the 'rolls' in Rome with the *ab epistulis*, who issued the commissions (*epistulae*). It was suggested above that even when appointments were not made directly by the emperor, but by his legates, the *epistulae* were issued in the form of letters-patent in order to ensure that their holders should enjoy equal status with the others. However, it is likely that in this case the 'rolls,' on which the name of the personal appointees of the legate were entered, were kept in the governor's provincial headquarters. But how then did the emperor ever come to learn the names of the tribunes who were, so to speak, 'his'? If there was any exchange of information between the centre and the provinces to bring the 'rolls' in the former up to date we are completely in the dark about it.

It stands to reason that it was necessary to apply in advance, that is, before the governor entered into office or at the beginning of his tenure: otherwise one might have to be satisfied with less, namely with a short-term tribunate – *tribunatus semestris*[42] – as seems to have happened in the case of Pliny's application

37 *Dig.* 29, 1, 42 (Ulpian) and cf. *Dig.* 24, 1, 4 and 38; 37, 13, 1, 2 for the expression '*in numeris.*'
38 *PIR* (1st ed.) M 435; Stein, *Die Präfekten von Ägypten in der römischen Kaiserzeit*, 49 f.
39 *P.Oxy.* 1022 = Fink, *Roman Military Records on Papyrus*, no. 87.
40 James Franklin Gilliam, "Enrolment in the Imperial Army," in *Symbolae Raphaeli Taubenschlag Dedicatae*, Vol. II (Vratislaviae-Varsaviae: Ossolineum, 1957), 209; see the whole argument there, 207–16. Cf. also R.W. Davies, "Joining the Roman Army," *Bonner Jahrbücher* 168 (1969): 221 f.; 229 f.
41 Gilliam, "Enrolment in the Imperial Army," 209, n. 12 is in favour of Rome rather than the governor's provincial headquarters, citing the *laterculum maius* and *minus* of the 'Notitia Dignitatum'; cf. A.H.M. Jones, *The Later Roman Empire*. Vol. II (Oxford: Blackwell, 1964), 574 f. (on the *primicerius* in charge of the *laterculum maius*) and 641 f. (on commissions issued to officers). From *Dig.* 4, 6, 32 (Modestinus) it seems that in the third century the names of *tribune militum*, *praefecti* and *comites legatorum* were referred to the *aerarium* of the imperial archives (*commentarii*).
42 Theodor Mommsen, *Gesammelte Schriften*, Vol. VIII (Berlin: Weidmann, 1913), 167 maintains that the salary of the *tribunus semestris* was equal to that of the annual tribune since his service lasted *maiore parte anni*. He makes his calculations on the basis of *Hist. Aug. Claud.* XIV. Brian Dobson, "Legionary Centurion or Equestrian Officer? A Comparison of Pay and Prospects," *An-*

on behalf of C. Calvisius to Q. Sosius Senecio (*Ep.* IV, 4). In AD 103 Senecio was not at the beginning of his tenure of Upper Moesia:[43] "*Multa beneficia in multos contulisti*" (*ibid.*). hence Pliny's request is more modest: "*Hunc rogo semestri tribunatu splendidiorem et sibi et avunculo suo facias.*" That a vacancy in a *tribunatus semestris* might occur in the middle of one's term of office can be inferred from the words of the governor of Lower Britain ca. AD 220 quoted above.

The consideration just mentioned may account for the vague and imprecise language used by Pliny in his solicitation of behalf of Voconius Romanus,[44] sent to the governor of Syria, L. Iavolenus Priscus ca. AD 101[45] (*Ep.* II, 13). It is generally assumed that in the clause "*quem rogo pro ingenio pro fortuna tua exornes*"[46] (§ 10) Pliny is requesting a military tribunate.[47] If so, how are we to account for the fact that contrary to his practice in other requests he here deliberately refrains from spelling it out to the governor? Perhaps this time it is not the military tribunate that he is requesting, but rather an inclusion in the governor's *cohors*. Pliny's vague language, it could be supposed, corresponds to the informality of a post on this amorphous body.[48] A pedantic literal interpretation of the expression, "*In primis ama hominem: nam licet tribuas ei quantum amplissimum potes, nihil autem amplius potes amicitia tua,*" may even construe it as the proper technical language in the context. However, it seems wrong to read so much into platitudes and phrases left deliberately vague, and for a good reason: Iavolenus Priscus was

---

cient Society 3 (1972): 196 admits that the only established fact about the pay-scales of equestrian officers is that the salary of a *tribunus semestris* ca. AD 220 was 25,000 sesterces. However, by various deductions he admirably reconstructs these pay-scales, suggesting (*ibid.*, 201) that the 25,000 sesterces reflect half the pay of the *prima militia* i. e. of the *praefectus cohortis* and not of the *secunda militia* i. e. of the *tribunus militum*.

43 Cf. Ronald Syme, "The Lower Danube under Trajan," *JRS* 49 (1959): 29; Ronald Syme, "Legates of Moesia," *Dacia* 12 (1968): 331–2 = *Danubian Papers*, 213; Christopher P. Jones, "Sura and Senecio," *JRS* 60 (1970): 102.

44 His full name is C. Licinius Marinus Voconius Romanus; cf. *CIL* II 3865–6; Géza Alföldy, *Flamines Provinciae Hispaniae Citerioris* (Madrid: C.S.I.C., 1973), no. 37.

45 Cf. Syme, *Tacitus*, Vol. II, 631–2, app. 3; Syme, "The Jurist Neratius Priscus," 487 f. = *Roman Papers*, Vol. I, 346 f.; Christopher P. Jones, "A New Commentary on the Letters of Pliny," *Phoenix* 22 (1968): 119–20.

46 *Exornare* like *ornare* may refer of course to 'commission' or 'promotion.' For *ornare* used to express the idea of 'commission' cf. Cicero, *Fam.* VII, 5, 2 ("*ornem*"); 3 ("*ornes*") quoted on p. 29.

47 Cf. above, n. 2.

48 Officially only a limited number was allowed: cf. *Dig.* 27, 1, 41, 2: "*Eorum qui rei publicae causa absunt comites, qui sunt intra statutum numerum, de tutela ... excusantur.*" But the composition of the body was still a matter of the governor's personal choice. For the complete freedom exercised by the governor in choosing his *cohors* cf. Fronto, *Ep. Ad Ant. Pium.* II, 8 (M.P.J. Van den Hout, ed., *M. Cornelii Frontonis Epistulae* (Leiden: Brill, 1954), 161).

not at the beginning of his tenure; it would be impertinent to ask for the specific post of *tribunus militum* at this late hour, when he had already recruited his staff. The most Pliny can do is to turn this fact, namely the governor's long term in office, to his own advantage (*Ep.* II, 13, 2): "*Regis exercitum amplissimum: hinc tibi beneficiorum larga materia, longum praeterea tempus, quo amicos tuos exornare potuisti. Convertere ad nostros nec hos multos.*" Another reason for rejecting a literal reading of the recommendation of Voconius Romanus to Iavolenus Priscus' *amicitia* would be the striking resemblance it bears to that of Trebatius Testa to Caesar's *benevolentia* and *liberalitas* cited above. By refraining from a request for a specific post or dismissing it (as Cicero does), both writers adroitly manage to pay the recipient a courteous compliment: a concrete favour in the form of a post is only secondary to the acquisition of his general goodwill and friendship.

The argument so far may be summed up as follows. *Ep.* III, 8 demonstrated that as long as the man's name was not entered on the rolls, a tribunate obtained for him could be transferred to someone else. It is likely that the rolls were completed shortly after the governor's entry into office. Therefore, a request for a tribunate submitted at a later date had perforce to be more modest: one might hope for a vacancy in a *tribunatus semestris* – perhaps invented for the very purpose of enlarging the range of opportunities for exercising the 'power of patronage' and for exchanges of favours between friends;[49] alternatively, one may omit all mention of a tribunate.

Yet a further problem is raised by *Ep.* III, 8: did Pliny obtain a tribunate from L. Neratius Marcellus unconditionally, that is, not specifically for Suetonius, but rather for whomsoever Pliny might have had in mind?[50]

This question receives a satisfactory answer from another request for a military tribunate. In AD 107 Pliny wrote to Q. Pompeius Falco, then governor of Judaea[51] (*Ep.* VII, 22): "*Minus miraberis me tam instanter petisse, ut in amicum meum conferres tribunatum, cum scieris quis ille qualisque. Possum autem iam tibi et nomen indicare et describere ipsum, postquam polliceris. Est Cornelius Minicianus.*" Evidently Pliny, on his side, petitioned for the post before divulging or even knowing for whom he was soliciting it; and Pompeius Falco, on his side,

---

49 Dobson, "Legionary Centurion or Equestrian Officer? A Comparison of Pay and Prospects," 196, n. 37 suggests that the post of *tribunus semestris* "was not taken by men who wished to have a serious military career." Perhaps in spite of Pflaum, *Le marbre de Thorigny*, 26–7, one may compare the *tribunatus semestris* to the *imaginariae militiae genus* of Claudius; cf. above, n. 29.
50 An affirmative answer to this question would be, incidentally, a strong presumption in favour of accepting Mommsen's hypothesis: see above, pp. 25 f.
51 Cf. Emil Schürer, *The History of the Jewish People in the Age of Jesus Christ*, Vol. I, ed. Fergus Millar and Géza Vermès (Edinburgh: Clark, 1973), 516–7.

promised to reserve a tribunate for a protégé of Pliny without requiring to know the name of the man and who he was.[52] There could hardly be a more palpable demonstration of how tribunates were kept in reserve for friends, and friends of friends. Furthermore, it was hardly necessary for a man to be in an official position to be able to dispense patronage and make appointments; it was sufficient for a *privatus* to have, like Pliny, friends in advantageous official positions.

52 Ronald Syme, "Consulates in Absence," *JRS* 48 (1958): 4 = *Roman Papers*, Vol. I, 383 puts Falco's entry into office in Judaea in 105. There could be several explanations for the fact that as late as 107 (for the book-date of Pliny's *Epistulae* VII see A.N. Sherwin-White, *The Letters of Pliny: A Historical and Social Commentary* (Oxford: Clarendon Press, 1966), 37–8; Syme, *Tacitus*, 661, app. 21) the name was not entered on the rolls, but it is hardly necessary to enter into them here. Likewise it is irrelevant whether or not C. Cornelius Minicianus actually served under Pompeius Falco. Syme, "Pliny's Less Successful Friends," 364 = *Roman Papers*, Vol. II, 479 identifies Cornelius Minicianus with his homonym of *ILS* 2722, who was *praef. coh. I Damascenorum, trib. leg. III Augustae* (in Africa). Hence he opines that he did not get (or accept) the post in Judaea. Against the identification see Birley, "The Equestrian Officers of the Roman Army," 141, n. 17.

The Concept of Indulgentia under Trajan

Even a casual reader of Pliny's letters to Trajan cannot fail to notice the frequency with which Pliny employs the term *indulgentia* – as well as various forms of the verb *indulgere* – to characterize the relationship between the Emperor and himself or between the Emperor and other people. This terminology appears without exception in all the letters recommending people to the notice of the Emperor – whether for promotion, for the grant of the Roman citizenship or for some other favour or privilege – as well as in those letters containing requests for privileges and favours for Pliny himself, or expressing gratitude on obtaining them. It also occurs in some of the letters mentioning concessions made to provincial communities.[1]

It may be admitted from the outset that the use of the 'indulgence' terminology in the contexts described above is by no means exclusive; comparable terms, such as *bonitas* and *beneficium*, are used as well.[2] Nevertheless, the 'indulgence' terminology predominates in these contexts. Moreover, it is absent from Pliny's letters in other contexts. And avoidance is often no less significant than use: it proves that for Pliny the terminology is still resonant with meaning, which makes its use fitting on specific occasions and not on others.

Indulgentia appears for the first time in our sources in the first century BC.[3] It is not, however, the purpose of the present inquiry to trace its long, intricate and fascinating career – not least because the work has already been undertaken by others[4] – but rather to concentrate first on the first stages of its association with the person of the emperor and secondly on the reasons for this association.

The first point calls for a survey of its occurrences up till its apparent establishment in the 'ideology of the principate,'[5] i.e. until Nerva's and Trajan's

---

1 Below, pp. 43 f.
2 Below, pp. 50 f.
3 Cicero, *Verr.* II, 1, 112; 5, 109.
4 Notably by Jean Gaudemet, *Indulgentia Principis* (Trieste: Instituto di storia del diritto, 1962) and Wolfgang Waldstein, *Untersuchungen zum römischen Begnadigungsrecht: Abolitio-Indulgentia-Venia* (Innsbruck: Universitätsverlag Wagner, 1964).
5 It is not claimed here that the ancients ever thought of it as such.

Article note: First published in *Chiron* 14 (1984): 245–266, with the following note: an earlier version of this paper was delivered at the annual meeting of the Society for the Promotion of Classical Studies in Israel held at the Hebrew University of Jerusalem in March 1983. The present version owes much to the constructive criticism and advice of F. Millar, J. Geiger, G. Clemente, D. Wasserstein, and A. Yakobson.

https://doi.org/10.1515/9783110770438-003

time.[6] It is then for the first time that the term is fully elaborated. The text of Pliny, the starting point for the present discussion, combined with the more scanty evidence of legal writings and inscriptions, gives us more than an insight into the cultural temper – or, into the political cant – of the period. Not only the persistence of certain themes, but also the recurrence of certain turns of phrase in connection with the term *indulgentia*, imply the rootedness of the term in the consciousness of the age.

The first step towards an understanding of the reasons for the emergence of the term *indulgentia* is to investigate its primary connotations and the specific aspect of the principate which its usage conveys. Secondly, *indulgentia* should be demarcated from other virtues of blessings[7] associated with the emperor whose frame of reference often overlaps with its own, and especially from *clementia* and *liberalitas*.[8] Only then may we be in a position to offer an answer – even if a tentative one – to the much larger question of why the aspect of the principate conveyed by *indulgentia* was emphasized when it was. However, the well-known hazards of transmission do not allow us to determine that the shift in emphasis occurred for the first time in the reign of Trajan. Thus, however much we may be tempted to do so, we are unable to connect its emergence then with contemporary events and intellectual currents with any degree of certainty.

Indulgentia was attributed to the master of Rome even before the establishment of the principate. In a letter to the oscillating Cicero, from March 49 BC,[9] Balbus and Oppius promise him that after having ascertained Caesar's intentions, they will give Cicero advice which will be commensurate both with his dignity and with his obligations towards Pompey. They conclude with an assurance: "*et hoc Caesarem pro sua indulgentia in suos probaturum putamus.*"[10]

---

6 Gaudemet's survey (above, n. 4) seems to suffer from the following shortcomings: 1) since he was interested in the later development of the term, the first stages are sketched briefly and no high-lights are pointed out; 2) the persistence of *indulgentia* in other contexts than that of remission of penalties and debts is neglected; 3) since the publication of Gaudemet's pioneer study other important evidence has come to light; 4) it has a number of inaccuracies worth correcting, e. g. in Cicero, *Att.* IX, 7a, 2 it is not Cicero who applies the term *indulgentia* to Caesar; see also below, nn. 79 and 112 for other examples.

7 The terms are used loosely throughout, and their meaning must not be pressed any further than common sense dictates.

8 Below, p. 54.

9 *Att.* IX, 9a, 2.

10 Cf. Caesar, *BGall.* VII, 63, 8.

The usage seems to disappear for a while, unless the restoration made by the editor of the much mutilated Augustan inscription is accepted.[11] It seems to be a dedication to Augustus by a colony.[12] The restored formula runs: *Ind[ulgentia] Ma[ximi principis]*.

Under Claudius *indulgentia* is once more associated with the ruler. In the *consolatio* to Polybius, Seneca expresses his confidence in the soothing properties of the Emperor's *mansuetudo* and *indulgentia*.[13] He reminds Polybius of the debt the latter owes to the Emperor's *indulgentia*.[14]

We would have had to wait until the reign of Domitian for *indulgentia* to be once more connected with the person of the emperor, were it not for the publication in 1960 of the only letter by Titus which has been preserved.[15] It was given to the *quattuor viti* and *decuriones* of the *municipium* of Munigua in Baetica on September 7, AD 79. The addressees had appealed to the Emperor against the verdict of the previous governor instructing the city to pay its debt to a man called Servilius Pollio. Having lost the appeal, the city should have paid the penalty of *iniusta appellatio*.[16] But as Titus now telling them, "*ego malui cum indulgentia mea quam cum temeritati (sic) vestra loqui et sestertia quinquaginta millia nummorum tenuitati publicae, quam praetexitis, remisi*" (ll. 6–9).

This is the first time that *indulgentia* is associated with the remission of money owed to the imperial treasury.[17] However, by implication the imperial *indulgentia* is also responsible for the other two concessions to the city: 1) absolving it from paying the interest accruing from the day of the original judgement; 2) deducting from its debt the sum of money owed to it and held back by the creditor.[18]

---

11 *AE* 1948, no. 91; published by Giuseppe Marchetti Longhi, "Scavi del largo argentina: Il materiale archeologico. I. Le epigrafi," *Bull. Com. Arch.* 71 (1943–1945): 66–7. The restoration is based on *AE* 1941, no. 73 (= *AE* 1973, no. 137, see below, p. 39 at n. 26).

12 For *indulgentia* in connection with colonies see below, p. 48.

13 *Nec dubito, cum tanta illi adversus omnes suos sit mansuetudo tantaque indulgentia, quin iam multis solaciis tuum istud vulnus obduxerit, iam multa, quae dolori obstarent tuo, congesserit* (XII, 4).

14 *Cum voles omnium rerum oblivisci, Caesarem cogita. Vide, quantam huius in te indulgentiae fidem, quantam industriam debeas* (VII, 1).

15 Herbert Nesselhauf, "Zwei Bronzeurkunden aus Munigua," *Madrider Mitteilungen* 1 (1960): 148 = *AE* 1962, no. 288.

16 See Tacitus, *Ann.* XIV, 28, 1.

17 For the later development see Gaudemet, *Indulgentia Principis*, 16 f.

18 That the compensation is in itself a concession since *ex dispari causa* is argued by Álvaro D'Ors, "Miscelánea epigráfica. Los bronces de Mulva," *Emerita* 29 (1961): 213.

Even if it is not necessary to go so far as to say that the declaration "*ego malui cum indulgentia mea ... loqui*" amounts to "un programme de gouvernement,"[19] nevertheless its presence calls for a modification of the view that *indulgentia* became an official attribute for the first time under Trajan.[20]

Under Domitian *indulgentia* re-emerges in both literary and non-literary sources. Statius, speaking through Venus, prophesies an early consulate for L. Arruntius Stella,[21] relying on the continuing *indulgentia* of the Emperor:

hunc et bis senos (sic indulgentia pergat
praesidis Ausonii) cernes attollere fascis
ante diem;
(*Silv.* I, 2, 174–6)

That the consulate emanates from the imperial *indulgentia* is made clear in what follows; the verb *indulgere* describes the gift of the curule chair and the purple dress:

iamque Parens Latius cuius praenoscere mentem
fas mihi, purpureos habitus iuvenique curule
indulgebit ebur,
(*ibid.*, 178–180)

This is not the last time that both the connection between *indulgentia* and senatorial office as well as the use of the title *parens* in this context will occur.[22]

In *Silvae* V, 2, 125 f. Statius advises Bolanus to enter on a military career: "*ergo iam magno ... surge animo, et fortis castrorum concipe curas.*" As incentives he mentions the Emperor's *indulgentia* and the successful career of the young man's brother: "*ducis indulgentia pulsat, certaque dat votis hilaris vestigia frater*" (ll. 125–6). The imperial *indulgentia* may stand for a general benevolent disposition of Domitian, relying on which the young man should be encouraged to apply for a commission; or it may refer to a particular favour shown to Bolanus himself.

19 *AE* 1962, no. 288 on p. 69.

20 This view is held by Paul Veyne, "La table des Ligures Baebiani et l'institution alimentaire de Trajan (2e Article)," *MÉFRA* 70 (1958): 223; 225, repeated in "Une hypothèse sur l'arc de Bénévent," *MÉFRA* 72 (1960): 199 and in Paul Veyne, *Les "Alimenta" de Trajan* (Paris: CNRS, 1965), 166.

21 *PIR* (2nd ed.) A 1151. He was praetor in 93. It is not known whether by the time the poem was written (after 89) he had already held any curule office; cf. ad loc. Friedrich Vollmer, ed., *P. Papinii Statii Silvarum Libri* (Leipzig: Teubner, 1898).

22 Below, pp. 43 and 55 f.

The phrase "*ducis indulgentia*" recurs later in Juvenal VII, 21 in the context of imperial patronage of the arts: "*circumspicit et stimulat uos materiamque sibi ducis indulgentia quaerit*,"[23] and in Suetonius' description of the relationship between Iulius Caesar and his soldiers: it was not so much the *auctoritas* as the *indulgentia ducis* which made them return to their duties after having mutinied.[24] *Ducis indulgentia*, unless a literary reminiscence, has perhaps become a common collocation by the second century AD, if not before.[25]

A dedication to Domitian by the Colonia Flavia Augusta Puteolana, erected sometime between 13 September 95 and 12 September 96,[26] mentions the *indulgentia gentia maximi divinique principis* which brought the colony nearer to Rome – *urbi eius admota*.[27] This last phrase probably refers to the construction of the Via Domitiana which connected Puteoli to the Via Appia.[28]

Indulgentissimus as an unofficial title[29] appears for the first time in another inscription from Domitian's reign.[30] In his letter of AD 82 to the people of Falerio in Picenum Domitian confirms their legal right (*ius possessorum*) over certain lands (*subpsiciva*), the ownership over which had for a long time been contested by the colony of Firmum. To justify his verdict Domitian recalls a letter of Augustus instructing Firmum to sell their lots; he had done so notwithstanding the fact of his being "*diligentissimus et indulgentissimus erga quartanos suos princeps*" (l. 21). The choice of *indulgentissimus* to describe the attitude of his predecessor towards the soldiers of the Fourth Legion whom Augustus had settled at Firmum may not be accidental; the same title appears in the Preface to the first book of the *Silvae*.

---

23 W.C. Helmbold and E.N. O'Neil, "The Form and Purpose of Juvenal's Seventh 'Satire,'" *CPhil.* 54 (1959): 106 take the phrase to refer to Domitian, to have a derogatory intention and to be a sarcastic reference to Statius and his relationship to this Emperor. E.J. Kenney, "The First Satire of Juvenal," *PCPS* 8 (1962): 31 and William S. Anderson, "The Programs of Juvenal's Later Books," *CPhil.* 57 (1962): 158–9, n. 17 argue successfully against each of these points. The latter protests against assigning a negative sense to *indulgentia* and to the phrase *indulgentia ducis* which he takes to be entirely conventional and not to have been invented by Juvenal.

24 Suet., *Iul.* 69; it should not be pressed too hard, however, since the context and the run of the sentence may have demanded it.

25 Cf. Anderson, "The Programs of Juvenal's Later Books," 158–9, n. 17.

26 *AE* 1941, no. 73 (dated to AD 86); for the date in the text see Kenneth D. Matthews, Jr., "Domitian: The Lost Divinity," *Expedition Magazine* 8 (1966): 30–36 = *AE* 1973, no. 137.

27 For this new reading of the last line see Matthews.

28 See Matthews.

29 For the concept see Leo Berlinger, "Beiträge zur inoffiziellen Titulatur der römischen Kaiser" (University of Breslau Thesis, 1935); Regula Frei-Stolba, "Inoffizielle Kaisertitulaturen im 1. und 2. Jahrhundert n. Chr.," *MH* 26 (1969): 18–39.

30 *CIL* IX 5420 = Salvatore Riccobono, ed., *Fontes Iuris Romani AnteIustiniani*, Vol. I (Florence: Barbèra, 1941), no. 75.

Statius calls Domitian "*indulgentissimus imperator*" in connection with the verses he wrote about the equestrian statue of the Emperor dedicated in the Forum.[31]

It is with Nerva's reign that *indulgentia* for the first time appears in an imperial proclamation addressed to the whole citizen body. In the edict cited by Pliny (*Ep.* X, 58, 7–9), Nerva published his intention to maintain all his predecessors' *beneficia*. The act of confirmation is presented as a manifestation of the imperial *indulgentia*. Its location in the document lends it a particular emphasis; it makes *indulgentia* into a programmatic term: "*Ne tamen aliquam gaudiis publicis adferat haesitationem vel eorum qui impetraverunt diffidentia vel eius memoria qui praestitit, necessarium pariter credidi ac laetum obviam dubitantibus indulgentiam meam mittere.*"

The other evidence for the use of *indulgentia* by Nerva is less certain. Ulpian traces the concession of *libera testamenti factio* to soldiers to Iulius Caesar. Being temporary, the concession was renewed by Titus, Domitian and Nerva; with Trajan it was inserted into the imperial *mandata*.[32] Whereas Titus and Domitian receive but a brief mention, Nerva's action is treated expansively: "*postea divus Nerva plenissimam indulgentiam in milites contulit.*" Despite the elaboration, the context makes it quite clear that Nerva added nothing of substance to what his predecessors had done. It may not be inconceivable, especially in view of the edict cited above, that Ulpian is using Nerva's own terminology.

Two references may be all that we can expect from Nerva's short reign. With Trajan's reign references to the imperial *indulgentia* abound in both official and non-official sources, in documentary and literary sources. That this may be merely an accident of transmission is not very likely. Yet one hesitates to postulate the guiding hand of imperial policy.

Indulgentia appears in the two big *alimenta* dedications in what looks like a formulaic context; hence Paul Veyne surmised that they come from the text of the *Lex Alimentorum*.[33] The introduction on the Table of Veleia has the fullest formulation: *Obligatio praediorum ob* $\overline{\textit{HS}}$ *deciens quadraginta quattuor milia, ut ex indulgentia optimi maximique principis imp. Caes. Nervae Traiani Aug. Germanici Dacici pueri puellaeque alimenta accipiant.*[34] A reference to an earlier *alimenta* scheme at some point between 98 and 102[35] uses identical words: *Item obligatio praediorum facta per Cornelium Gallicanum ab* $\overline{\textit{HS}}$ $\overline{\textit{LXXII}}$ *ut ex indulgentia optimi*

31 *Silv.* I, pr. 17 f. For the date – probably 91 – see Vollmer, *P. Papinii Statii Silvarum Libri*, 4–5.

32 *Dig.* 29, 1, 1.

33 Veyne, "La table des Ligures Baebiani et l'institution alimentaire de Trajan (2e Article)," 225, n. 8; 226.

34 *CIL* XI 1147 = *ILS* 6675.

35 The *Dacicus* is missing.

maximique principis imp. Caes. Nervae Traiani Augusti Germanici pueri puellaeq. alimenta accipiant (vii, 31f.). Despite the fragmentary state of the Table of the Ligures Baebiani, the same formula can be read here: *[imp. Caes.] Nerva Traiano Aug. G[ermanic]o IIII [Q.] Articuleio Paeto [cos.] .... [ex praecepto optim]i maximiq. principis obligarunt prae[dia] .... pto Ligures Baebiani .... [u]t*[36] *ex indulgentia eius pueri puuaellaeq. a[limenta a]ccipiant.*[37]

In an inscription from Ferentinum[38] the *municipium* records the motion to make T. Pomponius Bassus a patron of their community for having established the *alimenta* scheme in their town, a task given him by "the most indulgent emperor": *demandatam sibi curam ab indulgentissimo imp. Caesare Nerva Traiano Augusto Germanico, qua aeternitati Italiae suae prospexit, secundum liberalitatem eius ita ordinare, ut omnis aetas curae eius merito gratias agere debeat.*[39]

Admittedly, *indulgentia* in the alimentary inscriptions is interchangeable with *liberalitas*, as one learns from the "*secundum liberalitatem eius*"[40] of the Ferentine inscription quoted above. Later inscriptions prove the point even further: *Antonino Aug. Pio ... pueri puellae qui ex liberalitate eius alimenta accipiunt;*[41] *pueri et puillae qui ex liberalitate sacratissimi principis aliment(a) accipiunt.*[42] The increase of the *alimenta* by Hadrian is described in the Historia Augusta as an act of *liberalitas.*[43] Alternatively *munificentia* or *benificentia* – whichever the restoration may be – might be the source of the *alimenta.*[44] Or it may even be due to a virtue of an altogether different complexion, such as *providentia.*[45]

Nevertheless the use of *indulgentia* in the alimentary inscriptions is eminently appropriate in view of the primary meaning of *indulgentia* (to be explained

---

36 This is Dessau's (*ILS*) *reading*; the *CIL* reads *et.*
37 *CIL* IX 1455 = *ILS* 6509.
38 *CIL* VI 1492 = *ILS* 6106, 19 October 101.
39 Veyne, "Une hypothèse sur l'arc de Bénévent," 199 suggests that one of the two personified attributes assisting the Emperor Trajan in the alimentary scheme, portrayed on one of the panels of the Arch of Beneventum, represents the *indulgentia* of the Emperor.
40 Which refers to Trajan; cf. Hans Kloft, *Liberalitas Principis* (Köln: Böhlau, 1970), 97, n. 62.
41 *CIL* XI 5956, AD 139.
42 *CIL* XI 5395 = *ILS* 6620, probably from the time of M. Aurelius.
43 *Hist. Aug.*, *Hadr.*, VII, 8.
44 *CIL* IX 5825: *[Quod per mu-* or *be]nificentiam suam [robur* or *statum] subolemque Italiae c[onfirmavit]*; cf. Otto Hirschfeld, *Die kaiserlichen Verwaltungsbeamten bis auf Diocletian* (Berlin: Weidmann, 1905), 215, n. 1.
45 *CIL* X 6310 = *ILS* 282, Trajanic. On *providentia* see Martin Percival Charlesworth, "Providentia and Aeternitas," *Harv. Theol. Rev.* 29 (1936): 122.

below), and the fact that the *alimenta* scheme was directed towards providing means of subsistence for the children of the needy.[46]

There are three more inscriptions with the *indulgentia* terminology from the time of Trajan. The city of Aquileia records in AD 105 the successful career of its son C. Minicius Italus, who used his position to increase the honour and glory of his city of origin. The acts of his – perhaps different aspects of the same action – are singled out for special mention: *sacratissimum principem Traianum A[ugustum decrevisse rogatu ei]us, ut incolae, quibus fere censemur, muneri[bus nobiscum fungantur, e]t ut pleniorem indulgentiam maximi imper[atoris habeamus per eum cont]igisse.*[47]

Two more inscriptions use the title *indulgentissimus*. The fragmentary state of *CIL* IX 215 prevents us from ascertaining the context in which the title is used. *CIL* XI 3309 is a dedication to Trajan from Forum Claudii for financing from his own treasury a local aqueduct.[48]

In the period under discussion the term appears in legal writings for the first time. The jurist L. Iavolenus Priscus[49] propounds a rule: "*Beneficium imperatoris, quod a divina scilicet eius indulgentia proficiscitur, quam plenissime interpretari debemus*" (*Dig.* 1, 4, 3).[50] As the quotation clearly shows, we are still dealing with an abstract, general and non-technical term. More than a century will elapse before *indulgentia*, detached from the person of the emperor, designates in legal writings concrete and technical acts.[51] For Iavolenus *indulgentia* is still a personal quality, perhaps a general disposition; the *beneficia* are its manifest corollary.

The rich evidence of Pliny's correspondence with the Emperor Trajan faithfully records the predilection felt for the term and its ubiquity. Pliny invokes the Emperor's *indulgentia* in contexts familiar from before, but also in new contexts, in some of which the term will re-appear later on. In the following discussion the Plinian contexts will be surveyed, precedents will be pointed out and future developments delineated.

---

46 On the purpose of the *alimenta* see Veyne, *Les "Alimenta" de Trajan*, 166.; Richard Duncan-Jones, *The Economy of the Roman Empire* (Cambridge: Cambridge University Press, 1982), 294 f.

47 *CIL* V 875 = *ILS* 1374.

48 Below, pp. 46 f.

49 Cf. Wolfgang Kunkel, *Herkunft und soziale Stellung der römischen Juristen* (Graz: Bohlau, 1967), 138; Ronald Syme, "The Jurist Neratius Priscus," *Hermes* 85 (1957): 480 = *Roman Papers*, Vol. I (Oxford: Oxford University Press, 1979), 339.

50 See Álvaro D'Ors, *Epigrafía jurídica de la España romana* (Madrid: Instituto Nacional de Estudios Jurídico, 1953), 19–20.

51 Cf. Waldstein, *Untersuchungen zum römischen Begnadigungsrecht: Abolitio-Indulgentia-Venia*, 131 f.

The first time Pliny invokes the imperial *indulgentia* is in connection with the grant of the *ius trium liberorum* to himself.[52] The Emperor answered the entreaties of Pliny's patron, L. Iulius Ursus Servianus:[53] "*Iuli Serviani ... precibus indulseris*" (*Ep*. X, 2, 1). A short time before 100 or 101 Pliny obtained the same privilege for his own friend and protégé, Voconius Romanus: "*et nuper ab optimo principe trium liberorum ius impetravi*" (*Ep*. II, 13, 8).[54] Here too the 'indulgence' terminology is found: "*quod quamquam parce et cum delectu daret, mihi tamen tamquam eligeret indulsit*" (*ibid.*). About a decade later we find Pliny, this time in Bithynia, making the request on behalf of yet another protégé, Suetonius Tranquillus: "*Scio, domine, quantum beneficium petam, sed peto a te cuius in omnibus desideriis meis indulgentiam experior*" (*Ep*. X, 94, 3).

Nerva's permission to Pliny to transfer his private collection of statues of emperors to Tifernum Tiberinum with a statue of the living emperor included was also a demonstration of *indulgentia*: "*Quod quidem ille mihi cum plenissimo testimonio indulserat*" (*Ep*. X, 8, 2). In order to carry out the transfer as well as to put order in his private affairs in the district Pliny had to ask Trajan for leave from his duties as Prefect of the Aerarium Saturni: *indulgeas commeatum* (*ibid.*, § 4). A leave of 30 days would put Pliny in the debt of the Emperor's *indulgentia*: "*Debebo ergo, domine, indulgentiae tuae et pietatis meae celeritatem et status ordinationem*" (*ibid.*, § 6).

The contexts of promotions, honours and nominations yield a rich crop of *indulgentia* terminology. Statius had already associated it with an early grant of the consulate to L. Arruntius Stella and the entry of Crispinus Vettius Bolanus into a military career.[55] The Emperor's *indulgentia* (*indulgentia vestra*) put Pliny in charge of the Aerarium Saturni.[56] It is, therefore, hardly surprising that the imperial *indulgentia* is invoked when Pliny wishes the Emperor to enhance his dignity by nominating him for one of the more important priesthoods: "*rogo dignitati, ad quam me provexit indulgentia tua, vel auguratum vel septemviratum ... adicere digneris*" (*Ep*. X, 13).

Appeal is made to the Emperor's *indulgentia* to achieve promotions and honours for others as well. Voconius Romanus' sterling qualities combined with Pliny's entreaties on his behalf may win over Trajan's *indulgentia* and get the *latus*

52 *Ep*. X, 2, AD 98.

53 See Ronald Syme, *Tacitus*, Vol. II (Oxford: Clarendon Press, 1958), 636, app. 7. He was *cos*. I in 90 and II in 101.

54 For the date of this letter see Syme, *Tacitus*, Vol. II, 632, app. 3.

55 Above, pp. 38 f.

56 In AD 98: "*Ut primum me, domine, indulgentia vestra promovit ad praefecturam aerarii Saturni,*" *Ep*. X, 3a, 1.

clavus and the opening of a senatorial career for the man.[57] Having succeeded before in this type of request ("*quia tamen in hoc quoque indulsisti*"), Pliny asks the Emperor to bestow a praetorship on the impoverished senator, Accius[58] Sura: like other citizens this shy man was encouraged and summoned, by the "*felicitas temporum, ad usum indulgentiae tuae*" (*Ep.* X, 12). From Bithynia-Pontus Pliny requests Trajan to bestow his *indulgentia* on Pliny's former quaestor, Rosianus Geminus[59] ("*Cui, si quid mihi credis, indulgentiam tuam dabis*"), and enhance his dignity: "*pro dignitate eius precibus meis faveas* (*Ep.* X, 26, 2). The transfer of his mother-in-law's relative, Caelius Clemens, to Pliny's province – perhaps as a member of the governor's *cohors*[60] – is yet another demonstration of Trajan's *indulgentia* towards Pliny's entire household.[61] Recommending the homonymous son of the *primipilaris* Nymphidius Lupus[62] for further promotion in the equestrian career, Pliny assures the Emperor that the man "*suffecturum indulgentiae tuae*" (*Ep.* X, 87, 3). Finally the acephalous testimonial on behalf of an official who served with Pliny in the province expresses a similar assurance: "*indulgentia tua dignus est*" (*Ep.* X, 86b). The last quoted expression seems to have been a set phrase, as the description of the Prefect of the Pontic Coast, Gavius Bassus,[63] suggests: "*vir egregius et indulgentia tua dignus*" (*Ep.* X, 21, 1).

Not only in the letters but in the Panegyricus as well *indulgentia* appears in the context of the allocation of honours and promotions. The bestowal of the consulate on Pliny and Cornutus Terutullus[64] at the same time shows the 'indulgent' emperor "*indulgentissimus imperator in concordia nostra ea praestiterit ambobus, quae si tantum in alterum contulisset, ambos tamen aequaliter obligasset*" (*Pan.* XC, 4). Trajan's elevation of the nobility is also an act of *indulgentia:* "*Sunt in honore hominum, et in ore famae magna nomina <excitata> ex tenebris oblivionis indulgentia Caesaris, cuis haec intentio est ut nobiles et conservet et faciat*" (*Pan.* LXIX, 6). The grant of the highest honour of a third consulate to Iulius Frontinus

57 *Ep.* X, 4, 5.

58 See Ronald Syme, "People in Pliny," *JRS* 58 (1968): 139 = *Roman Papers*, Vol. II, 701.

59 See Ronald Syme, "Pliny's Less Successful Friends," *Historia* 9 (1960): 370 = Syme, *Roman Papers*, Vol II, 486.

60 Only a limited number of *comites* was allowed, cf. *Dig.* 27, 1, 41, 2; cf. 4, 6, 32.

61 *Ep.* X, 51.

62 See Brian Dobson, *Die Primipilares* (Köln: Rheinland-Verlag, 1978), 215, no. 215.

63 This man is mentioned in a newly discovered inscription from Ephesus, Dieter Knibbe, "Neue Inschriften aus Ephesos II," *JÖAI* 49 (supp.) (1968–1971): 15, no. 2 = *AE* 1972, no. 573.

64 See Syme, "Pliny's Less Successful Friends," 362 = *Roman Papers*, Vol. II, 478; Shelagh Jameson, "Cornutus Tertullus and the Plancii of Perge," *JRS* 55 (1965): 54; Stephen Mitchell, "The Plancii in Asia Minor," *JRS* 64 (1974): 27.

and probably to Vestricius Spurinna elicits from Pliny the following praise: "*Tanta tibi bene faciendi vis, ut indulgentia tua necessitates aemuletur*" (*Pan.* LXI, 8).

Suetonius' usage concurs. Vitellius' meteoric rise is attributed to "*trium principum indulgentia*" (Suet., *Vit.* 5). Tacitus uses the verb in the context of the grant of the "*insignia triumphalia*" to Corbulo (*Ann.* XI, 20), and in the context of promotions in the army (*Hist.* II, 94; III, 9).[65]

The *indulgentia* of Trajan is invoked in requests and acknowledgments of the grant of the Roman citizenship to foreigners and the *ius Quiritium* to *Latini Juniani.* Only by means of "*tuae indulgentiae beneficium*" could Pliny hope to repay his therapist Arpocras for his solicitude and devotion: "*Quare rogo des ei civitatem Romanam*" (*Ep.* X, 5, 1–2). The Emperor granted the request without delay ("*sine mora indulsisti,*" X, 6, 1), but Pliny had discovered in the meantime that the possession of Alexandrian citizenship is a prerequisite for obtaining the Roman one; he hastened to submit all the necessary information to the Emperor "*ne quid rursus indulgentiam tuam moraretur*" (X, 6, 2). In connection with the same request he addresses Trajan as "*indulgentissimus imperator*" (X, 10, 2). Pliny's obligation to yet another doctor could also be repaid "*si precibus meis ex consuetudine bonitatis tuae indulseris*" (X, 11, 1). Since the man is already in possession of Roman citizenship, Pliny requests it on behalf of the man's relative, in such a manner that they may retain their *patria potestas* in their sons and the *ius patronorum* in their freedmen.[66] In his covering letter to the *libellus* of the auxiliary centurion P. Accius Aquila Pliny describes the man's request for citizenship for his daughter as an appeal to the Emperor's *indulgentia:* "*libellum per quem indulgentiam pro statu filiae suae implorat*" (X, 106).

Mention should perhaps be made here of Panegyricus XXXIX, 2, where Trajan's 'indulgence' is expressed in the grant of the *cognationum iura* to people who obtained Roman citizenship *per Latium*, thereby freeing them of the obligation to pay inheritance tax when inheriting from peregrine relations. The remission of the inheritance tax recalls Titus' remission of a fine to the people of Munigua, with the difference that in the latter case the remission is indirectly granted by the creation of a legal situation (*cognationum iura*) which absolves the newly made citizens from the need to pay the tax.

The grant of the *ius Quiritium* to the freedmen of Pliny's friend is once again an act of *indulgentia*;[67] yet Pliny was careful not to abuse the Emperor's 'indul-

---

65 Cf. *Hist.* I, 52.

66 For the wider context see Fergus Millar, *The Emperor in the Roman World* (London: Duckworth, 1977), 483–6.

67 "*Ago gratias ... quod et ius Quiritium libertis necessariae mihi feminae ... sine mora indulsisti,*" *Ep.* X, 6, 1.

gence' in requesting the *ius Quiritium* for all and sundry: "*Vereor ... ne sit immodicum pro omnibus pariter invocare indulgentiam tuam*" (*Ep.* X, 104).

Pliny's usage is faithfully echoed in the recently discovered Tabula Banasitana. This document records the grant of Roman citizenship to a local dignitary in 177 as emanating directly from the *indulgentia principalis*: "*quamquam civitas Romana non nisi maximis meritis provocata in[dul]gentia principalis gentibus istis solita sit ...*".[68]

The use (or rather misuse) of an imperial *diploma* by an unqualified person and for a purpose other than that for which it was issued was yet another occasion for an appeal by Pliny to the imperial *indulgentia*; the fact that Pliny's request for permission is retrospective – his wife having already left for Rome to visit her lately bereaved aunt – only increases his debt to the Emperor's 'indulgence' (*Ep.* X, 120, 2): "*Haec tibi scripsi, quia mihi parum gratus fore videbar, si dissimulassem inter alia beneficia hoc unum quoque me debere indulgentiae tuae, quod fiducia eius quasi consulto te non dubitavi facere, quem si consuluissem, sero fecissem.*"

The 'indulgence' terminology appears also in the context of the relationship between the emperor and the communities in Pliny's province. The cities need the imperial licence for public building; its bestowal is yet another manifestation of the imperial *indulgentia*, although there is no question of imperial funding of their projects.

Pliny transmits Prusa's desire for a new bath-house with the observation that it could be accommodated: "*videris mihi desiderio eorum indulgere posse*" (*Ep.* X, 23, 1). The Emperor's replay is also cast in the 'indulgence' terminology: "*possumus desiderio eorum indulgere*" (X, 24). Later Pliny reminds him of his consent in identical terms: "*Quaerenti mihi ... Prusae ubi posset balineum quod indulsisti fieri ...*" (X, 70, 1). Similarly the Emperor is asked to give his consent to the building of an aqueduct in Sinope with the assurance that the funds for it will not be lacking: "*Pecunia curantibus nobis contracta non deerit, si tu, domine, hoc genus operis et salubritati et amoenitati valde sitientis coloniae indulseris*" (X, 90, 2).

Pliny's usage may be illuminated by the epigraphical evidence, since the invocation of the imperial *indulgentia* is nowhere more widespread than in inscriptions connected with public building. Mention has already been made of the dedication of Trajan from Forum Claudii (above, p. 42). It is addressed to *optimo [et*

68 For the text see William Seston and Maurice Euzennat, "Un dossier de la chancellerie romaine, la Tabula Banasitana: Étude de diplomatique," *CR Acad. Inscr.* 115 (1971): 470. The corrected reading *in[dul]gentia principalis* is supported by A.N. Sherwin-White, "The Tabula of Banasa and the Constitutio Antoniniana," *JRS* 63 (1973): 88, n. 6 against James H. Oliver's *in gente a principali* ("Text of the Tabula Banasitana, AD 177," *AJPhil.* 93 (1972): 336; 338–9). The present discussion, it is hoped, may strengthen the case for the reading offered by the original editors.

indul]gentissim[o principi] for having constructed an aqueduct and defrayed the expenses out of his own pocket. However, more akin in spirit to Pliny's usage are those inscriptions in which the imperial *indulgentia* is not expressed in material generosity but rather in the permission to carry out a project. Thus the inscription from Gortyn in Crete specifies that the reconstruction and redecoration of a *competus* is subsidised from funds sacred to the local goddess, but the project owes its existence to the *indulgentia* of Marcus Aurelius and Verus.[69] Similarly, although funds for road-building by the Milevitani of Numidia come from a tax imposed on vehicles, nevertheless the building of the road is attributed to the imperial 'indulgence': *ex auctoritate Imp. Caes. T. Aeli Hadriani Antonini Aug. Pii p. p., via a Milevitanis munita ex indulgentia eius de vectigali rotari.*[70] Successus Amoenianus, a public slave of Asisium, financed the building of a chapel with porches, an altar and a table to Iuppiter Paganicus "*ex indulgentia dominorum.*" This may refer to the reigning emperors rather than, as Dessau maintains, to his municipal masters.[71] In other inscriptions we cannot determine what the *indulgentia* stands for. A dedication from Verecunda (Lambesis) to Antoninus Pius speaks of an aqueduct built "*ex indulgentia (eius).*"[72] A third century inscription from Thysdrus (Africa) uses the same formula, "*ex indulgentia principis,*" to describe the supervision by Annius Rufinus of the building of an aqueduct in the colony.[73] The "*infatigabilis indulgentia*" of Severus Alexander is responsible for the fortification and extension of the walls of *castella* in Africa.[74]

On other occasions it seems that the emperor financed the project himself. Elagabalus is described as "*felicissimus adque*[75] *invictissimus ac super omnes retro principes indulgentissimus*" in two inscriptions celebrating his restoration of a road.[76] A market place (*macellum*) was restored "*ex indulgentia sacra*" of Severus Alexander.[77] The restoration of the Via Annia by the *providentissimus princeps* Maximinius is to be counted "*inter plurima indulgentiar(um) suar(um) in Aquileiens(es).*"[78] The Emperors Valerian and Gallienus, and the Caesar P. Cornelius Saloninus Valerianus "*indulgentia sua*" restored the bridge of Secula which had

---

69 *CIL* III 14120 = *IC* IV 333, AD 169.
70 *CIL* VIII 10327 = *ILS* 5874; 10328; 22391 – all from Antoninus Pius' time, not from Hadrian's as Gaudemet (*Indulgentia Principis*, 10) maintains.
71 *CIL* XI 5375 = *ILS* 3039.
72 *CIL* VIII 4205 = 18495 = *ILS* 5752, AD 160/4.
73 *CIL* VIII 51 = *ILS* 5777.
74 *CIL* VIII 20486; *AE* 1917/18, no. 68; *AE* 1966, nos. 593, 594.
75 *atque* in the second of these two otherwise identical inscriptions, see following note.
76 *CIL* VIII 10304 = *ILS* 471; 10308.
77 *CIL* V 1837 = *ILS* 5589.
78 *CIL* V 7992 = *ILS* 5860.

burnt down.[79] The city of Caesena rebuilt a bath-house "*ex liberalitate imp. Caes. M. Aureli*;"[80] but the funds came from the 'indulgence' of Aurelianus: "*servata indulgentia pecuniae eius, quam deus Aurelianus concesserat, facta usurarum exactione.*"[81] An inscription of the time of Constantine from Thignica in Africa speaks of "*fori holitori indulta pecunia.*"[82] Finally, "*ex indulgentia*" of Valentinus and Valens a "*forum transitorium*" in Lambesis which had collapsed was – probably, since the fragment breaks here – restored.[83]

Related to the subject of public building is that of favours shown to local senates. The imperial *indulgentia* is shown here in the permission granted to them to enrol supernumerary councillors in their *boulé*. Unlike ordinary councillors, these had to pay the *honorarium decurionatus*,[84] thereby increasing the local income: "*ii quos indulgentia tua quibusdam civitatibus super legitimum numerum adicere permisit, et singula milia denariorum et bina intulerunt*" (Pliny, *Ep.* X, 112, 1). In the next century the people and senate of Lanuvium built and dedicated spacious hot baths to replace their old bath-house. The funds came "*ex quantitatibus, quae ex indulgentia dominorum nn. principum* (i.e. Septimius Severus and Caracalla) *honorariarum summarum sacerdotiorum adquisitae sunt.*"[85] The resemblance is striking.

The emperor's *indulgentia* is also invoked in the context of the status of cities. Amisus in Pontus is a city both *libera* and *foederata*, and owing to the "*beneficium indulgentiae tuae*," as Pliny tells Trajan, it enjoys the use of its own laws (*Ep.* X, 92). In his replay (*Ep.* X, 93) Trajan puts it slightly differently: it is owing to the *beneficium foederis* that Amisus enjoys the use of its own laws. It is likely that Pliny is speaking loosely, referring all privileges to the *indulgentia* of the living emperor.[86] Trajan's rephrasing of Pliny's words shows that even if he is aware of Pliny's implied flattery, nevertheless he prefers to emphasize the objective legal situation.[87]

---

79 *CIL* XI 826 = *ILS* 539. Gaudemet's *pontem seculae VI ignis consumpt.* makes no sense; surely it should read *vi ignis.*

80 *CIL* XI 556 = *ILS* 5687.

81 For another instance of imperial permission to use *usurae*, see *CIL* XIV 2101 = *ILS* 5686.

82 *CIL* VIII 1408 = *ILS* 5359 = Alfred Merlin, *Inscriptions latines de la Tunisie* (Paris: Presses Universitaires de France, 1944), no. 1307.

83 *CIL* VIII 2772 = *ILS* 5358.

84 See Peter Garnsey, "Honorarium Decurionatus," *Historia* 20 (1971): 309 ff.

85 *CIL* XIV 2101 = *ILS* 5686.

86 Contra A.N. Sherwin-White, *The Letters of Pliny: A Historical and Social Commentary* (Oxford: Clarendon Press, 1966), 687–8.

87 See András Alföldi's illuminating remarks (*Die Kontorniaten* (Leipzig: Harrasowitz, 1943), 40) on the significance of the replacement of an objective, legal terminology by that of 'indulgence' and 'free gifts' in the later Roman Empire.

The connection between the confirmation of a *foedus* and the imperial *indulgentia* re-appears in a dedication from AD 210 from Camerinium in Umbria to Septimius Severus: *caelesti eius indulgentia in aeternam securitatem adque gloriam iure aequo foederis sibi confirmato.*[88] Four colonies documented their gratitude to the reigning emperor by whose *indulgentia* their status was confirmed and their prestige enhanced. We have already mentioned the dedication of an unknown colony to Augustus (above, p. 37). Ostia owed a debt to Hadrian: *colonia Ostia conservata et aucta omni indulgentia et liberalitate eius.*[89] The *indulgentia* of the same emperor is mentioned in an inscription from Colonia Canopitana in Africa Proconsularis: *[E]x indulgentia Imp(eratoris) Caes(aris) Hadriani Aug(usti) p(atris) p(atriae), term(inus) leguae col(oniae) Canopitanae (tria) mil(ia) pas(suum).*[90] The editor suggests that the borders were demarcated at the time that the colony was founded.[91] Thus the *indulgentia* applies both to the foundation of the colony and to the delimitation of its territory. And finally Colonia Alexandriana Augusta Uchi Maius in Africa was "*promota honorataque*" by "*indulgentia Augusti nostri,*" i. e. Severus Alexander.[92]

In 324–6 the people of Orcistus (on the borders of Phrygia and Galatia) were granted the *ius civitatis* by Constantine. The grant was conceived as "*indulgentiae nostrae munus*" as we learn from its re-confirmation in 331 against the claims of the city of Nacolea. These claims are "*ultra indulgentiae nostrae beneficia,*" and therefore the Emperor proceeds to instruct the *rationalis* of the Asian diocese to follow the "*forma indulgentiae concessae*" and forbid the exaction of money by Nacolea.[93]

However, neither in this inscription nor elsewhere is *indulgentia* used exclusively. Rather the contrary is true. We have already mentioned the case of the alimentary inscriptions. In the example just discussed the request for city status is said to have supplied the imperial *munificentia* with an object on which it could be exercised: *Incolae Orcisti ... iucundum munificentiae nostrae materiam praebuerunt.*[94] And although in their own petition the people of Orcistus appealed to the "*auxilium pietatis vestrae,*"[95] the Emperor speaks of an appeal to his *clem-*

88 *CIL* XIV 5631 = *ILS* 432.
89 *CIL* VI 972 = XIV 95, AD 133.
90 Azedine Beschaouch, "Éléments celtiques dans la population du pays de Carthage," *CR Acad. Inscr.* 123 (1979): 403–7 = *AE* 1979, no. 658.
91 Beschaouch, 405, n. 33.
92 *CIL* VIII 15447, AD 230.
93 *MAMA* IV 305, panel iii = André Chastagnol, "L'inscription constantinienne d'Orcistus," *MÉFRA* 93 (1981): 381–416.
94 *MAMA* IV 305, panel i, 9–12.
95 *MAMA* IV 305, panel ii, 18.

entia: "*Qui cum praecarentur, ut sibi ius antiquum nomenque civitatis concederet nostra clementia* ..."[96] Finally, it is the "*lenitas nostra*" (of the Emperor) which instructs the *rationalis* in the letter of 331 to defend Orcistus' rights.[97]

It can easily be demonstrated that for every context in which *indulgentia* occurs, cases may be found where it is altogether missing[98] or where comparable terms like *liberalitas*[99] and *munificentia*[100] appear instead. Sometimes the act being praised is seen from a totally different point of view and *providentia* is used.[101] But it is especially in the case of *indulgentissimus* that our information fails us. The context is almost always unspecified. However, the concatenation of several superlatives with *indulgentissimus* may tell against the existence of specific contexts in which it is especially likely to appear.[102] Indeed, there are cases where *indulgentissimus* seems interchangeable with any superlative.[103]

Since for Pliny the use of *indulgentia* was restricted to specific contexts, his variations are even more significant than those of a later age, when the term lost some of its original connotations and tended to merge with others. Thus we find Pliny using *bonitas tua* in the very same contexts in which he has used *indulgentia*: in the request of a *latus calvus* for Voconius Romanus (*Ep*. X, 4, 2), in requesting a *commeatus* for himself (X, 8, 5) and in his request for the *ius trium liberorum* for Suetonius (X, 94, 2). In one of the requests for citizenship "*consuetudine bonitatis tuae*" appears (X, 11, 1). "*Si premiseris*" occurs twice in requests for a building license, in the very same context in which *indulseris* has been used: once in reference to a bath-house built by the *indulgentia* of Trajan (X, 70, 3); and again in a request for permission to build a cover over a filthy stream (X, 98, 2). "*Permitteret*" crops up in the context of the request to transfer the collection of statues from Pliny's possession to that of the city of Tifernum Tiberinum (X, 8, 1).

---

96 *MAMA* IV 305, panel i, 42–4.

97 *MAMA* IV 305, panel iii, 25.

98 E.g., *ILS* 5685; 5818–25; Angelo Russi, "Contributo al CIL, XVII: i miliari della via Traiana presso Aecae (Troia)," *Epigraphica* 43 (1981): 109–10, frag. 2; 112, frag. 3 (Trajanic).

99 E.g., *ILS* 286; 703.

100 E.g., *ILS* 5885; 313.

101 E.g., *ILS* 5876; 613; 298 (*providentissumus*)

102 For examples see *Diz. Epigr.* IV s. v. *indulgentissimus*; cf. also the inscription in honour of Maxentius (G.M. Bersanetti, "Iscrizione leptitana in onore di Massenziop," *Epigraphica* 5–6 (1943–44.): 27–39): *[In]dulgentissimo ac libertatis restitutori victorissimoque Imperatori domino nostro Maxentio pio felici invicto Augusto.*

103 E.g., *CIL* VIII 12061–64, in which *nobilissimus* and *fortissimus* (12062 and 12064 respectively) come in exactly the same place in which *indulgentissimus* comes in the other two.

Beneficium, the outcome of the emperor's *indulgentia*, may replace it in requests for citizenship: *Rogo itaque, ut beneficio tuo legitime frui possim, tribuas ei et Alexandrinam civitatem [et Romanam]* (X, 6, 2; cf. X, 11, 1). The transfer of Caelius Clemens to Bithynia gives Pliny a "*mensura beneficii tui*" (X, 51, 2). The supernumerary senators enrolled in the city council are described as "*buleutae additi beneficio tuo*" (X, 39, 5). The term is also used to refer to the Emperor's permission to build a bath-house (X, 70, 3).

Having been nominated to the augurate in compliance with his request (X, 13), Pliny no longer speaks of the imperial *indulgentia* but rather of the *iudicium* of the Emperor revealed in the act of nomimating him (IV, 8, 1).

The above survey has yielded mainly negative results. So much is clear: *indulgentia* did not have the attributes of a technical term; its use was neither obligatory nor restricted to particular contexts. Nevertheless it did tend to appear in certain contexts, as we have shown, as well as in certain collocations in what seem to be common turns of phrase, forms of speech, or idioms. We have mentioned the '*indulgentia ducis*' (above, p. 39). Another collocation appears in Iavolenus' *dictum* (above, p. 42), namely that of *indulgentia* and various forms of the adjective *plenus* and forms of the derived adverb.[104] It recurs also in connection with Nerva's concession regarding the making of soldiers' wills (above, p. 40). This collocation is not restricted to the Digest text alone. A contemporary inscription from Aquileia exemplifies it as well: *ut pleniorem indulgentiam ... habeamus per eum contigisse.*[105] Pliny's usage concurs, as four places in his correspondence demonstrate, in three of which one also notices the collocation "*indulgentiam experiri.*" One of his letters to Trajan opens with: *Indulgentia tua ... quam plenissimam experior, hortatur me ...* (X, 4, 1); "*cum plenissimo testimonio indulserat,*" he says about Nerva's permission for the transfer of the emperors' statues (X, 8, 2); and again to Trajan: *Ex illo enim et mensuram beneficii tui penitus intellego, cum tam plenam indulgentiam cum tota domo mea experiar* (X, 51, 2); lastly in expressing his reservations about the request for *ius Quiritium*: *Vereor enim, ne sit immodicum pro omnibus pariter invocare indulgentiam tuam, qua debeo tanto modestius uti, quanto pleniorem experior* (X, 104). *Indulgentia* and *beneficium* are not only causally but also idiomatically connected, as "*beneficium indulgentiae tuae*" in Pliny's *Ep.* X, 51 and 92 shows (above, pp. 45 and 48 respectively). Finally there is the "*indulgentia tua dignus*" of *Ep.* X, 21 and 86b (above, p. 44).

---

104 Admittedly, the *plenissime* in Iavolenus' *dictum* goes with *beneficium interpretari*.
105 Above, p. 42 at n. 47.

We have now surveyed the history of *indulgentia* from Caesar to Trajan. Concentrating on the age of Trajan we have tried to indicate the lines of future development. We have not so far mentioned contexts in which *indulgentia* would appear in later periods, unless it had already been used in such contexts under Trajan.[106]

However, not only do the contexts in which *indulgentia* appears become more numerous, but further developments take place. Under Hadrian, *indulgentia*, like so many other virtues and blessings, also become a coin type.[107] It is represented as a Juno-type goddess with sceptre and the right hand extended in a gesture of generosity.[108] The personification and deification of the imperial *indulgentia* is also noticeable in such expressions as *indulgentia divina*,[109] *indulgentia sacra*[110] and *indulgentia caelestis*.[111] It is seen in a concrete form in the dedication from Cirta from the year 210. Caecilius Natalis as *triumvir* donated an *aedicula tetrastyla* with a "*statua aerea Indulgentiae domini nostri*."[112]

106 For other contexts see Gaudemet, *Indulgentia Principis*, 8–13. The survey is not complete. *PSI* 1026 is conspicuously absent: "*ex indulgentia divi Hadriani*" soldiers had been conferred from the fleet to the legions; also Fronto, *Ad M. Caes.* V, 50, where M. Aurelius in reply to Fronto's appeal on behalf of the tax-farmer Saenius Pompeianus, whose accounts are to be scrutinized by Antoninus Pius, expresses his hope that "*omnia ei ex indulgentia domini mei patris obsecundare*"; see Edward Champlin, *Fronto and Antonine Rome* (Cambridge, Mass.: Harvard University Press, 1980), 61.

107 On the multiplication of personified abstracts under the Emperor see Jean Beaujeu, *La religion romaine à l'apogée de l'empire* (Paris: Les Belles Lettres, 1955), 424 f.

108 See Henry Cohen, *Description historique des monnaies frappées sous l'empire romain*, Vol. II (Paris – London: Rollin & Feuardent, 1882), 126, no. 325; 176, nos. 845, 846; Paul L. Strack, *Untersuchungen zur römischen Reichsprägung des zweiten Jahrhunderts, Vol. II: Die Reichsprägung zur Zeit des Hadrian* (Stuttgart: Kohlhammer, 1933), 123 and nos. 198, 325; Harold Mattingly, *BMC* III, 305, nos. 518–21; 310, nos. 548, 549; 311, nos. 550, 551; 361, no. 594a; 455, no. 1420; 462, no. 1464a; Anne S. Robertson, *Roman Imperial Coins in the Hunter Coin Cabinet, University of Glasgow, Vol. II: Trajan to Commodus* (London: Oxford University Press, 1971), nos. 188, 189, 484, 485. The list is restricted to Hadrianic coins. The type appears later as well.

109 *Dig.* 1, 4, 3, cited above, p. 42 at n. 50.

110 *CIL* V 1837 = *ILS* 5589: *ex indulgentia sacra dom. n. invicti imp. M. Aur. Alexand. Aug. ...*; *CIL* VIII 23072: *ex indulgentia sacra dd. nn. Constantii et Constantis*; *CIL* VI 31776 (a+b): *ob insignem eius erga se benevolentiam qua sibi paravit indulgentiam sacram alloqui* (Elagabalus); *P.Ryl.* 614 (late second century) is too mutilated for us to know the context of *sacra indulgentia*.

111 *CIL* VI 31320: *ob maximam erga se domu[s divinae] caelestem indulgent[iam]*, AD 198–201; *CIL* XI 5631 quoted on p. 49 at n. 88.

112 *CIL* VIII 7095 = *ILS* 2933, cf. *CIL* VIII 6996 (probably the *titulus* to *indulgentia* that stood in the *aedicula tetrastyla*). *CIL* VIII 2194 reads *indulgentia* and not *indulgentiae* (cf. Gaudemet, *Indulgentia Principis*, 8, n. 28) and thus it is not a dedication to Caracalla's *indulgentia*, but only to the three deities mentioned at the beginning of the inscription.

Like other terms of its kind *indulgentia* too became a form of address and a common title. However, it seems to have retained its specific connotations even in later texts, and not to have been used indifferently.[113]

Indulgentia, however, developed some technical specialized meanings: from *indulgentia* as an abstract moral disposition of the emperor from which all *beneficia* could emanate; through an intermediate stage in which specific *beneficia* tended to be traced back to it; to the final stage in which *indulgentia*, detached from the person of the emperor, became the technical term for two concrete juristic institutions: remission of debts or taxes, and abolition of sentences, for which two titles stand in the Theodosian Code: "*de indulgentiis debitorum*" (XI, 28)[114] and "*de indulgentiis criminum*" (IX, 38).[115] *Indulgentia* in these two narrow technical senses coexisted with the more general meaning.[116]

We may return now to the end of the first century AD and address ourselves to the more complicated issue of the reason for the increasing association of *indulgentia* with the person of the emperor at that time. Pliny's letters document the term contemporaneously with its first appearance in legal writings and imperial proclamations, as well as with a significant increase in its use in dedicatory inscriptions. This cannot be a pure coincidence, especially in view of what we know about Pliny's conformity and his tendency to reflect faithfully the general currents of his time.

The first step towards the formulation of an answer can be sought in the precise connotations of *indulgentia*: the primary and original meaning of the term which is still very much present in its later occurrences. *Indulgentia* is first and foremost the natural affection and emotion which the parent feels towards a child, as one of its earliest uses makes clear: *si ferae partus suos diligunt, qua nos in liberos nostros indulgentia esse debemus?* (Cicero, *De oratore* II, 168). The parental *indulgentia* is the counterpart of the filial *pietas* as is manifest of the juxtaposition of the two terms in the final appeal to the jury in Cicero's *Pro Caelio* (79): *Quod cum huius (Caelius') vobis adulescentiam proposueritis, constituitote ante oculos etiam huius* (Caelius' father's) *miseri senectutem ... quem vos supplicem vestrae misericordiae ... vel recordatione parentum vestrorum vel liberorum iucunditate sustentate, ut in alterius dolore vel pietati vel indulgentiae vestrae serviatis.*

113 See the examples from the Theodosian Code collected in Richard M. Honig, *Humanitas und Rhetorik in spätrömischen Kaisergesetzen* (Göttingen: Schwartz, 1960), 110 f.

114 On which see Gaudemet, *Indulgentia Principis*, passim.

115 On which see Waldstein, *Untersuchungen zum römischen Begnadigungsrecht: Abolitio-Indulgentia-Venia*, 162 f.; 172 f.; 110 f.

116 Cf. Waldstein, 132.

The chiastic order stresses the point: those of you who are sons should feel *pietas* towards the elder Caelius and those of you who are fathers should feel *indulgentia* towards Caelius.[117]

Unlike the other virtues *indulgentia* is not a single exemplary quality but rather a disposition appropriate to anyone in a position of a parent. In fact it is a totality, for it represents a whole range of paternal emotions and attitudes. Therefore its meaning is likely to overlap with that of other attributes, but first and foremost with that of *liberalitas* (*munificentia*) on the one hand and *clementia* (*mansuetudo*) on the other. *Indulgentia* and *liberalitas* can appear in inscriptions as synonyms of each other, as in the formula applied twice to military *alae*[118] and once to a *cohors*;[119] "*indulgentiis eius aucta liberalitatibusque ditata*," or in that used by the colony of Ostia: "*colonia Ostia conservata et aucta omni indulgentia et liberalitate eius* (Hadrian)."[120] Tacitus seems not to make a distinction between them in describing Vespasian's gift of money to the poet Saleius Bassus: "*laudavimus nuper ut miram et eximiam Vespasiani liberalitatem, quod quingenta sestertia Basso donasset. Pulchrum id quidem, indulgentiam principis ingenio mereri*" (*Dialogus de oratoribus* 9, 5).[121]

The distinction between *liberalitas* and *indulgentia* is not easy to draw when they are both operating in the same sphere. On the whole, however, *liberalitas* seems to have taken on more concrete forms: *congiarium*, *donativum*, *remissio* of taxes and debts to the treasury, gifts to private people, building activity, aid after catastrophies, games and *alimentatio*.[122] True, some of these activities, as seen above, were attributed to the emperor's *indulgentia*. Yet *indulgentia* seems to transcend the sphere of material generosity,[123] especially when its meaning overlaps with that of *clementia*, in the sense of remission or mitigation of penalties.[124] The

---

117 Cf. Jacob van Wageningen's paraphrase in *M. Tulli Ciceronis Oratio pro M. Caelio* (Groningen: Noordhoff, 1908), 110.

118 *CIL* III 797; 1378.

119 *AE* 1979, no. 492; cf. Endre Tóth, *Porolissum: Das Castellum in Moigrad. Ausgrabungen von a. Radnóti, 1943* (Budapest: Magyar Nemzeti Múzeum, 1978), 22–4.

120 *CIL* VI 972 = XIV 95.

121 Cf. also Suetonius, *Tib.* 46.

122 Cf. Kloft, *Liberalitas Principis*, passim.

123 *Liberalitas* once did too, cf. Kloft, 61.

124 See Wilhelm Köhler, "Personifikationen abstrakter Begriffe auf römischen Münzen" (University of Königsberg Thesis, 1910), 69; Traute Adam, *Clementia Principis* (Stuttgart: E. Klett, 1970), 24–7. For the combination *'clementiae indulgentia'* see *Historia Apollonii Regis Tyri* 20 (on which see Elimar Klebs, *Die Erzählung von Apollonius aus Tyrus: Eine geschichtliche Untersuchung über ihre lateinische Urform und ihre späteren Bearbaitungen* (Berlin: G. Reimer, 1899), 235) and *Cod. Theod.* II, 6, 1, AD 316: *per indulgentiam nostrae clementiae.*

Emperor Domitian uses the verb *indulgere* in this sense for the first time in our sources (for Suetonius claims to be quoting him): "*Permittite, patres conscripti, a pietate vestra impetrari, quod scio me difficulter impetraturum, ut damnatis liberum mortis arbitrium indulgentis*" (*Dom.* 11, 3); and Suetonius in the same Life uses the verb again to describe the reduction of the death penalty to exile: "*praetorio viro ... exilium indulsit*" (*Dom.* 8, 4). From the second half of the second century *indulgentia* also appears in connection with remission of penalties imposed by criminal law.[125] In this sense it was to become one of the many links between the history of the Empire and that of the Church. But along the way it had lost much of the richness which made its application to the master of Rome so useful. We must turn now to the reasons for this application.

The association of *indulgentia* with the person of the emperor may have been bound up with an attempt to emphasize a particular aspect of the imperial regime, namely the imperial paternalism.[126] There is nothing novel of course in the attempt to liken the ruler to a father.[127] At an early stage the term *pater patriae* was inserted into the official nomenclature, although, true to its republican origins, it signified that the Princeps was the *servator* or *conservator* of his fellow citizens, and was associated with the *corona civica*.[128] Rhetorical and philosophical disquisitions on the title followed, as for example in Seneca: *Hoc, quod parenti, etiam principi faciendum est, quem appellavimus Patrem Patriae non adulatione vana adducti. Cetera enim cognomina honori data sunt; Magnos et Felices et Augustos diximus et ambitiosae maiestati quicquid potuimus titulorum congessimus illis hoc tribuentes; Patrem quidem Patriae appellavimus, ut sciret datam sibi potestatem patriam, quae est temperantissima liberis consulens suaque post illos reponens* (*De clementia* I, 14, 2).

Nor was Pliny one to miss an opportunity of elaborating on a title. Thus chapter XXI of the Panegyricus is devoted to the title *pater patriae*. Trajan was *pater patriae* even before assuming the title (§ 3). And from the moment he had taken it up: "*quod quidem nomen qua benignitate qua indulgentia exerces! ut cum civibus tuis quasi cum liberis parens vivis!*" (§ 4). This is in fact one of the few

125 Cf. Waldstein, *Untersuchungen zum römischen Begnadigungsrecht: Abolitio-Indulgentia-Venia*, 131 f.

126 Cf. Chaim Wirszubski, *Libertas as a Political Idea at Rome during the Late Republic and Early Principate* (Cambridge: Cambridge University Press, 1950), 167–71; Jean Béranger, *Recherches sur l'aspect idéologique du principat* (Basel: F. Reinhardt, 1953), 252–78.

127 Cf. András Alföldi, *Der Vater des Vaterlandes im römischen Denken* (Darmstadt: Wissenschaftliche Buchgesellschaft, 1978), 112 = "Die Geburt der kaiserlichen Bildsymbolik: Kleine Beiträge zu ihrer Entstehungsgeschichte," *MH* 11 (1954): 133.

128 Cf. Alföldi, *Der Vater des Vaterlandes im römischen Denken*, 40 = "Die Geburt der kaiserlichen Bildsymbolik: Kleine Beiträge zu ihrer Entstehungsgeschichte," *MH* 9 (1952): 204.

places in which *indulgentia* is mentioned in this speech.[129] Its absence from the list of virtues recorded at the opening of the speech[130] is conspicuous in view of its frequency in the letters to the Emperor. The contrast with the letters is intriguing. It is to be explained perhaps by the fact that the Panegyricus is the speech of the consul and the senator delivered before the senate; its *Leitmotif*, as observed by others,[131] is the *moderatio* and *modestia* of Trajan. Another explanation is that when the Panegyricus was delivered *indulgentia* had not yet established itself in the phraseology of the age as it was to do later on.[132]

Yet even if *indulgentia* is to a large extent absent from the Panegyricus, the insistence on the paternal aspect of the emperor is there. One of the most common ways of addressing Trajan (and referring to Nerva) is by the title *parens*. The note is struck right at the beginning when Pliny announces: "*non enim de tyranno, sed de cive; non de domino, sed de parente loquimur* (*Pan.* II, 3). "*Parens noster*" in IV, 2 is used in reference to the prohibition of private expressions of thanks. Nerva is "*imperator et parens generis humani*" in VI, 1. In VII, 4 it is asserted that "*eodemque animo divus Nerva pater tuus factus est, quo erat omnium*"; whereas in X, 6: "*ille nullo magis nomine publicus parens, quam quia tuus.*" Chapter XXI is devoted to the assumption of the title *pater patriae* by Trajan (see above). In connection with the remission of the inheritance tax Trajan is "*communis omnium parens*" (XXXIX, 5). Contrasting Trajan's attitude towards his slaves and freedmen with that of previous emperors, Pliny maintains that: "*Non enim iam servi nostri principis amici sed nos sumus, nec pater patriae alienis se mancipiis cariorem quam civibus suis credit*" (XLII, 3). Trajan is called "*parens publicus*" since he reorganized the corn distributions to children (XXVI, 3).[133] In LIII, 1 Pliny expresses his belief in the moral superiority of Trajan: "*longa consuetudine corruptos depravatosque mores principatus parens noster reformet et corrigat.*" His confidence in the good faith of Trajan is grounded on the manner and the content of the latter's words: "*Equidem hunc parentis publici sensum cum ex oratione eius tum pronuntiatione ipsa perspexisse videor*" (LXVII, 1). Trajan is called again "*parens publicus,*" when he is praised for not using force and for respecting liberty (LXXXVII, 1), or

129 For the other occasions in which *indulgentia* is mentioned see above, pp. 44 f. In *Pan.* LXXIV, 5 it refers to the gods: "*Civitas religionibus dedita semperque deorum indulgentiam pie merita nihil felicitati suae putat adstrui posse, nisi ut di Caesarem imitentur.*"

130 *Pan.* III, 4, where we find: *humanitas, frugalitas, clementia, liberalitas, benignitas, continentia, labor* and *fortitudo*.

131 E.g., Helen North, *Sophrosyne: Self-Knowledge and Self-Restraint in Greek Literature* (Ithaca: Cornell University Press, 1966), 306.

132 By the time Pliny reached Bithynia, cf. Syme, *Tacitus*, Vol. II, 659 f.

133 "*ut iam inde ab infantia parentem publicum munere educationis experirentur ... tantumque omnes uni tibi quantum parentibus suis quisque deberent.*"

when he is said to be on familiar terms with some of the senators (LXXXVII, 3). In electing Trajan Jupiter was giving a son to Nerva, a parent ("*parens*") to Rome and a priest to himself (XCIV, 4).

A contemporary official record echoes Pliny's usage: the Acts of the Arval Brethren of March 25, AD 101 insert the unofficial title *princeps parensque noster* after the cognomen Germanicus and before *pontifex maximus*, notwithstanding the *pater patriae* which appears later on.[134]

In being a *parens* the emperor was not forfeiting any power or authority. The *patria potestas* was absolute enough to satisfy the most autocratic of rulers.[135] The *potestas* of the father over his children was as unlimited as that of the master over his slaves.[136] Despite Panegyricus II, 3 (above, p. 56), the real contrast is not between a *dominus* and a *parens*, but rather between the two and a *civis*. The *indulgentia-pietas* bond is a bond between unequals.[137] In Panegyricus XLII, 2 a list of the proper emotions in the following relationship is offered: "*Reddita est amicis fides, liberis pietas, obsequium servis.*" *Pietas* is the proper emotion for a son to feel towards his parents, the paternal emperor and the gods;[138] nevertheless there is no real contrast between *pietas* and *obsequium* – the proper servile emotion – as Panegyricus X, 3 shows: "*neque aliud tibi ex illa adoptione quam filii pietatem filii obsequium adsereres.*"

Indeed the paternal aspect of the emperor may wear more than a single expression. *Indulgentia* is only one facet of the paternal emperor; it is the one chosen to soften the harsh aspects of the *patriae potestas*. It denotes the love,

---

134 Wilhelm Henzen, *Acta Fratrum Arvalium* (Berlin: G. Reimeri, 1874), cxl-cxliii; though Claudius too is called *divinus princeps parensque publicus* in the Acts of the Arval Brethern, cf. Henzen, lvii. Cf. Berlinger, "Beiträge zur inoffiziellen Titulatur der römischen Kaiser," 79 f. and Franz Sauter, *Der römische Kaiserkult bei Martial und Statius* (Stuttgart – Berlin: Kohlhammer, 1934), 28–31 for the application of the title *parens* to other emperors in non-official sources.

135 Cf. Alföldi, *Der Vater des Vaterlandes im römischen Denken*, 45 = "Die geburt Der kaiserlichen Bildsymbolik: Kleine Beiträge zu ihrer Entstehungsgeschichte" (1952), 209; Anton von Premerstein, *Vom Werden und Wesen des Prinzipats* (München: Beck, 1937), 166–75.

136 The combination *dominus indulgentissimus* occurs very often in the inscriptions, perhaps in order for the two words to qualify each other. *Indulgentia* is as desirable in a *dominus* as in a father, cf. *CIL* II 4909; III 4020, 5745, 5998, 6900; VI 1052, 1065, 1174. And recently *AE* 1977, no. 810: *[D]ominis indulgentissimis Pompon[(ius) ...]ianus proc(urator)*, cf. Stephen Mitchell, "R.E.C.A.M. Notes and Studies No. 1: Inscriptions of Ancyra," *Anatolian Studies* 27 (1977): 65.

137 Cf. *Pan.* XXIV, 5: "*... te civium pietas super ipsos principes vehunt*"; LV, 4: "*si quando pietas nostra silentium rupit et verecundiam tuam vicit*"; LXXIX, 4: "*Pietati certe senatus cum modestia principis ... certamen*"; *Ep.* X, 9 (Trajan to Pliny): "*ne impedisse cursum erga me pietatis tuae videar*"; X, 13: "*ut iure sacerdotii precari deos pro te publice possim, quos nunc precor pietate private.*"

138 Cf. *Pan.* LXXIV, 5 quoted above, n. 129.

affection, care and even indulgence that the parent entertains towards his children. It contrasts sharply with, and transcends, the legal bond between them. In this sense alone can one speak of it at an early date as an extra-legal term, not so much expressing the mitigation of law as going beyond it, to the sphere of gratuitous acts.[139] No *ius* or right could be invoked as a title to the emperor's favours, no claim can be made on him. The emperor's gifts are not deserved but freely given, not due but magnanimously bestowed. His *indulgentia* invites one to put a request to him, to which otherwise one has no innate, legitimate right: "*Indulgentia tua ... hortatur me ut audeam tibi etiam pro amicis obligari*" (Pliny, *Ep.* X, 4, 1); or with more elaboration: "*felicitas temporum ... ad usum indulgentiae tuae provocat et attollit*" (*Ep.* X, 12, 2). The most a man could do was to rely on the emperor's former favours as precedents for subsequent requests: "*peto a te cuius in omnibus desideriis meis indulgentiam experior*" (*Ep.* X, 94, 3). One notices that the request of a man who appeals to the emperor's *indulgentia* easily takes (or deteriorates into) the forms familiar from addresses to the gods[140] whom the emperors came more or less to resemble.[141] Indeed in being a *parens*, the emperor stood nearer to the gods than to his fellow men.

The process has its obverse and more sinister aspect. The likening of the emperor to a father and the insistence on his *indulgentia* conflicts with the image of the *princeps civilis*,[142] the *princeps* as a fellow-citizen, a fellow-senator, an equal, a friend-*amicus*. The *indulgentia-pietas* bond between the paternal *princeps* and his subjects excludes a relationship of reciprocity: it is the extinction of *amicitia* – in the old sense – between him and his subjects. The omnipotent *princeps* who monopolizes all *beneficia* doles them out to his subjects, not for a return in kind, which the latter cannot dream of ever being able to make, but in return for *pietas*,[143] and this perforce makes the beneficiary an inferior.[144]

---

139 Cf. Veyne, "La table des Ligures Baebiani et l'institution alimentaire de Trajan (2e Article)," 226 f.

140 Often in prayers a god is asked to help because he has done so in the past; for examples see R.G.M. Nisbet and Margaret Hubbard, *A Commentary on Horace: Odes, Book I* (Oxford: Clarendon Press, 1970), 360 on Ode I, 32, 1. For the relative clause following the name of a god, or a pronoun referring to the god ("*peto a te, cuius* ..." etc.) see Eduard Norden, *Agnostos Theos: Untersuchungen zur Formengeschichte religiöeser Rede* (Leipzig: Teubner, 1913), 168 f.

141 Cf. Pliny, *Pan.* IV, 3: "*cum interea fingenti formantique mihi principem, quem aequata dis immortalibus potestas deceret* ..."

142 For the concept see Andrew Wallace-Hadrill, "Civilis Princeps: Between Citizen and King," *JRS* 72 (1982): 32–48.

143 See above, n. 137.

144 Cf. Kloft, *Liberalitas Principis*, 178–82.

When reciprocity is stamped out so is equality, its natural concomitant. Futile empty rhetorical conceits might be used to argue "*a minore ad maius*" that the emperor is the best of all friends, since, as Pliny tells Trajan: "*tibi amicos tuos obligandi tanta facultas inest, ut nemo te possit nisi ingratus non magis amare*" (*Pan.* LXXXV, 8). But the over-embellished argument is its own undoing; it destroys the very relationship it set out to establish. For friendship is the happy mean and delicate balance which an infinite and unilateral *facultas obligandi* is all too apt to upset.

We started this discussion with Pliny; we may end it with him. If anywhere at all, it is in the correspondence between this ex-consul, specially appointed by the Emperor to govern a problematic province, that we would have expected to find the terminology of friendship, lip-service paid to the image of the *princeps civilis* and compliance with the demands supposedly laid down by 'egalitarian' social etiquette. In their stead we find the suppliant voice of the humble official appealing even in matters within his domain to the *indulgentia* of his master.

The Role of Cicero's Letters of Recommendation: *Iustitia* versus *Gratia*?

Cicero's letters of recommendation are mostly appeals to Roman officials in the provinces on behalf of people whose interests came within the officials' sphere of competence (*imperium; potestas*). Yet not only do the letters often fail to refer to the official authority vested in the recipient, but the paucity of references to it contrasts sharply with the multitude of appeals to the man's *humanitas, liberalitas, voluntas, integritas, mansuetudo, clementia, studium, officium* etc. All of these are patently personal qualities not derived from the man's official position.[1] Likewise few recommendations explicitly ask for an official act on the part of the addressee. Generally they are requests to extend his friendship (*fides, amicitia, necessitudo* and similar terms) to the person or persons recommended.[2] We may note also the non-committal verbs used, perhaps euphemistically but nonetheless constantly, in the context of the request.[3]

The informal language and the personal tone are altogether in tune with the nature of these letters: although in the main not intimate, they are neither official nor semi-official letters – as one writer describes them[4] – but private letters even when addressed to officials. It is the ties of friendship uniting the persons

1 E.g.: (to Caesar) "*Huic ego ... benevolentiam tuam et liberalitatem peto*" (*Fam.* VII, 5, 3); (to Silius) "*Id cum gratum mihi erit tum etiam existimabo te humanitate tua esse usum*" (*Fam.* XIII, 64, 1); (to Valerius Orca) "*Eorum ego domicilia, sedes, rem, fortunas ... tuae fidei, iustitiae bonitatique comendo*" (*Fam.* XIII, 4, 3); (to Sulpicius Rufus) "*quom ea facies Lacedaemoniorum causa quae tuafides, amplitudo, iustitia postulat ...*" (*Fam.* XIII, 28a, 2).

2 E.g.: (to Valerius Orca) "*Ipsum hominem, quem tibi commendo, perdignum esse tua amicitia ... credo*" (*Fam.* XIII, 6, 4); (to Allienus) "*Peto ... a te ut ... recipias eum in tuam fidem ... si ... dignum eum tua amicitia hospitioque cognoveris, peto ut eum complectare, diligas, in tuis habeas*" (*Fam.* XIII, 78, 2); (to Sulpicius Rufus) "*Lysonem in fidem necessitudinemque recipias*" (*Fam.* XIII, 19, 2); (to Gallus) "*Oppium igitur praesentem ut diligas*" (*Fam.* XIII, 43, 2); (to Marcus Brutus) "*Bonos viros ad tuam necessitudinem adiunxeris*" (*Fam.* XIII, 11, 3); (to Acilius) "*Peto ... abs te ut omnibus rebus ... ei commodes habeasque in numero tuorum*" (*Fam.* XIII, 35, 2).

3 E. g.: (to Silius) "*Peto ut quod habet in tua provincia negoti expedias*" (*Fam.* XIII, 63, 2); (to Sulpicius Rufus) "*T. Manlium ... quibuscumque rebus ... poteris, iuveris atqueornaveris*" (*Fam.* XIII, 22, 2); (to Brutus) "*operamque des ut per te quam commodissime negotium municipi administretur*" (*Fam.* XIII, 11, 2).

4 Friedrich Lossmann, *Cicero und Caesar im Jahre 54: Studien zur Theorie und Praxis der römischen Freundschaft* (Wiesbaden: F. Steiner, 1962), 15.

Article note: First published in *Hermes* 114 (1986): 443–460, with the following note: I would like to dedicate this paper to the memory of M.W. Frederiksen, who together with P.A. Brunt offered constructive criticism, which, I hope, improved my argument.

https://doi.org/10.1515/9783110770438-004

concerned which constitute the main justification for putting forward a recommendation.[5]

In what light are we to regard these personal and non-official interventions in the working of provincial government?

Perhaps the argument should be taken one step further and be made more specific. It is noticeable that most of the recommendations are written on behalf of Roman *negotiatores* and *publicani*[6] whose interests often, if not always, clashed with those of the provincials. In fact Cicero admits to his brother Quintus that reconciling the conflicting interests of these two groups is the hardest task facing the provincial governor: "*Atqui huic tuae voluntati ac diligentiae difficultatem magnam afferunt publicani: quibus si adversabimur, ordinem de nobis optime meritum et per nos cum re publica coniunctum et a nobis et a re publica diiungemus; sin autem omnibus in rebus obsequemur, funditus eos perire patiemur, quorum non modo saluti, sed etiam commodis consul<ere deb>emus. Haec est una, si vere cogitare volumus, in toto imperio tuo difficultas*" (*QFr.* I, 1, 32).

And if letters of recommendation were intended to tilt this delicate balance in favour of one group, may one not suggest that although the surface never so much as hints at them, the polite language of social intercourse conceals sinister appeals to coercion and the use of brute force? May one go even further and maintain that many of the acts of abuse, exploitation and oppression committed

5 On the paramount importance of the ties of friendship between recommender and recommended on the one hand and recommender and recipient on the other hand, see Roman Andrzejewski, "La structure de la lettre de recommandation antique a la lumière des principes de la rhetorique," *Roczniki Humanistyczne* 21, no. 3 (1973): 17 (in Polish with a résumé in French) and Hannah M. Cotton, *Documentary Letters of Recommendation in Latin from the Roman Empire* (Königstein/Ts.: Hain, 1981), 19; 50 f.

6 By *negotiatores* I mean anyone who has *negotia* in the province, even if not referred to by this title, see *Fam.* V, 5 (Atticus); XII, 21 (C. Anicius, a senator); XII, 24 (T. Pinarius, a procurator); XII, 26 and 27 (heirs of Q. Turius, a *negotiator*); XII, 29 (L. Aelius Lamia, *princeps equestris ordinis* in the 50s); XIII, 14 (C. Titius Strabo, a knight); XIII, 17 (M. Curius, a *negotiator*); XIII, 18 (Atticus); XIII, 21 and 27 (M. Aemilius Avianius, a *negotiator*, and C. Avianius Hammonius, his freedman procurator); XIII, 22 (T. Manlius, a *negotiator*); XIII, 23 (L. Cossinius, a cattle-raiser); XIII, 38 (L. Bruttius, a knight); XIII, 44; 45; 47; 73; 74 (L. Egnatius Rufus, a *negotiator*, L. Oppius, his procurator, and Anchialus, his slave); XIII, 53 (L. Genucilius Curvus); XIII, 55 and 57 (M. Anneius, Cicero's legate); XIII, 56 (M. Cluvius, a banker); XIII, 61 (T. Pinnius, money-lender); XIII, 63 (M. Laenius Flaccus, a knight); XIII, 66 (A. Caecina); XIII, 69 (C. Curtius Mithres, a freedman); XIII, 72 (an heir to the *negotiator*, C. Vennonius); XIII, 79 (C. and M. Avianius, sons of a corn-dealer). For publicans and public companies see *Fam.* XIII, 6 and 6a (P. Cuspius and the members of the African public company, especially L. Iulius and P. Cornelius); XIII, 9 (the Bithynian public company and especially, P. Rupilius and Cn. Pupius); XIII, 65 (P. Terentius Hispo, *promagister* of the public company which collects the *scriptura*).

by Roman officials in the provinces were initiated and perpetuated by such seemingly innocuous letters?

This and more. Where the vagueness and obscurity characteristic of such letters[7] give way to some detail, a matter of litigation or legal dispute is generally at hand. This comes out vividly in a complaint launched by a correspondent which Cicero mentions along with his own report: "*Itane? praeter litigatores nemo ad te meas litteras? Multae istae quidem; tu enim perfecisti, ut nemo sine litteris meis tibi se commendatum putaret*" (*Fam.* XII, 30, 1). This is hardly a cause for surprise. Jurisdiction, after all, was the main duty of the governor in a peaceful province, as Cicero points out to his brother Quintus, the governor of Asia at the time: "*Ac mihi quidem videtur non sane magna varietas esse negotiorum in administranda Asia, sed ea tota iurisdictione maxime sustineri*" (*QFr.* I, 1, 20).

It is precisely because these letters contain appeals to officials in matters concerning the latter's judicial competence that they may justly be held to reflect Roman attitudes towards the administration of justice. Any discussion of their role and function in the system of Roman provincial government must take into account the interpretation put on them by J.M. Kelly in his *Roman Litigation.*[8] To him these letters are "first-hand material on how *gratia* or *potentia* worked in practice."[9] He brands the appeals contained in them as "improper influences in Roman litigation,"[10] since they conflict with "the theory of an equal and objective justice" which "was perfectly familiar" to the Romans.[11] One may make his point even more strongly: *aequum ius* or *aequae leges*, namely equality before the law, one law binding on all, was regarded by the Romans as the essence and foundation of Republican *libertas*: "*Quare cuum lex sit civilis societatis vinculum, ius autem legis aequale, quo iure societas civium teneri potest, cum par non sit condicio civium? Si enim pecunias aequari non placet, si ingenia omnium paria esse non possunt; iura certe paria debent esse eorum inter se, qui sunt cives in eadem republica. Quid est enim civitas, nisi iuris societas?*" (Cicero, *Rep.* I, 49).[12]

These letters are, therefore, in Kelly's eyes an outright attempt to tamper with the working of the law, even though, on his own admission, "We never find in so

---

7 Cf. Hannah M. Cotton, "Cicero, Ad Familiares XIII, 26 and 28: Evidence for Revocatio or Reiectio Romae/Romam?," *JRS* 69 (1979): 41 [above, p. 7].

8 John Maurice Kelly, *Roman Litigation* (Oxford: Clarendon Press, 1966).

9 Kelly, 55.

10 This is the title of the second chapter of his book in which the letters of recommendation are discussed.

11 Kelly, *Roman Litigation*, 61.

12 See Chaim Wirszubski, *Libertas as a Political Idea at Rome during the Late Republic and Early Principate* (Cambridge: Cambridge University Press, 1950), 1 f.

many words the request that justice and the rules of law should be sidestepped or partially applied; only a request for favours so far as justice will permit." But he goes on to ask: "are not justice and favour mutually exclusive ideas, even in Latin?"[13] Consequently he dismisses the saving clause, usual in such letters, "so far as your dignity and justice will permit," as a stock phrase "which probably meant as little to the recipient as to the sender, as the broad wink of *gratia* passed between them."[14]

The incompatibility of favour (*gratia*) and justice (*iustitia*), observed by Kelly, is illustrated by a definition of the *ius civile* in Cicero's *Pro Caecina* 73: "*Quod enim est ius civile? Quod neque inflecti gratia neque perfringi potentia neque adulterari pecunia possit.*"[15] *Ius* and *gratia* are contrasted also in a letter of recommendation to Quintus Cicero, the governor of Asia. Cicero is rebuking his brother for acting unlawfully in the case of the praetor designate, L. Flavius, who was prevented by Quintus from coming into his inheritance in the province before the demands on it were met: "*Haec mihi veri similia non videntur; sunt enim a prudentia tua remotissima. Ne deminuat heres? quid, si infitiatur? quid, si omnino non debet? quid? praetor solet iudicare deberi? quid? ego Fundanio* (the claimant) *non cupio, non amicus sum, non misericordia moveor? Nemo magis; sed vis iuris eius modi est quibusdam in rebus ut nihil sit loci gratiae*" (*QFr.* I, 2, 10).

The exercise of *gratia* cannot be justified by the existence of *amicitia* between the recommender and the recommended person, or between the recommender and the recipient, for the judge himself is debarred from showing to a friend more favour than is compatible with the demands of impartial justice.[16] In fact, friendship itself should be renounced once wrongful claims are made in its name.[17]

Thus the exercise of *gratia* and the elevation of the claims of *amicitia* over those of justice are strongly condemned by Cicero himself as subversive and incompatible with the principle of *aequum ius*. Nevertheless, Cicero, with what looks like perverse inconsistency, by writing letters of recommendation lays himself open to this very charge of improper influence and fragrant subversion of justice. The inconsistency is not diminished, nor does the charge lose its force by the insertion of the saving clause. For, as Kelly sees it, the formula "so far as

---

13 Kelly, *Roman Litigation*, 58.

14 Kelly, 61.

15 Cf. Kelly, 32 f.

16 Cf. Cicero, *Off.* III, 43: "*At neque contra rem publicam neque contra ius iurandum ac fidem amici causa vir bonus faciet, ne si iudex quidem erit de ipso amico. Ponit enim personam amici cum induit iudicis.*"

17 Cicero, *Amic.* 33 f.

your dignity and justice will permit" merely pays lip service to an ideal of equal and objective justice which "no one reckoned on finding ... applied in practice."[18]

The argument is persuasive but not unassailable. Its main flaw is that it compels us to regard Cicero either as a hypocrite or as naive. He was the former if we accept Kelly's dismissal of the saving clause as mere lip service; and he was the latter if he was unaware of the difficulty of yoking together two disparate and incompatible concepts, *gratia* and *iustitia*, and trying to satisfy both the demands of justice and of friendship simultaneously. Cicero's correspondents, with whose connivance (or obtuseness) Cicero pays a specious tribute to an ideal of impartial justice while hoping to tamper with its application, are no less guilty of one of the aforementioned faults.

The first part of our reply to Kelly addresses the larger issue mentioned above, namely the role and function of letters of recommendation in the Roman system of government and the light in which such personal interventions in its working should be regarded. Therefore, we shall begin with general considerations of the principles underlying the working of Roman provincial government, the code of behaviour to which its officials subscribe and the discretion which we allow them to have had.

As is well known, the provincial governor enjoyed very wide discretionary powers. Cicero contrasts them once with those of the praetor at Rome: "*ubi tanta arrogantia est, tam immoderata libertas, tam infinita hominum licentia, denique tot magistratus, tot auxilia, tanta vis <plebis>, tanta senatus auctoritas*" (*QFr*. I, 1, 22). No such checks existed on the powers of the provincial governor; here, in the provinces "*tanta multitudo civium, tanta sociorum, tot urbes, tot civitates unius hominis nutum intuentur, ubi nullum auxilium est, nulla conquestio, nullus senatus, nulla concio*" (*ibid.*).[19]

The real constitutional checks on the almost untrammelled powers of the provincial governor seem to have amounted to a general supervision of the senate over the provinces,[20] the charters of the individual cities[21] and the constant threat

---

18 Kelly, *Roman Litigation*, 61.

19 However, the governors must have been bound by the terms of their own edicts; the wording of the *Lex Cornelia* of 67 BC which demanded "*ut praetores ex edictis suis perpetuis ius dicerent*" (Asconius, *Corn*. 52, ed. Clark) does not exclude them, since *praetor* was used as a generic term for provincial governors, see Theodor Mommsen, *Römisches Staatsrecht*, Vol. II (Graz: Akademische Druck- u. Verlagsanstalt, 1952), 240, n. 5. See, however, Peter A. Brunt, "Lex De Imperio Vespasiani," *JRS* 67 (1977): 108, n. 68.

20 See Mommsen, *Römisches Staatsrecht*, Vol. III, 1121 f.

21 For an example of such a treaty see now the *senatus consultum de Aphrodisiensibus* in Joyce Reynolds, *Aphrodisias and Rome* (London: Society for the Promotion of Roman Studies, 1982), 54–91, document 8.

of being put on trial at Rome for crimes committed during his term of office. The effectiveness of these measures and safeguards depended to a large extent on a nonconstitutional factor whose importance can hardly be overemphasized, namely the governor's concern for his reputation and prestige – his *existimatio*.[22]

In his famous advisory letter to his brother, on whose evidence we have drawn before, Cicero compares the province to a theatre in which one displays one's virtues and enhances one's *existimatio*: "*Qua re quoniam eius modi theatrum totius Asiae virtutibus tuis est datum, celebritate refertissimum, magnitudine amplissimum, iudicio eruditissimum, natura autem ita resonans, ut usque Romam significationes vocesque referantur, contende, quaeso, atque elabora, non modo ut his rebus dignus fuisse sed etiam ut illa omnia tuis artibus superasse videare*" (*QFr.* I, 1, 42).

The claim made here for the crucial importance of the governor's *existimatio* is fully substantiated by the tone and manner of Cicero's letters of recommendation to provincial governors. Here various locutions and formulae receive their explanation. In fact, regard for the governor's *existimatio* is one instance of the general regard of the recipient's interests which is the key to the *decorum* of letters of recommendation.[23] The list of saving clauses and formulae[24] shows clearly that no other obstacle to compliance with a request was assumed apart from the fear that the request might injure the governor's *existimatio*.

An elaborate expression of Cicero's desire to do justice to both claims, that of the recommended person's interests on the one hand and that of the governor's *existimatio* on the other hand, is found in a letter to P. Servilius Rufus, the governor of Asia in 46 BC, written on behalf of the sons of Antipater of Derbe:[25] "*A te autem pro vetere nostra necessitudine etiam atque etiam peto ut eius filios, qui in tua provincia sunt, mihi potissimum condones, nisi quid existimas in ea re violari existimationem tuam. Quod ego si arbitrarer, numquam te rogarem mihique tua fama multo antiquior esset quam illa necessitudo est; sed mihi ita persuadeo (potest fieri ut fallar) eam rem tibi laudi potius quam vituperationi fore*" (*Fam.* XIII, 73, 2).

22 Cf. Cotton, "Cicero, Ad Familiares XIII, 26 and 28: Evidence for Revocatio or Reiectio Romae/Romam?" 41 and n. 28 there [above, p. 8 and n. 29].

23 Cotton, 41 [above, p. 7].

24 See below, n. 26.

25 See Ronald Syme, "Observations on the Province of Cilicia," in *Anatolian Studies Presented to William Hepburn Buckler*, ed. W.M. Calder and Josef Keil (Manchester: Manchester University Press, 1939), 309–11 = *Roman Papers*, Vol. I (Oxford: Oxford University Press, 1979), 128–31.

No less eloquent are the briefer clauses inserted in most of the letters.[26] We learn indirectly from them the attributes necessary for the governor's *existimatio* or *dignitas*: *iustitia, fides, ius, aequitas, honestum* and *rectum* are the typical terms. More explicit definitions are offered to Quintus: "*Qua re sint haec fundamenta dignitatis tuae: tua primum integritas et continentia*" (*QFr*. I, 1, 18). And a little further: "*qua re sit summa in iure dicendo severitas, dum modo ea ne varietur gratia sed conservetur aequabilis*" (§ 20).[27] Atticus too regarded *continentia, diligentia,*[28] *summa modestia* and *summa abstinentia*[29] as the qualities on which Cicero's good name – for which he was most solicitous[30] – rested. And Cato praised Cicero after his governorship for just these qualities: *virtus, innocentia* and *diligentia*.[31]

But are not letters of recommendation, by their very nature, overt attempts to compromise the governor's integrity and impartiality, to sway him in favour of the person or the group whose interests they represent? May the letters not be the triggers for acts of oppression as suggested above?

In support of this view we may recall the famous incident of Marcus Brutus and the people of Salamis.[32] The letter of recommendation written to Cicero by Brutus on behalf of M. Scaptius and P. Matinius presumably read like any of Cicero's recommendations of money-lenders in the provinces, as might be gathered from the letters to Atticus where Cicero partly quotes, partly paraphrases its contents: "*familiares habet Brutus tuus quosdam creditores Salaminorum ex Cypro, M. Scaptium et P. Matinium, quos mihi maiorem in modum commendavit*" (*Att*. V, 21, 10); "*quin etiam libellum ipsius habeo in quo est 'Salamini pecuniam debent M. Scaptio et P. Matinio, familiaribus meis.' Eos mihi commendat; adscribit etiam et quasi calcar admovet intercessisse se pro iis magnam pecuniam*" (*Att*. VI, 1, 5).

---

26 E.g.: (to Brutus) "*operamque des, quoad tibi aequum et rectum vibebitur, ut ... negotium conficiant*" (*Fam*. XIII, 14, 2); (to Sulpicius Rufus) "*T. Manlium ... quibuscumque rebus honeste ac pro tua dignitate poteris, iuveris*" (XIII, 22, 2); (to the same) "*Illud... si non alienum tua dignitate putabis esse, feceris mihi pergralum*" (XIII, 26, 3); (to the same) "*cum ea feceris mihi pergratum*" (XIII, 26, 3); (to the same) "*cum ea facies Lacedaemoniorum causa quae tua fides, amplitudo, iustitia postulat ...*" (XIII, 28a, 2); (to Acilius) "*peto a te ... ut iis omnibus in rebus, quantum tua fides, dignitasque patietur, commodes*" (XIII, 32, 2); (to Silius) "*a teque ... peto ut quod habet in provincia negoti expedias, quod tibi videbitur rectum esse ipsi dicas*" (XIII, 63, 2). It is worth noting the non-formulaic expression in *Fam*. XIII, 55, 2, to Thermus: "*Ius enim quem ad modum dicas clarum et magna cum tua laude notum est. Nobis autem in hac causa nihil aliud opus est nisi te ius instituto tuo dicere.*"

27 Cf. "*sed via iuris eius modi est quibusdam in rebus ut nihil sit loci*" (*QFr*. I, 2, 10), cited above.

28 *Att*. V, 3, 3.

29 *Att*. V, 9, 1.

30 "*Flens mihi meamfamam commendasti; quae epistula tua est in qua mentionem non facias?*" (*Att*. VI, 1, 8).

31 *Fam*. XV, 5, 1.

32 *Att*. V, 21, 10–12; VI, 1, 3–8; VI, 2, 7–9; VI, 3, 5–7.

Cicero promised to comply with Brutus' request: "*Pollicitus ei sum curaturum me Bruti causa ut ei Salamini pecuniam solverent*" (*Att.* V, 21, 10). The request to confer a *praefectura* on Scaptius so as to enable him to use military force in order to exact the debt from the people of Salamis was not conveyed in writing; it was made orally by the recommended person: "*Egit (Scaptius) gratias; praefecturam petivit*" (*ibid.*). Thus it may be assumed that Cicero's recommendations too were accompanied by such oral requests – or that the governor was expected to read such a request between the lines – which patently gave the lie to the manner and content of the written appeal, which explicitly requested a peaceful intervention, limited by the demands of justice and equity, and recognized the need to preserve the governor's good name which rested on the possession of these qualities.

The sequel of the Salaminian affair, however, proves the opposite of what the above-mentioned opinion maintains: Cicero could not reconcile the request for a *praefectura* with his own *existimatio*, which rested, as he saw it, on not bestowing a *praefectura* on a *negotiator* and in abiding by the terms of his own *institutum*[33] (*Att.* VI, 1, 7).

We may use this incident as evidence that at least one governor refused to go beyond what could be honourably committed to writing and what befitted the *decorum* of a letter of recommendation, in order to rebut the view which cynically dismisses the courtesies and civilities in letters of recommendation as mere lip-service paid to a code of behaviour to which no one subscribed.

In fact, the evidence of these letters seems to redress the imbalance reflected in the traditional view of Roman provincial government: acts of abuse and maladministration may have eclipsed in their glaring and conspicuous brutality the more tranquil and regular conduct of provincial government.

There is much to be said for the view which regards letters of recommendation not as calls for coercion but as calls for an exercise of *auctoritas*, namely a call for the use of the governor's influence in order to convince the provincials to come to terms with the Roman publicans and money-lenders. However, the possibility of peaceful collaboration with the provincials seems to have depended on the governor's ability to have gained beforehand a reputation for integrity and clemency. Thus the governor's *existimatio* both prepares the way for collaboration with the provincials and is, in turn, enhanced by it.

The advisory letter to Quintus makes it quite clear that this is the only way in which the governor may hope to reconcile the almost incompatible interests of the

---

33 "*Negavi me cuique negotianti dare, quod idem tibi ostenderam (Cn. Pompeio petenti probaram institutum meum ...),*" *Att*, V, 21, 10; cf. VI, 1, 4; VI, 1, 6; VI, 2, 8 etc.

Greeks and the Romans in the province: "*remoto imperio ac vi potestatis et fascium publicanos cum Graecis gratia atque auctoritate coniungas ... et ab iis de quibus optime tu meritus es* (i. e. the Greeks) *et qui tibi omnia debent hoc petas, ut facilitate sua nos eam necessitudinem quae est nobis cum publicanis obtinere et conservare patiantur*" (*QFr.* I, 1, 35). Cicero used this very argument in order to convince the people of Salamis to pay their debt to their Roman money-lenders: "*petivi etiam pro meis in civitatem beneficiis ut negotium conficerent*" (*Att.* V, 21, 11).

It is not a coincidence, therefore, that it is those governors who are known to have conducted themselves most honourably, P. Silius and Q. Minucius Thermus,[34] who receive requests to use their personal influence with the provincials. Thermus' *auctoritas* is founded on his *integritas*, *gravitas* and *clementia* (*Fam.* XIII, 55, 2) and similarly that of Silius on his *integritas*, *humanitas* and *mansuetudo* (*Fam.* XIII, 65, 1). Cicero writes to the latter on behalf of the public company which farms the *scriptura*. He requests Silius' assistance in concluding the *pactiones* with the reluctant cities, confessing that he himself could not induce the cities to reach an agreement with the representative of the company, P. Terentius Hispo: "*sed quoniam, quem ad modum omnes existimant et ego intellego, tua cum summa integritate tum singulari humanitate et mansuetudine consecutus es ut libentissimis Graecis nutu quod velis consequare, peto a te in maiorem modum ut honoris mei causa hac laude Hisponem adfici velis*" (*ibid.*).

To read more sinister intentions into this language is to charge Cicero with downright hypocrisy. The onus of proof, particularly in the case of recommendations written to upright governors,[35] is on those who refuse to take the manner and the tone on the one hand and the terminology on the other hand at their face value.

The need for peaceful collaboration with the provincials is further explained by the essential passivity of the Roman provincial administration. On the whole one tends to accept Greenidge's formulation that "the amount of administrative work which the governor undertook was as much or as little as he pleased."[36] The governor's intervention in provincial affairs was bound to be fitful and intermit-

34 "*Thermum, Silium vere audis laudari*," *Att.* VI, 1, 13.

35 Less upright governors were not insensitive to the question of their *existimatio*, as Verres' efforts to keep it prove (see Zvi Yavetz, "Existimatio, Fama, and the Ides of March," *Harv. Stud.* 78 (1974): 42 and n. 23 there for references) or Appius Claudius Pulcher's indignation at the obstacles put in the way of the provincial legationes sent to sing his praises at Rome (*Fam.* III, 8, 1 f.; III, 10, 6 f.).

36 A.H.J. Greenidge, *Roman Public Life* (London: Macmillan, 1901), 324.

tent and often followed upon the exercise of initiative from below, not least among which are the letters of recommendation studied here.[37]

Another aspect of these letters is thereby revealed: they fulfilled an essential function in a system of government which left the governor with wide discretionary powers on the one hand, and without the machinery needed to carry out judicial and administrative transactions on a regular and impersonal basis on the other hand. Hence we may regard these letters as part and parcel of the Roman political system as opposed to the ancillary role which they have in modern bureaucracy. One can hardly regard letters of recommendation as irregular interferences in the regular working of government where no such regularity existed. There is room to suspect that whatever we might resolve into a well-defined system of government, may have been in reality a sequence of ad hoc decisions resulting from personal appeals, in the name of personal ties, to wide discretionary powers vested in the official addressed. This wide discretion of the Roman governor should deter us from too hastily branding the governor's bestowal of personal favours as illegal. At the same time it extended the realm of what was considered legal to cover all that was tolerated by public opinion and the governor's conscience, or rather his regard for his *existimatio*. Within this realm personal and non-official influence could be brought to bear.

Having thus delineated the general framework within which Cicero's letters of recommendation operated, we may now turn to the letters themselves to seek in them extenuating circumstances which would keep the exercise of *gratia* within the bounds of *iustitia* and allow it to be compatible with it.

The legal disputes mentioned in these letters do not necessarily imply court proceedings. More often than not Cicero's letter is aimed at something quite different from obtaining the governor's favour at the trial stage. Hence these letters should not be seen as attempts to bias the judge and influence the verdict itself.

Court proceedings were distasteful to the Romans and they tried to avoid them:[38] the recommendation was one way of doing so. This may take the form of a direct appeal to prevent litigation, as Cicero does in the case of his translator's son's mother in-law. Thermus is requested to help and bring about "*ut socrus*

---

37 For the administration of justice in the provinces under the Republic see Anthony J. Marshall, "Governors on the Move," *Phoenix* 20 (1966): 231, and for the Empire see G.P. Burton, "Proconsuls, Assizes and the Administration of Justice under the Empire," *JRS* 65 (1975): 92.

38 See John Maurice Kelly, *Studies in the Civil Judicature of the Roman Republic* (Oxford: Clarendon Press, 1976), 93 f. for some of the evidence. The distaste for the courts goes hand in hand with regarding *leges* as a necessary evil. Legislation, as Tacitus in the digression on law-making points out, reflects the breaking down of the old standards (*Ann.* III, 26–27): "*corruptissima respublica plurimae leges.*"

adulescentis rea ne fiat" (*Fam.* XIII, 54). On other occasions the governor's influence is enlisted as an alternative to legal remedies, to induce the other party to settle out of court. Thus P. Silius is asked, as we have seen above, to urge the Greek cities to conclude their *pactiones* with P. Terentius Hispo.[39]

In the case of the succession of Cicero's former quaestor, L. Mescinius Rufus, to the inheritance left to him by his cousin, M. Mindius, Servius Sulpicius Rufus is requested to threaten Mindius' widow, Oppia, with a remittal of the case to Rome as means of swiftly concluding the affair, presumably out of court: "*adiuves ineasque rationem quem ad modum ea mulier Romam perducatur. Quod si putarit illa fore, ut opinio nostra est, negotium conficiemus*" (*Fam.* XIII, 28, 2).[40]

An expeditious solution is desired in the case of Cicero's legate, whose services are indispensable to his superior (*Fam.* XIII, 57, 1). If legal proceedings have already begun, we may assume that Cicero attempts to prevent them from dragging on. But he could be asking for a swift solution out of court.[41] Finally, in his recommendation of T. Claudius Nero's protégé, Pausanias of Alabanda, Cicero is trying to delay legal proceedings pending Nero's arrival: "*de Pausania Alabandensi sustentes rem, dum Nero veniat*" (*Fam.* XIII, 64, 1).[42]

When Cicero requested a governor to refrain from action, he was not denying anyone his right – at least the Romans would not have seen it in this light. For it is well-known that classical law never formulated any idea of an individual's *right* to an action.[43] The presence of an *actio* does not necessarily imply that the man had a claim, but rather that there was a *formula* that could be adapted to his case, and the formula was a matter of agreement between the praetor (governor) and the two parties. This was another way in which the governor could, if he chose, remain passive without, however, depriving anyone of an inherent right.

---

39 *Fam.* XIII, 65, on which see Hannah M. Cotton, "A Note on the Organization of Tax-Farming in Asia Minor (Cicero, Fam. XIII, 65)," *Latomus* 45 (1986): 367–73.

40 For a full discussion of *Fam.* XIII, 26 and 28 see Cotton, "Cicero, Ad Familiares XIII, 26 and 28: Evidence for Revocatio or Reiectio Romae/Romam?" 39–50 [above, pp. 3–22].

41 *Controversia* in the previous letter concerning Cicero's legate and the people of Sardis, *Fam.* XIII, 55, 1 ("*Eum cum Sardinis habere controversiam scis*"), does not have to be used as a technical term to denote litigation and legal proceedings.

42 See Louis Harmand, "Note sur une lettre de Cicéron (Ad Fam., XIII, 64)," *Latomus* 6 (1947): 23; Elizabeth Rawson, "The Eastern Clientelae of Clodius and the Claudii," *Historia:* 22 (1973): 226. D.R. Shackleton Bailey, ed., *Cicero: Epistulae Ad Familiares*, Vol. I (Cambridge: Cambridge University Press, 1977), 476, suggests that "the heading is wrong and that this letter was really addressed to the governor of Asia"; cf. Rawson's review in *CR* 29 (1979): 51; Cotton, "A Note on the Organization of Tax-Farming in Asia Minor (Cicero, Fam. XIII, 65)."

43 See Michel Villey, "L'idée du droit subjectif et les systèmes juridiques romains," *RHDFÉ* 24 (1946–1947): 201.

Some letters have a prophylactic and provisory nature, as in the case of L. Genucilius Rufus, where Cicero requests Q. Minucius Thermus to hear in the assize centre of the area[44] any dispute which might arise in the future between this man and a provincial: "*si quid habebit cum aliquo Hellespontino controversiae, ut in illam* διοίκησιν *reicias*" (*Fam.* XIII, 53, 2). Similarly in the case of L. Manlius who inherited his brother's estate in Sicily, although no complications were foreseen at the time, it may safely be assumed that the recommendation was intended to provide for such an eventuality (*Fam.* XIII, 30). The same may be said about the recommendation of Lyso's son's right to inherit from the Roman exile, G. Maenius Gemellus, who adopted the young man in accordance with the local laws of Patrae (*Fam.* XIII, 19, 2).[45]

Cicero was perfectly aware of the existence of legislation which debarred the governor from taking cognizance in his court of debts (*pecuniae creditae*) incurred by free cities.[46] Nevertheless he writes on Atticus' behalf to two successive governors of Macedonia in order to help his friend to recover his debt from the free city of Sicyon.[47] He must have believed in the governor's ability to help, but he could hardly be thinking of court proceedings. The governor, it seems, could force the cities to send legal representatives (*ecdici*) to Rome (*Fam.* XIII, 56, 1), as we learn from the letter to Thermus on behalf of M. Cluvius of Puteoli: the governor is to issue an order to Alabanda and Mylasa, two free cities in Caria,[48] to send *ecdici* to Rome (*Fam.* XIII, 56, 1).

The variety of the requests surveyed here suggests a corresponding variety of means at the disposal of the governor. Whether these putative means are to be called judicial, administrative, extra-judicial, authoritative or by another name is often a matter of definition. These letters call on the governor to employ his discretion in the preliminaries, the procedure, the pace of the proceedings and so forth. Interference in these does not necessarily constitute a violation of justice,

44 On the assize system see Marshall, "Governors on the Move."

45 Since it has a bearing on the issue of 'double citizenship,' this seemingly modest request has been the subject of a fierce debate between Vincenzo Arangio-Ruiz, "Sul problema della doppia cittadinanza nella Repubblica e nell'impero romano," in *Scritti giuridici in onore di Francesco Carnelutti* (Padova: CEDAM, 1950), 59, n. 1 and Ernst Schönbauer, "Zur Entwicklung des 'Ius Publice Respondendi,'" *Iura* 4 (1953): 224–27.

46 See *Att.* I, 19, 9; 20, 4; *Prov. cons.* 6–7.

47 *Fam.* V, 5 to C. Antonius Hibrida. The letter to his successor, C. Octavius (cf. *Att.* XI, 1, 12) has not survived, but it is likely to have had the same purpose.

48 For their freedom see Pliny, *Naturalis historia* V, 108.

since the discretion of the governor was wide and the system was flexible: the use of discretion need not entail a reversal of justice.[49]

The language Cicero uses constitutes another proof; instead of the technical terms generally used in the context of jurisdiction we find in these letters vague and ambiguous terminology: "*Peto igitur a te ut in ea controversia, quam habet de fundo cum quodam Colophonio, et in ceteris rebus ... ei honoris mei causa commodes*" (*Fam.* XIII, 69, 2); "*Pergratum igitur mihi feceris ... si dederis operam ... ut quam plurimum pecuniae Pinnio solvatur Nicaeensium nomine*" (*Fam.* XIII, 61); "*Caunii ... debent, sed aiunt se depositam pecuniam habuisse. Id velim cognoscas et, si intellexeris eos neque ex edicto neque ex decreto depositam habuisse, des operam ut usurae Cluvio instituto tuo conserventur*" (*Fam.* XIII, 56, 3).[50] *Commodare, operam dare, cognoscere*[51] can hardly be described as legal terms. The rules of *decorum*[52] may go some way towards explaining the choice of terminology. However, the possibility cannot be excluded that Cicero does not use terms specifying strictly legal proceedings and judicial remedies because his mind was set on other measures.

We may test this assumption by examining the two letters to the praetors at Rome – *Fam.* XIII, 58 and 59 – where the exercise of jurisdiction is clearly in question. There are several features which set these letters apart. First, both letters stand out for their extreme formality and cordiality. In fact each letter is a series of set phrases and formulae. Secondly, although they are addressed to two different persons and written on behalf of two different litigants – one of whom, as we know from other evidence,[53] was a close friend of Cicero – nevertheless both letters use almost identical phraseology. No two letters addressed to the same governor bear such close resemblance to each other.[54]

---

49 *Off.* III, 43, cited above (n. 16), continues: "*Tantum dabit amicitiae, ut veram amici causam esse malit, ut orandae litis tempus, quoad per leges liceat, accommodet*"; it seems to be making an allowance for the use of discretion.

50 On deposit of money to stop the interest from accumulating see *Att.* VI, 1, 7.

51 "*Cognoscas*" in *Fam.* XIII, 56, 3, cited above, does not refer to the *cognitio* procedure, as maintained by Max Kaser, *Das römische Zivilprozessrecht* (München: Beck, 1966), 123, n. 57, but as in *Fam.* XIII, 55, 1 – "*cognosces*" – it means 'inquire into.'

52 Cf. Cotton, "Cicero, Ad Familiares XIII, 26 and 28: Evidence for Revocatio or Reiectio Romae/Romam?" 41 [above, p. 7].

53 We possess other letters written on his behalf: *Fam.* II, 14 (to M. Caelius Rufus), IX, 25, 2–3 (to L. Papirius Paetus) and XV, 14, 1 (to C. Cassius Longinus) – all probably occasioned by the same event that led to the writing of a recommendation to the praetor. *Fam.* VII, 23–27 are addressed to him.

54 The similarities suggest to Shackleton Bailey that they were written about the same time, *Cicero: Epistulae Ad Familiares*, Vol. I, 479. He may very well be right; however, if his explanation

Each of the two letters contains the following elements: 1) presentation of the recommended person and his relationship to Cicero; 2) a saving clause, somewhat expanded in the case of Cicero's friend, M. Fabius;[55] 3) the request itself, divided into three parts. The first of these is a request for accessibility. We find here two variants: "*ut facilis ad te aditus habeat*" (*Fam.* XIII, 58) and: "*ut quam facillimos ad te aditus habeat*" (XIII, 59). It is not easy to determine how this accessibility is to express itself. Should the praetor construe it as a modest plea to fix a date for hearing or as a more ambitious request to let the man 'jump the queue' of litigants trying to get a hearing at the praetor's court?[56] Perhaps here as elsewhere its indefiniteness is the formula's chief virtue: being vague it was less likely to give offence or meet with a rebuff. Thus not only the praetor's honour was safeguarded but Cicero's as well. The desire to make the recipient accessible is sometimes implicit in letters to governors, but never so explicitly stated.[57] The second part of the request proper is another saving clause; again we find two variants: "*quae aequa postulabit ut libente te impetret*" (XIII, 58) and "*quae erunt aequa libente te impetret*" (XIII, 59). Finally, there is a request that Cicero's absence and inability to deliver the request in person would not weaken its force and cogency. This is phrased, however, in a positive way: "*sentiatque meam sibi amicitiam, etiam*

---

is adopted exclusively, then one would have to conclude that no two other letters of recommendation were written at about the same time – which is clearly not the case.

55 For Fabius rather than Fadius see D.R. Shackleton Bailey, "Two Tribunes, 57 B. C.," *CR* 12 (1962): 195–96.

56 I know of no explicit evidence for the existence of such a queue; see, however, A.H.J. Greenidge, *The Legal Procedure of Cicero's Time* (Oxford: Clarendon Press, 1901), 135 f. for a discussion of the time at which court could be held: the comparatively few days assigned for this purpose permit us to assume the existence of such a queue. Perhaps one may draw on later evidence which explains the replacement of the public courts by that of the urban prefect as caused "*ob magnitudinem populi ac tarda legum auxilia*" (Tacitus, *Ann.* VI, 11, 3).

57 We learn from a letter to P. Servilius Isauricus, the governor of Asia, that the magnitude of affairs calling for the governor's attention compels Cicero to persist in recommending Caerellia's affairs to him (*Fam.* XIII, 72, 1). Numerous letters in our corpus repeat a recommendation made before either orally (*Fam.* XIII, 9, 1; 55, 1; 78, 1; *Att.* V, 20, 10) or in writing (*Fam.* XIII, 41 refers to 42; 28 refers to 26; 24 to 19; 57 to 55; 27 to 21; 44 to 43; cf. also 75, 1). The governor's business, slowness or inaccessibility may have occasioned some of these repeated appeals. Despite Cicero's protestations to the contrary, the repetition of a request served as a polite reminder, cf. *Fam.* XIII, 75. Cicero admits once to Servius Sulpicius Rufus that he often uses the expression of thanks as an opportunity to repeat and strengthen a previous request, cf. *Fam.* XIII, 27, 1.
The problem of access to the governor's court must have provided the occasion for praising the governor who showed "*facilitas in audiendo*" (see *QFr.* I, 1, 21; cf. ibid. § 32: "*facilem te ... in hominibus audiendis*") and grants "*faciles*" or "*facilissimi aditus*" to himself (*QFr.* I, 1, 25; *Att.* VI, 2, 5; *De imp. Cn. Pomp.* 41).

cum longissime absim,[58] *prodesse, in primis apud te*" (XIII, 58) and the variant: "*ut meam amicitiam sibi, etiam cum procul absim, prodesse sentiat, praesertim apud te*" (XIII, 59).

The formulaic similarity of the two letters to the praetors encourages us to think of two specimens of a special type with its own rules of *decorum*. These rules prescribe the tone, the manner, and, above all, the content of recommendations written to praetors. Only certain appeals are tolerated and the tactful writer will not go beyond these: facility of access, fair treatment, and due consideration for the recommender's friendship with the litigant even in the former's absence. When there is no room for exercising discretion, only jurisdiction, Cicero is held back from pressing his request beyond what the ideal of equal and objective justice as well as the rules of *decorum* permitted.

The disparity between the situation at Rome and that in the provinces is brought into further relief in the difference between letters of recommendation to praetors and those to provincial governors: the wide and almost untrammelled discretion of the provincial governor contrasts sharply with the competence of the praetors at Rome, circumscribed as it was by law and tradition. Cicero's tact and good taste lead him to adjust the content, the tone, and manner of his requests accordingly.

We have thus excluded a great many letters from the category of "improper influences in Roman litigation," but sometimes there is no denying that the letters addressed the governor in his capacity as judge. It is here that another consideration should be raised. Although the claims of friendship should not be put before those of justice, they may still be considered relevant to the case. The continual emphasis on the friendship between Cicero and the recommended person and the accompanying catalogue of the man's virtues are the most meaningful testimony to the credibility, trustworthiness, and good character of the litigant. These always had much weight in the Roman courts, and were to be seriously considered along with the facts themselves. In fact letters of recommendation fulfil the same function as that fulfilled by evidence of character, a *testimonium* or a *laudatio.*[59] The latter was considered a legitimate element in court proceedings: "*et laudare testem vel contra pertinet ad momentum iudiciorum, et ipsis etiam reis dare laudatores licet*" (Quintilian, *Inst.* III, 7, 2). In the absence of the *laudatores*, their *laudationes*, as we learn from Republican evidence, could be submitted in writing.[60]

---

58 This points to Cicero's proconsulate and dates the letter, cf. Shackleton Bailey, *Cicero: Epistulae Ad Familiares*, Vol. I, 479.

59 See Cotton, *Documentary Letters of Recommendation in Latin from the Roman Empire*, 5–6 and n. 28.

60 Asconius, *Pro Scauro* 25 (ed. Clark).

More than two centuries after Cicero, another writer of letters of recommendation, M. Cornelius Fronto, explicitly likens the *commendatio* to the *laudatio*, defending thereby the transfer of the *laudatio* from the court to a letter: "*Commendandi mos initio dicitur benivolentia ortus, cum suum quisque amicum ali amico suo demonstratum conciliatumque vellet. Paulatim denique iste mos progressus est, ut etiam eos qui publico vel privato iudicio disceptarent, non tamen improba res videretur iudicibus ipsis aut iis, qui consilio adessent, commendare, non, opinor, ad iustitiam iudicis labefactandam vel de vera sententia deducendam. Sed iste in ipsis iudiciis mos inveteratus erat causa perorata laudatores adhibere, qui quid de reo existimarent, pro sua opinione cumfide expromerent; item istae commendatium litterae laudationis munere fungi visae sunt*" (*Ep. ad Amicos* I, 1, 1).

Fronto's attempt to prove the legitimacy of a time-honoured institution and especially his assertion "*non opinor ad iustitiam iudicis labefactandam*" meet with Kelly's cynical scepticism: "perhaps not, but who would be so naive as to imagine that it could not have this effect?"[61] However, a recent discussion of Fronto's letters which does not lose sight of the moral character of both Fronto and his correspondent, Claudius Severus, both "highly honourable men, the latter an ardent student of philosophy," regards Kelly's allegation as misconceived: "this 'prooemium' of the orator on the custom of recommendation was surely intended to be not a plausible excuse for undue influence, but rather the reverse, a careful repudiation of anything dishonest."[62] It was included to prevent the judge, Claudius Severus, from taking the letter as a slight to his *gravitas* and *auctoritas*.

Clearly both the case of *laudatio* and that of *commendatio* should be studied against the background of the nature of the judicial proof in Roman litigation. All the studies devoted to the subject concur in stressing the prominent role played by evidence of character in the courts and the great weight, placed by the courts on the character of the parties and the witnesses alike.[63] The last was considered to have a direct bearing on the credibility of the witnesses' evidence:[64] "*Persona*

61 Kelly, *Roman Litigation*, 59.

62 Edward Champlin, *Fronto and Antonine Rome* (Cambridge, Mass.: Harvard University Press, 1980), 69.

63 Jean-Phillipe Lévy, "La formation de la théorie romaine des preuves," in *Studi in onore di Siro Solazzi* (Naples: Jovene, 1948), 418; Jean-Phillipe Lévy, "Cicéron et la preuve judiciaire," in *Droits de l'antiquité et sociologie juridique: mélanges Henri Lévy-Bruhl* (Paris: Sirey, 1959), 187; Jean-Phillipe Lévy, "Dignitas, gravitas, auctoritas testium," in *Studi in onore di Biondo Biondi* (Milano: Giuffrè, 1965), 29; Giovanni Pugliese, "La preuve dans le procès romain de l'epoque classique," in *La preuve: recueils de la société Jean Bodin*, Vol. I (Brussels: Librairie encyclopédique, 1965), 277; Kelly, *Roman Litigation*, 31 f.; Peter Garnsey, *Social Status and Legal Privilege in the Roman Empire* (Oxford: Clarendon Press, 1970), 210 f.

64 Lévy, "Cicéron et la preuve judiciaire," 194.

autem non qualiscumque est testimoni pondus habet; ad fidem enim faciendam auctoritas quaeritur" (Cicero, *Topica* 73). The insistence on *auctoritas* becomes so persistent that in many passages this word stands for 'evidence,' whereas *auctor* is used to refer to a witness.[65]

Once we agree that the *commendatio* may be regarded as evidence of character, we may legitimately apply to the recommender all that applies to the witness. His authority, his social and moral standing and his trustworthiness underwrote the *commendatio*. Similarly, the same criterion Cicero uses in one of his speeches to assess the defendant's guilt might be applied to that of the recommended person: "*nam perinde ut opinio est de cuiusque moribus, ita quid ab eo factum et non factum sit, existimari potest*" (*Pro Cluentio* 70). A *laudatio* or a *commendatio* becomes indispensable when character is listed among the judicial proofs: "*At vero in foro tabulas, testimonia, pacta conventa stipulationes, cognationes adfinitates, decreta responsa, vita denique eorum qui in causa versantur, tota cognoscenda est*" (Cicero, *De oratore* II, 100).

The principle of equality before the law in Roman eyes seems never to have excluded this emphasis on the *persona* of the litigants – and in *persona* one must include both moral and social standing.[66] Cicero, who solemnly upholds the principle of *aequum ius*, regards that equality which fails to recognize social distinctions as unequal: "*ipsa aequabilitas est iniqua, cum habet nutlos gradus Dignitatis*" (*Rep.* I, 43).[67] Perhaps it is not accidental that one of the most well-known definitions of justice in Roman law books, namely "*iustitia est constans et perpetua voluntas ius suum cuique tribuens*,"[68] can easily lend itself to an interpretation which includes the observance of social distinctions: "*Iustitia est habitus animi communi utilitate conservata suam cuique tribuens dignitatem*" (Cicero, *Inv. rhet.* II, 160).

Thus a plea can be made to the judge to do justice to both claims, that of the *dignitas* of the litigant on the one hand and that of the *veritas* of the case on the other hand: "*Illud quod tecum et coram et per litteras diligentissime egi, id et nunc etiam atque etiam rogo curae tibi sit, ut suum negotium, quod habet cum populo*

---

65 Lévy, "Dignitas, gravitas, auctoritas testium," 264–5.

66 Garnsey, *Social Status and Legal Privilege in the Roman Empire*, 210 f.

67 The Younger Pliny's advice to Calestrius Tiro, the proconsul of Baetica, echoes Cicero's statement: "*discrimina ordinum dignitatumque custodias; quae si confusa turbata permixta sunt, nihil est ipsa aequalitate inaequalius*" (*Ep.* IX, 5, 3).

68 *Inst. Iust.* I, 1, 1; cf. *Dig.* 1, 1, 10. Fritz Schultz, *History of Roman Legal Science* (Oxford: Clarendon Press, 1946), 136 maintains that such definitions came from the "Greek storehouse"; still they were adopted because they seemed adequate. For a rhetorical exposition see, Pseudo-Quintilian, *Declamationes Minores* 77, 14 f. (ed. Ritter), in the context of *aequatio patrimoniorum*.

Sardiano, pro causae veritatis et pro sua dignitate conficiat" (Cicero, *Fam.* XIII, 57, 2).

The tension we have detected between the two incompatible claims of *iustitia* and *gratia* is much reduced when we take into account the emphasis on *dignitas* and *persona* in the Roman notion of *aequitas*. At first these considerations were relevant to the trustworthiness of the person in his role as defendant or witness. Eventually it affected the penalties he might undergo. Social distinctions, as Peter Garnsey' study shows, were incorporated into the legal system itself, gradually hardening into a full-fledged system of discriminatory justice.[69]

We may conclude with a few cautionary remarks. It would be a mistake to regard a *commendatio* as an open attempt to override legitimate claims, to further illegal interests – in short to trample justice under foot. Conversely, it should not be assumed that were the request legitimate, the law unambiguous, and justice clearly on the side of the recommended person, a letter of recommendation would not have been written. The existence of a recommendation does not automatically make the man for whom it was written suspect, nor does it show the elevation of the claims of *gratia* and *amicitia* over those of *iustitia* – not even when Cicero himself says so, as in his letter to Q. Valerius Orca: "*Sed mihi minus libet multa de aequitate rei scribere, ne ca usa potius apud te valuisse videar quam gratia*" (*Fam.* XIII, 5, 3). Such a declaration would be scandalous indeed, did it not follow upon a detailed exposition of the merits of the case. In the context in which it appears one can hardly miss the facetious note.

Finally we may point to the more extraneous but no less significant evidence of publication. Perhaps book thriteen of the *Epistulae ad Familiares* was published in Cicero's lifetime.[70] But even if Tiro had published these letters, it is hardly credible that he would have included letters which might have damaged Cicero's posthumous reputation. Indeed the very fact that these letters were assembled in a book shows that they were to be held up as models. Fronto, for one, considered them such.

---

69 The incompatibility of *dignitas* and *ius aequum* had become complete under the dual penal system when social position influenced the verdict directly and not through the mediation of the notion of 'good character.' Influences which are branded by Kelly as improper were now considered perfectly proper: "It was considered perfectly proper that verdicts should be influenced in this way: justice and equity were thought thereby to have been achieved rather than compromised," Kelly, *Roman Litigation*, 213.

70 Ludwig Gurlitt, "De M. Tulli Ciceronis Epistulis Earumque Pristina Collectione" (University of Göttingen Thesis, 1879), 25.

Cassius Dio, Mommsen and the Quinquefascales

Few passages are more familiar to historians of the Augustan age than the chapters in Book 53 of Cassius Dio dealing with the constitutional settlement of 27 BC whose corollary was the division of the empire into public and imperial provinces.[1] This division, as Fergus Millar demonstrated long ago, was not one of responsibility and authority; rather, it boiled down to a formal distinction between the methods of appointment, the *insignia*, and the length of tenure of the proconsuls, i. e. governors of the public provinces on the one hand, and of the *legati Augusti pro praetore*, i. e. governors of imperial provinces on the other hand.[2] For all this, our most complete, explicit and detailed source is Cassius Dio.[3] Indeed, for some details he is our only source – as he is for the subject of the present discussion.

One of the formal distinctions between the two types of governors was reflected in the number of lictors assigned to the governors in each type. The proconsuls had the number of lictors corresponding to their rank as ex-praetors or ex-consuls: Ῥαβδούχοις τέ σφας ἑκατέρους ὅσοισπερ καὶ ἐν τῷ ἄστει νενόμισται χρῆσθαι (Cass. Dio 53, 13, 4). Not so the *legati Augusti pro praetore*: whether they were ex-praetors or ex-consuls, they all had the same number of lictors. Here is what we read in Dio's text, as we have it in Boissevain's authoritative edition: Ῥαβδούχοις δὲ δὴ πέντε πάντες ὁμοίως οἱ ἀντιστράτηγοι χρῶνται, καὶ ὅσοι γε οὐκ ἐκ τῶν ὑπατευκότων εἰσί, καὶ ὀνομάζονται ἐπ' αὐτοῦ τοῦ ἀριθμοῦ τούτου. (53, 13, 8; ed. Boissevain, Vol. II, 423).

This passage is rendered in modern translations as follows:

1. E. Cary's Loeb translation:[4] "All the propraetors alike employ five lictors, and indeed, all of them except those who were ex-consuls at the time of the appointment to the governorship receive their title from this very number."

---

1 Fergus Millar, "'Senatorial' Provinces: An Institutionalized Ghost," *Ancient World* 20 (1989): 93–97.

2 Fergus Millar, "The Emperor, the Senate and the Provinces," *JRS* 56 (1966): 156–66. In the course of time the absence of any but a formal distinction became even clearer.

3 Cass. Dio 53, 13; cf. Millar, "'Senatorial' Provinces: An Institutionalized Ghost," 93–97.

4 *Dio Cassius, Roman History, Volume VI: Books 51–55*, Loeb Classical Library (Cambridge, Mass.: Harvard University Press, 1980), 225.

Article note: First published in *Chiron* 30 (2000): 217–234, with the following note: for Géza Alföldy on his 65th birthday; I am grateful to Werner Eck for his generous help and advice throughout the many revisions of this article. Alexander Yakobson made insightful comments on an earlier draft and Dieter Hagedorn gave me sound advice. My student, Asaph Ben-Tov, by asking the right question inspired me to sit down and write it.

https://doi.org/10.1515/9783110770438-005

2. O. Veh's German Translation:[5] "Sämtliche Propraetoren verfügen gleichheitlich über fünf Liktoren und erhalten insgesamt, sofern sie nicht aus dem Kreis gewesener Konsuln genommen sind, von eben dieser Zahal her ihrem Titel."
3. J.W. Rich's English translation:[6] "All the propraetors alike employ five lictors, and those who are ex-consuls also get a title from this number."
4. A. Stroppa's Italian translation: "Ugualmente tutti i propretori dispongono di cinque littori e tutti costoro, tranne coloro che sono stati ex-consoli, ricevono il titolo in base al numero stesso di littori."[7]

All translations agree that although all *legati Augusti pro praetore* were assigned five lictors, only those whose rank was that of an ex-praetor derived their title from the number. This title, as the translations often add in a note, is that of *quinquefascalis*. Nothing could be stated more unequivocally.

What about the reality behind our sole literary source? Many hundreds of inscriptions (and some papyri) from all over the Roman world attest praetorian governors of imperial provinces with titles such as *legatus Augusti pro praetore*, *legatus pro praetore*, πρεσβευτὴς καὶ ἀντιστράτηγος, πρεσβευτὴς Σεβαστοῦ ἀντιστράτηγος, ἡγεμών and later *praeses*. In view of the common interpretation of Dio's text one is entitled to expect, especially in the epigraphic sources, praetorian governors with the title *quinquefascalis*, or πεντάραβδος, or, failing that, at least a circumlocution which would imply that this indeed was the title of praetorian governors in imperial provinces. Are our expectations met in the epigraphic material, i. e. in reality?

5 *Cassius Dio: Römische Geschichte. Band IV: Bücher 51 – 60* (Zürich – München: Artemis Verlag, 1986), 117.

6 *Cassius Dio: The Augustan Settlement (Roman History 53–55.9)* (Westminster: Aris and Phillips, 1990).

7 *Cassio Dione: Storia Romana. Libri 52–56* (Milano: Biblioteca universale Rizzoli, 1998), with notes by Francesca Rohr Vio. Note, though, that καὶ ὅσοι γε οὐκ ἐκ τῶν ὑπατευκότων εἰσί is not "tranne coloro che sono stati ex-consoli" but either: "tranne coloro che sono ex-consoli" or "tranne coloro che sono stati consoli" (I am grateful to Elio Lo Cascio for sending me the Italian translation, and for the suggested emendation).

I

I have assembled here what I believe to be all the available evidence about the so-called *quinquefascales* and *quinque fasces*, and their Greek equivalents, in official careers in the provincial context. What does it tell us?

I begin, despite me concern with the epigraphic material, with a case mentioned in the literary sources.

1) In 17 CE an ex-praetor with five lictors was assigned to the cities of the province of Asia which had suffered from an earthquake: Ταῖς ἐν τῇ Ἀσίᾳ πόλεσι ταῖς ὑπὸ τοῦ σεισμοῦ κακωθείσαις ἀνὴρ ἐστρατηγηκὼς σὺν πέντε ῥαβδούχοις προσετάχθη (Cass. Dio 57, 17, 7).

Tacitus identifies the man as M. Ateius[8] who was elected amongst the ex-praetors. As Tacitus explains, the choice fell on a praetorian rather than on a consular senator in order to avoid strife between equals, i. e. between the special envoy and the consular governor of Asia – a strife which would impede the giving of succour to the cities: "*delectus est M. Ateius e praetoriis, ne consulari obtinente Asiam aemulatio inter pares et ex eo impedimentum oreretur*" (*Ann.* II, 47, 4).

Unfortunately no honorific inscription has survived to tell us the title borne by the praetorian M. Ateius who was assigned five lictors on his special mission to Asia.[9] We do know though that he was not the governor of Asia. As is made quite clear by Tacitus, he was to fulfil his task while the proconsul of Asia was in office ("*consulari obtinente Asiam*").

2) *ILS* 8826 = *IGRom.* III 174, Ancyra:
Γ(αῖον) Ἰ(ούλιον) Σεουῆρον | βασιλέων καὶ | τετράρχων | ἀπόγονον | μετὰ πάσας τὰς ἐν | τῷ ἔνθει φιλοτιμία[ς] | καταταγέντα εἰς τοὺ[ς] | δημαρχ<ικ>ούς[10] ὑπὸ θεο[ῦ] | Ἀδριανοῦ, <στρατηγόν>,[11] πρεσβεύσα[ν]|τα ἐν Ἀσίᾳ ἐξ ἐπιστολῆς [καὶ] | κωδικίλλων θεοῦ Ἀδριαν[οῦ], | ἡγεμόνα λεγεῶνος δ' Σκ[υ]|θικῆς καὶ [δι]οικήσαντα τὰ ἐν | Συρίᾳ πράγματα, ἡνίκα Πουβλί|κιος Μάρκελλος διὰ τὴν κίνη|σιν τὴν

8 *PIR* (2nd ed.) A 1278.
9 But see the case of C. Pontius Paelignus (*CIL* V 4348) who was *legatus pro pr(aetore) iter[um] ex s(enatus) c(onsulto) et ex auctorit[ate] Ti(berii) Caesaris* in an unknown province; M. Ateius' appointment could have been described in similar, or even identical, terms, cf. Werner Eck, "Prosopographica II," *ZPE* 106 (1995): 249–51.
10 Cf. *IGRom.* III 175 for this reading.
11 This must be restored from *AE* 1923, no. 4 = Allen Brown West, "Latin Inscriptions, 1896–1926," *Corinth* 8 (1931): 38, no. 56.

Ἰουδαικὴν μεταβεβήκε[ι] | ἀπὸ Συρίας, ἀνθύπατον Ἀχα|ίας, πρὸς ε' ῥάβδους πεμφθέν|τα εἰς Βειθυνίαν διορθωτὴν | καὶ λογιστὴν ὑπὸ θεοῦ Ἀδριανοῦ, ...

(Gaius Iulius Severus, descendant of kings and tetrarchs, after discharging all the *honores* amongst his own people, was enrolled by the deified Hadrian amongst the former tribunes, <praetor>, (nominated) by letter and codicil of the deified Hadrian as legate in Asia, commander of the *legio IV Scythica* and in charge of affairs in Syria when Publicius Marcellus had left the province because of the insurrection in Judaea, proconsul of Achaia, sent with[12] five *fasces* to Bithynia as *corrector* and *curator* by the deified Hadrian ...).

This last commission of C. Iulius Severus[13] is mentioned in Cass. Dio 69, 14, 4: "He [Hadrian] sent Severus into Bithynia, which needed no armed force but a ruler (ἄρχων) and a leader (ἐπιστάτης) who was just and prudent and a man of rank. All these qualifications Severus possessed. And he managed and administered both their private and their public affairs in such a manner that we are still, even today, wont to remember him."

The language of the epitomiser is vague. However, any attempt to read 'governor' into the terms ἄρχων[14] and ἐπιστάτης with the implication that C. Iulius Severus was a governor when sent to Bithynia, is belied by the inscription which says explicitly that he was *corrector* and *curator*, and as such equipped with five lictors. No doubt a senatorial proconsul, as in the previous case, was in office there.[15]

---

12 πρὸς ε' ῥάβδους translates the Latin *ad quinque fasces* (see below, no. 3); cf. however *LSJ* s. v. πρός C. III.6 for πρός used in the sense of 'with', 'accompanied by'.

13 *PIR* (2nd ed.) I 573.

14 So in Loeb.

15 Despite Theodor Mommsen, *Gesammelte Schriften*, Vol. VIII (Berlin: Weidmann, 1913), 149. Needless to say, the traditional interpretation of *quinquefascalis* as a term interchangeable with the designation *legatus Augusti pro praetore* of a governor of a praetorian imperial province, leads Bernard Rémy, *Les carrières sénatoriales dans les provinces romaines d'Anatolie au Haut-Empire* (Istanbul – Paris: Institut Français d'Études Anatoliennes, 1989), 50 ff. to regard C. Iulius Severus as the governor of the province of Pontus-Bithynia, which, according to him, had been withdrawn by Hadrian from the senate's control and turned into an imperial province. This interpretation, which uses Pliny's position in the province under Trajan as a parallel, is not warranted by the text. Rémy seems to have been influenced by Hans-Georg Pflaum, "Légats impériaux à l'intérieur des provinces sénatoriales," in *Hommages à Albert Grenier*, ed. Marcel Renard (Bruxelles: Peeters, 1962), 1236, who rendered πρὸς ε' ῥάβδους πεμφθέντα εἰς Βειθυνίαν διορθωτὴν in Latin: *legatus Augusti pro praetore ad corrigendum statum provinciae Ponti et Bithyniae.*

3) *CIL* VIII 7044 = *ILS* 1163, Cirta:
M. Flauio T. fil. / Quir. Postumo / praef. aerari milit., / ordinato in Gal/lia at quinque fasces, / leg. leg. VI Ferratae, prae/tori, adlecto inter tri/bunicios ab / imp. Antonino Aug., ...

(To M. Flavius Postumus, son of Titus, of the tribe Quirina, prefect of the military treasury, appointed for Gallia with[16] five *fasces*, legate of the *legio VI Ferrata*, praetor, enrolled by the emperor Antoninus Augustus amongst the former tribunes ...)

M. Flavius Postumus[17] had indeed praetorian rank and five lictors when appointed for Gallia, but there is nothing in the inscription to suggest that he was made governor of any particular province. Gallia by itself without any further specification is not one of the provinces of Gallia, but all four of them (Aquitania, Lugdunensis, Belgica and Narbonensis) – a geographical, not an ordinary administrative, concept.[18] Nor does the inscription state for what purpose he was sent there.

4) *ILS* 8834[b] = *IC* IV 299, Gortyna:
[– – – ἐπὶ τοῦ] | σειτομετρίου τοῦ Ῥωμαίων ταχθέν[τα], | τειμηθέντα ἱερωσύνῃ τῶν ιε' ἀνδρῶ[ν, | λογιστὴν – – –]ριανῶν τῶν ἐν Ἰταλίᾳ, | [πρεσβευτὴν] Ἀφρικῆς, ἀνθύπατο[ν | – – –, πε]ντάραβδον Ῥαιτίας, | [Βολουμν]ία Κάληδα τὸν γλυκύτατ|[ον καὶ εὐ]σεβέστατον υἱόν

(Prefect of the corn supply, one of fifteen men in charge of sacrifices, *curator* of (a city, whose name is lost in the lacuna) ... in Italia, [legate] in the province of Africa, proconsul ...., *quinquefascalis* in Raetia, Volumnia Calida for her most sweet and pious son).

It is true that the Ignotus could have become governor of a praetorian province at the stage in his career occupied here by his post as *quinquefascalis Raetiae*. Nevertheless the absence of an earlier service as a legionary commander is disturbing: normally a governor in a praetorian province where a legion was sta-

16 *At* (i. e. *ad*), cf. πρός in the previous inscription.
17 *PIR* (2nd ed.) F 341. See there for the date.
18 Thus Dessau (*ILS*, III.1, Index VI, p. 372) is wrong to say: "*incertum cuius* [i. e., Galliae]", implying that the specification should have been there. Mommsen, however, rightly regards him as an extraordinary envoy, and not as a governor of one of the four Galliae: according to Mommsen he belonged to the "*genus*" of "*legati Augusti extra ordinem in provincias senatorias missi*," who were also entitled to five *fasces*, see Mommsen, *Gesammelte Schriften*, Vol. VIII, 228. The formulation "*in provincias senatorias missi*" is unfortunate since three of the Galliae were imperial; cf. below n. 51.

tioned – as was the case in Raetia since ca. 170[19] – had always commanded a legion before. This legionary command usually followed immediately after the prefecture of the corn supply (*praefectura frumenti dandi*) attested here as the man's first post.[20] It is only if we start with the premise that *quinquefascalis* is the formal title of a governor of a praetorian province that we are made to take the anonymous [πε]ντάραβδος Ῥαιτίας as the governor of the province. But there is nothing in this inscription itself which compels us to assume that the man was a governor of Raetia rather than on a special commission there as in other cases surveyed here.

5) *CIL* VI 41134 = 1546, Rome:
[– – –]VM[– – – | – – –]TEM GERM[– – – | – – –] VRATA•ED SA[– – – | – – –] SODALI ANTO[– – – | – – –]QUE P•ASCREG[– – – | – – –]IICL•F•PRAETOR[– – –]

The inscription itself is now lost. As restored by Géza Alföldy in *CIL* VI 41134 it reads as follows:[21] *[– – –,?comiti | Augustor]um [expeditionis | Parthicae i]tem Germ[anicae | et Sarmaticae c]urat(ori) aed(ium) sa[crarum | et oper(um) publicor(um) (?)], sodali Anto[niniano | leg(ato) Aug(usti) (?)*[22]*?quin]que fasc(ali) reg(ionis) [Transpad(anae)*[23] *| leg(ato) Aug(usti) leg(ionis) V]II Cl(audiae) <p(iae)> f(idelis), praetor[i, trib(uno) | plebis, quaestori – – –]*

(Companion of the (two) Augusti in the Parthian expedition as well as in the German and the Sarmatian expedition, in charge of the sacred temples and public buildings (?), priest of the (deified) Antoninus, imperial legate *quinquefascalis* (or: with *quinque fasces*) of the region of Transpadana (?), imperial commander of the *legio Claudia VII pia fidelis*, praetor, tribune of the plebs, quaestor ...).

It is possible that *[– – –]que fasc* should be expanded to yield *[quin]que fasc(ium)*,[24] i. e. we cannot be sure that the Ignotus indeed bore the title of *quinquefascalis*. Be this as it may, the place occupied by the post of *quinquefascalis* or *legatus Augusti quinque fascium* in the Ignotus' career is of course entirely compatible

19 See Ferdinand Haug in *RE*, Vol. I A.1 (1914), s. v. *Raetia*, col. 54; Bengt E. Thomasson, *Laterculi praesidum* (Göteborg: Radius, 1984), 80, assigns the Ignotus, whom he takes to be a governor, to the late second century; cf. Gerhard Winkler, "Die Statthalter der römischen Provinz Raetia unter dem Prinzipat," *Bayerische Vorgeschichtsblätter* 36 (1971): 79, n. 21.

20 Cf. Werner Eck, "Beförderungskriterien innerhalb der senatorischen laufbahn, dargestellt an der zeit von 69–138 n. chr.," in *Aufstieg und Niedergang der römischen Welt*, Vol. II.1 (Berlin: De Gruyter, 1974), 192 = *Tra epigrafia prosopografia e archeologia: Scritti scelti, rielaborati ed aggiornati* (Rome: Quasar, 1996), 40.

21 I am grateful to Géza Alföldy for allowing me to see the proofs of the new suppl. volume.

22 Or, less likely: [*Veriano*].

23 Restored before as *reg[(ni) Norici]*.

24 See no. 6.

with the assumption of it having been that of a provincial governorship in a praetorian province. Furthermore, in contrast to the case of the πεντάραβδος Ῥαιτίας (no. 4), a legionary command is attested in this descending career inscription as having preceded this post. Nonetheless, while the fragmentary condition of the inscription makes it unsafe to assume without further proof that the *legatus Augusti quinquefascalis* (or *quinque fascium*) was a provincial governor, the place (i. e. the *regio Transpadana*) taken together with the date renders this possibility altogether unlikely.[25]

The restoration: *sodali Anto[niniano leg(ato) Aug(usti) quin]que fasc(ali) or quin]que fasc(ium)* yields a date between 161–169. With *Veriano* (see note 22) instead of *leg(ato) Aug(utsti)* restored in the lacuna – *sodali Anto[niniano Veriano quin]que fasc(ali)* – the inscription is to be dated not before 169 and not after 180. The *regio Transpadana* suffered greatly from the German invasions and the plague at these dates, and Marcus Aurelius must have felt the need to send someone to look after matters in the afflicted region. However, precisely under Marcus Aurelius the presence in one of the regions of Italy of an official whose title would suggest that he was a provincial governor of praetorian rank is very unlikely. Hadrian's policy of sending *legati Augusti pro praetore* of consular rank whose title and competence were identical to those of the provincial governors into regions of Italy, thus creating the impression of treating an Italian *regio* like a province, had been abolished by Antoninus Pius. Marcus Aurelius revived it in a modified form meant to avoid the impression that a 'provincial' treatment was being given to an Italian *regio*; instead he sent there, when the situation called for it, *iuridici* of praetorian rank whose competence was much more limited than that of the Hadrianic *legati Augusti pro praetore*.[26] It would be inconsistent with Marcus Aurelius' attested policy to send to the Transpadane region an envoy whose title would

---

25 The old restoration *reg[(ni) Norici]* cannot stand. This concept occurs only in procuratorial inscriptions between 160 and 170, i. e. when the province was still governed by equestrian procurators; cf. Werner Eck cited in Dieter Knibbe, Helmut Engelmann, and Bülent Iplikçioglu, "Neue Inschriften aus Ephesos XII," *JÖAI* 62 (1993): 127 f. (no. 20 = *SEG* 43, 777). On the other hand, *regnum Noricum* is no longer attested when the legate of the *legio II Italica*, raised during the Marcomannic wars, became the senatorial *legatus Augusti pro praetore* of Noricum ca. 175 (for the date see Géza Alföldy, *Noricum* (London: Routledge, 1974), 156–8). Thus the fact that we have here a career inscription of a senator makes it unlikely that *regnum Noricum* stood here.

26 See Werner Eck, "Die italischen legati Augusti pro praetore unter Hadrian und Antoninus Pius," in *Historiae Augustae Colloquium Parisinum*, ed. Giorgio Bonamente and Noël Duval (Macerata: Università degli studi, 1991), 183–95 = *Die Verwaltung des römischen Reiches in der hohen Kaiserzeit. Ausgewählte und erweiterte Beiträge*, ed. Regula Frei-Stolba and Michael A. Speidel (Basel: F. Reinhardt, 1995), 315–26; cf. Werner Eck, *L'Italia nell'impero romano. Stato e amministrazione in epoca imperiale* (Bari: Edipuglia, 1999), 155 ff.

suggest that he was a normal provincial governor. Consequently the occurrence of *quinquefascalis* (or *legatus Augusti quinque fascium*) precisely in this inscription may be proof that it was not the normal title borne by the praetorian provincial governor.

6) *AE* 1917/18, no. 51, Lambaesis:
L. Iulio Apronio Ma[e]nio Pio Salamalliano trib(uno) latic(lavio) leg(ionis) X Gem(inae), adlect(o) inter qq(aestorios) praepos(ito) actis senatuus (sic), *aedili curuli, <praetori>, leg(ato) Aug(usti) vice <leg(ati) Aug(usti) pr(o) pr(aetore)> quinque fascium prov(inciae) Belgi[cae], leg(ato) leg(ionis) I Adiut(ricis) et leg(ato) Aug(usti) pr(o) pr(aetore) prov(inciae) Galatiae, <leg(ato)> leg(ionis) III Aug(ustae) Sever(ianae) et prov(inciae) Numid(iae), M. Aurelius Crescens p(rimi)p(ilus) leg(ionis) eiusd(em) praesidi rarissimo.*

Another inscription bearing an almost identical text attests (as was to be expected) *praetor* before the phrase containing the term which is the subject of this paper: *CIL* VIII 18270 = *ILS* 1196, Lambaesis:

L. Iul(io) Apronio Ma[e]nio Pio Salamalliano trib(uno) latic(lavio) leg(ionis) X Gem(inae), adlecto inter qq(aestorios), praeposito actis senat(us), aed(ili) curuli, praetori, leg(ato) Aug(usti) vice <leg(ati) Aug(usti) pr(o) pr(aetore)> quin[q]ue fascium prov(inciae) Belgi[cae, le]g(ato) leg(ionis) I Adiutric(is), leg(ato) Au[g](usti) pr(o) pr(aetore) prov(inciae) Ga[la]tiae item l[eg(ato) pr. pr. [– – –].

The translation unifies both versions for the man's career: "To L. Iulius Apronius Maenius Pius Salamallianus, laticlave tribune of the *legio X Gemina*, enrolled amongst the ex-quaestors, in charge of the official record of senatorial proceedings, curule aedile, praetor, imperial legate substituting <the governor with praetorian rank> with five *fasces* of the province of Belgica, commander of the *legio I Adiutrix*, governor with praetorian rank of the province of Galatia, legate of the *legio III Augusta Severiana* and (governor with praetorian rank) of the province of Numidia ..."

The case of L. Iulius Apronius Maenius Pius Salamallianus[27] calls for a more detailed discussion. At the crucial place the text reads: *leg. Aug. vice quinque fascium prov(inciae) Belgi[cae]*. Mommsen,[28] followed by others, understood *vice quinque fascium provinciae Belgicae* as equivalent to *vice quinquefascalis provinciae Belgicae* "in the place of (a deputy of) the *quinquefascalis* of the province of Belgica," thus finding here proof for his assumption that *quinquefascalis* was another title of a praetorian governor of an imperial province. Such an interpreta-

27 *PIR* (2nd ed.) I 161; cf. Thomasson, *Laterculi praesidum*, 45, no. 16 for his tenure in Belgica.
28 *Römisches Staatsrecht*, Vol. I (Graz: Akademische Druck- u. Verlagsanstalt, 1952), 388, n. 5.

tion indeed turns the term *quinquefascalis* into the proper and official title of the praetorian provincial governor whom our man was replacing.

However, this interpretation of the text runs into serious difficulties. First, if L. Iulius Apronius is assumed to have borne the title *legatus Augusti vice quinquefascalis prov(inciae) Belgi[cae]* – as the traditional interpretation would have it – it is to be inferred that the governor of a praetorian province like Belgica bore the title *quinquefascalis prov(inciae) Belgi[cae]*; however, in this very inscription we find that in the praetorian province of Galatia, where indeed L. Iulius Apronius was a praetorian governor, he was called *leg(atus) Aug(usti) pr(o) pr(aetore) prov(inciae) Galatiae* and not *quinquefascalis prov(inciae) Galatiae.*[29]

Secondly, *vice quinque fascium* does not mean *vice quinquefascalis* in normal Latin. The only way to make sense here of the *quinque fascium* is to take it as a qualitative genitive, a variation on *ad quinque fasces*, i. e. with five *fasces* (above, no. 3). True, this leaves the *vice* without its complementary genitive.[30] However, an omission of *leg. Aug. pr. pr.* after *vice* by the stonecutters (or the author of the text),[31] could easily be explained if both the governor and his deputy bore the title of *legatus Augusti* – for *legatus Augusti* by itself is not the title of a provincial governor exclusively. In other words the text should have read as proposed above: *leg(ato) Aug(usti) vice <leg(ati) Aug(usti) pr(o) pr(aetore)> quinque fascium prov(inciae) Belgi[cae].*

It could be argued that the *quinque fascium* qualifies the entire nominal group *vice leg(ati) Aug(usti) pr(o) pr(aetore)*, and not merely the *leg(ati) Aug(usti) pr(o) pr(aetore)*; thus serving as an attribute of the deputy governor, and not of the

29 Mommsen solved the difficulty by suggesting: "hier zeigt sich die erstere Titulatur [i. e. *quinquefascalis*] als die geringere," *Römisches Staatsrecht*, Vol. I, 388, n. 5; it would seem that Mommsen too was uncomfortable with equating *quinquefascalis* with the official title *legatus Augusti pro praetore.*

30 Unless one takes the *quinque fascium* together with the preceding nominal group, i. e. with the *leg. Aug.*, understanding the latter to be an abbreviation of *leg(ati) Aug(usti)* rather than of *leg(ato) Aug(usti)*, as the text is normally expanded. Admittedly *legati Augusti vice* is not the normal word order for expressing substitution of one official by another in the epigraphic sources; the only examples I have been able to find for this inverted order are taken from literary sources: e. g. Pliny, *Ep.* IV, 19, 7: "*matrem meam parentis vice [*loco] vererere*; Tacitus, *Ann.* VI, 21, 6: "*oracli vice accipiens*"; Pliny, *Naturalis historia* VIII, 184: "*bos in Aegypto etiam numinis vice colitur.*"

31 The source of both inscriptions – although the dedicants are different – is very likely to be the honorand himself, but in that case the text was probably changed at some point between its composition and execution, see Werner Eck, "'Tituli honorarii', Curriculum Vitae und Selbstdarstellung in der hohen Kaiserzeit," in *Acta Colloquii Epigraphici Latini : Helsingiae, 3.–6. Sept. 1991 Habiti*, ed. Heikki Solin, Olli Salomies, and Uta-Maria Liertz (Helsinki: Finnish Society of Sciences and Letters, 1995), 211 ff. (= *Tra epigrafia prosopografia e archeologia: Scritti scelti, rielaborati ed aggiornati,* 319 ff.).

governor himself, i. e. as if the text read *leg(ato) Aug(usti) quinque fascium vice <leg(ati) Aug(usti) pr(o) pr(aetore)> prov(inciae) Belgi[cae]*. But even if grammatically the *quinque fascium* qualifies the *legatus Augusti pro praetore*, i. e. the praetorian governor of Belgica, whom L. Iulius Apronius was replacing, it can hardly count as a title. In fact the only reason for mentioning it at all would be to define more closely the *potestas* of the deputy who would likewise be entitled to five *fasces*. Perhaps it is best to regard the *quinque fascium* as qualifying both the governor and his deputy.

Again, this inscription cannot be used as evidence that *quinquefascalis*, or rather *legatus Augusti pro praetore quinque fascium*, was the normal title of the praetorian governor of an imperial province.

7) *CIL* XIII 3162 = *ILTG* 341 = *AE* 1949, nos. 136 = 137 = 214 = *AE* 1959, no. 95.[32]

The famous tripartite inscription from Thorigny engraved on the base of a statue decreed by the Three Gauls in honour of their high priest, T. Sennius Sollemnis, on 16 December 238 (I 30), contains an honorific inscription (the main face of the base) and two letters of recommendation (left and right faces). The letter on the right-hand side of the base is a recommendation of the Viducassian Titus Sennius Sollemnis by the praetorian prefect, M. Aedinius Iulianus, and is addressed to the acting governor of Gallia Lugdunensis, Badius Comnianus:[33]

Exemplum epistulae Aedin[i] | Iuliani praefecti praet(orio) | ad Badium Comnianum pr[o]|cur(atorem) et vice praesidis agen[t(em)]. | Aedinius Iulianus Badio | Comniano sal(utem). In provincia | Lugduness(i) quinquefascal(em)[34] *| cum agerem plerosq(ue) bonos viros perspexi* etc.

(A copy of the letter of Aedinius Iulianus the praetorian prefect to Badius Comnianus, procurator and acting in the place of the governor. Aedinius Iulianus sends his greetings to Badius Comnianus: 'When I served in the province of Lugdunensis as *quinquefascalis*, I became aware of many good men ...').

Here for the first (and only) time we have a secure attestation of the term *quinquefascalis* in Latin, whereas before it was found either expressed in a roundabout way (nos. 1, 2, 3, 6), uncertainly restored (no. 5), or translated into Greek (no. 4).

---

32 See above all, Hans-Georg Pflaum, *Le marbre de Thorigny* (Paris: H. Champion, 1948).

33 See Hannah M. Cotton, *Documentary Letters of Recommendation in Latin from the Roman Empire* (Königstein/Ts.: Hain, 1981), 34 ff.

34 Pflaum expands: *quinquefascal(is)*, but see e. g. Suetonius, *Claud.* 29, 1: "*non principem sed ministrum egit*"; Tacitus, *Hist.* II, 83: "*socium magis imperii quam ministrum agens*"; cf. Raphael Kühner and Carl Stegmann, *Ausführliche Grammatik der lateinischen Sprache*, Vol. II.1 (Hannover: Hahn, 1976), 297, A. 3, and *TLL* s. v. *ago* 1399, e. g. l. 42.

However, the formulation *in provincia Lugduness(i) quinquefascal(em) cum agerem* must be juxtaposed with the different formulation of Aedinius Iulianus' position in Lugdunensis given in the central panel, where T. Sennius Solemnis is described by the *ordo* of the *civitas Viducassium* as "a greaty beloved client of Aedinius Iulianus, the imperial legate in Gallia Lugdunensis": *cliens probatissimus Aedini Iuliani leg(ati) Aug(usti) prov(inciae) Lugd(unensis)* (I 21).

What is the meaning of the two different formulations of Aedinius Iulianus' position in the province, i.e. *in provincia Lugduness(i) quinquefascal(em) cum agerem* and *legatus Augusti provinciae Lugdunensis*? Can they be reconciled or are they incompatible? And finally, does their co-existence support the assumption that *quinquefascalis* was the normal title of the praetorian imperial governor?

M. Aedinius Iulianus[35] served in Lugdunensis ca. 220; his predecessor in Lugdunensis,[36] Claudius Paulinus, is attested in Britannia Inferior in 220,[37] where "his term of office must have begun soon before."[38] However, as late as 223 M. Aedinius Iulianus still belonged to the equestrian order as is proven by his tenure of the prefecture of Egypt in 222–223,[39] from which position he moved directly to the praetorian prefecture in which he is attested under Alexander Severus in 223.[40] In other words Aedinius Iulianus did not yet belong to the senatorial order when acting as *quinquefascalis* in Lugdunensis in the early 220s,[41] despite the *leg. Aug.*

35 *PIR* (2nd ed.) A 113.
36 Cf. *decessori meo* in line 15 of the recommendation.
37 *CIL* VII 1045 + 1044 = *RIB* 1280.
38 Anthony R. Birley, *The Fasti of Roman Britain* (Oxford: Clarendon Press, 1981), 189.
39 Cf. Guido Bastianini, "Lista dei prefetti d'egitto dal 30ª al 299ᵖ," *ZPE* 17 (1975): 308 f.: 222–223 CE; cf. Guido Bastianini, "Lista dei prefetti d'egitto dal 30ª al 299ᵖ : aggiunte e correzioni," *ZPE* 38 (1980): 87 and Guido Bastianini, "Il prefetto d'Egitto (30 a.c. – 297 d.c.): addenda (1973 –1985)," in *Aufstieg und Niedergang der römischen Welt*, Vol. II.10/1 (Berlin: De Gruyter, 1988), 513; cf. Paul Bureth, "Le préfet d'Egypte (30 av.j.c.–297 ap. j.c.): etat présent de la documentation en 1973," in *Aufstieg und Niedergang der römischen Welt*, Vol. II.10/1 (Berlin: De Gruyter, 1988), 492: "été/automne 222-été 223."
40 This is the date of the '*album* of Canusium' (*CIL* IX 338), in which Aedinius Iulianus appears among the patrons of the city in the number of *clarissimi*, i.e. on becoming *praefectus praetorio* he was enrolled in the senatorial order; cf. *Hist. Aug., Alex. Sev.* XXI: "*Praefectis praetorii suis senatoriam addidit* [Alexander Severus] *dignitatem, ut viri clarissimi et essent et dicerentur.*" See next note.
41 Those, who, unlike Pflaum, *Le marbre de Thorigny*, 38–39, distinguish between the inclusion of Aedinius Iulianus in the senatorial order in 223 – after which he could hold the governorship of Lugdunensis as a senator – and his eventual nomination as praetorian prefect maintain that he served in Lugdunensis after 223 as a senatorial governor, and that *decessor meus* in our text (see n. 36) does not mean direct predecessor, cf. Arthur Stein, *Die Präfekten von Ägypten in der römischen Kaiserzeit* (Bern: Francke, 1950), 216, n. 391 and Guido Barbieri, *L'Albo senatorio da*

prov. Lugd. in line 21 of the central panel, with its ostensible implication that Aedinius Iulianus was a senatorial governor of Lugdunensis. It is possible of course to dismiss (with Pflaum) the expression *leg. Aug. prov. Lugd.* as a misunderstanding on the part of the provincials who assimilated Aedinius Iulianus' position to that of the normal senatorial governor.[42] For it seems extremely unlikely that M. Aedinius Iulianus, were he a senatorial governor, would refer to himself as *quinquefascalis* rather than as a *legatus Augusti pro praetore*. But how did an equestrian governor come by five *fasces* when normally, so far as we know, he would have none at all?[43]

Evidently M. Aedinius Iulianus was no ordinary equestrian governor, nor an equestrian deputy of a senatorial governor.[44] Therefore, one may suggest that perhaps the Viducassians made no mistake in calling him *leg. Aug. prov. Lugd.* One should seek the explanation for the two designations in the special circumstances prevailing under Elagabalus when equestrians are found serving in positions normally filled by senatorial governors, and the same person is found occupying indiscriminately both senatorial and equestrian positions.[45] It is precisely at this time that Aedinius Iulianus could have been appointed governor of Lugdunensis, designated *leg. Aug. prov. Lugd.*, and assigned five *fasces* – notwithstanding his equestrian status. However, the combination of *leg. Aug. prov. Lugd.* and *quinquefascalis* does not imply that *quinquefascalis* was the normal designation of a praetorian governor in the imperial provinces; quite the contrary: it suggests that even under Elagabalus a distinction was maintained between a senatorial and an equestrian governor. Only the latter would use the circumlocution *quinquefascalem cum agerem* to describe his position as governor in the province; only in his case was it necessary and important to stress that he held the five *fasces*, for normally they

---

Settimio Severo a Carino (193–285) (Rome: Signorelli, 1952), 190 no. 923; 615, n. ad 190, no. 923. Pflaum's reconstruction is adopted here as the most economic interpretation of the various texts.

42 Pflaum, *Le marbre de Thorigny*, 35–6.

43 Thomas Schäfer, *Imperii insignia. Sella curulis und Fasces: Zur Repräsentation römischer Magistrate* (Mainz: Philipp von Zabern, 1989), 214.

44 Despite Pflaum who maintains that had he been a governor, rather than a deputy governor, he would have said *esse* instead of *agere* (*Le marbre de Thorigny*, 20); but see above n. 34 on the grammatical construction. To me it seems that, had he been a deputy governor, he would probably have used about himself the same terms that he uses for his addressee, Badius Comnianus, namely "*procurator et vice praesidis agens*."

45 With Badius Comnianus we can see that we are back in the old order, for he is described as "*procurator vice praesidis agens*," i. e. an equestrian deputy to a senatorial governor. For an attempt to explain away irregularities in appointments under Elagabalus, see Benet Salway, "Fragment of Severan History: The Unusual Career of ...atus, Praetorian Prefect of Elagabalus," *Chiron* 27 (1997): 127 ff.

would not be allotted to an equestrian. In corroboration of this hypothesis one could point to the different titles given in the document to Aedinius Iulianus and to his predecessor, Claudius Paulinus: Aedinius Iulianus is called *legatus Augusti provinciae Lugdunensis* (I 21), whereas Claudius Paulinus is called *legatus Augusti pro praetore provinciae Lugdunensis* (I 15–16) and *provinciae Britanniae* (III 1–3) respectively, i. e. the normal official title of the senatorial provincial governor in an imperial province. The omission of *pro praetore* from Aedinius Iulianus' title may thus be no oversight on the part of the provincials, but a reflexion of an official designation intended to bring out the distinction between the two.

This inscription too cannot prove that *quinquefascalis* was the normal title of the praetorian governor of an imperial province.

II

Our evidence is restricted to a handful of testimonies: none of them discloses a praetorian governor of an imperial province; none of them proves or even implies that the governor of a praetorian imperial province, i. e. the *legatus Augusti pro praetore* with the rank of an ex-praetor, received his title from the number of lictors assigned to him, i. e. that he bore an (official) title of *quinquefascalis*. The epigraphic evidence shows in fact that it is a praetorian (or in one case an equestrian) official, sent to replace the governor or perform a special task in the province while the governor is still in office, who is said to be accompanied by five *fasces*. In fact the two officials, i. e. the normal praetorian governor of an imperial province and an official accompanied by five *fasces*, represented two different positions, and the so-called *quinquefascalis* occupied a lower rank than that of the praetorian governor. This is seen above all in the career of L. Iulius Apronius Maenianus Sallamallianus, whose term of office as a deputy governor in the province of Belgica preceded his legionary command (no. 6).

A brief survey may help:

No. 1: The praetorian M. Ateius was sent to Asia while the consular governor was in office there.

No. 2: C. Iulius Severus was *corrector* and *curator* in Bithynia, not its governor.

No. 3: M. Flavius Postumus was appointed (*ordinatus*) in Gaul, i. e. for all four Gallias, but was governor of none.

No. 4: The Ignotus who was πεντάραβδος in Raetia could have been a governor at this stage in his career, but the absence of a legionary command in his career makes this unlikely; furthermore, now that we know that none of the other so-called *quinquefascales* was a provincial governor, and that the position of the so-called *quinquefascalis* is to be distinguished from that of a governor, we can say that the very fact that he is called πεντάραβσος implies the opposite, namely that he was not the provincial governor of Raetia.

No. 5: The Ignotus who was probably in office in the Transpadane *regio* of Italy was not a provincial governor, but a special commissioner sent by Marcus Aurelius to the afflicted region.

No. 6: The governor of Belgica, whom L. Iulius Apronius Maenianus Sallamallianus was replacing, did not bear the title *quinquefascalis* of the province of Belgica; at most his title as *legatus Augusti pro praetore* could have been further qualified by the qualitative genitive *quinque fascium* – a qualification attested nowhere else; it was put there only in order to underline the rank of his deputy now in possession of an identical *potestas*.

No. 7: M. Aedinius Iulianus was an equestrian while serving as governor of Gallia Lugdunensis. The usual *pro praetore* is missing from his title as governor: *legatus Augusti provinciae Lugdunensis*, and the *quinque fasces* may in fact prove the uniqueness of his position.

Nor am I convinced that even in the case of these special envoys did *quinquefascalis* ever crystallize into an official title. The term is attested securely in Latin only once, in no. 7: *in provincia Lugduness(i) quinquefascal(em) cum agerem*; but even here it is not used as a title but is part of a circumlocution which describes the man's term of office as an equestrian governor in what used to be a praetorian province. It is restored in no. 5: *[?legatus Augusti quin]que fasc(ali) reg(ionis) [?Transpad(anae)]*, which could also read *[?legatus Augusti quin]que fasc(ium) reg(ionis) [?Transpad(anae)]*. Its Greek equivalent πεντάραβδος is also attested once only, in no. 4: [πε]ντάραβδον Ῥαιτίας. In the other four cases a periphrasis is used to convey the fact that the man held five *fasces*: ἀνὴρ ἐσετρατηγηκὼς σὺν πέντε ῥαβδούχοις (no. 1); πρὸς ε' ῥάβδους πεμφθέντα εἰς Βειθυνίαν (no. 2);[46] *ordinato in Gal/lia at quinque fasces* (no. 3); *<leg. Aug. pr. pr.> quinque fascium prov(inciae) Belgi[cae]* (no. 6). Nor does Dio come up with a title after his suggestive καὶ ὀνομάζονται ἐπ' αὐτοῦ τοῦ ἀριθμοῦ τούτου; one would have expected πεντάραβδοι or a Greek transliteration of *quinquefascales* to follow.

The scarcity of the epigraphic evidence suggests that not all imperial envoys were entitled to five *fasces*. Those who were, by emphasizing the five *fasces* in their career inscriptions, i. e. the symbol of the praetorian *potestas*, made themselves to some extent appear the equals of governors in imperial provinces. In the province into which they were sent, accompanied by five lictors, they looked no different from a praetorian or consular imperial governor.

---

46 This is the only case where a more specific definition of the praetorian's position follows: διορθωτὴν καὶ λογιστήν.

III

What about Dio's assertion that the praetorian governors of imperial provinces "also receive their name from that number," i. e. five: καὶ ὀνομάζονται ἐπ' αὐτοῦ τοῦ ἀριθμοῦ τούτου?

Editors of Dio must have puzzled over this statement. The first printed editions of Dio changed the πέντε ῥαβδούχοις to ἕξ ῥαβδούχοις. Of course they were unaware of the existence of the epigraphic evidence presented above, and could not use it to defend their correction. They must have suspected Dio's accuracy on the grounds adduced by Mommsen in a paper published for the first time in 1852,[47] namely their acquaintance with the six *fasces* of the republican propraetors (and of the proconsuls with praetorian rank), the existence of the term ἑξαπελέκεις in the literary sources,[48] and conversely, the absence in these sources of the term *quinquefascalis* and its Greek equivalent πεντάραβδος. However, the ἕξ, as Mommsen categorically states, has no manuscript authority.[49] Boissevain's edition dismisses this correction with *perperam* and gives the credit for the restoration of the original reading πέντε to Mommsen.[50] All subsequent editions follow Boissevain's.

Surely it was the epigraphic evidence quoted above, as well as the case of M. Ateius (Cass. Dio 57, 17, 7 together with Tacitus, *Ann.* II, 47, 4, no. 1), which led Mommsen to vindicate Dio's accuracy and reinstate the reading of the unanimous manuscript tradition. At the same time this epigraphic evidence suggested to Mommsen that not all *legati Augusti pro praetore* were called *quinquefascales*, but only those *legati Augusti pro praetore* who were ex-praetors.[51] The way in

---

47 Mommsen, *Gesammelte Schriften*, Vol. VIII, 147 (first published as no. 20 in "Epigraphische analekten: 18–28," *Ber. Sächs. Ges. Wiss.* 4 (1852): 213 ff.).

48 Although *sexfascalis* is absent from the literary sources, in the second half of the fourth century we find dozens of inscriptions attesting the governor of Numidia as *consularis sexfascalis provinciae Numidiae*: *AE* 1888, no. 30; 1885, no. 108; 1902, no. 166 (= *ILAlg* 2.620); 1909, no. 220; 1911, no. 110 (= 1946, no. 112); 1913, nos. 23, 35; 1917/18, no. 58; 1936, no. 30 (= 1937, no. 144); 1946, nos. 107 (= no. 111), 110; 1987, nos. 1062, 1082, 1083 (= 1911, no. 217); *CIL* VIII 7015 (= *ILAlg* 2.596), 7034 (= *ILAlg* 2.619), 7975 (= 19852 = *ILAlg* 2.379), 10870 (= 1487 = *ILAlg* 2.661), 17896, 19502 (= *ILAlg* 2.618); *ILAlg* 2.629; see Mommsen, *Gesammelte Schriften*, Vol. VIII, 149 f.; Mommsen, *Römisches Staatsrecht*, Vol. I, 385, n. 2.

49 One could conceivably argue that somewhere along the transmission of Dio's text, a *digamma* was misread as an *epsilon*, were it not for the fact that the reasons which made the editors of the printed editions change the πέντε of the mss. to ἕξ would have worked as a corrective.

50 See apparatus to vol. II, 423, line 28: "πέντε] ἕξ Xyl. perperam, cf. Mommsen, *Staatsrecht* I^2 369, 4."

51 Although he believed that the title was not restricted to praetorian governors but common to them and to special envoys, whom he designates *legati Augusti extra ordinem*, and wrongly

which he punctuated and translated Dio's text was meant to bring out the distinction between the consular and the praetorian *legati Augusti* – only the latter received their title from the reduced number of lictors.[52] This less than natural interpretation of the Greek text is reflected in all the translations quoted at the beginning of this paper, which were clearly influenced by Mommsen's: the first καί was taken in the sense of *et* (and), and the second καί in the sense of *etiam* (also): ῥαβδούχοις δὲ δὴ πέντε πάντες ὁμοίως οἱ ἀντιστράτηγοι χρῶνται· καὶ ὅσοι γε οὐκ ἐκ τῶν ὑπατευκότων εἰσί, καὶ ὀμάζονται ἐπ' ἀυτοῦ τοῦ ἀριθμοῦ τούτου ("Sämtliche kaiserliche Legaten haben nicht mehr als fünf Lictoren, und diejenigen von ihnen, welche nicht das Consulat bekleidet haben, entnehmen diesen fünf Fasces auch den Namen).[53]

However, once it is realized that the epigraphic evidence does not bear out the claim that *quinquefascalis* or πεντάραβδος was the title (if indeed, which is extremely dubious, it was a title at all) of the praetorian governors – we may attempt a more straightforward translation of the text. The translation offered below takes the first καί in the sense of *etiam* (also), and the second καί in the sense of *et* (and). The first καί will then put the clause ὅσοι γε οὐκ ἐκ τῶν ὑπατευκότων εἰσί in parenthesis, whereas the second καί[54] will connect the two verbs χρῶνται and ὀνομάζονται to each other: ῥαβδούχοις δὲ δὴ πέντε πάντες ὁμοίως οἱ ἀντιστράτηγοι χρῶνται – καὶ ὅσοι γε οὐκ ἐκ τῶν ὑπατευκότων εἰσί – καὶ ὀνομάζονται ἐπ' αὐτοῦ τοῦ ἀριθμοῦ τούτου ('All propraetors alike employ five lictors – indeed *also* those who are not ex-consuls – and receive their name from that number). This is in fact how the passage was translated into German in 1838 when the text still read ἕξ: "Alle Proprätoren ohne Unterschied haben sechs Lictoren, *auch wenn* sie früher keine Consuln gewesen waren, *und* werden von der Zahl der Beile [ἑξαπελέκεις Sechsbeilige] benannt."[55]

restricts it to the public (which he of course called 'senatorial') provinces, cf. Mommsen, *Gesammelte Schriften*, Vol. VIII, 228, see above n. 18.

52 No one seems to have asked himself why only the ex-praetors were thus called, although all the *legati Augusti pro praetore* had the same number of lictors.

53 Mommsen, *Gesammelte Schriften*, Vol. VIII, 147.

54 It could be argued that the second καί connects not the two verbs χρῶνται and ὀνομάζονται but the verbs εἰσί and ὀνομάζονται to each other with the result that we have two relative clauses following the first καί: 'All propraetors alike employ five lictors – *also* those who are not ex-consuls *and* (who) receive their name from that number,' but this makes poor sense.

55 In G.L.F. Tafel, C.N. Osiander, and Gustav Schwab, eds., *Griechische Prosaiker in neuen Uebersetzungen*, Vol. 176 (Stuttgart: Metzler, 1838), 1060. Mommsen too seems to have understood the Greek in this way at some point, cf. Mommsen, *Römisches Staatsrecht*, Vol. II, 245: "im Sprachgebrauch wird allerdings der gewesene Consul ausgezeichnet als *legatus consularis* oder *consularis*

True, in this translation and punctuation there is strong emphasis on the fact that even non-*consulares*, i. e. praetorians, receive five *fasces*: καὶ ὅσοι γε οὐκ ἐκ τῶν ὑπατευκότων εἰσί.[56] It may be objected that the emphasis should have been on the *consulares* who were deprived of more than half their *fasces*. Roman sensitivity for *discrimina ordinum dignitatumque* dictated otherwise: Dio anticipates here the 'natural' expectation that those who ranked as ex-praetors should have had fewer than five lictors. Indeed, in the case of the proconsuls of the public provinces the shared title did not result in allotting all proconsuls, whether consulars or praetorians, the same number of lictors. Each group kept the number of lictors commensurate with its rank in the city.

The negative formulation – καὶ ὅσοι γε οὐκ ἐκ τῶν ὑπατευκότων εἰσί – emphasizes the implied parallelism and contrast with the proconsuls of the public provinces.[57] In fact the passages dealing with these two groups are almost mirror images of each other. All the governors of the public provinces were called proconsuls, even those who were not ex-consuls, but ex-praetors: καὶ ἀνθυπάτους καλεῖσθαι μὴ ὅτι τοὺς δύο τοὺς ὑπατεθκότας ἀλλὰ καὶ τοὺς ἄλλους τοὺς ἐκ τῶν ἐστρατηγηκότων. Likewise, all governors of the imperial provinces were called *legati Augusti pro praetore*, even those who were ex-consuls: Τοὺς δὲ ἑτέρους ὑπό τε ἑαυτοῦ αἱρεῖσθαι καὶ πρεσβευτὰς αὑτοῦ ἀντιστρατήγους τε ὀνομάζεσθαι, κἂν ἐκ τῶν ὑπατευκότων ὦσι, διέταξε.[58] However, whereas the proconsuls kept the number of *fasces* befitting their rank in the city: ῥαβδούχοις τέ σφας ἑκατέρους ὅσοισπερ καὶ ἐν τῷ ἄστει νενόμισται χρῆσθαι, the imperial governors, in contrast, had all the same number, even those who were not *consulares*: ῥαβδούχοις δὲ δὴ πέντε πάντες ὁμοίως οἱ ἀντιστράτηγοι χρῶνται, καὶ ὅσοι γε οὐκ ἐκ τῶν ὑπατευκότων εἰσί. It is the sharp contrast with the case of the proconsuls – where proprieties were maintained to a certain extent – which offends Roman sensitivity and expectations, and accounts for the negative formulation: unlike the proconsuls, the governors of imperial provinces were not compensated for a title shared with people of a lower rank than their own by the preservation of the external appurtenances of their rank in the city.

---

schlechtweg, wogegen die ebenfalls der Umgangssprache angehörende Benennung *quinquefascalis* allen gemein ist."

56 See J.D. Denniston, *The Greek Particles* (Oxford: Clarendon Press, 1934), 157–8 on καὶ ... γε in the case both of a connective καί and of the adverbial καί.

57 Already noticed by Mommsen, *Gesammelte Schriften*, Vol. VIII, 148.

58 Cass. Dio 53, 13, 5.

IV

Are we now in a better position to explain Dio's passage? Although I believe that the passage as translated above is the correct interpretation of Dio's Greek, it must be admitted that it does not offer a more satisfactory explanation of its factual content than Mommsen's. There is not a shred of evidence for the claim that the senatorial governors of imperial provinces, whether they were ex-consuls or ex-praetors, received their title from the number of their *fasces*. With one exception, none of those attested as accompanied by five *fasces* can safely and without a reasonable doubt be identified as a provincial governor; in some of the cases this is absolutely excluded. The exception, M. Aedinius Iulianus, was an equestrian and thus can hardly count as proof for Dio's claim.

Therefore Cassius Dio could not have had an official title in mind when he said καὶ ονομάζονται ἐπ' αὐτοῦ τοῦ ἀριθμοῦ τούτου. It may be tentatively suggested that he meant a name used in colloquial language, as Mommsen already suggested,[59] and as such never recorded in career inscriptions. This informal name, derived from the number of the *fasces* carried by the *legati Augusti pro praetore*, could have been used in senatorial circles, in the provincial context or in both.

Appendix: Pliny's position in Pontus-Bithynia

Mommsen explained Pliny the Younger's unparalleled and highly anomalous appointment to an official position of a *legatus Augusti pro praetore* with a consular *potestas* in Pontus-Bithynia as motivated by the fact that it was inappropriate to have a *quinquefascalis* establish order in a province so far under the rule of a *sexfascalis*,[60] namely the praetorian proconsul. Although he does not say so explicitly, Mommsen is likely to have thought that Pliny held twelve *fasces* like any holder of consular imperium.[61]

A different conception of Pliny's position in Pontus-Bithynia has recently been offered by Géza Alföldy. Alföldy challenges Mommsen's authoritative reading of

---

59 *Römisches Staatsrecht*, Vol. II, 245, cited above, n. 55.

60 "Die einzige uns bekannte Abweichung von diesem Prinzip [i. e. the denial of consular *potestas* to a legate] ist die Sendung des Plinius nach Bithynien als *legatus Augusti pro praetore consulari potestate* ... der Sache nach begreiflich, da in einer bisher von Sexfascales regierten Provinz ein Quinquefascalis nicht wohl geeignet war Ordnung zu stiften, aber formell eine arge Anomalie," *Römisches Staatsrecht*, Vol. II, 245, n. 1.

61 *Römisches Staatsrecht*, Vol. I, 382.

consulari potestate in Pliny's famous inscription from Comum,[62] and convincingly reinstates E. Bormann's reading *[pro]consulari potesta[te]* there:[63] *legat(us) pro pr(aetore) provinciae Pon[ti et Bithyniae pro]consulari potesta[te] in eam provinciam e[x senatus consulto ab]*[64] *Imp(eratore) Caesar(e) Nerva Traiano Aug(usto) German[ico Dacico p(atre) p(atriae) missus].*

How many *fasces* was Pliny entitled to as *legatus Augusti pro praetore* and as holder of a *proconsularis potestas*?

Alföldy proposes six, assuming that thereby Pliny's rank was kept equal to that of the previous proconsul: "Als Inhaber der *proconsularis potestas* war Plinius, den bei seinen amtlichen Handlungen nicht fünf, sondern sechs Liktoren begleiteten, für jeden erkennbar mit den Prokonsuln gleichgestellt."[65] For Alföldy the possession of the *proconsularis potestas*, externally manifested in the proconsular six *fasces*, made it clear that although Pliny was a *legatus Augusti pro praetore*, Pontus-Bithynia did not change its status and did not become an imperial province.[66]

This is not the place to enter into this highly controversial issue. Pliny's position in Pontus-Bithynia as it emerges if one accepts Alföldy's restoration of *proconsularis potestas* in the inscriptions from Comum and Hispellum is unique and without any parallel. His correspondence with Trajan proves, however, that in all respects he was like the other *legati Augusti pro praetore*.[67] The *proconsularis potestas* in his titulature will therefore have to do with rank rather than with substance. As *legatus Augusti pro praetore* he was entitled to five *fasces* – one fewer than his predecessors in the province who had six. Alföldy's six would indeed put him on a par with his predecessors, implying however that like them he ranked as an ex-praetor. But Pliny's *proconsularis potestas*, unlike that of his predecessors, was not that of an ex-praetor but that of an ex-consul, and as such entitled him to twelve *fasces*.[68]

---

62 *CIL* V 5262 = *ILS* 2927 (Comum).

63 Géza Alföldy, "Die Inschriften des jüngeren Plinius und seine Mission in Pontus et Bithynia," in *Städte, Eliten und Gesellschaft in der Gallia Cisalpina* (Stuttgart: Steiner, 1999), 221 ff.; for the reconstruction see 229 and 243 (Abb. 17). See also the text of the inscription from Hispellum (*CIL* XI 1552) as restored by Alföldy, 234: *ex s(enatus) c(onsulto) pro[consulari potestate legatus pr(o) pr(aetore) provinciae Ponti] et Bithyniae.*

64 Bormann had *auctore*.

65 Alföldy, "Die Inschriften des jüngeren Plinius und seine Mission in Pontus et Bithynia," 240.

66 Alföldy, 236 ff.

67 Fergus Millar, *The Emperor in the Roman World* (London: Duckworth, 1977), 325.

68 See Cass. Dio 53, 13, 4 quoted at the beginning of this article.

The Evolution of the So-Called Provincial Law, or: Cicero's Letters of Recommendation and Private International Law in the Roman World

The sub-title to this paper, "Cicero's Letters of Recommendation and Private International Law in the Roman World," combines two pieces of autobiography. My unpublished doctorate was devoted to Latin letters of recommendation by Cicero, Pliny the Younger and Fronto.[1] It was much later that, quite by chance, I came across the concept of Private International Law and realized that it could be applied to the Roman Provincial scene, exploring this for the first time in a paper delivered in 2005 in a conference in honour of Professor Werner Eck. As befitted the honorand, this concentrated on the 'High Empire.'[2] It was only recently that I have come to see that the concept could be usefully applied to the early imperial period as well, the Republican Empire so to speak.

I

The letter of recommendation – *litterae commendaticiae* as it is called in the Ciceronian Corpus[3] – is by no means an exciting literary genre; nor are the *formulae* and the attempts to manipulate and challenge them so as to distinguish between routine and mechanical letters of recommendation and the unusual one which is

---

1 Hannah M. Cotton, "Letters of Recommendation: Cicero-Fronto," Unpublished DPhil. Dissertation, University of Oxford (1977), supervised by Professor Sir Fergus Millar.

2 It was published as "Private International Law or Conflict of Laws: Reflections on Roman Provincial Jurisdiction," in *Herrschen Und Verwalten. Der Alltag Der Römischen Administration in Der Hohen Kaizerzeit*, ed. Rudolf Haensch and Johannes Heinrichs (Köln: Böhlau, 2007), 234–55 [below, pp. 213–35].

3 *Fam*. XIII, 26, 3 with Hannah M. Cotton, "Cicero, Ad Familiares XIII, 26 and 28: Evidence for Revocatio or Reiectio Romae/Romam?," *JRS* 69 (1979): 48–50 [above, pp. 18–22]. See however *P.Mich*. 8.468, col. ii, ll. 39–40 with Hannah M. Cotton, *Documentary Letters of Recommendation in Latin from the Roman Empire* (Königstein/Ts.: Hain, 1981), 1 ff. and Silvia Strassi, *L'archivio di Claudius Tiberianus da Karanis* (Berlin – New York: De Gruyter, 2008), 178–79.

Article note: First published in *Integration in Rome and in the Roman World: Proceedings of the Tenth Workshop of the International Network Impact of Empire (Lille, June 23–25, 2011)*, ed. G. de Kleijn and Stéphane Benoist (Leiden – Boston: Brill, 2013), 43–56, with the following note: I am very grateful to Stéphane Benoist for his inexhaustible patience, and to Nicholas Horsfall and Alexander Yakobson for improving my text and my arguments.

https://doi.org/10.1515/9783110770438-006

meant in earnest, particularly arousing, nor do they ever surprise. Nevertheless these *formulae* are sometimes quite useful: I got into the habit of ending my letters of recommendation for outstanding students with a variation on Cicero's *formula* in a letter to Caesar (*Fam.* XIII, 15, 3): "*genere novo sum litterarum ad te usus ut intellegeres non vulgarem esse commendationem.*"

However, their interest for me had nothing to do with any theory of genre. Cicero's letters of recommendation are mostly appeals to Roman officials in the provinces on behalf of people whose interests fell within the officials' sphere of competence (*imperium*; *potestas*). Yet surprisingly the letters often fail to refer to the official authority vested in the recipient, and this paucity of references to it contrasts sharply with the multitude of appeals to the man's *humanitas, liberalitas, voluntas, integritas, mansuetudo, clementia, studium, officium*, etc. These are all patently personal qualities, not derived from the man's official position. Likewise few recommendations explicitly ask for an official act on the part of the addressee. Generally they are requests to extend his friendship (*fides, amicitia, necessitudo* and similar terms) to the person or persons recommended.

Where the vagueness and obscurity characteristic of such letters resolves to some detail, a matter of litigation or legal dispute is generally at hand. This is hardly a cause for surprise. Jurisdiction, after all, was the main duty of the governor in a peaceful province. It is precisely because these letters contain appeals to officials in matters concerning the latter's judicial competence that they may justly be held to reflect Roman attitudes towards the administration of justice in their empire. One is surely entitled to suspect, if not condemn, these letters, as blatant attempts to flout justice and make *gratia*, personal influence, tilt the balance in favour of a protégé. Or as J.M. Kelly put it in a nutshell: "are not justice and favour mutually exclusive ideas, even in Latin?" Consequently he dismissed the saving clause, usual in such letters, 'so far as your dignity and justice will permit,' as a stock phrase, "which probably meant as little to the recipient as to the sender, as the broad wink of *gratia* passed between them."[4] I have tried to save Cicero's reputation in an analysis of the realities and principles underpinning Roman provincial administration of justice.[5] David Daube was left unconvinced by what, in a private communication, he described as "special pleading," meaning sophistry, perhaps naïveté.

My main line of defence was that these letters fulfilled an essential function in a system of government, which left the governor with wide discretionary powers

4 John Maurice Kelly, *Roman Litigation* (Oxford: Clarendon Press, 1966), 58 and 61.
5 Hannah M. Cotton, "The Role of Cicero's Letters of Recommendation: Iustitia versus Gratia?," *Hermes* 114 (1986): 443–60 [above, pp. 61–78].

on the one hand, and on the other without the machinery needed to carry out judicial and administrative transactions on a regular and impersonal basis. Hence we may regard these letters as part and parcel of the Roman political system as opposed to the ancillary role, which they have in modern bureaucracy.[6] I also suggested that there were other safeguards, such as the need to preserve *decorum* on the recommender's part, and to protect his own *existimatio* on the governor's. Finally, I supplied plenty of extenuating circumstances. I claimed that the legal disputes mentioned in these letters do not necessarily imply court proceedings, and that more often than not Cicero's letter is aimed at something quite different than obtaining the governor's favour at the trial stage. Hence these letters should not be seen as attempts to bias the judge and influence the verdict itself. Furthermore, court proceedings were distasteful to the Romans and they tried to avoid them: the recommendation was one way of doing so. This may take the form of a direct appeal to prevent litigation, as Cicero does in the case of his translator's son's mother in-law: Q. Minucius Thermus proconsul in Asia in 50 BC is requested to help and bring about "*ut socrus adulescentis rea ne fiat*" (*Fam.* XIII, 54). On other occasions the governor's influence is enlisted as an alternative to legal remedies, i. e. to induce the other party to settle out of court (we are not told whose court of law: the governor's or a local court?). For example P. Silius, governor of Pontus-Bithynia in 50 BC is asked to urge the Greek cities to conclude their *pactiones* with the *promagister* of the public company which collects the *scriptura* in the province, P. Terentius Hispo (*Fam.* XIII, 65).[7] In the case of the succession of Cicero's former quaestor, L. Mescinius Rufus, to the inheritance left to him by his cousin, M. Mindius, Servius Sulpicius Rufus, governor of Achaia in 46 BC (*Fam.* XIII, 26) is requested to threaten Mindius' widow, Oppia, with a remittal of the case to Rome as means of swiftly concluding the affair, presumably out of court.[8] An expeditious solution is desired in the case of Cicero's legate, whose services are indispensable to his superior (*Fam.* XIII, 57, 1). If legal proceedings have already begun by the governor, Thermus, we may assume that Cicero attempts to prevent them from dragging on, but he could be asking for a swift solution out of court. Finally, in his recommendation of T. Claudius Nero's protégé Pausanias of

6 For its survival into the imperial period see Hannah M. Cotton, "Military Tribunates and the Exercise of Patronage," *Chiron* 11 (1981): 229–38 [above, pp. 23–34].
7 Hannah M. Cotton, "A Note on the Organization of Tax-Farming in Asia Minor (Cicero, Fam. XIII, 65)," *Latomus* 45 (1986): 367–73.
8 Cotton, "Cicero, Ad Familiares XIII, 26 and 28: Evidence for Revocatio or Reiectio Romae/Romam?," 48–50 [above, pp. 18–22].

Alabanda, Cicero is trying to convince Silius that he should delay legal proceedings pending Nero's arrival (*Fam.* XIII, 64, 1).[9]

When Cicero requested a governor to refrain from action, he was not denying anyone his right – at least this is not how the Romans would have seen it. For it is well known that classical law never formulated any idea of an individual's *right* to an action. The presence of an *actio* does not necessarily imply that the man had a claim, but rather that there was a *formula* that could be adapted to his case, and the *formula* was a matter of agreement between the praetor (governor) and the two parties. This was another way in which the governor could, if he chose, remain passive without, however, depriving anyone of an inherent right.

Some letters have a prophylactic and provisory nature, as in the case of L. Genucilius Rufus, where Cicero requests Thermus to hear in the assize centre of the area any dispute which might arise in the future between this man and a provincial (*Fam.* XIII, 53, 2). Similarly in the case of L. Manlius who inherited his brother's estate in Sicily, although no complications were foreseen at the time, it may safely be assumed that the recommendation was intended to provide for such an eventuality (*Fam.* XIII, 30). The same may be said about the recommendation of Lyso's son's right to inherit from the Roman exile, C. Maenius Gemellus, who adopted the young man in accordance with the local laws of Patrae (*Fam.* XIII, 19, 2). The last two cases have a bearing on the issue of 'double citizenship,' which will be discussed later.

The variety of the requests surveyed here suggests a corresponding variety of means at the disposal of the governor. Whether these putative means are to be called judicial, administrative, extra-judicial, authoritative, or by any other name is often a matter of definition. These letters call on the governor to employ his discretion in the preliminaries, the procedure, the pace of the proceedings and so forth. Interference in these, as it might be, 'phases' clearly implies that the discretion of the governor was wide, the system was flexible, and the use of discretion need not entail a reversal of justice, to go back to Kelly's doubts (above text to n. 4).

Although I have never published my doctoral dissertation but merely despoiled and looted it in a few articles, my interest in administration and jurisdiction – inseparable in ancient governments – remained a lifetime preoccupation.

---

9 For an imperial example of the delicate interplay between the governor's discretionary powers, the rights of cities and the influence of individuals see Christina Kokkinia, "Aphrodisias' 'Rights of Liberty': Diplomatic Strategies and the Roman Governor," in *Aphrodisias Papers 4: New Research on the City and Its Monuments*, ed. Ch. Ratté and R.R.R. Smith (Portsmouth: Journal of Roman Archaeology, 2008), 51–60.

However, as one sheds one's youth, the 'noble' principles governing a legal system seem to matter less than its operation: *wie es eigentlich gewesen ist.* And this new phase coincided by a happy serendipity with the re-distribution in 1992 of the documents from the Judaean Desert by the Advisory Committee for the Dead Sea Scrolls of the Israel Antiquities Authority, some of which now turned up, so to speak, on my desk, and invited me to the study of case law. I was back where I had started, but now equipped with authentic documents from real life – not that the letters assembled in Book XIII of the *Ad Familiares* are *not* authentic: they may have been published already in Cicero's own lifetime.[10] However, this time I had documents written by the litigants themselves, or their lawyers, and in some cases the protocol of court proceedings. I was admitted into the ancient courtroom.

II

This is where my second topic, private international law, or 'conflict of laws' enters the scene, and it seems necessary at this point to repeat here almost *verbatim* my introduction to the topic in the earlier article.[11]

I became acquainted with private international law almost by accident when one day my eyes fell on the opening anecdote in an article by a close friend, who is a well-known expert on the subject.[12] The expression 'private international law' suggests at first sight – quite wrongly as turns out – that there are two kinds of international law, private and public. But in fact 'private international law' does not mean 'international law' in the sense of a law common to all nations, but rather that part of the national law of a country which deals with cases where a foreign element intrudes in one form or another: e. g. one side to the contract or suit is a foreigner; or when the property in question is outside the country where the court operates; or if the contract is signed in a third country; or when all these and other factors come together – with many other variations. It is that set of rules which deals with what are known as 'conflicts of laws,' although its purpose is to resolve rather than to analyse the conflicts between legal systems.

---

10 Ludwig Gurlitt, "De M. Tulli Ciceronis Epistulis Earumque Pristina Collectione" (University of Göttingen Thesis, 1879).

11 Cotton, "Private International Law or Conflict of Laws: Reflections on Roman Provincial Jurisdiction," 234–35 [below, pp. 213–14].

12 Celia Wasserstein Fassberg, "On Time and Place in Choice of Law for Property," *The International and Comparative Law Quarterly* 51 (2002): 385–400, to whom I wish to thank for letting me read the general introduction to her then forthcoming book, in Hebrew, on the subject, which was published in 2013.

Thus both terms, private international law and conflicts of laws, are to a certain extent misnomers.

Broadly speaking, cases of conflict of laws revolve around two issues: 1) which court has jurisdiction in the matter; and 2) what law applies. It does not follow automatically – nor would it be fair and just that it should – that the court which has jurisdiction in the matter, will apply its own law. A third but closely related issue is the enforcement of a judgement of a foreign court by the national court. Finally, there is no 'harmony of laws' between private international laws of different countries, i. e. in the rules concerning conflicts of law – perhaps it is not even so desirable or beneficial to achieve such harmony.

Notwithstanding the reservation of one of the foremost authorities on the subject,[13] I believe that it is both legitimate and profitable to apply the conceptual framework called forth by private international law to the Roman Empire as early as republican times, even if it is true that local legal institutions owed their continued existence and their regulation to Roman toleration of their existence. On the other hand, nowhere do we witness that Rome, once she became the sovereign, tried to impose her own legal system, her own law and jurisdiction on the subject populations:[14] the *ius civile* was intended for *cives*; at most Rome extended to foreigners some provisions of its *ius civile* (e. g. by using the fiction *si ciuis Romanus esset*). Wolff's argument that "private international law can only establish itself where respect is shown for foreign law," which he takes to be the *sine qua non* for the development of private international law, is untenable.

Theoretically, with the exception of some communities who had a special treaty with Rome, all of Rome's provincial subjects were *de iure* under the jurisdiction (*iuris dictio*) of Roman officials. However, judicial autonomy, that is the use of local courts of law and of local law, especially in civil cases, may well have been taken for granted, or at least need not have called for a specific grant by the Roman government – at any rate in the case of self-governing communities, i. e. cities. Later, it seems to have become a tralatician part of the provincial edict, as

---

13 Hans Julius Wolff, "Nicht Gleichordnung, sondern Über- und Unterordnung bestimmte die Stellung der Normenkreise zu einander," in *Das Problem der Konkurrenz von Rechtsordnungen in der Antike* (Heidelberg: C. Winter, 1979), 7 and 66. I thank Professor Lucia Fanizza for discussing the issue with me, and drawing my attention to some pertinent bibliography. See also Hans Lewald's "Conflits de lois dans le monde grec et romain," *Ἀρχεῖον Ἰδιωτικοῦ Δικαίου* 13 (1946): 30–77 (reprinted in *Labeo* 5 (1959): 334–69 and in *Revue critique de droit international privé* 57 (1968): 419–40 and 615–39), for an early systematic attempt to analyse the legal evidence from the Graeco-Roman world from the point of view of 'private international law' or 'conflict of laws.'

14 Hartmut Galsterer, "Roman Law in the Provinces: Some Problems of Transmission," in *L'Impero romano e le strutture economiche e sociali delle province*, ed. Michael Crawford (Como: New Press, 1986), 13–27.

we know from Cicero's provincial edict in Cilicia where he was governor in 50 BC (*Att.* VI, 1, 15), and it is this wholesale, perhaps formerly implicit, grant of local autonomy, that introduced 'conflict of laws' into the scene; no more than the tacit admission of the foreign in legal contexts is needed for the private international law to become part and parcel of a legal system. The legal situation prevailing in Sicily as described by Cicero (*Verr.* II, 2, 31–32) adumbrated regulations which modern jurists would have recognised as belonging to the sphere of 'private international law' or 'conflict of laws,' as does Augustus' fourth Cyrene edict (*FIRA*, Vol. I, 409, no. 68). It is remarkable that with the exception of cases between citizens of the same city in Sicily who are to be tried *suis legibus* in the city's court, both Cicero and Augustus only refer to courts, i. e. the jurisdiction, but fail to specify the law to be exercised in the court. However, the principle of 'inalienability' of personal legal status (see more below) taken together with the absence of any sign for the imposition of a single juridical framework for the whole empire,[15] renders the question of the extent of local legal autonomy of secondary importance: limited and curtailed though local jurisdiction might have been, peregrines continued to enjoy the use of their personal law either in their own courts or in those provided by the Romans. A man could *not* have a choice between the personal laws of one legal system and another.[16] In republican times, the question concerned Roman citizens living in the provinces but even more so newly made citizens, those who certainly after 212, but also before, received the citizenship with the rider *saluo iure gentis*. True, with the spread of citizenship and the rapid increase in the number of mixed communities, *civitas*, citizenship, *did* change its character, but so far as personal law was concerned, it is hard to believe that the principle enunciated by Cicero in the *Pro Balbo* 28 suffered any derogation: "*Duarum ciuitatum ciuis noster esse iure ciuili nemo potest: non esse huius ciuitatis qui se alii ciuitati dicarit potest.*" The restriction implied by *saluo iure gentis* did not apply to personal status: it inserted a wedge between public duties and private status. The possession of Roman citizenship was inextricably bound up with the *ius civile* in matters concerning the law of persons, and denotes personal status in contrast to public duties.[17]

---

15 See Galsterer.

16 See on 'double citizenship' below.

17 Cf. A.N. Sherwin-White, *The Roman Citizenship* (Oxford: Clarendon Press, 1973), 273: "in the second century [CE] the status of a Roman citizen was, in private law, as clearly fixed and defined as ever it had been."

This is why one can, or rather should, look at these cases through the prism of the principles underlying modern Private International Law, which as we saw were not unknown, even if never formulated as such, in the Roman World.[18]

III

It is my intention to discuss a few cases taken from Cicero's letters of recommendation to republican provincial governors. A good starting point would be Cicero's letter to M. Acilius Glabrio, governor of Sicily in 46–45 BC (*Fam.* XIII, 30), where one witnesses the kind of 'conflict of laws' resulting from the acquisition of Roman citizenship by one member of the peregrine family:[19] "L. Manlius Sosis was formerly a citizen of Catina. He became eligible for Roman citizenship together with the rest of the Neapolitans, since his attachment to that town had preceded the grant of franchise to aliens and Latins. He also served as a town councillor there."[20] His brother had recently died at Catina, but Cicero did not expect any dispute to arise over his title to the estate, and indeed he was in possession of it at the time the letter was written:

> However, since he has some old affairs of business in his part of Sicily, I beg to recommend to your notice this matter of his brother's estate and all other concerns of his, above all the

18 One should take account now of the first two chapters of Clifford Ando, *Law, Language, and Empire in the Roman Tradition* (Philadelphia: University of Pennsylvania Press, 2011). As the reader of the present volume will realize, the themes raised in the present article intersect with Ando's "Pluralisme Juridique et Intégration de l'empire," in *Integration in Rome and in the Roman World: Proceedings of the Tenth Workshop of the International Network Impact of Empire (Lille, June 23–25, 2011)*, 5–19. I would subscribe to all the conclusions reached and summarized at the end of his article, but use his own words to insist: "sur le caractère à la fois centripète et centrifuge de ces pressions intégratrices, qui s'exerçaient non seulement d'en haut **mais aussi d'en bas**" (emphasis mine). For a salient example of the latter see Tiziana J. Chiusi, "IV. Zur Vormundschaft der Mutter," *ZSS* 111 (1994): 155–96 and Tiziana J. Chiusi, "Babatha vs. The Guardians of Her Son: A Struggle for Guardianship – Legal and Practical Aspects of P. Yadin 12–15, 27," in *Law in the Documents of the Judean Desert*, ed. Ranon Katzoff and David Schaps (Leiden: Brill, 2005), 105 ff. In both she demonstrates the legal measures proposed by Babatha (or rather, her lawyer) in the document to support resurface in third-century Roman legal writings.
19 For imperial examples and their interpretation see Fergus Millar, *The Emperor in the Roman World* (London: Duckworth, 1977), 484, referring to Pliny, *Pan.* XXXVII–XL.
20 "*Is fuit Catinensis, sed est una cum reliquis Neapolitanis ciuis Romanus factus decurioque Neapoli; erat enim adscriptus in id municipium ante ciuitatem sociis et Latinis datam.*" Unlike the poet Archias, who was a non-resident *adscriptus* of Heraclea, L. Manlius Sosis *did* reside in his adoptive *patria*, namely Naples, and became a citizen under the *lex Iulia*: see Sherwin-White, *The Roman Citizenship*, 151–52, on this letter in conjunction with Cicero, *Pro Archia* 7.

> man himself. He is an excellent person and a familiar friend of mine, conversant with the literary and scholarly pursuits in which I chiefly delight. Let me ask you (whether or not he goes to Sicily) to be aware that he is one of my closest and most intimate friends, and to let him understand by the way you treat him that my recommendation has been of substantial assistance to him.[21]

Cicero stresses that no dispute is hanging over the inheritance ("*nullam omnino arbitramur de ea hereditate controuersiam eum habiturum*"), and under Roman law the fact that "he is in possession" – *est hodie in bonis* – means that "if anyone wishes to disturb (it) ... he can only do so by means of a regular judicial proceeding in which he himself proves a title."[22] However, if a dispute arose, could a remedy be sought under Roman law? The testament, if it was a testate succession, or the remedies, if it was an intestate succession, would have been in both cases foreign instruments, and, as pointed out before (text to nn. 16 and 17 above), it is inconceivable that a Roman citizen could inherit (as well as disinherit, or marry, divorce, bequeath, adopt, etc.) according to one system or another, depending on the prospective jurisdiction, in accordance with his own free choice. L. Manlius was subject by the principle of personality to one legal system whereas his inheritance fell under another. How could he have realized it if a dispute arose, and which court of law would take cognizance of the case, a Roman court or a local court? This is a perfect case to which in modern times we would look for the provisions laid down by the private international law of each one of the two countries involved, which may or may not be in harmony with each other, e. g. one law may refer to the *lex situs* whereas the other to the personal law of the parties involved.[23]

In contrast to this case, the adoption of Lyso of Patrae's son by C. Maenius Gemellus (*Fam.* XIII, 19),[24] attracted the attention of modern jurists who dealt with the implications of the possession of 'dual citizenship.' It became a bone of contention between them, and thus received two mutually exclusive interpretations.

---

21 "*sed, quoniam habet praeterea negotia uetera in Sicilia tua, et hanc hereditatem fraternam et omnia eius tibi commendo in primisque ipsum, uirum optimum mihique familiarissimum, iis studiis litterarum doctrinaeque praeditum, quibus ego maxime delector. Peto igitur abs te, ut eum, siue aderit siue non uenerit in Siciliam, in meis intimis maximeque necessariis scias esse itaque tractes, ut intelligat meam sibi commendationem magno adiumento fuisse.*" D.R. Shackleton Bailey's translation in *Cicero's Letters to His Friends*, Vol. I (Harmondsworth: Penguin Books, 1978).
22 H.F. Jolowicz and Barry Nicholas, *A Historical Introduction to the Study of Roman Law* (Cambridge: Cambridge University Press, 1972), 259.
23 See Wasserstein Fassberg, "On Time and Place in Choice of Law for Property."
24 This letter written in 46 BC, like others written after the civil war, adumbrates the advent of a new era: a third party intrudes into the egalitarian relationship between recommender and recipient, that of the dictator, whose good will must be secured in advance, see Cotton, "Letters of Recommendation: Cicero-Fronto," chapter 4.

During the civil wars, C. Maenius Gemellus received the local citizenship of the city of Patrae where he spent his exile. As a citizen of Patrae he adopted Lyso's son in accordance with local law: "*[tibi commendo] filium eius (i. e. Pisonis) quem C. Maenius Gemellus, cliens meus, quum in calamitate exsilii sui Patrensis ciuis factus esset, Patrensium legibus adoptauit*" (ibid., § 3). Cicero requests from the governor of Achaia at the time, the celebrated jurist, S. Sulpicius Rufus, to take care of the adopted son's claims to the heritage: "*eius ipsius hereditatis ius causamque tuear.*"

Loyal to the principle of incompatibility, Arangio-Ruiz maintained that C. Maenius Gemellus, having returned to Rome after his exile, by regaining his Roman citizenship must have lost his Patrensian citizenship – at least so far as the Romans were concerned – and this resulted in the invalidation of the adoption made in accordance with the local law of Patrae: "e non sappiamo se la grande abilità di un Servio bastasse a venire a capo."[25] Schönbauer seizes triumphantly on this note of despair in his rival to assert that if one accepts the principles propounded by Arangio- Ruiz, Cicero's appeal to Servius would be futile: "Ciceros Ersuchen wäre einfach unverständlich, wenn es keine Möglichkeit der Erfullung seines Wunsches gab."[26] Accordingly he suggests that Gemellus should be treated as a citizen of Patrae who had just received (or been awarded) the Roman citizenship, rather than as a citizen of Patrae who had once held Roman citizenship and had lost it until regaining it, *postliminio*, when permitted to return to Italy; only in the first case, that of a newly-made Roman citizen, would legal transactions performed in accordance with the laws of his previous *polis* have remained valid after his having received Roman citizenship.[27]

---

25 Vincenzo Arangio-Ruiz, "Sul problema della doppia cittadinanza nella Repubblica e nell'impero romano," in *Scritti giuridici in onore di Francesco Carnelutti*, Vol. IV (Padova: CEDAM, 1950), 55–77.

26 Ernst Schönbauer, "Zur Entwicklung des 'Ius Publice Respondendi,'" *Iura* 4 (1953): 224–27 (reply to Arangio-Ruiz, above n. 25).

27 Schönbauer in *Iura* 4 (1953): 393–94 (Review of Arangio-Ruiz, above n. 25). However, even Fernand De Visscher, who generally shares Schönbauer's views on the principle of double citizenship, holds that compatibility applied only as long as the newly made citizen remained in his home-town, whereas a *mutatio civitatis* would have resulted in its loss, see "La dualité des droits de cité et la 'mutatio civitatis,'" *Bulletin de la Classe des Lettres et des Sciences Morales et Politiques* 40 (1954): 49–67; see Sherwin-White, *The Roman Citizenship*, 292–336.

The assumption shared by both Schönbauer and Arangio-Ruiz, that C. Maenius Gemellus returned to Rome, albeit reasonable, cannot be proved; it may be based on his being described by Cicero as "*cliens meus*" – a designation rarely used in Cicero's letters of recommendations, but which may well imply physical closeness. Nevertheless, C. Maenius Gemellus could hardly be the moving force behind this recommendation which is devoted entirely to promoting Piso's interests and his household's.

Be this as it may, Schönbauer is quite right to observe (n. 27) that it was obviously too early, in any case, for 'positive norms' to have emerged. I would even go further and claim that the very attempt to detect such norms is probably misconceived: by that time the Roman State (whatever we may mean by that) could hardly have formulated principles and made provisions to close the gap between the new reality and traditional theory and practice; under these circumstances the wide discretionary powers of the governor could legitimately be called upon (see text to nn. 4–6 above).

Furthermore: it would seem that even in cases where norms did exist, the concrete evidence we have in Cicero's letters of recommendation does not unequivocally imply that they were followed. Thus in *Fam*. XIII, 37, also addressed to the governor of Sicily at the time, M. Acilius, Cicero recommends Hippias, son of Philoxenus, from the city of Calacte, "whose property ... is being held by the state under a different name in violation of the laws of Calacte."[28]

This is an instance of a dispute between a private citizen and a city. The *Lex Rupilia* provides for such a case: "When an individual sues a community or a community sues an individual, the Council of some city is appointed to try the case, each party being entitled to challenge one council thus proposed" (Loeb translation).[29] Why was the governor's assistance sought when the law (of procedure) was unambiguous? Is the governor expected merely to enforce those provisions, or accelerate the process – or should we detect here an appeal for 'illegal' intervention? The cautious and courteous language suggests to me that Cicero was aware of the existence of norms, which did not permit a specific request which might compromise the governor's integrity (*existimatio*); he could ask only what was commensurate with the latter: "*Id si ita est, etiam sine mea commendatione ab aequitate tua res ipsa impetrare debet ut ei subuenias, and later on: tantumque ei commodes in hac re et in ceteris quantum tua fides dignitasque patietur.*"[30]

I shall conclude this survey with the case of Pausanias, a citizen of the free city of Alabanda[31] in the province of Asia,[32] which Cicero, acting for the patrician T.

28 "*Hippiam, Philoxeni filium, Calactinum ... tibi commendo ... eius bona, quem ad modum ad me delata res est, publice possidentur alieno nomine contra leges Calactinorum.*"

29 "*Quod priuatus a populo petit aut populus a priuata, senatus ex aliqua ciuitate qui iudicet datur, cum alternae ciuitates reiectae sunt.*" (*Verr*. II, 2, 32).

30 For a full discussion of the significance of the terms used here (*existimatio*, *aequitas*, *fides* and *dignitas*) and elsewhere in letters of recommendation see examples in Cotton, "The Role of Cicero's Letters of Recommendation: Iustitia versus Gratia?"

31 For Alabanda see Pliny, *Naturalis historia* V, 108.

32 Unless we accept Shackleton Bailey's conjecture that "the heading is wrong and that this letter was really addressed to the governor of Asia," in *Cicero: Epistulae Ad Familiares*, Vol. I (Cambridge: Cambridge University Press, 1977), 476.

Claudius Nero, brings to the attention of the governor of the province of Bithynia, P. Silius Nerva, in 50 BC: "*de Pausania Alabandensi sustentes rem, dum Nero ueniat*" (*Fam.* XIII, 64, 1). If Pausanias on trial before the governor, who could be requested to delay the case, or is it a request to interfere unofficially in legal proceedings held before another court? Be that as it may, I would suggest that the question as to what legal procedure was available in the case of a citizen of a free city sojourning in another province, would certainly have taxed the skills of a modern expert on private international law. In the Roman Empire, I would maintain, it meant that legal cases tended to gravitate towards the Roman courts, which would account for the long queues and the long delays attested in our sources.[33] Needless to say, this was not the sole reason for resort to the governor's court: Roman justice was more effective and could be more rigorously imposed on the antagonists. Consequently, even cases calling for the recourse to personal law may come before the governor, who could apply local law, as in the famous 'Complaint of Dionysia' (*P.Oxy*. 237, AD 186), or failing that, Roman civil law, as in *P.Oxy*. 706.[34]

The foregoing discussion has by no means attempted to do more than skim the surface of the issues raised in it. In conclusion, I wish to emphasize where precisely there is need for re-thinking and further investigation:

1) As in my earlier article (above n. 2, passim) I would like to insist on the distinction between choice of courts and choice of law, procedure as distinct from the substance. A Roman court of law may well use and enforce local law.
2) For our purpose, the Empire could be conceived as an extension of Italy: the first 'conflicts of laws' arose and were solved when Rome entered into various treaties with the cities of Italy. Whatever rules, or rather rules of thumb, had evolved in Italy up to 90/89 BC, would be applied in the provinces by the very same magistrates who later on went overseas. However, the evidence for Italy is mainly epigraphic, and contains statutes rather than court cases.[35]

---

33 E.g. *P.Euphr*. 1, l. 7 (= *SB* XXII 15496, AD 245): "spending eight months in attendance at your court" (to the governor of Koile-Syria); see Denis Feissel and Jean Gascou, "Documents d'archives romains inédits du Moyen Euphrate (IIIe s. Après J-C): I. Les pétitions (T. Euphr. 1 à 5)," *Journal des Savants*, no. 1 (1995): 65–119. On the queues see above all G.P. Burton, "Proconsuls, Assizes and the Administration of Justice under the Empire," *JRS* 65 (1975): 92–106; cf. Cotton, "Private International Law or Conflict of Laws: Reflections on Roman Provincial Jurisdiction," 244 ff. [below, pp. 224 ff.].

34 If this is how we should understand τοῖς ἀστικοῖς νόμοις in line 9, as I believe we should; cf. Naphtali Lewis, "Nouveau texte sur la juridicion du préfet d'Égypte," *RHDFÉ* 50 (1972): 10 citing *Dig*. 1, 3, 32 pr. I intend to discuss this papyrus elsewhere. I am obliged to Uri Yiftach and Egbert Koops for discussing it with me.

35 Cf. Michael Crawford, ed., *Roman Statutes* (London: Institute of Classical Studies, 1996). Not exclusively though; for wax tablets recording legal transactions, see e. g. G. Camodeca, *Tabulae*

3) One cannot a-priori assume that the judicial autonomy of the more privileged communities (Roman and Latin) in a province was wider than that enjoyed by peregrine communities, which stood, so to speak, altogether outside the entire framework of the Roman legal system; the contrary may prove to be true.[36]
4) Above all, it seems to me, one must be fully conscious of the crucial distinction between the statutes and the law-books on the one hand and the courtroom, the litigants and the lawyers on the other.[37] We must, at all costs, avoid a schematic legal approach which takes legal writings as a faithful depiction of what happened in the day to day 'to and fro' of litigants and litigators: such an approach removes us from the truth, and from reality.

Pompeianae Sulpiciorum (TPSulp.): Edizione critica dell' Archivio Puteolano dei Sulpicii (Rome: Quasar, 1999) with the review article by Gregory Rowe in "Trimalchio's World," *SCI* 20 (2001): 225–45.

36 Hannah M. Cotton, "Jewish Jurisdiction under Roman Rule: Prolegomena," in *Zwischen den Reichen: Neues Testament und römische Herrschaft. Vorträge auf der ersten Konferenz der European Association for Biblical Studies*, ed. Michael Labahn and Jürgen Zangenberg (Tübingen: Francke Verlag, 2002), 16 ff. [below, pp. 489 ff.].

37 I suppose this could be summed up, perhaps anachronistically, as case law. Needless to say, legal papyri constitute our best evidence. A huge amount of work has been done, and is being done by the papyrologists, but the historians of the Roman Empire are not fully cognizant of it.

B Documents, Languages, and Law

Subscriptions and Signatures in the Papyri from the Judaean Desert: The χειροχρήστης

One of the recently published documents from the Judaean desert, *XḤev/Ṣe Gr* 5 (= *DJD* XXVII, no. 61),[1] contains the conclusion to a land-declaration submitted in Rabbath-Moab during the census held in the province of Arabia in 127 CE by the governor of the province, Titus Aninius Sextius Florentinus.[2] The conclusion contains two subscriptions: 1) a sworn subscription of the declarant X son of Levi; 2) an official subscription of the Roman prefect who received the declaration, dated to the 25th of April 127:[3] The text reads as follows:

XḤev/Ṣe Gr 5 (see *ZPE* 99 (1993): plate XIIId)
μο[-ca.?-]ρ̣. *traces* λ̣ο̣ς
Λειουου ὄμνυμι τύχην Κυρίου Καίσαρος κ[α]λῇ πίστει ἀπογεγράφθαι ὡς προγέγραπται μηθὲν ὑποστειλάμενος. ἐ̣[γράφη διὰ[4]
χειροχρήστου Οναινου Σααδαλλου. Ἑρμην{ν}εία ὑπογραφῆ[ς τοῦ
ἐπάρχου. Πρεῖσκος ὕπαρχος ἐδεξάμην πρὸ ἑπτὰ κα[λανδῶν
Μαίων.

"I, X son of Levi, swear by the *tyche* of the Lord Caesar that I have in good faith registered as written above, concealing nothing. Written by the χειροχρήστης Onainos son of Sa'adalos. Translation of the subscription of the prefect: I, Priscus prefect, received [this] on the seventh day before the Kalends of May."

---

1 Hannah M. Cotton, "Another Fragment of the Declaration of Landed Property from the Province of Arabia," *ZPE* 99 (1993): 115–21; Cf. Hannah M. Cotton, "Fragments of a Declaration of Landed Property from the Province of Arabia," *ZPE* 85 (1991): 263–67.

2 See *P.Yadin* 16, ll. 11–13: ἀποτιμήσεως Ἀραβίας ἀγομένης ὑπὸ Τίτου Ἀνεινίου Σεξστίου Φλωρεντείνου πρεσβευτοῦ Σεβαστοῦ ἀντιστρατήγου, in Naphtali Lewis, *The Documents from the Bar Kokhba Period in the Cave of Letters. Greek Papyri* (Jerusalem: IES, 1989). Henceforth 'Lewis'. For the reasons for believing that it was submitted at the same date and place as *P.Yadin* 16 see Cotton, "Another Fragment of the Declaration of Landed Property from the Province of Arabia."

3 The alternative date, 25 April 128, suggested in Cotton, "Another Fragment of the Declaration of Landed Property from the Province of Arabia," 121 is no longer tenable after the publication of the entire archive to which this declaration belongs, see Hannah M. Cotton, "The Archive of Salome Komaise Daughter of Levi: Another Archive from the 'Cave of Letters,'" *ZPE* 105 (1995): 176.

4 In the first publication: διὰ τοῦ.

Article note: First published in *JJP* 25 (1995): 29–40, with the following note: the substance of this paper was presented to a seminar in the Department of Classics at Tel Aviv University in May 1995. I am grateful to the participants for their comments. I am greatly indebted to Roger Bagnall, Werner Eck and David Wasserstein for commenting on earlier drafts of this paper.

https://doi.org/10.1515/9783110770438-007

Whereas the prefect wrote the original Latin subscription himself, the declarant did not write his subscription himself; but had it written for him by Onainos son of Sa'adalos. This last person is called χειροχρήστης.

This is the earliest occurrence of the term χειροχρήστης in the Greek language, as far as I know. It is attested once in the fourth century CE, in Iamblichus, *Vita Pythagorae* 161, where we find χειροχρήστων τινῶν λόγων translated in the lexicons as 'manuals,' 'handbooks.'[5] More telling is the entry in (spurious) Athanasius (*Quaestiones ad Antiochum* 88 = M. 28.652B) that the χειροχρήστης is ὁ τὰ ἀλλότρια πιστευόμενος ἐπὶ τῷ διαδοῦναι τοῖς πένησιν,[6] that is a kind of trustee. The idea of representing someone else brings us closer to the function fulfilled by the χειροχρήστης in *XḤev/Ṣe Gr* 5; the latter's function, however, is far more circumscribed.

I shall try to show here that χειροχρήστης in *XḤev/Ṣe Gr* 5 stands for a precise and specific legal function,[7] one not attested elsewhere for the bearer of this title before the middle (perhaps the end) of the sixth century CE. Only at this late date does it occur in Latin letters in a group of papyri from Ravenna.[8] From the mid-eighth century it occurs again in this specific legal sense in Byzantine legal rules. In the papyri from Egypt this specific legal function is fulfilled by the ὑπογραφεῦς.[9] It is not without interest that the first and only occurrence of χειροχρήστης in this specific legal sense before the Byzantine age should be in

5 The apparatus (see Ludwig Deubner and Uhlrich Klein, eds., *Iamblichi De vita Pythagorica liber* (Stuttgart: Teubner, 1975), 91) mentions a proposal by Reinesius that the text be emended to read πυθοχρήστων; although the proposal has been rejected in modern editions, the fact that it could be made is a pointer to the rarity of the term.

6 The argument there runs: καὶ ἕτερος ὁ χειροχρήστης, ὁ τὰ ἀλλότρια πιστευόμενος i. e. 'and it is different in the case of him who ...'. The spelling χειροχρήστης here should be used to correct Du Cange's χειροχρῆστοι: see *Glossarium ad Scriptores Mediae et Infimae Graecitatis*, p. 1748, s. v. χειροχρῆστοι; also Tjäder (below, n. 8), 452 mistakenly writes ὁ χειρόχρηστος.

7 Obscured by the present writer's imprecise translations of the term in Cotton, "Another Fragment of the Declaration of Landed Property from the Province of Arabia," 117: 'scribe'; 118: 'scribe, an *amanuensis*.'

8 Jan-Olof Tjäder, *Die nichtliterarischen lateinischen Papyri Italiens aus der Zeit 445–700* (Lund: C.W.K. Gleerup, 1955), nos. 16 ("um 600?"), l. 34; 20 ("um 600?"), l. 72; 27 ("Mitte des 6. Jh.?"), l. 1. Nos. 16 and 20 are new editions of Gaetano Marini, *I papyri diplomatici* (Rome, 1805), nos. 90 and 93 respectively: no. 27 is not in Marini.

9 Cf. Ernst Rabel on *P.Bas.* 2 in Ernst Rabel and Wilhelm Spiegelberg, eds., *Papyrusurkunden der Öffentlichen Bibliothek der Universität zu Basel* (Berlin, 1917), 19–20. For the role of the ὑπογραφεύς see Herbert C. Youtie, "ὑπογραφεύς: The Social Impact of Illiteracy in Graeco-Roman Egypt," *ZPE* 17 (1975): 201–21.

a papyrus written by a Jew from the province of Arabia and found in the Cave of Letters in Naḥal Ḥever.[10]

XḤev/Ṣe Gr 5 is a copy of the original declaration as shown by the fact that the original subscription of the prefect, which was in Latin, is here missing, as well as by the fact that it is written by the same hand throughout.[11] The original was written in several hands and also in more than one language.[12] Because only traces of letters have survived of the line preceding the subscription of the declarant, X son of Levi, it is impossible to tell if the words ἑρμηνεία ὑπογραφῆς preceded also the first subscription; thus Onainos son of Sa'adalos may or may not have originally written the subscription in Greek.[13] This is of no consequence for our purpose, however, since it is maintained here that it is not *qua* scribe and/or translator that Onainos son of Sa'adalos is mentioned here. This claim can be supported by the verified copy of a complete declaration preserved almost intact in *P.Yadin* 16. I quote those parts of the outer text of *P.Yadin* 16 which are important for the present discussion:[14]

> ἐγγεγραμμένον καὶ ἀντιβεβλημένον ἀντίγραφον πιτακι̣ου ἀπογρα̣φῆς π̣ρ̣ο̣κ̣ει̣μένης ἐν τῇ ἐνθάδε βασιλικῇ, καὶ ἔστιν ὡς ὑποτέτακται· ἐπὶ Αὐτοκράτορος Καίσαρος θεοῦ Τραιανοῦ Παρθικοῦ υ̣ἱ̣οῦ θεοῦ Νέρουα υἱωνοῦ Τραιανοῦ Ἀδριανοῦ Σεβαστοῦ ἀρχιερέως μεγίστου δημαρχικῆς ἐξουσίας τὸ δωδέκατον ὑπάτου τὸ τρίτον, ἐπὶ ὑπάτων Μάρκου Γα<ου>ίου Γαλλικανοῦ καὶ Τίτου Ἀτειλίου Ῥούφου Τιτιανοῦ πρὸ τεσσάρων νωνῶν Δεκεμβρίων, κατὰ δὲ τὸν τῆς νέας

10 There can be little doubt that most of the so-called *P.Ṣe'elim*, to which *XḤev/Ṣe Gr* 5 belongs, originated in the caves of Naḥal Ḥever; see Jonas C. Greenfield, "The Texts from Naḥal Ṣe'elim (Wadi Seiyal)," in *The Madrid Qumran Congress*, ed. Julio Trebolle Barrera and Luis Vegas Montaner (Leiden: Brill, 1992), 662.

11 As is *P.Yadin* 16, which was written by the same hand throughout, see plate 13: the scribe seems to have sharpened his 'pencil' towards the end, which may explain Lewis' 'second hand' on pp. 65 and 67. See Marcel Hombert and Claire Préaux, *Recherches sur le recensement dans l'Egypte romaine* (Leiden: Brill, 1952), 85 and n. 4.

12 Cf. *P.Yadin* 11, ll. 29–30, where only the translation of Judah's Aramaic subscription into Greek is found: "the original copy of this loan, with Judah's signature in Aramaic was retained by the lender," Lewis, 42; contrast *P.Yadin* 27, which preserves an original receipt: the Aramaic subscription as well as its Greek translation preceded by the word ἑρμηνία{ς} are found here, ll. 11–18.

13 See the Greek signatures of Nabataeans in *P.Yadin* 16, l. 16; 19, l. 34; for the plausible suggestion that Soumaios, the writer (not the scribe) of a Greek letter to two of Bar Kokhba's commanders, was a Nabataean see Dirk Obbink, "Bilingual Literacy and Syrian Greek," *BASP* 28 (1991): 57, and Hayim Lapin, "Palm Fronds and Citrons: Notes on Two Letters from Bar Kosiba's Administration," *HUCA* 64 (1993): 115–16. The letter was first published by Baruch Lifshitz, "Papyrus grecs du désert de Juda," *Aegyptus* 42 (1962): 240, no. 1 (= *P.Yadin* 52; *SB* 9843).

14 The inner text is composed of two lines (ll. 1–2), identical to ll. 3–5 of the outer text.

ἐπαρχείας Ἀραβίας ἀριθμὸν ἔτους δευτέρου εἰκοστοῦ μηνὸς Ἀπελλαίου ἑκκαιδεκάτη ἐν Ῥαββαθμωβοις πόλει. ἀποτιμήσεως Ἀραβίας ἀ̣γ̣ομένης ὑπὸ Τίτου Ἀνεινίου Σεξστίου Φλωρεντείνου πρεσβευτοῦ Σεβαστοῦ ἀντιστρατήγου, Βαβθα Σίμωνος Μαωζηνὴ τῆς Ζοαρηνῆς περιμέτρου Πέτρας, οἰκοῦσα ἐν ἰδίοις ἐν αὐτῇ Μαωζ̣α̣, ἀπογράφομα̣ι̣ ἃ κέκτημαι, συνπαρόντος μοι ἐπιτρόπου Ἰουδάνου Ἐλαζάρου κώμης Αἰνγαδδῶν περὶ Ἰερειχοῦντα τῆς Ἰουδαίας οἰκοῦντος ἐν ἰδίοις ἐν αὐτῇ Μαωζ̣α̣·[15]

****

ἑρμηνεία ὑπογραφῆς· Βαβθα Σίμωνος ὄμνυμι τύχην κυρίου Καίσαρος καλῇ πίστει ἀπογεγ̣ρ̣ά̣φ̣θ̣α̣ι̣ ὡς προγέγρα̣π̣[τα]ι. Ἰ̣ουδάνης Ἐ̣λ̣αζάρο̣υ̣ ἐπιτρ̣ό̣πευ[σ]α̣ καὶ ἔγραψα ὑπὲρ αὐτῆς. ἑρμηνεία ὑπογραφῆς τοῦ ἐπάρχου· Πρεῖσκος ἔ̣π̣αρχος ἱππέων ἐδεξάμην τῇ πρὸ μιᾶς νωνῶν Δεκεμβρίων ὑπατίας Γαλλικ[αν]ο̣ῦ [καὶ Τιτιανο]ῦ̣.[16]

The copyist, whose name is missing, must have composed (not copied) lines 1–5 since they were not in the original declaration; they serve to confirm that this is a 'verified exact copy.' Lines 5–17 give the time and place of the declaration, the name of the declarant and her address and the name of her guardian and his address. Lines 17–33, not cited above, constitute the main body of the land-declaration: the name, size and abutters of each one of the date-groves owned by Babatha in Maḥoza, and the taxes in money and kind which each date-grove paid. It is likely that lines 5–33 were originally composed in Greek, but we do not know who wrote them in the original declaration. Whoever did so was acting merely as

15 "Verified exact copy of a document of registration which is displayed in the basilica here, and it is as appended below. In the reign of *Imperator Caesar divi Traiani Parthici filius divi Nervae nepos Traianus Hadrianus Augustus pontifex maximus tribuniciae potestatis XII consul III*, in the consulship of Marcus Gavius Gallicanus and Titus Atilius Rufus Titianus four days before the *nones* of December, and according to the compute of the new province of Arabia year twenty-second month Apellaios the sixteenth, in the city of Rabbath-Moab. As a census of Arabia is being conducted by Titus Aninius Sextius Florentinus, *legatus Augusti pro praetore*, I, Babtha daughter of Simon, of Maoza in the Zoarene [district] of the Petra administrative region, domiciled in my own private property in the said Maoza, register what I possess (present with me as my guardian being Judanes son of Elazar, of the village of En-gedi in the district of Jericho in Judaea, domiciled in his own private property in the said Maoza) ..."

16 Translation of subscription: "I, Babtha daughter of Simon, swear by the genius of our lord Caesar that I have in good faith registered as has been written above. I, Judanes son of Elazar, acted as guardian and wrote for her. [2nd hand] Translation of subscription of the prefect: I, Priscus, prefect of cavalry, received [this] on the day before the *nones* of December in the consulship of Gallicanus and Titianus."

a scribe and fulfilled no legal function. This is not the case with the subscription, which had to be written by the person submitting the declaration or by his representative.[17] Judah (here Judanes), son of Eleazar Khthousion, Babatha's second husband, wrote the subscription for her as her guardian (ll. 33–36). The term ἐπιτρόπευ[σ]α suggests that he wrote it for her not merely because she was illiterate,[18] but also because she was a woman.[19] Judah's original Aramaic subscription was not reproduced in the copy, only its translation into Greek preceded by ἑρμηνεία ὑπογραφῆς (ll. 33–36); nor was the original subscription of the Prefect, in Latin (written with his own hand), reproduced here: the words ἑρμηνεία ὑπογραφῆς τοῦ ἐπάρχου are followed by its translation into Greek (ll. 36–38).[20] It is patent that we have in the conclusion to Babatha's land-declaration the same sequence as in *XḤev/Ṣe Gr* 5.

Were Judah merely a scribe for Babatha, and not a 'legal representative,' his name would not be mentioned in this verified copy of the declaration, where the names of all the scribes – if they had ever been in the original – are omitted, even that of the copyist himself. The same is true of the χειροχρήστης Onainos son of Sa'adalos of *XḤev/Ṣe Gr* 5 who wrote for X son of Levi: his name is mentioned only because he fulfilled a specific legal function.[21] Were he merely the scribe of the

17 See Youtie, "Ὑπογραφεύς: The Social Impact of Illiteracy in Graeco-Roman Egypt," 212 and n. 28.

18 Elsewhere we hear: Ἐλεάζαρος Ἐλεαζάρου ἔγραψα ὑπὲρ αὐτῆς ἐρωτηθεὶς διὰ τὸ αὐτῆς μὴ ε<ἰ>δένα<ι> γράμματα, *P.Yadin* 15, ll. 36–7; see below.

19 It should be pointed out that the term ἐπίτροπος in the Greek of the Judaean Desert papyri is used both for the guardian of a woman as well as for that of a minor. In the Aramaic subscription, though, the guardian of a woman is called *adon* = κύριος: e. g. *P.Yadin* 15, l. 37: *yhwdh br ktwšyn 'dwn bbth*: "Judah son of Khthousion 'lord' of Babatha" (cf. Hans Julius Wolff, "Le droit provincial dans la province romaine d'Arabie," *RIDA* 23 (1976): 279–83). Hence the ἐπίτροπος of a woman here is no different from the κύριος in the Egyptian papyri. Judah's ἐπιτρόπευ[σ]α καὶ ἔγραψα is paralleled by μετὰ κυρίου or κύριος ἐπιγέγραμμαι in the Egyptian papyri, see Hombert and Préaux, *Recherches sur le recensement dans l'Egypte romaine*, 128 and n. 5. Here too as in Egypt though "Il est impossible de réduire à une règle unique la capacité des femmes comme auteurs de déclaration," Hombert and Préaux, 159; cf. 59–62.

20 Thus accepting Babatha's own assessment of the taxes she owes the Roman government; see now Benjamin Isaac, "Tax Collection in Roman Arabia: A New Interpretation of the Evidence from the Babatha Archive," *Mediterranean Historical Review* 9 (1994): 256–66. For official handling of census declarations in Egypt, see Hombert and Préaux, *Recherches sur le recensement dans l'Egypte romaine*, 129–35 and Roger S. Bagnall and Bruce W. Frier, *The Demography of Roman Egypt* (Cambridge: Cambridge University Press, 1994), 26.

21 Youtie, "Ὑπογραφεύς: The Social Impact of Illiteracy in Graeco-Roman Egypt," 210 speaks of the *hypographeus's* "special kind of responsibility," which I regard as 'a specific legal function.' For although the principal, as Youtie points out there, "is responsible for the content of the subscription," the handwriting is that of the *hypographeus*, and "he holds himself ready to testify

Greek translation of a subscription written in Aramaic,[22] his name would not have been mentioned: the name of the Greek translator of the Prefect's Latin subscription is not mentioned. Perhaps this should be stated positively: it was obligatory for the name of the χειροχρήστης, like that of the *hypographeus*, to be there, if one was used.[23]

X (son) of Levi was a male as μηθὲν ὑποστειλάμενος in l. 3 of *XḤev/Ṣe Gr* 5 proves; from the deed of renunciation of 127 CE in the archive of Salome Komaïse daughter of Levi, we learn that she had a brother who recently died – probably the declarant X son of Levi.[24] The presence of a χειροχρήστης may be explained either by minority or by illiteracy. In what follows I shall try to show that it is more likely to have been caused by the latter.

It is precisely in cases of illiteracy or some other cause which prevents a person from writing a subscription himself that the χειροχρήστης – as the etymology of the term suggests – is provided for in Byzantine legal writings. A *novella* of the Empress Irene from 797–802 CE reads: εἰ δὲ ὁ τὸ ἔγγραφον ποιῆσαι ἀπαιτούμενος ... ἀγράμματος ὑπάρχει ἢ ἐκ πάθους ἀδύνατως ἔχει τοῦ γράφειν, προτάσσειν αὐτὸν τὸν τίμιον σταυρὸν[25] καὶ τὰ λοιπὰ γράφεσθαι διὰ ταβουλαρίου ἢ νομικῶν ἢ ἑτέρων χειροχρήστων.[26] The same procedure is to be followed in the case of witnesses'

to this fact and to the circumstances in which he put his service as a writer at the disposal of his principal," 211. In that respect he is not unlike the witnesses, who also have a legal function to perform. Only the scribe lacks any legal attributes and can, therefore, remain anonymous.

22 Jews in Arabia used Aramaic in their subscriptions, see Y. Yadin and J.C. Greenfield, "Aramaic and Nabataean Subscriptions," in Lewis, *The Documents from the Bar Kokhba Period in the Cave of Letters. Greek Papyri*, 135 ff.

23 See Youtie, "Ὑπογραφεύς: The Social Impact of Illiteracy in Graeco-Roman Egypt," 209: "It was common practice for professional scribes to remain anonymous, but the hypographeis ... are never anonymous"; and further on: "since it was obligatory that he [the *hypographeus*] give his name, his function was different from that of the usual anonymous scribe, and more significant," 210; cf. Herbert C. Youtie, "Hypographeis and Witnesses of 2nd Century Tebtunis," *ZPE* 19 (1975): 191–201; Herbert C. Youtie, "Notes on Subscriptions," *BASP* 13 (1976): 81–84.

24 Cotton, "The Archive of Salome Komaise Daughter of Levi: Another Archive from the 'Cave of Letters,'" 177–83, no. III.

25 See Rabel in *Papyrusurkunden der Öffentlichen Bibliothek der Universität zu Basel*, 20 and Youtie, "Ὑπογραφεύς: The Social Impact of Illiteracy in Graeco-Roman Egypt," 211, n. 25 for the use of a series of crosses by illiterate persons in Christian papyri; cf. e. g. *P.Mich.* XI 607 (569 CE): Αὐρήλιος Μαγίστωρ Ὡρουωγχίου ἀπὸ Ἀντι(νόου) ἀξιωθ(εὶς) [ἔγ]ραψα ὑπ(ὲρ) αὐτοῦ γράμμ(ατα) μὴ εἰδότος σταυρία τρία προβαλόντος τῇ αὐτοῦ χειρί.

26 "And if he who wishes to make a written document ... happens to be illiterate or cannot write because of some ailment, let him make the holy cross and the rest will be written by the *tabularius*, the legal clerks or the other *chirocristai*," *Nov.* 27, 1, K.E. Zachariae von Lingenthal, *Ius Graecoromanum*, 1931, Vol. I, 58. ἢ ἑτέρων χειροχρήστων could also mean 'or the other (kind of clerks), namely the χειρόχρησται.'

subscriptions.[27] Further on in the same *novella* it is said explicitly about witnesses that if they happen to be illiterate, they too should affix the holy cross and let the rest of their subscription be written by the χειρόχρησται.[28] In the *Ecloga legum* (740 CE) 5.2 it is said of the testator that he must write the name of his heir in the subscription to the will, either with his own hand or use a χειροχρήστης for that purpose: τοῦ διατιθεμένου ὀφείλοντος διὰ τῆς ἰδίας ὑπογραφῆς ἢ διὰ χειροχρήστου τὸ ὄνομα τοῦ κληρονόμου ἐν αὐτῇ (*scil.* τῇ διαθήκῃ) ὑποσημειώσασθαι.[29]

As observed before, the term appears in Latin letters as – *chirocrista* – in several Byzantine papyri from Ravenna.[30] The most complete one, a document from 590–602(?) CE (Tjäder, no. 20), records a donation of part of an estate to the church of Ravenna, made by Sisivera, a Gothic freedwoman. The woman declares herself illiterate: *Quam donationis meae paginam ... Bono tabellioni huius civitatis Rav(ennae) ... dictavi, in qua subter propria manu pro ignorantia litterarum signum venerabilem s(an)c(t)ae crucis feci, et testibus a me rogitis optuli suscribendam* (ll. 55–60). The deed concludes with her signature: *Signum Sisiverae h(onestae) f(eminae), s(upra) s(crip)tae donatricis, omnia s(upra) s(crip)ta agnoscentis et consentientis cui et relecta est* (ll. 65–66, written by the scribe – *tabellio* – Bonus).[31] Subscriptions of six witnesses follow. The first of them describes himself as both *testes* and *chirocrista*: *Armatus v(ir) d(evotus), scolar(is), huic chartulae donationis ... fact(a)e ... a s(upra)s(crip)ta Sisivera h(onesta) f(emina), donatrice, quae me praesente signum s(an)c(t)e crucis fecit, et coram nobis ei relicta [relecta] est, rogatus ab eadem ad signum eius roborandum testes et chirocrista suscribsi* (ll. 67–72). The other five witnesses use the same phrasing in this part of their subscriptions: *quae me praesente signum s(an)c(t)e crucis fecit, et coram nobis ei relictum est, rogatus ab eade[m] testis suscribsi* (ll. 78–80; 93–95; 100–102; 109–11 1; in Greek letters in ll. 87–9) – with the significant omission of the words: *ad signum eius roborandum ... et chirocrista suscribsi*. After the subscriptions of the six witnesses comes the scribe's subscription: *Bonus, tabellio civitatis Rav(ennatis), scribtor huius chartulae donationis portionis in integro fundi ... post roboratam a testibus atque traditam complevi et absolvi* (ll. 115–119).

---

27 καὶ εἰ μέν ἐστιν ἀναγκαῖον τὸ ὑπογράψαι τοὺς μάρτυρας, γενέσθω οὕτως.

28 εἰ δὲ ἀγράμματοί εἰσι, ποιείτωσαν τοὺς τιμίους σταυρούς, καὶ τὰ λοιπὰ γραφέτωσαν διὰ χειροχρήστων, *Nov.* 27, 2, *Ius Graecoromanum*, Vol. I, 59.

29 von Lingenthal, *Ius Graecoromanum*, Vol. II, 30; K.E. Zachariae von Lingenthal, *Geschichte des griechisch-römischen Rechts* (Aalen in Wurttemberg: Scientia, 1955), 150 ff.; note the mistaken plural χειρόχρηστοι in n. 441 on p. 151 (above, n. 6).

30 Above, n. 8.

31 Tjäder, *Die nichtliterarischen lateinischen Papyri Italiens aus der Zeit 445–700*, 344, but see 477 on no. 27, l. 1.

A similar formula to that in no. 20 is used by the chirocrista in Tjäder, no. 16 (c. 600 CE), ll. 33–34: *rogatus ab eodem ad signum eius ro[boran]do chirocrista suscripsi.*[32] A different formula is preserved in Tjäder, no. 27 (middle of the sixth century CE?), where only the chirocrista's subscription is preserved: *[ad signum eius incl]udendum testis et chir[o]crista sus[cripsi]* (l. 1).[33]

Thus the function fulfilled by the *chirocristae* in the papyri from Ravenna is discrete and neatly distinguished from that of the scribe as well as from that of the other witnesses. He has the additional and concrete function of establishing the sign of the holy cross made by the illiterate party to an agreement as his/her authentic signature: *ad signum eius roborandum*. Since the Byzantine legal rules quoted above are later than the documents just mentioned, they are likely to be repetitions of earlier rules:[34] they seem to have been implemented to the letter. They also bear a striking resemblance to the legal procedure observable in the documents from the Judaean Desert.

The χειροχρήστης in *XḤev/Ṣe Gr* 5 is also, as we have seen before, to be distinguished from the scribe in being endowed with a legal power enabling him to write the only part of a census declaration which had to be written by the declarant himself/herself, namely the subscription with the oath engaging his/her good faith. I believe that, as in the Ravenna papyri, here too we have a case of illiteracy, rather than of minority: unlike Judah in *P.Yadin* 16, ll. 35–36, Onainos son of Sa'adalos is not said to be guardian of X son of Levi. Further proof for the distinction between the guardian and the χειροχρήστης (although the latter term does not appear there) seems to be contained in *P.Yadin* 15. This is a case of deposition against the guardians of Babatha's sons. Babatha's guardian for this matter, Judah son of Eleazar Khthousion, did *not* write the subscription for her; Eleazar son of Eleazar wrote it for her, since her illiteracy prevented her from doing it herself. The relevant lines are (ll. 33–37):

> [ἐμαρ]τυροποιήσατο ἡ Βαβαθα ὡς προγέγραπται διὰ ἐπιτρόπου αὐτῆς τοῦδε τοῦ πράγματ[ος Ἰούδου Χ]θουσίωνος ὃς παρὼν ὑπέγραψεν. (2nd hand) Βαβαθας Σίμωνος ἐμαρτυροποιησάμη<ν> κạτ̣ὰ Ἰωάνου Ἐγλα Ἀ<βδ>αοβδα Ἐλλουθα ἐπιτρώπων Ἠσους υ<ἱ>ο<ῦ> μου ὀρφανοῦ δι'

32 In this case the word 'testis' is absent; I suppose that nevertheless he counted as a witness here too; unfortunately only two more subscriptions are preserved.

33 See Tjäder, 477, attempting to explain the variation here.

34 For example, *Nov.* 73, 8, where, however, the term used is ταβουλάριος; see Herbert C. Youtie, "βραδέως γράφων: Between Literacy and Illiteracy," *GRBS* 12 (1974): 253 f. But see already Paulus in *Dig.* 48, 2, 3, 2 (about the accuser in the case of adultery): "*Item subscribere debebit is qui dat litteras se professum esse vel alius pro eo, si litteras nescit.*"

> ἐπιτρόπου μου Ἰούδα Χαθουσ̣ίωνος ἀκο̣λ̣[ο]ύθω̣ς τε͂ς προγεγραμμένες ἐρέσασιν. Ἐλεάζαρος Ἐλεαζάρ̣ου ἔγραψα ὑπὲρ αὐτῆς ἐρωτηθ̣εὶς διὰ τὸ αὐτ̣ῆς μὴ ε<ἰ>δένα<ι> γράμματα.[35]

It seems that διὰ τὸ αὐτ̣ης μὴ ε<ἰ>δένα<ι> γράμματα in Babatha's case does not mean that she could not write Greek,[36] but that she was illiterate in any language. A Greek subscription was not required: Judah son of Eleazar, her guardian, wrote his own subscription in Aramaic.[37] If Judah son of Eleazar did not write a subscription for Babatha, although he was her guardian and could write Aramaic, but Eleazar son of Eleazar did, then we have to look for some legal ground: evidently she was legally competent to do so, but incapable of doing so because of her illiteracy. This is where a *chirocrista*, not a guardian, steps in.

The χειροχρήστης of *XḤev/Ṣe Gr* 5 is the direct ancestor of the *chirocrista* of the Ravenna papyri of the early seventh century CE and the χειροχρήστης of the Byzantine legal rules of the following century. He fulfilled a distinct and specific function, which is to be distinguished from that of the scribe on the one hand and from that of the guardian on the other. Precisely like the *hypographeus*, the χειροχρήστης is the one who writes the subscription for those who are legally competent to do so, but who happen to be illiterate (or otherwise incapable of writing), when a subscription and/or a signature in their own hand is required to render a document valid. He lends his hand, or rather someone else borrows his hand.

In fact we can see how the term χειροχρήστης came into being in *P.Oxy.* L 3593 (238–44 CE, 'Instructions to a Rhodian bank about a slave sale'), ll.17–21 (cf. ll. 45–50): Αὐ[ρήλι]ο̣[ς] Κ̣[υεῖντο]ς̣ Εἰλάρο̣υ̣ χῖρα̣ [χ]ρ̣η[σάμενο]ς̣ π̣α̣ρ̣ὰ̣ Μά[ρκ]ο̣υ Αὐ<ρηλίου]> Ε̣ἰ̣ρ̣η̣[νίωνος το]ῦ̣ κα̣ὶ̣ Διο[νυσί]ου Ῥοδί̣[ου διὰ τὸ ἐμὲ] ἀ̣γ̣ρ̣ά̣μ̣μ̣α̣τ̣ο̣ν̣

35 "Babatha deposed as aforestated through her guardian for this matter, Judah son of Khthusion, who was present and subscribed. [2nd hand] I, Babatha daughter of Simon, have deposed through my guardian Judah son of Khthusion against John son of Eglas and 'Abdoöbdas son of Ellouthas, guardians of my orphan son Jesus, according to the aforestated conditions. I, Eleazar son of Eleazar, wrote for her by request, because of her being illiterate."

36 As is claimed by Youtie to be the case in Egyptian papyri: see "Αγραμματος: An Aspect of Greek Society in Egypt," *Harv. Stud.* 75 (1971): 162–3; Idem, "Because They Do Not Know Letters," *ZPE* 19 (1975): 101–8; cf. Roger S. Bagnall, *Egypt in Late Antiquity* (Princeton: Princeton University Press, 1993), 256–7, n. 142.

37 *yhwdh br ktwšyn 'dwn bbth bqmy hšrt bbth kkl dy 'l ktb yhwdh ktbh*: "Yehudah son of Khthousion lord of Babatha: in my presence Babatha confirmed all that is written above. Yehudah wrote this," *P.Yadin* 15, l. 37; cf. Yadin and Greenfield in Lewis, *The Documents from the Bar Kokhba Period in the Cave of Letters. Greek Papyri*, 139–40.

ὑπάρχειν.[38] The formula χεῖρα χρησάμενος παρὰ δεῖνος 'to borrow someone's hand' graphically describes the ὑπογραφεύς.[39] The next step would be to coin the term χειροχρήστης.

Similar formulae expressing the idea of borrowing someone else's hand on account of illiteracy occur in two legal contracts from the Aramaic Near East.[40] Recently the late J.C. Greenfield, in discussing illiteracy and subscriptions in Semitic legal documents, has drawn attention to the occurrence of the formula in a fourteen-line funerary inscription from Palmyra which is a copy of a legal document conceding the ownership of part of a tomb.[41] After the date, September 214, we read:

> *ywlys 'wrlys ydy'bl dy mtqr' mzbn' br ywlys 'wrlys 'ninws 'š'lt ktb ydy lywlys br 'wrlys 'gylw br 'prḥt br ḥry zbdbwl bdyldy l' yd' spr* (ll. 2–4).
>
> Iulius Aurelius Yedīʿbel who is called Mezabannā, son of Iulius Aurelius Anīnōs, I have lent my hand to Iulius son of Aurelius 'Ogeilū, son of Afraḥat freedman of Zabdibōl, because he did not know writing.[42]

These lines of the Palmyrene inscription help us in interpreting a difficult line in one of the so-called *P.Ṣelim* group (above, n. 10) from 134 or 135 CE: *XḤev/Ṣe Ar* 13 (= *DJD* XXVII, no. 13). This Aramaic document is interpreted by the editor as a quittance given by a woman, Shlamzion daughter of Yehosaf, on the occasion of her divorce.[43] The subscription in ll. 9–12 reads:

> *wqym 'lh 'n' šlmzin kwl dy 'l k[t]b šlmzin brt yhwsf 'l nfšh š'lh ktb mtt b[r] šm'wn mmr'.*
>
> I Shlamẓion stand by everything that is written above. Shlamẓion daughter of Yehosaf in person. She is borrowing the writing of Matat son of Shimeon (who wrote) what she said.[44]

---

38 "I, Aurelius Quintus son of Hilaros, having borrowed the handwriting of M. Aurelius Eirenion also called Dionysius, Rhodian, because I am myself illiterate ...".

39 Pointed out by Herbert C. Youtie, "A Rhodian Auction Sale of a Slave," *ZPE* 15 (1974): 146–47.

40 See now Hannah M. Cotton, W.E.H. Cockle, and Fergus Millar, "The Papyrology of the Roman near East: A Survey," *JRS* 85 (1995): 214–35.

41 Jonas C. Greenfield, "'Because He/She Did Not Know Letters': Remarks on a First Millennium C.E. Legal Expression," *JNES* 22 (1993): 39–44.

42 Harald Ingholt, "Palmyrene Inscription from the Tomb of Malkû," *Mélanges de l'Université Saint-Joseph* 38 (1962): 106–7.

43 Ada Yardeni, *Naḥal Ṣe'elim Documents* (Beer-Sheva: Ben-Gurion University of the Negev Press, 1995), 55–60, no. 13 (Hebrew).

44 I have taken *ktb* to be in the construct-state, i. e. 'the writing of'; if *ktb* is taken to be in the absolute state, i. e. 'the writing,' then a period should follow *ktb*, and the translation will be: 'She

The expression 'in person' – *'l nfšh* – implies that the principal "was one of the parties to the deed,"[45] even when he or she did not write the subscription himself or herself. It indicates his or her presence when the subscription was written.[46] The editor of the papyrus has now adopted the translation offered above for *š'lh ktb*.[47] As Ada Yardeni herself has pointed out to me, the same hand which wrote *š'lh ktb* also wrote *mtt b[r] šm'wn mmr'*. In other words Matat son of Shimeon must have written both *š'lh ktb* and *mtt b[r] šm'wn mmr'*. It is, therefore, better to take *š'lh* as a verb: 'is borrowing' and *ktb* as a noun: 'writing' rather than understanding *Š'lh* to be a name and translating the entire phrase as '*Š'lh* wrote it.' Shlamzion daughter of Yehosaf did precisely what Aurelius Quintus son of Hilaros did in *P.Oxy*. L 3593 quoted above: she borrowed a hand, that of Matat son of Shimeon to write for her.

Thus the same graphic notion of 'borrowing someone else's hand' appears both in Greek and in Aramaic. In Greek, though, at some point, the further step was taken of coining the descriptive term χειροχρήστης for the person whose hand was borrowed, but this is attested for the first time in an Aramaic speaking environment, in *XḤev/Ṣe Gr* 5.[48]

---

is borrowing the writing. Matat son of Shimeon (wrote) what she said.' In the absence of parallels, it is hard to know which is better. I am very grateful to Stephen Fassberg for his help.

45 See Yigael Yadin, "Expedition D – The Cave of the Letters," *IEJ* 12 (1962): 253 on the expression *'l nfšh* in the Judaean Desert documents; cf. Manfred R. Lehmann, "Studies in the Murabba'at and Naḥal Ḥever Documents," *Revue de Qumran* 4 (1963): 65; P.J. Sijpesteijn, "A note on P.Murabba'at 29," *IEJ* 34 (1984): 49–50.

46 As is implied by "at the request" of the principal and "in his presence" in Greek subscriptions, see Youtie, "'Ὑπογραφεύς: The Social Impact of Illiteracy in Graeco-Roman Egypt," 211 and n. 26, and above, n. 18.

47 See Yardeni, *Naḥal Ṣe'elim Documents*, 57, l. 11, and 60.

48 Perhaps the χ̣ε̣ιρ in *P.Yadin* 18, l. 76: "... [...]τιτος χ̣ε̣ιρ" (unfortunately not reproduced in Plate 19; I have looked at the photograph of the papyrus) is an abbreviation of χειροχρήστης, and "the raised horizontal line" is a "sign of abbreviation"; *contra* Lewis, *The Documents from the Bar Kokhba Period in the Cave of Letters. Greek Papyri*, 82, who admits though that "the end of the line clearly does not have μάρ(τυς)."
For the Aramaic speaking environment of the papyri from Naḥal Ḥever see now, Abraham Wasserstein, "Non-hellenized Jews in the Semi-hellenized East," *SCI* 14 (1995): 111–37, and 123, n. 36 (specifically on the papyri from the Judaean Desert).

The Languages of the Legal and Administrative Documents from the Judaean Desert

This discussion will be devoted to legal and administrative documents, including official letters, from the first and second centuries written in the Roman province of Judaea and in the Nabataean kingdom which became in 106 CE the province of Arabia. The great majority of the documents, but not all of them, whether letters or legal deeds, were written by or at least involve Jews.

The sources and the languages

The evidence consists of documents from the Judaean Desert found on Masada, in Wadi Murabba'at, Naḥal Ḥever, Naḥal Se'elim, Naḥal Mishmar, and Ketef Jericho. Some come from unknown provenance. The bulk of the material has been published only recently, and some of it remained unpublished to this day.[1] As it happens, the Greek documents have fared better than others: most of them are now published, or nearly so.[2] The Semitic documents include, besides documents

---

1 See surveys: Hannah M. Cotton, W.E.H. Cockle, and Fergus Millar, "The Papyrology of the Roman near East: A Survey," *JRS* 85 (1995): 214–35; a much shorter survey, restricted to the finds from the Judaean Desert, can be found in Hannah M. Cotton, "Documentary Texts," in *Encyclopedia of the Dead Sea Scrolls*, ed. Lawrence H. Schiffman and James VanderKam (New York: Oxford University Press, 2000), 212–15. These two surveys are limited to the documentary texts. The following two catalogues include the literary texts as well: Emanuel Tov, with the collaboration of Stephen J. Pfann, *Companion Volume to the Dead Sea Scrolls on Microfiche Edition* (Leiden: Brill, 1995); Stephen A. Reed, revised and edited by Marilyn J. Lundberg, with the collaboration of Michael B. Phelps, *The Dead Sea Scrolls Catalogue: Documents, Photographs, and Museum Inventory Numbers* (Atlanta: Scholars Press, 1994).

2 The three main collections of Greek documents from the Judaean Desert so far in print are P. Benoit, J.T. Milik, and R. de Vaux, *Les grottes de Murabba'at*, Discoveries in the Judaean Desert II (Oxford: Clarendon Press, 1961), (designated here *P.Mur*); Naphtali Lewis, *The Documents from the Bar Kokhba Period in the Cave of Letters. Greek Papyri*, with Aramaic and Nabatean Signatures

---

Article note: First published in *ZPE* 125 (1999): 219–231, with the following note: this is a revised version of a paper originally delivered at the conference on Aspects of Bilingualism in the Ancient World, held at Reading University, 2–4 April 1998. I am grateful to J.N. Adamas, M. Janse, and S. Swain for inviting me to participate in the Reading meeting and for permitting me not to publish this revised version of my text in the proceedings of that conference, and to the participants in the meeting, for their criticism and comments, most of which are reflected, I hope faithfully, in this final version of my paper. As always, I thank my friends David Wasserstein and Werner Eck for good advice and sound criticism.

https://doi.org/10.1515/9783110770438-008

in Hebrew, texts in Jewish Aramaic and in Nabataean Aramaic, both of which developed from the Reichsaramäisch, the *lingua franca* of the Persian period in what later became the Roman Near East. It was only with the advent of Hellenism and the absence of a central government to preserve it that the uniformity of the Aramaic language (and of its script) broke down and different 'national' dialects of Aramaic gradually emerged.[3] Nabataean Aramaic is distinguished from Jewish Aramaic externally by its script and otherwise by the recurrence in it of obtrusive elements, described by most Semitists as Arabic.[4] Jewish Aramaic and most of the documentary Hebrew is written in what is commonly known as 'Jewish script,' a form of script which developed from the common Aramaic script of the Persian period.[5]

Latin is omitted from this discussion although it does appear in documents from Masada (and in some fragments from Wadi Murabba'at). The Masada documents belong to soldiers of the Tenth Legion, the legionary garrison of the province of Judaea, which, together with auxiliary forces, besieged and conquered Masada in 73 (74) CE.[6] The evidence of the Masada papyri bears out H. Rosén's observation made before their publication that Latin was never more than the language of the Roman administration and army in Palestine, and was never integrated into the socio-linguistic fabric of the provincial population.[7] This is

---

and Subscriptions, edited by Y. Yadin and J.C. Greenfield, Judean Desert Studies II (Jerusalem: IES, 1989), (designated here *P.Yadin*); and Hannah M. Cotton and Ada Yardeni, *Aramaic, Hebrew, and Greek Documentary Texts from Naḥal Ḥever and Other Sites*, Discoveries in the Judaean Desert XXVII (Oxford: Clarendon Press, 1997), (designated in this paper by their number in *DJD* XXVII); The non-Greek letters from the Bar Kokhba archive were published in Yigael Yadin et al., *The Documents from the Bar Kokhba Period in the Cave of Letters: Hebrew, Aramaic and Nabatean-Aramaic Papyri*, Judean Desert Studies III (Jerusalem: IES, 2002).

3 Joseph Naveh and Jonas C. Greenfield, "Hebrew and Aramaic in the Persian Period," in *The Cambridge History of Judaism, Volume 1: Introduction: The Persian Period* (Cambridge: Cambridge University Press, 1984), 115–29; Joseph Naveh, *On Sherd and Papyrus* (Jerusalem: Magnes Press, 1992), 11 ff. (Hebrew).

4 It is assumed that the Nabataeans spoke Arabic and used their version of Aramaic in official documents; see Fergus Millar, *The Roman Near East, 31 BC-AD 337* (Cambridge, Mass.: Harvard University Press, 1993), 401 f. for objections to this view.

5 The term 'Jewish script' is the term used to describe the scripts used by Jews in order to write both Aramaic and Hebrew; see Frank Moore Cross, "The Development of the Jewish Scripts," in *The Bible and the Ancient Near East: Essays in Honor of William Foxwell Albright*, ed. G. Ernest Wright (Garden City, N.Y.: Doubleday, 1961), 133–202.

6 See Hannah M. Cotton and Joseph Geiger, *Masada II: The Latin and Greek Documents* (Jerusalem: IES, 1989). The documents are referred to in the text as *Doc. Mas.*

7 Haiim Rosén, "Die Sprachsituation im römischen Palästina," in *Die Sprachen im römischen Reich der Kaiserzeit*, ed. Günter Neumann and Jürgen Untermann (Köln: Rheinland-Verlag, 1980), 220 ff.; Fergus Millar, "Latin in the Epigraphy of the Roman Near East," in *Acta Colloquii Epigraph-*

also borne out by the epigraphical evidence.[8] Furthermore, in their dealings with the subject populations the Romans too used the medium of the Greek language (which does not mean that they themselves wrote Greek).[9]

Non-Aramaic documents: the problem

All scholars agree that Aramaic was the dominant language of the Jews in Palestine during the first and second centuries CE.[10] As was to be expected, the majority of the documents found in the Judaean Desert were written in Jewish Aramaic. Yet it can be shown that the same society represented in the Aramaic documents, and sometimes, the very same people, wrote documents, or had them written, in Hebrew and Greek as well. In other words it is not the case that documents in different languages represent different sections of Jewish society. Why, then, Hebrew and Greek in a society whose predominant language was Aramaic?

Non-Aramaic documents: The Hebrew documents from Wadi Murabba'at

First, Hebrew. This is not the place to enter into a discussion of whether or not Hebrew was spoken in Judaea at the time.[11] Nor will I discuss here texts of liturgical nature, as for example those attested on Masada between 66 and 73 (74) CE; the use of Hebrew as the language of worship and religious literature has never

ici Latini, ed. Heikki Solin, Olli Salomies, and Uta-Maria Liertz (Helsinki: Societas Scientiarum Fennica, 1995), 403 ff.

8 As demonstrated by Werner Eck in an unpublished lecture delivered in Jerusalem, December 1997: "The Reflection of Power: Latin Inscriptions in the Province of Judaea/Syria Palaestina"; see also Werner Eck, "Rom und die Provinz Iudaea/Syria Palaestina: Der Beitrag der Epigraphik," in *Jüdische Geschichte in hellenistisch-römischer Zeit. Wege der Forschung: Vom alten zum neuen Schürer*, ed. Aharon Oppenheimer (München: Oldenbourg, 1999), 237–64.

9 See Millar, "Latin in the Epigraphy of the Roman Near East," 403 ff.

10 Emil Schürer, *The History of the Jewish People in the Age of Jesus Christ*, Vol. II, ed. Fergus Millar and Géza Vermès (Edinburgh: Clark, 1979), 20 ff.

11 The difficulties involved in using written documents as evidence for spoken language are well expressed in a recent discussion of the languages in Palestine: "In some cases writing may reflect no more than scribal practice. And in all cases writing is necessarily related to speech in highly complex and sometimes highly attenuated ways," Seth Schwartz, "Language, Power and Identity in Ancient Palestine," *Past & Present* 148 (1995): 13.

been contested.[12] For a time, though, it was also the language of legal and administrative documents (among which we should include official letters), although the great majority of legal documents continued to be written in Aramaic.

The first Hebrew documents were discovered in Wadi Murabba'at and published in 1961.[13] Later more Hebrew documents were discovered in Naḥal Ḥever.[14] All the Hebrew documents from Naḥal Ḥever can be dated safely to the Bar Kokhba Revolt of 132–6 CE.[15] Yadin's suggestion that the revival of Hebrew as the official language may have been brought about by a decree of the leader seems attractive.[16] An official act seems to have been necessary, given the overwhelming evidence for the currency of Aramaic in legal documents before this period. It comes as no surprise therefore that all the Hebrew documents, both those from Wadi Murabba'at as well as those from Naḥal Ḥever, have so far been associated with the second revolt. At first sight, the dating formulae seem to leave no doubt that this is indeed so. However, in the case of some of the Hebrew documents from Wadi Murabba'at there are some problems with such an uncritical attribution, and as will be seen immediately the evidence of the dating formulae is not altogether unambiguous.[17]

P.Mur 29 and 30 are double documents, both containing deeds of sale. The declaration of the sale is made by the seller in front of four people who are said actually to be signing (חותמים) it (*P.Mur* 29 line 9 and *P.Mur* 30 line 9), although

12 See Yigael Yadin and Joseph Naveh, *Masada I: The Aramaic and Hebrew Ostraca and Jar Inscriptions* (Jerusalem: IES, 1989), 8–9; 32–9.

13 See n. 2.

14 See Yigael Yadin, "Expedition D," *IEJ* 11 (1961): 36–52; Yigael Yadin, "Expedition D – The Cave of the Letters," *IEJ* 12 (1962): 227–57.

15 For 136 see Werner Eck, "The Bar Kokhba Revolt: The Roman Point of View," *JRS* 89 (1999): 76–89; Werner Eck and Gideon Foerster, "Ein Triumphbogen für Hadrian im Tal von Beth Shean bei Tel Shalem," *JRA* 12 (1999): 294–313.

16 Yigael Yadin, *Bar-Kokhba: The Rediscovery of the Legendary Hero of the Second Jewish Revolt Against Rome* (London: Random House, 1971), 181, but not for the reason he gives there, namely that "the earlier documents are written in Aramaic while the later ones are in Hebrew"; we now know that the chronological division made by Yadin between Hebrew and Aramaic is false; cf. Rosén, "Die Sprachsituation im römischen Palästina," 225–6.

17 The most recent discussion of the date of the documents from Wadi Murabba'at by Hanan Eshel, Magen Broshi, and T.A.J. Jull reached me too late for their arguments and conclusions to be integrated into my text. It seems that they have arrived at similar conclusions to my own. However, their main interest is in the question of whether or not Jerusalem was in the hands of the rebels during the second revolt, whereas my concern here is with the linguistic aspect; see Hanan Eshel, Magen Broshi, and T.A.J. Jull, "Documents from Wadi Murabba'at and the Status of Jerusalem during the Bar Kokhba Revolt," in *The Refuge Caves of the Bar Kokhba Revolt*, ed. Hanan Eshel and David Amit (Jerusalem: IES, 1998), 233 ff. (Hebrew).

some of the signatures on the *verso* do not in fact belong to those four.[18] Both contracts are dated by the year of the revolt and said to be concluded in Jerusalem. The outer (lower) text of *P.Mur* 29 lines 9–10 reads: 'On fourteenth Ellul, Year Two of the redemption of Israel (ל[גא]לת ישׂ[רא]ל), in Jerusalem (בירשלים), Yehonathan son of Yehosaf, Shim'on son of Shabbai, Judah son of Judah, and Shim'on son of Zechariah are signing'; and in the first two lines of the inner (upper) text we read: 'Kalbos son of Eutroplos from Jerusalem (מירשלים) sold' etc. Similarly, the outer (lower) text of *P.Mur* 30 lines 8–9 reads: 'On twenty first Tishrei, Year Four of the redemption of Israel (לגאולת ישראל) in Jerusalem (בירשלים), Yehonathan son of Yehosaf, Shime'on son of Simai, Jonathan son of Ele'azar, and Jonathan son of Ḥananiah are signing ...'.

The presence of four signatories to the deed, although there is nothing in the document to suggest that they constituted a court,[19] makes it clear that the transaction was done in public. Thus as late as autumn 135 CE (the date of *P.Mur* 30) a public transaction dated by the year of the revolt could have taken place in Jerusalem. This would imply that Jerusalem recognized Bar Kokhba's sovereignty as late as autumn 135. No wonder that Milik hesitated – at first – to read Jerusalem in the relevant lines: Jerusalem does not appear in his published text but in a 'repentant' appendix.[20] However, the reading is now confirmed by Ada Yardeni (oral communication). In other words at least from August/September 133 CE (the date of *P.Mur* 29) to September/October 135 (the date of *P.Mur* 30) Bar Kokhba's sovereignty was recognized in Jerusalem.

It could be argued that despite the preposition 'in' (ב), the expression 'in Jerusalem' (בירשלים) does not stand for the place where the contract was signed, but is part of the dating formula – a dating formula which expresses political aspiration and a hope, as is claimed for formulae mentioning Jerusalem on coins from the time of the revolt,[21] or in *P.Mur* 25 line 1: 'Year Three of the freedom of Jerusalem' (ש[נ]ת תלת לחרות ירו{ן}שלים), which is clearly part of a dating formula, and cannot, without further proof, be taken as a reflection of reality. However, taking

18 Thus it is difficult to accept Milik's suggestion that they resemble the Egyptian six-witness document, see *DJD* II, 143; we may have here something resembling one of the forms of the Egyptian notarial instrument, see Hans Julius Wolff, *Das Recht der griechischen Papyri Ägyptens in der Zeit der Ptolemäer und des Prinzipats II: Organisation und Kontrolle des privaten Rechtsverkehrs* (München: Beck, 1978), 81 ff.

19 Cf. Haggai Misgav, "Jewish Courts of Law as Reflected in the Documents from the Dead Sea," *Cathedra* 82 (1996): 17–24 (Hebrew).

20 *DJD* II, 205.

21 See e.g. Leo Mildenberg, "Bar Kochba in Jerusalem?," *Schweizer Münzblätter* 27 (1977): 1–6, who interprets – 'for the freedom of Jerusalem' – לחרות ירושלים – as no more than an aspiration on the part of the rebels.

'in Jerusalem' in *P.Mur* 29 and 30 to be part of a dating formula used simply for propaganda purposes leaves the contracts, quite abnormally, without any reference to the place where they were concluded. Legal usage excludes such forced interpretation of 'in Jerusalem' in *P.Mur* 29 and 30. The implications seem to be inescapable: the Jews who concluded these contracts 'in Jerusalem' lived in this city and recognized the authority of a Jewish state there as late as September/October 135 – if indeed the dating to the second revolt is to be trusted at all.

This new geographical extension of the war is surprising, and in view of the silence of the Jewish sources about the conquest of Jerusalem by the rebels – the importance of which for Jewish nationalism in the second century cannot be exaggerated – it is highly disturbing.[22] However, while it is not necessary to take sides in the controversy waged for many years now over whether Jerusalem was conquered by the rebels or not, and if so when and for how long it was in the rebels' hands,[23] I should like to propose another date for these two documents. If accepted, this new dating has far reaching consequences for the use of languages in Jewish documents from the Judaean Desert. I propose to assign these documents to the first revolt of 66–70.

Some support for my suggestion can be found in their dating formula. Normally in Hebrew and Aramaic documents from the time of the second revolt the formula 'the freedom' or 'the redemption of Israel' is followed by the formula 'by'

22 Eshel, Broshi, and Jull, "Documents from Wadi Murabba'at and the Status of Jerusalem during the Bar Kokhba Revolt," 235 are also disturbed by the new chronological extension of the second revolt implied by Yardeni's new reading of the dating formula in yet another Hebrew document (*P.Mur* 22), which now reads: 'Fourteenth of Marheshvan Year Four of the redemption of Israel' (ב-14 למרחשון שנת ארבע לגאולת ישראל). The new dating extends the revolt to October/November 135, well after the fall of Beithar, traditionally dated to July 135 (cf. Emil Schürer, *The History of the Jewish People in the Age of Jesus Christ*, Vol. I, ed. Fergus Millar and Géza Vermès (Edinburgh: Clark, 1973), 551 ff.). However, in view of the epigraphic evidence which demonstrates that the *imperator iterum* is not attested in Hadrian's titulature before 136 (see Eck and Eck and Foerster in n. 15 above), it seems to me that a late date in 135 need not make us redate *P.Mur* 22 to the first revolt. However, Eshel, Broshi, and Jull believe that the results of a carbon 14 test carried out on *P.Mur* 22 date it safely to the first century CE. Although I also believe that there are good – historical and other – reasons for accepting such a dating, as will be seen below, it seems to me, in view of the margin of error inherent in any carbon 14 testing, and especially so given the brevity (in carbon 14 terms) of the period between the first revolt (66–70 CE) and the second revolt (132–136 CE), that any such results can only offer supportive testimony to historical evidence and arguments, and cannot be conclusive on their own.

23 For detailed discussion of the evidence see Menachem Mor, *The Bar Kochba Revolt: Its Extent and Effect* (Jerusalem: Yad Ben-Zvi Press, 1991), 146–71 (Hebrew), and now Eshel, Broshi, and Jull, "Documents from Wadi Murabba'at and the Status of Jerusalem during the Bar Kokhba Revolt."

(על ידי)[24] or 'in the name of' (לשם)[25] or 'in the days of' (על ימי)[26] 'Shim'on son of Kosibah [scil. Bar Kokhba], the Prince of Israel.' Alternatively the documents make mention only of the year of Bar Kokhba's rule: 'year so and so of Shim'on son of Kosibah, the Prince of Israel.'[27] In the two contracts from Wadi Murabba'at, just mentioned (*P.Mur* 29 and 30), however, 'the redemption of Israel' is not followed by a reference to Bar Kokhba.

That this is not altogether decisive can be shown by the absence of a reference to Bar Kokhba in *DJD* XXVII no. 8a dated to '20 Adar, year 3 of the freedom (חרת) of Israel.' This papyrus certainly dates to the time of the second revolt since it is written by the same hand and in the same place (Kefar *Bryw*)[28] as *DJD* XXVII no. 8 explicitly dated to the third year of the revolt: '[...] Adar, year 3 of the freedom (חרות) of Israel in the days of Shim'on son of Kosibah, the Prince of Israel.'

Against the attribution to the first revolt one may also enlist the legends on the coins of the first revolt. Until very recently only: 'to the freedom (חרות or חרת) of Zion' and 'to the redemption (גאלת) of Zion' were attested on the reverse of these coins, but not 'to the redemption of Israel' (as we find in *P.Mur* 22, 29 and 30). But as the numismatist of the Bar Kokhba revolt, L. Mildenberg, well puts it:

---

24 *DJD* XXVII no. 49 (Hebrew): '20 Kislev, year 2 of the redemption (גאלת) of Israel by Shim'on son of Kosibah, the Prince of Israel'; *DJD* XXVII no. 7 = *XḤev/Ṣe ar* 7: '14 Iyyar, year 3 of the freedom (חרת) of Israel by Shim'on son of [Kosibah, the Prince of Israel]'; *P.Yadin* 44 (lease, Hebrew): '28 Heshvan year 3 of the redemption (גאלת) of Israel by Shim'on son of Kosibah, the Prince of Israel.'

25 *DJD* XXVII no. 7 (deed of sale, Aramaic): '14 Iyyar, year 3 of the freedom (חרות) of Israel in the name of Shim'on son of Kosibah, the Prince of Israel'; *DJD* XXVII no. 13 (renunciation of claims, Aramaic): '20 Sivan, year 3 of the freedom (חרת) of Israel in the name of Shim'on son of Kosibah, the Prince of Israel.'

26 *DJD* XXVII no. 8 (sale, inner text in Aramaic; outer text in Hebrew): '[...] Adar, year 3 of the freedom (חרות) of Israel in the days of Shim'on son of Kosibah, the Prince of Israel'; *P.Yadin* 42 (lease, Aramaic): '1 Iyyar, year 3 of the redemption (גאלת) of Israel by (or in the days of) Shim'on son of Kosibah, the Prince of Israel'; note that in the Aramaic contract from Wadi Sdeir (*P.Sdeir* 2, I am grateful to Ada Yardeni for showing me a transcription of the text) 'On 6 Adar, year three of the redemption (גאולת) of Israel' there is room for 'by (or 'in the name of) Shim'on son of Kosibah, Prince of Israel.'

27 *P.Yadin* 47a (Aramaic contract): '14 Tevet, year 3 of Shim'on son of K[osibah, the Prince of Israe]l'; *P.Yadin* 43 (receipt, Aramaic): '5 ..., year ... Shim'on son of Kosibah'; *P.Yadin* 45 (lease, Hebrew): '2 Kislev year 3 of Shim'on son of Kosibah, the Prince of Israel'; *P.Yadin* 46 (lease, Hebrew): '2 Kislev year 3 of Shim'on son of Kosibah, the Prince of Israel.'

28 Identified by Magen Broshi and Elisha Qimron, "A House Sale Deed from Kefar Baru from the Time of Bar Kokhba," *IEJ* 36 (1986): 207, with Βαάρας of Josephus, *BJ* 7.180; 189 and the Βααρυ of the Madaba Map (see Michael Avi-Yonah, *The Madaba Mosaic Map* (Jerusalem: IES, 1954), 29, 39–40, pl.2) – a place in the Peraea (Transjordan). I am grateful to Boaz Zissu for discussing the identification of the place with me.

"Numismatic evidence is irrefutable, but not final."[29] In 1993 Robert Deutsch published a unique bronze coin (*prutah*) from the first year of the first revolt with the legend 'Israel' on the reverse, which he very reasonably restores: 'to the redemption (גאלת) of Israel.'[30] Thus it cannot be ruled out that the dating formulae 'to the freedom' or 'redemption of Israel' would signify the first revolt. In addition, the cursive script of the two documents from Wadi Murabba'at allows for an earlier date.[31]

The difference between Wadi Murabba'at and Naḥal Ḥever

No doubt the discoveries of Hebrew documents which certainly date to the Bar Kokhba revolt in the 'Cave of Letters' in Naḥal Ḥever in 1960–62, immediately after the publication of the documents from Wadi Murabba'at, strengthened the belief that the Hebrew documents from Wadi Murabba'at must date to the Bar Kokhba revolt as well. The drastic difference between the history of the caves of Wadi Murabba'at and that of the 'Cave of Letters' in Naḥal Ḥever was thereby overlooked. However, unlike the 'Cave of Letters' of Naḥal Ḥever, the caves of Wadi Murabba'at show human occupation from the early bronze age and well into the Arab period.[32] The first document, written in paleo-Hebrew, dates to the eighth century BCE (*P.Mur* 17). But more relevant for us is the survival of literary and documentary texts and coins from the first century CE. The 'Cave of Letters' on the other hand was occupied during the second revolt only,[33] and one can prove that earlier documents were brought thither at the time of the Bar Kokhba revolt. Thus it is entirely conceivable that the caves of Wadi Murabba'at should have served as a place of refuge also during the first revolt – a place to which documents from the time of the revolt, but also some which preceded it, came to be hidden.

---

29 Leo Mildenberg, "A Bar Kokhba Didrachm," *INJ* 8 (1984–85): 33–36.
30 Robert Deutsch, "A Unique Prutah from the First Year of the Jewish War against Rome," *INJ* 12 (1992–93): 71–72.
31 Oral communication by Ada Yardeni; cf. also Eshel, Broshi, and Jull, "Documents from Wadi Murabba'at and the Status of Jerusalem during the Bar Kokhba Revolt," 237 for the results of carbon 14 tests carried out on *P.Mur* 22 and 29.
32 *DJD* II, 14–49.
33 Yadin, "Expedition D," 36–52.

Aramaic documents from Wadi Murabba'at

A survey of the Aramaic legal documents from Wadi Murabba'at which date to the period before or during the first revolt, as well as of those which may well share this earlier date, strengthens the case for the early date of the Hebrew documents.

The earliest dated document, *P.Mur* 18, is dated by Nero's regnal year to 55/56 CE: 'Year 3 of Nero Caesar' (line 1). This is an Aramaic IOU note, likely to have arrived in Wadi Murabba'at at the time of the first revolt. *P.Mur* 19, an Aramaic deed of divorce which closely resembles the rabbinic deed of divorce, is dated to 'year six in Masada.' Milik understood 'year six' to refer to the era of the province of Arabia, thus dating it to 111 CE. However, "there is not a single instance of the Arabian era in a document clearly from Judaea";[34] so the era of Arabia cannot be applied here without further proof. In fact it is precisely because there is no era in *P.Mur* 19 that the only possible dating would be by the first Jewish revolt, i. e. 72 CE. After the fall of Jerusalem, one could hardly add after 'year 6' the formula 'to the freedom (or redemption) of Zion (or Israel).' The isolated *sicarii* on Masada made a virtue of necessity: 'in Masada' – במצדא – doubles up for the era and the place of the contract, i. e. the era of the revolt has become the era of Masada to the extent that it continued only on Masada. *P.Mur* 21, an Aramaic marriage contract, was tentatively assigned by Milik himself to the years before the first revolt. *P.Mur* 23, an extremely fragmentary double document in Aramaic, can be dated either to 'year 1' or to 'year 5 of the,' (שנת ח.. ל[]), where it breaks off. The letter ח in Aramaic is the initial letter of both 'one' (חדה) and 'five' (חמש). If we read 5 (ח[מש]), then it must refer to the first revolt. The Aramaic *P.Mur* 25 dated to 'Year Three of the freedom of Jerusalem' ([שנ]ת תלת לחרות יר{ו}שלים), where as we have seen 'Jerusalem' is clearly part of a dating formula, may also belong to the first revolt.

One notes also that the caves of Wadi Murabba'at contain documents of people who lived in Jerusalem and its surrounding countryside:[35] Hardona (*P.Mur* 20); Khisalon (*P.Mur* 18, perhaps *P.Mur* 30 line 11), Ẓuba (*P.Mur* 18),[36] Anablata (*P.Mur* 19) and Jerusalem (*P.Mur* 29, 30, 114). The early date of some of these may also suggest an early date for other documents from the same area. I think of two documents which would fit this category. The first is *P.Mur* 20, another Aramaic marriage contract, concluded in Hardona, 5 km from Jerusalem. The era is lost in the lacuna which follows '7 Adar, year 11' written in its first line. Again Milik

34 David Goodblatt, "Dating Documents in Provincia Iudaea: A Note on Papyri Murabba'at 19 and 20," *IEJ* 49 (1999): 253.

35 See Eshel, Broshi, and Jull, "Documents from Wadi Murabba'at and the Status of Jerusalem during the Bar Kokhba Revolt," 236.

36 For the reading of צובה instead of Milik's צויה see Naveh, *On Sherd and Papyrus*, 84.

assumed that 'year 11' refers to the era of the province of Arabia, thus yielding the year 116/7. Since Judaea did not have its own provincial era, 'year 11' is likely to refer to a regnal year of an emperor. Claudius or Nero could easily fill the lacuna, i. e. 51 CE or 65 CE. The second document is an undated Aramaic double document which consists of *P.Mur* 26 and a fragment designated *XḤev/Ṣe ar* 50, whose provenance is unknown. Both are published together now by Ada Yardeni in *DJD* XXVII.[37] This document was signed by a witness from Hebron and the scribe (or more likely a witness) from Jerusalem (*XḤev/Ṣe ar* 50 lines 29 (18) – 31 (20)). The provenance of the witness and the scribe may suggest a date going back to the first revolt or before. Finally, the very many fragments of documents in Hebrew and in Aramaic whose date cannot be recovered in any case could be associated either with the first revolt or with the second one.[38]

Conclusion: Hebrew and Jewish ideology

It may not be a coincidence therefore that there are no documents in Hebrew which date to the years before the first revolt,[39] or to the period between the two revolts. During the revolts Hebrew became, alongside Aramaic, the language of legal documents. The same ideology which inspired the decision to use Hebrew in legal documents of the second revolt may well have motivated also the freedom fighters of the first one. However, the Aramaic scribal tradition of writing such documents is often revealed in the language and the legal formulae of the documents. The reality is represented almost plastically in one of the double documents from the second revolt. The inner text of *DJD* XXVII no. 8, that is the part which is hidden, was written in Aramaic, whereas the outer text was written in Hebrew. In other words, the legally binding text, the inner one, is written in the

37 See *DJD* XXVII no. 50 (= *P.Mur* 26 and *XḤev/Ṣe ar* 50) and in more detail see Ada Yardeni, "Two in one? A Deed of Sale from Wadi Murabba'at," *Eretz Israel* 26 (1999): 64–70 (Hebrew).

38 From sites other than Wadi Murabba'at we have *DJD* XXVII no. 9, an Aramaic deed of sale, dated palaeographically to the first century CE; *DJD* XXVII no. 11 is an Aramaic marriage contract, dated to 'year 8' which could refer to any emperor in the first (or second) century whose reign exceeded seven years; the very fragmentary contracts *DJD* XXVII nos. 21–25; *DJD* XXVII no. 32 (= *XḤev/Ṣe ar* 32 + 4Q347), an Aramaic document, which like *DJD* XXVII no. 11 is dated to 'year 8'; the documents allegedly from Cave 4 in Qumran include a double document in Hebrew mentioning a high priest (כהן גדול) and dated palaeographically to the first century BCE (4Q348); finally a Nabataean letter in early Nabataean script (4Q343) is dated palaeographically to the late Herodian period. This list is not exhaustive.

39 With the exception of 4Q348 (see previous note).

normal language of legal documents at the time,[40] whereas the Hebrew, displayed on the outside, advertises the ideology of the now independent Jewish state. The same ideology stands behind the appearance of Hebrew legends on coins of the two revolts written in the already then obsolete paleo-Hebrew script. Hebrew became the symbol of Jewish nationalism, of the independent Jewish State.

Non-Aramaic documents: Nabataean and Greek documents

All the Nabataean documents and most of the Greek ones found in the Judaean Desert were written in the province of Arabia, which until 106 was the Nabataean kingdom. The same question which was addressed to the Hebrew documents applies here as well: why Nabataean and Greek and not (Jewish) Aramaic?

Nabataean documents from the Nabataean kingdom and the province of Arabia

Of the Nabataean documents found in the Judaean Desert, only one, popularly designated *P.Starcky* (and sometimes *XḤev/Ṣe nab* 1 or *P.Yadin* 36) has so far been published,[41] but we know that they are all legal contracts. *XḤev/Ṣe nab* 1 and the Nabataean *P.Yadin* 1, 2, 3, 4, 6, and 9 are part of the Babatha archive found by Yadin in the 'Cave of Letters' in Naḥal Ḥever.[42] The unpublished *XḤev/Ṣe nab* 2–5(6)[43] may belong to the archive of Salome Komaïse daughter of Levi,[44] whose

40 Naveh, *On Sherd and Papyrus*, 102.

41 Jean Starcky, "Un contrat nabatéen sur papyrus," *RB* 61 (1954): 161–81. See now also Ada Yardeni, "The Decipherment and Restoration of Legal Texts from the Judaean Desert: A Reexamination of Papyrus Stracky (P.Yadin 36)," *SCI* 20 (2001): 121–37.

42 The Babatha Archive (94–132 CE) consists of *P.Yadin* 1–35. *P.Yadin* 5, 11–35 (Greek) were published in Lewis, *The Documents from the Bar Kokhba Period in the Cave of Letters. Greek Papyri*; *P.Yadin* 1–4, 6–10 (Aramaic, Hebrew and Nabataean) were published by Yadin et al., *The Documents from the Bar Kokhba Period in the Cave of Letters: Hebrew, Aramaic and Nabatean-Aramaic Papyri*.

43 Only *XḤev/Se nab* 2 has been read and transcribed by Ada Yardeni, to whom I am indebted for showing me the transcription. See now Yardeni, *Textbook of Aramaic, Hebrew and Nabataean Documentary Texts from the Judaean Desert and Related Material*, Vol. I (Jerusalem: The Hebrew University Press, 2000), 290.

44 The archive of Salome Komaïse daughter of Levi (125 [113?] – 131 CE) consists of *DJD* XXVII no. 12, (no. 32?), nos. 60–65, published in Cotton and Yardeni, *Aramaic, Hebrew, and Greek Documentary Texts from Naḥal Ḥever and Other Sites*.

documents also come from the 'Cave of Letters.'[45] Both archives revolve around the legal affairs of Jewish families in Maḥoza/Maḥoz 'Aglatain, a village on the southern shore of the Dead Sea, in the province of Arabia which was the kingdom of Nabataea until 106 CE. Although, as far as we can see, not all the Nabataean documents directly involve the Jews present in the other documents from the archives, there is no doubt that they were brought to the 'Cave of Letters' in Naḥal Ḥever by the Jews who left Arabia at the time of the Bar Kokhba revolt, and thus may justifiably be considered documents belonging to them.

The earliest Nabataean document, *XḤev/Ṣe nab* 1, of the year 60 CE, is a declaration by a Jew called Ele'azar who is the heir of his father, Nikarkhos, and of his childless uncle Banai (?) son of Nabima. *P.Yadin* 1 is an IOU note from 94 CE, between husband and wife, both Nabataeans; *P.Yadin* 2 and 3, of 99 CE, are deeds of sale, written one month apart from each other by the same scribe. They describe the sale of the same date grove by a Nabataean woman, 'Abi'adan daughter of 'Aftaḥ daughter of Manigros, at first to a man called Archelaus son of 'Abd'amiyu (*P.Yadin* 2) and a month later to Shim'on – probably to be identified as Shim'on bar Menaḥem, Babatha's father – (*P.Yadin* 3);[46] the undated *XḤev/Ṣe nab* 2 and *P.Yadin* 4 also belong to the regal period in Arabia, since the king is mentioned in one of the clauses.[47] The first one is a deed of sale between a Jewish woman, Shalom and a Nabataean called Sh'adalahi.

Nabataean continued to be used as the language of legal documents after provincialization, even in contracts involving only Jews. Two contracts in Nabataean belong to the Roman period in Arabia: *P.Yadin* 6 of the year 119 CE is a deed of lease between two Jews from Ein Gedi who live in Maḥoz 'Aglatain in Arabia, and *P.Yadin* 8 of 122 CE which may be a deed of renunciation of claims mentions a Jew called Joseph. On the other hand there are *no* documents written in Jewish Aramaic or Greek from the Nabataean period. Both languages appear for the first time in legal documents from Arabia only after 106 CE. However, the use of Jewish Aramaic is limited to four documents only: *P.Yadin* 7, of 120 CE, is a deed of gift in contemplation of death between Babatha's parents, probably on the occasion of their daughter's first marriage.[48] Although written in Jewish Aramaic, this doc-

45 See Cotton and Yardeni, 3 ff.

46 On *P.Yadin* 2 and 3 see Ada Yardeni, "Notes on Two Unpublished Nabataean Deeds from Naḥal Ḥever – P.Yadin 2 and 3," in *The Dead Sea Scrolls: Fifty Years after their Discovery 1947–1997*, ed. Lawrence H. Schiffman, Emanuel Tov, and James C. Vanderkam (Jerusalem: IES, 2000), 862–74.

47 The clause says: ולמראנא רבאל מלכא כות: *XḤev/Se nab* 2 (ca. 99 CE?) line 22; *P.Yadin* 4 (99 CE) lines 17–18; cf. *P.Yadin* 2 (99 CE) lines 13–14 = line 40; *P.Yadin* 3 (99 CE) line 18 = lines 45–46.

48 Published by Yigael Yadin, Jonas C. Greenfield, and Ada Yardeni, "A Deed of Gift in Aramaic Found in Naḥal Ḥever: Papyrus Yadin 7," *Eretz Israel* 25 (1996): 383–403 (Hebrew); for the occa-

ument recalls Nabataean contracts both in its script, which closely resembles Nabataean cursive hands, and in its legal formulae and the intrusion of Arabic words; *P.Yadin* 8 of 122 CE is a sale of a white donkey; *P.Yadin* 10, the marriage contract of Babatha to her second husband, Judah son of Ele'azar, was written between 125 and 128 CE;[49] and finally there is *DJD* XXVII no. 12 of 131 CE, a receipt given to Salome Komaïse daughter of Levi in Maḥoz 'Aglatain. Although this is written in Aramaic, its striking resemblance to a receipt in Greek from 125 CE (*DJD* XXVII no. 60)[50] suggests that like the Greek receipt, the Aramaic receipt too was for tax or rent paid to the Emperor.[51]

Greek documents from the province of Arabia

As against two Nabataean contracts and four written in Jewish Aramaic we have altogether 32 Greek documents from the period between 106 and 132 CE in Arabia, that is in the first 25 years of the province. There are 26 Greek documents in the Babatha archive and 6 Greek documents in the archive of Salome Komaïse daughter of Levi.[52] The first safely dated Greek document is *P.Yadin* 5 from 110 CE[53] and the last one is *P.Yadin* 27 from 132 CE.

Thus the intimate connection between provincialization and the use of Greek in legal documents from Nabataea/Arabia is firmly established. It should be stressed that the same names which appear in the Nabataean and Aramaic documents reappear in the Greek documents, as well as in the subscriptions and

sion see Hannah M. Cotton and Jonas C. Greenfield, "Babatha's Property and the Law of Succession in the Babatha Archive," *ZPE* 104 (1994): 211–24.

49 Published by Yigael Yadin, Jonas C. Greenfield, and Ada Yardeni, "Babatha's Ketubba," *IEJ* 44 (1994): 75–99.

50 See Hannah M. Cotton, "Land Tenure in the Documents from the Nabataean Kingdom and the Roman Province of Arabia," *ZPE* 119 (1997): 258–59 [below, pp. 298–99].

51 The use of Aramaic in tax receipts is surprising, although it is clear that the tax collectors were local people: see commentary on *DJD* XXVII no. 60 in Cotton and Yardeni, *Aramaic, Hebrew, and Greek Documentary Texts from Naḥal Ḥever and Other Sites*; cf. Benjamin Isaac, "Tax Collection in Roman Arabia: A New Interpretation of the Evidence from the Babatha Archive," *Mediterranean Historical Review* 9 (1994): 265 f. (= *The Near East under Roman Rule: Selected Papers* (Leiden: Brill, 1997), 330 ff.). The bulk of tax receipts in Demotic from the Roman period in Egypt dates to the time of Augustus and Tiberius (the latest from the reign of Caligula) and they all come from Upper Egypt, particularly from the area around Thebes. Thus it would seem that the use of Greek was gradually imposed (I am grateful to Michael Sharp for this information).

52 A few other fragmentary Greek documents may also come from Arabia: *DJD* XXVII nos. 66, 68, 70–73.

53 There is no certainty about the provenance of *DJD* XXVII nos. 66 of 99 or 109 CE.

signatures to these documents. In other words we are talking of the very same section of the population. The signatures and subscriptions, with some notable exceptions, continue to be written in Jewish Aramaic when the signatories are Jews and in Nabataean when the signatories are Nabataeans. Sometimes though the signatures are in Greek letters; in such cases, more often than not they belong to Nabataeans.[54] However, the scribes of the Greek documents are Jews: Theenas son of Shimʿon, the scribe of *P.Yadin* 13, 14, 15, 17 and 18; X son of Shimʿon, the scribe of *P.Yadin* 19; Germanus son of Judah, the scribe of *P.Yadin* 20–27 and 34, and perhaps also Judah son of Reisha, the scribe of *DJD* XXVII no. 64 – if indeed he is to be identified as the scribe of one of the most ungrammatical Greek documents in our collection.[55]

At least one Jew seems to prefer Nabataean to Aramaic, although he is the scribe of an Aramaic document of the year 122 CE.[56] This is the intriguing Yoḥana son of Makhoutha. Everywhere else in the Babatha archive he uses Nabataean: he signs as a witness in Nabataean in three documents of the years 125, 127 and 130 CE;[57] he serves as Babatha's guardian in a deed of sale from 130 CE (*P.Yadin* 22), and since she is illiterate, he subscribes for her there in Nabataean.[58] These five lines of Nabataean constitute the only Nabataean subscription in the documents. Yoḥana's full patronymic is revealed in *P.Yadin* 16 line 42: 'Yoḥana son of 'Abdʿobdat Makhoutha.' It turns out that the unattested Makhoutha is a nickname;[59] and ʿAbdʿobdat (עבדעבדת – 'slave of ʿObdat') is the father's real name, in other words

54 *P.Yadin* 12 lines 16–17: Ἀβδερẹὺς Σọυμα̣[ί]ọυ̣ μά(ρτυς) corrected to Αβδερετας by Émile Puech, “Présence arabe dans les manuscrits de ‘la grotte aux lettres’ du Wadi Khabra,” in *Présence arabe dans le croissant fertile avant l'Hégire. Actes de la Table ronde internationale organisée par l'Unité de recherche associée 1062 du CNRS, Études sémitiques au Collège de France, le 13 novembre 1993*, ed. Hélène Lozachmeur (Paris: Éditions Recherche sur les Civilisations, 1995), 39, n. 8; *P.Yadin* 19 line 34: [Σ]ọυμαῖος Κα̣[.]αβαίου μάρ̣(τυς). Sometimes Jews also sign their names in Greek letters, e. g. *P.Yadin* 5; *P.Yadin* 14 line 47: Θ̣α̣δ̣αῖος Θα[δαίου] μάρ(τυς); cf. for the same person: *P.Yadin* 15 line 43; *P.Yadin* 20 line 50; *P.Yadin* 23 line 29.

55 See Introduction to *DJD* XXVII no. 64 and comments to line 44.

56 *P.Yadin* 8 where he is called Yoḥanan son of Makhoutha. He is mentioned for the first time in the fragmentary *P.Yadin* 5 fr. b (Greek) of 110 CE, but the context is lost.

57 In *P.Yadin* 14 of 125 CE, in *P.Yadin* 16, Babatha's census declaration of 127 CE, and in *P.Yadin* 20 of 130 CE.

58 See comments by Yadin and Greenfield on the subscription in Lewis, *The Documents from the Bar Kokhba Period in the Cave of Letters. Greek Papyri*, 147; for the difference between the subscriber and the guardian see Hannah M. Cotton, “The Guardian (ἐπίτροπος) of a Woman in the Documents from the Judaean Desert,” *ZPE* 118 (1997): 269 ff. [below, pp. 435 ff.].

59 There are other nicknames in the papyri: Eleʿazar Khthousion, Judah Kimber, Yoḥana son of Egla (*P.Yadin* 15, l. 33: יוחנה חברי בר עגלא). That Egla is a nickname emerges from *P.Yadin* 14 line 23 and 15 lines 3–4 (= line 18): Ἰωάνης Ἰωσήπου τοῦ Ἐγ̣λα. Somala (*P.Yadin* 16 lines 5 and 35) is

that he was Nabataean.[60] On the other hand, the theophoric Jewish name Yoḥana and the Aramaic *P.Yadin* 8 may suggest that the son is the issue of a mixed marriage between a Jew and a Nabataean.[61]

The Nabataean Onainos son of Saʿadalos – graphically described as 'the one who lends his hand': χειροχρήστης – wrote the subscription to the census declaration of Salome Komaïse's brother who was illiterate. The fragmentary document where he is said to have written the subscription[62] is a copy, written in Greek, of the original census declaration: the original was written in several hands and also in more than one language.[63] Thus it is hard to know whether Onainos son of Saʿadalos wrote the subscription in Greek or in Nabataean.

Greek documents from Judaea

Whereas the use of Greek by Jews in legal documents in the province of Arabia is connected with the advent of the Romans, and Romanization filters through the Greek prism,[64] no such association can be made for the use of Greek in Judaea whose provincialization dates to 6 CE. With the exception of inscriptions on Jewish ossuaries, the first Greek documents from Jewish circles come from Masada. The majority of the Greek material found on Masada is likely to have been written by no one but the *sicarii*, and therefore dates to the years 66–73(4).[65] The use of Greek by this group of Jewish extremists is not more surprising than the use of Greek by the Bar Kokhba administration in *P.Yadin* 52 and 59.[66] By now we should have

therefore likely to be Ananias' nickname and not the name of a grandfather, despite Lewis, *The Documents from the Bar Kokhba Period in the Cave of Letters. Greek Papyri*, 81.

60 But see *CIS* II, 1, 3 (1902) no. 486, lines 1–2: 'Ḥonainu (חנינו) son of Aba who is also called 'Abdallahi (עבדאלהי).'

61 Tal Ilan, "Yohana bar Makoutha and Other Pagans Bearing Jewish Names," in *These are the Names – Studies in Jewish Onomastics III*, ed. Aaron Demsky (Ramat-Gan: Bar-Ilan University Press, 2002), 109–20, as the title indicates takes Yohana son of Makhoutha to be a pagan.

62 *DJD* XXVII no. 61, lines 3–4: ἐ̣[γράφη διὰ] χειροχρήστου Οναινου Σααδαλλου.

63 See Hannah M. Cotton, "Subscriptions and Signatures in the Papyri from the Judaean Desert: The χειροχρήστης," *JJP* 25 (1995): 29–40 [above, pp. 115–25].

64 See Rosén, "Die Sprachsituation im römischen Palästina," 219 ff.

65 Cotton and Geiger, *Masada II: The Latin and Greek Documents*, 9–10.

66 First published by Baruch Lifshitz, "Papyrus grecs du désert de Juda," *Aegyptus* 42 (1962): 240–56. *P.Yadin* 52 has been re-edited many times since: G. Howard and J.C. Shelton, "The Bar-Kokhba Letters and Palestinian Greek," *IEJ* 23 (1973): 101–2; Rosén, "Die Sprachsituation im römischen Palästina," 224; Dirk Obbink, "Bilingual Literacy and Syrian Greek," *BASP* 28 (1991): 51–8; Hayim Lapin, "Palm Fronds and Citrons: Notes on Two Letters from Bar Kosiba's Administration," *HUCA* 64 (1993): 111–35; G. Wilhelm Nebe, "Die beiden griechischen Briefe des Jonatan

learnt, I think, that the use of Greek by Jews has no ideological implications: it should not be mistaken for the hellenization of the writer nor be taken as evidence for his political and national sentiments. However, the Greek documents from Masada cannot be considered legal documents, and will therefore be ignored in the following discussion.[67]

The first safely dated legal document written in Greek in Judaea thus comes from the Babatha archive. *P.Yadin* 11 of 6 May 124 CE was written in Ein Gedi. This double contract is an acknowledgement of a loan upon security, which Babatha's second husband, Judah son of Eleʿazar Khthousion, took from Magonius Valens, a centurion of the *cohors prima Thracum milliaria* then stationed in Ein Gedi. Lines 29–30 contain a translation, ἑρμηνεία, of Judah's subscription, which must have been written in Aramaic.[68] It is signed by seven witnesses; the first witness, Gaius Iulius Proclus, is a Roman soldier, the rest are likely to be fellow Ein Gedians. Curiously the signatures are in Greek and not in Latin and Aramaic respectively, as we might have expected. Lewis maintains that what we have is a copy, with the original being retained by the lender.[69]

P.Yadin 11 closely recalls *P.Mur* 114, another IOU document which involves a Roman soldier of the *legio X Fretensis* and a person whose name is lost in the lacuna. Unlike *P.Yadin* 11, *P.Mur* 114 is very fragmentary. The document is dated by its editor to 171 CE, since he quite reasonably identifies the Statilius Severus in line 2 with the *consul ordinarius* of that year, T. Statilius Severus. However, the fact that the document is said to be signed '[in] Jerusalem' (line 3–4), should give us pause. For the Romans, Jerusalem no longer existed in 171 CE, only Aelia Capitolina. One would surely have expected Aelia Capitolina to be given as the place where a contract, dated by the consular year and involving a Roman legionary, was concluded after 132 CE. A date between 70 and 132 CE is much to be preferred.

Archivs in Engedi aus dem zweiten jüdischen Aufstand 132–135 nach Chr.," *Revue de Qumran* 17 (1996): 275–89; for final publication see above n. 2 ad fin.

67 *Doc. Mas.* 740, which carried a date and is tentatively dated to 25–35 CE, is too fragmentary to betray its real nature.

68 *P.Yadin* 11, lines 29–30: ἑρμηνεία· Ἰ̣ο̣ύ̣δα̣ς Ἐλ[αζάρου] Χθο̣[υσίων]ος τ̣ὰ̣ ... ὑ̣πέθηκα ἀκ̣ολούθω[ς τοῖς προγεγρ]α̣μμ̣έ̣ν̣[οις. ἐγράφη διὰ] Ἰ̣ο̣υ̣σ̣τείν̣ο̣υ̣.

69 Lewis, *The Documents from the Bar Kokhba Period in the Cave of Letters. Greek Papyri*, 42. This is difficult for two reasons: first, one would have expected to find it stated that this is a verified copy, as is the practice in other documents (e.g. *P.Yadin* 16 lines 1–2 and *DJD* XXVII no. 62, frg. a lines 1–2); secondly, the courtyard given here as security is bestowed later in a deed of gift by Judah on his daughter Shlamzion (*P.Yadin* 19, 16 April 128 CE) which implies that the loan was paid back. One would then expect the original to be returned (perhaps cancelled) to Judah, rather than that he should keep a copy; on the courtyard see Hannah M. Cotton, "Courtyard(s) in Ein-Gedi: P.Yadin 11, 19 and 20 of the Babatha archive," *ZPE* 112 (1996): 197–201 [below, pp. 285–91].

It could be suggested that with caution the Statilius Severus of line 2 is to be identified as the suffect consul of the year 115 CE, T. Statilius Maximus Severus Hadrianus, who replaced M. Pedo Vergilianus when the latter died in the earthquake in Antiochia.[70] This suggestion, if correct, would make *P.Mur* 114 the earliest dated contract from Judaea written in Greek.[71]

To the same milieu belongs the very fragmentary and undated *P.Mur* 113 which describes a legal process, involving two Jewish women, Salome and Miriam, and a Roman veteran. However, the similarity to the proceedings documented in *P.Yadin* 26 of 130 CE may give us a clue to its nature.[72]

Marriage contracts between Jews in Greek

That Greek is used in contracts which involve Roman soldiers is hardly surprising. It is more intriguing to find three marriage contracts written in Greek in which both parties, in at least two, are Jews. The earliest dated one is *P.Mur* 115 of 124 CE, concluded at Bethbassi in the toparchy of Herodium, south of Jerusalem. This is a contract of re-marriage between Elaios son of Shimʿon, who came 'from the village of Galoda of Akrabatta, but [was] an inhabitant of Batharda of Gophna' – both in Samaria – and his former wife Salome daughter of Yohanan Galgoula. The second one is *DJD* XXVII no. 69 of 130 CE, contracted in Aristoboulias in the toparchy of Zif, south of Hebron between Selampios (Shelamzion) and Akabas (Aqiba or Akabia) son of Meir from Yaqim (or Yaqum) in the same toparchy. Both documents are dated by regnal and consular year. The acephalic *P.Mur* 116, dated palaeographically to the first half of the second century CE, records some of the clauses in a marriage contract between an Aurelius and Salome. 'Aurelius' does not have

70 This was E. Groag's suggestion in "Zu einem neuen Fragment der Fasti von Ostia," *JÖAI* 21 (1935): 177–204; a dating by a suffect consul outside Italy is also problematic. See Hannah M. Cotton and Werner Eck, "P.Murabba'at 114 und die Anwesenheit römischer Truppen in den Höhlen des Wadi Murabbaʿat nach dem Bar Kochba Aufstand," *ZPE* 138 (2002): 173–83.

71 Pierre Benoit, "Une reconnaissance de dette du IIe siècle en Palestine," in *Studi in onore di Aristide Calderini e Roberto Paribeni*, Vol. II (Milano: Ceschina, 1957), 257–72 makes the soldier the borrower. For a suggestion that he is the lender see Cotton and Eck, "P.Murabbaʿat 114 und die Anwesenheit römischer Truppen in den Höhlen des Wadi Murabbaʿat nach dem Bar Kochba Aufstand."

72 I hesitate to add *DJD* XXVII no. 66 of 99 or 109 CE, a deed loan with hypothec, to the list, since no typical Jewish names are mentioned in it; the Φιλαδελφẹ[ύς] (or Φιλαδελφε[ῖς]) in line 2 may indicate that it comes from Arabia rather than Judaea, see introduction to no. 66 in Cotton and Yardeni, *Aramaic, Hebrew, and Greek Documentary Texts from Naḥal Ḥever and Other Sites*, 239–40.

to be a sign that the bearer is a Roman citizen despite what the editor suggests.[73] At any rate the marriage seems to have followed local custom, for we find in the preserved portion of this document formulae so far attested only in marriage contracts between Jews written in Aramaic or in Greek, namely that in the event of the wife's prior death, her sons will inherit their mother's dowry whereas daughters are to be fed and clothed in the father's house until they get married. I deliberately avoid saying that 'the document follows Jewish law' since the provision for male sons to inherit from their mother in fact contravenes Biblical law which makes the husband the sole heir to his wife's property. It must have been introduced into Jewish law under the influence of other Near Eastern traditions, where the wife's children were her heirs in order to protect male sons in polygamous marriages against the loss of their mother's property to sons of another woman. This is in fact expressed in so many words in this document: '[And if Salome] dies [before Aurelius], the sons that she will have from him will inherit her dowry and the things written above ... [in addition] to inheriting all of Aurelius' property together with their future brothers [from another woman]' (*P.Mur* 116, lines 4–8).[74]

Although in their formulae and practices these marriage contracts resemble Greek marriage contracts from Egypt, the Jews of the documents cannot be described as assimilated Jews, living outside the pale, so to speak. For their documents to be found in Naḥal Ḥever and Wadi Murabbaʿat together with letters and leases of Bar Kokhba and his men, they too must have taken part in Bar Kokhba's national and religious revolt. That their marriage contracts resemble Greek contracts from various parts of the Roman Near East can only prove that Jewish society as a whole, at the time, shared the mixture of legal systems documented in the area.[75]

Conclusion: Greek documents and provincial jurisdiction

Greek became the language of legal documents in Arabia almost immediately upon provincialization, whereas more than a hundred years elapsed before it is first attested in legal documents from Judaea. Nevertheless, I believe that identical reasons motivated the adoption of Greek in legal documents in both provinces, namely the need to make the contracts valid in a court of law which had the power

73 *DJD* II, 254.
74 See in detail Hannah M. Cotton, "The Rabbis and the Documents," in *Jews in a Greco-Roman World*, ed. Martin Goodman (Oxford: Oxford University Press, 1998), 175 ff. [below, pp. 460 ff.].
75 See Cotton and Yardeni, *Aramaic, Hebrew, and Greek Documentary Texts from Naḥal Ḥever and Other Sites*, 153–7.

to enforce them when necessary, such as that of the governor of the province, of another Roman official,[76] or the court of a *polis*. An additional reason could be the need to deposit the deeds in a public archive, similar to what we know to have been the case in Egypt, where public archives were used to deposit private documents; having been registered there, these documents could later be produced in court as evidence.[77]

After 70 CE conditions prevailing in Judaea became similar to what conditions in Arabia had always been: there was no Jewish court which had the authority to enforce its decisions. In Arabia there had never been Jewish courts of law as the exclusive use of Nabataean in the regal period demonstrates.

Until the first revolt (66–70 CE) at least the Great Sanhedrin in Jerusalem with the high priest at its head must have enjoyed a large measure of judicial independence in both civil and criminal law. There is much evidence for that in Josephus, Philo and the New Testament. Even if officially the Sanhedrin's judicial competence did not extend beyond Judaea proper, its authority certainly did not know such bounds.[78] Things changed drastically after 70 CE. The destruction of Jerusalem and the Temple meant among other things the dissolution of the Great Sanhedrin. What measure of legal and administrative autonomy was left? How much of the earlier judicial autonomy remained?[79]

It would be absurd to claim that the Roman government took it upon itself to deal with all civil cases in the province of Judaea/Syria Palaestina. It is a remarkable fact though that no court, Jewish or non-Jewish – apart from that of the Roman governor of Arabia – is mentioned in any of the documents from the Judaean Desert – a great many of which are legal documents. However, we should not jump from this to the conclusion that the governor's court was the only court in

---

76 See Hannah M. Cotton and Werner Eck, "Roman Officials in Judaea and Arabia and Civil Jurisdiction," in *Law in the Documents of the Judaean Desert*, ed. Ranon Katzoff and David Schaps (Leiden – Boston: Brill, 2005), 23–44.

77 For the evidence Hannah M. Cotton, "The Guardianship of Jesus Son of Babatha: Roman and Local Law in the Province of Arabia," *JRS* 83 (1993): 101–2 [below, pp. 417–20], and Cotton, "The Rabbis and the Documents," 175 ff. [below, pp. 460 ff.].

78 Schürer, *The History of the Jewish People in the Age of Jesus Christ*, Vol. II, 197–8; 218 ff.

79 The rabbinic sources, accepted by some scholars, have a neat picture of an autonomous hierarchical Jewish jurisdiction: "a court of three sat in every village, a court of seven in a toparchy, of twenty three in a *meris*, and the great Sanhedrin of seventy-one was at the head of the whole system" (Michael Avi-Yonah, *The Holy Land: From the Persian to the Arab Conquests* (Grand Rapids: Baker Book House, 1966), 99 – rightly dismissed as a pure conjecture in Schürer, *The History of the Jewish People in the Age of Jesus Christ*, Vol. II, 188, n. 15). This picture, itself an idealization, is taken to have remained basically unchanged after 70 CE, despite the fact that the Great Sanhedrin no longer existed.

operation in a Roman province. Nevertheless, the absence of others is disturbing, especially in view of the host of references in rabbinic sources to courts of different sizes in towns and villages. Furthermore, the fact that we have dozens of contracts written in Aramaic means that there was some sort of Jewish jurisdiction in civil cases. Perhaps one should think in terms of courts of arbitration acceptable to both parties to the contract or the litigation.[80] In the course of time, the Romans, even if not officially recognizing these forms of Jewish jurisdiction, nonetheless came to tolerate them.[81]

However, even from the rabbinic sources one can show that Jews used non-Jewish courts. There are several discussions in the rabbinic sources about the validity of contracts made in Greek, about the use of gentile witnesses, courts and archives. Sometimes such activities are explicitly forbidden. The harsh language employed by the Rabbis in the prohibition on the use of gentile courts may well indicate that the Jews *did* use them; no less is implied when the Rabbis used conciliatory language and allowed what was in common use to have validity under Jewish law.[82]

Of course, as we have seen, Jews continued to write contracts in Aramaic after 70 CE in Judaea and after 106 CE in Arabia, but they could not expect the Roman courts to enforce these contracts. That the overwhelming majority of documents in the archives from Arabia are in Greek[83] is illustrative of the trust their writers put in non-Jewish courts, especially those of the Roman governor.[84] Perhaps it was with this in mind that Judah son of Ele'azar who had written with his own hand his own marriage contract with Babatha in Aramaic (*P.Yadin* 10)[85] employed a scribe to write a Greek marriage contract for his daughter (*P.Yadin* 18). This contract she could take to the Roman governor's court if necessary.

---

80 Misgav, "Jewish Courts of Law as Reflected in the Documents from the Dead Sea," 17 f.

81 As for the assumed rabbinic tribunals, I do not think anyone has ever refuted H.P. Chajes' arguments presented exactly a hundred years ago (1899) that when we examine the sources closely, we never find people approaching a proper tribunal, but rather a single rabbi ("Les juges juifs en Palestine, de l'an 70 à l'an 500," *Revue des études juives* 39, no. 77 (1899): 39–52).

82 See Cotton, "The Guardianship of Jesus Son of Babatha: Roman and Local Law in the Province of Arabia," 101–2 [below, pp. 417–20] and Cotton, "The Rabbis and the Documents," 169 ff. [below, pp. 455 ff.].

83 The ratio of Aramaic to Greek documents in Judaea does not reflect normal conditions in the Roman province: many of the Aramaic documents found in the Judaean Desert were written in the short period of national independence during the Bar Kokhba revolt.

84 The Babatha archive contains many examples of people's unshakeable confidence in the accessibility of the Roman governor; it was not unfounded, see Cotton, "The Guardianship of Jesus Son of Babatha: Roman and Local Law in the Province of Arabia," 106–7 [below, pp. 426–29].

85 Yadin, Greenfield, and Yardeni, "Babatha's Ketubba."

'Diplomatics' or External Aspects of the Legal Documents from the Judaean Desert: Prolegomena

The original title of the lecture, "Scribes, Notaries, Subscribers, Witnesses, Signatures, Dating, and Other External Aspects of Legal Contracts in Papyri and Rabbinic Sources" proved to be all too ambitious, especially now that the entire documentary corpus from the Judaean Desert has been published – and this has happened quite recently with the publication of all the Semitic material from Naḥal Ḥever, the letters and leases of Bar Kokhba and his men (*P.Yadin* 42–48) and the unpublished part of the Babatha archive (*P.Yadin* 1–4, 6–10).[1] In the light of these publications, I have come to realize that much of what I have written about the external aspect of the documents from the Judaean Desert and its implications for various other issues needs to be revised. Furthermore, the new book of our host, Catherine Hezser, on *Jewish Literacy in Roman Palestine*,[2] reached me too late to take full account of the very pertinent questions she raises there in her attempt to use the documents to address a whole plethora of social, legal, and administrative issues. For example: is it true that the language of documents dictated the nationality of the courts, and the law to be applied?[3] Does the existence of documents necessarily imply the existence of formal jurisdiction, that is, of a court endowed with formal jurisdiction, for which they were presumably intended? What is the relationship between the existence of private documents

1 Yigael Yadin et al., *The Documents from the Bar Kokhba Period in the Cave of Letters: Hebrew, Aramaic and Nabatean-Aramaic Papyri*, Judean Desert Studies III (Jerusalem: IES, 2002). The Greek part of the Babatha Archive, *P.Yadin* 5, 11–36, was published by Naphtali Lewis, *The Documents from the Bar Kokhba Period in the Cave of Letters. Greek Papyri* (with Aramaic and Nabataean Signatures and Subscriptions, edited by Y. Yadin and J.C. Greenfield), Judean Desert Studies II (Jerusalem: IES, 1989).
2 Catherine Hezser, *Jewish Literacy in Roman Palestine* (Tübingen: Mohr Siebeck, 2001).
3 Hezser, 156–7.

Article note: First published in Catherine Hezser, ed., *Rabbinic Law in its Roman and Near Eastern Context* (Tübingen: Mohr Siebeck, 2003), 49–61, with the following note: I dedicate this paper to Ada Yardeni from whom I have learnt everything I know about the matters discussed below. I am greatly indebted to Rudolph Haensch for criticizing and improving my arguments, and to Elizabeth Meyer for allowing me to see the relevant chapter in her then forthcoming book, *Legitimacy and Law in the Roman World* (Cambridge: Cambridge University Press, 2004). I have retained the original lecture style of the paper and kept the footnotes to a bare minimum. For the nomenclature used in this article for the papyri from the Judaean Desert, see Hannah M. Cotton, "Documentary Texts from the Judaean Desert: A Matter of Nomenclature," *SCI* 20 (2001): 113–19.

https://doi.org/10.1515/9783110770438-009

and the legal and administrative organs in a Roman province? Should not one consider the possibility of an alternative procedure, namely, that of informal arbitration by bodies lacking formal jurisdiction in the Roman sense of the word – a subject with wide ramifications?[4] And finally, to link it all to my present topic: what implications does the external format, the external aspect of documents, have for the courts and legal system operating in a Roman province? The emphasis is on 'a Roman province': those who owned the documents, both Jews and non-Jews, were part of the Roman Near East with its ancient traditions and new masters; like everyone else they tried to make their documents as effective as possible within the existing order. The need to conform to the powers that be is apparent everywhere.

The majority of the legal documents from the Judaean Desert belonged to Jews. There has been a tendency to study both their contents and their form against the background of Jewish sources, namely the rabbinic sources. A recent attempt to compare "the procedures for signing and witnessing contracts from the Judaean Desert to those described in Rabbinic law" shows, as could be expected, that "many of the practices in use here do follow what Rabbinic law prescribes. Yet others differ markedly."[5] This is hardly surprising. As pointed out elsewhere, the discrepancy between the Halakha and the documents goes well beyond the surface, beyond the realm of what the papyrologists call 'diplomatics,' into that of the substance of law – a discrepancy between legal systems.[6] These external features are no less significant, of course, for observing the incursion of different legal systems and detecting differences and similarities between them. The diplomatics of ancient documents can often give us important clues about the legal system (or systems) in operation in the documents themselves. Moreover, legal systems can intersect in one and the same document.

The study of diplomatics goes together with the study of legal formulae in the documents – the development of both "owed less to statutes than to notaries."[7]

4 See Hannah M. Cotton, "Jewish Jurisdiction under Roman Rule: Prolegomena," in *Zwischen den Reichen: Neues Testament und römische Herrschaft. Vorträge auf der ersten Konferenz der European Association for Biblical Studies*, ed. Michael Labahn and Jürgen Zangenberg (Tübingen: Francke Verlag, 2002), 13–28 [below, pp. 485–99].

5 So Lawrence H. Schiffman, "Witnesses and Signatures in the Hebrew and Aramaic documents from the Bar Kokhba Caves," in *Semitic Papyrology in Context: A Climate of Creativity*, ed. Lawrence H. Schiffman (Leiden – Boston: Brill, 2003), 165–86. I am grateful for the opportunity to study this manuscript in advance of publication.

6 See Hannah M. Cotton, "The Rabbis and the Documents," in *Jews in a Greco-Roman World*, ed. Martin Goodman (Oxford: Oxford University Press, 1998), 167–79 [below, pp. 453–65].

7 Elias J. Bickerman's formulation for the formulae in "Two Legal Interpretations of the Septuagint," in *Studies in Jewish and Christian History*, Vol. I (Leiden: Brill, 1976), 207.

True, at times the central government intervened and prescribed the format of documents, as happened in Rome for example in the case of a *SC* from 61 CE cited in Paulus, *Sententiae* V, 25, 6, which specifies the format of double documents. On the whole, however, we may safely assume that the diplomatics, like the legal formulae, were transmitted for generations through the scribes, and were available to all, Jews and non-Jews alike.

The present discussion is conceived to be *prolegomena* to a future study (not necessarily by the present author), which will cover all the external aspects of the legal documents from the Judaean Desert against the backdrop of the entire corpus of legal documents from the Roman Near East. Here I have decided to concentrate on two subjects: double documents and witnesses; at the end I shall say something about guardians and subscribers. My presentation will stay extremely close to the documents themselves, always emphasizing the language of composition of the single document and the language used by witnesses and subscribers. Once the technical aspects are fully appreciated, theoretical implications can be drawn. I am using this occasion to correct some of the mistakes I have made in the course of previous publications. Such mistakes constitute real pitfalls for the uninitiated, for those who, unfamiliar with the allusive nature of the raw material, place a complete trust in the editors of the documents.

Although my emphasis here is on documents written in the Roman period and which thus show the influence of the diplomatics of Roman law on provincial law, i. e. on documents written in Greek from the provinces of Judaea and Arabia, I shall not exclude documents – some under the Nabataean kings, others under the rule of Bar Kokhba – written in the Semitic languages.

Certain elements present in the Greek documents imply that they were intended for a Roman court of law. (As an aside one may observe that all this implies of course that non-citizens had recourse to Roman law and courts of law long before 212 CE, and that this does not seem to have required the grant of a special privilege). I am not sure one should infer from the language of the documents the legal system to be applied by the envisioned court.

First, the use of the Greek language – the language used *par excellence* as means of communication between rulers and subjects in the Roman Near East – in legal documents strongly suggests that the court envisioned was that of the Roman governor. One can easily demonstrate the intimate connection between the advent of Roman rule (i. e. provincialization) and the recourse to using Greek in legal documents in the case of the former kingdom of Nabataea, which in 106 CE became the Roman province of Arabia. Until 106 CE legal documents had been written in Nabataean, whereas from 106 CE onwards the Greek language takes over; we have ca. 32 Greek documents from the period between 106 and 132 CE in Arabia, that is, in the first 25 years of the province, as against four documents in Jewish Aramaic (*P.Yadin* 7, 8, 10 and *P.Ḥever* 12) and at least two, perhaps five, Nabataean documents (*P.Yadin* 6 and 9; there are still three unpublished ones which may belong to the Roman period). In Judaea, on the other hand, the first safely dated Greek documents, *P.Yadin* 11 and *P.Mur* 115, date to 124 CE.[8] Elsewhere, I claimed that the lack of synchronization between provincialization and the use of the Greek language in legal contracts from Roman Judaea is the direct result of the survival until 70 CE of a large measure of Jewish legal autonomy.[9]

Secondly, the use of the double document needs to be discussed. Deeds can be categorized according to their format into 'simple deeds' and 'double deeds.' The simple deed is a deed written only once, as distinguished from the double deed which contains two copies – not always entirely identical – of the same text, an upper or inner version and a lower or outer version. The upper (inner) text was the legally binding one. It was rolled and tied with a string, and signatures are found against the stitches on the *verso*. The use of double documents fell into disuse in Ptolemaic Egypt by the time it became a Roman province in 30 BCE, with the exception of documents submitted by Roman citizens. On the other hand in other parts of the Roman Near East, like Judaea and Arabia, the practice survived into the Roman period.[10] Therefore, one should hesitate before ascribing the overwhelming number of double documents in the archives from the Judaean Desert to Roman influence – let alone regard them as a requirement imposed by the Roman

8 Note also that *P.Mur* 114 should be predated to the period before 130 CE, cf. Hannah M. Cotton and Werner Eck, "P.Murabbaʿat 114 und die Anwesenheit römischer Truppen in den Höhlen des Wadi Murabbaʿat nach dem Bar Kochba Aufstand," *ZPE* 138 (2002): 173–83.

9 Hannah M. Cotton, "Die Papyrusdokumente aus der judäischen Wüste und ihr Beitrag zur Erforschung der jüdischen Geschichte des 1. und 2. Jh.s n. Chr.," *ZDPV* 115 (1999): 237 ff.

10 Most of the information can be found in Hannah M. Cotton, W.E.H. Cockle, and Fergus Millar, "The Papyrology of the Roman near East: A Survey," *JRS* 85 (1995): 214–35. For *P.Dura* see C.B. Welles, R.O. Fink, and J.F. Gilliam, *The Excavations at Dura-Europos Conducted by Yale University and the French Academy of Inscriptions and Letters, Final Report V, Part I: The Parchments and Papyri* (New Haven: Yale University Press, 1959), with Jonathan A. Goldstein, "The Syriac Bill of Sale from Dura-Europos," *JNES* 25 (1966): 1–16. The Greek *P.Euphr.* are published in: Denis Feissel and Jean Gascou, "Documents d'archives romains inédits du Moyen Euphrate (IIIe s. après J-C): I. Les pétitions (T. Euphr. 1 à 5)," *Journal des Savants* (1995): 65–119; Javier Teixidor, Denis Feissel, and Jean Gascou, "Documents d'archives romains inédits du Moyen Euphrate (IIIe siècle après J-C): II. Les actes de vente- achat (P. Euphr. 6 À 10)," *Journal des Savants*, (1997): 3–57; Denis Feissel and Jean Gascou, "Documents d'archives romains inédits du Moyen Euphrate (IIIe s. après J.-C.): III. Actes divers et Lettres (P. Euphr. 11 à 17)," *Journal des Savants*, 2000, 157–208; for the Syriac *P.Euphr.* Javier Teixidor, "Deux documents syriaques du IIIe siècle ap. J.-C., provenant du Moyen Euphrate," *CR Acad. Inscr.* 134 (1990): 144–66; Javier Teixidor, "Un document syriaque de fermage de 242 ap. J.-C.," *Semitica* 41–42 (1993): 195–208.

authorities.[11] Furthermore, the Semitic double documents, written under Roman rule in Arabia,[12] are not likely to have been intended specifically for a Roman court.[13] In the Nabataean Kingdom, later to become the province of Arabia, as will be demonstrated immediately, a local tradition of writing double documents with its own peculiar customs existed, which continued into the Roman period in a Jewish Aramaic document of 120 CE: *P.Yadin* 7. No Roman encouragement was needed to establish or resuscitate the use of the double document in this part of the Roman Near East.

In a new edition of the earliest Nabataean double document (58–67 CE), *P.Starcky* (= *P.Ḥever* 1), Ada Yardeni points out a phenomenon which, so far as I know, has never been observed before.[14] The inner (or upper) text starts already on the *verso*, towards its bottom. Then the papyrus was turned over foot to head, rather than merely being turned sidewise from back to front. This is in fact the only way to keep both parts of the inner text (the beginning on the *verso* and its continuation on the *recto*) on the same part of the papyrus so that both could later be rolled and tied. The purpose of this complicated arrangement was to prevent tampering with the contents of the inner text. Nothing could be added since the writing on the *verso* reached the very bottom of the papyrus before it was turned over. This contrasts sharply with the casual, even perfunctory, treatment of the inner text in some of the other texts in the archives from Naḥal Ḥever and from Dura Europos.[15] Unless this was a mere formality, the procedure indicates a great reliance on the written document, for although the signatures of the witnesses

11 Cf. Meyer, *Legitimacy and Law in the Roman World*, chapter 7.

12 *P.Yadin* 7 and 10. The same is true of the Syriac double documents written in Syriac in Mesopotamia: *P.Euphr.Syr.* A and B (full bibliography in Cotton, Cockle, and Millar, "The Papyrology of the Roman near East: A Survey," nos. 157 and 159) and *P.Dura* 28.

13 Meyer, *Legitimacy and Law in the Roman World*, believes that Rome exercised an influence on the format of documents in other languages as well.

14 See Ada Yardeni, "The Decipherment and Restoration of Legal Texts from the Judaean Desert: A Reexamination of Papyrus Stracky (P.Yadin 36)," *SCI* 20 (2001): 121–37. *P.Starcky* and *P.Ḥever* 2 belong to the so-called Seiyal Collection II, most of which must have come from the Cave of Letters in Naḥal Ḥever, like the Babatha archive. See General Introduction to *P.Ḥever* in Hannah M. Cotton and Ada Yardeni, *Aramaic, Hebrew, and Greek Documentary Texts from Naḥal Ḥever and Other Sites*, Discoveries in the Judaean Desert XXVII (Oxford: Clarendon Press, 1997), 1–6. *P.Ḥever* 2 was published without commentary in Ada Yardeni, *Textbook of Aramaic, Hebrew and Nabataean Documentary Texts from the Judaean Desert and Related Material*, Vol. I (Jerusalem: The Hebrew University Press, 2000), 290–1 (see Vol. II, 95 for the English translation). See Hanan Eshel, "Another Document from the Archive of Salome Komaïse Daughter of Levi," *SCI* 21 (2002): 169–71 for associating the two papyri with the archive of Salome Komaïse daughter of Levi.

15 For *P.Yadin* see Lewis, *The Documents from the Bar Kokhba Period in the Cave of Letters. Greek Papyri*, 9; cf. *P.Ḥever* 62 and *P.Dura* 26, 28, 29.

are there to ensure that no one will tamper with the contents of the inner text, only a close comparison between the upper (inner) text with the lower (outer) text would reveal discrepancies between them. We find the same practice in two more Nabataean papyri, *P.Yadin* 2, 3[16] as well as in *P.Yadin* 7 of 120 CE, a deed of gift from husband to wife, in Jewish Aramaic, which must be following the Nabataean procedure.[17]

Double documents are always accompanied by witnesses and their signatures. The signatures on the back, the *verso* of the deed, are found close to the tie, at right angles to the direction of the lines of the lower (outer) version on the *recto*. In Aramaic, Nabataean and Hebrew deeds, the first signature on the *verso* starts on the back of the right margin of the text on the *recto*, whereas in Greek deeds, the first signature on the *verso* starts on the back of the left margin of the *recto*. In other words, in both Greek and Semitic documents the first signature bears the same relationship to the margin of the lower (outer) text, whether it was written right to left or left to right. The direction of the signatures is also determined by the language of the deed: in the Aramaic, Nabataean, and Hebrew deeds, signatures written in these scripts were written downwards (away) from the stitching, while signatures in the Greek script were written upwards (towards) the stitching. In the Greek deeds on the other hand, the signatures in the Greek script were written downwards (away) from the stitching, while signatures in the Aramaic or Nabataean scripts were written upwards (towards) the stitches.[18]

---

16 See figures and plates in Yadin et al., *The Documents from the Bar Kokhba Period in the Cave of Letters: Hebrew, Aramaic and Nabatean-Aramaic Papyri.*

17 It shares other features with the Nabataean documents of the archive; see commentary to *P.Yadin* 7 in Yadin et al., esp. 73–4. It may be said in passing that even in simple texts we can find evidence for precautions against tampering with the text. Thus in *P.Yadin* 22 the interlinear addition in line 16: ἔτι δέ is mentioned again in the last line of the body of the document: ἐπιγραφή· ἔτι δέ. "textual addition: ἔτι δέ" as Lewis translates it, observing that its purpose was "similar to what is accomplished by the present-day practice of having parties to a contract place their initials alongside any addition to or alteration of the original text", Lewis, *The Documents from the Bar Kokhba Period in the Cave of Letters. Greek Papyri*, 101.

18 See for example plates in Yadin et al., *The Documents from the Bar Kokhba Period in the Cave of Letters: Hebrew, Aramaic and Nabatean-Aramaic Papyri*: *P.Yadin* 1: tied upper part; *recto* and *verso* with signatures in Nabataean; *P.Yadin* 20: six Semitic signatures and one in Greek (l. 5) on a Greek document; *P.Yadin* 12: four Nabataean signatures and one in Greek on a Greek document; *P.Yadin* 11: seven Greek signatures on a Greek document; *P.Yadin* 7: semitic signatures on a Semitic document. It would be edifying to compare closely the usage here with that in the bilingual archives from Mesopotamia and the Middle Euphrates (see above, n. 10). I am grateful to Denis Feissel for giving me details, not found in the publications, on the signatures on the *verso* of *P.Euphr*.

The number of signatures – which is not the same as the number of witnesses – on the *recto* and the *verso* of simple and double documents needs further study, and cannot be treated here.[19] According to the rabbis, the witnesses' signatures in a simple deed – two are prescribed – are found on the *recto*, whilst in a tied document, where three are prescribed, they appear on the *verso*. Assuming that the rabbis' 'simple deed' and 'tied deed' correspond to the modern definitions based on what was found in the Judaean Desert, their specifications are reflected to a certain extent in the papyri from the Judaean Desert.[20]

A certain type of Roman legal instrument tends to bear the signatures of seven witnesses. For example Roman wills and testaments called for seven signatures. In addition some documents, of both public and official character, needed to be in the form of double documents. Among the documents from the Judaean Desert there are five certain cases of Greek documents signed by seven witnesses – all of them double documents. *P.Yadin* 11 from 124 CE records a loan on hypothec between a resident of Ein Gedi and a centurion of a Roman unit posted there;[21] *P.Yadin* 19 is a deed of gift by a father to his daughter from 128 CE, *P.Ḥever* 64 is a deed of gift by a mother to her daughter from 129 CE;[22] *P.Yadin* 20 is a concession of rights of inheritance from 130 CE; finally *P.Yadin* 15, described in the document itself as μαρτυροποίημα, i. e. a Roman *testatio*, from 125 CE, records in the text the presence of seven witnesses (καὶ ἐπεβάλοντο μάρτυρες ἑπτά), who signed on the *verso*.

In terms of Roman law, *P.Yadin* 15, a *testatio*, is the only case in which the presence of seven witnesses was to be expected. On the other hand, as pointed out recently by Rudolf Haensch,[23] it is disturbing to find the presence of only five rather than seven witnesses in documents in which we would have expected the signatures of seven witnesses. Thus we find only five witnesses in *P.Yadin* 14, 23,

19 My treatment of the subject in the introduction to Greek documents in Cotton and Yardeni, *Aramaic, Hebrew, and Greek Documentary Texts from Naḥal Ḥever and Other Sites*, 141–3 suffers from some misconceptions (see below on *P.Ḥever* 64) and needs to be considerably revised.

20 In the case of *P.Mur* 18 the handwriting as well as the presence of signatures on the *verso* suggest that this is the outer version of a double document. However, to argue from the presence of signatures on the *verso* that this was a double document involves circular reasoning.

21 I once thought that the involvement of a Roman soldier accounts for the format. However, a similar IOU note between a Roman soldier of the *Legio X Fretensis* and a local resident of Judaea recorded in *P.Mur* 114, to be dated before 132 CE, is a simple document, where the signatures of the witnesses would have appeared at the bottom, which is now missing, see Cotton and Eck, "P.Murabba'at 114 und die Anwesenheit römischer Truppen in den Höhlen des Wadi Murabba'at nach dem Bar Kochba Aufstand."

22 See discussion below.

23 "Zum Verständnis von P.Jericho 16 gr.," *SCI* 20 (2001): 164 ff.

and 26 from the years 125, 130 and 131 CE respectively – all of them summons, *parangeliai*, to the court of the Roman governor, and in *P.Yadin* 16 and *P.Ḥever* 62, certified copies of census declarations from 127 CE. It is precisely in the case of the latter, in certified copies of official documents (like census declarations), that one could have expected seven witnesses to attach their signatures, rather than five. These all but resemble military diplomas on bronze tablets, which are copies of imperial constitutions displayed in Rome bestowing the privilege of Roman citizenship and *conubium* with their wives on soldiers who retired from service with *honesta missio*.

I would like to go back to *P.Ḥever* 64 which, contrary to what was said in its first publication,[24] is a seven-witness document. The papyrus is written in a most peculiar Greek. The ease with which the document could be literally translated, with no adaptation, into Aramaic[25] proves that whoever wrote it had an Aramaic *Urtext* before his eyes. I do not think, however, that an Aramaic version of the document ever existed. Nevertheless, the reconstruction of the witnesses' signatures on the *verso* in the first publication assumed that the practice here followed that of the Semitic double document with the first signature being that of the principal (i. e. the person in whose name the deed was written), and the second, if he/she was illiterate, that of someone else who signed for him/her. The first signature was thus completely reconstructed *ex nihilo*, and the commentary reads:

> There were eight signatures on the *verso* of this deed. The first two signatures belong to the subscription. The first signature ... is likely to have been that of the mother, Salome Gropte, the donor, although she did not write it herself. The second signature is probably that of her husband and guardian, Yosef son of Shimeon, who signed for her – the traces of ink are compatible with his name. Reisha son of Judah, whose signature follows in the third line, is not a witness; what remains of the two letters after his name is not compatible with the Aramaic word for witness שהד; he is likely to be the scribe. The last five signatures belong to the witnesses. Five witnesses are found in Greek, Aramaic and Nabataean documents from the Judaean Desert etc. (*DJD* XXVII, 220).

[Shalom daughter of Menahem in person]	42. [שלם ברת מנחם על נפשה]
Yose[f son of Shimeon wrote for her]	43. יהוס[ף בר שמעון ממרה]
Reisha son of Yehudah wr[ote?]	44. רישה בר יהודה כת[בה]
Malik son of A ...[, witness]	45. מליך בר א ...[שהד]
Yeshua son of Yohanan, wit[ness]	46. ישוע בר יוחנן שה[ד]
Timadushra son of ʻAbdhare[tat, witness]	47. תימדושרא בר עבדחר[תת שהד]
Yehosef son of Shullai, witness	48. יהוסף בר שולי שהד
Y[ohe]saf son of Hana[n]iah, wit[ness]	49. י[וה]סף בר חנ[נ]יה שה[ד]

24 Cotton in *DJD* XXVII, 142.

25 See *DJD* XXVII, 211.

In similar subscriptions in Semitic documents, the two signatures of the subscription normally stand in close proximity to each other in two successive lines, as for example in *P.Mur* 18.[26] Less often the two signatures appear in the same line, or the whole phrase containing the subscription is divided mechanically between two lines as in *P.Ḥever* 8a, the Kfar Baru deed of sale[27] in which the wife is signing because she has just given up all claims to the property, which must have been earmarked for paying her dowry in the case of divorce or death (line 14) '... Shalom daughter of Shimeon, for herself (על נפשה), wrote'; (line 15) 'Eleazar son of Mattata what she said (ממרה).'[28]

It was therefore assumed in the first edition of *P.Ḥever* 64 that the now-lost signature of the principal, Salome Grapte, was followed closely by that of her husband/guardian who 'wrote what she said.' Next came the name of Reisha son of Judah, whom I took to be the scribe – if only to avoid being left with six witnesses, a number unattested elsewhere in the papyri from the Judaean Desert. This consideration encouraged me to read 'wrote' after his name, thus leaving five signatures of five witnesses, which seemed to suit perfectly the general practice in the Roman Near East.

However, this Reisha son of Judah could hardly have been the scribe of this Greek document, since he should be identified with the Reisha of *P.Ḥever* 60, a tax receipt of 125 CE which involved Salome Komaise's first husband, Sammouos son of Shimeon. The receipt ends with two words in Aramaic: רישה כתבה which means literally: 'Reisha (the head, presumably, of the group of tax farmers) wrote it,' but should be interpreted as an authentication rather than as an acknowledgement by a scribe. For it makes no sense for such an acknowledgement to be written in Aramaic rather than in Greek. Thus for example, in *P.Yadin* 15, the scribe writes: 'The writer of this is Theenas son of Simon': ὁ δὲ γράψας τοῦτο Θεένας Σίμωνος; or in *P.Yadin* 17: 'Theenas son of Simon, *liblarius*. I wrote (it)': Θεένας Σίμωνος λιβλάριος ἔγραψα; or as in *P.Yadin* 20: 'was written by Germanus the *liblarius*': ἐγράφη διὰ [Γερ]μανοῦ λ̣ιβλ̣α̣ρ̣ίο[υ]. Reisha is not the scribe of the receipt, but the

26 Yardeni, *Textbook of Aramaic, Hebrew and Nabataean Documentary Texts from the Judaean Desert and Related Material*, 15, corrected Milik's first edition: (*verso*, line 1): 'Zecharia son of Yochanan for himself (על נפשה)'; (line 2): 'wrote Yehosef son of [what he said].'

27 *DJD* XXVII, 36–7 and Fig. 4.

28 This papyrus should have been used to interpret the enigmatic subscription in *P.Ḥever* 13, a concession of all rights by a divorced woman and "the most widely discussed of the papyri published in the last decade and a half," as Ranon Katzoff puts it in his review of *DJD* XXVII (*SCI* 19 (2000): 321). This is a simple deed. I now much prefer Ranon Katzoff's suggestion to my original interpretation. The subscription should read: 'Shlamzion daughter of Yoseph asked. Wrote Mattat son of Shimeon what she said.'

one who issued it. We have here the factitive use of the verb *k-t-b*, that is 'Reisha had it written.' The receipt had to be written in Greek, but Reisha, the man in charge of tax collection and a native of Mahoza, could not write Greek, and therefore needed to have it written by someone else. This observation, therefore, sits somewhat oddly, to say the least, with his being the scribe of *P.Ḥever* 64, as was suggested in the first edition, where it was argued that this may account for the highly Aramaic flavour of the document as well as its extremely ungrammatical Greek.

This entire conception, it can be seen, was wrong. It was borrowed from the Nabataean and Jewish Aramaic tradition. For example, in *P.Yadin* 3, a Nabataean contract from 99 CE, we find seven signatures on the *verso*, but not all of them belong to witnesses.[29] The first signature is of the owner of the deed, followed by the subscriber, afterwards five more signatures follow. The last one is that of the scribe, ספרא, who may or may not be a fifth witness.

Once we have freed ourselves from preconceptions about subscriptions, number of witnesses, etc., we can see *P.Ḥever* 64 for what it was: a seven-witness legal document which followed the Roman custom, and thus seemed to be more acceptable in a Roman court of law – and this should explain the great effort invested in the translation into awkward Greek. There was no subscription of the document on the back by the woman who made the document, executed by her guardian. No eighth signature should have been added beyond the seven signatures attested on the back.

Indeed, what about the first *real* signature of which only few traces are left? The traces could hardly belong to an Aramaic witness since his signature should have been written upwards, towards the knot, as is the custom with Semitic signatures to Greek documents, and as is the case with the six other signatures. Indeed the first signature seems to be a signature in Greek, which started at the knot and was written away from it. This is why so few traces of it are left.

The lesson is simple: one should work at the same time with two contradictory methods: while a conceptual understanding of the diplomatics behind these documents may offer better and safer restorations, one must beware of imposing this conception on a fragmentary text to restore its missing parts. *P.Ḥever* 64 thus conforms to the general legal tradition noticeable in the Greek double documents from the Judaean desert: the signatures on the back are those of witnesses and not of the parties. *P.Yadin* 18, the marriage contract of Shlamzion daughter of Yehuda

29 *P.Yadin* 3, plate 23 + text in Yadin et al., *The Documents from the Bar Kokhba Period in the Cave of Letters: Hebrew, Aramaic and Nabatean-Aramaic Papyri*, 240.

Khthousion to Yehuda Kimber, is the only exception: the signatures of the father and the groom precede the signatures of four or five witnesses.[30]

I would like to end this part of the discussion with a comment on seals. In Latin legal documents the presence of seals is implied by the fact that the witnesses' signatures appear in the genitive case, i. e. 'the seal of so and so.' This is not the formulation practiced in the witnesses' signatures in the papyri from the Judaean Desert. Furthermore, Yigael Yadin testified that in all the deeds found in the Cave of Letters not one – even of those found intact or rolled – was discovered bearing a sealing.[31] It is well known that the Babatha archive was found intact. No seals would have escaped Yadin's eyes. Nor, so far as I am aware, are there any impressions of sealings left on the papyri. The only exception is a sealing discovered in Murabba'at which belonged to *P.Mur* 29, a deed of sale from the first revolt.[32]

The absence of sealing is all the more baffling in view of the fact that in two of the documents which belong to the Babatha archive it is said explicitly – at least so it seems at first sight – that witnesses are attaching their seals: [ἐπὶ τῶν ἐπι]βεβλημένων καὶ ἐπισφραγισαμένων [μαρ]τ̣ύ̣ρ̣[ων π]α̣ρ̣[ήγιλ]ε̣ν̣ Ἰ̣ο̣υ̣[λία Κ]ρ̣[ισπῖν]α̣ θ̣[υ]γ̣ά̣τ̣ηρ̣ Βερνικιανοῦ [ἐπίσκο]π̣ο̣ς τ̣ῶν ⟦ν⟧ ὀ̣ρ̣φ̣α̣νῶ̣ν̣ Ἰησούου Χθουσίωνος Β̣α̣β̣α̣θ̣[α̣ Σί]μ̣ωνος (*P.Yadin* 25).[33] Lewis translates: "Before the attending witnesses who affixed their signatures, Iulia Crispina, daughter of Bernicianus, *episcopus* of the orphans of Yeshua son of Khthousion summons Babatha daughter of Shimeon." "Who affixed their signatures" is by no means a literal translation of ἐπισφραγισαμένων, which means of course: 'who attached their seals.' Lewis cites *P.Dura* 26 of 227 CE where the identical formula appears,[34] and where the editor is also not minded to take it literally. In both cases the names of the witnesses appear in the nominative, not the genitive. In other words, the signatures rather

30 The plate is missing in the Plates volume, and the third signature in Greek is not transcribed in Lewis' volume.

31 Yigael Yadin, *The Finds from the Bar Kokhba Period in the Cave of Letters* (Jerusalem: IES, 1963), 118. The two seal impressions which he discusses on 118 ff., and which can be seen on plate 14 of Yadin et al., *The Documents from the Bar Kokhba Period in the Cave of Letters: Hebrew, Aramaic and Nabatean-Aramaic Papyri*, were found together with the letters.

32 P. Benoit, J.T. Milik, and R. de Vaux, *Les grottes de Murabba'at*, Discoveries in the Judaean Desert II (Oxford: Clarendon Press, 1961), 140 ff. and plate XLIc. I am excluding of course the early seal impressions found in Wadi Daliyeh and published in Mary Joan Winn Leith, *Wadi Daliyah I: The Wadi Daliyeh Seal Impressions*, Discoveries in the Judaean Desert XXIV (Oxford: Clarendon Press, 1997).

33 The same formula occurs in *P.Yadin* 26; cf. *P.Dura* 26 and 18.

34 For another formula which appears in both collections see *P.Ḥever* 63, line 1 (127 CE) and *P.Dura* 30, line 1 (232 CE).

than the seals attest the presence of the witnesses. ['Επὶ τῶν ἐπι]βεβλημένων καὶ ἐπισφραγισαμένων [μαρ]τ̣ύ̣ρ̣[ων] is presumed to be a fossilized formula.

I would like to end with guardians and subscribers. I am afraid I have to repeat some of the things I have said elsewhere, in order to point out precisely where some modification is needed.[35]

A strong argument for thinking that documents written in Greek were intended for a Roman court of law is the presence of a male guardian to represent a woman, and his total absence from the Semitic documents. This argument gains force when we observe that a single term – *epitropos* – is used for both the guardian of a woman as well as for that of a minor. Roman law, at least originally, did not distinguish between the two. The documents may reflect the wording used in proclamations by the Roman authorities, e. g. in the provincial edict, which demanded the representation of a woman in court by a guardian and made provision for the nomination of guardians for orphans. Thinking in Latin but writing in Greek, the Roman authorities used the term ἐπίτροπος for both kinds of *tutor*. *P.Ḥever* 69 from Aristoboulias, near Hebron, shows that the confusion between the two was not confined to Arabia, but that the same usage prevailed in Judaea.

The presence of a legal representative of a woman is well attested in contemporary Egyptian papyri, where he is designated κύριος. The κύριος goes back to Greek law. As the term indicates, the κύριος was once the woman's lord and master. However, with time women could and did own property and the κύριος was no longer the person with (complete) authority over the woman. His function degenerated therefore into that of an assistant of the woman in the performance of certain legal actions, mere lip service to an older legal system. In this reduced and humble form he survived in Ptolemaic Egypt, but perhaps not in the Seleucid sphere of influence, since he is absent from the Greek papyri from Dura Europos and from the recently published papyri from Mesopotamia. He might have vanished altogether from Egyptian legal documents were it not for the Roman system which insisted on his formal presence, expressed by the common formula μετὰ τοῦ κυρίου 'with her guardian' in legal transactions performed by women – a formula never attested in the documents from the Judaean Desert.

For all these reasons the appearance of the guardian of a woman in the Greek documents from the Judaean Desert cannot be attributed to the influence of Greek

---

35 See above all Hannah M. Cotton, "Subscriptions and Signatures in the Papyri from the Judaean Desert: The χειροχρήστης," *JJP* 25 (1995): 29–40 [above, pp. 115–25].; Hannah M. Cotton, "The Guardian (ἐπίτροπος) of a Woman in the Documents from the Judaean Desert," *ZPE* 118 (1997): 267–73 [below, pp. 431–41].

law, but only to the advent of the Romans. Here, as in Egypt, his passive and formal role – only his presence is recorded in the formula συνπαρόντος αὐτῇ ἐπιτρόπου – makes it eminently clear that this is just a matter of formal procedure required by the courts for which the Greek contracts were intended, namely Roman courts of law where a woman could not appear without a male representative.

The ἐπίτροπος could double up as the subscriber – the ὑπογραφεύς, to use the Egyptian term, or χειροχρήστης, to use the picturesque term once found in a document from the Judaean Desert (*P.Ḥever* 61). The subscriber is the one who writes the subscription for those who are legally competent to do so, but who happen to be illiterate (or otherwise incapable of writing), when a subscription and/or a signature in their own hand is required to render a document valid. I think that the fact that a subscription by the woman was needed is proof that she was a legal personality and the guardian a mere formality. For example Babelis son of Menahem fulfils both functions for Babatha in *P.Yadin* 27: Βα̣βαθας Σίμω̣[ν]ος, συνπαρόντος αὐτῇ [ἐπιτρόπου] κ̣[α]ὶ̣ ὑπὲρ αὐτῆς ὑπογράφοντος Βα̣βελ̣ι̣[ς] Μαναήμου. However, the subscriber is to be distinguished from the *epitropos*, first in that he is found also in Semitic documents, as we have just seen, and secondly in that he is present also in documents in which the principal is a man. In other words, the subscriber is by no means unique to one legal tradition and his presence does not anticipate proceedings in a Roman court of law.

The same is true in the papyri from Egypt: the subscriber is distinguished from the guardian. He subscribes for the woman, and sometimes he is said to be subscribing for both the woman and her guardian since both are illiterate. The latter phenomenon is never found in the documents from the Judaean Desert. On the other hand, in *P.Yadin* 15 we find something for which I believe there is no Egyptian parallel.

In this Roman *testatio* Babatha's guardian for this matter, Judah son of Eleazar Khthousion, did not write the subscription for her; instead, Eleazar son of Eleazar wrote it for her, since her illiteracy prevented her from doing it herself: 'Babatha deposed as aforestated through her guardian for this matter, Judah son of Khthousion, who was present and subscribed. [second hand] I, Babatha daughter of Simon, have deposed through my guardian Judah son of Khthousion against John son of Eglas and 'Abdoöbdas son of Ellouthas, guardians of my orphan son Jesus, according to the aforestated conditions. I, Eleazar son of Eleazar, wrote for her by request, because of her being illiterate.'

It seems clear that διὰ τὸ αὐτῆ̣ς μὴ ε<ἰ>δένα<ι> γράμματα, 'because she did not know her letters' in Babatha's case, does not mean that she could not write Greek, but that she was illiterate in any language. A Greek subscription was not required: Judah son of Eleazar, her guardian, wrote his own subscription in Aramaic: 'Judah son of Khthousion lord of Babatha: in my presence Babatha confirmed all that is written above. Judah wrote this.' Why does the guardian subscribe as well? It would seem that this duplication is legally redundant. One wonders again and again, when reading the legal documents from the Judaean Desert, especially those written in Greek, whose legal advice had been sought and taken.

Survival, Adaptation and Extinction: Nabataean and Jewish Aramaic versus Greek in the Legal Documents from the Cave of Letters in Naḥal Ḥever

The genesis of much of the documentary material found in the caves of the Judaean Desert lay in the two Jewish revolts against Rome: the so-called Great Revolt of 66–70 CE and the Bar Kokhba revolt of 132–136 CE.[1] The upheavals caused by the two revolts drove scores of Jews from their homes in the provinces of Judaea and Arabia and made them hide their documents, mostly legal documents, in the caves of Wadi Murabba'at, Naḥal Ḥever, Naḥal Ṣe'elim (Wadi Seyâl), Naḥal Mishmar, Naḥal David (Wadi Sdeir), in two caves near Jericho, and in a cave above Ein Gedi.[2]

In this paper, devoted to the languages used in legal documents written in what was until 106 CE the Nabataean Kingdom, and after that date became the Roman province of Arabia,[3] I shall rely on the evidence of two family archives brought to the Cave of Letters in Naḥal Ḥever by Jews from the village of Maḥoz 'Eglatain (Maḥoza), probably located at the southern tip of the Dead Sea:[4] the

1 For the date of the conclusion of the Bar Kokhba revolt see Werner Eck and Gideon Foerster, "Ein Triumphbogen für Hadrian im Tal von Beth Shean bei Tel Shalem," *JRA* 12 (1999): 301 ff. and esp. 312–3.

2 See usefully Stephen J. Pfann, "History of the Judaean Desert Discoveries," and "Sites in the Judaean Desert where Texts have been found," in Emanuel Tov, with the collaboration of Stephen J. Pfann, *Companion Volume to the Dead Sea Scrolls on Microfiche Edition* (Leiden: Brill, 1995), 97–119. For Cave Abi'or and the Cave of the Sandal near Jericho see Hanan Eshel and Boaz Zissu, "Jericho: Archaeological Introduction," in *Miscellaneous Texts from the Judaean Desert*, Discoveries in the Judaean Desert XXXVIII (Oxford: Clarendon Press, 2000), 3–20. For the two Greek papyri found near Ein Gedi see Nahum Cohen, "New Greek Papyri from a Cave in the Vicinity of Ein Gedi," *SCI* 25 (2006): 87–95. For a survey of the final publications of all the documents from the Judaean Desert see Hannah M. Cotton, "Documentary Texts from the Judaean Desert: A Matter of Nomenclature," *SCI* 20 (2001): 113–19.

3 A discussion of the situation in Judaea is unavoidable, but is subordinate to this main theme.

4 For Maḥoz 'Eglatain (Maḥoza) see Hannah M. Cotton and Jonas C. Greenfield, "Babatha's Patria: Maḥoza, Maḥoz 'Eglatain and Ẓo'ar," *ZPE* 107 (1995): 126–34 [below, pp. 275–83].

Article note: First published in Leonhard Schumacher and Oliver Stoll, eds., *Sprache und Kultur in der kaiserzeitlichen Provinz Arabia: Althistorische Beiträgezur Erforschung von Akkulturationsphänomenen im römischen Nahen Osten* (St. Katharinen: Scripta Mercaturae Verlag, 2003), 1–11, with the following note: not for the first time I thank my friend David Wasserstein for his excellent suggestions.

https://doi.org/10.1515/9783110770438-010

Babatha archive[5] and the archive of Salome Komaïse daughter of Levi.[6] The material spans a period of just over 70 years (ca. 60 to 132 CE),[7] and the great majority of documents were written by, or at least involve, Jews. However, amongst the documents in the two archives we have the longest preserved legal texts in the Nabataean language[8] – some of them involving non-Jews.[9] The people attested in the documents belong to a village society at a time when the majority of the population in this area consisted of village dwellers and the papyri, like others from elsewhere in the Roman Near East, thus reflect the legal habits of the otherwise silent majority.

Three languages are represented in the archives from Nabataea/Arabia: Nabataean Aramaic, Jewish Aramaic and Greek. Until the annexation of the Nabataean realm to the Roman empire all legal documents, whether involving Jews or non-Jews, were written in Nabataean Aramaic.[10] There are *no* documents written either in Greek or in Jewish Aramaic from the Nabataean period. Nabataean continued

5 The Greek part of the Babatha archive, *P.Yadin* 5, 11–35, is published in Naphtali Lewis, *The Documents from the Bar Kokhba Period in the Cave of Letters. Greek Papyri*, Judean Desert Studies II (Jerusalem: IES, 1989); the Semitic part, *P.Yadin* 1–4, 6–10, is published in Yigael Yadin et al., *The Documents from the Bar Kokhba Period in the Cave of Letters: Hebrew, Aramaic and Nabatean-Aramaic Papyri*, Judean Desert Studies III (Jerusalem: IES, 2002).

6 The archive of Salome Komaïse, *P.Hever* 12, 32(?), 60–65, is published in Hannah M. Cotton and Ada Yardeni, *Aramaic, Hebrew, and Greek Documentary Texts from Naḥal Ḥever and Other Sites*, Discoveries in the Judaean Desert XXVII (Oxford: Clarendon Press, 1997). Five or six other Nabataean documents, not published in this volume, are thought to belong to this archive as well, and like all the papyri in this volume are designated *P.Ḥever*: 1) *P.Hever* 2, published as *XHevSe* 2 in Ada Yardeni, *Textbook of Aramaic, Hebrew and Nabataean Documentary Texts from the Judaean Desert and Related Material*, Vol. I (Jerusalem: The Hebrew University Press, 2000), 290–1 (see Vol. II, 95 for the English translation); 2) *P.Starcky* (= *P.Hever* 1), published originally by Jean Starcky, "Un contrat nabatéen sur papyrus," *RB* 61 (1954): 161–81, and rearranged by Ada Yardeni, "The Decipherment and Restoration of Legal Texts from the Judaean Desert: A Reexamination of Papyrus Stracky (P.Yadin 36)," *SCI* 20 (2001): 121–37; and 3) three or four unpublished Nabataean papyri, now at the Israel Museum, which were found together with *P.Starcky* (= *P.Hever* 1) and *P.Hever* 2. See in detail Hanan Eshel, "Another Document from the Archive of Salome Komaïse Daughter of Levi," *SCI* 21 (2002): 169–71.

7 The earliest is *P.Starcky* (= *P.Hever* 1) (see previous note), and the latest is the Greek *P.Yadin* 27 of 19 August 132 CE.

8 The only comparable legal texts in Nabataean Aramaic would be the legal texts found on the rock-cut tombs from Mada'in Salih, in the Hijaz (northern Saudi Arabia); see John F. Healey, *The Nabataean Tomb Inscriptions of Mada'in Salih* (Oxford: Oxford University Press, 1993).

9 *P.Yadin* 1 and 2. The latter records the sale to a Nabataean of the same piece of land sold in *P.Yadin* 3 to Babatha's father; there is no explanation for the presence of *P.Yadin* 1 in the Babatha archive.

10 *P.Yadin* 1–4; *P.Starcky* (= *P.Hever* 1), *P.Hever* 2 and three or four others (see above n. 6).

to be used by Jews as the language of legal documents after annexation,[11] and we also have a few documents in Jewish Aramaic, also written by Jews, from this period;[12] two of the latter bear strong resemblance in both script and idiom to the Nabataean documents.[13] However, as against two Nabataean contracts and three written in Jewish Aramaic, we have altogether 32 Greek documents from the period between 106 and 132 CE in Arabia, that is in the first 25 years of the province: 26 Greek documents in the Babatha archive[14] and 6 Greek documents in the archive of Salome Komaïse daughter of Levi.[15] The first safely dated Greek document is *P.Yadin* 5 from 110 CE[16] and the last one is *P.Yadin* 27 from 132 CE. Thus the intimate connection between provincialization and the use of Greek in legal documents from Nabataea/Arabia is firmly established. It is hard to know though whether or not Nabataean continued to serve alongside Greek as the language of legal documents in the province of Arabia. True, no Nabataean legal document has been found after *P.Yadin* 9 of 122 CE. However, there are no legal documents in any language from the area after 132 CE and until the 6th century CE: a gap of three hundred and eighty years separates the latest legal document in the Babatha archive, *P.Yadin* 27 of 132 CE, from the first safely dated legal contract from Nessana, *P.Nessana* 16 of 512 CE;[17] and over four hundred years separate it from *P.Petra* 1, of 538 CE, published very recently in the first volume of the Petra Papyri (ca. 140 rolls of documentary papyri, all dating to the 6th CE, discovered at the end of 1993 in a Byzantine church in Petra).[18] Both *P.Petra* 1 and *P.Nessana* 16 like most of the papyri in the corpus to which they belong are written in Greek.[19] All that can be said in confidence is that Greek is likely to have remained the lan-

11 *P.Yadin* 6 and 9 dated to the years 119/120 and 122 CE respectively.

12 *P.Yadin* 7, 8, 10 of the years 120, 122 and 125–128 CE respectively. *P.Hever* 12 of 131 CE, a receipt for tax or rent could be added.

13 *P.Yadin* 7 and *P.Yadin* 8; cf. Yadin et al., *The Documents from the Bar Kokhba Period in the Cave of Letters: Hebrew, Aramaic and Nabatean-Aramaic Papyri*, 73 f. and 109 respectively.

14 See above n. 5.

15 *P.Hever* 60–65 (see above n. 6). A few other fragmentary Greek documents may also come from Arabia, *P.Hever* 66, 68, 70–73.

16 There is no certainty about the provenance of *P.Hever* 66 of 99 or 109 CE.

17 Casper J. Kraemer, *Excavations at Nessana III: Non-Literary Papyri* (Princeton: Princeton University Press, 1958).

18 Jaakko Frösén, Antti Arjava, and Marjo Lentinen, *The Petra Papyri I* (Amman: ACOR, 2002). Both Nessana and Petra belonged in the 6th century CE to Palaestina Salutaris/Tertia, which included southern Jordan, the Negev and the Sinai – territories which belonged to the Nabataean kingdom when it was redacted into the province of Arabia.

19 Some of the 7th-century papyri from Nessana have Arabic as well; cf. Hannah M. Cotton, W.E.H. Cockle, and Fergus Millar, "The Papyrology of the Roman near East: A Survey," *JRS* 85 (1995): nos. 571–609: 'Appendix: Documents from Nessana of the Early Islamic Period.'

guage of legal documents from 106 CE to the 6th and 7th centuries in the territories which once belonged to Nabataea/Arabia. We do not know when it ousted Nabataean Aramaic altogether.

Surely the linguistic situation reflected in legal documents does not necessarily convey a true picture of the linguistic situation outside them.[20] The explanation for the use of languages in legal documents should be sought elsewhere than in the presumed spoken languages – if only to avoid a circular argument. Indeed, elsewhere I have argued that the use of Greek in legal documents in the Roman province of Arabia is one of the reasons for believing that these documents were intended for a Roman court of law.[21] As is well known, in their communications with the subject populations of the Roman Near East, the Romans too used the medium of the Greek language.[22]

Nevertheless, one observes a marked difference between the language used to pen the documents themselves and the language(s) used in the subscriptions and signatures accompanying them – in other words between the language used by the scribes and the language of the parties.[23] The latter must be closer to the spoken language of the society reflected in the documents. The employment of scribes and the existence of signatures and subscriptions in Nabataean and Jewish Aramaic in a legal document written in Greek strongly suggests that we are *not* dealing here with hellenized – not even with semi-hellenized – populations.

The question of the language spoken in the former Nabataean Kingdom is closely tied up with the hard to disentangle and highly controversial issue of the ethnic identity of the Nabataeans and their relationship to the Arabs with whom

---

20 The difficulties of using written documents as evidence for the spoken language are well expressed in a recent discussion of the languages in Palestine: "In some cases writing may reflect no more than scribal practice. And in all cases writing is necessarily related to speech in highly complex and sometimes highly attenuated ways," Seth Schwartz, "Language, Power and Identity in Ancient Palestine," *Past & Present* 148 (1995): 13.

21 Hannah M. Cotton, "Jewish Jurisdiction under Roman Rule: Prolegomena," in *Zwischen den Reichen: Neues Testament und römische Herrschaft. Vorträge auf der ersten Konferenz der European Association for Biblical Studies*, ed. Michael Labahn and Jürgen Zangenberg (Tübingen: Francke Verlag, 2002), 13–28 [below, pp. 485–99].

22 See Werner Eck, "The Language of Power: Latin in the Inscriptions of Judaea/Syria Palaestina," in *Semitic Papyrology in Context: A Climate of Creativity*, ed. Lawrence H. Schiffman (Leiden – Boston: Brill, 2003), 123–44.

23 See Hannah M. Cotton, "Subscriptions and Signatures in the Papyri from the Judaean Desert: The χειροχρήστης," *JJP* 25 (1995): 29–40 [above, pp. 115–25].; Hannah M. Cotton, "'Diplomatics' or External Aspects of the Legal Documents from the Judaean Desert: Prolegomena," in *Rabbinic Law in its Roman and Near Eastern Context*, ed. Catherine Hezser (Tübingen: Mohr Siebeck, 2003), 49–61 [above, pp. 147–60].

they are often identified, especially in the literary sources.[24] It is not my purpose here to get involved in this debate, nor to join forces with one camp or the other. Nor is it necessary to do so. Whatever language/languages was/were spoken in the area, the traditional language of legal documents in Nabataea/Arabia, as in Judaea, was Aramaic: Nabataean Aramaic in Arabia and Jewish Aramaic in Judaea. Both languages descended from the Reichsaramäisch, the *lingua franca* of the Persian period in what later became the Roman Near East.[25] Part of their inheritance included legal formulae transmitted for generations in this language by scribes and notaries. With the advent of the Greeks, but even more so with that of the Romans, the Greek language and the Hellenistic legal tradition entered the scene. From then on it competes successfully with Aramaic – but by no means ousts it in Judaea as we shall see[26] – for political reasons rather than linguistic ones: this is the language of the rulers, the judges and the courts.[27]

The prior claim of Aramaic to be the language of legal contracts in Arabia and Judaea, whether written by Jews or Nabataeans, and at least in Judaea both before and after provincialization, can be proved from the documents themselves as well as from the Jewish rabbinic sources. Let us start with the latter.[28]

The interchange between Hebrew and Aramaic in the Mishnaic text is well known to those who read it in the original languages, even if it is lost on those who read the texts in translation. Furthermore, its true significance, so far as I can tell, has never been pointed out. Probably because those 'in the know' take it for granted. The Rabbis certainly did not write contracts;[29] we do not have one single contract in the whole of the *Mishnah* or the *Toseftah*, only contractual formulae. These formulae, unlike the legal discussion in which they are embedded which is conducted in Hebrew,[30] are written in Aramaic – thus proving not only that they are of a much older vintage than the Hebrew interpretation, but also that the language of contracts in daily use at the time was Aramaic. Separating the

24 See most recently Jan Restö, *The Arabs in Antiquity* (London: Routledge, 2003), 364–91 ('The Nabataean Problem').

25 Joseph Naveh and Jonas C. Greenfield, "Hebrew and Aramaic in the Persian Period," in *The Cambridge History of Judaism, Volume 1: Introduction: The Persian Period* (Cambridge: Cambridge University Press, 1984), 115–29.

26 *Contra* Naphtali Lewis, "The Demise of the Aramaic Document in the Dead Sea Region," *SCI* 20 (2001): 178–81.

27 See above, text to n. 22.

28 I owe a great debt to Shlomo Naeh for the following discussion.

29 See Haggai Misgav, "Jewish Epigraphic Sources and the Traditions Reflected in Talmudic Literature" Unpublished PhD dissertation submitted to the Hebrew University of Jerusalem (1999), 118 ff. (Hebrew).

30 The so-called *leshon ḥakhamim* on which see below.

contractual formulae from their interpretation is easily done since the *Mishnah*, the interpretation, is written in Hebrew, whereas the quotation from the contract discussed there is in Aramaic. It is harder of course to bring it out in translation, although Danby[31] tried to use old English forms for the Aramaic. Thus, to take an example almost at random:

> (*mKet.* 4, 7) If the husband had not written out a *ketubba* [marriage contract] for his wife, she may still claim 200 [*zuz*] if she was a virgin or one *mina* if she was a widow, since that is a condition enjoined by the court [i.e. "tacit conditions, binding upon all, even if not written in a specific marriage contract"[32]]. If he assigned her a field worth one *mina* instead of 200 *zuz*, and did not write ...

After the word 'write' the text goes on in Aramaic to cite what the husband has written:

> 'All my goods are for thy *ketubba*.'

And immediately the text reverts to Hebrew:

> he is still liable, since that is a condition enjoined by the court.

Later on in the same chapter (*mKet.* 4, 10–11),[33] we read in Hebrew:

> If he had not written for her ...

And now we go into Aramaic:

> 'Male children which you will have by me shall inherit thy *ketubba* besides the portion which they received with their brethren'

And now back to Hebrew:

> he is still liable [thereto], since this is a condition enjoined by the court. [If he had not written for her],

31 Herbert Danby, *The Mishnah: Translated from the Hebrew with Introduction and Brief Explanatory Notes* (Oxford: Oxford University Press, 1933).
32 Mordechai Akiva Friedman, *Jewish Marriage in Palestine: A Cairo Geniza Study*, Vol. I (Tel Aviv: Tel Aviv University Press, 1980), 15.
33 Cf. *mKet.* 13, 3.

And again Aramaic:

> 'Female children which you will have by me shall dwell in my house and receive maintenance from my goods until they marry husbands,'

And now back to Hebrew:

> he is still liable [thereto], since this is a condition enjoined by the court.

This phenomenon is apparent not only in marriage contracts, but also in simple commercial contracts, such as a contract of lease (*mBM* 9, 3):

> If a man leased a field from a fellow and he let it lie fallow, they assess how much it was likely to have yielded and he must pay the owner accordingly, for this is how they write ...

And we go into Aramaic:

> 'If I shall suffer the land to lie fallow and do not till it, I will pay thee at the rate of its highest yield.'

The same principle appears in stipulations concerning the validity of any contract (*mBB* 10, 2):

> An unfolded document [simple document] requires two witnesses; a folded one [double document] three. If an unfolded document has but one witness or a folded one but two, both are invalid. If there was written ...

And now the text goes into Aramaic:

> '100 *zuz* which are 20 *selas*'

And back to Hebrew for the commentary:

> he can claim only 20 *selas*; and if [there was written] ...

Again we switch over to Aramaic:

> '100 *zuz* which are 30 *selas*'

And back to Hebrew:

> he can claim only 100 *zuz*.

Once the principle is grasped it does not come as a great surprise to find in two Aramaic documents from the Judaean Desert, one a writ of divorce and the other a renunciation of claims after a divorce, a divorce formula almost identical to the one found embedded inside the Hebrew text of the Mishnaic discussion of the deed of divorce. *mGitt.* 9, 3 reads:

> Let this be from me thy *writ of divorce* and *letter of dismissal* and *deed of liberation*, that thou mayest marry whatsoever man thou wilt.

In *P.Murabba'at* 19 of 71/2 CE the husband tells his wife: 'So that you will have a *writ of divorce* and *a deed of dismissal* from me,' using two of the synonyms for a divorce document mentioned in the *Mishnah*.[34] And in *P.Hever* 13 of 134/5 CE, the wife, in a deed of renunciation of all claims, uses yet another combination of the same formula to recall the deed of divorce she gave her husband: '[you] who (have) had *a deed of divorce and dismissal* from me.'[35]

The *Mishnah*'s use of multiplied synonyms is intended presumably to cover and exhaust the variations attested in various divorce contracts of its time, whereas the actual contracts, as we can see, use only two terms or even just one.

We may envisage the Mishnaic discussion as a process whereby the rabbis comment in Hebrew on contracts written from beginning to end in Aramaic. The commentary cites the formulae *verbatim* in the language in which they were written, namely Aramaic. The rabbinic discussions eventually redacted in the *Mishnah* and the *Toseftah* continued in this manner long after the documents had dried up. This fact alone should leave no doubt in our minds that contracts continued to be written in Aramaic in Judaea.[36]

The discovery of letters from real life written in Hebrew in Wadi Murabba'at and Naḥal Ḥever has discredited the view that the Hebrew of the Mishnah (*leshon ḥakhamim*) was an artificial language created for the purpose of the legal discussions contained in the rabbinic sources; and this is not only because of the similarity of the Hebrew in the letters to the Hebrew language of the *Mishnah*, but no less because it differs from it in grammar, vocabulary and syntax: in other words it was another register of Hebrew.[37] However, even if Hebrew was the language spoken in

---

34 See Reuven Yaron, "The Mesadah Bill of Divorce," in *Studi in onore di Edoardo Volterra VI* (Milano: Giuffrè, 1971), 433–55.

35 See Hannah M. Cotton and Elisha Qimron, "XḤev/Se ar 13 of 134 or 135 C.E.: A Wife's Renunciation of Claims," *JJS* 49 (1998): 108–118.

36 *Contra* Lewis, "The Demise of the Aramaic Document in the Dead Sea Region."

37 Eduard Yechezkel Kutscher, "The Hebrew and Aramaic Letters of Bar Koseba and his Contemporaries: Part II: The Hebrew Letters," *Lĕšonénu* 26 (1961): 7–23 = *Hebrew and Aramaic Studies* (Jerusalem: Magnes Press, 1977), 54–70 (Hebrew). Many new insights into the topic were pre-

Judaea at least until the end of the Bar Kokhba revolt, nonetheless the language of legal contracts remained Jewish Aramaic. The majority of legal contracts even at the time of the Bar Kokhba revolt, when the leader must have encouraged the use of Hebrew,[38] are written in Aramaic.[39] The reality is represented almost plastically in one of the double documents from the second revolt. The inner text of *P.Hever* 8 (135 CE), that is the part which is hidden, was written in Aramaic, whereas the outer text was written in Hebrew. In other words, the legally binding text, the inner one, is written in the normal language of legal documents at the time,[40] whereas the Hebrew, displayed on the outside, advertises the ideology of the now independent Jewish state.

The predominance of the Aramaic legal practice is often revealed in the language and formulae of the Greek and Hebrew contracts.[41] Even if most of the Greek contracts from the Judaean Desert were written by professional scribes whose Greek falls in with the post classical *Koine* familiar from the Old and New Testaments, inscriptions, and papyri from Hellenistic and Roman Egypt and other sites in the Near East, nonetheless sometimes the Aramaic *Urtext* comes very close to the surface, as in *P.Hever* 64.

P.Hever 64 is a deed of gift made in 129 CE by Salome Grapte in favour of her daughter Salome Komaïse. The Greek of this document is singularly ungrammatical and non-idiomatic. The scribe pays no attention to case endings and gender. The ease with which the document can be literally translated, with no adaptation, into the presumed Aramaic *Urtext* proves this point incontrovertibly.[42] I shall not

---

sented in a lecture given on 29 January 2003 at the Institute for Advanced Studies in Jerusalem by Dr. Yohanan Breuer of the Hebrew University.

38 Yigael Yadin, *Bar-Kokhba: The Rediscovery of the Legendary Hero of the Second Jewish Revolt Against Rome* (London: Random House, 1971), 181. It has now been shown in two independent studies that the Hebrew contracts *P.Murabba'at* 29 and 30 should be dated to the first revolt when a similar ideology encouraged the use of Hebrew rather than the normal Aramaic in legal contracts, see Hannah M. Cotton, "The Languages of the Legal and Administrative Documents from the Judaean Desert," *ZPE* 125 (1999): 220 ff. [above, pp. 129 ff.]; Hanan Eshel, Magen Broshi, and T.A.J. Jull, "Documents from Wadi Murabba'at and the Status of Jerusalem during the Bar Kokhba Revolt," in *The Refuge Caves of the Bar Kokhba Revolt*, ed. Hanan Eshel and David Amit (Jerusalem: IES, 1998), 233 ff. (Hebrew).

39 See Cotton, Cockle, and Millar, "The Papyrology of the Roman near East: A Survey," nos. 293–331.

40 Joseph Naveh, *On Sherd and Papyrus* (Jerusalem: Magnes Press, 1992), 102 (Hebrew).

41 In the case of the Semitic contracts I have to rely on the experts in the field. However, I have been assured by Dr. Ada Yardeni that the leases of the Bar Kokhba administration, *P.Yadin* 42–44, albeit written in Hebrew, all but betray the Aramaic *Vorlage* which they try to imitate.

42 See Cotton and Yardeni, *Aramaic, Hebrew, and Greek Documentary Texts from Naḥal Ḥever and Other Sites*, 207 for my exercise in translating the Greek deed of gift back into Aramaic. I

dwell on mistakes in Greek, but I would like to point out some glaring Semitisms which betray the writer's servile adherence to the Aramaic. In lines 6–7 we read: εἰς δόσιν ἀπὸ τῆς σήμερον δόσιν αἰωνίου. The odd expression δόσιν αἰωνίου seems to be a literal translation of the Aramaic phrase 'an eternal gift' / MTNT 'LM, here cast in the construct state[43] – a linguistic formation common to Semitic languages. In Greek one would say εἰς τὸν ἀεὶ χρόνον, or ἐπ' ἀεί, or μέχρ[ι] παντός, or εἰς τὸν ἅπαντα χρόνον. In fact the whole expression ἀπὸ τῆς σήμερον δόσιν αἰωνίου is probably an attempt to translate the Aramaic expression 'an eternal gift from this day and forever' (MTNT 'LM MYMH DNH WL 'LM) found in Aramaic deeds. This could be expressed in Greek simply by εἰς δόσιν ἀπὸ τοῦ νῦν εἰς τὸν ἀεὶ χρόνον.

In line 8 we find the tautology κῆπον φοινεικῶνος, namely 'an orchard of a date orchard' (even worse is the κῆπον φοινεικώνων of the outer text, line 26). Again the expression seems to be a literal translation of the construct state in Aramaic: 'orchard of dates' (GNT TMRY'), found in the Aramaic documents from Maḥoza.

Finally, the document specifies the water rights attached to the orchard: σὺν ὕδατος αὐτῆς ἐφ' ἡμερῶν ἑπτὰ εἰς ἑπτὰ ἡμέραν τετάρτῃ ἡ[μ]ιωρ<ί>αν μίαν (lines 8–9 and 27–28). The fantastic circumlocution ἐφ' ἡμερῶν ἑπτὰ εἰς ἑπτὰ ἡμέραν conveys the notion of a 'week' which could simply be expressed in Greek by the word ἑβδομάς. Thus the whole expression ἐφ' ἡμερῶν ἑπτὰ εἰς ἑπτὰ ἡμέραν τετάρτῃ 'on the fourth day of the week' renders YWM 'ARB'H BŠBT that we find in the Nabataean and Aramaic documents in the same context.

I would like to conclude with the Nabataean legal documents. The publication of the Nabataean papyri of the Babatha archive (*P.Yadin* 1–4, 6, 9) and the archive of Salome Komaïse[44] constitute a substantial addition to the body of Nabataean law – so far known only from the funerary legal documents from Mada'in Salih. This is certainly the beginning of a new epoch for the study of Nabataean law.[45]

---

plundered for parallels *P.Yadin* 7, an Aramaic deed of gift executed by Babatha's father in favour of her mother.

43 Two nouns dependent on each other; the second one is in the genitive case.

44 See above, n. 10.

45 Cf. Healey, *The Nabataean Tomb Inscriptions of Mada'in Salih*; cf. also John F. Healey, "Sources for the Study of Nabataean Law," *New Arabian Studies* 1 (1993): 203–14; Jonas C. Greenfield, "Studies in the Legal Terminology of the Nabatean Funerary Inscriptions," in *Henoch Yalon Memorial Volume*, ed. Eduard Yechezkel Kutscher, Saul Lieberman, and Menaḥem Zevi Kaddari (Jerusalem: Kiryat Sefer, 1974), 64–83 (Hebrew); I.Sh. Shiffman, "To the Character of the Nabataean Private Law according to the Epigraphic Sources," *Palestinski Sbornik* 11 (1964): 16–24 (Russian. I am grateful to Alexander Yakobson for the translation). Geoffrey Khan, "The Pre-Islamic Background of Muslim Legal Formularies," *ARAM* 6 (1994): 193–224 concludes that Arabic legal formularies had their roots in Jewish legal tradition; more likely they derive from a common Aramaic legal koiné.

Some beginnings have already been made. In an excellent article, recently published, Baruch Levine points out that Jewish Aramaic contracts and Nabataean Aramaic contracts "share a common vocabulary of Aramaic 'legalese' consisting of idioms and formulae that produce a similar effect on the reader."[46] However, they "differ in the way each proliferates legal formulas to embrace all sorts of conceivable, often redundant provisions. Normally, in Jewish Aramaic documents this is achieved by stringing along Hebrew or Aramaic terms of reference, usually derived from known Jewish sources" ... whereas "scribes writing in Nabataean-Aramaic proliferated legal formulas by using Arabic equivalents of the Aramaic terms of reference."[47]

Even looking from the outside, so to say, at the external aspect of a Nabataean legal document can prove the existence of a long-standing Nabataean legal tradition. Ada Yardeni's ground-breaking studies of the Nabataean documents have made me realise that in the Nabataean Kingdom, later to become the province of Arabia, there existed a local tradition of writing double documents with its own peculiar customs, which continued into the Roman period, as displayed in *P.Yadin* 7, a Jewish Aramaic document of 120 CE.[48] No Roman encouragement was needed to establish or resuscitate the use of the double document in this part of the Roman Near East.[49]

In a new edition of the earliest Nabataean double document, *P.Starcky* (= *P.Hever* 1), Ada Yardeni points out a phenomenon which, so far as I know, has never been observed before.[50] The inner (or upper) text starts already on the *verso*, towards its bottom. Then the papyrus was turned over foot to head, rather than merely being turned sideways from back to front. This is in fact the only way to keep both parts of the inner text (the beginning on the *verso* and its continuation on the *recto*) on the same part of the papyrus so that both could later be rolled and tied. The purpose of this complicated arrangement was to prevent tamper-

---

46 Baruch A. Levine, "The Various Workings of the Aramaic Legal Tradition: Jews and Nabateans in the Naḥal Ḥever Archive," in *The Dead Sea Scrolls: Fifty Years after their Discovery 1947–1997*, ed. Lawrence H. Schiffman, Emanuel Tov, and James C. Vanderkam (Jerusalem: IES, 2000), 851.

47 Levine, 844 and 845.

48 It shares other features with the Nabataean documents of the archive; see commentary to *P.Yadin* 7 in Yadin et al., *The Documents from the Bar Kokhba Period in the Cave of Letters: Hebrew, Aramaic and Nabatean-Aramaic Papyri*, esp. 73–4.

49 Contrary to other areas, where Elizabeth Meyer believes that Rome exercised an influence on the format of documents in other languages as well. I am grateful to Dr. Meyer for allowing me to see the relevant chapter in her then forthcoming book, *Legitimacy and Law in the Roman World* (Cambridge: Cambridge University Press, 2004).

50 See Yardeni, "The Decipherment and Restoration of Legal Texts from the Judaean Desert: A Reexamination of Papyrus Stracky (P.Yadin 36)."

ing with the contents of the inner text. Nothing could be added since the writing on the *verso* reached the very bottom of the papyrus before it was turned over. This contrasts sharply with the careless treatment of the inner text in many of the Greek texts in the archives from Naḥal Ḥever and from Dura Europos.[51] We find the same practice in three more Nabataean papyri, *P.Yadin* 2 and 3, and, as pointed out above, in the Jewish Aramaic *P.Yadin* 7.

To cap it all, we now have the singular opportunity – and challenge – to explore in the recently discovered, and in part already published, *P.Petra*, whether or not the Nabataean legal tradition survived into late antiquity in Greek attire.

51 For *P.Yadin* see Lewis, *The Documents from the Bar Kokhba Period in the Cave of Letters. Greek Papyri*, 9; cf. *P.Hever* 62 and *P.Dura* 26, 28, 29.

The Bar Kokhba Revolt and the Documents from the Judaean Desert: Nabataean Participation in the Revolt (*P.Yadin* 52)

Introduction

The principal contribution of the documentary material from the Judaean Desert – the bulk of which consists of legal deeds – is to improving our understanding of social and legal aspects of Jewish society in the Roman provinces of Arabia and Judaea in the first century and the first half of the second century CE. Above all they provide a corrective to the biassed view found in rabbinic texts, and consequently in modern accounts which rely solely on the evidence of these sources. The documents from the Judaean Desert are our best testimony for the state of Jewish law and for the legal procedures used by Jews, and, indirectly, for the authority exercised by the rabbis at the time. The deeds of sale, renunciations of claims, land registrations, receipts, mortgages, promissory notes, deeds of gift, deeds of divorce and marriage contracts from the Judaean Desert bear a striking resemblance to their counterparts in Egypt and the rest of the Roman Near East,[1] thereby revealing the remarkable degree to which Jewish society was integrated into its environment. I should go so far as to say that often it is only the names that identify the parties as Jews.[2]

And the documents are representative! Despite the fact that the documents span a period of under a hundred years, their geographical distribution makes it clear that they are representative of Jewish society as a whole.[3] Almost without

---

1 See Hannah M. Cotton, W.E.H. Cockle, and Fergus Millar, "The Papyrology of the Roman Near East: A Survey," *JRS* 85 (1995): 214–35.

2 For the most up to date statement of this view see Hannah M. Cotton, "Die Papyrusdokumente aus der judäischen Wüste und ihr Beitrag zur Erforschung der jüdischen Geschichte des 1. und 2. Jh.s n. Chr.," *ZDPV* 115 (1999): 228–47; cf. Hannah M. Cotton, "The Impact of the Documentary Papyri from the Judaean Desert on the Study of Jewish History from 70 to 135 CE," in *Jüdische Geschichte in hellenistisch-römischer Zeit: Wege der Forschung – von alten zu neuen Schürer*, ed. Aharon Oppenheimer (München: Oldenbourg, 1999), 221–36 [below, pp. 467–84] (= "L'impatto dei papiri documentari del deserto di Giudea sullo studio della storia ebraica dal 70 al 135/6 e.v.," in *Gli ebrei nell'impero romano*, ed. Ariel Lewin (Florence: Giuntina, 2001), 217–31).

3 There is no distinction of course between Jews from the province of Arabia and those from Judaea, see Hannah M. Cotton, "The Rabbis and the Documents," in *Jews in a Greco-Roman World*, ed. Martin Goodman (Oxford: Oxford University Press, 1998), 172–73 [below, pp. 458–59].

Article note: First published in Peter Schäfer, ed., *The Bar Kokhba War Reconsidered* (Tübingen: Mohr Siebeck, 2003), 133–152.

https://doi.org/10.1515/9783110770438-011

exception the Jews attested in the documents are village dwellers, and this at a time when the majority of the Jewish population lived in villages. Thus the evidence of these documents cannot be set aside as reflecting the habits of fringe groups or sects, as the documents from Qumran do. Even when the documents are written in Greek, their owners cannot and should not be regarded as assimilated Jews.[4] The reason for using Greek is *not* that the writers are Hellenized – not even semi-Hellenized Jews.[5]

At the same time the Jews found acting in these documents come from most densely populated Jewish areas, from the heartland of two religious and national revolts – areas which survived the first revolt of 66–70 CE, but were utterly destroyed in the second one.[6] In fact, the very presence of their documents in the caves together with documents which clearly belonged to Bar Kokhba and his men demonstrates their owners' participation in the Bar Kokhba revolt. Furthermore, the Jews who used the same legal formulae used elsewhere in the Roman Near East seem to have adhered strictly to their own religious ordinances.[7] As an example we may point to the fact, brilliantly demonstrated by R. Katzoff and B.M. Schreiber,[8] that not one of the transactions recorded in the documents from the Judaean Desert was dated to the Sabbath. Of course there is no inevitable or obvious contradiction between a society's harmonious integration into its environment on the one hand and its active participation in a religious and national war of independence on the other. Nonetheless, it is a remarkable fact, well worth pondering.[9]

As for the Bar Kokhba revolt, the direct evidence of the documents is anything but satisfactory – even after the recent publication of almost all the remaining

4 Perhaps the most palpable proof of this is that the Jews employ scribes to write their Greek documents, whereas they sign their names in Jewish Aramaic.

5 See in detail Hannah M. Cotton, "Jewish Jurisdiction under Roman Rule: Prolegomena," in *Zwischen den Reichen: Neues Testament und römische Herrschaft. Vorträge auf der ersten Konferenz der European Association for Biblical Studies*, ed. Michael Labahn and Jürgen Zangenberg (Tübingen: Francke Verlag, 2002), 13–28 [below, pp. 485–99]

6 A detailed survey of the area can be found in Boaz Zissu, "Rural Settlement in the Judaean Hills and Foothills from the Late Second Temple Period to The Bar Kokhba Revolt," Unpublished PhD Dissertation, Hebrew University of Jerusalem, 2002.

7 Of course the latter fact has been noticed before, cf. Saul Lieberman, "The Importance of the Bar-Kokhba Letters for Jewish History and Literature," in *Texts and Studies* (New York: Ktav Pub. House, 1974), 208 ff.

8 "Week and Sabbath in Judaean Desert Documents," *SCI* 17 (1998): 102–14, the sample is convincingly shown not to be due to chance.

9 For an analysis of Jewish village society before and after the two revolts see Fergus Millar, *The Roman Near East, 31 BC-AD 337* (Cambridge, Mass.: Harvard University Press, 1993), 337–86.

documents from the Judaean Desert.[10] In his address to the then president of the state of Israel, the documents' discoverer, Y. Yadin, said: "Your excellency, I am honored to be able to tell you that we have discovered fifteen dispatches written or dictated by the last president of ancient Israel, 1,800 years ago." Yadin's enthusiasm long ago gave way to general and scholarly disappointment born of the cantankerous tone of the leader and the prosaic and mundane, often trivial, contents of the letters from the so-called Bar Kokhba archives. True, the leases and sub-leases found in Wadi Murabba'at and Naḥal Ḥever give us an insight into Bar Kokhba's administration, and suggest that Bar Kokhba laid his hands on the imperial domain in the places recorded in the documents.[11] But as with the legal documents from the period mentioned above, this has little to do with the causes, the course and the results of this revolt that had such catastrophic consequences for the Jewish people.

Scarcity of hard facts and the familiar *horror vacui* often lead historians of the second Jewish revolt to cling desperately to every scrap of evidence and resort to over-interpretation of fragmentary texts lacking a safe context. Here as elsewhere we need to reign in our imagination. And yet, despite the need for caution, the facts we find in the documents cannot speak for themselves, but call for the historian's imagination to make sense of them and explore their ultimate significance.

As the sub-title of this essay reveals, I propose to offer here a new interpretation of a single letter, from the so-called Bar Kokhba archive, found in the Cave of Letters in Naḥal Ḥever. This is the Greek *P.Yadin* 52, published for the first time in 1962 and re-edited many times since. Before I do so, however, I should like to turn briefly to papyri from other sites which have also been given new interpretations and whose value for the history of the revolt deserves reassessment.

---

10 James Charlesworth et al., eds., *Miscellaneous Texts from the Judaean Desert*, Discoveries in the Judaean Desert XXXVIII (Oxford: Oxford University Press, 2000); Ada Yardeni, *Textbook of Aramaic, Hebrew and Nabataean Documentary Texts from the Judaean Desert and Related Material*, Vols. I–II (Jerusalem: The Hebrew University Press, 2000); Yigael Yadin et al., *The Documents from the Bar Kokhba Period in the Cave of Letters: Hebrew, Aramaic and Nabatean-Aramaic Papyri*, Judean Desert Studies III (Jerusalem: IES, 2002).

11 See Hannah M. Cotton, "Ein Gedi between the Two Revolts," *SCI* 20 (2001): 139–54 [below, pp. 347–61].

I *P.Murabba'at* 29 and 30 and the Use of Hebrew During the Two Revolts

So long as the Hebrew *P.Murabba'at* 29 and 30, both of which are legal deeds concluded in Jerusalem (בירשלים), and carry the dates year two and year four 'of the redemption of Israel' (לגאלת ישראל) respectively, were assigned to the Bar Kokhba revolt, the conclusion seemed inescapable not only that Jerusalem was in the hands of the rebels,[12] but that Bar Kokhba's sovereignty was recognized in the city as late as September/October 135 CE (the presumed date of *P.Murabba'at* 30). Needless to say, the silence of the Jewish sources about the conquest of Jerusalem by the rebels seemed highly disturbing.[13]

However, it has now been shown in two independent studies that the two documents should be assigned to the first revolt[14] – not least because it was the use of Hebrew in them and the similarity to Hebrew documents from the second revolt discovered in Naḥal Ḥever which made the attribution to the second revolt acceptable in the first place. It should not come as a surprise, though, that Hebrew was used in legal contracts during the first revolt as well, and it may not be a coincidence, therefore, that there are hardly any documents in Hebrew which date to the years before the first revolt, or to the period between the two revolts.[15] The same ideology which inspired the decision to use Hebrew, rather than Aramaic – the common legal language of the time – in legal documents of the second revolt may well have motivated also the participants in the first one.[16] Hebrew became the symbol of Jewish nationalism, of the independent Jewish State, and has remained so to this very day.

12 Although some denied it even then, flying in the face of the evidence, e. g. Menachem Mor, *The Bar-Kochba Revolt: Its Extent and Effect* (Jerusalem: Yad Ben-Zvi Press, 1991), 156–8 (Hebrew).
13 See Cotton, "The Impact of the Documentary Papyri from the Judaean Desert on the Study of Jewish History from 70 to 135 CE," 225–26 [below, pp. 472–73].
14 See Hanan Eshel, Magen Broshi, and T.A.J. Jull, "Documents from Wadi Murabba'at and the Status of Jerusalem during the Bar Kokhba Revolt," in *The Refuge Caves of the Bar Kokhba Revolt*, ed. Hanan Eshel and David Amit (Jerusalem: IES, 1998), 233 ff. (Hebrew); Hannah M. Cotton, "The Languages of the Legal and Administrative Documents from the Judaean Desert," *ZPE* 125 (1999): 220–23 [above, pp. 129–34].
15 With the exception of 4Q348 dated by Hanan Eshel to 46/47 CE, see Eshel, "4Q348, 4Q343 and 4Q345: Three Economic Documents from Qumran Cave 4?," *JJS* 52 (2001): 132–34; cf. Ph. Callaway, "Documentary Texts Allegedly from Qumran Cave 4," *The Qumran Chronicle* 8 (1998): 113–19.
16 Hannah M. Cotton, "The Aramaic Legal Tradition in Roman Judaea/Syria Palaestina," a lecture given at a conference held in Tel Aviv University under the title 'Synchysis and Polyglossia: Multiplicity of Tongues from the Ancient Near East to Medieval Europe' (23 February 1999).

II *P.Murabba'at* 114: Roman Presence in Wadi Murabba'at after the Second Revolt?[17]

ἐπὶ ὑπά[των]
Στατειλι̣ίου Σεο[υήρου Πανή]-
μου ὀγδόῃ κ̣[αὶ δεκάτῃ]
Ἱεροσολυμ[ ]
αυουαια[ ]
ὀρεινῆς π̣ρο.[ ]
λεγεῶνος δ̣[εκάτης]
νιου Σατοργ̣[είνου χαί]-
ρειν. ὁμολο[γῶ]
σοι ἀργυρίου Τ̣[υ]ρι̣[ου].[ ].[ ]
οἵ εἰσιν στατῆρες δεκ̣[α]δύω καὶ δηνάρια δύω, ἃ
καὶ ἀπέσχογ̣ καὶ ἠρίθμημε· ὃ ἀργύριον ἀποδώσω
τῇ πρὸ μιᾶς̣ καλανδῶν Σεπτεμβρίων πρώτων ταῖς
ἔνγιστα κατὰ μηδὲν ἀντιλέγων. ἐὰν δὲ μὴ ἀποδῶ
τῇ ὡρισμέν[ῃ] προθεσμίᾳ̣, τελέσω σοι τὸν ἐγ διατάγ-
ματος τόκ̣[ον] μέχρι οὗ ἂν ἀποδῶ ἢ ε̣ἰσπραχθῶ τὸ
πᾶν δ̣ά̣[νει]ον ἐκ πλήρους, τῆ[ς] πράξεώς σοι οὔσης
καὶ ἄλ[λῳ π]α̣ντ̣ι̣ τῶν διά σοῦ ἢ ὑπέρ σοῦ κυρίως προ-
φερ[όντων τόδε τὸ χ]ειρ̣όγραφον ἐκ τε ἐμοῦ καὶ ἐκ τ̣-
ῶν ὑ̣[παρχόντων μοι] π̣[ά]ντων καὶ ὧν ἂν ἐπεικτή-
[σωμαι] [κ]υρίως τ̣ροπ.]
[ ] ρου λόγου̣ [ ]
[four lines]
Verso:
κ̣α̣τ̣α̣ Φεγ̣φ̣ε̣. (δηνάρια) 50

The presence of Jerusalem in *P.Murabba'at* 114 (l. 4), an IOU note, dated by its first editor, Pierre Benoit, to the year 171 CE, raises a different chronological problem.[18] The dating was based on the consul's name in line 2. Clearly we should read there Statilius Severus (ἐπὶ ὑπά[των ... Τίτου] Στατειλι̣ίου Σεο[υήρου πρὸ η̅ (or ὀκτὼ) εἰδῶν Ἰουλίων Πανή]μου ὀγδόῃ κ̣[αὶ δεκάτῃ], lines 1–3). Pierre Benoit, assuming quite rightly that he should look for a *consul ordinarius* with that name,[19] opted

17 See now in detail Hannah M. Cotton and Werner Eck, "P.Murabba'at 114 und die Anwesenheit römischer Truppen in den Höhlen des Wadi Murabba'at nach dem Bar Kochba Aufstand," *ZPE* 138 (2002): 173–83.

18 P. Benoit, J.T. Milik, and R. de Vaux, *Les grottes de Murabba'at*, Discoveries in the Judaean Desert II (Oxford: Clarendon Press, 1961), 240–43.

19 Pierre Benoit, "Une reconnaissance de dette du IIe siècle en Palestine," in *Studi in onore di Aristide Calderini e Roberto Paribeni*, Vol. II (Milano: Ceschina, 1957), 260: "il est a priori peu probable que, dans la lointaine Palestine, on ait daté un document par le nom d'un consul suffect."

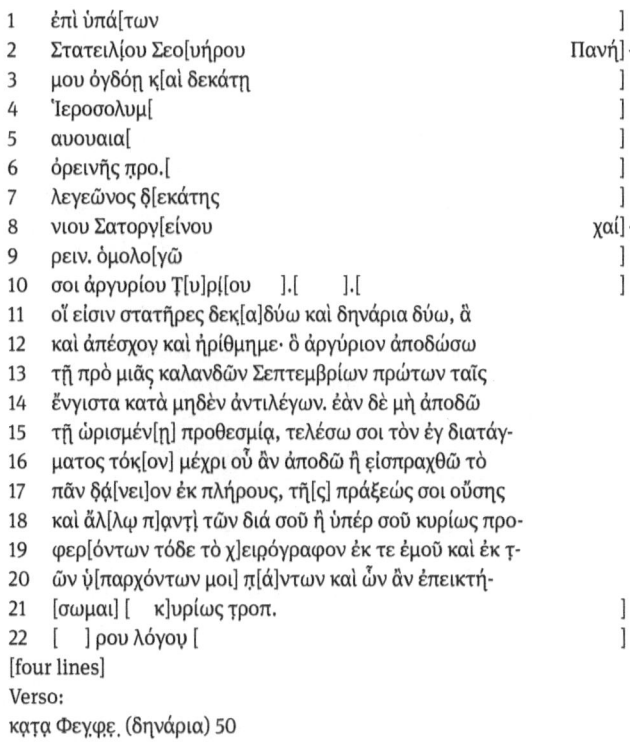

for Titus Statilius Severus attested as an *ordinarius* in 171 together with L. Alfidius Herennianus. He also believed that "the presence of a Roman garrison in the caves of Murabba'at cannot be explained before the Second Revolt."[20] It thus came to be commonly held and believed that the Roman authorities maintained a military presence in these caves in the later part of the second century CE, long after the Bar Kokhba revolt, although neither the archaeological nor the numismatic finds make this at all a necessary assumption – nor can I see any reasonable explanation for it.[21] The dating of *P.Murabba'at* 114 is probably the strongest support for this assumption. It thus seems to me all the more necessary to verify its precise date. As a result of the new dating we may be able to modify the current view of the presence of a Jewish population near Jerusalem between the two revolts.[22]

As in *P.Murabba'at* 29 and 30, here too Jerusalem is specified as the place where the transaction took place: [ἐν] Ἱεροσολυμ[(lines 3–4). However, in 171 Jerusalem no longer existed. It had ceased to exist already after 129/130, when on the occasion of Hadrian's visit the Colonia Aelia Capitolina was founded.[23] From then onwards, or at the latest from 132, in legal documents in particular, Jerusalem could not be named as the place where a legal transaction was concluded – especially not when a Roman soldier of the *legio decima Fretensis* (lines 7–8) was involved. Any date after 130, or at the latest 132 CE, for this document is thus *prima facie* unlikely.

Benoit assumed that this is a chirograph between two Roman soldiers, at least one of whom was on active service in the *legio X Fretensis* – which should make the use of the name of Jerusalem after 130 even less likely – but he never explained why Greek, rather than Latin, was used in such a case.[24] Finally, despite Benoit's hesitations and changes of mind, the epistolary form of the chirograph, suggested by [χαί]ρειν (ll. 9–10), clearly implies that the name of the writer, the borrower, preceded that of the creditor, and occupied lines 4–6, and therefore ὀρεινῆς is the last element in the description of the borrower's provenance.

Literally ἡ ὀρεινή is 'the hilly country' and refers in the sources to the Judaean hills near Jerusalem.[25] But Orine acquired a political significance after the first

20 Benoit; cf. idem in Benoit, Milik, and de Vaux, *Les Grottes de Murabba'at*, 241.
21 Benoit, Milik, and de Vaux, *Les grottes de Murabba'at*, 29–48, especially on p. 48.
22 See e. g. Yuval Shahar, "From Jerusalem to 'Orine' – Consequences of the First Revolt in the Vicinity of Jerusalem," in *New Studies on Jerusalem: Proceedings of the Sixth Conference*, ed. Avraham Faust and Eyal Baruch (Ramat-Gan: Bar-Ilan University Press, 2000), 187–201 (Hebrew).
23 *BMC Emp.* III 493 nos. 1655–1661; cf. Anthony R. Birley, *Hadrian: The Restless Emperor* (London: Routledge, 1997), 231–34.
24 See Cotton and Eck, "P.Murabba'at 114 und die Anwesenheit römischer Truppen in den Höhlen des Wadi Murabba'at nach dem Bar Kochba Aufstand," 176.
25 Cf. Joseph. *AJ* 12.7.

revolt. It became the political or administrative unit (toparchy) which included Jerusalem, or rather which once was Jerusalem.[26] Clearly the villages which once were within the toparchy of Jerusalem would now be described as belonging to Orine (hence Ὀρεινῆς not ὀρεινῆς should stand in l. 6).[27] The borrower, whose name was written in lines 4–5, in conformity with usage attested elsewhere in the Greek papyri from the Judaean Desert, is thus likely to have described himself as coming from a village in the district of Orine.[28] He was not a Roman soldier, but a native of Judaea, probably a Jew, and this is why the deed was written in Greek.[29] Were the borrower, like his creditor, a Roman soldier, as Benoit assumed, it is more likely than not that the document would have been drafted in Latin – especially if it was written in the colony of Aelia Capitolina, as it must have been if Benoit's dating of it to 171 is accepted.

Like Jerusalem, Orine too did not survive the second Jewish revolt. The occurrence of Jerusalem and Orine in a formal legal document, which is what *P.Murabba'at* 114 certainly is, speaks strongly against a date after 130 – and even more strongly against one after 132. Afterwards Jerusalem became Aelia Capitolina and Orine ceased to function as a toparchy. These facts establish, to my mind, an irrefutable chronological *post quem non*. Whatever the result of the attempts to locate the Statilius Severus of *P.Murabba'at* 114 in the consular *fasti*, and however we meet the objection that *normally* suffect consuls were not used to date legal documents in the provinces (in contrast to Italy), this consul must have been in office probably before the foundation of the colony and certainly before 132. However, there is nothing in the consular *fasti* to exclude a suffect consulship of a Statilius

---

26 Cf. Pliny, *NH* V, 70: *Orinen, in qua fuere Hierosolyma*; contrast with Josephus's list of toparchies in *BJ* 3.54–56, where Jerusalem is named in the first place, whereas Orine is omitted altogether – which makes it quite clear that his list predates the first revolt; cf. Hannah M. Cotton, "Some Aspects of the Roman Administration of Judaea/Syria-Palaestina," in *Lokale Autonomie und römische Ordnungsmacht in den kaiserzeitlichen Provinzen vom 1. bis 3. Jahrhundert*, ed. Werner Eck (München: Oldenbourg, 1999), 84 ff. [below, pp. 327 ff.].

27 Like Josephus, the documents describe the dependence of a village on the central village of the toparchy in terms identical to those which describe that of a village on the city to whose territory it belongs, see Cotton, 86 [below, p. 329].

28 Cf. Cotton, 82–89 [below, pp. 326–34].

29 The very same situation of a loan taken by a Judaean villager in Judaea from a Roman soldier is found in the opening lines of *P.Yadin* 11 of 125 CE, a deed of loan between Judah son of Eleazar Khthousion (who will become Babatha's second husband) from the village of Ein Gedi and Magonius Valens, centurion of the *cohors I milliaria Thracum*, also composed in Greek: ἐπ̣ὶ ὑ̣[πάτ]ω̣ν Μανείο̣υ Ἀκειλίου Γλαβρίωνος κα̣ὶ Τορκουά[του Θ]η̣βανιανο[ῦ πρὸ] μ̣ιᾶς νωγ̣ῶν Μαίω[ν] ἐν Ἐνγαδοῖς κώμη̣ κυρίου Καίσαρος, Ἰούδας Ἐλ̣[αζ]ά̣ρ̣ο̣υ̣ Χθο̣υ̣[σίω]ν̣ος Ἐ[ν]γ̣αδηνὸς Μαγωνίῳ Οὐά̣λ̣εντι (ἑκατοντάρ)χ(ῳ) σπείρης πρώτης μειλιαρίας Θρᾳκῶν χ[αί]ρ̣ε̣ιν (lines 12–14 = lines 1–2).

Severus prior to 130 or 132 in the month of July.[30] There are other Statilii Severi attested at the end of the Trajanic and the early Hadrianic period who can be fitted in quite comfortably. This is enough to satisfy the needs imposed by the internal dating of the document, namely the presence of Jerusalem and Orine in it.[31]

In view of all this *P.Murabba'at* 114 need not attest the presence of the Roman army in the caves of Murabba'at in the late second century, but testifies rather to that of Jewish refugees from the area near Jerusalem, who escaped into the cave with their documents during the second revolt[32] – not unlike *P.Murabba'at* 115 of 124 CE and probably also *P.Murabba'at* 113, described as 'actes d'un procès(?)', which seems to come from the same milieu as ours. It contains a report of an exchange between a *veteranus* and two Jewish women, Salome and Miriam. All the names are in the nominative. It thus closely resembles *P.Yadin* 26 where Babatha and Miriam (Judah's previous or second wife), exchange summonses with each other to appear before the governor of the province.[33] *P.Murabba'at* 113 may have also come from Jerusalem, which was not an unlikely place for legal transactions between Roman soldiers or veterans and Jews before 130. Jews were not forbidden to reside in Jerusalem or in its vicinity between the two revolts as they were to be later on.[34]

---

30 Even if my previous attempt to identify our Statilius Severus as a suffect consul in 115 CE no longer seems very probable, see Cotton and Eck, "P.Murabba'at 114 und die Anwesenheit römischer Truppen in den Höhlen des Wadi Murabba'at nach dem Bar Kochba Aufstand," 180 ff.

31 The use of suffect consuls for dating documents in the provinces, albeit rare, is nevertheless sometimes attested: see Werner Eck, "Consules ordinarii und consules suffecti als eponyme Amtsträger," in *Epigrafia. Actes du colloque de Rome (27–28 mai 1988) en mémoire de Attilio Degrassi* (Rome: École française de Rome, 1991), 15–44. Since one of the parties to the transaction was a Roman soldier, he may well have supplied the names of the *suffecti* in July from the office of the legion's commander in Jerusalem. Had he been in Italy at the time, he would certainly have used the *suffecti* to date a legal document.

32 There is no ready answer to the question why the deed was brought here by the borrower; see Cotton and Eck, "P.Murabba'at 114 und die Anwesenheit römischer Truppen in den Höhlen des Wadi Murabba'at nach dem Bar Kochba Aufstand,", 182; and see revised text of *P.Murabba'at* 114, lines 1–11 in Cotton and Eck, 177.

33 *P.Yadin* 26, line 1 ff: ẹ̓π̣ὶ [τῶν] ẹ̓π̣ιβẹβλ̣ημ[έ]νω̣ν̣ καὶ ἐπισφραγ̣ισαμέν̣ων μαρτύρων παρήνγιλεν Βαβαθας Σίμωνος Μα<ω>ζηνὴ Μαριάμην Βειανοῦ Ἠνγαδηνη<ν> συνεξέρχεσ̣θαι αὐτὴν ἐπὶ Ἀτέριον Νέπωταν πρε<σ>βευτου Σεβαστοῦ ἀντιστρατηγου ... ὃς δὲ ἀπεκρίθη Μαριάμη, λέγουσα· πρὸ τούτου παρήνγιλά σε μὴ ἐνγίσε εἰς τὰ ὑπάρ̣χοντά μοῳ <καί> [σο]υ ἀνδρὸς ἀ̣π̣[ο]γ̣ẹν̣[ομ]ẹ́[νου etc. Cf. especially Μαριάμη ἡ εἴπο̣[υσα] in *P.Murabba'at* 113, line 6.

34 For Jewish burials in the vicinity of Jerusalem in that period see Amos Kloner and Boaz Zissu, *The Necropolis of Jerusalem during the Hellenistic and Early Roman Periods* (Jerusalem: IES, 2003), chapter 45 (Hebrew). I am grateful to the authors for showing me the manuscript in advance of publication.

III *P.Se'elim* 4: A List Extracted from Census Declarations (and not a list of Bar Kokhba's Soldiers)[35]

Frg. a

col. i	col. ii	col. iii	col. i	col. ii	col. iii
1	[ἐτῶν] κε			[age] 25	
2	[ἐτ]ῶν ιγ	.[...].[		[ag]e 13	.[...].[
3	[ἐτ]ῶν ιθ	Ιησους Ληου.[		[ag]e 19	Yeshua son of Levi
4	[ἐτῶ]ν μα	[...]νῳρ.[		[ag]e 41	[...]nor [son]
5	[ ]	Ιωσηπος [		[age]	Yosepos [another son]
6	[ ]	Ιησους αλ[		[age]	Yeshua an[other son]
7 *trace of ink*	[ ]	Ιωσηπος .[	*trace of ink*	[age]	Yosepos [another son]
8]υ	ἐτῶν ξα	Ανεινας .[	son of [o]s	age 61	Aneinas [another son]
9]νος	ἐτῶν ξζ	Ελλῃλος ạλ̣[	Son of [Shim]on(?)	age 67	Ellelos an[other son]
10	[ ]	Γάιος α[		[ ]	Gaius a[nother son]
11	[ ].	Σẹ[.].ος Σειμạ[		[ ]	Se.os son of Seima[
12	[ἐτῶν] κβ	Α[		[age] 22	A[
13	[ἐτῶν] λς	Κ[		[age] 36	K[
14	[ἐτῶν] β			[age] [?]2	

P.Se'elim 4 from cave 34 in Naḥal Ṣe'elim, published for the first time by Baruch Lifshitz in 1961,[36] consists of six fragments surviving from a large document. The document contained at least four columns, in the form of two sets of two columns, the left one of each pair being a list of persons and the right one a list of their respective ages. This structure is revealed in frg. a (above) which preserves three columns, although the remains of the first column consist of only the ends of two names appearing in lines 7, 8 and 9. Cols. i and ii form a pair followed by col. iii which was paired presumably with the following column which has not survived. The preponderance of Jewish names inclines one to think that the papyrus comes from Judaea rather than from the province of Arabia.

There is no support for Lifshitz's speculation that this is a list of soldiers, a fraternity of warriors, who constituted the army of Bar Kokhba.[37] Not only is there

35 The papyrus was edited by Hannah M. Cotton in Charlesworth et al., *Misc. Texts from Judaean Desert*, 217–25 and Plate XXXIV; Hannah M. Cotton, "The Roman Census in the Papyri from the Judaean Desert and the Egyptian κατ' οἰκίαν ἀπογραφή," in *Semitic Papyrology in Context: A Climate of Creativity*, ed. Lawrence H. Schiffman (Leiden – Boston: Brill, 2003), 105–22 [below, pp. 363–78].

36 Baruch Lifshitz, "The Greek Documents from Naḥal Ṣeelim and Naḥal Mishmar," *IEJ* 11 (1961): 53–62.

37 Lifshitz, 60–1; his conclusion is based on an erroneous interpretation of the term ἀδελφός here, and elsewhere; see Baruch Lifshitz, "Papyrus grecs du désert de Juda," *Aegyptus* 42 (1962): 252 ff.

no apparent reason to associate the list with the Bar Kokhba revolt, but the idea of soldiers, as already pointed out by Benoit,[38] seems to be excluded by the presence of people aged thirteen years on the one hand and sixty-seven on the other.

The true nature of the list is revealed in the format of col. iii where a name and patronymic is followed by another name or names indented by slightly over 1 cm. It seems to be a roster of households listing the name of the head of the household followed by those of the other members (i. e. sons). Only males appear in what is preserved of the document; it seems therefore likely that the list was restricted to the male members of the household. Similar lists, drafted by local officials, are known from Egypt. They were derived, or rather abstracted, from the census declarations submitted every fourteen years at the house-by-house registration in Egypt, the κατ' οἰκίαν ἀπογραφή.[39] These synthesised lists omitted all details which were irrelevant for their purpose: liability to taxation or liturgies. However, the exclusion of women from the present list makes it unlikely to be a tax list, since women were probably liable for the poll tax in Judaea as in Syria.[40] I am therefore inclined to accept Dominic Rathbone's suggestion to me that "this is a list of men liable to one or several liturgies which were only imposed on men, probably therefore manual liturgies."

The official nature of the list is quite apparent, and is also implied by the fluent hand of the scribe. The use of Greek as the official language in a Roman province implies of course the active participation of local people in the routine of provincial administration. If the capital villages of the *toparchiae* in the Jewish region in Judaea fulfilled functions similar to those carried out by cities in other parts of the Roman Empire, then we can assume that these lists were prepared by the civic authorities in these villages.[41]

Such lists had to be kept up-to-date,[42] and therefore, one can be sure that, if such documents were deposited in the cave during the Bar Kokhba revolt, they were made not long before the outbreak of the revolt. A list of the sort we have here may give us an idea of how the Romans could have come by precise numbers for the casualties incurred by the Jews during the Bar Kokhba revolt. The number

---

38 Pierre Benoit, "Bulletin," *RB* 68 (1961): 467.

39 See Marcel Hombert and Claire Préaux, *Recherches sur le recensement dans l'Egypte romaine* (Leiden: Brill, 1952), 135–47; Roger S. Bagnall and Bruce W. Frier, *The Demography of Roman Egypt* (Cambridge: Cambridge University Press, 1994), 26 ff.

40 Judaea started its career as a Roman province as part of the province of Syria (see Cotton, "Some Aspects of the Roman Administration of Judaea/Syria-Palaestina," 75–9 [below, pp. 317–21], and in Syria, as we know from Ulpian, *Dig.* 50, 15, 3 pr., women were liable to the poll tax.

41 See Cotton, 87–9 [below, pp. 331–32].

42 See Bagnall and Frier, *The Demography of Roman Egypt*, 27–8.

given by Cassius Dio (39, 14, 1) of 580,000 Jews killed in the war has often been questioned as exaggerated.[43] It need not have been: the Romans could easily have compared the data summarized in the census returns from before and after the revolt by consulting such lists[44] – though of course this says nothing about what Cassius Dio did with his source, or about the reliability of the transmission of the number in our manuscripts of this writer.

IV *P.Yadin* 52 and Nabataean Participation in the Revolt

P.Yadin 52 is one of the two Greek letters in the so-called Bar Kokhba archive. The reason for its great fame lies in lines 12–15, for which many interpretations have been offered. It has often served as a springboard for discussions of the languages spoken in Palestine in the first two centuries CE, and the language likely to have been spoken by Jesus Christ. It is worth reproducing here side by side the first edition and most recent edition with translations.[45]

---

43 E.g. Peter Schäfer, *Der Bar Kokhba-Aufstand* (Tübingen: Mohr Siebeck, 1981), 131 ff.

44 For the romantic historian a fraternity of warriors fighting for Jewish freedom is probably a great deal more exciting than a list of people liable to one or several liturgies. However, it should not come as a great surprise that the refugees of the revolts hid in these caves those documents attesting the routine of daily life in a Roman province.

45 First edition: Lifshitz, "Papyrus grecs du gésert de Juda," 241 (reproduced in *SB* VIII 9843); Dirk Obbink, "Bilingual Literacy and Syrian Greek," *BASP* 28 (1991): 53–4; Hayim Lapin, "Palm Fronds and Citrons: Notes on Two Letters from Bar Kosiba's Administration," *HUCA* 64 (1993): 114; G. Wilhelm Nebe, "Die beiden griechischen Briefe des Jonatan Archivs in Engedi aus dem zweiten jüdischen Aufstand 132–135 nach Chr.," *Revue de Qumran* 17 (1996): 276–77; Luc Devillers, "La lettre de Soumaïos et les Ioudaioi johanniques," *RB* 105 (1998): 571–72 (in transliteration). In addition there have been several suggested corrections to lines 12–14: G. Howard and J.C. Shelton, "The Bar-Kokhba Letters and Palestinian Greek," *IEJ* 23 (1973): 101–2; Haiim Rosén, "Die Sprachsituation im römischen Palästina," in *Die Sprachen im römischen Reich der Kaiserzeit*, ed. Günter Neumann and Jürgen Untermann (Köln: Rheinland-Verlag, 1980), 224–26. A draft of a transcription of the text (perhaps made in consultation with H.J. Polotsky) was found among Yadin's personal papers. It is the basis for Yadin's translation of the text in his *Bar-Kokhba: The Rediscovery of the Legendary Hero of the Second Jewish Revolt Against Rome* (London: Random House, 1971), 130–2. See also Piero Capelli, "L'Epistola greca di Bar Kokhba e la questione del vernacolo giudaico nel II secolo," in *Biblische und judaistische Studien. Festschrift für Paolo Sacchi*, ed. Angelo Viviano (Frankfurt am Main: P. Lang, 1990), 271–78. Final publication by Hannah M. Cotton, "P.Yadin 52. Letter from Soumaios to Yonathes and Masabala in Ein Gedi," in *The Documents from the Bar Kokhba Period in the Cave of Letters: Hebrew, Aramaic and Nabatean-Aramaic Papyri*, ed. Yigael Yadin et al. (Jerusalem: IES, 2002), 351–62.

	Lifshitz 1962	Cotton 2002 with emendations[46]
m. 1	Σου[μαῖ]ος Ἰωναθῆι	Σου̣[μαι]ος Ι̣ωναθῆι
	Βαϊανοῦ καὶ Μα-	Β̣ε̣ι̣ανου καὶ Μα-
	[σ]αβάλα χαίρειν.	[σ]αβαλα[ι] χαίρειν.
	Ἐ̣[π]ηδη ἔπεμσα πρὸς	ἐ̣π̣ιδὴ ἔπεμσα πρὸς
	ὑμᾶς Ἀ[γ]ρίππαν σπου-	ὑ̣μᾶς Ἀ[γ]ρίππαν σπου-
	δ[άσα]τε πέμσε μοι	δ[άσα]τε πέμσε μοι
	σ[τε]λεοὺ[ς] καὶ κίτρια	θ̣[ύ]ρ̣σ̣ου[ς] καὶ κίτρια,
	α[ὐτὰ] δ' ἀνασθήσεται	ὅ[σον] δυ̣γασθήσεται,
	ἰς [κ]ιτρειαβολὴν Ἰου-	ἰς̣ [π]α̣ρεμβολὴν Ἰου-
	δαίων καὶ μὴ ἄλως	δ[αί]ων καὶ μὴ ἄλως
	ποιήσηται· ἐγράφη	π[οι]ή̣σηται. ἐγράφη
	δ[ὲ] Ἑληνιστὶ διὰ	δ[ὲ] Ἑληνεστὶ διὰ
	τ[ὸ ὁρ]μὰν μὴ εὑρη-	τ[ὸ ἡ]μᾶν μὴ εὑρη-
	θ[ῆ]ναι Ἑβραεστὶ	κ[έ]γαι Ἑβραεστί.
	γ[ρά]ψασθαι. Αὐτὸν	ἐ[.] ...αι αὐτὸν
	ἀπ[ο]λῦσαι τάχιον	ἀπ̣[ο]λῦσαι τάχιον
	δι[ὰ τ]ὴν Ἑορτὴν	δι[ὰ τ]ὴν ἑορτὴν
	κα[ὶ μ]ὴ ἄλλως ποιή-	κα[ὶ μ]ὴ̣ ἄλλως ποιή-
	ση[τα]ι	ση̣[ται].
m. 2	Σουμαῖος	Σουμαιος
	ἔρρωσο	ἔρρωσο

[4]ἐπιδὴ ἔπεμψα [6]πέμψαι [7]κίτρεια [8]δυγασθήσετε [9]εἰς [10]ἄλλως [11;18–19]ποιήσητε [12]Ἑλληνιστί [14]Ἑβραϊστί

46 I have preferred the alternative punctuation of lines 14–15 suggested to me by Dieter Hagedorn, and rejected the reading of ἐ[γγρ]ά̣ψ̣ασθαι in line 15, see Cotton, "P.Yadin 52. Letter from Soumaios to Yonathes and Masabala in Ein Gedi," 360 and n. 19 there.

	Lifshitz	Cotton
1st hand	Soumaïos à Jonathès fils de Banaïos et à Masabala salut. Attendu que j'ai envoyé à vous Agrippa empressez vous de m'envoyer des barres de bois et des citrons (c.-à-d. *ethrog*) et faites les arriver à la fête juive des Tabernacles et ne faites pas autrement. La lettre a été écrite en grec parce qu'on n'a pas en envoie d'écrire en hébreu. Fais le (scil. Agrippa) rentrer plus vite à cause de la Fête et ne faites pas autrement.	Soumaios to Yonathes son of Beianos and to Masabala greetings. Since I have sent you Agrippa, hurry to send me wands and citrons, as much as you will be able to, for the camp of the Jews, and do not do otherwise. It (the letter) was written in Greek because of our inability (to write) in Hebrew letters. [Make haste?] to release[47] him (Agrippa) quickly on account of the festival, and do not do otherwise.
2nd hand	Soumaïos porte toi bien.	Soumaios Farewell.

Detailed explanations for the new readings can be found in the final publication of the papyrus.[48] For the new interpretation of the papyrus, it is only important to point out that in line 7 θ̣[ύ]ρ̣σ̣ου[ς] is to be preferred to Lifshitz's σ[τε]λεού[ς][49] and in line 9 Yadin's reading, [π]α̣ρεμβολήν, namely 'camp,' is to be preferred to Lifshitz's [κ]ιτρειαβολήν, unattested as the name for the festival of Tabernacles,[50] especially in view of the Aramaic *P.Yadin* 57 which mentions a camp – מחניה – in the same context of sending the four species required for celebrating the festival of Tabernacles from Qiryat 'Arabayyah (or 'Arbayyah) 'to the camp' (למחניה).[51]

47 Naphtali Lewis in a private communication suggested restoring ἐ[υλ]ά̣β̣ε̣σ̣θ̣ε̣ καὶ αὐτὸν in line 15 and translating 'be sure to release also him.'
48 Cotton, "P.Yadin 52. Letter from Soumaios to Yonathes and Masabala in Ein Gedi."
49 See Lapin, "Palm Fronds and Citrons: Notes on Two Letters from Bar Kosiba's Administration," 128 ff.
50 Despite Devillers' vehement defense of Lifshitz's reading in "La lettre de Soumaïos et les Ioudaioi johanniques," 566 ff.
51 'Shim'on to Yehudah, son of Menasheh, at Qiryat 'Arabayyah (or 'Arbayyah): I have delivered to you two donkeys (in order) that you dispatch along with them two men to Yehonathan, son of Ba'yan, and to Masbalah (in order) that they pack up and deliver to the camp, to you, palm branches and citrons. And you are to send additional persons from your place and let them bring you myrtle branches and willows. And prepare them, and deliver them to the camp (למחניה), because the (or: its) population is large. Fare well'; see Cotton, "P.Yadin 52. Letter from Soumaios to Yonathes and Masabala in Ein Gedi," 357.

There are many suggestions for solutions to the famous crux in lines 12–14: Lifshitz's διὰ τ[ὸ ὀρ]μὰν μὴ εὑρηθ[ῆ]ναι 'because I do not feel like writing in Hebrew,' is logically unsatisfactory even after the unacceptable Doric form [ὀρ]μὰν is replaced with [ὀρ]μάς, for in any case the traces following the *alpha* are more compatible with a *sigma* than with a *nu*. The same goes for Nebe's τ[ὸ τι] μᾶ<ι>ν̣ μὴ εὑρηθ̣[ῆν]α̣ι 'because it did not seem worthwhile to write in Hebrew' – which also reads *nu* instead of *sigma* and yields an absurd sense. Howard and Shelton suggested [Ἑρ]μᾶν *exempli gratia*, i. e. 'the letter was written in Greek because [Her]mas could not be found to write in Hebrew (or Aramaic).' Rosén's διὰ τ[ὸ μὴ]δ̣[έν](α̣?) μὴ εὑρηθ[ῆ]ναι ignores the traces of letters preserved on the papyrus. Obbink's suggestion, to read here the familiar idiom "'to give, take, or have ἀφορμαί' in the sense of 'opportunity, chance, or means' of doing something (completed by the infinitive)," falls short for reasons of space: there is no room for four letters between the *tau* of τό and the μας.

Reading εὑρηθ[ῆ]ναι rather than εὑρηκ[έ]ναι seems to have bedevilled the entire reconstruction. Not only are the remains of the letter at the beginning of l. 14 compatible with *kappa* but they are incompatible with the kind of *theta* that we have in this document. The active εὑρίσκειν followed by an infinitive (or with the infinitive understood as suggested in the translation) in the sense of 'to get a chance of, to be able' is attested many times in the papyri,[52] but sometimes the combination means simply 'to be able to, to be capable of,' or rather together with the negative 'to be unable to,' with no need to add in our mind an unwritten ἀφορμάς 'opportunity.' Thus the sense here is clear and simple: 'because of our inability (to write)[53] Hebrew (or Aramaic).'[54]

Which language is designated by Ἑβραεστί: Hebrew or Aramaic? This old enigma has often been discussed in the context of several passages of the New Testament and Josephus, without a definite conclusion being reached. It would seem that Ἑβραεστί, τῇ Ἑβραίδι διαλέκτῳ and similar expressions can mean 'Aramaic' in certain contexts. But since both Hebrew and Aramaic are used in the correspondence of Bar Kokhba and his people, the expression may refer to either in the present context.

However, perhaps we should look at the identity of the writer, Soumaios. Lifshitz's identification of the Soumaios of our letter with the leader of the revolt,

52 See Cotton, 358–9.

53 'To write' is understood but not written; see above n. 46.

54 The Aramaic verb 'find' (מצא, מצי) also developed the meaning of 'to be able to' (see Marcus Jastrow, *A Dictionary of the Targumim, the Talmud Babli and Yerushalmi, and the Midrashic Literature* (London: Luzac, 1903), 825), but there is no need to suggest Semitic influence on Soumaios' Greek.

Shim'on son of Kosiba, can be dismissed out of hand: the form Soumaios is never used to transcribe the name Shim'on (שמעון),[55] and is certainly absurd when combined with his reading of ll. 11–15: ἐγράφη δ[ὲ] Ἑληνιστὶ διὰ τ[ὸ ὁρ]μὰν μὴ εὑρηθ[ῆ]ναι Ἑβραεστὶ γ[ρά]ψασθαι, i. e. 'written in Greek because we did not feel like writing in Hebrew' (Lifshitz understood *Ebraïsti* to mean Hebrew): it is inconceivable that the leader of the revolt, who, as Yadin plausibly suggested, brought about the revival of Hebrew as the official language by decree,[56] should not have felt like using it. Nor can the identification stand if we accept the reading suggested here: 'because we are unable to write Hebrew.' It is impossible that the leader of the revolt should have been unable to write *Ebraïsti* – whether it means Hebrew or Aramaic – and least of all that he should contrast 'us' (διὰ τ[ὸ ἡ]μᾶς, ll. 12–13) with 'the camp of the Jews' (ἰς [π]αρεμβολὴν Ἰουδ[αί]ων, ll. 9–10).[57]

The writer is not a Jew but a Nabataean, like his namesake in the Babatha archive, who signs his name in Greek in *P.Yadin* 19, l. 34: [Σ]ουμαιος Κα[.]αβαιου μάρ(τυς), and like the father of Αβδαρετας who gives his patronym in *P.Yadin* 12, ll. 16–17: Αβδαρετας Σουμα[ι]ου μά(ρτυς).[58] But it is not only the name which marks Soumaios as a Nabataean.[59] Nabataeans in the archives from the Roman province of Arabia, unless they sign their names in the Nabataean cursive script, do so in Greek letters, whereas Jews sign their names mostly in the Jewish script.

55 Lapin, "Palm Fronds and Citrons: Notes on Two Letters from Bar Kosiba's Administration," 115 ff.

56 Yadin, *Bar-Kokhba: The Rediscovery of the Legendary Hero of the Second Jewish Revolt Against Rome*, 181.

57 I do not find Obbink's "cultural distancing" ("Bilingual Literacy and Syrian Greek," 56, n. 18) convincing.

58 Lewis' Ἀβδερεὺς was corrected to Αβδαρετας by Émile Puech, "Présence arabe dans les manuscrits de 'La grotte aux lettres' du Wadi Khabra," in *Présence arabe dans le Croissant fertile avant l'Hégire. Actes de la Table ronde internationale organisée par l'Unité de Recherche Associée 1062 du CNRS, Études sémitiques au Collège de France, le 13 novembre 1993*, ed. Hélène Lozachmeur (Paris: Éditions Recherche sur les Civilisations, 1995), 39, n. 8.

59 Cf. Heinz Wuthnow, *Die semitischen Menschennamen in griechischen Inschriften und Papyri des vorderen Orients* (Leipzig: Dieterich, 1930), s. v. The localities where the name is attested, Kafer in Northern Arabia (*SEG* 7, 1146 = *LBW* III.5 2496: Σομα[ι]ου) and Schaqra in Southern Lebanon (*IGRom.* III 1152 = *LBW* III.6 2506: Σομαιου) support the claim that this is a Nabataean name; cf. Lapin, "Palm Fronds and Citrons: Notes on Two Letters from Bar Kosiba's Administration," 116 and n. 15 there. One may add *PPUAES* IIIA 795[3]: Σομαιος Μαλεχου ἐποίησεν τὸν βωμόν – a building inscription inside a tabula ansata. Most of these references are cited by Lifshitz, "Papyrus Grecs Du Désert de Juda," 243, n. 1, apparently without realizing their non-Jewish context; cf. Gerard Mussies, "Jewish Personal Names in Some Non-Literary Sources," in *Studies in Early Jewish Epigraphy*, ed. Pieter W. van der Horst and Jan Willem van Henten (Leiden: Brill, 1994), 252.

If Soumaios is a Nabataean, his admission that he and his men could not write *Ebraïsti* cannot be taken to mean that they did not know Aramaic. It may then be taken literally to mean that he did not know the Hebrew language, and that he was under the (false)[60] impression that Hebrew was the only acceptable language of communication among the Jewish rebels. Another solution is possible though: perhaps the whole debate on whether *Ebraïsti* means here Hebrew or Aramaic is misconceived; *Ebraïsti* in this context may mean something other than a language. As just observed, Soumaios as a Nabataean would have no problem with Jewish Aramaic – except for the script! It seems to me not impossible that *Ebraïsti* in this context refers to a script rather than to a language;[61] both Hebrew and Aramaic were written in the same script, namely what is generally designated 'Jewish Script.'[62] What Soumaios and his people are incapable of doing (διὰ τ[ὸ ἡ]-μᾶς μὴ εὑρηκ[έ]ναι Ἑβραεστί i. e. γράφειν) is communicating in writing, for Nabataean Aramaic is written in a script quite different from Jewish Aramaic.[63] I suggest therefore that Soumaios, Agrippa, the bearer of the present letter, as well as the writer of the other Greek letter from the so-called Bar Kokhba archives, *P.Yadin* 59 (especially if the latter is an Aelianus, as Yadin thought and not Annanos, as Lifshitz read)[64] – are all Nabataeans.

The pressing need for wands and citrons and the mention of the approaching festival imply that this letter, like *P.Yadin* 57, was written shortly before the festival of Tabernacles. It seems reasonable to assume that all the letters discovered in the Cave of Letters, although undated, belong to the very last months of the revolt, i. e. to the period immediately before the rebels left Ein Gedi and escaped to Naḥal

60 The majority of letters in Bar Kokhba's correspondence are in Aramaic: *P.Yadin* 50, 53, 54, 55, 57, 58, 62, 63, as against *P.Yadin* 49, 51, 60, 61.

61 Admittedly the meaning proposed here for the Greek adverbs is not the common one; normally the adverbs *Ebraïsti/Hellenisti* would designate both language and script, as they do for example in the inscription on the cross according to John 19:20 (ἦν γεγραμμένον Ἑβραιστί, Ῥωμαïστί, Ἑλληνιστί), and in line 12 of the present papyrus: ἐγράφη δ[ὲ] Ἑλληνιστί. For my interpretation to be consistent, the writer should have transcribed Nabataean Aramaic in Greek letters, rather than had it written in Greek – but this was hardly to be expected from people who were bilingual and could easily use both the Greek language and its script. A review of all the texts where these Greek adverbs ending in – στι to describe a language are used, may show us whether the meaning suggested here is admissible, but this could not be undertaken at present. I am very grateful to Eleonora Tagliaferro for raising all these issues with me, and encouraging me to re-think my original formulations.

62 See now above all Yardeni's *Textbook of Aramaic, Hebrew and Nabataean Documentary Texts from the Judaean Desert and Related Material*, Vol. II, 151–218.

63 See Yardeni, Vol. II, 219–63.

64 See Lifshitz, "Papyrus grecs du désert de Juda," 248–52 and Cotton, "P.Yadin 52. Letter from Soumaios to Yonathes and Masabala in Ein Gedi," 363–66.

Ḥever. This letter should therefore be dated to September or even early October 135 – depending of course on when Sukkot was celebrated that year – in the third year of the revolt. There should be no doubt that the revolt continued beyond the traditional date, the month of Ab (July/August) 135, perhaps even into 136.[65]

How are we to explain the participation of Nabataeans in the revolt, already nearing its end? How can we account for their presence in Judaea, albeit in their own camp, distinguished from that of the Jews?

One is reminded of Cassius Dio's statement that 'many outside nations too (πολλοί τε ἄλλοι καὶ τῶν ἀλλοφύλων) were joining them through eagerness for gain' (69, 13, 2). Nowadays we are more inclined to accept Werner Eck's exhortation that we should take Dio seriously, and understand him to mean that the revolt transcended the borders of Judaea and spread into the neighbouring provinces.[66] Nevertheless we still lack direct and tangible contemporary evidence for the revolt breaking out in other provinces, unless we accept the reading by S. Abbadi and F. Zayadine of a Safaitic inscription from North Eastern Jordan, where someone called Hlst son of M'n attests that he 'rebelled for three years against Nepos, who is a tyrant.'[67] If not – and the reading of the inscription is not beyond dispute – we are left with three indirect pieces of evidence for the revolt spilling over into the province of Arabia, which are open to alternative explanations: 1) the grant of the *ornamenta triumphalia* to the governors of Syria and Arabia at the conclusion of the revolt,[68] which could imply that they had to put down a revolt in their own provinces; 2) the departure of the Jews in massive numbers from Arabia; and 3) *P.Yadin* 52 as read and interpreted here.

There is no need to elaborate on the first point, exhaustively discussed by Werner Eck,[69] and we can pass immediately to the second one. Tal Ilan has recently alerted us to the fact that the signatures and subscriptions of witnesses in the archives from Arabia resurface in the documents from the so-called Bar Kokhba archives.[70] She rightly concludes that not only the families of Babatha

65 Cf. Werner Eck and Gideon Foerster, "Ein Triumphbogen für Hadrian im Tal von Beth Shean bei Tel Shalem," *JRA* 12 (1999): 301 ff. and esp. 312–13, and Werner Eck, "Hadrian, the Bar Kokhba Revolt, and the Epigraphic Transmission," in *The Bar Kokhba War Reconsidered*, ed. Peter Schäfer (Tübingen: Mohr Siebeck, 2003), 153–70.

66 Werner Eck, "The Bar Kokhba Revolt: The Roman Point of View," *JRS* 89 (1999): 76–89.

67 Sabri Abbadi and Fawzi Zayadine, "Nepos the Governor of the Provincia Arabia in a Safaitic Inscription?" *Semitica* 46 (1996): 157. This reading has been questioned by A. Knauf in a private communication.

68 Eck, "The Bar Kokhba Revolt: The Roman Point of View," 82 ff.

69 Eck, 82 ff.

70 Tal Ilan, "Witnesses in the Judaean Desert Documents: Prosopographical Observations," *SCI* 20 (2001): 169–78.

and Salome, whose archives were found in the Cave of Letters in Naḥal Ḥever, had left Arabia for Judaea; other Jews must have left as well. Some of them must have gone to the Peraea, where their signatures appear on one of the two deeds written there.[71] Close connections seem to have existed not only between families in Maḥoz Eglatain and Ein Gedi, but also between them and Jews from the Peraea: the second marriage of Salome Komaise daughter of Levi was to a man from a village in the *chora* of the *polis* of Livias in the Peraea, who owned land there, as is clear from *P.Hever* 65 (= *P.Yadin* 37).

The dating formulae in the two deeds from Kefar Baru, *P.Hever* 8 and 8a, prove that the Peraea, that part of the province of Judaea located in Transjordan, participated in the revolt; until the winter of the year 135,[72] the existence of an independent Jewish state with the Prince of Israel, Shim'on Bar Kokhba at its head, was recognised there. Both documents are dated to Adar of 'year three of the freedom of Israel in the days of Shim'on son of Kosiba, the prince of Israel in Kfar Baru.'[73] Later on the Jews of Kefar Baru left their village and sought shelter somewhere with their documents. The deeds from Kefar Baru were not found *in situ*. They belong to the so-called Seiyâl collection, which is more heterogeneous than the commonly accepted designation *P.Hever* would suggest.[74] These deeds may not have been found in Naḥal Ḥever at all, but in a place much closer to the village of Kefar Baru, now identified with Manyat Umm Hasan, above the hot springs of Hammat Ma'in, ca. 5 km northwest of Machaerus.[75]

Werner Eck, in a new interpretation of *P.Berol.* 21652 of 152 CE, has suggested that the Peraea took part in the revolt and as a result Jewish lands were confis-

---

71 See *P.Hever* 8a of 135 CE and commentary in Magen Broshi and Elisha Qimron, "A House Sale Deed from Kefar Baru from the Time of Bar Kokhba," *IEJ* 36 (1986): 201–14. Ele'azar son of Mattat and Ele'azar son of Shime'on witnessed *P.Yadin* 23 for Babatha in Maḥoza on 17 November 130. The third witness, Judah son of Judah, signed *P.Yadin* 19, a deed of gift written for Shlamzion by her father, Judah son of Ele'azar, Babatha's second husband, in 128 CE (*P.Yadin* 19). He may also have witnessed *P.Yadin* 26 of 131 CE.

72 Cf. Benjamin Isaac, "The Revolt of Bar Kokhba: Ideology and Modern Scholarship," in *The Near East under Roman Rule* (Leiden: Brill, 1998), 253 ("Postscript").

73 *P.Hever* 8, line, 1: [ב ...] לאדר שנת תלת לחרות ישראל על ימי שמעון בן כוסבא נשי ישראל; cf. *P.Hever* 8a, line, 1: בעשרה לא[ד]ר שנת תלת לחרת ישראל בכפר בריו: 'Ten of Adar, year three of the freedom of Israel in Kefar Baru.'

74 See the general introduction to Hannah M. Cotton and Ada Yardeni, *Aramaic, Hebrew, and Greek Documentary Texts from Naḥal Ḥever and Other Sites*, Discoveries in the Judaean Desert XXVII (Oxford: Clarendon Press, 1997), 1–6.

75 See Christa Clamer, "The Hot Springs of Kallirrhoe and Baarou," in *The Madaba Map Centenary 1897–1997*, ed. Michele Piccirillo and Eugenio Alliata (Jerusalem: Franciscan Printing Press, 1999), 221–25.

cated by the *fiscus* and distributed to retired veterans.[76] In this papyrus we find the freedman procurator, Aelius Amphigetes, continuing proceedings initiated before the procurator of the province, a Calpurnius Quintianus – now attested in a new inscription from Caesarea Maritima[77] – which involved the possession of a piece of land allotted to the veteran Valerius Serenus in the village of Meason in the Peraea.

Finally, it may be suggested that the papyri found in the caves of Ketef Jericho, and now published in *DJD* XXXVIII, also originated in the Peraea.[78]

The participation of the Peraea brings the revolt to Transjordan, but it still remains a Jewish affair. All three pieces of indirect evidence for the revolt spreading to Arabia enumerated above can be disposed of without involving non-Jews in the revolt.

1. T. Haterius Nepos, the governor of Arabia, and Publicius Marcellus, the governor of Syria, may have received their *ornamenta triumphalia* after the suppression of the Bar Kokhba revolt because they arrived in Judaea with their own armies without being made subordinate to the governor of Judaea, Iulius Severus, and not because they put down revolts in their own provinces.[79]
2. For the mass departure of Jews from Arabia more than one plausible explanation can be offered: a Jewish uprising in Arabia ended with the survivors escaping to Judaea; alternatively, the Jews were suspected of harbouring such plans, and therefore were driven out of the province. Or the Jews may have left Arabia of their own accord, cherishing the prospect of living in an independent Jewish state, or answering the call of a messianic leader.
3. The evidence of *P.Yadin* 52, attesting Nabataeans as present in their separate camp in Judaea towards the end of the revolt, may be taken to be describing mercenaries who joined Bar Kokhba in their greed for gain, as Cassius Dio says.

Nonetheless, we are bound to ask what mercenaries were doing in Judaea at the end of the revolt. Greed can no longer be the reason for it. Moreover, after 'many

76 Werner Eck, "Der Bar Kochba Aufstand, der kaiserliche Fiscus und die Veteranenversorgung," *SCI* 19 (2000): 139–48.

77 See Werner Eck and Hannah M. Cotton, "Inscriptions from the Financial Procurator's Praetorium in Caesarea," in *Man Near a Roman Arch: Studies Presented to Prof. Yoram Tsafrir*, ed. Leah Di Segni et al. (Jerusalem: IES, 2009), 100–102 (no. 2); for the identity of Quintianus, see Werner Eck, "Ein Prokuratorenpaar von Syria Palaestina in P. Berol. 21652," *ZPE* 123 (1998): 249–55.

78 *DJD* XXXVIII, nos. 1–19.

79 The inscriptions attesting their *ornamenta triumphalia* had been known for a long time, but were associated with the Bar Kokhba revolt for the first time by Eck, "The Bar Kokhba Revolt: The Roman Point of View."

outside nations too were joining them through eagerness for gain,' Cassius Dio adds: 'and the whole earth, one might almost say, was being stirred up over the matter.' (69, 13, 2). The whole *oikoumene* did not tremble because mercenaries came to join the Jews in Judaea. Moreover, the Jews who left their archives in the caves of the Judaean Desert were not messianic dreamers, eager to resettle in the Promised Land once it was freed from Roman yoke. Those who came equipped with legal deeds proving their ownership of plantations, houses and chattel in Arabia intended to claim this property on their return to the place they had come from.

I tend to think that both in the case of the Nabataeans and in that of the Jews from Arabia we are talking about refugees who left Arabia after the revolt had been put down there.

Why did the Nabataeans rise against Rome, having, as is commonly believed, accepted Roman rule so peacefully in 106? Why did it take them more than twenty-five years to rise up in arms against Rome? Could it be that they did not accept Roman rule so peacefully after all, and that the spectacular losses suffered by the Romans immediately after the revolt broke out in Judaea – one of the greatest military disasters ever suffered by Rome and seen as such by the Romans[80] – gave them the incentive to revolt?

Only speculations are possible, but once having made them we may be on the lookout for the evidence to prove them. Could it be that the Nabataeans, like the Jews with whom they lived in perfect harmony in Maḥoz Eglatain, shared not only legal formulae as the Jewish Aramaic and Nabataean Aramaic parts of the Babatha archive, now finally published, prove so well, but much more? The Aramaic-speaking populations of the Roman Near East shared a cultural inheritance and common sensitivities. Is it conceivable that the Jewish revolt against Rome triggered, for similar reasons, for similar susceptibilities, revolt also in Arabia? Did the inhabitants of that region, like the Jews, feel themselves threatened and excluded by the Cosmo-Hellenistic policy of the Emperor?

The foundation of Aelia Capitolina shattered the Jewish dream.[81] Did something occur in Arabia that shattered the Nabataean dream in similar fashion? We may think of the transfer of the capital from Petra to Bostra which, as we now know from the Babatha archive, did not take place immediately upon annexation. Various locutions in the Babatha archive strongly suggest that for a time Petra continued to function as the capital. It even received the title Hadriana

---

80 See above all Eck, "The Bar Kokhba Revolt: The Roman Point of View" for the evidence and its interpretation.

81 See Martin Goodman, "Trajan and the Origins of the Bar Kokhba War," in *The Bar Kokhba War Reconsidered*, ed. Peter Schäfer (Tübingen: Mohr Siebeck, 2003), 23–30.

upon annexation.[82] In *P.Yadin* 23 of 17 November 130 we hear Besas son of Yeshu'a summoning Babatha 'to meet him before Haterius Nepos, *legatus pro praetore*, in Petra or elsewhere in the province in the matter of a date orchard' etc. (lines 1–5 = lines 10–16). Clearly, if for some reason a litigant could not attend the assize centre (*conventus*) nearest to his place of residence, it was always possible to go to Petra where the governor resided on a more permanent basis.[83] This would explain why Titus Aninius Sextius Florentinus, governor of Arabia in 127, is buried in Petra. He must have died in office.[84]

We cannot know whether the transfer to Bostra caused a Nabataean uprising whose focus was Petra, but a date for this event close to the Jewish uprising would encourage such speculation. In the present state of our knowledge, we cannot go further.

82 Glen W. Bowersock, *Roman Arabia* (Cambridge, Mass.: Harvard University Press, 1983), 110.
83 Cf. Rudolf Haensch, *Capita Provinciarum* (Mainz am Rhein: von Zabern, 1997), 238 ff.
84 For the inscription set up by his son see *IGLS* XXI (= *Inscriptions de la Jordanie* IV), no. 51.

Language Gaps in Roman Palestine and the Roman Near East

Introduction

Whereas this entire paper will attempt to explain what I mean by 'language gaps,' I should confess right from the start that 'Roman Palestine' in my title is a bit of a red herring: Palestine has always been, and remains so to this day, a vague and far from uncontested concept; territories which may now be considered to be part of Palestine were in the period under discussion parts of the Roman provinces of Syria and Arabia, and the Roman province of Palestine never corresponded to any modern definition of the term. In any case precise borders are not terribly relevant to the present discussion; I wish to touch on linguistic phenomena common to many other parts of the Roman Near East.[1] I do not pretend here to do more than raise questions, examine the nature of our evidence and with the help of examples outline or merely adumbrate possible answers.

Here as elsewhere we face the same difficulty of having to rely on the direct or implied evidence of our written record as the sole evidence for the spoken languages.[2] Not infrequently these written sources, sometimes not inadvertently, hide the spoken language from our sight or obfuscate our vision. Granted that it

1 In recent years the Roman Near East has come into its own. Above all one should mention Fergus Millar's *The Roman Near East, 31 BC-AD 337* (Cambridge, Mass.: Harvard University Press, 1993) and a series of articles which constitute Fergus Millar, *Rome, the Greek World, and the East: Volume 3: The Greek World, the Jews and the East*, ed. Hannah M. Cotton and Guy M. Rogers (Chapel Hill: University of North Carolina Press, 2006); see also a review article by Ted Kaizer, "The Near East in the Hellenistic and Roman Periods between Local, Regional and Supra-Regional Approaches," *SCI* 22 (2003): 283–95.

2 Cf. Roger S. Bagnall, *Egypt in Late Antiquity* (Princeton: Princeton University Press, 1993), 240–41; Michael C.A. Macdonald, "Some Reflections on Epigraphy and Ethnicity in the Roman Near East," *Mediterranean Archaeology* 11 (1998): 177–78.

Article note: First published in Christian Frevel, ed., *Medien im antiken Palästina: Materielle Kommunikation und Medialität als Thema der Palästinaarchäologie* (Tübingen: Mohr Siebeck, 2005), 151–69, with the following note: the ideas in this paper were formed and developed during a year spent at the Institute for Advanced Studies in Jerusalem as a member of a research group called 'Greeks, Romans, Jews and Others in the Near East from Alexander to Muhammad: A Civilization of Epigraphy.' I owe a great debt to members of the group: Leah Di Segni, Robert Hoyland, Ernst Axel Knauf, Shlomo Naeh, Jonathan Price, Marijana Ricl, Seth Schwartz, and especially to David Wasserstein. I also wish to thank Werner Eck for insightful observations on my draft.

https://doi.org/10.1515/9783110770438-012

may be impossible to revoke the irrevocable, nonetheless one should be aware of questionable assumptions and unfounded modern constructs on the subject of spoken languages. Perhaps we can get nearer to the truth by eliminating some misconceptions.

Inscriptions seem at first sight to hold better promise for demonstrating the gap – or perhaps suggesting ways to close it – between spoken and written languages. However, historians using epigraphic material as their daily bread have been quick to point out the inherent optical distortion of the original linguistic map of the Roman Empire as a whole, and the Roman Near East in particular, caused by the evidence of the inscriptions themselves – a distortion which works in favour of the imperial languages, Latin and Greek, with their entrenched epigraphic habits, and against the spoken vernacular languages which often left no written record at all. Furthermore, the written record itself is hardly representative of reality since the material on which inscriptions were written determined their survival or conversely their extinction. The *Memorialepigraphik* meant to transcend the 'here and now' and be present for posterity was inscribed on durable materials. It thus stood a far better chance of surviving than the ephemeral epigraphy whose sole aim was to be understood by the people living then and there, to take effect in their 'here and now,' and which was consequently written on perishable materials. Inscriptions written on the latter no doubt far outnumbered those of the memorial epigraphy, and better documented the spoken languages at any given place and time.[3]

The apparent implication of the foregoing observations[4] is that the survival of that ephemeral epigraphy would have left us a more accurate picture of reality as it was then in that it would have 'given voice' to the spoken languages. This assumption can be shown to be patently false; it fails to take into account several important factors which have nothing to do with optimal physical conditions for survival. Even when it managed to survive, the ephemeral epigraphy, that written on papyri for example, may not attest faithfully the languages spoken in the place where such documents were written. This is certainly true of the materials with which I have been occupied in the last decade, namely the legal papyri from the

3 See Werner Eck, "Inschriften auf Holz. Ein unterschätztes Phänomen der epigraphischen Kultur Roms," in *Imperium Romanum. Studien zu Geschichte und Rezeption, Festschrift für Karl Christ zum 75. Geburtstag*, ed. Peter Kneissl and Volker Losemann (Stuttgart: F. Steiner, 1998), 203–17; Werner Eck, "Lateinische Epigraphik," in *Einleitung in die lateinische Philologie*, ed. Fritz Graf (Stuttgart: Teubner, 1997), 92–111.

4 Such reflexions can be found for example in Werner Eck, "The Presence, Role and Significance of Latin in the Epigraphy and Culture of the Roman Near East," in *From Hellenism to Islam: Cultural and Linguistic Change in the Roman Near East*, ed. Hannah M. Cotton et al. (Cambridge: Cambridge University Press, 2009), 15–42.

Judaean Desert. True, these documents may not be as representative of ephemeral epigraphy as graffiti, yet they were not intended to survive for the benefit of an anonymous future audience like the memorial epigraphy. I see no need to apologize for assigning a central place to these papyri for I regard them as pre-eminently representative of the sort of linguistic gaps which I am trying to explore here, namely those between written and spoken languages. A few words on this group of papyri are necessary.

Legal Papyri from the Judaean Desert and Other Places

The explanation for the presence of the documentary material found in the caves of the Judaean Desert lies in the two Jewish revolts against Rome: the so-called Great Revolt of 66–70 CE and the Bar Kokhba revolt of 132–136 CE.[5] The upheavals caused by the two revolts drove scores of Jews from their homes in the provinces of Judaea and Arabia and made them hide their documents, mostly legal documents, in the caves of Wadi Murabbaʿat, Naḥal Ḥever, Naḥal Se'elim (Wadi Seiyâl), Naḥal Mishmar, Naḥal David (Wadi Sdeir), in two caves near Jericho, and in a cave above Ein Gedi.[6] The material spans a period of just over 70 years (ca. 60 to 132 CE), and the great majority of the documents were written by, or at least involve, Jews. The people attested in the documents belong to a village society at a time when the bulk of the population in this area consisted of village dwellers, and the papyri, like others from elsewhere in the Roman Near East, thus reflect the legal habits of the otherwise silent majority.[7]

The legal documents from the Judaean Desert were composed in Jewish Aramaic, Nabataean Aramaic, Greek and Hebrew. The choice of language was determined by tradition and, as we shall see, also by utilitarian considerations. Up to a point Aramaic was the natural choice, not necessarily because it was the spoken language in the area – which cannot be proven even if probable – but because this was the language of legal documents from time immemorial in

5 On the Bar Kokhba revolt see now Peter Schäfer, ed., *The Bar Kokhba War Reconsidered* (Tübingen: Mohr Siebeck, 2003).

6 For surveys of the publications of papyri from the Judaean Desert see above all Hannah M. Cotton, "Die Papyrusdokumente aus der judäischen Wüste und ihr Beitrag zur Erforschung der jüdischen Geschichte des 1. und 2. Jh.s n. Chr.," *ZDPV* 115 (1999): 228–47; Hannah M. Cotton, "Documentary Texts from the Judaean Desert: A Matter of Nomenclature," *SCI* 20 (2001): 113–19; Hannah M. Cotton, W.E.H. Cockle, and Fergus Millar, "The Papyrology of the Roman Near East: A Survey," *JRS* 85 (1995): 214–35.

7 See Hannah M. Cotton, "The Guardianship of Jesus Son of Babatha: Roman and Local Law in the Province of Arabia," *JRS* 83 (1993): 94–108 [below, pp. 403–30].

this part of the world.[8] Most of the legal documents from the Judaean Desert are written in Aramaic, whether Nabataean Aramaic or Jewish Aramaic.[9]

I would like to mention here in brackets the use of Hebrew in legal documents, since, as argued elsewhere, this is found only during the two revolts – I suppose as a kind of nationalist manifesto: to advertise the ideology of the now independent Jewish state.[10] However, the Aramaic scribal tradition in writing such documents is often revealed in the language and the legal formulae of the documents.

Perhaps the best evidence for the use of Aramaic in legal documents are the *Mishnah* and the *Toseftah*, which contain Jewish civil law as redacted in the second and third centuries CE. Both of these collections are written in Hebrew.[11] We do not have one single contract in the whole of the *Mishnah* or the *Toseftah*, only contractual formulae. These formulae, unlike the legal discussion in which they are embedded which is conducted in Hebrew, are written in Aramaic – thus proving not only that they are of a much older vintage than the Hebrew interpretation, but also that the language of contracts in daily use at the time was Aramaic. We may

8 See above all Yochanan Muffs, *Studies in the Aramaic Legal Papyri from Elephantine* (Leiden: Brill, 1969); cf. observations in Elias J. Bickerman, "Two Legal Interpretations of the Septuagint," in *Studies in Jewish and Christian History*, Vol. I (Leiden: Brill, 1976), 201–224; Baruch A. Levine, "On the Origins of the Aramaic Legal Formulary of Elephantine," in *Christianity, Judaism, and Other Greco-Roman Cults: Studies for Morton Smith at Sixty*, ed. Jacob Neusner, Vol. III (Leiden: Brill, 1975), 37–54; Baruch A. Levine, "The Various Workings of the Aramaic Legal Tradition: Jews and Nabateans in the Naḥal Ḥever Archive," in *The Dead Sea Scrolls: Fifty Years after their Discovery 1947–1997*, ed. Lawrence H. Schiffman, Emanuel Tov, and James C. Vanderkam (Jerusalem: IES, 2000), 836–51; Abraham Wasserstein, "A Marriage Contract from the Province of Arabia Nova: Notes on Papyrus Yadin 18," *JQR* 80 (1989): 93–130; Abraham Wasserstein, "Non-Hellenized Jews in the Semi-Hellenized East," *SCI* 14 (1995): 111–37.

9 On the Aramaic dialects see Joseph Naveh and Jonas C. Greenfield, "Hebrew and Aramaic in the Persian Period," in *The Cambridge History of Judaism, Volume 1: Introduction: The Persian Period* (Cambridge: Cambridge University Press, 1984), 115–29.

10 See Hannah M. Cotton, "The Languages of the Legal and Administrative Documents from the Judaean Desert," *ZPE* 125 (1999): 219–31 [above, pp. 127–46]; cf. Hanan Eshel, Magen Broshi, and T.A.J. Jull, "Documents from Wadi Murabba'at and the Status of Jerusalem during the Bar Kokhba Revolt," in *The Refuge Caves of the Bar Kokhba Revolt*, ed. Hanan Eshel and David Amit (Jerusalem: IES, 1998), 233–39 (Hebrew).

11 The Hebrew language of the Mishnah used to be thought of as an artificial language, created for the purpose of the legal discussions contained in the rabbinic sources. This view has been discredited by the discovery of letters written in Hebrew in Wadi Murabba'at and Naḥal Ḥever, cf. Eduard Yechezkel Kutscher, "The Hebrew and Aramaic Letters of Bar Koseba and his Contemporaries: Part II: The Hebrew Letters," *Lĕšonénu* 26 (1961): 7–23 (Hebrew) = *Hebrew and Aramaic Studies* (Jerusalem: Magnes Press, 1977), 54–70. It is beyond my competence to take sides in the controversy on the use of Hebrew as a spoken language, but see sensible comments in Seth Schwartz, "Language, Power and Identity in Ancient Palestine," *Past & Present* 148 (1995): 3–47.

envisage the Mishnaic discussion as a process whereby the rabbis comment in Hebrew on contracts written from beginning to end in Aramaic. The commentary cites the formulae *verbatim* in the language in which they were written, namely Aramaic.[12] The rabbinic discussions eventually redacted in the *Mishnah* and the *Toseftah* continued in this manner long after the documents had dried up. This fact alone should leave no doubt in our minds that Jews continued to use Aramaic long after the introduction of Greek into legal contracts.[13]

The appearance of Greek in legal documents, at first sight surprisingly, but in fact not unexpectedly, coincides more or less with the advent of Rome. This is best seen in the case of the former Nabataean kingdom which in 106 CE became the Roman province of Arabia. There are *no* documents written in Greek (or Jewish Aramaic) from the Nabataean period. All legal documents from the Nabataean period are written in Nabataean Aramaic. Our corpus consists of two groups. The first is made up of tomb-inscriptions from Mada'in Salih.[14] That they are legal texts, and not warnings against interference with the tombs, is to be inferred *inter alia* from the fact that copies were deposited in the temple, as we read in one of the inscriptions.[15] There are a few more tomb-inscriptions of this sort in Petra and Madaba. The last dated one is from 74/75 CE. The second group is made up of the Nabataean papyri from Naḥal Ḥever which contain the longest texts of Nabataean law. All those from the Babatha archive – *P.Yadin* 1–4, 6 and 9 – have already been published.[16] There are five or six more contracts in Nabataean, of which two have been published, that most probably belong to the archive of Salome Komaïse.[17]

---

12 For examples see Hannah M. Cotton, "Survival, Adaptation and Extinction: Nabataean and Jewish Aramaic versus Greek in the Legal Documents from the Cave of Letters in Naḥal Ḥever," in *Sprache und Kultur in der kaiserzeitlichen Provinz Arabia: Althistorische Beiträgezur Erforschung von Akkulturationsphänomenen im römischen Nahen Osten*, ed. Leonhard Schumacher and Oliver Stoll (St. Katharinen: Scripta Mercaturae Verlag, 2003), 1–11 [above, pp. 161–72].

13 *Contra* Naphtali Lewis, "The Demise of the Aramaic Document in the Dead Sea Region," *SCI* 20 (2001): 178–81.

14 John F. Healey, *The Nabataean Tomb Inscriptions of Mada'in Salih* (Oxford: Oxford University Press, 1993).

15 Cf. Healey, H 36 l. 9.

16 *P.Yadin* 1–4, 6 and 9, published in Yigael Yadin et al., *The Documents from the Bar Kokhba Period in the Cave of Letters: Hebrew, Aramaic and Nabatean-Aramaic Papyri*, Judean Desert Studies III (Jerusalem: IES, 2002).

17 The Archive of Salome Komaïse was published as *P.Hever* 12, 32(?), 60–65 in Hannah M. Cotton and Ada Yardeni, *Aramaic, Hebrew, and Greek Documentary Texts from Naḥal Ḥever and Other Sites*, Discoveries in the Judaean Desert XXVII (Oxford: Clarendon Press, 1997). For the Nabataean contracts not published in this volume but thought to belong to the archive see: Cotton, "Survival, Adaptation and Extinction: Nabataean and Jewish Aramaic versus Greek in the Legal Documents from the Cave of Letters in Naḥal Ḥever," 2, n. 6 [above, p. 162, n. 6].

The dates of the Nabataean contracts from Naḥal Ḥever fall between 60 and 122 CE.

In 106 CE the Nabataean kingdom was annexed and made into the Roman province of Arabia. After 106 CE as against 2 Nabataean contracts and 4 written in Jewish Aramaic we have altogether 32 Greek documents from the period between 106 and 132 CE. The conclusion is inescapable that the Greek legal contract took over, not due to any language change, as proven from the fact that subscriptions and signatures of the parties to a contract continue to be written in Aramaic, but because the contract was intended for a Roman court of law.[18] There was no such requirement on the part of the Romans; rather, Greek was the language of communication between Rome and its subject populations of the Roman Near East (see below).

Elsewhere I have argued at some length that in Judaea contracts began to be written in Greek (alongside Aramaic) after the destruction of the Temple and the dissolution of the Sanhedrin. However, it was not merely the curtailment of legal autonomy which accounts for the transition to Greek, but also the intensive Romanization of the territory which now, under the Flavians, for the first time became a proper Roman province (perhaps, for the first time, no longer annexed to the province of Syria) with its own senatorial governor and equestrian procurator.[19]

Greek remained the language of legal documents up to the 6th and 7th centuries in the territories which once belonged to Nabataea/Arabia, as is shown by the Petra papyri[20] and by the Nessana Papyri of the 6th and 7th centuries CE.[21] Greek

---

18 Hannah M. Cotton, "Jewish Jurisdiction under Roman Rule: Prolegomena," in *Zwischen den Reichen: Neues Testament und römische Herrschaft. Vorträge auf der ersten Konferenz der European Association for Biblical Studies*, ed. Michael Labahn and Jürgen Zangenberg (Tübingen: Francke Verlag, 2002), 13–28 [below, pp. 485–99].

19 Hannah M. Cotton, "Some Aspects of the Roman Administration of Judaea/Syria-Palaestina," in *Lokale Autonomie und römische Ordnungsmacht in den kaiserzeitlichen Provinzen vom 1. bis 3. Jahrhundert*, ed. Werner Eck (München: Oldenbourg, 1999), 75–91 [below, pp. 317–35], and Hannah M. Cotton and Werner Eck, "Eine Provinz entsteht: Alte und neue lateinische Inschriften in Iudaea unter Vespasian," in *The Roman Near East and Armenia*, ed. Edward Dąbrowa (Krakow: Jagiellonian University Press, 2003), 25–37.

20 *P.Petra* are ca. 140 rolls of documentary papyri, all dating to the 6th century CE, which were discovered at the end of 1993 in a Byzantine church in Petra and published by scholars from Finland and the University of Michigan; see now Jaakko Frösén, Antti Arjava, and Marjo Lentinen, *The Petra Papyri I* (Amman: ACOR, 2002).

21 See Casper J. Kraemer, *Excavations at Nessana III: Non-Literary Papyri* (Princeton: Princeton University Press, 1958) (*P.Nessana*).

continued to be used in Nessana long after the Arab conquest – even by the Arab administration itself.[22]

The tenacity of the Greek legal tradition into the third century CE is strongly attested in Dura-Europos. Founded by the Macedonians ca. 300 BCE, and ruled in succession by the Seleucids in its first two hundred years, by the Parthians (from 100 BCE to 165 CE), and the Romans (from 165 to ca. 250 CE), the city of Dura-Europos retained the use of Greek in private legal transactions throughout its history.[23] The recently published *P.Euphr.*, the majority of which are written in Greek, show that the use of Greek in legal documents was by no means exclusive to a properly founded Greek city like Dura-Europos.[24]

The Greek Language and the Coming of Rome

A large vista opens before us: the presence of the Roman ruling power, which itself spoke Latin, promoted and prompted the use of Greek in the Near East, in a way which should remind us of the promotion of Aramaic under the Persian-speaking Achaemenids. Of course I am not the first to draw a parallel between the linguistic policies of the two empires. Both empires are likely to have relied on a widespread knowledge of Aramaic and Greek respectively. But how wide is far from obvious.

All over the Near East for hundreds of years literate notaries and scribes conducted legal and administrative affairs – the distinction between them is largely anachronistic – in a language that did not necessarily correspond to the vernacular of either ruler or subject. A group of recently discovered Aramaic documents of the fourth century BCE from Afghanistan attests that no matter what the identity of the ruling power at the time, whether it was the Persian Artaxerxes or the Macedonian Alexander, these administrative documents dispatched by a Persian

22 See Cotton, Cockle, and Millar, "The Papyrology of the Roman near East: A Survey," nos. 571–609.

23 Cf. Fergus Millar, "Dura-Europos under Parthian Rule," in *Das Partherreich und seine Zeugnisse*, ed. Josef Wiesehöfer (Stuttgart: F. Steiner, 1988), 473–92.

24 Denis Feissel and Jean Gascou, "Documents d'archives romains inédits du Moyen Euphrate (IIIe s. après J-C): I. Les pétitions (T. Euphr. 1 à 5)," *Journal des Savants*, 1995, 65–119; Javier Teixidor, Denis Feissel, and Jean Gascou, "Documents d'archives romains inédits du Moyen Euphrate (IIIe siècle après J-C): II. Les actes de vente- achat (P. Euphr. 6 À 10)," *Journal des Savants*, 1997, 3–57; Denis Feissel and Jean Gascou, "Documents d'archives romains inédits du Moyen Euphrate (IIIe s. après J.-C.): III. Actes divers et Lettres (P. Euphr. 11 à 17)," *Journal des Savants*, 2000, 157–208; Javier Teixidor, "Deux documents syriaques du IIIe siècle ap. J.-C., provenant du Moyen Euphrate," *CR Acad. Inscr.* 134 (1990): 144–66 (= Cotton, Cockle, and Millar, "The Papyrology of the Roman near East: A Survey," nos. 22–33).

Satrap to his Persian subordinate were written in the current Reichsaramäisch of the time. As was to be expected, the job was executed by a professional scribe whose name does not necessarily give us a clue to his ethnic affiliation: 'Daizaka the scribe is in charge of this document.'[25]

The Roman ruling power, with the exception of a short period in the late third century and the beginning of the fourth century CE (i. e. under the rule of emperors who hailed from Illyria and other Balkan provinces), never sought or wished to impose the use of Latin in the eastern provinces.[26] Greek was the language of communication between Rome and its subjects in the eastern part of the Empire. The presence of the governor or the financial procurator in a specific city seems never and nowhere to have induced the residents, not even the ambitious and the powerful, who had frequent intercourse with the powers that be, to resort more often to the use of Latin in the types of inscriptions preserved for posterity. When residents of a city, including members of its elite, raised monuments to honour the Roman emperors or Rome's highest representatives, this was done almost without exception in Greek.[27] The rare occasions on which Latin is used are signals for us to look for special reasons. Only within the immediate circle of the administration itself, among the *officiales* of the procurators and the subalterns of the governors, is Latin the norm.[28]

The almost exclusive use of Greek in communications with the ruling power is in evidence in the entire epigraphic corpus of the Greek communities in Asia Minor and Greece proper. But it is also true of the Roman Near East where Greek was far from being the spoken language of the majority of the population. This is demonstrated in the papyri from Egypt, as also in papyri and inscriptions found in other parts of the Roman Near East: in the Judaean Desert, near the Euphrates and in Bostra. Although many of these documents are addressed to representa-

---

25 Some of the documents were presented by Shaul Shaked in a seminar held at the Institute for Advanced Studies in Jerusalem in June 2003, and are now published by Joseph Naveh and Shaul Shaked, *Aramaic Documents from Ancient Bactria* (London: The Khalili Family Trust, 2012). The citation above comes from A 4, l. 6. On names and ethnic identity see more below.

26 Werner Eck, "The Language of Power: Latin in the Inscriptions of Judaea/Syria Palaestina," in *Semitic Papyrology in Context: A Climate of Creativity*, ed. Lawrence H. Schiffman (Leiden – Boston: Brill, 2003), 123–44.

27 Cf. Eck, "The Presence, Role and Significance of Latin in the Epigraphy and Culture of the Roman Near East."

28 Hannah M. Cotton and Werner Eck, "Governors and Their Personnel on Latin Inscriptions from Caesarea Maritima," *Proceedings of the Israel Academy of Sciences and Humanities* 7 (2001): 215–40; Werner Eck and Hannah M. Cotton, "Inscriptions from the Financial Procurator's Praetorium in Caesarea," in *Man Near a Roman Arch: Studies Presented to Prof. Yoram Tsafrir*, ed. Leah Di Segni et al. (Jerusalem: IES, 2009), 98–114.

tives of the Roman government, whether a *beneficiarius*,[29] a centurion,[30] a *praefectus alae*,[31] or the governor himself[32] – they are all written in Greek. The same is true of announcements made by Rome's representatives to her subjects – they are all in Greek. Not one of the edicts published by the prefects of Egypt uses Latin.[33]

There is some tension here, not to say a paradox: the advent of Rome brought with it considerable intensification of the process of Hellenization in the Near East as attested in the written corpus as well as in material culture. Until then, as pointed out by Fergus Millar, our evidence for the Greek presence in Syria for example is "limited, variable and erratic."[34] Nor do the indigenous local cultures express themselves much in writing until then. In fact, as pointed out by Fergus Millar throughout his book on the Roman Near East, the existence of such local cultures seems to have surfaced for the first time with the advent of Rome, mostly in Greek and sometimes in their own languages. This is true even of the pagan cults which "with the sole and notable exception of Palmyra ... did not find any written expression in languages other than Greek."[35] In other words, these local cultures owe their very appearance in the historical record to their adoption of the 'epigraphic habit' of the Graeco-Roman world. This 'epigraphic habit' seems

---

29 Jean Gascou, "Unités administratives locales et fonctionnaires romains. Les données des nouveaux papyrus du Moyen Euphrate et d'Arabie," in *Lokale Autonomie und römische Ordnungsmacht in den kaiserzeitlichen Provinzen vom 1. bis 3. Jahrhundert*, ed. Werner Eck (München: Oldenbourg, 1999), 71–3 (*P.Bostra* 1); cf. Cotton, "Some Aspects of the Roman Administration of Judaea/Syria-Palaestina," 90–1 [below, pp. 334–35].

30 E.g. *P.Euphr.* 5, published in Feissel and Gascou, "Documents d'archives romains inédits du Moyen Euphrate (IIIe s. Après J-C): I. Les Pétitions (T. Euphr. 1 à 5)."

31 *P.Yadin* 16, published in Naphtali Lewis, *The Documents from the Bar Kokhba Period in the Cave of Letters. Greek Papyri*, Judean Desert Studies II (Jerusalem: IES, 1989); *P.Hever* 61, published in Cotton and Yardeni, *Aramaic, Hebrew, and Greek Documentary Texts from Naḥal Ḥever and Other Sites.*

32 E.g. *P.Yadin* 13, 14, 15, published in Lewis, *The Documents from the Bar Kokhba Period in the Cave of Letters. Greek Papyri*; *P.Euphr.* 1–2, published in Feissel and Gascou, "Documents d'archives romains inédits du Moyen Euphrate (IIIe s. Après J-C): I. Les Pétitions (T. Euphr. 1 à 5)."

33 See Ranon Katzoff, "Sources of Law in Roman Egypt: The Role of the Prefect," in *Aufstieg und Niedergang der römischen Welt*, Vol. II.13 (Berlin: De Gruyter, 1980), 807–46; Gianfranco Purpura, "Gli editti dei prefetti d'Egitto, I sec. a.C. – I sec. d.C.," *Annali del seminario giuridico del Università di Palermo* 42 (1992): 487–671; to which add now: *SB* XVIII 13849; *BGU* XVI 2558; *P.IFAO* III 34; *P.Oxy.* 3613.

34 Fergus Millar, "The Problem of Hellenistic Syria," in *Hellenism in the East*, ed. Amélie Kuhrt and Susan Sherwin-White (London: Duckworth, 1987), 123.

35 Fergus Millar, "Ethnic Identity in the Roman Near East, AD 325–450: Language, Religion and Culture," *Mediterranean Archaeology* 11 (1998): 167.

to have been closely associated with the Greek language;[36] it offered a vehicle for the expression of the indigenous local cultures in the area.[37]

That the heyday of Greek epigraphy in the Near East belongs to the Roman period is well exemplified in the published volumes of the *Inscriptions grecques et latines de la Syrie* as also in the archives and the published volumes of the *Corpus Inscriptionum Iudaeae/Palaestinae*,[38] which contain so far 133 Hellenistic Greek inscriptions, as against thousands in Greek from the Roman period.

Nowhere are the complexities outlined above more sharply seen than in the re-foundations of local communities as new Greek *poleis* by Rome. Let me use the city of Petra as a salient example. Petra is attested as a *polis*, or rather as a *metropolis*, for the first time in an inscription on an arch dedicated to Trajan by the city of Petra in 114 CE, eight years after the annexation of the province, and already under its first governor:[39]

> [Αὐτοκράτορι Καίσα]ρ̣ι̣ θεοῦ [Νέρουα υἱῷ] Νέρουα̣ Τ̣ρ̣[αιανῷ Σεβαστῷ] | [Γερμανικῷ Δακικῷ Παρθικῷ Μαξίμ]ωι, ἀρχιερεῖ μεγίστῳ, δ[ημαρ]χικῆς ἐξουσίας τὸ [ι]η̣ʹ, αὐτοκράτορι τὸ ζʹ, ὑπ[άτῳ τὸ ςʹ, πάτρι πατρίδος] | [– – – ἡ μη]τρόπολις Πέτρα ἐπὶ Γαίου Κλ[αυδίο]υ Σεουήρου πρεσ̣β[ευτοῦ Σεβαστοῦ] ἀντιστρατήγου [– – –].

> To the Emperor Caesar, son of divus Nerva, Nerva Traianus Augustus Germanicus Dacicus Parthicus, pontifex maximus, holding the tribunician power for the eighteenth year, acclaimed imperator seven times, six times consul, Father of his Country, the *metropolis* of Petra at the time of Gaius Claudius Severus, legatus Augusti pro praetore.

There is nothing to suggest that Petra even had the constitution of a *polis* before 114 CE. It is thus all the more surprising to find ten years later a document in which Petra emerges as a Greek *polis* with a *boule* which publishes its decisions in Greek in *P.Yadin* 12 of 124 CE.[40]

> ἐγ<γ>εγραμμένον καὶ ἀντιβεβλημένον κεφαλαίου ἑνὸς \ἐπιτροπῆς/ ἀπὸ ἄκτων βου̣λῆς Πετραίω̣ν̣ τῆς μητ̣ροπόλεως προκειμένω<ν> ἐν τῷ ἐν Πέτρᾳ Ἀφροδεισίῳ καὶ ἔστιν

36 The point is emphasised in Ernst Axel Knauf, "Speaking and Writing in Galilee," in *Zeichen aus Text und Stein. Studien auf dem Weg zu einer Archäologie des Neuen Testaments*, ed. Stefan Alkier and Jürgen Zangenberg (Tübingen: A. Francke, 2003), 336–50.

37 See Glen W. Bowersock, *Hellenism in Late Antiquity* (Ann Arbor: University of Michigan Press, 1990).

38 See Hannah M. Cotton et al., "Corpus Inscriptionum Judaeae/Palaestinae," *ZPE* 27 (1999): 307–8.

39 Maurice Sartre, *Inscriptions de la Jordanie IV: Pétra et la Nabatène méridionale, du wadi al-Hasa au golfe de 'Aqaba*, *IGLS* XXI (Paris: P. Geuthner, 1993), no. 37.

40 *P.Yadin* 12 published in Lewis, *The Documents from the Bar Kokhba Period in the Cave of Letters. Greek Papyri.*

καθὼς ὑποτέτακται· καὶ Ἰασσούου Ἰουδαίου υἱοῦ Ἰασσούου κώμης Μαωζᾶ Ἀβδοβδας Ἰλλουθα καὶ Ἰωάνης Ἐγλα. ἐπράχθη ἐν Πέτρᾳ μητροπόλει τῆς Ἀραβ̣[ία]ς πρ[ὸ τεσσ]άρων καλανδῶṿ [. . . . ί]ων ἐπὶ ὑπάτῳν [Μ]αṿ[ί]ου Ἀκειλίου Γ̣λ̣ạβρίωνος κạὶ Γ̣ạίου Β̣ελ̣λ̣ικ<ί>ọṿ Ṭ[ο] ρκ̣ουάτοṿ . .σ[.] . .τọγοṿ. vacat (lines 4–11).

Verified exact copy of one item from the minutes of the council of Petra the metropolis, which were displayed in the temple of Aphrodite in Petra and it is appended below: 'And of Jesus, a Jew/Judaean, son of Jesus, of the village Mahoza, Abdobdas son of Illouthas and Iohanes son of Eglas [are appointed guardians].' Done in Petra, metropolis of Arabia, four days before the calends of ..., in the consulship of Manius Acilius Glabrio and Gaius Bellicius Torquatus ...

The καὶ Ἰασσούου ('and of Yeshua') clearly implies that there was a whole list of such appointments, all written in Greek. Are we to assume that the discussions in the *boule* took place in Greek as well? Hardly. However, all that can be said is that whether or not the discussion took place in Greek, the possession of a *polis*-constitution by a city in the Roman Near East implied the use of the Greek language in the public sphere. The decisions of the council had to be displayed in Greek in public, e. g. on a wall outside a temple as we see here. I do not know of any law or statute which said so, but it seems obvious that the use of Greek in the public sphere was part and parcel of the possession of this prestigious legal status in this part of the Roman world – with the obvious exception of the Roman colonies, where Latin had to be displayed in the public sphere, i. e. in decrees, coins etc.[41]

Some of the citizens of Petra may have known Greek before. It is hardly likely that a *polis* status would be conferred without this prerequisite.[42] But there is no way to prove this since the need to use Greek in the public sphere seems to have gone hand in hand with the introduction of the epigraphic habit little used before in the city; there are no Greek inscriptions in Sartre's corpus which can be dated safely to the royal period.[43]

---

41 For the published Latin inscriptions from Caesarea Maritima see Clayton Miles Lehmann and Kenneth G. Holum, *The Greek and Latin Inscriptions of Caesarea Maritima* (Boston: ACOR, 2000) with Hannah M. Cotton and Werner Eck, "A New Inscription from Caesarea Maritima and the Local Elite of Caesarea Maritima," in *What Athens Has to Do with Jerusalem. Essays on Classical, Jewish, and Early Christian Art and Archaeology in Honor of Gideon Foerster*, ed. Leonard V. Rutgers (Leuven: Peeters, 2002), 375–91.

42 Millar, "The Problem of Hellenistic Syria," 124, expresses strong doubt that "any ... existing communities could be made into Greek cities purely by the issue of some sort of charter or the granting of a Greek constitution, without either a settlement or building operations."

43 There are of course inscriptions in Nabataean from the period before annexation, but not recorded in Sartre, *Inscriptions de la Jordanie IV*, which does not record inscriptions in languages other than Latin and Greek.

However, there is another twist to the conclusions which can be drawn from the evidence of *P.Yadin* 12. Already its editor, Naphtali Lewis, now supported by Jim Adams,[44] suggested that "from beginning to end this document reads like a Greek translation of a Latin original." Lewis and Adams point to the expression ἐγ<γ>εγραμμένον καὶ ἀντιβεβλημένον rendering *descriptum et recognitum*; to the expression ἀπὸ ἄκτων βουλῆς Πετραίων which represents *ab/ex actis senatus Petraeorum*, especially since there is a threefold omission of the definite article (i. e. ἀπὸ τῶν ἄκτων τῆς βουλῆς τῶν Πετραίων); and to the expression ἐπράχθη ἐν Πέτρᾳ followed by the consular date just as in the *actum* in Roman legal documents. This piece of evidence joins others in establishing the Roman influence on the diplomatics of the legal texts here and elsewhere in the archives from the Judaean Desert.[45] Nonetheless the fact that this document was displayed in Greek is all that we need in order to prove that Greek was the *lingua franca* in the public domain of Petra. The epigraphic evidence from Petra offers us no proof whatsoever that Latin was used in the *boule* and by the *bouleutai*.

Language and Script

Those who speak of the 'epigraphic habit' seem to neglect altogether the correlation between epigraphic activity and literacy, or the existence of languages without script, like Arabic before it adopted and developed the Nabataean script, or spoken Arabic in our days, or Inuit whose script was invented by missionaries in the 19th century – to name but a few examples. In what follows I should like to suggest that the absence of uncomplicated script (or of any script altogether as for example among contemporary German and Pannonian peoples), no less than illiteracy, distorted the linguistic map of the Near East in favour of the imperial languages, or rather in favour of the languages for which there existed a large number of experienced and fluent professional scribes.

Some may think of an easy solution for the absence of script, namely transcription of the unwritten language in a different script, as happens for example in the case of Yiddish, a German dialect written in the Hebrew script, where we witness the transliteration *not* of single words or formulae, but full texts freely

44 J.N. Adams, *Bilingualism and the Latin Language* (New York: Cambridge University Press, 2003), 267–8.

45 Hannah M. Cotton, "'Diplomatics' or External Aspects of the Legal Documents from the Judaean Desert: Prolegomena," in *Rabbinic Law in its Roman and Near Eastern Context*, ed. Catherine Hezser (Tübingen: Mohr Siebeck, 2003), 49–61 [above, pp. 147–60].

composed in one language and written in the script of another. No doubt this is a very neat solution, but was it adopted by the ancients?

In their paper Shlomo Naeh and Jonathan Price[46] argue convincingly that throughout Antiquity language and script were perceived as an organic unity, not as separable entities. Transcription of freely composed texts was always in some way a marginal activity; there was always a compelling, exceptional reason when one language was written in the script of another. But this was not the norm.[47]

As a 'living' example of the perceived unity of a language and its script, Naeh and Price bring forward *P.Yadin* 52,[48] one of the two Greek letters in the so-called Bar Kokhba archive. The reason for its great fame lies in the crux in lines 11–15, for which many interpretations have been offered.[49] It has often served as a springboard for discussions of the languages spoken in Palestine in the first two centuries CE, and of the language likely to have been spoken by Jesus. I reproduce below the final edition with one modification:[50]

1st hand
1. Σου̣[μαι]ος Ι̣ωναθηι
2. Β̣ει̣ανου καὶ Μα-
3. [σ]αβαλα[ι] χαίρειν.
4. ἐ̣π̣ιδὴ ἔπεμσα πρὸς
5. ὑ̣μ̣ᾶς Ἀ[γ]ρίππαν σπου-
6. δ[άσα]τε πέμσε μοι
7. θ̣[ύ]ρ̣σ̣ου[ς] καὶ κίτρια,
8. ὅ[σον] δυ̣γ̣ασθήσεται,

46 Jonathan J. Price and Shlomo Naeh, "On the Margins of Culture: The Practice of Transcription in the Ancient World," in *From Hellenism to Islam: Cultural and Linguistic Change in the Roman Near East*, ed. Hannah M. Cotton et al. (Cambridge: Cambridge University Press, 2009), 257–88.
47 See two isolated cases of transliteration in Macdonald, "Some Reflections on Epigraphy and Ethnicity in the Roman Near East," 181.
48 Final edition in Hannah M. Cotton, "Greek Letters," in *The Documents from the Bar Kokhba Period in the Cave of Letters: Hebrew, Jewish Aramaic and Nabataean Aramaic Papyri*, Judean Desert Studies III, ed. Yigael Yadin et al. (Jerusalem: IES, 2002), 349–66, where the right solution presented above was missed, albeit it was observed there that normally the adverbs Ebraïsti/Hellenisti would designate both language and script, as they do for example in the inscription on the cross according to John 19:20 (ἦν γεγραμμένον Ἑβραϊστί, Ῥωμαϊστί, Ἑλληνιστί), and in line 12 of the present papyrus: ἐγράφη δ[ὲ] Ἑλληνιστί.
49 See Cotton.
50 I have preferred here, as also in Hannah M. Cotton, "The Bar Kokhba Revolt and the Documents from the Judaean Desert: Nabataean Participation in the Revolt (P.Yadin 52)," in *The Bar Kokhba War Reconsidered*, ed. Peter Schäfer (Tübingen: Mohr Siebeck, 2003), 144 [above, p. 184], the alternative punctuation of lines 14–15 suggested to me by Dieter Hagedorn, and rejected the reading of ἐ[γγρ]ά̣ψ̣ασθαι in line 15 of the final edition.

9. ἰς [π]αρεμβολὴν Ἰου-
10. δ[αί]ων καὶ μὴ ἄλως
11. π[οι]ήσηται. ἐγράφη
12. δ[ὲ] Ἑληνεστὶ διὰ
13. τ[ὸ ἡ]μᾶς μὴ εὑρη-
14. κ[έ]ναι Ἑβραεστὶ
15. ἐ[...] ...αι. αὐτὸν
16. ἀπ[ο]λῦσαι τάχιον
17. δι[ὰ τ]ὴν ἑορτὴν
18. κα[ὶ μ]ὴ ἄλλως ποιή-
19. ση[τα]ι.

2nd hand

20. Σουμαιος
21. ἔρρωσο

(1st hand) Soumaios to Yonathes son of Beianos and to Masabala greetings. Since I have sent you Agrippa, hurry to send me wands and citrons, as much as you will be able to, for the camp of the Jews, and do not do otherwise. It (the letter) was written in Greek because of our inability (to write) in Hebrew letters. [Make haste?] to release him (Agrippa) quickly on account of the festival, and do not do otherwise.
(2nd hand) Soumaios Farewell.

The crucial lines read: ... ἐγράφη δ[ὲ] Ἑληνεστὶ διὰ τ[ὸ ἡ]μᾶς μὴ εὑρηκ[έ]ναι Ἑβραεστὶ. 'It (the letter) was written in Greek because of our inability (to write) in Hebrew.' Which language is designated by Ἑβραεστί: Hebrew or Aramaic? This old enigma has often been discussed in the context of several passages of the New Testament and Josephus, without a definite conclusion being reached. It would seem that Ἑβραεστί, τῇ Ἑβραίδι διαλέκτῳ and similar expressions can mean Aramaic in certain contexts. But since both Hebrew and Aramaic are used in the correspondence of Bar Kokhba and his people, the expression may refer to either in the present context.

One may insist on Ἑβαεστί being taken literally to mean that Soumaios did not know the Hebrew language, and that he was under the (false) impression that Hebrew was the only acceptable language of communication among the Jewish rebels. I do not believe that he could have meant this, and another solution which relates to the issue of the inextricable association, between script and language at the time, is now at hand.

Soumaios, the author of this letter, is a Nabataean writing to Jews. Nabataeans and Jews in Palestine spoke mutually comprehensible Aramaic. His admission that he and his men could not write *Ebraïsti*, on this account alone, *cannot* refer even indirectly only to a language. Soumaios as a Nabataean would have no problem with Jewish Aramaic – except for the script. Both Hebrew and Aramaic were written by Jews in the same script, namely what is generally designated 'Jewish Script.' What Soumaios and his people are incapable of doing is communicating with Jews in writing, for Nabataean Aramaic is written in a script quite different from Jewish Aramaic.

It is precisely because he knew Aramaic that his writing in Greek called for an excuse. But what is important here is what the Nabataean Soumaios did not do: he did not write their common language, Aramaic, in Greek script. The author of the letter seems to feel instinctively that if he uses the Greek alphabet, he must also use the language associated with that alphabet. Thus the letter is written Ἑληνεστί, in Greek using Greek letters. When he says that his people cannot write Ἑβραεστί, he is thinking of script of course, but he does not conceive of separating language from script in actual writing practice: he will forfeit the more familiar language if he cannot write it in its cognate script.

There is a striking example of this from second century CE Roman Egypt. In Roman times Demotic script was used only by priests, and even they considered it cumbersome and difficult. The script was dying out, but the language continued to be used, probably by the majority of the Egyptian population who now and for some centuries to come used a language without a script.

A letter addressed by a man to his mother and sister opens with the following request:

> τὸν Σάραπιν, ὁ ἀναγιγνώσκων τὸ ἐπιστόλιον, τίς ἂν ἦς, κοπίασον μικρὸν καὶ μετερμήγευσεν ταῖς γυναιξὶ τὰ γεγραμμένα ἐν τῇ ἐπιστολῇ ταύτῃ καὶ μετάδος. Πτọλεμαῖος Ζ̣ωσίμῃ τῇ μητρὶ καὶ Ῥοδοῦτ[ι] τῇ ἀδελφῇ χαίριν ... (*P.Haun.* I 14, ll. 1–6).

> By Serapis! You, whoever you are, who are reading the letter, make a small effort and translate to the women what is written in this letter and tell them. Ptolemaios to his mother Zosime and his sister Rhodus, Greetings.[51]

The letter was not penned by the author himself; in fact he probably did not know Greek. But in Egypt at the time it was impossible for the majority of the population to record anything in their own language;[52] thus a letter had to be dictated in Egyptian, but then written in Greek, in order to be orally translated back into Egyptian for the recipient. It is surprising, as Roger Bagnall observes, that we do not have more evidence of this sort. A modern reader may find it surprising that it never occurred to anyone to transliterate the Demotic in Greek letters and thus save himself the task of translating. Again the organic connection between language and script seems to have imposed itself on the ancients. It took several

51 Adam Bülow-Jacobsen and Vincent P. McCarren, "P.Haun. 14, P.Mich. 679, and P.Haun. 15: A Re-Edition," *ZPE* 58 (1985): 71–79.
52 Bagnall, *Egypt in Late Antiquity*, 235.

hundreds of years for Coptic to be invented and remedy the situation by employing the alphabetic simplicity of an adapted Greek script.[53]

Spoken languages without scripts, or languages whose scripts were on their way out, increased the magnitude of illiteracy in antiquity.[54] The concomitant of this was an increased use of scribes, and those were in greater supply for the imperial languages, Aramaic and Greek, in the Near East. This observation makes one less confident when coming to assess the currency of Greek in the area despite the evidence of graffiti in Greek and of Greek inscriptions in the remotest villages:[55] did Greek indeed permeate every level of society in the Roman Near East, as Fergus Millar strongly maintains?[56] Are we allowed to speak of 'Greek-speaking villages' in the Near East just because of the presence of inscriptions in Greek? The 'epigraphic habit' which was associated with the imperial languages and the close association between language and script may account for much of the evidence. How much, we do not and cannot know.[57]

The Nabataean case may well be placed at the heart of the discussion.[58] It seems to me, as a non-expert, that whereas the majority of philologists strongly believe that the Nabataeans were Arabs and spoke Arabic in their daily life, the dissenting voices are those of the historians. We may leave out the question who were the Nabataeans and concentrate on their spoken language.[59] The claim that they spoke Arabic in their daily life rests on the intrusion of Arabic elements into written Aramaic Nabataean. Historians may remain unconvinced and pose some questions: why is it that Nabataean is attested not only in legal and formal documents, but also in thousands of graffiti from the Sinai, as well as in signatures

---

53 Bagnall, 235 ff.

54 We should beware of taking the admission of 'not knowing his/her letters' as a general admission of illiteracy, rather than of illiteracy in the particular language required at the time, cf. Herbert C. Youtie, "Αγραμματος: An Aspect of Greek Society in Egypt," *Harv. Stud.* 75 (1971): 161–76; Herbert C. Youtie, "Because They Do Not Know Letters," *ZPE* 19 (1975): 101–8; see the thoughtful discussion in Bagnall, *Egypt in Late Antiquity*, 230–60.

55 E.g. on Mt Hermon, cf. Shimon Dar and Nikos Kokkinos, "The Greek Inscriptions from Senaim on Mount Hermon," *PEQ* 124 (1992): 9–25.

56 Passim in Millar, *The Roman Near East, 31 BC-AD 337*, and related articles.

57 Cf. Macdonald, "Some Reflections on Epigraphy and Ethnicity in the Roman Near East," 180. David Wasserstein in his important article, "Why did Arabic Succeed Where Greek Failed? Language Change in the Near East after Muhammad," *SCI* 22 (2003): 257–72, questions the ubiquity of Greek.

58 A Round Table Discussion on 'Who were the Nabataeans' was held at the Institute for Advanced Studies on 20 November 2002; I am particularly grateful to the two main speakers, Robert Hoyland and Ernst Axel Knauf, as also to Simon Hopkins.

59 See however, David F. Graf, "The Origin of the Nabataeans," *ARAM* 2 (1990): 45–75 = *Rome and the Arabian Frontier: From the Nabataeans to the Saracens* (Aldershot: Ashgate, 1998), I.

and subscriptions to legal documents written in Greek?[60] The Jews who have their documents written in Greek sign on them and subscribe them, when necessary, in Jewish Aramaic, as anyone familiar with the family archives from Naḥal Ḥever knows.[61] The legal convention apparent everywhere is that signatures and subscriptions are written in one's native tongue and in one's own hand – unless one is illiterate or a child and needs a 'subscriber,' or 'one who lends his hand' (*cheirochrestes*).[62] On the other hand, the Nabataean witnesses and guardians who participate in these transactions sign and subscribe in Nabataean Aramaic (very rarely in Greek). If we were to draw on the example of the Jews, we should conclude that by the same token Nabataean Aramaic was indeed the native language of the Nabataeans – not Arabic.

The intrusion of Arabic elements, and one has no reason not to trust the philologists who maintain that these are elements foreign to Aramaic,[63] reflects, no doubt, the co-existence of another language, spoken by part of the population, or imported from outside; but why must we believe that Arabic was the only language spoken there? One is also entitled to ask whether the same language was spoken everywhere in this vast territory covered by the Nabataean kingdom: was the same language spoken and written in the Hijaz, in Sinai, in the Negev, around the Dead Sea, in Moab, around Petra, in Bostra and in Wadi Sirhan?

Over the entire discussion there always looms the attempt to use nomenclature as a means to establish or to define ethnic identities of different people and groups. However, as David Wasserstein demonstrated in his recent attempt to draw the linguistic map of the village of Nessana from the evidence of the papyri, this is an extremely unreliable method for identifying groups and, still more, individuals.[64]

---

60 These questions are raised in Millar, *The Roman Near East, 31 BC-AD 337*, 401 ff., and more poignantly in a private correspondence.

61 See Cotton, "'Diplomatics' or External Aspects of the Legal Documents from the Judaean Desert: Prolegomena" [above, pp. 147–60].

62 See Hannah M. Cotton, "Subscriptions and Signatures in the Papyri from the Judaean Desert: The χειροχρήστης," *JJP* 25 (1995): 29–40 [above, pp. 115–25].

63 But see the reservations of Macdonald, "Some Reflections on Epigraphy and Ethnicity in the Roman Near East," 186 ff.; Michael C.A. Macdonald, "Reflections on the Linguistic Map of Pre-Islamic Arabia," *Arabian Archaeology and Epigraphy* 11 (2000): 46–8.

64 "Sergius is just as likely as his brother Khalaf Allah to have spoken Arabic, and Khalaf Allah is just as likely as his brother Sergius to have been a Christian. In other words, the name 'Khalaf Allah' does not indicate an Arab, in the sense of someone who was neither Christian nor a user of Greek, just as a name like 'Victor', in the case of this particular man's brother, does not indicate a Christian, in the sense of someone who was not a user of Arabic. Names, and certainly names shorn of context, cannot easily be an infallible indication of very much", Wasserstein, "Why Did

The highly problematic three-fold association of language, script and ethnicity in the case of the Nabataeans comes to an end in the middle of the 4th century when Nabataean writing disappeared. From the second century onwards Greek became the public written language in the whole area of the former Nabataean kingdom, and from the fourth century onwards almost exclusively so. So far as we can tell Petra and Nessana of the sixth and seventh centuries CE wrote exclusively in Greek.[65]

But as we all know all this was about to change very soon. In contrast to Rome, the new empire of the Arabs soon used its own language exclusively as the language of communication with its subjects. "Arabic," to quote Wasserstein again, "replaced Greek and all the other languages not only at the levels of the social elite, in administration and in culture and religion. It replaced them also in the speech of virtually everyone in the region."[66] Whether or not this represented for those living in the Nabataean realm 'the return of the native' is probably impossible to know.

Arabic Succeed Where Greek Failed? Language Change in the Near East after Muhammad," 260; cf. Michael C.A. Macdonald, "Personal Names in the Nabataean Realm: A Review Article," *JSS* 44 (1999): 251–89, for similar scepticism.

65 Cf. *P.Nessana* 60–67 in Kraemer, *Excavations at Nessana III: Non-Literary Papyri* (Cotton, Cockle, and Millar, "The Papyrology of the Roman near East: A Survey," nos. 571–8): eight bilingual *entagia*, tax requisitions of wheat and oil, or money, by the Muslim government, dated to Oct./Nov. 674 – Aug./Sept. 689; the need to append a Greek translation only corroborates the impression that the tax payers understood Greek only.

66 Wasserstein, "Why Did Arabic Succeed Where Greek Failed? Language Change in the Near East after Muhammad," 262.

Private International Law or Conflict of Laws: Reflections on Roman Provincial Jurisdiction

Preliminary Remarks

I know of only one study which has *systematically* attempted to analyse the legal evidence from the Graeco-Roman world from the point of view of 'private international law' or 'conflict of laws.' This is Hans Lewald's[1] "Conflits de lois dans le monde grec et romain," published for the first time in 1946, and then reprinted again in 1959 and 1968.[2] It was dedicated, quite properly, to Ludwig Mitteis, whose *Reichsrecht und Volksrecht* of 1891 has never been superseded even if his conclusions are hotly disputed. Anyone familiar with Lewald's article will see immediately how much I am indebted to his pioneer study.

The expression private international law suggests at first sight – quite wrongly as we shall see – that there are two kinds of international law, private and public. But in fact 'private international law' does not mean 'international law' in the sense of a law common to all nations, even if at its inception it was thought of as some sort of supranational law. What we mean nowadays by private international law is that part of the national law of a country which deals with cases where a foreign element intrudes in one form or another: e. g. one side to the contract or

1 Singled out also by Hans Julius Wolff in *Das Problem der Konkurrenz von Rechtsordnungen in der Antike* (Heidelberg: C. Winter, 1979), 11.

2 Hans Lewald, "Conflits de lois dans le monde grec et romain," *Ἀρχεῖον ἰδιωτικοῦ δικαίου* 13 (1946): 30–77 = *Labeo* 5 (1959): 334–69; *Revue critique de droit international privé* 57 (1968): 419–40 and 615–39; but see complete bibliography in Wolff, *Das Problem der Konkurrenz von Rechtsordnungen in der Antike*, 8 ff.

Article note: First published in Rudolf Haensch and Johannes Heinrichs, eds., *Herrschen und Verwalten: Der Alltag der römischen Administration in der Hohen Kaiserzeit* (Köln: Böhlau, 2007), 234–55, with the following note: I fear that the attempt to apply a modern concept described as "a dismal swamp filled with quacking quagmires, and inhabited by learned but eccentric professors who theorise about mysterious matters in strange and incomprehensible jargon" may seem most alien to my friend Werner Eck, whose mind like his prose is characterized by simplicity, lucidity and precision. But this paper could not have been conceived without his own fresh and vigorous approach to Roman provincial government, and his generosity in sharing his ideas with me, as with others, over the years that I have known him.
My friend Celia Wasserstein-Fassberg introduced me to 'the fugal music' of private international law and my young colleague Uri Yiftach-Firanko put his expertise on legal papyri at my disposal. I am very grateful to both of them, as also to Dieter Hagedorn, Israel Shatzman and Bernard Stolte, and as always to David Wasserstein.

https://doi.org/10.1515/9783110770438-013

suit is a foreigner; or the property in question is outside the country where the court operates; or the contract is signed in a third country; or all these and other factors come together – with many other variations. It is that set of rules which deals with what are known as 'conflicts of laws,' although its purpose is to resolve rather than to analyse the conflicts between legal systems. Thus both terms, private international law and conflicts of laws, are to a certain extent misnomers.

Broadly speaking, cases of conflict of laws revolve around two issues: 1) which court has jurisdiction in the matter; and 2) what law applies. It does not follow automatically – nor would it be fair and just that it should – that the court which has jurisdiction will apply its own law. A third but closely related issue is the enforcement of a judgement of a foreign court by the national court. Before going any further I should stress that there is no 'harmony of laws' between private international laws of different countries, i. e. in the rules concerning conflicts of law – perhaps it is not even so desirable or beneficial to achieve such harmony.[3]

The concept of private international law is said to be of medieval origin; more precisely, its birth is dated to the thirteenth century. Did the classical world altogether lack the concept (and the practice) of private international law? This is precisely the question that H.J. Wolff poses at the beginning of his *Das Problem der Konkurrenz von Rechtsordnungen in der Antike* of 1979: "Kannte die klassische Antike *Begriff und Tatsache eines Internationalen Privatrecht*?," and his answer is an unqualified "Nein."[4] His tone becomes even harsher in the case of Roman provincial government: "*Nicht Gleichordnung* [which he takes to be the *sine qua non* for the development of private international law], *sondern Über- und Unterordnung* bestimmte die Stellung der Normenkreise zu einander."[5]

In this paper I should like, at the risk of opposing a great jurist, to examine the possibility that it is precisely in the Roman provincial context that something could be gained by applying the conceptual framework called forth by private international law; at the very least we can raise questions which may not have been asked otherwise.

One readily joins Wolff in dismissing the *ius gentium* as an equivalent of modern 'private international law.'[6] Gaius, clearly inspired by Greek thinking on the subject, speaks of the *ius gentium* as that 'which natural reason has appointed for all men' and consequently it is 'in force equally among all people' ... 'being

3 This brief exposition relies heavily on J.H.C. Morris, *The Conflict of Laws*, 3rd ed. (London: Stevens & Sons, 1984).

4 Wolff, *Das Problem der Konkurrenz von Rechtsordnungen in der Antike*, 7.

5 Wolff, 66.

6 Wolff, 67. I thank Bernard Stolte for showing me a draft of a paper in which he convincingly justifies this observation.

the law applied to all races. Thus the Roman people applies partly its own law, partly that common to all men.'[7] This general and theoretical definition of the *ius gentium*, assimilating it to natural law, does not take us very far for the simple reason that it denies, rather than deals with, conflicts of laws. The term *ius gentium* does not seem ever to have been applied to the rules which appeared in the edict of the *praetor peregrinus* nor to the edicts of the provincial governor. But even if it was so applied, these rules which could apply to Romans and foreigners alike are precisely those which do not emerge at all from conflicts of laws, that is from clashes between national laws. Furthermore, issues connected with the *ius gentium* fell under Roman jurisdiction. In other words, the *ius gentium* – a set of laws common to all people, whether Romans or non-Romans – has nothing whatsoever to do with private international law in its modern sense.[8]

It is true of course that, once Rome had become sovereign, local legal institutions owed their continued existence and their regulation to Roman toleration of their existence.[9] But nowhere do we witness that having become sovereign Rome tried to impose its own legal system, its own law and jurisdiction on the subject populations: the *ius civile* was intended for *cives*; at most Rome extended to foreigners the provisions of its *ius civile*.[10] Thus the explanation that "private international law can only establish itself where respect is shown for foreign law, where there is an atmosphere of equality such as pervaded legal thinking in the Italian city-states from the twelfth century"[11] clearly falls short of explaining anything at all.

Theoretically of course all of Rome's subjects were *de iure* under the jurisdiction (*iuris dictio*) of Roman officials in the provinces. However, judicial autonomy,

---

7 Gaius, *Institutiones* I, 1: *Nam quod quisque populus ipse sibi ius constituit, id ipsius proprium est vocaturque ius civile, quasi ius proprium civitatis; quod vero naturalis ratio inter omnes homines constituit, id apud omnes populos peraeque custoditur vocaturque ius gentium, quasi quo iure omnes gentes utuntur. Populus itaque Romanus partim suo proprio, partim communi omnium hominum iure utitur.*

8 Wolff, *Das Problem der Konkurrenz von Rechtsordnungen in der Antike*, 67; see H.F. Jolowicz and Barry Nicholas, *A Historical Introduction to the Study of Roman Law*, 3rd ed. (Cambridge: Cambridge University Press, 1972), 102 ff.

9 Wolff, *Das Problem der Konkurrenz von Rechtsordnungen in der Antike*, 66: "fremde Institutionen verdanken ihre Existenz ohnehin eigener Reglung durch die römische Regierung."

10 E.g. by using the fiction *si civis Romanus esset*, cf. Gaius, *Inst.* IV, 37 and Wolff, 68. On the use of the procedural forms of the *ius civile* in cases involving peregrines see J.S. Richardson, "The Tabula Contrebiensis: Roman Law in Spain in the Early First Century B.C.," *JRS* 73 (1983): 33–41; see further Peter Birks, Alan Rodger, and J.S. Richardson, "Further Aspects of the Tabula Contrebiensis," *JRS* 74 (1984): 45–73; J.S. Richardson, "The Reception of Roman Law in the West: The Epigraphic Evidence," in *Pouvoir et Imperium*, ed. Ella Hermon (Naples: Jovene, 1996), 65–75.

11 Martin Wolff, *Private International Law*, 2nd ed. (Oxford: Clarendon Press, 1950), 20.

that is the use of local courts of law and of local law, especially in civil cases, may well have been taken for granted, or at least need not have called for a specific grant by the Roman government – at any rate in the case of self-governing communities, i. e. cities.[12] Later it seems to have become a tralatician part of the provincial edict, as we know from Cicero's provincial edict in Cilicia where he was governor in 50 BCE:

> Indeed I have followed many of Scaevola's provisions, including that one which the Greeks regard as their charter of liberty (*libertas*), that cases between Greeks should be tried under their own laws (*ut Graeci inter se disceptent suis legibus*) (Cic. *Att.* VI, 1, 15).

It is precisely this wholesale, and formerly perhaps taciturn, grant of local autonomy which introduced 'conflict of laws' onto the scene and prevents it from becoming redundant.[13] Furthermore, whether Rome respected other legal systems or not is less relevant than the admission of the foreign in legal contexts which is at the core of private international law. As Hartmut Galsterer observed in an excellent article published in 1986,[14] Rome never attempted to create, nor was it interested in achieving, "a single juridical framework for the whole empire,"[15] but exercised a sort of negligent tolerance of local practice. Nor, as he observes there, would such an attempt to unify the legal systems of the empire have proven successful. One may add that no such attempt was undertaken even after the *Constitutio Antoniniana* of 212.[16]

I have no doubt that Galsterer cleared away a great amount of dead wood in his article, whose modest title may mislead the casual reader – perhaps he did so all too well, for he pre-empts many of my own conclusions. Therefore I shall try to concentrate on such documents as were not published fully at the time when Galsterer wrote his survey. One last caution: my jumping back and forth between the republican and the imperial periods in what follows should not be taken to mean that I am not aware of continuous evolution which may have taken place in the interval, introducing changes which had enormous repercussions on these, as on other, issues.

---

12 This must have happened already with the first province, Sicily; see below.

13 Wolff, *Das Problem der Konkurrenz von Rechtsordnungen in der Antike*, 66–7 and n. 203, in line with his argument above (text to n. 5), designates this as *Provinzialrecht* and therefore (subsumed into) *römisches Recht*; I fail to see what is gained by the 'hierarchical' terminology when in reality two different legal systems coexisted at the same place and at the same time.

14 Hartmut Galsterer, "Roman Law in the Provinces: Some Problems of Transmission," in *L'Impero romano e le strutture economiche e sociali delle province*, ed. Michael Crawford (Como: New Press, 1986), 13–27.

15 Galsterer, 23.

16 Lewald, "Conflits de lois dans le monde grec et romain," 1959, 355.

Courts and Laws

Here and there we do encounter in the Roman provinces regulations and practices which recall the rules set out by private international law. As pointed out above, the fact that this situation was created through a wholesale grant (or taciturn recognition) of local autonomy by Rome, that is to say under Roman occupation, does not, to my mind, invalidate this observation.[17] Thus I would suggest that the legal regulations prevailing in Sicily as described by Cicero in the famous passage in his speech against Verres (*Verr.* II.2, 32) adumbrated regulations which modern jurists would have recognized as belonging to the sphere of 'private international law' or 'conflict of laws':

> The legal procedure (*ius*) of the Sicilians is as follows: cases between citizens of the same city should be tried in that city's courts (*domi*) and by that city's laws (*suis legibus*); for cases between Sicilians of different cities, the praetor (i. e. governor) should appoint a court (*iudices*), choosing its members by lot in accordance with the statute (*decretum*) which Publius Rupilius enacted by the advice of ten commissioners, and which the Sicilians call the Rupilian law. When an individual sues a community or a community sues an individual, the council (*senatus*) of some city is appointed to try the case, each party being entitled to challenge one council thus proposed. A Sicilian is appointed to try a case where a Sicilian is sued by a Roman citizen, and a Roman citizen to try any case where a Roman citizen is sued by a Sicilian. In all other cases the regular procedure is to nominate the court from a panel of Roman citizens resident in the judicial district (*conventus*); except that cases between corn-farmers and collectors of the tithe are tried as is directed by the corn-law known as the law of Hiero.[18]

These regulations are commonly, but wrongly, subsumed under the rubric Lex Rupilia. However, as Mommsen observed long ago, no such law was ever enacted.[19] Rupilius, as the text cited above makes quite clear, dealt (probably in an edict) with

---

17 Text to n. 13 above.

18 *Siculi hoc iure sunt ut, quod civis cum cive agat, domi certet suis legibus, quod Siculus cum Siculo non eiusdem civitatis, ut de eo praetor iudices ex P. Rupili decreto, quod is de decem legatorum sententia statuit, quam illi legem Rupiliam vocant, sortiatur. Quod privatus a populo petit aut populus a privato, senatus ex aliqua civitate qui iudicet datur, cum alternae civitates reiectae sunt; quod civis Romanus a Siculo petit, Siculus iudex, quod Siculus a civi Romano, civis Romanus datur; ceterarum rerum selecti iudices ex conventu civium Romanorum proponi solent. Inter aratores et decumanos lege frumentaria, quam Hieronicam appellant, iudicia fiunt.* My translation follows in general that of the Loeb Classical Library, but *ius* here is certainly not 'rights,' which quite wrongly implies that the provisions were granted by Rome. It is correctly translated by Manfred Fuhrmann in *Marcus Tullius Cicero. Sämtliche Reden*, Vol. III (Zürich: Artemis Verlag, 1970), 202.

19 Theodor Mommsen, *Römisches Staatsrecht*, Vol. III (Graz: Akademische Druck- u. Verlagsanstalt, 1952), 315, n. 3

one single matter, the appointment of judges in cases between citizens of different cities. The composition of the relevant courts, as we read in the preceding passage, was based on the Sicilians' laws (*eorum legibus*).[20] Does *eorum legibus* refer to the legal situation inherited from the former sovereigns and sanctioned by Rome when the province was created or to a 'constitution' imposed by Rome itself?[21]

There is a faint echo of the provisions prevailing in Sicily in the first century BCE as described by Cicero in Augustus' fourth edict to Cyrene:

> Whatever disputes may arise between Greeks in the Cyrenaican province, except for those that concern capital offenses ... [which fall under the governor's jurisdiction] ... for all other matters it pleases me that Greek judges be granted to them, unless some defendant or accused wishes to have Roman citizens for judges. For the parties to whom Greek judges will be given in consequence of this decree of mine, it pleases me that no judge should be given from that city from which the plaintiff or accuser comes, or the defendant or accused.[22]

It is remarkable that with the exception of cases between citizens of the same city in Sicily who are to be tried *suis legibus* in the city's court, both Cicero and Augustus only refer to courts, i. e. the jurisdiction, but fail to specify the law to be exercised in the court. Was it obvious to contemporaries? It is also striking that Augustus leaves the choice of judges, i. e. courts, to the litigants without the slightest suggestion that choice of court is a privilege. This is in sharp contrast with republican documents where the latter concern is indeed presented as a privilege.

A choice between local courts and Roman courts and the courts of free cities was conferred on three Greek naval captains and their families – none of whom was a Roman citizen – in the *SC de Asclepiade sociisque* of 78 BCE:

> whatever lawsuits they, their children, their descendants, and their wives may bring against another person, and if other persons bring lawsuits against them, their children, their descendants, and their wives, these men and their children <and their descendants> and

---

20 § 31: *Siculos eorum legibus dari oporteret*, i. e. 'according to their laws Sicilians should have been appointed [as judges].'

21 Mommsen credits Rupilius with the establishment of "ein allgemeines Regulativ für die ganze Insel auf insbesondere hinsichtlich der zwischen Parteien verschiedener Nationalität stattfindenden Prozesse," *Römisches Staatsrecht*, Vol. III, 747; but nothing in our text implies this.

22 Αὐτοκράτωρ Καῖσαρ Σεβαστὸς ἀρχιερεὺς δημαρχικῆς ἐξουσίας τὸ ἑπτακαιδέκατον λέγει· Αἵτινες ἀμφιβητήσ(ε)ις ἀνὰ μέσον Ἑλλήνων ἔσονται κατὰ τὴν Κυρηναϊκὴν ἐπαρχήαν, ὑπεξειρημένων τῶν ὑποδίκων κεφαλῆς, ὑπὲρ ὧν ὃς ἂν τὴν ἐπαρχήαν διακατέχῃ αὐτὸς διαγεινώσκειν κ[αὶ] ἱστάναι ἢ συμβούλιον κριτῶν παρέχειν ὀφείλει, ὑπὲρ δὲ τῶν λοιπῶν πραγμάτων πάντων Ἕλληνας κριτὰς δίδοσθαι ἀρέσκει, εἰ μή τις ἀπαιτούμενος ἢ ὁ εὐθυνόμος πολείτας Ῥωμαίων κριτὰς ἔχειν βούληται· ὧν δ' ἂν ἀνὰ μέσον ἐκ τοῦδε τοῦ ἐμοῦ ἐπικρίματος Ἕλλην(ε)ς κριταὶ δοθήσονται, κριτὴν δίδοσθαι οὐκ ἀρέσκει ἐ(ξ) ἐκείνης τῆς πόλεως οὐδὲ ἕνα, ἐξ ἧς ἂν ὁ διώκων ἢ ὁ εὐθύνων ἔσται ἢ ἐκείν(η)ς ὁ ἀπαιτούμενος ἢ ὁ εὐθυνόμενος. The text follows *FIRA*, Vol. I, 409, no. 68, IV.

> their wives <are> to have the right and the choice of having the case decided in their own cities by their own laws (κατὰ τοὺς ἰδίους νόμους), if they wish, or before our magistrates by Italian judges, or in a free city, one which has remained constantly in the friendship of the People of the Romans – wherever they may prefer, there the trial about these matters is to be held (ll. 17–20).[23]

These are indeed sweeping privileges; but some interpret them as applicable only to those matters which arose as a result of their absence in service for Rome.[24]

Very similar are the privileges bestowed by Octavian on Seleucus of Rhosus and his family; however, unlike the three naval captains, Seleucus possessed the Roman citizenship:[25]

> [If anyone] wishes to accuse them and to introduce a complaint and to set up a trial against them and to join issue [–] for all these procedures [if] they wish the case to be tried at home (ἐν οἴκῳ) by their own [laws (τοῖς ἰδίοις [νόμοις]) – or in] free [cities] or before our magistrates or promagistrates [–] theirs shall be the choice, [–] and no one otherwise [than is written] herein shall act or shall judge concerning them or shall declare his opinion after having referred (the matter to another authority) (?). [And if any trial] takes place [about them] contrary to these (regulations), it [shall not be] legally binding (ll. 53–59).[26]

I find it peculiar that identical privileges are bestowed on peregrines and newly made Roman citizens without the slightest attention being paid to the implication of τοῖς ἰδίοις νόμοις or κατὰ τοὺς ἰδίους νόμους. Was Augustus using, or rather misusing, a formula lifted from a charter of privileges bestowed on friends of the Roman people without introducing the necessary changes? Did choice of courts

---

23 ὅσα τε ἂν αὐτοὶ, τέκνα, ἔκγονοι γυναῖκές τε αὐτῶν παρ' ἑτέρου μεταπορεύωνται, ἐάν τέ τι παρ' αὐτῶν τέκνων, ἐκγόνων γυναικῶν τε αὐτῶν ἕτεροι μεταπορεύωνται, ὅπως τούτων, τέκνων, <ἐκγόνων> γυναικῶν τε αὐτῶν ἐξουσία καὶ αἵρεσις <ἧι>· ἐάν τε ἐν ταῖς πατρίσιν κατὰ τοὺς ἰδίους νόμους βούλωνται κρίνεσθαι ἢ ἐ<π>ὶ τῶν ἡμετέρων ἀρχόντων ἢ ἐπὶ Ἰταλικῶν κριτῶν, ἐάν τε ἐπὶ πόλεως ἐλευθέρα[ς] τῶν διὰ τέλους ἐν τῆι φιλίᾳ τοῦ δήμου τοῦ Ῥωμαίων μεμενηκυιῶν, οὗ ἂν προαιρῶνται, ὅπως ἐκεῖ τὸ κρ<ι>τήριον περὶ τούτων τῶν πραγμάτων γίνηται. The text follows Robert K. Sherk, *Roman Documents from the Greek East* (Baltimore: Johns Hopkins Press, 1969), 127, no. 22, lines 17–20. The Latin text is too fragmentary and does not add much. See now Andrea Raggi, "Senatus consultum de Asclepiade Clazomenio sociisque," *ZPE* 135 (2001): 73–116.

24 E.g. Anthony J. Marshall, "Friends of the Roman People," *AJPhil.* 89 (1968): 44–5.

25 Sherk, *Roman Documents from the Greek East*, no. 58, lines 53–6.

26 [Ἐάν τις α]ὐτῶν κατηγορεῖν θέλ[ῃ ἔγκλημά τ[ε ἐν]άγειν κριτήριόν τε κατ' αὐτῶν λαμβά[νειν κρί]σιν τε συνίστασ[θαι --- ca. 20 ---]ειν, ἐπὶ τούτων τῶν πραγμάτων πάντων [ἐάν τε ἐ]ν οἴκῃ τοῖς ἰδίοις [νόμοις ἐάν τε ἐν πόλεσιν] ἐλευθέραις ἐάν τε πρὸς ἄρχοντας ἢ ἀν[τάρχοντα]ς ἡμετέρους [--- ca. 20 --- κρί[νεσθαι θέλωσιν, αὐτῶν τὴν αἵρεσιν εἶναι [...] μήτε τις ἄλλω[ς ἢ ἐν τ]ούτ[οις γεγραμμένον ἐστὶ ποιήσ]ῃ περί τε αὐτῶν κρίνη<ι> προσανε[ν]έγ[κας γνώ]μην τε εἰπῇ· [ἐάν δὲ κριτήριόν τι περὶ αὐτῶν ὑπ]εναντίως τούτοι[ς γεί]νηται τοῦτο κύριον [μὴ εἶνα]ι.

spell a choice between systems of law? What particular significance should be assigned to the third alternative open before the naval captains, namely using a free-city court? And again: what law was to be applied in the court of a free city? Finally, assuming that local autonomy was commonly (perhaps taciturnly) granted everywhere,[27] to what extent did it differ in the case of free cities?

We are told that free cities had full use of their courts and laws.[28] However, it would be naïve to speak of them as some kind of extra-territorial enclaves in the province, outside the direct control of the provincial governor. A close reading of Cicero's letters of recommendation to provincial governors seeking their intervention on behalf of Roman *negotiatores*, publicans and others in their dealings with free cities should disabuse one of any such notions.[29] True, a certain awareness of the privileged position of free cities is noticeable here and there and some lip-service is paid to their freedom, but the fact that these letters were written at all, flouting current legislation which attempted to prevent it, speaks for itself.[30] One suspects that faced with a stream of letters of recommendation from friends and acquaintances, the republican provincial governor would be using his own discretion and sense of *decorum*, rather than a set of impersonal legal rules, when making up his mind about interfering in the judicial affairs of provincial communities:[31] what should be the weight of the principle of *lex rei sitae* when a Roman citizen was involved; or in the case of a debt contracted with outrageous interest far exceeding what was allowed in the provincial edict, when the Roman creditor was backed by a *SC*?[32]

27 See text to nn. 12–13 above on Cicero's edict in Cilicia.
28 See now Raggi, "Senatus Consultum de Asclepiade Clazomenio Sociisque," 98 ff.; Andrew W. Lintott, *Imperium Romanum: Politics and Administration* (London: Routledge, 1993), 59 ff. See especially the discussions of the two inscriptions concerning the free city of Colophon, Jeanne Robert and Louis Robert, *Claros I: Décrets hellénistiques* (Paris: Éditions Recherche sur les Civilisations, 1989) and Jean-Louis Ferrary, "Le statut des cités libres dans l'Empire romain à la lumière des inscriptions de Claros," *CR Acad. Inscr.* 135 (1991): 557 ff. I have not been able to take in the full significance of Stephen Mitchell, "The Treaty between Rome and Lycia of 46 BC," in *Papyri Graecae Schøyen (Papyrologica Florentina XXXV)*, ed. Rosario Pintaudi (Florence: Edizioni Gonnelli, 2005), 163–258, although the author was kind enough to give it to me in advance of publication.
29 See Atticus and Sicyon: Cic. *Att.* I, 13, 1; I, 19, 9; I, 20, 4; II, 1, 12; II, 13, 2 and *Fam.* V, 5; Cluvius and Alabanda, *Fam.* XIII, 56.
30 I dealt with this subject in my doctoral dissertation (unpublished), "Letters of recommendation: Cicero-Fronto" (University of Oxford Thesis, 1977), 131 ff.
31 See on all this Hannah M. Cotton, "The Role of Cicero's Letters of Recommendation: Iustitia versus Gratia?," *Hermes* 114 (1986): 443–60 [above, pp. 61–78].
32 See the affair of M. Iunius Brutus and the people of Salamis: *Att.* V, 21, 10–13; VI, 1, 3–8; VI, 2, 7–9; VI, 3, 5.

So far I have dealt mainly with the Greek East. How do the Latin *municipia* of the West fare in comparison with peregrine communities? Chapters 84 and 89 of the municipal charter of the city of Irni in Baetica explicitly limit the jurisdiction (*iuris dictio*) of the magistrates (the *duoviri* and *aediles*) to private disputes with a value of up to 1,000 sesterces and no more, and specify certain actions which are altogether outside the competence of the local magistrates – unless both parties to the suit are willing to accept it. In other words, *a priori* there are serious limitations on the judicial autonomy of the *municipia*.[33]

Should we argue *a minore ad maius* that, if the judicial autonomy of Latin (as well as Roman[34]) communities was limited in such a way, there is all the more reason to believe that the judicial autonomy of peregrine communities was curtailed even further? In other words, did the provincials more often than not have to approach Roman courts of law (the governor's above all), as their own courts would not be competent to adjudicate cases exceeding a certain amount of money, or because of the character of the case? Or could it be argued that the limits set on the judicial autonomy of local courts in Roman and Latin communities are irrelevant for determining the scope of judicial autonomy in peregrine communities, since the latter were so to speak outside the entire framework of the Roman legal system? If so, the local autonomy of peregrine communities might conceivably have been wider than that of Roman and Latin ones.[35] This seems to me entirely plausible if one takes the republican point of view which regarded Roman and Latin communities in Italy as extensions of Rome herself and thus incapable of having more legal autonomy than the centre would grant.

---

33 For the text and translation see Julián González, "The Lex Irnitana: A New Copy of the Flavian Municipal Law," *JRS* 76 (1986): 147–243. The bibliography has grown enormously since, but see on these two chapters Alan Rodger, "Jurisdictional Limits in the Lex Irnitana and the Lex de Gallia Cisalpina," *ZPE* 110 (1996): 189–206. See also Umberto Laffi, "I limiti della competenza giurisdizionale dei magistrati locali," in *Estudios sobre la Tabula Siarensis*, ed. Julián González and Javier Arce (Madrid: Centro de Estudios Históricos, 1988), 141 ff.

34 For Roman charters see Lex de Gallia Cisalpina in Michael Crawford, ed., *Roman Statutes*, Vol. I (London: Institute of Classical Studies, 1996), no. 2, ch. 22, ll. 27–8, which stipulates a limit of 15,000 sesterces, and the Este Fragment, ibid. no. 16, ll. 4–7, which stipulates a limit of 10,000 sesterces on local jurisdiction.

35 See Hannah M. Cotton, "Jewish Jurisdiction under Roman Rule: Prolegomena," in *Zwischen den Reichen: Neues Testament und römische Herrschaft. Vorträge auf der ersten Konferenz der European Association for Biblical Studies*, ed. Michael Labahn and Jürgen Zangenberg (Tübingen: Francke Verlag, 2002), 17–8 [below, pp. 490–91]. But see the whole discussion there which overlaps with some of the points raised here.

The Principle of the Personality of the Law[36]

I should like to go back to choice of courts and the absence of any clear indication of the choice between systems of law entailed thereby. As we have seen, those documents which allow choice of courts fail sometimes to specify the law to be exercised in the court. Would such nonchalance and casualness characterise legal situations in which the law of persons, or personal law, is at stake? Is it at all conceivable that a man could have a choice between the personal laws of one legal system and another? Could a Roman citizen, for example, marry, divorce, inherit, bequeath, and disinherit, adopt, etc. according to one system or another, depending on the prospective jurisdiction, in accordance with his own free choice? The question concerns especially, and already in republican times, Roman citizens living in the provinces, but even more so newly made citizens,[37] those who later on, but already before 212 CE, as we learn from the Tabula of Banasa,[38] received the citizenship with the rider *salvo iure gentis*[39] – which clearly echoes Augustus' clarification in his third edict to Cyrene.[40]

True, with the spread of citizenship and the rapid increase in the number of mixed communities, *civitas*, citizenship, did change its character, but so far as personal law was concerned, it is hard to believe that the principle enunciated by Cicero in the *Pro Balbo* suffered any derogation:

> *Duarum civitatum civis noster esse iure civili nemo potest: non esse huius civitatis qui se alii civitati dicarit potest* (§ 28).

36 H.J. Wolff, it must be emphasised, contests strongly the existence of this principle in classical antiquity both in *Das Problem der Konkurrenz von Rechtsordnungen in der Antike* and elsewhere – at least in the sense given it in the context of private international law.

37 For a brief exposition of the controversies concerning the status of newly made citizens see Leopold Wenger, "Neue Diskussionen zum Problem 'Reichsrecht und Volksrecht,'" in *Mélanges Fernand de Visscher (RIDA III)*, ed. Lucien Caes, Vol. II (Bruxelles: Office international de librairie, 1949), 521 ff.; Jolowicz and Nicholas, *A Historical Introduction to the Study of Roman Law*, 71 ff.

38 William Seston and Maurice Euzennat, "Un dossier de la chancellerie romaine, la Tabula Banasitana: étude de diplomatique," *CR Acad. Inscr.* 115 (1971): 468 ff.; A.N. Sherwin-White, "The Tabula of Banasa and the Constitutio Antoniniana," *JRS* 63 (1973): 86 ff.; W. Williams, "Formal and Historical Aspects of Two New Documents of Marcus Aurelius," *ZPE* 17 (1975): 56–7; Fergus Millar, *The Emperor in the Roman World* (London: Duckworth, 1977), 130, 216, 223, 261–2, 473; Ute Schillinger-Häfele, "Der Urheber der Tafel von Banasa," *Chiron* 7 (1977): 323 ff.

39 Lines 19–20, 35: *his civitatem Romanam dedimus salvo iure gentis*.

40 Εἴ τινες ἐκ τῆς Κυρηναϊκῆς ἐπαρχήας πολιτήαι τετείμηνται, τούτους λειτουργεῖν οὐδὲν ἔλασσον ἐμ μέρει τῷ τῶν Ἑλλήνων σώματι, *FIRA*, Vol. I, 408, no. 68, III.

The restriction implied by *salvo iure gentis* did *not* apply to personal status: it inserted a wedge between public duties and private status. The possession of Roman citizenship was inextricably bound up with the *ius civile* in matters concerning the law of persons, and denotes personal status in contrast to public duties. To use Sherwin-White's formulation: "in the second century [CE] the status of a Roman citizen was, in private law, as clearly fixed and defined as ever it had been."[41] One need but glance at the *Gnomon* of the Idios Logos to be reassured of this.[42]

Recently the opposite has been claimed by Jane Gardner in connection with the Lex Irnitana.[43] Gardner believes with Fergus Millar[44] that no such status as Latinus, a half-breed between citizen and peregrine, was created by the grant of a municipal charter to Irni. Her implicit assumption of the wholesale application of Roman legal forms to a peregrine community need not detain us here; there are precedents for the fiction of treating peregrines as if they were Roman citizens.[45] But the corollary, a full and unqualified double citizenship for those who received the citizenship *per honorem*, i.e. ex-magistrates and their families, in the sense that these people could use two systems of private law, both Roman and local, is untenable – notwithstanding the observation that "Otherwise, there would be an unacceptable level of disruption to the personal lives of the local community, in marriages, family relationships, and transmission of property."[46] Indeed there always occurred such 'a level of disruption' whenever the emperor granted the citizenship to an individual, and the latter failed to ask at the same time for its extension to relatives. It is especially in these contexts that Fergus Millar can furnish ample proof of "how all rules, legal and otherwise, could be used as a framework against which to confer benefits and exceptions on individuals."[47] In Irni as elsewhere under the empire the citizenship was received *salvo iure gentis*, so that ex-magistrates and their sons could serve as magistrates in the future in the *municipium* of Irni; it did not turn them into Janus-like creatures.

---

41 A.N. Sherwin-White, *The Roman Citizenship* (Oxford: Clarendon Press, 1973), 273.

42 *BGU* 1210.

43 Jane F. Gardner, "Making Citizens: The Operation of the Lex Irnitana," in *Administration, Prosopography and Appointment Policies in the Roman Empire*, ed. Lukas de Blois (Leiden: Brill, 2001), 215 ff.

44 Millar, *The Emperor in the Roman World*, 406, 485–86, 630–35.

45 See above, n. 10.

46 Gardner, "Making Citizens: The Operation of the Lex Irnitana," 216.

47 Millar, *The Emperor in the Roman World*, 484 referring to Pliny, *Pan.* XXXVII–XL; see also Werner Eck and Andreas Pangerl, "Vater, Mutter, Schwestern, Brüder... Zu einer außergewöhnlichen Bürgerrechtsverleihung in einer Konstitution des Jahres 121 n. Chr," *Chiron* 33 (2003): 347–64.

The principle of 'inalienability' of personal legal status, taken together with Galsterer's rejection of 'a single juridical framework for the whole empire,' renders the question of the extent of local legal autonomy of secondary importance: limited and curtailed though local jurisdiction might have been, peregrines continued to enjoy the use of their personal law either in their own courts or in those provided by the Romans.

Roman Law and Local Law in Papyri

The legal status of a city or *polis* in the Roman Empire would normally go hand in hand with some measure of judicial autonomy, albeit occasionally quite limited. The city courts had jurisdiction over their own residents as well as over the city territory, the *chora*. But what about communities which did not enjoy a city status in regions organised along different lines, as was the case in Egypt[48] or in what is commonly called the 'Jewish region' of Palestine,[49] where there are very few cities and the majority of cities that were there were on the fringes, and in any case were not likely to have controlled the entire Jewish region as their city-territories. Many settlements referred to as cities in the Jewish sources, and taken as such by scholars, would not satisfy the criteria of a *polis* in the Roman empire. How seriously should one take the host of references in rabbinic sources to Jewish courts of different sizes in towns and villages?[50]

Elsewhere I have raised the possibility that one should not think in terms of formal *iuris dictio* of a court of law.[51] The restrictions on local judicial autonomy (or its absence) and the imperfections and deficiencies of the Roman assize system[52] – notwithstanding delegation of jurisdiction to lower officials (to *legati*, auxiliary officers, *strategoi* in Egypt, and others[53]) – may well have led the provin-

---

48 With the exception of the court of the Archidikastes in Alexandria, I cannot find any evidence for the existence of local courts with formal jurisdiction in Roman Egypt. Formal jurisdiction seems to have been almost exclusively in Roman hands, those of the Prefects and the Strategoi.
49 See Emil Schürer, *The History of the Jewish People in the Age of Jesus Christ*, Vol. II, ed. Fergus Millar and Géza Vermès (Edinburgh: Clark, 1979), 85–198.
50 See Hannah M. Cotton, "The Languages of the Legal and Administrative Documents from the Judaean Desert," *ZPE* 125 (1999): 230 f. [above, pp. 144 ff.].
51 See Cotton, "Jewish Jurisdiction under Roman Rule: Prolegomena," 19 ff. [below, pp. 493 ff.].
52 G.P. Burton, "Proconsuls, Assizes and the Administration of Justice under the Empire," *JRS* 65 (1975): 102: "whatever role we may finally ascribe to local courts," the evidence from different sources suggests that "any governor was faced with an immense amount of possible work."
53 Of course the governor was not the only official in a province who could exercise jurisdiction; see Hannah M. Cotton and Werner Eck, "Roman Officials in Judaea and Arabia and Civil Juris-

cials to seek other solutions, less cumbersome, less expensive and less time-consuming.[54] Private arbitration must have played a much greater role in the Roman Empire than is normally suspected, though it has left few traces. Thus recourse to the Roman tribunals could be a step taken from choice. Rome's subjects could and did seek Roman justice whenever they believed that it would be more effective, more advantageous and juster than what they could get either in the local courts or in front of the arbiter. One sees this at work in Egypt in the famous 'Complaint of Dionysia' (*P.Oxy.* 237), conducted before the Prefect, but concerned entirely with private Egyptian or Greek law: a father wishes to use the prerogative given him by local law to force his daughter, born in an unwritten marriage, to divorce her husband; a whole list of precedents is cited where previous prefects had dealt with similar cases.[55]

But now we witness the same phenomenon in the archives from the Judaean Desert. These were fully published only at the end of 2002, but already the first volume, containing the Greek papyri of the Babatha archive, published in 1989, gave us a foretaste of the overnight transition to Roman rule. Without coercion or attempts to impose uniformity, the very presence of the Romans as the supreme authority in the province invited appeals to their authority, to their courts, and partly to their laws. Babatha regards the advent of the Romans as the dawning of a new age; she wants her son 'to be raised in splendid style rendering thanks to *the[se] most blessed times* of the governorship of Julius Julianus.'[56] True, she

diction," in *Law in the Documents of the Judaean Desert*, ed. Ranon Katzoff and David Schaps (Leiden – Boston: Brill, 2005), 23 ff.

54 One gets the impression that the Roman courts were simply blocked; the queue must have been enormous if one had to wait 8 months in Antioch to see the governor and then be sent packing with nothing achieved: see *P.Euphr.* 1 in Denis Feissel and Jean Gascou, "Documents d'archives romains inédits du Moyen Euphrate (IIIe s. après J-C): I. Les pétitions (T. Euphr. 1 à 5)," *Journal des Savants*, 1995, 65–119.

55 If we take ἀ[κο]λούθως τοῖς ἀστικοῖς νόμοις in *P.Oxy.* 706 to mean the *ius civile*, as suggested by Hélène Cadell, "Pour une recherche sur 'astu' et 'polis' dans les papyrus grecs d'Égypte," *Ktema* 9 (1984): 23 f. and others, then we witness here an application of Roman law by the prefect in a case involving the duties of the freedman towards his patron, since as the prefect observes [ἐν μὲν τοῖς τῶν] Αἰγυπτίων νόμοις οὐδὲν περὶ τῆς ... relevant is to be found. Some clever jurist may have told the patron who waived all claims in a *cheirographon* (καὶ γεγρα[φέναι χειρόγρ]αφον περὶ τοῦ μηδὲν ἔξειν πρᾶγμα [πρὸς αὐτόν]) that he stood to gain by turning to a Roman court where such a waiver is void so far as the *operae* are concerned. This reminds one of the so called 'court stipulations' (TN'Y BYT DYN) in Jewish law, i. e. tacit conditions, binding upon all, even if not written in a specific contract.

56 ὅθεν λαμπρῶς διασωθῇ μου ὁ υἱὸς εὐχαριστῶν (εὐχαριστοῦντα) τοῖς μακαριωτάτοις καιροῖς ἡγεμωνίας Ἰουλίου Ἰουλιανοῦ ἡγεμόνος (*P.Yadin* 15, ll. 10–11 = ll. 26–27); cf. *Acts* 24:2 (the rhetor Tertullus to Felix): πολλῆς εἰρήνης τυγχάνοντες διὰ σοῦ, καὶ διορθωμάτων γινομένων τῷ ἔθνει

needs to propitiate the governor and her praise should be taken with a grain of salt, but it is not just empty phraseology either.[57]

The governor's court, it should be pointed out, is mentioned explicitly only in the Greek documents of the Babatha archive, in connection with the assize system prevailing in the Roman provinces.[58] Those Greek documents which are not slavish translations of an Aramaic *Urtext* greatly resemble the papyri from the rest of the Roman Near East (Dura Europos, the Euphrates, the Nessana papyri) including Egypt.[59] The legal procedure in the Greek papyri abounds in Roman elements. We find here petitions to the governor and summons of opponents to appear before his ambulatory tribunal, wherever that happened to be.[60] However, even when the Roman governor is not mentioned explicitly in the documents, the presence of certain formal elements, mainly (but not exclusively) of procedure rather than of substance, implies that these documents were intended for a Roman court of law. These are (in no particular order of importance): the use of the Greek language – the language used *par excellence* as a means of communication between rulers and subjects in the Roman Near East; the prevalence of the double-document format, which elsewhere was going out of fashion (although the Nabataean double-document before annexation exhibits diplomatic features which point to an independent local tradition);[61] the use of the *testatio* – a document signed by seven witnesses in front of whom the plaintiff makes his declaration;[62] the presence of a Roman legal instrument like the *actio tutelae* to be decided by a court of *recuperatores*, called here *xenokritai*;[63] the use of Roman

---

τούτῳ διὰ τῆς σῆς προνοίας: 'Seeing that by thee we enjoy great quietness and that very worthy deeds are done unto this nation by thy providence.'

57 As an aside I would like to call attention to the fact that in imperial times, in sharp contrast to republican times, it certainly called for no special grant for non-citizens to have recourse to Roman courts of law. Should we not rethink the implication of choice of court under the republic?

58 Cf. Burton, "Proconsuls, Assizes and the Administration of Justice under the Empire," 92–106; Rudolf Haensch, "Zur Konventsordnung in Aegyptus und den übrigen Provinzen des römischen Reiches," in *Akten des 21. Internationalen Papyrologenkongresses, Berlin, 13–19.8.1995*, ed. Barbara Kramer et al., Vol. I (Stuttgart – Leipzig: Teubner, 1997), 320–91.

59 See Hannah M. Cotton, W.E.H. Cockle, and Fergus Millar, "The Papyrology of the Roman Near East: A Survey," *JRS* 85 (1995): 214–35.

60 See Cotton and Eck, "Roman Officials in Judaea and Arabia and Civil Jurisdiction," 23 ff.

61 See Ada Yardeni, "The Decipherment and Restoration of Legal Texts from the Judaean Desert: A Reexamination of Papyrus Stracky (P.Yadin 36)," *SCI* 20 (2001): 121–37.

62 For the *testatio* see *P.Yadin* 15 and 24, and also *P.Jericho* 16 (*DJD* XXXVIII, 2000), as interpreted by Rudolf Haensch, "Zum Verständnis von P.Jericho 16 gr.," *SCI* 20 (2001): 155–67.

63 *P.Yadin* 28–30, cf. Dieter Nörr, "Zur condemnatio cum taxatione im römischen Zivilprozeß," *ZSS* 112 (1995): 51 ff.; Dieter Nörr, "The Xenokritai in Babatha's Archive (Pap. Yadin 28–30)," *Israel Law Review* 29 (1995): 83 ff.; Dieter Nörr, "Römisches Zivilprozeßrecht nach Max Kaser: Prozeß-

legal arguments in the documents; the use of the stipulation; and more. But so far as I am concerned the strongest argument for thinking that these documents were intended for a Roman court of law is the presence of a male guardian to represent a woman in the Greek documents, to be contrasted with his total absence from contemporary Aramaic (both Nabataean and Jewish Aramaic) documents. The passive role of this guardian – all he does is be present συμπαρόντος αὐτῇ ἐπιτρόπου – makes it eminently clear that this is just a matter of form and procedure, required by the court envisioned by the Greek documents, namely a Roman court of law where a woman could not appear without a male representative.[64]

P.Yadin 15

To conclude this discussion I should like to illustrate the convergence of the many strands and tendencies delineated above in a single Greek papyrus from the Babatha archive: this is *P.Yadin* 15 of October 125 CE, written twenty one years after the annexation. Unlike the rest of the Greek papyri, it was published as early as 1962 by Hans Jakob Polotsky,[65] and was therefore subjected to much learned discussion by Roman jurists, above all by Hans Julius Wolff.[66] He, like many others, was taken aback by the presence of so much 'Roman law' in a document from an until then unknown place called Maḥoz Eglatain, a village on the shores of the Dead Sea in the new province of Arabia. Nevertheless, Wolff continued to cling to his belief that there was no attempt to impose Roman law on the provincials, but that what we witness here is the introduction of a new procedure

recht und Prozeßpraxis in der Provinz Arabia," *ZSS* 115 (1998): 80–98.; Dieter Nörr, "Zu den Xenokriten (Rekuperatoren) in der römischen Provinzialgerichtsbarkeit," in *Lokale Autonomie und römische Ordnungsmacht in den kaiserzeitlichen Provinzen vom 1. bis 3. Jahrhundert*, ed. Werner Eck (München: Oldenbourg, 1999), 257 ff.

64 See Hannah M. Cotton, "The Guardian (ἐπίτροπος) of a Woman in the Documents from the Judaean Desert," *ZPE* 118 (1997): 267–73 [below, pp. 431–41].

65 Hans Jakob Polotsky, "Three Greek Documents from the Family Archive of Babatha," *Eretz Israel* 8 (1967): 46–51 (Hebrew) = *SB* 10288.

66 Hans Julius Wolff, "Römisches Provinzialrecht in der Provinz Arabia (Rechtspolitik als Instrument der Beherrschung)," in *Aufstieg und Niedergang der römischen Welt*, Vol. II.13 (Berlin: De Gruyter, 1980), 804 f. and Hans Julius Wolff, "Le droit provincial dans la province romaine d'Arabie," *RIDA* 23 (1976): 288 ff.; Arnaldo Biscardi, "Nuove testimonianze di un papiro arabogiudaico per la storia del processo provinciale romano," in *Studi in onore di Gaetano Scherillo*, Vol. I (Milano: Istituto editoriale cisalpino La Goliardica, 1972), 111 ff.; Maxime Lemosse, "Le Procés de Babatha," *Irish Jurist* 3 (1968): 363 ff.; Erwin Seidl, "Ein Papyrusfund zum klassischen Zivilprozessrecht," in *Studi in onore di Giuseppe Grosso*, Vol. II (Torino: Giappichelli, 1968), 345 ff.

designed to meet the requirements of a Roman court of law. More recently Tiziana Chiusi has demonstrated that the legal measures proposed by Babatha in the document to support her case against the appointed guardians of her son resurface in third-century Roman legal writings.[67] True, the Roman legal sources postdate our texts by many years, but the legal remedies reflected in them may well have been in force earlier; equally these legal remedies could have been the impact of local customs on later Roman law. For the time being the question must be left open.[68]

In what follows, however, I steer clear of substantive law and concentrate on the diplomatics of the document since I believe that important insights can be derived from the study of the minute details of external aspects of legal papyri.

P.Yadin 15 (11 or 12 October 125 CE)

Upper (Inner) Text

[ἔτους ἐν]άτου Αὐτοκράτορο[ς] Τ̣ραιαν̣οῦ Ἁδριανοῦ Καίσαρος Σεβαστοῦ, ἐπὶ ὑπάτων Μάρκου Οὐαλερίου Ἀ̣σιατικοῦ τὸ β καὶ Τιτίου Ἀκυλείνου πρὸ τεσσ̣[ά-]
[ρων εἰ]δ̣ῶν Ὀκ̣τ̣ω̣β̣ρίων, κ̣α̣τ̣ὰ̣ δὲ τὸν ἀριθμὸν τῆς ἐπαρχείας Ἀραβίας ἔτους εἰκοστοῦ μηνὸς Ὑπερβερεταίου λεγομένου Θεσρεὶ τετάρτῃ καὶ ε̣ἰ̣κὰς,
[ἐν Μα]ωζα̣ π̣ε̣ρ̣ὶ̣ Ζοαραν, ἐπὶ τῶν ἐπιβε̣β̣λ̣ημένων μαρτύρων ἐμαρτυροποιήσατο Βαβαθα Σίμωνος τοῦ Μαναή̣μου κατὰ Ἰωάνου̣ Ἰ̣ωσή-
[που το]ῦ̣ Ἐ̣γ̣λ̣α̣ [κ]αὶ Αβδοοβδ̣α̣ Ἐλλο̣υ̣θα ἐ̣π̣ιτρόπων Ἰησοῦ Ἰησοῦτος υἱοῦ αὐτῆς ὀρφανοῦ, κατασταθέντων τῷ αὐτῷ ὀρφανῷ ἐ̣π̣ιτρό-
πων ὑ̣[πὸ] β̣ο̣υ̣λ̣ῆς τῶν Πετ̣ρ̣α̣ί̣ων̣, π̣[α]ρ̣ό̣ν̣των τῶν αὐτῶν ἐπιτρόπων, λέγουσα· διὰ τ̣ὸ̣ ὑμᾶς μὴ δεδωκε̣ναι τῷ υἱῷ μο[υ ὀρφανῷ]
[. . . . .] τ̣ρ̣ο̣φ̣ῖ̣α πρὸς τ̣ὴ̣ν̣ δ̣[ύ]ν̣αμιν̣ \τ̣[όκ]ου/, ἀ̣ρ̣γ̣[υ]ρ̣ίου αὐτοῦ καὶ τῶν λοιπῶν ὑπαρχόντων αὐτοῦ καὶ μάλιστα πρὸς ὁμειλίαν ἣ̣ν̣ ε̣ἰκου̣[σα]
[. . . . . αὐ]τ̣ῷ [κ]αὶ μὴ χ[ορ]η̣[γ]εῖν αὐτῷ τόκον τοῦ ἀργυρίου εἰ μὴ τροπαιεϊκὸν ἕνα εἰς ἑκατὸν δηνάρια, ἔχουσα ὑπάρχοντα ἀξιό-

67 Tiziana J. Chiusi, "IV. Zur Vormundschaft der Mutter," *ZSS* 111 (1994): 155–96; Tiziana J. Chiusi, "Babatha vs. The Guardians of Her Son: A Struggle for Guardianship – Legal and Practical Aspects of P. Yadin 12–15, 27," in *Law in the Documents of the Judean Desert*, ed. Ranon Katzoff and David Schaps (Leiden: Brill, 2005), 105–32. On echoes of later Roman law in *P.Yadin* 15 see also Hannah M. Cotton, "The Guardianship of Jesus Son of Babatha: Roman and Local Law in the Province of Arabia," *JRS* 83 (1993): 108 [below, p. 430].

68 Chiusi, "Babatha vs. The Guardians of Her Son: A Struggle for Guardianship – Legal and Practical Aspects of P. Yadin 12–15, 27," 132.

[χρεα τούτ]ου τοῦ ἀρ[γυρίο]υ οὗ ἔχετε τοῦ ὀρφανοῦ, διὸ προεμαρτυροποίησα ἵνα εἰ δοκεῖ ὑμεῖν δοῦναί μοι τ̣ὸ ἀργύριον
[δι’ ἀσφαλείας περὶ ὑποθήκης τῶ]ν̣ ὑπαρχόντων μου χορηγοῦσα τόκον τοῦ ἀργυρίου ὡς ἑκ̣ατὸν δ̣ην[α]ρ̣ί̣ω[ν δηνάριον ἓν]
[ἥμισυ, ὅθεν λαμπρῶς διασω]θ̣ῇ μου ὁ υἱὸς εὐχ[αρι]σ̣τοῦν̣τα μακαριωτάτοις καιροῖς ἡγ̣[ε]μ̣ων[ί]α̣ς Ἰ̣[ουλίο]υ̣ [Ἰουλιανοῦ ἡγε-]
[μόνος, ἐπὶ οὗ περὶ τῆς ἀπειθαρ]χε̣[ί]α̣ς ἀποδόσεως τῶν τροφίων παρήν̣[γ]ε̣ιλ̣ε̣ γ̣ε̣ ἡ̣ Βαβαθα Ἰ̣ω̣ά̣ν̣η̣ [τ]ῷ̣ π̣ρ̣ο̣γ̣[εγ]ρ̣[αμμένῳ,]
[ἑνὶ τῶν ἐπιτρόπων τοῦ ὀρφαν]οῦ. ⟦και⟧ \ε̣ἰ̣ δὲ μή, ἔσται/ τοῦτο τὸ μαρτυροποίημα ⟦ἐγένετο⟧ εἰς δικαίωμα κέρδους ἀργυρίου τοῦ ὀρφα-
[νοῦ –ca.?–] vac.?

Lower (Outer) Text

ἔτου[ς ἐνάτου Αὐτοκράτορος] Τραιανοῦ Ἀδριανοῦ Καίσαρος Σε̣βαστο̣ῦ̣, ἐπὶ ὑπάτ[ω]ν̣ [Μάρκου Οὐαλερίου]
[Ἀσιατικοῦ τὸ β καὶ Τιτίου Ἀκυλεί]νου πρὸ τ̣[εσσάρων] ε̣ἰ̣δῶν [Ὀκ]τ[ωβρίων, κατὰ δὲ τὸν ἀριθμὸν τῆς ἐπαρχείας]
[Ἀραβίας ἔτους εἰκοστοῦ μηνὸς Ὑ]π̣ε̣ρ̣[βε]ρ̣[εταίου λεγομένου Θεσρε]ὶ̣ [τ]ε̣[τά]ρ̣[τῃ καὶ εἰκάδι, ἐν Μαωζα̣ περὶ]
[Ζοαραν, ἐπὶ τῶν ἐπιβεβλη]μ̣ένων μαρτύρων ἐμαρτυ̣ρ̣ο̣ποιήσατο̣ Βαβαθα Σίμωνος τοῦ Μανα-
[ήμου κατὰ Ἰωάνου Ἰωσή]που τοῦ Ἐγλα καὶ Ἀβδο̣οβδα Ἐλλουθα ἐπιτρόπων Ἰησοῦ Ἰησοῦτος
[υἱοῦ αὐτῆς ὀρφανοῦ κατασ]ταθέντων τῷ αὐτῷ ὀρφανῷ ὑπ̣ὸ̣ β̣ο̣υλῆ̣ς̣ τ̣ῶ̣ν̣ Π̣ε̣τ̣ραίω̣ν̣, παρόντω[ν]
[τῶν αὐτῶν ἐπιτρόπων,] λέγουσα· διὰ τὸ ὑ̣μ̣ᾶς μὴ δεδω̣κ̣έναι τῷ υἱῷ [μου ὀρ]φ̣α̣ν̣ῷ̣ δ .[.]ε-
[. . τροφεῖα πρὸς τὴν δύν]αμι̣ν̣ τόκου [ἀ]ρ̣γ̣υ̣ρ̣ί̣ο̣υ̣ [αὐ]τοῦ [κ]α̣ὶ [τῶν] λ̣ο̣ι̣πῶ[ν] ὑ̣[παρχόντων αὐτοῦ]
[κ]α̣[ὶ μ]ά̣λ̣[ιστα πρὸς ὁμιλία]ν̣ ἣ̣ν̣ [. .] . . .[.]α̣[. .] . .[. .] . [. καὶ μὴ χορηγεῖν αὐτῷ τόκον]
τ̣ο̣[ῦ] ἀρ[γυρ]ί̣ου ε̣[ἰ μὴ τροπαι]εϊκὸ̣ν̣ ἕ̣ν̣α̣ ε̣ἰ̣ς̣ ἑ̣κ̣α̣τ̣ὸ̣ν̣ δ̣η̣ν̣ά̣ρ̣ι̣α̣, ἔ̣[χουσ]α̣ ὑ̣π̣ά̣ρ̣χ̣[οντα] ἀ̣ξ̣ι̣[όχρεα]
τ̣ο̣[ύτ]ο̣υ̣ [τοῦ ἀργυρίου] ο̣ὗ̣ ἔχετε τοῦ ὀρφανοῦ, διὸ προεμαρτυροποίησα ἵνα εἰ δοκεῖ
ὑ̣με̣ῖν δ̣ο̣ῦ̣ναί μ[οι τὸ] ἀ̣ργύριον δι’ ἀσφαλίας \. . . ./ περὶ ὑποθήκης τῶν ὑπαρχόντων μου, χορη-
[γ]οῦσα τ̣ό̣κον τ̣ο̣ῦ̣ [ἀργυρίο]υ̣ ὡ̣ς ἑκατὸν δηνα̣ρ̣ίων δηνάριν ἓ̣ν ἥμισυ, ὅθεν λαμπρῶς διασω-

θ[ῆ μου] ọ υἱὸς εὐχạρịστῶν τοῖς μαḳαριωτάτοις καιροῖς ἡγεμωνε[ίας] Ἰουλ̣[ί]ọụ Ἰουλιανοῦ
ἡγεμώνος, ἐπὶ οὗ περὶ τῆς ἀπειθαρχείας ἀποδόσεως τῶν τροφίων παρήνγειλα ἐγὼ Βαβαθα Ἰωάνῃ τῷ προγεγραμμένῳ ἐνεὶ τῶν ἐπιτρόπων τοῦ ὀρφανοῦ. Ẹἰ δὲ μή, ἔσται
τοῦτ̣ọ [τὸ μαρτυρο]π̣ọίημα εἰς δικαίωμα κέρδους ἀργυρίου τοῦ ὀρφανοῦ εἰ διδόντες
. . .[.] . . . . [ἐμαρ]τυροποιήσατο ἡ Βαβαθα ὡς προγέγραπται διὰ ἐπιτρόπου αὐτῆς τοῦδε
τοῦ πράγματ[ος Ἰούδου Χ]θουσίωνος ὃς παρὼν ὑπέγραψεν. **[2nd hand]** Βαβαθας Σίμωνος ἐμαρτυροποιησάμη<ν>
κ̣ατ̣ὰ Ἰωάνου Ἔγλα Ἀ<βδ>αοβδα Ἐλλουθα ἐπιτρώπων Ἡσους υ<ἱ>ο<ῦ> μου ὀρφανοῦ δι' ἐπιτρόπου μου Ἰούδα
Χαθουσ̣ίωνος ἀκọλ̣[ο]ύθω̣ς τε̃ς προγεγραμμένες ἐρέσασιν. Ἐλεάζαρος Ἐλεαζάρ̣ου ἔγραψα ὑπὲρ αὐτῆς
ἐρωτηθ̣εὶς διὰ τὸ αὐτ̣ης μὴ ε<ἰ>δένα<ι> γράμματα. Vac.?
[1st hand] καὶ ἐπεβάλοντο μάρτυρες ἑπτά.
יהודה בר כתושין אדון בבתה בקמי השרת בבתה ככל די על כתב יהודה כתבה
עבדעבדת בר אילותא במקמי ובמקם יוחנה חברי בר עגלא כתיבת שהדתא דא כדי עלא כתיב עבדעבדת כתבה
ὁ δὲ γράψας τοῦτο Θεενας Σίμωνος λιβλάριος. יהותנן בר אלכס ביד יהוסף ברה

Signatures on the back

[ ]
[ ]
[ ]שהד
Θαδ̣ᾶις Θαδαίου μάρτ̣(υς)
יהוסף בר חננ[י]ה [ש]הד
תומה בר שמע[ון ש]הד
[י]שוע בר ישוע [שהד]

Translation

(*Upper [Inner] Text / Lower [Outer] Text*) In the ninth year of Imperator Traianus Hadrianus Caesar Augustus, in the consulship of Marcus Valerius Asiaticus for the second time and Titius Aquilinus, four days before the Ides of October and according to the compute of Arabia year twentieth on the twenty fourth of the month Hyperberetaios called Ṭishrei, in Maḥoza, Ẓoara district, before the attending witnesses Babatha daughter of Simon son of Menahem deposed against John son of Joseph Eglas and 'Abdoöbdas son of Ellouthas, guardians of her orphan son Jesus son of Jesus, appointed guardians for the said orphan by the council of Petra, in the presence of the said guardians, saying:

On account of your not having given my orphan son generous(?) maintenance money commensurate with the income from the interest on his money and the rest of his property, and commensurate in particular with a style of life which befits(?) him, and you contribute for him as interest on the money only one half-denarius per hundred denarii [per month], as I have property equivalent in value to this money of the orphan's that you have, therefore I previously deposed in order that you might decide to give me the money on security involving a hypothec of my property, with me contributing interest on the money at the rate of a denarius and a half per hundred denarii, wherewith my son may be raised in splendid style, rendering thanks to the[se] most blessed times of the governorship of Julius Julianus, our governor, before whom I, Babatha, summoned the aforesaid John, one of the guardians of the orphan, for his refusal of disbursement of the [appropriate] maintenance money. Otherwise this deposition will serve as documentary evidence of [your] profiteering from the money of the orphan (*Lower [Outer] Text*) by giving ...

Babatha deposed as aforestated through her guardian for this matter, Judah son of Khthousion, who was present and subscribed. **[2nd hand]** I, Babatha daughter of Simon, have deposed through my guardian Judah son of Khthousion against John son of Eglas and 'Abdoöbdas son of Ellouthas, guardians of my orphan son Jesus, according to the aforestated conditions. I, Eleazar son of Eleazar, wrote for her by request, because of her being illiterate.

[1st hand] And there were at hand seven witnesses.

[3rd hand, Aramaic] Yehudah son of Khthousion 'lord' of Babatha: In my presence Babatha confirmed all that is written above. Yehudah wrote it.

[4th hand, Nabatean] 'Abd'obdath son of Elloutha: In my presence and in the presence of Yoḥana, my colleague, son of 'Egla, this testimony is written according to what is written above. 'Abd'obdath wrote it.

[5th hand, Aramaic] Yeḥohanan son of Aleks, by the hand of Yehoseph his son.

[1st hand] The writer of this [is] Theënas son of Simon, *liblarius*.

On the back, individual signatures

[ ]

[ ]

... son of ..., witness

Thadeus son of Thadeus, witness

Yehosef son of Ḥanania

Tomah son of Shime'on, witness
Yeshu'a son of Yeshu'a, witness

P.Yadin 15, described in the document itself as μαρτυροποίημα, i.e. a Roman *testatio*, is a document in which the presence of seven witnesses was required; and indeed the presence of seven witnesses is recorded in the text (καὶ ἐπεβάλοντο μάρτυρες ἑπτά), and whatever is left of the seven signatures is found on the *verso*, close to the ties, at right angles to the direction of the lines of the lower (outer) version on the *recto*. The position of the signatures in relation to the text conforms to the diplomatics of the Greek double document in the archives from the Judaean Desert: whereas in Aramaic, Nabataean and Hebrew deeds the first signature on the *verso* starts on the back of the right margin of the text on the *recto*, in Greek deeds the first signature on the *verso* starts on the back of the left margin of the *recto*. In other words, in Greek and Semitic documents alike the first signature stands in the same relationship to the margin of the lower (outer) text, whether that text was written right to left or left to right. Further, the direction of the signatures was determined by the language of the deed: in the Aramaic, Nabataean, and Hebrew deeds, signatures writtten in these scripts were written downwards (away from the stitching), while signatures in the Greek script were written upwards (towards the stitching). In the Greek deeds on the other hand, the signatures in the Greek script were written downwards (away from the stitching), while signatures in the Aramaic or Nabataean scripts were written upwards (towards the stitches).[69]

I believe it is of paramount importance to observe the great care invested in executing signatures in documents written in two languages which go in different directions, but in which one or the other is dominant. Only microscopic investigation of this sort allows us to realize that no effort was spared by the scribe and the parties to ensure the validity of the document in a Roman court of law. The appalling Greek of another seven-witness document, *P.Hever* 64 of 129 CE, a deed of gift from the Salome archive,[70] is another example of the great effort spent by

---

69 I owe a great debt to Ada Yardeni for alerting me to these features of the double document from the Judaean Desert; see also Hannah M. Cotton, "'Diplomatics' or External Aspects of the Legal Documents from the Judaean Desert: Prolegomena," in *Rabbinic Law in its Roman and Near Eastern Context*, ed. Catherine Hezser (Tübingen: Mohr Siebeck, 2003), 49 ff. [above, pp. 147 ff.].
70 *P.Hever* 64 is published in Hannah M. Cotton and Ada Yardeni, *Aramaic, Hebrew, and Greek Documentary Texts from Naḥal Ḥever and Other Sites*, Discoveries in the Judaean Desert XXVII (Oxford: Clarendon Press, 1997), 203 ff. Note though that the reconstruction of signatures on the verso on p. 211 is wrong as is the whole conception there, wrongly borrowed from the Semitic diplomatic tradition; cf. Cotton, "'Diplomatics' or External Aspects of the Legal Documents from the Judaean Desert: Prolegomena," 56 ff. [above, pp. 154 ff.].

a scribe whose knowledge of Greek leaves much to be desired in making a document acceptable, that is comprehensible, in a Roman court of law.[71]

To go back to *P.Yadin* 15: on Babatha's side we find a guardian, here labelled ἐπίτροπος,[72] and a subscriber – not designated as such. The subscriber, i. e. ὑπογραφεύς, to use the normal Egyptian term, or χειροχρήστης, to use the picturesque term found once in a document from the Judaean Desert (*P.Hever* 61),[73] is the one who writes the subscription for those who are legally competent to do so, but who happen to be illiterate (or otherwise incapable of writing), when a subscription and/or a signature in their own hand is required to render a document valid. The guardian could double up as the subscriber, as we see in *P.Yadin* 27: Βα̣βαθας Σίμω̣[ν]ος, συμπαρόντος αὐτῇ [ἐπιτρόπου] κ̣[α]ὶ ὑπὲρ αὐτῆς ὑπογράφοντος Βα̣βελι̣[ς] Μαναήμου. However, the subscriber is to be distinguished from the *epitropos*, as is clear, first, from the fact that, unlike the latter, he is found also in Aramaic documents, and, secondly, in that he is present also in documents in which the principal is a man. The subscriber is by no means unique to one legal tradition and his presence does not anticipate proceedings in a Roman court of law. The same is true in the papyri from Egypt: the subscriber is distinguished from the guardian; he subscribes for the woman, and sometimes he is said to be subscribing for both the woman and her guardian since both are illiterate.

Babatha too was illiterate, but I cannot explain why her guardian for this matter, Judah son of Eleazar Khthousion, does not write the subscription for her – certainly not because he too was illiterate or because a subscription in Greek was required, for he writes his own subscription in Aramaic later on:

> Babatha deposed as aforestated through her guardian for this matter, Judah son of Khthousion, who was present and subscribed. [second hand] I, Babatha daughter of Simon, have deposed through my guardian Judah son of Khthousion against John son of Eglas and ʿAbdoöbdas son of Ellouthas, guardians of my orphan son Jesus, according to the aforestated conditions. I, Eleazar son of Eleazar, wrote for her by request, because of her being illiterate.

There seems to be a great deal of legal redundancy here. The fact that a subscription by the woman was needed is proof that she was a legal personality and the guardian a mere formality; the subscriber, as in other papyri, could easily have

---

71 I must confess that I was able to comprehend the Greek fully only after having translated it back into the Aramaic of its *Urtext*, cf. *DJD* XXVII, 207.

72 See Wolff, "Römisches Provinzialrecht in der Provinz Arabia," 792 ff. and Cotton, "The Guardian (ἐπίτροπος) of a Woman in the Documents from the Judaean Desert," 268 f. [below, pp. 432 f.].

73 *DJD* XXVII, 174 ff.; cf. Hannah M. Cotton, "Subscriptions and Signatures in the Papyri from the Judaean Desert: The χειροχρήστης," *JJP* 25 (1995): 29–40 [above, pp. 115–25].

doubled up as a guardian. But to make matters even more puzzling, Judah son of Eleazar, her guardian, writes his own subscription in Aramaic: 'Judah son of Khthousion lord of Babatha: in my presence Babatha confirmed all that is written above. Judah wrote this.' This would seem to be entirely uncalled for. Again and again one wonders, when reading the legal documents from the Judaean Desert, especially those written in Greek, whose legal advice had been sought and taken? It is clear though that the aim was to make the contract legally valid and enforceable in a Roman court of law.

A comparison with practice in Roman Egypt is inevitable. The late Naphtali Lewis argued already in 1993 that the advent of the Romans spelled the demise of the Demotic legal document.[74] This is fully substantiated in a new study by Marc Depauw.[75] For a document to be registered, a subscription in Greek as well as a summary in Greek became obligatory. "The new Roman policy eventually led to the complete obsolescence of Demotic as a forensic language in the third century AD."[76] Lewis went on to claim a parallel development for the Aramaic legal document as attested in the archives from the Judaean Desert.[77] True, here too Greek takes over as the language of legal documents: not only is the body of the document written in Greek, but, what is more crucial for the authentication of a legal document, the subscriptions are always translated into Greek.[78] It must be pointed out though that there are no safely dated contracts, either in Greek or in Aramaic, written by the Jewish population from either Judaea or Arabia, after 135 (or 136) CE.[79] Moreover, Aramaic continued to be written and used after the documents from the Judaean Desert dry up as we can infer from rabbinic sources – above all from the Mishnah, where formulae taken from living Aramaic contracts are embedded in the legal discussion round about which is conducted

---

74 Naphtali Lewis, "The Demise of the Demotic Document: When and Why," *JEA* 79 (1993): 276 ff. = *On Government and Law in Roman Egypt: Collected Papers* (Atlanta: Scholars Press, 1995), 351 ff. See now also Brian Muhs, "The Grapheion and the Disappearance of Demotic Contracts in Early Roman Tebtynis and Soknopaiou Neso," in *Tebtynis und Soknopaiu Nesos. Leben im römerzeitlichen Fajum*, ed. Sandra Lippert and Maren Schentuleit (Wiesbaden: Harrasowitz, 2005), 93–104.

75 Mark Depauw, "Autograph Confirmation in Demotic Private Contracts," *Chronique d'Égypte* 78 (2003): 89 ff.

76 Depauw, 105.

77 Naphtali Lewis, "The Demise of the Aramaic Document in the Dead Sea Region," *SCI* 20 (2001): 179 ff.

78 Cotton, "The Languages of the Legal and Administrative Documents from the Judaean Desert," 227 ff. [above, pp. 139 ff.].

79 The few Greek papyri mentioned in Cotton, Cockle, and Millar, "The Papyrology of the Roman Near East: A Survey," as nos. 333 ff., do not come from Jewish contexts, but either from Roman army circles or from the Greek *poleis*.

in Hebrew.[80] These Aramaic documents, representing common Aramaic law, may well have been used among the locals in cases which did not concern registration of property, property declarations etc., and could be resolved before a local arbiter, as suggested above.[81]

Is it at all useful to invoke here the modern concept of private international law? That the concept did not exist is clear enough. Furthermore, no separate set of rules was consistently developed to deal with cases nowadays dealt with by private international law. Nonetheless the principle seems certainly to have been recognized and acted upon that measures have to be invented and used when a foreign element enters into a legal conflict. The Roman provincial jurisdiction took cognizance of peregrine private law, and on occasion the fiction of *si civis Romanus esset* was used. The provincials sometimes more and sometimes less enthusiastically participated in this mode of mutual accommodation.[82]

---

80 See full discussion in Hannah M. Cotton, "Survival, Adaptation and Extinction: Nabataean and Jewish Aramaic versus Greek in the Legal Documents from the Cave of Letters in Naḥal Ḥever," in *Sprache und Kultur in der kaiserzeitlichen Provinz Arabia: Althistorische Beiträge zur Erforschung von Akkulturationsphänomenen im römischen Nahen Osten*, ed. Leonhard Schumacher and Oliver Stoll (St. Katharinen: Scripta Mercaturae Verlag, 2003), 1–11 [above, pp. 161–72].

81 Text to nn. 51–54 above.

82 It should be pointed out that the Romans were not the first to confront the issues posed by 'conflicts of laws' and react to them. There were precedents in classical Greece and the Hellenistic period, which have not been mentioned for reasons of space. See Lewald, "Conflits de lois dans le monde grec et romain," and Anthony J. Marshall, "The Survival and Development of International Jurisdiction in the Greek World under Roman Rule," in *Aufstieg und Niedergang der römischen Welt*, Vol. II.13 (Berlin: De Gruyter, 1980), 626–40. Above all one should mention the decree in *P.Teb.* I 5, ll. 207–20 = Mitteis, *Chr.* II, no. 1 (118 BCE), on which see Hans Julius Wolff, "Plurality of Laws in Ptolemaic Egypt'," *RIDA* 7 (1960): 191 ff. and Hans Julius Wolff, "The Political Background of the Plurality of Laws in Ptolemaic Egypt," in *Proceedings of the Sixteenth International Congress of Papyrology*, ed. Roger S. Bagnall et al. (Chico, California: Scholars Press, 1981), 313–18.

Continuity of Nabataean Law in the Petra Papyri: A Methodological Exercise

What do we know of Nabataean law? Or, rather, what are our sources for Nabataean law?[1]

Although some legal customs can be inferred and gleaned from literary sources about the Nabataeans,[2] most, if not all, the evidence derives from documentary texts, inscriptions and papyri, written in the Nabataean script in Nabataean Aramaic (and as will become clear later on, also in Greek). This documentary evidence, to use John Healey's phrase, "is not 'supported', so to speak, by the survival of any contemporary or later literature in Nabataean."[3] 'Unsupported' is indeed an understatement: in contrast to Roman or Jewish law for example, a vacuum exists outside the documents whose testimony cannot be enhanced, modified, explained or nuanced by a body of literary legal tradition. In this Nabataean shares the fate of several other Near Eastern Semitic languages represented by epigraphic documents alone. On the other hand the Nabataean legal document in the Nabataean script is part of the "Aramaic common-law tradition,"[4] and its formulae and provisions can be profitably compared and contrasted with sibling documents.[5] My aim in the present exercise, however, is *not* to detect identity,

---

1 See the pioneering study of John F. Healey, "Sources for the Study of Nabataean Law," *New Arabian Studies* 1 (1993): 203–14; see also John F. Healey, "The Writing on the Wall: Law in Aramaic Epigraphy," in *Writing and Ancient Near Eastern Society: Papers in Honour of Alan R. Millard*, ed. Piotr Bienkowski, Christopher Mee, and Elizabeth Slater (New York: T&T Clark, 2005), 128–41.

2 They are now collected, with a translation and a commentary in Ursula Hackl, Hanna Jenni, and Christoph Schneider, *Quellen zur Geschichte der Nabatäer* (Göttingen: Vandenhoeck & Ruprecht, 2003), 415–620.

3 Healey, "The Writing on the Wall: Law in Aramaic Epigraphy," 129; the observation cited is not restricted to legal texts, but, with some notable exceptions, describes the predicament of Semitic epigraphy in general.

4 For the concept see Yochanan Muffs, *Studies in the Aramaic Legal Papyri from Elephantine* (Leiden: Brill, 1969), especially 173–94.

5 See the incisive comparison of the formulae in Jewish and Nabataean legal documents in Baruch A. Levine, "The Various Workings of the Aramaic Legal Tradition: Jews and Nabateans in the Naḥal Ḥever Archive," in *The Dead Sea Scrolls: Fifty Years after their Discovery 1947–1997*, ed.

Article note: First published in Hannah M. Cotton et al., eds., *From Hellenism to Islam: Cultural and Linguistic Change in the Roman Near East* (Cambridge: Cambridge University Press, 2009), 154–74, with the following note: I owe many people many thanks for their criticism and encouragement: to my co-editors, Robert Hoyland, Jonathan Price and David Wasserstein, to Antti Arjava, Matias Buchholz and Robert Daniels of the *P.Petra* team, and last but not least to Joseph Geiger, Axel Knauf, Michael Macdonald, Arietta Papaconstantinou and Alex Yakobson.

https://doi.org/10.1515/9783110770438-014

similarity and continuity of formulae,[6] not even "to identify the diversity existing within commonality" of "heirs to a rich Aramaic tradition,"[7] but rather to isolate pieces of substantive Nabataean law, more precisely the Nabataean law of persons.[8] Paradoxically as it may seem at first sight, my task was rendered easier by the fact that I rely on documents written mostly in Greek rather than in Nabataean Aramaic.

Most of the texts written in Nabataean Aramaic predate the annexation of the Nabataean kingdom and its redaction into a Roman province in 106 CE. Our earliest sources are the tomb inscriptions, especially those from Mada'in Salih.[9] The realisation that they are legal texts, rather than epitaphs or warnings against interference with the tombs, came soon after their discovery in the last quarter of the nineteenth century:[10] this is to be inferred, *inter alia*, from the fact that a copy was deposited in the temple of a god, as we read in one of the inscriptions (H 36 l. 9: *nsḥt dnh yhyb [bb]yt qyš'*), but even more by the explicit reference to

Lawrence H. Schiffman, Emanuel Tov, and James C. Vanderkam (Jerusalem: IES, 2000), 836–51, pointing out the presence of repetitious clusters of legal terms meant to create an impression of all-inclusiveness; in the former "this is achieved by stringing along Hebrew or Aramaic terms of reference", whereas the scribes of the Nabataean documents use "Arabic equivalents of the Aramaic terms of reference" (Levine, 844–5). See Ludwig Koenen, "Preliminary Observations on Legal Matters in P.Petra 10," in *Atti del XXII Congresso internazionale di papirologia, Firenze, 23–29 agosto 1998*, ed. Isabella Andorlini et al. (Florence: Istituto papirologico G. Vitelli, 2001), 734–35 on the "traditional technique of accumulating words and formulas."

6 See the careful and exhaustive running commentary on the individual Nabataean documents in Yigael Yadin et al., *The Documents from the Bar Kokhba Period in the Cave of Letters: Hebrew, Aramaic and Nabatean-Aramaic Papyri*, Judean Desert Studies III (Jerusalem: IES, 2002).

7 The phrasing comes from Levine, "The Various Workings of the Aramaic Legal Tradition: Jews and Nabateans in the Naḥal Ḥever Archive," 851.

8 I am aware of only one systematic treatment of Nabataean law of persons on tomb inscriptions, namely I.Sh. Shiffman, "To the Character of the Nabataean Private Law according to the Epigraphic Sources," *Palestinski Sbornik* 11 (1964): 16–24 (Russian), which is mentioned only in Jonas C. Greenfield, "Studies in the Legal Terminology of the Nabatean Funerary Inscriptions," in *Henoch Yalon Memorial Volume*, ed. Eduard Yechezkel Kutscher, Saul Lieberman, and Menaḥem Zevi Kaddari (Jerusalem: Kiryat Sefer, 1974), 66, n. 13 (Hebrew) – *Russica non leguntur*. I am indebted to my friend Alexander Yakobson for its translation. I have not seen Hatoon Ajwad Al-Fassi, *Women in Pre-Islamic Arabia: Nabataea* (Oxford: Archaeopress, 2007) in its published version.

9 Introduced, edited, and translated with a commentary in John F. Healey, *The Nabataean Tomb Inscriptions of Mada'in Salih* (Oxford: Oxford University Press, 1993), 65–236 = H(egra) 1–38; for the other sites see Healey, 237–48.

10 For a survey of the research down to 1974 see Greenfield, "Studies in the Legal Terminology of the Nabatean Funerary Inscriptions," 64–6. For a succinct summary of their salient legal aspects see Healey, "The Writing on the Wall: Law in Aramaic Epigraphy," 136–8.

a legal document, *šṭr mwhbt'*, a deed of gift, in the hand of the beneficiary to be used as her legal claim, *dy bydh dy t'bd bh kl dy tṣb'* (H 27, l. 4).[11] The last dated tomb inscription is from 74/75 CE.

Our second category of sources are the papyri in Nabataean cursive script found in Naḥal Ḥever[12] in two archives, deposited there by refugees from the province of Arabia during the Bar Kokhba revolt (132–136 CE).[13] These papyri contain the longest legal texts in Nabataean Aramaic. The dates of these Nabataean contracts from Naḥal Ḥever fall between 60 and 122 CE. Eight documents have so far been published: *P.Yadin* 1–4, 6 and 9 which belong to the Babatha archive,[14] and two, *P.Hever* 1 and 2, out of five or six which probably belong to the archive of Salome Komaïse.[15] Six of those documents are from the royal period – only four of them with precise dates: *P.Hever* 1 (60 CE) and *P.Hever* 2; *P.Yadin* 1 (94 CE), *P.Yadin* 2–3 (both 99 CE), and *P.Yadin* 4; and two are from the Roman period: *P.Yadin* 6

11 Cf. also 'documents of consecration', *bšṭry ḥrmy'*, in the Wadi at-Turkmaniye inscription, *CIS* II 530, l. 4 = Healey, *The Nabataean Tomb Inscriptions of Mada'in Salih*, 238–42; see Hackl, Jenni, and Schneider, *Quellen Zur Geschichte Der Nabatäer*, 259: 'Weihungsurkunden.'

12 On the nomenclature of documentary texts from the Judaean Desert see Hannah M. Cotton, "Documentary Texts from the Judaean Desert: A Matter of Nomenclature," *SCI* 20 (2001): 113–19; see also Hannah M. Cotton in Lawrence H. Schiffman and James Vanderkam, eds., *Encyclopedia of the Dead Sea Scrolls* (New York: Oxford University Press, 2000), *s. v.* 'Documentary Texts,' 'Ḥever, Naḥal,' 'Ṣe'elim, Naḥal.'

13 See Yigael Yadin, *Bar-Kokhba: The Rediscovery of the Legendary Hero of the Second Jewish Revolt Against Rome* (London: Random House, 1971); Hanan Eshel and David Amit, eds., *The Refuge Caves of the Bar Kokhba Revolt* (Jerusalem: IES, 1998) (Hebrew).

14 Yadin et al., *The Documents from the Bar Kokhba Period in the Cave of Letters: Hebrew, Aramaic and Nabatean-Aramaic Papyri*.

15 However they were not published in Hannah M. Cotton and Ada Yardeni, *Aramaic, Hebrew, and Greek Documentary Texts from Naḥal Ḥever and Other Sites*, Discoveries in the Judaean Desert XXVII (Oxford: Clarendon Press, 1997), with the rest of the papyri which belong to this archive; as a result, *DJD* XXVII starts with no. 7. *P.Hever* 1 (= *P.Yadin* 36) was first published by Jean Starcky, "Un contrat nabatéen sur papyrus," *RB* 61 (1954): 161–81, and revised by Ada Yardeni, "The Decipherment and Restoration of Legal Texts from the Judaean Desert: A Reexamination of Papyrus Stracky (P.Yadin 36)," *SCI* 20 (2001): 121–37; for a preliminary publication of *P.Hever* 2 see Ada Yardeni, *Textbook of Aramaic, Hebrew and Nabataean Documentary Texts from the Judaean Desert and Related Material*, Vol. I (Jerusalem: The Hebrew University Press, 2000), 290–1 (Hebrew), (see Vol. II, 95, for English translation) with important observations in Hanan Eshel, "Another Document from the Archive of Salome Komaïse Daughter of Levi," *SCI* 21 (2002): 169–71. On Naḥal Ḥever as the provenance of the archive of Salome Komaïse as well, see Cotton and Yardeni, *Aramaic, Hebrew, and Greek Documentary Texts from Naḥal Ḥever and Other Sites*, 1–4.

(119 CE) and *P.Yadin* 9 (122 CE). The still unpublished *P.Hever* 3–5 may belong to either period.[16]

As indicated above, I am interested in isolating elements of substantive Nabataean law. However, a step forward in vindicating the distinctiveness of the Nabataean legal tradition has already been made in the study of its diplomatics. Ada Yardeni's new edition of the earliest Nabataean double document, *P.Hever* 1 (60 CE), is a veritable landmark.[17] Yardeni pointed out for the first time a phenomenon which, so far as I know, had never been observed before, whose implication is that there existed a unique and independent Nabataean tradition of writing double documents, unparalleled elsewhere, attested in *P.Hever* 1 and *P.Yadin* 2 and 3, all three from the royal period, and continuing into the Roman period, as exemplified in *P.Yadin* 7, a Jewish Aramaic document from 120 CE.[18]

I can do no better here than summarise her argument. What we see in these documents is that the inner (or upper) text starts already on the *verso*, towards its bottom. Then the papyrus was turned over foot to head, rather than merely being turned sideways from back to front. This is in fact the only way to keep both parts of the inner text (the beginning on the *verso* and its continuation on the *recto*) on the same part of the papyrus so that both could later be rolled and tied. The purpose of this complicated arrangement was to prevent tampering with the contents of the inner text. Nothing could be added since the writing on the *verso* reached the very bottom of the papyrus before it was turned over.[19]

No further legal documents written in Nabataean Aramaic after *P.Yadin* 9 of 122 CE have come to view. However, there are virtually no legal documents in any

---

16 Or rather 3–6 as, although they have been known since 1953, the fragments have to this day not been properly sorted out, see Roland de Vaux, "Fouille au Khirbet Qumrân," *RB* 60 (1953): 83–106.

17 Yardeni, "The Decipherment and Restoration of Legal Texts from the Judaean Desert: A Reexamination of Papyrus Stracky (P.Yadin 36)."

18 Elizabeth Meyer, "Diplomatics, Law and Romanisation in the Documents from the Judaean Desert," in *Beyond Dogmatics: Law and Society in the Roman World*, ed. John W. Cairns and Paul J. du Plessis (Edinburgh: Edinburgh University Press, 2007), 65, misjudges the fragmentary condition of the papyri; contrary to what she says, there is no sign of a shortening of the inner text in the Nabataean double document, but every reason to believe that the tradition was vibrant and tenacious.

19 This contrasts sharply with the cavalier treatment of the inner text in many of the Greek texts in the archives from Naḥal Ḥever and from Dura-Europos, see Naphtali Lewis, *The Documents from the Bar Kokhba Period in the Cave of Letters. Greek Papyri*, Judean Desert Studies II (Jerusalem: IES, 1989), 9; cf. *P.Hever* 62 and *P.Dura* 26, 28, 29. Uri Yiftach-Firanko, "Who killed the Double Document in Ptolemaic Egypt," *Arch. Pap.* 54 (2008): 203–18 offers a radical revision of the common explanation for the demise of the double document in Egypt.

script or language from the area of Syria Palaestina and Arabia[20] after 135/136 and until the sixth century CE:[21] a gap of 380 years separates the latest legal document in the Babatha archive, *P.Yadin* 27 of 132 CE, from the first safely dated legal contract from Nessana, *P.Nessana* 16 of 512 CE; and over 400 years separate it from *P.Petra* 1, of 537 CE, published in the first volume of the Petra Papyri.[22] Both *P.Petra* 1 and *P.Nessana* 16, like most of the papyri in the corpora to which they belong, are written in Greek.[23] However, the peculiar circumstances responsible for the preservation of the Nabataean papyri, namely the flight of Jews from Arabia to the caves of Naḥal Ḥever, would make it quite unsafe to say that by that date the Nabataean Aramaic contract was ousted altogether by the Greek contract. All that can be said with confidence is (1) that we know of no Nabataean contracts after 122 CE and (2) that Greek is likely to have remained the language of legal documents from 106 down to the sixth and seventh centuries in the territories which once belonged to Nabataea/Arabia.

Not everyone agrees. The late Naphtali Lewis, whose swift and authoritative publication of the Greek part of the Babatha archive in 1989 marks a new era in the study of Jewish life and law under Roman rule,[24] believed in the demise of the Aramaic legal document, both Jewish and Nabataean, whose fate he compares to that of the Demotic contract in Egypt, where "the Roman reorganization of the administration of Egypt denied such documents the recognition or status they had previously enjoyed."[25] Of course there was no policy of suppression of the native languages. But they were starved out of existence: "the 'natives' were generally free to continue their customs and practices so long as these did not conflict with governmental requirements. In the eastern provinces that meant conducting

20 But see below for 'Greater Syria.'

21 I no longer accept the dating in Hannah M. Cotton, W.E.H. Cockle, and Fergus Millar, "The Papyrology of the Roman Near East: A Survey," *JRS* 85 (1995): 214–35 of no. 332 (*P.Mur* 116) and nos. 336–7 (*P.Mur* 113 and 114) – all of them in Greek – to the period after 135 CE; they should be dated to the period before the end of the Bar Kokhba revolt in 135/136 (see Hannah M. Cotton and Werner Eck, "P.Murabba'at 114 und die Anwesenheit römischer Truppen in den Höhlen des Wadi Murabba'at nach dem Bar Kochba Aufstand," *ZPE* 138 (2002): 173–83); the other documents, nos. 333–5 and nos. 338–42 – in Latin and Greek – are either doubtful cases or come from Roman military circles, where the use of Aramaic cannot be expected anyway.

22 Both Nessana and Petra belonged in the sixth century to Palaestina Salutaris/Tertia, which included southern Jordan, the Negev and the Sinai – territories which belonged to the Nabataean kingdom when it was redacted into the province of Arabia.

23 Some of the seventh-century papyri from Nessana have Arabic as well: see Cotton, Cockle, and Millar, "The Papyrology of the Roman Near East: A Survey," nos. 571–609: 'Appendix: Documents from Nessana of the Early Islamic Period.'

24 See Hannah M. Cotton, "Naphtali Lewis 1911–2005," *SCI* 27 (2007): 253–56.

25 Naphtali Lewis, "The Demise of the Demotic Document: When and Why," *JEA* 79 (1993): 277.

official business in Greek, which in turn diminished the socio-economic viability of the vernaculars."[26]

Lewis was wrong. The Aramaic legal contract in Syria Palaestina remained alive and vibrant – at least in some form – for centuries to come, as must be inferred from the running commentaries in Hebrew on its formulae in the Mishnah and the Toseftah. It will resurface, for example, in the late contracts of the Cairo Genizah.[27] Elsewhere too, legal documents in the Semitic languages continued to be written, as is shown in the use of Syriac for legal transactions in Osrhoene in the mid-third century: *P.Dura* 28, a deed of sale,[28] and two other parchments, *P.Euphr.Syr* A and B, an acknowledgement of receipt of debt from a third party and a lease of land respectively – all of them written under direct Roman rule.[29]

This is not to deny that the overwhelming majority of legal documents in the Roman Near East were written in Greek.[30] As it happens, the impact of the transition from native to direct Roman rule is nowhere better attested than in the province of Arabia, the former Nabataean realm: there are *no* documents written

---

26 Naphtali Lewis, "The Demise of the Aramaic Document in the Dead Sea Region," *SCI* 20 (2001): 181.

27 See Hannah M. Cotton, "Survival, Adaptation and Extinction: Nabataean and Jewish Aramaic versus Greek in the Legal Documents from the Cave of Letters in Naḥal Ḥever," in *Sprache und Kultur in der kaiserzeitlichen Provinz Arabia: Althistorische Beiträge zur Erforschung von Akkulturationsphänomenen im römischen Nahen Osten*, ed. Leonhard Schumacher and Oliver Stoll (St. Katharinen: Scripta Mercaturae Verlag, 2003), 5–8 [above, pp. 165–68]; Lewis, "The Demise of the Aramaic Document in the Dead Sea Region," relied partly on the dating in Cotton, Cockle, and Millar, "The Papyrology of the Roman Near East: A Survey," nos. 332–42, on which see n. 21 above.

28 *P.Dura* 28, Edessa (243 CE) = Cotton, Cockle, and Millar, "The Papyrology of the Roman Near East: A Survey," no. 160 = Han J.W. Drijvers and John F. Healey, *The Old Syriac Inscriptions of Edessa and Osrhoene* (Leiden: Brill, 1999), 232–6 (Appendix 1, P1); *P.Euphr.Syr.* A (240 CE) and B (242 CE) = Cotton, Cockle, and Millar, nos. 157 and 159 = Drijvers and Healey, 237–48 (Appendix 1, P2 and P3). See bibliography in Cotton, Cockle, and Millar, ad loc.

29 On the wider context see Fergus Millar, *The Roman Near East, 31 BC-AD 337* (Cambridge, Mass.: Harvard University Press, 1993), 452–81.

30 Apart from the three documents mentioned in note 28, all the other documents in the archives from Mesopotamia, *P.Euphr.* 1–17, are in Greek with the exception of some of the signatures, on which see Hannah M. Cotton, "'Diplomatics' or External Aspects of the Legal Documents from the Judaean Desert: Prolegomena," in *Rabbinic Law in its Roman and Near Eastern Context*, ed. Catherine Hezser (Tübingen: Mohr Siebeck, 2003), 54 [above, p. 153]. For the final publication see Denis Feissel and Jean Gascou, "Documents d'archives romains inédits du Moyen Euphrate (IIIe s. après J-C): I. Les pétitions (T. Euphr. 1 à 5)," *Journal des Savants*, 1995, 65–119; Javier Teixidor, Denis Feissel, and Jean Gascou, "Documents d'archives romains inédits du Moyen Euphrate (IIIe s. après J-C): II. Les actes de vente- achat (P. Euphr. 6 À 10)," *Journal des Savants*, 1997, 3–57; Denis Feissel and Jean Gascou, "Documents d'archives romains inédits du Moyen Euphrate (IIIe s. après J.-C.): III. Actes divers et Lettres (P. Euphr. 11 à 17)," *Journal des Savants*, 2000, 157–208.

in Greek (or Jewish Aramaic) from the Nabataean period; whereas after 106 CE as against two Nabataean contracts and four written in Jewish Aramaic we have altogether thirty-two Greek documents from the period between 106 and 132 CE.[31] True, the number of documents is small and restricted to a few family archives, and at this level statistical interpretations must be meaningless – but one can work only with what one has.

The phenomenon observed here – the faint reflection[32] of the vernacular in legal and administrative documents and its eclipse by the current Reichssprache – is by no means unique to the province of Arabia, as emerges from the case of the Demotic language in Egypt mentioned above, nor is it unique to the Roman phase in the Near East. All over the Near East for hundreds of years literate notaries and scribes conducted legal and administrative affairs in a language that did not necessarily correspond to the vernacular of either ruler or subject. A striking example are the Aramaic documents from north-central Afghanistan, ancient Bactria, which date to the second half of the fourth century BCE: regardless of the identity of the ruling power at the time, whether it was the Persian Artaxerxes or the Macedonian Alexander, these administrative documents are written in the *Reichsaramäisch* of the time by a Persian Satrap to his Persian subordinate. The job is executed by a scribe: 'Daizaka the scribe is in charge of this document' (A4, l. 6).[33]

One should 'mind the gap' between reality and its epigraphic representation.[34] What is no longer available to us has to be taken into account no less than what

31 See Meyer, "Diplomatics, Law and Romanisation in the Documents from the Judaean Desert," 79–82, accounting for the different pace of Romanization in Judaea and Arabia; for another explanation see Hannah M. Cotton, "The Languages of the Legal and Administrative Documents from the Judaean Desert," *ZPE* 125 (1999): 230–31 [above, pp. 144–46].

32 On signatures and subscriptions, see Hannah M. Cotton, "Subscriptions and Signatures in the Papyri from the Judaean Desert: The χειροχρήστης," *JJP* 25 (1995): 29–40 [above, pp. 115–25] and Lawrence H. Schiffman, "Witnesses and Signatures in the Hebrew and Aramaic documents from the Bar Kokhba Caves," in *Semitic Papyrology in Context: A Climate of Creativity*, ed. Lawrence H. Schiffman (Leiden – Boston: Brill, 2003), 165–86.

33 The documents were presented in summer 2003 at the Institute for Advanced Studies in Jerusalem by Shaul Shaked and published by Joseph Naveh and Shaul Shaked, *Aramaic Documents from Ancient Bactria* (London: The Khalili Family Trust, 2012). I am grateful to Shaul Shaked for the information. See Shaul Shaked, *Le satrape de Bactriane et son gouverneur. Documents araméens du IVe s. avant notre ère provenant de Bactriane* (Paris: de Boccard, 2004).

34 See Hannah M. Cotton, "Language Gaps in Roman Palestine and the Roman Near East," in *Medien im antiken Palästina: Materielle Kommunikation und Medialität als Thema der Palästinaarchäologie*, ed. Christian Frevel (Tübingen: Mohr Siebeck, 2005), 151–69 [above, pp. 195–212], conceived in tandem with the present article.

has reached us, as Werner Eck reminds us at the beginning of this volume.[35] The written record is neither self-evident, nor necessarily representative.[36] The imperial period in the Near East is marked by the advent of the Greek language which penetrates everywhere. This is masterfully surveyed and displayed in Fergus Millar's *The Roman Near East 31 BC-AD 332*: in the smallest out-of-the-way villages we find Greek inscriptions. Many of the contributions in this volume bear witness to this. The indigenous languages, above all the several variants of Aramaic, seem to be on the wane – so far as can be gathered from the written record, and more than anywhere else in legal and administrative documents. This is only to be expected in view of the fact that the Roman Empire communicated with its subjects in the Near East in Greek. The use of Greek increased with the impact of empire.[37] But how deep must one probe beneath the written surface to discover the vernacular and the indigenous?[38]

Thus it seems to me pertinent and legitimate to ask: what happened to the Nabataean legal system with the disappearance of the Nabataean legal document? What happened to the indigenous law? Fergus Millar, discussing the Babatha archive (*P.Yadin*) observes: "So far as this archive can show, a legal system using Nabataean ceased almost at once when the area became a province."[39] Can this

---

35 See Werner Eck, "The Presence, Role and Significance of Latin in the Epigraphy and Culture of the Roman Near East," in *From Hellenism to Islam: Cultural and Linguistic Change in the Roman Near East*, ed. Hannah M. Cotton et al. (Cambridge: Cambridge University Press, 2009), 15–42.

36 To quote Seth Schwartz, "Language, Power and Identity in Ancient Palestine," *Past & Present* 148 (1995): 13: "In some cases writing may reflect no more than scribal practice. And in all cases writing is necessarily related to speech in highly complex and sometimes highly attenuated ways"; even more intriguing and surprising are the manifestations of 'literacy in an oral environment', see Michael C.A. Macdonald, "Literacy in an Oral Environment," in *Writing and Ancient Near Eastern Society: Papers in Honour of Alan R. Millard*, ed. Piotr Bienkowski, Christopher Mee, and Elizabeth Slater (New York: T&T Clark, 2005), 49–118.

37 See Werner Eck, "Latein als Sprache politischer Kommunikation in Städten der östlichen Provinzen," *Chiron* 30 (2000): 641–60; Werner Eck, "Lateinisch, Griechisch, Germanisch ...? Wie sprach Rom mit seinen Untertanen?," in *Roman Rule and Civic Life: Local and Regional Perspectives*, ed. L. de Ligt, E.A. Hemelrijk, and H.W. Singor (Leiden: Brill, 2004), 3–19; Werner Eck, "Befund und Realität. Zur Repräsentativität unserer epigraphischen Quellen in der römischen Kaiserzeit," *Chiron* 37 (2007): 49–64.

38 See the masterful vindication of the tenacity of Aramaic in the Near East against both Greek and Arabic in Robert G. Hoyland, "Language and Identity: The Twin Histories of Arabic and Aramaic (and: Why did Aramaic Succeed where Greek Failed?)," *SCI* 23 (2004): 183–99, modifying David J. Wasserstein, "Why did Arabic Succeed Where Greek Failed? Language Change in the Near East after Muhammad," *SCI* 22 (2003): 257–72.

39 Fergus Millar, "Empire, Community and Culture in the Roman Near East: Greeks, Syrians, Jews and Arabs," *JJS* 38 (1987): 153, but see Millar, *The Roman Near East, 31 BC-AD 337*, 400–28 in great detail on the linguistic situation in Nabataea/Arabia.

be the whole truth? Did Nabataean law die out with the disappearance of the Nabataean legal document, i. e. with the disappearance of the legal document written in the Nabataean language? Are we to assume that the language change brought about a total change of legal practices? Was the Greek legal instrument a vehicle of a new legal system, and if so, what system? Certainly, despite some formal features visible in the documents from the Judaean Desert, it was not likely to have been the law of the Roman ruling power, the *ius civile* formulated in Latin and designed exclusively for Roman citizens,[40] especially in branches of the law of persons including the law of marriage, divorce and succession.[41]

The example of the Coptic legal document springs to mind. The invention of the Coptic script, which uses 'the alphabetic simplicity of Greek,' did not occur merely to remedy the fact that it was impossible for the majority of the population to record anything in their own language.[42] The linguistic reality is far more complex, not least because Coptic contains a large quantity of Greek words, and assumes some knowledge of Greek. Nevertheless the appearance of Coptic is a remarkable fact.[43] The Coptic legal document becomes common only after the end of Roman rule and the arrival of the Arabs, that is in the mid-seventh century CE.[44] Does the Coptic legal document take up where the Demotic legal document had left off?[45] Is there continuity after a hiatus of c. 350 years,[46] not only in language

40 I am aware of course that this is a sweeping statement that should be slightly modified by such observations as those made in Andreas Wacke, "Gallisch, Punisch, Syrisch oder Griechisch statt Latein?," *ZSS* 110 (1993): 14–59.

41 See now Hannah M. Cotton, "Private International Law or Conflict of Laws: Reflections on Roman Provincial Jurisdiction," in *Herrschen und Verwalten. Der Alltag der römischen Administration in der Hohen Kaizerzeit*, ed. Rudolf Haensch and Johannes Heinrichs (Köln: Böhlau, 2007), 236 [above, p. 215 f.].

42 Roger S. Bagnall, *Egypt in Late Antiquity* (Princeton: Princeton University Press, 1993), 235.

43 See Tonio Sebastian Richter, "Greek, Coptic and the 'Language of the Hijra': The Rise and Decline of the Coptic Language in Late Antique and Medieval Egypt," in *From Hellenism to Islam: Cultural and Linguistic Change in The Roman Near East*, ed. Hannah M. Cotton et al. (Cambridge: Cambridge University Press, 2009), 405–7.

44 Although a few are dated to the sixth, see Tonio Sebastian Richter, *Rechtssemantik und forensische Rhetorik* (Leipzig: Wodtke & Stegbauer, 2002), 20–4.

45 On the Demotic legal document and its disappearance see Mark Depauw, "Autograph Confirmation in Demotic Private Contracts," *Chronique d'Egypte* 78 (2003): 66–111 and Brian Muhs, "The Grapheion and the Disappearance of Demotic Contracts in Early Roman Tebtynis and Soknopaiou Neso," in *Tebtynis und Soknopaiu Nesos. Leben im römerzeitlichen Fajum*, ed. Sandra Lippert and Maren Schentuleit (Wiesbaden: Harrasowitz, 2005), 93–104.

46 See Roger S. Bagnall and Klaas A. Worp, "Dating the Coptic legal documents from Aphrodite," *ZPE* 148 (2004): 247–52; Tonio Sebastian Richter, *Rechtsemantik und forensische Rhetorik*, 2nd Ed. (Wiesbaden: Harrasowitz, 2008): 'Vorwort zur 2. Auflage' (kindly sent me by the author in advance of publication).

but also in legal formulae and content; or is the Coptic document no more than a Greek legal document in Coptic dress? Those who uphold the idea of continuity suggest two ways in which the Demotic legal tradition could have been preserved without being written for hundreds of years. It is suggested that oral transmission somehow kept the Demotic legal tradition alive. Alternatively, it may have been preserved in the Greek documents of the succeeding ages to re-appear later in the Coptic document.[47] The whole subject lay virtually dormant for nearly half a century[48] following Schiller's monograph of 1957, to be picked up again and examined in detail in Richter's new study – with negative results: there was no line of continuity between the Demotic and the Coptic legal document.[49]

For my purpose here, however, the questions are far more important than the answers. To some extent the situation with Nabataean law parallels that of Egyptian law, although the material at our disposal is far more limited. The equivalent of the Demotic and Coptic documents would be the Nabataean and early Arabic legal documents respectively. The Nabataean legal tradition could be expected to resurface in early Arabic documents, if indeed at least part of the Nabataean population in the province of Arabia used Arabic in their daily life.[50] Healey for example concludes his paper on 'Sources for the Study of Nabataean Law' with the surmise that: "much of this legal tradition survived in northern Arabia into

47 Arthur A. Schiller, "Coptic Documents: A Monograph on the Law of the Coptic Documents and a Survey of Coptic Legal Studies 1938–1956," *ZVglRWiss* 60 (1957): 190–211.

48 But see Erich Lüddeckens, "Demotische und koptische Urkundenformeln," *Enchoria* 2 (1972): 21–31 and Gonnie van den Berg-Onstwedder, "The Use of Demotic Phrases from Legal Texts of the Ptolemaic Period in Coptic Legal Texts," *BSAC* 35 (1996): 101–16.

49 Richter, *Rechtssemantik und forensische Rhetorik*, 28–57, esp. 31–6.

50 I do not wish to enter here into the vexed question of 'Who were the Nabataeans?,' the topic of a roundtable discussion held at the Institute for Advanced Studies in Jerusalem on 20 November 2002, in which some of the contributors to this volume took part. That some of the Nabataeans were Arabic speakers is accepted by everyone, and this is sufficient for the present discussion. See Fergus Millar's contribution to the volume, "Introduction: Documentary Evidence, Social Realities and the History of Language," in *From Hellenism to Islam: Cultural and Linguistic Change in The Roman Near East*, ed. Hannah M. Cotton et al. (Cambridge: Cambridge University Press, 2009), 3; Michael C.A. Macdonald, "Some Reflections on Epigraphy and Ethnicity in the Roman Near East," *Mediterranean Archaeology* 11 (1998): 177–90, Michael C.A. Macdonald, "Reflections on the Linguistic Map of Pre-Islamic Arabia," *Arabian Archaeology and Epigraphy* 11 (2000): 28–79, and Michael C.A. Macdonald, "Languages, Scripts, and the Uses of Writing Among the Nabataeans," in *Petra Rediscovered: Lost City of the Nabataeans*, ed. Glenn Markoe (New York: Harry N. Abrams, 2003), 50–1, and Ernst Axel Knauf, "Arabo-Aramaic and 'Arabiyya: From Ancient Arabic to Early Standard Arabic, 200 CE – 600 CE," in *The Quran in Context*, ed. Angelika Neuwirth, Nicolai Sinai, and Michael Marx (Leiden – Boston: Brill, 2010), 197–254.

the Byzantine and early Islamic periods. The potential of this material in relation to the study of the historical roots of Islamic law is considerable."[51]

However, continuity cannot be taken for granted. Continuity has to be proven, and its exact manifestations, whether in vocabulary, formulae or legal norms, have to be sought out. Comparison between the Nabataean and early Arab/Muslim legal documents is quite beyond my skills and expertise.[52] The theme is touched upon again and again, mainly through terminology and formulae, in the extensive commentary to the Nabataean papyri from Nahal Hever by Ada Yardeni and Baruch Levine, which has laid the foundation for many discussions to come.[53]

Since, as stated at the beginning of this exercise, my aim is to seek out continuity of substantive Nabataean law, rather than of legal terminology and formulae, it seems legitimate, and as we shall soon see profitable, to tap also legal documents written in Greek from Arabia.[54] A native legal system using Greek rather than Nabataean Aramaic may have survived the demise of the Nabataean legal document,[55] especially that part of the Nabataean, as of any, legal system which is more tenacious than others, namely the law of persons: the law of marriage, divorce and succession.

One way by which we could reach positive results is to find a distinctive legal norm present in both the early Nabataean and the Greek documents from the first two centuries of our era in Arabia resurfacing in one or both of the two bodies of later documents from the area that was once part of Nabataea and later of the province of Arabia, that is the Greek papyri from Petra and Nessana.[56] Such detective work is far from easy in view of the process of standardization of law which took place in late antiquity, when Roman law, having absorbed local variations, was codified, with the result that the notaries and scribes could be expected to

51 Healey, "Sources for the Study of Nabataean Law," 210.

52 See Geoffrey Khan, "The Pre-Islamic Background of Muslim Legal Formularies," *ARAM* 6 (1994): 193–224, whose conclusions I do not find convincing.

53 See Yadin et al., *The Documents from the Bar Kokhba Period in the Cave of Letters: Hebrew, Aramaic and Nabatean-Aramaic Papyri*, 405–10 for Nabataean-Aramaic glossary with Arabic loan words; see Levine, "The Various Workings of the Aramaic Legal Tradition: Jews and Nabateans in the Naḥal Ḥever Archive."

54 Albeit written in Greek, they too may on occasion reflect faithfully the legal formulae of an Aramaic *Urtext* of which the Greek text is but a servile translation; see Cotton's commentary on *P.Hever* 64 in Cotton and Yardeni, *Aramaic, Hebrew, and Greek Documentary Texts from Naḥal Ḥever and Other Sites*.

55 Cf. Millar quoted above at text to note 39.

56 Although at the time they were written both Petra and Nessana were part of Palaestina Salutaris/Tertia.

reproduce in their legal contracts a more or less unified legal pattern.[57] However, this trend was not total and local variations were not altogether stamped out, certainly not as far as the formal aspects of the contracts (its diplomatics) are concerned, as already pointed out long ago by Hans-Julius Wolff.[58] I shall deliberately steer clear of the diplomatics of legal contracts, in which I would include the legal formulae, which distinguish the Greek papyri from Arabia from those of the Greek papyri in Egypt.[59] Semitisms and closer resemblances to the papyri from the rest of the Roman Near East, from Dura-Europos, the Euphrates, Bostra, etc. rather than to the Egyptian counterparts are only to be expected. On the other hand it is obvious that even the early Greek contracts, I mean those which are written immediately after annexation, are not, with one or two exceptions,[60] literal translations of Aramaic legal texts, but the creations of scribes fluent in Greek and familiar with the style of the Greek document. Thus on two occasions we find a groom agreeing, in exchange for the dowry, to carry out his obligations towards his wife and children 'in accordance with *nomos hellenikos*' (ἑλληνικῷ νόμῳ) in the Babatha archive,[61] expanded to 'in accordance with *nomos hellenikos* and *hellenikos tropos*' (ν̣ό̣μ̣[ῳ ἑλληνικ]ῷ καὶ ἑλλ̣[η]ν̣ικ̣ῷ τρόπῳ) in the Salome Komaïse archive.[62] This 'Hellenismus' as was pointed out long ago by H.-J. Wolff,[63] and rearticulated by Abraham Wasserstein, was "a *koine* of private law arising from

57 See Antti Arjava, "Everyday Life and Law in Byzantine Petra," *Acta Byzantina Fennica* 2 (2003/04): 7–17.

58 Hans Julius Wolff, "Der byzantinische Urkundenstil Ägyptens im Lichte der Funde von Nessana und Dura," *RIDA* 8 (1961): 115–54. See now Antti Arjava, "Physical Format and Notarial Conventions in the Petra Papyri," in *The Petra Papyri III*, ed. Antti Arjava, Matias Buchholz, and Traianos Gagos (Amman: ACOR, 2007), 1–5.

59 See Koenen, "Preliminary Observations on Legal Matters in P.Petra 10."

60 Above note 54.

61 The Babatha archive, *P.Yadin* 18 (128 CE), lines 14–17 = lines 47–52: ἃ ὡμολόγησεν [Ιουδα Κίμβερ] δοῦναι αὐτῇ πρὸς τ̣ὰ̣ τῆς προγεγραμμένης προσφορᾶς αὐτῆς πάντα εἰς λόγον προι{ο}κὸς αὐτῆς ἀκολούθως αἱρέσει τροφῆς καὶ ἀμφιασμοῦ αὐτῆς τε καὶ τῶν μελλόντων τέκνων ἑλληνικῷ νόμῳ ἐπὶ τῆς τοῦ αὐτοῦ Ἰούδα Κίμβ[ε]ρ̣ο[ς] π̣ίστ̣εως καὶ κ̣ινδύνου κτλ.

62 *P.Hever* 65 (131 CE), lines 7–10: [ἃ ὡμολογήσατο ὁ γήμας ὁ αὐ]τὸς Ιησου̣ς/ [ἀπ]ε̣σχηκ̣[έν]αι παρ̣' α̣ὐτῆς τῇ̣ [οὔ]σῃ ἡμέρᾳ τειμογ̣[ρ]αφίαν κοσμίας γυναικίας ἐν ἀ̣[ργύρῳ καὶ χρυσῷ καὶ ἱμα]τισμῷ καὶ ἑταίροις γυ[ναι]κίοις ἀ̣ξι[οχρέαν] . . . . . τ̣ο̣υ̣ ἀργυρίου, σὺν αἱρέσει τρ̣οφῆ̣ς [καὶ ἀμφιασμοῦ αὐτῆς] τ̣ε καὶ τῶν μελ̣λόντ̣ῳ[ν τέκ]ν̣ῳ̣ν̣ ν̣ό̣μ̣[ῳ] [ἑλληνικ]ῷ καὶ ἑλλ̣[η]ν̣ικ̣ῷ τρόπῳ ἐ̣π̣ὶ̣ τ̣ῆ̣ς τ̣[οῦ αὐτοῦ Ιησουου πίστεω]ς καὶ κινδ̣ύ̣νου πά̣ν̣[των ὑπα]ρ̣χόντων̣.

63 Wolff, "Der byzantinische Urkundenstil Ägyptens im Lichte der Funde von Nessana und Dura," 142–3: "Übrigens muss in diesem Zusammenhang [i. e. of the Greek legal contract in the East] der Ausdruck 'Hellenismus' wohl in dem weiten Sinne verstanden werden, dass er Institute umfasste, die ihren Ursprung in anderen Volksrechten des Ostens hatten, aber von den griechischen Urkundenschreibern aufgegriffen, griechischen Denk- und Sprachformen angepasst worden."

the amalgam of Greek and oriental institutes."[64] To my mind, notwithstanding the fact that by the sixth century the contractors were all Roman citizens and formally subject to the *ius civile*, the *ethos Romaikos* (ἔθει Ῥωμαικῷ) in *P.Nessana* 18, l. 20 and *P.Nessana* 20, l. 21, both marriage contracts, from 537 and 558 CE respectively, carries the same connotation as the *nomos hellenikos* of the much earlier papyri, as is clear from their presence in an identical context; both phrases are the underpinning of the groom's obligations consequent upon receiving the dowry.[65]

I can envision one objection to using *P.Yadin* and *P.Hever* as evidence for Nabataean law: seeing that these papyri were written for Jews and by Jews, I could be charged with mistaking for Nabataean law what was in reality Jewish law. But Jewish law in its halakhic or rabbinic form was still in the process of evolving, let alone becoming canonic. Any points of contact the Greek – and also the Semitic – documents from Naḥal Ḥever share with later rabbinic civil law were, when they were composed, part of a common law of the Graeco-Roman Near East. In other words, what we witness is *not* the impact of Jewish law on the documents but rather the reverse: the *halakha* adopted the legal usage reflected in the documents.[66]

What follows is devoted to the examination of a single legal item in *P.Petra* 1, which suggests a possible continuity of the pre-Roman Nabataean law of persons into late antique Petra, now 'the Antonine imperial colony, the distinguished and native mother of colonies, Hadrianic Petra, Metropolis of the Third Palestine Salutaris.'[67]

P.Petra 1 of 537 CE is a post-nuptial agreement, described in the text itself as an ἔνγραφος ἀσφάλια (l. 6), "which can mean any kind of a written agreement,"[68]

---

64 Wolff, 142–3, and see Abraham Wasserstein, "A Marriage Contract from the Province of Arabia Nova: Notes on Papyrus Yadin 18," *JQR* 80 (1989): 120.

65 I cite the context from the more complete *P.Nessana* 18, lines 16–20: ὁμολογ̣[ε]ῖ̣ [δὲ τῇ Ανιᾳ ὁ εἰρημένος Αλγεβ Αλοβαιου(?) τὸν] γαμετὴν ὀφίλειν τε αὐτῇ κ̣α̣ὶ̣ κλ[ηρονόμοις αὐτῆς καὶ διαδόχοις(?) c. 8] τὰς π̣ρογεγραμμένας τῆς προικ[ὸς χρυσοῦ οὐγκίας ἓξ καὶ τὰ προγεγραμμένα(?)] νομίσματα ἓξ ὄφλημα π̣ροικιμ[αῖον ὃ καὶ παραδώσει(?) c. 19] τιας ἔθει Ῥωμαικῷ καὶ χωρεὶς π̣ά̣[σης ἀντιλογίας καὶ ζητήσεως](?)

66 See Hannah M. Cotton, "The Rabbis and the Documents," in *Jews in a Greco-Roman World*, ed. Martin Goodman (Oxford: Oxford University Press, 1998), 167–79 [below, pp. 453–65]; see Peter Schäfer, "Bar Kokhba and the Rabbis," in *The Bar Kokhba War Reconsidered*, ed. Peter Schäfer (Tübingen: Mohr Siebeck, 2003), 21–2; *contra* Ranon Katzoff, "Review: Hannah M. Cotton and Ada Yardeni eds., Aramaic, Hebrew and Greek Documentary Texts from Nahal Hever and Other Sites," *SCI* 19 (2000): 324–27.

67 Lines 4–5: ἐν Αὐγουστοκολων[ί̣ᾳ̣ [Ἀ]ν̣τωνιανῇ ἐ[π]ι̣[σ]ήμ[ῳ καὶ] ἐ[γγεν]ε[ῖ] [μ]η[τρὶ] κ̣[ολωνιῶν] Ἀδριανῇ Πέτρᾳ μητροπόλει τῆς Τρίτης Παλαιστίνης Σαλουτ[αρίας]

68 See Jaakko Frösén, Antti Arjava, and Marjo Lentinen, *The Petra Papyri I* (Amman: ACOR, 2002), 24.

between Theodoros son of Obodianos, and his maternal uncle, Patrophilos, son of Bassos. Theodoros is married to his cousin Stephanous, who is Patrophilos' daughter. I am interested in the legal situation revealed in ll. 11–16 where we are told that the dowry of Theodoros' mother has been ceded to her son by his maternal uncle, Patrophilos, who has just become his father in-law. The syntax of these lines is unfortunately obscure:

11. ... ἐ̣π̣είπερ θ̣[– ca. 10 –]
12. προικὸς τῆς [μ]α̣καρι̣ο̣τάτης .ερε[. . . .γε]ναμέ[ν]ης Θεοδ̣ώρου̣ τ̣[οῦ]
13. εὐδοκιμοτάτου μητρὸς ἐξεχωρή[θη] ὁ αὐ̣τ̣ὸ̣ς εὐδοκιμότ̣α̣τ̣ο̣ς Θ̣[εό]δ̣[ωρος]
14. παρὰ τοῦ εἰρημένου εὐδοκιμοτάτου Πατροφί̣λ̣ου Βάσ̣σ̣ο̣υ̣ ... [– ca. 7 –]
15. τὰ[69] καὶ περιεχόμενα̣ τ̣ῇ γ̣ε̣νομέ[ν]η̣ [ἐν]γ̣ρ̣άφ̣[ῳ] ἐ[κ]χωρ̣ήσει εἰ̣ς [τὸν αὐτὸν]
16. εὐδοκιμότατον Θεόδωρον·

Because ... the dowry of the most blessed Hiereia(?), the deceased mother of the most honourable Theodoros was ceded (had been ceded?) to the same most honourable Theodoros by the said most honourable Patrophilos, son of Bassos, [which were ...] and also included in a written deed of cession in favour of the ... [same] most honourable Theodoros.

Why did the mother's dowry end up in the hands of her brother in the first place when, as the editor, Antti Arjava, observes: "according to the normal rules of inheritance, Theodoros should have inherited it immediately following his parents' death"?[70] Arjava offers three solutions as to why the mother's dowry was ceded to her son by his maternal uncle:

1. That the mother's dowry was returned to her father Bassos (Theodoros' grandfather and Patrophilos' father) after her death in compliance with a contract between the couple which stipulated the return of the dowry upon the dissolution of the marriage. In this way Patrophilos inherited it from his father (Bassos).
2. That Patrophilos only administered the dowry for his nephew.
3. That Theodoros had ceded to his uncle his mother's dowry which is now being ceded back to him.

---

69 τὰ; in the first edition, but here τα is taken to be the last syllable of a word in the previous line. As a result my translation differs somewhat from that of the first edition. The editor tells me that "the scribe does not seem to divide words between lines (except compounds), so it is less likely that τα could be the end of a word." However, such a word division occurs in lines 56–7 of the present document: [τοῦ εἰρη-] / μένου Πατροφί̣λου. Robert Daniel (personal communication) does not think that there is sufficient evidence to prove that "the scribes imposed on themselves the rule that they may divide only compounds."

70 Frösén, Arjava, and Lentinen, *The Petra Papyri I*, 25.

The second option is unacceptable since a formal deed of cession (ἐκχώρησις, l. 15) could hardly be needed in such a case. The third option is syntactically inadmissible: reading something like [τῆς] προικὸς ἐξεχώρη[σεν] ὁ αὐτὸς εὐδοκιμότατος Θ[εό]δ[ωρος], leaves the παρὰ τοῦ εἰρημένου εὐδοκιμοτάτου Πατροφίλου unaccounted for, as the editor himself admits, whereas ἐξεχωρή[θη] may have as its grammatical subject the person to whom something is given. Thus we are left with the first possibility only, which is also unsatisfactory since as the editor himself admits "usually such agreements did not interfere with the children's inheritance right."[71] This at least was the norm according to Roman law. However, perhaps another legal system, or its remnant, is lurking here. Is it possible that some norms of Nabataean personal law, or, to be precise, of the Nabataean law of succession, were still observed despite the imposed uniformity in that part of the Roman world?

The fact that the mother's dowry was in the hands of the maternal uncle and was ceded by him to his nephew evokes the legal situation in *P.Yadin* 5, the earliest Greek document from the Babatha archive from the Roman period. It is dated to 110 CE, only four years after the annexation of the Nabataean kingdom. It attests the existence of joint property between two brothers, one of whom had recently died. The property includes the dowry, or bride money, of the wife of the deceased brother – presumably because of the minority of the orphaned nephew. The document itself is an acknowledgment of debt by the paternal uncle, Joseph son of Joseph, made to his nephew, Babatha's first husband, Jesus son of Jesus (and not, as was once thought, to her orphaned son, who was also Jesus son of Jesus):

> I, Joseph son of Joseph, also called Zabouda, of Maḥoza, acknowledge to you Jesus son of my brother Jesus, from the same place that you have with me a thousand and a hundred and twenty silver 'blacks' as a deposit of all the property/assets of silver and deeds of debt, investment in a workshop, value of figs, value of wine, value of dates, value of oil and of every manner [of thing] large and small, from everything which was found [to belong] to your father and me, between me and him (πάντω[ν] ὧν εὑρέθη πατρεί σ[ο]υ καί μοι μεταξύ μου καὶ α[ὐ]τοῦ) [namely] one thousand and a hundred and twenty 'blacks', in addition to seven hundreds and ten 'blacks' of silver which your mother had from your father as her wedding silver, and which she had [as a lien] against Jesus, your father (ὑπὲρ ἀργυρίου μέλανας ἑπτακοσίους καὶ δέκα οὓς εἴλ[η]φεν ἡ μήτηρ σου ἀργύριον γαμικὸν αὐτῆς [ὃ]ν εἶχ[ε]ν κατ[ὰ] Ἰησοῦ πατ[ρ]ός σου) (*P.Yadin* 5, lines 5–16).

That the 'wedding silver,' and hence the legal system which governed it, goes back to the Nabataean period is clear from the fact that the sums of money are

71 *The Petra Papyri I*, 25

stated in 'blacks,' which is the old Nabataean silver.[72] There is another Nabataean feature in this document: the fine to the Roman emperor καὶ Καίσαρι ὡ̣σ̣αύτ̣ω̣ς (*P.Yadin* 5, *Frag*. A, col. II, l. 10), which substitutes for the fine to the Nabataean king in the Nabataean legal document: ולמראנא רבאל מלכא כות ('and to our lord Rab'el the king likewise', e. g. *P.Yadin* 1, ll. 9–19, 42, 43).[73] However, in this case it would seem that the nephew, once he has come of age, could call back the debt now in the possession of his paternal uncle. Unfortunately we do not have the sequel: both nephew and uncle disappear subsequently from the archive.[74]

Were this the only piece of evidence for the special role played by an uncle in questions of inheritance and succession, I would admit that I have hardly a leg to stand on. However, some of the documents give the clear impression that uncles, and more specifically paternal uncles (or agnatic brothers to use the Roman terminology), held a strong position, at least against daughters, in these early archives.[75] Various claims and counter-claims suggest that the brother of the deceased, and consequently also his descendants, who happen to be males, have a better claim to the inheritance than the children, who happen to be females.

In *P.Yadin* 20 of 130 CE the guardians of the orphans of her paternal uncle, Jesus son of Eleazar Khthousion, concede to Shelamzion daughter of Judah son of Eleazar Khthousion (the orphans' uncle) a courtyard in Ein Gedi which belonged to their common grandfather:

> We acknowledge that we have conceded to you, from the property of Eleazar, also known as Khthousion, son of Judah, your grandfather, a courtyard with all its rights in Ein Gedi and the rooms with it (lines 27–30 = lines 6–10).[76]

---

72 See Wolfram Weiser and Hannah M. Cotton, "'Gebt dem Kaiser, was des Kaisers ist …': Die Geldwährungen der Griechen, Juden, Nabatäer und Römer in syrisch-nabatäischen Raum unter besonderer Berücksichtigung des Kurses von Sela'/Melaina und Lepton nach der Annexion des Königreiches der Nabatäer durch Rom," *ZPE* 114 (1996): 237–87.

73 See the excellent discussion of the phrase in Hillel Newman, "Old and New in the Documentary Papyri from the Bar Kokhba Period," *SCI* 23 (2004): 247–51.

74 Although Joseph is mentioned again in Babatha's petition to the governor in *P.Yadin* 13, l. 8, but the context is obscure.

75 See Hannah M. Cotton and Jonas C. Greenfield, "Babatha's Property and the Law of Succession in the Babatha Archive," *ZPE* 104 (1994): 211–24; Hannah M. Cotton, "Deeds of Gift and the Law of Succession in Archives from the Judaean Desert," in *Akten des 21. Internationalen Papyrologenkongresses, Berlin, 13–19.8.1995*, ed. Barbara Kramer et al., Vol. I (Stuttgart – Leipzig: Teubner, 1997), 179–88; modified in Hannah M. Cotton, "The Law of Succession in the Documents from the Judaean Desert Again," *SCI* 17 (1998): 115–23 [below, pp. 443–51].

76 ὁμολογοῦμεν ⟦παρα⟧συγκεχωρηκέναι σ̣[οι ἐξ ὑ]παρχόντων Ἐλεαζάρου τοῦ καὶ Χθουσίωνος τοῦ Ἰ̣ο̣ύ̣δ̣ο̣[υ π]ά̣π̣ου σου αὐλὴν σὺν παντὶ δικαίοις αὐτῆς ἐν{ε} Ἡνγα̣δ̣ο̣ῖ̣ς καὶ τοῦς σὺν αὐτῆς οἰκίαι.

Either the grandfather, Eleazar Khthousion, outlived his son, Judah, or Shelamzion came into the possession of her grandfather's courtyard due to her father's recent death. The fact that Judah's nephews appear to have disputed Shelamzion's ownership may suggest that in the prevailing legal system, the granddaughter did not automatically acquire her father's right to the inheritance.[77]

In *P.Yadin* 23 and 24 of 130 CE the guardian of the same orphans (i. e. sons of Jesus son of Eleazar Khthousion) sue Babatha for 'confiscating' three orchards owned by her late second husband, Judah son of Eleazar Khthousion, who was their paternal uncle. Besas son of Judah threatens Babatha that he will register three date orchards of her dead husband in Maḥoza in the nephews' name, unless she produces written evidence that she has a right to them:

> I, therefore, summon you to disclose to me what document you possess as proof ([π]ọ[ί]ῳ δịκạịώματι) that you have the right to hold the said entities. If you refuse to disclose know that I am registering them (ἀπογράφο[μαι]) in the ἀπογραφή in the name of the said orphans (*P.Yadin* 24, lines 6–9).[78]

In *P.Yadin* 25 Iulia Crispina, who describes herself as the *episcopos* of the same orphans, insists that Babatha is distraining property which belongs by law to the orphans.[79] It is striking that nothing whatsoever is said about the claims of Judah's own daughter Shelamzion. She was still alive on 19 June 130 CE (*P.Yadin* 20), five months before Besas charges Babatha with illegal distraint of her late husband's property. Unless we assume that she died between 19 June and 17 November of 130 CE, or that Judah wrote a will in favour of his nephews,[80] we can infer that the law of succession in force at that time in the province of Arabia did not automatically grant a daughter the right to inherit from her father when in competition with sons of her father's brother or his male descendants.[81]

Combining the evidence for preferring the claims of uncles and their male descendants in these documents with the presence of deeds of gift in favour of

---

77 See Hannah M. Cotton, "Courtyard(s) in Ein-Gedi: P.Yadin 11, 19 and 20 of the Babatha archive," *ZPE* 112 (1996): 197–201 [below, pp. 285–91].

78 See Cotton, "Deeds of Gift and the Law of Succession in Archives from the Judaean Desert," 184 on the meaning of ἀπογραφή, ἀπογράφομαι and δικαίωμα in this context.

79 *P.Yadin* 25 lines 9–10: ... ὑπ̣ạρ̣χ̣όν̣τῳṿ τῶν αὐτῶν ọρ̣φ̣ạν[ῶ]ν β̣ίạ διακρατῖς ἃ οὐκ ἀνῆκέν σοι.

80 An assumption made by Lewis, *The Documents from the Bar Kokhba Period in the Cave of Letters. Greek Papyri*, 107 who suggests that we restore ἐν τῇ διαθήκῃ αὐτοῦ in *P.Yadin* 24, line 6.

81 All this is argued at much greater length in the articles mentioned above, in note 75.

females *only* in the archives,[82] I have gone so far as to say that "the deed of gift was the only way in which property could devolve on women in this society. The law of intestate succession simply sidestepped wives and daughters, even in the absence of a male heir, and the deed of gift came to mitigate the rigour of rules of succession which were prejudicial to women. To use Roman legal terminology: wives and daughters were not the *sui heredes* of their husbands and fathers."[83]

Now these preferences were not imposed by Jewish law; on the contrary they stand in flat contradiction to Jewish law, both biblical and rabbinic, which always preferred the children of the deceased, whether male or female, to siblings of the deceased and their children on the father's side.[84] In other words, what we see in operation in these archives is neither Jewish law, nor Roman law, both of which put the claims of children before those of any other blood relations. In all likelihood then it is the local law of the Nabataeans which is reflected in the papyri from the Judaean Desert, and what we read in lines 11–16 of *P.Petra* 1 suggests that it had survived into the sixth century, not necessarily as part of a legal code, perhaps merely as a compelling social custom. Antti Arjava rightly insists[85] on the *mutatis mutandis*: in *P.Yadin* it is the paternal uncles, or rather their male descendants, who make the claims against female descendants, whereas here we have a maternal uncle of a male descendant. Furthermore, in the *dialysis*, it is

---

82 There is also a deed of gift from a man to his wife among the tomb inscriptions from Mada'in Salih: 'And he gave this tomb to Amah, his wife, daughter of Gulhumu, from the date of the deed of gift which is in her hand, that she might do with it whatever she wishes,' Healey, *The Nabataean Tomb Inscriptions of Mada'in Salih*, H 27 (Healey's translation), see note 11 above, and see Shiffman, "To the Character of the Nabataean Private Law According to the Epigraphic Sources," 19.

83 Cotton, "Deeds of Gift and the Law of Succession in Archives from the Judaean Desert," 185–6. But I went too far: I now accept Oudshoorn's qualifications. Her idea that the change of legal status from a non-married to a married woman is at issue, and that only married daughters were denied intestate inheritance, accounts better for the fact that the three deeds of gifts in the archives were written on the occasion of a marriage; it also fits into the wider geographical context of the Ancient Near East; see Jacobine G. Oudshoorn, "Obtemperare legibus nostris Traianus conpulit imperator? The Relationship between Roman and Local Law in the Babatha and Salome Komaise Archives" (University of Groningen Thesis, 2005), chapter 4. Now published as *The Relationship between Roman and Local Law in the Babatha and Salome Komaise Archives: General Analysis and Three Case Studies on Law of Succession, Guardianship and Marriage* (Leiden: Brill, 2007) (*non vidi*); see also the interesting study of Zafrira Ben-Barak, *Inheritance by Daughters in Israel and the Ancient Near East* (Jaffa: Archaeological Center Publications, 2003).

84 *Numbers* 27:8: 'When a man dies leaving no son, his patrimony shall pass to his daughter. If he has no daughter, you shall give it to his brothers'; and again in *mBaba Bathra* 8.2: 'The son precedes the daughter, and all the son's offspring precede the daughter; the daughter precedes the brothers (of the deceased).'

85 In correspondence.

made clear that Stephanous will be inheriting her father's entire property. "There was no problem in having a female heir, quite in accordance with imperial law."[86]

Be this as it may, the paramount importance of the mother's dowry ceded by Patrophilos to his nephew and son-in-law, Theodoros, in *P.Petra* 1 is very obvious, and must reflect its great value: it included immovables (ἀκεί̣[ν]ητα πράγμα̣[τα], line 21), in all likelihood land or houses. It occupies the first two of the four conditions of the agreement (διάλυσις) reached between the parties before the present document,[87] and constitutes its core:[88] in the event of Theodoros' death the dowry will go either to his wife, Stephanous, or, if she too dies, to her father, Patrophilos.

1. (lines 18–22): If it should happen that the most honourable Theodoros dies without a child while his spouse, the most virtuous Stephanous, survives him, all the immovable property which her father, the said most honourable Patrophilos, had ceded to him [to Theodoros] shall go and devolve upon the same most virtuous Stephanous.[89]
2. (lines 22–26): If the same most virtuous Stephanous dies and after her also the same most honourable Theodoros – let this not happen – [all the property which had been ceded] shall devolve upon [his most honourable uncle] Patrophilos or his heirs.[90]
3. (lines 26–30): If it should happen that the said most honourable Patrophilos himself dies [and] leaves behind [the same Stephanous], the most virtuous spouse of Theodoros and the daughter of [Patrophilos] himself, it was agreed that all (the property) of the same most honourable Patrophilos shall go and devolve upon the same Stephanous.[91]

86 Arjava, "Everyday Life and Law in Byzantine Petra," 15.

87 I think that the restoration of πάντα τὰ ἐκχωρηθέντα at the end of line 24 must be correct.

88 καὶ ἐν τοῖς [μ]εταξὺ αὐτῶν κατὰ τὸν κα[ιρὸν] τῆς διαλύσεως λαλου̣μένοις συνεῖ̣δ̣ον σ̣[υμ]-φωνή̣σ̣[αντες ἀλλήλοις] ὡς κτλ, lines 16–18.

89 εἰ μὲν σ̣υμβῆ̣ Θε[ό]δ̣ωρο[ν] τὸν εὐδοκ[ιμό]τ̣ατ̣[ο]ν ἄπαιδα τελ[ευτῆσαι] περιούσης τῆς κοσμιοτάτης Σ[τε]φανοῦς αὐτοῦ γαμε[τῆς, πάντα τὰ] ἐκχωρηθέντα αὐτῷ παρὰ τοῦ̣ [εἰρημένου] ε[ὐ]δοκιμ̣[οτάτου] Πατροφίλ̣ο̣υ αὐτῆς πατρὸς ἀκεί̣[ν]ητα πράγμα̣[τα] ἔρχεσθαι κ̣[αὶ] καταντᾶν εἰς τὴν κοσμιοτά̣[τ]ην Στεφανοῦν.

90 εἰ δ̣ὲ̣ [τελευτήσει] ἡ αὐτὴ κοσμιοτάτη Στεφανοῦς, τελε[υτ]ήσει̣ δὲ με[τ' αὐτὴν καὶ] ὅπερ ἀπείη ὁ αὐτὸς εὐδοκιμ[ό]τατο̣ς Θ̣[εόδωρος, πάντα τὰ ἐκχωρηθέντα] ἔρχεσ̣θ[αι] ε̣ἰ̣ς Π̣[α]τ̣ρ̣[ό]φι[λον] τ̣[ὸν εὐδοκιμότατον] θ̣[εῖον αὐτοῦ ἤγουν] εἰς κληρονόμους αὐτοῦ.

91 ε̣[ἰ] δ̣ὲ συμβῆ̣ τὸν εἰρημέν[ον εὐ]δοκιμ̣[ότατον] Πατρόφιλον καὶ αὐτὸν τελευτ̣[ησα] . ̣α .[. . κα]τ̣[α]λεῖψαι τ̣[ὴν αὐτὴν Στεφανοῦν] τὴν κοσμιοτάτην γαμετὴ̣ν̣ [μ]ὲν Θεο̣[δ]ώρου, αὐτοῦ δὲ [Πατροφίλου] θυγατέραν, ἔδοξεν εἰ[ς] α̣ὐτὴν Σ̣[τ]εφ[α]νο̣ῦ̣ν ἔρχεσ[θα]ι κ̣αὶ κ[αταντᾶν] τὰ αὐτοῦ Πατροφίλο̣υ τοῦ εὐδοκιμοτά̣του πά[ντα.]

4. (lines 30–35): But if the most virtuous Stephanous [dies] while the [said] most honourable Patrophilos and [Theodoros both survive her] and (later) the same most honourable Patrophilos departs from life without a child altogether, his property shall go and devolve upon the said [most honourable] Theodoros, his nephew and son-in-law.[92]

Why was the dowry so important? Why is Theodoros's paternal inheritance[93] not mentioned in the *dialysis*? We know something of the paternal property,[94] but obviously Patrophilos had no standing to make conditions about that. At any rate, the dowry is the only asset mentioned in the *dialysis*: were Theodoros to die, what used to be his mother's dowry would go to his wife Stephanous (lines 18–22), and if she is no longer alive, it would go back to her father. I therefore suspect that the ceded dowry was the cause and the purpose of the marriage. I would even go so far as to maintain that, as implied by the term διάλυσις,[95] the agreement was reached because Patrophilos, the maternal uncle, refused at first to hand over the maternal dowry. Thus the marriage could be seen as a compromise between Patrophilos and Theodoros: the uncle was prepared to yield the dowry on condition that the nephew marry his daughter. Whether or not Patrophilos's refusal to cede the dowry was buttressed by law is hard to know; at least local custom may have been on his side, and we know that the dowry was in his hands.

92 εἰ δὲ τελευτήσει] ἡ κοσμιοτάτη Στεφανοῦς πẹ[ριόντων ἀμφοτέρ]ωγ [τῶν εἰρημένων] εὐδοκιμοτάτων Πατροφί[λου καὶ Θεοδώρου καὶ] ἄπ̣αις παν[τελῶς τὸν] βίογ κ[α]ταλῦσαι ὁ αὐτὸς εὐδ[οκιμ]ότατος Πατρόφιλ[ο]ς, ἔρχεσθ[αι καὶ] καταντᾶν τὰ αὐτοῦ π[ρ]άγμ[ατα εἰς] ṭὸν εἰ[ρημένον εὐδοκιμότατον] Θεόδωρον αὐτοῦ ἐξάδ[ελφον καὶ] γ̣αμ[βρὸν . . . . .]υπ̣εις . .[– ca.10 –].

93 His father died before 537 CE, and a curator, Eustathios son of Theon, is present at the signing of *P.Petra* 1 (Εὐσ̣[τα]θ[ί]ο̣[υ] Θ[έ]ωνο̣[ς τοῦ] ẹ[ὐ]δ̣[ο]κ[ιμοτάτου] αὐτοῦ κουράτο̣ρο̣ς π̣ερὶ τῶν ὑποτεταγμένων, lines 10–11).

94 It is mentioned in *P.Petra* 19 (vineyard), 22 (vineyard and other land), and 39 (house). In addition, a year after the present document Theodoros appears as one of the parties to 'an agreement concerning inherited property' in Gaza in the fragmentary *P.Petra* 2 (538 CE); two years later in *P.Petra* 18 (539 CE): 'Change of dowry agreement', we hear of a dowry he had received from Stephanous. Presumably there was a bridegift (πρὸ γάμου δωρεά), but it is "nowhere specifically mentioned", see Antti Arjava, Matias Buchholz, and Traianos Gagos, eds., *The Petra Papyri III* (Amman: ACOR, 2007), 21.

95 Which may well be used here in the sense of a compromise reached out of court, and not 'division' as in the first edition (Frösén, Arjava, and Lentinen, *The Petra Papyri I*, 24): see Orsolina Montevecchi, *La Papirologia* (Torino: Societe editrice internazionale, 1973), 231–3; Raphael Taubenschlag, *The Law of Greco-Roman Egypt in the light of the Papyri, 322 BC–640 AD* (Warsaw: Państwowe Wydawnictwo Naukowe, 1955), 403–6; Max Kaser, *Das römische Zivilprozessrecht* (München: Beck, 1966), 481–2.

Change and Continuity in Late Legal Papyri from Palaestina Tertia: *Nomos Hellênikos* and *Ethos Rômaikon*

This short study relies almost exclusively on the documentary evidence contained in four documents, all written in Greek. Two of them – *P.Yadin* 18 and *P.Yadin* 37 (= *P.Hever* 65) – were written in Arabia in 128 and 131 CE, respectively.[1] The other two – *P.Nessana* 18 and 20 – were written in Palaestina Tertia in 537 and 558 CE, respectively.[2] Palaestina Tertia included at the time those parts of Arabia and Judaea that in the early second century belonged to two different Roman provinces. Indeed, all four were written under Roman rule in the area.

---

1 The two, *P.Yadin* 18 and *P.Yadin* 37 (= *P.Hever* 65; see below), were published in Naphtali Lewis, *The Documents from the Bar Kokhba Period in the Cave of Letters. Greek Papyri*, Judean Desert Studies II (Jerusalem: IES, 1989). However, Lewis realized that *P.Yadin* 37 did not belong with the other documents, all of which were part of the celebrated Babatha Archive (see there p. 130). It was later identified as part of the less well known archive of Salome Komaïse daughter of Levi. A revised edition of the papyrus appeared first in Hannah M. Cotton, "The Archive of Salome Komaise Daughter of Levi: Another Archive from the 'Cave of Letters,'" *ZPE* 105 (1995): 204–7 (where it is still *P.Yadin* 37), and in its final form, now designated *P.Hever* 65, in Hannah M. Cotton and Ada Yardeni, *Aramaic, Hebrew, and Greek Documentary Texts from Naḥal Ḥever and Other Sites*, Discoveries in the Judaean Desert XXVII (Oxford: Clarendon Press, 1997), 224–37. See detailed explanation for the genesis of the so-called Seiyâl Collection in the general introduction to the volume, 1–6. All the papyri designated *P.Hever* belong to this volume, to distinguish them from *P.Yadin*, also found in Naḥal Ḥever but designated after their discoverer; see Hannah M. Cotton, "Documentary Texts from the Judaean Desert: A Matter of Nomenclature," *SCI* 20 (2001): 114–17.
2 These are *P.Nessana* 18 and 20, respectively, published in Casper J. Kraemer, *Excavations at Nessana III: Non-Literary Papyri* (Princeton: Princeton University Press, 1958).

Article note: First published in Natalie B. Dohrmann and Annette Yoshiko Reed, eds., *Jews, Christians, and the Roman Empire: The Poetics of Power in Late Antiquity* (Philadelphia: University of Pennsylvania Press, 2013), 209–221, with the following note: in memory of my teacher Abraham (Addi) Wasserstein. I wish to thank the two editors of the volume for their undefeatable patience and the Herbert D. Katz Center for Advanced Judaic Studies at the University of Pennsylvania for the wonderful term spent in distinguished company on the top floor of the center in 2008. I owe a great debt to Rachel Stroumsa for sharing with me the manuscripts of two lectures – "Greek and Arabic in Nessana" (now published in *Documents and the History of the Early Islamic World*, ed. Petra Sijpesteijn and Alexander T. Schubert (Leiden: Brill, 2015), 143–57) and "Imperial Presence in Flux: Changes and Continuities in Nessana, before and after the Arab Conquest" – and for discussing with me in detail the present chapter. She has been a source of inspiration.

https://doi.org/10.1515/9783110770438-015

The early two documents record marriage settlements entered into by Jews, as the names, but not much more, attest. Nothing in the two Greek marriage contracts from Arabia reflects what came to be the normative Jewish marriage contract, commonly known as the *ketubah* – above all, they lack the formula that would place them solidly in a Jewish framework and under the sanction of Jewish law: 'that you will be my wife according to the law of Moses and the Jews' (כדין מושה ויהודאי די תהוה לי לאנתה). And it is not as though the formula could not be expressed in Greek. However, we do find this formula in the opening lines of three Aramaic marriage contracts from the Judaean Desert: *P.Mur* 20 and 21 and *P.Yadin* 10.[3] Thus, if the rabbinic marriage contract had by then developed its own special form, it seems not to have become normative.[4] Therefore, I maintain that these two documents, *P.Yadin* 18 and *P.Hever* 65, albeit written by and for Jews, nevertheless can be legitimately used, not least for lack of other evidence, to trace continuity and change in legal practice and formulas in this part of the Roman world over the centuries.

Something similar was attempted in a recently published article on "Continuity of Nabataean Law in the Petra Papyri: A Methodological Exercise."[5] Starting from the observation that the law of succession reflected in second-century Jewish

3 For *P.Mur* 20 and 21, see P. Benoit, J.T. Milik, and R. de Vaux, *Les grottes de Murabba'at*, Discoveries in the Judaean Desert II (Oxford: Clarendon Press, 1961). For *P.Yadin* 10, see Yigael Yadin et al., *The Documents from the Bar Kokhba Period in the Cave of Letters: Hebrew, Aramaic and Nabatean-Aramaic Papyri*, Judean Desert Studies III (Jerusalem: IES, 2002).

4 This conclusion is supported by three more marriage contracts written in Greek from the Judaean Desert: *P.Mur* 115 (124 CE) and 116 (unknown date, probably second century CE) and *P.Hever* 69 (130 CE) – none of which can be said to be a translation of an Aramaic *ketubah*. All of them resemble in spirit and in phraseology contemporary Greek marriage contracts from Egypt. The crucial formula 'that you will be my wife according to the law of Moses and the Jews' is absent from all of them; cf. Hannah M. Cotton, "A Cancelled Marriage Contract from the Judaean Desert, XHev/Se Gr. 2," *JRS* 84 (1994): 64–86 (*XHev/Se Gr.* 2 was the Rockefeller Museum inventory number for *P.Hever* 69). It must be acknowledged that, unlike the Greek documents from Arabia (*P.Yadin* 18 and *P.Hever* 65), the three Greek marriage contracts from Judaea, as well as the Aramaic marriage contracts from Arabia and Judaea (*P.Yadin* 10 and *P.Mur* 20 and 21), draw a distinction between male and female children as heirs to their mother's property. I believe that the provision concerning male children as heirs to their mother's property entered Jewish law under the influence of other Near Eastern traditions and was meant to protect sons in polygamous marriages against the loss of part of their mother's property to sons of another woman; see Cotton on *P.Hever* 69 in Cotton and Yardeni, *Aramaic, Hebrew, and Greek Documentary Texts from Naḥal Ḥever and Other Sites*, 270–73.

5 Hannah M. Cotton, "Continuity of Nabataean Law in the Petra Papyri: A Methodological Exercise," in *From Hellenism to Islam: Cultural and Linguistic Change in the Roman Near East*, ed. Hannah M. Cotton et al. (Cambridge: Cambridge University Press, 2009), 154–74 [above, pp. 237–56].

papyri written in Arabia and found in the archives from Naḥal Ḥever is neither Jewish law nor Roman law, I concluded that this must have been Nabataean law.[6] Furthermore, it would seem that the latter had survived into the sixth century and resurfaced in the recently discovered *P.Petra* of the sixth century.

I would like to examine one instance of the Greek legal tradition that had become the common law – a legal koine, if you wish – of the Roman Near East, just as the Greek language became its lingua franca, without ousting the Aramaic legal tradition or the use of Aramaic in its various dialects in daily life. Seemingly paradoxical, the advent of Rome brought with it a considerable intensification of the process of Hellenization in the Near East, as attested in the written corpus as well as in material culture, a claim made long ago, especially by Fergus Millar in "The Problem of Hellenistic Syria," where he draws attention to the limits of Hellenization.[7]

Despite the fact that the majority of legal documents found in the Judaean Desert are in Greek, the peculiar circumstances responsible for the preservation of the legal contracts from Judaea and Arabia – the flight of the Jews from their villages to the caves of the Judaean Desert – would make it unsafe, and probably wrong, to say, even if the figures support it, that by the second century CE, the Aramaic legal contract had been altogether ousted by the Greek contract.[8] On the contrary, the Aramaic legal contract remained alive and vibrant in the Roman Near East – at least in some form – for centuries to come, as must be inferred from the running commentaries in Hebrew on its formulas in the *Mishnah* and the *Tosefta*.[9] It would resurface, for example, in the late contracts of the Cairo Genizah.

---

6 Although I still believe this conclusion to be true, I have now come to prefer Jacobine Oudshoorn's explanation – that women were the sole recipients of deeds of gifts in the documents from the Judaean desert – to the one I offer there (above n. 5) and elsewhere; rather than deny them the right to inherit, she claims – rightly, I believe – that the change of legal status from an unmarried to a married woman was at stake. Cf. Jacobine G. Oudshoorn, *The Relationship between Roman and Local Law in the Babatha and Salome Komaise Archives: General Analysis and Three Case Studies on Law of Succession, Guardianship and Marriage* (Leiden: Brill, 2007), chap. 4.

7 Fergus Millar, "The Problem of Hellenistic Syria," in *Hellenism in the East*, ed. Amélie Kuhrt and Susan Sherwin-White (London: Duckworth, 1987), 110–33, reprinted in Fergus Millar, *Rome, the Greek World, and the East: Volume 3: The Greek World, the Jews and the East*, ed. Hannah M. Cotton and Guy M. Rogers (Chapel Hill: University of North Carolina Press, 2006), 3–31; cf. Hannah M. Cotton, "Language Gaps in Roman Palestine and the Roman Near East," in *Medien im antiken Palästina: Materielle Kommunikation und Medialität als Thema der Palästinaarchäologie*, ed. Christian Frevel (Tübingen: Mohr Siebeck, 2005), 165–67 [above, pp. 211–12].

8 So Naphtali Lewis, "The Demise of the Aramaic Document in the Dead Sea Region," *SCI* 20 (2001): 178–81.

9 Cf. Hannah M. Cotton, "Survival, Adaptation and Extinction: Nabataean and Jewish Aramaic versus Greek in the Legal Documents from the Cave of Letters in Naḥal Ḥever," in *Sprache und*

There are virtually no firmly dated legal documents from our area in any script or language between the last document from the Babatha archive (132 CE)[10] and the sixth century: a gap of 380 years separates the latest legal document in the Babatha archive, *P.Yadin* 27 of 132 CE, from the first safely dated legal contract from Nessana, *P.Nessana* 16 of 512 CE; and over 400 years separate it from *P.Petra* 1 of 537 CE.[11] But the fortuitous survival of two significant legal corpora of Greek in the village of Nessana and in the city of Petra allows us to say with confidence what we cannot say about the Aramaic legal tradition: that Greek is likely to have continued as the language of legal documents down to the sixth and seventh centuries in what had been Roman Arabia and Judaea/Syria Palaestina and was now Palaestina Tertia.

Nomos Hellênikos in Second-Century Documents from Arabia

P.Yadin 18 (128 CE) was published for the first time in 1987 by Naphtali Lewis, Ranon Katzoff, and Jonas Greenfield.[12] Katzoff's painstaking legal commentary and, above all, his *interpretatio Hebraica* (p. 240) were taken to pieces, to put it mildly, by Abraham Wasserstein in an article published in 1989,[13] which laid

Kultur in der kaiserzeitlichen Provinz Arabia: Althistorische Beiträge zur Erforschung von Akkulturationsphänomenen im römischen Nahen Osten, ed. Leonhard Schumacher and Oliver Stoll (St. Katharinen: Scripta Mercaturae Verlag, 2003), 1–11 [above, pp. 171–72].

10 Although I accept 140 CE as the date of the recently published Hebrew *P.Beit Israel*, certainty is denied; see Esther Eshel, Hanan Eshel, and Ada Yardeni, "A Document from 'Year Four of the Destruction of the House of Israel,'" *Cathedra* 132 (2009): 5–24 (Hebrew; for an English version, see *Dead Sea Discoveries* 18 (2011): 1–28). Unlike the first editors, Moshe Bar-Asher, "The Language of the Beit 'Amar Document," *Cathedra* 132 (2009): 25–32 (Hebrew), maintains that the document is written in Aramaic rather than Hebrew. I no longer accept the dating in Hannah M. Cotton, W.E.H. Cockle, and Fergus Millar, "The Papyrology of the Roman Near East: A Survey," *JRS* 85 (1995): 214–35, of no. 332 (*P.Mur* 116) and nos. 336–37 (*P.Mur* 113 and 114), all in Greek, to the period after 136 CE: see Hannah M. Cotton and Werner Eck, "P.Murabba'at 114 und die Anwesenheit römischer Truppen in den Höhlen des Wadi Murabba'at nach dem Bar Kochba Aufstand," *ZPE* 138 (2002): 173–83; the other documents, nos. 333–35 and nos. 338–42 – in Latin and Greek – are doubtful cases.

11 Nessana and Petra belonged in the sixth century to Palaestina Salutaris/Tertia, which included southern Jordan, the Negev, and the Sinai – territories that had belonged to the Nabataean kingdom when it was redacted into the province of Arabia.

12 Naphtali Lewis, Ranon Katzoff, and Jonas C. Greenfield, "Papyrus Yadin 18," *IEJ* 37 (1987): 229–50.

13 Abraham Wasserstein, "A Marriage Contract from the Province of Arabia Nova: Notes on Papyrus Yadin 18," *JQR* 80 (1989): 93–130.

the groundwork and created the context for all future work on the legal documents from the Judaean Desert; the latter, as he claims there "fit into the picture of a well-integrated multi-ethnic society, whose cultural, social and legal life has absorbed many and various elements from different sources."[14] For Wasserstein, the idea of "a *koine* of private law"[15] is encapsulated into the single phrase *Hellênikos nomos* in *P.Yadin* 18 (from the Babatha Archive) and, in the reverse order, *nomos Hellênikos* in *P.Hever* 65 (from the Salome Komaïse Archive). Both are marriage contracts between Jews in Arabia. However, the scenario at the background of the two documents is very different.

In *P.Yadin* 18 (a double document with inner and outer texts),[16] a father, Judah son of Eleazar Khthousion (Babatha's second husband), gives his daughter Shelamzion in marriage to Judah Cimber son of Ananias for her to be his wedded wife according to the laws (*kata tous nomous*). She brings a dowry of gold, silver, and clothing with the value of 200 silver denarii; the bridegroom, having acknowledged that he has received all this from her father and that he owes it to his wife after adding to it another 300 denarii, 'takes upon himself the obligation to provide for his wife and for the children to come in accordance with the *Hellênikos nomos*; his entire property, both present and future, is placed in lien to guarantee this undertaking.'[17]

In *P.Hever* 65, a very damaged inner text of a double document, the scenario is totally different, if one accepts my interpretation and revised reading of Lewis's

14 Wasserstein, 130: "Its various ethnic elements are affected both by each other and by their common heritage, and after the irruption of Greek power and civilization they become, in various degrees 'Hellenized.' But 'Hellenism' as a cultural phenomenon differs from its classical Greek antecedent in the fact that it has itself absorbed vastly important elements of local culture, which it clothed with the name and the language of the Hellenes. This is true in many fields; it is particularly evident in law and custom." For, as Wasserstein claims in "Non-Hellenized Jews in the Semi-Hellenized East," *SCI* 14 (1995): 130, "Alongside [Hellenistic civilization] ... and sometimes intermingling with it, there existed another supra-natural civilization, influenced indeed by the encounter with the Greeks (and, later, with the Romans), but formed, and informed and characterised by the common Aramaic inheritance that had existed for many centuries before then as an international and supra-national bond for people of many nations, not all of them Semitic."

15 Wasserstein, "A Marriage Contract from the Province of Arabia Nova: Notes on Papyrus Yadin 18," 120.

16 See Appendix 1 of this chapter for the outer text and translation.

17 The above is a paraphrase of lines 32–54 of the outer text = lines 3–19 of the inner text, but the crucial lines, quoted above (47–54, outer text = 14–19, inner text) should be given in Greek as well: ἃ ὡμολόγησεν (the groom) δοῦναι αὐ̣[τῇ] (the bride) ... ἀ[κολούθως αἱρέσει τρο]φῆς καὶ ἀμφιασμοῦ αὐτῆς τε καὶ τῶν μελλόν̣[των τέ]κνων ἑλληνικῷ νόμῳ ἐπὶ τῆς τοῦ αὐτοῦ Ἰού̣[δα Κίμ]βερος πίστε̣ως καὶ κινδύνου καὶ πάντων ὑπα̣ρ̣[χόν]των ὧν τε ἔχει ἐν τῇ αὐτῇ πατρίδι αὐτοῦ καὶ ἐνθ[ά]δε καὶ ὧν ἂν ἐπικτήσηται πάντῃ πάντων κυρίω̣ς.

editio princeps.[18] Yeshu'a son of Menaḥem, from [the village] of Soffathe ... in the district of the city of Livias of the Peraea is already married to Salome Komaïse daughter of Levi in an unwritten marriage, *agraphos gamos*, as it is called, which was, as its name implies, a marriage without a contract, but whose legal validity was indistinguishable from that of the written marriage, the *engraphos gamos*, and it was practiced among Jews, as well as among others, at that time.[19] How do we know that? The groom, who addresses the bride as his wife, says so in so many words in lines 3– 6: 'Yeshu'a son of Menaḥem ... agreed with Salome also called Komaïse, daughter of Levi, his wife, who is from Maḥoza, that they continue life together as also before this time.'[20]

The occasion for drawing up the contract is the belated receipt of a dowry consisting in feminine adornment in silver, gold, and clothing for the amount of ninety-six denarii, which the groom now acknowledges, and reciprocates by taking upon himself the obligation to support his wife and children to come, in accordance with the *nomos Hellênikos* and the *Hellênikos tropos*, while his entire property, both present and future, guarantees this undertaking – and all this in terms almost identical to those we have just seen in *P.Yadin* 18.[21]

The fact that *nomos Hellênikos* (*P.Yadin* 18) and its variant *Hellênikos nomos kai Hellênikos tropos* (*P.Hever* 65) appear in two marriage contracts from the Judaean Desert in the same context – they are preceded by the acknowledgment by the groom of the receipt of a dowry and the undertaking to provide for the wife and children, and are followed by the liability clause, the entailment of his property to support the wife and children to come – is highly significant, given that the circumstances and the occasion, as was pointed out above, differ considerably. I believe that the sequence of acknowledgment and obligation, underlined

18 See Appendix 2 of this chapter for my edition of *P.Hever* 65 and translation.

19 See bibliography in Cotton ad *P.Hever* 65 (Cotton and Yardeni, *Aramaic, Hebrew, and Greek Documentary Texts from Naḥal Ḥever and Other Sites*), esp. Hans Julius Wolff, *Written and Unwritten Marriages in Hellenistic and Post-Classical Roman Law* (Haverford: American Philological Association, 1939).

20 ὡμολογήσ]ạτο Ιησους Μαναημου τ[ῶν ἀπὸ κώμης . . . .] Σοφφαθẹ[. .] . . . . π̣ẹρ̣ὶ πόλιν Λιουιάδος τῆς Π̣[εραίας – ca.9 – π̣ρ̣ὸ̣ς Σαλ]ωμην κ̣αλο̣υ̣μένην Κ̣[ομαΐσην Ληουειου τὴν] γυ̣ν̣αῖκα, Μ̣[α]ωζηνὴν ὥστε αὐτο̣ὺ̣ς [– ca.17 –].ετ̣ . . . . συμβιως̣ . . .[– ca.14 –] αὐ̣τῆς ὡ̣[ς κ]αὶ πρὸ τούτου τοῦ χρόνου (lines 3–6).

21 [ἃ ὡμολογήσατο ὁ γήμας] [ἀπ]ẹσχηκ̣[έν]αι παρ̣' α̣ὐτῆς ... σὺν αἱρέσει τρ̣οφῆ̣ς [καὶ ἀμφιασμοῦ αὐτῆς] τ̣ε καὶ τῶν μελ̣λόντ̣ω̣[ν τέκ]ν̣ω̣ν̣ ν̣ό̣μ[ῳ] [ἑλληνικ]ῷ̣ καὶ ἑλλ̣[η]ν̣ι̣κ̣ῷ̣ τρόπῳ ẹ̣π̣ὶ̣ τ̣ῆ̣ς τ̣[οῦ αὐτοῦ Ιησουου πίστεω]ς καὶ κινδύ̣νου πά̣ν̣[των ὑπα]ρ̣χόντων̣ αὐτοῦ α̣ὐ̣τ̣ο̣ῦ̣ ὧ̣ν̣ τ̣ε ἔχει ἐν̣ τ̣ῇ α̣ὐ̣τ̣ῇ π̣ατρίδι Σ̣οφφ[αθε . . .] [. . . . . καὶ ὧν ἂν] ἐπικτήσηται . . .[– ca.10 –] Σ[. . . . . . ἀπὸ] τοῦ αὐτ̣ο̣[ῦ Ι]η̣σ̣ουου καὶ ἐκ τ̣[ῶν ὑπαρχόντων αὐτοῦ πάντ]η (lines 7–12). The massive restorations are safe: there is no difference between Lewis and Cotton editions.

by the formula 'according to Hellenic law' (or its variant 'according to Hellenic law and custom') and guaranteed by the liability clause, constituted a fixed legal clause susceptible to slight variations, which the local scribe, following standard notarial practice, would insert into the marriage contract at precisely this point.[22]

The first editor of the two papyri, the late Naphtali Lewis, dismissed the edifice raised by Wasserstein on and around the phrase *Hellênikos nomos*, on the grounds that nowhere in the Roman Near East is the expression attested in any language, nor is there "a single occurrence of the expression *Hellênikos nomos* in all the thousands of Greek papyri from Egypt."[23] This argument does not carry much weight. Wasserstein is right to be less concerned with the precise meaning of the term than with the highly significant evidence "that the obligation to provide for the wife and the children to be born is taken upon himself by the [Jewish] husband in accordance with Greek *nomos*."[24] This bears witness to the remarkable degree of assimilation visible here, without Hellenizing its users: "not necessarily an assimilation to Hellenism *tout court* but an assimilation to an environment that in spite of not being Hellenized uses Hellenic elements; and conversely, to an environment that in spite of using Hellenic elements, is not by virtue of that use to be thought of as Hellenized."[25]

Hellênikos nomos should be equated with 'local custom' – with the rabbis' כמנהג המדינה or with the Syrian-Roman law book's כל אתרא איך נמוסא דילה. It recalls the so-called court stipulations (תנאי בית דין) of the Jewish *ketubah* (*mKet* 4.6–12): "tacit conditions, binding upon all, even if not written in a specific marriage contract."[26] It certainly implies the existence of other options, but this is the default, to use today's idiom.[27] It must be admitted that the expression is absent from two marriage contracts written in Greek from Judaea – *P.Mur* 115 (124 CE?) and 116 (second century CE)[28] – and cannot be restored in a third one, *P.Hever* 69 (130 CE),[29] a cancelled marriage contract from Judaea in which the mother gives

22 A study of the role of the notaries in shaping the law is still to be written, as pointed out long ago by Elias J. Bickerman, "Two Legal Interpretations of the Septuagint," in *Studies in Jewish and Christian History*, Vol. I (Leiden: Brill, 1976), 201–224, at 207.

23 Naphtali Lewis, "The World of P.Yadin," *BASP* 28 (1991): 40–41.

24 Wasserstein, "A Marriage Contract from the Province of Arabia Nova: Notes on Papyrus Yadin 18," 125.

25 Wasserstein, 125.

26 Mordechai Akiva Friedman, *Jewish Marriage in Palestine: A Cairo Geniza Study*, Vol I (Tel Aviv: Tel Aviv University Press, 1980), 15.

27 The insight and the phrasing are Rachel Stroumsa's, in a private exchange.

28 Both published in Benoit, Milik, and de Vaux, *Les grottes de Murabba'at*.

29 Published like the rest of *P.Hever* in Cotton and Yardeni, *Aramaic, Hebrew, and Greek Documentary Texts from Naḥal Ḥever and Other Sites*.

her daughter in marriage to Akiba son of Meir from the village of Yakim in the territory of Zephene – despite the many similarities that the last one shares with the contracts from Arabia.[30]

Ethos Rômaikon in the Sixth-Century Papyri from Nessana

P.Nessana 18 and 20 belong to the sixth century,[31] over 400 hundred years after the marriage contracts that we have just looked at were written. Unfortunately, there are no plates of the two papyri in the publication of the Nessana papyri, and the second one, in a bad state of preservation, was partly restored from the first one.[32] The corpus of papyri from Nessana has been unaccountably neglected by scholars, perhaps because of the need for cooperation between classicists, Arabists, and historians of Late Antiquity and early Islam. Recently, though, they seem to have attracted more attention: an important article by David Wasserstein elicited a response by Robert G. Hoyland, which he modestly describes as a footnote to Wasserstein's;[33] and in 2008, Rachel Stroumsa defended a doctoral dissertation on this fascinating and difficult corpus.[34]

I cannot go into detail here about complicated questions of ethnicity, religion, and language. However, the language of legal documents – marriage contracts, to be precise – is still Greek. If any other language was used by the natives of Nessana, if it was other than Greek, it did not survive in a written form until well into the Islamic conquest. Nevertheless, Rachel Stroumsa's assumption of an overall Semitic background lurking behind the Greek veneer or substance of the papyri is surely correct. Put differently: there is enough evidence in the papyri themselves, aside from the onomasticon, the place names, and the nicknames, for a widespread use of Arabic as the spoken language. The written documentation, overwhelmingly in Greek, does not mean that the people who wrote the docu-

30 Unfortunately, it does not seem possible to restore the 'in accordance with Greek law' after the acknowledgment of the handsome dowry and the obligation to look after her and the children, and before the liability clause that earmarks the husband's entire property as security for his wife's maintenance.

31 537 CE and 558 CE, respectively.

32 To the extent that it was restored at all.

33 David J. Wasserstein, "Why did Arabic Succeed Where Greek Failed? Language Change in the Near East after Muhammad," *SCI* 22 (2003): 257–72; and Robert G. Hoyland, "Language and Identity: The Twin Histories of Arabic and Aramaic (and: Why did Aramaic Succeed where Greek Failed?)," *SCI* 23 (2004): 183–99.

34 Rachel Stroumsa, "People and Identities in Nessana" (Duke University Thesis, 2008); the author very kindly bestowed on me a copy of her unpublished dissertation.

ments or had them written for them were necessarily Hellenized – and it does not mean that Greek was the commonly spoken language.

What we find in the marriage contract from Nessana is no longer *nomos Hellênikos* but *ethos Rômaikon* (also spelled *êthos Rômaikon*), Roman custom.[35] I suggest that *ethos Rômaikon* in the two marriage contracts from Nessana has the same connotation that the *nomos Hellênikos* had in the papyri from Arabia. After hundreds of years of Roman rule, this was the prevailing custom; however, it was not pure Roman law, any more than the *nomos Hellênikos* was pure Greek law, but was heavily diluted with local legal provisions. Lines 1–11 of *P.Nessana* 18 read as follows:[36]

> In the consulate following that of the most illustrious Flavius Belisarius, the year 432 to the provincial era, day [unknown] in the month of Daisios [May-June], the fifteenth year of the indiction, in the village of Nessana, in the territory of the city of Elousa. In the name of everything good. [...] Flavius Alobaios son of Elias, a soldier [acknowledges that he has given?] Aniya, his younger daughter, she being subject to his legal power, [for the partnership of marriage] to Flavius Valens son of Alobaius Algeb, both [Flavius] Alobaius and [Flavius] Valens being natives of the aforementioned village of Nessana, and received from [the groom] six ounces of gold and in feminine adornment (i. e. jewellery or clothes) six solidi ... which he has sent to Aniya as bridal gifts [and premarital gifts – *donatio ante nuptias*].

The next paragraph repeats the contents of the dowry from the groom's point of view, followed by: 'The aforesaid Al-Ghubb son of Al-Ubayy covenants with Āniyah that he, the bridegroom, is indebted to her and to her heirs and assigns for the dowry of six ounces of gold and the aforesaid six solidi, a debt that he will repay according to Roman custom, without any dispute of legal action' (line 20: *ethei Rômaikôι kai chôreis pa[sês antilogias kai zêtêseôs?]*). This is followed by an extremely lacunose passage that seems to be a version of what, in the earlier documents, was the liability, or entailment clause. The same phrase 'according to Roman custom, without any dispute of legal action' reappears in the very damaged marriage contract attested in *P.Nessana* 20, which, despite its parallels with no. 18, the editor did not even attempt to restore. However, there is no doubt that the order of the clauses closely followed the one in *P.Nessana* 18, and the

---

35 Cf. *SEG* 31, 122 (Attica, ca. 121/2 AD): τὸν ἐξ ἔθουϲ τριῶν μυριάδων; Modest. *Dig.* 50, 12, 10: κατὰ τὰ Ῥωμαίων.

36 See Appendix 3 of this chapter for text and translation. For the first eleven lines, I offer a new and precise translation, based on Ranon Katzoff and Naphtali Lewis's excellent emendations in "Understanding P.Ness. 18," *ZPE* 84 (1990): 211–13. For the rest, I have left the paraphrase of the first edition.

restoration in *P.Nessana* 20, lines 20–21 of *[chôris pasês zêtêseôs kai antilog]ias êthei Rômai[kôi]*, seems safe enough.

To my mind the use of *ethos Rômaikon* in Nessana vindicates the accuracy of Wasserstein's reading of *nomos Hellênikos* – and this is not trivial, for it shows that, in the second century, as later in the sixth century, there existed a society in the Roman Near East which considered itself bound by the law of the land. They could call it Greek law or Roman law, however diluted and contaminated it was, and Jews and others used it in their legal contracts.

Appendix 1

P.Yadin 18
Outer text, lines 29–67

ἐ[πὶ ὑ]π̣άτων Πο̣υ̣[β]λ̣ε̣ί̣[ο]υ̣ Μετειλ̣ί̣[ου] Ν̣έ̣π̣ωνος τὸ β καὶ Μάρκου
Ἀ̣γ̣γ̣ί̣ου Λίβωνος [νώναις Ἀπριλίαις], ἀ[ρ]ιθμῷ δὲ τῆς νέας
ἐ̣π̣α̣ρ̣χ̣ε̣ί̣α̣ς Ἀραβ̣ί̣α̣ς [ἔτους τρίτου εἰκοστοῦ] μη[νὸς] Ξ̣α̣γ̣-
δ̣ι̣κοῦ π̣[ε]ντεκ̣α̣ι̣δεκ[ά]τῃ ἐν Μ̣α[ωζ̣α̣][περὶ Ζ]ο̣α̣[ραν], ἐ̣ξ̣[έδ]ο̣-
τ[ο Ἰούδα]ς Ἐ̣λ̣ε̣αζάρου τοῦ καὶ [Χθουσί]ω̣ν[ος Σ]ελαμψ̣[ι-
ώ̣ν̣η̣ν̣ τ̣ὴ̣ν̣ ἰδίαν θυγατέραν αὐτο̣ῦ̣ παρθ̣έ̣ν̣ο̣ν Ἰου̣-
δατι ἐπικαλουμένῳ Κίμβερι υἱῷ Ἀνανίου τοῦ Σ̣ω̣μ̣α̣-
λα, ἀμφότεροι ἀπ̣ὸ̣ κ̣ώ̣μης Αἰνγαδῶν τῆς Ἰου̣δαία[ς]
ἐνθάδε καταμένοντ̣[ες], ε̣ἶ̣ν̣α̣ι̣ τ̣ὴ̣ν̣ Σ̣ε̣λ̣αμψιών[ην]
Ἰούδατι Κίμβερι γυν̣α̣ῖκαν γαμετὴν π̣ρ̣ὸ̣ς γάμου κ[οι-
νωνίαν κατὰ τοὺς νόμους, προσφερομένην αὐτ̣[ῷ
εἰς λόγον προσφορᾶς κοσμίαν γυναικίαν ἐν ἀργύρῳ κα[ὶ
χρυσῷ καὶ ἱματισμῷ διατετειμένην ἐν ἀλλήλοις, ὡς
λέγουσιν οἱ ἀμφότεροι, ἀξιοχρέαν εἶναι ἀργυρίου δη[ναρίων
διακοσίων, ἣν τειμο̣γ̣[ρ]α̣φίαν ὡμολόγησεν ὁ γήμ[ας Ἰούδας ὁ καλούμενος Κίμβε̣ρ̣ ἀπειληφέναι παρ' αὐτῆ̣[ς διὰ] χ[ει-
ρὸς παραχρῆμα παρὰ Ἰούδου πατρὸς αὐτῆς καὶ ὀφε̣ί̣λ̣[ειν
αὐτὸν τῇ αὐτῇ Σελαμψιώνῃ γυναικὶ αὐτοῦ ἅμα δη[να-
ρίων ἄλλων τριακοσίων ἃ ὡμολόγησεν δοῦναι αὐ̣[τῇ
πρὸς τὰ {τα} τῆς προγεγραμμένης προσφορᾶς [α]ὐ̣τ[ῆς
πάντα εἰς λόγον προικὸς αὐτῆς ἀ[κολούθως αἱρέσει τροφῆς καὶ ἀμφιασμοῦ αὐτῆς τε καὶ τῶν μελλόν̣[των τέκνων ἑλληνικῷ νόμῳ ἐπὶ τῆς τοῦ αὐτοῦ Ἰου̣[δα Κίμβερος πίστ̣ε̣ως καὶ κινδύνου καὶ πάντων ὑπα̣ρ̣[χόν-
των ὧν τε ἔχει ἐν τῇ αὐτῇ πατρίδι αὐτοῦ καὶ ἐνθ[ά-
δε καὶ ὧν ἂν ἐπικτήσηται πάντῃ πάντων κυρίως, [τρό-

πῳ ᾧ ἂν αἱρῆται ἡ Σελαμψιώνη γυνὴ αὐτοῦ ἢ ὃς δ̣[ι' αὐτῆς
ἢ ὑπὲρ αὐτῆς πρ̣ά̣σσων αἱρῆται τὴν εἴσπραξιν π̣[οιεῖσθαι.
ἀλλάξει δὲ Ἰούδας ὁ καλούμενος Κίμβε̣ρ̣ [τῇ γυ]ν̣αι̣[κὶ αὐτοῦ
Σελαμψιώνῃ τὴν συνγραφὴν ταύτην ἐν ἀργ̣[ύρῳ ἠσφαλισμένῳ ὡς καθῆκει ὁ̣π̣ό̣ταν αὐτὸν ἀπαιτή̣σ̣[ῃ
ταῖς ἑαυτοῦ δαπάναις κατὰ μηδὲν ἀντιλέγων. εἰ δ̣[ὲ
μή γε, ἐκτίσει αὐτῇ τὰ προγεγραμμένα δηνάρια [πάν-
τα διπλοῦν, καὶ τῆς πράξεως γεινομένης αὐτ[ῇ ἀπό
τε Ἰούδ[ο]υ Κίμβερος ἀνδρὸς αὐτῆς καὶ ἐκ τῶν ὑπ̣[αρχόν-
των αὐτοῦ κυρίως, τρόπῳ ᾧ ἂν αἱρῆτα̣[ι Σε]λ̣αμψ[ιώνη ἢ ὃς
δι' αὐτῆς ἢ ὑπὲρ αὐτῆς πράσσων τὴν ε̣ἴ̣σ̣π̣ρ[αξιν ποιεῖσθαι. π̣ί̣σ̣τ̣[ε]ι̣ [ἐπη]ρωτήθη καὶ ἀν̣θ̣ω̣μ̣ο̣λ̣ο̣γ̣ή̣θ̣[η ταῦτα οὕτως καλῶς γείνεσθαι.

Appendix 2

P.Hever 65 (*olim P.Yadin* 37)
Inner text

ἐπὶ ὑπάτ̣[ων] Σ̣ε̣ρ̣γ̣ί̣ο̣υ̣ Ὀκταουίου Λαίνα Ποντι[ανοῦ καὶ Μάρκου Ἀντων]-
ί̣ου Ῥουφείνου πρὸ ἑπτὰ εἰ̣δ̣[ῶν Αὐγούστων, κατὰ δὲ]
τὸν τῆς [νέ]ας ἐ̣παρχείας Ἀραβίας ἀριθμ̣ὸν ἔτο[υς ἕκτου καὶ εἰκοστοῦ
μην]ὸς Λῴ[ο]υ̣ ἐ̣ν̣ν̣ε̣ακαιδεκ̣ά̣[τῃ ἐν Μαωζα τῆς Ζο-]
αρηνῆς.[...] ... Πέτραν μητρόπολιν τῆ[ς Ἀραβίας, *c.4 letters* ὡμολογήσ]α̣το
Ιησους Μαναημου τ[ῶν ἀπὸ κώμης *c.9 letters*]
Σοφφαθε̣[.] ... π̣ε̣ρ̣ὶ πόλιν Λιουιάδος τῆς Π̣[εραίας *c.9 letters* π̣ρ̣ὸ̣ς̣(?) Σαλ]-
ωμην κ̣αλ̣ο̣υ̣μένην Κ̣[ομαϊσην Ληουειου τὴν]
γ̣υ̣ναῖκα, Μ̣[α]ωζηνὴν ὥστε αὐτ̣ο̣ὺ̣ς {ὥ̣σ̣τ̣ε̣ α̣[ὑτοὺς} *c.17 letters*].ετ̣ ...
συμβιως ... [*c.14 letters*]
α̣ὐ̣τῇ\ς/ ὡ̣[ς κ]αὶ πρὸ τούτου τοῦ χρόνου . .[καὶ ὀφείλειν̣ (?) *c.10 letters*] . . .
. . τῇ αὐτῇ Κομ̣α̣ι̣σ̣[ῃ τὴ]ν̣ προῖ{ο}κα
αὐτῆς ἀ[ρ]γ̣υρίου δηνάρια ἐνανήκ̣ο̣ντα ἕξ, [ἃ ὡμολογήσατο ὁ γήμας] \[ὁ
αὐ]τὸς Ιησους/ [ἀπ]ε̣σχηκ̣[έν]αι παρ' α̣ὐτῆς τῇ [οὔ]σῃ ἡ̣μέρα̣
τειμογ̣[ρ]αφίανκοσμίας γυναικίας ἐν ἀ̣[ργύρῳ καὶ χρυσῷ καὶ ἱμα]τισμῷ καὶ
ἑταίροις γυ[ναι]κίοις ἀ̣ξι-
[οχρέαν] . . . . .τ̣ο̣υ̣ ἀργυρίου, σὺν αἱρέσει τ̣ρ̣οφῆ̣ς [καὶ ἀμφιασμοῦ αὐτῆς] τ̣ε
καὶ τῶν μελ̣λόντ̣ω̣[ν τέκ]ν̣ω̣ν̣ ν̣ό̣μ[ῳ]
[ἑλληνικ]ῷ καὶ ἑλ̣λ̣[η]ν̣ι̣κ̣ῷ τρόπῳ ἐ̣π̣ὶ̣ τ̣ῆ̣ς τ̣[οῦ αὐτοῦ Ιησουου πίστεω]ς
καὶ κινδ̣ύ̣ν̣ου π̣ά̣ν̣[των ὑπα]ρχόντων̣ αὐτοῦ

α̣ὐ̣τ̣ο̣ῦ̣ ὧ̣ν̣ τ̣ε ἔχει ἐ̣ν̣ τ̣ῇ̣ α̣ὐ̣τ̣ῇ̣ π̣ατρίδι Σ̣οφφ[αθε . . .] [. . . . . . . καὶ ὧν ἂν]
ἐπικτήσηται . . .[*c.10 letters*]
Σ[. . . . . . ἀπὸ] τοῦ αὐτ̣ο̣[ῦ Ι]η̣σ̣ουου καὶ ἐκ τ̣[ῶν ὑπαρχόντων αὐτοῦ πάντ]η
[. . . .] . . . .[. . . .]ς τρόπ̣ῳ ᾧ̣
ἂ̣ν̣ αἰ̣ρ̣ῆ̣τ̣α̣ι̣ ἡ̣ αὐτὴ Κομαϊ[ση] ἢ̣ ὃ̣ς̣ [δι' αὐ]τῆς ἢ̣ [ὑπὲρ αὐτῆς πράσσων τὴν
εἴσπραξιν ποιεῖσθαι, περὶ τοῦ]
ο̣ὕ̣τ̣ω̣ς̣ [κ]α̣λ̣ῶ̣ς̣ γείνεσθαι πίσ̣τεως ἐπηρω̣[τημένης καὶ ἀνθωμολογημένης·
συμπαρόντος *c.8 letters*]
Μα[ναημο]υ̣ ἐπιτρόπου τῆ[ς αὐ]τ̣ῆ̣ς Κομαΐσης̣. Ἐπ[ιγραφή(?) *letters?*]

l. 8. τιμογραφίαν; ἑτέροις

In the consul[ship] of Sergius Octavius Laenas Pontia[nus and Marcus Anton]ius Rufinus, the seve[nth] of August, and according to the computation of the ne[w] province of Arabia year [twenty-six] on the nineteenth of month Loos, [in Maḥoza in the district of Z]o'ar [of the administrative region of] Petra, metropolis of Arabia, Yeshu'a son of Menaḥem, from [the village] of Soffathe ... in the district of the city of Livias of the administrative region of P[eraea ... agreed with Sal]ome also called K[omaïse, daughter of Levi], his wife, who is from Maḥoza, [that they continue] life together ... as also before this time ..., [and that he owes?] the above-mentioned Komaïse, as her dowry, ninety-six denarii of silver, [which the bridegroom], the above-mentioned Yeshu'a, [acknowledged] to have received from her on the present day, as the written evaluation of feminine adornment in sil[ver and gold and clo]thing and other feminine articles equivalent to the above-mentioned amount of money, (combined) with his undertaking to feed [and clothe both her] and her children to come in accordance with Greek custom and Greek manner upon [the above-mentioned Yeshu'a's good faith] and on peril of all his [posses]sions, both those which he possesses in his home village of Soffathe ... [and those which he has here(?) as well as those which he may in addition] acquire. [She has the right of execution both upon] the above-mentioned Yeshu'a and [upon all(?)] his [validly] held possessions [everywhere], in whatever manner the above-mentioned Komaïse, or whoever [acts] through her or [for her, may choose to carry out the execution,] regarding this being thus rightly done, the formal question having in good faith been as[ked and acknowledged, in reply. X] son of Menaḥem, guardian of the above-mentioned Komaïse was present with her.

Appendix 3

P.Nessana 18
Marriage settlement

ὑ[πατ]ί̣ᾳ̣ τῇ μετ̣ὰ τ̣ὶν ὑπατια Φλ(αουίου) Βελι̣[σαρίου τοῦ ἐνδοξοτ(άτου) ἔτους τετρακοσιοστοῦ]
τριακοστοῦ δευτέρ̣ο̣υ̣ μ̣η̣ν̣ὸ̣ς̣ {ο} Δα̣ι̣[σίου *letters?* χρόνων ἰνδικτίωνος ιε ἐν κώμῃ Νεσσάνοις]
[ὁρίο]υ̣ π̣όλεως Ἐλούσης· ἐπὶ πᾶσιν ἀγ[αθοῖς ὁμολογοῦσιν ἀλλήλοις *c.11 letters*]
νιων Φλ(άουιος) Αλοβαιος Ἡ̣λίου σ̣[τρ]α̣[τιώτης τοῦ ἐνθάδε κάστρου δεδωκέναι(?)]
Α̣νιαν ὑπεξουσίαν αὐτοῦ θυγατήρα ν[εωτέραν πρὸς γάμου κοινωνίαν Φλαουίῳ(?) *letters?*]
Οὐάλεντι τοῦ Αλοβαιου, Αλγεβ Αλ[οβαίου δὲ καὶ Οὐάλης *c.10 letters* καὶ αὐ-]
τῶν ὁρμωμένων ἐκ τ̣ῆς προει̣[ρημένης κώμης Νεσσάνων δεδωκέναι χρυσοῦ(?)]
οὐγκίας ἓξ καὶ ἐν κοσμ̣ίοις νο[μίσματα ἓξ *c.26 letters*]
αἱ πρὸ γάμου ἀποσταλῖσαι τῇ [Ανιᾳ δωρεαί(?) *c.25 letters* ἐξ ὑποστάσεως]
Σεργίου εἰς λόγον ἕδνων καὶ προμ[*c.36 letters*]
χρ̣υ̣σαίο̣ις νομίσματα ἕξ, εἰσ̣ὶ̣ν̣ [νο(μίσματα)ς (?) *c.12 letters* ἀνθ' ὧν ἐστὶν ἡ προὶξ τῆς]
γ̣αμεθείσης Ανιας ἐξ ὑποστάσεω̣[ς τοῦ εἰρημένου Αλοβαιου Ἡλίου *c.9 letters*]
τῆς προικὸς πάσης χρυσοῦ οὐ̣[γκίας ἓξ *c.28 letters*]
σταθμῷ καὶ δοκ̣ιμασίᾳ παρ' Αλο[βαιου Ἡλίου(?) *c.30 letters*]
π̣α̣ρά τε τῆς γαμεθείσης Ανιας κ̣[αι(?) *c.39 letters*]
ἐκ πλήρους διὰ χει[ρ]ὸς· ὁμολογ̣[ε]ῖ [δὲ τῇ Ανιᾳ ὁ εἰρημένος Αλγεβ Αλοβαιου τὸν(?)]
γαμετὴν ὀφίλειν τε αὐτῇ κα̣ὶ̣ κλ[ηρονόμοις αὐτῆς καὶ διαδόχοις(?) *c.8 letters*]
τὰς π̣ρογεγραμμένας τῆς προικ[ὸς χρυσοῦ οὐγκίας ἓξ καὶ τὰ προγεγραμμένα(?)]
νομίσματα ἓξ ὄφλημα π̣ροικιμ[αῖον ὃ καὶ παραδώσει(?) *c.19 letters*]
τιας ἔθει Ῥωμαικῷ καὶ χωρεὶς πά̣[σης ἀντιλογίας καὶ ζητήσεως(?) *c.12 letters*]
καὶ ἔ̣στε κύρια βέβαια τ̣[ὰ γράμματα ταῦτα αὐτῇ τε Ανιᾳ καὶ κληρονόμοις]
αὐτῆς καὶ διαδόχοις κ[αὶ αὐτῷ Οὐάλεντι τῷ Αλοβαιου καὶ πάντων]

αὐτοῦ κληρονόμων καὶ διαδόχω[ν ὑποθεμένων εἰς τοῦτο τὰ ὑπάρχοντα αὐτοῖς πάντα ἐν παντὶ]
εἴδι καὶ γένει ετιπ .ọσενετι[*c.37 letters*]
ἐξουσίαν ἐκ̣ παρφερνιμαί[ων] [*c.40 letters*]
[Ανι]ạς αὐτῆς καὶ τὴν ὑπ' αὐ[τῆς *c.40 letters*]
χρυ̣σωχρόων τ̣[*c.50 letters*]
κạβαλλαρικọ̀ν[*c.50 letters*]
τ̣αβλ̣ωρọυ̣[*c.55 letters*]
.[. .] σ̣ὺν ε .[*c.55 letters*]
δέκα πλουμάκ[ια *c.50 letters*]
ἡ γαμεθεῖσα Ανια καὶ [*c.45 letters*]
φριạ τρία ἔτι π[*c.50 letters*]
λεμ̣η̣ . . . .[*c.50 letters*]
.ανιạτιχαρην λευκὸν .[*c.45 letters*]
[δ]έ[κα] π̣λ̣ου̣μακην τρίạ [*c.45 letters*]
[δυ]ọ ἔτι βαφωρι[*c.50 letters*]
[.] .δ̣ιạκιν λιτὸν ν[*c.50 letters*]
[οὔ]σης τε καὶ ἐσσομέν[ης][*c.25 letters* εἰ δὲ συμβαίη̣]
τελευτᾶν ἡ γαμεθεῖσ̣[α] [Ανια *c.38 letters*]
καὶ ἔχει̣ κατ̣ὰ τὴν θίαν [διάταξιν *c.34 letters*]
π̣ạ[. . . κ]αὶ τῷν ὑ̣[παρχόντων αὐτῇ(?) *c.35 letters*]
αὐτοῦ καὶ κληρονόμο[ις αὐτοῦ *c.30 letters* ἐν παντὶ]
εἴδι καὶ γένει ἀπαιτήσ̣[εως γενομένης(?) *c.29 letters*]
[. .]ε̣[. . .]της .[*letters?*]
χρυσαίοις νομίσμ[ασι *letters?*]
[. . . . .] .π . . .[*letters?*]
[.] . . .ειν ἡ γạμεθ[εῖ]σ̣ạ [Ανια *letters?*]
σεν ἡ γαμεθεῖσα Ανια [*letters?*]
Σέργιον ὁμολογη[*letters?*]

I reproduced the text as it appears in the first edition. However, in view of Ranon Katzoff and Naphtali Lewis's excellent emendations in "Understanding P.Ness. 18" (note 36), making lines 6–7 read: Οὐάλεντι τοῦ Ἀλοβαῖος Ἀλγεβ, Ἀλ[οβαίου δὲ καὶ Οὐάλεντος ἀμφοτέρων καὶ αὐ]τῶν ὁρμωμένων ἐκ τῆς προει[ρημένης κώμης Νεσσάνων, ... κτλ.], getting rid of the idea of minority and the resulting need for a curator, and pointing out that ὑπεξουσίαν in line 5 means *in potestate*, I offer below a new and precise translation of lines 1– 11. For the rest, I leave the paraphrase of the first editor.

Lines 1–11

In the consulate following that of the most illustrious Flavius Belisarius, the year 432 to the provincial era, day [unknown] in the month of Daisios [May–June], the fifteenth year of the indiction, in the village of Nessana, in the territory of the city of Elousa. In the name of everything good .... Flavius Al-Ubayy son of Elias, a soldier [acknowledges that he has given?] Aniya, his younger daughter, she being subject to his legal power, [for the partnership of marriage] to Flavius Valens son of Al-Ubayy Algeb, both [Flavius] Al-Ubayy and [Flavius] Valens being natives of the aforementioned village of Nessana, and [that he received from the groom] six ounces of gold, and in feminine adornment [jewelry or clothes] six solidi ... which he has sent to Aniya as bridal gifts [and premarital gifts– *donatio ante nuptias*].

The counterpart of the above is the dowry of the wedded ʻĀniyah, coming from the property of the aforesaid al-Ubayy son of Elias. This dowry consists in full of six ounces of gold and six gold solidi guaranteed pure and of proper weight by al-Ubayy son of Elias and his wedded daughter ʻĀniyah and paid in full and in cash.

The aforesaid al-Ghubb son of al-Ubayy covenants with ʻĀniyah that he, the bridegroom, is indebted to her and to her heirs and assigns for the aforesaid dowry of six ounces of gold and the aforesaid six solidi, a debt which he will repay according to Roman practice, without any dispute or legal action.

This contract will be valid and binding both upon ʻĀniyah and her heirs and assigns and upon Valens son of al-Ubayy and all of his heirs and assigns and in support thereof they pledge their belongings of every sort and kind.

The bride ʻĀniyah's dowry consists of the following: gold-colored objects, ten pillows, and so on.

In the event of the death of the bride ʻĀniyah, her property shall pass according to the imperial decree, etc.

C Land, Army, and Administration

Babatha's 'Patria': Maḥoza, Maḥoz 'Eaglatain and Ẓo'ar

Partial citations in various publications of the Nabataean and Aramaic documents from the Babatha archive[1] have led people to assume that Babatha's village – Maḥoza, מחוזא – belonged under Nabataean rule to the larger unit of Maḥoz 'Eglatain. The word *maḥoz* in this phrase was taken to mean 'district,' as it does in modern Hebrew,[2] and the phrase as a whole was understood to mean 'the administrative district of 'Eglatain.' In the Semitic documents, which begin in 59–69 CE, both names Maḥoz 'Eglatain[3] and Maḥoza[4] occur, whereas in the Greek part of the Babatha archive[5] the name Maḥoz 'Eglatain never turns up, only the name Maḥoza (Μαωζα), which belongs here to the larger unit of Ẓo'ar.[6] Since the Greek documents begin after the annexation of the Nabataean kingdom (the first one is dated to 110 CE, *P.Yadin* 5a and 5b), it seemed very natural to assume that Ẓo'ar replaced Maḥoz 'Eglatain as the administrative district to which Maḥoza belonged.

1 E.g. Yigael Yadin, "Expedition D – The Cave of the Letters," *IEJ* 12 (1962): 238–246; Yigael Yadin, "The Nabataean Kingdom, Provincia Arabia, Petra and Ein-Geddi in the Documents from Naḥal Ḥever," *Ex Oriente Lux* 17 (1963): 229–34.
2 This is not insignificant, as will be seen below.
3 For Maḥoz 'Eglatain see *P.Yadin* 36 = Jean Starcky, "Un contrat nabatéen sur papyrus," *RB* 61 (1954): 163–65 (59–69 CE), Frag. A, l. 2: *'l šqy'* (שקיא) *bmḥwz 'gltyn*; Frag. C, l. 5: *dy bšwk mḥwz 'gltyn*. Ada Yardeni kindly showed me her reconstruction of the text, where these are now ll. 8 and 35 respectively (another contract from 43 CE is mentioned in the papyrus). Maḥoz 'Eglatain occurs also in the following papyri: *P.Yadin* 2 (99 CE), ll. 2–3 = ll. 20 + 22; *P.Yadin* 3 (99 CE), ll. 22–24; *P.Yadin* 6 (119 CE), l. 4; *P.Yadin* 7 (120 CE), l. 2 = l. 32; *XḤev/Se Nab.* 2 (c. 100? CE), ll. 4–5.
4 Maḥoza occurs only once in the Semitic documents – in *P.Yadin* 7, l. 3 = l. 33, see below.
5 Naphtali Lewis, *The Documents from the Bar Kokhba Period in the Cave of Letters. Greek Papyri*, Judean Desert Studies II (Jerusalem: IES, 1989).
6 E.g. *P.Yadin* 5, ll. 4–5: ἐ[ν] Μαω[ζοις τ]ῶν περὶ Ζ[οα]ρα.

Article note: First published with Jonas C. Greenfield in *ZPE* 107 (1995): 126–34, with the following note: my friend and colleague Jonas Greenfield died suddenly on the 13th of March 1995 before he could see the last draft of this paper. I sorely miss his friendship and learning. תנצב"ה.
I am much indebted to Simon Hopkins for his generous help with the Semitic material. I alone am responsible for the mistakes which still remain.
Because of the lack of a single authoritative and accepted scheme for transliteration of Semitic words into Latin script, and also because of citations from a variety of secondary sources, there will appear to be some slight inconsistencies in the transcription of these words below.

https://doi.org/10.1515/9783110770438-016

The argument was first put in these terms by Yadin: "It is interesting to note that this term [i. e. Maḥoz 'Eglatain] which does not appear in the Greek documents, possesses a parallel in the words ἐν Μαωζα περὶ Ζοάραν, hence it is to be concluded that מחוז עגלתין [Maḥoz 'Eglatain] is the Nabataean and perhaps also the ancient Moabite administrative term – later thus modified after the Roman conquest."[7]

Bowersock, in his review article of Lewis (n. 5),[8] simply makes Yadin's equation of Ẓo'ar with Maḥoz 'Eglatain more explicit: "Babatha's village of Maoza appears as Maḥôz in the Semitic documents. The district to which it belongs is the well-known Zoar in Greek, but – as we knew from the Starcky text as long ago as 1954 – it was called 'Egaltein in Aramaic." The nickname 'Eglas' in the name of Joseph Eglas, father of one of the guardians of Babatha's son "is transparently a local hypocoristic of a man from Zoar-'Egaltein."[9] The 'moschantic estate of our Lord the Emperor' in *P.Yadin* 16, l. 24 – μοσχαντικὴ κυρίου Καίσαρος – "is simply an imperial estate in 'Egaltein, which is Zoar south of the Dead Sea", since the μοσχ-element translates the element 'Egla (she-calf – עגלא ;עגלתא) in the place-name 'Eglatain.

As early as 1970 Y. Kutscher disputed the interpretation given by Yadin on purely linguistic grounds, but his protest seems to have remained unheeded: he proves beyond doubt that the original meaning of *maḥoz* in Aramaic is 'port' or 'city' or 'market' – 'district' is an altogether later accretion.[10] The meaning 'district' so prominent in the modern Hebrew word *maḥoz* seems to have imposed the anachronistic translation of Maḥoz 'Eglatain as 'the district of 'Eglatain.' It may still be maintained, however, that the construct state Maḥoz 'Eglatain could mean 'the port (in the district) of 'Eglatain': "The name Maḥôza or 'port' reflects the area of the district in which the village was located. ... The determinative word

---

7 Yadin, "The Nabataean Kingdom, Provincia Arabia, Petra and Ein-Geddi in the Documents from Naḥal Ḥever," 231; cf. Yadin, "Expedition D – The Cave of the Letters," 251: "in 'The Greek Documents' ... as already noted, Maḥoza (in the Nabataean and Aramaic documents part of 'the coastal district of 'Aglatain' [sic]) is included in the region of Zoar."

8 Glen W. Bowersock, "The Babatha Papyri, Masada, and Rome," *JRA* 4 (1991): 340–41.

9 Note though that it is Ἰωάνης Ἰωσήπου τοῦ Ἐγλα 'Yohanes son of Joseph Egla' only in *P.Yadin* 14, l. 23 and 15, ll. 3–4 = l. 18, whereas elsewhere the nickname replaces the name completely: Ἰωάνης Ἐγλα, 'Yohanes son of Egla,' *P.Yadin* 12, l. 8; 13, ll. 21–22; 27, l. 6, as well as in the Aramaic subscription of *P.Yadin* 15, l. 33: יוחנה חברי בר עגלא 'my colleague Yoḥanna son of Egla.' See now Βορκ.. Αγ̣λ̣α ἐπιτρόπ[ου] in *XḤev/Ṣe Gr.* 2, l. 4 in Hannah M. Cotton, "A Cancelled Marriage Contract from the Judaean Desert, XHev/Se Gr. 2," *JRS* 84 (1994): 69 (= *DJD* XXVII, no. 69).

10 Edward Yechezkel Kutscher, "Ugaritica Marginalia," *Lěšonénu* 34 (1969): 5–19 (Hebrew); see now J. Hoftijzer and K. Jongeling, *Dictionary of the North-West Semitic Inscriptions*, Vol. II (Leiden: Brill, 1995), 611. See end note.

'Egaltain most probably is a regional name referring to the northern part of the peninsula."[11]

Now that the Greek part of the archive has been published, and more is known about the Semitic documents,[12] it is possible to prove what Kutscher merely stated,[13] namely that Maḥoza and Maḥoz 'Eglatain are one and the same locality and that there was no region called 'Eglatain, just a village[14] variously called Maḥoza and Maḥoz 'Eglatain. The element 'Eglatain in the construct state Maḥoz 'Eglatain is no longer a partitive genitive which describes the whole of which Maḥoz is part, i. e. 'Mahoz in the district of 'Eglatain'; rather 'Eglatain here determines the word Maḥoz, i. e. it has become part of the name,[15] as *forum* is in Forum Clodii and Forum Sempronii, and *be'er* (i. e. 'well') in Be'er-Sheva and *'ein* (i. e. 'spring') in 'Ein-gedi.[16] Maḥoz 'Eglatain, 'the Port (or City) of 'Eglatain,' is sometimes abbreviated to Maḥoza, i. e. 'the Port' or 'the City' (the suffix aleph – א – at the end of a word stands for the definite article in Aramaic) by a process of *antonomasia*, as for example in *urbs Roma* becoming *Urbs*; *Glil Goyim* becoming *HaGalil* (Galilee), Portus Traiani becoming Portus.[17]

In the Greek documents the definite article 'the' (i. e. the Aramaic suffix, *aleph* – א – after Maḥoz – מחוז) has become part of the name, and is no longer felt to be the definite article. Hence Μαωζα rather than ὁ Μαωζ.[18] In other words, the Greek transliterates the Aramaic rather than translates it.[19]

---

11 Siegfried Mittmann, "The Ascent of Luhith," *Studies in the History and Archaeology of Jordan* 1 (1982): 178. It is not relevant to the argument presented here that he locates Maḥoza in the Al-Lisān.

12 For *P.Yadin* 10 (Aramaic) see Yigael Yadin, Jonas C. Greenfield, and Ada Yardeni, "Babatha's Ketubba," *IEJ* 44 (1994): 75–99; For *P.Yadin* 7 see Yigael Yadin, Jonas C. Greenfield, and Ada Yardeni, "A Deed of Gift in Aramaic Found in Naḥal Ḥever: Papyrus Yadin 7," *Eretz Israel* 25 (1996): 383–403 (Hebrew).

13 Kutscher, "Ugaritica Marginalia," 8–9; 11.

14 That it was a village we know from *P.Yadin* 12, l. 7: καὶ Ἰασσούου Ἰουδαίου υἱοῦ Ἰασσούου κώμης Μαωζᾶ Ἀβδοβδας Ἰλλουθα καὶ Ἰωάνης Ἐγλα.

15 The distinction is well illustrated in English by the difference between 'the City of Oxford' (i. e., the city that is Oxford) as against 'The City of David' (i. e., the city that David built).

16 Cf. 'port' in Port-Sa'id, 'cape' in Capetown and 'mouth' in Portsmouth.

17 See Jean-Louis Maier, *L'Episcopat de l'Afrique romaine, vandale et byzantine* (Neuchâtel: Institut suisse de Rome, 1973), 102 ff. for other examples of *antonomasia*, e. g., Aquae (125 ff.), Castellum (153 ff.), Horrea (240 ff.).

18 In the Greek documents Μαωζα, as pointed out by Lewis, *The Documents from the Bar Kokhba Period in the Cave of Letters. Greek Papyri*, 20, is usually "treated as a feminine singular," apart from *P.Yadin* 5 and 16 where "it is treated as a neuter plural."

19 See on Bagalgala in Lewis, 70 and below, n. 24.

The identity of Maḥoza and Maḥoz ʻEglatain is established by (1) the text of the Aramaic *P.Yadin* 7 and (2) simple logic:

1) *P.Yadin* 7, a deed of gift by Babatha's father to her mother, is the only document in which both Maḥoz ʻEglatain and Maḥoza occur. Here, therefore, we must look for the clue: the context itself must tell us whether or not these are two different locations or one and the same. First, however, it should be pointed out that although we are already in 120 CE, that is to say fourteen years after the annexation of the Nabataean kingdom, the name Maḥoz ʻEglatain still occurs, and Ẓoʻar – which had already appeared in the first Greek document[20] – is not mentioned here at all.

The papyrus begins with the date and place: 'In the consulship of Lucius Catilius Severus for the second time and of Marcus Aurelius Antoninus, in the third year of the Imperator (Autokrator) Caesar Traianus Hadrianus Augustus, and according to the era of the province on the twenty-fourth of Tammuz year fifteen in **Maḥoz ʻEglatain**' (ll. 1–2 = ll. 30–32),[21] immediately followed by: 'I, Simeon son of Menaḥem who lives in **Maḥoza** (מחוזא) gives you Miriam my wife, daughter of Joseph, son of Menashe, all that I own in **Maḥoza**' (l. 3 = l. 33).[22]

The run of the sentences and the context both show clearly that in the transition from line 2 (=32) to line 3 (=33) Maḥoza i. e. 'The Maḥoz' replaces Maḥoz ʻEglatain i. e. Maḥoz of ʻEglatain. In other words the definite article *aleph* (א) at the end of Maḥoza (מחוזא) has replaced the determinative ʻEglatain; Maḥoz becomes Maḥoza, 'The Port' or 'The City' and there is no longer any need to use ʻEglatain.

2) In the Nabataean document *P.Yadin* 3 of 99 CE a date grove bought by Babatha's father is said to be situated in Galgala which in turn is located in Maḥoz ʻEglatain: 'a date grove which belongs to ʼAbiʻadan called Gh... in the Galgala in Maḥoz ʻEglatain,' (ll. 2–3 = ll. 23–24).[23] Among the date groves which Babatha

---

20 *P.Yadin* 5a, ll. 4–5: ἐν Μαω[ζοις τ]ῶν περὶ Ζ[οα]ραν.

21 *ʻl hpṭyt lyqys qṭwlys swrs tnynyt' wmrqs 'wrlys 'nṭwnyns šnt tlt l'wṭqrṭwr qsr ṭryns hdryns sbsṭs wʻl mnyn hprkyh d' bʻśryn w'rbʻh btmwz šnt ʻśr wḥmš* ***bmḥwz ʻgltyn***. And again in ll. 12–13 = l. 48: Simeon adds: 'and also – [inner text: another gift] – all my dates and trees scattered in Maḥoza ... and also – another gift – my courtyards and houses in Maḥoza.'

22 *'n' šmʻwn br mnḥm dy ʻmr* ***bmḥwz'*** *lky 'nty mrym 'ntty brt ywsf br mnšh yt kl mh dy 'yty ly* ***bmḥwz'***. The outer text, l. 33, does not have 'all that I own in **Maḥoza**.'

23 *gnt tmry' dy l'byʻdn d' dy mtqryh gh.' dy bglgl' dy bmḥwz ʻgltyn*; see also *P.Yadin* 2 (Nabataean), l. 3 = l. 22, of the same year: 'a date grove in the Galgala in Maḥoz ʻEglatain.' This same grove, now part of Babatha's property, reappears in the Greek *P.Yadin* 16 of 127 CE. There is no doubt that we are dealing here with the same date grove since it is abutted by the same properties. It is one of the first two groves mentioned there: (1) κῆπον φοινικῶνος ἐν ὁρίοις Μαωζων λεγόμενον Αλγιφιαμμα ... γείτονες ὁδὸς καὶ θάλασσα, (2) κῆπον φοινικῶνος ἐν ὁρίοις Μαωζων λεγόμενον Αλγιφιαμμα ... γείτονες μοσχαντικὴ κυρίου Καίσαρος καὶ θάλασσα. See Hannah M. Cotton and

declared in the census of 127 CE, there was one said to be located in Galgala – this time said to be in Maḥoza: κῆπον φοινικῶνος ἐν ὁρίοις Μαωζων λεγόμενον Βαγαλγαλὰ[24] (*P.Yadin* 16, ll. 24–25). There is no reason to deny that the Galgala of *P.Yadin* 2 and 3 is the same as the Galgala of *P.Yadin* 16; consequently Maḥoz 'Eglatain must be identical with Maḥoza. If so, why should Maḥoz 'Eglatain and Maḥoza stand for two different places in *P.Yadin* 7?

Given that Maḥoza and Maḥoz 'Eglatain are one and the same in the documents, and given also that Maḥoza is a village (κώμη, *P.Yadin* 12, l. 7), we face the problem that the village of Maḥoza/Maḥoz 'Eglatain seems to contain several units within it.[25] Galgala is not the only unit located there. In one of Bar Kokhba's Hebrew contracts two men who now reside in 'En-gedi are said to come originally from the Luḥit in Maḥoz 'Eglatain: 'Teḥinnah son of Simeon and Alma son of Judah both of the Luḥit in Maḥoz 'Eglatain now resident in 'En-gedi.'[26] What kind of village is Maḥoza/Maḥoz 'Eglatain which contains both Galgala and Luḥit, and perhaps other units as well?[27]

It could be suggested that Maḥoza/Maḥoz 'Eglatain was an important regional centre, or an agglomeration of once independent villages. But this explanation is somewhat hard to reconcile with Maḥoza/Maḥoz 'Eglatain's obvious inferiority vis-à-vis Ẓo'ar in whose territory it is subsumed.[28] In fact everything about the phrasing suggests that Maḥoza/Maḥoz 'Eglatain was subordinate to Ẓo'ar in much

---

Jonas C. Greenfield, "Babatha's Property and the Law of Succession in the Babatha Archive," *ZPE* 104 (1994): 211–24.

24 Bagalgala – בגלגלא – means literally 'in the Galgala': the preposition 'in' (*beth* – ב), as well as the definite article 'the' (the suffix *aleph* – א) have become part of the name in Greek, see Lewis, *The Documents from the Bar Kokhba Period in the Cave of Letters. Greek Papyri*, 70. *P.Yadin* 6 (Nabataean), l. 4 reads 'which you have in Galgala in ...' (*dy lk bglgl' dy* ...), but Ada Yardeni tells us that there is no room for Maḥoz 'Eglatain in the gap which follows.

25 This difficulty, too, had been pointed out by Kutscher, "Ugaritica Marginalia," 11–13, but his solution does not seem convincing to me.

26 Yadin, "Expedition D – The Cave of the Letters," 251–2, no. 44 (134 CE): *tḥnh bn šm'wn w'lm' bn yhwdh šnyhm mhlwḥit šbmḥwz 'gltyn ywšbym b'yn gdy*. Yadin suggests cautiously that Teḥinnah son of Simeon could be Θεαννας Σιμονος of the Greek part of the Babatha archive, who no doubt resided in Maḥoza, for he is the scribe of many of the documents written there: *P.Yadin* 5 (110 CE); 15 (125 CE); 17 (128 CE); 18 (128 CE).

27 I suspect that Βηθφααραια – Bethphaararaia – of *P.Yadin* 16, l. 30 may be another one.

28 Above, n. 6, and see also *P.Yadin* 14, l. 20; 15, l. 3 = 16–17; 17, ll. 2–3 = 19–20; 18, l. 3 = 32: ἐν Μαωζᾳ περὶ Ζοαραν; *P.Yadin* 25, l. 28 = 64: ἐν Μαωζᾳ περὶ Ζοορων; *P.Yadin* 19, ll. 10–11: ἐν Μαωζας τῆς περὶ Ζοαρα; *P.Yadin* 20, ll. 22–23; 21, ll. 5–6; 22, ll. 5–6; 26, l. 18; 27, ll. 3–4: ἐν Μαωζᾳ περιμέτρῳ Ζοορων; *XḤev/Ṣe Gr.* 1, l. 3 in Hannah M. Cotton, "The Archive of Salome Komaise Daughter of Levi: Another Archive from the 'Cave of Letters,'" *ZPE* 105 (1995): 183: ἐ̣ν̣ Μ̣ᾳ̣ωζας τῆς π̣ε̣ρὶ Ζ[ο]ᾳ̣ρ̣ω̣ν (= *P.Hever* 64).

the same way as a village in Judaea was subordinate to the capital village which gave its name to the toparchy to which it belonged. Even if the term *toparchia* never appears in the Babatha archive or in the province of Arabia,[29] one cannot help noticing the striking resemblance between ἐν Μαωζᾳ περὶ Ζοαραν of *P.Yadin* 14. l. 20 for example and the locutions describing the hierarchical relationship between a capital village and a subordinate one in Judaea: ἐν Βαιτοβαισσαιας ... τοπαρχείας Ἡρωδείο[υ] ... ἀπὸ κ(ώμης) Γαλωδῶν τῆς περὶ Ἀκραβατῶν οἰκῶν ἐν κώμῃ Βαιτοάρδοις τῆς περὶ Γοφνοῖς of *DJD* II, no. 115, ll. 2–3;[30] and in the Babatha archive itself: κώμης Ἐνγαδδῶν περὶ Ἱερειχοῦντα of *P.Yadin* 16, l. 16; and in the so-called *P.Se'elim*: ἐν Ἀριστοβουλιάδι τῆς Ζẹιφηνῆς ... τῶν ἀπ̣ὸ κώμης Ἰακείμων τ̣[ῆς Ζειφηνῆς] of *XḤev/Ṣe Gr.* 2, ll. 3–5.[31] We cannot be sure of what is implied by the subordination of villages to each other (or to a city),[32] nor do we know the functions performed by central villages such as Ẓo'ar, Gophna, Akrabatta, Herodion, Jericho and Zif vis-à-vis their subordinate villages, Maḥoza, Bethbassi, Galoda, Batharda, Yaqim and Aristoboulias respectively, but there can be no doubt that something more than a merely geographical relationship is intended.[33]

Conclusion

We have thus eliminated the non-existent district of 'Eglatain, and the assumption that it was re-named Ẓo'ar under Roman rule. However, we cannot be sure that the inclusion of villages – like Maḥoza/Maḥoz 'Eglatain – in the district of other villages – like Ẓo'ar – originated only with the Roman re-organization of the new province: although the subordination of Maḥoza to Ẓo'ar is recorded for the first time after the annexation of Arabia (*P.Yadin* 5, 110 CE), it does not appear in

29 As Naphtali Lewis reminds us in "The Babatha Archive: A Response," *IEJ* 44 (1994): 244. For toparchies in Judaea see Emil Schürer, *The History of the Jewish People in the Age of Jesus Christ*, Vol. II, ed. Fergus Millar and Géza Vermès (Edinburgh: Clark, 1979),184–198.

30 'at Bethbassi in the toparchy of Herodion ... from the village of Galoda of Akrabatta, but is an inhabitant of Batharda of Gophna.'

31 'in Aristoboulias of the Zephene ... from the village of Yaqim [of the Zephene],' see Cotton, "A Cancelled Marriage Contract from the Judaean Desert, XHev/Se Gr. 2," 67, and discussion there, 73–77 (= P.Hever 69).

32 Petra is mentioned three times as the centre to which both Ẓo'ar and its subordinate village, Maḥoza, belonged. See *P.Yadin* 16, l. 13–14: Βαβθα Σίμωνος Μαωζηνὴ τῆς Ζοαρηνῆς περιμέτρου Πέτρας; *P.Yadin* 37, ll. 2–3: ἐν Μαωζᾳ τῆς Ζοαρηνῆς τῆς π[ερὶ] Πέτραν; cf. Naphtali Lewis, "A Jewish Landowner from the Province of Arabia," *SCI* 8–9 (1985/88): 134: l. 12: Σ̣ίμων[ο]ς Μαωζηὸς τῆς Ζοαρηνῆς περιμέτρου Πέτρας.

33 See Benjamin Isaac, "The Babatha Archive: A Review Article," *IEJ* 42 (1992): 67–70.

the Aramaic *P.Yadin* 7, written in 120 CE. It may be argued that the convention of attributing a village to the district is tied up with the language of the document – Semitic or Greek.

The exact location of Maḥoza also remains a puzzle. Whether *maḥoz* means 'a port' or 'a city,' Maḥoza/Maḥoz 'Eglatain lay by the sea shore.[34] The proof is in the documents themselves which mention two date groves in Maḥoza named Algiphiamma, which is a Greek transliteration of Aramaic *'l gif ym'* 'on the sea shore': κῆπον φοινικῶνος ἐν ὁρίοις Μαωζων λεγόμενον Αλγιφιαμμα ... γείτονες ὁδὸς καὶ θάλασσα, κῆπον φοινικῶνος ἐν ὁρίοις Μαωζων λεγόμενον Αλγιφιαμμα ... γείτονες μοσχαντικὴ κυρίου Καίσαρος καὶ θάλασσα (*P.Yadin* 16, ll. 17–24).[35] And indeed the sea, or rather the sea shore,[36] is said here to be one of the abutters of these date groves. Another clue to the location of Maḥoza/Maḥoz 'Eglatain is that dates constitute the main, if not the only, product of the area: they are mentioned in census declarations,[37] deeds of gift[38] and tax receipts.[39] Hence we must look for

34 Thus, an identification with Kh. Galgul (cf. Alois Musil, *Arabia Petraea I: Moab* (Wien: A. Hölder, 1907), 365 and 381, n. 1) or with Kh. el-Gillime (cf. Félix-Marie Abel, *Géographie de la Palestine*, Vol. II (Paris: J. Gabalda, 1938), 310, s. v. Eglaïm) is impossible since both are located inland. See the illuminating discussion of biblical 'Eglat (עגלת – Isaiah 15:5; Jeremiah 48:5) in Abraham Schalit, "Die Eroberungen des Alexander Jannäus in Moab," *Theokratia: Jahrbuch des Institutum Judaicum Delitzschianum* 1 (1970): 12 ff. (an earlier version of this article appeared in Hebrew as "Alexander Yannai's Conquests in Moab," *Eretz Israel* 1 (1951): 104–21).

35 Since Luḥit is explicitly said to be in Maḥoza/Maḥoz 'Eglatain, it should be located by the seashore. Any attempt to identify it with one or another of its namesakes must start from this fact. Biblical 'ascent of Luḥit' (Isaiah 15:5 and Jeremiah 48:5) is identified by Eusebius as a village lying between Areopolis and Ẓo'ar: καὶ ἔστι μεταξὺ Ἀρεωπόλεως καὶ Ζοορῶν κώμη νῦν καλουμένη Λουεθά (*Onomasticon* 122, 28, ed. Klostermann). A commander of an army camp in Lḥytw (*rb mšryta dy blḥytw*) is mentioned in a Nabataean inscription from 37 CE (of which two identical copies were found: *CIS* II.i, no. 196 = *RES* 674). See Antoine-Raphael Savignac and Jean Starcky, "Une inscription nabatéenne provenant du Djôf," *RB* 64 (1957): 200–203; Willy Schottroff, "Horonaim, Nimrim, Luhith und der Westrand des 'Landes Ataroth': Ein Beitrag zur historischen Topographie des Landes Moab," *ZDPV* 82 (1966): 196 ff.; Schalit, "Die Eroberungen des Alexander Jannäus in Moab," 40–41 and n. 4 there; Mittmann, "The Ascent of Luhith," 178.

36 In the Nabataean *P.Yadin* 3, where one of these two groves is mentioned, the word used is *rqq'* (l. 5 = l. 27), i. e. 'shoals,' a word used elsewhere for the shallow water near the shore of a lake or sea, cf. *bShabbat* 100b; *b'Erubim* 43a.

37 *P.Yadin* 16 and Lewis, "A Jewish Landowner from the Province of Arabia," 134, l. 12.

38 *P.Yadin* 7 and *XḤev/Ṣe Gr.* 1 (n. 28).

39 *XḤev/Ṣe Gr.* 5 (= *P.Hever* 64), see Hannah M. Cotton, "Rent or Tax Receipt from Maoza," *ZPE* 100 (1994): 547–57 = Cotton, "The Archive of Salome Komaise Daughter of Levi," 174–5, no. I; *XḤev/Ṣe* 12 (Aramaic), see Ada Yardeni, *Naḥal Ṣe'elim Documents* (Beer-Sheva: Ben-Gurion University of the Negev Press, 1995) (Hebrew); for an English translation of this document see Cotton, "The Archive of Salome Komaise Daughter of Levi," 204, no. V.

a place with climatic and water conditions similar to those prevailing in Ẓo‘ar[40] and ‘Ein-gedi. The Ģhor al-Safi, south of the Dead Sea, with Wadi al-Ḥasa nearby, would fit Maḥoza/Maḥoz ‘Eglatain admirably.[41]

End Note:
Even if *maḥoz* does mean ‘district,’ the identification of Maḥoza and Maḥoz ‘Eglatain remains unaffected; even then the word *maḥoz* in Maḥoz ‘Eglatain cannot mean ‘district’ literally. My colleague Simon Hopkins kindly supplied a similar example: the town Siirt in Southern Turkey is the capital of Siirt Province (*vilayet* in Turkish = Arabic *wilāya(t)*), but in the local Arabic *əl-wilāye*, i. e. ‘the province’ is used for the town Siirt itself, *not* ‘the province’; see Otto Jastrow, *Die mesopotamisch-arabischen qəltu-Dialekte* I (Wiesbaden: Steiner, 1978), 16; II (1981), 217; 220, n. 16; 274, n. 20. A good example is II, 226 § 1 *qaẓa əlwalāye* which means literally “the district of the province,’ i. e. ‘the district of Siirt.’

Concordance of the papyri mentioned in this article (with the exception of those published by Naphtali Lewis, n. 5) with Hannah M. Cotton, W.E.H. Cockle, and Fergus Millar “The Papyrology of the Roman Near East: A Survey,” *JRS* 85 (1995):
P.Yadin 2 = no. 182.
P.Yadin 3 = no. 183.
P.Yadin 6 = no. 186.
P.Yadin 7 = no. 187.
P.Yadin 12 = no. 175.
P.Yadin 36 = no. 180.
N. Lewis, *SCI* 8–9 (1985/88) (n. 32) = no. 179.
Y. Yadin, *IEJ* 12 (1962): 251–2, no. 44 (n. 26) = no. 303.

40 Ẓo‘ar is ‘the city of palms,’ see *Mishnah*, *Yebamot*, 16.7; see Magen Broshi, “Agriculture and Economy in Roman Palestine: Seven Notes on the Babatha Archive,” *IEJ* 42 (1992): 233: “The heat, the extreme low humidity and the abundant water are prerequisites for cultivating the date palm. The salinity ... is no hindrance”, cf. Broshi, 231–2. Note that in the two biblical passages mentioned above (n. 34) ‘Eglat is mentioned together with Ẓo‘ar.

41 The ‘big river’ – *nhr’ rb’* – mentioned in *P.Yadin* 7, l. 8 = l. 42 and the ‘water from the Wadi’ – *my wdy’* – mentioned in l. 43 may point to Wadi al-Ḥasa. Note also the ‘desert’ – *mdbr’* – as one of the abutters in l. 5. Cf. Nelson Glueck’s first impression of the Ghor al-Ṣafi area: “ ...We pushed on to Ghōr eṣ-Ṣāfi, near the south-eastern end of the Dead Sea. The waters of the Seil el-Qurāḥi, as the lower end of the Wādi el-Ḥesā is called, irrigate an extensive area, part of which is in a swampy state [cf. above, n. 36, the ‘shoals’ – *rqq’*] ... The large green fields of eṣ-Ṣāfi were a welcome relief after the waste stretches traversed from the time we left the plantations of the el-Mezra‘ah,” Nelson Glueck, “Explorations in Eastern Palestine II,” *Annual of the American Schools of Oriental Research* 15 (1934): 7.

XḤev/Ṣe Gr. 1 = no. 204.
XḤev/Ṣe Gr. 2 = no. 292.
XḤev/Ṣe Gr. 5 = no. 191.
XḤev/Ṣe Gr. 12 = no. 205.[42]
XḤev/Ṣe Nab. 2 = see Emanuel Tov, with the collaboration of Stephen J. Pfann, *The Dead Sea Scrolls on Microfiche: A Comprehensive Facsimile Edition of the Texts from the Judean Desert, Companion Volume* (Leiden: Brill, 1993), 66 (I am grateful to Ada Yardeni for giving me the information cited above in n. 3, on ll. 4–5 of the papyrus).

42 Greek and Aramaic papyri said to come from Naḥal Ṣe'elim and designated *XḤev/Ṣe* were published in a final form by Hannah M. Cotton and Ada Yardeni, *Aramaic, Hebrew, and Greek Documentary Texts from Naḥal Ḥever and Other Sites*, Discoveries in the Judaean Desert XXVII (Oxford: Clarendon Press, 1997).

Courtyard(s) in Ein-Gedi: P.Yadin 11, 19 and 20 of the Babatha Archive

In three papyri from the Babatha archive a courtyard in Ein-Gedi is described, *P.Yadin* 11, *P.Yadin* 19 and *P.Yadin* 20. The editor, Naphtali Lewis, considered all three documents to be describing one and the same courtyard.[1] Since the owner and neighbours of each courtyard are specified, it should be possible to find out whether or not the same courtyard is the subject of all three papyri. This, as we shall see, touches directly on questions of inheritance and succession. After setting out the evidence, I shall give it in the form of a table. A discussion of the case for and against identification will follow.

The courtyard(s) belong to the family of Babatha's second husband, Judah son of Eleazar Khthousion, whose family tree is given below:

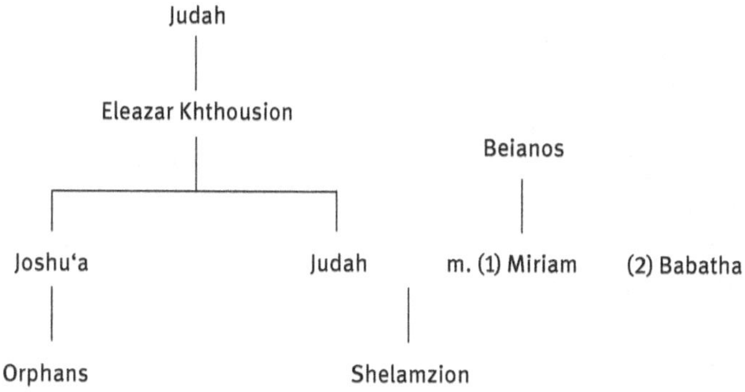

1) *P.Yadin* 11 (6 May 124, Ein-Gedi):
Judah son of Eleazar Khthousion takes a loan from Magonius Valens, a centurion of a detachment of the *cohors I milliaria Thracum* stationed in Ein-Gedi,[2] and mortgages a courtyard in Ein-Gedi, which belongs to his father, but which he has the legal right to mortgage and lease out. The neighours are as follows: east –

1 Naphtali Lewis, *The Documents from the Bar Kokhba Period in the Cave of Letters. Greek Papyri*, Judean Desert Studies II (Jerusalem: IES, 1989), 41–2; 83–4; 89; henceforth 'Lewis.'

2 On the unit see Michael P. Speidel, "A Tile Stamp of Cohors I Thracum Milliaria from Hebron/Palestine," *ZPE* 35 (1979): 170–72; Benjamin Isaac takes him to be the commander of the detachment, *The Limits of Empire: The Roman Army in the East* (Oxford: Clarendon Press, 1990), 137, 174, 430.

Article note: First published in *ZPE* 112 (1996): 197–201.

https://doi.org/10.1515/9783110770438-017

tents and workshop of Joshu‘a son of Mandron; west – tents and workshop of Eleazar Khthousion, Judah’s father; south – market and Shimeon son of Mathaios; north – road and *praesidium* (a military post).[3]

αὐλῆ ἐν Ἐνγαδοῖς Ἐλαζάρῳ Χθου̣σιω̣ν̣ο̣ς π̣α̣τ̣ρί μο̣υ̣ ἧς ἔχω ἐπιτ̣ρ̣ο̣πὴν̣ ὑ̣π̣ο̣τιθέ̣[ν]αι καὶ ἐγμισθοιν παρὰ τοῦ αὐτοῦ Ἐλα̣[ζάρο]υ̣, ἧς αὐλῆ̣ς γεί̣τ̣[ο]ν̣ες ἀπὸ ἀνατ[ο]λ̣ῶ̣ν σκ̣ηναὶ καὶ Ἰησοῦς Μαν̣δ[ρ]ῶ̣ν̣ο̣ς, δύσεος σκ̣η̣ν̣[αὶ καὶ] ἐ̣ρ̣γασ̣τ̣ήριον τοῦ αὐτοῦ Ἐλαζάρ<ο>υ πατρός μου, νότου ἀγορὰ καὶ Σ[ί]μ̣ω̣ν Μαθθ̣αίου, βο̣ρ̣[ρᾶ ὁ]δὸς [καὶ πρ]α[ισ]ί̣δ̣[ι]ο̣ν (ll. 16–19 = ll. 3–6).

2) *P.Yadin* 19 (16 April 128, Maḥoza):
Judah son of Eleazar Khthousion gives his daughter Shelamzion everything he owns in Ein-Gedi: a courtyard with the rooms in it. Shelamzion is to receive one half immediately, and the other half she will get after his death. The neighbours are as follows: east – Joshu‘a son of Madaronas and empty space; west – the donor; south – market; north – road.

[δι]έ̣θ̣ε̣τ̣[ο Ἰο]ύ̣δ̣ας Ἐ̣λ[αζά]ρου Χθουσ[ίω]ν̣ο̣ς Ἠ̣νγ̣α̣δη̣[νὸ]ς̣ οἰκῶν ἐν Μαωζᾶς [Σελ]αμψιο̣ῦ̣ς θυ[γατ]ερ̣ π̣ά̣ν̣[τα τὰ ὑ]πάρ[χον]τ̣α αὐ̣[τ]ῷ̣ [ἐ]ν Ἠνγ̣αδῆς ἥ[μισ]υ̣ α[ὐ]λ̣ῆς ... ἥμισυ οἰκοιμάτων̣ καὶ ὑπερωαις ἐνο[υ]σι χωρὶς αὐ̣λῆς μικκῆς π̣αλ̣εαν ἐ̣νγὺς τῆς α̣ὐτ̣[ῆ]ς̣ αὐλῆς, καὶ τ[ὸ] ἄλλ̣ο̣ ἥμισυ τῆς αὐλῆς καὶ οἰκο̣ιμ̣ά̣των διέθετο̣ . .[. Ἰ]ο̣ύ̣δας τ̣ῇ αὐ̣[τ]ῇ̣ [Σελ]α̣μψιοῦ[ς] μετὰ τὸ αὐτὸ[ν] τ̣ε<λε>υτῆσαι, ὧν γεί̣τ̣ω̣νες [τ]ῆ̣ς αὐλῆς καὶ οἰκοιμά[των ἀν]α̣τολῶ̣ν Ἰησοῦ Μαδδαρωνα καὶ αὐ̣ρίχω̣ρον, δυσμῶν ὁ διεθετῶν, νότου ἀγ̣ορά, βορρᾶ ὁδός (ll. 11–18).

3) *P.Yadin* 20 (19 June 130, Maḥoza):
The guardians of the nephews of Judah son of Eleazar Khthousion (i. e. the guardians of the sons of his brother Joshu‘a) are conceding a courtyard in Ein-Gedi with the rights attached to it to Shelamzion daughter of Judah. This courtyard belonged to her grandfather, Eleazar Khthousion. The neighhbours of this courtyard are as follows: east – market; west – Mathetos son of Zabbaios; south – market; north – lane of Aristion.

ὁμολογοῦμεν ⟦παρα⟧ συν̣κεχωρηκέναι σ̣[οι ἐξ ὑ]παρχόντων Ἐλεαζάρου τοῦ καὶ Χθουσίωνος Ἰούδ̣ο[υ π]άπ̣ου σου αὐλὴν σὺν παντὶ δικαιοις αὐτῆς ἐν{ν} Ἠνγ̣α̣δ̣ο̣ῖ̣ς καὶ τοὺς σὺν αὐτης οἰκιαι ... γίτονες ἀνατολῆς ἀγορά, δυσμῶν Μαθ̣θε[θο]ς Ζαββ̣α̣[ίου,] βορρᾶ ἀμφόδιον Ἀριστίωνος, νότου ἀγορὰ δημοσία (ll. 27–34 ≈ ll. 6–11).

3 Not ‘headquarters’ as translated by Lewis, *The Documents from the Bar Kokhba Period in the Cave of Letters. Greek Papyri*, 44.

Papyrus	*P.Yadin* 11	*P.Yadin* 19	*P.Yadin* 20
Date	**6 May 124 CE**	**16 April 128 CE**	**19 June 130 CE**
Owner	**Eleazar Khthousion, Judah's father**	**Judah son of Eleazar**	**Eleazar Khthousion, Judah's father**
East	tents and Joshu'a Mandron	Joshu'a Madaronas and empty space	market
West	tents and workshop of Eleazar, Judah's father	Judah son of Eleazar	Mathetos son of Zabbaios
South	market and Shimeon son of Mathaios	market	market
North	road and *praesidium*	road	lane of Aristion

Not only do the owners of the courtyard change from one papyrus to another, but so do the abutters.

I shall start with the discrepancies between the abutters and the owners in *P.Yadin* 11 and *P.Yadin* 19.

Between 6 May 124 CE, the date of *P.Yadin* 11, and 16 April 128 CE, the date of *P.Yadin* 19, four changes took place: 1) the tents disappeared from the east and west. In the east they were replaced by an empty space; 2) Judah son of Eleazar Khthousion, the donor (ὁ διεθετῶν) replaced his father, Eleazar Khthousion, in the west; 3) Shimeon son of Mathaios disappeared from the south (but the market remained); 4) the *praesidium* disappeared from the north.

If the tents – σκηναί – were, as Lewis and others believe, soldiers' quarters,[4] then the first and the fourth change are in fact one: that detachment of the military unit which was stationed in Ein-Gedi moved out between the two dates.

4 See Lewis, 45 ad ll. 5 and 18, especially the reference to Bärbel Kramer and Dieter Hagedorn, "Zwei ptolemäische Texte aus der Hamburger Papyrussammlung," *Archiv für Papyrusforschung* 33 (1987): 13, ad l. 5; Isaac, *The Limits of Empire: The Roman Army in the East*, 430; Benjamin Isaac, "The Babatha Archive: A Review Article," *IEJ* 42 (1992): 62–3; Hans Jakob Polotsky, "The Greek Papyri from the Cave of Letters," *IEJ* 12 (1962): 259 is cautious: "flanked by (presumably military) tents." I think that it is remarkable to find a private courtyard almost inside a Roman military camp.
A Roman bathhouse, dated by the coins to the period between 79 and 117/8, was excavated in Ein-Gedi in 1964 (see Benjamin Mazar and Immanuel Dunayevsky, "En-Gedi: Third Season of Excavations: Preliminary Report," *IEJ* 14 (1964): 128–30). It is thus almost contemporary with the Roman military presence in Ein-Gedi as attested in *P.Yadin* 11 of 6 May 124. Renewed excavations in Ein-Gedi, directed by Yizhar Hirschfeld, under the auspices of the Institute of Archaeology of the Hebrew University and University of Hartford, Connecticut, have so far reached only the late

Lewis (p. 83) assumed that Judah stepped into his father's property in the west (*P.Yadin* 19, l. 18), namely the 'workshop' of *P.Yadin* 11, l. 5 = l. 18.[5] How can this be reconciled with Judah's declaration that he is giving Shelamzion everything he owns in Ein-Gedi (π̣ά̣ν̣[τα τὰ ὑ]πάρ[χον]ṭα αὐ̣[τ]ῷ̣ [ἐ]ν Ἡνγα̣δῆς, *P.Yadin* 19, l. 12)? Two solutions suggest themselves: 1) Judah's possession in the west is the small old courtyard excluded from the gift (χωρὶς αὐ̣λῆς μικκῆς π̣α̣λ̣εαν ἐ̣νγὺς τῆς α̣ὐτ̣[ῆ]-ς̣ αὐλῆς, ll. 14–15); perhaps we should identify it as the 'workshop' of *P.Yadin* 11; 2) Judah abuts on the courtyard because until his death he owns its other half. In other words the list of neighbours in *P.Yadin* 19 does not represent the neighbours of the entire courtyard but only of the half which Shelamzion is getting now.[6] This is very difficult in view of the fact that the abutters are said to be those of the 'courtyard' and not just of its half: ὧ̣ν γείτ̣ω̣νες̣ [τ]ῆ̣ς αὐλῆς καὶ οἰκοιμά[των] κτλ. (ll. 16–17). I prefer, therefore, the first solution.

However this may be, it seems that only one significant change took place in as far as the abutters are concerned in the time which elapsed between *P.Yadin* 11 and *P.Yadin* 19: the Roman army has left. In view of the overall identity of the abutters, it is very likely that we are dealing with the same courtyard. How then are we to account for the discrepancy between the owners? The courtyard in *P.Yadin* 11 belongs to Eleazar Khthousion, Judah's father (although Judah could mortgage and lease it), whereas the courtyard in *P.Yadin* 19 belongs to Judah himself, as he himself declares. And there is no good reason to doubt Judah's statement in *P.Yadin* 19, ll. 11 ff. that he is giving his daughter his own property in Ein-Gedi. The discrepancy as to the owners can be solved by the possibility that Judah may have received the courtyard during the span of four years separating the two papyri either as a gift from his father, Eleazar Khthousion, or as part of an inheritance upon the latter's death.

In discussing the discrepancies between *P.Yadin* 19 and *P.Yadin* 20, I shall start with the owners and then pass on to the abutters.

Roman and Byzantine village. It is to be hoped that when the excavations, planned for the next ten years, reach the Roman bathhouse the area referred to in the Babatha Archive will be uncovered.

5 ἐ̣ργασ̣τ̣ήριον τοῦ αὐτοῦ Ἐλαζάρ<ο>υ πατρός μου.

6 Unfortunately another deed of gift of half a courtyard cannot help us decide whether the neighbours of the whole or of the half are usually given, see *XḤev/Ṣe Gr* 1 (= *P.Hever* 64) in Hannah M. Cotton, "The Archive of Salome Komaise Daughter of Levi: Another Archive from the 'Cave of Letters,'" *ZPE* 105 (1995): 186–87, Doc. IV, ll. 13–15 = ll. 33–36. It is true that the neighbours there do not include the donor, but this does not prove that the neighbours of the entire courtyard are given; possibly the mother did not own more than half a courtyard which she is now bestowing on her daughter. In *P.Yadin* 47b (Jan./Feb. 134 CE) the seller is one of the abutters to half a garden sold in Ein-Gedi (l. 8); again we cannot know whether by virtue of owning the other half or of owning another property there.

The courtyard in *P.Yadin* 19 belongs to Judah son of Eleazar Khthousion whereas the courtyard in *P.Yadin* 20 belongs to his father, Eleazar Khthousion. The only way to resolve the discrepancy, and uphold the identity of the courtyard, is to say that the sons of Eleazar Khthousion, Joshu‘a (the orphans' father) and Judah (Shelamzion's father), had not divided their father's property between them after their father's death. This was common practice as we learn from the papyri; it has left its mark in the frequency of the locution κληρονόμοι τοῦ δεῖνος to refer to joint owners of real property.[7] Such a situation might last for years.[8] If this were the case, the courtyard had never been registered in Judah's name. Presumably, though, the two brothers had agreed between them that the courtyard under discussion belonged to Judah's share of the inheritance. Judah was less than precise when he referred to the courtyard in the deed of gift (*P.Yadin* 19) as his own. However, since it was earmarked as his part of the as yet undivided inheritance in the consensual agreement between himself and his brother, Joshu‘a, he certainly had a reason to assume that this was so. We may recall that in 124 CE this courtyard was his to lease and mortgage. After Judah's death Judah's daughter Shelamzion, relying on the deed of gift, claimed her property. The nephews in *P.Yadin* 20, through their guardians, had not been disputing the validity of the gift, but Judah's legal right to bestow the courtyard, since it was not formally his but belonged to both brothers. *P.Yadin* 20 demonstrates that the nephews had at last agreed to accept the consensual agreement between the brothers, Joshu‘a and Judah, that in the final division of property the courtyard belonged to Judah's share, and he had the right to give it to his daughter: ὁμολογοῦμεν ⟦παρα⟧ συγκεχωρηκέναι σ̣[οι ἐξ ὑ]παρχόντων Ἐλεαζάρου τοῦ καὶ Χθουσίωνος Ἰούδο[υ π]άπ̣ου σου αὐλὴν σὺν παντὶ δικαιοις αὐτῆς ἐν{ν} Ἡνγ̣α̣δ̣ο̣ῖ̣ς καὶ τοὺς σὺν αὔτης οἰκιαι (ll. 27–30 ≈ ll. 6–10).

7 E.g. *P.Yadin* 16, l. 28: γ̣ε̣ί̣τ̣ο̣ν̣ε̣[ς κλ]η̣ρ̣ο̣ν̣ό̣μοι Θησαίου Σαβακα; cf. Hans Kreller, *Erbrechtliche Untersuchungen auf Grund der graeco-aegyptischen Papyrusurkunden* (Leipzig: Teubner, 1919), 63 ff.; Cotton, "The Archive of Salome Komaise Daughter of Levi," 198; in *XḤev/Ṣe Gr* 7 (= Naphtali Lewis, "A Jewish Landowner from the Province of Arabia," *SCI* 8–9 (1985/88): 134–37), the declarant, X son of Simon, is one of two brothers holding properties in partnership (μετοχῆ) in Maḥoza (Lewis, "A Jewish Landowner," 135, ll. 15 and 19). I suppose that as neighbours they could be described as κληρονό̣μ]ο̣ι Σιμωνος, although they do not make a joint declaration.

8 Kreller, *Erbrechtliche Untersuchungen auf Grund der graeco-aegyptischen Papyrusurkunden*, 65. The heirs of Joseph son of Baba, found in the Aramaic *P.Yadin* 7 from 120 CE (*yrty ywsf br bb'*, ll. 6, 11 = ll. 38, 45) as neighbours to two pieces of land owned by Babatha's father, reappear nine years later in *XḤev/Ṣe Gr* 1, ll. 11 (= ll. 32–33) dated to 129 CE (Cotton, "The Archive of Salome Komaise Daughter of Levi," 186–7), still as a single body of owners: κληρονόμοι Ἰωσηπος Βαβα, i. e. the property remained undivided for at least nine years.

Thus the change in the owner's name does not necessarily cast doubt on the identity of the courtyard described in the two papyri. The guardians' proposal to register the courtyard with the authorities (*P.Yadin* 20, l. 12 = ll. 35–36) can be reconciled with Judah's promise in *P.Yadin* 19, ll. 25–27 to do so whenever Shlemazion would summon him to do so:[9] father and daughter might not have got around to doing so before Judah's death.

But if the discrepancy as to the owners in *P.Yadin* 19 and *P.Yadin* 20 can be resolved in this way, is it possible to get around the discrepancies between the abutters in the two papyri?

I am assuming that the neighbours of the entire courtyard are given in *P.Yadin* 19, and that Judah was one of the abutters – not because he owned the other half – but because he owned other property there, namely the small old courtyard he excluded from the deed of gift (*P.Yadin* 19, ll. 14–15). This assumption brings the number of changes in the abutters between *P.Yadin* 19 and *P.Yadin* 20 to three: three out of four abutters have changed between 16 April 128 and 19 June 130: 1) in the east a market replaced the property of Joshu'a Madaronas (Mandron in *P.Yadin* 11, l. 5 = l. 18); 2) in the west Mathetos son of Zabbaios replaced Judah son of Eleazar; 3) in the north Aristion's lane replaced the road. The one abutter which did not change is the market in the south – an abutter which might well have bordered on more than one courtyard.

There appear to be too many changes in the abutters over a period which lasted no more than twenty-six months. *P.Yadin* 19 and *P.Yadin* 20 do not describe, therefore, the same courtyard. Hence there are two different courtyards in the three papyri under discussion: one in *P.Yadin* 11 and 19 and the other in *P.Yadin* 20.

The fact that the courtyard described in *P.Yadin* 11 and the one described in *P.Yadin* 20 share the same owner (Eleazar Khthousion) is not an argument for the identity of the courtyards described in them, since *P.Yadin* 11 and *P.Yadin* 19 describe an identical courtyard whereas *P.Yadin* 19 and *P.Yadin* 20 describe two different courtyards.

The courtyard in *P.Yadin* 20 is, therefore, not the subject of the deed of gift of Judah son of Eleazar Khthousion to his daughter Shelamzion (*P.Yadin* 19). We no longer need to say that the courtyard in *P.Yadin* 20 passed to Shelamzion's hands through the mediation of a deed of gift by her father. She could have got it directly from her grandfather, either in her father's lifetime or after his death.[10] It is possible that the grandfather, Eleazar Khthousion, outlived his son, Judah. In

9 ὅταν δὲ παραγγείλει Σελα<μ>ψιοῦς τῷ αὐτῷ Ἰούδατι, τευχίζ{ζ}ει αὐτὴν διὰ δημοσίων.
10 *P.Yadin* 20 was written on 19 June 130 CE; by the 11 September of that year Judah was dead, see *P.Yadin* 21, ll. 8–9: Ἰούδου Χθουσίωνος ἀνδρός σου ἀπογενομένου; cf. *P.Yadin* 22, ll. 8–9.

addition Shelamzion received in a deed of gift from her father (*P.Yadin* 19) half of another courtyard in Ein-Gedi during her father's lifetime, and after his death she was going to get the other half. It should be noticed that although Shelamzion is married at the time of both *P.Yadin* 19 and *P.Yadin* 20,[11] this real estate bestowed on her does not pass into the husband's hands, but is treated as her own.[12]

On the other hand it is possible that Shelamzion came into the possession of her grandfather's courtyard due to her father's recent death (see n. 10). The fact that Judah's nephews appear to have disputed Shelamzion's ownership may suggest that in the prevailing legal system, the granddaughter did not automatically acquire her father's right to the inheritance. I suspect in view of other indications in this archive as well as in that of Salome Komaïse daughter of Levi (above, n. 6) that the daughter was not even the *suus heres* of her own father, even in the absence of sons. The only way to transfer property to a daughter was through a deed of gift. Perhaps this is what her grandfather, Eleazar Khthousion, had done.[13]

11 *P.Yadin* 19 is written eleven days after her marriage and in *P.Yadin* 20 her husband represents her (ll. 5–6 = ll. 25–26).

12 For the wider context see Hannah M. Cotton, "Deeds of Gift and the Law of Succession in Archives from the Judaean Desert," in *Akten des 21. Internationalen Papyrologenkongresses, Berlin, 13–19.8.1995*, ed. Barbara Kramer et al., Vol. I (Stuttgart – Leipzig: Teubner, 1997), 179–88.

13 See Hannah M. Cotton and Jonas C. Greenfield, "Babatha's Property and the Law of Succession in the Babatha Archive," *ZPE* 104 (1994): 211–24 and Cotton, "Deeds of Gift and the Law of Succession in Archives from the Judaean Desert."

Land Tenure in the Documents from the Nabataean Kingdom and the Roman Province of Arabia

Land tenure in the documents from the Nabataean kingdom and after 106 CE from the Roman province of Arabia is a slippery issue. The documents contain indirect and not unambiguous information concerning the status of land in Nabataea/Arabia. What was the exact legal status of land said to be leased from the Nabataean king? Did the transition from independent kingdom to Roman province affect the status of this land? Did such land become private in the transition, or was it now leased from the Roman emperor? Is the payment mentioned in the documents that of rent or of tax?[1]

The documents to be discussed here are of different nature: deeds of sale, *P.Yadin* 2 and 3 (Nabataean, 99 CE);[2] receipts, *XḤev/Se gr* 60 (125 CE) and *XḤev/Se ar* 12 (131 CE); land declarations for the census, *XḤev/Se gr* 62 and *P.Yadin* 16 (127 CE); and a deed of gift, *XḤev/Se gr* 64 (129 CE).[3]

---

1 I do not take into account here the clauses mentioning a fine to be paid to the king/emperor if the terms of the contract are changed found in *P.Yadin* 2 (99 CE) lines 13–14 = line 40; *P.Yadin* 3 (99 CE) line 18 = lines 45–46; *XḤev/Se nab* 2 (ca. 99), line 22; *P.Yadin* 4 (99 CE) lines 17–18; *P.Yadin* 5 (110 CE, frg a, col. ii line 10); on the *Fiskalmult* see Adolf Berger, *Die Strafklauseln in den Papyrusurkunden* (Leipzig: Teubner, 1911 [1965]), 31 ff.; 93 ff.

2 See Ada Yardeni, "Notes on Two Unpublished Nabataean Deeds from Naḥal Ḥever – P.Yadin 2 and 3," in *The Dead Sea Scrolls: Fifty Years after their Discovery 1947–1997*, ed. Lawrence H. Schiffman, Emanuel Tov, and James C. Vanderkam (Jerusalem: IES, 2000), 862–74.

3 The papyri cited here as *XḤev/Se ar* or *XḤev/Se gr* are published in Hannah M. Cotton and Ada Yardeni, *Aramaic, Hebrew, and Greek Documentary Texts from Naḥal Ḥever and Other Sites*, Discoveries in the Judaean Desert XXVII (Oxford: Clarendon Press, 1997); the Greek part of the Babatha archive was published in Naphtali Lewis, *The Documents from the Bar Kokhba Period in the Cave of Letters. Greek Papyri* (with Aramaic and Nabatean Signatures and Subscriptions, edited by Y. Yadin and J.C. Greenfield), Judean Desert Studies II (Jerusalem: IES, 1989). The Aramaic and Nabataean part of the Babatha archive was published by Yigael Yadin et al., *The Documents from the Bar Kokhba Period in the Cave of Letters: Hebrew, Aramaic and Nabatean-Aramaic Papyri*, Judean Desert Studies III (Jerusalem: IES, 2002). All the papyri found by Yadin in Naḥal Ḥever, both published and unpublished, are designated *P.Yadin*.

Article note: First published in *ZPE* 119 (1997): 255–265, with the following note: the text and translation of the Nabataean *P.Yadin* 2 and 3 were put at my disposal by Ada Yardeni, who also discussed them with me, and rightly insisted on understanding them literally before trying to interpret them. I am grateful to her for her collaboration in this article as well as in our joint publication of the so-called Seiyâl collection (see note 3).
Not for the first time I am indebted to Dieter Hagedorn and Werner Eck for improving my arguments and correcting my misconceptions. The imperfections still left are my own responsibility.

https://doi.org/10.1515/9783110770438-018

P.Yadin 2 and 3 of 99 CE, two Nabataean deeds of sale, were written one month apart from each other by the same scribe. They describe the sale of the same date grove by a Nabataean woman, ʼAbiʻadan daughter of ʼAftaḥ daughter of Manigros, at first to a man called Archelaus son of ʻAbdʻamiyu (*P.Yadin* 2) and a month later to Shimʻon – probably to be identified as Shimʻon bar Menaḥem, Babatha's father – (*P.Yadin* 3).[4] Both deeds contain a clause about an annual and fixed share to be paid to the Nabataean king. This clause can be reconstructed as follows from the inner and outer texts of the two almost identical contracts (*P.Yadin* 2 lines 13–14 = lines 37–38; *P.Yadin* 3 lines 15–16 = lines 41–42):

כדנה פלקת אביעדן דא על גנתא דא חלק מראנא
אכרי[5] לשנתא כות בה סאין עשרה[6] עד די יהוא אסר
חדת ותתמנא גנתא דא באתר ארכלס (שמעון) דנא
בשטרא דנה.

In such a way this (same) ʼAbiʻadan divided for this grove the share of our Lord, lease-rent for the year, in like manner ten *se'ah* therein, until there will be a new binding agreement and this grove will become part of this Archelaus' (Shimʻon's) property by the present contract.

By 19 November and 18 December, the respective dates of *P.Yadin* 2 and 3, the lease-rent (אכרי) due for the current year has not yet been paid. However, now that the date grove is changing hands, the lease-rent ought to be divided between seller and buyer. ʼAbiʻadan is saying that she divided the share to the king for the current year, presumably between herself and the buyer (פלקת ... חלק מראנא). The meaning of the phrase כות בה סאין עשרה ('in like manner ten *se'ah* therein') in this context is obscure. Assuming that the בה ('therein') refers to the 'share of our Lord,' it could be cautiously suggested that the ten *se'ah* constitute ʼAbiʻadan's part in the 'share of our Lord'; alternatively if it refers to the 'grove,' it may stand for the entire yearly share of the king in the grove. Be this as it may, this is to be done until a new agreement is made (עד די יהוא אסר חדת), and the date grove

4 I do not have an explanation for the presence of the two deeds of sale in the Babatha archive, since the latter deed must have nullified the first one.

5 אכרי is Yardeni's new reading. It is crucial of course for the interpretation offered here, but see already Cotton and Yardeni, *Aramaic, Hebrew, and Greek Documentary Texts from Naḥal Ḥever and Other Sites*, 222. The Arabic term אכרי (*'akry*) to describe a lease is attested in early Arabic legal documents, see Geoffrey Khan, "The Pre-Islamic Background of Muslim Legal Formularies," *ARAM* 6 (1994): 193–224; Yardeni, "Notes on Two Unpublished Nabataean Deeds from Naḥal Ḥever – P.Yadin 2 and 3"; see also Baruch A. Levine, "The Various Workings of the Aramaic Legal Tradition: Jews and Nabateans in the Naḥal Ḥever Archive," in *The Dead Sea Scrolls: Fifty Years after their Discovery 1947–1997*, ed. Lawrence H. Schiffman, Emanuel Tov, and James C. Vanderkam (Jerusalem: IES, 2000), 836–51.

6 Note עשרה and not עשר: for the gender of *se'ah* see Yardeni, "Notes on Two Unpublished Nabataean Deeds from Naḥal Ḥever – P.Yadin 2 and 3."

bought in the present contract actually becomes the possession of the buyer (ותתמנא גנתא דא באתר ארכלס [שמעון]).

What is meant by a ‘new binding agreement’ (אסר חדת)? It could refer to an individual private contract between the king and the new owner (Archelaus or Shim‘on) which would change or confirm the current terms of leasing and the rates. It seems more likely though that what is meant by a ‘new binding agreement’ is ‘a new order’, i. e. a periodic reorganization of all land leased from the king which was likely to be accompanied by a readjustment of the terms of lease. If this latter suggestion is accepted, it follows that ’Abi‘adan will go on paying her share to the king for as long as the ‘old order’ is still in force. The new order will confirm new owners in their possession; only then will the present contract take its final effect.[7] Unfortunately, in the absence of further information, neither suggestion can be considered more than a working hypothesis.

The status of this date grove, leased from the Nabataean king, must have been different – although we do not know in what way – from that piece of land designated in the description of the abutters as ‘the land (the garden) of our Lord, king Rab’el’ (ארע [גנת] מראנא רבאל מלכא, *P.Yadin* 2 line 4 = line 24; *P.Yadin* 3 line 5 = lines 26–27). What we know from these two documents is that Nabataean legal practice allowed for land leased from the king to be alienated and sold (twice) on the open market, and transmitted to heirs (*P.Yadin* 2 line 9 = line 31; *P.Yadin* 3 line 10 = line 33). If the explanation suggested above for the ‘new binding agreement’ is accepted, then leased land could be alienated during the ‘present order’ – even if it takes its legal effect only when ‘a new order’ is established.

Was all land in the Nabataean kingdom, unless said to belong to the king (ארע [גנת] מראנא), conceived to be on lease from him? If so, then lease-rent could be considered as equivalent to tax.

What happened after 106 CE with the advent of the Romans? Did the status of the land undergo any changes?

The date grove of *P.Yadin* 2 and 3, as has been argued elsewhere, was given to Babatha by her father probably in 120 CE, and is to be identified with one of the two Algiphiammas described in Babatha’s land declaration during the census conducted in the Roman province of Arabia in 127 (*P.Yadin* 16 lines 17–24):[8]

7 One is reminded of the periodic redistribution (*diamisthosis*) of public land in Egypt, see Jane Rowlandson, *Landowners and Tenants in Roman Egypt* (Oxford: Oxford University Press, 1996), 81 ff. The expression μέχρι τῆς ἐσομένης κοινῆς γεωργῶν διαμισθώσεως, *P.Tebt.* II 376 (162 CE) lines 14–15 recalls עד די יהוא אסר חדת of *P.Yadin* 2 and 3; cf. Dieter Hagedorn, “Flurbereinigung in Theadelpheia?,” *ZPE* 65 (1986): 93–100.

8 Hannah M. Cotton and Jonas C. Greenfield, “Babatha’s Property and the Law of Succession in the Babatha Archive,” *ZPE* 104 (1994): 211–24.

1) κῆπον φοινικῶνος ἐν ὁρίοις Μαωζων λεγόμενον Αλγιφιαμμα σπόρου κρειθῆς σάτου ἑνὸς κάβων τριῶν τελοῦντα φοίνικος συρίου καὶ μείγματος σάτα δεκαπέντε πατητοῦ σάτα δέκα στεφανικοῦ[9] μέλαν ἓν λεπτὰ[10] τριάκοντα γείτονες ὁδὸς καὶ θάλασσα; 2) κῆπον φοινικῶνος ἐν ὁρίοις Μαωζων λεγόμενον Αλγιφιαμμα σπόρου κρειθῆς κάβου ἐνό<ς> τελοῦντα τῶν γεινομένων καθ' ἔτος καρπῶν μέρος ἥμισυ γείτονες μοσχαντικὴ κυρίου Καίσαρος καὶ θάλασσα

1) A date grove within the boundaries of Maḥoza called Algiphiamma, the area of sowing one *se'ah* and three *qab* of barley, paying fifteen *se'ah* of mixed and Syrian dates, ten *se'ah* of 'splits' and as *stephanikon* one 'black' and thirty lepta, abutted by the road and the sea; 2) a date grove within the boundaries of Maḥoza called Algiphiamma, the area of sowing one *qab* of barley, paying a half share of the crops produced every year, abutted by the Moschantic estate of the emperor and by the sea.

The abutters of the date grove in *P.Yadin* 2 and 3 are 'to the east the road, and to the west the houses of *Tḥa* daughter of 'Abdḥaratat and to the south the land of our Lord, king Rab'el, who maintained life and brought deliverance to his people, and to the north the swamp': למדנחא ארחא ולמערבא בתי תחא ברת עבדחרתת ולימינא ארע מראנא רבאל מלכא די אחיי ושיזב עמה ולשמאלא רקקא (*P.Yadin* 2 lines 4–5 = lines 23–24; *P.Yadin* 3 lines 4–5 = lines 25–27).[11] Thus this date grove (whose name cannot be recovered in *P.Yadin* 3 line 3 = line 24) can be identified either as the first Algiphiamma abutted by the road and the sea (ὁδὸς καὶ θάλασσα), or as the second Algiphiamma abutted by the Moschantic estate of the emperor and the sea (μοσχαντικὴ κυρίου Καίσαρος καὶ θάλασσα), assuming that the Nabataean king's property to the south of the date grove mentioned in *P.Yadin* 2 and 3 was transformed into imperial property after the creation of the province,[12] and the 'shoals' to the north of that date grove are to be equated with the sea in *P.Yadin* 16. The ten *se'ah* of *P.Yadin* 2 and 3 do not favour one or the other of the two Algiphiammas. As was suggested above, the ten *se'ah* may represent only the seller's ('Abi'adan's) part in the yearly rent; as such they could be part of the φοίνικος συρίου καὶ μείγματος σάτα δεκαπέντε πατητοῦ σάτα δέκα στεφανικοῦ μέλαν ἓν λεπτὰ τριάκοντα of the first Algiphiamma, or part of τῶν γεινομένων καθ' ἔτος καρπῶν μέρος ἥμισυ of the second Algiphiamma. Alternatively, the annual

---

9 For the *stephanikon* see Hannah M. Cotton, "Rent or Tax Receipt from Maoza," *ZPE* 100 (1994): 553 and n. 23 there.

10 For the money units see Wolfram Weiser and Hannah M. Cotton, "'Gebt dem Kaiser, was des Kaisers ist …': Die Geldwährungen der Griechen, Juden, Nabatäer und Römer in syrisch-nabatäischen Raum unter besonderer Berücksichtigung des Kurses von Sela'/Melaina und Lepton nach der Annexion des Königreiches der Nabatäer durch Rom," *ZPE* 114 (1996): 237–87.

11 In *P.Yadin* 3, a Ḥaninu son of Taim'alahi is added on the west side, see Yardeni, "Notes on Two Unpublished Nabataean Deeds from Naḥal Ḥever – P.Yadin 2 and 3."

12 Cf. Benjamin Isaac, "The Babatha Archive: A Review Article," *IEJ* 42 (1992): 70–71.

payment in *P.Yadin* 16 may represent the 'new binding agreement' (אסר חדת) of *P.Yadin* 2 and 3, which may have changed the terms of the lease when the date grove was sold to Shim'on, Babatha's father.

The participle of τελεῖν ('paying') applied to date groves in *P.Yadin* 16 (lines 19, 22–23, 26, 30–31) as in the other land declaration from Arabia, *XḤev/Se gr* 62 (frg. a line 16; frg. b line 3; frgs. c-m lines 8, 12, 16), is taken to refer to the annual tax paid by the provincial population.[13] But does it?

In fact two locutions in *XḤev/Se gr* 62 favour an annual lease. Twice the participle τελοῦν comes together with φόρου (e. g. μέρος ἥμισυ χώρας ... τελοῦν φόρου μέλαν ἕν, etc. frg. a lines 16–17; cf. frgs. c-m line 8). Φόρος, even if it may stand for tax, is the usual term for rent.[14] Even more cogent is the presence of the term [ἐ]γ̣ιαύσιον to describe the field declared in *XḤev/Se gr* 62:

ἀπο̣γράφομαι ἐμαυτὸν ἐτῶν τριάκοντ̣α̣
[...]η̣λ̣γ̣ι̣ογ̣ [ἐ]γ̣ιαύσιον μέρος ἥμισυ χώ̣ρας
ἐν ὁρίοις Μαωζων τῆς προγ̣ε̣γραμμέ̣ν̣ης̣
λ̣εγ̣ο̣μ̣έ̣νης Αρενοαραθα μετ̣οχῆς τῆς πρὸς
Ἰωναθην Σιμωνος ὃ μέρ̣ο̣ς ἥμισύ ἐστιν σπόρο̣υ̣
κρ̣ειθῆς σάτου ἑ̣[ν]ὸ̣ς κάβων τριῶ̣ν̣ τελοῦν
φόρου μέλαν ἓν λεπτὰ τεσ̣σ̣α̣ράκοντα πέντε.

I register myself, thirty years old, [as owner of?] a yearly half share of a field, called Arenoaratha, within the boundaries of the aforesaid Maḥoza, in partnership with Ionathes son of Shim'on, which half share is (the area) of sowing one *se'ah* three *qab* of barley, paying as tax one 'black' and forty-five *lepta*.

Unfortunately it is impossible to restore the word before [ἐ]γ̣ιαύσιον μέρος ἥμισυ χώ̣ρας, but the [ἐ]γ̣ιαύσιον strongly suggests 'a yearly lease,' or rather 'a lease for one year.'

If the date groves declared in *P.Yadin* 16 and *XḤev/Se gr* 62 were on lease from the emperor, then the payments mentioned in them are of rents and not of taxes, though it may seem odd at first sight that rent rather than tax is declared at the census. Nevertheless, the status of the land declared must have been different from that described in *P.Yadin* 16 as 'the Moschantic estate of the emperor' (μοσχαντικὴ κυρίου Καίσαρος), in the same way that the land sold by 'Abi'adan daughter of 'Aftaḥ to Shim'on bar Menaḥem, Babatha's father, although it paid

13 And so it is translated by Lewis, *The Documents from the Bar Kokhba Period in the Cave of Letters. Greek Papyri*, 68: 'paying as tax'; it is used wrongly as an argument for postulating that the annual payment mentioned in *XḤev/Se gr* 64 lines 28–30 is that of tax and not of rent, see Cotton and Yardeni, *Aramaic, Hebrew, and Greek Documentary Texts from Naḥal Ḥever and Other Sites*, 223; see more below.

14 Cf. Sherman Leroy Wallace, *Taxation in Egypt from Augustus to Diocletian* (Princeton: Princeton University Press, 1938), 71–2; Herbert C. Youtie, *Scriptiunculae*, Vol. II (Amsterdam: Hakkert, 1973), 751 (reprint of a review of Wallace's book); Hans-Albert Rupprecht, *Studien zur Quittung im Recht der graeco-ägyptischen Papyri* (München: Beck, 1971), 30.

lease-rent to the Nabataean king (see above on אכרי) is likely to have been of a different status from the piece of land designated in *P.Yadin* 2 and 3 as 'the land (the garden) of our Lord, king Rab'el' (ארע [גנת] מראנא רבאל מלכא).[15]

Similarly, it is hard to decide whether tax or rent is the subject of two very similar receipts from the archive of Salome Komaïse daughter of Levi: one is in Greek from 29 January 125 (*XḤev/Se gr* 60) and the other one, in Aramaic, was written exactly six years later, on 30 January 131 (*XḤev/Se ar* 12). The text and a translation of both follow:

XḤev/Se gr 60:

1. [–ca.?–] .θ.[–ca.?–]
2. [–ca.?–]ε̣τ̣[–ca.?–]
3. α[. . .]ς̣ Ιουδα κ̣αὶ ἑτα[ῖρ]ο̣ι̣ Μ[α]να[ημῳ]
4. Ι[ωα]ν̣ου χαίρ̣ι̣[ν]. ἀ̣πέσ̣[χ̣]α̣μεν π̣[αρὰ σοῦ]
5. τειμὴν φο̣ί̣ν̣ι̣κο̣ς οὗ ὀ̣φείλεις Κ̣[υ]ρ̣ίῳ
6. Καίσαρι ἐν Μαώζα̣ ἔτους ὀκτωκαι-
7. δεκάτου, ἐξ ὧν ἀπειλήφαμεν παρὰ
8. σοῦ ἐ̣κ χερὸς Σ̣α̣μμούου Σίμωνος μέ-
9. λανες τέσσαρε̣ς. \λεπτὰ πεντήκοντα ὀκτώ/ ἐγράφη ἐν Μαώζα̣ ἐπὶ
10. [ὑ]πάτων τῶν μετ̣ὰ̣ ὑ̣πατίαν Γλ̣α̣βρίωνος
11. [κ]αὶ Θη̣βανιανοῦ, ἔ̣τ̣ο̣[υ]ς̣ ἐννεακαιδε̣[κάτ]ου
12. μη̣ν̣ὸ̣ς [Π]ε̣ρειτ̣ί̣ου τ[εσσα]ρ[εσκ] α̣ιδε[κάτη]
13. רישה כתבה

[Names and patronyms] [ ] son of Judah and colleagues to Menaḥem son of Iohannes greetings. We received from you the amount due for dates, which you owe to our Lord the Emperor in Maḥoza for the eighteenth year (of the province). On account of which we have now received from you through Sammouos son of Shim'on four blacks (and) fifty-eight lepta-units. Written in Maḥoza in the year of the consulate which comes after that of Glabrio and Thebanianus, the nineteenth year (of the province), the fourteenth day in the month of Peritios. Reisha wrote this.

15 *P.Yadin* 2 line 4 = line 24; *P.Yadin* 3 line 5 = lines 26–27.

XḤev/Se ar 12:

1.	*Šlm*, daughter of Levi; your brother	שלם ברת לוי אחוך	.1
2.	*Yḥ* ... son of *T h*, and my friend	יח°° בר תשה וחברי	.2
3.	*Šm*[...,] we received from you the value in money of	שמ[ ]קבלן צ/ד מי	.3
4.	dates – *se'ah* ten	תמרין סאין עשר	.4
5.	and nine and a *qab* and a half,	ותשע וקב ופלג	.5
6.	which is with you(?), from ... Levi	ע°/די עמד מן בב לוי	.6
7.	your father, in the year	אבוך בשנת	.7
8.	twenty-four (or: And as such)	עשר[י]ן ו /// כזא	.8
9.	in the day ten and fi-	ביום עשרה וח	.9
10.	ve of Shevat,	משה בשבט	.10
11.	year twenty-	שנת עשרין	.11
12.	fi[ve] of the Eparch[y.]	וח[מ]ש להפרכ[יה].	.12
13.	*Td/ḥ*[...] wrote it.	ת ד/ח °°כתבה	.13

In both receipts we find more than one tax or rent collector described as 'colleagues'; the dates, 29 and 30 January respectively, imply that the tax or rent was collected at that time of year. The doubtful word דמי in line 3 of the Aramaic receipt is the construct-state of the word דמין (price, money, value), which is here the exact equivalent of τιμή of the Greek receipt.[16] Thus lines 3–5 of the Aramaic receipt קבלן מנך דמי תמרין סאין עשר ותשע וקב ופלג 'We received from you the value in money (דמי) for nineteen and a quarter *se'ah* of dates,' are the exact equivalent of Ἀπέσ[χ]αμεν π[αρὰ σοῦ] τειμὴν φοίνικος of lines 4–5 of the Greek receipt. The expression דמי תמרין suggests that an *adaeratio* took place, i. e. the nineteen and a quarter *se'ah* of dates were paid in cash – like the procedure in the Greek receipt – rather than in kind, even though the sum in money is not specified. It is very tempting to interpret the three vertical strokes with a horizontal stroke going through them, following the 'twenty' (עשרין) and the *waw* in line 8 of the Aramaic receipt as standing for the digit 4 (rather than for the doubtful וכזא) – thus 'in the twenty-fourth year.' The parallel with the Greek receipt will then be complete: just as in the Greek receipt, where the tax or rent due for 'the eighteenth year of the province' is paid in the 'nineteenth year of the province,' in the Aramaic receipt the tax or rent for 'the twenty-fourth year' is paid in the 'twenty-fifth year of the province' (lines 11–12). Finally, the date in both receipts comes at the end. This is unlike all other Aramaic deeds from the Judaean Desert; it seems to follow the conventions of receipts in Greek.

16 τιμή is sometimes transliterated as טימי in Aramaic; see Michael Sokoloff, *A Dictionary of Jewish Palestinian Aramaic of the Byzantine Period* (Ramat-Gan: Bar-Ilan University Press, 1990), 223.

The striking resemblance between the two receipts suggests that the land for which tax or rent was paid was of the same status. The apparent presence of more than one revenue collector might suggest that both receipts deal with a body of *conductores* on an imperial estate.[17] In Egypt, however, ordinary taxes were often collected by a group of people.[18] We have no information about the system of taxation which operated in Arabia before or after 106 CE. The crucial question seems to be whether ὀ̣φείλεις Κ̣[υ]ρ̣ίῳ Καίσαρι in lines 5–6 of the Greek receipt could be used to describe the public purse, i. e. the ordinary taxes, or whether it signifies exclusively the emperor's private property, i. e. the lease-rent.

The same doubts are raised by the payment mentioned in *XḤev/Se gr* 64, a deed of gift from 129 CE, which belongs to the same archive.[19] In this document written in singularly ungrammatical and non-idiomatic Greek the mother Salome Gropte (or Grapte)[20] makes an immediate gift of a date grove in Maḥoza to her daughter Salome Komaïse:

Inner text: lines 6–11
ὁμολογῶ ἐνεγο̣χ̣[έ]ν̣αι σ̣ο̣ι̣ ε̣ἰ̣ς̣ δόσιν ἀπὸ τῆς
σήμερον δόσιν αἰωνίου τὰ ὑπάρχοντά μοι
ἐν Μαωζας ἃ εἴδη ὑποτεταγμένα· κ̣ῆ̣πον
φοινεικῶνος κ̣α̣λούμενον Γαννα̣θ Ασαδαια
σὺν ὕδατος αὐτῆς ἐφ' ἡ̣μερῶν ἑπτὰ εἰς
ἑπτὰ ἡμέραν̣ τετάρτη ἡ̣[μ]ι̣ωρ<ί>αν μ̣ί̣α̣ν·
ἧ̣ς γείτωνες ἀνα[το]λῶν κῆπον κυρ̣ι̣α̣κὸν
καλο̣ύ̣μ̣ενον Γανναθ Αββ̣α̣ιδαια δυσμῶν
κληρον̣ό̣[μ]ο̣ι Αρετας νότου ὁδὸς̣ βορρᾶ
κληρονόμοι Ιωσηπος Βαβα

Outer text: lines 26–33
τὰ ὑπάρχοντα αὐτῆ̣ς ἃ ε̣ἴ̣δη ἐ̣γ̣ [Μ]αωζας
ὑποτεταγμ<έν>α· κ̣ῆπον φοινεικώνων
καλούμεν̣ον Γ̣α̣νναθ Ασαδαια σὺν ὕδατος
το̣ῦ αὐτοῦ κήπου ἐφ' [ἡ]μερῶν ἑπτὰ εἰς ἑπτὰ
ἡμ̣έραν τετάρτη̣ ἡμιωρ<ί>αν μίαν <ἣ> τελέσει
καθ ἔτος εἰς λόγον κυριακοῦ φίσκου {καθ
ἔτος} φοίνεικος πατη̣τοῦ σάτα δέκα καὶ συροῦ
καὶ ναα̣ρου σάτα ἕξ, ἧ̣ς γείτωνες ἀν̣ατολῶν
κῆπον κυριακὸν καλούμενον Γαννα̣θ
Αββα̣ιδαια δυσμῶν κληρονό̣μοι Αρετας νότου
ὁδὸς βορ̣ρ̣ᾶ̣ [κλ]ηρονόμοι Ιωσηπος Βαβα.

17 On the three-tiered administration of imperial estates in Egypt see George M. Parássoglou, *Imperial Estates in Roman Egypt* (Amsterdam: Hakkert, 1978), 52; 57; Dennis P. Kehoe, *Management and Investment on Estates in Roman Egypt during the Early Empire* (Bonn: Habelt, 1992), 16 ff.; for North Africa see Dennis P. Kehoe, *The Economics of Agriculture on Roman Imperial Estates in North Africa* (Göttingen: Vandenhoeck & Ruprecht, 1988), 117–53. A general survey in Dorothy J. Crawford, "Imperial Estates," in *Studies in Roman Property*, ed. Moses I. Finley (Cambridge: Cambridge University Press, 1976), 57–70.

18 See Wallace, *Taxation in Egypt from Augustus to Diocletian*, 286 ff.

19 The Excursus on these lines in Cotton and Yardeni, *Aramaic, Hebrew, and Greek Documentary Texts from Naḥal Ḥever and Other Sites*, 221–23, has some misconceptions which I have tried to correct here.

20 It is Gropte in *XḤev/Se gr* 64 line 3, but Grapte in *XḤev/Se gr* 63 line 9 – a deed of renunciation by the daughter, Salome Komaïse, to her mother.

(In the translation the inner text is written in Roman font; the outer text is written in italics; when the texts coincide, it is written in bold): 'I acknowledge that I have given you as a gift from this day and for ever my (*her*) **property in Maḥoza, which items are listed as follows: a date orchard called the Garden of Asadaia with** its [*the*] **water [allowance]** (*of that orchard*), **once a week on the fourth day, for one half-hour** *which will pay every year to the account of the fiscus of our Lord ten se'ah of 'splits', and six se'ah of the Syrian and the na'aran dates.* **The abutters on the east the orchard of our Lord [the emperor] called the Garden of 'Abbaid-aia, on the west the heirs of Aretas, on the south a road and on the north the heirs of Yosef son of Baba.'**

The crucial lines appear only in the outer text (lines 28–30):

<ἣ> τελέσει καθ ἔτος εἰς λόγον κυριακοῦ φίσκου φοίνεικος πατητοῦ σάτα δέκα καὶ συροῦ καὶ ναaρου σάτα ἕξ.	It (i. e. the date grove) will pay every year to the account of the *fiscus* of our Lord ten *se'ah* of 'splits', and six *se'ah* of the Syrian and the na'aran dates.

Does the annual payment in kind 'to the account of the *fiscus* of our Lord' imply that the date grove given in gift was on lease from the emperor?

Several expressions suggest at first sight that we are dealing in *XḤev/Se gr* 64 with private property: first, the use of the term τὰ ὑπάρχοντα, and, more particularly, τὰ ὑπάρχοντά μοι (αὐτῆς) ἐν Μαωζας (lines 7 and 25), to describe the property given in gift.[21] Secondly, the fact that the date grove is said to be given as a gift forever – εἰς δόσιν ἀπὸ τῆς σήμερον δόσιν αἰωνίου (lines 6–7) – repeated in different terms in the concluding declaration – ἔχειν τὴν π̣ρ̣ο̣[γ]εγραμμένην Κομαΐ[σην τὴν] προ̣γ̣εγραμμένην δόσ[ι]ν κ̣υ̣ρίως καὶ βεβ̣[αίως] ε̣ἰ̣ς τ̣ὸ̣ν ἄππαν[τα χρόνον] (lines 39–41) – also seems to point to private ownership.

However, these objections to the lease theory can easily be met. The verb ὑπάρχειν, i. e. 'possess,' is used by tenants on the *ge basilike* in Egypt to refer to the land they are cultivating; people came to think of land held for many generations in their families as their own. Nor should the assertions that the land is given forever be taken too literally. Similar expressions (e. g. ἀπὸ τοῦ νῦν ἐπὶ τὸν ἅπαντα χρόνον) occur in Egypt in division of 'public land' (βασιλικὴ γῆ) between brothers (e. g. *P.Mich.* IX 556–7); presumably no more is meant than 'as long as we lease the land,' which *de facto* might well be forever.

Finally the presence of an imperial orchard as one of the abutters of the date grove given in gift could be taken to imply that this date grove is not a κῆπος

21 See Friedrich Preisigke, *Wörterbuch der griechischen Papyrusurkunden* (Berlin: Erben, 1925), s. v. ὑπάρχω.

κυριακός.[22] But this reasoning too is not compelling. We may be witnessing here a wholesale transfer of Nabataean terms of ownership. The Roman emperor stepped into the Nabataean king's possessions without altering the terms of ownership: the expression κῆπος κυριακός describes what used to be ארע [גנת] מראנא – of which it is a literal translation – under the Nabataean king, whereas the date grove given in gift was of the same status as the land sold by 'Abi'adan on the open market in 99 CE (*P.Yadin* 2 and 3 discussed above), i. e. on lease from the emperor.

Pieces of land which belonged to what is commonly and vaguely called the 'imperial estate' may well have possessed different statuses, thereby faithfully reflecting their pre-Roman status. It is a fact that land owned by the *fiscus* was exploited in different ways: between land leased to tenants and land worked by slaves under a *vilicus*, "there was still an infinite range of local variations."[23] It is possible, therefore, that a date grove described as κῆπος κυριακός would be cultivated directly by the *fiscus*, whereas others would be leased to tenants – probably to hereditary tenants who would speak of it as their own property. There are examples of 'perpetual leaseholds' from other parts of the empire: in Egypt the lease of οὐσιακὴ γῆ could be transmitted to heirs.[24] An inscription attests hereditary leaseholds on an imperial estate in Lydia.[25] We also have the evidence of the North African inscriptions for 'perpetual leaseholds' held under the terms of the Lex Manciana: '*[Qui in f(undo) Vill<a>e Magn<a>e Varia]n<a>e siv<e> Mappali<a>e Sig[<a>e ficetum olivetum vineas se]verunt severin[t, eis eam superficiem heredibus], qui e legitim[is matrimoniis nati sunt eruntve], testamento relinquere permittitur*,' *CIL* VIII 25902 (the Henchir-Mettich inscription), col. IV lines 2–6.[26]

22 κῆπον κυριακὸν καλούμμενον Γανναθ Αββαιδαια, lines 10 and 31–32.

23 Crawford, "Imperial Estates," 44; cf. Dieter Flach, *Römische Agrargeschichte* (München: Beck, 1990), 82 ff. For complexity of land tenure see for example K.T.M. Atkinson, "A Hellenistic Land-Conveyance: The Estate of Mnesimachus in the Plain of Sardis," *Historia* 21 (1972): 45–74. (I am grateful to I. Shatzman for pointing this out to me).

24 On *Erbpacht*, see Hans-Christian Kuhnke, "Οὐσιακὴ γῆ. Domänenland in den Papyri der Prinzipatszeit" (Universität zu Köln Thesis, 1971), 99: "Nach allem gibt es bei ... οὐσιακὴ γῆ keine Eigentumsübertragung. Sie sind res extra commercium. Möglich ist allein eine Vergabe in Erbpacht," and see nn. 2 and 3 there; cf. Otto Eger, *Zum ägyptischen Grundbuchwesen in römischer Zeit* (Leipzig and Berlin: Teubner, 1909), 32.

25 Frank Frost Abbott and Allan Chester Johnson, *Municipal Administration in the Roman Empire* (Princeton: Princeton University Press, 1926), p. 478, no. 142, 200–250 CE.

26 The quotation follows Dieter Flach's text, "Inschriftenuntersuchungen zum römischen Kolonat in Nordafrika," *Chiron* 8 (1978): 480 (this paragraph defines the *usus proprius* of col. I, lines 9–10 of the Lex Manciana, cf. Flach, 445–6); cf. *CIL* VIII 25943 (Ain Wassel inscription), col. I, lines 7–13 (Flach, 487): *<i>isque qui occupaverint possidendi ac fru<en>di{i} eredique suo relinquendi id ius datur quod e<s>t lege Ha<drian>a comprehensum de rudibus agris et iis, qui per X an<n>os continuos inculti sunt*; see Dennis P. Kehoe, "Lease Regulations for Imperial Estates in

The *Tablettes Albertini* (*FIRA*, Vol. III, no. 139) prove that this was still true many years later, when private landlords replaced the emperor as owner of these lands. Thus, the fact that the date grove is spoken of as privately owned and given as 'a gift forever' does not, in itself, force us to regard it as private property *stricto sensu*.

The fact that the annual payment is in kind rather than in cash could have been adduced as further support for the view that this deed involves the lease of imperial land and the annual payment of rent for it – but the argument is not unassailable. It is certainly true that, in Egypt, taxes on vineyard and garden-land (which includes date groves) were converted into money terms (*adaeratio*),[27] whereas in leases of date groves one finds both kinds of payment.[28] However, the Romans may have inherited the evaluation, and perhaps also the payment, of taxes in kind from the Nabataean kings, just as they seem to have inherited from them the payment designated *stephanikon*, whatever this term represented.[29] Furthermore, taxes in the Roman empire were sometimes paid in kind.[30] Alternatively, an *adaeratio* might have followed later, as is likely to have happened for the rent or tax for dates (דמי תמרין) mentioned in the Aramaic receipt (*XḤev/Se ar* 12, lines 3–4): the φοίνεικος πατητοῦ σάτα δέκα καὶ συροῦ καὶ ναaρου σάτα ἕξ may have been converted into cash when actual payment took place. Thus we cannot use the payment in kind to buttress the suggestion that the land in question was on lease from the emperor.

Nor can the straightforward implication of the text that the yearly payment went into the imperial *fiscus* (εἰς λόγον κυριακοῦ φίσκου) determine incontrovertibly whether the date grove given in gift is private property or on lease from the emperor. Even those who claim that in the first two centuries the annual taxes (even from the imperial provinces) did not go into the imperial *fiscus*,[31] and con-

North Africa. Part II," *ZPE* 59 (1985): 156–59; Kehoe, *The Economics of Agriculture on Roman Imperial Estates in North Africa*, 39; Kehoe, *Management and Investment on Estates in Roman Egypt during the Early Empire*, 50.

27 Wallace, *Taxation in Egypt from Augustus to Diocletian*, 47 ff.

28 Nicolas Hohlwein, "Palmiers et palmeraies dans l'Égypte romaine," *Études de Papyrologie* 5 (1939): 65–74.

29 See above n. 8.

30 E.g. the *frumentum mancipale* in Sicily; cf. also the *Lex Portorii Asiae* from 62 CE which attests the payment of the *decuma* in kind: Helmut Engelmann and Dieter Knibbe, *Das Zollgesetz der Provinz Asia* (Bonn: Habelt, 1989), 25, lines 72–73 (*AE* 1989, no. 681). See the general survey of taxation in money and kind in the Roman Empire in Richard Duncan-Jones, *Structure and Scale in the Roman Economy* (Cambridge: Cambridge University Press, 1991), 187–98.

31 Fergus Millar, "The Fiscus in the First Two Centuries," *JRS* 53 (1963): 29 ff. Millar mentions possible exceptions to his claim on pp. 40–41 and in *The Emperor in the Roman World* (London:

sequently that the date grove must be part of the imperial estate, i. e. part of the *patrimonium*, would concede that in εἰς λόγον κυριακοῦ φίσκου as well as in the ὀφείλεις Κ[υ]ρίῳ Καίσαρι in the receipt from 125 CE (*XḤev/Se gr* 60 lines 5–6) we have a case of "loose terminology":[32] whoever wrote the deed of gift or the receipt was convinced that the monies belonged to the emperor. In other words, the fact that the yearly payment is said to go to the *fiscus* cannot be used to support the claim that the date grove is on lease from the emperor; nor, if the date grove was private property on which there was an annual tax in kind, can we use this text to record a stage in the process of the development of the imperial *fiscus* into the public chest any more than we can use for this purpose the evidence of the New Testament, where people speak about the annual taxes, κῆνσος and φόρος, as being paid 'to the emperor.'[33]

This last point gains force from the following considerations: the imperial procurator in Arabia, whose seat was in faraway Gerasa,[34] was in charge of both the annual tax and the rent from the imperial estates; both tax and rent are likely to have been collected by the same local tax collectors. Neither the tax collectors of *XḤev/Se gr* 60 nor the scribe of *XḤev/Se gr* 64 were necessarily aware of the division between private and public monies which may well have taken place in the office of the procurator in Gerasa, or later on in Rome.

Can the evidence concerning land tenure found in the papyri from the Judaean Desert gain from a comparison with the situation in Egypt?

Roman Egypt was divided into two principal land categories – public and private. Both categories were administered by the *dioikesis*.[35] The private property of the emperor, the imperial estates, "began to be administered as a category of the public land" when the Flavians formed the *ousiakos logos*.[36] All public land paid rent; private land paid tax. In addition private land could be freely disposed

Duckworth, 1977), 623 ff.; see Michael Alpers, *Das nachrepublikanische Finanzsystem: Fiscus und Fisci in der frühen Kaiserzeit* (Berlin: De Gruyter, 1995), 1–20 for a survey of opinions. A brief and lucid discussion in Werner Eck, Antonio Caballos, and Fernando Fernández, *Das senatus consultum de Cn. Pisone patre* (München: Beck, 1996), 179–80.

32 Millar, *The Emperor in the Roman World*, 625.

33 To the question ἔξεστι δοῦναι κῆνσον Καίσαρι; ἢ οὔ (Matt 22:17) Jesus answers with the famous: Ἀπόδοτε οὖν τὰ Καίσαρος Καίσαρι (Matt 22:21; cf. Mark 12:14; 12:17; φόρος replaces κῆνσος in Luke 20:22: ἔξεστι ὑμᾶς Καίσαρι φόρον δοῦναι). See also Luke 23:2, where Jesus is charged with obstructing the payment of the tribute: κωλύοντα Καίσαρι φόρους διδόναι.

34 Cf. Benjamin Isaac, *The Limits of Empire: The Roman Army in the East*, 2nd ed. (Oxford: Clarendon Press, 1992), 345 f.

35 See Rowlandson, *Landowners and Tenants in Roman Egypt*, 29 ff. I shall be using her lucid distinctions in what follows.

36 Rowlandson, 30.

of through sale, gift or inheritance.[37] The rates of rent on public land were significantly higher than tax rates on private land.[38]

Certain locutions found in the papyri from the Judaean Desert imply that land once leased from the Nabataean kings was now leased from the Roman emperor. Such expressions and practices as seem to imply that the land in question was privately owned, i. e. the alienation of such land through sale, gift or succession, can be reconciled, albeit uncomfortably, with hereditary tenancy. The wholesale adaptation of modes of Nabataean land tenure by the Romans is not uncharacteristic. Far more disturbing are the declarations of leased land, if that is what it was, in the census of 127 CE. That the land declaration was part of a provincial census is made clear in the two declarations which use almost identical language to describe it:

P.Yadin 16 lines 11–15
ἀποτιμήσεως Ἀραβίας ἀ̣γ̣ομένης ὑπὸ Τίτου
Ἀνεινίου Σεξστίου Φλωρεντείνου πρεσβευτοῦ
Σεβαστοῦ ἀντιστρατήγου, Βαβθα Σίμωνος
Μαωζηνὴ τῆς Ζοαρηνῆς περιμέτρου
Πέτρας, οἰκοῦσα ἐν ἰδίοις ἐν αὐτῇ Μαωζα̣,
ἀπογράφομα̣ι̣ ἃ κέκτημαι.

XḤev/Se gr 62 frg. a lines 10–13
ἀποτειμήσεως Ἀραβίας ἀγομένης ὑ̣[πὸ Τ]
[ι]τ̣[ο]υ̣ Ἀ̣[νεινίου Σεξτίου] Φ̣λ̣ω̣ρ̣ε̣ν̣τ̣είνο[υ]
π̣ρ̣ε̣σ̣β̣ευτ̣ο̣ῦ̣ Σ̣εβαστ̣ο̣ῦ̣ ἀ̣γτιστρατ̣ή̣γ̣ο̣υ.
Σ̣α̣μμ̣ο̣υος Σ̣ιμων[ο]ς Μαωζηνὸς τῆς Ζοαρηνῆς
περιμέτρου Πέτρας, ο̣ἰ̣κῶν [ἐ]ν ἰδίοις ἐν αὐτῇ
Μαωζα̣, ἀπ̣ο̣γράφομαι ἐμαυτὸν ... etc.

No other land declarations from the Roman world have survived. The Egyptian fourteen-year cycle census declarations[39] involve only people and house property, never agricultural land. Thus no comparison is to hand. Is it possible that land on lease from the emperor and the rents paid on it were declared in the provincial census? Or is the declaration itself a good enough reason to postulate that we are dealing here with taxes on private land? If the latter is the case, then those expressions which suggest lease and rent are in fact fossilized juristic terms inherited from the Nabataeans but now stripped of all meaning.

---

37 Rowlandson, 29.

38 Rowlandson, 71 ff.

39 The basic study on which is still Marcel Hombert and Claire Préaux, *Recherches sur le recensement dans l'Egypte romaine* (Leiden: Brill, 1952); see Roger S. Bagnall and Bruce W. Frier, *The Demography of Roman Egypt* (Cambridge: Cambridge University Press, 1994). Egyptian property returns, ἀπογραφαί, even if required by an official order, were not intended for the purpose of taxation, see Austin M. Harmon, "Egyptian Property-Returns," in *Yale Classical Studies, Vol. IV*, ed. Austin M. Harmon (New Haven: Yale University Press, 1934), 135–234 with Herbert C. Youtie, "Review: Egyptian Property-Returns by Austin M. Harmon," *AJA* 40 (1936): 282–84 and Claire Préaux, "Déclarations de propriété foncière dans l'Égypte romaine," *Chronique d'Egypte* 10 (1935): 393–96.

Appendix: Land Units and their Taxes or Rents

The table below is an update of a table which appeared in Wolfram Weiser and Hannah M. Cotton, "'Gebt dem Kaiser, was des Kaisers ist ...': Die Geldwährungen der Griechen, Juden, Nabatäer und Römer im syrisch-nabatäischen Raum unter besonderer Berücksichtigung des Kurses von Sela'/Melaina und Lepton nach der Annexion des Königreiches der Nabatäer durch Rom', *ZPE* 114 (1997): 238. It is based on data found in five papyri from the Province of Arabia: *P.Yadin* 16 and *XḤev/Se gr* 60, 62, 64 and *XḤev/Se ar* 12. It attempts to convey the relations between size of land and the amount of tax or rent, both in kind and in cash, on them. Only for the two land declarations, *P.Yadin* 16 and *XḤev/Se gr* 62, do we have both size of land and rates of tax or rent.

It seems that the land declared in *XḤev/Se gr* 62 was made up of small plots. Babatha's plots, declared in *P.Yadin* 16, were generally much larger. The fact that each piece of land, in *P.Yadin* 16 as well as in *XḤev/Se gr* 62 and 64, has its own name (and thus, presumably, its own history), suggests that land was accumulated by one family over time.[40]

The size of land is conveyed in the documents in *bet se'ah*, i. e. the size of land sown by a *se'ah* of wheat. The tax or rent, when paid in kind, is conveyed in units of volume, i. e. the *se'ah*, translated in Greek as σάτον. There is disagreement about the area corresponding to *bet se'ah* and the capacity of the *se'ah*.

There does not seem to be any constant ratio between the rate of tax and the size of land, in as far as we have these. The rates are in Αλγιφιαμμα (*P.Yadin* 16 lines 17 ff.): 1:10; 1:6.66; and 1:0.86; Βαγαλγαλα (*P.Yadin* 16 lines 24 ff.): 1:10; 1:10; and 1:1.1; Βηθφααραια (*P.Yadin* 16 lines 29 ff.): 1:4.5; 1:3; and 1:0.42; Αρενοαραθα (*XḤev/Se gr* 62 frg. a lines 14 ff.): 1:0.96; Χαφφουρα (*XḤev/Se gr* 62 frgs. c-m lines 7 ff.): 1:1.1; and Χαφφουρα (*XḤev/Se gr* 62 frgs. c-m lines 14 ff.): 1:3.12; 1:3.12.

The only remarkable fact is the low rates paid by Βηθφααραια (*P.Yadin* 16 lines 30 ff.) in contrast with the high rates paid by Χαφφουρα (*XḤev/Se gr* 62 frgs. c-m lines 14 ff.), which may be due to the quality of the soil and the resultant yields.[41] The monetary tax or rent is variously described as τειμὴ φοίνικος (*XḤev/Se gr* 60 line 5), φόρος[42] (*XḤev/Se gr* 62 frg. a line 16, frgs. c-m line 8), and sometimes στεφανικόν (e. g. *P.Yadin* 16 lines 20, 27, 32; *XḤev/Se* 62 frgs. c-m lines 17–18).[43] The

40 See Magen Broshi, "Agriculture and Economy in Roman Palestine: Seven Notes on the Babatha Archive," *IEJ* 42 (1992): 240.

41 Cf. Hyginus Gromaticus, *Constitutio limitum*, in Carl Olof Thulin, ed., *Corpus agrimensorum Romanorum I: Opuscula agrimensorum veterum* (Leipzig: Teubner, 1913), 168 f.

42 Indicated in the table by #.

43 Indicated in the table by *; on the *stephanikon*, see note 9 above.

monetary tax or rent seems to be loosely related to the size of land and the tax or rent in kind. Our estimation of the rate is further hampered by our ignorance of the respective value of 'blacks' and *lepta*: how many *lepta* made up one 'black'?[44]

44 See note 10 above.

	Name of Grove	Size (*Bet Se'ah*)	Tax or Rent in *Se'ah* on Dates[45]	Tax or Rent in *Se'ah* on 'Splits'[46]	Monetary Tax or Rent * = στεφανικόν # = φόρος	Other Kind of Tax or Rent
XḤev/Se gr 60	–	–	–	–	4 blacks; 58 lepta	
P.Yadin 16	Αλγιφιαμμα	1.5 *bet se'ah*	15 *se'ah*	10 *se'ah*	* 1 black; 30 lepta	
	Αλγιφιαμμα	1/6 *bet se'ah*			none	half–share of the crops
	Βαγαλγαλα	3 *bet se'ah*	30 *se'ah*	30 *se'ah*	* 3 blacks; 30 lepta	
	Βαγαλγαλα	20 *bet se'ah*	90 *se'ah*	60 *se'ah*	* 8 blacks; 45 lepta	
XḤev/Se gr 62 frg. a	Αρενοαραθα	1.5 *bet se'ah*	none	none	# 1 black; 45 lepta	
	Χαφφουρα	–	–	–	–	
XḤev/Se gr 62 frg. b	?	0.125 *bet se'ah*	–	–	–	
	Γανναθ ...χ.βασα	less than 1 *bet se'ah*	–	–	–	
XḤev/Se gr 62 frg. c-m	Χαφφουρα	1 *bet se'ah*	none	none	# 1 black; 10 lepta	
	Γανναθ.οραθ	–	unknown amount of Syrian dates	–	–	
	Χαφφουρα	0.08 *bet se'ah*	2.5 *se'ah*	2.5 *se'ah*	* unknown amount	
XḤev/Se gr 64	Γανναθ Ἀσαδαια	–	6 *se'ah*	10 *se'ah*	none	
XḤev/Se ar 12	–	–	none	none	none	19.25 *se'ah* of dates, kind not specified

45 This category includes Syrian, mixed, and/or na'aran dates which are taxed together in the documents. For na'aran dates see Broshi, "Agriculture and Economy in Roman Palestine: Seven Notes on the Babatha Archive," 233.

46 Πατητός in Greek. This is a particularly juicy variety of dates which bursts open on the tree itself; see Hohlwein, "Palmiers et palmeraies dans l'Égypte romaine," 18–22.

Ἡ νέα ἐπαρχεία Ἀραβία: The New Province of Arabia in the Papyri from the Judaean Desert

The era of the Roman province of Arabia began on 22 March 106 CE.[1] The earliest document which bears the provincial year in its dating formula is the Greek *P.Yadin* 5 from 2 June 110 CE: τῆς δὲ κατ̣[αστ]ά̣σ̣ε̣ω̣[ς τῆς] ἐπαρχείας ἔτους πέμπτου (lines 3–4).[2] The next four documents bear the formula על מנין הפרכיה דא, 'according to the era of this hyparchia' (i. e. the province of Arabia) in their opening: *P.Yadin* 6 (119 CE, Nabataean) line 1; *P.Yadin* 7 (120 CE, Aramaic) lines 1–2 = lines 31–32;[3] *P.Yadin* 8 (122 CE, Aramaic) lines 2–3; *P.Yadin* 9 (122 CE, Nabataean) line 2. Then we have *XḤev/Se gr* 60 from 29 January 125 CE,[4] where the provincial year, without τῆς ἐπαρχείας (or τῆς ἐπαρχείας Ἀραβίας),[5] is given at the end: ἔ̣τ̣ο̣[υ]ς ἐννεακαιδε̣[κάτ]ου (line 11). Two Greek papyri from the Babatha archive from 11 or 12 October 125 CE bear an identical formula at the opening: κατὰ δὲ τὸν ἀριθμὸν τῆς ἐπαρχείας Ἀραβίας ἔτους εἰκοστοῦ (*P.Yadin* 14 lines 17–18; 15 line 2 = lines 15–16).

1 See Rudolf Ernst Brünnow and Alfred von Domaszewski, *Die Provincia Arabia*, Vol. III (Strasbourg: Trübner, 1909), 303; Glen W. Bowersock, "The Annexation and Initial Garrison of Arabia," *ZPE* 5 (1970): 37–47; Glen W. Bowersock, "A Report on Arabia Provincia," *JRS* 61 (1971): 231.

2 Cf. *IGLS* XXI.2 26 ('year 43,' Madaba). The *P.Yadin* so far published can be found in Naphtali Lewis, *The Documents from the Bar Kokhba Period in the Cave of Letters. Greek Papyri*, Judean Desert Studies II (Jerusalem: IES, 1989); Yigael Yadin et al., *The Documents from the Bar Kokhba Period in the Cave of Letters: Hebrew, Aramaic and Nabatean-Aramaic Papyri*, Judean Desert Studies III (Jerusalem: IES, 2002).

3 See Yigael Yadin, Jonas C. Greenfield, and Ada Yardeni, "A Deed of Gift in Aramaic Found in Naḥal Ḥever: Papyrus Yadin 7," *Eretz Israel* 25 (1996): 383–403 (Hebrew, with an English résumé on p. 103*).

4 Olim *XḤev/Se gr* 5, see Hannah M. Cotton, "Rent or Tax Receipt from Maoza," *ZPE* 100 (1994): 550 = Hannah M. Cotton, "The Archive of Salome Komaise Daughter of Levi: Another Archive from the 'Cave of Letters,'" *ZPE* 105 (1995): 174. The Aramaic, Hebrew and Greek *XḤev/Se* are published in Hannah M. Cotton and Ada Yardeni, *Aramaic, Hebrew, and Greek Documentary Texts from Naḥal Ḥever and Other Sites*, Discoveries in the Judaean Desert XXVII (Oxford: Clarendon Press, 1997).

5 The convention of dating by the provincial era without in any way referring to the province is very common in inscriptions from this area as well as in the Nessana papyri, see Philip Freeman, "The Era of the Province of Arabia: Problems and Solution?," in *Studies in the History of the Roman Province of Arabia: The Northern Sector*, Henry Innes MacAdam (Oxford: B.A.R. 1986), 39.

Article note: First published in *ZPE* 116 (1997): 204–8, with the following note: to my daughter Tor for her birthday.

https://doi.org/10.1515/9783110770438-019

From 4 December 127 CE onwards, a new element enters the formula which expresses the provincial year: the adjective νέα modifies ἡ ἐπαρχεία in the dating formula, thus no longer ἡ ἐπαρχεία Ἀραβία but ἡ νέα ἐπαρχεία Ἀραβία. It is attested for the first time in the two land declarations from that date *P.Yadin* 16 and *XḤev/Se gr* 62.[6] The better preserved *P.Yadin* 16 reads in lines 9–10: κατὰ δὲ τὸν τῆς νέας ἐπαρχείας Ἀραβίας ἀριθμὸν ἔτους δευτέρου εἰκοστοῦ μηνὸς Ἀπελλαίου ἐκκαιδεκάτῃ (cf. *XḤev/Se gr* 62 frg. a lines 8–9). The addition proves tenacious: it occurs, in one of two formulas, in all the Greek documents which employ a provincial dating in the next five years, until the documents stop altogether in 132 CE: ἀριθμῷ δὲ τῆς νέας ἐπαρχείας (*P.Yadin* 17, 21 February 128 CE, line 2 = lines 18–19; *P.Yadin* 18, 5 April 128 CE, lines 30–31) or κατὰ τὸν ἀριθμὸν τῆς νέας ἐπαρχίας Ἀραβίας (*P.Yadin* 19, 16 April 128 CE, lines 9–10; *P.Yadin* 20, 19 June 130 CE, lines 3–4 = lines 21–22; *XḤev/Se gr* 65, 7 August 131 CE, lines 1–2;[7] *P.Yadin* 21 and 22, 11 September 130 CE, lines 4–5; *P.Yadin* 27, 19 August 132 CE, lines 2–3).

Two papyri seem at first sight to throw doubt on the clear-cut division between documents written before and after December 127 CE:

i) *P.Yadin* 31 reads τῆς νέας ἐ̣π̣α̣ρ̣[χίας] in line 2, but is dated tentatively by Lewis to 110 CE on the basis of the fragmentary consular date in lines 15–16 of the outer text:

ἐπὶ ὑπ̣ά̣τ̣ω[ν] Μ̣[άρκου Σαλουειδιηνοῦ Ὀρφίτου καὶ Κοίντου Πεδ-]
ουκ̣α̣ί̣ου Π̣ρ̣[ι]σ̣κ[εί]ν̣ο̣υ̣

In the time since Lewis' work the papyrus has deteriorated, and I have not been able to verify any of the letters beyond ουκ̣α̣ι̣ in line 16. It could be suggested that we have here ου κ̣α̣ι̣, i. e. the ου is the last syllable of the cognomen of the first consul, and is followed by καί, which introduces the name of the second consul. The fact that the formula ἡ νέα ἐπαρχία Ἀραβία occurs without exception in all Greek documents from 127 CE onwards in which the date can be safely read, together with the fact that the element νέα is never found in the documents before 127 CE, makes it *a priori* more likely that *P.Yadin* 31 belongs in the years

6 Frg. a of *XḤev/Se gr* 62 was published originally by Naphtali Lewis, "A Jewish Landowner from the Province of Arabia," *SCI* 8–9 (1985/88): 132–37; for a final publication which includes the other fragments see Cotton and Yardeni, *Aramaic, Hebrew, and Greek Documentary Texts from Naḥal Ḥever and Other Sites*.

7 Originally published by N. Lewis as *P.Yadin* 37, but it is now known to belong to the archive of Salome Komaïse daughter of Levi; see Cotton, "The Archive of Salome Komaise Daughter of Levi," 204–7, and the new edition of the papyrus in Cotton and Yardeni, *Aramaic, Hebrew, and Greek Documentary Texts from Naḥal Ḥever and Other Sites*.

127 CE onwards;[8] at least it puts the onus of proof on those who would postulate 110 CE as the date of this document. What remains of the consular date in line 16 can be comfortably accommodated to the names of the consuls known to us for the years 127, 130, 131 or 132 CE:[9] 1) ἐπὶ ὑπάτων Μάρκου Γαουίου Γαλλικανοῦ καὶ Τίτου Ἀτειλίου Ῥούφου Τιτιανοῦ, as in *P.Yadin* 16 for the year 127 CE; 2) ἐπὶ ὑπάτων Κοείντου Φαβίου Κατηλίνου καὶ Φλαουίου Ἄπερου for 130 CE;[10] 3) ἐπὶ ὑπάτων Σεργίου Ὀκταουίου Λαίνα Ποντιανοῦ καὶ Μάρκου Ἀντωνίου Ῥουφείνου, as in *XḤev/Se* 65 for the year 131 CE; 4) ἐπὶ ὑπάτων Γαίου Σερρίου Αὐγορείνου καὶ Πουπλίου Τρεβίου Σεργιανοῦ, as in *P.Yadin* 27 for the year 132 CE.[11]

ii) The Aramaic *XḤev/Se ar* 12 from 30 January 131 CE does not have the word 'new' in its dating formula:[12] 'year twenty-five to the hyparchia' שנת עשרין וח[מ]ש להפרכ[יה]. However, this absence may be attributed to the nature of the document, a receipt; or, alternatively, to the different diplomatics of the Semitic documents, noticeable for example in the varying order of the several dating formulas (the regnal, the consular and the provincial).[13]

The fact that the term νέα modifies ἐπαρχεία and not Ἀραβία – 'the new province,' not *Nova Arabia* – as rightly emphasized by Lewis,[14] shows clearly that there is no question of the creation of a new province called Νέα Ἀραβία under

8 Abraham Wasserstein, "Review: Lewis, Yadin and Greenfield, 'Documents from the Cave of Letters,'" *JQR* 84 (1993): 374–75.

9 The consuls of the year 128 and 129 CE are excluded since a β̄, for the iteration of the consulate of the first named consul, would have stood between the ου and the καί, e. g. *XḤev/Se gr* 64 (129 CE, olim *XḤev/Se gr* 1, see Cotton, "The Archive of Salome Komaise Daughter of Levi," 183 ff.) line 1: [ἐ]π̣ὶ ὑπά̣τ̣ων̣ Πο̣[πλ]ί̣ο̣υ̣ Ἰ̣ο̣υ̣[ο]υ̣εντ̣ί̣ου Κέ̣λ̣σου τὸ β̄ κ̣α̣ὶ̣ Λ̣[ο]υ̣κ̣ί̣ο̣υ̣ Νηρατίου Μαρκέλλου τὸ β̄.

10 This is the order of names in *P.Yadin* 20, and 23, but not in *P.Yadin* 21 and 22: Μάρκου Φλαουίου Ἄπερος καὶ Κοείντου Φαβίου Κατηλίνου, unless Aper in the genitive is written Ἄπρου as in *XḤev/Se gr* 69 line 2.

11 We do not have the line length for the outer text in this document. The reconstructions offered above have 30, 30, 37 and 29 letters per line respectively. In comparison with other documents in the Babatha Archive the line length in the first, second and fourth reconstruction falls below the average. Note though that the outer texts of *P.Yadin* 23 (130 CE), *P.Yadin* 25 (131 CE) and *P.Yadin* 26 (131 CE) have ca. 34, 37 and 34 letters per line respectively. I would, therefore, opt for the third reconstruction: ἐπὶ ὑπάτων Σεργίου Ὀκταουίου Λαίνα Ποντιανοῦ καὶ Μάρκου Ἀντωνίου Ῥουφείνου, i. e. the year 131 CE, as the date of *P.Yadin* 31.

12 For an English translation see Cotton, "The Archive of Salome Komaise Daughter of Levi," 204.

13 See in detail Cotton, "Introduction to the Greek Documentary Texts: The Calendar" in Cotton and Yardeni, *Aramaic, Hebrew, and Greek Documentary Texts from Naḥal Ḥever and Other Sites*, 146–49.

14 Naphtali Lewis, "The World of P.Yadin," *BASP* 28 (1991): 35–6 against Abraham Wasserstein, "A Marriage Contract from the Province of Arabia Nova: Notes on Papyrus Yadin 18," *JQR* 80 (1989): 98, n. 15.

Hadrian. The dating formula says explicitly 'the new province,' not *Nova Arabia*.[15] The νέα, therefore, has nothing to do with the name, only with the 'province.' This is further proved by the fact that the counting of the provincial years continues uninterrupted from 106 CE.[16] One notes also that although the dating formula in the two land declarations says τῆς νέας ἐπαρχίας Ἀραβίας (*P.Yadin* 16 lines 9–10; cf. *XḤev/Se gr* 62 frg. a lines 8–9), the text itself says Ἀραβίας with no modification: ἀποτιμήσεως Ἀραβίας ἀγ̣ομένης ὑπὸ Τίτου Ἀνεινίου Σεξστίου Φλωρεντείνου πρεσβευτοῦ Σεβαστοῦ ἀντιστρατήγου (*P.Yadin* 16 lines 11–13; cf. *XḤev/Se gr* 62 frg. a lines 10–12).

How to explain the change in the dating formula?

Lewis was right to point out that the change in the dating formula took place at the time of the census held in the province in 127 CE.[17] The expression of the rate of taxation in terms of the old Nabataean monetary unit – the *melaina*,[18] as well as the presence in the declarations of the Nabataean royal tax – the *stephanikon*,[19] make it likely that this was the first census conducted in Arabia since its annexation in 106 CE.[20]

---

15 And thus the association with the fourth century Νέα Ἀραβία in *P.Oxy*. L 3471 (Wasserstein, "A Marriage Contract from the Province of Arabia Nova," 96 ff.) is quite irrelevant here. For the controversy over Νέα Ἀραβία in *P.Oxy*. L 3471 see Timothy D. Barnes, *The New Empire of Diocletian and Constantine* (Cambridge, Mass.: Harvard University Press, 1982), 205–6, 211, 213–15; Glen W. Bowersock, *Roman Arabia* (Cambridge, Mass.: Harvard University Press, 1983), 145–46; Philip Mayerson, "P.Oxy. 3574: 'Eleutheropolis of the New Arabia,'" *ZPE* 53 (1983): 251–58 (= *Monks, Martyrs, Soldiers and Saracens. Papers on the Near East in Late Antiquity (1962–1993)* (Jerusalem: IES, 1994), 204–11); Philip Mayerson, "'Palaestina' vs. 'Arabia' in the Byzantine Sources," *ZPE* 56 (1984): 223–30 (= *Monks, Martyrs, Soldiers and Saracens*, 224–31); Glen W. Bowersock, "Naming a Province: More on New Arabia," *ZPE* 56 (1984): 221–22; Philip Mayerson, "Nea Arabia (P.Oxy. 3574): An Addendum to ZPE 53," *ZPE* 64 (1986): 139–40 (= *Monks, Martyrs, Soldiers and Saracens*, 256–7).

16 A point raised by Wasserstein himself ("A Marriage Contract from the Province of Arabia Nova," 101) and dismissed.

17 Lewis, "The World of P.Yadin," 36.

18 See *P.Yadin* 16 lines 20, 27, 32; *XḤev/Se gr* 62 frg. a lines 16–17; frgs. c-m line 8.

19 See *P.Yadin* 16 lines 20, 27, 32; *XḤev/Se gr* 62 frgs. c-m lines 17–18.

20 For the *melaina* and the *stephanikon* see Wolfram Weiser and Hannah M. Cotton, "'Gebt dem Kaiser, was des Kaisers ist ...': Die Geldwährungen der Griechen, Juden, Nabatäer und Römer in syrisch-nabatäischen Raum unter besonderer Berücksichtigung des Kurses von Selaʿ/Melaina und Lepton nach der Annexion des Königreiches der Nabatäer durch Rom," *ZPE* 114 (1996): 237–87.

The fact that this was the first census in Arabia is crucial for the explanation of the new dating formula given below. It is, therefore, important to dispel at this point the notion that a provincial census followed immediately upon the annexation of a territory to the Roman empire. Such a claim has been made for example in respect of the annexations of Judaea, of Cappadocia and of Dacia.[21]

Judaea happened to be annexed to the province of Syria[22] at the same time that the latter's governor, P. Sulpicius Quirinius, was conducting a census there;[23] naturally the census spread to the newly annexed area: παρῆν δὲ καὶ Κυρίνιος εἰς τὴν Ἰουδαίαν προσθήκην τῆς Συρίας γενομένην ἀποτιμησόμενός τε αὐτῶν τὰς οὐσίας καὶ ἀποδωσόμενος τὰ Ἀρχελάου χρήματα (Joseph., *AJ* 18.2).[24] Nor does Tac. *Ann.* VI, 41, 1 prove that "the annexation of ... Cappadocia by Tiberius [was] ... followed by [a census]."[25] Cappadocia was annexed in 17 CE (Tac. *Ann.* II, 42, 4) or 18 CE (*Ann* II, 56, 4); whereas *Ann.* VI, 41, 1 tells us that the Cietae revolted against the census à la mode romaine (*nostrum in modum ... census*) imposed on them shortly before 36 CE by the young Archelaus, whose subjects they were ('*Cietarum natio Cappadoci Archelao subiecta*').[26] Finally, Lactant. *De mort. pers.* XXIII, 5 does not imply at all a census following directly upon the reduction of Dacia to a province: '*Quae veteres adversus victos iure belli facerant, et ille adversus Romanos et Romanis subiectos facere ausus est, quia parentes eius censui subiugati fuerant, quem Traianus Daciis assidue rebellantibus poenae gratia victor imposuit.*' Lactantius means that Trajan made the Dacians subject to Roman taxes, not that he held a census there: the *poena* consisted in the payment of taxes, not in the census.

Significantly not only the formula expressing the provincial era was modified in the land declarations of 127 CE, but also the formula expressing the regnal year is unlike anything we encounter before or after. Hadrian's full titulature appears in the dating formula:

---

21 E.g. Peter A. Brunt, "The Revenues of Rome," in *Roman Imperial Themes* (Oxford: Clarendon Press, 1990), 330. On the provincial census see Lutz Neesen, *Untersuchungen zu den direkten Staatsabgaben der römischen Kaiserzeit 27 v. Chr. bis 284 n. Chr.* (Bonn: Habelt, 1980), 39 ff; Anna Aichinger, "Zwei Arten des Provinzialcensus? Überlegungen zu neu-publizierten israelischen Papyrusfunden," *Chiron* 22 (1992): 35–45.

22 That it did not become an independent province, as the *communis opinio* maintains, will be argued elsewhere.

23 Joseph., *AJ* 18.1 and *ILS* 2683; on P. Sulpicius Quirinius see now Edward Dąbrowa, *The Governors of Roman Syria from Augustus to Septimius Severus* (Bonn: Habelt, 1998).

24 Cf. Joseph., *BJ* 2.117.

25 Brunt, "The Revenues of Rome," 330.

26 See Emil Schürer, *The History of the Jewish People in the Age of Jesus Christ*, Vol. I, ed. Fergus Millar and Géza Vermès (Edinburgh: Clark, 1973), 414.

ἐπὶ Αὐτοκράτορος Καίσαρος θεοῦ Τραιανοῦ Παρθικοῦ υ̣ἱοῦ θεοῦ Νέρουα υἱωνοῦ Τραιανοῦ Ἁδριανοῦ Σεβαστοῦ ἀρχιερέως μεγίστου δημαρχικῆς ἐξουσίας τὸ δωδέκατον ὑπάτου τὸ τρίτον (*P.Yadin* 16 lines 5–7 = *XḤev/Se gr* 62 frg. a lines 4–7).

The appearance of the emperor's full titulature in the dating formula (i.e. following ἐπί) is quite exceptional; nowhere else in the papyri is the full titulature attested as part of the dating formula.[27] On the two occasions in which Hadrian's full titulature appears in the papyri, it occurs in the nominative, since it is the beginning of an edict and of an epistle. There are, as far as I know, only two other examples of the full form of Hadrian's imperial titulature in the papyri: *SB* III 6944 (two copies of an edict from 136 CE); *P.Oslo* III 78 (another copy of the same edict),[28] and *P.Würzb.* 9 (a letter to the city of Antinoopolis, between 130 and 135 CE).[29] A much shorter form of the imperial titulature occurs when it is part of the dating formula, as here, i.e following ἐπί.[30]

The explanation offered below attempts, therefore, to explain both the νέα in the formula expressing the provincial date as well as the unusual appearance of the full form of the imperial titulature in the formula expressing the regnal years.

The land declarations *P.Yadin* 16 and *XḤev/Se gr* 62 reflect in their dating formula the language used by emperor Hadrian, in an *edictum* or an *epistula*, ordering the census in a new province. In Hadrian's *edictum* or *epistula* the imperial titulature appeared in the nominative and not as part of the dating formula. Furthermore, since this was the first census, it was only natural that Hadrian will order a census in 'the New Province.' The *edictum* or *epistula* was then published by the provincial governor together with his own edict ordering the census. It is true that there is no example of an edict from Egypt ordering the census, but many declarations after 89 CE refer to it in the formula κατὰ τὰ κελευσθέντα or κατὰ τὰ προστεταγμένα followed by the name of the prefect.[31] The procedure of attach-

27 I suppose this is what Lewis means when he says "This is the imperial titulature of Hadrian in its fullest form, found hitherto only in inscriptions," *The Documents from the Bar Kokhba Period in the Cave of Letters. Greek Papyri*, 68.

28 See James H. Oliver, *Greek Constitutions of Early Roman Emperors from Inscriptions and Papyri* (Philadelphia: American Philosophical Society, 1989), no. 88A, B, C.

29 See Oliver, no. 164; see Paul Bureth, *Les titulatures impériales dans les papyrus, les ostraca et les inscriptions d'Égypte (30 a.C.-284 p.C.)* (Bruxelles: Fondation égyptologique reine Elisabeth, 1964), 63.

30 Cf. Bureth, *passim.*

31 See Marcel Hombert and Claire Préaux, *Recherches sur le recensement dans l'Egypte romaine* (Leiden: Brill, 1952), 53; see 53–6; 76–7; Roger S. Bagnall and Bruce W. Frier, *The Demography of Roman Egypt* (Cambridge: Cambridge University Press, 1994), 11. *W.Chr.* 202 (*P.Lond.* III 904) is an edict calling people to return home after the census has been declared: τῆς κατ' οἰ[κίαν ἀπογραφῆς ἐ]νεστώ[σης] (line 20).

ing the emperor's communication to the governor's edict is attested for Claudius' epistle to the Alexandrians, published by the prefect of Egypt, Lucius Aemilius Rectus, together with his own edict in 41 CE.[32] The prefect's edict ends with the normal dating formula:

> (ἔτους) β Τιβερίου Κλαυδίου Καίσαρος Σεβαστοῦ Γερμανικοῦ Αὐτοκράτορος, μηνὸς Νέου Σεβαστο(ῦ) ιδ (col. I lines 11–12).

The imperial letter follows in the second column with the full nomenclature of the emperor in the nominative:

> Τιβέριος Κλαύδιος Καῖσαρ Σεβαστὸς Γερμανικὸς Αὐτοκράτωρ ἀρχ{ι}ιερεὺς μέγιστος δημαρχικῆς ἐξουσίας ὕπατος ἀποδεδιγμένος (col. II lines 14–15).

What we have in the land declarations from Arabia is both the imperial titulature and the order to conduct a census in the 'new province.' Both were translated into the dating formula by the official scribes who translated the original declarations into Greek and prepared the authorized copies.[33] Thus there is no longer a reason to postulate a reorganization of the province of Arabia, "occasioned by, or connected with, the antecedents ... of the Bar Kokhba rebellion,"[34] nor "a reform of the provincial administration."[35]

As has been seen, the intrusion of the νέα element into the provincial dating formula proves tenacious. It is present in documents written in two different locations and by different scribes. The land declarations *P.Yadin* 16 and *XḤev/Se gr* 62 were written in 127 CE in Rabbath-Moab by two different, though unknown, scribes. The other documents bearing the new provincial dating formula were written in Maḥoza, also by different scribes: *P.Yadin* 18 (marriage contract) was written in 128 CE by Theënas son of Shim'on; *P.Yadin* 19 (deed of gift) was written in 128 CE by a son of Shim'on (not to be identified with Theënas son of Shim'on);[36] *XḤev/Se gr* 64 (deed of gift) was written in 129 CE by Reisha son of Judah;[37] *P.Yadin* 20 (concession of rights), *P.Yadin* 21 and 22 (complementary deeds of sale) and

32 Oliver, *Greek Constitutions of Early Roman Emperors from Inscriptions and Papyri*, no. 19 (= *P.Lond.* VI 1912).
33 See Hannah M. Cotton, "Subscriptions and Signatures in the Papyri from the Judaean Desert: The χειροχρήστης," *JJP* 25 (1995): 29 ff. [above, pp. 115 ff.].
34 J. Geiger apud Wasserstein, "A Marriage Contract from the Province of Arabia Nova," 101, n. 27.
35 Lewis, "The World of P.Yadin," 36.
36 See Lewis, *The Documents from the Bar Kokhba Period in the Cave of Letters. Greek Papyri*, 83.
37 Note though that the νέα in line 2 is a restoration. For the scribe see commentary ad *XḤev/Se gr* 64 line 44 in Cotton and Yardeni, *Aramaic, Hebrew, and Greek Documentary Texts from Naḥal Ḥever and Other Sites.*

P.Yadin 27 (receipt) were written in 130 CE by Germanus son of Judah; *XḤev/Se gr* 65 (marriage contract) was written in 131 CE; the scribe's name is not preserved since only the inner text survived. This uniformity of usage gives us an insight into scribal practices in the province of Arabia: dating formulae invented in administrative centers for copying official documents were later incorporated into private documents by local scribes.[38]

38 The role of the scribe in influencing the form and content of legal and non-legal documents is a fascinating subject, much neglected, see Elias J. Bickerman, "Two Legal Interpretations of the Septuagint," in *Studies in Jewish and Christian History*, Vol. I (Leiden: Brill, 1976), 207.

Some Aspects of the Roman Administration of Judaea/Syria-Palaestina

This paper falls into two parts: in the first part I discuss the provincialization of the territory that came to be called the province of Judaea, and later Syria-Palaestina;[1] in the second part I look at the administration of the so-called 'Jewish region' of Judaea in the light of the recently published documents from the Judaean Desert.

I

Judaea came under direct Roman rule only in 6 CE with the exile of Herod's son, the Tetrarch Archelaus. From the conquest of Judaea by Pompey in 63 BCE until 6 CE, Judaea was ruled first by descendants of the Hasmonaean house without royal title and later by the Herodian dynasty. Pompey reduced the extent of Jewish territory by annexing all the coastal cities and those of the Decapolis to the new province of Syria.[2] Judaea included then Judaea proper, Idumaea, Samaria, the Peraea and the Galilee. Under Herod the districts of Batanea, the Trachonitis and Auranitis were added to his kingdom.[3] After Herod's death the kingdom was divided between his three sons. Archelaus had Judaea proper, Idumaea, and Samaria including the cities of Caesarea, Samaria-Sebaste, Jerusalem and Joppa – this part came under direct Roman rule upon his exile in 6 CE. Philip received Batanea, the Trachonitis and Auranitis – districts with mixed population where the non-Jewish element prevailed. It is little wonder that after his death they were attached to

1 This is part of the prolegomena to the once projected *Fasti* of Judaea/Syria-Palaestina by H.M. Cotton and W. Eck. See Hannah M. Cotton, "The Roman Fasti of Judaea/Syria Palaestina," in *Memorial for Menachem Stern* (Jerusalem: Israel Academy of Sciences and Humanities, 2002), 55–69 (Hebrew).
2 See Emil Schürer, *The History of the Jewish People in the Age of Jesus Christ*, Vol. I, ed. Fergus Millar and Géza Vermès (Edinburgh: Clark, 1973), 240.
3 Schürer I, 291.

Article note: First published in Werner Eck, ed., *Lokale Autonomie und römische Ordnungsmacht in den kaiserzeitlichen Provinzen vom 1. bis 3. Jahrhundert* (München: Oldenbourg, 1999), 75–91, with the following note: the citation of bibliographical references in the notes has been deliberately reduced to a minimum, both to preserve the form of a lecture, and because of exigencies of space.
I am grateful to Werner Eck and David Wasserstein for helpful criticism of earlier versions. The research for this article was supported by a grant from the Israel Science Foundation.

https://doi.org/10.1515/9783110770438-020

the province of Syria. Herod Antipas received the Galilee and the Peraea. He was deposed in 37 CE and his territory was granted to Agrippa I who later received from Claudius the whole of Herod the Great's earlier kingdom together with a royal title. Agrippa's reign lasted only three years, from 41 to 44 CE.[4] After his death Judaea was once more under direct Roman rule. In the 50s the territory that had been subject to Philip (Batanea, the Trachonitis and Auranitis), with parts of the Peraea and the Galilee was bestowed on Agrippa II. The non-Jewish parts were incorporated once more into the province of Syria upon his death in 93/4, whereas the Jewish were joined to the rest of the Jewish territory.[5]

I have deliberately used the expression 'came under direct Roman rule' for Archelaus' ethnarchy and for Agrippa's kingdom and refrained from saying 'it became the province of Judaea,' since this seems to me a moot point, one which needs to be discussed once more.

Josephus' statement in *BJ* 2.117 about the fate of Judaea after Archelaus' deposition – τῆς δὲ Ἀρχελάου χώρας εἰς ἐπαρχίαν περιγραφείσης ἐπίτροπος τῆς ἱππικῆς παρὰ Ῥωμαίοις τάξεως Κωπώνιος πέμπεται – which implies that Archelaus' former kingdom was reduced to a province, does not decide the issue, for this is in stark contradiction to what he himself says in *AJ* 17.355 – τῆς δ' Ἀρχελάου χώρας ὑποτελοῦς προσνεμηθείσης τῇ Σύρων – and in *AJ* 18.2 – παρῆν δὲ καὶ Κυρίνιος εἰς τὴν Ἰουδαίαν προσθήκην τῆς Συρίας – namely that Judaea was annexed to the province of Syria.[6]

There is no doubt at all that a part of the Herodian kingdom was provincialized in 6 CE, but was it from the beginning the *provincia Iudaea*? Was it from the beginning an independent province with its independent provincial governor? We may not use the fact that it later became an independent province as proof that it was so from the very beginning.

The current consensus is that from the beginning there existed an independent Roman province of Judaea,[7] first ruled by a governor with the title of *praefec-*

4 Schürer I, 442–53.

5 Schürer I, 330–57.

6 Abraham Schalit, who believes that Judaea was annexed to Syria from 6 till 66 CE (*The Roman Administration in Palestine* (Jerusalem: Mosad Bialik, 1937), 11 (Hebrew)), explains away the contradiction by maintaining that Judaea constituted an independent administrative unit within the province of Syria, Schalit, 89 and 149, n. 97.

7 Cf. Martin Goodman, "Judaea," in *The Cambridge Ancient History, Volume 10*, ed. Alan K. Bowman, Edward Champlin, and Andrew Lintott, 2nd ed. (Cambridge: Cambridge University Press, 1996), 750 ff.; see the admirably cautious exposition of Menahem Stern, "The Province of Judaea," in *The Jewish People in the First Century, Volume 1*, ed. Shmuel Safrai and Menahem Stern (Assen: Van Gorcum & Comp. B.V., 1974), 308 ff. Stern's final judgement, however, is that Judaea was an independent province from 6 CE. There are some dissenting voices, e. g. Maurizio Ghiretti,

tus,[8] who later on was designated *procurator*,[9] and that the difference was merely semantic: "the difference between *praefectus* and *procurator* in imperial provinces was one in name only."[10]

It is quite possible that this became true later, but were early *praefecti* distinguished from the later *procuratores* in only name? Perhaps. Nonetheless, it seems more likely that the change of name coincided with a change in the status of the former *praefecti*. This assumption may account for the fact that no praesidial procurators are attested in the provinces before Claudius. Furthermore, were all early *praefecti* of the same status? It is tacitly assumed that the presence of a *praefectus* in Judaea means that Augustus restructured the province of Judaea on the Egyptian model.[11] I believe that Egypt in any case should not be taken as a model since this province was created in the special circumstances prevailing after Actium. A special law was passed in the *comitia* to regulate the unusual appointment of an equestrian.[12] Egypt remained unusual to the extent that three and later two legions were stationed there under the command of an equestrian. This happened in no other province: nowhere else were legions under the command of an equestrian governor. Later, when a legion was stationed in Judaea, the status of its governor changed to that of a senator.[13]

There are good reasons to equate the *praefectus* of Judaea with prefects of 'civitates' and 'gentes,' about whom we know that they were dependent on provincial governors; in their case the evidence is based solely on inscriptions.[14] These *prae-*

"Lo «status» della Giudea dall'età Augustea all'età Claudia," *Latomus* 44 (1985): 751–66, some of whose arguments agree with those presented here.

8 This is established by the inscription of Pontius Pilatus from Caesarea, in: *AE* 1963, no. 104; see Gilbert Labbé, "Ponce Pilate et la munificence de Tibère. L'inscription de Césarée," *Revue des Études Anciennes* 93 (1991): 277–97 and Laura Boffo, *Iscrizioni greche e latine per lo studio della Bibbia* (Brescia: Paideia, 1994), 217–33, no. 25.

9 For this designation there is no epigraphical evidence in Judaea.

10 Schürer, *The History of the Jewish People in the Age of Jesus Christ* I, 359.

11 See Alan K. Bowman, "Provincial Administration and Taxation," in *The Cambridge Ancient History, Volume 10*, 346.

12 *Dig.* 1, 17, 1 (Ulpian): *Praefectus Aegypti non prius deponit praefecturam et imperium, quod ad similitudinem proconsulis lege sub Augusto ei datum est, quam Alexandriam ingressus sit successor eius ...*

13 Cf. Cappadocia: it was governed by procurators with auxiliary forces under their command until Vespasian, when it was united with Galatia under a consular *legatus Augusti pro praetore* with two legions under him; see Werner Eck, *Senatoren von Vespasian bis Hadrian: Prosopographische Untersuchungen mit Einschluß der Jahres- und Provinzialfasten der Statthalter* (München: Beck, 1970), 2–3.

14 E.g. the *praefecti* in Spain: *CIL* II 4616 = *ILS* 6948: *praefectus Asturiae, tribunus militum legionis secundae*; *CIL* II 3271: *praef. Gallaeciae*; in Numidia: *CIL* V 5267 = *ILS* 2721: *praefectus coh. VII*

fecti did not govern autonomous provinces, but parts of provinces where special circumstances called for the presence of a special functionary. I assume that unlike independent governors these prefects would normally not be vested with full authority to judge provincials in capital cases.[15] It is in the light of this assumption that we should understand Josephus' explicit statement in the case of the first prefect of Judaea, Coponius: Κωπώνιός τε αὐτῷ (Κυρινίῳ) συγκαταπέμπεται τάγματος τῶν ἱππέων, ἡγησόμενος Ἰουδαίων τῇ ἐπὶ πᾶσιν ἐξουσίᾳ (*AJ* 18.2).[16] And indeed we find both in Josephus as well as in the New Testament the prefects making full use of their absolute penal jurisdiction.[17] However, there would have been no need to specify the grant of such competence had Coponius been an independent governor.

Considerations of size may well have contributed to the decision not to turn a territory into an independent province. "Archelaus' ethnarchy was too small to demand the creation of an independent province."[18] The smallest province, Cyprus with its 8,500 square km was bigger than the combined size of what had earlier been Archelaus' ethnarchy. "The simplest way, on the face of it, was to annex the ethnarchy to the neighboring province of Syria."[19] The appointment of a prefect subordinate to the governor of Syria fits in well with the size of territories put elsewhere under the command of a *praefectus*.

The census of 6 CE in Judaea is taken as a proof for the inauguration of Judaea as a new independent province. The notion that a provincial census followed immediately upon the annexation of a territory to the Roman empire is not, however, well founded.[20] That a census took place in Judaea at the time of its provincialization was a mere coincidence: at the time, as we know both from

---

Lusitanorum et nationum Gaetulicarum sex quae sunt in Numidia; in Sardinia *CIL* XIV 2954 = *ILS* 2684: *praef. coh. Corsorum et civitatium Barbariae*; on the Danube and the Alps: *CIL* V 1838/9 = *ILS* 1349: *primopilus leg. V Macedonic., praef. civitatium Treballiae, praef. civitatium in Alpibus Maritimis*; *CIL* IX 3044 = *ILS* 2689: *pra[ef(ectus)] Raetis Vindolicis valli[s P]oeninae et levis armatur(ae)*. On these early prefects see Hans Zwicky, "Zur Verwendung des Militärs in der Verwaltung des römischen Kaiserzeit" (University of Zurich Thesis, 1944), 11 ff.

15 See Ghiretti, "Lo «status» della Giudea dall'età Augustea all'età Claudia," 765.

16 Cf. *BJ* 2.117: Κωπώνιος πέμπεται μέχρι τοῦ κτείνειν λαβὼν παρὰ Καίσαρος ἐξουσία. I do not accept Stern's explanation for Josephus' statement ("The Province of Judaea," 337).

17 Schürer, *The History of the Jewish People in the Age of Jesus Christ*, Vol. I, 367 ff.

18 Stern, "The Province of Judaea," 309.

19 Stern, 309.

20 See in detail Hannah M. Cotton, "Ἡ νέα ἐπαρχεία Ἀραβία: The New Province of Arabia in the Papyri from the Judaean Desert," *ZPE* 116 (1997): 204–8 [above, pp. 309–16].

Josephus and from *ILS* 2683,[21] a census was conducted in Syria by the governor P. Sulpicius Quirinius; naturally the census spread into the newly *annexed* territory. Josephus explicitly combines the fact of annexation with the administration of the census: Κυρίνιος δὲ ... ἐπὶ Συρίας παρῆν, ὑπὸ Καίσαρος δικαιοδότης τοῦ ἔθνους ἀπεσταλμένος καὶ τιμητὴς τῶν οὐσιῶν γενησόμενος, Κωπώνιός τε αὐτῷ συγκαταπέμπεται τάγματος τῶν ἱππέων, ἡγησόμενος Ἰουδαίων τῇ ἐπὶ πᾶσιν ἐξουσίᾳ. παρῆν δὲ καὶ Κυρίνιος εἰς τὴν Ἰουδαίαν προσθήκην τῆς Συρίας γενομένην ἀποτιμησόμενός τε αὐτῶν τὰς οὐσίας καὶ ἀποδωσόμενος τὰ Ἀρχελάου χρήματα (*AJ* 18.1–2).[22] The Judaea-centered view of the census as the inauguration of a new province distorts the true picture.

On the other hand, the assumption that the prefect of Judaea, although appointed by the emperor,[23] was a subordinate of the governors of Syria would explain the constant interventions of the latter in Judaea in matters which were not purely military[24] – an intervention that cannot always be explained by special authorization.[25]

All this seems to me to justify a reconsideration of what Josephus says – namely that Judaea was subordinate to the province of Syria – before we conclude that Judaea became an independent province in 6 CE. Josephus says so in so many words in *AJ* 18.2 (τὴν Ἰουδαίαν προσθήκην τῆς Συρίας γενομένην), and in *AJ* 17.355 (τῆς δ' Ἀρχελάου χώρας ὑποτελοῦς προσνεμηθείσης τῇ Σύρων).[26]

---

21 *Q. Aemilius Q. f. Pal. Secundus [in] castris divi Aug. s[ub] P. Sulpi[c]io Quirinio le[gato] C[a]esaris Syriae honoribus decoratus, pr[a]efect. cohort. Aug. I, pr[a]efect. cohort. II classicae; idem iussu Quirini censum egi Apamenae civitatis millium homin. civium CXVII...* See Boffo, *Iscrizioni greche e latine per lo studio della Bibbia*, 182–203, no. 23.

22 Cf. *AJ* 17.355: τῆς δ' Ἀρχελάου χώρας ὑποτελοῦς προσνεμηθείσης τῇ Σύρων πέμπεται Κυρίνιος ὑπὸ Καίσαρος ἀνὴρ ὑπατικὸς ἀποτιμησόμενός τε τὰ ἐν Συρίᾳ καὶ τὸν Ἀρχελάου ἀποδωσόμενος οἶκον.

23 Stern, "The Province of Judaea," 319.

24 E.g. the vestments of the High Priest.

25 As pointed out by Stern, "The Province of Judaea," 313, and see the whole discussion there.

26 Tacitus, *Ann.* II, 42, 5: '*et provinciae Syria atque Iudaea fessae oneribus deminutionem tributi orabant*,' for 18 CE, seems at first sight to imply that Judaea, like Syria, was an independent province. However, the term *provinciae* could have been added by Tacitus himself, in view of Judaea's status in his own time. Thus there is all the more reason to give credence to what he says in *Ann.* XII, 23, 1 cited below.

When did Judaea become an independent province?

There are reasons to believe that this happened in 44 CE with the death of Agrippa I, and the provincialization of his kingdom. This time the territory in question was much larger than in 6 CE. Furthermore, under Claudius the equestrian procurator as a praesidial governor makes his appearance elsewhere in the Empire.[27] Two of the governors of Judaea, unlike the earlier prefects, are known to have served in other procuratorial posts before and after their governorship of Judaea. Ti. Iulius Alexander had served as *epistrategus* of the Thebaid in Egypt[28] before becoming governor of Judaea in 46–8, and in 66 was appointed prefect of Egypt.[29] Lucceius Albinus proceeded directly from Judaea, where he was governor in 62–64, to the governorship of Mauretania Caesarensis to which Tingitana was added later.[30] All these facts would suggest that by now Judaea had become an independent procuratorial province. This, however, cannot be easily reconciled with what Tacitus says about the status of Judaea in 49 CE (*Ann.* XII, 23, 1): '*Ituraeique et Iudaei defunctis regibus Sohaemo atque Agrippa provinciae Syriae additi.*'[31] This he could not have invented, but must have found in his sources, for in his own time Judaea was an independent praetorian (or already consular) province (see below).

During the Great Revolt of 66–70 the Roman field commanders ruled Judaea, and Antonius Iulianus, the procurator mentioned in Josephus (*BJ* 6.238) as taking part in Titus' war council, must now have been in charge of finance only. After the revolt Judaea became a one-legion praetorian province ruled by a *legatus Augusti pro praetore* in charge of the province as well as of the legion – the *Legio Decima Fretensis*. In fact, it was the first province to have a *legatus Augusti pro praetore* of praetorian rank in charge of a legion.[32] Before the Bar Kokhba revolt the status of

27 For Raetia, see H. Wolff in *The Cambridge Ancient History, Volume 10*, 541 f.; for Noricum see J.J. Wilkes, "The Danubian and Balkan Provinces," in *The Cambridge Ancient History, Volume 10*, 568; for Thrace, Wilkes, 567; for Mauretania Caesariensis and Tingitana see C.R. Whittaker, "Roman Africa: Augustus to Vespasian," in *The Cambridge Ancient History, Volume 10*, 598–9.

28 Hans-Georg Pflaum, *Les carrières procuratoriennes équestres sous le haut-empire romain* (Paris: P. Geuthner, 1960), 1091.

29 *PIR* (2nd ed.) J 139; E.G. Turner, "Tiberius Iulius Alexander," *JRS* 44 (1954): 54–64.

30 Tac. *Hist.* II, 58; *PIR* (2nd ed.) L 354.

31 Note, though, that *Ann.* XII, 23, 1 echoes *Hist.* V, 9: '*Claudius defunctis regibus aut ad modicum redactis, Iudaeam provinciam equitibus Romanis aut libertis permisit*,' which seems to imply that Claudius reduced Judaea to a province, unless the renewal of provincialization after Agrippa's death is all that is implied here.

32 B.E. Thomasson, "The One-Legion Provinces of the Roman Empire during the Principate," *Opuscula Romana* 9, no. 7 (1973): 63. The other one-legion provinces (Hispania Citerior and Dalmatia) were consular; a *legatus legionis* of praetorian rank was in charge of the one legion. In

the governor of Judaea changed once more – thus not as a result of the revolt. At an unknown date, a second legion, first the *Legio II Traiana*, later permanently replaced by the *Legio VI Ferrata*, was stationed in Judaea and a consular governor was put in charge. The exact date of the change is unknown. If we accept the argument of Isaac and Roll that the second legion is already attested in 120 CE, then this must be the date *ante quem* Judaea became a consular province.[33] It has been suggested that the change could have come about already under Pompeius Falco,[34] and that a likely date for the transfer of the *Legio II Traiana* to Judaea was after the second Dacian War, i. e. 107–108. It seems prudent though, in the absence of compelling evidence, to suspend our final dating of the change from praetorian to consular status.

After the Bar Kokhba revolt, if not already before its conclusion, the name of the province was changed from Judaea to Syria-Palaestina – thus suppressing the Jewish identity of the province. The province remained under a senator of consular rank since he was in charge of two legions at least until the reign of Probus (276–82): two governors of senatorial rank from this reign are now attested on two columns from Caesarea Maritima.[35] At the latest by 293–305 the governor became an equestrian as twice attested on the same columns for Aufidius Priscus *v(ir) p(erfectissimus) pr(aeses) prov(inciae) Pal(aestinae)*.[36] This brings us down to the end of the third century.

In conclusion of this part, I should like to re-emphasize two facts. First, from 63 BCE to the end of the first century CE, the area of Judaea/Syria-Palaestina was subject to fluctuation between direct Roman and dynastic rule. Secondly, even

Hispania Citerior the second legion was removed at the latest in 63, Géza Alföldy, "Spain," in *The Cambridge Ancient History, Volume 10*, 454; in Dalmatia, the second legion was removed in 58 or 59, see Emil Ritterling, "Legio," in *RE*, Vol. XII.1 (1924), 1225.

33 Benjamin Isaac and Israel Roll, "Legio II Traiana in Judaea," *ZPE* 33 (1979): 149–56; contra J.R. Rea, "Ordinatus," *ZPE* 38 (1980): 217–19; Benjamin Isaac and Israel Roll, "Legio II Traiana in Judaea: A Reply," *ZPE* 47 (1982): 131–32.

34 Werner Eck, "Zum konsularen Status von Iudaea im frühen 2. Jh," *BASP* 21 (1984): 55–67. His conjecture is based on this governor's two career inscriptions: *CIL* X 6321 = *ILS* 1035 (prope Tarracinam) and *CIL* III 12117 = *ILS* 1036 = E.L. Hicks, "Inscriptions from Eastern Cilicia," *JHS* 11 (1890): 253, no. 28 (Hierapolis Castabala); note the *consularis* in the second inscription: *leg. Aug. leg. X Fret. et leg. pr. pr. [pr]ovinciae Iudaeae consularis*.

35 Barbara Burrell, "Two Inscribed Columns from Caesarea Maritima," *ZPE* 99 (1993): 288–89, column I, insc. 2 = *AE* 1993, no. 1620, ll. 5–6: *(v)ir c(larissimus) praes(es) prov(inciae) Syr(iae) Pal(estinae)*; for the senatorial status of Acilius Cleobulus (Burrell, 292–93, column II, insc. 2 = *AE* 1993, no. 1623) see Werner Eck, "Zu lateinischen Inschriften aus Caesarea in Iudaea / Syria Palaestina," *ZPE* 113 (1996): 141 ff.

36 Burrell, "Two Inscribed Columns from Caesarea Maritima," 290–91, column I, insc. 3 = *AE* 1993 no. 1621; Burrell, 293–94, column II, insc. 3 = *AE* 1993, no. 1624.

after the introduction of direct Roman rule, the history of the province of Judaea/Syria-Palaestina is characterized by violent political, administrative, and military changes reflected in the changing ranks of its officials.

The unique sources at our disposal, as well as other factors – not to be admitted by the impartial historian – have conspired to create the notion of the special and unique status of the province of Judaea/Syria-Palaestina within the Roman empire.[37] Was it so regarded by the Romans? To a certain extent the answer is that it was – at least in practice; we cannot explain otherwise the violent changes in the status of the territory in the period described above. Its provincialization began in 6 CE, when it is likely to have been annexed to the Roman province of Syria; it may have become an independent procuratorial province between 44 and 67; it was promoted to a praetorian province in 70 CE; finally, at an unknown date in the early second century it became a consular province, with two legions as well as three cavalry *alae* and twelve cohorts at the disposal of the governor[38] – and all that in what was after all an exceedingly small province. The Romans must have felt themselves faced with special problems calling for special administrative and military measures.[39]

II

Having discussed the more external aspect of Roman rule in Judaea/Syria-Palaestina, I devote the second part of this presentation to the local organization of the area with special emphasis on the papyrological evidence now coming to light. Following Emil Schürer I distinguish the so-called 'Hellenistic cities' from

---

37 There is a striking similarity to the fate of Roman Egypt: the 'Sonderstellung Ägyptens' is the direct corollary of the availability of the papyrological material; but see now the corrective views of Naphtali Lewis, "'Greco-Roman Egypt': Fact or Fiction?," in *Proceedings of the Twelfth International Congress of Papyrology, Ann Arbor, Michigan, 12–17 August 1968*, ed. Deborah H. Samuel (Toronto: Hakkert, 1970), 3–14; James G. Keenan, "Papyrology and Roman History: 1956–1980," *Classical World* 76 (1982): 30–31; Naphtali Lewis, "The Romanity of Roman Egypt: A Growing Consensus," in *Atti del XVII Congresso internazionale di papirologia* (Napoli: Centro internazionale per lo studio dei papiri ercolanesi, 1984), 1077–1084; Alan K. Bowman and Dominic Rathbone, "Cities and Administration in Roman Egypt," *JRS* 82 (1992): 107–27; Dominic Rathbone, "Egypt, Augustus and Roman Taxation," *Cahiers du Centre Gustave Glotz* 4 (1993): 81–112.

38 *CIL* XVI 87, 139 CE.

39 However, the Romans could not, and did not, realize the special problems facing them in Judaea from the beginning, as those who postulate the creation of an independent province with an independent governor already in 6 CE seem to suggest; see e.g. Stern, "The Province of Judaea," 309.

the 'Jewish region.'[40] Assuming that these cities functioned in a similar way to other cities in the Roman Empire, i. e. in their relations to the sovereign power and the villages within their boundaries, I have decided to concentrate on the Jewish region only. I can foresee many objections: their history was often entwined; some cities had mixed populations of Jews and non-Jews; the populations of a few cities were preponderantly Jewish. Although to the extent that they are *poleis* they could be seen as Hellenistic foundations, the history of many of these cities goes back far beyond the Hellenistic age, whereas other cities were recent Herodian and Roman foundations. Nor is it quite accurate to speak of the Hellenistic cities as cities of Judaea/Syria-Palaestina, since, as we have seen, one of the first acts of Roman rule was to free the cities from Jewish rule and attach them to the province of Syria. At different times many of the Hellenistic cities belonged to Syria and to Arabia. Altogether the artificiality of the provincial borders is apparent in the fluctuations between native dynastic rule and direct Roman rule, and in the parceling and re-parceling of the territories. The expression of Jewish nationality and the Hellenic pretensions of the cities paid little attention to provincial borders. The Great Revolt involved Jews across the borders and I suspect that the Jews of Arabia were involved in some way in the Bar Kokhba revolt, and, that this is the reason why their archives were found in Naḥal Ḥever in Judaea.[41] A good example of the Hellenic pretensions of the Greek cities is the formula 'a Greek city of Koile Syria' on coins and inscriptions of six cities of the Decapolis incorporated into the 'Barbaric' provinces of Judaea/Syria-Palaestina and Arabia by the mid-second century CE. 'Koile Syria' was neither an administrative entity nor a *koinon*, nor even a geographical reference, but merely an attempt at showing off the 'Hellenic credentials' of these cities, as a recent study describes it.[42] While I admit that the objections enumerated above are valid, I have nevertheless decided to exclude a treatment of the Hellenistic cities here.

---

40 Emil Schürer, *The History of the Jewish People in the Age of Jesus Christ*, Vol. II, ed. Fergus Millar and Géza Vermès (Edinburgh: Clark, 1979), 85–198.

41 I refer to the Babatha archive and the archive of Salome Komaïse daughter of Levi. The Greek part of the former was published by Naphtali Lewis, *The Documents from the Bar Kokhba Period in the Cave of Letters. Greek Papyri*, Judean Desert Studies II (Jerusalem: IES, 1989) (*P.Yadin*); for the latter see Hannah M. Cotton and Ada Yardeni, *Aramaic, Hebrew, and Greek Documentary Texts from Naḥal Ḥever and Other Sites*, Discoveries in the Judaean Desert XXVII (Oxford: Clarendon Press, 1997) (*XḤev/Ṣe ar.* and *XḤev/Ṣe gr.*); see now Werner Eck, "The Bar Kokhba Revolt: The Roman Point of View," *JRS* 89 (1999): 76–89.

42 Alla Stein, "Studies in Greek and Latin Inscriptions on Palestinian Coinage under the Principate" (Tel-Aviv University Thesis, 1990), 260–91.

The Jewish region

We are talking here of Judaea proper, Samaria, the Galilee and the Peraea. There are very few cities in these areas and the majority of cities that are there are on the fringes, and in any case are not likely to have controlled the entire Jewish region as their city-territories. Many settlements referred to as cities in the Jewish sources would not pass the criteria of a *polis*. The Jewish region was composed then of villages of different sizes. The Jewish sources speak of 'a large city' (כרך), 'a town' (עיר) and 'a village' (כפר or חצר).

It is generally assumed, as far as I can tell, that there was a relationship of subordination between the settlements of different size in the Jewish region. The new Schürer for example assumes that the subordination of villages to a 'town,' indicated already in the Old Testament, where it is reflected in such locutions as 'the cities and their villages' (הערים וחצריהן) or 'the city and its daughters' (העיר ובנותיה), must have continued into our period.[43] It has been suggested that one can trace at least economic dependence of smaller villages on larger ones both in the rabbinic sources and in aerial surveys of patterns of settlement and communication in the Jewish region.[44]

A parallel is often drawn between the so-called 'towns' of the Jewish region and the 'mother villages' μητροκωμίαι in the Trachonitis – a territory which like the Jewish region lacked cities.[45] It is argued that the 'mother villages' were administrative and judicial centers like cities in other parts of the Roman world. A letter of Iulius Saturninus, the governor of Syria in 185–87, to Phaena, in which the city is described as the '*metrokomia* of the Trachon' (μητροκωμία τοῦ Τράχωνος),[46] illustrates, to cite Fergus Millar, "the city-like function of the major villages of this region."[47] This may well be so, but the letter, which addresses the inhabitants of Phaena only (Ἰούλιος Σατουρνῖνος Φαινησίοις μητροκωμίᾳ τοῦ Τράχωνος χαίρειν), does not give us any information about the range and nature of Phaena's responsibilities vis-à-vis its lesser neighbours. Moreover, as MacAdam points out: "Apart from the paucity of inscriptions which testify to *metrocomiai*,

43 Schürer, *The History of the Jewish People in the Age of Jesus Christ* II, 189.
44 Ze'ev Safrai, "The Village in the Time of the Mishnah and the Talmud," in *Nation and History: Studies in the History of the Jewish People*, ed. Menahem Stern (Jerusalem: Zalman Shazar Center, 1983), 173–95 (Hebrew); Ian W. J. Hopkins, "The City Region in Roman Palestine," *PEQ* 112 (1980): 19–32.
45 Schürer, *The History of the Jewish People in the Age of Jesus Christ* II, 189 f.
46 *IGRom.* III 1119 = *OGIS* 609.
47 Fergus Millar, *The Roman Near East, 31 BC-AD 337* (Cambridge, Mass.: Harvard University Press, 1993), 426.

not a single community is yet attested twice as a *metrocomia*."[48] It seems to me idle, therefore, to talk, as MacAdam does, about the "extent of [their] territoriy" and "[their] duties and responsibilities ... regarding the *komai*,"[49] since we do not really know whether they possessed either or both attributes. After all the title of *metropolis* which *metrocomia* closely resembles is merely honorific. There is abundant epigraphic evidence for village officials, village assemblies and public building undertaken by the villages in the Trachonitis, the Auranitis and Batanea. This evidence argues for a large measure of independence of the single village. Harper is right to point out that "had the villages become dependent parts of city territories, it is not probable that they would have retained such an elaborate organization of their own";[50] the same could be said about putative dependence on the *metrocomiai*. I think that Jones was right to suggest that "the village was the normal social and administrative unit in this area."[51] The village then must have been in direct contact with the Roman governor. Whether this was done through an official appointed by the governor of Syria we do not know. The one and only piece of evidence for such a link are the centurions who figure in nine or eleven inscriptions from the area. But since they all fall between the years 169–189, this may be no more than a temporary measure.[52]

It seems to me that we may be on safer ground in understanding the administration of the Jewish region if we examine the evidence for the existence of administrative divisions in Judaea in Roman times. Gabinius' division of the country into five regions ruled by *synhedria* was an episode (57 BCE) – we do not hear of it later.[53] A much older division of Judaea proper into *toparchiai* survived into the Roman period. The origin of some of the toparchies seems to have been Ptolemaic; the Seleucids maintained them, the Hasmoneans increased their number and they continued into Herod's time.[54] Josephus (*BJ* 3.55) and Pliny (*NH* V, 70) as

48 Henry Innes MacAdam, *Studies in the History of the Roman Province of Arabia: The Northern Sector* (Oxford: B.A.R., 1986), 82.

49 MacAdam, 82.

50 George McLean Harper, *Village Administration in the Roman Province of Syria*, Yale Classical Studies, Vol. I (New Haven: Yale University Press, 1928), 141; cf. 145.

51 A.H.M. Jones, *The Cities of the Eastern Roman Provinces*, rev. Michael Avi-Yonah, 2nd ed. (Oxford: Clarendon Press, 1971), 285.

52 Jones, 465, n. 79; MacAdam, *Studies in the History of the Roman Province of Arabia: The Northern Sector*, 54 f., 91 ff.

53 Schürer, *The History of the Jewish People in the Age of Jesus Christ* I, 268–69; Schürer, *The History of the Jewish People in the Age of Jesus Christ* II, 190.

54 Abraham Schalit, *King Herod: Portrait of a Ruler* (Jerusalem: Mosad Bialik, 1960), 101 ff. (Hebrew).

well as the documents from the Judaean Desert confirm the survival of *toparchiai* into the Roman period, both before and after the Great Revolt of 66–70.

With the exception of Idumaea – which is an ethnic name – the *toparchia* was named after one of its villages, presumably the most important or central village in the *toparchia*. Adora and Beth Govrin have each been proposed as the central village for Idumaea.

Josephus gives the following list of κληρουχίαι or τοπαρχίαι for Judaea proper: (1) Jerusalem (2) Gophna (3) Acrabeta (4) Idumaea (5) Thamna (6) Lydda (7) Emmaus (8) Pella i. e. Betholeptephene (9) Ein Gedi (10) Herodion (11) Jericho (*BJ* 3.55). Pliny names ten toparchies: (1) Jericho (2) Emmaus (3) Lydda (4) Jopica (5) Acrabeta (6) Gophna (7) Thamna (8) Betholeptephene (9) Orine (10) Herodion (Pliny, *NH* V, 70). There are two significant discrepancies between Josephus' and Pliny's lists: 1) Ein Gedi and Idumaea are absent from Pliny's list; 2) Jamnia and Joppa are not included in Josephus' list, but added as an appendix,[55] whereas Pliny includes Joppa in his list, but omits Jamnia.

The omission of Ein Gedi and Idumaea from Pliny's list led people to the conclusion that he used a source which goes back to Herod's time when Idumaea and Ein Gedi had not yet been made part of Judaea.[56] However, all this was before the recent publication of the archives from the Judaean Desert. It now seems certain that Pliny's list reflects the situation after the revolt. The village of Ein Gedi, sacked by the *sicarii* of Masada and possibly also by the Romans in the battles over the balsam groves,[57] became like Jerusalem 'a heap of ashes' (*nunc alterum bustum*, Pliny, *NH* V, 73), and, as we now know from the papyri, ceased to be the central village of a toparchy, and was itself subsumed in the toparchy of Jericho. In *P.Yadin* 16 from 127 CE, Babatha's second husband Judah son of Eleazar is said to come from 'the village of Ein Gedi in the district of Jericho in Judaea' (Ἰουδάνου Ἐλαζάρου κώμης Αἰνγαδδῶν περὶ Ἱερειχοῦντα τῆς Ἰουδαίας, lines 14–15). Perhaps Ein Gedi lost its status as a capital village of a toparchy as it became 'a village of our Lord the Caesar,' as attested in the opening lines of *P.Yadin* 11 of 124 CE: ἐπ̣ὶ ὑ̣[πάτ]ω̣ν Μανείο̣υ Ἀκειλίου Γλαβρίωνος κ̣α̣ὶ Τορκουά[του Θ]η̣βανιανο[ῦ πρὸ] μ̣ιᾶς

55 μεθ' ἃς Ἰάμνεια καὶ Ἰόππη τῶν περιοίκων ἀφηγοῦνται, Joseph. *BJ* 3.56.

56 Menahem Stern, "The Description of Palestine by Pliny the Elder and the Administrative Division of Judea at the End of the Period of the Second Temple," *Tarbiz* 37 (1978): 215–29 (Hebrew), reprinted in *Studies in Jewish History. The Second Temple Period*, ed. Yeshayahu Gafni, Moshe David Herr, and Moshe Amit (Jerusalem: Yad Ben-Zvi Press, 1991), 246–60.

57 Hannah M. Cotton and Werner Eck, "Ein Staatsmonopol und seine Folgen: Plinius, Naturalis Historia 12,123 und der Preis für Balsam," *Rheinisches Museum für Philologie* 140 (1997): 153–61.

νωγῷν Μαίω[ν] ἐν Ἐνγαδοῖς κώμῃ κυρίου Καίσαρος; cf. *XḤev/Ṣe gr.* 67, line 2: [Ἐν] γαδῶν κυρίου Κ[αίσαρος].[58]

As for Idumaea, it could be suggested that it too suffered such devastation that it disappeared as an independent toparchy.[59] At some point though between the late 70s and 130 a new toparchy was created at least in part of what had previously been the toparchy of Idumaea: the toparchy of Zif or Zephine. This is biblical Zif situated south-east of Hebron. The new toparchy is attested for the first time in a marriage contract from the Judaean Desert from 130 CE. The marriage was contracted ἐν Ἀριστοβουλιάδι τῆς Ζ̣ε̣ι̣φ̣η̣νῆς, and the groom is Ἀκαβας Μηειρω τῶν ἀ̣π̣ὸ κώμης Ἰακείμων τ̣[ῆς Ζειφηνῆς], *XḤev/Ṣe* 69 (= *XḤev/Ṣe gr.* 2), lines 3–5.[60] The two villages, Aristoboulias and Yaqim (or Yakum),[61] belonged to the new toparchy of Zif. It is true that the term *toparchia* does not appear in this papyrus[62] but the expression ἐν Ἀριστοβουλιάδι τῆς Ζ̣ε̣ι̣φ̣η̣νῆς describes the relationship between a central village and another village, typical of the toparchy structure.

Another marriage contract from the Judaean Desert, *DJD* II, no. 115, from 124 CE, was concluded 'at Bethbassi in the toparchy of Herodium' – ἐν Βαιτοβαι̣σσαιας ... τ̣ο̣παρχείας Ἡρωδείο[υ]; the groom, Eleaios son of Simon, came 'from the village of Galoda of Akrabatta, but [was] an inhabitant of Batharda of Gophna': τῶν ἀπὸ κ(ώμης) Γαλωδῶν τῆς περὶ Ἀκραβαττῶν οἰκῶν ἐν κώμῃ Βαιτοα̣ρδοις τῆς περὶ Γοφνοῖς. It thus attests the survival of three of the old toparchies into the period after the Great Revolt. Finally, Orine (Ὀρεινή), the toparchy which replaced Jerusalem according to Pliny (*Orinen in qua fuere Hierosolyma*), is attested in *DJD* II, no. 114 (an acknowledgement of debt), line 6.

In conclusion, the papyri and the 'rehabilitated' Pliny prove that the system of toparchies, i. e. the division of Judaea proper into districts, which took their names from their capital villages, remained virtually unchanged after the First Revolt.

---

58 Hannah M. Cotton, "Ein Gedi between the Two Revolts," *SCI* 20 (2001): 139–54 [below, pp. 347–61].

59 *BJ* 4.231–5.

60 See preliminary publication in Hannah M. Cotton, "A Cancelled Marriage Contract from the Judaean Desert, XHev/Se Gr. 2," *JRS* 84 (1994): 64–86.

61 Yakim or Yakum is mentioned also in the Aramaic *XḤev/Ṣe ar.* 9.

62 In fact the term appears but once in the papyri from the Judaean Desert to describe Herodion: τοπαρχείας Ἡρωδε[ί̣ο̣][υ], *DJD* II, no. 115, line 2.

What about the rest of the Jewish region, namely Samaria, Galilee and the Peraea?

Stern, as well as others, believed that the system of *toparchiai* was not restricted to Judaea proper: it is maintained that although we have full lists only for Judaea proper, nevertheless there is enough evidence to prove that *toparchiai* were to be found elsewhere in Judaea/Syria-Palaestina as well. This belief is based on Josephus' use of the term *toparchia* to describe administrative units outside Judaea proper.[63] Moreover, the term *toparchia* is used by Josephus to describe what at first sight at least seems a totally different regional division.[64] Josephus attaches the name of toparchy not only to a cluster of villages, of which the most important or central one gives its name to the toparchy, but also to cities with their territories. Joppa and Jamnia, as we have seen, are added as an appendix to Josephus' list of toparchies in Judaea proper.[65] Joppa is included in Pliny's list of toparchies, and is mentioned in the same breath with Lydda and Emmaus, two of the toparchies of Judaea proper, as centers to which commanders were assigned by the war council in Jerusalem on the eve of the Great Revolt.[66] In *AJ* 18.31 we are told that Salome, Herod's sister, bequeathed to Livia, Augustus' wife, Jamnia and its *toparchia*: Ἰάμνειάν τε ... καὶ τὴν τοπαρχίαν πᾶσαν. Even more revealing is the evidence of *BJ* 2.252, where we are told that Nero annexed to Agrippa II's kingdom 'four cities with their *toparchiai* (*πόλεις ... σὺν ταῖς τοπαρχίαις*). The cities were Abila and Julias (that is Livias) in the Peraea and Trachinae and Tiberias in the lower Galilee. The parallel passage in *AJ* explains to us the meaning of the expression 'a city with its toparchy': 'he (Nero) gave him also Livias (Julias), a *polis* of the Peraea, with its fourteen villages' (δίδωσι δὲ [Nero] καὶ Ἰουλιάδα πόλιν τῆς Περαίας καὶ κώμας τὰς περὶ αὐτὴν δεκατέσσαρας, 20.159). In other words, the fourteen villages constituted Livias' toparchy.

The expression καὶ κώμας τὰς περὶ αὐτὴν to describe the relationship between a city and the villages within its territory is attested now in a document from the Judaean Desert, *XḤev/Ṣe gr.* 65 (olim *P.Yadin* 37), which belongs to the archive of Salome Komaïse daughter of Levi. This is a marriage contract concluded between

63 E.g. Narbata in Samaria is called *toparchia* in Joseph., *BJ* 2.509. Narbata, like the *toparchiai* in Judaea, was named after its central village, Narbata, see Stern, *Studies in Jewish History. The Second Temple Period*, 256.

64 The same conclusions have been reached independently by Yuval Shahar, "Josephus' Geography of Eretz Israel and its Relation to Talmudic Traditions and Hellenistic and Roman Literature" (Tel-Aviv University Thesis, 1996), 181 f. (Hebrew).

65 Above n. 55.

66 *BJ* 2.567.

Salome Komaïse and 'Yeshu'a son of Menaḥem from the village of Soffathe… in the district of the city of Livias of the administrative region of P[eraia]' – Ἰησοῦς Μαναήμου τ[ῶν ἀπὸ κώμης …] Σοφφαθε̣[.]… π̣ε̣ρ̣ὶ πόλιν Λιουιάδος τῆς Π̣[εραίας] (lines 3–4).

Furthermore, like Josephus, the documents too describe the dependence of a village on the central village of the toparchy in terms identical to those which describe that of a village on the city to whose territory it belongs: the dependence of the village of Soffathe[…] on the city of Livias just quoted is expressed in the same terms as that of the village of Ein Gedi vis-à-vis Jericho (also a village) in *P.Yadin* 16 line 16: Ἰουδάνου Ἐλαζάρου κώμης Αἰνγαδδῶν περὶ Ἱερειχοῦντα τῆς Ἰουδαίας;[67] that of Bethbassi vis-à-vis Herodion – ἐν Βαιτοβαι̣σσαιας … τ̣ο̣παρχείας Ἡρῳδε̣ί̣ο̣[υ]; Galoda vis-à-vis Akrabatta – ἀπὸ κ(ώμης) Γαλωδῶν τῆς περὶ Ἀκραβα̣τ̣ῶν, and Batharda vis-à-vis Gophna – ἐν κώμῃ Βαιτοα̣ρδοις τῆς περὶ Γοφνοῖς – all in *P.Mur.* 115 lines 2–3; and finally that of Aristoboulias and Yaqim (or Yaqum) vis-à-vis Zif in *XḤev/Ṣe gr.* 69 lines 3–5 cited above.[68]

Does the identity of language imply an identity of function: would it be legitimate to maintain that the central village performed the same functions fulfilled by cities both in respect of their subordinate villages and in respect of the Roman authorities?

It is tempting to draw parallels between the administrative arrangement in Egypt, so richly documented, and that of the Jewish region of Judaea/Syria-Palaestina, where the documentation is so scarce and lacunose, when it exists at all. Such an approach gains force from the assumption that the toparchy is an inheritance from Ptolemaic times (note though that the Egyptian *toparchia* is a subdivision of the *nomos* which is the real equivalent of the Jewish *toparchia*). Thus the central or capital village which gives its name to the toparchy could be assimilated to the *metropoleis* of the Egyptian *nomoi*. A recent study of the Egyptian *metropoleis* by Alan Bowman and Dominic Rathbone convincingly demonstrates that already in the Julio-Claudian period "the *metropoleis* were to a significant degree functioning and behaving like the Greek *poleis* of other eastern provinces."[69] Were the central villages of the *toparchiai* in Judaea the equivalent to these *metropoleis*? The enslavement of Gophna, Emmaus, Lydda and Thamna – all of them capital villages of toparchies – by Cassius (Caesar's murderer) in 43 BCE for failing to raise the amount of money imposed on them is often adduced as evidence that taxes were imposed and collected at the level of the toparchy, and

67 Judaea here means Judaea proper, not the province.
68 Above ad n. 60.
69 Bowman and Rathbone, "Cities and Administration in Roman Egypt," 125

that the central village (or rather its officials or council) was therefore responsible for their collection. What we lack in Judaea/Syria-Palaestina altogether is the centrally appointed *strategoi*. Shalit believes that the *strategoi* stood at the head of the toparchies under Herod.[70] Furthermore two passages from the Jerusalem and Babylonian Talmuds have been interpreted as if there were *strategoi* in charge of the *toparchiai*, but I accept Alon's argument that the *estrategi* (אס[ט]רטגי) mentioned there are the *duoviri* of a *colonia*.[71]

The circumstantial evidence for the role of the capital village of the toparchy is strong; and yet one must not lose sight of the fact that there is evidence for a large measure of independence and administrative autonomy of the individual village – not unlike our evidence for the village in southern Syria mentioned above. Josephus mentions for the late Herodian period κωμογραμματεῖς in *AJ* 16.203 and κωμῶν γραμματεῖς in the parallel passage in *BJ* 1.479. We also hear in the New Testament of πρεσβῦτεροι, βουλαί and συνεδρία – located in villages. Needless to say, the Jewish sources abound in manifestations of self-rule, and administrative, religious and judicial autonomy. The people of a town were competent to control their synagogue, their market prices, the wages of their workers, to impose fines, check roads, dig public cisterns, mark boundaries of cemeteries etc. The sources speak of assemblies where decisions were taken and of local village courts, to handle civil and criminal cases; in particular, these courts were responsible for appointment of guardians for orphans and widows. The sources attest the existence of *agoranomoi* in charge of market prices, weights, and measures. *Parnasim* (פרנסים) and *gabbaim* (גבאים) are mentioned in the sources as the village magistrates, handling moneys and building projects. *Parnasim* are also attested in the Bar Kokhba documents as being in charge of leasing and sub-leasing public land in Ein Gedi. Taxes seem to have been collected by local people. This is evident in Josephus, in the New Testament,[72] as well as in the documents from the Judaean desert.[73] The *mochsin* (מוכסין) of the Jewish sources stand for

---

70 Schalit, *King Herod: Portrait of a Ruler*, 116 f.

71 Gedaliah Alon, "The στρατεγοί in the Cities of Palestine during the Roman Period," in *Studies in Jewish History*, Vol. II (Tel-Aviv: Hakibuz Hameuchad, 1958), 74–87 (Hebrew).

72 Herbert C. Youtie, "Publicans and Sinners," *ZPE* 1 (1967): 1–20 (originally, 1937).

73 Two receipts from Maḥoza, *XḤev/Ṣe gr.* 60 (125 CE, see Hannah M. Cotton, "Rent or Tax Receipt from Maoza," *ZPE* 100 (1994): 547–57) and the Aramaic *XḤev/Ṣe* 12 (131 CE, for an English paraphrase see Hannah M. Cotton, "The Archive of Salome Komaise Daughter of Levi: Another Archive from the 'Cave of Letters,'" *ZPE* 105 (1995): 204), both from the archive of Salome Komaïse daughter of Levi, demonstrate that local people, fellow-villagers, collected the taxes; see Benjamin Isaac, "Tax Collection in Roman Arabia: A New Interpretation of the Evidence from the Babatha Archive," *Mediterranean Historical Review* 9 (1994): 256–66. Susan Weingarten rightly suggests, "presumably the use of local middlemen who knew the properties ... concerned meant

collectors of taxes. We cannot determine whether the job of the collector of taxes was a liturgy, as in Egypt, or handled by *publicani* (τελῶναι).[74]

In conclusion, Josephus, Pliny and the papyri prove that the Jewish region was divided into administrative units with central villages or cities at their head. Only about Judaea proper can we be sure that these units were called *toparchiai*. There is no evidence for local officials at the head of these capital villages, nor for centrally appointed officials in charge of the *toparchiai* – but the existence of one kind or another of local officials must be assumed. There are some hints that the *toparchiai* were in charge of taxation. Above all it is hard to believe that nothing beyond a merely geographical relationship is intended by the description of the dependence of a village on a central village, especially since the dependence of the single village on the central village is described both in the papyri and in Josephus in terms identical to those describing the dependence of the *chora* on its *polis*. Furthermore, we know that under the Severi some of these central villages received the status of a *polis*: thus Lydda became Diospolis in 199/200, and Emmaus became Nicopolis in 219 or 220. In 199/200 Beth Govrin – about which we do not know that it was a capital village – received the status of a *polis* and was renamed Eleutheropolis.[75] The accelerating urbanization of Judaea (now called Syria-Palaestina) resulted in the eventual disappearance of the toparchies and their replacement by *poleis* with their territories. This is the picture conveyed by the fourth century Onomasticon of Eusebius.[76] But if we are right to think that the capital villages achieved a degree of local autonomy and administrative responsibilities already in the first and second centuries, then this urbanization was but a logical development. On the other hand, one must also take into account

---

that the central authorities had a built-in mechanism for verifying the census declaration" (apud Isaac, 266, n. 26). Evidently the display of the land declarations in the basilica of Rabbath-Moab (*P.Yadin* 16 lines 1–2 = lines 3–4; *XḤev/Ṣe gr.* 62 frg. a lines 1–2 = lines 3–4) also served as a deterrent to false declarations.

74 It is hard to interpret the scene described in *BJ* 2.405 of tax collection by the ἄρχοντες καὶ βουλευταί of Jerusalem in 66 CE: εἰς δὲ τὰς κώμας οἵ τε ἄρχοντες καὶ βουλευταὶ μερισθέντες τοὺς φόρους συνέλεγον. Was it an emergency measure? To what extent were they personally involved in the collection of taxes?

75 See A.H.M. Jones, "The Urbanization of Palestine," *JRS* 21 (1931): 82 ff.

76 Aharon Oppenheimer, "Urbanization and City Territories in Roman Palestine," in *The Jews in the Hellenistic-Roman World: Studies in Memory of Menahem Stern*, ed. Isaiah M. Gafni, Aharon Oppenheimer, and Daniel R. Schwartz (Jerusalem: Zalman Shazar Center, 1996), 220 ff. (Hebrew). For example, the village of Zif which was the capital of its toparchy to which both Aristoboulias and Yaqim belonged (*XḤev/Ṣe gr.* 69 lines 3–5) is now described as 'a κώμη in the Daromas in the territory of Eleutheropolis, near Hebron, eight miles to the south,' Eusebius, *Onomasticon*, p. 92, line 15 (ed. Klostermann).

the social and demographic changes, or rather upheavals, consequent upon the failure of the Bar Kokhba revolt: the heavy losses suffered by the Jewish population and its severe dislocation. The change of name from Judaea to Syria-Palaestina which reflects the suppression of the Jewish element symbolizes a new reality. The urbanization of Palestine in the centuries following the Revolt is concurrent with the strengthening of the non-Jewish element in the province, first the pagan and later on the Christian.

Appendix: Administrative divisions in Arabia

The hierarchical relationship between Maḥoza and Ẓo‘ar has been known to us from the Babatha archive, where it takes the following variants: ἐν Μαω[ζοις τ]ῷν περὶ Ζ[οα]ρα;[77] ἐṿ Μαωζα̣ περὶ Ζοαραν;[78] ἐν Μαωζα̣ περὶ Ζοορων;[79] ἐṿ Μ̣α̣ω̣ζας τῆς πε[ρὶ Ζοα]ρ̣α;[80] ἐν Μαωζα̣ περιμέτρῳ Ζοορων.[81] It is attested also in the archive of Salome Komaïse daughter of Levi: ἐ̣ṿ Μ̣α̣ω̣ζας τῆ̣ς π̣ερ̣ὶ Ζ[ο]α̣ρ̣ω̣ν (*XḤev/Ṣe gr.* 64 line 3). The phrasing in all its different variations strongly resembles the locutions describing the hierarchical relationship between central villages and subordinate ones in Judaea: ἐν Βαι̣τοβαισσαιας ... τ̣ο̣παρχείας Ἡρῳδεί̣ο̣[υ] ... ἀπὸ κ(ώμης) Γαλωδῶν τῆς περὶ Ἀκραβα̣τ̣τῶν οἰκῶν ἐν κώμη̣ Βαιτοα̣ρδοις τῆς περὶ Γοφνοῖς (*P.Mur* 115 lines 2–3); κώμης Αἰνγαδδῶν περὶ Ἱερειχοῦντα (*P.Yadin* 16 line 16); ἐν Ἀριστοβουλιάδι τῆς Ζε̣ι̣φη̣νῆς ... τῶν ἀπ̣ὸ κώμης Ἰακείμων τ̣[ῆς Ζειφηνῆς] (*XḤev/Ṣe gr.* 69 lines 3–5). The similarity suggests that Maḥoza was subordinate to Ẓo‘ar in much the same way as a village in Judaea was subordinate to the central village which gave its name to the toparchy to which it belonged – even if the term *toparchia* never appears in the archives from the province of Arabia.[82]

Yet, as we now know, Arabia was organized differently. In the section on Judaea it was demonstrated that the province was divided into toparchies, the center of which could be either a city (*polis*) or a village. In Arabia, on the other hand, there was double subordination: both Maḥoza and Ẓo‘ar were subsumed in

---

77 *P.Yadin* 5a col. i lines 4–5.
78 *P.Yadin* 14 line 20; 15 line 3 = lines 16–17; 17 lines 2–3 = lines 19–20; 18 line 3 = line 32.
79 *P.Yadin* 25 line 28 = line 64.
80 *P.Yadin* 19 lines 10–11.
81 *P.Yadin* 20 line 4 = lines 22–23; 21 lines 5–6; 22 lines 5–6; 26 line 18; 27 lines 3–4.
82 As Naphtali Lewis reminds us in "The Babatha Archive: A Response," *IEJ* 44 (1994): 244; however, one notes that it is also absent in *XḤev/Ṣe gr.* 69 quoted above as well as in two out of three dependencies described in *DJD* II, no 115 quoted above.

the territory of Petra, which possessed the legal status of a *polis*.[83] This is attested in Babatha's land declaration, *P.Yadin* 16: Βαβθα ... Μαωζηνὴ τῆς Ζοαρηνῆς περιμέτρου Πέτρας (lines 13–14), as well as in that of Sammouos son of Shim'on, Salome Komaïse's first husband, *XḤev/Ṣe gr*. 62 (olim *XḤev/Ṣe gr*. 7):[84] Σ̣α̣μμ̣ο̣υ̣ος Σ̣ιμων[ο]ς Μαωζηνὸς τῆς Ζοαρηνῆς περιμέτρου Πέτρας (frg. a line 12). It also occurs in Salome Komaïse's contract of marriage to her second husband mentioned above: [ἐν Μαωζ̣α̣ τῆς Ζο]αρηνῆς.[...]... Πέτραν μητρόπολιν τῆ[ς Ἀραβίας] (*XḤev/Ṣe gr*. 65 lines 2–3). The fact that the double subordination is recorded in land declarations (*XḤev/Ṣe gr*. 62 and *P.Yadin* 16) lends the subordination an official status. That this was – or came to be – the administrative structure in the whole province of Arabia is now proved by *P.Bostra* 1.[85] The Bostra papyrus dates to 260 CE. It is a petition addressed to a *beneficarius* by a woman called Aurelia Thopheise, daughter of Azeizos, from the village Azzeira, which belongs to Aianatis in the territory of Bostra, Augusta Colonia and Metropolis: παρὰ Αὐρηλίας Θοφ̣ε̣ισης Ἀζειζου κώμης Ἀζζειρων τῆς Αἰανείτιδος ὁρίου Αὐγουστοκολ(ωνίας) μητροπόλεως Βόστρων (lines 2–4). The three concentric circles familiar to us from the southern part of the province are reproduced in its northern part.[86] As in the case of Petra, the vastness of Bostra's territory should be seen to account for the inclusion of villages in a subdivision of the city's territory.

83 The evidence for its status as a *polis* is *P.Yadin* 12 lines 1–2 (= lines 4–5, 114 CE): ἐγγεγραμμένον καὶ ἀντιβεβλημένον κεφαλαίου ἑνὸς ἀπὸ ἄκτων βουλῆς Πετραίων τῆς μητροπόλεως.

84 Frg. a of *XḤev/Ṣe gr*. 62 was published by Naphtali Lewis, "A Jewish Landowner from the Province of Arabia," *SCI* 8–9 (1985/88): 132–37.

85 I am much obliged to Jean Gascou for allowing me to see the text and the commentary on it in advance of publication. A preliminary edition of *P.Bostra* 1 can be found in his "Unités administratives locales et fonctionnaires romains. Les données des nouveaux papyrus du Moyen Euphrate et d'Arabie," in *Lokale Autonomie und römische Ordnungsmacht in den kaiserzeitlichen Provinzen vom 1. bis 3. Jahrhundert*, ed. Werner Eck (München: Oldenbourg, 1999), 71–3.

86 The editors regard Aianatis as a name of a district rather than that of a village. In that case the district of Aianatis, unlike that of Zo'ar, is not called after its capital village.

The Legio VI Ferrata

Ritterling's account of the history of the *legio VI Ferrata* in his Legio article of 1925[1] is on the whole still valid. Many questions which Ritterling left open have remained unsolved. Thus we still do not know where the legion's permanent quarters in Syria were for as long as it was stationed there.[2] In the province of Iudaea, later Syria Palaestina, the legion had its camp in Lajjun. However, we still know nothing about the camp's layout, since to this day no excavations have been carried out on the site.[3] Nor are we in a better position to answer definitely the question of whether or not the legion was transferred to Syria Phoenice in the middle of the third century CE. This possibility – which Ritterling did not wish to rule out – is based on the evidence of coins from the colony of Damascus which display the name of the legion together with a *vexillum*, suggesting thereby that veterans of the legion were settled in this colony.[4] Ritterling considered it more likely than not that the settled veterans belonged to the garrison of Syria Phoenice at the time.[5] However, there was nothing unusual about settling veterans outside

1 Emil Ritterling, "Legio," in *RE*, Vol. XII.2, 1925, 1587–96.
2 Perhaps in Raphanea, see Lawernce Keppie, "Legions in the East from Augustus to Trajan," in *The Defence of the Roman and Byzantine East: Proceedings of a Colloquium Held at the University of Sheffield in April 1986*, ed. Philip Freeman and David Kennedy, Vol. II (Oxford: B.A.R., 1986), 413.
3 The first epigraphic monument of the legion from this area – an altar dedicated to Iuppiter Sarapis by the *primipilus* Iulius Isidorianus from the time of Elagabal – was discovered about 2.5 km to the north-west of the camp (now in the Rockefeller Museum, Jerusalem), cf. *AE* 1948, no. 145.
4 *BMC* Syria, 286, no. 25; cf. Meir Rosenberger, *The Coinage of Eastern Palestine and Legionary Countermarks, Bar-Kochba Overstrucks* (Jerusalem: M. Rosenberger, 1978), 29 no. 41. See further Novella Vismara, *Monetazione provinciale Romana, II: Collezione Winsemann Falghera, 4: Maximinus-Aemilianus* (Milano: Edizioni Ennerre, 1992), 980 no. 2355. Another type from Damascus from the time of Trebonianus Gallus displays a *vexillum* with the legend *LEG III GAL*. Are we to understand that within a short span of time two legions were stationed in Damascus? Or, rather, that such *vexilla* with names of legions do not imply that the legion was stationed near the minting city? Furthermore, such legends may refer to past events, and in the case of the *legio VI Ferrata* the coins might well have recalled the time before the departure of the legion for Arabia or Judaea (see below). I am grateful to Wolfram Weiser for the numismatic references.
5 Ritterling, "Legio," 1594.

Article note: First published in Yann Le Bohec, ed., *Les legions de Rome sous le haut-empire: actes du congres de Lyon (17–19 septembre 1998)*, Vol. I (Lyon: Centre d'etudes romaines et gallo-romaines, 2000), 351–357, with the following note: this research was supported by the Israel Science Foundation.

https://doi.org/10.1515/9783110770438-021

the province in which they were serving,[6] and consequently there is no cogent reason to move the *legio VI Ferrata* out of Syria Palaestina in the second half of the third century CE. As far as our present knowledge goes there is no evidence that the legion, so long as it existed, was ever transferred from Syria Palaestina to another province.

Ritterling already knew of the legion's participation in Trajan's Parthian war.[7] Further confirmation is found in the decoration of its legate, C. Bruttius Praesens L. Fulvius Rusticus, in this war.[8]

The only substantial revision of Ritterling's account[9] concerns the time at which the legion left Syria to become the second legion in the garrison occupying the neighboring province of Judaea, later Syria Palaestina.

Ritterling believed that it was only towards the end of Hadrian's reign, following the heavy losses incurred in putting down the Jewish revolt, that we can be sure that the *legio VI Ferrata* was transferred from Syria. The revolt demonstrated that a second legion was needed to keep order in Judaea, now Syria Palaestina. That legion was the Syrian *legio VI Ferrata*. A military diploma from 139 CE (*CIL* XVI 87) which shows that the governor of the province was now of consular rank, i.e. at the head of an army of more than one legion, led Ritterling to believe that the transfer followed the revolt. The list of legions and their dispositions from the 160s (*CIL* VI 3492 = *ILS* 2288)[10] shows that the *legio VI Ferrata* no longer belonged to the Syrian army. Dio names the legion as one of the two legions serving in Judaea in his time (55, 23, 3). Finally, several undated inscriptions explicitly connect the legion with Caparcotna in the valley of Jezreel in Syria Palaestina (*CIL* III 6814–16; *AE* 1920, no. 78).[11]

However, we now know that the change in the status of the province, from praetorian to consular, was not the corollary of the Bar Kokhba revolt, but had occurred already some time earlier.[12] Q. Tineius Rufus, who was governor at the time of the revolt (but may well have become so as early as 130, as an inscription

---

6 Cf. for example *SEG* 17, 584 (time of Hadrian).

7 Ritterling, "Legio," 1590–1.

8 *AE* 1950, no. 66; *IRT* 545.

9 However, we now know that a *vexillatio* of the *legio VI Ferrata* took part in the second Dacian War, see *AE* 1983, no. 825 and Karl Strobel, "Zu Fragen der frühen Geschichte der römischen Provinz Arabia und zu einigen Problemen der Legionsdislokation im Osten des Imperium Romanum zu Beginn des 2. Jh.n.Chr.," *ZPE* 71 (1988): 251–53.

10 Ritterling dated it to the time of Antoninus Pius.

11 Ritterling, "Legio," 1591–2.

12 See Michael Avi-Yonah, "When Did Judea Become a Consular Province?," *IEJ* 23 (1973): 209–13; Lawernce Keppie, "The Legionary Garrison of Judaea under Hadrian," *Latomus* 32 (1973): 859–64; Werner Eck, "Zum konsularen Status von Iudaea im frühen 2. Jh," *BASP* 21 (1984): 55–67.

from Caesarea suggests),[13] was consul in 127. However, the consular status of its governor is no longer the sole evidence for the presence of a second legion in the province; nor the promotion of its procurator to a *ducenarius* in late Trajanic or early Hadrianic time.[14]

Two milestones found on the military road from Caparcotna to Sepphoris, and dated by Hadrian's tribunician power to 120 CE[15] – one of them giving Caparcotna as a *caput viae*[16] – show that Caparcotna was important for the military road-system by then, and therefore likely to be the permanent camp of a legion. In other words, a second legion was in Judaea by 120. Of course all this does not reveal the identity of the second legion at this time. In fact, another milestone published by Isaac and Roll, if we accept their reading, attests the *legio II Traiana* as active in building the road from Sepphoris to Ptolemais, which is the continuation of the road from Caparcotna to Sepphoris just mentioned.[17]

The camp in Caparcotna/Lajjun (near Meggido) has not been excavated, but the strategic position of the site which commands the valley of Jezreel and sits on the natural access from the Mediterranean coast to Damascus is very obvious. It also, as has been observed, could be used to drive a wedge between the inhabitants of Judaea to the south and the Galilee to the north.[18]

About 25–30 km to the southeast another Roman camp was discovered in recent years, in Tel Shalem, 12 km south of Scythopolis, on the road from Scythopolis to Jericho. The camp is dated by the archaeologists to the first half of the second century CE.[19] It certainly was occupied in Hadrian's times, as is proved by a cuirassed statue of Hadrian found there. Nearby a gigantic arch was raised after the Bar Kokhba revolt to celebrate Hadrian's victory over the Jews. Fragments of a monumental inscription may suggest that the arch was dedicated by

---

13 A dedication by the *beneficiarii* of Tineius Rufus was found in excavations in Caesarea by Y. Porath and published in *CIIP* II 1276.

14 Hans-Georg Pflaum, "Remarques sur le changement de statut administratif de la province de Judée: À propos d'une inscription récémment découverte a Sidé de Pamphylie," *IEJ* 19 (1969): 232–33.

15 Benjamin Isaac and Israel Roll, "Judaea in the Early Years of Hadrian's Reign," *Latomus* 38 (1979): 56.

16 Another milestone, from the 130s, and also giving Caparcotna as a *caput viae*, is mentioned in Isaac and Roll, 57.

17 Benjamin Isaac and Israel Roll, "Legio II Traiana in Judaea," *ZPE* 33 (1979): 149–56; J.R. Rea, "The Legio II Traiana in Judaea?," *ZPE* 38 (1980): 220–21; Benjamin Isaac and Israel Roll, "Legio II Traiana in Judaea: A Reply," *ZPE* 47 (1982): 131–32.

18 Shimon Applebaum, *Prolegomena to the Study of the Second Jewish Revolt A.D. 132–135* (Oxford: B.A.R., 1976), 23; Isaac and Roll, "Judaea in the Early Years of Hadrian's Reign," 61 f.

19 Gideon Foerster, "A Cuirassed Bronze Statue of Hadrian," *Atiqot* 17 (1985): 139 f.

the S.P.Q.R.[20] Finally a building inscription of a *vexillatio* of the *legio VI Ferrata* was discovered nearby some thirty years ago.[21] Assuming that all these pieces of information are interconnected, it might be suggested, with caution, that already under Hadrian, for a time, part of the *legio VI Ferrata* was stationed in the smaller camp in Tel Shalem; of course we cannot know whether its presence there preceded the Bar Kokhba revolt or not.

Thus we still do not know when the *legio VI Ferrata* arrived in Judaea/Syria Palaestina. However, unlike Ritterling who merely toyed with the idea that the *legio VI Ferrata* did not move directly from Syria to Judaea/Syria Palaestina, but did so via the new province of Arabia,[22] we can actually prove that the *legio VI Ferrata* replaced the *legio III Cyrenaica* in Arabia some time before 119 (see below). This piece of information is revealed by an inscription from Gerasa, often mentioned in this context but never, to my mind, satisfactorily read and fully exploited for this purpose.[23]

Few will dispute now that the first legionary garrison in Arabia was the *legio III Cyrenaica* from Egypt which was put under the command of a senatorial legate, Claudius Severus, who was to become the first governor of the annexed province, once A. Cornelius Palma returned to Syria.[24] The *legio III Cyrenaica* remained outside Egypt for some time: it took part in the Parthian war,[25] where the *tribunus*

---

20 Werner Eck and Gideon Foerster, "Ein Triumphbogen für Hadrian im Tal von Beth Shean bei Tel Shalem," *JRA* 12 (1999): 294 ff.

21 Nehemia Tzori, "An Inscription of the Legio VI Ferrata from the Northern Jordan Valley," *IEJ* 21 (1971): 53–54.

22 Ritterling, "Legio," 1591, who suggests that one of the Syrian legions, perhaps the *legio VI Ferrata*, belonged to the first garrison of the new province of Arabia.

23 See Appendix 1: The inscription from Gerasa. Less decisive is the republication by Maurice Sartre, "Note sur la première légion stationnee en Arabie romaine," *ZPE* 13 (1974): 85–89 of an epitaph of an *optio hastati* of the *legio VI Ferrata* found at Bostra.

24 To mention the more important contributions: Claire Préaux, "Une source nouvelle sur l'annexion de l'Arabie par Trajan : les papyrus de Michigan 465 et 466," *Phoibos* 5 (1950): 123–39; David L. Kennedy, "Legio VI Ferrata: The Annexation and Early Garrison of Arabia," *Harv. Stud.* 84 (1980): 283–309; Strobel, "Zu Fragen der frühen Geschichte der römischen Provinz Arabia und zu einigen Problemen der Legionsdislokation im Osten des Imperium Romanum zu Beginn des 2. Jh.n.Chr." For the auxiliary units from Egypt, *I Hispanorum* and *I Thebaeorum*, which perhaps together with the *legio III Cyrenaica* belonged to the first garrison of Arabia, see Michael P. Speidel, "The Roman Army in Arabia," in *Aufstieg und Niedergang der römischen Welt*, Vol. II.8 (Berlin: De Gruyter, 1978), 709 f.

25 S. Gould, "Inscriptions. I. The Triumphal Arch," in *The Excavations at Dura-Europos conducted by Yale University and the French Academy of Inscriptions and Letters*, Vol. IV (New Haven: Yale University Press, 1933), 56 ff.; S. Gould, "Supplementary Inscriptions. I. An Addition to the Inscriptions of the Arch of Trajan," in *The Excavations at Dura-Europos conducted by Yale University and the French Academy of Inscriptions and Letters*, Vol. VI (New Haven: Yale University

militum laticlavius Q. Voconius Saxa Fidus won the *dona militaria*,[26] and a *vexillatio* of the *legio III Cyrenaica* was in Jerusalem ca. 116, perhaps as part of the force sent with Lusius Quietus to quell riots in Judaea.[27] By 119 the legion was back in its camp in Egypt together with the *legio XXII Deiotariana*.[28] Its place in Arabia, as pointed out above, was taken before 119 by the *legio VI Ferrata*.

As is well known, Egypt was not to be the final station for the *legio III Cyrenaica*, nor was Arabia to be the final stop for the *legio VI Ferrata*. However, the precise date of their arrival at their final destination, Judaea/Syria Palaestina and Arabia respectively, is unknown. In fact any conjecture about their movements after 119 is based on the hypothesized movements of the *legio II Traiana* and the *legio XXII Deiotariana*. As we have seen the *legio II Traiana*, whose whereabouts since the conclusion of the Dacian wars are unknown, is attested in Judaea in 120.[29] By 127 it is present in Egypt.[30] Its arrival there would have raised the number of legions in Egypt to three. There was no military reason to justify the presence of three legions in Egypt in this period: consequently the arrival of the *legio II Traiana* in Egypt must have meant that it replaced there either the *legio XXII Deiotariana* or the *legio III Cyrenaica*.

It is thus possible that the *legio XXII Deiotariana* moved now to Judaea.[31] There might be some evidence for its presence there on an erased inscription from the

Press, 1936), 480 ff.: *Imp. Ca[es]ari divi N[er]vae f. Nervae | Traiano [Opt. Au]g. Ge[rm. D]ac. p[o]nt. max. tri. | po[t. XX?, imp. IX?, cos. VI p.p. le]gio [I]II Cyr.*

26 The restoration of lines 11–14 of the Latin inscription published by Ismail Kaygusuz, "Eine neue Ehrung für Quintus Voconius Saxa Fidus in Perge," *Epigraphica Anatolica* 2 (1983): 37–39 is supported by the Greek inscription from Phaselis published by David J. Blackman in Jörg Schäfer, ed., *Phaselis: Beiträge zur Topographie und Geschichte der Stadt und ihrer Häfen* (Tübingen: Wasmuth, 1981), 154–59: χειλίαρχον πλατύσημον λεγεῶνος γ' Κυρηναικῆς καὶ λεγεῶνο[ς δ]ωδε[κά]της κε[ρ]α[υν]οφόρου, δώροις στρατιωτικοῖς ὑπὸ θεοῦ Τραιανοῦ ἐν τῷ Παρθικῷ πολέμῳ δωρηθέντα; *[trib(unum) mil](itum) lato clavo leg(ionis) III Cyr(enaicae) [et leg(ionis XII] Fulm(inatae), donis mil(itaribus) [donatum a div]o Traiano [ob] expeditionem Parthicam.*

27 *CIL* III 13587 = *ILS* 4393: *Iovi. m. Sarapidi pro salute et victoria imp. Nervae Traiani Caesaris optumi Aug. Germanici Dacici Parthici et populi Romani, vexill. Leg. III Cyr. fecit.*

28 *BGU* I 130 = James H. Oliver, *Greek Constitutions of Early Roman Emperors from Inscriptions and Papyri* (Philadelphia: American Philosophical Society, 1989), no. 70.

29 See above n. 17; it is attested also on the aqueduct in Caesarea, Clayton Miles Lehmann and Kenneth G. Holum, *The Greek and Latin Inscriptions of Caesarea Maritima* (Boston: ACOR, 2000), no. 47 (*CIIP* II 1202); a soldier of the legion was buried in Sidon in 117/8, Emil Ritterling, "Zur Geschichte der leg. II Traiana unter Traian," *Rheinisches Museum für Philologie* 58 (1903): 476–80.

30 *CIL* III 42 (19 April 127); *CIL* III 79 = 14147(6), p. 2300 (5 February 128).

31 Lawrence Keppie, "The History and Disappearance of the Legion XXII Deiotariana," in *Greece and Rome in Eretz Israel: Collected Essays*, ed. Aryeh Kasher, Uriel Rappaport, and Gideon Fuks (Jerusalem: Yad Ben-Zvi Press, 1990), 59 f.

Caesarea aqueduct.[32] As Keppie puts it, "it remained there only to be destroyed in 132."[33] It was replaced during the revolt or after by the *legio VI Ferrata* which came from Arabia and was replaced in its turn by the *legio III Cyrenaica*. Alternatively, the *legio II Traiana* could have replaced the *legio III Cyrenaica* in Egypt, and the latter replaced the *legio VI Ferrata* in Arabia. In this reconstruction the *legio VI Ferrata* moved into Judaea before the Bar Kokhba revolt. It should be admitted that neither scenario can be proved; and indeed, perhaps both are wrong.

Appendix 1: The Inscription from Geresa

It is principally on account of this inscription that it is commonly assumed that the *legio VI Ferrata* replaced the *legio III Cyrenaica* in Arabia some time before 119, and stayed there until, replaced by the *legio III Cyrenaica*, it moved into Judaea, which might already have become Syria Palaestina. The readings and interpretations of the inscription from Gerasa offered so far do not categorically prove the presence of the entire legion in Arabia at the time. However, as read and interpreted below, this is precisely what can be inferred from this inscription. Furthermore, some of the previous readings and restorations are palpably false. Nevertheless, so long as the actual inscription cannot be traced and photographed, the following reconstruction is offered as no more than an attempt to make sense of this partially preserved text.[34]

The first publication by A.H.M. Jones[35] was reproduced with some corrections by C.B. Welles:[36]

pr]aef(ecto) coh
trib(uno) mil(itum) leg(ionis) X] piae fideli[s
proc(uratori) provinc(iae)] Arabiae
milites?] leg(ionis) VI Ferr(atae)
imp(eratore) Caes(are) T]raiano Hadriano
Aug(usto) trib(unicia) pot(estate) XI]V III co(n)s(ule)
fece]runt ex AVN

32 See Isaac and Roll, "Judaea in the Early Years of Hadrian's Reign," 60–1 = Lehmann and Holum, *The Greek and Latin Inscriptions of Caesarea Maritima*, no. 46 (*CIIP* II 1201).
33 Keppie, "The History and Disappearance of the Legion XXII Deiotariana," 59–60.
34 I wish to thank Werner Eck for inspiring suggestions.
35 "Inscriptions from Jerash," *JRS* 18 (1928): 146–47.
36 In Carl H. Kraeling, ed., *Gerasa: City of the Decapolis* (New Haven: American Schools of Oriental Research, 1938), 435, no. 171.

D.L. Kennedy[37] rejects Welles's reconstruction of the inscription as a *cursus* inscription but has to admit that the precise nature of the inscription eludes him. He reconstructs it as follows:

U]lpiae fideli ...
provinciae?] Arabiae
vexill(ationis)] leg. VI Ferr(atae)
imp(eratore) Caes(are) T]raiano Hadriano
Aug(usto) trib.pote]st. III cos [III]
...]runt ex Alex[andria]

His revised reading of *piae fideli[s* as *U]lpiae fideli[---]* is meaningless. My starting point is in fact the *piae fideli[s]* which, with Welles, I take to be the title of a legion (there are several candidates: *legio I Adiutrix, legio I Minervia, legio II Adiutrix, legio VII Macedonica, legio XI Claudia, legio XIII Gemina* and *legio XXII Primigenia*). Combined with *Arabiae* in the following line, a *cursus* is suggested. However, unlike Welles, I do not wish to restore here an equestrian *cursus*, but a senatorial one. Not only because the dedication by soldiers to their commander (rather than to the provincial procurator) should be our first choice, but also because the equestrian *cursus* suggested by Welles is hardly probable: the provincial procuratorship in Arabia is not likely to have followed immediately after a military tribunate, a post in the *militia secunda*.[38] I propose therefore to restore a legionary command: *legato legionis* (number and name of legion) *piae fidelis*. The governorship of the province of Arabia then follows: *[legato Augusti pro praetore provinciae] Arabiae*. And since I accept Kennedy's suggestion that the *III* stands for the tribunician power, the date under Hadrian must be between 10/12/118 and 9/12/119. The next known governor after Claudius Severus is Q. Gargilius Antiquus,[39] consul in 119.[40] He could be the governor honored by a group of soldiers from the *legio VI Ferrata*. Therefore I restore at the beginning of the

---

37 Kennedy, "Legio VI Ferrata: The Annexation and Early Garrison of Arabia," 297–99.
38 In the list of procurators from Arabia given by Hans-Georg Pflaum, *Les carrières procuratoriennes équestres sous le haut-empire romain* (Paris: P. Geuthner, 1960), 1083 there is not one case of the direct promotion of an equestrian holding a post in the *tertia militia* – to say nothing of one holding a post in the *secunda militia* – to the post of provincial procurator of the province of Arabia. The promotion from a *praefectus alae* to the post of financial procurator of Arabia in the case of L. Valerius Firmus is merely a restoration of *AE* 1930, no. 92 = Welles in Kraeling, *Gerasa: City of the Decapolis*, no. 173.
39 *AE* 1973, no. 551 = *IGLS* XIII.1 9063, Bostra.
40 *AE* 1979, no. 62.

inscription his name; his nomenclature is given here as in the inscription from Bostra[41] and not as in the inscription from Dor.[42]

Finally the last line: if *[---]runt ex Alex[---]* is the correct reading, then the restoration of *[redie]runt ex Alex[andria]* seems very likely. But if a unit of the *legio VI Ferrata* is now returning from Alexandria, where it was sent in all likelihood in order to help with putting down the Jewish revolt, then the legion as a whole reached Arabia some time before 119 – perhaps when the *legio III Cyrenaica* set off for the Parthian campaign.[43] The *legio VI Ferrata* at this time is the permanent legion of Arabia. It is hardly surprising that soldiers of the legion are dedicating a statue to their governor on their return to their home province.

I propose tentatively the following reconstruction:

[Q. Coredio Q. f. Quir.]
[Gallo Gargilio Antiquo]
[– – – – – –]
[– – – – – –]
[– – – – – –]
[.....................................legato leg.]
[................ a]e piae fideli[s, legato Aug.]
[pr. pr. provinciae] Arabiae, [cos. designat.]
[milites] leg. VI Ferr[at(ae)]
[qui Imp. Caes. T]raiano Hadriano [Aug.]
[tribunic. pote]st. III cos. [III]
[feliciter redie]runt ex Alex[andria]
[ob merita]

Appendix 2: Officers of the *legio VI Ferrata*

1. *Legati legionis*

– See in general for *legati legionis* in the first and early second century CE: Thomas Franke, *Die Legionslegaten der römischen Armee in der Zeit von Augustus bis Traian* (Bochum: Brockmeyer, 1991), 127–49; Edward Dąbrowa, "The Commanders of Syrian Legions, 1st to 3rd c. A.D.," in *The Roman Army*

41 *AE* 1973, no. 551
42 *AE* 1991, no. 1576
43 However, the date must not be close to the beginning of this campaign since the *legio VI Ferrata* too took part in the Parthian war, as Ritterling already noted (cf. Ritterling, "Legio," 1590–91), and as is now demonstrated in the career of its legate C. Bruttius Praesens L. Fulvius Rusticus, decorated at the time, cf. *AE* 1950, no. 66; *IRT* 545.

in the East, ed. David L. Kennedy (Ann Arbor: Journal of Roman Archaeology, 1996), 277–96, esp. 285–88.

- Add the following to Ritterling, "Legio," 1594:

  Mentioned in Ritterling:

  To the *Ignotus* of *CIL* XIII 5089 see Michael Alexander Speidel, "Ein unbekannter Patronus der Helvetier-Stadt Aventicum: Überlegungen zu CIL XIII 5089," *MH* 47 (1990): 149–62.

  To the *Ignotus* of *CIL* XIV 3617 cf. Géza Alföldy, "Epigraphica Tiburtina," *Epigraphica* 28 (1966): 3 f. = *AE* 1967, no. 80.

  To Q. Antistius Adventus see *AE* 1914, no. 281 and *CIL* VI 41119.

  Not mentioned in Ritterling:

  C. Bruttius Praesens L. Fulvius Rusticus, *AE* 1950, no. 66; *IRT* 545.

  ? T. Settidius Firmus [--]cianus, *AE* 1984, no. 426 = *AE* 1987, no. 421.

2. *Tribuni militum*

- Add the following to Ritterling, "Legio," 1595:

  a. *laticlavii*:

  T. Calestrius Tiro, *AE* 1965, no. 320.

  Q. Cornelius Aquinus, *AE* 1938, no. 178 = *IGLS* III 813.

  ?*Ignotus*, *AE* 1969/70, no. 606.

  b. *angusticlavii*:

  Mentioned in Ritterling:

  To T. Statilius Optatus cf. *CIL* VI 41272 (= 31863 = *ILS* 9011).

  To C. Iulius Demosthenes see Wörrle, Michael, *Stadt und Fest im kaiserzeitlichen Kleinasien* (München: Beck, 1988), 55 ff.

  Not mentioned in Ritterling:

  L. Conetanius Proculus, *AE* 1950, no. 190.

  C. Iulius [---]tus, *IGRom.* IV 1422 = Louis Robert, *Études anatoliennes* (Paris: de Boccard, 1937), 134 ff. (repr. Amsterdam: Hakkert, 1970).

  L. O[---], *AE* 1947, no. 127.

  [---] Cl(audia tribu) Proculus, *AE* 1976, no. 265.

  L. Valerius Martialis, *tribunus militum* in the *legio VI Ferrata* or in the *Legio X Fretensis*, *CIIP* II 1228.

3. *Praefecti legionis*

- Add the following to Ritterling, "Legio," 1595:

  Cl(avius) Potens, *AE* 1962, no. 269 = Lehmann and Holum, *The Greek and Latin Inscriptions of Caesarea Maritima*, no. 146 (*CIIP* II 1351).

4. *Primi ordines*

- See in general to the *primi ordines* Brian Dobson, *Die Primipilares* (Köln: Rheinland-Verlag, 1978), 356 f.
- Add the following to Ritterling, "Legio," 1595:

Q. Anatius Ga[lli]o Stellatina (tribu) Paulus, *primipilaris*, *IGLS* IV 1804 = *AE* 1992, no. 1687.

Iulius Isidorianus, *p.p.*, *AE* 1948, no. 145.

Q. Mucius Q. f. Fab(ia tribu) Scaeva, *primuspilus*, *AE* 1934, no. 61.

[Annatius] Rufus, *hastatus primus*, *IGLS* IV 1804 = *AE* 1992, no. 1687.

Q. Flavius Marcianus was not an *hastatus* but rather an *op(tio) hast(ati)* of the legion, *AE* 1974, no. 659.

5. *Centuriones*

– Add the following to Ritterling, "Legio," 1595:

[?M. Aurelius Pa]latina Iustus, Géza Alföldy, *Die römischen Inschriften von Tarraco* (Berlin: De Gruyter, 1975), 177 = *AE* 1977, no. 467.

Cl(audius) Protianus, *AE* 1962, no. 269 = Lehmann and Holum, *The Greek and Latin Inscriptions of Caesarea Maritima*, no. 146 (*CIIP* II 1351).

[---] Celestinus, *AE* 1947, no. 172.

Mevius Romanus, *AE* 1985, no. 829 = Lehmann and Holum, no. 4 (*CIIP* II 1284).

P. Mucius Q. f. Vol., *AE* 1934, no. 62.

[P]ompeius [-]ullus, *AE* 1948, no. 146.

M. Pulfennius Sex. f. Arn., *AE* 1941, no. 105.

C. Valerius Strabo, *AE* 1961, no. 16.

Postscript:
The results of an autopsy of the inscription from Gerasa carried out on 8 April 2000 cannot, unfortunately, be taken into account here, and will have to be published elsewhere.

Ein Gedi between the Two Revolts

Ein Gedi in the documents – ‘an imperial village’

Ein Gedi is mentioned for the first time in the documents from the Judaean Desert on 6 May 124 CE in a deed of acknowledgement of debt by Babatha’s second husband, Judah son of Eleazar Khthousion (*P.Yadin* 11 lines 12–13 = lines 1–2):[1]

> ἐπὶ ὑ[πάτ]ων Μανείου Ἀκειλίου Γλαβρίωνος καὶ Τορκουά[του Θ]ηβανιανο[ῦ πρὸ] μιᾶς νωνῶν Μαίω[ν] ἐν Ἐνγαδοῖς κώμῃ κυρίου Καίσαρος ....
>
> In the consulate of Manius Acilius Glabrio and Torquatus Thebanianus on 6 May in Ein Gedi, the village of our Lord the Emperor.

An undated fragmentary document which belongs to the so-called Seiyâl collection[2] describes Ein Gedi in the same way (*P.Hever* 67 lines 1–3):

> Μολιμας...[...τῶν ἀπὸ Ἐν]γαδων Κυρίου Κ[αίσαρος κώμης] χαίρειν.
>
> Molimas [to X from Ein] Gedi, [the village] of our Lord [the Emperor].

Notwithstanding the sorry condition of *P.Hever* 67, the Roman dating at the end of this document, [. ν]ώνων Μαίω[ν], combined with the language of the document, implies that we are in the same environment as that of the other documents from the archives found in Naḥal Ḥever.

---

1 Naphtali Lewis, *The Documents from the Bar Kokhba Period in the Cave of Letters. Greek Papyri* (Jerusalem: IES, 1989) (henceforth Lewis). The papyri are referred to in this article as *P.Yadin*, as are the other papyri found in Naḥal Ḥever in 1960–61, cf. Yigael Yadin, “Expedition D,” *IEJ* 11 (1961): 36–52; Yigael Yadin, “Expedition D – The Cave of the Letters,” *IEJ* 12 (1962): 227–57.
2 Hannah M. Cotton and Ada Yardeni, *Aramaic, Hebrew, and Greek Documentary Texts from Naḥal Ḥever and Other Sites*, Discoveries in the Judaean Desert XXVII (Oxford: Clarendon Press, 1997), 244 ff.

Article note: First published in *SCI* 20 (2001): 139–54, with the following note: this paper is based on a lecture delivered (in Hebrew) in spring of 1995 at a colloquium held at the Hebrew University of Jerusalem in memory of my teacher and friend Professor Abraham (Addi) Wasserstein. An English version was presented at the Judaean Desert Documents Workshop organised by Ranon Katzoff at Bar Ilan University, 3–5 June 1998.
I am greatly indebted to Peter Eich and Rudolph Haensch for discussing with me the problem of imperial estates, and to Magen Broshi and Gideon Hadas for enlightening me on the agricultural aspect.

https://doi.org/10.1515/9783110770438-022

When and why did Ein Gedi become 'a village of our Lord the Emperor' and what status is implied by this title? It seems self-evident that this is not merely an honorific title like 'Hadrianic Petra' in *P.Yadin* 25 line 26 = line 48.[3] What then is the reality behind the title?

I know of only one other village in the Roman empire similarly designated: this is the village of Beth Phoura in Syria attested thus in a petition from 28 August 245:[4]

> Ἰουλίῳ Πρείσκῳ τῷ διασημοτάτῳ ἐπάρχῳ Μεσοποταμίας διέποντι τὴν ὑπατείαν [i.e of Syria] παρὰ Ἀρχώδου Φαλλαιου καὶ Φιλώτα Νισραιαβου καὶ Ουορωδου Συμιοσβαραχου καὶ Αβεδσαυτα Αβεδιαρδα ὄντων ἀπὸ κώμης Βηφφούρης κυριακῆς τῆς περὶ Ἀππάδαναν (*P.Euphr.* 1 lines 3–5).
>
> To Iulius Priscus, prefect of Mesopotamia, exercising the function of a consular governor (i.e. of Syria), from Archodes son of Phallaios, Philotas son of Nisraiabos, Ouorodes son of Symiosbarachos and Abedsautas son of Abediardas – all from the imperial village of Beth Phoura in the region of Appadana.

Κώμη κυριακή is translated by the editors as 'village impériale.' Was Beth Phoura part of the imperial domain (*praedia fiscalia*) attested in *P.Dura* 64 (221 CE) as existing near Appadana,[5] the district to which Beth Phoura belonged (κώμης Βηφφούρης κυριακῆς τῆς περὶ Ἀππάδαναν)? Such an interpretation is rendered very likely by the villagers' request to the governor of Syria Koele for the intervention of the imperial procurator who has his seat in Appadana:[6]

> διὰ τοῦτο κατεφύγομεν ἐπί σε καὶ δεόμεθά σου κελεῦσαι δι' ὑπογραφῆς σου Κλαυδίῳ Ἀρί<σ>τωνι τῷ κρατίστῳ ἐπιτρόπῳ τῷ ἐν Ἀππαδάνᾳ, ὑφ' ὃν ἡ διοίκησις ἐστίν,[7] ἐν ἀκεραίῳ πάντα τηρηθῆναι καὶ βίαν κωλυθῆναι μέχρι τῆς σῆς εἰς τοὺς τόπους ἐσομ[έ]νης σου εὐτυχῶς ἐπιδεμίας (lines 13–16)

---

3 As claimed by Naphtali Lewis, "The Babatha Archive: A Response," *IEJ* 44 (1994): 244; Brigitte Galsterer-Kröll, "Untersuchungen zu den Beinamen der Stadte des Imperium Romanum," *Epigraphische Studien* 9 (1972): 55–7 (on titles of peregrine cities).

4 Denis Feissel and Jean Gascou, "Documents d'archives romains inédits du Moyen Euphrate (IIIe s. après J-C): I. Les pétitions (T. Euphr. 1 à 5)," *Journal des Savants* (1995): 71; Denis Feissel and Jean Gascou, "Documents d'archives romains inédits du Moyen Euphrate (IIIe s. après J.-C.): III. Actes divers et Lettres (P. Euphr. 11 à 17)," *Journal des Savants* (2000): 159, no. 11, ll. 4–5.

5 '*Et peto compellas ordinatum Aug(ustorum) n(ostrorum) lib(ertum) equitibus siv[e] mulionibfus q]u[i] in vexill(atione) Appadanensfi] deg(unt) horde[u]m ex praedis fiscalib[u]s dare,*' C.B. Welles, R.O. Fink, and J.F. Gilliam, *The Excavations at Dura-Europos Conducted by Yale University and the French Academy of Inscriptions and Letters, Final Report V, Part I: The Parchments and Papyri* (New Haven: Yale University Press, 1959), 231.

6 The *procuratores* of imperial estates did not necessarily reside in the properties but in cities, see e.g. *CIL* VIII 20570 col. lii line 10 (for Africa).

7 Cf. *P.Euph.* 2 line 16: τῷ ἐν Ἀπ[πα]δάνᾳ ἐπιτρόπῳ Κλ(αυδίῳ) Ἀρίστωνι.

> Therefore, we had recourse to you and request that in your subscription you order Claudius Ariston, the 'egregius' procurator in Appadana, who is in charge of the *dioikesis*, to preserve the status quo and prevent violence until your joyful visit to these places takes place.[8]

In fact the meaning of κώμη κυρίου Καίσαρος and κώμη κυριακή is not in doubt: a village which belongs to the emperor, part of his private property, the *patrimonium*. But what does this imply about the legal status of the residents of the village and their property; what implications, if any, does the status of 'imperial village' have for its provincial status?[9] "The insoluble problem of the juridical status of imperial property in the established empire"[10] cannot be resolved here. However, we should be wary of projecting backwards our own notions and preconceptions – or misconceptions – of the legal consequences entailed by the status of 'an imperial village.' Thus for example one notes that the petitions to the governor in *P.Euph.* 1 and 2 clearly imply the existence in Beth Phoura and in Birtha Okbanon[11] of private property: χώρα (*P.Euph.* 1 line 11) and ἄμπελος (*P.Euph* 2 lines 8, 15). Similar issues, as we shall see, arise in the case of Ein Gedi. Perhaps the documents at hand are the best evidence we have for the reality behind the title.[12]

---

8 The editors, however, dismiss the possibility that Ariston is approached "en tant que procurateur des domaines impériaux de Syrie"; instead, they regard Ariston as "un procurateur purement judiciaire, gérant le *conventus* entre deux visites du gouverneur, comparable, à certains égards, à l'épistratège égyptien." Lastly, they understand διοίκησις to mean 'judicial assize' rather than 'financial administration,' Feissel and Gascou, "Documents d'archives romains inédits du Moyen Euphrate (IIIe s. après J-C): I. Les pétitions (T. Euphr. 1 à 5)," 83–4. See the objections to their interpretation of the evidence in Rudolf Haensch, *Capita Provinciarum* (Mainz am Rhein: von Zabern, 1997), 254–5, n. 139. Fara Nasti, "Un nuovo documento dalla Siria sulle competenze di governatori e procuratori provinciali in tema di interdetti," *Index* 21 (1993): 365–80 also seems to exclude the possibility that Claudius Ariston is a procurator in charge of the imperial domain.

9 Rainer Wiegels, "'Solum Caesaris' – Zu einer Weihung im römischen Walheim," *Chiron* 19 (1979): 61–102 is not helpful. He addresses the question on p. 92: "in welchem Verhältnis der *saltus* zum Umland stand," without offering any satisfactory discussion.

10 This is Fergus Millar's formulation in *The Emperor in the Roman World* (London: Duckworth, 1977), 177, but see the whole chapter there pp. 175–89. The subject is worthy of serious treatment even if it serves only to show the limitations of our knowledge. See now Maurice Sartre, "Les Metrokomiai de Syrie du Sud," *Syria* 76 (1999): 219 ff. on the judicial status of the *metrokômiai* in the imperial estate in Batanea in the third century CE.

11 It is true that Birtha Okbanon is not described as 'an imperial village,' but this is an altogether different kind of document by an illiterate person (see line 20).

12 Cf. Millar, *The Emperor in the Roman World*, 175: "we are hopelessly ignorant of the patterns of private ownership and exploitation of land ... which prevailed in the different regions of the empire"; cf. Hannah M. Cotton, "Land Tenure in the Documents from the Nabataean Kingdom and the Roman Province of Arabia," *ZPE* 119 (1997): 255–65 [above, pp. 293–308].

Before we investigate this, however, we should ask when and why Ein Gedi became 'the village of our Lord the Emperor.'

Ein Gedi as part of a royal domain. The balsam groves

The first editor of *P.Yadin* 11 offers the following explanation: "The oasis of En-gedi and its surroundings were a flourishing part of the royal domain under the Hasmonaean and Herodian dynasties. ... As such they might reasonably be expected to have become part of the Roman emperor's estates after the suppression of the Jewish Revolt in A.D. 70. That *a priori* assumption is confirmed by the characterization of En-gedi in this document ... as κώμη κυρίου Καίcαρος."[13] Lewis, as he acknowledges there, embraces the theory propounded by the archaeologists who excavated Ein Gedi in the 1960s.[14]

It must be said in warning that no literary or epigraphic source supports the archaeologists' assertions that it was John Hyrcanus who turned the oasis into "a royal Hasmonean domain" and settled "tenant farmers there," and that Ein Gedi continued its life as a royal/imperial domain into the Byzantine period. It is only for the balsam plantations that we have Pliny's explicit testimony that they were always in royal hands: *Sed omnibus odoribus praefertur Balsamum, uni terrarum Iudaeae concessum, quondam in duobus tantum hortis, utroque regio, altero iugerum viginti non amplius, altero pauc-orum* (*NH* XII, 111).[15] It seems that of the two plantations mentioned in other sources as well, one was located in Jericho[16] and the other one in Ein Gedi.[17] The reference to royal possession (*utroque regio*),

13 Lewis, *The Documents from the Bar Kokhba Period in the Cave of Letters. Greek Papyri*, 42; Lewis, "The Babatha Archive: A Response," 244.

14 Benjamin Mazar, Trude Dothan, and Immanuel Dunayevsky, *En-Gedi: The First and Second Seasons of Excavations, 1961–1962*, Atiqot 5, 1966, 4–7. These theories were first formulated by Joseph Naveh in an unpublished MA dissertation – based on the author's survey of Ein Gedi in 1956–57 – submitted to the Hebrew University in 1958, and then published for internal use in Hebrew by the Ein Gedi Field School in 1966 as *The History of Ein Gedi in light of the Archaeological Survey*.

15 Cf. Menahem Stern, *Greek and Latin Authors on Jews and Judaism*, Vol. I (Jerusalem: Israel Academy of Sciences and Humanities, 1976), no. 213 (henceforth Stern). It is obvious that by Pliny's time the balsam grew in more than two places in Palestine; cf. Galen, *De Antidotis* 1.4, p. 25 (ed. Kühn) = Stern, no. 391, cited in the text at note 32.

16 For Jericho see Strabo 16.2.41, p. 763 (ed. Kramer) = Stern, no. 115; Joseph., *BJ* 1.138 (= *AJ* 14.54); *BJ* 1.361–2 (= *AJ* 15.95–6); *BJ* 4.469.

17 For Ein Gedi see Joseph., *AJ* 9.7 and below n. 28. Pliny's *quondam in duobus tantum hortis* implies that in his time there were more than two, but this does not concern us here.

is likely to refer to the Seleucid(?),[18] Hasmonean and Herodian dynasties. Royal monopoly is also implied by the artificial attempts to limit the balsam's growth in order to ensure that demand always exceeded supply and the price always remained high.[19]

However, even if direct royal/imperial control was restricted to the balsam groves, it is still hard to see why they should have become imperial property only in 70 CE. If, as Lewis' interpretation seems to imply, the Roman emperor was the legal heir to the 'royal domain' of the Hasmonaean and Herodian dynasties, as he very likely was, then the taking over of the balsam groves would have happened not in 70, but long before. As early as 34 BCE Mark Antony bestowed the balsam together with the dates of Jericho on Cleopatra, from whom Herod leased them.[20] After Actium they may have been returned to Herod; or else the lease continued, this time between Octavian/Augustus and Herod. The rule of the Herodian dynasty came to an end with Archelaus' exile in 6 CE. Josephus informs us that at that time 'his property was absorbed by the imperial treasury': ἡ οὐσία δ' αὐτοῦ (Archelaus') τοῖς Καίσαρος θησαυροῖς ἐγκατατάσσεται (*BJ* 2.111).[21] Thus if not already earlier, then at the latest in 6 CE, when Archelaus was exiled and Judaea provincialized,[22] the balsam groves must have become part of the *patrimonium*.[23]

---

18 Possibly Alexander had already taken possession of the balsam gardens; see Pliny, *NH* XII, 117 = Stern, no. 213.

19 Strabo tells us that in Egypt those who wished to obtain greater profits from the papyrus imitated Jewish practice with the balsam: οὐ γὰρ ἐῶσι πολλαχοῦ φύεσθαι, τῇ δὲ σπάνει τιμὴν ἐπιτιθέντες τὴν πρόσοδον οὕτως αὔξουσι, Strabo, 17.1.15 = Stern, no. 121; this explains τίμιος οὖν ἐστι καὶ διότι ἐνταῦθα μόνον γεννᾶται in Strabo 16.2.41 = Stern, no. 115; see in general Hannah M. Cotton and Werner Eck, "Ein Staatsmonopol und seine Folgen: Plinius, Naturalis Historia 12,123 und der Preis für Balsam," *Rheinisches Museum für Philologie* 140 (1997): 153–61.

20 Joseph., *BJ* 1.361–2; cf. *AJ* 15.96. Herod leased the entire domain taken from him for 200 talents a year. See Emil Schürer, *The History of the Jewish People in the Age of Jesus Christ*, Vol. I, ed. Fergus Millar and Géza Vermès (Edinburgh: Clark, 1973), 298–300 and especially n. 36 there.

21 Cf. *AJ* 17.344: Augustus exiled Archelaus and τὰ δὲ χρήματα ἀπηνέγκατο; see Fergus Millar, "The Fiscus in the First Two Centuries," *JRS* 53 (1963): 30; Michael Alpers, *Das nachrepublikanische Finanzsystem: Fiscus und Fisci in der frühen Kaiserzeit* (Berlin: De Gruyter, 1995), 295 ff.; see Cotton and Eck, "Ein Staatsmonopol und seine Folgen: Plinius, Naturalis Historia 12,123 und der Preis für Balsam," 155, n. 12.

22 For its annexation to Syria, see Hannah M. Cotton, "Some Aspects of the Roman Administration of Judaea/Syria-Palaestina," in *Lokale Autonomie und römische Ordnungsmacht in den kaiserzeitlichen Provinzen vom 1. bis 3. Jahrhundert*, ed. Werner Eck (München: Oldenbourg, 1999), 75–91 [above, pp. 317–35]; Hannah M. Cotton, "Ἡ νέα ἐπαρχεία Ἀραβία: The New Province of Arabia in the Papyri from the Judaean Desert," *ZPE* 116 (1997): 204–8 [above, pp. 309–16].

23 Contra Paolo Baldacci, "Patrimonium e ager publicus al tempo dei Flavi," *La parola del passato* 128 (1969): 355 ff.

And yet, at first sight, this seems to stand in direct contradiction to Pliny's claim that the balsam had become only in his days subject to taxation: 'it is enslaved now and pays tribute together with its people': *servit nunc haec* (i. e. the balsam) *ac tributa pendit cum sua gente* (*NH* XII, 111 = Stern, no. 213),[24] and only *now* has there begun the cultivation of the balsam by the *fiscus*, 'now the *fiscus* plants it, and it has never been in such quantity': *seritque nunc eum fiscus, nec umquam fuit numerosior* (*NH* XII, 113 = Stern, no. 213).

In an attempt to solve this difficulty it has been suggested that Pliny is referring here to drastic changes which were introduced in his time into the methods of cultivating and exploiting the balsam – perhaps as a consequence of the Jewish attempt to destroy the balsam groves ('The Jews assaulted and ravaged it just as they assaulted and ravaged their own life; the Romans warded off the attack, and they battled over the fruit').[25] The new methods were aimed at significantly increasing the quantity of the balsam, presumably without lowering its price. They faithfully reflect Vespasian's economic policy of expanding, saving, and exploiting resources untapped before.[26] Pliny's *inplet* (i. e. the balsam) *colles vinearum modo* ('it covers hillsides as vineyards do') as well as Jerome's *balsamum quod nascitur in vineis Engaddi*[27] may well describe the expansion by the Romans of the area over which the balsam grew after the revolt, as against the previous small dimensions of the two gardens: twenty *iugera* in one case and less than twenty *iugera* in the other.[28] Furthermore, the *colles* are likely to be the terraced

24 In addition, the balsam was displayed in the triumphal procession of 71 CE, see *NH* XII, 111 = Stern, no. 213: *Ostendere *arbutum* hanc urbi imperatores Vespasiani, clarumque dictu, a Pompeio Magno in triumpho arbores quoque duximus.*

25 *Saeviere in eam Iudaei sicut in vitam quoque suam; contra defendere Romani, et dimicatum pro frutice est*, *NH* XII, 113 = Stern, no. 213. See Cotton and Eck, "Ein Staatsmonopol und seine Folgen,"155 ff.; cf. Joseph Patrich, "Agricultural Development in Antiquity: Improvements in the Cultivation and Production of the Balsam," in *Hikrei Eretz: Studies in the History of the Land of Israel Dedicated to Prof. Yehuda Felix*, ed. Ze'ev Safrai, Yvonne Friedman, and Joshua Schwartz (Ramat-Gan: Bar-Ilan University Press, 1997), 143 ff. (Hebrew).

26 E.g. the utilization of the twigs of the balsam, which used to be thrown away, for producing the *xylobalsamum*; this earned the *fiscus* 800,000 sesterces in the five years following the end of the revolt: Pliny, *NH* XII, 118 = Stern, no. 213. Two Latin papyri mentioning the *xylobalsamum* were found on Masada, and thus are to be dated ca. 73/74, see Hannah M. Cotton and Joseph Geiger, *Masada II: The Latin and Greek Documents* (Jerusalem: IES, 1989), nos. 725 and 749b. On the new methods of growing the balsam see in detail Cotton and Eck, "Ein Staatsmonopol und seine Folgen," 160 f.

27 *Comm. in Hiezechielem* 27:17 (*PL* XXV, col. 256); recalling Canticum Canticorum 1:13: *dilectus meus mihi in vineis Enggadi* (דודי לי בכרמי עין גדי).

28 *altero iugerum viginti non amplius, altero pauciorum*, Pliny, *NH* XII, 111 = Stern, no. 213. It is generally assumed that the grove in Jericho was the bigger one.

hills above ancient Ein Gedi. The elaborate water supply system discovered in archaeological surveys of the hills facing ancient Ein Gedi, the terraces, the aqueducts, the water reservoirs, the pools, the cisterns, and the canals – all date from the Roman and Byzantine periods, not before.[29] The later sources on balsam do not mention Jericho as one of its centers, but only Ein Gedi.[30] This may indicate that Ein Gedi, rather than Jericho, became the center of large-scale production of the balsam. It is therefore not insignificant that already in the second century, Galen expressly connects the balsam with Ein Gedi. He tells us that the Syrian *opobalsamum* has another name derived from the place where it grows most plentifully and most beautifully: 'for it is named 'Ein Gedian'; because it is superior to that which grows in other places in Palestine': τὸ Ἐγγαδηνὸν γὰρ ὀνομάζεται, κρεῖττον ὂν τῶν ἐν ἄλλοις χωρίοις τῆς Παλαιστίνης γινομένων.[31] And Jerome, as we saw, speaks of the *balsamum quod nascitur in vineis Engaddi.*

Ein Gedi during and after the first revolt: its status

Since the real change in Ein Gedi's status seems to be the consequence of the first revolt, this must be the starting point of any discussion. Ein Gedi fared badly during the first revolt. The *Sicarii* who had occupied Masada since 66 CE[32] raided the village in Passover 68: after driving away the men and killing seven hundred women and children who could not escape, they plundered the victims' homes, removing all fresh supplies which they took with them to Masada.[33] In June 68 Vespasian arrived in Jericho where he was joined by M. Ulpius Traianus, the commander of the Tenth Legion Fretensis.[34] Vespasian remained in the area for

---

29 See the works cited in note 14, and esp. Naveh, *The History of Ein Gedi in Light of the Archaeological Survey*, 17 ff. The date has been confirmed in recent excavations in Ein Gedi by Gideon Hadas (oral communications by the archaeologist).

30 Above, n. 28 and Patrich, "Agricultural Development in Antiquity: Improvements in the Cultivation and Production of the Balsam," 143.

31 Galen, *De Antidotis* I, 4 – p. 25 (ed. Kühn) = Stern, no. 391. Aelius Aristides (*Orat.* XXXVI, 82 = Stern, no. 370) must also be referring to Ein Gedi since the balsam which he mentions grows near the Dead Sea. Cf. from the fourth century the testimony of Eusebius: Ἐνγγάδι, παρακειμένη τῇ νεκρᾷ θαλάσσῃ, ὅθεν τὸ ὀποβάλσαμον, *Onomasticon*, p. 86 (ed. Klostermann), and that of Jerome quoted in the text at n. 27.

32 Not the Zealots, as our sole source, Josephus, makes quite clear, whereas ideological discussions tend to obfuscate; see Hannah M. Cotton and Jonathan J. Price, "Who Conquered Masada in 66 CE, and Who Lived There until the Fortress Fell?," *Zion* 55 (1990): 449–54 (Hebrew).

33 Joseph., *BJ* 4.402–4.

34 Joseph., *BJ* 4.450.

a while, establishing a camp in Jericho.[35] We may assume that the pitched battles over the balsam groves described by Pliny[36] took place at this time. Ein Gedi, which had suffered the attacks of the *Sicarii* earlier on, was now in ruins:

> *Infra hos* (i.e. the Essenes) *Engada oppidum fuit, secundum ab Hierosolymis fertilitate palmetorumque nemoribus,*[37] *nunc alterum bustum* (Plin. *NH* V, 73 = Stern, no. 204).
>
> Lying below the Essenes was (formerly) the town of Ein Gedi, second only to Jerusalem in the fertility of its land and its groves of palm-dates, but now, like Jerusalem, a heap of ashes.

When we next hear of Ein Gedi in *P.Yadin* 11 of May 124 it has become a κώμη κυρίου Καίcαρος and part (or the whole) of the *cohors I milliaria Thracum* is stationed there.[38]

> *P.Yadin* 11, lines 13–15 = lines 2–3: Ἰούδας Ἐλ̣[αζ]ά̣ρ̣ο̣υ̣ Χθο̣υ̣[σίω]ν̣ος Ἐ[ν]γ̣αδηνὸς Μαγωνίῳ Οὐά̣λ̣εντι (ἑκατοντάρ)χ(ῳ) σπείρης πρώτης μειλιαρίας Θρ̣ακῶν χ[αί]ρ̣ε̣ιν· ὁμ̣ο̣λ̣ο̣γ̣ῶ ἔ̣χειν καὶ ὀφείλειν σοι ἐν δάνει ἀργυρίου Τυρίου δηνάρια ἑ̣ξ̣ήκοντα, οἵ εἰσι̣ν̣ [σ]τ̣α̣τ̣ῆρες δεκ̣απέντε.
>
> Judah son of Eleazar Khthousion of Ein Gedi to Magonius Valens, centurion of the *cohors I milliaria Thracum* greetings. I acknowledge that I have from you and I owe you 60 denarii of Tyrian silver, which are 15 staters.

The Jewish attempt to destroy the balsam during the revolt and the intensive cultivation of the orchards after 70 fully account for the presence of a military force in Ein Gedi. The unit could not have arrived there before 91 since it is attested in Syria in this year.[39] It may have replaced another unit.[40] The unit (or part of it)

---

35 Joseph., *BJ* 4.450. Josephus' description of Vespasian's sojourn in the Dead Sea area, exploring it and preparing his next moves (*BJ* 4.451–90), implies that he spent more than a few days there. He heard of Nero's death (which occurred on 9 June 68) only when he returned to Caesarea (*BJ* 4.491). For Roman and Jewish chronology in book 4 of the *Jewish War* see Jonathan J. Price, *Jerusalem under Siege: The Collapse of the Jewish State 66–70 CE* (Leiden: Brill, 1992) 218–23.
36 Above in text at n. 25.
37 Something seems to have dropped out, since the sentence as it stands makes little sense. For an attempt to use this source to identify the archaeological remains above Ein Gedi as an Essene settlement see Yizhar Hirschfeld, "A Community of Hermits above Ein Gedi," *Cathedra* 96 (2000): 8–40 (Hebrew); contra David Amit and Jodi Magness, "The Essenes Did Not Live above Ein Gedi: A Reply to Y. Hirschfeld," *Cathedra* 96 (2000): 57–68 (Hebrew).
38 This is the only unit which we know for certain was stationed in Judaea both before and after the Bar Kokhba revolt, see James Russell, "A Roman Military Diploma from Rough Cilicia," *Bonner Jahrbücher* 195 (1995): 88–100.
39 Margaret M. Roxan, *Roman Military Diplomas 1954 to 1977* (London: Routledge, 1978), no. 4.
40 Its transfer to Judaea may suggest the enlargement of the Roman garrison in Judaea as a result of the coming of a second legion, see brief summary in Hannah M. Cotton, "The Legio VI

seems to have been stationed right in the middle of the village,[41] as emerges from the description of the abutters of the courtyard given as security for the loan Judah son of Eleazar contracted from the Roman centurion, Magonius Valens:

> ἧς αὐλῆς γείτ̣[ο]ν̣ες ἀπὸ ἀνατ[ο]λ̣ῶν σκ̣ηναὶ καὶ Ἰησοῦς Μαν̣δ[ρ]ῶν̣ο̣ς̣, δύσεος σκ̣η̣ν̣[αὶ καὶ] ἐ̣ρ̣γασ̣τ̣ήριον τοῦ αὐτοῦ Ἐλαζάρ<ο>υ πατρός μου, νότου ἀγορὰ καὶ Σ[ί]μ̣ω̣ν Μαθθ̣αίου, βο̣ρ̣[ρᾶ ὁ]δὸς [καὶ πρ]α[ισ]ί̣δ̣[ι]ο̣ν (lines 17–19 = lines 4–6).
>
> the abutters of the said courtyard being to the east tents and Joshua son of Mandron, to the west tents and the workshop of the said Eleazar, my father, to the south a market and Shime'on son of Mathaius, to the north a road and a *praesidium* (a military post).[42]

Lewis reasonably suggests that σκηναί refers to military tents.[43] If so, then the soldiers were camping right in middle of the village, since the courtyard is flanked by them on three sides. A long and narrow Roman bath house excavated in Ein Gedi is dated by the coins to the years between the two revolts;[44] it is likely to have served the unit. Four years later the unit must have moved. In *P.Yadin* 19 of April 128 Judah son of Eleazar bestows the same courtyard on his daughter Shlamzion. A comparison between the abutters of the courtyard in May 124 and those described in April 128 reveals that in the period of four years which elapsed between the writing of the two documents both the tents and the *praesidium* have disappeared, as the following table makes clear:[45]

Ferrata," in *Les legions de Rome sous le haut-empire: actes du congres de Lyon (17–19 septembre 1998)*, ed. Yann Le Bohec, Vol. I (Lyon: Centre d'etudes romaines et gallo-romaines, 2000), 351 ff. [above, pp. 337 ff.].

41 For military units inside cities in the Roman East see Benjamin Isaac, *The Limits of Empire: The Roman Army in the East*, 2nd ed. (Oxford: Clarendon Press, 1992), 269–80.

42 Not 'headquarters' as translated by Lewis, *The Documents from the Bar Kokhba Period in the Cave of Letters. Greek Papyri*, 44.

43 See Lewis, 45 ad lines 5 and 18, especially the reference to Bärbel Kramer and Dieter Hagedorn, "Zwei ptolemäische Texte aus der Hamburger Papyrussammlung," *Archiv für Papyrusforschung* 33 (1987): 13, ad line 5; Hans Jakob Polotsky, "The Greek Papyri from the Cave of Letters," *IEJ* 12 (1962): 259 is cautious: "flanked by (presumably military) tents."

44 Benjamin Mazar and Immanuel Dunayevsky, "En-Gedi: Third Season of Excavations: Preliminary Report," *IEJ* 14 (1964): 128–30; Benjamin Mazar and Immanuel Dunayevsky, "En-Gedi: Fourth and Fifth Seasons of Excavations: Preliminary Report," *IEJ* 17 (1967): 142–43. The latest coin is dated to 117/18 CE.

45 ὧν γείτ̣ω̣νε̣ς [τ]ῆς αὐλῆς καὶ οἰκοιμά[των ἀν]α̣τολῶν Ἰησοῦ Μαδδαρωνα καὶ αὐρίχ̣ω̣ρον, δυσμῶν ὁ διεθετῶν, νότου ἀγ̣ορά, βορρᾶ ὁδός ('the abutters of the courtyard and the rooms are on the east Joshua' son of Maddaron and an empty lot, on the west the donor, on the south a market, on the north a road,' ll. 16–18); see Hannah M. Cotton, "Courtyard(s) in Ein-Gedi: P.Yadin 11, 19 and 20 of the Babatha archive," *ZPE* 112 (1996): 197–201 [above, pp. 285–91].

Papyrus no.	*P.Yadin* 11, 6 May 124 CE	*P.Yadin* 19, 16 April 128 CE
East	tents and Joshua Mand<a>ron	Joshua Maddaron and empty space
West	tents and workshop of Eleazar, Judah's father	Judah son of Eleazar
South	market and Shime'on son of Mathaios	market
North	road and *praesidium*	road

The presence of an empty space (αὐρίχωρον) where the tents once were and just a road where once there was also a *praesidium* makes it likely, to my mind, that the unit will have left Ein Gedi altogether, rather than merely changed its location inside the village. Later on it is attested in Hebron by a tile stamp of the *cohors I milliaria Thracum* and a military diploma from 186 whose recipient belonged to the unit.[46]

Babatha's land declaration of December 127, *P.Yadin* 16, reveals to us that since the first revolt Ein Gedi had lost its status as the central village of a toparchy and was subsumed into the toparchy of Jericho:[47]

> συνπαρόντος μοι ἐπιτρόπου Ἰουδάνου Ἐλαζάρου κώμης Αἰνγαδδῶν περὶ Ἱερειχοῦντα τῆς Ἰουδαίας (lines 15–16).

> present with me my guardian Judah son of Eleazar of the village of Ein Gedi in the district of Jericho in Judaea.[48]

It is not insignificant that despite the title κώμη κυρίου Καίσαρος – which we have no reason to believe Ein Gedi had lost by 127 – which implies that Ein Gedi was part of the imperial *patrimonium*, Ein Gedi was not an enclave administratively and juridically detached from the toparchy to which it now belonged. On the contrary, as B. Isaac puts it, "Ein Gedi was somehow administered from Jericho."[49] This fact harmonizes well with the existence of private property in Ein Gedi as attested in *P.Yadin* 11, 19 and 20 which, as I have shown elsewhere, refer to two different court-

46 See Roxan, *Roman Military Diplomas 1954 to 1977*, ad no. 69.

47 See Josephus, *BJ* 3.55 with Cotton, "Some Aspects of the Roman Administration of Judaea/Syria-Palaestina," 82 ff. [above, pp. 326 ff.] on the administrative divisions of Judaea (and see following note).

48 Judaea here is a geographical notion, Judaea proper, rather than the province; cf. *P.Hever* 65 lines 3–4: Ιησους Μαναημου τ[ῶν ἀπὸ κώμης *c.8 letters*] Σοφφαθε̣[.]... π̣ε̣ρὶ πόλιν Λιουιάδος τῆς Π̣[εραίας].

49 Benjamin Isaac, "The Babatha Archive," in *The Near East under Roman Rule* (Leiden: Brill, 1998), 177 (Postscript).

yards both of which became the property of Shlamzion, the daughter of Babatha's second husband: she received one in a deed of gift from her father (*P.Yadin* 19) and the other from her grandfather (*P.Yadin* 20).[50] The possession of private property can also be assumed for the abutters to these courtyards.[51] This private property was registered in the public archives.[52] Thus the residents of Ein Gedi could own real estate in their village, and I suspect therefore that not all the land in Ein Gedi was the property of the *patrimonium*. But even land owned by the *fiscus* was exploited in different ways: between land leased to tenants and land worked by slaves under a *vilicus* "there was still an infinite range of local variations."[53] Furthermore, if one can take the Bar Kokhba documents to reflect earlier conditions, then the sale of half a garden in Ein Gedi attested in *P.Yadin* 47 of 134[54] reveals also the existence of productive land in private hands in Ein Gedi. The people attested in the Babatha Archive in connection with Ein Gedi are not serfs, as is shown by their mobility and the fact that they could own land outside Ein Gedi.

The leases and sub-leases found among the documents from Wadi Murabba'at and Naḥal Ḥever (as well as implied in some of Bar Kokhba's letters to his men in Ein Gedi)[55] suggest that Bar Kokhba took over the imperial domain in the

50 Two courtyards not one, see Cotton, "Courtyard(s) in Ein-Gedi: P.Yadin 11, 19 and 20 of the Babatha Archive" [above, pp. 285–91] Hannah M. Cotton, "The Law of Succession in the Documents from the Judaean Desert Again," *SCI* 17 (1998): 120–22 [below, pp. 448–50]; contra Naphtali Lewis, "In the World of P.Yadin," *SCI* 18 (1999): 127 ff.

51 Joshua Mandron (Maddaron), Eleazar Khthousion, Shime'on son of Mathaius and Judah son of Eleazar in *P.Yadin* 11 and 19 and Mathethos son of Zabbaios (perhaps also Aristion of 'lane of Aristion') in *P.Yadin* 20.

52 *P.Yadin* 19 lines 25–27: ὅταν δὲ παρᾳνγείλει Σελα<μ>ψιοῦς τῷ αὐτῷ Ἰούδατι, τευχιζζει αὐτὴν διὰ δημοσίων; *P.Yadin* 20 lines 12–13 = lines 35–36: ταύτην δὲ τὴν αὐλὴν ὅπου ἂν βουληθῇς τευχίσω σοι διὰ δομηςοίωγ, σοῦ διδούσης τὸ ἀνάλωμα; for the registration of private property in Egypt in the βιβλιοθήκη ἐγκτησέων, see Hans Julius Wolff, *Das Recht der griechischen Papyri Ägyptens in der Zeit der Ptolemäer und des Prinzipats II: Organisation und Kontrolle des privaten Rechtsverkehrs* (München: Beck, 1978), 46 ff.

53 Dorothy J. Crawford, "Imperial Estates," in *Studies in Roman Property*, ed. Moses I. Finley (Cambridge: Cambridge University Press, 1976), 44; cf. Dieter Flach, *Römische Agrargeschichte* (München: Beck, 1990), 82 ff.

54 See Ada Yardeni, *Textbook of Aramaic, Hebrew and Nabataean Documentary Texts from the Judaean Desert and Related Material*, Vol. I (Jerusalem: The Hebrew University Press, 2000), 62–3 (English translation in Vol. II, p. 32). All the Bar Kokhba documents mentioned in the following notes, with the exception of the Greek ones, are now published in Yardeni's magnificent edition with English translations in vol. II; note though that they are designated there *Naḥal Ḥever* rather than *P.Yadin*.

55 Leases: *P.Mur* 24A-L (134 CE), and *P.Yadin* 42 (132 CE), 43 (132 CE), 44, 45 and 46 (all three from 134 CE); letters: *P.Yadin* 52 (Greek = *SB* 9843); *P.Yadin* 49, 50, 54–58, 60; *P.Mur* 46; *P.Yadin* 51, 53; *P.Yadin* 59 (Greek = *SB* 9844).

places recorded. Was the system of leasing and sub-leasing reflected in the Bar Kokhba documents taken over from the imperial *fiscus*? In some, but not all, of the documents (e.g. not in *P.Mur* 24A-L), the first lessees are *parnasim* of Bar Kokhba who sublease to others.[56] Should we assume that there was always a sub-layer of tenants left unrecorded in the documents, those who actually tilled the land? Such a three-tiered administration is typical for example of imperial estates in Egypt.[57] On the other hand the sub-lessees in the Bar Kokhba leases are not share-croppers, but pay for the lease in money. This was not the method employed by the *fiscus*, at least for the balsam in Judaea – and there are hints in some of the Bar Kokhba documents that, as might have been expected, Bar Kokhba took over the precious balsam groves.[58] We know from Pliny that the *fiscus* itself sold the balsam to retailers, who in their turn sold it to others for less than a third of what they had paid for it, and yet made a profit by adulterating the pure balsam:[59]

> *nec manifestior alibi fraus, quippe millibus denarium sextarii empti vendente fisco, trecenis denariis veneunt: in tantum expedit augere liquorem* (Pliny, *NH* XII, 123).
>
> Nowhere is there more visible fraud, since sextarii (of balsam) bought from the *fiscus* for 1000 denarii are sold again for 300 denarii (each). To such a degree is it feasible to increase the quantity of balsam.

---

56 In *P.Yadin* 46 (134 CE) line 5 there is a reference to a Hananiah who had once 'held' (החזיק) the property now being sub-leased. If the man 'held' the property before the revolt, then the same system of sub-leasing (presumably by the imperial procurator who would be the equivalent of Bar Kokhba's *parnasim*) may have prevailed when the land belonged to the imperial domain as well. I am grateful to Ada Yardeni and Baruch Levine for showing me their commentary to this document before its publication in Yigael Yadin et al., *The Documents from the Bar Kokhba Period in the Cave of Letters: Hebrew, Aramaic and Nabatean-Aramaic Papyri* (Jerusalem: IES, 2002).
57 On the three-tiered administration of imperial estates in Egypt see George M. Parássoglou, *Imperial Estates in Roman Egypt* (Amsterdam: Hakkert, 1978), 52, 57; Dennis P. Kehoe, *Management and Investment on Estates in Roman Egypt during the Early Empire* (Bonn: Habelt, 1992), 16 ff.; for Africa see Dennis P. Kehoe, *The Economics of Agriculture on Roman Imperial Estates in North Africa* (Göttingen: Vandenhoeck & Ruprecht, 1988), 117–53, and for the provinces of Anatolia see Stephen Mitchell, *Anatolia: Land, Men, and Gods in Asia Minor*, Vol. I (Oxford: Clarendon Press, 1993), 162 ff.
58 The balsam is not mentioned in the Bar Kokhba documents. However, one should probably identify the *lotem* in *P.Yadin* 50 with the λῆδος, the shrub from which the gum called λάδανον (or λήδανον) exudes: ולוטמה די לא יקרב בה אנש ('no one should get near the Lotem'). For the identification of the *lotem* with the *ladanum* see Felix Yehuda, *Trees: Aromatic, Ornamental, and of the Forest in the Bible and Rabbinic Literature* (Jerusalem: Reuven Mass, 1997), 86 f.
59 Pliny, *NH* XII, 123 (= Stern, no. 213); cf. Cotton and Eck, "Ein Staatsmonopol und seine Folgen," 159: "Denn die für je 1000 Denare gekauften (*empti*) sextarii Balsam, wobei der Fiscus der Verkäufer ist, werden für je 300 Denare (weiter-)verkauft. So sehr ist es möglich, den Balsamsaft zu vermehren" (this passage has always been misunderstood and mistranslated).

The answers to the foregoing questions must await the commentaries to the Bar Kokhba documents.[60] On the other hand there is precious evidence in the documents already published for the fate of the Jewish population of Ein Gedi after the first revolt.

The ties between Ein Gedi and Maḥoza (Maḥoz 'Eglatain): one Jewish community

The existence of intimate ties between families in Ein Gedi in the province of Judaea and those living in Maḥoza (Maḥoz 'Aglatain) in the province of Arabia strikes one immediately on reading the Babatha archive. Very often we find the expression 'from Ein Gedi residing in Maḥoza,'[61] or vice versa, as in one of Bar Kokhba's leases: 'Alma son of Judah and Tahnah son of Shime'on from the Luḥit in Maḥoz 'Aglatain, residing in Ein Gedi.'[62] Judah son of Eleazar, Babatha's second husband, is attested in Ein Gedi in 124 in *P.Yadin* 11, but by 125 (*P.Yadin* 15) he is already in Arabia. Between 125 and 128 he marries Babatha of Maḥoza. He continues to hold property in Ein Gedi (*P.Yadin* 19), but also owns date groves in Maḥoza (*P.Yadin* 21–22, 24–26). Judah's other or former wife, Miriam daughter of Beianos,[63] although called an Ein Gedian, is likely to have lived in Maḥoza.[64] Both his daughter, Shlamzion, and her new husband, Judah son of Hananiah, are Ein Gedians now living in Maḥoza.[65] On one occasion we find an Ein Gedian residing in Mazra'a in the so-called Lysna (al-Lisân). Since he is serving as the guardian of Judah son of Eleazar's orphaned nephews,[66] it is possible that the orphans

---

60 Above n. 56.

61 E.g. *P.Yadin* 19 (128 CE), lines 11–12: [Ἰο]ύ̣δ̣ας Ἐ̣λ[αζά]ρου Χθουσ[ίω]ν̣ο̣ς Ἠ̣νγ̣α̣δη̣[νὸ]ς̣ οἰκῶν ἐν Μαωζᾶς.

62 *P.Yadin* 44 (November 134), lines 4–6: אלמא בן יהודה ותחנה בן שמעון מן הלוחית שבמחוז עגלתין שניהם יושבים בעין גדי.

63 For the controversy over evidence for polygamy in the documents see R. Katzoff (denying it) in "Polygamy in P.Yadin?," *ZPE* 109 (1995): 128–32; contra Naphtali Lewis, "Judah's Bigamy," *ZPE* 116 (1997): 152; see also Adiel Schremer, "How much Jewish Polygyny in Roman Palestine?," *Proceedings of the American Academy for Jewish Research* 63 (1997–2001): 181–223.

64 *P.Yadin* 26 line 3: Μαριάμη̣ν Βειανοῦ Ἡνγαδηνη̣. I am corrected by Naphtali Lewis who points out that Miriam too is likely to have resided in Maḥoza: "In the World of P.Yadin: Where did Judah's Wife Live?," *IEJ* 46 (1996): 256–57.

65 *P.Yadin* 18 (128 CE), lines 32–37 = lines 3–6: ἐ̣ξ̣[έδ]ο̣τ[ο Ἰούδα]ς̣ Ἐ̣λ̣ε̣αζάρου τοῦ καὶ [Χθουσί]-ω̣ν[ος Σ]ελαμψ̣[ι]ώνη̣ν̣ τὴ̣ν ἰδίαν θυγατέραν αὐτο̣ῦ παρθ̣έ̣ν̣ο̣ν Ἰούδατι ἐπικαλουμένῳ Κίμβερι υἱῷ Ἀνανίου τοῦ Σ̣ωμ̣α̣λα, ἀμφότεροι ἀπ̣ὸ κ̣ώμης Αἰνγαδῶν τῆς Ἰο̣υδαία[ς] ἐνθάδε καταμένον̣τ̣[ες].

66 *P.Yadin* 20 (130 CE), lines 4–5 = lines 23–24: Βησᾶς Ἰησούου Ἠνγαδηνὸς οἰκῶν ἐν Μαζρα̣α̣ ἐ<πί>τροπος ὀρφανῶν Ἰησούου Χθουσ̣ίωνος.

too lived in Mazra‘a. Thus the two brothers, Judah and Joshua, sons of Eleazar Khthousion, both originally hailing from Ein Gedi, settled in two different villages in Arabia. Ein Gedians not only reside in Maḥoza but also own property there and intermarry with the Jews of Maḥoza. It is just possible that Yadin was right to identify Beianos, father of Miriam of the Babatha archive, with the father of one of Bar Kokhba's men in Ein Gedi, namely Jonathan son of Beianos, and that she brought his archive to the 'Cave of Letters' in Naḥal Ḥever.[67]

The impression that people who belonged to the same families lived on both sides of the so-called provincial border is so strong that one is bound to ask: when were they separated? I believe that the families were separated during the first revolt. After the raids by the *Sicarii* in Passover 68 CE[68] and the battles over the balsam between the Jews and the Roman army in that year,[69] Ein Gedi must have been practically abandoned, at least for a while. The Jewish families who escaped from Ein Gedi settled in a place with similar climatic conditions, similar cultivation, a similar watering system, where other Jewish families had settled before: in Maḥoz 'Aglatain – a village in what was then and until 106 the Nabataean kingdom. But the ties with the home village remained. Communication was facilitated by sea travel: both villages were situated on the seashore, and the Dead Sea was navigable.[70]

The very fact that documents of people from Ein Gedi and of families from Arabia were found in the same cave is the best testimony to the survival of close ties between the families. These ties with the mother community go a long way to explaining why the well-off Jews of Arabia, notwithstanding their excellent relations with their neighbours the Nabataeans (who serve as guardians, witnesses

67 E.g. *P.Yadin* 52 (*SB* VIII 9843), lines 1–3: Σου[μαῖ]ος Ἰωναθῆι Βαιανοῦ καὶ Μα[σ]αβάλα χαίρειν; *P.Yadin* 49, lines 1–2: משמעון בר כוסבא לאנשי עינגדי למשבלא וליהונתן בר בעין שלום בטב, cf. Yadin, "Expedition D – The Cave of the Letters," 247–48.

68 Joseph., *BJ* 4.402.

69 Pliny, *NH* XII, 112.

70 Two of Babatha's date groves in Maḥoz 'Aglatain were named Algiphiamma, which is a Greek transliteration of Aramaic על גיף ימא: 1) κῆπον φοινικῶνος ἐν ὁρίοις Μαωζων λεγόμενον Αλγιφιαμμα ... γείτονες ὁδὸς καὶ θάλασσα; 2) κῆπον φοινικῶνος ἐν ὁρίοις Μαωζων λεγόμενον Αλγιφιαμμα ... γείτονες μοσχαντικὴ κυρίου Καίσαρος καὶ θάλασσα, *P.Yadin* 16 lines 17–24; cf. *P.Hever* 62 frg. a lines 14–17: Sammouos son of Shime'on, Salome Komaïse's first husband, declares 'a field, called Arenoaratha, within the boundaries of the aforesaid Maḥoza' which is abutted by the sea: μέρος ἥμισυ χώρας ἐν ὁρίοις Μαωζων τῆς προγ̣ε̣γραμμέν̣ης λ̣ε̣γ̣ο̣μ̣ένης Αρενοαραθα ... γείτ̣[ον]ες Μαγ̣ᾳης Μαναη καὶ θάλασσα, lines 14–17; *P.Yadin* 49, sent to Masabala and Yehonatan in Ein Gedi, mentions loading the fruit on/from a boat (שפינא) as well as harbour; see boats sailing on the Dead Sea in the Madaba Map, cf. Michael Avi-Yonah, *The Madaba Mosaic Map* (Jerusalem: IES, 1954); Gideon Hadas, "Where was the Harbour of 'En-Gedi Situated?," *IEJ* 43 (1993): 45–49.

and subscribers in the Jewish documents), left their property behind and crossed over to Judaea soon after the beginning of the Bar Kokhba revolt.[71] This event may tell us as much about the nature of the Bar Kokhba revolt as do the documents left behind by the leader of the revolt and his men. Perhaps the revolt spread into Arabia, something for which there may be now indirect evidence;[72] or else Jews from Arabia responded to some sort of call and returned home. Was it a messianic hope or what seemed like the renewal of Jewish sovereignty that made them come home? The Bar Kokhba Revolt reunited the families whom the first revolt had rent asunder – tragically, they were reunited in death.

71 The last dated document is *P.Yadin* 27 of 19 August 132.

72 See Werner Eck, "The Bar Kokhba Revolt: The Roman Point of View," *JRS* 89 (1999): 76–89.

The Roman Census in the Papyri from the Judaean Desert and the Egyptian κατ' οἰκίαν ἀπογραφή

I should like to start with a well-known passage from the New Testament which has been the subject of endless discussions and controversies in the attempt to salvage the tradition about Jesus' year of birth:

> In those days a decree (δόγμα) was issued by Caesar Augustus for the whole inhabited world to register (in a census) (ἀπογράφεσθαι πᾶσαν τὴν οἰκουμένην). This census (ἀπογραφή) took place for the first time (πρώτη) when Quirinius was governor of Syria. And everyone made his way to be registered, each to his own city (Luke 2:1–3).[1]

Ever since the discovery of papyri recording house-to-house censuses at fourteen-year intervals in Egypt (the κατ' οἰκίαν ἀπογραφή), we can be sure that a hard core of historical fact lies behind the passage from Luke, even if we cannot reconcile the time of the census with the traditional date of Jesus' birth.[2]

Although one can show that there was never a general census of the entire Roman empire, i. e. one held simultaneously in all provinces, nevertheless it is true that provincial censuses were an Augustan innovation, as was the general imposition of the provincial poll tax, *tributum capitis*, intimately connected with the census, albeit not the only reason for it.[3] There is therefore good reason to believe that

1 Ἐγένετο δὲ ἐν ταῖς ἡμέραις ἐκείναις ἐξῆλθεν δόγμα παρὰ Καίσαρος Αὐγούστου ἀπογράφεσθαι πᾶσαν τὴν οἰκουμένην. αὕτη ἀπογραφὴ πρώτη ἐγένετο ἡγεμονεύοντος τῆς Συρίας Κυρηνίου. καὶ ἐπορεύοντο πάντες ἀπογράφεσθαι, ἕκαστος εἰς τὴν ἑαυτοῦ πόλιν.

2 See now Bernhard Palme, "Die ägyptische κατ' οἰκίαν ἀπογραφή und Lk 2,1–5," *Protokolle zur Bibel* 2 (1993): 1–24; Bernhard Palme, "Neues zum ägyptischen Provinzialzensus. Ein Nachtrag zum Artikel PzB 2 (1993) 1–24," *Protokolle zur Bibel* 3 (1994): 1–7; Klaus Rosen, "Jesu Geburtsdatum, der Census des Quirinius und eine jüdische Steuererklärung aus dem Jahr 127 nC.," *Jahrbuch für Antike und Christentum* 38 (1995): 5–15; cf. Hans-Albert Rupprecht, "Ein Münchner Papyrus zum Provinzial-Zensus," in *Bayern und die Antike. 150 Jahre Maximilians-Gymnasium in München*, ed. Wolf-Arnim Frhr. V. Reitzenstein (München: Beck, 1999), 262–71; Michael Wolter, "Erstmals unter Quirinius! Zum Verständnis von Lk 2,2," *Biblische Notizen* 102 (2000): 35–41.

3 Lutz Neesen, *Untersuchungen zu den direkten Staatsabgaben der römischen Kaiserzeit 27 v. Chr. bis 284 n. Chr.* (Bonn: Habelt, 1980), 39–45; cf. Peter A. Brunt, "The Revenues of Rome," in *Roman*

Article note: First published in Lawrence H. Schiffman, ed., *Semitic Papyrology in Context: A Climate of Creativity* (Leiden – Boston: Brill, 2003), 105–122, with the following note: this revised version of the lecture delivered in New York in March 2000 in honour of Baruch Levine owes much to detailed criticism provided by Dominic Rathbone, who kindly allowed me to see in advance of publication his "PSI XI 1183: A Record of a Roman Census Declaration of AD 47/8," in *Essays and Texts in Honor of J. David Thomas*, ed. Traianos Gagos and Roger S. Bagnall (Cincinnati: American Society of Papyrologists, 2001), 99–113.

https://doi.org/10.1515/9783110770438-023

the census which took place in year 6 CE under P. Sulpicius Quirinius was indeed the first provincial census to be conducted in the province of Syria – and naturally the first census was ordered by Augustus and not by the governor.[4] Quirinius did no more than transmit the imperial order in his edict; he may even have cited the emperor's *ipsissima verba* in his edict commanding the people to register.[5] It is also entirely credible that the same edict, or perhaps rather a later one, ordered the provincials to go back to their 'legal domicile' to be registered there, as did the often-quoted edict of C. Vibius Maximus, the prefect of Egypt in 104 CE, where one notices that the wording implies that the census had already started:

> The house-to-house census having started, it is essential that all persons who for any reason whatsoever are absent from their homes be summoned to return to their own hearths, in order that they may perform the customary business of registration and apply themselves to the cultivation which concerns them (*P.Lond.* III 904 = *W.Chr.* 202, lines 20–28).[6]

We have independent epigraphic evidence for a census in Syria in 6 CE in the inscription of Quintus Aemilius Secundus, who as prefect of an auxiliary cohort conducted a census in Apamea:

> Quintus Aemilius Secundus, son of Quintus, of the tribe Palatina, I received honours in the camps of the Divine Augustus under Publius Sulpicius Quirinius, legate of Caesar in Syria, as prefect of the First Cohort Augusta, as prefect of the Second Cohort Classica; I also conducted by Quirinius' command a census in the city of Apamea (counting) 117,000 citizens ... (*ILS* 2683).[7]

It was precisely in the year 6 CE, when a census was conducted in Syria by the governor P. Sulpicius Quirinius, that Archelaus was banished from Judaea, which

---

Imperial Themes (Oxford: Clarendon Press, 1990), 329–30; Dominic Rathbone, "Egypt, Augustus and Roman Taxation," *Cahiers du Centre Gustave Glotz* 4 (1993): 86–99.

4 Thus there is no reason to reject Luke's statement on the ground that a census was ordered by the governor and not by the emperor.

5 Somewhat in this vein, see Hannah M. Cotton, "Ἡ νέα ἐπαρχεία Ἀραβία: The New Province of Arabia in the Papyri from the Judaean Desert," *ZPE* 116 (1997): 206–8 [above, pp. 312–16].

6 τῆς κατ' οἰ[κίαν ἀπογραφῆς ἐ]νεστώ[σης] ἀναγκαῖόν [ἐστιν πᾶσιν τοῖ]ς καθ' ἥ[ντινα] δήποτε αἰτ[ίαν ἀποδημοῦσιν ἀπὸ τῶν] νομῶν προσα[γγέλλε]σθαι ἐπα[νελ]θεῖν εἰς τὰ ἑαυ[τῶν ἐ]φέστια ἵν[α] καὶ τὴν συνήθη [οἰ]κονομίαν τῆ[ς ἀπο]γραφῆς πληρώσωσιν καὶ τῇ προσ[ηκού]σῃ αὐτοῖς γεωργίαι προσκαρτερήσω[σιν]. There is often a reference to the prefect's edict in the declaration itself (κατὰ τὰ κελευσθέντα or τὰ προστεταγμένα *vel sim.*): 'I register myself ... as ordered by the prefect ... etc.'

7 *Q(uintus) Aemilius Q(uinti) f(ilius) Pal(atina) Secundus [in] castris divi Aug. s[ub] P(ublio) Sulpi[c]io Quirinio le[gato] C[a]esaris Syriae honoribus decoratus, pr[a]efect. Cohort(is) Aug(ustae) I, pr[a]efect. cohort. II classicae; idem iussu Quirini censum egi Apamenae civitatis millium homin. civium CXVII. ...*

became at that time part of the Roman province of Syria under its own prefect.[8] Naturally the census spread into the newly annexed territory.[9] Josephus explicitly combines the fact of annexation with the administration of the census:

> Quirinius ... arrived in Syria, dispatched by Caesar to be governor of the people and to be the assessor of their properties. Coponius, a man of equestrian rank, was sent along with him to rule over the Jews with full authority. Quirinius was also present in Judaea, which had been made subject to Syria, in order to make an assessment of their property and liquidate the estate of Archelaus (*AJ* 18.2).[10]

That a census took place in Judaea at the time of its provincialization was a mere coincidence and does not constitute proof for the inauguration of Judaea as a new independent province. The notion that a provincial census followed immediately upon the annexation of a territory to the Roman empire is not well founded.[11]

Josephus gives little further information about the course and form which the census took in Judaea, except to observe that the Jews found it hard to tolerate the judicial (?) hearing, perhaps disputes, which accompanied the registrations (τὴν ἐπὶ ταῖς ἀπογραφαῖς ἀκρόασιν, *AJ* 18.3), and that the more seditious claimed that the property assessment (ἀποτίμησις) was no better than downright slavery (*AJ* 18.4).[12] No doubt the Jews found the tax itself offensive, but the passages from *Antiquities* suggest that they also resented the assessment of their property and the examination of the verity of their statements – perhaps also the need to take an oath.[13]

---

8 Cf. *AJ* 17.355: τῆς δ' Ἀρχελάου χώρας ὑποτελοῦς προσνεμηθείσης τῇ Σύρων; cf. *AJ* 18.2: παρῆν δὲ καὶ Κυρίνιος εἰς τὴν Ἰουδαίαν προσθήκην τῆς Συρίας with Hannah M. Cotton, "Some Aspects of the Roman Administration of Judaea/Syria-Palaestina," in *Lokale Autonomie und römische Ordnungsmacht in den kaiserzeitlichen Provinzen vom 1. bis 3. Jahrhundert*, ed. Werner Eck (München: Oldenbourg, 1999), 76–9 [above, pp. 318–21].

9 Fergus Millar, "State and Subject: the Impact of Monarchy," in *Caesar Augustus: Seven Aspects*, ed. Fergus Millar and Erich Segal (Oxford: Clarendon Press, 1984), 44 (= *Rome, the Greek World, and the East: Volume 1: The Roman Republic and the Augustan Revolution*, ed. Hannah M. Cotton and Guy M. Rogers (Chapel Hill: University of North Carolina Press, 2002), 299).

10 Κυρίνιος δὲ ... ἐπὶ Συρίας παρῆν, ὑπὸ Καίσαρος δικαιοδότης τοῦ ἔθνους ἀπεσταλμένος καὶ τιμητὴς τῶν οὐσιῶν γενησόμενος. Κωπώνιός τε αὐτῷ συγκαταπέμπεται τάγματος τῶν ἱππέων, ἡγησόμενος Ἰουδαίων τῇ ἐπὶ πᾶσιν ἐξουσίᾳ. παρῆν δὲ καὶ Κυρίνιος εἰς τὴν Ἰουδαίαν προσθήκην τῆς Συρίας γενομένην ἀποτιμησόμενός τε αὐτῶν τὰς οὐσίας καὶ ἀποδωσόμενος τὰ Ἀρχελάου χρήματα.

11 See Cotton, "Ἡ Νέα Ἐπαρχεία Ἀραβία: The New Province of Arabia in the Papyri from the Judaean Desert," 206–8 [above, pp. 312–16].

12 τήν τε ἀποτίμησιν οὐδὲν ἄλλο ἢ ἄντικρυς δουλείαν ἐπιφέρειν λέγοντες.

13 On the oath in census declarations see Marcel Hombert and Claire Préaux, *Recherches sur le recensement dans l'Egypte romaine* (Leiden: Brill, 1952), 123 ff. On the taking of the oath by Jews in census declarations see Hannah M. Cotton, "Fragments of a Declaration of Landed Property

How was the provincial census carried out? Was it universal – even if not simultaneous – and uniform?

It seems reasonable to assume that the provincial census would be patterned on the model of the Roman census in republican times which, at least in theory, took place every five years to determine fiscal and military liability and, indirectly, political rights.[14] None of these features was relevant under the Empire and the census of Roman citizens as such lapsed altogether after the Flavian period, if not already after Augustus.[15] However, already from the middle of the last century of the republic the conduct of the census of Roman citizens in Italy was decentralized. The local magistrates of each city took the census and forwarded the census-returns to Rome. The Tabula Heracleensis from the mid-first century BCE[16] gives us the official republican formula of the census:

> And he (i.e. the magistrate) is to receive from them (the citizens) under oath their *nomina*, their *praenomina*, their fathers or patrons, their tribes, their *cognomina*, and how many years old each of them shall be and an account of their property (*rationem pecuniae*), according to the form of the census (*ex formula census*), which shall have been published at Rome by whoever is then about to conduct the census of the people; and he is to see that it all is entered in the public records of his *municipium* (*FIRA*, Vol. I, no. 13, lines 146–149).[17]

Local censuses in Italy continued in imperial times, but the returns were no longer forwarded to Rome. They were used to determine fiscal and liturgical duties of their own citizens. It seems that the Roman type of census extended to Roman colonies and Latin communities in the provinces as well.[18]

What about the rest of the empire, the non-citizens, the peregrine subjects and communities? The documentation is patchy and incomplete. Apart from some references in the literary and legal sources we are left with the sporadic evidence,

---

from the Province of Arabia," *ZPE* 85 (1991): 266–67. Josephus mentions a census again in *BJ* 2.385 as means of obtaining statistics about the population: ὡς ἔνεστιν ἐκ τῆς καθ' ἑκάστην κεφαλὴν εἰσφορᾶς τεκμήρασθαι.

14 However, in the east the provincial censuses may have owed much to Hellenistic practices.

15 But see now Rathbone, "PSI XI 1183: A Record of a Roman Census Declaration of AD 47/8," 111–13.

16 For the date see Michael Crawford, ed., *Roman Statutes*, Vol. I (London: Institute of Classical Studies, 1996), 360–62; cf. also Elio Lo Cascio, who believes that the Tabula Heracleensis is of the time of Caesar and the decentralised census is a novelty introduced by Caesar: Elio Lo Cascio, "Le professiones della Tabula Heracleensis e le procedure del census in età cesariana," *Athenaeum* 78 (1990): 287–318; Elio Lo Cascio, "Le procedure di recensus dalla tarda repubblica al tardo antico e il calcolo della popolazione di Roma," in *La Rome impériale. Démographie et logistique* (Rome: École Française de Rome, 1997), 3–76.

17 Translation from Crawford, *Roman Statutes*, Vol. I, 377.

18 See Claude Nicolet, "Control of the Human Sphere: the Census," in *Space, Geography, and Politics in the Early Roman Empire* (Ann Arbor: University of Michigan Press, 1991), 123–47.

unevenly distributed between the different provinces, of career inscriptions of senators and equestrians involved in taking the census. It would seem that the provincial governors in the imperial provinces administered the provincial census in their provinces. However, whereas some of them mention their having taken the census in their career inscriptions, others do not.[19] To determine the frequency of the census in some provinces and their absence in others on the basis of these career inscriptions would be hazardous indeed. As Peter A. Brunt put it: "If we were to trust arguments *e silentio* in relation to Roman taxation, we should have to conclude that there were provinces in which Rome extracted not a single penny from her subjects!"[20]

Recently Elio Lo Cascio proposed that whereas the census in imperial provinces was conducted by the governor and the individual was directly responsible to Rome, in the public provinces, those governed by proconsuls, on the other hand, the cities conducted the census, and it was they who were responsible to Rome for the payment of taxes. To put it in a nutshell: communal assessment and liability in the public provinces as against central assessment and individual liability in the imperial provinces.[21]

However, evidence for the involvement of the cities in taking the census is not restricted to the public provinces, nor is the concept of communal responsibility. Furthermore, although we find imperial officials, e.g. equestrians and some military personnel (like the prefect Quintus Aemilius Secundus in Apamea), involved in taking the census in the imperial provinces,[22] it is clear that the Roman provincial government did not dispose of the necessary manpower to process the declarations, make the lists and the evaluations as well as collect the taxes. As far as the collection of taxes is concerned there is no doubt that responsibility for collecting them devolved on the cities, where these existed, or, as in Egypt, on other autonomous local bodies and institutions – and later on it was done through the liturgical system which operated under the supervision of state officials.[23]

---

19 See Anna Aichinger, "Zwei Arten des Provinzialcensus? Überlegungen zu neu-publizierten israelischen Papyrusfunden," *Chiron* 22 (1992): 35–45.

20 Brunt, "The Revenues of Rome," 336.

21 Elio Lo Cascio, "Census provinciale, imposizione fiscale e amministrazioni cittadine nel Principato," in *Lokale Autonomie und römische Ordnungsmacht in den kaiserzeitlichen Provinzen vom 1. bis 3. Jahrhundert*, ed. Werner Eck (München: Oldenbourg, 1999), 197–212.

22 For more examples of soldiers taking the census see Hans Zwicky, "Zur Verwendung des Militärs in der Verwaltung des römischen Kaiserzeit" (University of Zurich Thesis, 1944), 75–6, and Brunt, "The Revenues of Rome," 334–35.

23 See now Michael Sharp, "Shearing Sheep: Rome and the Collection of Taxes in Egypt, 30 BC–AD 200," in *Lokale Autonomie und römische Ordnungsmacht in den kaiserzeitlichen Provinzen vom 1. bis 3. Jahrhundert*, ed. Werner Eck (München: Oldenbourg, 1999), 213–42.

We have to admit that we simply do not know enough about the taking of the census and its processing in any province apart from Egypt. The most recent treatment of the Egyptian census declarations by R. Bagnall and B. Frier is based on just over 300 declarations,[24] dating from 12 to 259 CE with fourteen-year intervals between each census.[25] These declarations were submitted to officials in the villages and the *metropoleis*. The declaration includes personal details (name, identifying features, age, status) of the declarant(s) and other people living in the same household, including slaves. These 'household' declarations are registrations of people but not of property. Houses and other living quarters are mentioned solely for the purpose of registering the people domiciled in them.[26] All this strengthens the impression of the existence of an intimate connection between these declarations and liability to the poll tax, with which they shared the name of *laographia*,[27] even if women, men above 62 and children under 14 – all of whom not liable to the poll tax – were also declared in the census. The glaring absence in the Egyptian census returns of the declaration of property, not to mention its evaluation, makes it clear that taxation on property in Egypt was not done through the census process. It must have been done in some other way.[28] The registration of land in Egypt in the βιβλιοθήκη ἐγκτήσεων was intermittent and unsystematic; the language of the property returns submitted, whether 'regular' or 'general,' hardly encourages a belief in their effectiveness as a means for anything like assigning taxes and liturgies.[29]

---

24 The number has increased since to almost four hundred, see Rathbone, "PSI XI 1183: A Record of a Roman Census Declaration of AD 47/8," n. 37.

25 Roger S. Bagnall and Bruce W. Frier, *The Demography of Roman Egypt* (Cambridge: Cambridge University Press, 1994).

26 Rathbone, "PSI XI 1183: A Record of a Roman Census Declaration of AD 47/8," 106–7: "*Oikia* here also carried the connotation of civil domicile ... for a man could only be liable in one place for dues on the person, and a multiple property owner would only register himself as a resident of his 'home' property."

27 Rathbone, "Egypt, Augustus and Roman Taxation," 88. Consequently Roman citizens, being exempt from the poll tax, need not have filed these declarations in Egypt, as now convincingly argued by Rathbone, "PSI XI 1183"; contra Bagnall and Frier who take the view that the function of the census in Egypt was not merely to facilitate exaction of fiscal and liturgical dues which fell on a person, but first and foremost to control the population, and in the case of Egypt to maintain "a rigidly fixed social structure, in which Romans, citizens of Greek cities, metropolitans, and other Egyptians (not to mention freedmen and slaves) were kept clearly distinct and barred by a complex of rules from many forms of interaction," *The Demography of Roman Egypt*, 29.

28 See Rathbone, "PSI XI 1183," 106 and n. 27.

29 Austin M. Harmon, "Egyptian Property-Returns," in *Yale Classical Studies, Vol. IV*, ed. Austin M. Harmon (New Haven: Yale University Press, 1934), 135–234; Hans Julius Wolff, *Das Recht der griechischen Papyri Ägyptens in der Zeit der Ptolemäer und des Prinzipats II: Organisation und Kontrolle des privaten Rechtsverkehrs* (München: Beck, 1978), 222–55. See recently Jane Rowland-

Both omissions, i. e. of landed property and of its evaluation in the Egyptian provincial census declarations, are striking in view of the explicit provisions for the declaration of landed property and its evaluation in the 'census form' (the *forma censualis*) cited by Ulpian in the third book *On Censuses* – a form which must have been used in the provincial census as well:[30]

> The census form (*forma censualis*) provides that lands should be registered as follows: the name of each farm, the *civitas* and *pagus* in which it is situated and the names of its two closest neighbours. As regards a field, which shall have been sown within the last ten years, how many *iugera* it measures; as regards a vineyard, how many *iugera* it measures and how many vines it contains; as regards olives, how many *iugera* there are and how many trees; as regards meadow land, which shall have been cut in the last ten years, how many *iugera*; as regards pasture land, how many *iugera* there seem to be, and the same with woodland with trees suitable for felling. In all cases the person making the return is himself to make the evaluation (*omnia ipse qui defert aestimet*) (*Dig.* 50, 15, 4pr.).

No ἀπογραφαί of the Egyptian kind were found amongst the papyri from the Judaean Desert. On the other hand two land declarations, *P.Yadin* 16 (completely preserved)[31] and *P.Hever* 62,[32] and the subscription to a third one, *P.Hever* 61[33] – all three submitted at the census of 127 CE in the province of Arabia – were found in the Cave of Letters in Naḥal Ḥever. The two land declarations preserved in *P.Yadin* 16 and in *P.Hever* 62 evince a striking correspondence to the *forma censualis* of the Digest cited above. The declarants, Babatha and Samouos respectively, after identifying themselves and their domicile, declare their landed property giving the name of each plot, its size, the amount of tax it pays and two of its abutters. The following table brings out this striking correspondence:[34]

---

son, *Landowners and Tenants in Roman Egypt* (Oxford: Oxford University Press, 1996), 127–28, 145–47; and the introductions to *P.Hamb.* IV 241 and 300 in Bärbel Kramer and Dieter Hagedorn, *Griechische Papyri der Staats- und Universitätsbibliothek Hamburg (P.Hamb.IV)* (Stuttgart – Leipzig: Teubner, 1998).

30 Horst Braunert, "Cives Romani und κατ' οἰκίαν ἀπογραφαί," in *Antidoron Martino David oblatum*, ed. E. Boswinkel, B.A. van Groningen, and P.W. Pestman (Leiden: Brill, 1968), 11.

31 This is Babatha's land declaration, see Naphtali Lewis, *The Documents from the Bar Kokhba Period in the Cave of Letters. Greek Papyri* (Jerusalem: IES, 1989), 65–70.

32 This is Samouos son of Shime'on's land declaration found with the documents of his wife, Salome Komaïse daughter of Levi, see Hannah M. Cotton and Ada Yardeni, *Aramaic, Hebrew, and Greek Documentary Texts from Naḥal Ḥever and Other Sites*, Discoveries in the Judaean Desert XXVII (Oxford: Clarendon Press, 1997), 181–94.

33 The declarant is probably Salome Komaïse's brother, see Cotton and Yardeni, 174–80.

34 On the entire procedure see the excellent paper by Benjamin Isaac, "Tax Collection in Roman Arabia: A New Interpretation of the Evidence from the Babatha Archive," *Mediterranean Historical Review* 9 (1994): 256–66 = *The Near East under Roman Rule: Selected Papers* (Leiden: Brill, 1997), 322–333.

Land Declarations from the Judaean Desert

Dig. 50, 15, 4pr.	*P.Yadin* 16	*P.Hever* 62, frag. A
Forma censuali cavetur ut agri sic in censum referantur:	Βαβθα Σίμωνος Μαωζηνὴ τῆς Ζοαρηνῆς περιμέτρου Πέτρας, οἰκοῦσα ἐν ἰδίοις ἐν αὐτῇ Μαωζᾳ, ἀπογράφομαι ἃ κέκτημαι	Σ̣α̣μμ̣ο̣υ̣ος Σ̣ιμων[ο]ς Μαωζηνὸς τῆς Ζοαρηνῆς περιμέτρου Πέτρας, ο̣ἰκῶν [ἐ]ν ἰδίοις ἐν αὐτῇ Μαωζᾳ, ἀπ̣ογράφομαι ἐμαυτὸν ἐτῶν τριάκον̣τ̣α̣
The census form provides that lands should be registered as follows:	I, Babtha daughter of Simon, of Maḥoza in the district of Zoar of the administrative region of Petra, domiciled in my own private property in the said Maḥoza, register what I possess:	I, Sammouos son of Simon, of Maḥoza in the district of Zoar of the administrative region of Petra, domiciled in my own private property in the said Maḥoza, register myself, thirty years old, [as owner of?]
Nomen fundi cuiusque: et in qua civitate et in quo pago sit: et quos duos vicinos proximos habeat. Et arvum, quod in decem annos proximos satum erit, quot iugerum sit: vinea quot vites habeat etc. ... Omnia ipse qui defert aestimet.	κῆπον φοινικῶνος ἐν ὁρίοις Μαωζων λεγόμενον Αλγιφιαμμα σπόρου κρειθῆς σάτου ἑνὸς κάβων τριῶν τελοῦντα φοίνικος συρου καὶ μείγματος σάτα δεκαπέντε πατητοῦ σάτα δέκα στεφανικοῦ μέλαν ἓν λεπτὰ τριάκοντα γείτονες ὁδὸς καὶ θάλασσα	με̣τ̣οχῆς τῆς πρὸς Ιωναθην Σιμωνος ὃ μέ̣ρ̣ο̣ς ἥμισύ ἐστιν σπόρ̣ο̣υ̣ κ̣ρειθῆς σάτου ἑ̣[ν]ὸ̣ς̣ κάβων τριῶ̣ν̣ τελοῦν φόρου μέλαν ἓν λεπτὰ τε̣σ̣σ̣αράκοντ̣α̣ πέντε, γείτ̣[ον]ες Μαν̣α̣ης Μαναη καὶ θάλασσα
the name of each farm, the *civitas* and *pagus* in which it is situated and the names of its two closest neighbours. As regards a field, which shall have been sown within the last ten years, how many *iugera* it measures; as regards a vineyard, how many *iugera* it measures and how many vines it contains ... In all cases the person making the return is himself to make the estimate.	a date orchard called Algiphimma, the area of sowing one saton three kaboi of barley, paying as tax, in dates, Syrian and mixed fifteen sata, 'splits' ten sata, and for the crown tax one 'black' and thirty *lepta*, abutters a road and the sea.	half share of a field, called Arenoaratha, within the boundaries of the aforesaid Maḥoza, in partnership with Ionathes son of Shimeon, which half share is (the area) of sowing one *se'ah* three qabs of barley, paying as tax one 'black' and forty-five *lepta*, abutters (being) Manaes son of Manaes and the sea.

Nothing like these two land declarations has ever been found in Egypt prior to Diocletian's reforms.[35] In 297 an imperial edict ordered a general imperial census. In 298–300 *censitores* make their appearance in land declarations from Egypt which closely resemble those from the first half of the second century CE in Arabia. As Wilcken observed long ago this is something completely new in Egypt.[36] Until then, so far as we know, land declarations were not made in connection with the census, nor addressed to the officials in charge of the census. In fact even after Diocletian's reforms personal declarations in Egypt were still separate.[37]

The discrepancy in the wording of the two land declarations from Arabia[38] gave rise to the hypothesis that the land declaration served also as a registration of persons for the purpose of the poll tax. Like the ἀπογραφαί from Egypt, the land declarations from Arabia begin with the first person ἀπογράφομαι. However, whereas Babatha merely says ἀπογράφομ̣α̣ι̣ ἃ κέκτημαι: 'I register what I possess' (*P.Yadin* 16, line 15), Samouos son of Simon introduces the registration of landed property with his age at the time: ἀπ̣ογράφομαι ἐμαυτὸν ἐτῶν τριάκον̣τ̣α̣: 'I register myself thirty years old' (*P.Hev*er 62 frg. a, line 13). It has been argued that women in Arabia, as in Egypt, were not subject to the *tributum capitis*, and thus Babatha, unlike Samouos, had no need to register herself.[39] This does not convince: too many of the features recurrent in the Egyptian ἀπογραφαί are missing here to make Samouos' a personal declaration similar to what we have in Egypt. Furthermore, women's exemption from the poll tax in Egypt did not dispense them from being registered properly together with others who resided in the same household; the orphan, Yeshua' son of Yeshua', Babatha's first husband, who was still a minor at the time[40] and seems to have resided with his mother,[41] should have been mentioned in her declaration, if it was intended also to serve as a declaration of

35 The old κατ' οἰκίαν ἀπογραφή system seems to have been discontinued after the census of 257/8, cf. Bagnall and Frier, *The Demography of Roman Egypt*, 9–11.

36 *W.Chr.*, Vol. I, Pt. I, 226.

37 E.g. *P.Cair.Isid.* 8 (= *ChLA* XLI, 1201) from 309 CE.

38 Pointed out by Naphtali Lewis, "A Jewish Landowner from the Province of Arabia," *SCI* 8–9 (1985/88): 136.

39 Cf. Lo Cascio, "Census Provinciale, Imposizione Fiscale e Amministrazioni Cittadine Nel Principato," 201: there was no need to mention exemption or liability to pay the poll tax: the mere fact that someone was a thirty-year-old male was sufficient to make him automatically liable to it; and since the amount was probably a fixed annual cash levy, unlike the *tributum soli*, it did not have to be mentioned in the declaration itself.

40 Cf. *P.Yadin* 27 of 19 August 132.

41 Hannah M. Cotton, "The Guardianship of Jesus Son of Babatha: Roman and Local Law in the Province of Arabia," *JRS* 83 (1993): 94–108 [below, pp. 403–30].

persons. Finally, we cannot be sure that women were exempt from the poll tax in Arabia. They were liable to it in the Syrian provinces in Ulpian's time.[42]

It must be stated categorically, then, that just as information concerning property is lacking from ca. 400 declarations submitted in the house-to-house censuses in Egypt between 18/19 and 257/8 CE, so is all information concerning persons lacking from the two land declarations taken at the census of 127 in Arabia. Since it is impossible both that property was not declared and assessed in Egypt, and that there was no registration of persons in Arabia, it would seem that people and property were registered separately in the two provinces – in contrast to the old republican custom which combined the two.[43] We should expect to find separate land declarations from Egypt and separate person declarations from Arabia. The fact that no record of the latter has survived from Arabia is far less disturbing than the total absence of property declarations from Egypt between 18/19 and 257/8 CE. With the exception of the two Bostra papyri,[44] there are no papyri from the province of Arabia between *P.Yadin* 27 of 19 August 132 and the Petra papyri of the sixth century CE.[45] The three papyri mentioned above (*P.Yadin* 16 and *P.Hever* 61 and 62) are the only written records connected with a census to have survived from the province of Arabia. In the case of Arabia, we can easily assume that people and property were declared separately during the census, and that none of the declarations of persons has survived. On the other hand, the absence of details about property in the ἀπογραφαί from Egypt combined with the fact that no property census declarations have survived there strongly suggests, as stated above, that the assessment of property for the purpose of taxation and exacting liturgies in Egypt was totally divorced from the census process; but we have no clear idea of

42 Ulpian, *On Censuses*, book 2: 'It is necessary to record one's age in the census since their age dispenses some people from the tribute; for example in the provinces of Syria men are liable to the poll tax (*tributum capitis*) from age 14 and women from age 12, until they both reach 65. The relevant age is that which is recorded at the time of taking the census,' *Dig.* 50, 15, 3pr.

43 For the republican form see text above ad n. 17; personal details and property are combined in Lucius Pompeius Niger's declaration, see Rathbone, "PSI XI 1183," 111–13.

44 For the Bostra papyri see Jean Gascou, "Unités administratives locales et fonctionnaires romains. Les données des nouveaux papyrus du Moyen Euphrate et d'Arabie," in *Lokale Autonomie und römische Ordnungsmacht in den kaiserzeitlichen Provinzen vom 1. bis 3. Jahrhundert*, ed. Werner Eck (München: Oldenbourg, 1999), 71–73 and Cotton, "Some Aspects of the Roman Administration of Judaea/Syria-Palaestina," 90–1 [above, pp. 334–35]; cf. Hannah M. Cotton, W.E.H. Cockle, and Fergus Millar, "The Papyrology of the Roman Near East: A Survey," *JRS* 85 (1995): nos. 171–72.

45 For the Petra papyri see the various articles by A. Arjava, R. Daniel, J. Frösén, T. Gagos, M. Kaimio, L. Koenen, M. Lehtinen, and M. Vesterinen in Isabella Andorlini, ed., *Atti del XXII Congresso internazionale di papirologia: Firenze, 23–29 agosto 1998* (Florence: Istituto papirologico G. Vitelli, 2001); Jaakko Frösén, Antti Arjava, and Marjo Lentinen, *The Petra Papyri I* (Amman: ACOR, 2002).

the process which determined the level of taxation and liturgies on properties.[46] Registration of property existed in both provinces but its main purpose seems to have been the establishment of ownership.[47]

The striking similarity between the *formula censualis* of the provincial census and the two land declarations from Arabia makes us realize once again how swift the new province of Arabia was to assimilate Roman forms twenty-one years after its annexation.[48] In fact we witness in these two land declarations a fascinating interplay between Romanization in the shape of the faithful adoption of the *formula censualis*, and traditional localism expressed in the preservation of local standards and units of measurement. The Roman authorities must have imposed the former and tolerated the latter.

In one feature, however, the land declarations from Arabia diverge sharply from the *formula censualis*. The jurist's injunction that 'in all cases the person making the return is himself to estimate its value' (*omnia ipse qui defert aestimet*) can hardly refer to an assessment by the declarant himself or herself of the amount of tax to be paid. But this is precisely what we find in the land declarations from Arabia; in addition to giving the measurements of the plots and their two linear neighbours, the declarants from Arabia state how much each plot pays as tax both in kind and in cash: e. g. τελοῦντα (i. e. κῆπον φοινικῶνος) φοίνικος συρου καὶ μείγματος σάτα δεκαπέντε πατητοῦ σάτα δέκα στεφανικοῦ μέλαν ἓν λεπτὰ τριάκοντα (Babatha's declaration in *P.Yadin* 16, lines 19–21), and: τελοῦν (i. e. ὃ μέρ̣ο̣ς ἥμισύ) φόρου μέλαν ἓν λεπτὰ τεσ̣σ̣αράκοντα̣ πέντε (Samouos' declaration in *P.Hever* 62, frg. a, lines 16–17). The expression of the rate of taxation in terms of the old Nabataean monetary unit, the *melaina*,[49] combined with the fact that cash payments are described as *stephanikon*, crown money,[50] i. e., the old Naba-

46 See text above ad nn. 28–29.

47 For Egypt see above all Harmon, "Egyptian Property-Returns." For Arabia one may cite *P.Yadin* 24 of 130 CE lines 4–6: ἐπιδὴ ἀπεγράψατο Ἰούδας Ἐλεαζά̣ρ̣ο̣[υ Χθουσίωνος] ἀ̣π̣ο̣γ̣ενομενου σου ἀνὴρ ἐπ' ὀνόματός σου ἐν τ̣ῇ̣ ἀπ̣[ο]γ̣ρ̣αφῇ κήπους φοινικῶνος ἐν Μαωζα̣. The ἀπογραφή here has nothing to do with the census, *pace* Naphtali Lewis, "In the World of P.Yadin," *SCI* 18 (1999): 126.

48 Cf. Cotton, "The Guardianship of Jesus Son of Babatha: Roman and Local Law in the Province of Arabia," 94 [below, p. 403].

49 See Wolfram Weiser and Hannah M. Cotton, "'Gebt dem Kaiser, was des Kaisers ist …': Die Geldwährungen der Griechen, Juden, Nabatäer und Römer in syrisch-nabatäischen Raum unter besonderer Berücksichtigung des Kurses von Sela'/Melaina und Lepton nach der Annexion des Königreiches der Nabatäer durch Rom," *ZPE* 114 (1996): 237–87.

50 Which is not *aurum coronarium*, which was not an annual tax and would not be declared in a census. Note though that in *P.Hever* 62 cash payments are not described as *stephanikon*, except in frgs. a-m, lines 17–18.

taean royal tax, implies that the Romans adopted without much ado the rates of taxation prevailing in the Nabataean realm. This may lend force to the claim made elsewhere that this was the first census to be conducted in Arabia after its annexation in 106.[51] The rate of taxation seems to have been part and parcel of the description of a piece of land in Arabia, as implied by the phrasing found in a deed of gift from 129 CE from the archive of Salome Komaïse daughter of Levi:[52]

> a date orchard called the Garden of Asadaia with its [the] water [allowance] (of that orchard), once a week on the fourth day, for one half-hour which will pay every year to the account of the *fiscus* of our Lord ten *se'ah* of 'splits,' and six *se'ah* of the Syrian and the na'aran dates. The abutters on the east the orchard of our Lord [the emperor] called the Garden of 'Abbaidaia, on the west the heirs of Aretas, on the south a road and on the north the heirs of Yosef son of Baba (*P.Hever* 64, lines 26–33).[53]

Neither in the Diocletianic land declarations from Egypt[54] nor in the census declaration of Roman citizens in Egypt under the Empire[55] do we find the declarant giving the amount of tax on the piece of land declared in the census. The census in Arabia may have been influenced by patterns of describing property in the Nabataean kingdom or by the status of the land and the nature of landholding there.[56] Thus not only was the provincial census different from the republican census and the census of Roman citizens under the Empire in that persons and property were declared separately, as we have seen before, but in addition it may be assumed that the nature of the provincial census, determined as it was by conditions in each province, may have varied from province to province. By 127 CE, when Titus Aninius Sextius Florentinus conducted the census in Arabia, over

---

51 Cf. Cotton, "Ἡ Νέα Ἐπαρχεία Ἀραβία: The New Province of Arabia in the Papyri from the Judaean Desert," 206–8 [above, pp. 312–16].

52 Admittedly this is not true of the lots described in *P.Yadin* 7, a deed of gift in Jewish Aramaic of 120 CE, see Yigael Yadin et al., *The Documents from the Bar Kokhba Period in the Cave of Letters: Hebrew, Aramaic and Nabatean-Aramaic Papyri* (Jerusalem: IES, 2002), 73–108.

53 κ̣ῆπον φοινεικώνων καλούμεν̣ον Γ̣α̣νναθ Ασαδαια σὺν ὕδατος τοῦ̣ αὐτοῦ κήπου ἐφ' [ἡ]μερῶν ἑπτὰ εἱς ἑπτὰ ἡμέραν τετάρτῃ ἡμιωρ<ί>αν μίαν <ἥ> τελέσει καθ ἔτος εἰς λόγον κυριακοῦ φίσκου {καθ ἔτος} φοίνεικος πατητοῦ σάτα δέκα καὶ συροῦ καὶ ναα̣ρου σάτα ἕξ, ἧς γείτωνες ἀνατολῶν κῆπον κυριακὸν καλούμενον Γανν̣α̣θ Αββ̣α̣ιδαια δυσμῶν κληρονό̣μοι Αρετας νότου ὁδὸς βορρ̣ᾶ̣ [κλ]ηρονόμοι Ιωσηπος Βαβα.

54 See e. g. *P.Cair.Isid*. 2 and 3.

55 See *PSI* XI 1183 in Rathbone, "PSI XI 1183: A Record of a Roman Census Declaration of AD 47/8," 100–1 and 111–13

56 See Hannah M. Cotton, "Land Tenure in the Documents from the Nabataean Kingdom and the Roman Province of Arabia," *ZPE* 119 (1997): 255–65 [above, pp. 293–308], with no positive conclusions.

150 years had elapsed since the first provincial census in Gaul in 27 BCE under Augustus. Nevertheless it is quite likely that there was no norm, represented by the *forma censualis* of Ulpian: the latter, if not reflecting some local variation, may have been 'an idealized type.'[57]

What system operated in Judaea? Did the declarations of 6 CE resemble the Egyptian ἀπογραφαί or the Arabian land declarations? A new interpretation of a Greek papyrus from Naḥal Ṣe'elim, published for the first time by Baruch Lifshitz in 1961,[58] may throw some light on the census process in Judaea.[59]

The papyrus consists of six fragments surviving from a large document. The extent of the loss cannot be established. Only one of the two largest fragments, frag. a, is reproduced below.

The document contained at least four columns, consisting of two sets of two columns, the left one of each pair being a list of persons and the right one a list of their respective ages. This structure is revealed in frag. a which preserves three columns, although the remains of the first column consist of only the ends of two names appearing in lines 7, 8 and 9. Cols. i and ii form a pair followed by col. iii which was paired with the following column, which has not survived.

The official nature of the list is quite apparent, and is also implied by the fluent hand of the scribe. If we exclude the Bar Kokhba documents, this is one of the few official documents found in the Judaean Desert, where most of the documents are private. The only other group of official documents are the parchment fragments from Wadi Murabba'at (*P.Mur.* 89–107), which on the most plausible interpretation are lists of taxes in money and kind received by the administration.[60] Like the present document and the land declarations from Arabia they are written in Greek. The use of Greek as the official language in a Roman province implies of course the active participation of local people in the routine of provincial administration.

The date and place of writing of the present document are unknown. If, as is argued reasonably by the archaeologists, the documents found in cave 34 of Naḥal Ṣe'elim were hidden there by refugees of the Bar Kokhba revolt, then the present document should be dated most probably to the first half of the second

---

57 The conclusions reached here owe a great deal to my discussions with Dominic Rathbone.

58 Baruch Lifshitz, "The Greek Documents from Naḥal Ṣeelim and Naḥal Mishmar," *IEJ* 11 (1961): 53–62.

59 The papyrus is re-edited by the present author as '34Ṣe papCensus List from Judaea or Arabia gr' in James Charlesworth et al., eds., *Miscellaneous Texts from the Judaean Desert*, Discoveries in the Judaean Desert XXXVIII (Oxford: Oxford University Press, 2000), 217–25.

60 See introduction to *P.Mur.* 89–107 in P. Benoit, J.T. Milik, and R. de Vaux, *Les grottes de Murabba'at*, Discoveries in the Judaean Desert II (Oxford: Clarendon Press, 1961).

col. i	col. ii	col. iii	col. i	col. ii	col. iii
1	[ἐτῶν] κε			[age] 25	
2	[ἐτ]ῶν ιγ	.[...].[		[ag]e 13	.[...].[
3	[ἐτ]ῶν ιθ	Ιησους Ληου.[		[ag]e 19	Yeshua son of Levi
4	[ἐτῶ]ν μα	[...]νῳρ.[		[ag]e 41	[...]nor [son]
5	[ ]	Ιωσηπος [		[age]	Yosepos [another son]
6	[ ]	Ιησους αλ[		[age]	Yeshua an[other son]
7 *trace*	[ ]	Ιωσηπος.[	*trace*	[age]	Yosepos [another son]
8]υ	ἐτῶν ξα	Ανεινας.[	son of [o]s	age 61	Aneinas [another son]
9]νος	ἐτῶν ξζ	Ελληλος ạḷ[	Son of [Shim]on(?)	age 67	Ellelos an[other son]
10	[ ]	Γάιος α[		[ ]	Gaius a[nother son]
11	[ ].	Σẹ[.].ος Σειμạ[		[ ]	Se.os son of Seima[
12	[ἐτῶν] κβ	Α[		[age] 22	A[
13	[ἐτῶν] λς	Κ[		[age] 36	K[
14	[ἐτῶν]β̣			[age] [?]2	

century CE. There are at least fourteen names in cols. i and ii and a minimum of thirteen in col. iii. Together with the twenty-one names appearing in frags. b-f, the list must have contained the names and ages of at least forty-nine persons. The preponderance of Jewish names inclines one to think that the papyrus comes from Judaea rather than from the province of Arabia.

There is no support for Lifshitz's speculation that this is a list of soldiers, a fraternity of warriors, who constituted the army of Bar Kokhba.[61] Not only is there no apparent reason to associate the list with the Bar Kokhba revolt, but the idea of soldiers, as pointed out already by Benoit,[62] seems to be excluded by the presence of people aged thirteen years on the one hand and sixty-seven on the other.[63]

The true nature of the list is revealed in the format of col. iii where a name and patronymic is followed by another name or names indented by slightly over 1 cm.

---

61 Lifshitz, "The Greek Documents from Naḥal Ṣeelim and Naḥal Mishmar," 60–1; his conclusion is based on an erroneous interpretation of the term ἀδελφός here, and elsewhere; see Baruch Lifshitz, "Papyrus grecs du désert de Juda," *Aegyptus* 42 (1962): 252–54.
62 Pierre Benoit, "Bulletin," *RB* 68 (1961): 467.
63 Cf. frag. a, col. ii, line 9.

It seems to be a roster of households listing the name of the head of the household followed by those of the other members (i.e. sons). Only males appear in what is preserved of the document; it is therefore likely that the list was restricted to the male members of the household. Similar lists, drafted by local officials, are known from Egypt. They were derived, or rather abstracted, from the census declarations submitted every fourteen years at the house-by-house registration in Egypt, the κατ' οἰκίαν ἀπογραφή.[64] Some of these lists are clearly intended solely for the purpose of taxation; summarizing the material contained in the declarations, they omit all details which are irrelevant to that purpose, such as the names of persons who were exempted from the poll tax, and thus contain only males between fourteen and sixty-two. In Egypt, women were exempt from the poll tax which males between the ages of fourteen and sixty-two had to pay.

However, it is precisely the exclusion of women from the present list which makes it unlikely to be a tax list. It is more likely than not that women were liable for the poll tax in Judaea, and this is for the following reason. The first census in Judaea in 6 CE, as pointed out before, was an extension of the census carried on in Syria at the time into the annexed territory.[65] Consequently the same rules of liability to the poll tax prevailing in the province of Syria at the time must have been applied to the annexed territory. Now, unless a change occurred between 6 CE and the first quarter of the third century CE, the exclusion of women from the poll tax cannot be reconciled with what Ulpian tells us about the Syrian provinces in his time, where males from the age of fourteen, females from the age of twelve, and both till they reached the age of sixty-five, were liable for the poll tax.[66] I am therefore inclined to accept Dominic Rathbone's suggestion to me that "this is a list of men liable to one or several liturgies which were only imposed on men, probably therefore manual liturgies."[67]

Such lists had to be kept up-to-date,[68] and therefore, we can be sure that, if deposited in the cave during the Bar Kokhba revolt, they were made not long before the outbreak of the revolt. If I am right in thinking that this is a list from Judaea from before the Bar Kokhba revolt, we must conclude that lists based on census declarations, like the ἀπογραφαί in Egypt, were prepared by local officials in Judaea using the Greek language. If the capital villages of the *toparchiae* in the

---

64 See Hombert and Préaux, *Recherches sur le recensement dans l'Egypte romaine*, 135–47; Bagnall and Frier, *The Demography of Roman Egypt*, 26–7.

65 Above text ad nn. 8–11.

66 Cited above in n. 42.

67 Like the πενθήμερος in Egypt, on which see P.J. Sijpesteijn, *Penthemeros-Certificates in Graeco-Roman Egypt* (Leiden: Brill, 1964).

68 See Bagnall and Frier, *The Demography of Roman Egypt*, 27–8.

Jewish region in Judaea fulfilled functions similar to those carried out by cities in other parts of the Roman Empire, then we can assume that these lists were prepared by the civic authorities in these villages.[69] But it is entirely possible that, as in Egypt, the Romans employed in Judaea too the liturgical system with local people working under state officials.[70]

Unfortunately this is as far as one can go with the fragmentary evidence. Some lessons can be learnt though.

Although we probably owe the presence of papyri in the caves of the Judaean Desert to the two great revolts in 66–73 and 132–136, these papyri should be studied dispassionately and in context – always bearing the Egyptian example in mind – that is without attempting to read into them the unique history of the Jewish people. For the romantic historian a fraternity of warriors fighting for Jewish freedom is probably a great deal more exciting than a list of people liable to one or several liturgies. However, it should not come as a great surprise that the refugees of the revolts hid in these caves those documents attesting the routine of daily life in a Roman province, demonstrating once again that Judaea was a normal province and Jewish society part and parcel of the society of the Roman Near East.[71]

---

69 On capital villages see discussion and bibliography in Cotton, "Some Aspects of the Roman Administration of Judaea/Syria-Palaestina," 82 ff. [above, pp. 326 ff.].

70 For Egypt see Friedrich Oertel, *Die Liturgie: Studien zur Ptolemäischen und Kaiserlichen Verwaltung Aegyptens* (Leipzig: Teubner, 1917) (reprinted, Aalen: Scientia-Verlag, 1965); John D. Thomas, "Compulsory Public Service in Roman Egypt," in *Das römischbyzantinische Ägypten*, ed. Günter Grimm, Heinz Heinen, and Erich Winter (Mainz: von Zabern, 1983), 35–40; Naphtali Lewis, *The Compulsory Public Services of Roman Egypt*, 2nd ed. (Florence: Edizioni Gonnelli, 1997).

71 See Hannah M. Cotton, "Introduction to the Greek Documentary Texts," in Cotton and Yardeni, *Aramaic, Hebrew, and Greek Documentary Texts from Naḥal Ḥever and Other Sites*, 153–57 with Ranon Katzoff's Review of the volume in *SCI* 19 (2000): 323–27.

The Administrative Background to the New Settlement Recently Discovered near Giv'at Shaul, Ramallah-Shu'afat Road

Archaeological evidence for a continued but brief (down to ca. 130 CE) Jewish presence in a planned settlement in the environs of Jerusalem after the destruction of the Temple leads one to reconsider the aftermath of the Great Revolt in terms different from those used so far. With a legionary camp stationed in Jerusalem, such a settlement must have been tolerated, if not approved, by the Roman government. Its short-lived existence on the other hand is bound to shed some light on the fatal implications of the foundation of a Roman colony in Jerusalem which to my mind was the main cause for the outbreak of the Bar Kokhba revolt. But it is too soon to draw conclusions and indulge in speculation. Nevertheless, the new excavations throw into high relief some evidence from the literary sources, normally neglected, although recently reinforced by the papyri from the Judaean Desert.

To put it in a nutshell: the settlement just excavated was situated in the toparchy of Orine, the administrative unit which replaced Jerusalem after the first revolt; it may or may not have been its administrative centre. Once the colony of Aelia Capitolina was founded, Orine no longer could exist as an administrative unit; what had been Orine would become the *territorium* of the Roman colony, whose centre was Aelia Capitolina. Perhaps this would not have entailed the cession of Jewish presence then, but this may well have happened once the revolt broke out.

In what follows I would like to talk about the toparchies in general and Orine in particular, in order to give a concrete administrative context to what we see on the ground.

The so-called Jewish Region[1] of the province of Judaea, which included Judaea proper, Samaria, the Galilee and the Peraea, was composed on the whole of villages of different sizes, and divided into *toparchiai*. The origin of some of the toparchies seems to have been Ptolemaic; the Seleucids maintained them, the Hasmoneans increased their number and they survived into the Roman period. Their existence both before and after the first revolt of 66–70 CE is attested in Josephus (*BJ* 3.55) and the Elder Pliny (*NH* V, 70), and is now vindicated by the documents from the Judaean Desert.

1 The concept is taken from Emil Schürer, *The History of the Jewish People in the Age of Jesus Christ*, ed. Fergus Millar and Géza Vermès, Vol. II (Edinburgh: Clark, 1979), 184 ff.

Article note: First published in Joseph Patrich and David Amit, eds., *New Studies in the Archaeology of Jerusalem and its Region, Volume I* (Jerusalem: IAA, 2007), 12*–18*.

https://doi.org/10.1515/9783110770438-024

Josephus (*BJ* 3.54) gives the following list of κληρουχίαι or τοπαρχίαι for Judaea proper: (1) Jerusalem,[2] (2) Gophna, (3) Acrabeta, (4) Idumaea, (5) Thamna, (6) Lydda, (7) Emmaus, (8) Pella, i.e. Betholeptephene, (9) Ein Gedi, (10) Herodion, (11) Jericho (*BJ* 3.55). Pliny names ten toparchies: (1) Jericho, (2) Emmaus, (3) Lydda, (4) Jopica, (5) Acrabeta, (6) Gophna, (7) Thamna, (8) Betholeptephene, (9) Orine, (10) Herodion (*NH* V, 70).

With the exception of Idumaea – which is an ethnic name – the *toparchia* was named after one of its villages, presumably the most important or central village in the *toparchia*. Adora and Beth Govrin have each been proposed as the central village for Idumaea.

There are three significant discrepancies between Josephus' and Pliny's lists: 1) Ein Gedi and Idumaea are absent from Pliny's list; 2) Jamnia and Joppa are not included in Josephus' list, but added as an appendix, whereas Pliny includes Joppa in his list, but omits Jamnia; 3) and most importantly for us, Jerusalem disappears and is replaced by Orine (Pliny, *NH* V, 70).

With the publication of the documents from the Judaean Desert it has become evident that Pliny's list reflects the situation after the revolt. The village of Ein Gedi, sacked by the *sicarii* of Masada and possibly also by the Romans in the battles over the balsam groves,[3] became like Jerusalem 'a heap of ashes' (*nunc alterum bustum*, Pliny, *NH* V, 73), and, as we now know from *P.Yadin* and *P.Hever*, it ceased to be the central village of a toparchy, and was itself subsumed in the toparchy of Jericho. Perhaps Ein Gedi lost its status as a capital village of a toparchy as it became 'a village of our Lord the Caesar.'[4]

As for Idumaea, it could be suggested that it too suffered such devastation that it disappeared as an independent toparchy (*BJ* 4.231–5). At some point though between the late 70s and 130 a new toparchy was created at least in part of what had previously been the toparchy of Idumaea: the toparchy of Zif or Zephine. This is biblical Zif situated south-east of Hebron. The new toparchy is attested for the first time in a cancelled marriage contract from the Judaean Desert from 130 CE. The marriage was contracted ἐν Ἀριστοβουλιάδι τῆς Ζ̣ε̣ι̣φ̣η̣νῆς, and the groom is Ακαβας Μηειρω τῶν ἀ̣π̣ὸ κ̣ώμης Ἰακείμων τ̣[ῆς Ζειφηνῆ̣ς̣], *P.Hever* 69, lines

2 Μερίζεται δ' είς ἕνδεκα κληρουχίας, ὧν ἄρχει μὲν βασίλειον τὰ Ἱεροσόλυμα προανίσχουσα τῆς περιοίκου πάσης ὥσπερ ἡ κεφαλὴ σώματος

3 Hannah M. Cotton and Werner Eck, "Ein Staatsmonopol und seine Folgen: Plinius, Naturalis Historia 12,123 und der Preis für Balsam," *Rheinisches Museum für Philologie* 140 (1997): 153–61.

4 In *P.Yadin* 16 of 127 CE, Babatha's second husband Judah son of Eleazar is said to come from 'the village of Ein Gedi in the district of Jericho in Judaea' Ἰουδάνου Ἐλαζάρου κώμης Αἰνγαδδῶν περὶ Ἱερειχοῦντα τῆς Ἰουδαίας, lines 15–16; *P.Yadin* 11 of 124 CE, line 1: ἐν Ἐνγαδοῖς κώμῃ κυρίου Καίσαρος; cf. *P.Hever* 67, line 2: [Εν]γαδων Κυρίου Κ[αίσαρος κώμης].

3–5.[5] The two villages, Aristoboulias and Yaqim (or Yakum),[6] belonged to the new toparchy of Zif. It is true that the term toparchia does not appear in this papyrus,[7] but the expression ἐν Ἀριστοβουλιάδι τῆς Ζ̣ε̣ιφηνῆς describes the relationship between a central village and another village, typical of the toparchy structure.

Another marriage contract from the Judaean Desert, known for a while, *P.Mur* (*DJD* II), no. 115, from 124 CE, was concluded 'at Bethbassi in the toparchy of Herodium' – ἐν Βαιτοβα̣ι̣σσαιας ... τ̣ο̣παρχείας Ἡρῳδε[ί̣ο̣[υ]; the groom, Eleaios son of Simon, came 'from the village of Galoda of Akrabatta, but [was] an inhabitant of Batharda of Gophna': τῶν ἀπὸ κ(ώμης) Γαλωδῶν τῆς περὶ Ἀκραβ̣α̣τ̣τ̣ῶν οἰκῶν ἐν κώμῃ Βαιτοα̣ρδοις τῆς περὶ Γοφνοῖς. It thus attests the survival of three of the old toparchies into the period after the first revolt.

Finally Orine (Ὀρεινή), the toparchy which replaced Jerusalem according to Pliny (*Orinen in qua fuere Hierosolyma*), is attested in *DJD* II, no. 114 (an acknowledgement of debt), line 6. But I shall come back to it at the end.

The term *toparchia* is used by Josephus to describe what at first sight at least seems a totally different regional division.[8] Josephus attaches the name of toparchy not only to a cluster of villages, of which the most important or central one gives its name to the toparchy, but also to cities with their territories. In *AJ* 18.31 we are told that Salome, Herod's sister, bequeathed to Livia, Augustus' wife, Jamnia and its *toparchia*: Ἰάμνειάν τε ... καὶ τὴν τοπαρχίαν πᾶσαν. Even more revealing is the evidence of *BJ* 2.252, where we are told that Nero annexed to Agrippa II's kingdom 'four cities with their *toparchiai*' (τέσσαρας πόλεις ... σὺν ταῖς τοπαρχίαις). The cities were Abila and Julias (that is Livias) in the Peraea and Trachinae and Tiberias in the lower Galilee. The parallel passage in *AJ* explains to us the meaning of the expression 'a city with its toparchy': 'he (Nero) gave him also Livias (Julias), a *polis* of the Peraea, with its fourteen villages' (δίδωσι δὲ [Nero] καὶ Ἰουλιάδα πόλιν τῆς Περαίας καὶ κώμας τὰς περὶ αὐτὴν δεκατέσσαρας, *AJ* 20.159). In other words, the fourteen villages constituted Livias' toparchy.

The expression καὶ κώμας τὰς περὶ αὐτὴν to describe the relationship between a city and the villages within its territory is attested now in a document from the Judaean Desert, *P.Hever* 65 (= *P.Yadin* 37), which belongs to the archive of Salome

5 Cf. Hannah M. Cotton, "A Cancelled Marriage Contract from the Judaean Desert, XHev/Se Gr. 2," *JRS* 84 (1994): 64–86 = *DJD* XXVII, no. 69.

6 Yakim or Yakum is mentioned also in the Aramaic *P.Hever* 9, published by Ada Yardeni in *DJD* XXVII.

7 In fact the term appears but once in the papyri from the Judaean Desert to describe Herodion: τ̣ο̣παρχείας Ἡρῳδε[ί̣ο̣[υ], *P.Mur*. 115, line 2 (*DJD* II).

8 The same conclusions have been reached independently by Yuval Shahar, *Josephus Geographicus: The Classical Context of Geography in Josephus* (Tübingen: Mohr Siebeck, 2004).

Komaïse daughter of Levi. This is a marriage contract concluded between Salome Komaïse and 'Yeshu'a son of Menahem from the village of Soffathe[...] in the district of the city of Livias of the administrative region of P[eraia]' (lines 3–4: Ιησους Μαναημου τ[ῶν ἀπὸ κώμης *c.7 letters*] Σοφφαθε̣[. .] . . . . π̣ε̣ρ̣ὶ πόλιν Λιουιάδος τῆς Π̣[εραίας]). Note that as in Josephus, the dependence of the village of Soffathe[...] on the city of Livias just quoted is expressed in the same terms as that of the village of Ein Gedi vis-à-vis Jericho (also a village) in *P.Yadin* 16 line 16: Ἰουδάνου Ἐλαζάρου κώμης Αἰνγαδδῶν περὶ Ἱερειχοῦντα τῆς Ἰουδαίας; that of Bethbassi vis-à-vis Herodion – ἐν Βαιτοβαι̣σσαιας ... τ̣ο̣παρχείας Ἡρω̣δε̣ί̣ο̣[υ]; Galoda vis-à-vis Akrabatta – ἀπὸ κ(ώμης) Γαλωδῶν τῆς περὶ Ἀκραβα̣τ̣τῶν, and Batharda vis-à-vis Gophna ἐν κώμῃ Βαιτοα̣ρδοις τῆς περὶ Γοφνοῖς – all in *P.Mur* 115 lines 2–3; and finally that of Aristoboulias and Yaqim (or Yaqum) vis-à-vis Zif in *P.Hever* 69 lines 3–5 cited above.

Does the identity of language imply an identity of function: would it be legitimate to maintain that the central village performed the same functions fulfilled by cities both in respect of their subordinate village and in respect of the Roman authorities? The circumstantial evidence for the role of the capital village of the toparchy is strong; and yet one must not lose sight of the fact that there is evidence for a large measure of independence and administrative autonomy of the individual village. Josephus mentions for the late Herodian period κωμογραμματεῖς in *AJ* 16.203 and κωμῶν γραμματεῖς in the parallel passage in *BJ* 1.479. We also hear in the New Testament of πρεσβύτεροι, βουλαί and συνεδρία – located in villages. Needless to say, the Jewish sources abound in manifestations of self-rule, and administrative, religious and judicial autonomy. The people of a town were competent to control their synagogue, their market prices, the wages of their workers, to impose fines, check roads, dig public cisterns, mark boundaries of cemeteries etc. The sources speak of assemblies where decisions were taken and of local village courts, to handle civil and criminal cases; in particular these courts were responsible for appointment of guardians for orphans and widows. The sources attest the existence of *agoranomoi* in charge of market prices, weights and measures. *Parnasim* (פרנסים) and gabbaim (גבאים) are mentioned in the sources as the village magistrates, handling moneys and building projects. *Parnasim* are also attested in the Bar Kokhba documents as being in charge of leasing and sub-leasing public land in Ein Gedi. Taxes seem to have been collected by local people. This is evident in Josephus, in the New Testament,[9] as well as in the documents

9 Herbert C. Youtie, "Publicans and Sinners," *ZPE* 1 (1967): 1–20 (originally, 1937).

from the Judaean desert.[10] The *mochsin* (מוכסין) of the Jewish sources stand for collectors of taxes.

In conclusion, Josephus, Pliny and the papyri prove that the Jewish region was divided into administrative units with central villages or cities at their head. Only about Judaea proper can we be sure that these units were called *toparchiai*. There is no evidence for local officials at the head of these capital villages, nor for centrally appointed officials in charge of the *toparchiai* – but the existence of one kind or another of local officials must be assumed. There are some hints that the *toparchiai* were in charge of taxation. Above all it is hard to believe that nothing beyond a merely geographical relationship is intended by the description of the dependence of a village on a central village, especially since the dependence of the single village on the central village is described both in the papyri and in Josephus in terms identical to those describing the dependence of the *chora* on its *polis*. Furthermore, we know that under the Severi some of these central villages received the status of a *polis*: thus Lydda became Diospolis in 199/200, and Emmaus became Nicopolis in 219 or 220. In 199/200 Beth Govrin – about which we do not know that it was a capital village – received the status of a *polis* and was renamed Eleutheropolis.[11]

Now back to Orine, where the newly discovered settlement is located. A few years ago I reedited lines 1–11 of *P.Mur* 114 first published by P. Benoit in *DJD* II, 1961, pp. 240–43 (see attached figure).[12] *P.Mur* 114 was dated by its first editor to the year 171 CE. The dating was based on the consul's name in line 2, where we should read Statilius Severus. Assuming quite rightly that he should look for a *consul ordinarius* with that name, Benoit opted for Titus Statilius Severus attested as an *ordinarius* in 171, together with L. Alfidius Herennianus. Before the Macedonian date, I have also restored the Roman date, since we now know that this double dating was normal in the Greek papyri from the Judaean desert. In line 4 however, we read: Ἱεροσολύμ[...]. This must be the name of the place where the transaction took place.

And it is here that one must pause to reflect on the date suggested by the first editor. In 171 Jerusalem no longer existed. In fact it has not existed as a place name which legal documents could use since 129/130, when on the occasion of

10 Two receipts from Maḥoza in *DJD* XXVII, nos. 12 and 60, both from the archive of Salome Komaïse daughter of Levi, demonstrate that local people, fellow-villagers, collected the taxes.

11 See A.H.M. Jones, "The Urbanization of Palestine," *JRS* 21 (1931): 82 ff.

12 Hannah M. Cotton and Werner Eck, "P.Murabba'at 114 und die Anwesenheit römischer Truppen in den Höhlen des Wadi Murabba'at nach dem Bar Kochba Aufstand," *ZPE* 138 (2002): 173–83.

Hadrian's visit the Colonia Aelia Capitolina was founded.[13] But other factors come also to the fore to reject the late dating of this papyrus. The first editor assumed that this is a chirograph between two Roman soldiers, at least one of whom on active service in the *legio X Fretensis* – which should make the use of the name of Jerusalem after 130 even less likely – but he never explained the use of the Greek language in such a case. A chirograph between two Roman soldiers of the *legio X Fretensis* would have been written in Latin like other soldiers' chirographs.[14] The Greek can be explained by its being a chirograph between a native of Palestine and a Roman soldier, like *P.Yadin* 11 and *P.Mich.inv.* 256.[15] Of course Benoit could not have known these two documents in 1961. Furthermore, despite Benoit's hesitations and change of mind, it must be the case that the name of the borrower preceded that of the creditor, and therefore there is no doubt that the creditor is the soldier of the *legio X Fretensis* mentioned in lines 6–8, whereas the borrower was mentioned in lines 4–6, and not in the space between Σατοργ[είνου] and [χαί]ρειν. Ὀρεινή is therefore the place of origin of the borrower.[16]

Literally ἡ ὀρεινή is 'the hilly country' and refers in the sources to the Judaean hills near Jerusalem.[17] Orine is mentioned in *AJ* 12.7 as synonymous to the area around Jerusalem: 'Now Ptolemy, after taking many captives both from the hill country of Judaea and the district round Jerusalem.'[18] But Orine has acquired a political significance after the first revolt. Now that Jerusalem was in ruins, the name of the toparchy which had taken its name from Jerusalem was changed to 'Orine.' This is exactly what the elder Pliny tells us: *Orinen, in qua fuere Hierosolyma longe clarissima urbium orientis, non Iudaeae modo* (*NH* V, 70). Clearly the villages which once were within the toparchy of Jerusalem would now be described as belonging to Orine.

13 *BMC* Emp. III, 493, nos. 1655–1661; cf. Anthony R. Birley, *Hadrian: The Restless Emperor* (London: Routledge, 1997), 231–34.

14 R.S.O. Tomlin, "The Twentieth Legion at Wroxeter and Carlisle in the First Century: The Epigraphic Evidence," *Britannia* 23 (1992): 148, n. 33; True *BGU* 69 = Mitteis, *Chr.* 142 is in Greek although it is a contract between soldiers too, but they are auxiliaries and may not even possess Roman citizenship, despite their names.

15 Nancy E. Priest, "A Loan of Money with Some Notes on the Ala Mauretana," *ZPE* 51 (1983): 65–70.

16 And the word must be capitalised, as I do in my new edition of *P.Mur.* 114.

17 See Schürer, *The History of the Jewish People in the Age of Jesus Christ*, Vol. II, 191, where it is wrongly identified with *HR HMLK*, and see now Shahar, *Josephus Geographicus: The Classical Context of Geography in Josephus*; Yuval Shahar, "Har Hamelekh – A New Solution to an Old Puzzle," *Zion* 65 (2000): 275–306 (Hebrew).

18 I take the καὶ to be explicative in: ἀπό τε τῆς ὀρεινῆς Ἰουδαίας καὶ τῶν περὶ Ἱεροσόλυμα τόπων, and this is clear from the next phrase (see ad loc.).

I expect that the borrower, whose name was written in lines 4–5, came from a village in the toparchy of Orine. This, as we have seen above, would conform to usage elsewhere in the Greek (not Aramaic!) papyri from the Judaean Desert.

To sum up: the presence of Jerusalem as the place name, where a legal document was signed, combined with the reference to Orine as the toparchy of the creditor is enough to date the document between 70 and 130 or 132. Orine did not exist before or after as a toparchy, and Jerusalem became Aelia Capitolina at the latest in 132. Jerusalem cannot be used in a transaction involving a Roman soldier of the *legio X Fretensis* (lines 7–8) during or after the Bar Kokhba revolt. Any date after 130, or at the latest 132 CE, for this document is thus excluded. Whatever the result of the attempts to date the Statilius Severus of *P.Mur* 114 in the consular *Fasti* may be, and whichever way we meet the objection that normally suffect consuls were not used to date legal documents in the provinces (in contrast to Italy), this consul must have been in office probably before the foundation of the colony and certainly before 132.

Was the new settlement discovered in Giv'at Shaul, Ramallah-Shu'afat road, the capital village of the new toparchy of Orine, or one village among others? I do not think we shall ever know.

***P.Mur.* 114, lines 1–11**

	P. Benoit in *DJD* II (1961), 240–43		**H.M. Cotton in *ZPE* 138 (2002), 173–83, ll. 1–11**	
1	ἐπὶ ὑπά[των	]	ἐπὶ ὑπά[των	Τίτου]
2	Στατειλίου Σεο[υήρου	πανέ-]	Στατειλίου Σεο[υήρου πρὸ η̅ εἰδῶν Ἰουλίων	Πανέ-]
3	μου ὀγδόῃ κ[αὶ δεκάτῃ	]	μου ὀγδόῃ κ[αὶ δεκάτῃ	ἐν]
4	Ἱεροσολύμ[	]	Ἱεροσολύμ[ᾳ *name of the debtor*	]
5	αυουαια[	]	αυουαια[*debtor's village*	]
6	ὀρεινῆς προ.[	]	Ὀρεινῆς προς [*Praenomen?, Nomen and Cognomen, rank or* στρατιώτην?]	
7	λεγεῶνος δ[εκάτης	]	λεγεῶνος δ[εκάτης Φρετηνσίας ἑκατονταρχίας *name of centurion*]	
8	νιου Σατορν[είνου	χαί-]	νιου Σατορν[είνου	χαί-]
9	ρειν. ὁμολο[γῶ	]	ρειν. ὁμολο[γῶ ἔχειν καὶ ὀφείλειν ἐν δάνει]	
10	σοι ἀργυρίου Τ[υ]ρί[ου].[ ].[	]	σοι ἀργυρίου Τ[υ]ρί[ου δηνάρια πεντήκοντα]	
11	οἵ εἰσιν στατῆρες δεκ[α]δύω καὶ δηνάρια δύω, ἃ		οἵ εἰσιν στατῆρες δεκ[α]δύω καὶ δηνάρια δύω, ἃ	
12	καὶ ἀπέσχον καὶ ἠρίθμημε· ὃ ἀργύριον ἀποδώσω		For the rest = Benoit's text.	
13	τῇ πρὸ μιᾶς καλανδῶν Σεπτεμβρίων πρώτων ταῖς			
14	ἔνγιστα κατὰ μηδὲν ἀντιλέγων. Ἐὰν δὲ μὴ ἀποδῶ			
15	τῇ ὡρισμέν[ῃ] προθεσμίᾳ, τελέσω σοι τὸν ἐγ διατάγ-			
16	ματος τόκ[ον] μέχρι οὗ ἂν ἀποδῶ ἢ εἰσπραχθῶ τὸ			
17	πᾶν δά[νει]ον ἐκ πλήρους, τῆ[ς] πράξεώς σοι οὔσης			
18	καὶ ἄλ[λῳ π]αντὶ τῶν διά σοῦ ἢ ὑπέρ σοῦ κυρίως προ-			
19	φερ[όντων τόδε τὸ χ]ειρόγραφον ἐκ τε ἐμοῦ καὶ ἐκ τ-			
20	ῶν ὑ[παρχόντων μοι] π[ά]ντων καὶ ὧν ἂν ἐπεικτή-			
21	[σωμαι κ]υρίως τροπ.[	]		
22	[ ] ̣ρου λόγου[	]		
	[four lines]			

The Impact of the Roman Army in the Province of Judaea/Syria Palaestina

The impact of empire may include such things as culture, language, religion, the imperial cult, law, etc. The army was always involved in the transmission of all of these. However, in the case of the province of Judaea/Syria Palaestina, we should stress first and above all the antagonism, the disastrous clashes; all other forms of intercourse pale against the crude fact of the suppression twice, within the span of 70 years, of two major national and religious revolts – two great catastrophes which changed the history of this province – indeed the entire course of Jewish history.

The Romans could not have foreseen the existence of special problems here, and indeed the integration of the province of Judaea into the *Imperium Romanum* was not different from that of other parts of the Roman Near East. Like the rest of the Roman Near East, so far as the Romans were concerned, Judaea came into their sphere of influence already in the second century BCE, that is long before its so-to-speak 'official' provincialization.[1] True, at the beginning there were fluctuations between direct Roman and dynastic native rule, but there was nothing unique about this. Identical patterns can be discerned in the case of Commagene for example, as demonstrated recently by Michael Speidel, to the extent that here too opposing factions in the native population favoured direct Roman rule or their own dynasty.[2] So far as the governor of Syria was concerned, there was no fundamental difference in status between Judaea as a client kingdom or as part of the province of Syria under its own prefect: the ultimate responsibility rested with the consular governor of the neighbouring province, even though the territory was administered separately or differently from the rest of the province under his control.[3] The *praefectus* of Judaea should be equated with these prefects of *civitates* and *gentes*, known to us solely from inscriptions in northern Spain and the lower

---

1 I subscribe to Israel Shatzman's view expressed in great detail in "The Integration of Judaea into the Roman Empire," *SCI* 18 (1999): 49 ff. Thus what happened in 63 BCE was in no way something "bearing on the new political reality."

2 Michael Alexander Speidel, "Early Roman Rule in Commagene," *SCI* 24 (2005): 85 ff.

3 See Hannah M. Cotton, "Some Aspects of the Roman Administration of Judaea/Syria-Palaestina," in *Lokale Autonomie und römische Ordnungsmacht in den kaiserzeitlichen Provinzen vom 1. bis 3. Jahrhundert*, ed. Werner Eck (München: Oldenbourg, 1999), 75–91 [above, pp. 317–35].

Article note: First published in Lukas de Blois and Elio Lo Cascio, eds., *The Impact of the Roman Army (200 B.C. – A.D. 476): Economic, Social, Political, Religious and Cultural Aspects* (Leiden – Boston: Brill, 2007), 393–407.

https://doi.org/10.1515/9783110770438-025

Danube provinces, who had a few auxiliary units under their command. Special circumstances – like distrust of the local elites or some structural anomalies from the Roman perspective – called for the presence of a special functionary between the Syrian governor and the local units.[4] There is no Josephus for these areas to flesh out the lapidary evidence of the inscriptions. And the disparate character of the evidence, epigraphic in the case of the *praefecti civitatium* or *gentium*, and literary in the case of the prefects of Judaea, seems to have blinded people to the similarity between them.

The history of Judaea as an independent province may have begun in 44 CE with the death of Agrippa I, and the provincialization of his kingdom. This time the territory in question was much larger than in 6 CE. Furthermore, under Claudius the equestrian *procurator* as a praesidial governor makes his appearance elsewhere in the Empire. Nonetheless, whereas the title *praefectus* is epigraphically attested for Pontius Pilatus, the title *procurator* or *epitropos* is not attested in an inscription for any of the equestrians serving as so-called governors in Judaea. We cannot be sure that a praesidial *procurator* ever made his appearance here. The history of the independent province of Judaea may well begin only after the end of the revolt, unless (which is very likely) this has already taken place during the suppression of the revolt.[5]

If this is true, then it would prove that nothing short of a full scale revolt jolted the Romans into the realization that this territory could neither be annexed to the province of Syria, nor made subordinate to the Syrian governor either as a prefecture or as a client kingdom, but had to be made into an independent province with its own governor. The need to keep a legion in Judaea led Vespasian to create here an altogether new kind of provincial organization: the one-legion province, not by reduction,[6] governed by a governor with praetorian rank in charge of the province as well as of the legion. Although the new arrangement is attested for the first time in the titulature of the third governor, the conqueror of Masada, L. Flavius Silva, we may safely assume after Werner Eck's restoration of the name and title of the

4 E.g. the *praefecti* in Spain: *CIL* II 4616 = *ILS* 6948: *praefectus Asturiae, tribunus militum legionis secundae*; *CIL* II 3271: *praef. Gallaeciae*; on the Danube and the Alps: *CIL* V 1838/9 = *ILS* 1349: *primopilus leg. V Macedonic., praef. civitatium Treballiae, praef. civitatium in Alpibus Maritimis*; *CIL* IX 3044 = *ILS* 2689: *pra[ef(ectus)] Raetis Vindolicis valli[s P]oeninae et levis armatur(ae)*. On these early prefects see Hans Zwicky, "Zur Verwendung des Militärs in der Verwaltung des römischen Kaiserzeit" (University of Zurich Thesis, 1944), 11 ff.

5 See the presence of a procurator, Antonius Iulianus, in Titus' war council during the siege of Jerusalem, Josephus, *BJ* 6.238.

6 B.E. Thomasson, "The One-Legion Provinces of the Roman Empire during the Principate," *Opuscula Romana* 9, no. 7 (1973): 61–66.

second governor, Sex. Lucilius Bassus, in the inscription from Abu Gosh,[7] that this was the arrangement from the very beginning.

But even before the outbreak of the second revolt, at an unknown date in the early second century Judaea became a consular province,[8] with two legions as well as three cavalry *alae* and twelve cohorts at the disposal of the governor, as a military *diploma* from 139 shows[9] – and all that in what was after all an exceedingly small province.

We have come a long way as far as military force is concerned since the provincialization of Judaea in 6 CE, when the prefect inherited the Herodian army numbering one cavalry *ala* and five infantry cohorts.[10] Their names, *Kaisareis* and *Sebastenoi*, indicate that they were locally recruited amongst the non-Jewish population of Caesarea and Sebaste and their territories (Josephus, *AJ* 20.176). At the outbreak of the Great Revolt there were Roman units stationed at various places: at Ascalon (where a cohort and an *ala* are attested, Josephus, *BJ* 3.12), Kypros, above Jericho, Machaerus (*BJ* 2.484–5), Masada (*BJ* 2.408), perhaps also in Samaria (*BJ* 3.309) and the Great Valley (known in English as the Jezreel Valley) (Josephus, *Vita* 115). It is reasonable to assume that the presence of units in different key positions in the province was not just an emergency measure, but represents the current situation from the establishment of the province.[11]

After the fall of Jerusalem, Josephus tells us: 'Titus decided to leave the Tenth Legion, along with some squadrons of cavalry and companies of infantry, as the local garrison.'[12] The *legio X Fretensis* which had belonged to the Syrian army since at least 6 CE, and perhaps even before, participated in the subjugation of the Galilee and was part of the force employed by Titus in the siege of Jerusalem. Its presence in Jerusalem is supported by the evidence of inscriptions, coins and brick stamp impressions.

A newly published *diploma* from 90 CE identifies for us the 'squadrons of cavalry and companies of infantry' mentioned by Josephus as two *alae* and seven

---

7 Werner Eck, "Sextus Lucilius Bassus, der Eroberer von Herodium, in einer Bauinschrift von Abu Gosh," *SCI* 18 (1999): 109 ff. = *CIIP* I 712.

8 Hannah M. Cotton and Werner Eck, "Governors and Their Personnel on Latin Inscriptions from Caesarea Maritima," *Proceedings of the Israel Academy of Sciences and Humanities* 7 (2001): 215–40.

9 *CIL* XVI 87, 139 CE.

10 Josephus, *AJ* 19.365; cf. *BJ* 3.66.

11 Hannah M. Cotton and Joseph Geiger, *Masada II: The Latin and Greek Documents* (Jerusalem: IES, 1989), 14.

12 *BJ* 7.5.

cohorts.[13] They replaced the *Kaisareis* and *Sebastenoi* which were deported from the province (*AJ* 19.366). Bearing in mind that military *diplomata* list only those units whose veterans are the subject of the constitution recorded in them, the nine units mentioned in the *diploma* from 90 CE may not have constituted the entire auxiliary force in the province of Judaea at that time. However, two considerations buttress the assumption that we probably have here the full auxiliary force in Judaea at the time. First, the *diploma* records eight quingenary units (ca. 500 soldiers each) and one military unit, thus roughly a force of 5,000 soldiers which is more or less what one would have expected in a one-legion province, if it is true that the size of the auxiliary in a province was more or less commensurate with that of the citizen force. Secondly, two more *diplomata* from 86 and 87 CE mention six and eight units respectively out of the nine units known from the *diploma* of 90.[14] It is extremely unlikely that a unit which was stationed in the province at the time would not be mentioned in at least one of the three constitutions issued for this particular province in the course of the four years 86–90. As pointed out before, this entire force was doubled when the rank of the governor and of the province was raised from praetorian to consular sometime in the early years of Hadrian, if not already under Trajan: perhaps already in 117. Lusius Quietus, who had put down the Jewish revolt in the eastern provinces, became the first consular governor of Judaea for a short period.[15] I resist the temptation to go into the causes for the 'promotion' of the province. This is likely to have been connected with the Jewish revolts in the diaspora in 115–117. All that needs to be said at this point is that by a process of trial and error – if one may thus describe the two revolts – the Romans discovered the unique problems presented by this province and addressed them by increasing considerably the military force stationed here.

It is important to emphasize how great these two revolts were, by any standards. For the first revolt, culminating in the siege of Jerusalem which lasted some five months, the Romans marshalled four legions, with detachments (*vexillationes*) of two others, twenty infantry cohorts, eight mounted *alae*, and 18,000 men, supplied by four dependent kings. The victory was celebrated in a magnif-

13 *Ala I Thracum Mauretana, Ala Veterana Gaetulorum, Cohors I Augusta Lusitanorum, Cohors I Damascena Armeniaca, Cohors I milliaria sagittariorum, Cohors I Thracum, Cohors II, Thracum, Cohors II Cantabrorum, Cohors III Callaecorum Bracaraugustanorum*, see Hannah M. Cotton, Werner Eck, and Benjamin Isaac, "A Newly Discovered Governor of Judaea in a Military Diploma from 90 CE," *Israel Museum Studies in Archeology* 2 (2003): 17–31.

14 *CIL* XVI 33 from 86 CE and a *diploma* from 87 CE, see Werner Eck and Peter Weiß, "Eine Konstitution für die Truppen Iudaeas aus dem Jahr 87," *ZPE* 170 (2009): 201–206.

15 Cotton and Eck, "Governors and Their Personnel on Latin Inscriptions from Caesarea Maritima," 222f.

icent triumph and in a series of monuments which partly transformed the center of Rome. In a recent article Fergus Millar rightly emphasizes that we should count as war records not only the two arches erected to Titus on top of the Veleia and in the Circus Maximus but also the two greatest monuments of the Flavian period, namely the Temple of Peace and the Colosseum.[16] Thus the victory over the Jews was monumentalized; it left an indelible imprint on the architecture of the city of Rome. The *Templum Pacis*, displaying as it did among its other treasures also the spoils from the temple in Jerusalem, symbolized not merely an end to the civil wars of the long year 69, but the reestablishment of peace in the empire – thus rivalling Augustus' celebration of his two parallel achievements in the *Forum Augusti* and the Temple of Mars Victor.

True, the Bar Kokhba revolt left no such monumental record on the public sphere in the city of Rome.[17] However, even the 'minimalists' concede that in addition to the two legions of the Judaean garrison, at least seven more legions in full force or represented by *vexillationes* took part in suppressing the revolt. There must have been more, even if not all at the same time. Given the province's size, this was a huge military force. Werner Eck's "Roman point of view" on the Bar Kokhba Revolt should leave us in no doubt as to its magnitude. Let me quote from his conclusion:[18]

> The Bar Kokhba revolt, with its initial heavy losses in manpower, must have dealt a heavy blow to Roman power, pride, and sense of security – all the more so since the war was not restricted to Judaea itself, but spilled over the borders into Arabia and perhaps also into Syria. The extraordinary measures taken by Hadrian to put down the revolt ... vindicate the truthfulness of this claim. ... Hadrian accepted for the first time an imperatorial acclamation for a military victory; and no less than three senatorial generals who had contributed to this final victory and thereby to the restoration of Roman pride and self-confidence, received exceptional distinctions – the *ornamenta triumphalia*. A huge arch was erected near Tel Shalem, in the defeated province itself, probably by order of *senatus populusque Romanus*, to commemorate the victory. From the Roman perspective ... the extraordinary measures

16 Fergus Millar, "Last Year in Jerusalem: Monuments of the Jewish War in Rome," in *Flavius Josephus and Flavian Rome*, ed. Jonathan Edmondson, Steve Mason, and James Rives (Oxford: Oxford University Press, 2005), 101 ff.

17 Although the two fragmentary inscriptions, found not far from the *Templum divi Vespasiani*, certainly justify Werner Eck's claim that they were displayed on monuments which presented Hadrian as Vespasian's successor in Rome's war against its Jewish rebels, see Werner Eck, "Hadrian, the Bar Kokhba Revolt, and the Epigraphic Transmission," in *The Bar Kokhba War Reconsidered*, ed. Peter Schäfer (Tübingen: Mohr Siebeck, 2003), 165.

18 Werner Eck, "The Bar Kokhba Revolt: The Roman Point of View," *JRS* 89 (1999): 89. This has become the consensus nowadays, see Peter Schäfer's Preface to *The Bar Kokhba War Reconsidered* (2003), xx.

> and the exceptional distinctions bestowed on three senatorial generals prove more than anything else the gravity of the Bar Kokhba Revolt, the reality of the threat.

Finally, we may recall, the name of the province was changed from Judaea to Syria Palaestina. Our familiarity with the new name may have jaded us as to the significance of the change, but Eck rightly points out that although the Romans changed provinces' names quite often, never before (or after) was an old name of a province changed as a corollary of a revolt.[19] It was a kind of *damnatio memoriae*: Judaea was washed out, air-brushed out of the map of Roman provinces.

Although the change of name was not due to demographic factors, the suppression of this revolt brought with it a dramatic reduction in the size of the Jewish population in the province. Dio's numbers need not be exaggerated: 'Fifty of their most important outposts and 985 villages of their most famous villages were razed to the ground and 580,000 men were slain in the various raids and battles, and the number of those that perished by famine, disease and fire was past finding out.'[20] Nor need we doubt Dio's summing up: 'nearly the whole of Judaea was made desolate.' Recent archaeological excavations and surveys conducted by the Israeli archaeologist Boaz Zissu[21] in Judaea proper (i.e. the area covered by the Judaean Hills, the Shephela and the Judaean desert) – the very territory where an independent Jewish State survived for over three and a half years – attest major and profound destruction in the wake of the revolt. The second revolt thus had long-term repercussions on the pattern of Jewish settlement in the province – far exceeding those of the so-called Great Revolt of 66–70 CE. To the destruction of Jerusalem and the Temple in the first revolt, a major dislocation had now been added: Judaea proper ceased to be populated by Jews and the center of Jewish life moved to the Galilee.

My presentation so far is quite rightly open to criticism: my association of Judaea/Syria Palaestina with the history of the Jewish people assumes a total overlap between the province and the Jewish *ethnos* who lived here. Such overlap did not exist even before the two revolts. As an aside I may point out that one of the problems encountered by the editors of the current project, the *Corpus Inscriptionum Iudaeae/Palaestinae* (*CIIP*), has been to define the territory from

---

19 "Iudaea, derived from Iudaei, ceased to exist for the Roman government after the Bar Kokhba revolt. ... The change of name was part of the punishment inflicted on the Jews; they were punished with the loss of a name. This is the clear message of this exceptional measure, the one and only example of such a measure in the history of the empire," Eck, "The Bar Kokhba Revolt: The Roman Point of View," 89.

20 Cassius Dio 69, 14, 3.

21 Boaz Zissu, "Rural Settlement in the Judaean Hills and Foothills from the Late Second Temple Period to The Bar Kokhba Revolt" (Hebrew University of Jerusalem Thesis, 2002).

which inscriptions should be collected. During the time span covered by this multilingual corpus, that is the millennium between Alexander and Muhammad, the borders of the territory one has in mind were never static; moreover this area never coincided with any ancient Roman or Byzantine province – let alone matched the territory of any national or ethnic unit.[22] Nonetheless, I am sure that it can be agreed that it is the more complex encounter between the Jewish people and the Roman army, as the spearhead of Roman government and civilization, that is intriguing in this context, rather than the encounter between Rome and the other peoples who lived within the borders of what we may call the province of Judaea/Syria Palaestina. It can be safely assumed, although there is no definite evidence at present for it,[23] that Hadrian's *adventus* in 130 was celebrated in the Greek cities of Judaea in a way not unlike what took place across the provincial border, in the city of Gerasa in Arabia. The city erected a triumphal arch ὑπὲρ σωτηρίας of the Emperor in accordance with the terms of the testament of one of its citizens, Flavius Agrippa. Three other statues of the emperor were raised in the city, two by the city itself (ἡ πόλις) and one by a private person – all dated by the 14th tribunician power to the year 130, and hence dedicated on the same occasion.[24] Parallel examples of such a reception of an emperor on the move could be adduced from all over the empire.[25] In sheer and significant contrast, for the Jewish people this visit spelled dire disaster; it shattered once and for all any hope of rebuilding the Temple in Jerusalem, for on this occasion Hadrian decided on the foundation of Aelia Capitolina – a pagan Roman colony on the site of Jerusalem. This act, to quote Martin Goodman's deliberately provocative formulation,

---

22 On the *Corpus Inscriptionum Iudaeae/Palaestinae (CIIP)* see the notes in *SCI* 18 (1999): 175 f. and *ZPE* 127 (1999): 307 f.

23 But see Leah Di Segni, "A New Toponym in Southern Samaria," *Liber Annuus* 44 (1994): 579–84; *SEG* 44, 1361; *AE* 1994, no. 1781. For a slightly revised edition see Leah Di Segni, "The Hadrianic Inscription from Southern Samaria (?) – A Palinode," *Liber Annuus* 53 (2003): 335–40. However, as observed by Pierre-Louis Gatier already on the occasion of the first publication (*BE* 1996, 649–50, no. 486), it would be hazardous to revise our view of the relationship between the imperial power and villages in Judaea solely on the basis of an inscription found in suspicious circumstances.

24 For the arch see C.B. Welles, "The Inscriptions" in Carl H. Kraeling, ed., *Gerasa: City of the Decapolis* (New Haven: American Schools of Oriental Research, 1938), no. 58 and for the others nos. 143–145; cf. Werner Eck, "Vier mysteriöse Rasuren in Inschriften aus Gerasa: Zum 'Schicksal' des Statthalters Haterius Nepos," in *Ἐπιγραφαί. Miscellanea epigrafica in onore di Lidio Gasperini*, ed. Gianfranco Paci, Vol. I (Rome: Tipigraf, 2000), 347–62.

25 Cf. Helmut Halfmann, *Itinera principum: Geschichte und Typologie der Kaiserreisen im römischen Reich* (Stuttgart: Steiner, 1986), 129 ff.; Joachim Lehnen, *Adventus principis: Untersuchungen zu Sinngehalt und Zeremoniell der Kaiserankunft in den Städten des Imperium Romanum* (Frankfurt am Main: Peter Lang, 1997), 85 ff.

was the "final solution for Jewish rebelliousness";[26] it served as the direct cause for a second revolt, as Dio tells us: 'At Jerusalem he founded a city in place of the one which had been razed to the ground, naming it Aelia Capitolina, and instead of the temple he raised a new temple to Jupiter.[27] This brought on a war of no slight importance nor of brief duration for the Jews deemed it intolerable that foreign races should be settled in their city and foreign religious rites planted there' (69, 12, 1–2).

Nowhere is the conflict more extremely present and the rivalling forces more sharply delineated than in the story of Masada, where modern historiography turned the Jewish resistance and suicide on the one hand and the Roman siege and conquest of the fortress on the other into symbols – indeed into a myth.[28] The *sicarii*, a group of fanatical extremists, banned by the Jewish rebels themselves and forced to flee from Jerusalem in 66[29] – never to take part in the revolt again – came to represent the whole Jewish people, whereas the Roman siege has been turned into a most impressive engineering feat, one of the greatest sieges the Romans ever embarked on: the greater the siege, the more admirable the Jewish resistance and final martyrdom. Eventually Edward Luttwack, taking the Roman point of view, gave the story of Masada a respectable 'scientific' wrapping. In his study the siege and capture of Masada – extended to three years – became the capstone of Roman imperial strategy, the clue to Rome's success and her long survival as a mighty world empire:

> Above all, the Romans clearly realized that the dominant dimension of power was not physical but psychological – the product of others' perceptions of Roman strength rather than the use of this strength. And this realization alone can explain the sophistication of Roman strategy at its best. The siege of Masada in A.D. 70–73 [sic!] reveals the exceedingly subtle workings of a long-range security policy based on deterrence. Faced with the resistance of a few hundred Jews on a mountain in the Judean desert, a place of no strategic or economic

26 Martin Goodman, "Trajan and the Origins of the Bar Kokhba War," in *The Bar Kokhba War Reconsidered* (2003), 28; cf. Martin Goodman, "Trajan and the Origins of Roman Hostility to the Jews," *Past & Present* 182 (2004): 3–29.

27 On the passage see Yaron Z. Eliav, "Hadrian's Actions in the Jerusalem Temple Mount According to Cassius Dio and Xiphilini Manus," *JSQ* 4 (1997): 125–44; cf. now Yaron Z. Eliav, *God's Mountain. The Temple Mount in Time, Place, and Memory* (Baltimore: Johns Hopkins University Press, 2005), 85 ff.

28 See for example Nachman Ben-Yehuda, *The Masada Myth: Collective Memory and Mythmaking in Israel* (Madison: University of Wisconsin Press, 1995), and review by Jonathan Roth in *SCI* 17 (1998): 252–55.

29 On the *sicarii* and Masada see Hannah M. Cotton and Jonathan J. Price, "Who Conquered Masada in 66 CE, and Who Lived There until the Fortress Fell?," *Zion* 55 (1990): 449–54 (Hebrew); Daniel R. Schwartz, "Once Again: Who Captured Masada? On Doublets, Reading Against the Grain, and What Josephus Actually Wrote," *SCI* 24 (2005): 75–83.

> importance, the Romans could have insulated the rebels by posting a few hundred men to guard them ... Alternatively, the Romans could have stormed the mountain fortress.
> The Romans did none of these things ... Instead, at a time when the entire Roman army had a total of only twenty-nine legions to garrison the entire empire, one legion was deployed to besiege Masada, there to reduce the fortress by great works of engineering, including a huge ramp reaching the full height of the mountain. This was a vast and seemingly irrational commitment of scarce military manpower – or was it? The entire three-year operation [sic!], and the very insignificance of its objective, must have made an ominous impression on all those in the East who might otherwise have been tempted to contemplate revolt: the lesson of Masada was that the Romans would pursue rebellion even to mountain tops in remote deserts to destroy its last vestiges regardless of cost.[30]

There it is in a nutshell. However, grave doubts begin to gather as soon as we recall that Rome maintained complete and utter silence about this great victory, which can hardly be reconciled with a desire to transmit a message to its conquered peoples. No source apart from Josephus tells us about the siege of Masada and its fall. There are no inscriptions, no decorations for Roman soldiers who participated in this great siege, nothing at all. Even in the inscriptions from the hometown of the Roman general who conquered Masada, L. Flavius Silva, which recount his entire career[31] – not a word is said about the conquest of Masada. One may counter this with the observation that after the fall of Jerusalem, the destruction of the Temple and the magnificent triumphal procession of 71 mentioned above, it was no longer possible or even desirable to celebrate the fall of Masada, but it was considered more prudent to play down as much as possible the fact that some cells of resistance had remained in Judaea after the fall of Jerusalem. As for the conqueror of Masada, L. Flavius Silva Nonius Bassus became *consul ordinarius* in 81 CE. A glance at the crowded consular *Fasti* under Vespasian and Titus makes it clear that his victory did not go unrewarded.

Nonetheless, I do not believe in Luttwack's grand lesson which Rome desired to teach its subject nations. Thus we should welcome Jonathan Roth's reassessment of the siege of Masada, which cuts the siege down to its real historical dimensions.[32] This notion had been adumbrated earlier by several modern historians, but their caution and comments had disappeared from the books of history.

Roth bases his conclusion that the siege could not have lasted for more than 8 weeks, perhaps merely 4 weeks, on known and verifiable facts about the military

---

30 Edward N. Luttwak, *The Grand Strategy of the Roman Empire From the First Century CE to the Third* (Baltimore – London: Johns Hopkins University Press, 1976), 3 f.

31 Maria Federica Fenati, *Lucio Flavio Silva Nonio Basso e la città di Urbisaglia* (Macerata: Pubblicazioni dell'Istituto di storia antica, 1995).

32 Jonathan Roth, "The Length of the Siege of Masada," *SCI* 14 (1995): 87–110.

capability of the Roman army in laying siege to cities and fortresses. These facts can be substantiated by Josephus' own descriptions of the siege works in Yodfat, Gamla and Jerusalem. We know the size of the Roman force which laid siege to Masada, both from Josephus as well as from the size and nature of the camps: the Tenth legion numbered about 4800 soldiers and the auxiliary units about 3400 – altogether 8200 soldiers – although I would suggest fewer since I cannot believe that the country was completely stripped of its garrison – to which one must add local militia and Jewish slaves occupied with carrying supplies for the army. One can calculate with a great deal of accuracy – checking the results against information obtained from other sources – how long it would take such a force to put together the camps, the circumvallation, the ramp and the battering ram. The Romans wanted to break down the casemate wall, not to starve the Jews into submission; they directed all their efforts to this main purpose. As Roth concludes:

> A combination of Josephus' dramatic rhetoric and the striking topography of Masada (as well as perhaps the influence of politics) have misled scholars on the length of the siege of Masada. A careful analysis of the narrative account, an understanding of the parameters of Roman engineering capabilities and the recognition that the siege ramp lies on top of a sloping natural spur suggest that the siege was a relatively short one.[33]

Cutting the siege down to a realistic size makes it commensurate with everything we know about the Roman army and its methods, its experience, and its use of manpower. The conquest of Masada was a reaction to resistance to Roman rule on a local level; it was a lesson administered locally – not an expression of Roman grand strategy. Nor do I agree with Luttwack's view of Joesphus' role: "And as if to ensure that the message was duly heard, and duly remembered, Josephus was installed in Rome where he wrote a detailed account of the siege, which was published in Greek, the acquired language of Josephus, and that of the Roman East."[34] The fact that the story of Masada makes the climax of the last book of the Jewish War,[35] that the book was written in Greek, the *lingua franca* of the Roman Near East, that it was presented to both Vespasian and Titus (Josephus, *Vita* 361), and signed by the latter's own hand (*Vita* 363)[36] with the order to have it published, does *not* turn Josephus into the spokesman of the Roman government. All that

33 Roth, 110.
34 Luttwak, *The Grand Strategy of the Roman Empire From the First Century CE to the Third*, 110.
35 See Seth Schwartz, "The Composition and Publication of Josephus's Bellum Iudaicum Book 7," *Harv. Theol. Rev.* 78 (1986): 373–86.
36 Cf. Christopher P. Jones, "Towards a Chronology of Josephus," *SCI* 21 (2002): 113–21; see now Hannah M. Cotton and Werner Eck, "Josephus' Roman Audience? Josephus and the Roman Elites," in *Flavius Josephus and Flavian Rome*, 37–52.

one can say is that it was a Jewish historian who *qua* Jew, and not *qua* spokesman of the Roman government, laid the foundations for the haunting and ominous myth of Masada. Subsequently, the story of Masada acquired a life of its own, but already in the *Jewish War* it seems to have risen on its creator and thwarted his original intention, or perhaps rather, it thrived on the deep divide in its author's soul: like Balaam the son of Be'or who came to curse and remained to bless, so Josephus who starts with a stark condemnation of the *sicarii*, goes on to put two noble speeches in the mouth of Eleazar Ben Yair in which he extols freedom and consecrates martyrdom – καλῶς καὶ ἐλευθέρως ἀποθανεῖν – both condemned by the same Josephus as utter folly and transgression in three other speeches, which no less than Eleazar's speech reflect the historian's convictions – only that in them his rationality has gained the upper hand. I refer to the speech he puts in the mouth of Agrippa II on the eve of the revolt[37] – to which I shall return later – and to the one he himself delivers after the fall of Jotapata,[38] not to mention his speech under the walls of the besieged Jerusalem.[39]

Even more disturbing to my mind is the view which sees in the Roman siege and conquest of Masada the key to understanding Rome's success in keeping its Empire under control. The long survival of Roman power is not to be explained merely by the use of military force – not even by the sophisticated use of such force. The Roman Empire survived for as long as it did not because it successfully put down local revolts, but because it did not have to do so: there were very few revolts. Roman rule was on the whole acceptable to its subjects, especially to the local elites. The absence of revolts is not to be explained by the exercise of force: after all not all provinces had much of a military presence in them. Rome managed to obtain the co-operation of those subjects who at the end of the process received Roman citizenship, shared the benefits of the empire and finally came to identify with Rome's history and ideology.[40] This is not to belittle the military threat that Rome presented; the Roman army's efficiency, superiority and cruelty were familiar to Rome's subjects, at least in the first years after the conquest. But if Rome had to use its force in the way it used it to suppress two successive revolts

37 *BJ* 2.345–404.

38 *BJ* 3.361–391

39 *BJ* 5.362–423.

40 Sometimes producing a magnificent fusion of local cultures and Roman government embodied in figures like the Greek historian Cassius Dio or the Greek jurist M. Cn. Licinius Rufinus, see Fergus Millar, *A Study of Cassius Dio* (Oxford: Clarendon Press, 1964), 189 f., and Fergus Millar, "The Greek East and Roman Law: The Dossier of M. Cn. Licinius Rufinus," *JRS* 89 (1999): 90 ff. = *Rome, the Greek World, and the East: Volume 2: Government, Society, and Culture in the Roman Empire*, ed. Hannah M. Cotton and Guy M. Rogers (Chapel Hill: University of North Carolina Press, 2004), 435 ff.

in Judaea rather than merely display it, holding it out as an ever-present threat, its empire would have fallen apart long before it did. The second half of the last century taught us the limits of the use of military force in keeping down hostile and rebellious populations. Rome would not have survived for hundreds of years as a world empire had its rule not been acceptable to its subjects, sometimes more than acceptable – desirable.

It is precisely the benefits which the empire offered its subjects that the Jews – not all of them, and not everywhere, of course[41] – in contradistinction to everyone else, seem to have remained at best indifferent to and at worst rejected out of hand. Full participation in reaping the benefits of empire held no attraction for them. This is surely the root cause of Jewish-Roman antagonism and the explanation for the fact that here in Judaea/Syria Palaestina the impact of empire for the first two hundred years was *par excellence* the impact of the Roman army and the use of brutal military force. Here and nowhere else the lesson which Luttwack speaks of had to be inculcated – twice. Thus it does not come as a surprise that the only argument which the 'Roman citizen, Flavius Josephus', puts in the mouth of yet another 'Roman citizen, Julius Agrippa', to persuade his fellow Jews in Jerusalem not to rise against Rome is, in a nutshell, that 'Rome is invincible and all opposition is futile.' As observed long ago by the late Menahem Stern in a little-known article,[42] what strikes the reader of Agrippa's speech in 66 CE (*BJ* 2.345–404) is the absence of "any expression of appreciation of the civilizing achievements of Rome or some expression of good will and awareness of aspirations and ideals common to provincials as well as rulers. The speech reflects no awareness of the benefits of the 'Imperial Peace,' the renowned Pax Romana which provides security for all the inhabitants of the empire in sharp contrast to earlier periods when a more or less permanent state of war prevailed over the Mediterranean basin."

This, to continue Stern's argument, contrasts sharply with Cerialis's speech to the Gauls in 70 CE, as reported by Tacitus. The Roman general dissuades them from joining the Batavian revolt in 70, not because it is futile to attempt a revolt, but because they have no cause for revolt: Rome has saved them from endemic intestine war and periodic German invasions and shared with them the benefits of her empire:

---

41 Surely one must not lose sight of the Jewish diaspora; there we know only of the revolts of 115–117 CE.

42 Menahem Stern, "Josephus and the Roman Empire as Reflected in The Jewish War," in *Josephus, Judaism, and Christianity*, ed. Louis H. Feldman and Gohei Hata (Detroit: Wayne State University Press, 1987), 71–80.

> Gaul always had its petty kingdoms and intestine wars, till you submitted to our authority. We, though so often provoked, have used the right of conquest to burden you only with the cost of maintaining peace. For the tranquility of nations cannot be preserved without armies; armies cannot exist without pay; pay cannot be furnished without tribute; all else is common between us. You often command our legions. You rule these and other provinces. There is no privilege, no exclusion (*nihil separatum clausumve*).[43]

No such sharing and solidarity ever existed or could exist between Romans and Jews, at least in their own land. No Jew from Judaea/Syria Palaestina was to command Roman legions unless he first ceased to be a Jew (like Tiberius Alexander). The integration of the local elite into the imperial elite was possible only in the non-Jewish sector of the population of Judaea/Syria Palaestina. The hope that future excavations in the province or elsewhere in the Roman world may produce the first Roman senator to originate from one of the cities of Syria Palaestina can go no further than the Greek cities and the Roman *coloniae* of the province.[44]

I would like to end on a more cheerful note, or at least by introducing a ray of light into the gloom which the hostility and intransigence inherent in the Roman-Jewish relationship have surely caused. In one of the documents from the Judaean Desert, the now rightly celebrated Babatha,[45] a Jewish woman from the Roman province of Arabia who somehow got involved in the Bar Kokhba revolt, tells the Roman governor of Arabia of her fondest wish that her son 'be raised in splendid style rendering thanks to *the[se] most blessed times* of the governorship of Julius Julianus.'[46] This should be taken with a grain of salt, like a similar expression used by the rhetor Tertullus in his address to Felix: 'Seeing that by thee we enjoy great quietness and that very worthy deeds are done unto this nation by thy providence.'[47] Both statements hail the advent of Rome as the dawning of a

---

43 Tacitus, *Hist.* IV, 74: *Regna bellaque per Gallias semper fuere donec in nostrum ius concederetis. nos, quamquam totiens lacessiti, iure victoriae id solum vobis addidimus, quo pacem tueremur; nam neque quies gentium sine armis neque arma sine stipendiis neque stipendia sine tributis haberi queunt: cetera in communi sita sunt. ipsi plerumque legionibus nostris praesidetis, ipsi has aliasque provincias regitis; nihil separatum clausumve.*

44 Cf. Hannah M. Cotton and Werner Eck, "A New Inscription from Caesarea Maritima and the Local Elite of Caesarea Maritima," in *What Athens Has to Do with Jerusalem. Essays on Classical, Jewish, and Early Christian Art and Archaeology in Honor of Gideon Foerster*, ed. Leonard V. Rutgers (Leuven: Peeters, 2002), 375–91.

45 The Greek part of the Babatha Archive is published by Naphtali Lewis, *The Documents from the Bar Kokhba Period in the Cave of Letters. Greek Papyri* (Jerusalem: IES, 1989).

46 *P.Yadin* 15, ll. 10–11 = ll. 28–29: [ὅθεν λαμπρῶς διασω]θῇ μου ὁ υἱὸς εὐχ[αρι]στουντα μακαριωτάτοις καιροῖς ἡγ[ε]μων[ί]ας Ἰ[ουλίο]υ [Ἰουλιανοῦ ἡγεμόνος].

47 *Acts* 24:2: πολλῆς εἰρήνης τυγχάνοντες διὰ σοῦ καὶ διορθωμάτων γινομένων τῷ ἔθνει τούτῳ διὰ τῆς σῆς προνοίας.

new age of peace and felicity. True, both Babatha and Tertullus, in their attempts to propitiate a Roman official, may have resorted to self-congratulatory Roman propaganda, but their sincerity should not be dismissed out of hand. For the repeated petitions to the governor of Arabia in the Babatha archive – all of them answered by the governor – reveal a complete adjustment to and reconciliation with Roman rule: it is in his court that justice is expected to be administered. Furthermore, nowhere in the documents is Babatha's confidence in the Roman governor's accessibility seen to be unfounded or misguided.[48] How are we to reconcile this with the fierce rebellions motivated by religious and national motives against everything which the empire represented?

48 See Hannah M. Cotton, "The Guardianship of Jesus Son of Babatha: Roman and Local Law in the Province of Arabia," *JRS* 83 (1993): 94–108 [below, pp. 403–30]; Hannah M. Cotton, "Private International Law or Conflict of Laws: Reflections on Roman Provincial Jurisdiction," in *Herrschen und Verwalten. Der Alltag der römischen Administration in der Hohen Kaizerzeit*, ed. Rudolf Haensch and Johannes Heinrichs (Köln: Böhlau, 2007), 234–55 [above, pp. 213–35].

D Law, Custom, and Provincial Life

The Guardianship of Jesus Son of Babatha: Roman and Local Law in the Province of Arabia

The Babatha archive contains documents of a Jewish woman who lived in the village of Maoza situated on the southern shore of the Dead Sea, in what had been the kingdom of Nabataea and became in 106 CE the Roman province of Arabia. The first dated document in the archive dates to 22 Elul (August/September) 94 and the last to 19 August 132; some of the documents therefore precede the annexation of Arabia, but the majority follow it. This offers a rare opportunity to examine the consequences of Roman annexation: by examining in detail the changes effected by the Roman presence in the newly acquired province of Arabia, we may improve our picture of Roman provincial government and the relationship between Roman law and native local law, as well as our understanding of the reaction of the provincial population to Roman rule.

Although I have not attempted to do so, I believe that the results of the investigation could usefully be compared with what is known about the annexation of Egypt in 30 BCE, since the answer bears directly on the question of the alleged special status of Egypt: to what extent was Egypt different from other provinces?[1]

1 Naphtali Lewis, "'Greco-Roman Egypt': Fact or Fiction?," in *Proceedings of the Twelfth International Congress of Papyrology, Ann Arbor, Michigan, 12–17 August 1968*, ed. Deborah H. Samuel (Toronto: Hakkert, 1970), 3–14; James G. Keenan, "Papyrology and Roman History: 1956–1980," *Classical World* 76 (1982): 30–31; Naphtali Lewis, "The Romanity of Roman Egypt: A Growing Consensus," in *Atti del XVII Congresso internazionale di papirologia* (Napoli: Centro internazionale per lo studio dei papiri ercolanesi, 1984), 1077–1084. For the legal situation in Egypt in the first two centuries after the Roman conquest see Joseph Modrzejewski, "La règle de droit dans l'Egypte romaine," in *Proceedings of the Twelfth International Congress of Papyrology, Ann Arbor, Michigan, 12–17 August 1968*, 317–77; and see now Alan K. Bowman and Dominic Rathbone, "Cities and Administration in Roman Egypt," *JRS* 82 (1992): 107–27 and Dominic Rathbone, "Egypt, Augustus and Roman Taxation," *Cahiers du Centre Gustave Glotz* 4 (1993): 81–112.

Article note: First published in *JRS* 83 (1993): 94–108, with the following note: this article was given as a paper in the Annual Meeting of the Society for the Promotion of Classical Studies in Israel, held in Jerusalem in May 1992, as well as in seminars held in University College London and in the University of Newcastle upon Tyne (Phoenix Society) in October 1992. I am grateful to the participants for their useful comments. I am greatly indebted to my colleagues, J.C. Greenfield, J. Geiger, D. Wasserstein and A. Wasserstein, and to Ari Paltiel. Shlomo Naeh gave me invaluable help with the Jewish legal sources. Finally, the Editorial Committee of the Journal made my biases clear to me. No one but I is responsible for the imperfections that still remain.

https://doi.org/10.1515/9783110770438-026

The remarkable rate of Romanization in the new province of Arabia struck scholars first introduced to the archive.[2] How were we to account for the fact that a young province which had previously been ruled by vassal kings was so swift to adopt Roman forms? The publication of the Greek part of the archive by Lewis only strengthened the first impression.[3] "The most prominent Roman elements" are now conveniently summed up for us in the General Introduction; special emphasis is rightly put on the adoption of the Roman pattern of dating by consuls.[4]

Romanization, however, is not the only issue at stake. The owner of the archive was a Jewish woman. Although the term Ἰουδαίου is mentioned only in connection with her orphaned son by her first husband (*P.Yadin* 12, l. 7), there can be no doubt that she is Jewish.[5] And so are her second husband and his wife and children, as well as most of her adversaries. How is their Jewishness expressed in the archive?

I propose here to concentrate on a single issue, that of the guardianship of Babatha's orphaned son, Jesus (Joshua), her son by her first husband,[6] and to examine its implications for the questions raised above, namely the extent of Romanization and its nature seen against the background of the local Nabataean and Jewish milieu.

---

2 E.g. Hans Julius Wolff, "Römisches Provinzialrecht in der Provinz Arabia (Rechtspolitik als Instrument der Beherrschung)," in *Aufstieg und Niedergang der römischen Welt*, Vol. II.13 (Berlin: De Gruyter, 1980), 763–806, most poignantly on 785: "Wie konnte ein so spezifisch römisches Gebilde wie eine Prozessformel überhaupt in das peregrine Rechtsleben dieser entlegenen und erst kürzlich eingerichteten Provinz gelangen?"

3 Naphtali Lewis, *The Documents from the Bar Kokhba Period in the Cave of Letters. Greek Papyri* (Jerusalem: IES, 1989) = *P.Yadin*; henceforth 'Lewis.' This volume contains also 'Aramaic and Nabataean Subscriptions' to the Greek documents edited by Y. Yadin and J.C. Greenfield. The Aramaic and Nabataean documents themselves – *P.Yadin* 1–4; 6–10 – have been published by Yigael Yadin et al., *The Documents from the Bar Kokhba Period in the Cave of Letters: Hebrew, Aramaic and Nabatean-Aramaic Papyri* (Jerusalem: IES, 2002).

4 Lewis, 16 ff. and 27 ff. It should be noted that the Aramaic documents (*P.Yadin* 6–10), as I am kindly informed by J.C. Greenfield, also carry consular dates, in addition to the era of the province and the regnal year of the emperor (the latter replaces the regnal year of the Nabataean kings of the Nabataean documents *P.Yadin* 1–4; see also Jean Starcky, "Un contrat nabatéen sur papyrus," *RB* 61 (1954): 163, frag. a, l.1 with note 9 below).

5 Martin Goodman's arguments in his review of Lewis for her possible non-Jewishness ("Babatha's Story," *JRS* 81 (1991): 170 [her name]; 175) seem to me far less convincing than the genealogical table in Lewis, 25.

6 It is interesting to note that the deeds concerning his guardianship were tied together in the leather purse where the archive was found; see Yigael Yadin, "Expedition D – The Cave of the Letters," *IEJ* 12 (1962): 235. One would like to know if *P.Yadin* 28–30, the three copies of the *actio tutelae*, were tied together with them.

I

The guardianship of Jesus is mentioned for the first time in a document of 124 CE (*P.Yadin* 12, ll. 4–8),[7] which is an extract from the minutes of the city council of Petra: ἐκ<γ>εγραμμένον καὶ ἀντιβεβλημένον κεφαλαίου ἑνὸς \ἐπιτροπῆς/ ἀπὸ ἄκτων βου̣λῆς Πετραίω̣ν τῆς μη̣τροπόλεως ... καὶ ἔστιν καθὼς ὑποτέτακται· καὶ Ἰασσούου Ἰουδαίου υἱοῦ Ἰασσούου κώμης Μαωζᾶ Ἀβδοβδας Ἰλλουθα καὶ Ἰωάνης Ἐγλα.[8] The καί "copied from the minutes indicates that other items preceded this one" (Lewis ad loc.); the omission of the predicate after the genitive Ἰασσούου Ἰουδαίου υἱοῦ Ἰασσούου and the nominatives Ἀβδοβδας Ἰλλουθα καὶ Ἰωάνης Ἐγλα suggest very strongly that the predicate was common to a list of items, and thus it must have read: 'have been appointed as guardians.'[9] Hence it is quite likely that the minutes contained a list of similar appointments, and as a whole could be described as a 'Register of guardians.'[10]

The appointment of guardians by the city council: οἱ ... κατασταθέντες ἐπίτροποι ὑπὸ βουλῆς τῶν Πετραίων (*P.Yadin* 13, ll. 19–21) recalls immediately the Roman institution of *tutoris datio* (appointment of guardian) by a magistrate.[11] It fits well with the Roman character of the entire document, which is in fact a

7 *P.Yadin* 7 assumes that Babatha was still married to her first husband on 24 Tammuz 120: it declares that if she were to become a widow she could live in one of the houses on her father's property. There is no mention of a son. Since she acknowledges the receipt of money from guardians on 19 April 132, the boy must have been quite young in 124, when the guardians were first appointed. It is less likely that by then she had already been married to her second husband.

8 'Verified exact copy of one item of [guardianship] from the minutes of the council of Petra the metropolis ... and it is as appended below: 'And of Jesus, a Jew, son of Jesus of the village Maoza, 'Abdobdas son of Illouthas and John son of Eglas [are appointed guardians].''

9 Cf. e.g. *P.Yadin* 13, l. 20 (οἱ ... κ̣ατασ̣ταθ̣ἐ̣ντες ἐπίτροποι [ὑπ]ὸ βουλῆς τῶ̣[ν] Πετρ̣α̣[ί]ων Αβδοοβδα<ς> Ελλουθα καὶ Ἰω̣ά̣νης [Ἐγλ]α̣); *P.Yadin* 14, ll. 23–24; *P.Yadin* 15, ll. 4–5 = 18–19. The verb καθίστημι is commonly used in Egyptian papyri for the appointment of guardians: e.g. *P.Ryl.* 121 (2nd century CE), ll. 11–12: καὶ ἐπίτροπος [α]ὑτοῦ οὐ κατεστάθη; ll. 15–6: [ἐ]πίτροπον αὐτῷ καταστα[θῆ]ναι; *P.Oxy.* 898 (123 CE), ll. 28–29: ἕτερόν μου ἐπίτροπον κατασταθῆναι.

10 So Hans Jakob Polotsky, "The Greek Papyri from the Cave of Letters," *IEJ* 12 (1962): 260, but not for the whole province, as assumed by Wolff, "Römisches Provinzialrecht in der Provinz Arabia," 789 f. The occurrence of 'metropolis' in the title of Petra does not make it into the capital of the province, see Glen W. Bowersock, "The Babatha Papyri, Masada, and Rome," *JRA* 4 (1991): 340, n. 7 summing up his previous references. On administrative divisions and boundaries see Benjamin Isaac, "The Babatha Archive: A Review Article," *IEJ* 42 (1992): 63–4; 67–70.

11 The need to appoint a guardian by a magistrate arose only when no guardian had been nominated in the will of the deceased (*tutor testamentarius*) and there was no agnate available to be *tutor legitimus*, see Alan Watson, *The Law of Persons in the Later Roman Republic* (Oxford: Oxford University Press, 1967), 114–30.

literal translation when it is not a transcription into Greek (e.g. ἀπὸ ἄκτων)[12] of a Latin document. It is true that the testimony of the *Digest* does not speak of the appointment of guardians by the city council, but rather by the city magistrates: *Ius dandi tutores [tutorem?] datum est omnibus magistratibus municipalibus* (Ulpian, *Dig.* 26, 5, 3).[13] However, the Lex Municipii Salpensani,[14] and now also the Lex Irnitana[15] – IIIC <29>: *De tutorum datione* – demonstrate that the appointment of guardians to children under age (*impuberes*) by city magistrates, in their case *duoviri*, is done – in certain circumstances[16] – *ex decreto decurionum.*[17] The same phrasing appears in a wax tablet from Herculaneum (albeit in a case of a guardian for a woman):[18] '*Cassius Cr[ispu]s IIvir ex decurionum decre[to, quo ne ab] iusto tutore [tutela abeat, ex] lege Iulia [et Titia dixit Aresc]usae Q. Vibidius [A]mpliatus sit tuto[r].*' Thus the phrase κατασταθέντες ἐπίτροποι ὑπὸ βουλῆς τῶν

---

12 For Latinisms in the archive see Lewis, 16 ff. (Introduction III.2). However, we do find ἀπὸ ἄκτων βουλῆς elsewhere, e.g. *OGIS* 595 (Tyre, 174 CE); for more examples for the use of *acta* in connection with a *boule* see Hugh J. Mason, *Greek Terms for Roman Institutions* (Toronto: Hakkert, 1974), 20, *s. v.*; see now ἐπὶ τὰ ἄκτ[α] in Shimon Dar and Nikos Kokkinos, "The Greek Inscriptions from Senaim on Mount Hermon," *PEQ* 124 (1992): 13, no. 2, line 4, and p. 16.

13 Cf. *Dig.* 26, 5, 24; *Dig.* 38, 17, 2, 23: *quoniam et magistratibus municipalibus dandi [scil. tutores] necessitas iniungitur*, and the whole tenor of *Dig.* 27, 8 (suits against magistrates). Admittedly there are texts which suggest that the municipal magistrates had but a limited authority for appointing guardians: e.g. *Dig.* 26, 7, 46, 6: *praesidis provinciae praecepto a magistratibus alius tutor datus est*; *Dig.* 27, 8, 1, 5: *Si curatores fuerunt minus idonei dati, dicendum est teneri magistratus oportere, si ex suggestu eorum vel nominibus ab eis acceptis praeses dederit*; *Dig.* 26, 5, 24 (when the city magistrates have to look elsewhere for suitable guardians): *nomina praesidi provinciae mittere, non ipsos arbitrium dandi sibi vindicare*; *Dig.* 27, 10, 2; *CJ* 5, 34, 6.

14 *FIRA*, Vol. I, no. 23.

15 Julián González, "The Lex Irnitana: A New Copy of the Flavian Municipal Law," *JRS* 76 (1986): 157.

16 The city council participates in the *duovir*'s appointment of guardians only in cases in which he was unable to make the appointment in consultation with his fellow-magistrates, González, "The Lex Irnitana, " 157, ll. 22 ff. For the participation of the decurions see *Dig.* 26, 5, 19 pr.; *Dig.* 6, 3; *Dig.* 27, 8, 1 pr.

17 González, "The Lex Irnitana, " 157, ll. 25–29: *Is a quo ... postulatum erit, causa cognita in diebus X proxumis, ex decreto decurionum ... eum, qui nominatus erit ... ei [scil. pupillo pupillaeve] tutorem dato*; 'the person from whom the request has been made, once the case has been examined, within ten days, *according to the decree of the decurions* ... is to grant as guardian to him (or her) the person who has been nominated.'

18 M. Della Corte, "Tabelle cerate Ercolanesi," *La parola del passato* 6 (1951): 228, no. 13; for the reconstructed text see Vincenzo Arangio-Ruiz, "Due nuove tavolette di Ercolano relative alla nomina di tutori muliebri," in *Studi in onore di P. De Francisci*, Vol. I (Milano: Giuffrè, 1956), 3–12.

Πετραίων is not incompatible with the interpretation that here too the magistrates acted "according to a decree of the council."[19]

The application of Roman legal forms to Petra is surprising: translated into Latin, the document could have been issued by a municipality with Latin rights in the West. Since it is impossible to believe that Petra possessed Latin status, the document assumes a high degree of Romanization in a native city that had just come within the Roman sphere of influence.[20]

If we compare the situation with that in Egypt[21] we discover that it was the Strategos,[22] the Grammateus[23] or the Exegetes[24] who appointed guardians for peregrine orphans.[25] This could well reflect the absence of city councils and magistrates there.[26] It would be interesting to know the practice in other cities in the eastern part of the Empire where these did exist.

In Egypt we find the mother exercising guardianship alongside a male guardian and sometimes alone – obviously a remnant of peregrine law,[27] perhaps mod-

---

19 Naphtali Lewis, "Two Greek Documents from Provincia Arabia," *Illinois Classical Studies* 3 (1978): 110 rightly cites Ulpian *Dig.* 27, 8, 1: *si a magistratibus municipalibus tutor datus sit, non videtur per ordinem electus*, for "possible involvement" of the entire city council.

20 There is nothing to suggest that Petra even had the constitution of a Greek *polis* before 114 CE, see Glen W. Bowersock, "Review of A. Spijkerman, The Coins of the Decapolis and Provincia Arabia," *JRS* 72 (1982): 198. Note, however, that it became a *colonia* under Elagabalus, see Stella Ben-Dor, "Petra Colonia," *Berytus* 9 (1948–9): 41–43; Fergus Millar, "The Roman Coloniae of the Near East: A Study of Cultural Relations," in *Roman Eastern Policy and other Studies in Roman History*, ed. Heikki Solin and Mika Kajava (Helsinki: Finnish Society of Sciences and Letters, 1990), 51.

21 Raphael Taubenschlag, *The Law of Greco-Roman Egypt in the light of the Papyri, 322 BC–640 AD* (Warsaw: Państwowe Wydawnictwo Naukowe, 1955), 161; Mitteis, *Chr.* I, 254.

22 *P.Brem.* 39 (113/120 CE); *P.Oxy.* 898 (123 CE).

23 *P.Oxy.* 487 = *M.Chr.* 322 (156 CE), but see Hunt's reservation in *P.Ryl.* 121 about the *grammateus*' authority to appoint guardians (*Catalogue of the Greek papyri in the John Rylands Library, Volume II: Documents of the Ptolemaic and Roman Periods* (Manchester: The University Press, 1915), 114 f.)

24 *P.Mich.* 232 = A.E.R. Boak, "A Petition to an Exegetes, AD 36," *JEA* 19 (1933): 139 = *SB* 7568; *P.Ryl.* 121 (2nd century CE); *M.Chr.* 323 (218 CE).

25 Cf. Naphtali Lewis, "Instructions for Appointing a Guardian," *BASP* 7 (1970): 116–18.

26 But see now Bowman and Rathbone, "Cities and Administration in Roman Egypt."

27 Max Kaser, *Das römische Privatrecht*, 2nd ed. (München: Beck, 1971), § 85 and n. 5; Taubenschlag, *The Law of Greco-Roman Egypt in the Light of the Papyri*, 153–55; 158 f.; Mitteis, *Chr.* I, 253. By virtue of provisions laid down in the father's will or in the marriage contract, the mother could either share the guardianship with a male relative, or even exercise it alone: for appointment by will see e. g. *SB* 9065 (1st century BCE), ll. 5–8 = E.P. Wegener, "Petition concerning the Dowry of a Widow (P. Berl. Inv. 16.277)," *Mnemosyne* 13 (1947): 302–16; and for marriage contracts see, *P.Oxy.* 265 (81–95 CE), ll. 28–30, *P.Oxy.* 496 (127 CE), l. 12 and *P.Oxy.* 497 (2nd century CE), ll. 12–13. In *BGU* 1813 (62/1 BCE), *P.Mich.* 232 (=*SB* 7568, 36 CE) and *P.Oxy.* 898 (123 CE) the mother is designated ἐπίτροπος with no mention of a will or a marriage contract.

ified under Roman influence.[28] Roman law, as we shall see below in greater detail, barred women from the exercise of guardianship in no uncertain terms.[29]

Nevertheless, we do have another woman in the archive, who seems to share the duties of a guardian with a Jew called Besas. I refer to the 'mysterious' Iulia Crispina.[30] She appears for the first time with Besas in *P.Yadin* 20: 'Besas son of Jesus, En-gedian domiciled in Mazraä, guardian – ἐ<πί>τροπος – of the orphans of Jesus son of Khthousion, and Iulia Crispina, supervisor – ἐπίσκοπος' (ll. 4–5; see ll. 23–25). Together they concede rights over a courtyard: 'We acknowledge that we have conceded to you, from the property of Eleazar (also known as Khthousion) son of Judah, your grandfather, a courtyard ... etc';[31] and promise to register it with the authorities: 'This courtyard I will register for you with the public authorities wherever you wish,'[32] as well as defend it against any counterclaim: 'And if anyone enters a counterclaim for the said courtyard, we will conduct a firm legal defence and will clear it for you of any counterclaimant at our own expense.'[33] In *P.Yadin* 23–24 Besas acts alone, disputing Babatha's right to a date orchard that had belonged to her late second husband. But in *P.Yadin* 25, because of her partner's ailment, Iulia Crispina is on her own, launching a παραγγελία.[34]

It is true that she is called ἐπίσκοπος rather than ἐπίτροπος. Ἐπίσκοπος is used in a technical legal sense only once – so far as I know – in pre-Christian

28 See Orsolina Montevecchi, "Una donna 'prostatis' del figlio minorenne in un papiro del IIa," *Aegyptus* 61 (1981): 114 and see below at n. 36.

29 "There was no exception," see W.W. Buckland and Peter Stein, *A Text-Book of Roman Law from Augustus to Justinian*, 3rd ed. (Cambridge: Cambridge University Press, 1966), 150.

30 Yigael Yadin, *Bar-Kokhba: The Rediscovery of the Legendary Hero of the Second Jewish Revolt Against Rome* (London: Random House, 1971), 247; and see the ingenious reconstruction by Tal Ilan, "Julia Crispina, Daughter of Berenicianus, a Herodian Princess in the Babatha Archive: A Case Study in Historical Identification," *JQR* 82 (1992): 361–81.

31 ὁμολογοῦμεν̣ συνκεχωρηκέναι σοι ἐξ ὑπαρχόντων Ἐλεαζάρου τοῦ καὶ Χθουσίωνος τοῦ̣ Ἰ̣ο̣ύ̣δ̣ο̣υ πά̣π̣ου σου αὐλὴν (ll. 6–8, see ll. 27–29).

32 ταύτην δὲ τὴν αὐλὴν ὅπου ἂν βουληθῇς τευχίσω σοι διὰ δομησ̣οίων̣ (ll. 12–13, see ll. 34–36).

33 ἐὰν δέ τις ἀντιποιήσῃ τῆς προγεγραμμένης αὐλῆς σταθόντες ἐγδικήσωμεν καὶ θαροποιησωμεν ἀπὸ παντὸς ἀντιποιουμέν̣ου ταῖς εἰδίαις ἀναλώμ̣α̣σ̣ι̣ν̣ (ll. 13–16, see ll. 36–39). The switch from plural to singular (i. e. from 'we' to 'I') may be nothing more than inadvertence; it is quite common in Egyptian papyri (as pointed out to me by N. Lewis); thus the τευχίσω may not prove that, unlike Besas, Iulia Crispina could not register land with the authorities.

34 [ἐπὶ τῶν ἐπι]βεβλημένων καὶ ἐπισφραγισαμένων [μαρ]τ̣ύ̣ρ̣[ων π]α̣ρ̣[ήγγειλ]ε̣ν̣ Ἰ̣ο̣υ̣[λία Κ]ρ̣[ισπῖν]α̣ θ̣[υ]γ̣α̣τ̣ὴ̣ρ̣ Βερνικιανοῦ [ἐπίσκο]π̣ο̣ς τ̣ῶν ⟦ν⟧ ὀ̣ρ̣φ̣α̣ν̣ῶ̣ν̣ Ἰησούου Χθουσίωνος Β̣α̣β̣α̣θ̣[α̣ Σί]μωνος· ἐπιδὴ ὁ ἐπίτροπος Βησᾶς Ἰησούου τῶν αὐτῶν [ὀρ]φ̣ανῶ̣ν̣ ἀσ̣θενέστε̣ρ̣ός ἐστιν καὶ οὐκ ἠδυνάσθη πα̣ρ̣[αγγεῖλαι] ἐ̣σ̣[ὲ σ]ὐ̣[ν] ἐ̣[μο]ί̣ (ll. 1–6).

Egyptian papyri:[35] this is too early to have any relevance to our case. Perhaps it is because the term lacks a technical legal sense, that it could be applied to Iulia Crispina in order to describe her position *vis-à-vis* the orphans:[36] she is their caretaker, she looks after them and their interests.[37] John Rea has recently pointed out the similarity between Iulia Crispina and the Egyptian ἐπακολουθήτρια,[38] or

35 In *P.Petr.* III 36 V(a) (= *M.Chr.* 5), ll. 16–17: ἐπὶ τῶν ἀποδεδειγμένων ἐπισκόπων. It is used "to describe the judges specially qualified to judge complaints made against officials" (so Turner in *The Hibeh Papyri, Part II* (London: Egypt Exploration Society, 1955), 109), but this belongs to the 3rd century BCE, as does *P.Hib.* II 198, l. 242, where ἐπισκοπεῖν ... is said to "evoke the idea of an administrative enquiry" (p. 109). Cf. also ἐπισκοπεί{τ}[ω ὁ οἰκονόμος] in *P.Rev.* (259 BCE), col. 33, l. 2 (re-edited by Jean Bingen, *Papyrus Revenue Laws*, *SB* Beiheft 1 (Göttingen: Hubert, 1952)) and ἐπισκοπεῖν in *P.Tebt.* III.1 703, ll. 47; 183 (late 3rd century BCE) instructions of the *dioiketes* to the *oikonomos* 'to look into controversies between the farmers and the village scribes or the *comarch*.' Finally περὶ τῶν τοιούτων ἐπισκ[οποῦσι] [οἱ] δικασταὶ in *P.Oxy.* 46 3285, l. 34 appears in a 2nd century CE copy of a Greek translation of a demotic legal code which itself goes back to the Pharaonic period; see J. Rea's introduction in *The Oxyrhynchus Papyri*, Vol. 46 (London: Egypt Exploration Society, 1978), 30–1.

We find ἐπίσκοποι as municipal or village magistrates in the inscriptions (e.g. Maurice Sartre, *Bostra: des origines à l'Islam* (Paris: Geuthner, 1985), 81–2 and Henry Innes MacAdam, *Studies in the History of the Roman Province of Arabia: The Northern Sector* (Oxford: B.A.R., 1986), 169 f., 3rd century CE, Trachonitis). See also *Dig.* 50, 4, 18, 7 (Arcadius Charisius' list of civil liturgies): '*item episcopi, qui praesunt pani et ceteris venalibus rebus, quae civitatium populis <ad> cotidianum victum us<ui> sunt, personalibus muneribus funguntur*' ('The *episcopi*, in charge of the daily supply of bread and other victuals to the population of the cities, also perform personal liturgies'). But I do not think that Iulia Crispina was a magistrate.

36 As suggested by Montevecchi, "Una donna 'prostatis' del figlio minorenne in un papiro del IIa," 107 to explain the term προστάτις acquired by the mother of an orphan by the terms of her marriage contract: προστάτιδος τῆς οὔσης αὐτοῦ (*sc.* ὀρφανοῦ) ἀπὸ συγγραφῆς συνοικισίου τῆς αὐτοῦ μητρὸς (*P.Med.Bar.* 1 [142 BCE], ll. 4–6): "*Prostatis* è usato qui ad indicare una funzione di responsiblità della donna nei riguardi del figlio, un potere su di lui, che si avvicina alla tutela pur senza averne il carattere giuridico." (Montevecchi, 107).

37 Like the faithful shepherd, ἐπίσκοπος, of the New Testament, on which see Gerhard Kittel, *Theologisches Wörterbuch zum Neuen Testament*, Vol. II (Stuttgart: Kohlhammer, 1935), 611 ff. For the association of ἐπίσκοπος and Hebrew 'Mebaqqer' (מבקר, e.g. *Damascus Covenant* 14:12–16), see now Jonas C. Greenfield and Michael E. Stone, "Two Notes on the Aramaic Levi Document," in *Of Scribes and Scrolls: Studies on the Hebrew Bible, Intertestamental Judaism, and Christian Origins, Presented to John Strugnell on the Occasion of his Sixtieth Birthday*, ed. Harold W. Attridge, John J. Collins, and Thomas H. Tobin (Lanham: University Press of America, 1990), 153–61, esp. 158–61.

38 For example in *P.Mich.Inv.* 2922 (A.E.R. Boak, "A Petition for Relief from a Guardianship. P. Mich. Inv. No. 2922," *JEA* 18 (1932): 70 [172/3 CE] = *SB* 7558 = *FIRA*, Vol. III, no. 30) a grandmother is appointed in the father's will joint guardian with two other men; they are designated ἐπίτροποι (l. 6) whereas she is called ἐπακολουθήτρια (l. 7).

παρακολουθήτρια,[39] who also appears accompanied by a male guardian, but who is attested in Egyptian papyri only from the second half of the second century.[40] If indeed, as seems quite likely, the later institution was created to satisfy the strictures imposed by Roman law on the exercise of guardianship by women,[41] then we may have in Arabia the first example for such an adaptation of local custom, and another expression of Romanization. Admittedly, this contrasts sharply with Babatha's total exclusion from the guardianship. There may be circumstances unknown to us which may explain the special status enjoyed by Iulia Crispina. One notices immediately that she is not represented by a male guardian[42] like the other women in the archive.[43]

---

39 *P.Oxy*. 3921, ll. 6; 49 (219 CE) and see J. Rea ad loc. (*The Oxyrhynchus Papyri*, Vol. 58 (London: Egypt Exploration Society, 1991)). I find it hard to believe, though, that she is the mother of the orphans and the widow of Jesus, son of Eleazar. In the Egyptian papyri the relationship of the ἐπακολουθήτρια/παρακολουθήτρια to the ward(s) is always pointed out. I agree, though, that she may not be a Roman citizen. Had she been one, it would have made it less, rather than more, likely that she would be exercising the duties of a guardian. For her Roman name, see Rea.

40 See Montevecchi, "Una donna 'prostatis' del figlio minorenne in un papiro del IIa," 109 and nn. there for a full list.

41 So Montevecchi, 111 ff. She points out that all the occurrences of a female ἐπίτροπος come from peregrine contexts, and that the terms ἐπίτροπος and ἐπακολουθήτρια do not overlap: there is no female ἐπίτροπος after 123 CE.

42 Note that in the archive the word ἐπίτροπος is used both for the guardian of minors and for that of women; in Greek speaking lands the traditional term for the latter was κύριος. See Hans Julius Wolff, "Le droit provincial dans la province romaine d'Arabie," *RIDA* 23 (1976): 279–83 for the significance of the confusion here. Note, however, that in the Aramaic the guardian of a woman is called אדון – Adon – κύριος: e.g. *P.Yadin* 15, l. 37: יהודה בר כתושין אדון בבתה 'Yehudah son of Khthousion 'lord' of Babatha.'

43 Babatha is represented by her second husband, Judah son of Khthousion (*P.Yadin* 14, ll. 22–23; *P.Yadin* 15, ll. 31–32; *P.Yadin* 16, ll. 35–36), by Jacob son of Joseph (*P.Yadin* 17, ll. 4–5 = ll. 22–23), by John son of Makhouthas (*P.Yadin* 22, ll. 28–29) and by Babelis son of Menahem (*P.Yadin* 27, ll. 4–5; *P.Yadin* 18). Salome (*alias* Komais) is represented by X son of Menahem (*P.Yadin* 37, l. 15). Could the mere fact of her literacy – she signs her name in Greek (*P.Yadin* 20, ll. 43–44) – have made the difference between Iulia Crispina and the other women in the archive? There is no simple answer to this question, see Raphael Taubenschlag, "La compétence du kurios dans le droit gréco-égyptien," in *Opera Minora*, Vol. II (Warsaw: Panstwowe Wydawn Naukowe, 1959), 353–77; Herbert C. Youtie, "Αγραμματος: An Aspect of Greek Society in Egypt," *Harv. Stud.* 75 (1971): 166 = *Scriptiunculae*, Vol. II (Amsterdam: Hakkert, 1973), 616.

II

If Babatha's legal position *vis-à-vis* her orphaned son is not easily explained by the so-called 'law of the papyri,' this is hardly a cause for surprise, since the latter was to a large extent shaped by a mixture of Egyptian and Greek legal practices and customs.[44] Whether her situation as well as her course of action could be accounted for by Nabataean legal practices, we have no means of knowing. Whatever there is to know about Nabataean law is enshrined in the 'Semitic' part of the archive. But in view of Babatha's Jewishness, it is legitimate to ask what rights she would have had under Jewish law and practices. In other words, what do we know about the rules governing the appointment of a guardian as well as about the status of the mother of an orphan in Jewish law of the time? I shall then use the information contained in the archive itself, namely Babatha's own awareness and behaviour, in order to address the more fundamental question of whether there was any operative Jewish legal system in the period concerned.[45] Traditionally interpreted, the Jewish legal texts from this period (see below) give us the biased view that Rabbinic or Halakhic Judaism as we know it has always been there and that Rabbinic Judaism was the only manifestation of Judaism.[46]

Naturally I shall base my study of the principles governing the Jewish law on guardianship in this period only on Tannaitic sources,[47] that is sources that roughly belong to the period 70 CE – the destruction of the Temple – and the end of the second century CE – the redaction of the *Mishnah* by Judah the Patriarch

---

44 Joseph Modrzejewski, "La Règle de droit dans l'Egypte ptolémaïque," in *Essays in Honor of C. Bradford Welles* (New Haven: American Society of Papyrologists, 1966), 125–73.

45 See above all Martin Goodman, *State and Society in Roman Galilee, AD 132–212* (Totowa, N.J.: Rowman and Allanheld, 1983), *passim*, but esp. 3–24; 93–118; 155–71; 178–81, who thinks that the authority of the Rabbis was slow in evolving and became dominant only from mid-third century onwards. See also Erwin Ramsdell Goodenough, *Jewish Symbols in the Greco-Roman Period*, Vol. 12 (New York: Pantheon Books, 1965), 184–98; *contra* Morton Smith, "Goodenough's Jewish Symbols in Retrospect," *Journal of Biblical Literature* 86 (1967): 53–68; Ephraim E. Urbach, "The Laws of Idolatry in the Light of Historical and Archaeological Facts in the Third Century," *Eretz Israel* 5 (1958): 189–205 = *The World of the Sages: Collected Studies* (Jerusalem: Magnes Press, 1988), 125–78 (Hebrew); Lee I. Levine, *The Rabbinic Class of Roman Palestine in Late Antiquity* (Jerusalem – New York: Yad Ben-Zvi and Jewish Theological Seminary of America, 1989), chapter 3.

46 H.L. Strack and Günter Stemberger, *Introduction to the Talmud and Midrash* (Edinburgh: T & T Clark, 1991), 54–5.

47 "Aramaic *tanna*, from Hebrew *shanah* 'to repeat, learn,'" *tannaim*: "the masters of teaching transmitted by continual oral repetition," Strack and Stemberger, 7. The *Tannaim* were active in the first two and half centuries of our era and were followed "by the *Amoraim* (*amar*, 'to say,' comment: the commentators of the Tannaitic teachings) up to *c.* 500" (Strack and Stemberger, 7).

(R. Yehudah *ha-Nasi*).[48] The *Mishnah* is the authoritative collection of religious law which had been formulated in the rabbinic schools during that period. There is, however, Tannaitic material outside it. *Barayta*[49] "designates all Tannaitic teachings and sayings outside the *Mishnah*,"[50] and thus assumed to be roughly contemporary with it.[51] A special collection of *baraytot* is the *Tosefta* ('addition, supplement'), which is much more extensive than the *Mishnah*;[52] the relationship between the two is still far from clear.[53] Greater precision for individual passages can sometimes be achieved on the basis of rabbinic names cited in them.[54]

Jewish law does not have its own term for the institution of guardianship, but borrowed the Greek term ἐπίτροπος to describe a guardian.[55] Gulak assumed that the institution developed under the influence of Hellenistic and Roman law.[56] On the other hand the conceptual differences between the Roman and the Jewish forms of guardianship put this assumption in question.[57] At all events, by the

48 Strack and Stemberger, 123; 155–6.

49 "Lit. the 'outside' teaching (short for Aramaic *matnita baraita*)," Strack and Stemberger, 195.

50 Strack and Stemberger, 195. The term usually refers to Tannaitic teachings quoted verbatim and commented on in the Palestinian and Babylonian Talmuds.

51 This assumption sometimes proves to be wrong: some *baraytot* were either mistakenly or falsely ascribed to the Tannaim, see Strack and Stemberger, 216–17, see also 54.

52 Strack and Stemberger, 168–9.

53 Strack and Stemberger, 168–77. Both the *Mishnah* and the *Tosefta* as we now have them consist of six main divisions or orders (*sedarim*), each of which consists of tractates, subdivided into chapters and sentences. The method of citation is by work (*m* or *t*), tractate, chapter and sentence, but the 'order' is omitted. The two Talmuds are also cited by work (*y* for *Yerushalmi*, i.e. the Palestinian Talmud and *b* for the Babylonian Talmud), and respective Mishnaic tractate. In the Babylonian Talmud tractate is followed by page-number, with the front and back of each leaf counted as *a* and *b*; in the Palestinian Talmud (the Venice edition) the tractate is followed by page number; each page has four columns (*a-d*). The Talmuds, being later commentaries on Tannaitic material by the *Amoraim* (see above, n. 46), are cited here only to corroborate Tannaitic traditions, but never as evidence for the status of Jewish law in the earlier period.

54 There are no absolute dates; chronology is determined by the relationship of one rabbi to another as his teacher: "in this way generations of rabbis can be co-ordinated" Strack and Stemberger, 63; however attributions are not always reliable or certain, Strack and Stemberger, 63 ff.

55 Rendering it אפיטרופוס – *epitropos*; אפוטרופוס – *apotropos*; אפיטרופא – *epitropa*, etc. see Daniel Sperber, *A Dictionary of Greek and Latin Legal Terms in Rabbinic Literature* (Ramat-Gan: Bar-Ilan University Press, 1984), 56 ff. This is the term used to this very day in modern Hebrew.

56 Asher Gulak, *Principles (Institutions) of Jewish Law III: Family Law* (Jerusalem: Dvir, 1922), 146 (Hebrew); Z.W. Falk, "Zum fremden Einfluss auf das jüdische Recht," *RIDA* 18 (1971): 11–23, is much more affirmative.

57 See Y.K. Reinitz, "The Guardian of Orphans in Jewish Law: His Responsibility, Methods of Supervision" (Hebrew University of Jerusaelm Thesis, 1984), ivf. and bibliography cited in the notes (Hebrew); Moses Bloch, *Die Vormundschaft nach mosaisch-talmudischem Rechte* (Budapest: A. Alkalay Pressburg, 1904).

second half of the second century CE the main lines of the institution had already been drawn.[58]

There is no doubt that a woman could serve as a guardian, if appointed by her husband in his lifetime, whether as guardian of his property[59] or of that of his orphans.[60] The *Tosefta* adds the restriction that the courts would not appoint a woman as a guardian, unless she had already served in this capacity in her husband's lifetime: 'the courts should not take the initiative (לכתחילה – *lekhathilah*) and appoint women and slaves as guardians, but if the father had appointed any of them in that capacity during his lifetime, the courts should confirm the appointment' (*tTerumoth*[61] 1.11).[62] Neither in the *Mishnah* nor in the *Tosefta* is it suggested that a man could appoint his wife a guardian of their common children in his will. However, a *barayta* in the Babylonian Talmud, while repeating the restriction on the courts to appoint a woman as guardian, can be interpreted in such a way as to mean that a man could make his wife a guardian of their common children in his will: 'Women, slaves and minors[63] should not be made

58 Reinitz, "The Guardian of Orphans in Jewish Law," ix puts it earlier: "by the first half." In evidence he mentions the controversy between Abba Saul and R. Eliezer b. Jacob about the taking of the oath by the guardian of orphans at the end of his term of office (*bGittin* ('divorce certificates') 52b); however, R. Eliezer b. Jacob (the Younger) and Abba Saul belonged to the third generation of Tannaites, *c.* 130–160 CE, see Strack and Stemberger, *Introduction to the Talmud and Midrash*, 83–6; see also A.M. Heiman, *History of the Tannaim and Amoraim*, Vol. I (Jerusalem: Kirya Neemana, 1964), *s.vv.* (Hebrew).

59 Cf. *mKetubboth* (= *Ket.* 'marriage contracts') 9.4: 'If a man set up his wife as a shopkeeper or appointed her as a guardian (*epitropa*) he may exact of her an oath whensoever he will.' The presence of Rabbi Eliezer ben Hyrcanus in this *Mishnah* dates it to the early 2nd century, see Strack and Stemberger, *Introduction to the Talmud and Midrash*, 77; cf. *tKet.* 9.6; *bKet.* 86b; *yKet.* 54a; cf. *bBaba Bathra* (= *BB* 'last gate' i.e. the last tractate of Seder *Neziqin* 'Damages') 131b: 'If a [dying] man gave all his property to his wife in writing, he [thereby] only appointed her guardian (אפוטרופא – *apotropa*)'; cf. *bBB* 144a; *bGittin* 14a. See also *yShevu'ot* ('oaths') 93a, where both the guardian and the woman who manages her husband's property are required to take an oath: 'And these [must] take an oath [even] when there is no claim [laid against them]: (1) partners (2) tenants (3) guardians (4) a woman who manages her household and (5) son of the household.'

60 Cf. *mKet.* 9.6: 'If she was made a guardian [i.e. in her husband's lifetime], the heirs may exact an oath from her concerning [her trust during] the time after [her husband's death], but not the time before.' After her husband's death, the widow is entitled to continue holding the guardianship over his property which has now become the orphans'; cf. *bKet.* 86b-88b; *yKet.* 55a.

61 *Ter.* 'levies' or 'heave offerings' (e.g. priestly heave offering).

62 I have adopted Boaz Cohen's translation, *Jewish and Roman Law: A Comparative Study*, Vol. I (New York: Jewish Theological Seminary of America, 1966), 243; see Saul Lieberman, *Tosefta Ki-fshutah. Part I: Order Zera'im ('Seeds')* (New York: Jewish Theological Seminary Press, 1955), 304 (Hebrew, the most important modern commentary on the *Tosefta*); cf. *tBB* 8.17.

63 'Minors' must be a mistake, see Lieberman, *Tosefta Ki-Fshutah. Part I: Order Zera'im ('Seeds')*, 303.

guardians: if, however, the father of the orphans chooses to appoint one, he is at liberty to do so – 'ואם מינן אבי יתומין הרשות בידו' (lit. 'it is in his hand,' *bGittin* 52a).[64] It seems to have remained the rule that the courts were prohibited from initiating the appointment of a woman.[65]

It is likely that the orphan Jesus was living with Babatha, his mother, at the time documented in the archive, for the guardians hand her the money for his upkeep.[66] We do not know whether or not she insisted on having him with her. A Jewish mother could indeed demand that the orphan be left with her. For many reasons she may have appeared more trustworthy than those entitled to be the orphan's heirs.[67] And in fact such a claim was accepted by the Jewish courts: 'If a man dies leaving a son, and the mother says: 'let him be brought up by me' and the heirs say: 'let him be brought up by us,' then the son may not be brought up by those who are entitled to be his heirs' (*tKet.* 11.4).[68]

It seems that boarding with his mother did not have the legal consequence of turning Babatha into the guardian of her orphaned son, Jesus. This needs to be said since in Jewish law not only did there exist two legal ways of creating a guardianship (appointment by the father in his lifetime or in his will, and appointment by the court); there also existed a *de facto* sort of guardianship: guardianship acquired by virtue of 'orphans boarding with the householder' (סמיכה *semikhah*).[69] This form may well have been the original and authentic Jewish form of guardi-

---

64 The Rashba (R. Shlomo b. Abraham b. Aderet, 1235–1310) in his *Commentary on the Babylonian Talmud* (חידושי הרשב"א על הש"ס – *Ḥiddushim on the SHAS*) on *bGittin* 52a suggests to read '*they* are at liberty to do so (lit. 'in their hands' בידן) i. e. the courts, thus bringing the *barayta* into line with *tTer.* 1.11. His reading of the *Barayta* leaves us with no Tannaitic authority for the appointment of a woman as a guardian in the father's will. His proposed correction of the text of *bGittin* 52a from בידו ('in his hand,' i. e. the father's) to בידן ('in their hands,' i. e. the courts') is minuscule: the mere lengthening of the *waw* (ו) to produce a final *nun* (ן).

65 See Simcha Assaf, "The Appointment of Women as Guardians," *Ha-Mishpat Ha-'Ivri* 2 (1927): 75–81 (Hebrew); Y.K. Reinitz, "Appointment of a Woman as a Guardian," *Bar-Ilan Law Studies* 4 (1985): 167–203 (Hebrew).

66 *P.Yadin* 13–15 (124–125 CE); *P.Yadin* 27 (132 CE).

67 Note that a similar provision for the children to stay with their mother till they come of age is found in Egyptian marriage contracts: e. g. *P.Oxy.* 497 (early 2nd century CE), l. 13: [τῶν τέκνων] διαιτωμένων παρὰ τῇ [μ]ητρὶ μέχρι τοῦ εἰς ἡλικίαν ἐλθεῖν; see also *P.Oxy.* 496 (127 CE), l. 12; Roman orphans also tended to be brought up by their mothers, see Jane F. Gardner, *Woman in Roman Law and Society* (London: Croom Helm, 1986), 147.

68 In the *barayta* it says explicitly: 'they leave him with his mother,' *bKet.* 102b.

69 *mGittin* 5.4: 'If orphans were supported (סמכו *samkhu*) by a householder, or if their father appointed a guardian for them, he must give tithe from the produce that belongs to them. If a guardian was appointed by the orphans' father he must take an oath; if he was appointed by the court he need not take an oath. Abba Saul says: The rule is to the contrary etc.'; cf. *tTer.* 1.12; *tBB* 8.13.

anship.[70] This could offer a way for women to become *de facto* guardians of their children.[71]

We may mention in passing that one of Jesus' guardians was not a Jew.[72] It is hard to know why the *boule* of Petra appointed a non-Jew as one of the guardians of the Jewish orphan Jesus. The indifference to the principle of personality could be a local custom,[73] as has been suggested for the naming of two guardians instead of one.[74]

None of the Jewish practices and rules delineated above regarding the orphan's mother is present in this archive. Indeed there is nothing to show that Babatha was aware of any of them.

The example of the Jews of Egypt springs to mind. The editors of the *Corpus Papyrorum Judaicarum* expressed their surprise at the absence of any documents reflecting the existence of Jewish courts in Egypt and of the exercise of Jewish law

---

70 See Falk, "Zum fremden Einfluss auf das jüdische Recht," 14: "Das erste Verhältnis, das man vielleicht *proto-epitropé* nennen kann ..." and *passim*; cf. Y.K. Reinitz, "Guardianship by Virtue of 'Orphans Boarding with the Householder,'" *Bar-Ilan Law Studies* 1 (1980): 219–50 (Hebrew). Gradually this *de facto* sort of guardianship was assimilated into the legal institution of guardianship and made equal with the other two forms: 'The householder with whom the orphans boarded has all the legal rights possessed by guardians appointed by the court or by the orphans' father,' R. Asher b. Yeḥiel (1250–1327), *Responsa*, 87a; cf. Reinitz, "The Guardian of Orphans in Jewish Law," 93 ff.

71 As some interpret the famous story of the old woman ('ההיא סבתא'), *bGittin* 52a: 'Certain orphans who boarded with an old woman had a cow which she took and sold. Their relatives appealed to R. Nahman (third generation of *Amoraim* in Babylonia) saying: what right had she to sell it? He said to them: we learn 'if orphans boarded with the householder." See the Rashba's (see above, n. 64) *Responsa* (שאלות ותשובות) II, no. 49: 'And even if they boarded with a woman whom the court does not appoint as guardian ... she is like a guardian to them, as we learn from the story of the old woman [*bGittin* 52a], and it seems to be the same in the case of a mother ...'; see also the Rashba's *Responsa* II, no. 285; cf. Reinitz, "Guardianship by Virtue," 223–24, and esp. 243–47: "The Guardianship of the widow by virtue of the orphans boarding with her."

72 Ἀβδοβδας Ἰλλουθα of *P.Yadin* 12 is clearly a Nabataean: see *P.Yadin* 15, l. 38; Lewis, 139 ("Aramaic and Nabataean Subscriptions" by Y. Yadin and J.C. Greenfield) and pls. 10–12.

73 It thus contrasts with Roman law which demands that the guardian should come from the same nationality as his ward, see Taubenschlag, *The Law of Greco-Roman Egypt in the Light of the Papyri*, 158; Mitteis, *Chr.* I, 252–53, on Egypt. Jean Juster, *Les Juifs dans l'Empire romain: leur condition juridique, economique et sociale*, Vol. II (Paris: Geuthner, 1914), 24, n. 1 takes *Dig.* 27, 1, 15, 6: Ἰουδαῖοι τῶν μὴ Ἰουδαίων ἐπιτροπεύσοσιν, ὥσπερ καὶ τὰ λοιπὰ λειτουργήσουσιν, to refer to Jews who possessed Roman citizenship, and thus not to constitute an infringement of the principle of personality; see Juster, 62–4; Amnon Linder, *The Jews in Roman Imperial Legislation* (Detroit: Wayne State University Press, 1987), no. 4.

74 See Lewis, *The Documents from the Bar Kokhba Period in the Cave of Letters. Greek Papyri*, 48 on *P.Yadin* 12. See below Appendix I.

there;[75] not even for Alexandria, where we know that a Jewish tribunal existed, do we possess any evidence.[76] "On the other hand, the papyri contain rich evidence of Jews using freely the common Hellenistic law."[77] They conclude, therefore, that "the laws and regulations forming the legal basis for the business life of the Jews are the common laws of the Greeks in Egypt ... the family life of Alexandrian Jews, their marriages and divorces, were regulated by Greek contracts in accordance with the principles of Hellenistic law."[78]

Thus not even in Egypt where documents do exist, do we possess any proof that Jews did use their own courts and laws. What is, therefore, the precise meaning of the privilege successfully sought and granted to Jews by the Roman government, namely to live according to their ancestral laws or customs (νόμοι or ἔθη)?[79] Surely the papyri from Egypt and Arabia render the evidence for legal autonomy elsewhere very difficult to interpret.[80]

Finally but most importantly: what conclusions should be drawn about the authority and influence of the Rabbis and of Halakhic Judaism at the time from the

75 The one clear exception is *CPJ* II 143, ll. 7–8, which mentions the depositing of a will (διαθήκην) in the τὸ τῶν Ἰουδαίων ἀρχεῖον; for Jewish archives in Asia Minor see *CIJ* 741 (burial inscription from Smyrna): ταύτης τῆς ἐπιγραφῆς τὸ ἀντίγραφον ἀπόκειται εἰς τὸ ἀρχεῖον; *CIJ* 775 (Hierapolis) mentions τῷ ἀρχίῳ τῶν Ἰουδαίων; see also *CIJ* 776; 778; 779. See also Joseph., *BJ* 6.354.

76 Strabo apud Joseph., *AJ* 14.117 = Menahem Stern, *Greek and Latin Authors on Jews and Judaism*, Vol. I (Jerusalem: Israel Academy of Sciences and Humanities, 1976), no. 105; *tKethubboth* 3.1 = *tPeah* ('corner') 4.6; *CPJ* II, pp. 4–5; Bowman and Rathbone, "Cities and Administration in Roman Egypt," 117.

77 *CPJ* I, p. 33 (*Prolegomena*); see also *CPJ* II, pp. 4–5.

78 *CPJ* I, pp. 33–4; cf. Victor A. Tcherikover, *The Jews in Egypt in the Hellenistic-Roman Age in the Light of the Papyri* (Jerusalem: Magnes Press, 1963), 103–15 (Hebrew).

79 See Tessa Rajak, "Was There a Roman Charter for the Jews?," *JRS* 74 (1984): 107–23.

80 I refer of course to the famous charters mentioned in Joseph., *AJ* 14.185–267. Admittedly an explicit grant of judicial autonomy is attested only for Sardis, where the Jews claimed before L. Antonius that they used to adjudicate cases between themselves in a court of their own: (σύνοδον ἔχειν ἰδίαν κατὰ τοὺς πατρίους νόμους ἀπ' ἀρχῆς καὶ τόπον ἴδιον, ἐν ᾧ τά τε πράγματα καὶ τὰς πρὸς ἀλλήλους ἀντιλογίας κρίνουσιν, Joseph., *AJ* 14.235); as a result of this appeal the city council issued a ruling that the Jews were to: κατὰ τὰ νομιζόμενα ἔθη συνάγωνται καὶ πολιτεύωνται καὶ διαδικάζωνται πρὸς αὑτούς (Joseph., *AJ* 14.260). I find it hard to believe with Rajak, 116 and n. 35 there, that this was unique to Sardis. See Leah Roth-Gerson, "The Civil and Religious Status of the Jews in Asia Minor from Alexander the Great to Constantine BC 336 – AD 337" (Hebrew University of Jerusalem Thesis, 1972), 65–92 (Hebrew); Tessa Rajak, "Jewish Rights in the Greek Cities under Roman Rule: A New Approach," in *Approaches to Ancient Judaism, V: Studies in Judaism and Its Greco-Roman Context*, ed. W.S. Green (Atlanta: Scholars Press, 1985), 19–36.

fact that Jews in this corner of Arabia, close to the border with Judaea,[81] although not Hellenized Jews – for most of them sign in Aramaic – did not resort to Jewish laws and practices in matters that concerned personal law[82] and property? How shall we account for the total absence of Jewish law and Jewish law courts in the Greek part of the archive?[83]

The answer must be that the existence of a coherent and operative Jewish system of law at the time is thereby called into question. Such a system, if already being formulated in the schools of the Rabbis, has yet to become normative. It has certainly left no trace here. "It was only through centuries of development that [Rabbinic Judaism] became the 'normative' Judaism which it has often been assumed to have been for the entire period."[84]

This conclusion, although based solely on the Greek part of the archive, seems to me hardly likely to change with the publication of the rest of the archive. It is true of course that Babatha's own marriage contract is written in Aramaic,[85]

81 ʿEn-gedi – the patria of Babatha's second husband, Judah son of Eleazar, where he owned property (*P.Yadin* 11; 19–20) and where his first wife was living (*P.Yadin* 26) – is already in the province of Judaea: κώμης Αἰνγαδδῶν περὶ Ἱερειχοῦντα τῆς Ἰουδαίας (*P.Yadin* 16, l. 16).

82 The two marriage contracts in the archive (*P.Yadin* 18 and 37) have nothing distinctly Jewish about them; see Abraham Wasserstein, "A Marriage Contract from the Province of Arabia Nova: Notes on Papyrus Yadin 18," *JQR* 80 (1989): 105–130 and Joseph Geiger, "A Note on P.Yadin 18," *ZPE* 93 (1992): 67–68; contra R. Katzoff in Naphtali Lewis, Ranon Katzoff, and Jonas C. Greenfield, "Papyrus Yadin 18," *IEJ* 37 (1987): 236–47; N. Lewis rallies to Katzoff's defence in "The World of P.Yadin," *BASP* 28 (1991): 35–41; see also Ranon Katzoff, "Papyrus Yadin 18 Again: A Rejoinder," *JQR* 82 (1991): 171–76 (where the *interpretatio Hebraica* is modified); Ranon Katzoff, "P. Yadin 19: A Gift after Death from the Judaean Desert," in *Proceedings of the World Congress of Jewish Studies* 10, Div. C, Vol. 1 (1989): 1–8 (Hebrew); Ranon Katzoff, "Interpretation of P. Yadin 19: A Jewish Gift after Death," in *Proceedings of the 20th International Congress of Papyrologists, Copenhagen, 23–29 August, 1992*, ed. Adam Bülow-Jacobsen (Copenhagen: Museum Tusculanum Press, 1994), 562–65.

83 See also the Greek remarriage contract from Wadi Murabbaʿat (*DJD* II, no. 115 of 124 CE): although it comes from Judaea itself, it has nothing to mark it as Jewish apart from the names; the same is true of another marriage contract in Greek (said to come from Wadi Seiyal, but in all likelihood also from Naḥal Ḥever), now in the Rockefeller Museum in Jerusalem (published as no. 69 in *DJD* XXVII). *DJD* II, no. 116 is too fragmentary, but I suspect that the same applies to it (see below, n. 89).

84 Strack and Stemberger, *Introduction to the Talmud and Midrash*, 5 f. Furthermore, we still find unresolved disputes in the *Mishnah*, see Shaye J.D. Cohen, "The Significance of Yavneh: Pharisees, Rabbis, and the End of Jewish Sectarianism," *HUCA* 55 (1984): 27–53 *passim*.

85 *P.Yadin* 10. This contract is of her second marriage, to Judah son of Eleazar Khthousion, between 122 and 125 CE.

and is said to be in harmony with the rules formulated in *Mishnah Ketubboth*.[86] It seems though that the Greek language takes over with time: types of contract that were written before in Aramaic and Nabataean[87] are now written in Greek.[88] The marriage contract of Shelamzion, Babatha's second husband's daughter from his other wife (*P.Yadin* 18, 5 April 128), is written in Greek and so is that of Salome-Komais of *P.Yadin* 37 (7 August 131).[89] And when the document is written in Greek, the rules formulated in the Rabbinic schools seem no longer to apply. It reads then like a Greek legal instrument.[90]

Once we accept, however, that the Jews often used foreign laws and practices – alongside their own – the absence of documents with a distinctly Jewish flavour from the Greek part of the archive is not as striking as it seemed at first. The Jews used the Greek language for the same reason that they used Greek diplomatics, Greek practices and Greek laws: they had to make sure that their documents were valid and acceptable in non-Jewish courts of law, and that they

---

86 See Yadin, "Expedition D – The Cave of the Letters," 244–45. See Léonie J. Archer, *Her Price is Beyond Rubies. The Jewish Woman in Graeco-Roman Palestine* (Sheffield: Academic Press, 1990), 171–88 on the development of the Jewish Ketubba in Tannaitic times. I do not accept, however, her interpretation of *DJD* II, no. 115 as a Jewish instrument.

87 The Nabataean contract published sometime ago by Starcky, "Un contrat nabatéen sur papyrus," may well have been part of the archive; see Yadin, "Expedition D – The Cave of the Letters," 228–29; 242, n. 21, and Bowersock, "The Babatha Papyri, Masada, and Rome," 340, since it mentions property (גנתא – *ganatha* – 'orchard') which belonged to Babatha's second husband's family and which later on passed into her hands; *P.Yadin* 21, l. 10 and *P.Yadin* 22, l. 11: γαννα θ Νικαρκος. This document was republished as *P.Yadin* 36 by Ada Yardeni, "The Decipherment and Restoration of Legal Texts from the Judaean Desert: A Reexamination of Papyrus Stracky (P.Yadin 36)," *SCI* 20 (2001): 121–37.

88 With the exception of *P.Yadin* 6–10, but these belong to the early 120s.

89 Cf. also the marriage contracts in *DJD* II: two marriage contracts in Aramaic: no. 20 is from 116/7 CE ('the eleventh year of the Province,' i.e. Arabia); no. 21 is probably from 126/7 CE (assuming that 'twenty-one' refers to the province); and two marriage contracts in Greek: no. 115 (124 CE) and 116 (first half of 2nd century CE according to the editors); the marriage contract in the Rockefeller Museum in Jerusalem (*DJD* XXVII, no. 69) dates from 130 CE (see above, n. 83). On Jewish marriage contracts see Mordechai Akiva Friedman, *Jewish Marriage in Palestine: A Cairo Geniza Study* (Tel Aviv: Tel Aviv University Press, 1980).

90 I use 'Greek' here in the sense used by Wasserstein, "A Marriage Contract from the Province of Arabia Nova: Notes on Papyrus Yadin 18," to explain the use of ἑλληνικὸς νόμος in *P.Yadin* 18 and 37, namely as that amalgam of laws of various origins which seems to be called Hellenic in the Roman East. I suppose Goodman, *State and Society in Roman Galilee*, means something similar by "simple Semitic common law" (p. 160) "into which some Greek ideas had crept" (p. 161).

could be deposited 'with the public authorities,'[91] which must refer to the city archives (ἀρχεῖα). That these were frequently used by Jews we learn for example from *mGittin* 1.5: 'Any writ is valid that is drawn up in the registries of the gentiles except a writ of divorce or a writ of emancipation. R. Simeon[92] says: 'These, too, are valid; they were not mentioned [as invalid] unless they were prepared by such as were not [authorized] judges.''[93]

I have been able to find only two Tannaitic passages which explicitly discourage Jews from using gentile courts. Rabbi Tarfon, who lived before the Bar Kokhba revolt,[94] is cited in a *barayta* in *bGittin* 88b: 'In any place where you find gentile law courts,[95] even though their judgements [דינים] are the same as those of Israel, you must not resort to them since it says 'These are the judgements which thou shalt set before them' [*Ex.* 21:1], that is to say, 'before them' and not before gentiles.' This follows a discussion of whether or not a deed of divorce given under compulsion by a gentile court is valid. The second passage is again a commentary on *Ex.* 21:1, by Rabbi Eleazar ben Azariah,[96] cited in the *Mekhilta d'R. Ishmael*:[97] 'If the gentiles pronounce judgements in accordance with Jewish law [דנו כדיני ישראל], are their judgements valid? No, for it is written: 'These are the judgements': you judge them but they do not judge you.'[98] The harsh language employed by the Rabbis in the prohibition on using gentile courts may well indi-

91 See the τευχίζει διὰ δημοσίων of *P.Yadin* 19, ll. 26–27 and the τευχίσω σοι διὰ δημοσίων of *P.Yadin* 20, l. 13 = ll. 35–6.

92 R. Simeon without patronym means R. Simeon ben Yohai (= Yohanan), third generation of *Tannaim*, c. 130–160 CE, see Strack and Stemberger, *Introduction to the Talmud and Midrash*, 83–4, but he is clearly referring to an earlier rule (לא הוזכרו 'they were not mentioned').

93 Cf. *tGittin* 1.4; *bGittin* 11a; See Gedaliah Alon, *The Jews in Their Land in the Talmudic Age 70–640 CE*, Vol. II (Jerusalem: Magnes Press, 1984), 553–57; Asher Gulak, *Towards a Study of the History of Jewish Law in the Talmudic Period* (Jerusalem: Hasefer, 1929), 54 ff. (Hebrew).

94 See Strack and Stemberger, *Introduction to the Talmud and Midrash*, 80; Heiman, *History of the Tannaim and Amoraim*, Vol. II, 524–29.

95 The Hebrew has Agorai'oth (אגוריאות) from ἀγορά.

96 He belonged to the second generation of *Tannaim* (90–130 CE); contemporary of Rabban Gamliel II, the leader of rabbinic Judaism between 80/90–110, whom he replaced temporarily, Strack and Stemberger, *Introduction to the Talmud and Midrash*, 76; 78.

97 *Mekhilta* "is the Aramaic equivalent of Hebrew *midda* or *kelal*, 'rule, norm' ... the derivation of halakhah ['law'] from Scripture according to certain rules,' Strack and Stemberger, 275. The *Mekhilta d'R. Ishmael* is a commentary on some chapters of Exodus "with a core going back to the school of R. Ishmael" [middle of the second century], although its final redaction took place "in the second half of the third century," Strack and Stemberger, 278–79.

98 H.S. Horovitz and I.A. Rabin, eds., *Mekhilta d'R. Ishmael*, 2nd ed. (Jerusalem: Wahrman, 1960), 246. The two passages, however, are not unrelated: both refer to *mGittin* 9.8 and to *Ex.* 21:1; see Juster, *Les Juifs dans l'Empire romain*, Vol. II, 95 f.

cate that the Jews *did* use them. We may assume that in the absence of a Jewish court in Maoza or its vicinity, the parties had to attend non-Jewish courts where local customs were followed. Alternatively, perhaps these Jews preferred non-Jewish courts. However that may be, these local customs seem at times extremely Roman in character, and the courts preferred by the parties turn out to be Roman. The rest of the discussion will be devoted to the form and shape Romanization took soon after the annexation of Arabia as revealed in this archive.

III

We have discovered (above, Sections I and II) that neither the 'law of the papyri' nor Jewish law explains Babatha's situation. We may look therefore more closely at Roman law.[99]

Women were excluded by Roman law from the exercise of guardianship: '*Feminae tutores dari non possunt*' (*Dig*. 26, 1, 18); the father cannot make the mother a guardian of their common children in his will: '*Iure nostro tutela communium liberorum matri testamento patris frustra mandatur*' (*Dig*. 26, 2, 26). The fact that Babatha seems to be excluded from the guardianship of her son also fits the Roman legal practice – this time substantive law rather than procedure.[100]

Although excluded from the guardianship of her children, the mother is expected to take interest in their welfare, and the guardians would do well to heed the mother's advice, if instructed to do so by the testator – with no diminution of their competence and responsibility (*Dig*. 26, 7, 5, 8).[101] The *Senatus Consultum Tertullianum* of Hadrianic date, which gave a mother (with *ius trium liberorum*) the right to inherit from her children in case of intestacy, made it her duty under sanction to ensure that guardians are legally appointed; should she fail to do so, she loses her claim to the inheritance.[102] However, the law stopped short of saying that it was the duty of a mother to prosecute a guardian who failed in his

99 The following discussion benefited a great deal from the pertinent criticism of J.F. Gardner.

100 I refer to the manner of appointing guardians, the *tutoris datio* described above.

101 '*Viris bonis conveniet salubre consilium matris admittere ...*' etc.

102 *Dig*. 38, 17, 2, 23 (Ulpian): '*Si mater non petierit tutores idoneos filiis suis vel prioribus excusatis reiectisve non confestim aliorum nomina ediderit, ius non habet vindicandorum sibi bonorum intestatorum filiorum*'; cf. *Dig*. 26, 6, 2, 2 (Modestinus); *Dig*. 26, 6, 4, 2 (Tryphoninus); Gardner, *Woman in Roman Law and Society*, 149 has a different interpretation for the purpose of the injunction; cf. *CJ* 5, 31, 6: '*Matris pietas instruere te potest, quos tutores filio tuo petere debes, sed et observare, ne quid secus quam oportet in re filii pupilli agatur*' (224 CE, 'Your maternal piety can instruct you which guardians to request for your son, but also to see to it that his property is being looked after properly'); *CJ* 5, 31, 8; 9; 11 (even unmarried mothers).

duty (*Dig.* 26, 6, 4, 4).[103] Finally and most crucially for the discussion here: 'even women are admitted [to bring a charge of untrustworthiness],[104] but only those who take this step as a family duty, as for example a mother' (*Dig.* 26, 10, 1, 7).[105]

We may examine Babatha's behaviour in the light of these statements. Shortly after the appointment of the guardians by the city council of Petra, Babatha took the case against them to the governor of the province.[106] *P.Yadin* 13 is a petition (ἀξίωμα) to the governor, and *P.Yadin* 14 is the actual summons of one of them to his court.[107] It is only in *P.Yadin* 15 that we get the full grounds for her complaint against her son's guardians: (1) that they did not give her son 'the maintenance money commensurate with the income from the interest on his money and the rest of his property,'[108] but only half a percent (l. 7 = l. 22–23), which as we learn elsewhere came to two denarii per month;[109] (2) that the amount was insufficient to maintain the style of life the boy was accustomed to (or his social standing?);[110]

---

103 '*Quae autem suspectum tutorem non fecit, nec verbis nec sententia constitutionis incidit, quod eiusmodi facta diiudicare et aestimare virilis animi est et potest etiam delicta ignorare mater ...*', see below on the *crimen suspecti tutoris*.

104 The *crimen suspecti tutoris*, see *Dig.* 26, 10; *Inst. Just.* I, 26. Kaser, *Das römische Privatrecht*, 364, § 88, cautions that the *accusatio suspecti* may have applied in classical times to testamentary guardians only and not to those appointed by the magistrates.

105 '*Quin immo et mulieres admittuntur [suspectos postulare], sed hae solae, quae pietate necessitudinis ductae ad hoc procedunt, ut puta mater,*' but also a nurse, a grandmother, a sister as well as others motivated by *pietas necessitudinis*; cf. *Inst. Just.* I, 26, 3.

106 About four months later: see *P.Yadin* 13, ll. 19–21.

107 *P.Yadin* 14, ll. 28–9 seem to suggest that 'Abdobdas son of Ellouthas was not guilty of the same offence in Babatha's eyes; and although *P.Yadin* 15 is directed against both (ἐπὶ τῶν ἐπιβε̣βλ̣ημένων μαρτύρων ἐμαρτυροποιήσατο Βαβαθα Σίμωνος τοῦ Μαναήμου κατὰ Ἰωάνου̣ Ἰ̣ωσή[που το]ῦ̣ Ἐ̣γ̣λ̣α̣ [κ]αὶ Αβδοοβδ̣α̣ Ἐλλο̣υ̣θα ἐ̣π̣ιτρόπων Ἰησοῦ Ἰησοῦτος υἱοῦ αὐτῆς ὀρφανοῦ ('before the attending witnesses Babatha daughter of Simon son of Menahem deposed against John son of Joseph Eglas and 'Abdoöbdas son of Ellouthas, guardians of her son Jesus son of Jesus, appointed guardians for the said orphan') ll. 3–4 = ll. 17–19; cf. ll, 32–33), the actual summons is given only against John son of Eglas: ἐπὶ οὗ (the governor) περὶ τῆς ἀπειθαρχείας ἀποδόσεως τῶν τροφίων παρήνγειλα ἐγὼ Βαβαθα Ἰωάνη τῷ προγεγραμμένῳ, ἑνεὶ τῶν ἐπιτρόπων τοῦ ὀρφανοῦ ('before whom I, Babatha, summoned the aforesaid John, one of the guardians of the orphan, for his refusal of disbursement of the [appropriate] maintenance money') ll. 11–12 = ll. 28–29. Perhaps at this point she has to serve separate summons to each of them.

108 διὰ τ̣ὸ̣ ὑμᾶς μὴ δεδωκέ̣ναι τῷ υἱῷ μο[υ ὀρφανῷ] τ̣ρ̣ο̣φῖ̣α πρὸς τ̣ὴ̣ν̣ δ̣[ύ]ναμιν̣ τ̣[όκ]ου, ἀ̣ρ̣γ̣[υ]ρ̣ίου αὐτοῦ καὶ τῶν λοιπῶν ὑπαρχόντων αὐτοῦ, ll. 5–7 = ll. 20–21.

109 From *P.Yadin* 13, ll. 19–23: καὶ οἱ πρ̣ὸ̣ μ̣η̣νῶν τεσ̣σ̣[άρ]ων̣ κ̣[α]ὶ̣ πλείω κ̣αταστ̣αθ̣έ̣ντες ἐπίτροποι [ὑπ]ὸ βουλῆς τῷ[ν] Πετρ̣α̣[ί]ων Αβδοοβδα<ς> Ελλουθα καὶ Ἰω̣ά̣νης [Ἐγλ]α̣ οὐ̣δ[ὲ] α[ὐτοὶ τρ]ο̣φ̣ῖα τ̣ο̣[ῦ ὀρ]φ̣ανοῦ ἔδωκα[ν] ε̣ἰ̣ μὴ μ̣[όν]ον δ̣η̣νάρια δυ̣ω̣ [κατὰ μ]ῆ̣ν̣α, it follows that they had 400 denarii to invest; see also a receipt for six denarii for three months, *P.Yadin* 27.

110 *P.Yadin* 15, ll. 6–7 = l. 22: καὶ μάλιστα πρὸς ὁμειλίαν ἣν̣ ε̣ἰκου̣[σα] [... αὐ]τ̣ῷ (for the reading see Lewis, *The Documents from the Bar Kokhba Period in the Cave of Letters. Greek Papyri*, 63–3

(3) that if they gave her the money on security, she could invest it in such a way as to get 'a denarius and a half [per month] per hundred denarii' (ll. 9–10 = l. 26).

We do not know at what rate the guardians had invested the money; they may have invested it at the usual rate of 12 per cent per annum and added to the capital whatever was left over after they gave the boy his allowance, unless we take the words ẹἰ δὲ μή, ἔσται τοῦṭọ [τὸ μαρτυρο]π̣ọίημα εἰς δικαίωμα κέρδους ἀργυρίου τοῦ ὀρφανοῦ εἰ διδόντες ... (ll. 31–32) to mean that they appropriated the profits.[111] At any event her last offer seems to imply that they had made a poor investment with the money; she could get 18 per cent per annum.[112] With such an income she could ensure that her 'son ... be raised in splendid style rendering thanks to *the[se] most blessed times* of the governorship of Julius Julianus.'[113]

It is somewhat surprising to find here an echo of the imperial advertisement of the good times ushered in by Nerva and Trajan. When Pliny the Younger asked Trajan to bestow the praetorship on Attius Sura, he assured the Emperor that his friend 'is encouraged to hope for such an honour by his distinguished antecedents, his exceptional integrity in the midst of poverty, and, above all, by the *happiness of your times* which encourages your best citizens to make use of your paternal indulgence' (Pliny, *Ep*. X, 12).[114] This is not the only Roman sentiment in this

ad loc.). The recent publication of 'Annual Account of a Guardian' from 219 CE (*P.Oxy*. 3921–2, see above, n. 39), allows us to compare Jesus' allowance with that of an early third century one: the two boys' maintenance came to 99 dr. per month = roughly 8 denarii, i. e. 4 denarii per child; twice as much as that provided for Babatha's son. Babatha might have had grounds for complaint.

111 Lewis, 61 translates: 'Otherwise this deposition will serve as documentary evidence of [your] profiteering from the money of the orphan by giving ...'; see also Lewis, "Two Greek Documents from Provincia Arabia," 111: "[she] is here accusing the guardians of profiting from their trust by pocketing the rest of the interest themselves."

112 The usual rate seems to be 12 per cent per annum, see *P.Yadin* 11, ll. 6–7 = ll. 20–22. Lewis, 41 suspects that "a usurious squeeze" is concealed in the erasure of forty and the interlinear insertion of sixty in l. 3 of the inner text: "he was compelled to sign the note for sixty denarii but actually received only forty denarii in hand." This would yield an interest of more than 60 per cent per annum, see Magen Broshi, "Agriculture and Economy in Roman Palestine: Seven Notes on the Babatha Archive," *IEJ* 42 (1992): 239–40.

113 ὅθεν λαμπρῶς διασωθῇ μου ὁ υἱὸς εὐχαριστῶν (ll. 10–11: εὐχαριcτοῦντα) *τοῖς μακαριωτάτοις καιροῖς* ἡγ̣εμωνίας Ἰουλίοụ Ἰουλιανοῦ ἡγεμόνος (ll. 10–11 = ll. 26–27). Fergus Millar reminds me of *Acts* 24:2 (the rhetor Tertullus to Felix): πολλῆς εἰρήνης τυγχάνοντες διὰ σοῦ, καὶ διορθωμάτων γινομένων τῷ ἔθνει τούτῳ διὰ τῆς σῆς προνοίας ('Seeing that by thee we enjoy great quietness and that very worthy deeds are done unto this nation by thy providence').

114 '*Ad quam spem [sc. praeturae] ... hortatur et natalium splendor et summa integritas in paupertate et ante omnia felicitas temporum, quae bonam conscientiam civium tuorum ad usum indulgentiae tuae provocat et attollit*'; cf. Pliny, *Ep*. X, 58, 7: '*Quaedam sine dubio, Quirites, ipsa felicitas temporum edicit*'; Tacitus, *Agr*. 3, 1: '*augeatque cotidie felicitatem temporum Nerva Traianus*'; Tacitus, *Hist*. I, 1: '*rara temporum felicitate ubi sentire quae velis et quae sentias dicere licet*.'

document. Babatha's demand for an income befitting 'the style of life the boy is accustomed to'[115] is familiar from the Roman juristic sources dealing with guardianship: 'Since a guardian is put in charge not only of his ward's property, but also of his conduct and character, he should not assign the lowest possible wages to the teachers, but [pay them] *in accordance with the resources of the inheritance and the rank of the family*; he will provide maintenance for the slaves and freedmen, sometimes even for those outside the household if this will be advantageous to the ward etc.' (*Dig.* 26, 7, 12, 3);[116] 'a guardian has to consider the rank and the resources of his ward in estimating the number of slaves who are to be in attendance' (*Dig.* 26, 7, 13 pr.).[117] It looks as if whoever composed the document was familiar with Roman turns of thought and sentiment, and perhaps with Roman legal argumentation; he was certainly acquainted with the imperial propaganda of 'these most blessed times.'

We may well inquire into her reasons for not approaching the city council of Petra:[118] was it her fear that they might not prove impartial, since it was they who had appointed the guardians, or was there some other, technical or legal, obstruction? Were charges against guardians within the exclusive competence of the governor of the province?

The legal sources offer some help here. As pointed out above, a mother could lay charges against an untrustworthy guardian and ask for his removal under the *crimen suspecti tutoris*.[119] "There was no definite list of grounds of removal; it was at the discretion of the Court."[120] 'The right of removing untrustworthy (*suspectos*) tutors' was granted 'at Rome to the praetors and in the provinces to their

115 Above, n. 110.

116 '*Cum tutor non rebus dumtaxat, sed etiam moribus pupilli praeponatur, imprimis mercedes praeceptoribus, non quas minimas poterit, sed pro facultate patrimonii, pro dignitate natalium constituet, alimenta servis libertisque, nonnumquam etiam exteris, si hoc pupillo expediet, praestabit* ... etc.'; cf. *CJ* 5, 50, 2: '*ut arbitrio praetoris alimenta pro modo facultatum pupillis vel iuvenibus constituantur*'; and *Dig.* 27, 2, 1: '*si vero praetor non est aditus, pro modo facultatium pupilli debet arbitrio iudicis aestimari.*'

117 '*Tutor secundum dignitatem facultatesque pupilli modum servorum aestimare debet.*' Lewis, "Two Greek Documents from Provincia Arabia," 110 cites *CGL* III, 36, ll. 5–14: '*Adrianus dixit curatori: 'propter hoc ergo datus es, ut fame neces pupillum? pro modo ergo facultatis alimenta ei praesta*'' ('Hadrian said to a guardian: Was it for this purpose that we appointed you, so that you would starve your ward to death? Give him provisions in accordance with his (your) means!').

118 Assuming that nomination implies jurisdiction in matters arising from it, see Isaac, "The Babatha Archive," 63–4.

119 At nn. 99–100.

120 See Buckland and Stein, *A Text-Book of Roman Law from Augustus to Justinian*, 160.

governors' (*Dig.* 26, 10, 1, 3).[121] Further on in the same source we are told that 'a guardian who does not use his resources to provide for his ward is untrustworthy and can be removed' (*Dig.* 26, 10, 3, 14).[122] The instruction in *CJ* 5, 50, 1 fits our case admirably: 'If a guardian does not provide maintenance to his ward, the latter may approach the provincial governor.'[123] Although the rule postdates our text by almost a hundred years (it dates from 215 CE), it may well have been in force earlier. Whether aware of these legal niceties or not (or alerted to them by her lawyers), Babatha confidently approaches the governor of the province, and no one else, with her complaint against the guardians.

It has to be emphasized that at no stage does she contest the guardianship or ask to be made guardian herself. Z.W. Falk[124] and B. Klein[125] are wrong to maintain that Babatha's first offer (which the guardians must have rejected) to lend her the orphan's money on security[126] is tantamount to a request to have the guardians removed so as to be made guardian herself. On the contrary this proposal demonstrates that she recognized their ultimate authority.[127] If anything she was seeking compensation, as the presence of the *actio tutelae* in *P.Yadin* 28–30 seems to suggest.[128] Admittedly the presence of these documents here is disconcerting;

121 '*Damus autem ius removendi suspectos tutores Romae praetoribus, in provinciis praesidibus earum*' (Ulpian, *Ad Edictum* 35); cf. *Inst. Just.* I, 26, 1.

122 '*Tutor, qui ad alimenta pupillo praestanda copiam sui non faciat, suspectus est poteritque removeri,*' Ulpian, *Ad Edictum* 35.

123 '*Pupillus, si ei alimenta a tutore suo non praestantur, praesidem provinciae adeat*', see Maxime Lemosse, "Le Procés de Babatha," *Irish Jurist* 3 (1968): 372 ff., who finds in this claim the explanation for her approaching the governor rather than the *boule* who appointed the guardians. Lewis maintains that she is charging the guardians with fraud (see above, n. 111).

124 Ze'ev W. Falk, *Introduction to Jewish Law of the Second Commonwealth*, Vol. II (Leiden: Brill, 1978), 330.

125 Birgit E. Klein, "Die Stellung der Frau in Judentum: Rabbinische Initiative oder Legitimation? Demonstriert am Beispiel des jüdischen Vormundschaftsrechts" (Heidelberg, Hochschule für Jüdische Studien, Magisterarbeit, 1991), 44–5.

126 P.*Yadin* 15, ll. 7–10 = ll. 23–26: ἔχουσα ὑπάρχοντα ἀξιό[χρεα τούτ]ου τοῦ ἀρ[γυρίο]υ οὗ ἔχετε τοῦ ὀρφανοῦ, διὸ προεμαρτυροποίησα ἵνα εἰ δοκεῖ ὑμεῖν δοῦναί μοι τ̣ὸ ἀργύριον [δι' ἀσφαλείας περὶ ὑποθήκης τῶ]ν ὑπαρχόντων μου κτλ. ('as I have property equivalent in value to this money of the orphan's that you have, therefore I previously deposed in order that you might decide to give me the money on security involving a hypothec of my property,' etc.).

127 Wolff, "Römisches Provinzialrecht in der Provinz Arabia," 801; Wolff, "Le droit provincial dans la province romaine d'Arabie," 287.

128 A similar case of tutors refusing to pay the amount of maintenance money stipulated in the will to the person with whom the orphans are living is mentioned in *Dig.* 33, 1, 7 pr., discussed by Watson, *The Law of Persons in the Later Roman Republic*, 143 f; but the implication of the ruling there, if I understand it correctly, is that such conduct does not give rise to *actio tutelae*; in fact, the legal proceedings and remedies envisioned in them are quite distinct from those of the *crimen suspecti tutoris*, so far discussed.

The use of the formulary system, in a provincial setting, between *peregrini* – and to make matters more complicated, in a newly-created province – has naturally invited much speculation.[129] In addition, the language of the textbooks leaves no room for doubt that actions on tutelage became available only when the tutelage has ended: it could be ended either when the ward came of age or by the death of either the guardian or the ward (*Dig.* 27, 3, 4 pr.).[130] This certainly is not the case here. We know that Jesus was a minor as late as 19 August 132, the date of *P.Yadin* 27, the latest dated document in the archive. There his mother acknowledges the receipt of maintenance money from his guardian, Simon 'the hunchback.' The latter is, as we learn, the son of John son of Eglas, one of Jesus' two guardians; he had been appointed by the council of Petra to replace his father.[131] Thus neither the death of one of the guardians nor Jesus' coming of age can account for the presence of three copies of the *actio tutelae* in our archive. Various explanations have been offered.[132] It has been claimed that we have evidence from Egypt that "the *actio tutelae* may also be entered *durante tutela*."[133] This is tantamount to saying

---

the tutors run the risk (*periculum*) of being sued by means of the *actio* if they spend too much on living expenses.

129 For the norm, see Max Kaser, *Das römische Zivilprozessrecht* (München: Beck, 1966), 119 f.; for speculations on *P.Yadin* 28–30, see Wolff, "Römisches Provinzialrecht in der Provinz Arabia," 784–88 with the older literature cited in the notes.

130 '*Nisi finita tutela sit, tutelae agi non potest: finitur autem non solum pubertate, sed etiam morte tutoris vel pupilli*'; cf. *Dig.* 27, 3, 9, 4.

131 Βạβαθας Σίμφ[ν]ος ... Σίμωνι κυρτῷ Ἰωάνου Ἐγλα [τῆ]ς αὐτ[ῆ]ς Μαωζας χαίρι[ν]. σοῦ δευτέρου ἐπιτρόπου κατασταθέντος [*c.* 16 letters missing] ὑπ[ὸ βουλῆς Πετρ]αίων Ἰησο[ύ]ου Ἰησούου ὀρφανοῦ υ[ἱοῦ] μου, ll. 4–8 ('Babathas (*sic*) daughter of Simon ... to Simon the hunchback son of John son of Eglas, of the said Maoza, greetings. You having been appointed by the council of Petra to be the second guardian of my orphan son Jesus son of Jesus'). Lewis, *The Documents from the Bar Kokhba Period in the Cave of Letters. Greek Papyri*, 117 rightly holds that "the lacuna is likely to have been ἀντὶ τοῦ πατρός σου. Even without that explicit statement, the names alone are sufficient to reveal that the son had succeeded the father as the second guardian of Babatha's son."

132 Lemosse, "Le procés de Babatha," 375–76; Erwin Seidl, "Ein Papyrusfund zum klassischen Zivilprozessrecht," in *Studi in onore di Giuseppe Grosso*, Vol. II (Torino: Giappichelli, 1968), 345–61.

133 Taubenschlag, *The Law of Greco-Roman Egypt in the Light of the Papyri*, 168 and n. 60. However, only one of the examples cited there is of an *actio tutelae*, and even this one (*BGU* 136 [135 CE] = *M.Chr.* 86) takes place after the ward came of age, see O. Gradenwitz, "Ein Protocoll von Memphis aus hadrianischer Zeit," *Hermes* 28 (1893): 321–34; Arnaldo Biscardi, "Nuove testimonianze di un papiro arabogiudaico per la storia del processo provinciale romano," in *Studi in onore di Gaetano Scherillo*, Vol. I (Milano: Istituto editoriale cisalpino La Goliardica, 1972), 116–17 has no other evidence.

that there were no fixed rules and that the system accommodated more than the legalists would assume. At the very least the presence of the three copies of the *actio tutelae* suggests that whoever supplied Babatha with them acted in the belief that they could be put to use.[134] Since they are Roman legal instruments, they were intended for a Roman court of law, that is for the governor's court.[135]

Babatha may well have been misinformed about the applicability of the *actio tutelae* in her case; was she also wrong about the accessibility of the Roman governor? In the next section the role of Roman authority as arbitrator will be examined.

IV

Babatha first (*P.Yadin* 13, second half of 124 CE) approaches the governor (πρεσβευτῇ Σεβαστοῦ ἀντιστρατήγῳ) with a petition (ἀξίωμα), the exact content of which is now lost. Nevertheless, the sequel demonstrates that her petition was answered and that she was instructed to proceed. In *P.Yadin* 14 Babatha uses the *parangelia* procedure, known to us from Egyptian papyri: a summons to appear before the governor's court; in the Egyptian papyri, however, the petition is addressed to the *strategos* who serves it on the plaintiff through his subordinate (the ὑπηρέτης).[136] Here these links in the chain are missing; Babatha herself serves the summons on the defendants:[137] 'before the attending witnesses Babatha daughter of Simon, son of Menahem ... summoned (παρήνγειλεν) John son of Joseph Eglas ... saying: on account of your not having given ... etc. ... I summon (παρανγέλλω) you to attend at the court of the governor Julius Julianus in Petra [the metropolis of] Arabia [until we are heard] at the tribunal in Petra.'[138]

---

134 See Biscardi, "Nuove testimonianze di un papiro arabogiudaico per la storia del processo provinciale romano," 140–51 for conjectures on the origin of such copies.

135 See below, Appendix II.

136 On the *parangelia* in Egypt see Kaser, *Das römische Zivilprozessrecht*, 374; Taubenschlag, *The Law of Greco-Roman Egypt in the Light of the Papyri*, 500 ff.; Giuliana Foti Talamanca, *Ricerche sul processo nell'Egitto grecoromano II.1: Introduzione del giudizio* (Milano: Giuffrè, 1979), 65 ff. and 81–2, n. 72 for a list.

137 A much later example of this is *P.Nessana* 29 (590 CE), where the editor observes that "The document is unique, since παραγγελίαι have hitherto been known only by reference, principally in petitions containing a request that a summons to appear in court be served to the accused," Casper J. Kraemer, *Excavations at Nessana III: Non-Literary Papyri* (Princeton: Princeton University Press, 1958), 89.

138 *P.Yadin* 14 (11 or 12 October 125): [ἐπὶ τῶν ἐπιβεβλημένων] μαρτύρων παρήγγει[λεν Βαβαθα Σίμωνος τοῦ Μανα]ήμου ... διὸ παρανγέλλω σοι παρεδρεῦσαι [ἐπὶ βήμα]τος Ἰουλίου Ἰουλιανοῦ

It seems that as a rule a petition to the governor preceded a summons. This we learn from a later suit in which Babatha was involved. In *P.Yadin* 25 (9 July 131) Iulia Crispina summons Babatha to appear before the governor in Petra: 'I now summon (παρανγέλλω) you pursuant to the subscription (ὑ[πογρα]φή) of his Excellency the governor to accompany me to Petra.'[139] Clearly the governor's subscription was affixed to a petition submitted to him previously by Iulia Crispina. Babatha replies that seeing that she has been summoned to the governor, she too has given (ἔδωκα) a petition (πιττάκιν) to the governor and he has written under it a subscription ([ὑπέγρα]ψέν μοι) to perform the legal formalities in Petra.[140]

Thus the sequence 'petition – subscription – summons' should be assumed to have existed also in Babatha's suit against the guardians, even though the middle stage is not explicitly present. Furthermore, everywhere in the archive it is assumed by the litigants that they can present themselves or call on others to attend, whenever they wish and in whichever assize centre the governor might be.[141] Thus Besas son of Jesus summons Babatha 'to meet him before Haterius Nepos legate and propraetor in Petra or elsewhere in his province ...';[142] and Babatha forestalls Iulia Crispina's summons to appear before the governor in Petra later in the year (*P.Yadin* 25, 9 July 131, ll. 7–20 = ll. 37–54), by summoning her to appear before him now in Rabbath-Moab.[143] Finally Babatha summons Miriam, her late husband's first wife, to appear with her before the governor Haterius Nepos 'wherever he happens to be exercising justice in the province ... and to attend before the said Nepos until judgement.'[144]

ἡγεμώνος ἐγ̣ Πέ̣τρα̣ [μητροπόλει τῆ]ς̣ Ἀ̣ρ̣αβ̣ί̣α̣ς̣ [μέχρι οὗ διακουσθῶμεν ἐ]ν̣ τ̣ῷ ἐν Π̣έ̣[τρα̣ τριβουναλίῳ] (ll. 20–32). A reference to the summons served in *P.Yadin* 14 can be found in *P.Yadin* 15 (of the same date): ἐπὶ οὗ [*sc.* Ἰουλίου Ἰουλιανοῦ ἡγεμόνος] περὶ τῆς ἀπειθαρ̣χείας ἀποδόσεως τῶν τροφίων παρήνγειλα ἐγὼ Βαβαθα Ἰωάνῃ τῷ προγεγραμμένῳ, ἐνεὶ τῶν ἐπιτρόπων τοῦ ὀρφανοῦ (ll. 30–31 = 11–12, see above, n. 107).

139 [π]αρανγέλλω σοι κατὰ τὴν ὑ̣[πογραφ]ὴ̣ν̣ τοῦ κρατίστου ἡγεμόνος συνεξελθῖν αὐτὴ<ν> εἰς̣ [Π]έ̣[τραν] (ll. 6–8).

140 ἐπὶ πρὸ τού<του> παρήνγιλ̣έ̣ς με εἰς [Ἀδριανὴν Πέτραν πρὸς τὸν] κ̣ρ̣ά̣τ̣[ι]σ̣[τ]ο̣ν̣ [ἡ]γ̣[ε]μ̣ό̣ν̣α̣ ... [καὶ ἔδωκα καθ' ὑμ]ῶ̣ν̣ π̣ι̣τ̣τ̣ά̣κ̣ι̣ν τ̣ῷ κρ̣[ατί]σ̣τῳ ἡ̣γ̣ε̣μ̣ό̣νι κ̣α̣ὶ̣ [ὑπέγρα]ψ̣έ̣ν μοι [εἰς Π]έ̣τ̣ρ̣[αν σὺν ὑμ]-ῖ̣[ν τ]ὰ [νόμι]μα χ̣ρ̣ᾶ̣[σ]θ̣α̣ι̣ (ll. 15–21).

141 Thus I cannot agree with Isaac, "The Babatha Archive," 64–5 that "this demonstrates the hardships caused by the Roman judicial system, which *forced* provincials to travel to assize cities" (italics mine); there does not seem to be any question of coercion.

142 *P.Yadin* 23 (17 November 130), ll. 1–5 = ll. 10–16: 'Besas son of Jesus ... [εἰς] Πέτραν ἢ̣ ἄλλου ἐν τῇ αὐτοῦ̣ ἐπαρχίᾳ̣.'

143 See Lewis, *The Documents from the Bar Kokhba Period in the Cave of Letters. Greek Papyri*, 112, notes on ll. 21 and 55.

144 *P.Yadin* 26, ll. 2–11: 'Babatha ... summoned Miriam ... to accompany her in person before Haterius Nepos ... ὅπου ἂν ᾖ̣ ὑπ' αὐτοῦ ὑπαρχ[εί]α̣ ... καὶ παρεδρεύιν̣ ἐ̣π̣ὶ̣ τ̣ὸ̣ν̣ α̣ὐ̣τὸ̣ν̣ Ν̣έπωτα μέχρι

P.Yadin 27, from 19 August 132, the latest dated document from the archive and the last one to deal with the guardianship of Jesus, shows Babatha acknowledging the receipt of maintenance money in the amount of six denarii of silver for a period of three months: the sum of money had not been increased.[145] Either she dropped her charges against the guardians or the governor ruled against her. Whichever explanation we choose to accept, there seems no good reason to assume that Babatha's confidence in the governor's accessibility was unfounded or misguided.[146]

Was the recourse to Roman law and Roman courts required by the Roman authorities?[147] This would be out of character with the rest of the archive – as well as with much evidence to the contrary from other parts of the Roman world – where the initiative is seen to be taken by the subjects. There is nothing in the documents we have reviewed here to suggest that recourse to Roman law and Roman courts was anything but voluntarily adopted. Without coercion or attempts to impose uniformity, the very presence of the Romans as the supreme authority in the province invited appeals to their authority, to their courts as well as to their laws. The provincials seem more than willing to let the central government handle their disputes; they take the trouble of preparing blank forms of the *actio tutelae*, of searching for Roman legal arguments and of introducing into their personal claims Roman propaganda slogans of 'the most blessed times.' They are active and enterprising in inviting intervention. Having previously used Aramaic and Nabataean, they now resort to Greek in their legal documents, for no other reason, it seems, than to make them valid in a Roman court of law. No other courts occur in this archive, and there is no good reason for assuming that Nabataean and Aramaic could not be used in a local court.

διαγνώσεως.' I translate ὅπου ἂν ᾖ ὑπ' αὐτοῦ ὑπαρχ[εί]α by 'wherever he happens to be exercising justice in the province' in agreement with Lewis, 115: it does not mean here a subdivision of the province, and *pace* Isaac it can hardly be used as evidence that "Arabia was divided into districts called *hyparcheia*," cf. Isaac, "The Babatha Archive," 69. One would have expected something like παρουσία here, as in *P.Yadin* 14, l. 14: ᾖ εἰς τὴν αὐτοῦ ἔγγιστα παρ[ουσίαν] (cf. ll. 32–33 and Lewis, 57, notes on ll. 14 and 33, on παρουσία), but the υ before παρ[is very clear.

145 See above, at n. 109.

146 Goodman, "Babatha's Story," 172, quite rightly draws attention to the absence from the documents of evidence "for an effective local ruling class interposed between ordinary provincials and the machinery of the Roman state"; this observation should make it easier to accept the view of the governor's accessibility and involvement in the legal affairs of the *peregrini* in the provinces put forward some time ago by G.P. Burton, "Proconsuls, Assizes and the Administration of Justice under the Empire," *JRS* 65 (1975): esp. 101–2. As far as jurisdiction is concerned, no distinction should be made between proconsuls and *legati*.

147 Cf. Wolff, "Römisches Provinzialrecht in der Provinz Arabia," 788 ff; Isaac, "The Babatha Archive," 64–5 and see n. 141 above.

Most of the people involved in this archive are Jews; but, as there is nothing specifically Jewish about the Greek part of the archive, we are perfectly justified in regarding the Jews as representative of the provincials in general. Moreover, they represent that part of the provincial population which was less tainted by the 'epigraphic habit' of the Graeco-Roman world, i. e. they come from the less Hellenized section of the provincial population, those who would have left us no inscriptions – in this case the great majority of the population. Precisely because of this we can be sure that their dealings with the Roman authorities constitute a faithful picture of the realities of life in the province.

Appendix I

Having explored the Roman legal system for explaining Babatha's appeal to the governor of the province, I would like to raise, with all due caution, an altogether different hypothesis, namely that under Nabataean law such cases came before the King; the Roman governor, therefore, replaced in this instance royal authority. We know very little about Nabataean legal practices – and most of our knowledge derives from this archive, to which as we have seen (above, n. 87) the Nabataean contract published sometime ago by J. Starcky belongs; but it seems that royal authority was involved in private contracts, as witnessed by *P.Yadin* 1–3 where all three contracts end with "a specification of the fine to be paid, in the event of the purchaser's non-observance of the contract, both to the vendor and to the Nabataean king: ('ולמראנא רבאל מלכא כות – and to our lord Rabel the king likewise')."[148] This formula is rendered into Greek and applied to the Emperor in *P.Yadin* 5 (2 June 110), frg. a, col. ii, ll. 9–11: δ[ι]π̣λοῦ̣[ν] τ̣ῶν [-ca.?-] καὶ Καίσαρι ὡ̣σ̣αύτ̣ω̣ς κ[-ca.?-] προγέγραπ̣ται ....[149] One need not go here into any extended argument to prove that the Romans frequently accepted and continued local practices, especially when they did not directly contradict their own.[150] Likewise, royal property became imperial property as witnessed by a comparison of *P.Yadin* 2 (from 99 CE): ולִימינא גַנת מראנא רבאל מלך נבטו – 'to the south the grove of our lord Rabel the king of the Nabataeans'[151] and *P.Yadin* 16, ll. 23–4: γείτονες μοσχαντικὴ κυρίου Καίσαρος.[152]

---

148 Yadin, "Expedition D – The Cave of the Letters," 241.

149 Pointed out by Bowersock, "The Babatha Papyri, Masada, and Rome," 340.

150 For private contracts containing clauses for the benefit of the fiscus, see Fergus Millar, "The Fiscus in the First Two Centuries," *JRS* 53 (1963): 37–8.

151 Yadin, "Expedition D – The Cave of the Letters," 240–41.

152 On the meaning of μοσχαντικὴ see Bowersock, "The Babatha Papyri, Masada, and Rome," 341.

Appendix II

There is some evidence for limitations on the competence of local courts in cases involving *tutela*. The Lex Irnitana IXA <84>, ll. 10–11[153] makes it quite clear that the local *duovir* who is in charge of the administration of justice ('*qui ibi iure dicundo praeerit*') does not have jurisdiction in cases involving *tutela*.[154] Further on, though, there is a mitigating circumstance in which the *duovir* can exercise jurisdiction (ll. 17–18): 'and even about these matters if each of the two parties is willing' ('*de is rebus etiam, si uterque inter quos ambig{er}etur volet*'). One could mention also the provision in the municipal charter known as the *Fragmentum Atestinum* to the effect that municipal magistrates might appoint a judge in cases involving *tutela* only when the sum of money involved does not exceed 10,000 sesterces, or 2,500 denarii.[155] This sum of money happens to be mentioned twice as the upper limit in the *actio tutelae* contained in *P.Yadin* 28–30: judges are to be appointed only if the matter involves up to 2,500 denarii; and again: their judgement cannot involve a sum of money which will exceed 2,500 denarii. But see the *Edictum Augusti de Aquaeductu Venafrano*,[156] which mentions the same sum of money; perhaps the sum of 10,000 sesterces was used arbitrarily for convenience, and no special significance should be attached to it.[157] Moreover, assuming that it is the governor rather than local magistrates who would issue the *actio tutelae*, it is hard to see why a limit was set at all in the present case.

---

153 González, "The Lex Irnitana: A New Copy of the Flavian Municipal Law," 175.

154 See Alan Rodger, "The Jurisdiction of Local Magistrates: Chapter 84 of the Lex Irnitana," *ZPE* 84 (1990): 147–51.

155 *FIRA*, Vol. I, no. 20, ll. 1–7

156 *FIRA*, Vol. I, no. 67, ll. 65 ff.

157 I owe both the observation and the reference to M. Crawford.

The Guardian (ἐπίτροπος) of a Woman in the Documents from the Judaean Desert

The documentary texts from the Judaean Desert are mostly legal texts. They were written in a number of languages: Hebrew, Jewish Aramaic, Nabataean Aramaic and Greek. However, regardless of the language in which they were composed, with very few exceptions all of them were written by Jews or at least involve Jews.[1] Those Jews who wrote their documents in Greek are by no means Hellenized Jews. This is amply demonstrated by their Aramaic subscriptions and signatures, and sometimes by the faulty Greek they use.[2] What does the use of different languages tell us about this society? Does the use of one language, as against others, reflect no more than the diplomatics of the documents, or does it reveal to us the coexistence of different legal systems within this society? It seems to me that the topic

1 For surveys see Hannah M. Cotton, W.E.H. Cockle, and Fergus Millar, "The Papyrology of the Roman Near East: A Survey," *JRS* 85 (1995): 214–35; Hannah M. Cotton, "The Impact of the Documentary Papyri from the Judaean Desert on the Study of Jewish History from 70 to 135 CE," in *Jüdische Geschichte in hellenistisch-römischer Zeit: Wege der Forschung – von alten zu neuen Schürer*, ed. Aharon Oppenheimer (München: Oldenbourg, 1999), 221–36 [below, pp. 467–84]; Hannah M. Cotton, "Documentary Texts," in *Encyclopedia of the Dead Sea Scrolls*, ed. Lawrence H. Schiffman and James VanderKam (New York: Oxford University Press, 2000), 212–15.

2 See Abraham Wasserstein, "A Marriage Contract from the Province of Arabia Nova: Notes on Papyrus Yadin 18," *JQR* 80 (1989): 124 f.; Abraham Wasserstein, "Non-Hellenized Jews in the Semi-Hellenized East," *SCI* 14 (1995): 111–37. For their 'faulty Greek' see Cotton and Yardeni, *Aramaic, Hebrew, and Greek Documentary Texts from Naḥal Ḥever and Other Sites*, 136 f.; 206 ff.

Article note: First published in *ZPE* 118 (1997): 267–273, with the following note: this paper is based on a lecture given at the International Congress on 'The Dead Sea Scrolls – Fifty Years after their Discovery' held at The Israel Museum, Jerusalem, July 20–25, 1997; I am grateful to the participants for their comments, and to Dieter Hagedorn and Werner Eck for insightful criticism of an earlier version.

The papyri cited here as *XḤev/Se ar* or *XḤev/Se gr* are published in Hannah M. Cotton and Ada Yardeni, *Aramaic, Hebrew, and Greek Documentary Texts from Naḥal Ḥever and Other Sites*, Discoveries in the Judaean Desert XXVII (Oxford: Clarendon Press, 1997) (henceforth Cotton and Yardeni); the Greek part of the Babatha archive was published in Naphtali Lewis, *The Documents from the Bar Kokhba Period in the Cave of Letters. Greek Papyri* (with Aramaic and Nabatean Signatures and Subscriptions, edited by Y. Yadin and J.C. Greenfield) (Jerusalem: IES, 1989) (henceforth Lewis), and are designated *P.Yadin*; the Hebrew, Aramaic, and Nabatean Documents found by Yadin in the Cave of Letters in Naḥal Ḥever, also designated *P.Yadin*, were published in Yigael Yadin et al., *The Documents from the Bar Kokhba Period in the Cave of Letters: Hebrew, Aramaic and Nabatean-Aramaic Papyri* (Jerusalem: IES, 2002). I am grateful to Ada Yardeni and Jonas Greenfield for showing me the texts in advance of publication.

https://doi.org/10.1515/9783110770438-027

of this paper, the presence or absence of a guardian of a woman in a document, can profitably be used to address these questions.

The legal representative, the guardian of a woman, appears only in the Greek documents, and never in the Hebrew, Aramaic or Nabataean ones. What is the implication of this absence? That the legal system reflected in the Semitic documents did not recognize, or did not call for, the institution of a guardian for a woman? In that case what legal system is reflected in the Greek documents? I deliberately take no account here of the evidence of the rabbinic sources. In defence of this, it should be said that in view of the late date of the redaction of the Jewish legal code in the Mishnah, reliance on these sources would involve us in a vicious circle: we are totally dependent on the papyri for evaluating the influence exercised by the rabbis on the law used by Jews at the time.[3]

We may start with a random example from the Babatha archive: in *P.Yadin* 17 of 21 February 128 Judah son of Eleazar Khthousion, Babatha's second husband, acknowledges that he has received 300 *denarii* from her as a deposit to be paid on demand; her guardian is present with her: ὡμολογήσατο Ἰούδας Ἐλεαζάρου τοῦ καὶ [Χ]θ̣ο̣υ̣σίωνος Αἰνγαδηνὸς πρ[ὸς] Βαβαθα̣ν̣ Σίμωνος ἰδίαν γυναῖκαν αὐτοῦ, συνπαρόντ̣[ος α]ὐτῇ ἐπιτρόπου το̣ῦ̣δε τοῦ π̣ρ̣ά̣γμ̣α̣τος χάριν Ἰακώβου Ἰησοῦ̣ ... ὥστε̣ τὸν Ἰούδαν ἀπε[σ]χηκ̣έναι παρ' αὐτῆς \εἰς λόγον π̣α̣ραθήκης/ ἀργ̣[υ]ρ̣ίου καλοῦ δοκίμ[ο]υ νομ[ίσμα]τος δηνα̣ριων τριακοσ[ι]ω̣ν \ἐπὶ το αὐτὸν/ ἔχειν αὐτ̣ὰ καὶ ὀφείλ̣ε̣[ι]ν ἐν παραθήκη̣ μέχρι οὗ ἂ̣ν χ̣ρ̣ό̣ν̣[ου δόξη̣ τῇ Βαβαθα̣] etc.[4]

The presence of a legal representative of a woman is well attested in contemporary Egyptian papyri. But there is a difference of usage: the term used for the guardian of a woman in the passage just quoted and elsewhere in the papyri from the Judaean Desert is ἐπίτροπος; in the Greek papyri from Egypt, however, the guardian of a woman is designated κύριος. The term ἐπίτροπος is reserved in the Egyptian papyri for the guardian of a minor; and for good reason too. The two terms are not synonyms; they stand for two distinct legal concepts. The ἐπίτροπος can only refer to the person who administers someone else's patrimony.[5] The κύριος on the other hand was in the old Attic law from which the term derives the master of

3 See Hannah M. Cotton, "The Rabbis and the Documents," in *Jews in a Greco-Roman World*, ed. Martin Goodman (Oxford: Oxford University Press, 1998), 167–79 [below, pp. 453–65].

4 'Judah son of Eleazar Khthousion from Ein Gedi acknowledged to Babatha daughter of Shim'on, his own wife, present with her as her guardian for the purpose of this matter Jacob son of Yeshu'a ... that he has received from her on account of a deposit three hundred *denarii* of silver in coin of genuine legal tender, on condition that he hold them and owe them on deposit until such time as it may please Babatha ... etc.,' *P.Yadin* 17 lines 3–5 = 22–24.

5 "ἐπίτροπος ... kann sich niemals auf eine andere Person beziehen als einen Verwalter fremden Vermögens," Hans Julius Wolff, "Römisches Provinzialrecht in der Provinz Arabia (Rechtspolitik als Instrument der Beherrschung)," in *Aufstieg und Niedergang der römischen Welt*, Vol. II.13 (Ber-

a person who could not own property. It is a fossilized remnant of an older social structure in which the woman lacked altogether the competence to own property. The κύριος, as the term indicates, was the woman's lord and master. With time women could and did own property and the κύριος was no longer the person in whose power the woman was. His function degenerated therefore into that of an assistant of the woman in the performance of certain legal actions, mere lip service to an older legal system.[6] He survived thus in Ptolemaic Egypt, but perhaps not in the Seleucid sphere of influence, since he is absent from the Greek papyri from Dura-Europos and from the recently published papyri from Mesopotamia.[7]

In the Greek papyri from the Judaean Desert the term ἐπίτροπος is used – even in a single document – both for the guardian of a woman and for the guardian of a minor, as in the following example: Βησᾶς Ἰησούου Ἠνγαδηνὸς οἰκῶν ἐν Μαζρ̣α̣α̣ ἐ̣[πί]τροπος ὀρφανῶν Ἰησο̣ύου Χθουσίωνος, ... Σελαμσιοῦ Ἰούδου Ἠνγαδηνῇ διὰ ἐπιτρόπου αὐτῆς Ἰουδᾶς ὃς κ̣α̣ὶ Κίνβ̣ε̣ρ̣ Ἀ̣ν̣α̣ν̣ί̣ο̣υ Ἠ̣ν̣[γ]αδηνοῦ τ̣ο̣ῦ̣δ̣ε̣ τοῦ πράγματος χάριν.[8] But the identity of terms does not in fact reflect an identity of function. As I hope to prove in the following discussion, the low profile kept by the guardian of a woman in the Greek documents from the Judaean Desert is conspicuous. It contrasts sharply with that of the guardian of the minor[9] but resembles that of the κύριος in the Egyptian papyri.

---

lin: De Gruyter, 1980), 794; as the *tutor* in Roman law, see Max Kaser, *Das römische Privatrecht*, 2nd ed. (München: Beck, 1971), 85–86.

6 For the κύριος in Egyptian papyri see Raphael Taubenschlag, "La compétence du kurios dans le droit gréco-égyptien," in *Opera Minora*, Vol. II (Warsaw: Panstwowe Wydawn Naukowe, 1959), 353–77; Claire Préaux, "Le statut de la femme à l'époque hellenistique principalement en Égypte," *Recueils de la Société Jean Bodin* 11 (1959): 139 ff.; Hans-Albert Rupprecht, "Zur Frage der Frauentutel im römischen Ägypten," in *Festschrift für Arnold Kränzlein: Beiträge zur antiken Rechtsgeschichte*, ed. Gunter Wesener (Graz: Leykam, 1986), 95–102.

7 *P.Dura* 28–32, see also C.B. Welles, R.O. Fink, and J.F. Gilliam, *The Excavations at Dura-Europos Conducted by Yale University and the French Academy of Inscriptions and Letters, Final Report V, Part I: The Parchments and Papyri* (New Haven: Yale University Press, 1959), 12; in *P.Euphr.* 6–7 the brother of Maththabeine, daughter of Abbas son of Goras, who subscribes for her, is not called κύριος, see Javier Teixidor, Denis Feissel, and Jean Gascou, "Documents d'archives romains inédits du Moyen Euphrate (IIIe s. après J-C): II. Les actes de vente- achat (P. Euphr. 6 À 10)," *Journal des Savants*, 1997, 3–57.

8 'Besas son of Yeshu'a from Ein Gedi residing in Mazra'a, the *epitropos* of the orphans of Yeshu'a son of Khthousion ... to Shlamzion daughter of Judah from Ein Gedi through Judah also known as Kimber son of Hananiah from Ein Gedi, her *epitropos* for this matter,' *P.Yadin* 20 lines 23–27.

9 For the guardian of the minor in the Babatha archive see Hannah M. Cotton, "The Guardianship of Jesus Son of Babatha: Roman and Local Law in the Province of Arabia," *JRS* 83 (1993): 94–108 [above, pp. 403–30]; see also Tiziana J. Chiusi, "IV. Zur Vormundschaft der Mutter," *ZSS* 111 (1994): 155–96.

That the lack of distinction was not due to the influence of the Aramaic environment is proved by the fact that in the Aramaic subscriptions the distinction is made: the guardian of a woman is called אדון = κύριος,[10] as in *P.Yadin* 15 line 37: יהודה בר כתושין אדון בבתה,[11] and in *P.Yadin* 22 line 34: יוחנא בר מכותא אדונה כתבת,[12] whereas for the guardian of the minor the Aramaic borrowed the Greek term ἐπίτροπος: אפטרפא, as in *P.Yadin* 20 line 41: בסא בר ישוע אפט<ר>פא דיתמ<י>א.[13] Judah son of Eleazar Khthousion is attested for the first time as Babatha's husband in *P.Yadin* 17 of 21 February 128. We do not know if he was already married to her at the time that *P.Yadin* 15 was written, i. e. October 125.[14] However, even if he were married to her by then, Yoḥana son of Makhoutha of *P.Yadin* 22 is certainly not married to her at the time. Thus אדון cannot mean 'husband' but must stand for κύριος. The distinction between אדון and אפטרפא in the Aramaic subscriptions is all the more striking since as I pointed out above the guardian of a woman is absent from the Semitic documents.

It was, therefore, suggested with great plausibility by the late Hans Julius Wolff that the use of a single term for the two kinds of guardians is due to the influence of the Roman legal system, where at least originally no legal distinction existed between the guardian of a minor and that of a woman, and, consequently, the same term, *tutor*, was used for both. Both, if they were not *sui iuris*, were represented by the *tutor*.[15] Why did the local notaries writing in Greek adopt the Roman terminology, when, as we see from the Aramaic subscriptions, they must have been familiar with the term κύριος which they translated by אדון? Again, it was suggested that the notaries copied from the proclamations of the Roman authorities, which demanded the representation of a woman in court by a guardian, and made provision for the nomination of guardians for orphans.[16] The Roman authorities, thinking in Latin, even if writing in Greek, may well have used the term ἐπίτροπος for the two kinds of *tutor*.[17]

---

10 Note אדון i. e. the Hebrew term for κύριος and not מרא, i. e. the Aramaic term. On אדון see Yadin and Greenfield in Lewis, *The Documents from the Bar Kokhba Period in the Cave of Letters. Greek Papyri*, 139, n. 6.

11 'Judah son of Khthousion, Babatha's κύριος.'

12 'Yoḥana son of Makhoutha, her κύριος, wrote this.'

13 'Besa son of Yeshu'a ἐπίτροπος of the orphans.'

14 No date is preserved in *P.Yadin* 10, Babatha's marriage contract: see Yigael Yadin, Jonas C. Greenfield, and Ada Yardeni, "Babatha's Ketubba," *IEJ* 44 (1994): 75–99.

15 Wolff, "Römisches Provinzialrecht in der Provinz Arabia," 796–97; cf. Lewis, *The Documents from the Bar Kokhba Period in the Cave of Letters. Greek Papyri*, 17.

16 These are likely to have been mentioned in the provincial edict.

17 "Es scheint nicht einmal undenkbar, dass die römische Provinzialregierung selbst in griechisch herausgebrachten, aber römische gedachten, wenn nicht geradezu aus dem Lateinischen

Hans Julius Wolff in his pioneer study of the legal system in the documents from the Judaean Desert could not know that the confusion in terminology was not unique to documents from the new province of Arabia which came under Roman rule only in 106, and whose accelerated Romanization is so well attested in the archives from Maḥoza/Maḥoz ʻAglatain, but is present also in documents from the province of Judaea, which was under Roman rule from 6 CE. In a cancelled marriage contract of 130 CE written in Aristoboulias, 7 km south of Hebron, a mother who gives her daughter in marriage is assisted by a guardian designated ἐπίτροπος and not κύριος: ἔτους τεσερεσκαιδεκάτου̣ Αὐ̣τ̣[ο]κράτ̣ο̣ρ̣ος Τ̣ρ̣α̣ι̣[ανοῦ Ἁδριανοῦ Καίσαρος Σεβαστοῦ ἐπὶ ὑπά]τω̣ν Μάρκου Φλα<ου>ι̣ου Ἄπρ̣ου κ̣αὶ Κο̣ίν̣τ{ι}ου Φαβί̣ο̣υ̣ [Κατουλλίνου *c.19 letters*] ἐν Ἀριστοβουλιάδι τῆς Ζε̣ι̣φη̣νῆς ἐξέδετο Σελα .ε[*c.30 letters*] δι̣ὰ̣ Βορκ . . Αγ̣λ̣α ἐπ̣ιτρόπ̣[ου] α̣ὐτῆς τοῦδε τοῦ πράγμ̣α̣[τος χάριν].[18] The absence of the ἐπίτροπος of a woman in *P.Mur* 115, a contract of remarriage from Judaea, written in 124 CE, might be explained by the role of the bride in this contract in contrast to that of the mother, in *XḤev/Se gr* 69: the latter is the subject of the *homologia* (see below).

The person who is often found signing for the woman in the Semitic documents from the Judaean Desert must be carefully distinguished from the ἐπίτροπος. This is the subscriber, designated in the Egyptian papyri by the term ὑπογραφεύς[19] and in one of the Greek papyri from the Judaean Desert by the term χειροχρήστης:]λ̣ο̣ς Λειουου ὄμνυ̣μι τύχην Κυρίου Καίσ̣α̣ρος κ[α]λῇ πίστει ἀπογεγράφθαι ὡς προγέγραπται μηθὲν ὑποστειλάμενος. ἐ̣[γράφη διὰ] χειροχρήστου Οναινου Σααδαλλου.[20] The latter term χειροχρήστης is revealing of the true function of this person: he lends his hand by signing for someone who is legally competent to do so, but who happens to be illiterate (or otherwise incapable of writing), when a subscription and/or a signature in his or her own hand is required to render a document valid. No technical term exists for this person

übersetzten, Verlautbarungen beide Arten der Tutel in dieser vom Standpunkt der griechischen Sprache her anfechtbaren Weise gleich benannt hatte," Wolff, "Römisches Provinzialrecht in der Provinz Arabia," 796; see also his comments there on the ἐπίτροπος τοῦδε τοῦ πράγμαστος.

18 'In the fourteenth year of the Emperor Tra[jan Hadrian Caesar Augustus, in the consulship of Marcus Flavius Aper and Quintus Fabius [Catullinus ...] in Aristoboulias of the Zeiphênê. Sela.e[...] gave in marriage [her daughter (?) Selampious ...] through Bork. Agla, her guardian for this matter [...],' *XḤev/Se gr* 69 lines 1–4.

19 See Herbert C. Youtie, "ὑπογραφεύς: The Social Impact of Illiteracy in Graeco-Roman Egypt," *ZPE* 17 (1975): 201–21.

20 'X son of Levi, swear by the *tyche* of the Lord Caesar that I have in good faith registered as written above, concealing nothing. W[ritten by] the *chirocrista* Onainos son of Sa'adallos,' *XḤev/Se gr* 61 lines 1–4.

in the Semitic documents,[21] but the graphic notion of borrowing someone else's hand is present in the Aramaic *XḤev/Se ar* 13, where a woman called Shlamzion daughter of Yehosef renounces all claims against her former husband. She is said to have 'borrowed the hand of Mattat so[n] of Shim'on, who wrote what she said': שלמצין ברת יהוסף ... שאלה כתב מֿתֿת ב[ר] שמעון מֿמרא. The subscriber is present also in documents in which the principal is a man, probably in cases of illiteracy, as is the case in *XḤev/Se gr* 61.[22]

The ἐπίτροπος could fulfill the function of the subscriber at the same time as he served as an ἐπίτροπος, in which case the verbs γράφω or ὑπογράφω are used to describe his action. Thus Judah son of Eleazar Khthousion is both an ἐπίτροπος and a subscriber in Babatha's land declaration: Ἰ̣ουδάνης Ἐ̣λ̣αζάρ̣ο̣υ̣ ἐπιτρ̣ό̣πευ[σ]α̣ καὶ ἔγραψα ὑπὲρ αὐτῆς (*P.Yadin* 16 lines 35–36), as is Iohannes son of Makhoutha in Babatha's deed of sale: [δι]ὰ̣ ἐ[πιτρ]ό̣που αὐτῆς καὶ ὑπογράφοντος Ἰωαανης Μαχχουθας τῆς αὐ[τῆ]ς Μαωζα<ς> (*P.Yadin* 22 lines 28–29), and Babelis son of Menaḥem in Babatha's receipt: Βα̣βαθας Σίμω̣[ν]ος, συνπαρόντος αὐτῇ [ἐπιτρόπου] κ[α]ὶ̣ ὑπὲρ αὐτῆς ὑπογράφοντος Βα̣βελ̣ι̣[ς] Μαναήμου (*P.Yadin* 27 lines 4–5).[23] And yet the ἐπίτροπος is to be distinguished from the subscriber, as is apparent in *P.Yadin* 15 where both an ἐπίτροπος and a subscriber take part in the legal proceedings. This is a case of deposition against the guardians of Babatha's son. Babatha's guardian for this matter, Judah son of Eleazar Khthousion, did not write the subscription for her; instead, Eleazar son of Eleazar wrote it for her, since her illiteracy prevented her from doing it herself: [ἐμαρ]τυροποιήσατο ἡ Βαβαθα ὡς προγέγραπται διὰ ἐπιτρόπου αὐτῆς τοῦδε τοῦ πράγματ[ος Ἰούδου Χ]θουσίωνος ὃς παρὼν ὑπέγραψεν. (second hand) Βαβαθας Σίμωνος ἐμαρτυροποιησάμη<ν> κα̣τ̣ὰ Ἰωάνου Ἐγλα Ἀ<βδ>αοβδα Ἐλλουθα ἐπιτρώπων Ἠσους υ<ἱ>ο<ῦ> μου ὀρφανοῦ δι' ἐπιτρόπου μου Ἰούδα Χαθουσ̣ίωνος ἀκο̣λ̣[ο]ύθω̣ς τε̃ς προγεγραμμένες ἐρέσασιν.

21 Nor does the term ὑπογραφεύς appear in the Greek papyri from the Judaean Desert, only the verb, see *P.Yadin* 22 line 29 and *P.Yadin* 27 line 5, quoted in the text. See Hannah M. Cotton, "Subscriptions and Signatures in the Papyri from the Judaean Desert: The χειροχρήστης," *JJP* 25 (1995): 29–40 [above, pp. 115–25].

22 Cf. Yardeni's new reading of *P.Mur* 18 lines 9–10: [זכ]ריה בר יהוח[נן ע]ל נפשה [כת]ב יהוסף ב[ר]◦ מֿמֿרֿהֿ. Ada Yardeni, *Textbook of Aramaic, Hebrew and Nabataean Documentary Texts from the Judaean Desert and Related Material*, Vol. I (Jerusalem: The Hebrew University Press, 2000), 15 (Hebrew; for English see Vol. II, 19).

23 Likewise in the verso of *XḤev/Se gr* 64 the first signature, of which only traces are left, is likely to have been that of the mother, Salome Gropte, the donor, although she did not write it herself. The second signature is probably that of her husband and guardian, Joseph son of Shim'on, who signed for her – the traces of ink are compatible with his name, see Cotton and Yardeni, *Aramaic, Hebrew, and Greek Documentary Texts from Naḥal Ḥever and Other Sites*, 220 ad *XḤev/Se gr* 64 lines 42–43.

Ἐλεάζαρος Ἐλεαζάρ̣ου ἔγραψα ὑπὲρ αὐτῆς ἐρωτηθεὶς διὰ τὸ αὐτ̣ης μὴ ε<ὶ>δένα<ι> γράμματα.[24]

It seems clear that διὰ τὸ αὐτ̣ης μὴ ε<ὶ>δένα<ι> γράμματα, 'because she did not know her letters' in Babatha's case, does not mean that she could not write Greek, but that she was illiterate in any language. A Greek subscription was not required: Judah son of Eleazar, her guardian, wrote his own subscription in Aramaic: יהודה בר כתושין אדון בבתה בקמי השרת בבתה ככל די על כתב יהודה כתבה.[25] If Judah son of Eleazar did not write a subscription for Babatha, although he was her guardian and could write Aramaic, but Eleazar son of Eleazar did, then we must look for some legal reason: evidently she was legally competent to do so, but incapable of doing so because of her illiteracy. This is where a subscriber, and not a guardian, must have been used.

What was then the function of the guardian of a woman? As observed above the low profile kept by the guardian of a woman in the Greek documents from the Judaean Desert is conspicuous. Nevertheless, he seems to be taking a more active part in those contracts in which the woman is the one in whose name the *homologia* is written or another kind of legal obligation is undertaken. Here, with one exception[26] we find the formula διὰ ἐπιτρόπου αὐτῆς, that is 'through her ἐπίτροπος.' Thus a mother gives her daughter in marriage δι̣ὰ̣ Βορκ. Ἀγ̣λ̣α ἐπ̣ιτρόπ̣[ου] α̣ὐτῆς τοῦδε τοῦ πράγμ̣α̣[τος χάριν].[27] Babatha summons Iohannes son of Joseph, her son's guardian, to appear before the governor (παρ̣ήγγ̣ε̣ι̣[λεν Βαβαθα Σίμωνος τοῦ Μανα]ήμου): διὰ ἐπιτρόπου αὐ̣τ̣[ῆς τ]ο̣ῦ̣δε τοῦ πράγμ̣[ατος] Ἰούδα Χθουσίωνος etc. (*P.Yadin* 14 lines 22–23). Similarly Babatha writes a deposition against her son's guardians 'through her guardian for that matter, Judah son of Khthousion, who was present and subscribed': [ἐμαρ]τυροποιήσατο ἡ Βαβαθα ὡς προγέγραπται διὰ ἐπιτρόπου αὐτῆς τοῦδε τοῦ πράγματ[ος Ἰούδου Χ]θουσίωνος ὃς παρὼν ὑπέγραψεν (*P.Yadin* 15 lines 31–32). On the occasion of selling the date crop of three date groves to Shim'on son of Yeshu'a, Babatha uses

---

24 'Babatha deposed as aforestated through her guardian for this matter, Judah son of Khthousion, who was present and subscribed, [second hand] I, Babatha daughter of Shim'on, have deposed through my guardian Judah son of Khthousion against John son of Eglas and 'Abdoöbdas son of Ellouthas, guardians of my orphan son Jesus, according to the aforestated conditions. I, Eleazar son of Eleazar, wrote for her by request, because of her being illiterate,' lines 31–35.

25 'Judah son of Khthousion lord of Babatha: in my presence Babatha confirmed all that is written above. Judah wrote this,' *P.Yadin* 15, line 37.

26 The exception is *P.Yadin* 20, where Besas son of Yeshu'a and Julia Crispina concede a courtyard in Ein Gedi to Shelamṣion, the daughter of Babatha's second husband, who is said to act through her guardian: Σελαμσιοῦ Ἰούδου Ἡνγαδηνῇ διὰ ἐπιτρόπου αὐτῆς Ἰουδᾶς ὃς κ̣α̣ὶ Κινβε̣ρ̣ Ἀ̣γ̣α̣ν̣[ο̣]υ Ἡ̣γ[γ]αδ̣ηνοῦ τ̣ο̣ῦ̣δ̣ε̣ τοῦ πράγματος χάριν, lines 25–27 = lines 5–6.

27 'Through Bork., her *epitropos* for that matter,' *XḤev/Se gr* 69 line 4.

Iohannes son of Makhoutha as guardian and subscriber: [δι]ạ̀ ἐ[πιτρ]ọ́που αὐτῆς καὶ ὑπογράφοντος Ἰωαανης Μαχχουθας: 'through her ἐπίτροπος who also subscribed Iohannes son of Makhouthas' (*P.Yadin* 22 lines 28–29). Babatha summons Julia Crispina to come before the governor in Rabbath-Moab: 'through her *epitropos*, Maras son of Abdalgas from Petra (*P.Yadin* 25 lines 46–47): διὰ ἐπ̣ι̣τ̣ρ̣ό̣π̣ου ạὐτῆς Μαρας Ἀβ[δ]αλγου Πετρạῖος. Finally Babatha acknowledges the receipt of maintenance money for her orphaned son through her ἐπίτροπος, Babelis son of Menaḥem: [διὰ ἐπιτ]ρ̣ό̣π̣ου αὐτῆς Βαβελις Μαναημου (*P.Yadin* 27 line 18).

In contrast, in those contracts in which the woman is the recipient of an *homologia* – in all but one of the cases[28] – we have merely the formula recording the presence of the ἐπίτροπος. Thus in *P.Yadin* 17, where Judah son of Eleazar Khthousion, Babatha's second husband, acknowledges that he has received 300 *denarii* from her as a deposit to be paid on demand, only the presence of the *epitropos* is recorded: ὡμολογήσατο Ἰούδας Ἐλεα]ζάρου τ̣οῦ καὶ Χθουσίω̣ν̣[ο]ς Α̣[ἰνγα]δ̣[ηνὸς] πρὸς Βαβ̣α̣θαν Σ̣ίμ̣ω̣νος ἰδίαν γυναῖκα αὐτ̣[ο]ῦ̣, συ̣ναρ̣[ό]ντ̣ο̣ς ạὐτῆς ẹ̀[πιτρόπ]ο̣υ̣ τοῦδε τοῦ πράγματος χάριν Ἰακώβ[ο]υ̣ Ἰησοῦ (lines 21–24).[29] A similar case is that of *XḤev/Se gr* 65 (= *P.Yadin* 37): in this marriage contract the husband acknowledges the receipt of a dowry which transforms the union from an unwritten marriage (ἄγραφος γάμος) into a written marriage (ἔγγραφος γάμος). This is one of the reasons for restoring the text in the lacuna in lines 14–15 so as to record simply the presence of the ἐπίτροπος: [συμπαρόντος *c.8 letters*] Μα[ναημο]υ̣ ἐπιτρόπου τῆ[ς αὐ]τ̣ῆς Κομαΐσης (lines 14–15).[30]

It should be pointed out that in the last two cases the ἐπίτροπος of the woman is not her husband, for the obvious reason that *P.Yadin* 17 and *XḤev/Se gr* 65 involve the husband and wife as the two opposing parties to a contract creating a state of obligation between them.[31]

The opposite rule, however, does not seem to hold: the formula διὰ τοῦ ἐπιτρόπου αὐτῆς 'through her ἐπίτροπος' does not always occur in contracts in which the woman is the one in whose name the *homologia* is written or another kind of legal obligation is undertaken; here too, the mere presence of the *epitropos* can be recorded. In *P.Yadin* 16 Babatha declares her lands in the census held in the province of Arabia by its governor in 127, recording that her ἐπίτροπος, her second

28 *P.Yadin* 20, see above n. 26.

29 The συμπαρόντος αὐτῇ ἐπιτρόπου may be considered the equivalent of μετὰ κυρίου of the Egyptian papyri, see Rupprecht, "Zur Frage der Frauentutel im römischen Ägypten," 98 and n. 47 there.

30 'X son of Menaḥem, the ἐπίτροπος of the above-mentioned Komaïse, was present with her.'

31 See comments ad *XḤev/Se gr* 65 lines 14–15 in Cotton and Yardeni, *Aramaic, Hebrew, and Greek Documentary Texts from Naḥal Ḥever and Other Sites*, 235–37.

husband Judah son of Eleazar, is present with her: Βαβθα Σίμωνος Μαωζηνὴ τῆς Ζοαρηνῆς περιμέτρου Πέτρας, οἰκοῦσα ἐν ἰδίοις ἐν αὐτῇ Μαωζᾳ, ἀπογράφομαι ἃ κέκτημαι, συνπαρόντος μοι ἐπιτρόπου Ἰουδάνου Ἐλαζάρου κώμης Αἰνγαδδῶν περὶ Ἱερειχοῦντα τῆς Ἰουδαίας οἰκοῦντος ἐν ἰδίοις ἐν αὐτῇ Μαωζᾳ.[32] In *XḤev/Se gr* 64, the mother, Salome Gropte, writes a deed of gift in favour of her daughter, Salome Komaïse, with her guardian merely recorded as present: Σα[λω]μ̣η̣ ἡ καὶ Γροπτη Μαναημου συνπαρ̣ό̣ν̣τ̣ο̣ς α̣ὐ̣τ̣[ῆ̣ ἐ]πιτρόπ̣ο̣[υ τοῦδε τοῦ πρά]γ̣μ̣α̣τ̣ο̣ς χάριν Ιωσηπου Σιμ̣ω̣ν̣ο̣ς [ἀ]νὴρ αὐτῆς.[33]

The presence of the formula διὰ ἐπιτρόπου αὐτῆς in a case where the woman is not the subject of the *homologia*, but the receiver of one,[34] combined with its absence in contracts in which she is the one in whose name the *homologia* is written casts doubt on the attempt to draw a legal distinction between διὰ ἐπιτρόπου αὐτῆς and συμπαρόντος αὐτῇ ἐπιτρόπου; the two formulae might have been used interchangeably. If so, this further accentuates the minor role played by the guardian of a woman in these documents.[35]

Furthermore, there are documents where a woman is involved, but no ἐπίτροπος accompanies her: in *P.Yadin* 19 Shlamzion receives a gift from her father; in *P.Yadin* 21 Shim'on son of Yeshu'a acknowledges purchase of a date crop from Babatha; in *P.Yadin* 23 Babatha receives a summons from Besas son of Eleazar to appear before the governor's court; in *P.Yadin* 24 Besas son of Eleazar challenges Babatha to prove that she is entitled to the date groves of her late husband which she has seized; in *P.Yadin* 26 Babatha and Miriam summon each other to appear before the governor's court; in *XḤev/Se gr* 63 Salome Grapte

---

32 'I, Babtha daughter of Simon, of Maḥoza in the Zoarene [district] of the Petra administrative region, domiciled in my own private property in the Maḥoza, register what I possess, present with me as my guardian being Judah son of Elazar, of the village of En-Gedi in the district of Jericho in Judaea, domiciled in his own private property in the said Maḥoza ...' lines 13–17.

33 'Salome who is also known as Gropte, present with her her ἐπίτροπος for this matter, Josephus son of Shim'on, her husband,' lines 3–5.

34 I.e. *P.Yadin* 20 (see above, n. 26) lines 6–7 = line 27: ὁμολογοῦμεν̣ συνκεχωρηκέναι σοι ἐξ ὑπαρχόντων Ἐλεαζάρου τοῦ καὶ Χθουσίωνος τοῦ̣ Ἰ̣ο̣ύ̣δ̣ο̣υ πάπ̣ου σου αὐλὴν σὺν παντὶ δικαιοις αὐτῆς ... etc.

35 Further proof may be 'the rapid turnover' of ἐπίτροποι in the documents; in addition to Judah son of Eleazar Khthousion, her second husband, Babatha is represented by no less than four different ἐπίτροποι between 128 and 132: Jacob son of Yeshu'a (*P.Yadin* 17), Yoḥana son of Makhoutha (*P.Yadin* 22), Maras son of Abdaglos of Petra, a Nabataean (*P.Yadin* 25) and Babelis son of Menaḥem (*P.Yadin* 27). None of them is said to be related to her; see Émile Puech, "Présence arabe dans les manuscrits de 'La grotte aux lettres' du Wadi Khabra," in *Présence arabe dans le Croissant fertile avant l'Hégire. Actes de la Table ronde internationale organisée par l'Unité de Recherche Associée 1062 du CNRS, Études sémitiques au Collège de France, le 13 novembre 1993*, ed. Hélène Lozachmeur (Paris: Éditions Recherche sur les Civilisations, 1995), 37–46.

receives a renunciation of claims from her daughter Salome Komaïse; in *XḤev/Se gr* 64 Salome Komaïse receives a deed of gift from her mother Salome Grapte; finally in *P.Mur* 115 Elaios son of Shim'on acknowledges that he has been paid the two hundred *drachmae* of dowry by Salome son of Iohannes Galgoula: ὡμολό[γη]-σεν ὁ αὐτὸς Ἐλαῖος Σίμωνος ἠριθμ[ῆσθαι] [*c.34 letters*] π[ρογε]γρ̣αμμ[έναι] σ̅ ε̣ἰ̣ς λόγον προικὸς παρὰ Σαλ̣ώμης Ἰωάν̣[ο]υ̣ Γαλγ̣ο̣[υλ]ᾶ̣, lines 6–7.[36] In none of these cases is there an ἐπίτροπος present with the woman.

To conclude the argument so far: in the majority of cases where the woman is the one in whose name the *homologia* is written or another kind of legal obligation is undertaken, she is said to be acting 'through her ἐπίτροπος' (διὰ τοῦ ἐπιτρόπου αὐτῆς), but sometimes even here his presence is merely recorded (συμπαρόντος αὐτῇ ἐπιτρόπου), as it is in transactions in which the woman is not the one in whose name the *homologia* is written or another kind of legal engagement is undertaken. And sometimes in such cases no ἐπίτροπος appears at all. There is certainly no question of the ἐπίτροπος, who is normally her husband except in the cases in which he is himself one of the parties to the transaction, managing the woman's property; and there is no doubt at all that women could own property and dispose of it as they wished.

In view of the conspicuous passivity of the ἐπίτροπος of a woman in the Greek documents, it would seem that his absence from the Semitic documents is just a matter of form and procedure required by the courts for which the Greek contracts were intended. Which courts are these? One notices that all Greek documents in which a woman appears with her guardian, both in Arabia and in Judaea, were written under Roman rule, and, as suggested above, under the influence of Roman law. Does the presence of an ἐπίτροπος of a woman show incontrovertibly that the Greek documents were intended for a Roman court of law, and his absence from the Semitic documents that they were intended for other courts? In order to claim this we should have to prove that the Semitic documents too were written under Roman rule. Unfortunately the nature of the evidence hampers us in this attempt: 1) in some of the documents the date is missing;[37] 2) others are too lacunose for

---

36 In *XḤev/Se gr* 63, where the daughter renounces her rights vis-à-vis her mother, we could have expected the formula διὰ τοῦ ἐπιτρόπου αὐτῆς 'through her ἐπίτροπος.' However, this formula fails to fill the entire space in the lacuna in line 1, and the longer formula which records the presence of the ἐπίτροπος has to be restored there: [ἐξωμολο]γ̣ήσατο καὶ συνεγρ[άψατο Σαλ]ωμη Λησυει τ̣ο̣υ̣[. . . συμπαρόντος αὐτῇ ἐπιτρόπου *c.7 letters*]υ̣ Σιμωνος ἀνδρὸς α[ὐτῆ]ς τοῦδε τοῦ { . . }π̣ρ̣[άγματος χάριν πρὸς Σαλωμην τὴν καὶ Γραπτ]η̣ν Μαναημο[υ]: '[Sal]ome daughter of Levi ... [present with her as her guardian for the purpose] of this matter, her husband [Sammou]os(?) son of Shim'on – [acknow]ledged and agreed in w[riting], vis-à-vis Salome also (called) [Grapt]e daughter of Menaḥem,' lines 1–2.

37 *P.Mur* 20 (marriage contract); *XḤev/Se ar* 50 + *P.Mur* 26 (deed of sale).

us to know if an ἐπίτροπος was present there;[38] 3) the absence of the ἐπίτροπος in Semitic documents dated to the Roman period may be due to the role played by the woman in them: *P.Mur* 19 (18 October 111 CE) is a writ of divorce given to the wife by her husband; *P.Mur* 20 (117 CE) is a marriage contract, and in fact an acknowledgement by the husband of the debt of the *ketubba*; *XḤev/Se ar* 12 (30 January 131) is a receipt given to Salome Komaïse by the tax or rent collectors – all three documents might not have called for the presence of an ἐπίτροπος even under Roman rule; 4) other Semitic documents in which a woman takes part in the proceedings were not written under Roman rule: the Nabataean *P.Yadin* 1 (94 CE) and *P.Yadin* 2–3 (99 CE), *XḤev/Se nab* 2 (ca. 100 CE) were written under Nabataean rule; *P.Mur* 29 (133 CE), *P.Mur* 30 (135 CE), *XḤev/Se ar* 7 (135 CE), *XḤev/Se ar* 8a (134 or 135 CE) and *XḤev/Se ar* 13 (134 CE) were all written during the Bar Kokhba revolt. The dating by the year of the revolt shows clearly that the contractors recognized the rebels as the only legitimate government. In some of these documents we find the women acting together with their husbands: in *XḤev/Se ar* 7 the wife is selling property together with her husband; in *P.Mur* 30 and *XḤev/Se ar* 8a (perhaps also *P.Mur* 29) the wife waives all claims on the property sold by her husband, presumably because it guaranteed the return of her *ketubba* or dowry. Consequently, it could be claimed that the absence of a guardian may well be due to the fact that he would be superfluous, even under Roman legal procedures.

A single document belonging to the last-mentioned group shows a woman unaccompanied by an ἐπίτροπος as the principal to an action: *XḤev/Se ar* 13 of 134 CE is a deed of renunciation of all claims on the wife's part after a divorce.[39] Three times, in different variations, the phrase 'I have no claim against you' recurs. In lines 8–9 we find: [מ]לת מדעה ל[א] איתי לי עמך א[נת] אלעזר על צבת כל מדעם. We know from *XḤev/Se gr* 63, a deed of renunciation of all claims, which repeats twice or three times the same phrasing in Greek: μηδένα λόγον ἔχειν πρὸς αὐτήν (lines 4, 8, 11), that under Roman rule such a deed required the presence of the ἐπίτροπος of a woman.[40] It seems obvious that under Bar Kokhba's rule a woman did not need an ἐπίτροπος. What remains obscure is whether a similar deed, although written in Aramaic, if written under Roman rule, would have required the presence of an ἐπίτροπος.

---

38 *XḤev/Se ar* 11 (marriage contract, perhaps of 113/4 CE).

39 Contra Tal Ilan, "On a Newly Published Divorce Bill from the Judaean Desert," *Harv. Theol. Rev.* 89 (1996): 195–202, this document is not a writ of divorce, even though it refers to such an instrument.

40 See Cotton and Yardeni, *Aramaic, Hebrew, and Greek Documentary Texts from Naḥal Ḥever and Other Sites*, 195–96 (Introduction to *XḤev/Se gr* 63).

The Law of Succession in the Documents from the Judaean Desert Again

In a series of articles written over the last four years I have claimed that the law of succession reflected in the documents from the Judaean Desert seems not to have been in harmony with Jewish law on the subject.[1] I have now come to believe that there are considerations and circumstances, not taken into account before, which may undermine, or at least weaken, this claim – they may even remove the apparent discrepancy between the law of the papyri and Jewish law.

Jewish law, both biblical and rabbinic, preferred the claims of children, whatever their sex, to those of the man's brother or of his brother's children. We read in Numbers 27:8: 'When a man dies leaving no son, his patrimony shall pass to his daughter. If he has no daughter, you shall give it to his brothers'; and again in *mBaba Bathra* 8.2: 'The son precedes the daughter, and all the son's offspring precede the daughter; the daughter precedes the brothers (of the deceased).'

My argument that the law of the papyri differed from Jewish law of succession was based – perhaps impressionistically – on the indirect evidence of three deeds of gift[2] in the archives from Maḥoza/Maḥoz 'Aglatain[3] and on the direct evidence

1 Hannah M. Cotton and Jonas C. Greenfield, "Babatha's Property and the Law of Succession in the Babatha Archive," *ZPE* 104 (1994): 211–24; Hannah M. Cotton, "Deeds of Gift and the Law of Succession in the Papyri from the Judean Desert," *Eretz Israel* 25 (1996): 410–15 (Hebrew). For a revised English version see Hannah M. Cotton, "Deeds of Gift and the Law of Succession in Archives from the Judaean Desert," in *Akten des 21. Internationalen Papyrologenkongresses, Berlin, 13–19.8.1995*, ed. Barbara Kramer et al., Vol. I (Stuttgart – Leipzig: Teubner, 1997), 179–88.

2 1) *P.Yadin* 7 published by Yigael Yadin, Jonas C. Greenfield, and Ada Yardeni, "A Deed of Gift in Aramaic Found in Naḥal Ḥever: Papyrus Yadin 7," *Eretz Israel* 25 (1996): 383–403 (Hebrew); 2) *P.Yadin* 19 published in Naphtali Lewis, *The Documents from the Bar Kokhba Period in the Cave of Letters. Greek Papyri* (with Aramaic and Nabatean Signatures and Subscriptions, edited by Y. Yadin and J.C. Greenfield) (Jerusalem: IES, 1989) (henceforth Lewis, *Documents*); 3) *XḤev/Se gr* 64 published in Hannah M. Cotton and Ada Yardeni, *Aramaic, Hebrew, and Greek Documentary Texts from Naḥal Ḥever and Other Sites*, Discoveries in the Judaean Desert XXVII (Oxford: Clarendon Press, 1997) (henceforth Cotton and Yardeni). All *P.Yadin* mentioned in this article were published in Lewis, *Documents* unless otherwise indicated. All *XḤev/Se gr* were published in Cotton and Yardeni.

3 See Hannah M. Cotton and Jonas C. Greenfield, "Babatha's Patria: Maḥoza, Maḥoz 'Eglatain and Ẓo'ar," *ZPE* 107 (1995): 126–34 [above, pp. 275–83].

Article note: First published in *SCI* 17 (1998): 115–123, with the following note: this paper is dedicated to the memory of Abraham Wasserstein, to whose warning 'Hold your horses' I never paid enough attention. I thank Ranon Katzoff for reading this paper and for making valuable suggestions for improvement.

https://doi.org/10.1515/9783110770438-028

of *P.Yadin* 23, 24 and 25 of 130 and 131 CE. Let me start with the first. Two facts stand out as soon as one reads the three deeds of gift: 1) the beneficiaries of the gifts in all these documents are wives or daughters; 2) in all three cases there is no sign of a male heir whose existence might have called forth the writing of the deed of gift. These two facts suggested to me that the law of succession sidestepped wives and daughters, even in the absence of a male heir, and the deed of gift came to mitigate the rigour of rules of succession which were prejudicial to women. The deed of gift was the only way in which property could devolve on women in this society. To use Roman legal terminology: wives and daughters were not the *sui heredes* of their husbands and fathers. I am not suggesting that the mere existence of deeds of gift in favour of daughters and wives is the proof that without such legal instruments the property would not have devolved on them, even when there were no male heirs. But I did think that the existence of such instruments creates a strong presumption that this was so. The writing of a deed of gift, like the writing of a will and testament, was intended to emend the legal state otherwise created by the law of succession. In denying the claims of the wife to her husband's property this law seems to have been not unlike the Jewish law of succession. It differs from Jewish law in preferring the claims of the man's brother or his brother's children to those of the daughter.

The force of the foregoing conclusions is weakened by the following two considerations:[4]

1) There could be other reasons to write a will or a deed of gift – for the latter amounts to the same thing as a will. For example a second marriage of the father or the mother might lead to it. Judah son of Eleazar was married to Babatha[5] when he wrote *P.Yadin* 19 in favour of his daughter from a previous marriage, Shelamzion,[6] and Salome Grapte (or Gropte) was married to Joseph son of Shim'on when she wrote *XḤev/Se gr* 64 in favour of Salome Komaïse, her daughter from her marriage to Levi.[7] It could be argued, therefore, that they wrote deeds of gift in favour of their daughters in anticipation of the birth of a male child who would deprive the daughter of their previous marriage of her right to inherit.

2) At least in one instance, and perhaps also in two, the occasion for the bestowal of property in a deed of gift seems to have been the marriage of the daughter. Thus Judah son of Eleazar writes the deed of gift *P.Yadin* 19 on 16 April

4 These were but briefly mentioned in previous studies.

5 Between 125 and 128 CE; the marriage contract *P.Yadin* 10 was published by Yigael Yadin, Jonas C. Greenfield, and Ada Yardeni, "Babatha's Ketubba," *IEJ* 44 (1994): 75–99.

6 Nowhere in the archive is it said that she is the daughter of Miriam daughter of Beianos, his other (or previous) wife; see family tree at the end.

7 Levi was dead by 127 CE, see *XḤev/Se gr* 63 in Cotton and Yardeni.

128, eleven days after Shelamzion's marriage to Judah Kimber, attested in *P.Yadin* 18 written on 5 April 128. Likewise, Salome Grapte (Gropte) may have written *XḤev/Se gr* 64 of 9 November 129 CE in favour of her daughter, Salome Komaïse, when the latter started her *agraphos gamos* with Yeshua' son of Menaḥem, which the couple turned into an *engraphos gamos* only on 7 August 131.[8] Like the property given *en prosphora* in Egypt, the property given in a deed of gift was meant for immediate use, to help the new household;[9] and, as in the case of the *prosphora*, the daughter gains absolute ownership over this property.[10] In other words the deed of gift does not imply in itself that daughters could not inherit; it simply makes the devolution of property immediate. Thus deeds of gift need tell us nothing about the law of succession.

What direct evidence is there for the assertion that a daughter did not have the right to inherit from her father when in competition with sons of her father's brother?

I believed that direct evidence could be found in *P.Yadin* 23, 24 where, after the demise of Judah son of Eleazar (Babatha's second husband), the guardian of the children of his dead brother (Yeshua'), Besas son of Judah, threatens Babatha that he will register three date orchards of her dead husband in Maḥoza in the nephews' name, unless she produces written evidence that she has a right to them:[11]

> I, therefore, summon you to disclose to me what document you possess as proof (π̣ο̣[ί]ῳ [δ]ι̣κα̣[ι]ώ̣μα̣τ̣ι̣) that you have the right to hold the said entities. If you refuse to disclose know that I am registering them (ἀπογράφο[μαι]) in the ἀπογραφή in the name of the said orphans (*P.Yadin* 24 lines 6–9).[12]

8 The unwritten marriage, ἄγραφος γάμος, was, as its name implies, a marriage without a contract: it did not require a contract in order to become valid. Its legal validity was no different from that of the written marriage, the ἔνγραφος γάμος; see Hans Julius Wolff, *Written and Unwritten Marriages in Hellenistic and Post-Classical Roman Law* (Haverford: American Philological Association, 1939), 66–7; see Cotton and Yardeni's introduction to *XḤev/Se gr* 65 on Salome Komaïse daughter of Levi's marriage.

9 See Jane Rowlandson, *Landowners and Tenants in Roman Egypt* (Oxford: Oxford University Press, 1996), 164.

10 The dowry or *ketubba* recorded in the documents, whether written in Greek or in Aramaic, consists exclusively of valuables (jewellery and clothes) or sums of money; real property is never recorded as part of the dowry.

11 παρανγέλλω σοι ἀποδ̣ῖξ̣ε̣ μ̣[οι π]ο̣[ί]ῳ δ̣ι̣κ̣α̣ι̣ώματι διακ̣[ρ]α̣τ̣ῖ̣ς τὰ αὐτὰ εἴδη. ε̣ἰ̣ δ̣ὲ̣ ἀ̣π̣ι̣[θῖς] [τοῦ μὴ ἀ]π̣ο̣δ̣ε̣ῖ̣ξαι [γί]γωσκε ὅτι ἀπογράφο[μαι] α̣ὐ̣τ̣ὰ̣ [ἐν τῇ *c.8 letters* ἀπο]γ̣ρ̣α[φῇ ἐ]π' ὀνόματος τῶν αὐτ̣ῶ̣ν̣ [ὀρ]φ̣[ανῶν *? letters*].

12 See Cotton, "Deeds of Gift and the Law of Succession in Archives from the Judaean Desert," 184 on the meaning of ἀπογραφή, ἀπογράφομαι and δικαίωμα in this context.

In *P.Yadin* 25 Iulia Crispina, who describes herself as the *episcopos* of the same orphans, insists that Babatha is detaining property which belongs by law to the orphans.[13] It is striking that nothing whatsoever is said about the claims of Judah's own daughter Shelamzion. She was still alive on 19 June 130 (*P.Yadin* 20), five months before Besas charges Babatha with illegal distraint of her late husband's property. Unless we assume that she died between 19 June and 17 November of 130, or that Judah wrote a will in favour of his nephews,[14] we can infer that the law of succession in force at that time (at least among the Jews) in the province of Arabia did not automatically grant a daughter the right to inherit from her father when in competition with sons of her father's brother.[15]

Is this argument unassailable? The legal status of the date groves of *P.Yadin* 23 and 24[16] of November 130 may not have been unambiguous on Judah son of Eleazar's death (by 11 September 130).[17] It is possible that the sons of Eleazar Khthousion,[18] Yeshua' (the orphans' father) and Judah (Shelamzion's father), had not divided their father's property between them after their father's death,[19] but continued to hold them in joint ownership. This was common practice as we learn from the papyri; it has left its mark in the frequency of the locution κληρονόμοι τοῦ δεῖνος to refer to joint owners of real property.[20] Such a situation might last for years.[21] The heirs of Yosef son of Baba – ירתי יוסף בר בבא – found in *P.Yadin* 7 (lines 6, 11 = lines 38, 45) of 120 CE[22] as neighbours to two pieces of land owned by Babatha's father, reappear nine years later in *XḤev/Se gr* 64, line 11 (= lines 32–33)

---

13 *P.Yadin* 25 lines 9–10: ... ὑ̣π̣ạρ̣χ̣ό̣ν̣τ̣ω̣ν̣ τῶν αὐτῶν ὀ̣ρ̣φ̣ạν[ῶ]ν βίᾳ διακρατῖς ἃ οὐκ ἀνῆκέν σοι.

14 An assumption made by Lewis (*Documents*, 107) who suggests that we restore ἐν τῇ διαθήκῃ αὐτοῦ in *P. Yadin* 24, line 6.

15 All this is argued at much greater length in the articles mentioned in n. 1.

16 In fact it is only in *P.Yadin* 24 that the plural appears.

17 See *P.Yadin* 21 lines 8–9: Ἰούδου Χθουσίωνος ἀνδρός σου ἀπογενομένου; cf. *P.Yadin* 22 lines 8–9.

18 See family trees at the end.

19 I assume he was dead by the time of *P.Yadin* 20, see below on *P.Yadin* 20.

20 E.g. *P.Yadin* 16 line 28: γ̣ẹ[ί]τ̣ο̣ν̣ẹ[ς κλ]η̣ρ̣ο̣ν̣ό̣μοι Θησαίου Σαβακạ; *XḤev/Se gr* 64 lines 9–11 (= lines 30–33): ἧς γεί[τ]ωνες ... δυσμῶν κληρογό̣[μ]ο̣ι Αρετας ... βορρᾶ κληρονόμοι Ιωσηπος Βαβα; cf. Hans Kreller, *Erbrechtliche Untersuchungen auf Grund der graeco-aegyptischen Papyrusurkunden* (Leipzig: Teubner, 1919), 63 ff. In *XḤev/Se gr* 62 the declarant, Sammouos son of Shim'on, is one of two brothers holding properties in partnership (μετοχῇ) in Maḥoza. I suppose that as neighbours they could be described as [κληρογό̣μ]ο̣ι Σιμωνος, although they do not make a joint land declaration.

21 Kreller, 65.

22 Above n. 2.

dated to 129 CE, still as a single body of owners: κληρονόμοι Ιωσηπος Βαβα, i.e. the property remained undivided for at least nine years.[23]

I assume that the date groves of *P.Yadin* 23 and 24 are the three date groves mentioned by name in *P.Yadin* 21 and 22,[24] which Babatha distrained after Judah son of Eleazar's death: 'in lieu of my dowry and a debt' (ἀντὶ τῆς προοικός μου καὶ ὀφιλῆς),[25] i.e. for the debt of her *ketubba* money attested as 400 *zuzim* (= 400 *denarii*) in *P.Yadin* 10,[26] and for the three hundred *denarii* which Judah borrowed from her in a deed of deposit (*P.Yadin* 17) on 21 February 128, a few months before the marriage of his daughter Shelamzion.[27] The terms of the marriage contract (*P.Yadin* 10) and the deposit (*P.Yadin* 17) gave her the right of execution upon Judah's possessions everywhere. This 'pledging clause' has been preserved in *P.Yadin* 17:[28]

> γε[ινο]μένης δὲ τῆς πράξεως τῇ αὐτῇ Βαβαθα ἢ τῷ ὑπ<ὲρ> αὐτῆς προφ[έ]ροντι τὴν συνγραφὴν ταύτην ἀπό τε Ἰούδου καὶ τῶν ὑπαρχόντων αὐτοῦ πάντῃ πάντων, ὧν τε ἔχει καὶ ὧν ἂν ἐπικτήσηται κυρίως (lines 33–37 = lines 12–15).

However, Babatha claims that her late husband had registered the date groves in her name:

> ἐπιδὴ ἀπεγράψατο Ἰούδας Ἐλεαζάρο[υ Χθουσίωνος] ἀπογενομενου σου ἀνὴρ ἐπ' ὀνόματός σου ἐν τῇ ἀπ[ο]γραφῇ κήπους φοινικῶνος ἐν Μαωζα (*P.Yadin* 24 lines 4–6).

In other words, notwithstanding the wording of the 'pledging clause' that all of Judah's property was put in lien to pay his debt to Babatha,[29] it seems that specific properties were earmarked to guarantee its return. Babatha's claim to

23 There must have been sound economic reasons for avoiding the parcelling of land into smaller units, but this is not the place to go into these.

24 *P.Yadin* 21 lines 7–12: ὁμολογῶ ἠγορακέναι παρά σου καρπίαν φοινικῶνος κήπων Ἰούδου Χθουσίωνος ἀνδρός σου ἀπογενομένου ἐν Μαωζα λεγόμεναι γανναθ Φερωρα καὶ γανναθ Νικαρκος καὶ ἡ τρίτη λεγομένη τοῦ Μολχαίου, ἃ κατέχις, ὡς λέγις, ἀντὶ τῆς σῆς προοικὸς καὶ φιλῆς; cf. *P.Yadin* 22 lines 7–11.

25 *P.Yadin* 22 line 10; cf. *P.Yadin* 21 lines 9–10.

26 *P.Yadin* 10 line 6 'and I owe you the sum of four hundred *denarii* (*zuzim*) which equal one hundred tetradrachms (*ṣorin*).'

27 Unless ἀντὶ τῆς προοικός μου καὶ ὀφιλῆς is to be construed as hendiadys for 'the debt of my dowry.'

28 It is missing in *P.Yadin* 10 but we know that the 'pledging clause' was a standard feature in contemporary marriage contracts: *P.Mur* 20 line 12, *P.Mur* 115 line 17, *P.Yadin* 18 lines 24–26 (= lines 62–64), *XḤev/Se gr* 65 lines 11–12.

29 Cited above ad n. 28.

have the groves registered in her name as security for her *ketubba* money and the debt seems plausible enough: we have evidence for dowries being secured on specific pieces of property in documents from Egypt, and some evidence that this was practiced elsewhere.[30] The objection that Judah would not have registered in her name property which he, at least formally, shared with his brother, could be met by pointing out that on 6 May 124 he mortgaged a courtyard in Ein Gedi which belonged to his father Eleazar Khthousion as security for a loan which he took from Magonius Valens, a centurion of a detachment of the *Cohors I milliaria Thracum* then stationed in Ein Gedi.[31]

However, the guardians of Judah's nephews may not have known of any consensual agreement between the brothers concerning the date groves in question. This is precisely the reason for Besas son of Judah to demand from Babatha that she produce proof (δικαίωμα) that the groves were registered in her name, as she maintained.[32] Having been appointed to guard the interests of the orphans, Besas need not, at this stage at least, be concerned with Judah's own daughter's claims to these properties. This would fully account for her name not being mentioned in this context, and no inferences should be drawn about the daughter's right of succession.

At first sight *P.Yadin* 20 of 19 June 130 seems to favour my former argument about the law of succession in force in the papyri. There we find the guardians of Judah's nephews conceding a courtyard in Ein Gedi with the rights attached to it to Shelamzion daughter of Judah:

> We acknowledge that we have conceded to you, from the property of Eleazar, also known as Khthousion, son of Judah, your grandfather, a courtyard with all its rights in Ein Gedi and the rooms with it (lines 27–30 = lines 6–10).[33]

Lewis identified that courtyard with the one mentioned in the deed of gift, *P.Yadin* 19.[34] If so, then despite the existence of a deed of gift, Judah's nephews tried to

---

30 E.g. *P.Oxy.* 907 (a will of 276 CE); *P.Bostra* 1; I am grateful to Jean Gascou for providing me with the text of *P.Bostra* 1 before its publication in Gascou, "Unités administratives locales et fonctionnaires romains. Les données des nouveaux papyrus du Moyen Euphrate et d'Arabie," in *Lokale Autonomie und römische Ordnungsmacht in den kaiserzeitlichen Provinzen vom 1. bis 3. Jahrhundert*, ed. Werner Eck (München: Oldenbourg, 1999), 71–74.

31 *P.Yadin* 11 lines 14–16 (= lines 2–4): ὁμ̣ο̣λ̣ο̣γ̣ῶ ἔ̣χειν καὶ ὀφείλειν σοι ἐν δάνει ἀργυρίου Τυρίου δηνάρια ἑξήκοντα, οἵ εἰσι̣ν [σ]τ̣α̣τ̣ῆρες δεκ̣απέντε, ἐπὶ ὑποθήκῃ τῇ ὑπαρχούσῃ αὐλῇ ἐν Ἐνγαδοῖς Ἐλαζάρῳ Χθου̣σιω̣ν̣ο̣ς̣ π̣α̣τρί μο̣υ̣.

32 See *P.Yadin* 24 lines 6–9 quoted in n. 11.

33 ὁμολογοῦμεν ⟦παρα⟧ συγκεχωρηκέναι σ̣[οι ἐξ ὑ]παρχόντων Ἐλεαζάρου τοῦ καὶ Χθουσίωνος Ἰούδο[υ π]ά̣π̣ου σου αὐλὴν σὺν παντὶ δικαιοις αὐτῆς ἐν Ἠνγ̣α̣δ̣ο̣ῖ̣ς καὶ τοὺς σὺν αὔτης οἰκιαι.

34 Lewis, *Documents*, 89.

dispute the validity of the gift, and finally had to concede the cession of his property to his daughter. It could be assumed, therefore, that they were his heirs according to the current law of succession.

However, the identification of the courtyard in *P.Yadin* 20 with the one given to Shelamzion in *P.Yadin* 19 is far from certain. The neighbours are not the same,[35] nor is the original owner: the courtyard in *P.Yadin* 20 formerly belonged to Shelamzion's grandfather, Eleazar Khthousion, not to her father. To maintain Lewis' identification of the courtyard in *P.Yadin* 19 and 20 it could be suggested as above that the two brothers, Judah and Yeshua', had not formally divided their father's property between them, the courtyard had never been registered in Judah's name, and that this was the reason for the nephews' implicit counterclaim: they disputed not the validity of the gift but Judah's legal right to bestow the courtyard. This calls for some ingenuity. It would require still more ingenuity to get rid of the discrepancy between the neighbours of the two courtyards.[36]

But if the courtyard in *P.Yadin* 20 is not the subject of the deed of gift of Judah son of Eleazar to his daughter Shelamzion (*P.Yadin* 19), we no longer need to say that the courtyard in *P.Yadin* 20 passed into Shelamzion's hands through the mediation of a deed of gift by her father. She could have got it directly from her grandfather, either in her father's lifetime or after his death. It is possible of course that the grandfather, Eleazar Khthousion, outlived his son, Judah. It seems more likely though that Shelamzion came into possession of her grandfather's courtyard as a result of her father's recent death (though it is attested for the first time only three months later).[37] As long as Judah was alive the grandfather's property must have remained undivided between uncle and nephews. Furthermore, until then Judah may have served as their guardian, or at least looked after the common property. A similar situation is reflected in the fragmentary *P.Yadin* 5 of 110 CE, the first Greek document from the Babatha archive, where an uncle, Yosef son of Yosef, acknowledges to his nephew, Yeshua' son of Yeshua' (Babatha's first husband) monies and assets on deposit with him:

> I Yosef son of Yosef surnamed Zaboudos, inhabitant of Maḥoza, acknowledge to Yeshua' son of Yeshua' my brother, of the same place, that you have with me a thousand and a hundred and twenty 'blacks' of silver as deposit of all assets of silver, contracts of debt, investment in factory, value of figs, value of wine, value of dates, value of oil and of every manner [of thing] small and large, from everything which was found [to belong] to your father and me,

---

35 Three out of four abutters changed between 16 April 128 and 19 June 130.

36 See in great detail Hannah M. Cotton, "Courtyard(s) in Ein-Gedi: P.Yadin 11, 19 and 20 of the Babatha archive," *ZPE* 112 (1996): 197–201 [above, pp. 285–91].

37 Cf. *P.Yadin* 21, of 11 September 130, lines 8–9 quoted in n. 17 above.

> between me and him, [namely] one thousand and a hundred and twenty 'blacks' of silver ... etc. (*P.Yadin* 5 frg. a col. i lines 5–14).[38]

After Judah's death, adjustments had to be made, and these are reflected in *P.Yadin* 20. The fact that Shelamzion did get the courtyard in the end may imply that the granddaughter acquired her father's right to the inheritance.

The material which I have looked at here is the same material which I have studied in the articles published over the last four years. However, in this paper I have tried to look at the material and the question from a slightly different angle, and in addition I have taken into account a number of new considerations and arguments. While I still suspect that the deeds of gift were indeed intended to bypass the existing law of succession to the benefit of daughters, it now seems to me, in particular on the basis of these newer considerations, that it is not possible to demonstrate this conclusively from the evidence at our disposal at present. In consequence, therefore, I submit, we must consider this a *non liquet*.

Family Trees

1) Family tree of Babatha and her two husbands

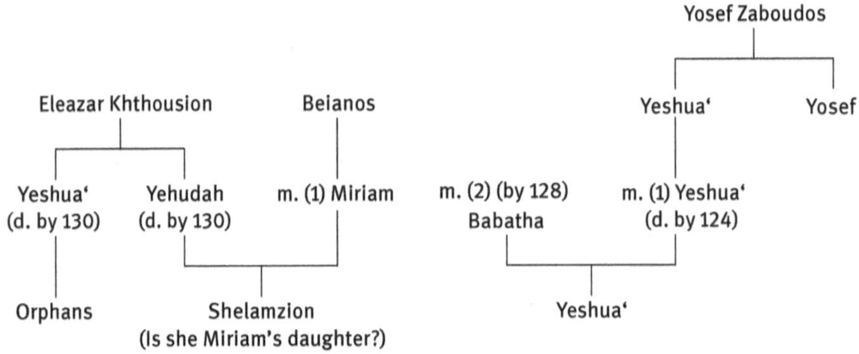

38 ὁμοḷογῶ ẹγὼ Ἰώσηπọς τοῦ̣ Ἰωσήπ[ου ἐπι]ḳαλουμ[ένου] Ζαβούδο[υ] τῶṿ ἀπὸ̣ Μαωζων [σο]ὶ Ἰη[σοῦ τ]ọῦ̣ Ἰησ[οῦ τοῦ] ἀδελφοῦ̣ μου ạὐτόθεν ἔχ[ει]ν σε παρ' ẹ̓μ[οὶ ἀργυρ]ίου μέ[λανας] χείλια καὶ [ἑ]κατὸν εἴκọσι παραθήκη[ν] π̣άṿτων ὑ̣[παρχόν]των καὶ ἀ[ρ]γυρίου καὶ χ[ει]ρογράφων ὀφ̣[ει]λήματος κα[ὶ δ]απ̣άγ̣ης ἐργαστη̣ρίου κ̣α̣ὶ τειμῆς [ὀ]λύνθων κα[ὶ] τειμῆς οἴνου κ̣α̣ὶ τ̣ε̣ιμῆς φοίṿικος καὶ τε[ι]μῆς ἐλαίοṳ καὶ ἐκ παντὸς τ̣ρόπ̣ọυ μ̣ειкροῦ καὶ μ̣εγάλου ἐκ πάντω[ν] ὧν εὑρέθη π̣α̣τρεί σ[ο]υ καί μοι μετ̣α̣ξύ μου καὶ α[ὐ]τοῦ ἀ̣ργυρίου μέλανες χείλ[ι]ον ἓν καὶ ἑκ̣ατὸν ẹ̓ίκοσι etc.

2) Family tree of Salome Komaïse daughter of Levi

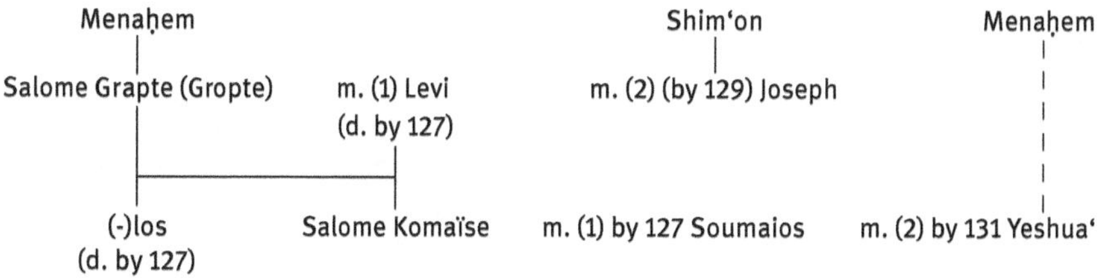

The Rabbis and the Documents

On 2 December 127 CE Babatha daughter of Shim'on had her guardian, Judah son of Eleazar Khthousion, write the following sworn subscription to her land declaration, submitted in Rabbath-Moab on the occasion of the census held in the Roman province of Arabia by the governor, Titus Aninius Sextius Florentinus: 'I, Babatha daughter of Shim'on, swear by the genius (*tyche*) of the Lord Caesar that I have in good faith registered as has been written above. I, Judanes son of Eleazar, acted as guardian and wrote for her.' This subscription has survived only in its Greek translation in the verified copy of Babatha's land declaration.[1] Seven months earlier, around 25 April, another Jew, whose name has not been preserved, but whose patronymic is Levi, thus X son of Levi, because he was illiterate had his sworn declaration written for him by the Nabataean Onainos son of Sa'adalos.[2] The wording is almost identical: 'I, X son of Levi, swear by the genius of the Lord Caesar that I have in good faith registered as written above, concealing nothing.'[3]

We find similar oath formulas in census returns of the fourteen-year census cycle in Egypt, the κατ' οἰκίαν ἀπογραφή.[4] The oath does not appear on all declarations: the presence or absence of the oath depends entirely on local custom.[5] The oath is by the reigning emperor or his *tyche* as well as by local divinities. We do not possess an example of a Jew affixing an oath by the *tyche* of the emperor to a census declaration from Egypt, but we do have an example of a Jew from the

1 Βαβθα Σίμωνος ὄμνυμι τύχην κυρίου Καίσαρος καλῇ πίστει ἀπογεγράφθαι ὡς προγέγραπ[τα]-ι. Ἰουδάνης Ἐλαζάρου ἐπιτρόπευ[σ]α καὶ ἔγραψα ὑπὲρ αὐτῆς, *P.Yadin* 16, ll. 33–35 in Naphtali Lewis, *The Documents from the Bar Kokhba Period in the Cave of Letters. Greek Papyri* (Jerusalem: IES, 1989), 67.

2 See Hannah M. Cotton, "Subscriptions and Signatures in the Papyri from the Judaean Desert: The χειροχρήστης," *JJP* 25 (1995): 34–8 [above, pp. 119–23].

3 [Ὁ δεῖνα] Λειουου ὄμνυμι τύχην Κυρίου Καίσαρος κ[α]λῇ πίστει ἀπογεγράφθαι ὡς προγέγραπται μηθὲν ὑποστειλάμενος in Hannah M. Cotton, "Another Fragment of the Declaration of Landed Property from the Province of Arabia," *ZPE* 99 (1993): 117, ll. 2–3 = Hannah M. Cotton, "The Archive of Salome Komaise Daughter of Levi: Another Archive from the 'Cave of Letters,'" *ZPE* 105 (1995): 176 = *DJD* XXVII, no. 61.

4 On which see Marcel Hombert and Claire Préaux, *Recherches sur le recensement dans l'Egypte romaine* (Leiden: Brill, 1952) and Roger S. Bagnall and Bruce W. Frier, *The Demography of Roman Egypt* (Cambridge: Cambridge University Press, 1994).

5 Hombert and Préaux, *Recherches sur le recensement dans l'Egypte romaine*, 125.

Article note: First published in Martin Goodman, ed., *Jews in a Greco-Roman World* (Oxford: Oxford University Press, 1998), 167–179, with the following note: dedicated to the memory of my teacher and friend Abraham (Addi) Wasserstein. It is my pleasure to thank my friend David Wasserstein for his incisive criticisms.

https://doi.org/10.1515/9783110770438-029

Fayyûm, Soteles son of Josepos, affixing an oath by the emperor to the notification of the death of his son (Josepos), which he is submitting to the authorities.[6] It is true that *tyche* is not mentioned here. However, the editors of the *Corpus Papyrorum Judaicarum* are right to argue that this omission is not "on account of the Judaism of Soteles," but is explained by the fact that "the Roman oath 'by the genius of the emperor' was not yet familiar in Egypt." And at any rate "an oath by the emperor presupposes his superhuman origin, which contradicts the principles of Judaism."[7] It would seem that the Jews of this period were less conscious – even oblivious – of the religious implication of an oath by the emperor or by his *tyche* from the standpoint of a monotheistic Jewish theology. It is not necessary to assume that they felt coerced into using the formula. One's expectations of what Jews would or would not do at certain periods of their history are often belied by the evidence. Babatha and X son of Levi swore by the *tyche* of the emperor as a matter of course. In this as well as in their other contacts with the authorities, they simply followed local custom.[8]

It could be objected that those Jews who swear by the *tyche* of the emperor are Hellenized Jews. This is patently not true of the men and women who people the Babatha archive and the archive of Salome Komaïse daughter of Levi, the sister of the declarant mentioned above.[9] On the contrary: they sign and subscribe in Aramaic, and when they need their contracts written in Greek, they employ scribes.[10] And even the latter are not very proficient in Greek. Perhaps the most glaring example is a deed of gift from the archive of Salome Komaïse daughter of Levi.[11] The scribe pays no attention whatever to case endings and gender.[12] He cannot be said to know the language; he translates from the Aramaic word for word and literally. At times the Aramaic *Urtext* is so close to the surface that the

---

6 Σωτέλης Ἰωσήπου ὁ πρωγεγραμένος ὠμνύω Ạὐτοκράτορα Κạίσ̣α[ρα Νέρουα] Τραιαν[ὸν] Σεβα̣[στόν], *BGU* IV 1068 = *CPJ* II 427, ll. 18–24 (101 CE).

7 *CPJ* II 427, on ll. 18 ff.

8 It may be suggested that this was facilitated by another social phenomenon described by Saul Lieberman, *Greek and Hellenism in Jewish Palestine* (Jerusalem: Mosad Bialik, 1984) (Hebrew), namely the abusive use of the practice of oath taking in daily life in Palestine.

9 See Hannah M. Cotton and Ada Yardeni, *Aramaic, Hebrew, and Greek Documentary Texts from Naḥal Ḥever and Other Sites*, Discoveries in the Judaean Desert XXVII (Oxford: Clarendon Press, 1997), 160–62.

10 For scribes in the Babatha archive see *P.Yadin* 11: Iustinus; *P.Yadin* 14, 15, 17, 18: Theenas son of Simon; *P.Yadin* 19: X son of Simon; *P.Yadin* 20–27: Germanus son of Joudah.

11 See Cotton, "The Archive of Salome Komaise Daughter of Levi," 183–203 = *DJD* XXVII, no. 64.

12 See text and apparatus in Cotton, "The Archive of Salome Komaise Daughter of Levi," 185–87 = Cotton and Yardeni, *Aramaic, Hebrew, and Greek Documentary Texts from Naḥal Ḥever and Other Sites*, 206–207.

text can be understood only when translated back into the original Aramaic. For example: in lines 6–9 the mother, Salome Gropte, declares: 'I acknowledge that I have given you as a gift from this day and forever my property in Maḥoza, which items are listed as follows: a date orchard called the Garden of Asa'adaia with water [allowance], once a week on the fourth day for one half-hour.' The Greek reads:

> ὁμολογῶ ἐνενοχ[έ]ναι σοι εἰς δόσιν ἀπὸ τῆς σήμερον δόσιν αἰωνίου τὰ ὑπάρχοντά μοι ἐν Μαωζας ἃ εἴδη ὑποτεταγμένα· κῆπον φοινεικῶνος καλούμενον γανναθ Ἀσαδαια σὺν ὕδατος αὐτῆς ἐφ' ἡμερῶν ἑπτὰ εἰς ἑπτὰ ἡμέραν τετάρτη ἡ[μ]ιωρ<ί>αν μίαν.

My proposed translation into Aramaic is based entirely on the Aramaic deed of gift written for Babatha's mother, Miriam, by her husband in 120:[13]

> אנא יהבת לכי מן יומא דנה ולעלם מתנת עלם דאיתי לי במחוזא ... כדי כתיבין גנת תמריא די מתקריא גנת חצדית? אסאדיה? וענימיה יום ארבעה בשבת פלגות שעה ...

The use of Greek in my opinion is to be explained by the desire to make the deed of gift valid and enforceable in a Greek-speaking court, such as that of the governor of the province. Babatha, for example, as well as her opponents, were in the habit of approaching this court on their own initiative, as any reader of the Greek part of the archive immediately discovers.[14] Another reason could be the need to deposit the deeds in a public archive, similar to what we know to have been the case in Egypt, where public archives were used to deposit private documents; having been registered there, these documents could later be produced in court as evidence.[15] We have a reference to such archives in the Babatha archive. A deed of gift by Judah son of Eleazar Khthousion to his daughter from his first wife concludes with: 'And whenever Shelamzion summons the said Judah he will register it with the public archives.'[16] Again, in a deed of concession of inherited property, Besas son of Yeshu'a and Julia Crispina, promise Shelamzion to register with the public

---

13 *P.Yadin* 7, published in Yigael Yadin, Jonas C. Greenfield, and Ada Yardeni, "A Deed of Gift in Aramaic Found in Naḥal Ḥever: Papyrus Yadin 7," *Eretz Israel* 25 (1996): 383–403 (Hebrew), ll. 1–5 = ll. 30–36; ll. 14–16 = ll. 50–54. I am grateful to the editors for allowing me to see and use the text in advance of publication.
14 See Hannah M. Cotton, "The Guardianship of Jesus Son of Babatha: Roman and Local Law in the Province of Arabia," *JRS* 83 (1993): 106 ff. [above, pp. 426 ff.].
15 See W.E.H. Cockle, "State Archives in Graeco-Roman Egypt from 30 BC to the Reign of Septimius Severus," *JEA* 70 (1984): 116; see also Fabienne Burkhalter, "Archives locales et archives centrales en Egypte romaine," *Chiron* 20 (1990): 191–216.
16 ὅταν δὲ παρᾳνγείλει Σελα<μ>ψιοῦς τῷ αὐτῷ Ἰούδατι, τευχιζζει αὐτὴν διὰ δημοσίων, *P.Yadin* 19, ll. 25–7.

archives in her name at her expense a courtyard in Ein-Gedi which had belonged to her paternal grandfather.[17] In both cases, since the property is located in Ein-Gedi, it is likely that the public archive operating in Greek is to be located there. A fragmentary papyrus from the same archive tells us that Babatha's late husband had registered date-groves in her name in the *apographe*.[18] *Apographe* here – as we can see from what follows – cannot refer to the census,[19] and thus must refer to an official registration of property, presumably in the public archives.

That Jews registered their contracts with the public authorities is neither surprising nor unknown. We hear in the rabbinic sources of these 'non-Jewish archives' – ערכאות הגויים, in which the term ערכאות is simply a transliteration of the Greek word ἀρχεῖα. That these were frequently used by Jews we learn for example from *mGittin* 1:5: 'Any deed is valid that is registered in the registries of the gentiles (ערכאות הגויים), although witnessed by gentiles, except a deed of divorce or a deed of emancipation. R. Sim'on [c. 130–160 CE] says: 'These, too, are valid; they were mentioned [as invalid] only when they were prepared by unauthorized people (נעשׂו בהדיוט).'' The language of the deed is not important as we learn from *t. Baba Bathra* 11:8: 'They change the language of deeds from Hebrew to Greek and from Greek to Hebrew and make it valid (ועושׂין לו קיום בית דין).'[20]

There are several discussions in the rabbinic sources on the validity of contracts made in Greek, on the use of gentile witnesses, courts and archives. Sometimes such activities are explicitly forbidden. I have been able to find only two tannaitic passages which explicitly discourage Jews from using gentile courts. These two passages are not unrelated. The harsh language employed by the Rabbis in the prohibition on using gentile courts may well indicate that the Jews *did* use them; no less is implied when the Rabbis used conciliatory language and allowed what was in common use to have validity under Jewish law.

It is a remarkable fact that no court, Jewish or non-Jewish – apart from that of the Roman governor of Arabia – is mentioned in any of the documents from the Judaean Desert – a great many of which are legal documents. We should not jump from this to the conclusion that the governor's court was the only court in operation in a Roman province. Still the absence of others is disturbing, especially

17 ταύτην δὲ τὴν αὐλὴν ὅπου ἂν βουληθῇς τευχίσω σο[ι] διὰ δημοσίων, σοῦ διδούσης τὸ ἀνάλωμα, *P.Yadin* 20, ll. 34–6.

18 ἀπεγράψατο Ἰούδας Ἐλεαζάρο[υ Χθουσίωνος] ἀπογενομενου σου ἀνὴρ ἐπ' ὀνόματός σου ἐν τῇ ἀπ[ο]γραφῇ κήπους φοινικῶνος ἐν Μαωζα, *P.Yadin* 24, ll. 4–6.

19 So Lewis, *The Documents from the Bar Kokhba Period in the Cave of Letters. Greek Papyri*, 105–7.

20 Saul Lieberman, *Tosefta Ki-fshutah. Part X: Order Nezikin* (New York: Jewish Theological Seminary Press, 1988), 168–69 (Hebrew): "the court approves the translation."

in view of the host of references in rabbinic sources to courts of different sizes in towns and villages.[21]

Non-Hellenized Jews were using the Greek language – sometimes a very faulty version of it – in their contracts, for a variety of reasons: perhaps in the absence of Jewish courts and archives; perhaps in order to leave their options open: with their contracts written in Greek they could go to the court of their choice, Jewish or gentile – perhaps that of the Roman governor. But we can go further than this: not all the contracts are written in faulty Greek, nor are they all literal translations from the Aramaic, as is the deed of gift in favour of Salome Komaïse daughter of Levi cited above. Some of them use a language not different from the *koine* used in the papyri from Egypt. Even the script is similar, and this in itself is significant.[22] The external resemblance is paralleled by internal similarities: not only the Greek script and Greek diplomatics but often the very phrases, the entire ethos of the Greek contract was taken over by the Jewish scribes. Thus we find deeds of sale, petitions, land registrations, receipts, mortgages, promissory notes and even marriage contracts, all of which bear a striking resemblance to their Egyptian counterparts.

What makes a contract Jewish is not its language, content, or particular ingredients. Jewish civil law, as we have it in the tannaitic and later sources (as well as in the Pentateuch), was not created *in vacuo*, but absorbed very many local, or, better, regional traditions which are reflected in its rules. But unless we wish to describe everything used by Jews as Jewish, we need to find some criteria which will distinguish what is Jewish from what is not. I have not found a better definition for what is Jewish than such material that eventually received halakhic sanction, and is present in the halakhic sources. Conversely, what is not there, or explicitly forbidden, I would designate non-Jewish. I wish to emphasize that in the period reflected in the documents from the Judaean Desert – after the destruction of the Temple in 70 CE and before the end of the Bar Kokhba Revolt in 135/6 CE – Jewish civil law was in the process of being created in the rabbinic schools, but had yet to receive its final shape – let alone the authority it was to acquire after its formal redaction at the end of the second century CE. Thus to say that Jews are using 'non-Jewish' contracts is to say no more than that the legal

21 Emil Schürer, *The History of the Jewish People in the Age of Jesus Christ*, ed. Fergus Millar and Géza Vermès, Vol. II (Edinburgh: Clark, 1979), 184–88; Gedaliah Alon, *The Jews in Their Land in the Talmudic Age 70–640 CE*, Vol. II (Jerusalem: Magnes Press, 1984), 553–57; Asher Gulak, *Towards a Study of the History of Jewish Law in the Talmudic Period* (Jerusalem: Hasefer, 1929), 54 ff. (Hebrew); less sceptical is Ze'ev Safrai, *The Jewish Community in the Talmudic Period* (Jerusalem: Zalman Shazar Center, 1995), 76 ff. (Hebrew).

22 See Edoardo Crisci, *Scrivere greco fuori d'Egitto* (Florence: Gonnelli, 1996).

usage reflected in the documents is not in harmony with what eventually came to be normative Jewish law. The diversity and fluidity manifested in the documents from the Judaean Desert are the best evidence we have, I believe, for the state of Jewish law and the authority exercised by the rabbis at the time.

Objections could be made to my exclusive reliance on these documents to evaluate the state of Jewish law and the authority exercised by the rabbis at this time. Three points need to be made in defence of my position.

First, the Jews represented in the documents from the Judaean Desert are not a fringe group, even if the presence of their documents in the caves of the Judaean Desert was caused by the upheaval resulting from the outbreak of the Bar Kokhba Revolt and is thus limited both in place – to those parts of Judaea and the province of Arabia that were near the caves – and in time – to the period 70–135/6 CE. These are Jews from villages as scattered as Maḥoza and Mazra'a in the southern part of the Dead Sea area in the Province of Arabia, Sophathe[.] from the Peraea in Transjordan, which belonged to the province of Judaea, Ein-Gedi near the Dead Sea, Yaqim and Aristoboulias in the area south-east of Hebron, Bethbassi near Herodium, Galoda in eastern Samaria and Batharda in southern Samaria. They are by no means restricted to one locality. I maintain, therefore, that they are representative of Jewish society as a whole in the period under discussion. They present a faithful picture of the realities of life at the time that they were written.

Second, any notion of a distinction between Jews from the Province of Arabia and those from Judaea should be dispelled; we are talking about areas which are very close to each other (a day's walk or two days at most between the furthest destinations), and where borders had very little inhibiting effect on movement. The official names, Arabia, Judaea and Syria-Palaestina, represent artificial divisions which did not seem to matter very much in reality. The archives amply demonstrate that the Jews living in Arabia and the Jews living in the province of Judaea belonged to a single Jewish society whose internal ties overrode provincial boundaries: they disregarded the provincial boundaries in their residence, marriages, and property holdings.

Lastly, the Jews represented in these documents come from densely populated Jewish areas, from the heartland of the Bar Kokhba Revolt, a religious and national movement. Many of the Greek documents were written close to the time when the revolt broke out – a revolt which was carefully prepared some years in advance. In fact the very presence of their documents in the caves demonstrates their owners' participation in the revolt. The writers of these documents cannot and should not be regarded as assimilated Jews.[23]

---

23 See above.

I should like to illustrate the state of fluidity in the legal habits and traditions manifest amongst Jews in the period between 70 and 135 CE through one kind of contract: the marriage contract. I choose this particular contract for several reasons. First of all because we have by now no less than eight (perhaps nine) such contracts from the Judaean Desert.[24] Second, because it is in the sphere of marriage law that rabbinic traditions claim to go back to a period long before the destruction of the Temple, and by implication to have become normative by the time of our documents. I refer to the artificial reconstruction of how the biblical *mohar* was transformed from an immediate payment, a bride-gift to the wife's father, into an 'endowment pledge, a divorce payment,' which was due to the wife upon the dissolution of the marriage, and as such written into the marriage contract, the *ketubba*. The traditional and almost universally accepted view is that the process reached its conclusion when Shim'on b. Shetah – who was active in the first half of the first century BCE – put into the *ketubba* a clause to the effect that the husband's entire property is held liable for the payment of the *mohar*. We find the story in several versions.[25] I use the term 'artificial' to describe this process deliberately, since I believe that among other things this narrative was constructed to account for the fact that the term *mohar* simply disappeared from current usage. In the earliest *ketubboth*, that of Babatha published recently and that in *DJD* II, no. 21, the payment in question is referred to simply, but equivocally, as 'the money of your *ketubba*' – כסף כתבתך.[26] Third, and lastly, I choose the marriage contract because the *ketubba*, the Jewish marriage contract – unlike other contracts – includes, in addition to financial arrangements, formulae which place it solidly within a Jewish framework and under the sanction of Jewish law. I refer of course to the formula 'that you will be my wife according to the law of

---

24 (1) *DJD* II, no. 20, 1st or 2nd century CE, Ḥardona, Aramaic; (2) *DJD* II, no. 115, 124 CE, Bethbassi, Judaea, Greek; (3) *P.Yadin* 10 (Yigael Yadin, Jonas C. Greenfield, and Ada Yardeni, "Babatha's Ketubba," *IEJ* 44 (1994): 75–99), 125–128 CE, Maḥoza, Arabia, Aramaic; (4) *P.Yadin* 18, 128 CE, Maḥoza, Arabia, Greek; (5) *XḤev/Ṣe Gr* 2 (Hannah M. Cotton, "A Cancelled Marriage Contract from the Judaean Desert, XHev/Se Gr. 2," *JRS* 84 (1994): 64–86 = *DJD* XXVII, no. 69), 130 CE, Aristoboulias, Judaea, Greek; (6) *P.Yadin* 37 (=*DJD* XXVII, no. 65), 131 CE, Maḥoza, Arabia, Greek; (7) *DJD* II, no. 116, first half of 2nd century CE, unknown place, Greek; (8) *DJD* II, no. 21, no date, unknown place, Aramaic.

25 *bKet*. 82b; *yKet*. 8.11, 32b; *tKet*. 12.1; Mordechai Akiva Friedman, *Jewish Marriage in Palestine: A Cairo Geniza Study*, Vol. I (Tel Aviv: Tel Aviv University Press, 1980), 257 ff.; Markham J. Geller, "New Sources for the Origins of the Rabbinic Ketubah," *HUCA* 49 (1978): 227–37; Léonie J. Archer, *Her Price is Beyond Rubies. The Jewish Woman in Graeco-Roman Palestine* (Sheffield: Academic Press, 1990), 159–63.

26 *P.Yadin* 10, l. 16 (Yadin, Greenfield, and Yardeni, "Babatha's Ketubba," 78) and *DJD* II, no. 21, l. 10.

Moses and the Jews' – די תהוא לי לאנתה כדין משה ויהודאי – a formula that we find in the opening lines of two almost contemporary Aramaic marriage contracts, *DJD* II, no. 20 and *P.Yadin* 10 (see above, n. 24, nos. 1 and 3 respectively).[27]

The three Aramaic marriage contracts from the Judaean Desert reveal to us that the rabbinic marriage contract had indeed by then developed its own special form. But had it become normative? Surely not. Not one of the five marriage contracts written in Greek can be said to be a translation of an Aramaic *ketubba*. All of them resemble both in spirit and in phraseology contemporary Greek marriage contracts from Egypt.[28] The crucial formula 'that you will be my wife according to the law of Moses and the Jews' is absent from all of them.

I have laid much emphasis in the past on the fact that whereas the *ketubba* is centred around the sum of money that the husband pledges to the wife, which was once called *mohar* and is now called (by the rabbis) *ketubba*, the Greek marriage contract is an acknowledgment by the groom that he has received the dowry from the bride or her family.[29] I have now come to believe that the difference is more apparent than real. I am not sure that I fully understand the expression 'the money of your *ketubba*' in the documents. If the fictitious *mohar* is meant, then it must be said that it is treated in the very same way as what we may call the 'gentile' dowry is treated: the husband's entire property is put in lien to secure the return of that money on the dissolution of the marriage, and it is stipulated that the wife's sons will inherit that money, if she dies before the husband. There is nothing whatsoever in the text of *DJD* II, no. 21 and in *P.Yadin* 10 – where the phrase 'the money of your *ketubba*' occurs – which forces us to think that 'the money of your *ketubba*' is the rabbinic fictitious *mohar*, rather than the dowry of the Greek marriage contracts.[30]

I have been able to find only one exception to the 'non-Jewish character' of the Greek marriage contract between Jews, i.e. the absence of features in them which set marriage contracts between Jews apart from marriage contracts between non-

27 *DJD* II, no. 20, l. 3: [ד]י תהוא לי לאנתה כדין מ[שה ויהודאי] (revised reading of Ada Yardeni); *P.Yadin* 10, l. 5: לאנת[ה כדי]ן משה ויה[ו]דאי [...].

28 See Cotton, "A Cancelled Marriage Contract from the Judaean Desert, XHev/Se Gr. 2," 68 ff. for a detailed survey of the Egyptian parallels.

29 Cotton, 82 ff.

30 Elias J. Bickerman, "Two Legal Interpretations of the Septuagint," in *Studies in Jewish and Christian History*, Vol. I (Leiden: Brill, 1976), 212–15, in fact comes very close to suggesting that 'the money of the *ketubba*' may refer to the dowry; cf. Baruch A. Levine, "Comparative Perspectives on Jewish and Christian History," *JAOS* 99 (1979): 85; Michael Satlow, "Reconsidering the Jewish Ketubah Payment," in *The Jewish Family in Antiquity*, ed. Shaye J.D. Cohen (Atlanta: Scholars Press, 1993), 137 ff.: the documentary marriage contracts support Satlow's claim that "The rabbinic *ketubah* payment was a rabbinic innovation of around the late first century CE," 146.

Jews. I have in mind the stipulation that the sons will inherit the dowry or *ketubba* money of their mother. This stipulation is present in all four marriage contracts from Wadi Murabba'at, both Aramaic and Greek (*DJD* II, nos. 20, 21, 115, 116),[31] in the Aramaic *P.Yadin* 10 (Babatha's *ketubba*),[32] as well as in the Greek marriage contract from Aristoboulias (*DJD* XXVII, no. 69). Sometimes it is accompanied by the phrase that the daughters are to be provided for out of the husband's property (*DJD* II, nos. 20, 21, *P.Yadin* 10 and *DJD* XXVII, no. 69). The specific clauses which distinguish between male and female children are attested so far only in the Jewish marriage contract tradition, and, as it seems, already in the early Mishnaic period. The phrase 'The sons inherit and the daughters are provided for' – הבנים ירשו והבנות יזונו (*mKet.* 4:6) is said there to have been expounded on by R. Eleazar b. Azarya, a second generation Tanna (90–130 CE), and thus must have existed for a while.

It cannot be denied, therefore, that this particular clause unites marriage contracts between Jews written both in Greek and in Aramaic. However, these clauses are absent from *P.Yadin* 18 (from the Babatha archive) and from *DJD* XXVII, no. 65 (from the archive of Salome Komaïse daughter of Levi). Furthermore, the order of the relevant clauses concerning provision for the children in the case of the prior death of the wife, and sometimes without reference to it, varies a great deal.[33]

The stipulation that the daughters are to be fed and clothed may have replaced an earlier one which provided for all children to be fed and clothed from the father's property.[34] This original situation is reflected in one of the two Greek marriage contracts from Wadi Murabba'at (*DJD* II, no. 115) as well as in the two marriage contracts from Arabia, both of which use an almost identical terminology: 'with his undertaking to feed and clothe both her and the children to come in accordance with Greek custom upon the said Judah Cimber's good faith and peril and security of all his possessions, both those which he now possesses in his said home village and here and all those which he may in addition acquire.'[35]

It should also be pointed out, though, that the provision concerning male children as heirs to their mother's property had entered Jewish law under the influence of other Near Eastern traditions, where – unlike the situation under

31 Cf. Cotton, "A Cancelled Marriage Contract from the Judaean Desert, XHev/Se Gr. 2," 80–1.
32 See the editors' comments on ll. 11–14: Yadin, Greenfield, and Yardeni, "Babatha's Ketubba," 93 ff.
33 Cf. Cotton, "A Cancelled Marriage Contract from the Judaean Desert, XHev/Se Gr. 2," 80–1.
34 Friedman, *Jewish Marriage in Palestine: A Cairo Geniza Study*, Vol. I, 369.
35 ἀκολούθως αἱρέσει τροφῆς καὶ ἀμφιασμοῦ αὐτῆς τε καὶ τῶν μελλόντων τέκνων ἑλληνικῷ νόμῳ ἐπὶ τῆς τοῦ αὐτοῦ Ἰούδα Κίμβ[ε]ρ̣ο[ς] π̣ίστ̣εως καὶ κινδύνου καὶ πάντων ὑπαρχόντων ὧν τε ἔχει ἐν τῇ α̣ὐ̣τ̣ῇ [πα]τ̣ρ̣ί̣δ̣ι αὐ̣τ̣ο̣ῦ̣ καὶ ὧδε καὶ ὧν ἐπικτήσηται, *P.Yadin* 18, ll. 16–18 = ll. 49–51; almost identical phrasing in *DJD* XXVII, no. 65, ll. 9–10.

Jewish law – the wife's children were her heirs. The provision certainly contravenes the biblical law of inheritance which made the husband sole heir to his wife's property; upon his death all his sons, including those from another woman, would divide his property equally between them. Thus the provision for male sons to inherit their mother's dowry or her *ketubba* was meant to protect male sons in polygamous marriages against the loss of part of their mother's property to sons of another woman.[36] This can be safely read in *DJD* II, no. 116, ll. 4–8: '[And if Salome] dies [before Aurelius], the sons that she will have from him will inherit her dowry and the things written above ... [in addition] to inheriting all of Aurelius' property together with their future brothers [from another woman].'[37]

I have deliberately emphasized the variation, the lack of uniformity, even when the provisions seem unique to marriage contracts between Jews; this needs to be emphasized even more with regard to provisions which disappeared from the later *ketubba* tradition.[38] There was no normative, authoritative and uniform marriage contract which Jews knew that they had to use. Neither may we assume that for every marriage contract in Greek which diverges from the rabbinic *ketubba* which has been preserved, a '*kosher*' Jewish Aramaic *ketubba* has been lost. Obviously the Jews who wrote these documents felt free to use the legal instrument that seemed to them most effective.

We can perhaps take this argument one step further and question the assumption that a written marriage contract was a *sine qua non* for the conclusion of marriage between Jews.

In *DJD* XXVII, no. 65 (= *P.Yadin* 37), which we now know to be the marriage contract of Salome Komaïse daughter of Levi of the archive mentioned above, we find the following clause: 'Yeshu'a son of Menaḥem, domiciled in the village of Sophathe[.] in the district of the city of Livias of the administrative region of P[eraea] agreed with Salome also called Komaïse [daughter of Levi], his wife who is from Maḥoza, [that they continue] life together *as also before this time*.'[39]

---

36 Friedman, *Jewish Marriage in Palestine: A Cairo Geniza Study*, Vol. I, 380–82; Ze'ev W. Falk, "The Right of Inheritance of a Daughter and Widow in Bible and Talmud," *Tarbiẓ* 23 (1952): 9–15 (Hebrew).

37 [ἐὰν δὲ ἡ Σαλώμη πρὸ τοῦ Αὐρηλίου] τὸν βίον μ[ε]τ̣αλλάξει υ̣[ἱοὺ]ς̣ οὓς ἂν ἕ̣ξε̣ι̣ ἀπ̣' α̣ὐ̣τ̣[οῦ ... κληρονομήσουσιν] τὴν φ̣ε̣ρ̣νὴν κ̣α̣ὶ τὰ πρ[ογε]γραμμέ̣ν̣α̣ [*c.40 letters missing*] τ̣ῆ̣ς τ̣οῦ Αὐρ̣η̣λ̣ί̣ου ο̣ὐ̣[σ]ί̣ας π̣ᾶσ̣α̣[ν κλ]ηρονομί̣αν με̣θ' ὧν ἂ̣ν ἕξωσιν ἀ̣[δ]ελφῶν.

38 E.g. the need to provide for all children.

39 [ὡμολογήσ]α̣το Ιησους Μαναημου τ[ῶν ἀπὸ κώμης c.8 letters] Σοφφαθε̣[. .] . . . . π̣ε̣ρ̣ὶ πόλιν Λιουιάδος τῆς Π̣[εραίας *c.9 letters* π̣ρ̣ὸ̣ς(?) Σαλ]ωμην κ̣αλο̣υ̣μένην Κ̣[ομαϊσην Ληουειου τὴν] γ̣υ̣ναῖκα, Μ̣[α]ωζηνὴν ὥστε αὐτο̣ὺ̣ς {ὥ̣σ̣τ̣ε̣ α̣[ὐτοὺς]} [*c.17 letters*].ετ̣ . . . . συμβιως̣ . . .[*c.14 letters*] αὐ̣τῆ\ς/ ὡ̣[ς κ]αὶ πρὸ τούτου τοῦ χρόνου, ll. 3–6.

In his introduction to the papyrus Lewis quite rightly cites the parallel of the 'unwritten marriage' ἄγραφος γάμος recorded in Egyptian papyri,[40] a union which was "sometimes later converted by a written contract into ἔγγραφος γάμος." But he rejects this interpretation in favour of an *interpretatio Hebraica*: "Close as the parallel may be, however, ... the expression 'as also before this time' more likely implies that the bride and groom had been living together since the day of their betrothal, in keeping with a Jewish practice of the time when the bride was an orphan and a minor."[41]

We now know a great deal more about Salome Komaïse: she was indeed an orphan in 131 CE, but not a minor. Already in 127 CE (if not before) she had been married to Sammouos son of Shim'on who represented her in the deed of renunciation.[42] Yeshu'a son of Menaḥem of *DJD* XXVII, no. 65 is her second husband. In 129 CE she received a gift from her mother, unaccompanied, as far as we can tell, by either a husband or guardian.[43] Thus putative minority cannot explain their having lived together before the contract was drawn up, even if we assume that they followed Jewish customs – an assumption unwarranted by the marriage contract concluded between them: this marriage contract, in which the groom undertakes to follow Greek law and custom in providing for her and the children to come, cannot be described as a Jewish *ketubba*.[44] Neither can I accept the suggestion propounded recently that we have here a case of premarital cohabitation peculiar to and common in Judaea.[45] This so-called radical approach assumes just as does the 'apologetic approach' of Lewis that by this time there existed a coherent and operative system of Jewish law which had already become normative. In this system 'a man may not keep his wife even one hour without a *ketubba*' (*bBK* 89a), and life together without a *ketubba* must be branded 'premarital cohabi-

40 Cf. above all Hans Julius Wolff, *Written and Unwritten Marriages in Hellenistic and Post-Classical Roman Law* (Haverford: American Philological Association, 1939).

41 Lewis, *The Documents from the Bar Kokhba Period in the Cave of Letters. Greek Papyri*, 130.

42 Cotton, "The Archive of Salome Komaise Daughter of Levi," 177–83, Doc. III = *DJD* XXVII, no. 63.

43 Cotton, 183–203, Doc. IV = *DJD* XXVII, no. 64; but the occasion did not call for the presence of a husband in the role of a guardian.

44 σὺν αἱρέσει τρ̣οφῆ̣ς̣ [καὶ ἀμφιασμοῦ αὐτῆς] τ̣ε καὶ τῶν μελ̣λόντ̣ω̣[ν τέκ]ν̣ων̣ νό̣μ̣[ῳ ἑλληνικ]ῷ καὶ ἑλλ̣[η]νι̣κ̣ῷ τρόπῳ (*DJD* XXVII, no. 65, ll. 9–10); see Abraham Wasserstein, "A Marriage Contract from the Province of Arabia Nova: Notes on Papyrus Yadin 18," *JQR* 80 (1989): 117 ff. against Katzoff in Naphtali Lewis, Ranon Katzoff, and Jonas C. Greenfield, "Papyrus Yadin 18," *IEJ* 37 (1987): 241 f.; Katzoff modified his views in "Papyrus Yadin 18 Again: A Rejoinder," *JQR* 82 (1991): 173–74.

45 Tal Ilan, "Premarital Cohabitation in Ancient Judea: The Evidence of the Babatha Archive and the Mishnah (Ketubbot 1.4)," *Harv. Theol. Rev.* 86 (1993): 247–64.

tation' or 'sex out of wedlock.' If we go by halakha, *DJD* XXVII, no. 65 is not the *ketubba* which would turn 'premarital cohabitation' into a proper Jewish marriage. Lewis's original suggestion of 'unwritten marriage' – ἄγραφος γάμος – is surely the right solution.

Thus even the writing of a marriage contract had not yet become the norm. Yeshu'a son of Menaḥem from the Peraea and Salome Komaïse daughter of Levi from Maḥoza had been married for a while by the time their marriage contract was written, as the verb συμβιόω demonstrates: the verb does *not* mean 'to live together' in the modern sense of experimenting at life together before finalizing the bond, but is used in Egyptian papyri to describe life together in wedlock. Likewise the adjective σύμβιος means 'spouse' and συμβίωσις means 'marriage.' The two last terms are used in these very senses in *DJD* II, no. 115 which is a contract of remarriage, where we read: 'Eleaios son of Shim'on from the village of Galoda of Akrabatta ... an inhabitant of Batharda of Gophna came into a written agreement with Salome daughter of Yoḥanan Galgoula, who used to be his wife (σύμβιον) ...' and later: 'For the sake of marriage (σ̣[υ]ν̣βιώσεος χάριν) now the same Eleaios son of Shim'on agrees to be reconciled and take again Salome daughter of Yoḥanan Galgoula as wedded wife' (ll. 2–5).[46]

There are other branches of personal law, such as the law of succession[47] and the law of guardianship,[48] in which similar discrepancies between the documents and halakhic law are apparent, and the incursion of other legal systems can sometimes be seen and sometimes be assumed. For an appreciation of the polyethnic society of Aramaic-speaking people, into which these documents fit – a society whose cultural, social and legal life absorbed many and various elements from different sources, only one of which was Hellenism – one should consult two recent studies by Abraham Wasserstein, to whose memory this paper is ded-

46 ἐ̣ξομο̣λ̣[ογ]ή̣σα̣[το καὶ σ]υνεγ̣ράψατο Ἐ̣λ̣ε̣α̣ῖ̣ος Σίμωνος τῶν ἀπὸ κ(ώμης) Γαλωδῶν τῆς περὶ Ἀκραβα̣τ̣τῶν οἰκῶν ἐν κώμῃ Βαιτοα̣ρδοις τῆς περὶ Γοφνοῖς πρὸς [Σα]λ̣ώμην [Ἰ]ωά[νου Γαλγ]ο̣υ̣λ̣ὰ π̣ρογενομέ[νην] α̣ὐτοῦ Ἐλαίο̣υ̣ σύνβιον ... σ̣[υ]γ̣βιώσεος χάριν, νυνεὶ ὁμολογεῖ ὁ αὐτὸς Ἐλαῖος Σίμω̣[νος] ἐξ ἀνανεώσεος καταλλάξαι κ[αὶ] π̣ροσλαβέσθαι τὴν αὐ̣τ̣ὴν Σαλώ[μην Ἰω]άγ̣[ο]υ Γ̣[αλγο]υ̣λὰ ε̣ἰ̣[ς γυναῖ]κα γαμετὴν, *DJD* II, no. 115, ll. 2–5.

47 Hannah M. Cotton and Jonas C. Greenfield, "Babatha's Property and the Law of Succession in the Babatha Archive," *ZPE* 104 (1994): 211–24; Hannah M. Cotton, "Deeds of Gift and the Law of Succession in Archives from the Judaean Desert," in *Akten des 21. Internationalen Papyrologenkongresses, Berlin, 13–19.8.1995*, ed. Barbara Kramer et al., Vol. I (Stuttgart – Leipzig: Teubner, 1997), 179–88; Hannah M. Cotton, "The Law of Succession in the Documents from the Judaean Desert Again," *SCI* 17 (1998): 115–23 [above, pp. 443–51].

48 See Cotton, "The Guardianship of Jesus Son of Babatha: Roman and Local Law in the Province of Arabia" [above, pp. 403–30].

icated.[49] Rabbinic law itself acquired its shape in the same environment: that it reflects the documents is only to be expected. We should be wrong, though, to assume without compelling proof that the documents reflect the still-to-be-codified halakha. These documents are the raw material of which life is made, and on which the rabbis wished to put their own stamp.[50]

49 Wasserstein, "A Marriage Contract from the Province of Arabia Nova: Notes on Papyrus Yadin 18"; Abraham Wasserstein, "Non-Hellenized Jews in the Semi-Hellenized East," *SCI* 14 (1995): 111–37.

50 Hayim Lapin, "Early Rabbinic Civil Law and the Literature of the Second Temple Period," *JSQ* 2 (1995): 149–83, using as a test case the Mishnaic tractate *Baba Meṣi'a* is able to show that Mishnaic economic and contract law is not reflected in the literature of the Second Temple period, nor in the documents which postdate the destruction. I am grateful to Professor Lapin for letting me see his manuscript in advance of publication.

The Impact of the Documentary Papyri from the Judaean Desert on the Study of Jewish History from 70 to 135 CE

We are now in possession of inventories of almost the entire corpus of documents discovered in the Judaean Desert.[1] Obviously the same cannot be said about the state of publication of the documents. We still lack a great many documents. I propose to give here a short review of those finds which are relevant to the study of Jewish history between 70 and 135 CE. The survey will include the state of publication of texts from each find.[2] After that an attempt will be made to draw some interim, and necessarily tentative, conclusions about the contribution that this fairly recent addition to the body of our evidence can make to the study of different aspects of Jewish history between 70 and 135 CE.

This material can be divided into several groups:

1) The first documents came from the caves of Wadi Murabba'at in 1952. They were published without much delay in 1961.[3] The collection consists of documents written in Aramaic, Hebrew, Greek, Latin and Arabic, and contains, among other

---

1 For a complete list till the Arab conquest see Hannah M. Cotton, W.E.H. Cockle, and Fergus Millar, "The Papyrology of the Roman Near East: A Survey," *JRS* 85 (1995): 214–35. A much shorter survey, restricted to the finds from the Judaean Desert, can be found in Hannah M. Cotton, "Documentary Texts," in *Encyclopedia of the Dead Sea Scrolls*, ed. Lawrence H. Schiffman and James VanderKam (New York: Oxford University Press, 2000), 212–15. These two surveys, like the present paper, are limited to the non-literary, the documentary texts. The following two catalogues include the literary texts as well: Emanuel Tov, with the collaboration of Stephen J. Pfann, *Companion Volume to the Dead Sea Scrolls on Microfiche Edition* (Leiden: Brill, 1995); see also Stephen A. Reed, revised and edited by Marilyn. J. Lundberg with the collaboration of Michael B. Phelps, *The Dead Sea Scrolls Catalogue: Documents, Photographs, and Museum Inventory Numbers* (Atlanta: Scholars Press, 1994).

2 In the present survey meaningless fragments and scraps are ignored.

3 P. Benoit, J.T. Milik, and R. de Vaux, *Les grottes de Murabba'at*, Discoveries in the Judaean Desert II (Oxford: Clarendon Press, 1961). The papyri published in this volume are referred to as *P.Mur*.

Article note: First published in Aharon Oppenheimer, ed., *Jüdische Geschichte in hellenistisch-römischer Zeit: Wege der Forschung – von alten zu neuen Schürer* (München: Oldenbourg 1999), 221–36, with the following note: as always I am grateful to my friend David Wasserstein for his sensitive criticism and generous help.

https://doi.org/10.1515/9783110770438-030

texts, letters and leases of the Bar Kokhba administration[4] as well as private documents[5] from our period.

2) The most important documents for our period were discovered in Naḥal Ḥever in the course of two seasons of excavations in 1960 and 1961, as part of a large scale Judaean Desert Survey, which included Naḥal Ḥever, Naḥal Ṣe'elim, Naḥal David (Wadi Sdeir), Naḥal Mishmar and Naḥal Hardof (Wadi Mardif).[6] In the Cave of Letters in Naḥal Ḥever was found the rightly celebrated Babatha archive, which contains legal documents in Nabataean,[7] Aramaic,[8] and Greek[9] belonging to a Jewish woman who lived in the village of Maḥoza/Maḥoz 'Aglatain on the southern shore of the Dead Sea, in what used to be the Nabataean Kingdom and in 106 CE became the Roman province of Arabia.[10] The Greek part of the Babatha archive was published in 1989.[11] In the same cave were found letters of Bar Kokhba, in Hebrew, Aramaic and Greek, the majority of which were dictated by the leader himself,[12] as well as leases from the Bar Kokhba administration.[13] Preliminary publications of the Bar Kokhba letters and leases were made by Yadin,[14] and more recently two Aramaic documents from the Babatha archive were published.[15] Two Greek letters were published in 1962.[16] It is to be hoped that the entire material,

---

4 *P.Mur* 24A-L (a lease); *P.Mur* 42–44 (letters); the fragmentary *P.Mur* 45–52 may belong to the Bar Kokhba circle as well.

5 *P.Mur* 18–23, 25, *XḤev/Se* 50 + *P.Mur* 26, *P.Mur* 27–33, 89–97, 113–116. *P.Mur* 18 is before our period, 55/6 CE.

6 See Stephen J. Pfann, "History of the Judaean Desert Discoveries and Sites in the Judaean Desert where Texts have been found," in: Tov, *Companion Volume to the Dead Sea Scrolls on Microfiche Edition*, 97–119. See below on texts from the other sites mentioned above.

7 *P.Yadin* 1–4, 6 and 9.

8 *P.Yadin* 7–8 and 10.

9 *P.Yadin* 5; 11–35.

10 For *XḤev/Se nab* 1 see below n. 61.

11 Naphtali Lewis, *The Documents from the Bar Kokhba Period in the Cave of Letters. Greek Papyri*, Judean Desert Studies II (Jerusalem: IES, 1989).

12 *P.Yadin* 49–63, the majority of these letters are addressed to Jonathan son of Baianos and sometimes to him and Masabalah (*P.Yadin* 49–56, 58–59); none of the letters is dated.

13 *P.Yadin* 42–46, leases; *P.Yadin* 47a+b seems to be a private deed.

14 Yigael Yadin, "Expedition D," *IEJ* 11 (1961): 36–52; Yigael Yadin, "Expedition D – The Cave of the Letters," *IEJ* 12 (1962): 227–57; Yigael Yadin, "The Nabataean Kingdom, Provincia Arabia, Petra and Ein-Geddi in the Documents from Naḥal Ḥever," *Ex Oriente Lux* 17 (1963): 227–41.

15 *P.Yadin* 7, published by Yigael Yadin, Jonas C. Greenfield, and Ada Yardeni, "A Deed of Gift in Aramaic Found in Naḥal Ḥever: Papyrus Yadin 7," *Eretz Israel* 25 (1996): 383–403 (Hebrew) and *P.Yadin* 10, published by Yigael Yadin, Jonas C. Greenfield, and Ada Yardeni, "Babatha's Ketubba," *IEJ* 44 (1994): 75–99.

16 *P.Yadin* 52 and 59 (= *SB* 9843 and 9844), published by Baruch Lifshitz, "Papyrus grecs du désert de Juda," *Aegyptus* 42 (1962): 240–56, and often discussed later: G. Howard and J.C. Shel-

Aramaic, Nabataean, Hebrew and Greek, will be published soon.[17] All the papyri found by Yadin in Naḥal Ḥever are designated *P.Yadin*.

3) The so-called Seiyâl collection II[18] is composed of documents that were not discovered in the course of controlled excavations, but were found by Bedouin and brought in August 1952 and July 1953 to the Palestine Archaeological Museum (subsequently known as the Rockefeller Museum), where they are kept to this day. The plates were labelled 'Se,' i. e. Wadi Seiyâl (Naḥal Ṣe'elim).[19] Although the labelling suggests that the papyri came from Naḥal Ṣe'elim, those directly in charge of the documents at the time of their discovery have never made this claim anywhere in print. We can safely assume, even when we do not have tangible proof, that most of the documents in this lot came from the caves of Naḥal Ḥever in the early fifties. This is why the documents are described as *XḤev/Se*. The X stands for the fact that the cave number is not known for certain, although most of them probably come from the Cave of Letters. Depending on the language in which they were written, the documents are designated *Ḥev/Se* for the Hebrew documents, *XḤev/Se ar* for the Aramaic documents, *XḤev/Se nab* for the Nabataean documents and *XḤev/Se gr* for the Greek documents. Single documents from this lot have been published in preliminary publications. The entire corpus

ton, "The Bar-Kokhba Letters and Palestinian Greek," *IEJ* 23 (1973): 101 f.; Haiim Rosén, "Die Sprachsituation im römischen Palästina," in *Die Sprachen im römischen Reich der Kaiserzeit*, ed. Günter Neumann and Jürgen Untermann (Köln: Rheinland-Verlag, 1980), 224–26; Dirk Obbink, "Bilingual Literacy and Syrian Greek," *BASP* 28 (1991): 51–58; Hayim Lapin, "Palm Fronds and Citrons: Notes on Two Letters from Bar Kosiba's Administration," *HUCA* 64 (1993): 111–35; and most recently, G. Wilhelm Nebe, "Die beiden griechischen Briefe des Jonatan Archivs in Engedi aus dem zweiten jüdischen Aufstand 132–135 nach Chr.," *Revue de Qumran* 17 (1996): 275–89.

17 The papyri were published by Yigael Yadin et al., *The Documents from the Bar Kokhba Period in the Cave of Letters: Hebrew, Aramaic and Nabatean-Aramaic Papyri*, Judean Desert Studies III (Jerusalem: IES, 2002).

18 The Seiyâl collection I contains the Greek translation of the Minor Prophets (8ḤevXIIgr). The fragments of this translation discovered by Y. Aharoni in 1960 in the 'Cave of Horror' of Naḥal Ḥever established that the larger fragments of the text designated on the plates in the Rockefeller Museum as coming from Wadi Seiyâl also come from Cave 8 of Naḥal Ḥever. Thus the entire Seiyâl collection I originated in Naḥal Ḥever.

19 *XḤev/Ṣe*: surveys: J.T. Milik, "Le travail d'édition des manuscrits du Désert de Juda," in *Volume du Congrès International pour l'étude de l'Ancien Testament, Strasbourg 1956* (Leiden: Brill, 1957), 17–26; Jonas C. Greenfield, "The Texts from Naḥal Ṣe'elim (Wadi Seiyal)," in *The Madrid Qumran Congress*, ed. Julio Trebolle Barrera and Luis Vegas Montaner, Vol. II (Leiden: Brill, 1992), 661–66. This last survey is based on a preliminary sorting and identification of the Aramaic and Hebrew texts by Ada Yardeni.

(with the exception of the Nabataean documents) appeared in 1997.[20] Among the papyri designated *XḤev/Se* in this publication, there are several which were not part of the original Seiyâl collection, but which like them were not discovered in a controlled excavation. The Seiyâl collection contains the only surviving letter addressed to Bar Kokhba (written in Hebrew),[21] as well as private legal deeds in Aramaic and Greek, seven (or eight) of which belong to the archive of Salome Komaïse daughter of Levi who, like Babatha, lived in the village Maḥoza/Maḥoz 'Aglatain in the province of Arabia.[22]

In addition to these texts this volume includes an Appendix with some Qumran texts, said to come from cave 4.[23] The derivation of documentary texts from Qumran would be a sensation indeed,[24] had their provenance not been cast into doubt; it is for this reason that they are published as 'alleged Qumran Texts.'[25]

4) Very few documents were found in other sites in the course of the Judaean Desert Survey mentioned above: one Greek text was found in cave 8, Cave of Horror, in Naḥal Ḥever,[26] a few Greek papyri were found in cave 34, Cave of the Scrolls, in Naḥal Ṣe'elim and one Greek papyrus was found in Naḥal Mishmar; the last two finds were published by Lifshitz in 1961, and corrected by Benoit and

---

20 Hannah M. Cotton and Ada Yardeni, *Aramaic, Hebrew, and Greek Documentary Texts from Naḥal Ḥever and Other Sites*, Discoveries in the Judaean Desert XXVII (Oxford: Clarendon Press, 1997).

21 *XḤev/Se* 30.

22 *XḤev/Se ar* 12, *XḤev/Se gr* 60–65, perhaps also *XḤev/Se ar* 32 and 4Q347 as well as some of the as-yet undeciphered *XḤev/Se nab* 2–5(6) which undoubtedly come from the Cave of Letters in Naḥal Ḥever; see below. The other substantial, or at least meaningful, documents published in Cotton and Yardeni, *Aramaic, Hebrew, and Greek Documentary Texts from Naḥal Ḥever and Other Sites*: *XḤev/Se ar* 7, 8, 8a, 9, 10, 11, 13, 49, 50, *XḤev/Se gr* 66–73.

23 4Q342–346a, 348, 351–354, 356–360b.

24 Such as was rightly caused by the ostracon found at the site of Qumran by James F. Strange, and published by Frank Moore Cross and Esther Eshel, "Ostraca from Khirbet Qumrân," *IEJ* 47 (1997): 17–28. According to the editors' interpretation this is a deed of gift by a neophyte in favour of the community of the Yaḥad. The reading of 'Yaḥad' (יחד) in line 8 is crucial for this interpretation. However, Ada Yardeni has now convincingly demonstrated that the reading of 'Yaḥad' (יחד) in line 8 is wrong. Thus the ostracon can no longer serve to silence those who dispute the close connection between the community which lived on the site and the scrolls found in the adjacent caves; cf. Ada Yardeni, "A Draft of a Deed on an Ostracon from Khirbet Qumrân," *IEJ* 47 (1997): 233–37.

25 See Cotton and Yardeni, *Aramaic, Hebrew, and Greek Documentary Texts from Naḥal Ḥever and Other Sites*, 283 f.

26 *8Ḥev* 4, transcribed by Baruch Lifshitz, "The Greek Documents from the Cave of Horror," *IEJ* 12 (1962): 206 f.

Schwartz,[27] one Aramaic document and a few documents in Greek were discovered in Wadi Sdeir; Excavations in 1986 and 1993 in Cave Abi'or and the Cave of the Sandal in the vicinity of Jericho yielded Aramaic and Greek papyri,[28] of which only two fragments in Aramaic have so far been published.[29]

5) The papyri, jar-inscriptions and ostraca in Hebrew, Aramaic, Latin and Greek found on Masada during the excavations conducted there in 1963–4 and 1964–5, and published in 1989,[30] have a *terminus ante quem* of 73 or 74 CE,[31] and thus are only marginally relevant to the present survey. More documents were discovered in the course of excavations conducted on Masada in 1995–7, but these are so far unpublished.[32] The Latin texts from Masada constitute a unique find in the Roman province of Judaea: we have *tituli picti* on jars from Italy and Spain imported by King Herod (or brought, perhaps, by the besieging Roman army),[33] papyri and ostraca written by legionaries of the Tenth Legion *Fretensis* as well as Aramaic and Greek papyri and ostraca which originated in all likelihood among the *Sicarii* who occupied the fortress from 66 until its fall in 73 or 74.

What then do these documents contribute to the study of Jewish history for the period which they mostly record, i. e. 70 to 135? Since not all the documents have been published, any conclusions to be drawn from them are bound to be partial and tentative. This is especially true of the mostly unpublished letters

27 Baruch Lifshitz, "The Greek Documents from Naḥal Ṣeelim and Naḥal Mishmar," *IEJ* 11 (1961): 53–62; Pierre Benoit, "Bulletin," *RB* 68 (1961): 466 f.; Jacques Schwartz, "Remarques sur des fragments grecs du Désert de Juda," *RB* 69 (1962): 61–63.

28 See Hanan Eshel and Boaz Zissu, "Ketef Jericho, 1993," *IEJ* 45 (1995): 292–98.

29 Esther Eshel and Hanan Eshel, "Fragments of Two Aramaic Documents which were Brought to Abi'or Cave during the Bar-Kokhba Revolt," *Eretz Israel* 23 (1992): 276–85 (Hebrew). All the documents mentioned in this category were published (or republished – as the case may be) in James Charlesworth et al., eds., *Miscellaneous Texts from the Judaean Desert*, Discoveries in the Judaean Desert XXXVIII (Oxford: Oxford University Press, 2000).

30 Yigael Yadin and Joseph Naveh, *Masada I: The Aramaic and Hebrew Ostraca and Jar Inscriptions* (Jerusalem: IES, 1989); Hannah M. Cotton and Joseph Geiger, *Masada II: The Latin and Greek Documents* (Jerusalem: IES, 1989). The documents are designated *Doc.Mas.*

31 See Hannah M. Cotton, "The Date of the Fall of Masada: The Evidence of the Masada Papyri," *ZPE* 78 (1989): 157–62.

32 See Ehud Netzer, "The Rebels' Archives at Masada," *IEJ* 54 (2004): 218–29.

33 See Hannah M. Cotton and Joseph Geiger, "The Economic Importance of Herod's Masada: the Evidence of the Jar Inscriptions," in *Judaea and the Greco-Roman World in the Time of Herod in the Light of Archaeological Evidence*, ed. Gideon Foerster and Klaus Fittschen (Göttingen: Vandenhoeck & Ruprecht, 1996), 163–70; Hannah M. Cotton, Omri Lernau, and Yuval Goren, "Fish Sauces from Herodian Masada," *JRA* 9 (1996): 223–38. For the possibility that the Roman army brought some of the Latin inscribed amphorae to Masada during the siege, see J.R. Rea, "Masada and Pompeii: Another Link," *SCI* 18 (1999): 121–24 (on *Doc.Mas.* 820).

and leases which originate from Bar Kokhba and his men. These are sure to shed further light on this poorly documented revolt which had such catastrophic consequences for the history of the Jewish people.

Three pieces of evidence are relevant to the question of the geographical and chronological extent of the Bar Kokhba Revolt.

1) First, Jerusalem: was Jerusalem occupied by the rebels, or to put it more circumspectly: was Jewish sovereignty recognized there? The relevant lines of *P.Mur* 29 and 30, two deeds of sale dated by the era of the revolt, as corrected by Milik himself in an 'addendum,'[34] and confirmed by Ada Yardeni, seem to establish that Jewish sovereignty was recognized in Jerusalem at least from Aug./Sept. 133 and until Sept./Oct. 135.[35] *P.Mur* 29 (Aug./Sept. 133) lines 9–10 (outer text) read:

בארבעה עשׂר באלול
שנת שתים ל[גאלת] ישׂ[ראל] בירושלים חותמים יהונתן בר יהוסף שמעון בר שבי

'On fourteenth Elul, Year Two of the redemption of Israel, in Jerusalem, Yehonathan son Yehosaf and Shime'on son of Shabbai are signing ...'.

Later on, lines 10–11 read:

מכר קלבוס בר אוטרפלוס מירושלים

'Kalbos son of Eutroplos from Jerusalem sold etc.'.

P.Mur 30 (Sept./Oct. 135), lines 8–9 (outer text) reads:

בעשׂרים ואחד לתשרי
שנת ארבע לגאולת ישׂראל בירושלים חותמים יהונתן בר יהוסף שמעון בר סימי ...

'On twenty first Tishrei, Year Four of the redemption of Israel in Jerusalem, Yehonathan son Yehosaf and Shime'on son of Simai are signing ... '.

Now it could be argued that despite the preposition 'in' (ב), the expression 'in Jerusalem' (בירושלים) does not stand for the place where the contract was signed, but is part of the dating formula – a dating formula which expresses political

34 Benoit, Milik, and de Vaux, *Les grottes de Murabba'at*, 205.

35 Contra Menachem Mor, *The Bar-Kochba Revolt: Its Extent and Effect* (Jerusalem: Yad Ben-Zvi Press, 1991), 146–171, esp. 156 f (Hebrew). Contrary to what he assumes (p. 133, n. 5 and p. 157, n. 72) there is no independent evidence for Iulius Severus' arrival in Judaea (which might have become already Syria-Palaestina), see Anthony R. Birley, *The Fasti of Roman Britain* (Oxford: Clarendon Press, 1981), 106 ff.

aspiration and a hope, as is claimed for formulae mentioning Jerusalem on coins from the time of the revolt.[36] However, taking 'in Jerusalem' in these documents to be part of a dating formula used simply for propaganda purposes will leave the contracts, quite abnormally, without any reference to the place where they were concluded.[37] Legal usage excludes such a forced interpretation. The implications seem to be inescapable: Jerusalem recognized the authority of a Jewish state as late as Sept./Oct. 135.[38]

2) *P.Mur* 22 (a deed of sale in Hebrew) line 1 used to read: 'Fourteenth of Marḥeshvan year one (שׂנת אחת) of the freedom of Israel.' The new reading of the line, for which full credit should be given to Ada Yardeni, makes this the latest dated document from the time of the revolt (later than *P.Mur* 30 just discussed): 'Fourteenth of Marḥeshvan year four (שׂנת ארבע) of the freedom of Israel,' that is, Oct./Nov. 135.

The cumulative weight of these late documents must arouse doubts about the traditional date for the fall of Beithar and the conclusion of the revolt with it. Otherwise we have to assume that the revolt continued in other areas well after the fall of Beithar, traditionally dated to July 135.[39] We should take it that people in these areas continued to date their documents as if Israel were still independent. Additional evidence for the continuation of the revolt at least to the end of 135 CE seems to be supplied by the absence of *imperator iterum* from Hadrian's titulature until his twentieth *tribunicia potestas*, i. e. after 10 December 135.[40]

The most obvious contribution of the documents which come from Bar Kokhba's own circles is to a better understanding of the exploitation of land which fell into the rebels' hands. The leases and sub-leases found among the documents from Wadi Murabba'at and Naḥal Ḥever, as well as some of Bar Kokhba's letters to

---

36 See e. g. Leo Mildenberg, "Bar Kochba in Jerusalem?," *Schweizer Münzblätter* 27 (1977): 1–6.

37 One has to draw a distinction between לגאולת ישראל בירושלים in *P.Mur* 29 and 30 and שׁנ]ת] תלת לחרות ירו{ו}שלים ('Year Three of the freedom of Jerusalem') in *P.Mur* 25 (134/5 CE) line 1, which is clearly part of a dating formula, and cannot, without further proof, be taken as a reflection of reality.

38 The alternative is to take the date in *P.Mur* 29 and 30 as referring to the first revolt. In support of this it could be said that in both documents the formula 'to the redemption of Israel' is not followed by a reference to Bar Kokhba as it is in *P.Mur* 24 A-I; *XḤev/Se ar* 7, 8, 13, 49 and in *P.Yadin* 42, 44. Hanan Eshel and myself propose to deal with these documents in more detail elsewhere.

39 Emil Schürer, *The History of the Jewish People in the Age of Jesus Christ*, ed. Fergus Millar and Géza Vermès, Vol. I (Edinburgh: Clark, 1973), 551 ff.

40 See Werner Eck, "The Bar Kokhba Revolt: The Roman Point of View," *JRS* 89 (1999): 76–89 and Werner Eck and Gideon Foerster, "Ein Triumphbogen für Hadrian im Tal von Beth Shean bei Tel Shalem," *JRA* 12 (1999): 294–313.

his administrators (*parnasim*) in Ein Gedi,[41] imply that Bar Kokhba laid his hands on parts of the imperial domain in the places recorded. Land owned by the *fiscus* was exploited in different ways: between land leased to tenants and land worked by slaves under a *vilicus* "there was still an infinite range of local variations."[42] Was the system of leasing and sub-leasing reflected in the Bar Kokhba documents taken over from the imperial *fiscus*? In some, but not all, of the documents (e. g. not in *P.Mur* 24A-L), the first lessees are *parnasim* of Bar Kokhba who sublease to others. Should we assume that there was always a sub-layer of tenants left unrecorded in the documents, those who actually tilled the land? Such a three-tiered administration is typical for example of imperial estates in Egypt. On the other hand the sub-lessees in the Bar Kokhba leases are not share-croppers, but pay for the lease in money. This was not the method employed by the *fiscus*, at least for the balsam in Judaea, about which we know from Pliny that the *fiscus* itself sold the balsam to retailers, who in their turn sold it to others for less than a third of what they had paid for it, and yet made a profit by adulterating the pure balsam.[43] I believe that there are hints in some of the Bar Kokhba documents that, as might have been expected, Bar Kokhba took over the precious balsam groves.[44]

Since I have mentioned the imperial *fiscus* and the evidence for the existence of imperial domains in Ein Gedi, let me say something parenthetically about the possible interpretation of Jewish documents from the province of Arabia as evidence for Jews having perpetual leaseholds on imperial estates in Maḥoza. Three land declarations from 127 CE, two receipts from 124 and 131 respectively, and a deed of gift from 129, may all be describing rent rather than tax paid to the imperial *fiscus*. Were the date groves in Maḥoza part of an imperial domain and an imperial monopoly like the balsam groves in Ein Gedi?[45]

---

41 Leases: *P.Mur* 24A-L (134 CE), and the *P.Yadin* 42 (132 CE), 43 (132 CE), 44, 45 and 46 (all three from 134 CE); letters: *P.Yadin* 52 (Greek = *SB* 9843); *P.Yadin* 49, 50, 54–58, 60; *P.Mur* 46; *P.Yadin* 51, 53; *P.Yadin* 59 (Greek = *SB* 9844).

42 Dorothy J. Crawford, "Imperial Estates," in *Studies in Roman Property*, ed. Moses I. Finley (Cambridge: Cambridge University Press, 1976), 44; Dieter Flach, *Römische Agrargeschichte* (München: Beck, 1990), 82 ff.

43 Pliny, *NH* XII, 123: *nec manifestior alibi fraus quippe millibus denarium sextarii empti vendente fisco trecenis denariis veneunt: in tantum expedit augere liquorem*; Hannah M. Cotton and Werner Eck, "Ein Staatsmonopol und seine Folgen: Plinius, Naturalis Historia 12,123 und der Preis für Balsam," *Rheinisches Museum für Philologie* 140 (1997): 153–61.

44 See *P.Yadin* 50: ולטמה די לא יקרב בה אנש ('no one should get near the Lotem(?)').

45 Land declarations: *P.Yadin* 16; *XḤev/Se gr* 61 and *XḤev/Se gr* 62; receipts: *XḤev/Se gr* 60 and *XḤev/Se ar* 12; deed of gift: *XḤev/Se gr* 64, see esp. lines 28–30: <ἥ> (i. e. the date grove) τελέσει

Documents which did not originate in Bar Kokhba's circles may also have something to tell us, albeit indirectly, about the revolt. The existence of intimate ties between families in Ein Gedi in the province of Judaea and those living in Maḥoza (Maḥoz 'Aglatain) in the province of Arabia strikes one immediately on reading the Babatha archive. Very often we find the expression 'from Ein Gedi residing in Maḥoza,' or vice versa, as in one of Bar Kokhba's leases: 'from the Luhit in Maḥoz 'Aglatain, residing in Ein Gedi'.[46] Ein Gedians reside in Maḥoza, own property there and intermarry with the Jews of Maḥoza. It is just possible that Yadin was right to identify Beianos, father of Miriam of the Babatha archive, with the father of one of Bar Kokhba's *parnasim* in Ein Gedi.[47] People who belonged to the same families lived on both sides of the so-called provincial border. When were they separated? I believe that the families were separated during the Great Revolt. After the raids by the *sicarii* in Passover 68[48] and the battles over the balsam between the Jews and the Roman army in that year,[49] Ein Gedi must have been practically abandoned, at least for a while: 'Ein Gedi is now another ruin' says Pliny the Elder in the late 70s.[50] Ein Gedi ceased being the capital of a toparchy, became subsumed in the toparchy of Jericho,[51] and in 124 is attested as 'a village of

καθ ἔτος είς λόγον κυριακοῦ φίσκου {καθ ἔτος} φοίνεικος πατητοῦ σάτα δέκα καὶ συροῦ καὶ ναaρου σάτα ἕξ; see Hannah M. Cotton, "Land Tenure in the Documents from the Nabataean Kingdom and the Roman Province of Arabia," *ZPE* 119 (1997): 255–65 [above, pp. 293–308].

46 For the expression 'from Ein-Gedi, residing in Maḥoza': *P.Yadin* 18 (128 CE), ll. 32–37 = ll. 3–6: ἐ̣ξ[έδ]ο̣τ[ο Ἰούδα]ς Ἐ̣λ̣εαζάρου τοῦ καὶ [Χθουσί]ω̣ν[ος Σ]ελαμψ̣[ι]ώγ̣η̣ν τὴν ἰδίαν θυγατέραν αὐτο̣ῦ παρθ̣έ̣ν̣ο̣ν Ἰοὐ̣δατι ἐπικαλουμένῳ Κίμβερι υἱῷ Ἀνανίου τοῦ Σ̣ω̣μ̣α̣λα, ἀμφότεροι ἀπὸ̣ κ̣ώ̣μης Αἰνγαδῶν τῆς Ἰου̣δαία[ς] ἐνθάδε καταμένοντ̣[ες]; *P.Yadin* 19 (128 CE), ll. 11–12: [Ἰο]ύ̣δ̣ας Ἐ̣λ[αζά]ρου Χθουσ[ίω]ν̣ο̣ς Ἡ̣νγ̣α̣δη̣[νὸ]ς οἰκῶν ἐν Μαωζᾶς; cf. *P.Yadin* 20 (130 CE), ll. 4–5 = ll. 23–24: Βησᾶς Ἰησούου Ἡνγαδηνὸς οἰκῶν ἐν Μαζραᾳ ἐ<πί>τροπος ὀρφανῶν Ἰησούου Χθουσ̣ίωνος; *P.Yadin* 44 (November 134 CE), ll. 4–6: אלמא בן יהודה ותחנה בן שמעון מן הלוחית שבמחוז עגלתין שניהם יושבים בעין גדי: ''Alma son of Judah and Taḥna son of Shime'on from the Luḥit in Maḥoz 'Aglatain, both residing in Ein Gedi.'

47 *P.Yadin* 26, l. 3: Μαριάμην Βειανοῦ Ἡνγαδηνη; *P.Yadin* 52 (= Lifshitz, "Papyrus grecs du désert de Juda," 240, no. 1 = *SB* VIII, 9843), ll. 1–3: Σου[μαῖ]ος Ἰωναθῆι Βαιανοῦ καὶ Μα[σ]αβάλα χαίρειν; *P.Yadin* 49, ll. 1–2: משמעון בר כוסבא לאנשי עינגדי למשבלא וליהונתן בר בעין שלום, cf. Yadin, "Expedition D – The Cave of the Letters," 247 f.

48 Joseph., *BJ* 4.402.

49 Pliny, *NH* XII, 112.

50 Pliny, *NH* V, 73: '*Infra hos* (i.e. the Essenes) *Engada oppidum fuit, secundum ab Hierosolymis fertilitate palmetorumque nemoribus, nunc aiterum bustum.*'

51 *P.Yadin* 16 (127 CE) line 16: Ἰουδάνου Ἐλαζάρου κώμης Αἰνγαδδῶν περὶ Ἰερειχοῦντα τῆς Ἰουδαίας; note that Ein Gedi is absent from Pliny's list of toparchies, *NH* V, 70, which is more updated than that of Josephus, *BJ* 3.55.

our Lord Caesar.'[52] At least the balsam groves must have become part of the imperial domain. The Jewish families who escaped from Ein Gedi settled in a place with similar climatic conditions, similar cultivation, a similar watering system, where other Jewish families had settled before: in Maḥoz 'Aglatain – a village in what was then and until 106 the Nabataean kingdom. But the ties with the home village remained. I believe that communication was facilitated by sea travel: both villages were situated on the seashore, and the Dead Sea was navigable.[53] The very fact that documents of people from Ein Gedi and of families from Arabia were found in the same cave is the best testimony to the survival of close ties between the families. It seems not unreasonable to assume that the close ties with the mother community go a long way to explain why the well-off Jews of Arabia, notwithstanding their excellent relations with their neighbours the Nabataeans (who serve as guardians, witnesses and subscribers in the Jewish documents), left their property behind and crossed over to Judaea soon after the beginning of the Bar Kokhba revolt. This event may tell us as much about the nature of the Bar Kokhba revolt as the documents left behind by the leader of the revolt and his administrators themselves. Unless the revolt spread into Arabia – for which there is not a shred of evidence – we must assume that Jews from Arabia responded to some sort of call and returned home. Was it a messianic hope or what seemed like the renewal of Jewish sovereignty that made them come home? The Bar Kokhba Revolt reunited the families whom the First Revolt had rent asunder – tragically, they were reunited in death.[54]

Elsewhere in the series of *Kolloquien des Historischen Kollegs* I discussed at great length the contribution of the documents from the Judaean Desert to our understanding of the Roman administration of the province of Judaea/Syria-Palaestina. I shall therefore limit myself here to a brief summary.[55] Schürer and his new editors distinguish between the 'Greek cities' and the 'Jewish region.'[56]

---

52 *P.Yadin* 11 (6/5/124 CE), ll. 12–13 = ll. 1–2: ἐπ̣ὶ ὑ̣[πάτ]ω̣ν Μανείο̣υ Ἀκειλίου Γλαβρίωνος κα̣ὶ Τορκουά[του Θ]ηβανιανο[ῦ πρὸ] μιᾶς νωγῶν Μαίω[ν] ἐν Ἐνγαδοῖς κώμῃ κυρίου Καίσαρος; *XḤev/Se gr* 67 lines 1–2: [Ἐν]γαδων Κυρίου Κ[αίσαρος κώμης].

53 Gideon Hadas, "Where was the Harbour of 'En-Gedi Situated?," *IEJ* 43 (1993): 45–49; see boats sailing on the Dead Sea in the Madaba Map.

54 For the possibility that the revolt spread to the province of Arabia see Eck, "The Bar Kokhba Revolt: The Roman Point of View."

55 See Hannah M. Cotton, "Some Aspects of the Roman Administration of Judaea/Syria-Palaestina," in *Lokale Autonomie und römische Ordnungsmacht in den kaiserzeitlichen Provinzen vom 1. bis 3. Jahrhundert*, ed. Werner Eck (München: Oldenbourg, 1999), 75–91 [above, pp. 317–35].

56 Emil Schürer, *The History of the Jewish People in the Age of Jesus Christ*, ed. Fergus Millar and Géza Vermès, Vol. II (Edinburgh: Clark, 1979), 85–198. I do not propose to enter here into the question of the validity of this division.

The Jewish region includes Judaea proper, Samaria, the Galilee and the Peraea. There are very few cities in these areas and the majority of cities that are there are on the fringes, and in any case are not likely to have controlled the entire Jewish region as their city-territories. The documents enable us now to confirm, revise and reinterpret the evidence about the administrative divisions in the Roman province of Judaea contained in the literary sources, namely Josephus and Pliny the Elder. Josephus, Pliny and the papyri prove that the Jewish region was divided into administrative units with central villages or cities at their head. Only about Judaea proper can we be sure that these units were called *toparchiai*. There is no evidence for local officials at the head of these capital villages, nor for centrally appointed officials in charge of the *toparchiai* – but the existence of one kind or another of local officials must be assumed. There are some hints that the *toparchiai* were in charge of taxation. Above all it is hard to believe that nothing beyond a merely geographical relationship is intended by the description of the dependence of a village on a central village, especially since the dependence of the single village on the central village is described both in the papyri and in Josephus in terms identical to those describing the dependence of the *chora* on its *polis*.[57] Furthermore, we know that under the Severi some of these central villages received the status of a *polis*: thus Lydda became Diospolis in 199/200, and Emmaus became Nicopolis in 219 or 220. In 199/200 Beth-Govrin – about which we do not know that it was a capital village – received the status of a *polis* and was renamed Eleutheropolis. The accelerating urbanization of Judaea (now called Syria-Palaestina) resulted in the eventual disappearance of the toparchies and their replacement by *poleis* with their territories.[58] This is the picture conveyed by the fourth century *Onomasticon* of Eusebius. But if we are right to think that the capital villages achieved a degree of local autonomy and administrative respon-

57 Cf. the dependence of the village of Soffathe [...] on the city of Livias in the Peraea described in *XḤev/Se gr* 65 (olim *P.Yadin* 37): Ἰησοῦς Μαναήμου τ[ῶν ἀπὸ κώμης ...] Σοφφαθẹ[. .] . . . . π̣ẹρ̣ὶ πόλιν Λιουιάδος τῆς Π̣[εραίας] (lines 3–4), and the dependence of the village of Ein Gedi on the central village of its toparchy, Jericho, in *P.Yadin* 16 line 16: Ἰουδάνου Ἐλαζάρου κώμης Αἰνγαδδῶν περὶ Ἱερειχοῦντα τῆς Ἰουδαίας; or that of Bethbassi vis-à-vis Herodion – ἐν Βαιτοβαι̣σσαιας ... τ̣ο̣παρχείας Ἡρω̣δεί̣ο̣[υ]; Galoda vis-à-vis Akrabatta – ἀπὸ κ(ώμης) Γαλωδῶν τῆς περὶ Ἀκραβạττῶν, and Batharda vis-à-vis Gophna – ἐν κώμῃ Βαιτοα̣ρδοις τῆς περὶ Γοφνοῖς – all in *P.Mur* 115 lines 2–3; and finally that of Aristoboulias and Yaqim (or Yaqum) vis-à-vis Zif in *XḤev/Se gr* 69 lines 3–5: ἐν Ἀριστοβουλιάδι τῆς Ζẹιφηνῆς ... Ακαβας Μηειρω τῶν ἀπ̣ὸ κ̣ώμης Ἰακείμων τ̣[ῆς Ζειφηνῆ̣ς].
58 See A.H.M. Jones, “The Urbanization of Palestine,” *JRS* 21 (1931): 82 ff.; Aharon Oppenheimer, “Urbanization and City Territories in Roman Palestine,” in *The Jews in the Hellenistic-Roman World: Studies in Memory of Menahem Stern*, ed. Isaiah M. Gafni, Aharon Oppenheimer, and Daniel R. Schwartz (Jerusalem: Zalman Shazar Center, 1996), 220 ff. (Hebrew).

sibilities already in the first and second centuries, then this urbanization was but a logical development.[59]

The main contribution, however, of the growing corpus of documentary texts from the Judaean Desert is towards a better understanding of legal and social aspects of Jewish society in the Roman provinces of Judaea and Arabia in the first half of the second century CE. All the documents from the time of the Bar Kokhba Revolt, whether written by Bar Kokhba and his people or by individuals who somehow got entangled in the revolt, can be utilized for this purpose. Especially in the case of the latter, only the dating formula and the use of Hebrew single them out from contracts in Aramaic concluded before the outbreak of Bar Kokhba Revolt. The impression is that the private-law procedures visible in these documents are continuous with those from the immediately preceding 'provincial' period. Nevertheless, in the absence of a final publication of this corpus of evidence, I am naturally reluctant to reach final conclusions about the state of law at the time as reflected in Aramaic and Hebrew contracts from the Judaean Desert and its relationship to rabbinic sources.

More intractable and far less accessible are the Nabataean documents.[60] These documents raise a host of technical and theoretical problems. One would like to know what is uniquely Nabataean about them apart from the script. We know that they are all contracts, that is legal documents, and that at least some of them involve Jews: what is the relationship between contracts written in Nabataean and those written in Jewish Aramaic? What conclusions can we reach about the use of Nabataean script, diplomatics and perhaps law by Jews? The Nabataean *P.Yadin* 1, 2, 3, 4, 6, and 9 belong to the Babatha archive. The last two were written in 119 and 122 respectively. Thus as many as 16 years after the annexation of Arabia contracts continued to be written in Nabataean. Of the other Nabataean documents, only one, *XḤev/Se nab* 1 has so far been published.[61] Since fragments of this papyrus were found by Yadin in the Cave of Letters in Naḥal Ḥever, we can be pretty sure that this papyrus as well as the other five Nabataean papyri found with it, *XḤev/Se nab* 2–6, also come from the Cave of Letters in Naḥal Ḥever. *XḤev/Se nab* 1 may belong to the Babatha archive if the γανναθ Νικαρκος in the possession of Babatha's second husband, Judah son of Eleazar Khthousion, is named after the Nikarchos (ניקרכס), who was the father of the author of the Nabataean

59 Cf. the metropoleis of Roman Egypt in Alan K. Bowman and Dominic Rathbone, "Cities and Administration in Roman Egypt," *JRS* 82 (1992): 107–27.
60 I am grateful to Ada Yardeni for making transcriptions of the Nabataean documents available to me.
61 Jean Starcky, "Un contrat nabatéen sur papyrus," *RB* 61 (1954): 161–81.

contract. The seller in *XḤev/Se nab* 2[62] is Shalom, perhaps the mother of Salome Komaïse daughter of Levi, and may belong to the latter's archive.[63] Do the other (still unread) Nabataean contracts also belong to one or both archives? If they do, then this, I submit, would change completely the ratio of Nabataean documents in the two archives.

As it happens we have fared better with the Greek papyri, most of which are now published, or nearly so. These Greek papyri are with very few exceptions all written by Jews or at least involve Jews. However, the Jews who wrote the papyri are by no means Hellenized Jews. This is amply demonstrated by their Aramaic subscriptions and signatures,[64] and sometimes by the faulty Greek they use. One or two of the Greek papyri can be shown to be almost certainly literal translations from an Aramaic *Urtext.*[65] Furthermore, the same people have recourse to both languages in their legal documents. Thus for example, Judah son of Eleazar Khthousion, Babatha's second husband, writes his wife, Babatha, a marriage contract in Aramaic, which one may choose to call *Ketubba* (*P.Yadin* 10),[66] whereas for his own daughter, Shelamṣion, he employs a scribe to write a marriage contract in Greek (*P.Yadin* 18).

There are no Greek documents which can be dated safely to the Nabataean period, that is before 106 when the Nabataean Kingdom was annexed. The use of Greek by Jews in the province of Arabia is thus connected with the advent of the Romans. No such association can be made for the use of Greek in Judaea whose provincialization dates to 6 CE. With the exception of inscriptions on Jewish ossuaries, the first Greek documents from Jewish circles come from Masada.[67] The earliest one, *Doc.Mas.* 740, tentatively dated to 25–35 CE, is too fragmentary to betray its origin. However, the majority of the Greek material found on Masada is likely to have been written by no one but the *sicarii*. This is no more surprising than the use of Greek by the Bar Kokhba administration in *P.Yadin* 52 and 59 (mentioned in note 16). By now we should have learnt that the use of Greek by Jews has no ideological implications: it should not be mistaken for the Hellenization of the writer

---

62 Published in Ada Yardeni, *Textbook of Aramaic, Hebrew and Nabataean Documentary Texts from the Judaean Desert and Related Material* Vol. I (Jerusalem: The Hebrew University Press, 2000), 290 (Hebrew; for English see Vol. II, 95).

63 See above n. 22.

64 See Aramaic and Nabatean Signatures and Subscriptions, edited by Yigael Yadin and Jonas C. Greenfield, in Lewis, *The Documents from the Bar Kokhba Period in the Cave of Letters. Greek Papyri*, 136–149.

65 See the attempted translation back into Aramaic of *XḤev/Se gr* 64 in Cotton and Yardeni, *Aramaic, Hebrew, and Greek Documentary Texts from Naḥal Ḥever and Other Sites*, 207.

66 See Yadin, Greenfield, and Yardeni, "Babatha's Ketubba."

67 See introduction to Cotton and Geiger, *Masada II: The Latin and Greek Documents*, 9 f.

nor as evidence for his political and national sentiments. The Jews represented in some of the Greek documents come from densely populated Jewish areas, from the heartland of the Bar Kokhba Revolt, a religious and national movement. Some of the Greek documents were written close to the time when the Revolt broke out – a revolt which was carefully prepared some years in advance. In fact the very presence of their documents in the caves demonstrates their owners' participation in the Revolt. The writers of these documents cannot and should not be regarded as assimilated Jews.

Nor is there any reason to draw a distinction between Jews from the province of Arabia and those from Judaea; the areas in question are very close to each other (a day's walk or two days at most between the furthest destinations involved in our documents), and borders in the region had very little inhibiting effect on movement. The official names, Arabia, Judaea and later Syria-Palaestina, represent artificial divisions which do not seem to have mattered very much in reality. As was pointed out above, it is very likely that the Jews living in Maḥoza originally came from Ein Gedi. The archives demonstrate clearly that the Jews living in Arabia and the Jews living in the province of Judaea belonged to a single Jewish society whose internal ties overrode provincial boundaries.

Finally it should be stressed that the Jews represented in the documents from the Judaean Desert – whatever their language – are not a fringe group. This corpus owes its preservation to the upheaval caused by the Bar Kokhba Revolt. Most of it, it is true, is thus limited in time to the years immediately preceding the Bar Kokhba Revolt and those of the Revolt itself (although some documents are much earlier, e. g. *P.Mur* 18, an acknowledgement of debt in Aramaic, from 55/6 CE, and *XḤev/Se nab* 1 from 60 CE). On the other hand, the people attested in the documents come from villages as scattered as Mazra'a and Maḥoza/Maḥoz 'Aglatain in the Dead Sea area in the Province of Arabia, Sophathe[...] in the Peraea in Transjordan, which belonged to the province of Judaea, Ein Gedi on the western shore of the Dead Sea, Kesalon and Hardona in the vicinity of Jerusalem, Kaphar Barucha, Yaqim (or Yaqum) and Aristoboulias in the area south-east of Hebron, Bethbassi near Herodium, Galoda in eastern Samaria and Batharda in southern Samaria. The great majority of the documents, whether letters or legal deeds, were written by, or at least involve Jews, thus giving us glimpses of Jewish village society in the Roman provinces of Arabia and Judaea at the time that they were written. I consider it legitimate to rely on them in order to evaluate the state of Jewish law and society at the time, and more particularly, the authority exercised on Jewish law by the rabbis.[68]

---

68 By 'Jewish law' here I mean the forms of law used by Jews.

However, the rabbinic sources are not the only background against which these documents should be assessed. We should not lose sight of the general environment in which they were written, namely the Roman Near East. Although written by Jews, these papyri must be seen in the context of the papyri of the Roman Near East as a whole, including Egypt.[69] The area concerned is that covered by the Roman provinces of Syria (divided in the 190s into 'Syria Coele' and 'Syria Phoenice'); Mesopotamia (created in the 190s); Arabia; and Judaea, which in the 130s became 'Syria Palaestina,' and to which in the 290s the southern part of the former province of Arabia, the Negev and Sinai, were added. Greek is the dominant language in the papyri from the Roman Near East, alongside Latin (especially in Roman army circles), several Aramaic dialects (Palestinian Aramaic, Nabataean, Syriac, and Palmyrene), Hebrew, as well as Parthian and Middle Persian (a few scraps). A salient feature of the papyrology of the Roman Near East is the variety of languages employed, but more particularly "the presence of two or more languages in the same archive, or even in the same document: for instance Greek and Syriac in the texts from Mesopotamia and the Middle Euphrates; Nabataean, Aramaic and Greek in the archive from Arabia; and Hebrew, Aramaic and Greek in the Bar Kokhba documents."[70]

The double document, which fell into desuetude in Egypt in the first century BCE (with the exception of documents submitted by Roman citizens), is very typical of the texts from other parts of the Roman Near East. Although the Romans used the double document, one cannot simply attribute to their influence the use of the double document in Near Eastern societies.[71] Unlike the Roman double document which required the signature of seven witnesses, the majority of double documents from the Judaean Desert, as well as many of the documents from elsewhere in the Roman Near East, carry the signatures of five witnesses. On the other

---

69 Which is excluded in Cotton, Cockle, and Millar, "The Papyrology of the Roman Near East: A Survey."

70 Cotton, Cockle, and Millar, 214. For Mesopotamia and the Middle Euphrates see C.B. Welles, R.O. Fink, and J.F. Gilliam, *The Excavations at Dura-Europos Conducted by Yale University and the French Academy of Inscriptions and Letters, Final Report V, Part I: The Parchments and Papyri* (New Haven: Yale University Press, 1959); and recently: Javier Teixidor, "Deux documents syriaques du IIIe siècle ap. J.-C., provenant du Moyen Euphrate," *CR Acad. Inscr.* 134 (1990): 144–66; Javier Teixidor, "Un document syriaque de fermage de 242 ap. J.-C.," *Semitica* 41 (1993): 195–208; Denis Feissel and Jean Gascou, "Documents d'archives romains inédits du Moyen Euphrate (IIIe s. après J-C): I. Les pétitions (T. Euphr. 1 à 5)," *Journal des Savants*, 1995, 65–119; Javier Teixidor, Denis Feissel, and Jean Gascou, "Documents d'archives romains inédits du Moyen Euphrate (IIIe s. après J-C): II. Les actes de vente- achat (P. Euphr. 6 À 10)," *Journal des Savants*, 1997, 3–57.

71 See Lewis, *The Documents from the Bar Kokhba Period in the Cave of Letters. Greek Papyri*, 6–10; Elisabeth Koffmahn, *Die Doppelurkunden aus der Wüste Juda* (Leiden: Brill, 1968), 10–30.

hand Roman influence is detectable in the dating formulae: private documents from Arabia and Judaea, like those from Syria and Mesopotamia, and in contrast to those from Egypt, use consular dates and Roman months, often in addition to regnal years of the Roman emperor and the provincial era.

Roman legal requirements seem also to lie behind the representation of women by a guardian, for whom the term ἐπίτροπος – the technical term for the guardian of minors – rather than κύριος is used. The use of a single term for the two kinds of guardians is due to the influence of Roman law, and not to the influence of the Aramaic environment. The Aramaic subscriptions make the distinction: the guardian of a woman is called אדון = κύριος; for the guardian of the minor the Aramaic borrowed the Greek term ἐπίτροπος: אפטרפא. In none of the Hebrew, Aramaic and Nabataean papyri from the Judaean Desert do we find a woman represented by a guardian. Are we in the presence of two different legal systems, or is this merely a question of the language of the document? Unfortunately the evidence is not sufficient to allow us to give an unequivocal answer. The low profile kept by the guardian of a woman even in the Greek documents is conspicuous. The four deeds in languages other than Greek which would have required the presence of a guardian of a woman under Roman law were not written under Roman rule. Is it merely a coincidence that we do not have a document written under Roman rule in Aramaic, Nabataean or Hebrew with a guardian representing a woman, or does this prove incontrovertibly that the Greek deeds, unlike the Semitic ones, were meant for Roman courts, or at least had to conform to Roman legal formalities?[72]

Finally, beyond the language and the diplomatics, the documents attest to recourse to Roman courts of law and the use of Roman legal instruments. Without dwelling on this issue here,[73] I wish merely to point out here that the recourse to Roman law and Roman courts was not required by the Roman authorities. This would be out of character, and against much evidence to the contrary from other parts of the Roman world – where the initiative in such actions is seen to be taken voluntarily by the subjects. Without coercion or attempts to impose uniformity, the simple presence of the Romans as the supreme authority in the province invited appeals to their authority, to their courts as well as to their laws. The Babatha

---

72 See in detail Hannah M. Cotton, "The Guardian (ἐπίτροπος) of a Woman in the Documents from the Judaean Desert," *ZPE* 118 (1997): 267–73 [above, pp. 431–41].

73 Most recently, Dieter Nörr, "Prozessuales aus dem Babatha-Archiv," in *Mélanges de droit romain et d'histoire ancienne: hommage à la mémoire de André Magdelain*, ed. Michel Humbert and Yan Thomas (Paris: Panthéon-Assas, 1998), 317–41, with all previous bibliography. I am grateful to Dieter Nörr for showing me the ms. in advance of publication. See also Tiziana J. Chiusi, "IV. Zur Vormundschaft der Mutter," *ZSS* 111 (1994): 155–96.

archive shows us provincials who seem more than willing to let the representative(s) of the central government and its legal system handle their disputes, who take the trouble to prepare blank forms of the *actio tutelae*, to search for Roman legal arguments and to introduce into their personal claims Roman propaganda slogans of 'the most blessed times.' They are active and enterprising in inviting intervention. Having previously used Aramaic and Nabataean, they now resort to Greek in their legal documents, for no other reason, it seems, than to make them valid in a Roman court of law. No other courts are mentioned in this archive, and there is no good reason to assume that Nabataean and Aramaic could not be used in a local court.[74]

It is thus, indirectly, that the documents from the Judaean Desert reveal to us a facet of the Roman-Jewish relationship not often in evidence: we are all too familiar with the Jewish-Roman antagonism, and much less with a day-to-day routine of good working relations. And if we may venture beyond the Jewish perspective of this colloquium, a substantial contribution to the study of Roman provincial history is at hand: we are perfectly justified in regarding the Jews as representative of provincials in general. Moreover, they represent that part of the provincial population which was less tainted by the 'epigraphic habit' of the Graeco-Roman world, i. e., they come from the less Hellenized section of the provincial population, those who would have left us no inscriptions – in this case the great majority of the population. Precisely because of this we can be sure that their dealings with the Roman authorities constitute a faithful picture of the realities of life in the province.

To conclude: what we witness in the Greek texts from the Judaean Desert – it is sometimes true of the Aramaic and Hebrew documents as well – is not merely the use of Greek and Greek diplomatics by non-Hellenized or semi-Hellenized Jews, but the absence of anything which would mark them as Jewish apart from the identity of the parties as disclosed by their names. Thus we find deeds of sale, renunciations of claims, land registrations, receipts, mortgages, promissory notes, deeds of gift and even marriage contracts – all of which bear a striking resemblance to their Egyptian and other Near Eastern counterparts, thereby revealing the remarkable degree of integration of Jewish society into its environment. The influence of Roman law and diplomatics that we detect in the documents is only one manifestation of this integration: it is likely to have been absorbed by Jewish society by virtue of the fact that that society was part of the Near Eastern civilization in which it lived – that Near Eastern civilization which was the same prism

74 See Hannah M. Cotton, "The Guardianship of Jesus Son of Babatha: Roman and Local Law in the Province of Arabia," *JRS* 83 (1993): 94–108 [above, pp. 403–30].

through which Jewish society and culture absorbed the impact of Hellenism over the centuries.[75] It could be, and has been, argued that there is a discrepancy between the law of the documents and halakhic law in the various branches of personal law applied in the documents, namely the law of marriage and divorce, the law of succession and the law of guardianship. This is sometimes true of contract law as well.[76] But to say that Jews are writing 'non-Jewish' contracts is merely to say that the legal usage current in these contracts is not always in harmony with what eventually came to be normative Jewish law. The diversity and fluidity manifested in the documents from the Judaean Desert, the incursion of different legal systems sometimes, but not always, overlapping with what came to be halakhic law, are the best evidence we have for the state of Jewish law and the authority exercised by the rabbis at the time.

---

75 See above all Abraham Wasserstein, "A Marriage Contract from the Province of Arabia Nova: Notes on Papyrus Yadin 18," *JQR* 80 (1989): 93–130 and Abraham Wasserstein, "Non-Hellenized Jews in the Semi-Hellenized East," *SCI* 14 (1995): 111–37.

76 Marriage law: Wasserstein, "A Marriage Contract from the Province of Arabia Nova: Notes on Papyrus Yadin 18"; Hannah M. Cotton, "A Cancelled Marriage Contract from the Judaean Desert, XHev/Se Gr. 2," *JRS* 84 (1994): 64–86; Hannah M. Cotton, "The Rabbis and the Documents," in *Jews in a Greco-Roman World*, ed. Martin Goodman (Oxford: Oxford University Press, 1998), 167–79 [above, pp. 453–65]; for divorce see Hannah M. Cotton and Elisha Qimron, "XḤev/Se ar 13 of 134 or 135 C.E.: A Wife's Renunciation of Claims," *JJS* 49 (1998): 108–118; law of succession: Hannah M. Cotton, "Deeds of Gift and the Law of Succession in the Papyri from the Judean Desert," *Eretz Israel* 25 (1996): 410–15 (Hebrew); for an English version see "Deeds of Gift and the Law of Succession in Archives from the Judaean Desert," in *Akten des 21. Internationalen Papyrologenkongresses, Berlin, 13–19.8.1995*, ed. Barbara Kramer et al., Vol. I (Stuttgart – Leipzig: Teubner, 1997), 179–88; Hannah M. Cotton, "The Law of Succession in the Documents from the Judaean Desert Again," *SCI* 17 (1998): 115–23 [above, pp. 443–51]; law of guardianship: Cotton, "The Guardianship of Jesus Son of Babatha: Roman and Local Law in the Province of Arabia" [above, pp. 403–30]; contract law: Hayim Lapin, "Early Rabbinic Civil Law and the Literature of the Second Temple Period," *JSQ* 2 (1995): 149–83.

Jewish Jurisdiction under Roman Rule: Prolegomena

The study of the day-to-day aspect of Roman rule in a province has normally to rely on non-literary sources, mainly on epigraphy; sometimes, as in the case of Egypt, it can tap the rich resources of papyrology. The historian of the province of Judaea, later on Syria Palaestina, on the other hand, is in the fortunate position of being able to draw on literary sources: above all Josephus, the New Testament and rabbinic literature. However, these literary sources have conspired to create the biased notion of the special and unique status of the province of Judaea/Syria Palaestina within the Roman empire. Some corrective of this bias is supplied by the inscriptions, all of which – and their number has increased considerably recently – are now collected for the first time in the comprehensive multi-lingual *Corpus Inscriptionum Iudaeae Palaestinae*.[1] The documentary papyri from the Judaean Desert supply yet another corrective to the traditional view – especially now that almost the entire evidence from the Judaean Desert has been published.[2] True, many of the documents were written in the Nabataean kingdom which in 106 CE became the province of Arabia. However, the patterns of the relationship between the Jews of Arabia and the Roman authorities documented in the papyri cannot be assumed to have been very different from those current in the province of Judaea/Syria Palaestina.

---

1 See Werner Eck, "Die Inschriften Judäas im 1. und frühen 2. Jh. n. Chr. als Zeugnisse der römischen Herrschaft," in *Zwischen den Reichen: Neues Testament und römische Herrschaft. Vorträge auf der ersten Konferenz der European Association for Biblical Studies*, ed. Michael Labahn and Jürgen Zangenberg (Tübingen: Francke Verlag, 2002), 47. On the *CIIP* see Hannah M. Cotton et al., "Corpus Inscriptionum Judaeae/Palaestinae," *ZPE* 27 (1999): 307–8 and in *SCI* 18 (1999): 175–76.
2 For an exhaustive survey see Hannah M. Cotton, "Die Papyrusdokumente aus der judäischen Wüste und ihr Beitrag zur Erforschung der jüdischen Geschichte des 1. und 2. Jh.s n. Chr.," *ZDPV* 115 (1999): 228–47, to which add Hannah M. Cotton, "Documentary Texts from the Judaean Desert: A Matter of Nomenclature," *SCI* 20 (2001): 113–19.

Article note: First published in Michael Labahn and Jürgen Zangenberg, eds., *Zwischen den Reichen: Neues Testament und römische Herrschaft. Vorträge auf der ersten Konferenz der European Association for Biblical Studies* (Tübingen: Francke Verlag, 2002), 13–28, with the following note: For my sister, Ruth, on her Birthday. I am very grateful to Peter Eich of the University of Köln for an ongoing dialogue on the issues discussed in this paper, and also to Werner Eck (Köln), Ulrich Manthe (Passau), and Derek Roebuck (Oxford) for useful suggestions; and, as always, to David Wasserstein.

https://doi.org/10.1515/9783110770438-031

Elsewhere I have tried to determine the precise status of the province of Judaea within the Roman empire.[3] The following discussion, triggered off by the striking resemblance between the papyrology of the Judaean Desert and that of Egypt,[4] should be conceived as no more than preliminary remarks on the extent of local judicial autonomy in Judaea/Syria Palaestina under Roman rule. This issue has, I believe, suffered the greatest distortion under the overwhelming impact of rabbinic legal sources. The documents do not bear out many of the assumptions commonly held.

It has been observed:[5]

> It is a remarkable fact that no court, Jewish or non-Jewish, other than that of the Roman governor of Arabia, is mentioned in any of the documents from the Judaean Desert, a great many of which ... are legal documents. We should not therefore conclude, however, that the governor's court was the only court in operation in a Roman province. Nonetheless, the absence of any reference to other courts is disturbing, especially in view of the host of references in rabbinic sources to courts of different sizes in towns and villages.[6]

The governor's court, it should be pointed out, is mentioned explicitly only in the Greek documents of the Babatha archive.[7] There we watch the provincials making use of the assize system prevailing in the Roman provinces[8] to make petitions to the governor[9] or summon their opponents to appear before his

---

3 Hannah M. Cotton, "Some Aspects of the Roman Administration of Judaea/Syria-Palaestina," in *Lokale Autonomie und römische Ordnungsmacht in den kaiserzeitlichen Provinzen vom 1. bis 3. Jahrhundert*, ed. Werner Eck (München: Oldenbourg, 1999), 75–91 [above, pp. 317–35].

4 See Hannah M. Cotton, "The Guardianship of Jesus Son of Babatha: Roman and Local Law in the Province of Arabia," *JRS* 83 (1993): 94–108 [above, pp. 403–30].

5 Hannah M. Cotton and Ada Yardeni, *Aramaic, Hebrew, and Greek Documentary Texts from Naḥal Ḥever and Other Sites* (Oxford: Clarendon Press, 1997), 154.

6 See Emil Schürer, *The History of the Jewish People in the Age of Jesus Christ*, ed. Fergus Millar and Géza Vermès, Vol. II (Edinburgh: Clark, 1979), 184–88; Gedaliah Alon, *The Jews in Their Land in the Talmudic Age 70–640 CE*, Vol. I (Jerusalem: Magnes Press, 1984), 553–57; Asher Gulak, *Towards a Study of the History of Jewish Law in the Talmudic Period* (Jerusalem: Hasefer, 1929), 54 ff. (Hebrew); less sceptical is Ze'ev Safrai, *The Jewish Community in the Talmudic Period* (Jerusalem: Zalman Shazar Center, 1995), 76 ff. (Hebrew).

7 Edited by Naphtali Lewis, *The Documents from the Bar Kokhba Period in the Cave of Letters. Greek Papyri* (Jerusalem: IES, 1989). The papyri are referred to as *P.Yadin*.

8 Cf. G.P. Burton, "Proconsuls, Assizes and the Administration of Justice under the Empire," *JRS* 65 (1975): 92–106; Christian Habicht, "New Evidence on the Province of Asia," *JRS* 65 (1975): 64–91; Rudolf Haensch, "Zur Konventsordnung in Aegyptus und den übrigen Provinzen des römischen Reiches," in *Akten des 21. Internationalen Papyrologenkongresses, Berlin, 13–19.8.1995*, ed. Barbara Kramer et al., Vol. I (Stuttgart – Leipzig: Teubner, 1997), 320–91.

9 E.g. *P.Yadin* 13.

ambulatory tribunal, wherever that happened to be.[10] However, even when the Roman governor is not mentioned explicitly in the documents, certain elements present in them imply that these documents were intended for a Roman court of law. The following list does not attempt to be exhaustive but records the more salient features of Romanization in the documents:

- the use of the double document, probably under Roman influence[11] since elsewhere it was going out of fashion;[12]
- the use of *testatio*, a document signed by seven witnesses in front of whom the plaintiff makes his declaration;[13]
- the presence of three copies of a Roman instrument, namely the *actio tutelae* in the Babatha archive;[14]
- the use of Roman legal arguments in the documents;[15]
- and finally the use of the stipulation.[16]

A strong argument for thinking that these documents were intended for a Roman court of law is the presence of a male guardian to represent a woman in the Greek documents and his total absence from the Semitic documents. The passive role of the guardian (in general it is merely his presence which is recorded συμπαρόντος

---

10 E.g. *P.Yadin* 26, lines 2–11: 'Babatha ... summoned Miriam ... to accompany her in person before Haterius Nepos ... ὅπου ἂν ὑπ' αὐτοῦ ὑπαρχία ('wherever he happens to be exercising justice in the province') ... καὶ παρεδρεύιν ἐπὶ τὸν αὐτὸν Νέπωτα μέχρι διαγνώσεως. See Cotton, "The Guardianship of Jesus Son of Babatha: Roman and Local Law in the Province of Arabia," 106 f. [above, pp. 426 f.], for a detailed survey of all references to summons to the governor's court in the Babatha archive.

11 Roman military diplomas, copies made on bronze tablets of the constitutions granting privileges to individual soldiers which were displayed in Rome, are double documents, as are the deeds on wooden tablets from pre-Vesuvian Campania; on the latter see now the review article by Gregory Rowe, "Trimalchio's World," *SCI* 20 (2001): 225–45.

12 See Lewis, *The Documents from the Bar Kokhba Period in the Cave of Letters. Greek Papyri*, 6–10.

13 *P.Yadin* 15 and 24, and probably also *P.Jericho* 16, as interpreted by Rudolf Haensch, "Zum Verständnis von P.Jericho 16 gr.," *SCI* 20 (2001): 155–67.

14 See Dieter Nörr, "Prozessuales aus dem Babatha-Archiv," in *Mélanges de droit romain et d'histoire ancienne: hommage à la mémoire de André Magdelain*, ed. Michel Humbert and Yan Thomas (Paris: Panthéon-Assas, 1998), 317–41; Tiziana J. Chiusi, "IV. Zur Vormundschaft der Mutter," *ZSS* 111 (1994): 155–96; Tiziana J. Chiusi, "Babatha vs. The Guardians of Her Son: A Struggle for Guardianship – Legal and Practical Aspects of P. Yadin 12–15, 27," in *Law in the Documents of the Judean Desert*, ed. Ranon Katzoff and David Schaps (Leiden: Brill, 2005), 105–32.

15 See above all Chiusi in the two papers cited in n. 14; Cotton, "The Guardianship of Jesus Son of Babatha: Roman and Local Law in the Province of Arabia," 102–5 [above, pp. 420–26].

16 H.L.W. Nelson and Ulrich Manthe, *Gai Institutiones III 88–181. Die Kontraktsobligationen: Text und Kommentar* (Berlin: Duncker & Humblot, 1999), 475 ff.

αὐτῇ ἐπιτρόπου) makes it eminently clear that this is just a matter of form and procedure required by the courts for which the Greek contracts were intended, namely Roman courts of law where a woman could not appear without a male representative.[17]

Last but not least the use of the Greek language – the language used *par excellence* as means of communication between rulers and subjects in the Roman Near East – in legal documents strongly suggests that the court envisioned was that of the Roman governor; admittedly, the alternative explanation of a Greek-speaking court of a *polis* cannot be excluded.

As an aside one may observe that all this implies of course that non-citizens had recourse to Roman courts of law and Roman law long before 212 CE, and that this does not seem to have required the grant of a special privilege.[18]

One can easily demonstrate the intimate connection between the advent of Roman rule (i. e. provincialization) and the recourse to using Greek in legal documents in the case of Nabataea, which in 106 CE became the Roman province of Arabia. Until 106 legal documents had been written in Nabataean, whereas from 106 onwards the Greek language takes over; as against two Nabataean contracts and four written in Jewish Aramaic we have altogether 32 Greek documents from the period between 106 and 132 CE in Arabia, that is in the first 25 years of the province.[19]

No such association can be made for the use of Greek in Judaea whose provincialization dates to 6 CE:[20] more than a hundred years elapsed before Greek

17 See Hannah M. Cotton, "The Guardian (ἐπίτροπος) of a Woman in the Documents from the Judaean Desert," *ZPE* 118 (1997): 267–73 [above, pp. 431–41]. The use of a single term – *epitropos* – for the two kinds of guardians is due to the influence of Roman law, where at least originally no legal distinction existed between the guardian of a minor and that of a woman, and, consequently, the same term, *tutor*, was used for both. Both, if they were not *sui iuris*, had to be represented by the tutor, see Hans Julius Wolff, "Römisches Provinzialrecht in der Provinz Arabia (Rechtspolitik als Instrument der Beherrschung)," in *Aufstieg und Niedergang der römischen Welt*, Vol. II.13 (Berlin: De Gruyter, 1980), 796–97.

18 A choice between local courts and Roman courts, conferred on three Greek naval captains and their families – none of whom is a Roman citizen – is presented as a special privilege in the *SC de Asclepiade sociisque* of 78 BCE: Robert K. Sherk, *Roman Documents from the Greek East* (Baltimore: Johns Hopkins Press, 1969), no. 22. The same is true of the privileges bestowed by Octavian on Seleucus of Rhosus: Sherk, no. 58, lines 53–56.

19 See Hannah M. Cotton, "The Languages of the Legal and Administrative Documents from the Judaean Desert," *ZPE* 125 (1999): 225 ff. [above, pp. 136 ff.].

20 See n. 3 above. With the exception of inscriptions on Jewish ossuaries, the first Greek documents from Jewish circles come from Masada, i. e. 66–73(4) CE, see Hannah M. Cotton and Joseph Geiger, *Masada II: The Latin and Greek Documents* (Jerusalem: IES, 1989), 9 f.

is first attested in legal documents from Judaea.[21] This could be a coincidence: our documentation is anything but complete; but it is probably not just a coincidence. Elsewhere I have suggested[22] that the same explanation could be offered for the immediate recourse to Greek in legal documents in Arabia and its somewhat delayed use in Judaea: in both provinces the recourse to Greek may well have been the corollary of the extent of local judicial autonomy granted by the Romans. The provincialization of Judaea in 6 CE left the Great Sanhedrin in Jerusalem with the high priest at its head a large measure of judicial independence in civil and criminal law alike.[23] There is much evidence for this in Josephus, Philo and the New Testament.[24] Even if officially the Sanhedrin's judicial competence did not extend beyond Judaea proper, its authority certainly did not know such bounds. Things must have changed drastically after the revolt (66–70 CE). The destruction of Jerusalem and the Temple meant among other things the dissolution of the Great Sanhedrin. It is to be assumed that after 70 conditions in Judaea bore a strong resemblance to those current in Arabia in 106: these included a more limited local judicial autonomy under Roman rule.[25]

I have now come to realize that the argument which I offered in 1999 may be faulted on the ground of being circular: it would seem that I posit limited local judicial autonomy in order to explain the use of, or the transition to, the employment of the Greek language in legal documents; and, conversely, that I infer the existence of a limited local judicial autonomy from the use of Greek. We should,

---

21 This is if we accept 115 CE for *P.Mur* 114, dated by Benoit to 171 CE (P. Benoit, J.T. Milik, and R. de Vaux, *Les grottes de Murabba'at*, Discoveries in the Judaean Desert II (Oxford: Clarendon Press, 1961)), but see Hannah M. Cotton and Werner Eck, "P.Murabba'at 114 und die Anwesenheit römischer Truppen in den Höhlen des Wadi Murabba'at nach dem Bar Kochba Aufstand," *ZPE* 138 (2002): 173–83. See in general Cotton, "The Languages of the Legal and Administrative Documents from the Judaean Desert," 228 f. [above, pp. 139 f.].

22 In Cotton, "The Languages of the Legal and Administrative Documents from the Judaean Desert," 230 f. [above, pp. 144 f.].

23 See Joseph., *BJ* 2.22; *AJ* 17.227; *BJ* 2.80; *AJ* 17.300; *BJ* 2.91; *AJ* 17.314; *AJ* 17.303. See below Appendix 2, on criminal jurisdiction.

24 Schürer, *The History of the Jewish People in the Age of Jesus Christ*, Vol. II, 197 f.; 218 ff.

25 The Nabataean documents from the Babatha archive recently published by Ada Yardeni, *Textbook of Aramaic, Hebrew and Nabataean Documentary Texts from the Judaean Desert and Related Material* (Jerusalem: The Hebrew University Press, 2000), imply to my mind limited local autonomy under the Nabataean kings; see also her new reading of *P.Starcky* in Ada Yardeni, "The Decipherment and Restoration of Legal Texts from the Judaean Desert: A Reexamination of Papyrus Stracky (P.Yadin 36)," *SCI* 20 (2001): 121–37. The Romans were likely to leave matters as they were, see Cotton, "The Guardianship of Jesus Son of Babatha: Roman and Local Law in the Province of Arabia," 107, Appendix I [above, p. 429].

therefore, cast our net wider and enquire about the extent of local judicial autonomy under Roman rule.

Theoretically all of Rome's subjects were *de iure* under the jurisdiction (*iuris dictio*) of Roman officials in the provinces. Judicial autonomy, that is the use of local courts of law, invariably called for a special grant by the Roman government. Of course some measure of judicial autonomy was almost always allowed, and very early on had become a tralatician part of the provincial edict, as we know from Cicero's provincial edict in Cilicia where he was governor in 50 BCE:

> *Multaque sum secutus Scaevolae, in iis illud in quo sibi libertatem censent Graeci datam, ut Graeci inter se disceptent suis legibus ... Graeci vero exsultant quod peregrinis iudicibus utuntur. 'Nugatoribus quidem' inquies. Quid refert? Ii se* αὐτονομίαν *adeptos putant* (Cic. *Att.* VI, 1, 15).
>
> Indeed I have followed many of Scaevola's provisions, including that one which the natives regard as their charter of liberty (*libertas*) that cases between natives should be tried under their own laws ... The natives are jubilant because they have foreign judges.[26] 'Triflers,' you may say, well, what of it? They feel they have won *autonomia* just the same.

What was the extent of local judicial autonomy in the imperial period? Was it uniform or did it vary from one province to another, or even from one community to the next, depending on their status?

This is not the place to discuss the ancient evidence for uniformity and variation in local judicial autonomy – far less the vast array of modern opinions about the subject. I shall therefore claim for the views expounded here no more than the status of working hypotheses which may account for and explain the legal situation in Judaea and Arabia.

As a starting point we may take chapters 84 and 89 of the municipal charter of the city of Irni in Baetica which established the city as a Latin *municipium* subject to Roman law and legal procedure in the Flavian period.[27] In these two chap-

26 See Charles Crowther, "Foreign Judges from Priene: Studies in Hellenistic Epigraphy" (King's College London Thesis, 1990); Dieter Nörr, "Zu den Xenokriten (Rekuperatoren) in der römischen Provinzialgerichtsbarkeit," in *Lokale Autonomie und römische Ordnungsmacht in den kaiserzeitlichen Provinzen vom 1. bis 3. Jahrhundert*, ed. Werner Eck (München: Oldenbourg, 1999), 257–301; Derek Roebuck, *Ancient Greek Arbitration* (Oxford: Holo Books, 2001), 269 ff.

27 For text and translation see Julián González, "The Lex Irnitana: A New Copy of the Flavian Municipal Law," *JRS* 76 (1986): 147–243. The bibliography has grown enormously since, but see on these two chapters Alan Rodger, "Jurisdictional Limits in the Lex Irnitana and the Lex de Gallia Cisalpina," *ZPE* 110 (1996): 189–206. See also Umberto Laffi, "I limiti della competenza giurisdizionale dei magistrati locali," in *Estudios sobre la Tabula Siarensis*, ed. Julián González and Javier Arce (Madrid: Centro de Estudios Históricos, 1988), 141–56.

ters it is explicitly stated that the magistrates in a Latin *municipium* (the *duoviri* and *aediles*) have jurisdiction (*iuris dictio*) in respect of any private dispute with a value up to 1,000 sesterces and no more, and that certain actions are altogether outside the competence of the local magistrates – unless both parties to the suit are willing to accept it. To the possibilities which are opened up by this derogation from the general rule I shall return later.

Should we argue *a minore ad maius* that if the judicial autonomy of Roman[28] and Latin communities was limited in such a way, there is all the more reason to believe that the judicial autonomy of peregrine communities was curtailed even further? In other words, did the provincials more often than not have to approach Roman courts of law (the governor's above all), for their own courts would not be competent to adjudicate cases exceeding a certain amount of money, or due to the character of the case? Or could it be argued that the limits set on the judicial autonomy of local courts in Roman and Latin communities are irrelevant for determining the scope of judicial autonomy in peregrine communities since the latter were so to speak outside the entire framework of the Roman legal system? If so, the local autonomy of peregrine communities might conceivably have been wider than that of Roman and Latin ones.

There are no cut and dried answers to these questions. A thorough examination of the relevant *documentary* evidence from the entire empire is necessary. This cannot be attempted here. However, we must also at all costs avoid a schematic legal approach which takes legal writings, both Roman and Jewish, as a reflection of what happened in reality: such an approach removes us from the truth, and from reality. Perhaps an elucidation of the legal situation in Judaea and Arabia can be offered without taking a firm stand on the question of the scope of local judicial autonomy. After all, limited local judicial autonomy need not have been the only reason for approaching the Roman tribunals in the province. G.P. Burton in his seminal article on the administration of justice in proconsular provinces rightly observes that "whatever role we may finally ascribe to local courts," the evidence from different sources suggests that "any governor was faced with an immense amount of possible work."[29] The recourse to the Roman tribunals, which in Judaea and Arabia is attested in the use of Greek in documents[30] clearly

28 For Roman charters see *Lex de Gallia Cisalpina* in Michael Crawford, ed., *Roman Statutes*, Vol. I (London: Institute of Classical Studies, 1996), no. 28, ch. 22, ll. 27–28, which stipulates a limit of 15,000 sesterces, and the Este Fragment, Crawford, no. 16, ll. 4–7, which stipulates a limit of 10,000 sesterces on local jurisdiction.

29 Burton, "Proconsuls, Assizes and the Administration of Justice under the Empire," 102.

30 Of course an additional reason could be the need to deposit the deeds in a public archive, similar to what we know to have been the case in Egypt, where public archives were used to de-

meant for a Roman court of law, may not have been the corollary of limited local autonomy. In other words it may not have been a matter of necessity to go to a Roman court,[31] but a step taken out of choice. Rome's subjects could and would seek Roman justice whenever they believed that it would be more effective, more advantageous and more just than the local one.[32] This is clearly the impression one gets from the Babatha archive: "Without coercion or attempts to impose uniformity, the very presence of the Romans as the supreme authority in the province invited appeals to their authority, to their courts as well as to their laws."[33] Babatha seems to regard the Roman advent as the dawning of a new age; she wants her son 'to be raised in splendid style rendering thanks to *the[se] most blessed times* of the governorship of Julius Julianus.'[34] True, she needs to propitiate the governor and her praise should be taken with a grain of salt, but it is not just empty phraseology either.

And yet the majority of documents from the Judaean Desert are written in Jewish Aramaic.[35] Moreover, contracts in Aramaic continued to be written and used after the documents from the Judaean Desert dried up.[36] This we can infer

posit private documents; having been registered there, these documents could later be produced in court as evidence.

31 For officials other than the governor see Hannah M. Cotton and Werner Eck, "Roman Officials in Judaea and Arabia and Civil Jurisdiction," in *Law in the Documents of the Judaean Desert*, ed. Ranon Katzoff and David Schaps (Leiden – Boston: Brill, 2005), 23–44.

32 The best example are marriage contracts: five out of eight (or nine) marriage contracts found in the Judaean Desert are written in Greek and cannot be said to be translations of Aramaic contracts, since they contain a different legal tradition (see Hannah M. Cotton, "Marriage Contracts from the Judaean Desert," *Materia giudaica* 6 (2000): 2–6). However, the choice of Greek could hardly have been dictated by limited local judicial autonomy, for the Romans are unlikely to have interfered with peregrine marriage arrangements.

33 Cotton, "The Guardianship of Jesus Son of Babatha: Roman and Local Law in the Province of Arabia," 107 [above, p. 429].

34 ὅθεν λαμπρῶς διασωθῇ μου ὁ υἱὸς εὐχαριστῶν (εὐχαριστοῦντα) τοῖς μακαριωτάτοις καιροῖς ἡγεμωνίας Ἰουλίου Ἰουλιανοῦ ἡγεμῶνος (*P.Yadin* 15, ll. 10–11 = ll. 26–27); cf. *Acts* 24:2 (the rhetor Tertullus to Felix): πολλῆς εἰρήνης τυγχάνοντες διὰ σοῦ καὶ διορθωμάτων γινομένων τῷ ἔθνει τούτῳ διὰ τῆς σῆς προνοίας: 'Seeing that by thee we enjoy great quietness and that very worthy deeds are done unto this nation by thy providence.'

35 For Hebrew see Cotton, "The Languages of the Legal and Administrative Documents from the Judaean Desert," 220–25 [above, pp. 129–36].

36 There are no safely dated contracts, either in Greek or in Aramaic, after 135 CE. The few Greek papyri mentioned in Hannah M. Cotton, W.E.H. Cockle, and Fergus Millar, "The Papyrology of the Roman Near East: A Survey," *JRS* 85 (1995): 214–35 as nos. 333 ff. do not come from Jewish contexts, but either from Roman army circles or from the Greek *poleis*. They are irrelevant for my discussion here. But see Naphtali Lewis, "The Demise of the Aramaic Document in the Dead Sea Region," *SCI* 20 (2001): 178–81.

from rabbinic sources, and above all from the Mishnah, where formulae taken from living Aramaic contracts are embedded in the legal discussion which is conducted in Hebrew.[37] Although, as pointed out before, no courts are ever mentioned in the Aramaic documents from the Judaean Desert,[38] the existence of legal contracts anticipates the possibility of legal proceedings. Where would these legal proceedings be conducted? Where should one look for courts exercising *iuris dictio* (in the Roman sense of the word)[39] in Judaea/Syria Palaestina? Again we should look at patterns current everywhere in the empire.

The legal status of a city or *polis* in the Roman empire would normally go hand in hand with some measure of judicial autonomy, albeit occasionally quite limited as we have just seen in the Tabula Irnitana of the city of Irni in Spain. The city courts had jurisdiction over their own residents as well as over the city territory, the *chora*. However, this was not the principle of local organization in what is commonly called the 'Jewish region' of Palestine, where there are very few cities and the majority of cities that are there are on the fringes, and in any case are not likely to have controlled the entire Jewish region as their city-territories. Many settlements referred to as cities in the Jewish sources, and taken as such by scholars, would not pass the criteria of a *polis* in the Roman empire. The Jewish region as we know from Josephus, Pliny and now also from the documents from

37 See Hannah M. Cotton, "Survival, Adaptation and Extinction: Nabataean and Jewish Aramaic versus Greek in the Legal Documents from the Cave of Letters in Naḥal Ḥever," in *Sprache und Kultur in der kaiserzeitlichen Provinz Arabia: Althistorische Beiträge zur Erforschung von Akkulturationsphänomenen im römischen Nahen Osten*, ed. Leonhard Schumacher and Oliver Stoll (St. Katharinen: Scripta Mercaturae Verlag, 2003), 1–11 [above, pp. 161–72].

38 Haggai Misgav, "Jewish Courts of Law as Reflected in the Documents from the Dead Sea," *Cathedra* 82 (1996): 17–24 (Hebrew), maintains that *P.Mur* 29–30 contain reference to the presence of four people before whom the contracts are written who are unlikely to constitute a court of law. Nevertheless, they seem to resemble the Egyptian *synchoresis*, and thus may well be described as something like notarized legal instruments. However these documents have now been predated to the time of the Great Revolt – see Cotton, "The Languages of the Legal and Administrative Documents from the Judaean Desert," 220–23 [above, pp. 129–34] and Hanan Eshel, Magen Broshi, and T.A.J. Jull, "Documents from Wadi Murabba'at and the Status of Jerusalem during the Bar Kokhba Revolt," in *The Refuge Caves of the Bar Kokhba Revolt*, ed. Hanan Eshel and David Amit (Jerusalem: IES, 1998), 233 ff. (Hebrew) – whereas I am concerned here mainly with jurisdiction under Roman rule. Thus those legal documents written at the time of the two revolts, i.e. at the time of Jewish independence, remain largely outside the scope of the present discussion – unless they too betray the use of what I shall designate here arbitration.

39 A practical definition of a court of law with formal jurisdiction, meant for historians rather than for jurists, is a court of law whose decisions are binding and backed up by the powers that be – by the Roman government in our period – who will enforce them if the parties fail to do so themselves.

the Judaean Desert, was composed of villages of different sizes and divided into administrative units with central villages at their head. Only about Judaea proper can we be sure that these units were called *toparchiai*. There is no evidence for local officials at the head of these capital villages, nor for centrally appointed officials in charge of the *toparchiai* – but the existence of one or another kind of local officials must be assumed. There are some hints that the *toparchiai* were in charge of taxation. Above all it is hard to believe that nothing beyond a merely geographical relationship is intended by the description of the dependence of a village on a central village, especially since the dependence of the single village on the central village is described both in the papyri and in Josephus in terms identical to those describing the dependence of the *chora* on its *polis*. It is either here in the capital villages or in the smaller villages – which enjoyed a large measure of independence – that one should try to locate judicial autonomy in so far as it was allowed by the Romans.

However, we may be on the wrong track after all. Perhaps it is altogether misleading to think in terms of formal *iuris dictio* of a court of law. The restrictions on local judicial autonomy and the imperfections and deficiencies of the Roman assize system[40] – notwithstanding delegation of jurisdiction to lower officials (to *legati* in the public provinces and to *strategoi* and others in Egypt for example) – may well have led the provincials to seek other solutions, less cumbersome, less expensive and less time-consuming.[41] I should like to raise the option of private arbitration to account for the presence of contracts in Aramaic among the documents from the Judaean Desert and in the background of the Mishnaic legal discussion. It is worth recalling that the charter of Irni contained a derogation from the general rule, to wit that if both parties to a suit are willing, the local magistrates could adjudicate cases which go beyond their normal competence.[42]

---

40 See Burton, "Proconsuls, Assizes and the Administration of Justice under the Empire," 99 ff.
41 One gets the impression that the Roman courts were simply blocked; the queue must have been enormous if one had to wait 8 months in Antioch to see the governor and then be sent packing with nothing achieved: see *P.Euphr* 1 in Denis Feissel and Jean Gascou, "Documents d'archives romains inédits du Moyen Euphrate (IIIe s. après J-C): I. Les pétitions (T. Euphr. 1 à 5)," *Journal des Savants*, 1995, 65–119.
42 See Tabula Irnitana, ch. 84 and 89 (above, n. 27); cf. *Dig*. 50, 1, 28: *Inter convenientes et de re maiori apud magistratus municipiales agetur*. In the case of a Roman or Latin community such consent between the two parties may lead to that kind of arbitration recognised and provided for by the Roman lawyers. The parties could make a contract of arbitration (*compromissum*), in the form of a stipulation which (1) obliged the parties to follow the sentence of a private (non-official) *arbiter* and not to go to the public court, and (2) stipulated a *poena* (fine) for acting against the *compromissum*. The defendant could not be compelled to accept the sentence of the *arbiter*; if sued at court, he would merely forfeit the fine. The *compromissum* was valid only if the proposed

Whatever courts we hear about in the rabbinic sources, I suggest, may have been no more than forms of private arbitration, not backed by the powers that be, i. e. the Roman authorities in the province.[43] Thus you could not force your opponent to appear before an arbiter, nor – which is crucial – enforce his verdict.[44] The one and only sanction would then have been the authority of the arbiter, that is the social and moral standing of the arbiter in the community and the social pressure exercised by the community in which one lived. The effectiveness of those should not be underestimated.

This could be an explanation for the absence of any mention of courts in the Aramaic documents; but far more importantly it could account for the fact that, as observed more than a hundred years ago by H.P. Chajes and never refuted, when you examine the rabbinic sources closely, you never find people approaching a proper tribunal, but rather a single rabbi.[45] This would imply a private arbiter rather than a court of law.

Private arbitration must have played a much greater role in the Roman empire than is normally suspected, though it has left few traces.[46] It was, of its nature, rarely accompanied by documents, and thus in most cases the process and the results alike are hidden from our sight. But for all that, I believe that we possess now three documents from the Judaean Desert which attest the results of private arbitration and the renunciation of further claims by the plaintiff: the Greek *P.Hever* 63 (127 CE) from the archive of Salome Komaïse daughter of Levi,[47]

arbiter committed himself to giving a sentence in a contract called *receptum arbitri*; see in general *Dig.* 4, 8 and examples in G. Camodeca, *Tabulae Pompeianae Sulpiciorum (TPSulp.): Edizione critica dell' Archivio Puteolano dei Sulpicii* (Rome: Quasar, 1999), nos. 34 ff.

43 Contra Aharon Oppenheimer, "Jewish Penal Authority in Roman Judaea," in *Jews in a Graeco-Roman World*, ed. Martin Goodman (Oxford: Oxford University Press, 1998), 181–91.

44 As such it differs from that recognised in the late legislation of 398 CE (*Cod. Theod.* II, 1, 10): 'the governors of the provinces shall even execute their sentences as if they were appointed arbiters through a judge's award.' This is no longer pure private arbitration.

45 H.P. Chajes, "Les juges juifs en Palestine, de l'an 70 à l'an 500," *Revue des études juives* 39, no. 77 (1899): 39–52. The one case I know of what might be a court of three is so confused and problematic that no sense can be made of it, although it is so often quoted; I refer of course to the case of Tamar in *yMegillah* ('scroll') 3.3 p. 74a. Shalom Albeck, *Law Courts in Talmudic Times* (Ramat-Gan: Bar-Ilan University Press, 1980), who also disputes the existence of formal Jewish courts, shows no awareness of the existence of Roman rule in Judaea/Syria Palaestina at the time when the rabbinic sources were written.

46 Cf. Roger S. Bagnall, *Egypt in Late Antiquity* (Princeton: Princeton University Press, 1993), 161: "Actual litigation is only the tip of the iceberg; most disputes were handled (not necessarily 'settled' or 'resolved') in other ways."

47 First published in Hannah M. Cotton, "The Archive of Salome Komaise Daughter of Levi: Another Archive from the 'Cave of Letters,'" *ZPE* 105 (1995): 171–208, as no. III; final publication in

the Nabataean *P.Yadin* 9 (122 CE)[48] and the Aramaic *P.Hever* 13 (134 or 135 CE).[49] *P.Hever* 13 was written under Jewish rule at the time of the Bar Kokhba revolt, whereas my main concern here is with jurisdiction under Roman rule. *P.Yadin* 9 is badly damaged and its content is practically irretrievable.[50] I shall therefore give here only the text and translation of *P.Hever* 63, and refer to the other two in my discussion.

1 [ἐξωμολο]γ̣ήσατο καὶ συνεγρ[άψατο Σαλ]ωμη Ληουει τ̣ο̣υ̣[... συμπαρόντος αὐτῇ ἐπιτρόπου]
2 [*c. 7 letters*]υ̣ Σιμωνος ἀνδρὸς α[ὐτῆ]ς τοῦδε τοῦ { ...}π̣ρ̣[άγματος χάριν πρὸς Σαλωμην τὴν]
3 [καὶ Γραπτ]ηγ Μαναημο[υ *c. 6 letters*]λου θυγατέρα, ἰ̣δ̣ί̣α̣ν̣ [δὲ μητέρα αὐτῆς *c. 13 letters*]
4 [πάντες Μα]ωζηνοι· καὶ ἡ [Σαλωμη Λ]ηουει μηδένα λ[όγον ἔχειν *c. 17 letters*]
5 [*c. 8 letters*].α̣ ἐξ ὀνόματος αὐ̣[τῆς πρὸς Σ]α̣λωμην τὴν καὶ [Γραπτην *c. 19 letters*]
6 [*c. 3 letters* περὶ τ]ῶ̣ν καταλειφθέντω̣[ν ὑπὸ Λ]η̣ουει γενομένου σ̣υ̣[μβίου αὐτῆς *c. 13 letters* καὶ]
7 [ὑπὸ *c. 4 letters*]λου γενομένου αὐ[τῆς υἱοῦ] ἀδελφοῦ δὲ τῆς ὁμ[ολογούσης *c. 17 letters*]
8 [*c. 7–8 letters*]α̣ ἔτι δὲ ὁμολογεῖ ἡ̣ [Σαλωμ]η Ληουει μηδένα λ[όγον ἔχειν *c. 17 letters*]
9 [πρὸς Σαλωμη]ν̣ τὴν καὶ Γ̣ραπτην̣[*c. 4–5 letters*]η κληρονόμους αὐ[τῆς περὶ *c. 19 letters*]
10 [*c. 7–8 letters*]. παρῳχημέν[ης ἀμφισβ]ητήσεως ὅρκου ἐπ̣[ιδοθέντος *c. 17 letters*]
11 [*c.? letters*] . . . .[.] . . .[*c. 10 letters*].ε . . π̣ρὸς αὐτὴν̣[*c. 26 letters*]
12 [*c. 26 letters*]υμενης στᾶσα δ̣[ὲ *c. 25 letters*]
13 [πίστει ἐπηρωτήθη καὶ ἀνθωμολογήθη ο]ὕτως καλῶς γενέσ̣[θαι *vacat?*]
14 [*vacat?*] *vacat*
15 (hand 2) [ἐπὶ ὑπάτων Μάρκου Γαουίου Γαλλικανο]ῦ̣ καὶ Τίτ[ου Ἀτιλίου Ῥούφου Τιτιανοῦ *vacat?*]
16 [*day and month? place?*] vacat

Cotton and Yardeni, *Aramaic, Hebrew, and Greek Documentary Texts from Naḥal Ḥever and Other Sites*, 195 ff. The papyri in Cotton and Yardeni are referred to as *P.Hever*; for the reference see now Cotton, "Documentary Texts from the Judaean Desert: A Matter of Nomenclature."

48 See Yardeni, *Textbook of Aramaic, Hebrew and Nabataean Documentary Texts from the Judaean Desert and Related Material*, Vol. I, 297 (Hebrew; for an English translation see Vol. II, 97). For commentary see Yigael Yadin et al., *The Documents from the Bar Kokhba Period in the Cave of Letters: Hebrew, Aramaic and Nabatean-Aramaic Papyri* (Jerusalem: IES, 2002), 268–76.

49 Published in Cotton and Yardeni, *Aramaic, Hebrew, and Greek Documentary Texts from Naḥal Ḥever and Other Sites*, 65 ff. Its claim to fame rests though on the face that the wife seems to refer in it to a deed of divorce she had given her husband, cf. Hannah M. Cotton and Elisha Qimron, "XḤev/Se ar 13 of 134 or 135 C.E.: A Wife's Renunciation of Claims," *JJS* 49 (1998): 108–118. Contra Adiel Schremer, "Divorce in Papyrus Ṣe'elim 13 Once Again: A Reply to Tal Ilan," *Harv. Theol. Rev.* 91 (1998): 193–202.

50 Thus the editors of the commentary, see n. 48 above.

Translation:

> [Sal]ome daughter of Levi, the son of X (or: son of Tou[?) – [present with her as her guardian for the purpose] of this matter, her husband [Sammou]os son of Shim'on – [acknow]ledged and agreed in w[riting], vis-á-vis Salome also (called) [Grapt]e daughter of Menahem, [son of]*los* (or]*las*), her own [mother ... – all of them living in Ma]hoza: 'and also [(she) Salome] daughter of Levi has no [claims ...] in her name [towards S]alome who is also (called) [Grapte ... regarding] the properties left [by L]evi, her late hus[band ... and by]*los* (or]*las*), her late [son] and brother of her who ag[rees ...]. Likewise [Salom]e daughter of Levi agrees that she has no [claims ... vis-á-vis Salom]e also (called) Grapte ... her heirs [regarding ..., the cont]roversy which has now been solved, an oath having been gi[ven] ... towards her ... while standing firm (?) [... In faith[51] the formal question was asked and it was agreed in reply] that this was thus rightly done. [*vacat*]
> (second hand) [In the consulate of Marcus Gavius Gallican]us and Tit[us Atilius Rufus Titianus] *vacat?* [day and month? place?] *vacat.*

The recent death of Salome's brother[52] – perhaps also of her father – was the likely occasion for writing this deed. We cannot be certain about the nature of the controversy – (line 10) – which preceded the deed, but it is likely to have concerned the property left after the death of both father and son: [περὶ τ]ῷν καταλειφθέντῳ[ν ὑπὸ Λ]ῃουει γενομένου σ̣υ̣[μβίου αὐτῆς ... καὶ ὑπὸ ...]λου γενομένου αὐ[τῆς υἱοῦ] ἀδελφοῦ δὲ τῆς ὁμ[ολογούσης] (lines 6–7). The καὶ ἡ [Σαλωμη Λ]ηουει, '*and* also Salome daughter of Levi' (line 4), implies that there was a separate deed of renunciation of claims by the mother, Salome Grapte, who, for her part, had written a deed of renunciation in favor of the daughter. The settlement of the dispute (παρῳχημέν[ης ἀμφιβσ]ητήσεως) accompanied by the taking of the oath (ὅρκου ἐπ̣[ιδοθέντος]) preceded the act of writing down the deed, and are likely to have taken place before a private arbiter. The waiver of all claims expressed by the formula μηδένα λόγον ἔχειν πρὸς αὐτήν, repeated twice (or even three times) in the present document (lines 4, 8, 11) cannot but call to mind the parallel Aramaic formula כל מדעם לא איתי לי עמך: 'I have no claim against you' which is repeated in three variations in *P.Hever* 13, where the wife renounces all claims against her former husband. The same formula recurs also in the fragmentary Nabataean *P.Yadin* 9, lines 6–7: ולא... עמך מנדעם לא זעיר [ולא שגיא].

51 I stand corrected by U. Manthe: πίστει means of course *fide* not *bona fide*, see Nelson and Manthe, *Gai Institutiones III 88–181. Die Kontraktsobligationen: Text und Kommentar*, 477.
52 He was still alive on the 25th of April 127 CE, see *P.Hever* 61.

The fact that the deed was written down in Greek and the use of the *stipulatio* imply to my mind that the parties left themselves the option of going to court – to a Roman court – in case one of them did not stand by the terms of the arbitration.[53]

Appendices

1. Judicial Autonomy in the Diaspora

Evidence for judicial autonomy in the Jewish Diaspora could be used as an *argumentum ex minore ad maius* for the existence of judicial autonomy in Judaea/Syria Palaestina. I do not find this argument very compelling. Not even in Egypt, where documents do exist, do we possess any proof that Jews used their own courts (or their own laws for that matter), despite evidence to the contrary in the rabbinic sources. In fact the editors of the *Corpus Papyrorum Judaicarum* expressed their surprise at the absence of any documents reflecting the existence of Jewish courts in Egypt and the exercise of Jewish law there. As for the famous charters mentioned in Josephus, *AJ* 14.185–267 which contain privileges successfully sought and granted to Jews in the diaspora by the Roman government permitting them to live according to their ancestral laws or customs (νόμοι or ἔθη), it should be observed that an explicit grant of judicial autonomy is attested only for Sardis (Joseph., *AJ* 14.235), and might well be unique to this city, as suggested by Tessa Rajak.[54] Otherwise we hear only of religious privileges, namely the freedom to observe the Sabbath, the right not to appear in court on the Sabbath (which must refer to a non-Jewish court of course), the right to collect and dispatch the Temple Tax until 70 CE etc. The evidence in the newly published archive from Herakleopolis in Egypt dated to the middle of the second century BCE[55] suggests that under the Ptolemies there existed real autonomous Jewish jurisdiction, and we may well ask whether it disappeared in Roman times.[56]

---

53 See detailed commentary and comparison with the Egyptian evidence in Cotton and Yardeni, *Aramaic, Hebrew, and Greek Documentary Texts from Naḥal Ḥever and Other Sites*, ad no. 63 with bibliography on this type of deed. Derek Roebuck suggests to me that "the use of *stipulatio* and Greek could just be borrowings by a legalistic arbitrator'; hence hardly "good evidence of the parties' intentions to resort to another tribunal."

54 See Tessa Rajak in another context: "Was There a Roman Charter for the Jews?," *JRS* 74 (1984): 116 and n. 35.

55 James M. S. Cowey and Klaus Maresch, eds., *Urkunden des Politeuma der Juden von Herakleopolis (144/3–133/2 v. Chr.) (P. Polit. Iud.)* (Wiesbaden: Westdeutscher Verlag, 2001).

56 An exhaustive discussion of Jewish rights and privileges under Roman rule is now available in Miriam Pucci Ben Zeev, *Jewish Rights in the Roman World* (Tübingen: Mohr Siebeck, 1998).

2. Criminal Jurisdiction

It must be clear that so far as criminal jurisdiction is concerned, it was much curtailed, if not altogether removed. However, even from the Jewish sources themselves one could demonstrate Roman 'total monopoly' so to speak in the sphere of criminal law. This is precisely what Saul Lieberman did in an important article published in 1944.[57] In that article Lieberman shows convincingly that the rabbinic sources faithfully describe the legal procedure in Roman courts in Judaea/Syria Palaestina in penal cases. The very terminology betrays the non-Jewish context. The judge is the 'king,' the ἔπαρχος (*eparchos*), the ἡγεμών (*hegemon*), the ἄρχων (*archon*) and the Hebrew equivalent 'government' (*shilton*). The place of judgement is the basilica or the βῆμα (*bema*) and the defendant was put on a *gradus* (*gardom*). The sources are familiar with the interrogation during the trial, the tortures applied, the speech of the lawyer for the defendant, the *elogium* of the συνήγορος or the ῥήτωρ, the sentence (ἀπόφασις *apophasis* or *periculum – pericula*) and finally the execution. The picture which emerges seems highly authentic. But, so far as I am aware, there are no similar scenes describing criminal procedure in Jewish courts. And as for the later period, the famous letter of Origen to Julius Africanus[58] shows, as I read it, the opposite of what A. Oppenheimer claims for it.[59] If anything, it shows that, as late as the first half of the third century CE, the right to try in criminal cases was usurped by Jews, not granted them by the Roman government. Anyone familiar with the principles of Roman provincial administration could hardly have expected anything different to take place in a province. And Judaea/Syria Palaestina was no exception.

---

57 Saul Lieberman, "Roman Legal Institutions in Early Rabbinics and in the Acta Martyrum," *JQR* 35 (1944): 1–57.

58 Origen, *Epist. ad Africanum de Historia Susannae datae*, ch. 14 (*PG* XI, cols. 81–3).

59 Oppenheimer, "Jewish Penal Authority in Roman Judaea."

Women and Law in the Documents from the Judaean Desert

In a rightly famous survey, published in 1959, Claire Préaux outlined in a masterly way various aspects of the status of women in the Hellenistic period, basing herself on information contained in the papyri from Egypt.[1] Since then many specialized and general studies have considerably enlarged and deepened our understanding and knowledge of the subject. The study of the papyrology of the Judaean Desert is still in its infancy: the bulk of the material has been published only recently. But we are in the fortunate position of being able to use profitably the methods developed for Egyptian papyrology. In what amounts to the first survey of the status of women as it emerges from the papyri from the Judaean Desert, I have decided to imitate the structure of Claire Préaux's pioneer study, in addition to sharing her preoccupation with the legal aspects of the subject. And this is not merely because of personal inclinations (which I will not deny), but also because of the nature of the material at hand: most of the documentary material from the Judaean Desert consists of legal documents.

The Material

Some brief comments on the documentary material from the Judaean Desert are necessary. The genesis of much of the documentary material found in the caves of the Judaean Desert lay in the two Jewish revolts against Rome: the so-called Great Revolt of 66–70 and the Bar Kokhba revolt of 132–135/136 CE. These upheavals drove scores of Jews from their homes in the provinces of Judaea and Arabia, and made them hide their documents, especially their legal documents, in the caves

1 Claire Préaux, "Le statut de la femme à l'époque hellenistique principalement en Égypte," *Recueils de la Société Jean Bodin* 11 (1959): 127–75.

Article note: First published in Henri Melaerts and Leon Mooren, eds., *Le rôle et le statut de la femme en Égypte hellénistique, romaine et byzantine: actes du colloque international, Bruxelles-Leuven 27–29 novembre 1997* (Leuven: Peeters, 2002), 123–147, with the following note: I have deliberately retained the lecture form and minimized my references to modern works. For an abbreviated version of this paper see "Recht und Wirtschaft. Zur Stellung der jüdischen Frau nach den Papyri aus der judäischen Wüste," *Zeitschrift für Neues Testament* 3, no. 6 (2000): 23–30. See also Hannah M. Cotton, "Women: The Texts," in *Encyclopedia of the Dead Sea Scrolls*, ed. Lawrence H. Schiffman and James VanderKam (New York: Oxford University Press, 2000), 984–87.

https://doi.org/10.1515/9783110770438-032

of Naḥal Ḥever, Wadi Murabba'at, Naḥal Ṣe'elim, Naḥal Mishmar, Ketef Jericho, Wadi Sdeir (Naḥal David), Wadi Ghweir, and other sites. This material is thus limited in time to a period of less than a hundred years. On the other hand, the people attested in the documents come from villages as scattered as Ein Gedi on the western shore of the Dead Sea, Kesalon and Ḥardona in the vicinity of Jerusalem, Jerusalem itself, Kaphar Barucha, Yaqim (or Yaqum) and Aristoboulias in the area south-east of Hebron, Bethbassi near Herodium, Galoda in eastern Samaria and Batharda in southern Samaria, Mazra'a and Maḥoza/Maḥoz 'Aglatain in the Dead Sea area in the Province of Arabia and finally Sophathe[...] near Livias in the Peraea, which although in Transjordan belonged to the province of Judaea.[2] The great majority of the documents, whether letters or legal deeds, were written by or at least involved Jews, thus affording us glimpses of Jewish village society in the Roman provinces of Judaea and Arabia at the time when they were written. There are no city dwellers in the documents, but at that time the majority of Jewish society in these provinces consisted of village dwellers. Thus like other papyri from elsewhere in the Roman Near East these documents give voice to the otherwise silent majority. There is no doubt that the Jews of the two provinces belonged to a single Jewish society whose ties overrode the provincial borders, as demonstrated in their marriages, property holdings and residence. The documents are written in Jewish Aramaic, Hebrew (during the two revolts), Nabataean Aramaic, and Greek; often two or more languages are present in the same archive, or even in the same document – a feature shared with other documents from the Roman Near East, for example the recently published papyri from Mesopotamia and the Middle Euphrates.[3] The resort to Greek does not reveal Hellenized or even semi-Hellenized Jews – a fact that is amply demonstrated by their Aramaic signatures and subscriptions, and by the very faulty version of the Greek language which they occasionally use.

The foregoing remarks are meant to suggest that the documents from the Judaean Desert are representative, that they contain an authentic picture of Jewish

---

2 See Emil Schürer, *The History of the Jewish People in the Age of Jesus Christ*, ed. Fergus Millar and Géza Vermès, Vol. II (Edinburgh: Clark, 1979), 12–13.

3 Denis Feissel and Jean Gascou, "Documents d'archives romains inédits du Moyen Euphrate (IIIe s. ap. J.-C.)," *CR Acad. Inscr.* 133 (1989): 535–61; Denis Feissel and Jean Gascou, "Documents d'archives romains inédits du Moyen Euphrate (IIIe s. après J-C): I. Les pétitions (T. Euphr. 1 à 5)," *Journal des Savants*, 1995, 65–119; Javier Teixidor, Denis Feissel, and Jean Gascou, "Documents d'archives romains inédits du Moyen Euphrate (IIIe s. après J-C): II. Les actes de vente- achat (P. Euphr. 6 À 10)," *Journal des Savants*, 1997, 3–57; Denis Feissel and Jean Gascou, "Documents d'archives romains inédits du Moyen Euphrate (IIIe s. après J.-C.): III. Actes divers et Lettres (P. Euphr. 11 à 17)," *Journal des Savants*, 2000, 157–208.

law and society as a whole at the time, that they do not represent fringe groups, or sects (as the sectarian documents from Qumran do). The map I have drawn shows that the Jews represented in the documents come from densely populated Jewish areas, some of them from the heartland of the religious and national movements incarnated in the two revolts.

The juxtaposition of the picture of Jewish society and law as it emerges from the papyri with contemporary and later legal texts which have survived from Palestine, namely the rabbinic sources, and above all with the Mishnah, redacted at the end of the second century CE, is unavoidable. Thus, whereas Claire Préaux ponders throughout her paper as to whether the divergences from classical Greek law are the result of later development of this law or reflect the influence of Egyptian law on it, my inquiry will have to grapple with the relationship between the position of women at law as it is found in the papyri and what is known from the rabbinic sources. Needless to say, not all aspects of women's life are covered by these documents, nor can an exhaustive legal code be drawn from them. I believe though that what we can learn from them is authentic and representative. Furthermore, I can think of no better criterion for evaluating the historical realities behind the rabbinic sources and for appraising the influence exercised by the rabbis on the law used by Jews at the time.

The documentary material on women from the Judaean Desert consists of two women's archives found in Naḥal Ḥever: the Babatha archive[4] and the archive of Salome Komaïse daughter of Levi.[5] Both archives revolve around the legal affairs of Jewish families in Maḥoza/Maḥoz 'Aglatain, a village on the southern shore of the Dead Sea, in what was the Nabataean Kingdom and in 106 CE became the Roman province of Arabia.[6] In addition to these two archives we have single documents which belonged to women or mention them. Some of these were found in

4 The Babatha Archive (94–132 CE) = *P.Yadin* 1–36. *P.Yadin* 5, 11–36 (Greek), published in Naphtali Lewis, *The Documents from the Bar Kokhba Period in the Cave of Letters. Greek Papyri*, Aramaic and Nabataean Signatures and Subscriptions, edited by Y. Yadin and J.C. Greenfield (Jerusalem: IES, 1989). *P.Yadin* 1–4, 6–10 (Aramaic and Nabataean), published in Yigael Yadin et al., *The Documents from the Bar Kokhba Period in the Cave of Letters: Hebrew, Aramaic and Nabatean-Aramaic Papyri* (Jerusalem: IES, 2002).

5 The archive of Salome Komaïse daughter of Levi (125 [113?]-131 CE) = *P.Hever* 12, (perhaps also *P.Hever* 32) and *P.Hever* 60–65, published in Hannah M. Cotton and Ada Yardeni, *Aramaic, Hebrew, and Greek Documentary Texts from Naḥal Ḥever and Other Sites*, Discoveries in the Judaean Desert XXVII (Oxford: Clarendon Press, 1997). See also n. 11 below.

6 See family trees in Lewis, *The Documents from the Bar Kokhba Period in the Cave of Letters. Greek Papyri*, 25 and Cotton and Yardeni, *Aramaic, Hebrew, and Greek Documentary Texts from Naḥal Ḥever and Other Sites*, 160.

Wadi Murabba'at; others belong to the so-called Seiyâl collection,[7] and are likely, therefore, to come from Naḥal Ḥever like the two archives just mentioned.[8] These documents too involve Jewish women from the province of Judaea and perhaps also from the province of Arabia.

Economic Activity

One is struck immediately by the intensive and independent economic and legal activity of the women encountered in the documents. The women, whether married or not, own real estate – houses, courtyards and date orchards – and are free to dispose of it as they wish. Some of this property was acquired via deeds of gift from parents or husbands.[9]

Documents written in the Nabataean kingdom reveal women selling property on their own. *P.Yadin* 2 and 3 from 99 CE, written in Nabataean Aramaic, describe the sale of the same date grove by a Nabataean woman, 'Abi'adan daughter of 'Aftah daughter of Manigros, first to a man called Archelaus son of 'Abd'amiyu (עבדעמיו) and a month later to Shim'on – probably to be identified as Shim'on bar Menaḥem, Babatha's father.[10] Another unpublished deed of sale in Nabatean, probably of the same date, belongs to the so-called Seiyâl collection: a Jewish woman called Shalom sells land to a Nabataean called Sh'ad'alhy.[11] On two occasions we find

7 Single documents: *P.Mur* 19, 20, 21, *P.Hever* 50 + *P.Mur* 26, *P.Mur* 29, 30, 113, 115, 116, published in P. Benoit, J.T. Milik, and R. de Vaux, *Les grottes de Murabba'at*, Discoveries in the Judaean Desert II (Oxford: Clarendon Press, 1961) (for *P.Hever* 50 + *P.Mur* 26 see below n. 12); *P.Hever* 7, 8a, 11, 13 and *P.Hever* 69.

8 It is just possible that two other archives which contain most of the documents of Bar Kokhba's administrators – both letters and leases – were brought to the Cave of Letters in Naḥal Ḥever and Wadi Murabba'at respectively by their womenfolk, whom we know by name from other documents left in the cave: Miriam daughter of Beianos of *P.Yadin* 26, Babatha's second husband's first (or other) wife, might be the sister of Jonathan son of Beianos of Ein Gedi, to whom *P.Yadin* 49–56, 58–60 are addressed, and Salome daughter of Iohannes Galgula, the wife in the Greek marriage contract from Wadi Murabba'at (*P.Mur* 115 = *SB* X 10305 of 124 CE), might be the sister or niece of Yeshu'a son of Galgula, to whom *P.Mur* 42–44 are addressed.

9 *P.Hever* 64 and *P.Yadin* 19 (parents); *P.Yadin* 7 (husband).

10 *P.Yadin* 2–3 from 99 CE.

11 *P.Hever* 2 (olim *XḤev/Se nab* inv. 2), published without commentary in Ada Yardeni, *Textbook of Aramaic, Hebrew and Nabataean Documentary Texts from the Judaean Desert and Related Material*, Vol. I (Jerusalem: The Hebrew University Press, 2000), 290–292 (Hebrew; English translation in Vol. II, p. 95). This document may belong to the archive of Salome Komaïse, see now Hanan Eshel, "Another Document from the Archive of Salome Komaïse Daughter of Levi," *SCI* 21 (2002): 169–71.

women selling property together with their husbands.[12] Finally in two deeds of sale, one in Aramaic and one in Hebrew, the wife waives all claims on the property just sold, presumably because it guaranteed the return of her *ketubba* or dowry.[13]

A woman could dispose of her property also in a deed of gift, as does Salome Grapte in 129 in favour of her daughter, Salome Komaïse daughter of Levi, to whom she gives a date orchard and half a courtyard in Maḥoz ‘Aglatain.[14] The presence of her husband as her guardian – συνπαρọ́ντọς ạὐτ̣[ῇ ἐ]πιτρόπọ[υ τοῦδε τοῦ πρά]γ̣μ̣ạτ̣ọς χάριν Ιωσηπου Σιμ̣ẉνọς [ἀ]νὴρ αὐτῆς – shows that she was married at the time when the deed was drawn up.

A land declaration submitted to the Roman authorities by a woman constitutes proof of full ownership. Although we cannot be entirely sure if Babatha was already married to Judah son of Eleazar Khthousion when she made her land declaration at the census of Arabia in 127,[15] his presence there as her ἐπίτροπος is a strong presumption that she was. However, her complete ownership of the four date groves she declares is not in question: ἀπογράφομạ ̣ι ἃ κέκτημαι: ‘I declare what I own.’ Unlike Sammouos son of Shim‘on, the declarant in *P.Hever* 62, Babatha does not give her age at the census.[16]

Money lending offers yet another instance of economic activity. In February 128, a few months before the marriage of his daughter Shlamzion, Judah son of Eleazar, Babatha’s second husband – who might have been short of ready cash – borrows from his wife Babatha in a deed of deposit three hundred *denarii*.[17] After his death, following the terms of the deposit which gave her the right of execution upon Judah’s possessions everywhere, she distrains three date groves which he owned in Maḥoza ‘in lieu of my dowry and a debt’: κατ̣ẹ́χẉ αὐτὰ ἀντὶ τῆς προ<ο>ικός μου καὶ ὀφịλ̣ῆς[18] – perhaps to be construed as hendiadys for ‘the

12 *P.Hever* 50 + *P.Mur* 26 and *P.Hever* 7; on *P.Hever* 50 + *P.Mur* 26 see Ada Yardeni, “Two in one? A Deed of Sale from Wadi Murabba‘at,” *Eretz Israel* 26 (1999): 64–70 (Hebrew; English resumé on p.*230).

13 *P.Mur* 30 and *P.Hever* 8a.

14 *P.Hever* 64.

15 *P.Yadin* 16.

16 *P.Hever* 62 lines 12–13: Σ̣ạμμọụος Σ̣ιμων[ο]ς Μαωζηνὸς τῆς Ζοαρηνῆς περιμέτρου Πέτρας, ọἰκῶν [ἐ]ν ἰδίοις ἐν αὐτῇ Μαωζạ, ἀπọγράφομαι ἐμαυτὸν ἐτῶν τριάκοντ̣ạ etc.; contrast with *P.Yadin* 16 lines 13–15: Βαβθα Σίμωνος Μαωζηνὴ τῆς Ζοαρηνῆς περιμέτρου Πέτρας, οἰκοῦσα ἐν ἰδίοις ἐν αὐτῇ Μαωζạ, ἀπογράφομạι̣ ἃ κέκτημαι. For women’s liability to the poll tax in Arabia and Judaea see Hannah M. Cotton, “The Roman Census in the Papyri from the Judaean Desert and the Egyptian κατ’ οἰκίαν ἀπογραφή,” in *Semitic Papyrology in Context: A Climate of Creativity*, ed. Lawrence H. Schiffman (Leiden – Boston: Brill, 2003), 105–22 [above, pp. 363–78].

17 *P.Yadin* 17.

18 *P.Yadin* 22 lines 9–10; cf. *P.Yadin* 21 lines 11–12.

debt of my dowry.' However this may be, she claimed that her late husband had registered the groves in her name,[19] but the representatives of her late husband's nephews maintained that she had detained them by force.[20] The issue is never settled, but Babatha's claim to have the groves registered in her name as security for a debt or for her dowry seems plausible enough: we have evidence for dowries being secured on specific pieces of property in documents from Egypt, and some evidence that this was practiced elsewhere.[21]

Babatha exercises economic initiative and much resourcefulness – to no avail as it turned out – in her dealings with her orphaned son's appointed guardians. She implies in *P.Yadin* 15 that her son's guardians had made a poor investment with his money, as a result of which his income is not commensurate with the style of life which the boy was accustomed to (or his social standing), one which would allow him to be raised splendidly and render thanks to the '*the[se] most blessed times* of the governorship of Julius Julianus' as she tells the Roman governor of Arabia, using phrases all too familiar from Roman imperial propaganda of the time.[22] She, on the other hand, could get 18 % per annum if they entrusted her with the boy's capital.[23] She is prepared to give her own property as security:

> as I have property equivalent in value to this money of the orphan that you have, therefore, I previously deposed in order that you might decide to give me the money on security involving a hypothec of my property.[24]

In this as in her attempt to indict the guardians as untrustworthy and thus have them removed, she must have sought the advice of people well versed in Roman legal practice, since as has been shown elsewhere her actions and proposals are in harmony with what is later attested in the Roman legal sources as remedies open to the mother of a ward.[25]

---

19 *P.Yadin* 24 lines 4–6.
20 *P.Yadin* 25 lines 9–10.
21 For a different interpretation see Naphtali Lewis, "In the World of P.Yadin," *SCI* 18 (1999): 125–27.
22 ὅθεν λαμπρῶς διασωθ[ῇ μου] ọ υἱὸς εὐχ̣α̣ρ̣ι̣σ̣τ̣ῶν (εὐχαριστοῦντα) τοῖς μακ̣αριωτάτοις καιροῖς ἡγεμωνε[ίας] Ἰουλ̣[ί]ọυ̣ Ἰ̣ουλιανοῦ ἡγεμώνος (*P.Yadin* 15 lines 10–11 = lines 26–27).
23 'A denarius and a half [per month] per hundred denarii' (*P.Yadin* 15 lines 9–10 = line 26).
24 *P.Yadin* 15 lines 7–9 = lines 23–25.
25 See Hannah M. Cotton, "The Guardianship of Jesus Son of Babatha: Roman and Local Law in the Province of Arabia," *JRS* 83 (1993): 94–108 [above, pp. 403–30]; Tiziana J. Chiusi, "IV. Zur Vormundschaft der Mutter," *ZSS* 111 (1994): 155–96; Dieter Nörr, "Prozessuales aus dem Babatha-Archiv," in *Mélanges de droit romain et d'histoire ancienne: hommage à la mémoire de André Magdelain*, ed. Michel Humbert and Yan Thomas (Paris: Panthéon-Assas, 1998), 317–41, with all previous bibliography. I am grateful to Dieter Nörr for showing me the ms. in advance of publication.

Neither Babatha nor her adversaries feel any qualms about approaching the Roman governor and summoning their rivals to appear before him at any time and place, and initiating litigation over what at times seem trivial claims, such as the chattel removed from Judah son of Eleazar's house after his death by Miriam daughter of Beianos, his other (or previous) wife, in the face of Babatha's vehement protests.[26]

Against this background of married women freely disposing of their property, one should examine the varying degrees of control of the married woman's property by her husband in Jewish law. The sages differed over the question whether the husband had title to property *not* recorded in the marriage contract (*ketubba*) – either such property as was owned by the woman before she was married or that acquired after marriage; on the other hand such property as is recorded in the marriage contract itself passes into the husband's control during the marriage. This is implied in the documents themselves as well. However, we notice that the dowry or *ketubba* recorded in the documents, whether written in Greek or in Aramaic, consists exclusively of valuables (jewellery and clothes) or sums of money; real property is never recorded as part of the dowry. It was not by chance, therefore, that Judah son of Eleazar waited eleven days after he had given his daughter Shlamzion in marriage to Judah Kimber (*P.Yadin* 18) before bestowing on her in a deed of gift (*P.Yadin* 19) half a courtyard in Ein Gedi; nor that Salome Komaïse daughter of Levi receives real property from her mother in a deed of gift (*P.Hever* 64) either during her marriage to her first husband, Sammouos son of Shim'on, or before her marriage to her second husband, Yeshu'a son of Menaḥem (*P.Hever* 65). Safeguarding the daughter's title to her parents' real property in this way has notable parallels in Egyptian papyri in the institution of the *prosphora* and the so-called 'parental apportionment.' Jewish practice seems to have been no different.[27]

Legal Competence

Economic activity leads us naturally to consider women's legal competence, skills and education. The only literate woman we encounter in the documents is the mysterious Iulia Crispina whom I shall have occasion to mention later on. In her

26 *P.Yadin* 16.

27 See Jane Rowlandson, *Landowners and Tenants in Roman Egypt* (Oxford: Oxford University Press, 1996), 165: "there were sound reasons, perhaps legal as well as practical, that the *pherne* never seems to have included land or house property. It is notable that, where such property is given by the bride's parents through a marriage contract, it is always the bride herself who obtains ownership of it"; cf. the whole discussion there, 160 ff.

function as *episcopos* of the orphans of Yeshu'a son of Eleazar she writes a Greek subscription, whereas the male guardian writes his subscription in Aramaic.[28] Babatha, on the other hand, 'did not know her letters,' and therefore someone else wrote a subscription for her.[29] Her signature on the back of her land declaration is that of a person laboriously and mechanically copying someone else's writing. Illiteracy may be assumed even in those cases where it is not set out as the reason for the employment of a subscriber.[30] It is quite obvious in the case of Shlamzion daughter of Yehosef who says in the subscription to her deed of renunciation that, although present, she 'borrowed the writing of Matat son of Shimeon (who wrote) what she said': שלמצין ברת יהוסף על נפשה שאלה כתב מתת ב[ר] שמעון ממרא.[31] The subscriber fulfilled merely a technical function: he subscribed for a person, who was legally competent to do so, whether male or female, but who happened to be illiterate (or otherwise incapable of writing), when a subscription and/or a signature in his or her own hand was required to render a document valid.[32] The question that naturally arises is therefore: is the presence of a male guardian in a legal transaction involving a woman a sign of real restriction on a woman's freedom of action?[33]

The presence of a guardian for a woman is attested only in legal documents written in the Greek language. The guardian of a woman is designated here an ἐπίτροπος;[34] in the Greek papyri from Egypt, however, the guardian of a woman

---

28 *P.Yadin* 20 lines 43–44.

29 Βαβαθας Σίμωνος ἐμαρτυροποιησάμη<ν> κạṭὰ Ἰωάνου Ἐγλα Ἀ<βδ>αοβδα Ἐλλουθα ἐπιτρώπων Ἠσους υ<ἱ>ο<ῦ> μου ὀρφανοῦ δι' ἐπιτρόπου μου Ἰούδα Χαθουσ̣ίωνος ἀκọλ̣[ο]ύθῳς τὲς προγεγραμμένες ἐρέσασιν. Ἐλεάζαρος Ἐλεαζάρ̣ου ἔγραψα ὑπὲρ αὐτῆς ἐρωτηθ̣εὶς διὰ τὸ αὐṭης μὴ ε<ἰ>δένα<ι> γράμματα, *P.Yadin* 15 lines 34–37.

30 E.g. *P.Hever* 8a, 13, *P.Mur* 50 + *P.Hever* 26, *P.Mur* 21, 29, *P.Hever* 64.

31 *P.Hever* 13 lines 11–12; for the expression cf. Harald Ingholt, "Palmyrene Inscription from the Tomb of Malkû," *Mélanges de l'Université Saint-Joseph* 38 (1962): 106–107: אשאלת כתב ידי ליוליס בר אורליס עגילו בר אפרהט בר חרי זבדבול בדילדי לא ידע ספר 'I have lent my hand to Iulius son of Aurelius 'Ogeilu, son of Afrahat, freedman of Zabdibol, because he did not know writing.' However, I prefer now Ranon Katzoff's punctuation and translation of the lines: 'Shelamsion daughter of Yehosaf asked; Matat son of Shim'on wrote what she said'; see Katzoff, "Review: Hannah M. Cotton and Ada Yardeni eds., Aramaic, Hebrew and Greek Documentary Texts from Nahal Hever and Other Sites," *SCI* 19 (2000): 322.

32 Cf. *P.Yadin* 15 where both an ἐπίτροπος and a subscriber take part in the legal proceedings; on the subscriber in the documents from the Judaean Desert see Hannah M. Cotton, "Subscriptions and Signatures in the Papyri from the Judaean Desert: The χειροχρήστης," *JJP* 25 (1995): 29–40 [above, pp. 115–25].

33 Cf. Hannah M. Cotton, "The Guardian (ἐπίτροπος) of a Woman in the Documents from the Judaean Desert," *ZPE* 118 (1997): 267–73 [above, pp. 431–41].

34 Ἐπίτροπος of a woman in Greek documents: *P.Yadin* 14–17, 20–22, 25, 27, *P.Hever* 63–65, 69.

is designated κύριος. The term ἐπίτροπος is reserved in the Egyptian papyri for the guardian of a minor; and for good reason too. The two terms are not interchangeable; they stand for two distinct legal concepts. The ἐπίτροπος can only refer to the person who administers someone else's patrimony.[35] The κύριος on the other hand was in the old Attic law from which the term derives the master of a person who could not own property. That the lack of distinction was not due to the influence of the Aramaic environment is proved by the fact that in the Aramaic subscriptions the distinction is made: the guardian of a woman is called אדון (*'dwn*) = κύριος;[36] whereas for the guardian of the minor the Aramaic borrowed the Greek term ἐπίτροπος: אפטרפא (*'ptrp'*). And this is all the more striking since in none of the Hebrew, Aramaic and Nabataean papyri from the Judaean Desert do we find a woman represented by a guardian. As was suggested with great plausibility by the late Hans Julius Wolff the use of a single term (*epitropos*) for the guardian of a woman as well as for that of a minor in the papyri from the Judaean Desert is due to the influence of Roman law, where at least originally no legal distinction existed between the guardian of a minor and that of a woman, and, consequently, the same term, *tutor*, was used for both. Both, if they were not *sui iuris*, were represented by the *tutor*. The requirement for a woman to be represented by a guardian seems to have been imposed by the Roman authorities.[37] On the other hand, the low profile kept by the guardian of the woman in the Greek documents is conspicuous: a woman is said to be acting 'through her ἐπίτροπος' (διὰ τοῦ ἐπιτρόπου αὐτῆς) only in cases in which she is the one in whose name the *homologia* is written or another kind of legal obligation is undertaken; but sometimes even in these cases his presence is merely recorded (συμπαρόντος αὐτῇ ἐπιτρόπου); and sometimes no ἐπίτροπος appears at all. There is certainly no question of the ἐπίτροπος, who is normally her husband, except in the cases in which he is himself one of the parties to the transaction,[38] managing the woman's property; and, as we have just seen, there is no doubt at all that women could own property and dispose of it as they wished.

---

35 "Ἐπίτροπος ... kann sich niemals auf eine andere Person beziehen als einen Verwalter fremden Vermögens," Hans Julius Wolff, "Römisches Provinzialrecht in der Provinz Arabia (Rechtspolitik als Instrument der Beherrschung)," in *Aufstieg und Niedergang der römischen Welt*, Vol. II.13 (Berlin: De Gruyter, 1980), 794; in contrast to the *tutor* in Roman law, see Max Kaser, *Das römische Privatrecht*, 2nd ed. (München: Beck, 1971), 85–6.

36 *P.Yadin* 15 line 37: יהודה בר כתושין אדון בבתה: 'Judah of Khthousion, Babatha's κύριος'; *P.Yadin* 20 line 41: בסא בר ישוע אפט<ר>פא דיתמ<י>א: 'Besa son of Yeshua' ἐπίτροπος of the orphans.'

37 See Wolff, "Römisches Provinzialrecht in der Provinz Arabia," 796–97.

38 As he is in *P.Yadin* 17 and *P.Hever* 65; see Cotton and Yardeni, *Aramaic, Hebrew, and Greek Documentary Texts from Naḥal Ḥever and Other Sites*, 236–37.

It would seem that the presence of the guardian of a woman in the Greek documents is just a matter of form and procedure required by the courts for which the Greek contracts were intended. Which courts are these? One notices that all Greek documents in which a woman appears with her guardian, both in Arabia and in Judaea, were written under Roman rule, and, as suggested above, under the influence of Roman law. Does the presence of an ἐπίτροπος of a woman show incontrovertibly that the Greek documents were intended for a Roman court of law, and his absence from the Semitic documents that they were intended for other courts? In order to claim this we should have to prove that the Semitic documents too were written under Roman rule. Unfortunately the nature of the evidence hampers us in this. The four Semitic deeds which would have required the presence of a guardian of a woman under Roman law were not written under Roman rule: the Nabataean *P.Yadin* 2–3 and *P.Hever* 2 were written before the annexation of the Nabataean kingdom and the creation of the province of Arabia, and *P.Hever* 13 was written in Ein Gedi at the time of the Bar Kokhba revolt. Nevertheless, I do not believe that it is merely a coincidence that we do not have a document written under Roman rule in Aramaic, Nabataean or Hebrew with a guardian representing a woman.[39]

It is noteworthy that women do not figure as witnesses to any of the documents, many of which are double documents which require five to seven witnesses.[40] Could they serve as guardians? A certain Iulia Crispina appears in *P.Yadin* 20 and 25, calling herself an *episkopos* – whatever the title means – of Yeshua' son of Eleazar's orphans. She is acting together with, and once instead of, a proper male *epitropos* of the orphans. Since the *epitropos* was appointed by the city council of Petra,[41] is it conceivable that Iulia Crispina too was officially nominated to serve as such by the city authorities? John Rea has recently pointed out the similarity between Iulia Crispina and the Egyptian ἐπακολουθήτρια, or παρακολουθήτρια, who also appears accompanied by a male guardian, but who is attested in Egyptian papyri only from the second half of the second century.[42] If indeed, as seems quite likely, the later institution was created to satisfy the strictures imposed by Roman law on the exercise of guardianship by women, then we may have

39 Hannah M. Cotton, "Jewish Jurisdiction under Roman Rule: Prolegomena," in *Zwischen den Reichen: Neues Testament und römische Herrschaft. Vorträge auf der ersten Konferenz der European Association for Biblical Studies*, ed. Michael Labahn and Jürgen Zangenberg (Tübingen: Francke Verlag, 2002), 15 [above, pp. 487 f.].

40 See Cotton and Yardeni, *Aramaic, Hebrew, and Greek Documentary Texts from Naḥal Ḥever and Other* Sites, 141–43; but see the reservations of Rudolf Haensch, "Zum Verständnis von P.Jericho 16 gr.," *SCI* 20 (2001): 162–67.

41 *P.Yadin* 11.

42 Ad *P.Oxy.* LVIII 3921, lines 6 and 49 (219 CE).

in Arabia the first example of such an adaptation of local custom, and another expression of Romanization. Admittedly, this contrasts sharply with Babatha's total exclusion from the guardianship of her orphaned son – an exclusion which cannot be accounted for by Jewish law. A woman could serve as a guardian of their common children if appointed by her husband in his lifetime. There also existed a *de facto* sort of guardianship, probably the original and authentic Jewish form of guardianship: guardianship acquired by virtue of 'orphans boarding with the householder' (סמיכה). This could offer a way for women to become *de facto* guardians of their children, but it seems that as the result of the strict application of Roman legal practice, boarding with his mother did not have the legal consequence of turning Babatha into the guardian of her orphaned son, Yeshua'.[43]

Family Law: Marriage, Re-marriage, Polygamy, Widowhood, Divorce and the Law of Succession

Marriage

We possess nine documentary marriage contracts, five in Greek and four in Aramaic:

DOCUMENT	DATE	PLACE	LANGUAGE
P.Mur 20	1st century CE?	Ḥardona, Judaea	Aramaic
P.Mur 115	124 CE	Bethbassi, Judaea	Greek
P.Yadin 10 (*IEJ* 44, 1994, 75–99)	125 CE	Maḥoza, Arabia	Aramaic
P.Yadin 18	128 CE	Maḥoza, Arabia	Greek
P.Hever 69	130 CE	Aristoboulias, Judaea	Greek
P.Hever 65 (= *P.Yadin* 37)	131 CE	Maḥoza, Arabia	Greek
P.Mur 116	first half of 2nd century CE	unknown	Greek
P.Mur 21	1st century CE?	unknown	Aramaic
P.Hever 11	1st or 2nd century CE	unknown	Aramaic

43 For a detailed discussion of the Jewish sources see Cotton, "The Guardianship of Jesus Son of Babatha: Roman and Local Law in the Province of Arabia," 97–100 [above, pp. 411–15].

In addition to the marriages attested in the marriage contracts we know from the documents of dozens of married couples. It seems evident from the names that at least the Jews represented in these documents married among themselves. I deliberately underscore this fact in order to set it off against my claim that the marriage contracts in Greek lack anything which would mark them out as Jewish apart from the identity of the parties as disclosed by their names: all of them resemble both in spirit and in phraseology contemporary Greek marriage contracts from Egypt. The Aramaic marriage contracts, on the other hand, reveal to us that the rabbinic marriage contract, the *ketubba*, had indeed by then developed its own special form, but it had not yet become normative, since not one of the five marriage contracts written in Greek can be said to be a translation of an Aramaic *ketubba*. Above all they lack the well-known formula, found in the opening line of at least two of the Aramaic contracts, namely the statement of the groom 'that you will be my wife according to the law of Moses and the Jews': די תהוא לי לאנתה כדין משה ויהודאי (*P.Mur* 20 line 3).[44] This formula places the marriage firmly within a Jewish framework and imposes on it the sanction of Jewish law. The claim that the conventional phrase κατὰ τοὺς νόμους found in the Greek marriage contract of Babatha's stepdaughter, Shelamzion, replaces the traditional Jewish formula cited above is, of course, unfounded.[45] It appears here as part of the *ekdosis* formula pronounced by the father of the bride:

> Judah son of Eleazar also known as Khthousion gave away (ἐξέδετο) Shelamzion his own daughter, a virgin, to Judah surnamed Cimber ... for Shelamzion to be a wedded wife to Judah Cimber for the partnership of marriage according to the laws (κατὰ τοὺς νόμους) ... etc.[46]

In papyri from Egypt the phrase συνεῖναι γυναικὶ κατὰ τοὺς νόμους means no more than to live with her lawfully, even when there is no marriage contract.[47] The

---

44 Cf. *P.Yadin* 10 line 5 לאנת[ה כדי]ן משה ויהודאי 'for a wife [according to the la]w of Moses and the Jews.'

45 So R. Katzoff, in Naphtali Lewis, Ranon Katzoff, and Jonas C. Greenfield, "Papyrus Yadin 18," *IEJ* 37 (1987): 241; modified in Ranon Katzoff, "Papyrus Yadin 18 Again: A Rejoinder," *JQR* 82 (1991): 173. The phrase is now attested in a marriage contract from Bostra (*P.Bostra* 2) dated to the third century, in connection with the dowry; but the context is unclear. I am grateful to J. Gascou for showing me the text.

46 *P.Yadin* 18 lines 32–39 = lines 3–7: ἐ̣ξ̣[έδ]ο̣τ[ο Ἰούδα]ς Ἐ̣λ̣ε̣αζάρου τοῦ καὶ [Χθουσί]ω̣ν[ος Σ]-ελαμψ̣[ι]ώ̣νη̣ν̣ τ̣ὴν ἰδίαν θυγατέραν αὐτο̣ῦ̣ παρθ̣έ̣ν̣ο̣ν Ἰο̣ύ̣δατι ἐπικαλουμένῳ Κίμβερι υἱῷ Ἀνανίου τοῦ Σω̣μ̣α̣λα, ἀμφότεροι ἀπ̣ὸ̣ κώ̣μης Αἰνγαδῶν τῆς Ἰο̣υ̣δαία[ς] ἐνθάδε καταμένον̣τ̣[ες], ε̣ἶ̣ν̣α̣ι̣ τ̣ὴν Σ̣ε̣λ̣αμψιών[ην] Ἰούδατι Κίμβερι γυν̣α̣ῖκαν γαμετὴν π̣ρ̣ὸς γάμου κ̣[οι]νωνίαν κατὰ τοὺς νόμους.

47 Cf. Hans Julius Wolff, *Written and Unwritten Marriages in Hellenistic and Post-Classical Roman Law* (Haverford: American Philological Association, 1939), *Addenda*, p. vi (*P.Cair.Cat.* 10388, 5);

term ἐξέδετο occurs in another Greek marriage contract from the Judaean Desert, where the mother is giving away the bride. The *ekdosis* is certainly not a Jewish institution. On the contrary it is only in the case of minority that Jewish law speaks of the giving away of the daughter by one of the parents.[48]

In the Greek contracts the groom acknowledges the receipt of a dowry from the bride (προσφορά; προίξ), whereas in the Aramaic contracts he acknowledges the debt of *ketubba* money to her. By 'the money of your *ketubba*'[49] it is commonly assumed that the fictitious *mohar* is meant, i. e. the rabbinic 'endowment pledge, the divorce payment' due to the wife upon the dissolution of the marriage, which replaced the biblical *mohar* which was an immediate payment, a bride-gift to the wife's father. If this is so, then it must be said that 'the money of the *ketubba*' is treated in exactly the same way as what we may call the 'gentile' dowry is treated: the husband's entire property is put in lien to secure the return of that money on the dissolution of the marriage, and it is stipulated that the wife's sons will inherit the money if she dies before the husband. However, there is nothing whatsoever in the text of the Aramaic contracts which compels us to think that 'the money of your *ketubba*' is the rabbinic fictitious *mohar*, rather than the dowry of the Greek marriage contracts.[50]

The acknowledgement of a dowry is also the occasion of undertaking the nourishment of the wife in four marriage contracts,[51] and twice also that of the children to come.[52] The undertaking to feed and clothe the wife is a recurrent element in marriage contracts in Greek from Egypt, and, as here, it often follows immediately upon the groom's acknowledgement of receipt of the dowry. On the other hand, there is only indirect evidence for the inclusion of the obligation to

---

pp. 28–29, n. 96 (*P.Grenf.* 21, 126 BCE = Mitteis, *Chr.*, no. 302 lines 4 and 13, and see Mitteis there, p. 341, n. 1); p. 54, n. 192a; p. 67, n. 238 (*BGU* I 232, 108 CE, lines 2 ff.: ὁμ[ολογεῖ] Ἀπολλώνιος ... τῇ προούσῃ κ[αὶ συν]ούσῃ αὐτῷ κατὰ νόμους γυναικεί); Joseph Modrzejewski, "La Règle de droit dans l'Egypte ptolémaïque," in *Essays in Honor of C. Bradford Welles* (New Haven: American Society of Papyrologists, 1966), 154.

48 For the Jewish sources see Cotton and Yardeni, *Aramaic, Hebrew, and Greek Documentary Texts from Naḥal Ḥever and Other Sites*, 266.

49 'כסף כתבתך,' *P.Mur* 21 line 13; *P.Yadin* 10 line 16.

50 Elias J. Bickerman, "Two Legal Interpretations of the Septuagint," in *Studies in Jewish and Christian History*, Vol. I (Leiden: Brill, 1976), 212–215, in fact comes very close to suggesting that "the money of the *ketubbah*" may refer to the dowry; the documentary marriage contracts support M. Satlow's claim that "the rabbinic *ketubah* payment was a rabbinic innovation of around the late first century" ("Reconsidering the Jewish Ketubah Payment," in *The Jewish Family in Antiquity*, ed. Shaye J.D. Cohen (Atlanta: Scholars Press, 1993), 146); see also Hannah M. Cotton, "Marriage Contracts from the Judaean Desert," *Materia giudaica* 6 (2000): 2–6.

51 *P.Yadin* 10, 18, *P.Hever* 65 and 69.

52 *P.Yadin* 18 and *P.Hever* 65.

provide for the wife in rabbinic marriage contracts of the early Mishnaic period. In three Greek marriage contracts from the Judaean Desert[53] the maintenance clause is followed by a liability clause which earmarks the husband's entire property as security for his wife's maintenance. No such clause is found, as far as I know, in Greek marriage contracts from Egypt, where it is generally stated that the husband will provide for all that is necessary (τὰ δέοντα πάντα) according to his means (κατὰ δύναμιν or κατὰ δύναμιν τῶν ὑπαρχόντων), and where the liability clause, as in the other marriage contracts from the Judaean Desert, is used simply to guarantee the return of the dowry or *ketubba* in the event of a divorce or death. However, in demotic marriage contracts from Egypt we find that "the husband repeatedly pledges everything he possesses and will acquire as security for honouring the obligations which he has taken upon himself by a deed drawn up in view of a marriage."[54] The similarity to demotic contracts extends even to the particular wording used to apply the liability clause not only to the property possessed by the husband at the time of concluding the contract, but also to property acquired after its conclusion.[55]

In fact all the practices and obligations discussed so far are frequently documented in dozens of Greek marriage contracts from Egypt and other parts of the Roman Near East, and are certainly not unique to Jewish marriage contracts. There was no normative, authoritative and uniform marriage contract which Jews knew that they had to use. Neither may we assume that for every marriage contract in Greek which has been preserved, a '*kosher*' Jewish Aramaic *ketubba* accompanying it has been lost. Obviously the Jews who wrote these documents felt free to use the legal instrument that seemed to them most effective.

Perhaps the most striking evidence of the remarkable degree of assimilation of Jewish society to its environment is the documentation of the existence of the institution of unwritten marriage (*agraphos gamos*) in this society. This is recorded in a badly preserved inner part of a double document, which was first published by N. Lewis as *P.Yadin* 37, and then republished, revised and reinterpreted, together with the other documents of the archive of Salome Komaïse

---

53 *P.Yadin* 18 and *P.Hever* 65 and 69; but see also the Aramaic *P.Yadin* 10 lines 7–10 (Babatha's marriage contract).

54 P.W. Pestman, *Marriage and Matrimonial Property in Ancient Egypt* (Leiden: Brill, 1961), 115; See Pestman, 115–17; 133–36.

55 In *P.Mich.* inv. 4526 (Philadelphia, 199 BCE) we find almost a translation of lines 10–11 of our document: 'Everything that I possess and that I shall acquire is security for your above-mentioned food-and-clothing allowance'; see Erich Lüddeckens, *Ägyptische Eheverträge* (Wiesbaden: Harrasowitz, 1960), 148–51, no. 4D; cf. Pestman, *Marriage and Matrimonial Property in Ancient Egypt*, 115 ff.

daughter of Levi, in *DJD* XXVII as no. 65. The groom, Yeshua‘ son of Menaḥem, from the Peraea, declares that:

> [he agreed with Sal]ome also called K[omaïse, daughter of Levi], his wife, who is from Maḥoza, [that they continue] life together ... as also before this time ..., [and that he owes?] the above-mentioned Komaïse, as her dowry, ninety-six denarii of silver, [which the bride-groom], the above-mentioned Yeshua‘, [acknowledged] to have received from her on the present day, as the written evaluation of feminine adornment in sil[ver and gold and clo]-thing and other feminine articles equivalent to the above-mentioned amount of money, (combined) with his undertaking to feed [and clothe both her] and her children to come in accordance with Greek custom and Greek manner.[56]

The most straightforward implication of various formulas in this passage, familiar from similar Egyptian contracts, is that the couple had been married for some time in an unwritten marriage when the document was drawn up. The unwritten marriage was, as its name implies, a marriage without a contract, but its legal validity was no different from that of the written marriage, the ἔνγραφος γάμος. Whatever its origins,[57] the institution is known to have existed outside Egypt as well. *P.Dura* 31 from 204 CE attests its existence in the village of Ossa, in what was then Syria Coele. In the majority of cases, the receipt of a dowry constituted the occasion for drawing up a contract. The presence of the formula: ‘the above-mentioned Yeshua‘, [acknowledged] to have received from her on the present day etc.’ suggests that in this case too it was the receipt of a dowry which called forth the present contract.

However, in an attempt to reconcile ‘living together’ without a marriage contract with Jewish law, N. Lewis rejected the Egyptian parallels in favour of an *interpretatio Hebraica*: “Close as the parallel may be, however, ... the expression ‘as also before this time’ more likely implies that the bride and groom had been

56 ὡμολογήσ]ạτο Ιησους Μαναημου ... [π̣ρ̣ὸ̣ς(?) Σαλ]ωμην κ̣αλο̣υ̣μένην Κ̣[ομαϊσην Ληουειου τὴν] γυ̣ν̣αῖκα, Μ̣[α]ωζηνὴν ὥστε αὐτο̣ὺ̣ς {ὥ̣σ̣τ̣ε̣ α̣[ὐτοὺς]} [*c. 17 letters*].ετ̣ . . . . συμβιως . . .[*c. 14 letters*] αὐ̣τῇ\ς/ ὡ̣[ς κ]αὶ πρὸ τούτου τοῦ χρόνου . .[καὶ ὀφείλειν̣ *c. 10 letters*] . . . . . τῇ αὐτῇ Κομα̣ι̣σ̣[η τὴ]ν̣ προῖ{ο}κα αὐτῆς ἀ[ρ]γ̣υ̣ρίου δηνάρια ἐνανήκο̣ν̣τα ἕξ, [ἃ ὡμολογήσατο ὁ γήμας] \[ὁ αὐ]τὸς Ιησους/ [ἀπ]ε̣σχηκ[έν]αι παρ̣’ α̣ὐτῆς τῇ̣ [οὔ]ση ἡμέρα̣ τειμογ̣[ρ]αφίαν κοσμίας γυναικίας ἐν ἀ̣[ργύρῳ καὶ χρυσῷ καὶ ἱμα]τισμῷ καὶ ἑταίροις γυ[ναι]κίοις ἀ̣ξι[οχρέαν] . . . . .τ̣ο̣υ̣ ἀργυρίου, σὺν αἱρέσει τ̣ρ̣οφῆ̣ς [καὶ ἀμφιασμοῦ αὐτῆς] τ̣ε καὶ τῶν μελ̣λόντ̣ω̣[ν τέκ]ν̣ω̣ν̣ νό̣μ[ῳ] [ἑλληνικ]ῷ καὶ ἑλλ̣[η]ν̣ι̣κῷ τρόπῳ.

57 There is no need to enter here into a discussion of its origins; see Wolff, *Written and Unwritten Marriages in Hellenistic and Post-Classical Roman Law*, 48 ff., 83 ff.; Raphael Taubenschlag, *The Law of Greco-Roman Egypt in the light of the Papyri, 322 BC–640 AD* (Warsaw: Państwowe Wydawnictwo Naukowe, 1955), 115 ff.; Joseph Modrzejewski, “Note sur P. Strasb. 237,” in *Symbolae Raphaeli Taubenschlag Dedicatae III* (Vratislaviae-Varsaviae: Ossolineum, 1957), 152 ff. See Hans-Albert Rupprecht, “Marriage Contract Regulations and Documentary Practice in the Greek Papyri,” *SCI* 17 (1998): 60–76.

living together since the day of their betrothal, in keeping with a Jewish practice of the time when the bride was an orphan and a minor."[58] After the discovery of the archive of Salome Komaïse daughter of Levi we know that she was not a minor at the time this contract was written. The radical approach which takes the phrase to be referring to 'premarital cohabitation,' and claims, on the basis of this marriage contract, that "premarital cohabitation was a local practice particular to and common to Judaea"[59] is not much better; it assumes no less than the 'apologetic approach' that, by this time, there existed a coherent and operative Jewish system of law which had already become normative. In such a system, 'a man may not keep his wife even one hour without a *ketubba*,' (*bBK* 89a),[60] and life together without a *ketubba* must be branded 'premarital cohabitation' or 'sex out of wedlock.' Even if this were so, this marriage contract is not the *ketubba* which would turn 'premarital cohabitation' into a proper Jewish marriage.

Re-marriage, Polygamy and Widowhood

The documents give us a few glimpses of the conditions of re-marriage, polygamy and widowhood. A second marriage is attested for three women in the two archives, Babatha, Salome Komaïse, and her mother, Salome Grapte. *P.Mur* 115 is a contract of re-marriage, where the groom acknowledges a fresh dowry to his former wife, a feature which is also attested in Egyptian papyri. Jewish law allowed a man to marry his divorced wife as long as she had not married another man in the meantime, but the document does not allow us to see whether this rule was accepted by Jewish society of the time.[61] On the evidence of *P.Yadin* 26 and 34, where another wife of Babatha's second husband, Judah son of Eleazar Khthousion, makes her appearance after his death, and where both women refer to Judah as 'my and your dead husband,'[62] the editor, N. Lewis, posited that polygamy was

---

58 Lewis, *The Documents from the Bar Kokhba Period in the Cave of Letters. Greek Papyri*, 130; the suggestion is R. Karzoff's, who defends it in his "Review: Hannah M. Cotton and Ada Yardeni Eds., Aramaic, Hebrew and Greek Documentary Texts from Nahal Hever and Other Sites," 324–25.

59 Tal Ilan, "Premarital Cohabitation in Ancient Judea: The Evidence of the Babatha Archive and the Mishnah (Ketubbot 1.4)," *Harv. Theol. Rev.* 86 (1993): 247–64.

60 Quoted by Ilan, 254.

61 On re-marriage of one's former wife see Mordechai Akiva Friedman in *Saul Lieberman Memorial Volume*, ed. Shamma Friedman (New York – Jerusalem: Jewish Theological Seminary of America, 1993), 189–232 (Hebrew).

62 E.g. *P.Yadin* 26, lines 7–8: Ἰούδου Ἐλεαζάρου Χθουσίωνος ἀνδρός μου καί σου ἀ[πογενομένου]. See Ranon Katzoff, "Polygamy in P.Yadin?," *ZPE* 109 (1995): 128–32 and contra Naphtali Lewis, "Judah's Bigamy," *ZPE* 116 (1997): 152.

practiced by Jews in Arabia at the time. Lewis' interpretation of the document has been disputed by Ranon Katzoff, who argues that Jewish society was essentially monogamous in the second century CE. Adi Shremer makes the important point that for a society to be polygamous (or as he puts it, polygynous) not every male member has to be married to more than one woman – which would be economically hard to bear. Polygamy can rarely be practiced even in a society which accepts it.[63] Four marriage contracts[64] show that the widow had a right to remain in her husband's house and to be supported from his estate (while her dowry/*ketubba* remained intact), either as long as she wished[65] or until the heirs repaid the money of her dowry/*ketubba*.[66] The rabbinic sources attribute the former practice to the people of Jerusalem, followed by the Galileans, whereas the latter is said to be the practice in Judaea.[67] Finally a deed of gift in contemplation of death by a husband to his wife provides the married daughter with a hut on her parents' estate, in case she becomes a widow and as long as she does not remarry – exactly as recorded in the rabbinic sources.[68]

Divorce

P.Mur 19 of 72, published in 1961, is a deed of divorce given by a man to his wife which reflects to a great extent the wording of the rabbinic deed of divorce.[69] A complete and irreconcilable divergence from rabbinic law on divorce is now attested in the *P.Hever* 13 from 134 or 135 CE. This papyrus attracted attention even before it was published. In his commentary on *P.Mur* 19, Milik mentions an unpublished 'letter of divorce' given by a wife to her husband in stark contradiction to Jewish law. Milik's interpretation was rejected in the preliminary publication of *P.Hever* 13 in favour of 'a receipt for a *ketubba*,' where the offending clause

63 See Adiel Schremer, "How much Jewish Polygyny in Roman Palestine?," *Proceedings of the American Academy for Jewish Research* 63 (1997): 181–223. I am grateful to Dr. Schremer for letting me see the ms. in advance of publication.
64 *P.Mur* 20, 21, 116 and *P.Yadin* 10.
65 *P.Mur* 20, 21 and 116.
66 *P.Yadin* 10.
67 See *mKet*. 4:12; on the widow see Mordechai Akiva Friedman, *Jewish Marriage in Palestine: A Cairo Geniza Study*, Vol. I (Tel Aviv: Tel Aviv University Press, 1980), 427 ff.
68 See *mKet*. 2:6–7.
69 Reuven Yaron, "The Mesadah Bill of Divorce," in *Studi in onore di Edoardo Volterra VI* (Milano: Giuffrè, 1971), 433–55.

of repudiation was conveniently made to come from the husband's mouth.[70] In the final publication Ada Yardeni wavers between 'waiver of claims' and 'a divorce document written by the wife?'[71] Yardeni's indecision becomes an affirmative in Tal Ilan who goes back to Milik's interpretation of the document as a writ of divorce.[72] The wheel has come full circle. Elisha Qimron and myself argue that *P.Hever* 13 is neither 'a receipt for a *ketubba*' nor a 'writ of divorce,' but indeed a renunciation of all claims on the part of the wife who had in strict contradiction to rabbinic law given her husband a deed of divorce, using phrases which closely echo the essential part of the rabbinic writ of divorce found in Aramaic – unlike the rest of the Mishnaic text – in *mGitt.* 9.3 and those used in *P.Mur* 19 mentioned above.[73] The crucial lines in *P.Hever* 13 run as follows:

> I, Shlamzion daughter of Yehosef *Qbšn* from Ein-Gedi, have no claim against you, Eleazar son of Ḥananiah, who previously were my husband (די הוית בעלה מן קדמת דנן) and who had (have) a deed of abandoning and expulsion from me (די הוא לך מנה גט שבקין ותרכין). You Eleazar, owe me nothing concerning anything whatsoever. And I accept as binding on me, I, Shlamzion daughter of Yehosef, all (the obligations) written above (lines 3–10).

The use of the so-called 'rabbinic' formulae in reference to a writ of divorce given by a wife, combined with the fact that the writ of divorce is mentioned in passing as a background to the wife's renunciation of claims – it is by no means the core of the document, even if it is its most interesting and provoking message – convinced us that this is a matter of routine to be taken for granted. This is irreconcilable with the Halakha, Jewish law, which makes the dissolution of a marriage the prerogative of the husband. One may argue along the lines of Bernadette Brooten,[74] and

---

70 Ada Yardeni and Jonas C. Greenfield, "A Receipt for a Ketubba," in *The Jews in the Hellenistic-Roman World: Studies in Memory of Menahem Stern*, ed. Isaiah M. Gafni, Aharon Oppenheimer, and Daniel R. Schwartz (Jerusalem: Zalman Shazar Center, 1996), 197–208 (Hebrew) = Ada Yardeni, *Naḥal Ṣe'elim Documents* (Beer-Sheva: Ben-Gurion University of the Negev Press, 1995), 54–60 (Hebrew).

71 Cotton and Yardeni, *Aramaic, Hebrew, and Greek Documentary Texts from Naḥal Ḥever and Other Sites*, 65.

72 Tal Ilan, "On a Newly Published Divorce Bill from the Judaean Desert," *Harv. Theol. Rev.* 89 (1996): 195–202.

73 Hannah M. Cotton and Elisha Qimron, "XḤev/Se ar 13 of 134 or 135 C.E.: A Wife's Renunciation of Claims," *JJS* 49 (1998): 108–118; *contra* Adiel Schremer, "Divorce in Papyrus Ṣe'elim 13 Once Again: A Reply to Tal Ilan," *Harv. Theol. Rev.* 91 (1998): 193–202 and Robert Brody, "Evidence for Divorce by Jewish Women?," *JJS* 50 (1999): 230–34.

74 Though one may start with David Daube, "The New Testament Terms for Divorce," *Theology* 47 (1944): 65–67 and Ernst Bammel, "Markus 10 11 f. und das jüdische Eherecht," *Zeitschrift für die neutestamentliche Wissenschaft* 61 (1970): 95–101. Many of the latter's arguments are reiterated and expanded by Bernadette J. Brooten, "Konnten Frauen im alten Judentum die Scheidung

long before her of Joseph Modrzejewski,[75] that alongside the rabbinic legal rules there existed other customs documented in Josephus, the Elephantine papyri, Samaritan and Karaite sources, as well as in the famous NT passage Mark 10:11–12, about which so much has been written. It does not seem necessary to rehearse the arguments here. Either these Jews went against the Halakha or the Halakha had not yet become normative. I believe though that it is not insignificant that the divorce formula in *mGitt.* 9.3: דיהוי ליכי מנאי ספר תרוכין ואגרת שבקין וגט פטורין: 'Let this be from me thy writ of divorce and letter of dismissal and deed of liberation,' is an Aramaic formula embedded in a Hebrew text; it is likely to be much older than the rest of the text – a formula current before Halakha made the dissolution of marriage the prerogative of the husband alone.[76] Some support for this earlier legal condition may be reflected in an almost contemporary marriage contract between two Jews from Ein Gedi who get married in Maḥoz 'Aglatain in the Roman province of Arabia, which attests that the woman could demand at any time the return of her dowry, and presumably thus initiate a divorce:

> Judah called Cimber shall redeem this contract for his wife Shelamzion, whenever she may demand it of him, in silver secured in due form, at his own expense, interposing no objection.[77]

But is the demand for a return of the dowry tantamount to a dissolution of the marriage initiated by the wife? If the answer to this question is positive, one may still ask why it does not say so explicitly in the document.

---

betreiben?: Überlegungen zu Mk 10, 11–12 und 1Kor 7, 10–11," *Evangelische Theologie* 42 (1982): 65–80, criticised by Eduard Schweizer, "Scheidungsrecht der jüdischen Frau?: Weibliche Jünger Jesu?," *Evangelische Theologie* 42 (1982): 294–300; Hans Weder, "Perspektive der Frauen?," *Evangelische Theologie* 43 (1983): 175–78; cf. Brooten's reply, "Zur Debatte über das Scheidungsrecht der jüdischen Frau," *Evangelische Theologie* 43 (1983): 466–78.

75 Joseph Modrzejewski, "Les juifs et le droit hellénistique: Divorce et égalité des époux (CP Jud. 144)," *Iura* 12 (1961): 162–93. See also the discussion in Friedman, *Jewish Marriage in Palestine: A Cairo Geniza Study*, Vol. I, 312 ff., who mentions *P.Hever* 13 on p. 319, n. 26 – only to dismiss it as inconclusive.

76 The Biblical evidence in Deut. 24:1–4 is less unambiguous than usually interpreted: it deals with a particular case, and it does not exclude the possibility of divorce given by a woman, even if it was thus interpreted by the rabbis. Nor is Joseph., *AJ* 15.259 free from problem: he also denies that a divorced woman could marry without her ex-husband's consent.

77 *P.Yadin* 18 from 128 CE: ἀλ̣λ̣άξ̣[ει] δ̣[ὲ Ἰο]ύδας ὁ κ̣αλούμ̣ε̣νος Κίμβε̣[ρ τῆ γυνα]ι̣[κὶ] α̣ὐτοῦ Σελαμψιώνῃ τὴ[ν] σ̣υνγ̣ρ̣α̣[φ]η [τ]αύτην ἐν ἀ̣[ργύρ]ῳ ἠσφαλισμένῳ ὡς καθήκει ὁπόταν αὐτὸν ἀπα̣ι̣τήσει ταῖς ἑαυτοῦ δαπ̣[άναις] κατὰ μηδ̣ὲ̣ν [ἀ]ντιλέγων (lines 21 ff. = lines 57 ff.).

Law of Succssion

Contrary to my method so far I shall start with Jewish law on the subject and then pass on to the documents. Jewish law, both biblical and rabbinic, preferred the claims of children, whatever their sex, to those of the man's brother or of his brother's children. We read in *Numbers* 27:8: 'When a man dies leaving no son, his patrimony shall pass to his daughter. If he has no daughter, you shall give it to his brothers'; and again in *mBaba Bathra* 8.2: 'The son precedes the daughter, and all the son's offspring precede the daughter; the daughter precedes the brothers (of the deceased).'

My conclusion that the law of the papyri differed from Jewish law of succession is based – perhaps impressionistically – on the indirect evidence of three deeds of gifts in the archives from Maḥoza[78] and on the direct evidence of *P.Yadin* 23, 24 and 25 of 130 and 131 CE. Let me start with the first. Two facts stand out as soon as you read the three deeds of gift: 1) The beneficiaries of the gifts in all these documents are wives and daughters; 2) In all three cases there is no sign of a male heir whose existence might have called forth the writing of the deed of gift. These two facts suggested to me that the law of succession sidestepped wives and daughters, even in the absence of a male heir, and the deed of gift came to mitigate the rigour of rules of succession which were prejudicial to women. The deed of gift was the only way in which property could devolve on women in this society. To use Roman legal terminology: wives and daughters were not the *sui heredes* of their husbands and fathers. I am not suggesting that the mere existence of deeds of gift in favour of daughters and wives is the proof that without such legal instruments the property would not have devolved on them, even when there were no male heirs. But I do think that the existence of such instruments creates a strong presumption that this was so. The writing of a deed of gift, like the writing of a will and testament, was intended to emend the legal state otherwise created by the law of succession.

Nonetheless I admit there could be other reasons to write a will or a deed of gift – for the latter of course amounts to the same thing as a will. For example a second marriage of the father or the mother might lead to it: it could be argued that Judah son of Eleazar and Salome Grapte wrote deeds of gift in favour of their daughters in anticipation of the birth of a male son who would deprive the daughter of their previous marriage of her right to inherit.

Alternatively, one notices that the proper occasion for the bestowal of property in a deed of gift seems to have been the marriage of the daughter. Like the property given *en prosphora* in Egypt, the property given in a deed of gift was

---

78 *P.Yadin* 7, 19 and *P.Hever* 64.

meant for immediate use, to help the new household; and, we saw that, as in the case of the *prosphora*, the daughter gains absolute ownership over this property. In other words the deed of gift does not imply that daughters could not inherit; it simply makes the devolution of property immediate. Thus deeds of gift need tell us nothing about the law of succession.

I believe though that direct evidence can be found in *P.Yadin* 23, 24 where, after Judah son of Eleazar's demise, the guardian of his dead brother's children threatens Babatha that he will register three date orchards of her dead husband in Maḥoza in the nephew's name, unless she produces written evidence that she has a right to them. In *P.Yadin* 25, Iulia Crispina insists that Babatha is detaining property which belongs by law to the orphans. It is striking that nothing whatsoever is said about the claims of Judah's own daughter Shelamzion. She was still alive on 19 June 130, five months before Besas charges Babatha with illegal distraint of her late husband's property.[79] Unless we assume that she died between 19 June and 17 November of 130, or that Judah wrote a will in favour of his nephews,[80] we must believe that the law of succession in force at that time (at least among the Jews) in the province of Arabia did not automatically grant a daughter the right to inherit from her father when in competition with sons of her father's brother. In denying the claims of the wife to her husband's property this law seems to have been not unlike the normative Jewish law of succession. It differs from such Jewish law in preferring the claims of the man's brother or his brother's children to those of the daughter. Like Jewish law, however, the legal system reflected in these documents recognized a legal instrument which mitigated the rigour of rules of succession which were so prejudicial to women: the deed of gift.[81]

Devolution of property is effected also in the mother's marriage contract. It is stipulated there that the sons inherit their mother's dowry, whereas daughters are to be fed and clothed from their father's estate until they get married.[82] The provision concerning male children as heirs to their mother's property had entered Jewish law under the influence of other Near Eastern traditions, where – unlike the situation under Jewish law – the wife's children were her heirs. The provision

79 *P.Yadin* 20 lines 1–4 = lines 18–22.

80 An assumption made by Lewis, who suggests that we restore ἐν τῇ διαθήκῃ αὐτοῦ in *P.Yadin* 24, line 6.

81 See in detail Hannah M. Cotton, "Deeds of Gift and the Law of Succession in Archives from the Judaean Desert," in *Akten des 21. Internationalen Papyrologenkongresses, Berlin, 13–19.8.1995*, ed. Barbara Kramer et al., Vol. I (Stuttgart – Leipzig: Teubner, 1997), 179–88; for some reservations see now Hannah M. Cotton, "The Law of Succession in the Documents from the Judaean Desert Again," *SCI* 17 (1998): 115–23 [above, pp. 443–51].

82 Mother's dowry: *P.Mur* 20, 21, 116, *P.Yadin* 10, *P.Hever* 69.

certainly contravenes the biblical law of inheritance which made the husband sole heir to his wife's property; upon his death all his sons, including those from another woman, would divide his property equally between them. Thus the provision for male sons to inherit their mother's dowry or her *ketubba* was meant to protect male sons in polygamous marriages against the loss of part of their mother's property to sons of another woman. This can be safely read in *P.Mur* 116, lines 4–8:

> [And if Salome] dies [before Aurelius], the sons that she will have from him will inherit her dowry and the things written above ... [in addition] to inheriting all of Aurelius' property together with their future brothers [from another woman].[83]

It should be pointed out that the specific clauses distinguishing between male and female children are so far attested only in the Jewish *ketubba* tradition and, apparently, already in the early Mishnaic period; they unite marriage contracts between Jews written both in Greek and in Aramaic.[84] It needs to be emphasized though that they are absent from some of the marriage contracts, and that the order of the relevant clauses concerning provision for the children in the case of the prior death of the wife, and sometimes without reference to it, varies a great deal. The variation, the lack of uniformity, even when the provisions seem unique to marriage contracts between Jews, shows that we are in a state of flux. This is further demonstrated by the disappearance from the later *ketubba* tradition of provisions attested in the documents. Thus the stipulation that the daughters are to be fed and clothed seems to have replaced an earlier one which provided for all children to be fed and clothed from the father's property. This original situation is reflected in one of two Greek marriage contracts from Murabba'at as well as in two marriage contracts from Arabia.[85] I cite from one of the documents from Arabia:

> pursuant to his undertaking to feed and clothe both her and the children to come in accordance with Greek custom upon the said Judah Cimber's good faith and peril and security of all his possessions, both those which he now possesses in his said home village and here and all those which he may in addition acquire.[86]

83 *P.Mur* 116, lines 4–8: [ἐὰν δὲ ἡ Σαλώμη πρὸ τοῦ Αὐρηλίου] τὸν βίον μ[ε]ταλλάξει υ̣[ἱοὺ]ς οὓς ἂν ἕ̣ξε̣ι̣ ἀπ̣' αὐ̣τ̣[οῦ ... κληρονομήσουσιν] τὴν φ̣ε̣ρ̣νὴν κ̣α̣ὶ τὰ πρ[ογε]γραμμέ̣ν̣α̣ [c. 40 letters] τ̣ῆ̣ς τ̣οῦ Αὐρ̣η̣λ̣ί̣ου ο̣ὐ̣[σ]ί̣ας π̣ᾶσ̣α̣[ν κλ]ηρονομί̣αν μ̣ε̣θ' ὧν ἂγ̣ ἕξωσιν ἀ̣[δ]ελφῶν.

84 *P.Mur* 20, 21, 115, 116; *P.Yadin* 10; *P.Hever* 69.

85 *P.Mur* 115; *P.Yadin* 18 and *P.Hever* 65.

86 ἀκολούθως αἱρέσει τροφῆς καὶ ἀμφιασμοῦ αὐτῆς τε καὶ τῶν μελλόντων τέκνων ἑλληνικῷ νόμῳ ἐπὶ τῆς τοῦ αὐτοῦ Ἰούδα Κίμβ[ε]ρ̣ο[ς] π̣ίστε̣ως καὶ κ̣ινδύνου καὶ πάντων ὑπαρχόντων ὧν τε ἔχει ἐν τῇ α̣ὐ̣τ̣ῇ̣ [πα]τ̣ρ̣ί̣δ̣ι αὐ̣τ̣ο̣ῦ̣ καὶ ὧδε καὶ ὧν ἐπικτήσηται, *P.Yadin* 18 lines 15–18 = lines 49–53; identical phrasing in *P.Hever* 65 lines 9–11.

Conclusion

For less than a century, roughly between 50 and 135/136, the curtain is raised, and we are able to observe how Jewish women behaved and acted within the legal system operating in the Roman provinces of Judaea and Arabia at the time. My concentration on legal issues has been dictated by the nature of the evidence, as it is their bias which allows me to put women in the limelight. However, the conclusions to be drawn from the documents apply to Jewish society as a whole. I have tried to show that the documents from the Judaean Desert bear an extraordinary similarity to their Egyptian and other Near Eastern counterparts, thereby revealing the remarkable degree of integration of Jewish society into its environment. I have tried to emphasize the diversity and fluidity manifested in the documents from the Judaean Desert: the incursion of different legal systems sometimes, but not always, overlapping with what came to be halakhic law. The discrepancies that we have detected between the law of the papyri and halakhic law seem to me to prove that what eventually came to be normative Jewish law has not yet become so. At this stage it would be right to regard Jewish society as part and parcel of a Near Eastern civilization which as a whole had absorbed the impact of Hellenism over the centuries, and yet retained its own multifarious culture.

After ca. 136 the documents dry up and the curtain falls. After the Bar Kokhba revolt we are almost exclusively at the mercy of the legal sources: did the society reflected in the rabbinic sources, and the code of law to which it subscribed, ever exist in reality? Is it true that after the Bar Kokhba revolt Judaism turned inwards and interaction with the broader environment ceased? And how did women then fare in a society which presumably accepted rabbinic law as binding? A large vista opens up, but it is outside the scope of the present study.

Eleuthera and *Brat Horin*: Another Look at Babatha's Ketubba, *P.Yadin 10*

The date of *P.Yadin* 10 has not been preserved, but the document must have been written between AD 124, when Babatha is attested for the first time as the mother of an orphan (*P.Yadin* 12–13), and AD 128, when Judah son of Eleazar Khthousion is attested for the first time as Babatha's (second) husband (*P.Yadin* 17).[1] The document was written by the bridegroom himself in Aramaic. It is in fact the first Jewish *ketubba* of which we possess more than fragments.[2] Its close resemblance to later Jewish *ketubbot* from the Cairo Genizah,[3] as well as to modern documents, is striking and instructive. The presence in it of a unique phrase not found in any other *ketubba* – or even mentioned in any of the sources which deal with *ketubbot* – is all the more striking.

Despite the fragmentary state of *P.Yadin* 10, we can safely reconstruct what the husband undertakes to provide for his wife in ll. 6–11. A single phrase is repeated there twice (ll. 6–8 and 9–10 respectively), namely Judah's undertaking to provide Babatha with 'your food, and your clothing, and your bed, the (fitting) sustenance of a *free* woman/wife': עם דין לחמך וכסותך ופרשך מזון אנתה ברת חורין.

The qualifying/restrictive phrase '[as befits] a free woman/wife' (אנתה ברת חורין)[4] is not found in any other *ketubba*; nor is it mentioned in any of the ancient sources which deal with marriage. Are we to understand that these are the distinct privileges of a free, as distinct from a non-free, woman?

The biblical passage in Exodus 21:7–11 about the female slave in fact implies the opposite: 'When a man sells his daughter as a slave, she shall not go out as the male slaves do. (1) If she does not please her master, who has designated her for himself, then he shall let her be redeemed. He shall have no right to sell her to a

---

1 Acknowledgement of a loan taken by Judah from Babatha 'his own wife,' *P.Yadin* 17, ll. 4 and 22.

2 The latter is the case of *P.Mur* (*DJD* II) 20, 21 and *P.Ḥever/Se* (*DJD* XXVII) 11, but see Ada Yardeni, *Textbook of Aramaic, Hebrew and Nabataean Documentary Texts from the Judaean Desert and Related Material*, Vol. I (Jerusalem: The Hebrew University Press, 2000), 119–24 (Hebrew).

3 Mordechai Akiva Friedman, *Jewish Marriage in Palestine: A Cairo Geniza Study*, Vol. I (Tel Aviv: Tel Aviv University Press, 1980), 167.

4 Aramaic אנתה like Hebrew אשה has both meanings.

Article note: First published in *JJS* 68 (2017): 225–33, with the following note: this article is dedicated to my teacher and friend Miriam Griffin, in fond memory of our Bible reading over the years, which included the notoriously difficult passage in Exodus 21:7–11, at the core of this article. It was delivered as a lecture on the occasion of her eightieth birthday, celebrated on 30 May 2015 in Somerville College, Oxford. A preliminary version in Hebrew was presented at the Hebrew University on 3 March 2013 in memory of Professors Y.N. Epstein and A.Sh. Rosenthal.

https://doi.org/10.1515/9783110770438-033

foreign people, since he has broken faith with her. (2) If he designates her for his son, he shall deal with her as with (free) maidens (כְּמִשְׁפַּט הַבָּנוֹת). (3) If he takes another wife to himself, he shall not diminish (i) her food, (ii) her clothing, or (iii) her marital rights. And if he does not do these three things for her, she shall go out for nothing, without payment of money.'

It would seem from this that the rights of the female slave were not any different from those of the free woman. Indeed so far as I know there is not a shred of evidence in the Jewish sources that such a distinction ever existed. According to R. Yoshia's exegesis of the biblical phrase 'as with (free) maidens' (כְּמִשְׁפַּט הַבָּנוֹת), the contrary seems to be true: 'What have we learned about the practice with free maidens? ... Just as one must *not* withhold from this one (the slave girl taken in marriage) her food, her clothing and her conjugal rights, likewise he must not withhold from a [free] Israelite woman her food, her clothing and her conjugal rights' (*Mekhilta d'R. Ishmael*, ed. Horovitz and Rabin, 258).

The occurrence of this phrasing in Babatha's *ketubba* could be seen as an affirmation through an *argumentum a minore ad maius* of these three obligations towards the wife who is a free woman: if the slave should receive her food, clothing and her marital rights, all the more reason to expect that the free woman should receive them as well. The latter consideration may lead us to suppose that what we see in Babatha's *ketubba* is a reflection of rabbinic exposition on a biblical verse.

Mordechai Friedman,[5] who raises this conjecture, withdraws it forthwith – and correctly: "Such apparent employment of literary sources is noteworthy, since the marriage contract, like other legal documents, is primarily based on customary law. The *ketubba* was referred to by the Tannaim as לשון הדיוט, 'a layman's formulary,' and from antiquity through the Middle Ages its essentials had a large degree of independence from legal rabbinic literature." Indeed, what we find in the *Mekhilta* sounds more like an exegesis of the rabbis on the formulas in a contemporary marriage contract than the other way round. Furthermore, not only was the *ketubba* 'a layman's formulary' (לשון הדיוט), but all contracts were so as well: the rabbis did not write contracts; they wrote commentary on them.[6]

---

5 Mordechai Akiva Friedman, "Babatha's Ketubba: Some Preliminary Observations," *IEJ* 46 (1996): 55–76.

6 We do not have even a single contract in the whole of the Mishnah or the Tosefta, only contractual formulas. These formulas – unlike the legal discussion in which they are embedded, which is conducted in Hebrew – are all in Aramaic, thus proving not only that they are of a much older vintage than the Hebrew interpretation, but also that the language of contracts in daily use at the time was Aramaic. We may envisage the Mishnaic discussion as a process whereby the rabbis comment in Hebrew on contracts written from beginning to end in Aramaic by scribes. See

One may raise (as Friedman does) the possibility that *ben* or *brat ḥorin* means a nobleman or a noble woman respectively, citing Rabbi Akiva, who says in *mBab Kama* 8.6: 'Even the poor of Israel, we see them as if they are free people [*bnei horin*] who have lost their property, because they are children of Abraham, Isaac and Jacob.' However, what Rabbi Akiva says goes back to the biblical text which reflects a society made up solely of *bnei horin* who are therefore all noblemen.[7] Moreover, as we have just observed, in that society, so far as marital rights were concerned, the female slave did not differ from the free woman. In other words, what Rabbi Akiva says has no legal implications bearing on the present discussion.

On the other hand, when such terms make their appearance in a legal document, like *P.Yadin* 10, one would expect them to have a legal significance: the rights of the *brat horin*, the free woman, if made thus explicit, should differ from the rights of those who are not free. If it is not explicable in the light of the Jewish sources, could the formula have been adopted from non-Jewish sources, could it be a foreign import?

The earliest of all marriage contracts in Greek from Egypt, *P.Elephantine* 1 (310 BC), tells us the following: 'Heraklides takes Demetria of Kos, a respectable woman (γυναῖκα γνησίαν) from her father Leptinus of Kos and her mother Philotis, *[he being] a free man, [taking] a free woman* (ἐλεύθερος ἐλευθέραν), who is bringing to him clothes and jewelry valued at 1,000 drachms. Heraklides will provide Demetria with all that is befitting *a free woman* (παρεχέτω δὲ Ἡρακλείδης Δημητρίαι ὅσα προσήκει γυναικὶ ἐλευθέραι πάντα).'

However, in this document we can make no mistake as to the meaning of ἐλευθέρα. The contract emphasizes the free origin, the non-servile origin, of both bride and groom. In the newly settled Greek society in Egypt, a society of first generation immigrants, such an emphasis was necessary, even indispensable, in order to make the marriage legitimate. In other words, *P.Elephantine* 1 implies a contrast between the free woman and the unfree woman, the slave. This distinction, as we have just seen, does not exist in Jewish sources, and therefore the

---

Hannah M. Cotton, "Language Gaps in Roman Palestine and the Roman Near East," in *Medien im antiken Palästina: Materielle Kommunikation und Medialität als Thema der Palästinaarchäologie*, ed. Christian Frevel (Tübingen: Mohr Siebeck, 2005), 151–69 [above, pp. 195–212]; Hannah M. Cotton, "Survival, Adaptation and Extinction: Nabataean and Jewish Aramaic versus Greek in the Legal Documents from the Cave of Letters in Naḥal Ḥever," in *Sprache und Kultur in der kaiserzeitlichen Provinz Arabia: Althistorische Beiträge zur Erforschung von Akkulturationsphänomenen im römischen Nahen Osten*, ed. Leonhard Schumacher and Oliver Stoll (St. Katharinen: Scripta Mercaturae Verlag, 2003), 1–11 [above, pp. 161–72].

7 I am grateful to Steve Fassberg for drawing my attention to the distinctions pointed out in the text.

language used in *P.Elephantine* 1 cannot be used to illustrate or to elucidate the use of the term ברת חורין (= ἐλευθέρα) in *P.Yadin* 10.

Perhaps a clue is to be found in the context of the appearance, rather than in the literal meaning, of the term ברת חורין (= ἐλευθέρα). We notice that the term ברת חורין in Babatha's *ketubba* follows (twice in l. 8 and in l. 10) the bridegroom's acknowledgement of the dowry and the obligations it puts on him towards his wife: 'and I will feed you and cover you and I will bring you into [my house] by [means of] your *ketubba*, and I owe you the sum of silver [in the amount of] four hundred denarii (*zuzim*), which equal one hundred T[y]rian[8] [tetradrachms], whatever you may wish to take and to ... from the *dowry*, together with the rightful allocation of your food, and your clothing and your *bed* [?], the fitting sustenance of a free woman (אנתה ברת חורין).'[9]

Although the text is fragmentary, and the syntactic connection between the acknowledgment of the debt (i.e. the dowry) and the duties of Judah towards Babatha are not crystal clear, there is no doubt that these items follow each other – even if there is no causal connection between them.

As in Babatha's *ketubba*, the acknowledgement of a dowry in Greek marriage contracts from Egypt already from the second century BC onwards preceded the section describing the duties owed by the husband to his wife. As an example one may take *P.Tebt.* I 104 (= *M.Chr.* 285) of 92 BC: the acknowledgement of the dowry in ll. 9–13 is followed by the commitment of the husband to support his wife (ll. 16–18): Τὰ δὲ [δ]έοντα π[ά]ντα καὶ τὸν [ἱμ]ατισμὸν καὶ τἆλλα ὅσα προσ[ήκει γυναικὶ γαμετῆ πα]ρεχέτω Φιλίσκος Ἀπολλωνίαν ἐνδημῶν καὶ ἀποδημῶν κατὰ δύναμιν τῶν ὑπαρχόντων αὐτοῖς ('And all that is owed, clothing and the rest, as fitting/appropriate to a wedded wife [γυναικὶ γαμετῆ] will Philiskos provide Apollonia with, inside and outside').

True, what we have here is *not* a 'free woman,' as in Babatha's *ketubba*, but γυνὴ γαμετή, normally translated as 'wedded wife.'[10] This common English translation, admittedly a fossilized and meaningless phrase, quite rightly implies that the Greek phrase which it is translating has become so as well. However, there is no doubt at all that the γυνὴ γαμετή had started its career as a meaningful term.

8 For Tyrian money, see Wolfram Weiser and Hannah M. Cotton, "Neues zum 'Tyrischen Silbergeld' herodianischer und römischer Zeit," *ZPE* 139 (2002): 235–50.

9 וקים <ע>לך עֹלי כסף זוזין ארבע מאֹה מֹה אנון צ[ו]רין מאה מה די תצבא למשב ולמס[ ]נֹה מן פֹרנֹה עם דין לחמך וכסותך ופֹרשך מזון אנתה ברת חורין או\די שוֹם כסף זו[ז]ין[א]רבֹע מאה די היֹמון סלעין מאה >אֹ<ה די תצב[י]ן למשב ולמ[ס:נה מן פ]רֹן עם דין[לחמ]ךֹ ופֹרשך וכסתך כ״נתה ברת חורין.

10 γυνὴ γαμετή hardly ever occurs in the nominative case in the papyri, but in general either in the accusative or in the dative case.

Γυνὴ γαμετή is the antonym of the γυνὴ κτητή, the 'bought woman,' the concubine (so the *LSJ*). However, in the context of the marriage contract the γυνὴ γαμετή was a woman who was legally able to marry a man – that is, no legal objections stood in the way of her doing so – as opposed to one who was already married, a minor, or one without a valid deed of divorce. In other words, the expression γυνὴ γαμετή described the woman who was *legally free* to marry; at least before it had turned into a standard formula.[11]

The term γυνὴ γαμετή appears also in marriage documents[12] from the Judaean Desert. In *P.Hever* 69 (AD 130) a mother gives her daughter in marriage:

> [προσφερομένην] αὐτῷ εἰς λόγον προσφορᾶς πρ̣ο̣ικ̣[ὸς] ἐ̣ν ἀργ̣ύ[ρῳ καὶ χρυσῷ [*approx. 15 letters*] δηνάρια πεν]τακόσιαι οἵ εἰσιν στατῆρε̣[ς ἑκατὸν εἰκο]σιπέ̣[ντε *approx. 29 letters* παρ'] αὐτῆς ἀ̣πεσκηκέναι καὶ ἔχ[ειν] .[. . .] .[. . .] . . . .[*approx. 33 letters*] δηνάρια πεντακόσιαι παραχρῆμα διὰ χερὸς χω .[*approx. 23 letters* γυναῖκα] γαμετὴν ἐφ' ᾧ ἔσται ἡ Σελαμπιους τρεφομένη καὶ ἀμφ[ιαζο]μ̣[ένη] (ll. 5–10).
>
> She [bringing] to him on account of bridal gift of the dowry(?) in sil[ver and gold ... all appraised in money value as five] hundred *denarii* which are the equivalent of [one hundred and twenty-fi]ve staters, [and the groom acknowledges] to have received and to ho[ld from her ...] five hundred *denarii* forthwith by hand [...] wedded wife ([γυναῖκα] γαμετὴν) so that Selampious is nourished and cloth[ed ... upon the security of all his posse]ssions, both those which he has now and those which he will acquire.

It also crops up in *P.Mur* 115 (AD 124):

> ὁμολογεῖ ὁ αὐτὸς Ἐλαῖος Σίμ̣ω̣[νος] ἐξ ἀνανεώσεος καταλλάξαι κ[αὶ] π̣ροσλαβέσθαι τὴν αὐ̣τ̣ὴν Σαλώ[μην Ἰω]άν̣[ο]υ Γ̣[αλγο]υ̣λὰ ε̣ἰ̣[ς γυναῖ]κ̣α γαμετὴν κτλ. (ll. 4–5).
>
> And the same Elaios, son of Simon, agrees to make it up with Salome daughter of Jonathan Galgoula, and take her again as his wedded wife.

Finally, the same expression appears in *P.Yadin* 18 (AD 128), where Judah son of Eleazar, Babatha's second husband, here as a father, gives his own daughter, Shelamzion, in marriage to the groom, Judah Kimber:

---

11 Two more examples should suffice, although there are many more: <ἐφ' ᾧ> τὸν Διονύσιον ἀπεσχηκότα τὴν προκειμένην φερνὴν τρέφειν καὶ ἱματίζειν τὴν Ἰσιδώραν ὡς γυναῖκα γα[μετὴν] κατὰ δύναμιν κτλ. (*BGU* 1050 = *M.Chr.* 286, 13 BC, ll. 12–14); τοῦ Σουχάμμωνος ἐπαρκ[ο]ῦντος αὐ̣τ̣ῇ τὰ [δέοντα πάντα καὶ τὸ]ν ἱματισμὸν καὶ τὰ ἄλλα ὅσα π̣ροσήκει γυναικὶ γαμετῇ κατὰ δύναμιν (*Stud. Pal.* XX, 5, ll. 21–22 [AD 136]).

12 I deliberately avoid the label 'marriage contracts' for the Greek contracts; see following note.

> ἐξ[έδ]οτ[ο Ἰούδα]ς Ἐλεαζάρου τοῦ καὶ [Χθουσί]ων[ος Σ]ελαμψ[ι]ώνην τὴν ἰδίαν θυγατέραν αὐτοῦ παρθένον Ἰούδατι ἐπικαλουμένῳ Κίμβερι ... εἶναι τὴν Σελαμψιών[ην] Ἰούδατι Κίμβερι γυναῖκαν γαμετὴν (ll. 32–38 = ll. 3–7).
>
> Judah son of Eleazar, also known as Khthusion, gave Shelamzion, his very own daughter, a virgin, to Judah surnamed Cimber ... to be his wedded wife.[13]

Thus, in a marriage document in Greek written almost at the same time by the same person who wrote an Aramaic *ketubba* for his wife Babatha, we find an intimate connection between the acknowledgement of the dowry and the undertaking of obligations towards the wife as a 'wedded wife': γυνὴ γαμετή.

One cannot ignore the existence of the close parallel between Babatha's Aramaic marriage contract and contemporary marriage documents in Greek, written for Jews, in the phrasing of the crucial formula linking the status of the wife to the obligations undertaken by the husband. The phrase ברת חורין (*brat ḥorin*) 'free woman' in *P.Yadin* 10, an Aramaic marriage document written among Jews, seems to be the equivalent of γυνὴ γαμετή, mentioned in contemporary Greek marriage documents written among Jews, namely: a woman on whose marriage there exists no legal restrictions, one who is legally capable of marrying a man, as opposed to one who was already married, a minor, or one without a valid deed of divorce. In other words, γυνὴ γαμετή described the woman who was free, in the sense of being at liberty, to marry. It has nothing to do with the status as a slave/free woman as such.

True, both in the marriage contracts from Egypt cited above, and in their Judaean Desert counterparts, γαμετή seems to have lost this legal or even quasi-legal significance. It is no longer used in order to distinguish between those women who are legally capable and those who are legally incapable of getting married. The woman who is giving herself in marriage in *P.Giss.* I 2 (173 BC), ll. 8–12: Ἐξέδοτο ἑαυτὴν Ὀλυμπιὰς ... Ἀνταίωι ... [εἶναι] γυναῖκα γαμετὴν φερνὴν

13 *P.Yadin* 18, written by the father of the bride, is *not* a marriage contract *stricto sensu* because the document did not create a new legal status. As Abraham Wasserstein suggested long ago in his seminal article ("A Marriage Contract from the Province of Arabia Nova: Notes on Papyrus Yadin 18," *JQR* 80 (1989): 93–130), it is quite likely that a proper *ketubba*, written by the groom, like *P.Yadin 10*, preceded this document (Wasserstein, 120); the same is true of *P.Yadin* 37 = *DJD* XXVII, no. 65, where it is made clear that the bride and groom had been living together before the writing of the present document. The latter is not a case of unwritten marriage or living together outside the marriage bond, as Tal Ilan will have it ("Premarital Cohabitation in Ancient Judea: The Evidence of the Babatha Archive and the Mishnah (Ketubbot 1.4)," *Harv. Theol. Rev.* 86 (1993): 247–64), but like *P.Yadin* 18 it relates to the marriage which may well have followed upon the betrothal, an oral ceremony or an Aramaic document like *P.Yadin* 10.

προσφερομένην κτλ. was using a fixed and jaded formula, rather than declaring herself legally capable of getting married. In late Greek the noun ἡ γαμετή meant simply 'a wife.'

I suggest that אנתה ברת חורין (*anth brt ḥorin*), a free woman, in *P.Yadin* 10 was simply the Aramaic equivalent of the phrase γυνὴ γαμετή in the Greek marriage documents from the Judaean Desert, even if the latter had by then lost its original meaning of being 'legally free to marry,' and never meant 'a free woman' as opposed to a slave. That the husband, Judah son of Eleazar, as the scribe of his own Aramaic marriage contract (*ketubba*), was influenced by the Greek terminology used by the scribe he himself had employed to write a marriage document for his own daughter in *P.Yadin* 18 is perfectly reasonable in this Jewish society where both languages were used in contracts written by or for the same people.

I would like to conclude with an interesting development: from the fourth century AD onwards the term ἡ ἐλευθέρα also became a synonym for a married woman, a wife – especially, so it seems, in Christian sources. Two epigraphic examples suffice: Κύριε ἐλέησον Ἀβραμα ΟΒΔ καὶ [τὴν] ἐλευθέραν [καὶ τὰ] τέκνα [not 'Ἐλευθέραν!];[14] καὶ κίτη (ἡ ἐ)λευθέρα αὐτοῦ Θεκλα.[15] Juan Chapa quite rightly rejected the translation of ἐλευθέρα as 'widow' which one finds in the dictionaries.[16] In all the examples given in Lampe's dictionary for ἐλευθέρα it seems to be the equivalent of 'a noble woman,' 'a lady.' It is not difficult to understand that someone of noble birth might be called ἐλεύθερος/ἐλευθέρα, but, as Juan Chapa points out, it does not explain how the word took on the specific meaning of a married woman. He admits that its seemingly Christian use may point towards a religious origin, but he cannot trace it. Instead he suggests that "the use of the adjective ἐλευθέρα in marriage contracts to define the social condition of a woman ... may have influenced its later use as a noun."[17]

It seems to me that the same process observed in the case of the adjective γαμετή has now taken place in that of the adjective ἐλευθέρα: γαμετή, once used to express the status of the marriageable wife, had become meaningless

---

14 Avraham Negev, *The Inscriptions of Wadi Haggag, Sinai*, Qedem Reports 6 (Jerusalem: Institute of Archaeology, Hebrew University of Jerusalem, 1977), 36, no. 113, but see Denis Feissel, "Béroia," *Bulletin de correspondance hellénique. Supplément* 8 (1983): 60–78, esp. 61.

15 *ICUR* II 567 (San Paolo fuori le mura).

16 Juan Chapa, *Letters of Condolence in Greek Papyri* (Florence: Edizioni Gonnelli, 1998). The present article owes much to Juan Chapa's encouragement and help.

17 Chapa. Cf. *SB* I 4658, where four citizens of Arisone act as surety for the husband that αὐτὸν φιλιοθῆναι τῇ [αὐ]τοῦ γαμετῇ Μαρίᾳ καὶ θάλπειν αὐτὴν ὡς ἄξιό[ν ἐστι]ν τῶν ἐλευθέρων γυναικῶν. The same is true of Mitteis, *Chr.*, no. 290: ἀλλὰ πάντα τὰ πρέποντα ἐλευθέραις γυναῖξιν παρὰ ἀνδράσι σεμνοῖς ἐνδείξασθαι εἰς αὐτὴν, and finally, *P.Lond.* 1711: προσομολογῶ ... μὴ δύνασθαι μή ποτε καιρῷ ἢ χρόνῳ ἐνεγκεῖν ἀλλοδαπὰς γυναῖκας ἐπάνω τῆς ἐμῆς ἐλευθέρας.

and redundant in the phrase γυνὴ γαμετή (as in 'wedded wife' – i. e. not merely marriageable), and ended up as a noun: ἡ γαμετή is the wife. The same seems to have taken place with ἐλευθέρα: the adjective has come to denote what the noun once did and eventually replaced it. Without doubt Chapa is right to believe that the marriage contract had a significant role in bringing this about: the term which originally pointed to a high social status eventually came to mean merely a married woman.[18]

18 Michael Zaken's suggestion in his unpublished M.A. dissertation "Rabbinic Marriage Adjudication in the Second Century in Light of the Babatha Archives and Rabbinic Law" (Columbia University, 2016), that the phrase discussed here, '[as befits] a free woman/wife,' was a way of ensuring that Babatha has a claim to a specific style of maintenance, can be reconciled with the present discussion. Note that despite its many similarities to *P.Yadin* 10, the fifth-century AD *ketubba* from Cologne also does not include the phrase discussed in this paper; cf. Colette Sirat et al., *La Ketouba de Cologne: Un contrat de mariage juif à Antinoopolis* (Opladen: Westdeutscher Verlag, 1986).

'The Conception of Jesus'

In every society the legal status of children depends on the legal status of the parents, as well as on the legitimacy of the marriage. There is a fundamental difference between the status of a child born altogether outside the marriage bond and that of a child born in what one may call a 'defective marriage,' i. e. when the two people who conceived the child were forbidden by the laws of the land or of their religion to enter into a legal marriage. The first would be a fatherless child and inherit the legal status of the mother (sometimes with grim consequences); the latter, however, should not have been conceived in the first place, and the stigma of its birth could become a legal liability for the rest of its life.

An instance of a forbidden relationship is that between a man and a married woman, i. e. another man's wife. At what point is a woman considered to be legally married to a man under Jewish law?

Under biblical (as well as under rabbinic) law marriage is effected in two stages, betrothal and marriage proper. The English term betrothal renders loosely the legal institution designated *'erusin* in the Bible and *qiddushin* in rabbinic sources.[1] Betrothal in biblical and rabbinic law is constitutive: it creates a new

1 For identifying references to editions of Jewish sources one may consult H.L. Strack and Günter Stemberger, *Introduction to the Talmud and Midrash* (Edinburgh: T & T Clark, 1991). The following description relies heavily on and borrows freely from the authoritative discussion in Mordechai Akiva Friedman, *Jewish Marriage in Palestine: A Cairo Geniza Study*, Vol. I (Tel Aviv: Tel Aviv University Press, 1980), 192–215.

Article note: First published in Laïla Nehmé and Ahmad Al-Jallad, eds., *To the Madbar and Back Again: Studies in the Languages, Archaeology, and Cultures of Arabia Dedicated to Michael C.A. Macdonald* (Leiden: Brill, 2018), 581–598, with the following note: Dear Michael: you have heard my 'Conception of Jesus' more than once, and on several continents, but having now been turned into an article and gone through the superlative editing of David Wasserstein and Ari Paltiel, it is yours exclusively and forever: *donum auctor dedit!*
Over the years of conceiving the Conception, I have incurred very many debts, only two of which can be acknowledged here: I am indebted to Sacha Stern for a thorough and wonderful editing and criticism of an early draft, and for drawing my attention to a plethora of issues I had not been aware of, and to Alanna Nobbs of Macquarie University who must have liked the Conception well enough to bring me over to Australia to hear it once again.
Needless to say, this article only skims the surface of the formidable issues of betrothal, marriage and divorce in Jewish law of the Second Temple period and its aftermath, to say nothing of the story of the Nativity and Early Christianity. The bibliography, intimidating for the expert, let alone for the layman, is poorly represented here.
I was always amazed and intrigued by my audience's response. I suspect that as a Jew I failed to take for granted what a born Christian would have done.

https://doi.org/10.1515/9783110770438-034

legal status. Deuteronomy 22: 23–29 assumes throughout that there is a difference between the violation of the betrothed and that of the un-betrothed virgin:

> When a virgin is betrothed (μεμνηστευμένη, LXX) to a man and another man comes upon her in the town and lies with her, you shall bring both of them out to the gate of that town and stone them to death; the girl because, although in the town, she did not cry for help, and the man because he dishonored another man's wife (τὴν γυναῖκα τοῦ πλησίον, LXX) ... [on the other hand] ... when a man comes upon a virgin who is not pledged in marriage (ἥτις οὐ μεμνήστευται i. e. not betrothed) and forces her to lie with him, and they are discovered, then the man who lies with her will give the girl's father fifty pieces of silver, and she shall be his wife because he has dishonored her.

The *'arusa*, i. e., the 'betrothed' woman (from the same root as *'erusin*, 'betrothal') normally continued to live in her parents' home,[2] but otherwise, as pointed out above, her legal status approximated that of a married woman. There is nothing in biblical law about the option of terminating a betrothal (as distinct from marriage) with a deed of divorce, although this becomes commonplace in rabbinic literature.[3]

The second stage, the *nissu'in*, or marriage, is associated with the taking of the bride by the groom to his home.

Some, not unreasonably, cast doubt on the existence of the two-stage marriage during the Second Temple period.[4] Michael Satlow, for example, singles out the story of Miriam's betrothal to Joseph in the gospel of Matthew (which he names "a form of inchoate marriage"), as our sole evidence for the existence of a legal status for the act of betrothal before the first half of the second century

---

2 The difference in customs between Judaea (where the betrothed couple could have intimate relations in the bride's parents' house) and the Galilee need not concern us here; cf. *Mishnah, Ketubbot* 1.5; *Mishnah, Yebamot*, 4.10, and see Vered Noam, "The Seventeenth of Elul in Megillat Ta'anit," *Zion* 59 (1994): 433–44 (Hebrew). Variety does not end there; one should also consider the evidence in sectarian writings which cannot be taken into account here, e. g. the fascinating article by Aharon Shemesh, "4Q271.3: A Key to Sectarian Matrimonial Law," *JJS* 49 (1998): 244–63.

3 Ranon Katzoff, "Philo and Hillel on Violation of Betrothal in Alexandria," in *The Jews in the Hellenistic-Roman World: Studies in Memory of Menahem Stern*, ed. Isaiah M. Gafni, Aharon Oppenheimer, and Daniel R. Schwartz (Jerusalem: Zalman Shazar Center, 1996), 39–59, makes the interesting observation that Roman law makes adultery punishable also in the case of betrothal: *impune in ea stuprum committeretur: Divi Severus et Antoninus rescripserunt etiam in sponsa hoc idem vindicandum, quia neque matrimonium qualecumque nec spem matrimonii violare permittitur, Dig.* 48, 5, 14 (13), 2–3.

4 As distinct from the rabbinic period, although no precise dates can be given.

AD, i.e. before the so-called rabbinic period, and dismisses the story in the New Testament as a sign of the provincialism of Jews in rural Galilee.[5]

It is quite true that rabbinic Judaism as commonly conceived emerged later than the Second Temple period. The legal documents from the Judaean Desert, the latest of which coincided with the outbreak of the Bar Kokhba Revolt in 132,[6] still display a variety of legal customs and the incursion of different legal systems which do not always overlap with what came to be halakhic law.[7]

Thus, the dismissal of the constitutive force of 'betrothal' as a legal stage in the creation of a Jewish marriage, i.e. that it was impossible for a betrothed woman to marry another man without having first secured a deed of divorce from her fiancé, need not be *prima facie* unreasonable, especially since there is no mention in the Bible of a deed of divorce in the case of dissolving a betrothal. It could be argued that in post-biblical times the constitutive nature of betrothal faded – if it was at all observed. If the passage in Matthew were the sole evidence for betrothal being constitutive (which as we shall see is not the case), skepticism could not be ruled out. It could even be argued that the passage in Matthew reflects Deuteronomy rather than contemporary usage. However, skepticism should not be taken too far: the New Testament, although not a book of history, may well reflect current legal practice – and precisely where it wishes to convey its new message.

---

5 Cf. Michael Satlow, *Jewish Marriage in Antiquity* (Princeton: Princeton University Press, 2001), 69–73. He states categorically that post-biblical Judaism did not practise the two-stage marriage: "during the entire Second Temple period (most?) Jews neither customarily betrothed ... nor did they even have a firm understanding of what such a betrothal would mean. Instead they followed Greek practices, and understood the biblical institution of betrothal within their own Hellenistic contexts' (p. 69).

6 Cf. *P.Yadin* 27 (19 August 132); unless 'year 4 to the destruction of the House of Israel' dates to 140 rather than to 74; see Esther Eshel, Hanan Eshel, and Ada Yardeni, "A Document from 'Year Four of the Destruction of the House of Israel,'" *Cathedra* 132 (2009): 5–24 (Hebrew) = Esther Eshel, Hanan Eshel, and Ada Yardeni, "A Document from 'Year 4 of the Destruction of the House of Israel,'" *Dead Sea Discoveries* 18 (2011): 1–28 (English).

7 Hannah M. Cotton, "The Rabbis and the Documents," in *Jews in a Greco-Roman World*, ed. Martin Goodman (Oxford: Oxford University Press, 1998), 167–79 [above, pp. 453–65]; Hannah M. Cotton and Ada Yardeni, *Aramaic, Hebrew, and Greek Documentary Texts from Naḥal Ḥever and Other Sites* (Oxford: Clarendon Press, 1997), 133–157. Scepticism concerning the authority of the Rabbis could go too far; see below n. 35 on *P.Hever* 13.

The story of the nativity is found only in the gospels of Matthew and Luke.[8] There is no conception narrative in the other two gospels.[9] However, the birth narratives in the two gospels are not just different; they are irreconcilable. Merely in the light of historical information from external sources the sequence of events in Matthew is possible, but that in Luke is impossible. Perhaps both are *post eventum* fictions. However, to my mind these reservations do not affect the argument I wish to put forward here.

Both accounts contain two premises: 1) that Maria/Miriam had already been betrothed to Joseph (μνηστευθείσῃ), but was not yet married to him, and 2) that she was a virgin (παρθένος) when Jesus was conceived.

Matthew 1:18–25:[10]

> And the birth of Jesus was like this. His mother, Maria, was betrothed (μνηστευθείσης τῆς μητρὸς αὐτοῦ) to Joseph, and before they came together (πρὶν ἢ συνελθεῖν αὐτοὺς), she was found to be pregnant by the holy spirit (εὑρέθη ἐν γαστρὶ ἔχουσα ἐκ Πνεύματος Ἁγίου). Joseph, her husband, being a righteous/law-abiding man (δίκαιος ὤν), and at the same time not wishing to put her to shame in public, decided to divorce her quietly (λάθρᾳ). When he had resolved on this – lo and behold! – an angel of God appeared to him in a dream saying: 'Joseph, son of David, be not afraid to take Maria, your wife (τὴν γυναῖκά σου). The child was begotten in her of the holy spirit (τὸ γὰρ ἐν αὐτῇ γεννηθὲν ἐκ Πνεύματός ἐστιν Ἁγίου). She will bear a son, and you will call him Jesus, for he will save his people from their sins.[11] All this has happened in order to fulfill what was said by the Lord through his prophet: 'Behold

8 For the evaluation of the individual gospels, see Fergus Millar, "Reflections on the Trial of Jesus," in *A Tribute to Geza Vermes: Essays on Jewish and Christian Literature and History*, ed. Philip R. Davies and Richard T. White (Sheffield: JSOT Press, 1990), 355–81 = *Rome, the Greek World, and the East: Volume 3: The Greek World, the Jews and the East*, ed. Hannah M. Cotton and Guy M. Rogers (Chapel Hill: University of North Carolina Press, 2006), 139–63.

9 Michael Macdonald pointed out to me the existence of slightly different genealogies in Matthew 13:55: οὐχ οὗτός ἐστιν ὁ τοῦ τέκτονος υἱός; οὐχ ἡ μήτηρ αὐτοῦ λέγεται Μαριὰμ καὶ οἱ ἀδελφοὶ αὐτοῦ Ἰάκωβος καὶ Ἰωσὴφ καὶ Σίμων καὶ Ἰούδας ('Is not this the carpenter's son? Is not his mother called Mary? And his brethren, James, and Joseph, and Simon, and Judas?), and in Mark 6:3: οὐχ οὗτός ἐστιν ὁ τέκτων, ὁ υἱὸς τῆς Μαρίας καὶ ἀδελφὸς Ἰακώβου καὶ Ἰωσῆτος καὶ Ἰούδα καὶ Σίμωνος; καὶ οὐκ εἰσὶν αἱ ἀδελφαὶ αὐτοῦ ὧδε πρὸς ἡμᾶς; καὶ ἐσκανδαλίζοντο ἐν αὐτῷ 'Is not this the (son of the) carpenter, the son of Mary, the brother of James, and Joseph, and of Juda, and Simon? and are not his sisters here with us?'

10 See commentary in Ulrich Luz, *Das Evangelium nach Matthäus, EKK I/1 (Mt 1–7)* (Düsseldorf: Benziger, 2002) and Herbert Basser, *The Mind Behind the Gospels: A Commentary to Matthew 1–14* (Boston: Academic Studies Press, 2010).

11 The impact of the divine intervention is greatly enhanced if one recalls Genesis 22:11–13, where the angel stays Abraham's hand when he is about to slaughter his own son: μὴ ἐπιβάλῃς τὴν χεῖρά σου ἐπὶ τὸ παιδάριον μηδὲ ποιήσῃς αὐτῷ μηδέν (And he said: 'Lay not thy hand upon the lad, neither do thou any thing unto him').

> the virgin will conceive and bear a son (Ἰδοὺ ἡ παρθένος ἐν γαστρὶ ἕξει καὶ τέξεται υἱόν), and they will call him Emmanuel,' which means 'God is with us.'' After Joseph woke up he did as he was instructed by the angel; he took his wife home with him.

Luke 1:25–35:

> And in the 6th month the angel Gabriel was sent by God to a city of the Galilee, called Nazareth, to a virgin, betrothed to a man (πρὸς παρθένον μεμνηστευμένην ἀνδρί) called Joseph from the house of David. And the name of the virgin was Miriam. Coming to her he said: 'Greetings, blessed one, the Lord is with you.' She was disturbed by his saying and asked what this greeting meant. And the angel told her: 'Be not afraid, for you have found favor with God. (31) Behold, you will conceive and bear a son, and you will call him Jesus etc. ...' (34) And Miriam said to the angel: 'How can (will) this be since I do not know a man/a husband?' (Πῶς ἔσται τοῦτο, ἐπεὶ ἄνδρα οὐ γινώσκω). And the angel said to her in reply: 'The holy spirit will come upon you and the power of the most high will cast his shadow over you. It is on this account that the child to be born will be called holy, son of God.'

It is true that the fact of Miriam being a betrothed virgin who has not yet 'known' a husband is played down in Luke; it seems to be there in order to emphasize the miraculous nature of her pregnancy. Nevertheless here too we are told that she was pregnant during her betrothal – and before her marriage. Joseph goes to Bethlehem 'in order to register together with Miriam who was betrothed to him, who was pregnant' (Luke 2:5: ἀπογράψασθαι σὺν Μαριὰμ τῇ μεμνηστευμένῃ αὐτῷ, οὔσῃ ἐγκύῳ).

We should overlook the improbable need for those living in Nazareth to register in Bethlehem. The parallel with Egyptian census-returns indicates that the order was to return to one's normal place of residence.[12] But as we know there are good reasons – into which we need not enter here – for sending them to Bethlehem; but why make her engaged and pregnant?

Finally, in Matthew in contrast to Luke, there are elements which clearly imply that her betrothal to Joseph had obvious legal implications. The angel who dissuades the latter from divorcing her, treats them as man and wife: 'Joseph, son of David, be not afraid to take (home?) Maria, your wife' (μὴ φοβηθῇς παραλαβεῖν Μαριὰμ τὴν γυναῖκά σου, Matt 1:20), and this becomes a fact: 'he took his wife home with him' (καὶ παρέλαβε τὴν γυναῖκα αὐτοῦ, Matt 1:24).

---

12 For the census see Hannah M. Cotton, "The Roman Census in the Papyri from the Judaean Desert and the Egyptian κατ' οἰκίαν ἀπογραφή," in *Semitic Papyrology in Context: A Climate of Creativity*, ed. Lawrence H. Schiffman (Leiden – Boston: Brill, 2003), 105–22 [above, pp. 363–78] and Hannah M. Cotton, "Some Aspects of the Roman Administration of Judaea/Syria-Palaestina," in *Lokale Autonomie und römische Ordnungsmacht in den kaiserzeitlichen Provinzen vom 1. bis 3. Jahrhundert*, ed. Werner Eck (München: Oldenbourg, 1999), 75–91 [above, pp. 317–35].

Once Miriam's pregnancy was discovered, Joseph, who had not known her in the biblical sense of the word (πρὶν ἢ συνελθεῖν αὐτούς), and certain that the child was not his, decided to divorce her. He chose a course which, as we have seen above, went *against* the biblical injunction specified in Deut. 22:24: 'When a virgin is betrothed to a man and another man comes upon her in the town and lies with her, you shall bring both of them out to the gate of that town and stone them to death.' One may regard this as an indication that the biblical injunction was no longer in force, or no longer practiced. At all events, he decided to divorce her. Nevertheless, being a righteous/law-abiding man (δίκαιος ὢν),[13] and wishing to spare her honor (καὶ μὴ θέλων αὐτὴν παραδειγματίσαι),[14] Joseph chose to divorce her away from the public eye (λάθρα ἀπολῦσαι αὐτήν), but divorce her nonetheless. This implies of course that they were already legally bound together (Matt. 1:19), although, as pointed out earlier, nowhere in the Bible is divorce mentioned as a means to dissolve a betrothal, and certainly not when the woman became pregnant by someone other than the man who had betrothed her. Until very recently (see below), one would have assumed that divorce as a means of breaking up an engagement was a rabbinic invention, if only for the lack of any evidence to the contrary.[15]

However, what the angel instructs him to do: Ιωσήφ, υἱὸς Δαβίδ, μὴ φοβηθῇς παραλαβεῖν Μαριὰμ τὴν γυναῖκά σου, was surely more compromising than a divorce, for 'taking her home' meant passing over to the second stage in Jewish marriage; from now on it would be assumed that Joseph was the father of the child, even though the author, who without doubt wishes to establish the paternity of God, informs us that Joseph had no marital relations with her until she gave birth (οὐκ ἐγίνωσκεν αὐτήν, ἕως οὗ ἔτεκεν υἱόν).[16]

---

13 There are very many different interpretations of δίκαιος ὢν which we need not get into here.

14 However, it is hard to see how he could have spared her since divorce was not a private matter which could be performed away from the public eye. But again there is no need to enter into this here.

15 As pointed out by Peter Zaas, "Matthew's Birth Story: An Early Milepost in the History of Jewish Marriage Law," *Biblical Theological Bulletin* 39 (2009): 127: "This makes the Gospel of Matthew ... a key in the history of Jewish law. There is no earlier literary text, biblical or otherwise, that specifies a divorce for a broken engagement, whether this is an innovation in rabbinic law or not." See also Peter Zaas, "Spiritus Ex Machina: Jewish Legal Aspects of the Matthean Birth Narrative," *Jewish Law Association Studies* 16 (2005): 295–302. These two papers will be published (with others) in his forthcoming book, *Mary's Divorce: Jewish-Legal Aspects of the Matthean Birth Narrative.*

16 I owe the last observation to John Curran. The full text in Matthew 1:24–25 reads: ἐγερθεὶς δὲ ὁ Ἰωσὴφ ἀπὸ τοῦ ὕπνου ἐποίησεν ὡς προσέταξεν αὐτῷ ὁ ἄγγελος Κυρίου, καὶ παρέλαβε τὴν γυναῖκα αὐτοῦ· καὶ οὐκ ἐγίνωσκεν αὐτήν, ἕως οὗ ἔτεκεν υἱόν; 'he did as the angel of the Lord commanded him; he took her as his wife, but he did not know her (i. e. had no marital relations with her) until she had borne a son ...'.

By entering upon the second stage of marriage, Joseph will become the legal father of the son in her womb. He will acknowledge the child as his by giving him a name – an indirect, or symbolic, act of adoption so to speak. Adoption, as we know, did not exist as a legal institution in Jewish law at that time.[17]

The concept of virginal conception, i. e. a non-biological conception with no human intervention, strains belief. Nevertheless, this offers no reason to give preference to the new "feminist theological interpretation of the infancy narratives" for which "The New Testament Infancy Narratives incorporate the tradition of Jesus' illegitimate conception," i. e. that behind the story of the nativity lurks an intervention in the form of rape or adultery.[18] There is in fact nothing new about this interpretation except the association with the new feminism: already in the Jewish sources and in Origen's *Contra Celsum* we find allegations of adultery with a Roman soldier, named Panthera,[19] and Jesus is called Ben Pantera/Pandera and Ben Stada in Talmudic sources. There are many versions of the Jewish story of the nativity, designated תולדות ישו or מעשי ישו, which were collected by Samuel Krauss in *Das Leben Jesu nach jüdischen Quellen*.[20] All of them have allegations of rape, adultery and so forth. The 'new feminists,' like the old Jewish detractors of Jesus, argue that both gospels – whether by playing down the pregnancy of a betrothed woman, as Luke does, or by confronting it directly as does Matthew – are in fact replying to charges of adultery and illegitimacy.[21]

---

17 See Yigal Levin, "Jesus, 'Son of God' and 'Son of David': The 'Adoption' of Jesus into the Davidic Line," *Journal for the Study of the New Testament* 28 (2006): 415–42, who takes the combination of θεοῦ υἱός and son of David to reflect the dynastic adoptions of the Julio-Claudians.

18 E.g. the late Jane Schaberg, *The Illegitimacy of Jesus: A Feminist Theological Interpretation of the Infancy Narratives* (San Francisco: Harper & Row, 1987).

19 Cf. *Contra Celsum* 1.32. However, his *Homiliae in Lucam* VI (*PG* XIII, cols. 1314–1315) (= *PL* XXVI, cols. 230–231) shows that he makes no distinction between betrothal and marriage, and is no longer aware of the betrothed being forbidden to her husband: *Debuit de ea virgine nasci, quae non solum sponsum habet, sed ut Mattheus scribit, iam viro tradita fuerat, licet eam vir necdum noscat, ne turpitudinem virginis habitus ipse monstraret, si virgo videretur utero tumenti.*

20 The bibliography is immense. For a convenient recent introduction see Peter Schäfer, Michael Meerson, and Yaacov Deutsch, eds., *Toledot Yeshu ('The Life Story of Jesus') Revisited* (Tübingen: Mohr Siebeck, 2011). I am grateful to Michael Meerson for allowing me to read before publication his paper "Illegitimate Jesus: Family Matters with 'Toledot Yeshu,'" in *When West Met East. The Encounter of Greece and Rome with the Jews, Egyptians, and Others. Studies Presented to Ranon Katzoff in Honor of his 75th Birthday* (Trieste: Edizioni Università di Trieste, 2016), 91–114.

21 I am not sure whether the definition of *mamzer* (ממזר) as the offspring of a betrothed or legally married woman, who conceived from another man, had entered Jewish law by that time. Nothing in the biblical passages mentioning the exclusion of the *mamzer* from the community actually defines how that status was achieved. All they tell us is the dire legal consequences of being one. Thus the strength at that time of the charge against Jesus' illegitimate conception cannot be

But why should we assume that the concept of virginal conception represents Christian 'apologetics' in response to those allegations, rather than accept, with no less plausibility, that these allegations took their cue from the narrative of virginal conception?

For indeed if the subtext was an illegitimate conception, one wonders why the 'incriminating' details were not left out of the two gospels altogether. The best way to meet allegations of adultery and illegitimacy would have been to hide the fact that Maria was pregnant between betrothal and marriage, and to find another way to make the child born to married parents a child of God through a different form of divine intervention.[22] There are certainly examples in the Old Testament and the apocrypha which endow the child of a mortal but barren woman with godlike provenance.[23] Luke (chapter 1) does precisely this with John the Baptist and his mother Elizabeth. For some reason, it would seem, the two gospels chose not to omit the 'incriminating' details in the case of the conception of Jesus. Even Luke, who does very little with them, leaves them there notwithstanding, *en passant*. I suspect that what was left was retained, or at least was not removed, for a reason.

It makes much better sense to assume that the story, as we have it, with the so-called incriminating details, seemed the best way to make virginal conception plausible, or, even better, possible. A precondition – albeit insufficient without the miracle – for virginal conception was the fact that the couple, Joseph and Mary, were betrothed but not yet married, and thus forbidden to each other. Admittedly,

meaningfully evaluated. See for example Bruce Chilton, "Jésus, le mamzer (Mt 1.18)," *New Testament Studies* 47 (2001): 222–27, and a response by Charles Quarles, "Review: Jesus as Mamzer: A Response to Bruce Chilton's Reconstruction of the Circumstances Surrounding Jesus' Birth in Rabbi Jesus," *Bulletin for Biblical Research* 14 (2004): 243–55.
I have learnt much from an unpublished paper by Yonathan Sagiv submitted to Professor Shlomo Naeh at the Hebrew University of Jerusalem.

22 I cannot attempt here to put the Conception of Jesus in the context of miraculous conceptions and births in the Jewish, Christian and Pagan traditions. See for example the intriguing article by Christfried Böttrich, "Die vergessene Geburtsgeschichte: Mt 1–2 / Lk 1–2 und die wunderbare Geschichte des Melchisedek in slHen 71–72," in *Jüdische Schriften in ihrem antik-jüdischen und urchristlichen Kontext*, ed. Hermann Lichtenberger and Gerbern S. Oegema (Gütersloh: Gütersloher Verlagshaus, 2002), 222–48.

23 Although after Genesis 6:1–4, all intercourse between the 'sons of God and the daughters of men' seems to have come to an end: 'And it came to pass, when men began to multiply on the face of the earth, and daughters were born unto them, that the sons of God saw the daughters of men that they were fair; and they took them wives of all which they chose. And the Lord said, my spirit shall not always strive with man, for that he also is flesh: yet his days shall be a hundred and twenty years. There were giants in the earth in those days; and also after that, when the sons of God came in unto the daughters of men, and they bare children to them, the same became mighty men which were of old, men of renown'.

this precondition would also constitute the ground for a claim of illegitimacy.[24] Were she properly married, her pregnancy would arouse no suspicion; no allegation of illegitimacy could be made, and conversely, no virginal conception would be believed. Were she not betrothed, her subsequent marriage to Joseph would imply that he is the biological father – since this is the remedy offered in Deut. 22:29 in such cases – and this too would be no good for sustaining the claim of virginal conception: 'When a man comes upon a virgin who is not pledged in marriage (ἥτις οὐ μεμνήστευται, LXX) and forces her to lie with him, and they are discovered, then the man who lies with her will give the girl's father fifty pieces of silver, and she shall be his wife because he has dishonored her.'

Thus, *only* in the case of a betrothed virgin, who was expected to remain a virgin until her marriage, virginal conception or illegitimacy are possible alternatives. For the virginal conception the concept of betrothal meant that the woman was for the period between betrothal and marriage *in a chastity vacuum*; and for the illegitimacy charge – to maintain the argument of equal plausibility – it meant that she *ought to have remained* in a chastity vacuum.

Of course we must not forget that Joseph, the fiancé/husband, came from the house of David, for only in this way could the combination of virginal conception be combined with descent from the house of David: 'And Jacob bore Joseph, Maria's husband, of whom Jesus called Christus was born' (Matt. 1:16). Perhaps this and no other was the *raison d'être* for the entire construct: a son of God whose legal father is a descendant from the house of David, for only he could be the Messiah.

Because of the crucial importance of the betrothal element, I believe that the evidence of the stories of the gospel for the existence at that time of the two-stage marriage, i. e. for the constitutive force of betrothal, is far stronger than one would have otherwise thought. The existence of the two-stage marriage should not be dismissed as restricted to some rustic Jews and to parochial Galilee (to use the terms employed by those who reject its existence).

This was the state of the evidence until 2001. Since then we have new documentary evidence for the legal status of betrothal in Jewish law from second-century BC Egypt: the two-stage marriage is now confirmed in *P.Polit.Iud.* 4.[25]

The publication by James Cowey and Klaus Maresch in 2001 of twenty papyri from the *politeuma* of the Jews in Herakleopolis in Middle Egypt written between

---

24 For the difference between Judaea and the Galilee see above n. 2.

25 James M. S. Cowey and Klaus Maresch, eds., *Urkunden des Politeuma der Juden von Herakleopolis (144/3–133/2 v. Chr.) (P. Polit. Iud.)* (Wiesbaden: Westdeutscher Verlag, 2001). Cf. Thomas Kruse, "Das jüdische politeuma von Herakleopolis und die Integration fremder Ethnien im Ptolemäerreich," in *Volk und Demokratie im Altertum*, ed. Vera Dement'eva and Tassilo Schmitt (Göttingen: Edition Ruprecht, 2010), 93–105.

144/3 and 133/2 BC marks a turning point in the study of the history of Jewish settlement in Egypt: it constitutes our first unambiguous evidence for the use of Jewish law by Jews in Egypt. The absence of such evidence led the editors of the *Corpus Papyrorum Judaicarum* to conclude that "the laws and regulations forming the legal basis for the business life of the Jews are the common laws of the Greeks in Egypt ... the family life of Alexandrian Jews, their marriages and divorces, were regulated by Greek contracts in accordance with the principles of Hellenistic law."[26] The new archive demonstrates clearly that they were wrong; Jewish law was used by Jews as their νόμος πολιτικός – certainly in cases which involved family and personal law as here.[27] *P.Polit.Iud.* 4 vindicates the claim that the two-stage marriage was practiced long after the Biblical period: betrothal created a new legal status and its dissolution called for a deed of divorce.

P.Polit.Iud. 4[28] is a petition by a Jew named Philotas son of Philotas to the archons of the Jewish *Politeuma* of Herakleopolis from 134 BC, recounting in some detail his betrothal to a woman called Nikaia daughter of Lysimachos[29] and his subsequent betrayal: he was promised the bride, and a sworn agreement was made according to the law, but: 'Not long afterwards, Lysimachos, without justification joined Nikaia to another man before having received from me the customary bill of divorce': μετ' οὐ π̣[ολὺν χ]ρ̣ό̣νον ὁ Λυσί[μ̣α̣χ̣ο̣ς συνήρμοκεν ἄγ̣ε̣υ̣ λόγου ἑ̣τ̣έ̣ρωι ἀ̣ν̣δ̣ρὶ τὴν Νε̣ίκαιαν̣ πρὶν ἢ λαβεῖν παρ' ἐμοῦ τ̣ὸ̣ εἰθισμένον τοῦ ἀποσ̣τ̣ασίου τὸ βυβλ̣ίο̣ν. The phrase τὸ βιβλίον τοῦ ἀποστασίου is the technical term (so to speak) used in the Bible for a deed of divorce given by a husband to his wife.[30] Admittedly, the Bible as pointed out above, does not mention a deed of divorce for the dissolution of betrothal.[31]

Be this as it may, this papyrus makes it clear that the betrothal created a legal bond which could only be dissolved by a deed of divorce, given by the fi-

26 *CPJ* I, pp. 33–4, but see the whole discussion on 33–47 (the Ptolemaic period) as well as the commentary on *P.Enteux.* 23 = *CPJ* I 128 (218 BCE).

27 As already claimed by Joseph Modrzejewski, "Jewish Law and Hellenistic Legal Practice in the Light of Greek Papyri from Egypt," in *An Introduction to the History and Sources of Jewish Law*, ed. N.S. Hecht et al. (Oxford: Clarendon Press, 1996), 75–99.

28 See text and translation in the Appendix at the end.

29 I once thought that this might have been a case of intermarriage, that Nikaia and her father were not Jews and thus unaware of the need to obtain a deed of repudiation from the man to whom she was engaged before getting involved with another one. But even if this were the case, there is no doubt at all that the betrayed groom did not make such an allowance for the gentiles. Philotas takes it for granted that he should have given her a deed of divorce before she could become free to marry the next man.

30 Cf. Deut. 24:1 and 24:3: καὶ γράψει αὐτῇ βιβλίον ἀποστασίου καὶ δόσει εἰς τὰς χεῖρας αὐτῆς; cf. Jeremiah 3:8 βιβλίον ἀποστασίου and Isaiah 50:1 τὸ βιβλίον τοῦ ἀποστασίου.

31 See notes 2 and 3 above.

ancé.[32] On the basis of this text, we should now accept the reconstruction of the fragmentary first lines of *P.Enteux.* 23 (= *CPJ* I 128, ll. 2–3), [κατὰ τὸν νόμον π]ọḷιτικὸν τῶν ['Ιου]δαίων ἔχειν με γυν[αῖκα], which shows that Jewish law was paramount in marriage contracts in Hellenistic Egypt (Cowey and Maresch, 60, n. 22).

Another justification for the emphasis placed on the two-stage marriage, which does not contradict the one pursued so far, but rather complements it, may be suggested. It is possible that the first impulse for creating the entire construct came from the LXX text of Isaiah 7:14. The verse is cited by Matthew in 5:23: Ἰδού, ἡ παρθένος ἐν γαστρὶ ἕξει, καὶ τέξεται υἱόν, καὶ καλέσουσι[33] τὸ ὄνομα αὐτοῦ Ἐμμανουήλ ('Behold: the virgin will conceive in her womb and give birth to a son, and they will call him Immanuel'). The Greek παρθένος translates here the Hebrew term *'alma* (עלמה), an ambiguous term which can mean νεᾶνις as well as παρθένος, that is to say, a young woman as well as a virgin. However, the Septuagint παρθένος can only mean the latter. Having used the Greek text, Matthew understood that for the prophecy to be accurate Jesus/Emmanuel must be born of a virgin. The two-stage marriage, which required the preservation of the virginity of the mother in the time gap between betrothal and marriage (for as has been pointed out above, the betrothed woman was forbidden to her fiancé as well as to everyone else) suited the prerequisite for a virgin-mother for the messiah to perfection – in fact, it was indispensable for maintaining the divine conception in a Jewish context. Matthew did not need to invent a complex narrative device; in the two-stage marriage he had at hand one which was part of everyday life.

Conclusion

There is no room here to look at the question of the identity of the authors and intended readers of the Gospels, nor of any earlier sources that the Gospels were drawing on. We cannot be certain of the cultural milieu and the traditions that the narratives in the Gospels used and reflect: the Galilee, the Jewish Diaspora, or particular pagan audiences in the Roman empire? These questions have been discussed endlessly without reaching definite conclusions. However, it is no longer the case that we have no evidence for the two-stage marriage outside the conception story in the New Testament, and that the story is strictly localized in cultural terms to provincial Galilee.[34] On the contrary, the structure of the story, as related

32 See below, n. 35.

33 Matthew uses the plural although the Septuagint like the Hebrew text הנה העלמה הרה וילדת בן וקראת שמו עמנואל uses the 2nd person singular.

34 One can apply here Fergus Millar's double-negative form of argument ("Epigraphy," in

in the Gospels, appears to reflect a very particular context in which the nature and portentous consequences of betrothal were clearly understood, and heighten the narrative.

Unlike the marriage contract which is merely a financial transaction with no constitutive power, acts of betrothal – and divorce[35] – are decidedly crucial for the legal status of the children born to a couple. And it stands to reason that the society concerned would pay more attention to these than to financial transactions, which are the essence of marriage contracts. The lack of uniformity in marriage contracts is hardly disturbing, and there is no need to follow some scholars in proselytizing every single marriage contract written in Greek.[36] But the constitutive force of betrothal in post-biblical Jewish society is vindicated by the evidence: by *P.Polit.Iud.* 4, by *Tosefta Ket.* 4:9[37] – and by the stories of the nativity.

Sources for Ancient History, ed. Michael Crawford (Cambridge: Cambridge University Press, 1983), 92–97 = *Rome, the Greek World, and the East: Volume 1: The Roman Republic and the Augustan Revolution*, ed. Hannah M. Cotton and Guy M. Rogers (Chapel Hill: University of North Carolina Press, 2002), 48–51): it is not the case that we do not have a single piece of evidence from real life, i. e. documentary one, for the existence of the two-stage marriage in post-biblical Jewish society.

35 The deed of divorce was always to be given by the fiancé/husband, as the editors of *P.Polit. Iud.* 4 (Cowey and Maresch, *Urkunden Des Politeuma Der Juden von Herakleopolis*, 57) quite rightly point out. *P.Hever* 13 can no longer be used against the clear evidence of *P.Mur* 19, and in strict contradiction to rabbinic law, as though referring to a deed of divorce given by a wife to her husband, as once claimed by Hannah M. Cotton and Elisha Qimron, "XḤev/Se ar 13 of 134 or 135 C.E.: A Wife's Renunciation of Claims," *JJS* 49 (1998): 108–118. This claim has been convincingly refuted once and for all in an unpublished paper by Hillel Newman (given on 15 May 2014 in Haifa University) who has kindly allowed me to refer to his ms. We must return to Yardeni's reading of the document as referring to a deed of divorce given, as expected, by the husband (*DJD* XXVII, no. 13). Despite Joseph Modrzejewski, "Les juifs et le droit hellénistique: Divorce et égalité des époux (CP Jud. 144)," *Iura* 12 (1961): 162–93, I agree with Reuven Yaron, "CPJud. 144 et Alia," *Iura* 13 (1962): 170–75, that *CPJ* II 144 of the year 13 BC is not a Jewish document, but a mutual agreement between the couple to dissolve their marriage. See also Bernard S. Jackson, "Marriage and Divorce: From Social Institution to Halakhic Norms," in *The Dead Sea Scrolls: Texts and Context*, ed. Charlotte Hempel (Leiden: Brill, 2010), 339–64.

36 See Abraham Wasserstein, "A Marriage Contract from the Province of Arabia Nova: Notes on Papyrus Yadin 18," *JQR* 80 (1989): 93–130, who dismisses the interpretation of Ranon Katzoff of the papyrus in 'II: Legal Commentary' in Naphtali Lewis, Ranon Katzoff, and Jonas C. Greenfield, "Papyrus Yadin 18," *IEJ* 37 (1987): 236–47, and response in Ranon Katzoff, "Papyrus Yadin 18 Again: A Rejoinder," *JQR* 82 (1991): 173–74. See now Hannah M. Cotton, "Continuity of Nabataean Law in the Petra Papyri: A Methodological Exercise," in *From Hellenism to Islam: Cultural and Linguistic Change in the Roman Near East*, ed. Hannah M. Cotton et al. (Cambridge: Cambridge University Press, 2009), 154–74 [above, pp. 237–56].

37 On which see Menahem Kister, "From Philotas to Hillel: 'Betrothal' Contracts and their Violation," *SCI* 21 (2002): 57–60.

As for the latter: scholars can express no opinion about virginal conception. In this essay I have tried to explain the historical ingredients which contribute to the making of the narrative of the conception, the myth, the miracle or whatever one chooses to call it. A miracle is the interference of the supernatural with mundane reality. But how can one appreciate the miraculous without knowing the ordinary, the normal, the routine? I have therefore attempted to reveal the hard core of legal reality behind the New Testament conception narrative, which to my mind makes it all the more powerful on a symbolic plane. For those who believe that God could intervene in human affairs, this explanation takes nothing away; on the contrary, it makes the miracle all the more clear and striking. It supplies the nuances which would have been perfectly understood by contemporaries.

Appendix: *P.Polit.Iud.* 4: Greek Text and Translation[38]

1 (ἔτους) λς Χο(ιὰκ) ιθ̄ π̣ε̣ρ̣ὶ̣ γ̣ά̣μ̣ο̣υ̣. συ(νετάξαμεν) παρα(γγεῖλαι).
2 τοῖς ἄρχο̣υ̣[σι]
3 π̣α̣ρ̣ὰ Φ̣ι̣λ̣ώ̣τ̣ο̣υ̣ τ̣ο̣ῦ̣ Φ̣ι̣λώτου
4 τῶν ἐκ τοῦ πολιτεύματος.
5 ἐν τῶι ἐνεστῶτι ἔ[τ]ει ἐμνησ-
6 τευσάμην Ν̣ε̣[ίκ]α̣[ι]α̣ν̣ Λ̣υ̣σ̣ι̣μ̣ά̣-
7 χου καὶ τοῦ ση̣μ̣α̣[ι]ν̣ο̣μένο̣υ̣
8 αὐτῆς πατρὸς ὀ̣μ̣[ό]σαντος
9 δώσ̣ε̣ι̣ν̣ ἐμοὶ αὐτ[ὴ]ν καὶ τὴν
10 σταθε̣ῖ̣σ̣αν ἐπ' α̣[ὐ]τῆι̣ φ̣ε̣ρ̣ν̣ήν,
11 ἐφ' ἧι κἀ̣μοῦ εὐδοκοῦντος
12 οὕτως οὐ̣ μ̣ό̣ν̣ο̣[ν] ὁ̣ρισμῶν
13 γενομέν̣ω̣ν̣ κα̣[τ]ὰ̣ κοινὸν
14 ἀλλὰ καὶ τῆς κα̣τ̣ὰ τὸν νό-
15 μον αποκα̣ . .[.] .ς̣ γ̣ενη-
16 θείσης κα̣ὶ̣ \είς δεδ̣η̣λ̣ο̣υ̣[. .] . . ./ ἐ̣π̣ὶ̣ [τ]ο̣ύτοις
17 ἀπαλλαγέντ̣ω̣ν̣ ἡμῶν

(1–4) Year 36. 19 Choiak. Regarding a marriage.

We have given an order to issue a summons.

To the archons from Philotas son of Philotas, (4) a member of the *Politeuma*.

(5–17) In the current year I betrothed Nikaia daughter of Lysimachos. Her said father swore to give her to me along with the dowry laid down for her, and with which I was in agreement. So after not only vows(?) were exchanged between us but also the ... according to the law (or the Law) ... We parted on those terms.

38 The images of *P.Polit.Iud.* 4 that appear in the original publication of this paper (on pp. 593–94) were not reproduced here, but can be viewed through the website papyri.info.

18 **μετ’ οὐ π̣[ολὺν χ]ρ̣ό̣νον**
19 **ὁ Λυσί̣μ̣α̣χο̣ς συνήρμοκεν**
20 **ἄν̣ε̣υ̣ λόγου ἑ̣τ̣έ̣ρωι ἀ̣ν̣δ̣ρὶ**
21 **τὴν Νε̣ίκαιαν πρὶν ἢ̣ λα-**
22 **βεῖν παρ’ ἐμοῦ τ̣ὸ̣ εἰθ̣ισμέ-**
23 **νον τοῦ ἀποσ̣τ̣ασίου**
24 **⟦τὸ⟧ β̣υβλ̣ίο̣ν.** διὸ ἀξιῶ,
25 ἐὰν φανη̣ται, συντάξαι
26 γ̣ρ̣άψ̣αι τοῖς ἐν τῆι̣ κώμηι̣
27 Ἰουδαίοις π̣αραγγεῖλαι τῶι
28 Λυσιμάχωι ἀπαντᾶν
29 ἐφ’ ὑμᾶς ἵν’ ἐ̣ὰν ἦ̣ι ⟦ .α̣ι̣⟧ οἷα
30 [γ]ρ̣ά̣φ̣ω δ̣ι̣α̣λ̣η(φθῆι) περὶ αὐ(τοῦ)
κα(τὰ) τὸν νό(μον) ἐμ̣ο̣ὶ δ’ ἐπ̣α̣ναγ-
31 [κάσαι . . . .] .[. .] .[. .] . . .ψ̣. . . . . . .χ

(18–24) **Not long afterwards, Lysimachos without justification joined Nikaia to another man before having received from me the customary bill of divorce.**

(24–31) Therefore, I request, if you think it right, that you give the order to write to the Jews in the village to summon Lysimachos to appear before you, so that if the matter is as I write, his case may be decided according to the law (or the Law), and at the same time [he] may be forced ... to me ...

Map of Judaea and Arabia

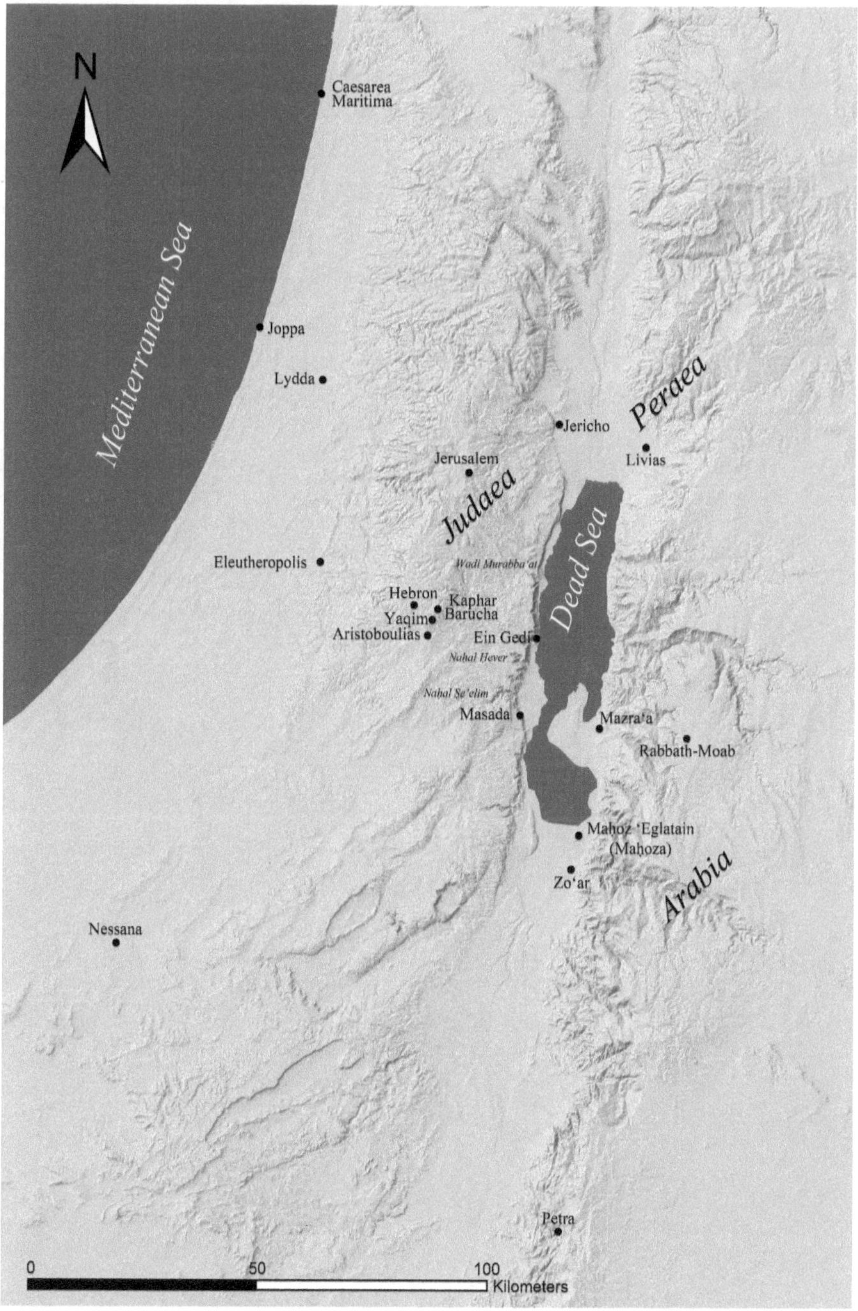

https://doi.org/10.1515/9783110770438-036

Bibliography

Abbadi, Sabri, and Fawzi Zayadine. "Nepos the Governor of the Provincia Arabia in a Safaitic Inscription?" *Semitica* 46 (1996): 155–64.
Abbott, Frank Frost, and Allan Chester Johnson. *Municipal Administration in the Roman Empire*. Princeton: Princeton University Press, 1926.
Abel, Félix-Marie. *Géographie de la Palestine*. Vol. II. Paris: J. Gabalda, 1938.
Adam, Traute. *Clementia Principis*. Stuttgart: E. Klett, 1970.
Adams, J.N. *Bilingualism and the Latin Language*. New York: Cambridge University Press, 2003.
Aichinger, Anna. "Zwei Arten des Provinzialcensus? Überlegungen zu neu-publizierten israelischen Papyrusfunden." *Chiron* 22 (1992): 35–45.
Al-Fassi, Hatoon Ajwad. *Women in Pre-Islamic Arabia: Nabataea*. Oxford: Archaeopress, 2007.
Albeck, Shalom. *Law Courts in Talmudic Times*. Ramat-Gan: Bar-Ilan University Press, 1980 (Hebrew).
Alföldi, András. *Der Vater des Vaterlandes im römischen Denken*. Darmstadt: Wissenschaftliche Buchgesellschaft, 1978.
Alföldi, András. "Die Geburt der kaiserlichen Bildsymbolik: Kleine Beiträge zu ihrer Entstehungsgeschichte." *MH* 11 (1954): 133–69.
Alföldi, András. "Die Geburt der kaiserlichen Bildsymbolik: Kleine Beiträge zu ihrer Entstehungsgeschichte." *MH* 9 (1952): 204–43.
Alföldi, András. *Die Kontorniaten*. Leipzig: Harrasowitz, 1943.
Alföldy, Géza. "Die Inschriften des Jüngeren Plinius und seine Mission in Pontus et Bithynia." In *Städte, Eliten und Gesellschaft in der Gallia Cisalpina*, 221–244. Stuttgart: Steiner, 1999.
Alföldy, Géza. *Die römischen Inschriften von Tarraco*. Berlin: De Gruyter, 1975.
Alföldy, Géza. "Epigraphica Tiburtina." *Epigraphica* 28 (1966): 3–17.
Alföldy, Géza. *Flamines Provinciae Hispaniae Citerioris*. Madrid: C.S.I.C., 1973.
Alföldy, Géza. *Noricum*. London: Routledge, 1974.
Alföldy, Géza. "Spain." In *The Cambridge Ancient History, Volume 10*, edited by Alan K. Bowman, Edward Champlin, and Andrew Lintott, 449–63. Cambridge: Cambridge University Press, 1996.
Alon, Gedaliah. *The Jews in Their Land in the Talmudic Age 70–640 CE*. 2 Vols. Jerusalem: Magnes Press, 1980–84.
Alon, Gedaliah. "The στρατεγοί in the Cities of Palestine during the Roman Period." In *Studies in Jewish History*, Vol. II, 74–87. Tel-Aviv: Hakibuz Hameuchad, 1958 (Hebrew).
Alpers, Michael. *Das nachrepublikanische Finanzsystem: Fiscus und Fisci in der frühen Kaiserzeit*. Berlin: De Gruyter, 1995.
Amit, David, and Jodi Magness. "The Essenes Did Not Live above Ein Gedi: A Reply to Y. Hirschfeld." *Cathedra* 96 (2000): 57–68 (Hebrew).
Anderson, William S. "The Programs of Juvenal's Later Books." *CPhil.* 57 (1962): 145–60.
Ando, Clifford. *Law, Language, and Empire in the Roman Tradition*. Philadelphia: University of Pennsylvania Press, 2011.
Ando, Clifford. "Pluralisme juridique et intégration de l'empire." In *Integration in Rome and in the Roman World: Proceedings of the Tenth Workshop of the International Network Impact*

Note: Hannah M. Cotton's publications, including those written or edited with others, are listed at the beginning of this volume.

https://doi.org/10.1515/9783110770438-035

of Empire (Lille, June 23–25, 2011), edited by G. de Kleijn and Stéphane Benoist, 5–19. Leiden – Boston: Brill, 2013.

Andorlini, Isabella, ed. *Atti del XXII Congresso internazionale di papirologia: Firenze, 23–29 agosto 1998*. Florence: Istituto papirologico G. Vitelli, 2001.

Andrzejewski, Roman. "La structure de la lettre de recommandation antique a la lumière des principes de la rhetorique." *Roczniki Humanistyczne* 21, no. 3 (1973): 17–24.

Applebaum, Shimon. *Prolegomena to the Study of the Second Jewish Revolt A.D. 132–135*. Oxford: B.A.R., 1976.

Arangio-Ruiz, Vincenzo. "Due nuove tavolette di Ercolano relative alla nomina di tutori muliebri." In *Studi in onore di P. De Francisci*, Vol. I, 1–18. Milano: Giuffrè, 1956.

Arangio-Ruiz, Vincenzo. "Sul problema della doppia cittadinanza nella Repubblica e nell'Impero romano." In *Scritti giuridici in onore di Francesco Carnelutti*, 55–77. Padova: CEDAM, 1950.

Archer, Léonie J. *Her Price is Beyond Rubies. The Jewish Woman in Graeco-Roman Palestine*. Sheffield: Academic Press, 1990.

Arjava, Antti. "Everyday Life and Law in Byzantine Petra." *Acta Byzantina Fennica* 2 (2003): 7–17.

Arjava, Antti. "Physical Format and Notarial Conventions in the Petra Papyri." In *The Petra Papyri III*, edited by Antti Arjava, Matias Buchholz, and Traianos Gagos, 1–5. Amman: ACOR, 2007.

Arjava, Antti, Matias Buchholz, and Traianos Gagos, eds. *The Petra Papyri III*. Amman: ACOR, 2007.

Assaf, Simcha. "The Appointment of Women as Guardians." *Ha-Mishpat Ha-'Ivri* 2 (1927): 75–81 (Hebrew).

Atkinson, K.T.M. "A Hellenistic Land-Conveyance: The Estate of Mnesimachus in the Plain of Sardis." *Historia* 21 (1972): 45–74.

Avi-Yonah, Michael. *The Holy Land: From the Persian to the Arab Conquests*. Grand Rapids: Baker Book House, 1966.

Avi-Yonah, Michael. *The Madaba Mosaic Map*. Jerusalem: IES, 1954.

Avi-Yonah, Michael. "When Did Judea Become a Consular Province?" *IEJ* 23 (1973): 209–13.

Bagnall, Roger S. *Egypt in Late Antiquity*. Princeton: Princeton University Press, 1993.

Bagnall, Roger S., and Bruce W. Frier. *The Demography of Roman Egypt*. Cambridge: Cambridge University Press, 1994.

Bagnall, Roger S., and Klaas A. Worp. "Dating the Coptic legal documents from Aphrodite." *ZPE* 148 (2004): 247–52.

Baldacci, Paolo. "Patrimonium e ager publicus al tempo dei Flavi." *La parola del passato* 128 (1969): 349–67.

Bammel, Ernst. "Markus 10 11f. und das jüdische Eherecht." *Zeitschrift für die neutestamentliche Wissenschaft* 61 (1970): 95–101.

Bar-Asher, Moshe. "The Language of the Beit 'Amar Document." *Cathedra* 132 (2009): 25–32 (Hebrew).

Barbieri, Guido. *L'Albo senatorio da Settimio Severo a Carino (193–285)*. Rome: Signorelli, 1952.

Barnes, Timothy D. *The New Empire of Diocletian and Constantine*. Cambridge, Mass.: Harvard University Press, 1982.

Basser, Herbert. *The Mind Behind the Gospels: A Commentary to Matthew 1–14*. Boston: Academic Studies Press, 2010.

Bastianini, Guido. "Il prefetto d'Egitto (30 a. C. – 297 d. C.): Addenda (1973 –1985)." In *Aufstieg und Niedergang der römischen Welt*, Vol. II.10/1, 503–17. Berlin: De Gruyter, 1988.

Bastianini, Guido. "Lista dei prefetti d'Egitto dal 30a al 299p : Aggiunte e correzioni." *ZPE* 38 (1980): 75–89.
Bastianini, Guido. "Lista dei prefetti d'Egitto dal 30a al 299p." *ZPE* 17 (1975): 263–328.
Beaujeu, Jean. *La religion romaine à l'apogée de l'empire*. Paris: Les Belles Lettres, 1955.
Ben-Barak, Zafrira. *Inheritance by Daughters in Israel and the Ancient Near East*. Jaffa: Archaeological Center Publications, 2003.
Ben-Dor, Stella. "Petra Colonia." *Berytus* 9 (1948–49): 41–43.
Ben-Yehuda, Nachman. *The Masada Myth: Collective Memory and Mythmaking in Israel*. Madison: University of Wisconsin Press, 1995.
Benoit, P., J.T. Milik, and R. de Vaux. *Les grottes de Murabba'at*. Discoveries in the Judaean Desert II. Oxford: Clarendon Press, 1961.
Benoit, Pierre. "Bulletin." *RB* 68 (1961): 464–67.
Benoit, Pierre. "Une reconnaissance de dette du IIe siècle en Palestine." In *Studi in onore di Aristide Calderini e Roberto Paribeni*, Vol. II, 257–72. Milano: Ceschina, 1957.
Béranger, Jean. *Recherches sur l'aspect idéologique du principat*. Basel: F. Reinhardt, 1953.
Berg-Onstwedder, Gonnie van den. "The Use of Demotic Phrases from Legal Texts of the Ptolemaic Period in Coptic Legal Texts." *BSAC* 35 (1996): 101–16.
Berger, Adolf. *Die Strafklauseln in den Papyrusurkunden*. Leipzig: Teubner, 1911 [1965].
Berlinger, Leo. "Beiträge zur inoffiziellen Titulatur der römischen Kaiser." University of Breslau Thesis, 1935.
Bernhardt, Rainer. "Imperium und Eleutheria: die römische Politik gegenüber den freien Städten des griechischen Ostens." University of Hamburg Thesis, 1971.
Bersanetti, G.M. "Iscrizione leptitana in onore di Massenziop." *Epigraphica* 5–6 (1943–44): 27–39.
Beschaouch, Azedine. "Éléments celtiques dans la population du pays de Carthage." *CR Acad. Inscr.* 123 (1979): 394–409.
Bickerman, Elias J. "Two Legal Interpretations of the Septuagint." In *Studies in Jewish and Christian History*, Vol. I, 201–224. Leiden: Brill, 1976.
Bingen, Jean. *Papyrus Revenue Laws* (*SB* Beiheft 1). Göttingen: Hubert, 1952.
Birks, Peter, Alan Rodger, and J.S. Richardson. "Further Aspects of the Tabula Contrebiensis." *JRS* 74 (1984): 45–73.
Birley, Anthony R. *Hadrian: The Restless Emperor*. London: Routledge, 1997.
Birley, Anthony R. *The Fasti of Roman Britain*. Oxford: Clarendon Press, 1981.
Birley, Anthony R. "The Roman Governors of Britain." *Epigraphische Studien* 4 (1967): 63–102.
Birley, Eric. "Promotions and Transfers in the Roman Army, II: The Centurionate." *Carnuntum Jahrbuch*, 1963–64, 21–33.
Birley, Eric. "The Equestrian Officers of the Roman Army." In *Roman Britain and the Roman Army: Collected Papers*, 133–53. Kendal: T. Wilson, 1953.
Biscardi, Arnaldo. "Nuove testimonianze di un papiro arabogiudaico per la storia del processo provinciale romano." In *Studi in onore di Gaetano Scherillo*, Vol. I, 111–52. Milano: Istituto editoriale cisalpino La Goliardica, 1972.
Bloch, Moses. *Die Vormundschaft nach mosaisch-talmudischem Rechte*. Budapest: A. Alkalay Pressburg, 1904.
Blois, Lukas de, and Elio Lo Cascio, eds. *The Impact of the Roman Army (200 B.C. – A.D. 476): Economic, Social, Political, Religious and Cultural Aspects*. Leiden – Boston: Brill, 2007.
Boak, A.E.R. "A Petition for Relief from a Guardianship. P. Mich. Inv. No. 2922." *JEA* 18 (1932): 69–76.

Boak, A.E.R. "A Petition to an Exegetes, A.D. 36." *JEA* 19 (1933): 138–42.
Boffo, Laura. *Iscrizioni greche e latine per lo studio della Bibbia*. Brescia: Paideia, 1994.
Bohec, Yann Le, ed. *Les legions de Rome sous le haut-empire: actes du congres de Lyon (17–19 septembre 1998)*. 3 Vols. Lyon: Centre d'etudes romaines et gallo-romaines, 2000.
Böttrich, Christfried. "Die vergessene Geburtsgeschichte: Mt 1–2 / Lk 1–2 und die wunderbare Geschichte des Melchisedek in slHen 71–72." In *Jüdische Schriften in ihrem antik-jüdischen und urchristlichen Kontext*, edited by Hermann Lichtenberger and Gerbern S. Oegema, 222–48. Gütersloh: Gütersloher Verlagshaus, 2002.
Bowersock, Glen W. "A Report on Arabia Provincia." *JRS* 61 (1971): 219–42.
Bowersock, Glen W. *Hellenism in Late Antiquity*. Ann Arbor: University of Michigan Press, 1990.
Bowersock, Glen W. "Naming a Province: More on New Arabia." *ZPE* 56 (1984): 221–22.
Bowersock, Glen W. "Review of A. Spijkerman, The Coins of the Decapolis and Provincia Arabia." *JRS* 72 (1982): 197–98.
Bowersock, Glen W. *Roman Arabia*. Cambridge, Mass.: Harvard University Press, 1983.
Bowersock, Glen W. "The Annexation and Initial Garrison of Arabia." *ZPE* 5 (1970): 37–47.
Bowersock, Glen W. "The Babatha Papyri, Masada, and Rome." *JRA* 4 (1991): 336–44.
Bowman, Alan K. "Provincial Administration and Taxation." In *The Cambridge Ancient History, Volume 10*, edited by Alan K. Bowman, Edward Champlin, and Andrew Lintott, 2nd ed., 344–70. Cambridge: Cambridge University Press, 1996.
Bowman, Alan K. "Roman Military Records from Vindolanda." *Britannia* 5 (1974): 360–73.
Bowman, Alan K., and Dominic Rathbone. "Cities and Administration in Roman Egypt." *JRS* 82 (1992): 107–27.
Bowman, Alan K., and J. David Thomas. "The Vindolanda Writing Tablets and Their Significance: An Interim Report." *Historia* 24 (1975): 463–78.
Braunert, Horst. "Cives Romani und κατ' οἰκίαν ἀπογραφαί." In *Antidoron Martino David oblatum*, edited by E. Boswinkel, B.A. van Groningen, and P.W. Pestman, 11–21. Leiden: Brill, 1968.
Breeze, David. "The Organization of the Legion: The First Cohort and The Equites Legionis." *JRS* 59 (1969): 50–55.
Brody, Robert. "Evidence for Divorce by Jewish Women?" *JJS* 50 (1999): 230–34.
Brooten, Bernadette J. "Konnten Frauen im alten Judentum die Scheidung betreiben?: Überlegungen zu Mk 10, 11–12 und 1Kor 7, 10–11." *Evangelische Theologie* 42 (1982): 65–80.
Brooten, Bernadette J. "Zur Debatte über das Scheidungsrecht der jüdischen Frau." *Evangelische Theologie* 43 (1983): 466–78.
Broshi, Magen. "Agriculture and Economy in Roman Palestine: Seven Notes on the Babatha Archive." *IEJ* 42 (1992): 230–40.
Broshi, Magen, and Elisha Qimron. "A House Sale Deed from Kefar Baru from the Time of Bar Kokhba." *IEJ* 36 (1986): 201–14.
Broughton, T. Robert S. *The Magistrates of the Roman Republic*. 2 Vols. New York: American Philological Association, 1952–1960.
Bruna, F.J. *Lex Rubria: Caesars Regelung für die Richterlichen Kompetenzen der Munizipal-magistrate in Gallia Cisalpina*. Leiden: Brill, 1972.
Brünnow, Rudolf Ernst, and Alfred von Domaszewski. *Die Provincia Arabia*. 3 Vols. Strasbourg: Trübner, 1904–1909.
Brunt, Peter A. "Lex De Imperio Vespasiani." *JRS* 67 (1977): 95–116.

Brunt, Peter A. "Review: Peter Garnsey, Social Status and Legal Privilege in the Roman Empire. Oxford: the Clarendon Press, 1970." *JRS* 62 (1972): 166–70.
Brunt, Peter A. "The Revenues of Rome." In *Roman Imperial Themes*, 324–46. Oxford: Clarendon Press, 1990.
Buckland, W.W., and Peter Stein. *A Text-Book of Roman Law from Augustus to Justinian*. 3rd ed. Cambridge: Cambridge University Press, 1966.
Bülow-Jacobsen, Adam, and Vincent P. McCarren. "P.Haun. 14, P.Mich. 679, and P.Haun. 15: A Re-Edition." *ZPE* 58 (1985): 71–79.
Bureth, Paul. "Le préfet d'Egypte (30 av.J.C.–297 ap. J.C.): Etat présent de la documentation en 1973." In *Aufstieg und Niedergang der römischen Welt*, Vol. II.10/1, 472–502. Berlin: De Gruyter, 1988.
Bureth, Paul. *Les titulatures impériales dans les papyrus, les ostraca et les inscriptions d'Égypte (30 a.C.-284 p.C.)*. Bruxelles: Fondation égyptologique reine Elisabeth, 1964.
Burkhalter, Fabienne. "Archives locales et archives centrales en Egypte romaine." *Chiron* 20 (1990): 191–216.
Burrell, Barbara. "Two Inscribed Columns from Caesarea Maritima." *ZPE* 99 (1993): 287–95.
Burton, G.P. "Proconsuls, Assizes and the Administration of Justice under the Empire." *JRS* 65 (1975): 92–106.
Cadell, Hélène. "Pour une recherche sur 'astu' et 'polis' dans les papyrus grecs d'Égypte." *Ktema* 9 (1984): 235–46.
Callaway, Ph. "Documentary Texts Allegedly from Qumran Cave 4." *The Qumran Chronicle* 8 (1998): 113–19.
Camodeca, G. *Tabulae Pompeianae Sulpiciorum (TPSulp.): Edizione critica dell' Archivio Puteolano dei Sulpicii*. Rome: Quasar, 1999.
Campbell, John K. *Honour, Family and Patronage: A Study of Institutions and Moral Values in a Greek Mountain Community*. Oxford: Clarendon Press, 1964.
Capelli, Piero. "L'Epistola greca di Bar Kokhba e la questione del vernacolo giudaico nel II secolo." In *Biblische und judaistische Studien. Festschrift für Paolo Sacchi*, edited by Angelo Viviano, 271–78. Frankfurt am Main: P. Lang, 1990.
Casavola, Franco. *Actio petitio persecutio*. Napoli: Jovene, 1965.
Cascio, Elio Lo. "Census provinciale, imposizione fiscale e amministrazioni cittadine nel Principato." In *Lokale Autonomie und römische Ordnungsmacht in den kaiserzeitlichen Provinzen vom 1. bis 3. Jahrhundert*, edited by Werner Eck, 197–212. München: Oldenbourg, 1999.
Cascio, Elio Lo. "Le procedure di recensus dalla tarda repubblica al tardo antico e il calcolo della popolazione di Roma." In *La Rome impériale. Démographie et logistique*, 3–76. Rome: École Française de Rome, 1997.
Cascio, Elio Lo. "Le professiones della Tabula Heracleensis e le procedure del census in età cesariana." *Athenaeum* 78 (1990): 287–318.
Cassio Dione: Storia Romana. Libri 52–56. Milano: Biblioteca universale Rizzoli, 1998.
Cassius Dio: Römische Geschichte. Band IV: Bücher 51 – 60. Translated by Otto Veh. Zürich – München: Artemis Verlag, 1986.
Cassius Dio: The Augustan Settlement (Roman History 53–55.9). Translated by J.W. Rich. Westminster: Aris and Phillips, 1990.
Chajes, H.P. "Les juges juifs en Palestine, de l'an 70 à l'an 500." *Revue des études juives* 39, no. 77 (1899): 39–52.
Champlin, Edward. *Fronto and Antonine Rome*. Cambridge, Mass.: Harvard University Press, 1980.

Chapa, Juan. *Letters of Condolence in Greek Papyri*. Florence: Edizioni Gonnelli, 1998.
Charlesworth, James, et al., eds. *Miscellaneous Texts from the Judaean Desert*. Discoveries in the Judaean Desert XXXVIII. Oxford: Oxford University Press, 2000.
Charlesworth, Martin Percival. "Providentia and Aeternitas." *Harv. Theol. Rev.* 29 (1936): 107–32.
Chastagnol, André. "L'inscription constantinienne d'Orcistus." *MÉFRA* 93 (1981): 381–416.
Chilton, Bruce. "Jésus, le mamzer (Mt 1.18)." *New Testament Studies* 47 (2001): 222–27.
Chiusi, Tiziana J. "Babatha vs. The Guardians of Her Son: A Struggle for Guardianship – Legal and Practical Aspects of P. Yadin 12–15, 27." In *Law in the Documents of the Judean Desert*, edited by Ranon Katzoff and David Schaps, 105–32. Leiden: Brill, 2005.
Chiusi, Tiziana J. "IV. Zur Vormundschaft der Mutter." *ZSS* 111 (1994): 155–96.
Clamer, Christa. "The Hot Springs of Kallirrhoe and Baarou." In *The Madaba Map Centenary 1897–1997*, edited by Michele Piccirillo and Eugenio Alliata, 221–25. Jerusalem: Franciscan Printing Press, 1999.
Cockle, W.E.H. "State Archives in Graeco-Roman Egypt from 30 BC to the Reign of Septimius Severus." *JEA* 70 (1984): 106–22.
Cohen, Boaz. *Jewish and Roman Law: A Comparative Study*. New York: Jewish Theological Seminary of America, 1966.
Cohen, Henry. *Description historique des monnaies frappées sous l'empire romain*. 8 Vols. Paris – London: Rollin & Feuardent, 1880–1892.
Cohen, Nahum. "New Greek Papyri from a Cave in the Vicinity of Ein Gedi." *SCI* 25 (2006): 87–95.
Cohen, Shaye J.D. "The Significance of Yavneh: Pharisees, Rabbis, and the End of Jewish Sectarianism." *HUCA* 55 (1984): 27–53.
Cowey, James M. S., and Klaus Maresch, eds. *Urkunden des Politeuma der Juden von Herakleopolis (144/3–133/2 v. Chr.) (P. Polit. Iud.)*. Wiesbaden: Westdeutscher Verlag, 2001.
Crawford, Dorothy J. "Imperial Estates." In *Studies in Roman Property*, edited by Moses I. Finley, 35–70. Cambridge: Cambridge University Press, 1976.
Crawford, Michael, ed. *Roman Statutes*. London: Institute of Classical Studies, 1996.
Crisci, Edoardo. *Scrivere greco fuori d'Egitto*. Florence: Gonnelli, 1996.
Crook, John. "Sponsione Provocare: Its Place in Roman Litigation." *JRS* 66 (1976): 132–38.
Cross, Frank Moore. "The Development of the Jewish Scripts." In *The Bible and the Ancient Near East: Essays in Honor of William Foxwell Albright*, edited by G. Ernest Wright, 133–202. Garden City, N.Y.: Doubleday, 1961.
Cross, Frank Moore, and Esther Eshel. "Ostraca from Khirbet Qumrân." *IEJ* 47 (1997): 17–28.
Crowther, Charles. "Foreign Judges from Priene: Studies in Hellenistic Epigraphy." King's College London Thesis, 1990.
D'Ors, Álvaro. *Epigrafía jurídica de la España Romana*. Madrid: Instituto Nacional de Estudios Jurídico, 1953.
D'Ors, Álvaro. "Miscelánea epigráfica. Los bronces de Mulva." *Emerita* 29 (1961): 203–18.
Dąbrowa, Edward. "The Commanders of Syrian Legions, 1st to 3rd c. A.D." In *The Roman Army in the East*, edited by David L. Kennedy, 277–96. Ann Arbor: Journal of Roman Archaeology, 1996.
Dąbrowa, Edward. *The Governors of Roman Syria from Augustus to Septimius Severus*. Bonn: Habelt, 1998.
Danby, Herbert. *The Mishnah: Translated from the Hebrew with Introduction and Brief Explanatory Notes*. Oxford: Oxford University Press, 1933.

Dar, Shimon, and Nikos Kokkinos. "The Greek Inscriptions from Senaim on Mount Hermon." *PEQ* 124 (1992): 9–25.

Daube, David. *Roman Law: Linguistic, Social and Philosophical Aspects.* Edinburgh: Edinburgh University Press, 1969.

Daube, David. "The New Testament Terms for Divorce." *Theology* 47 (1944): 65–67.

Davies, R.W. "Joining the Roman Army." *Bonner Jahrbücher* 168 (1969): 208–32.

Della Corte, M. "Tabelle cerate Ercolanesi." *La parola del passato* 6 (1951): 224–30.

Denniston, J.D. *The Greek Particles.* Oxford: Clarendon Press, 1934.

Depauw, Mark. "Autograph Confirmation in Demotic Private Contracts." *Chronique d'Égypte* 78 (2003): 66–111.

Deubner, Ludwig, and Uhlrich Klein, eds. *Iamblichi De vita Pythagorica liber.* Stuttgart: Teubner, 1975.

Deutsch, Robert. "A Unique Prutah from the First Year of the Jewish War against Rome." *INJ* 12 (1992–93): 71–72.

Devillers, Luc. "La lettre de Soumaïos et les Ioudaioi johanniques." *RB* 105 (1998): 556–81.

Dio Cassius, Roman History, Volume VI: Books 51–55. Translated by Earnest Cary. Loeb Class. Cambridge, Mass.: Harvard University Press, 1980.

Di Segni, Leah. "A New Toponym in Southern Samaria." *Liber Annuus* 44 (1994): 579–84.

Di Segni, Leah. "The Hadrianic Inscription from Southern Samaria (?) – A Palinode." *Liber Annuus* 53 (2003): 335–40.

Dobson, Brian. *Die Primipilares.* Köln: Rheinland-Verlag, 1978.

Dobson, Brian. "Legionary Centurion or Equestrian Officer? A Comparison of Pay and Prospects." *Ancient Society* 3 (1972): 193–207.

Dohrmann, Natalie B., and Annette Yoshiko Reed, eds. *Jews, Christians, and the Roman Empire: The Poetics of Power in Late Antiquity.* Philadelphia: University of Pennsylvania Press, 2013.

Domaszewski, Alfred von. *Die Rangordnung des römischen Herres.* Köln: Böhlau, 1967.

Drijvers, Han J.W., and John F. Healey. *The Old Syriac Inscriptions of Edessa and Osrhoene.* Leiden: Brill, 1999.

Drumann, W.K.A., and P. Groebe, eds. *Geschichte Roms in seinem Übergange von der republikanischen Verfassung.* Hildesheim: G. Olms, 1964.

Duncan-Jones, Richard. *Structure and Scale in the Roman Economy.* Cambridge: Cambridge University Press, 1991.

Duncan-Jones, Richard. *The Economy of the Roman Empire.* Cambridge: Cambridge University Press, 1982.

Eck, Werner. "Beförderungskriterien innerhalb der senatorischen Laufbahn, dargestellt an der Zeit von 69–138 n. Chr." In *Aufstieg und Niedergang der römischen Welt*, Vol. II.1, 158–228. Berlin: De Gruyter, 1974.

Eck, Werner. "Befund und Realität. Zur Repräsentativität unserer epigraphischen Quellen in der römischen Kaiserzeit." *Chiron* 37 (2007): 49–64.

Eck, Werner. "Consules ordinarii und consules suffecti als eponyme Amtsträger." In *Epigrafia. Actes du colloque de Rome (27–28 mai 1988) en mémoire de Attilio Degrassi*, 15–44. Rome: École française de Rome, 1991.

Eck, Werner. "Der Bar Kochba Aufstand, der kaiserliche Fiscus und die Veteranenversorgung." *SCI* 19 (2000): 139–48.

Eck, Werner. "Die Inschriften Judäas im 1. und frühen 2. Jh. n. Chr. als Zeugnisse der römischen Herrschaft." In *Zwischen den Reichen: Neues Testament und römische Herrschaft. Vorträge auf der ersten Konferenz der European Association for Biblical Studies*, edited by Michael Labahn and Jürgen Zangenberg, 29–50. Tübingen: Francke Verlag, 2002.

Eck, Werner. "Die italischen legati Augusti pro praetore unter Hadrian und Antoninus Pius." In *Historiae Augustae Colloquium Parisinum*, edited by Giorgio Bonamente and Noël Duval, 183–95. Macerata: Università degli studi, 1991.

Eck, Werner. *Die Verwaltung des römischen Reiches in der hohen Kaiserzeit. Ausgewählte und erweiterte Beiträge*. Edited by Regula Frei-Stolba and Michael A. Speidel. Basel: F. Reinhardt, 1995.

Eck, Werner. "Ein Prokuratorenpaar von Syria Palaestina in P. Berol. 21652." *ZPE* 123 (1998): 249–55.

Eck, Werner. "Hadrian, the Bar Kokhba Revolt, and the Epigraphic Transmission." In *The Bar Kokhba War Reconsidered*, edited by Peter Schäfer, 153–70. Tübingen: Mohr Siebeck, 2003.

Eck, Werner. "Inschriften auf Holz. Ein unterschätztes Phänomen der epigraphischen Kultur Roms." In *Imperium Romanum. Studien zu Geschichte und Rezeption, Festschrift für Karl Christ zum 75. Geburtstag*, edited by Peter Kneissl and Volker Losemann, 203–17. Stuttgart: F. Steiner, 1998.

Eck, Werner. *L'Italia nell'impero romano. Stato e amministrazione in epoca imperiale*. Bari: Edipuglia, 1999.

Eck, Werner. "Latein als Sprache politischer Kommunikation in Städten der östlichen Provinzen." *Chiron* 30 (2000): 641–60.

Eck, Werner. "Lateinisch, Griechisch, Germanisch ...? Wie sprach Rom mit seinen Untertanen?" In *Roman Rule and Civic Life: Local and Regional Perspectives*, edited by L. de Ligt, E.A. Hemelrijk, and H.W. Singor, 3–19. Leiden: Brill, 2004.

Eck, Werner. "Lateinische Epigraphik." In *Einleitung in die lateinische Philologie*, edited by Fritz Graf, 92–111. Stuttgart: Teubner, 1997.

Eck, Werner, ed. *Lokale Autonomie und römische Ordnungsmacht in den kaiserzeitlichen Provinzen vom 1. bis 3. Jahrhundert*. München: Oldenbourg, 1999.

Eck, Werner. "Prosopographica II." *ZPE* 106 (1995): 249–54.

Eck, Werner. "Rom und die Provinz Iudaea/Syria Palaestina: Der Beitrag der Epigraphik." In *Jüdische Geschichte in hellenistisch-römischer Zeit. Wege der Forschung: Vom alten zum neuen Schürer*, edited by Aharon Oppenheimer, 237–64. München: Oldenbourg, 1999.

Eck, Werner. *Senatoren von Vespasian bis Hadrian: Prosopographische Untersuchungen mit Einschluß der Jahres- und Provinzialfasten der Statthalter*. München: Beck, 1970.

Eck, Werner. "Sextus Lucilius Bassus, der Eroberer von Herodium, in einer Bauinschrift von Abu Gosh." *SCI* 18 (1999): 109–20.

Eck, Werner. "The Bar Kokhba Revolt: The Roman Point of View." *JRS* 89 (1999): 76–89.

Eck, Werner. "The Language of Power: Latin in the Inscriptions of Judaea/Syria Palaestina." In *Semitic Papyrology in Context: A Climate of Creativity*, edited by Lawrence H. Schiffman, 123–44. Leiden – Boston: Brill, 2003.

Eck, Werner. "The Presence, Role and Significance of Latin in the Epigraphy and Culture of the Roman Near East." In *From Hellenism to Islam: Cultural and Linguistic Change in the Roman Near East*, edited by Hannah M. Cotton, Robert G. Hoyland, Jonathan J. Price, and David J. Wasserstein, 15–42. Cambridge: Cambridge University Press, 2009.

Eck, Werner. "'Tituli honorarii', curriculum vitae und Selbstdarstellung in der Hohen Kaiserzeit." In *Acta colloquii epigraphici latini : Helsingiae, 3.–6. sept. 1991 habiti*, edited by Heikki

Solin, Olli Salomies, and Uta-Maria Liertz, 211–37. Helsinki: Finnish Society of Sciences and Letters, 1995.
Eck, Werner. *Tra epigrafia prosopografia e archeologia: Scritti scelti, rielaborati ed aggiornati*. Rome: Quasar, 1996.
Eck, Werner. "Vier mysteriöse Rasuren in Inschriften aus Gerasa: Zum 'Schicksal' des Statthalters Haterius Nepos." In *Ἐπιγραφαί. Miscellanea epigrafica in onore di Lidio Gasperini*, edited by Gianfranco Paci, Vol. I, 347–62. Rome: Tipigraf, 2000.
Eck, Werner. "Zu lateinischen Inschriften aus Caesarea in Iudaea / Syria Palaestina." *ZPE* 113 (1996): 129–43.
Eck, Werner. "Zum konsularen Status von Iudaea im frühen 2. Jh." *BASP* 21 (1984): 55–67.
Eck, Werner, Antonio Caballos, and Fernando Fernández. *Das senatus consultum de Cn. Pisone patre*. München: Beck, 1996.
Eck, Werner, and Gideon Foerster. "Ein Triumphbogen für Hadrian im Tal von Beth Shean bei Tel Shalem." *JRA* 12 (1999): 294–313.
Eck, Werner, and Andreas Pangerl. "Vater, Mutter, Schwestern, Brüder... Zu einer außergewöhnlichen Bürgerrechtsverleihung in einer Konstitution des Jahres 121 n. Chr." *Chiron* 33 (2003): 347–64.
Eck, Werner, and Peter Weiß. "Eine Konstitution für die Truppen Iudaeas aus dem Jahr 87." *ZPE* 170 (2009): 201–206.
Eger, Otto. *Zum ägyptischen Grundbuchwesen in römischer Zeit*. Leipzig and Berlin: Teubner, 1909.
Ehrenberg, Victor. "Imperium Maius in the Roman Republic." *AJPhil.* 74 (1953): 113–36.
Eliav, Yaron Z. *God's Mountain. The Temple Mount in Time, Place, and Memory*. Baltimore: Johns Hopkins University Press, 2005.
Eliav, Yaron Z. "Hadrian's Actions in the Jerusalem Temple Mount According to Cassius Dio and Xiphilini Manus." *JSQ* 4 (1997): 125–44.
Engelmann, Helmut, and Dieter Knibbe. *Das Zollgesetz der Provinz Asia*. Bonn: Habelt, 1989.
Eshel, Esther, and Hanan Eshel. "Fragments of Two Aramaic Documents which were Brought to Abi'or Cave during the Bar-Kokhba Revolt." *Eretz Israel* 23 (1992): 276–85 (Hebrew).
Eshel, Esther, Hanan Eshel, and Ada Yardeni. "A Document from 'Year 4 of the Destruction of the House of Israel.'" *Dead Sea Discoveries* 18 (2011): 1–28.
Eshel, Esther, Hanan Eshel, and Ada Yardeni. "A Document from 'Year Four of the Destruction of the House of Israel.'" *Cathedra* 132 (2009): 5–24 (Hebrew).
Eshel, Hanan. "4Q348, 4Q343 and 4Q345: Three Economic Documents from Qumran Cave 4?" *JJS* 52 (2001): 132–35.
Eshel, Hanan. "Another Document from the Archive of Salome Komaïse Daughter of Levi." *SCI* 21 (2002): 169–71.
Eshel, Hanan, and David Amit, eds. *The Refuge Caves of the Bar Kokhba Revolt*. Jerusalem: IES, 1998 (Hebrew).
Eshel, Hanan, Magen Broshi, and T.A.J. Jull. "Documents from Wadi Murabba'at and the Status of Jerusalem during the Bar Kokhba Revolt." In *The Refuge Caves of the Bar Kokhba Revolt*, edited by Hanan Eshel and David Amit, 233–39. Jerusalem: IES, 1998 (Hebrew).
Eshel, Hanan, and Boaz Zissu. "Jericho: Archaeological Introduction." In *Miscellaneous Texts from the Judaean Desert*, Discoveries in the Judaean Desert XXXVIII, 3–20. Oxford: Clarendon Press, 2000.
Eshel, Hanan, and Boaz Zissu. "Ketef Jericho, 1993." *IEJ* 45 (1995): 292–98.
Falk, Z.W. "Zum fremden Einfluss auf das jüdische Recht." *RIDA* 18 (1971): 11–23.

Falk, Ze'ev W. *Introduction to Jewish Law of the Second Commonwealth*. Vol. II. Leiden: Brill, 1978.

Falk, Ze'ev W. "The Right of Inheritance of a Daughter and Widow in Bible and Talmud." *Tarbiẓ* 23 (1952): 9–15 (Hebrew).

Feissel, Denis. "Béroia." *Bulletin de correspondance hellénique. Supplément* 8 (1983): 60–78.

Feissel, Denis, and Jean Gascou. "Documents d'archives romains inédits du Moyen Euphrate (IIIe s. ap. J.-C.)." *CR Acad. Inscr.* 133 (1989): 535–61.

Feissel, Denis, and Jean Gascou. "Documents d'archives romains inédits du Moyen Euphrate (IIIe s. après J-C): I. Les pétitions (T. Euphr. 1 à 5)." *Journal des Savants*, 1995, 65–119.

Feissel, Denis, and Jean Gascou. "Documents d'archives romains inédits du Moyen Euphrate (IIIe s. après J.-C.): III. Actes divers et Lettres (P. Euphr. 11 à 17)." *Journal des Savants*, 2000, 157–208.

Fenati, Maria Federica. *Lucio Flavio Silva Nonio Basso e la città di Urbisaglia*. Macerata: Pubblicazioni dell'Istituto di storia antica, 1995.

Ferrary, Jean-Louis. "Le statut des cités libres dans l'Empire romain à la lumière des inscriptions de Claros." *CR Acad. Inscr.* 135 (1991): 557–77.

Fink, Robert O. *Roman Military Records on Papyrus*. Cleveland: APA, 1971.

Flach, Dieter. "Inschriftenuntersuchungen zum römischen Kolonat in Nordafrika." *Chiron* 8 (1978): 441–92.

Flach, Dieter. *Römische Agrargeschichte*. München: Beck, 1990.

Foerster, Gideon. "A Cuirassed Bronze Statue of Hadrian." *Atiqot* 17 (1985): 139–57.

Foti Talamanca, Giuliana. *Ricerche sul processo nell'Egitto grecoromano II.1: Introduzione del giudizio*. Milano: Giuffrè, 1979.

Franke, Thomas. *Die Legionslegaten der römischen Armee in der Zeit von Augustus bis Traian*. Bochum: Brockmeyer, 1991.

Frederiksen, M.W. "The Lex Rubria: Reconsiderations." *JRS* 54 (1964): 129–34.

Freeman, Philip. "The Era of the Province of Arabia: Problems and Solution?" In *Studies in the History of the Roman Province of Arabia: The Northern Sector*, Henry Innes MacAdam, 38–46. Oxford: B.A.R., 1986.

Frei-Stolba, Regula. "Inoffizielle Kaisertitulaturen im 1. und 2. Jahrhundert n. Chr." *MH* 26 (1969): 18–39.

Frevel, Christian, ed. *Medien im antiken Palästina: Materielle Kommunikation und Medialität als Thema der Palästinaarchäologie*. Tübingen: Mohr Siebeck, 2005.

Friedman, Mordechai Akiva. "Babatha's Ketubba: Some Preliminary Observations." *IEJ* 46 (1996): 55–76.

Friedman, Mordechai Akiva. *Jewish Marriage in Palestine: A Cairo Geniza Study*. 2 Vols. Tel Aviv: Tel Aviv University Press, 1980.

Friedman, Mordechai Akiva. In *Saul Lieberman Memorial Volume*, edited by Shamma Friedman, 189–232. New York – Jerusalem: Jewish Theological Seminary of America, 1993 (Hebrew).

Frösén, Jaakko, Antti Arjava, and Marjo Lentinen. *The Petra Papyri I*. Amman: ACOR, 2002.

Fuhrmann, Manfred, ed. *Marcus Tullius Cicero. Sämtliche Reden*. Vol. III. Zürich: Artemis Verlag, 1970.

Gallet, Léon. "Essai sur le sénatus-consulte 'de Asclepiade sociisque.'" *RHDFÉ* 16 (1937): 242–93.

Galsterer-Kröll, Brigitte. "Untersuchungen zu den Beinamen der Stadte des Imperium Romanum." *Epigraphische Studien* 9 (1972): 44–145.

Galsterer, Hartmut. "Roman Law in the Provinces: Some Problems of Transmission." In *L'Impero romano e le strutture economiche e sociali delle province*, edited by Michael Crawford, 13–27. Como: New Press, 1986.

Gardner, Jane F. "Making Citizens: The Operation of the Lex Irnitana." In *Administration, Prosopography and Appointment Policies in the Roman Empire*, edited by Lukas de Blois, 215–29. Leiden: Brill, 2001.
Gardner, Jane F. *Woman in Roman Law and Society*. London: Croom Helm, 1986.
Garnsey, Peter. "Honorarium decurionatus." *Historia* 20 (1971): 309–25.
Garnsey, Peter. *Social Status and Legal Privilege in the Roman Empire*. Oxford: Clarendon Press, 1970.
Garnsey, Peter. "The Criminal Jurisdiction of Governors." *JRS* 58 (1968): 51–59.
Garnsey, Peter. "The Lex Iulia and Appeal under the Empire." *JRS* 56 (1966): 167–89.
Gascou, Jean. "Unités administratives locales et fonctionnaires romains. Les données des nouveaux papyrus du Moyen Euphrate et d'Arabie." In *Lokale Autonomie und römische Ordnungsmacht in den kaiserzeitlichen Provinzen vom 1. bis 3. Jahrhundert*, edited by Werner Eck, 61–74. München: Oldenbourg, 1999.
Gaudemet, Jean. *Indulgentia Principis*. Trieste: Instituto di storia del diritto, 1962.
Geiger, Joseph. "A Note on P.Yadin 18." *ZPE* 93 (1992): 67–68.
Geller, Markham J. "New Sources for the Origins of the Rabbinic Ketubah." *HUCA* 49 (1978): 227–45.
Ghiretti, Maurizio. "Lo «status» della Giudea dall'età Augustea all'età Claudia." *Latomus* 44 (1985): 751–66.
Gilliam, James Franklin. "Enrolment in the Imperial Army." In *Symbolae Raphaeli Taubenschlag Dedicatae*, 207–16. Vratislaviae-Varsaviae: Ossolineum, 1957.
Gilliam, James Franklin. "Paganus in BGU 696." *AJPhil.* 73 (1952): 75–78.
Gilliam, James Franklin. "The Appointment of Auxiliary Centurions (P.Mich. 164)." *TAPA* 88 (1957): 155–68.
Goldstein, Jonathan A. "The Syriac Bill of Sale from Dura-Europos." *JNES* 25 (1966): 1–16.
González, Julián. "The Lex Irnitana: A New Copy of the Flavian Municipal Law." *JRS* 76 (1986): 147–243.
Goodblatt, David. "Dating Documents in Provincia Iudaea: A Note on Papyri Murabbaʿat 19 and 20." *IEJ* 49 (1999): 249–59.
Goodenough, Erwin Ramsdell. *Jewish Symbols in the Greco-Roman Period*. Vol. 12. New York: Pantheon Books, 1965.
Goodman, Martin. "Babatha's Story." *JRS* 81 (1991): 169–75.
Goodman, Martin, ed. *Jews in a Greco-Roman World*. Oxford: Oxford University Press, 1998.
Goodman, Martin. "Judaea." In *The Cambridge Ancient History, Volume 10*, edited by Alan K. Bowman, Edward Champlin, and Andrew Lintott, 2nd ed., 737–81. Cambridge: Cambridge University Press, 1996.
Goodman, Martin. *State and Society in Roman Galilee, AD 132–212*. Totowa, N.J.: Rowman and Allanheld, 1983.
Goodman, Martin. "Trajan and the Origins of Roman Hostility to the Jews." *Past & Present* 182 (2004): 3–29.
Goodman, Martin. "Trajan and the Origins of the Bar Kokhba War." In *The Bar Kokhba War Reconsidered*, edited by Peter Schäfer, 23–30. Tübingen: Mohr Siebeck, 2003.
Gould, S. "Inscriptions. I. The Triumphal Arch." In *The Excavations at Dura-Europos conducted by Yale University and the French Academy of Inscriptions and Letters*, Vol. IV, 56–65. New Haven: Yale University Press, 1933.
Gould, S. "Supplementary Inscriptions. I. An Addition to the Inscriptions of the Arch of Trajan." In *The Excavations at Dura-Europos conducted by Yale University and the French*

Academy of Inscriptions and Letters, Vol. VI, 480–82. New Haven: Yale University Press, 1936.
Gradenwitz, O. "Ein Protocoll von Memphis aus hadrianischer Zeit." *Hermes* 28 (1893): 321–34.
Graf, David F. *Rome and the Arabian Frontier: From the Nabataeans to the Saracens*. Aldershot: Ashgate, 1998.
Graf, David F. "The Origin of the Nabataeans." *ARAM* 2 (1990): 45–75.
Greenfield, Jonas C. "'Because He/She Did Not Know Letters': Remarks on a First Millennium C.E. Legal Expression." *JNES* 22 (1993): 39–44.
Greenfield, Jonas C. "Studies in the Legal Terminology of the Nabatean Funerary Inscriptions." In *Henoch Yalon Memorial Volume*, edited by Eduard Yechezkel Kutscher, Saul Lieberman, and Menaḥem Zevi Kaddari, 64–83. Jerusalem: Kiryat Sefer, 1974 (Hebrew).
Greenfield, Jonas C. "The Texts from Naḥal Ṣe'elim (Wadi Seiyal)." In *The Madrid Qumran Congress*, edited by Julio Trebolle Barrera and Luis Vegas Montaner, Vol. II, 661–66. Leiden: Brill, 1992.
Greenfield, Jonas C., and Michael E. Stone. "Two Notes on the Aramaic Levi Document." In *Of Scribes and Scrolls: Studies on the Hebrew Bible, Intertestamental Judaism, and Christian Origins, Presented to John Strugnell on the Occasion of his Sixtieth Birthday*, edited by Harold W. Attridge, John J. Collins, and Thomas H. Tobin. Lanham: University Press of America, 1990.
Greenidge, A.H.J. *Roman Public Life*. London: Macmillan, 1901.
Greenidge, A.H.J. *The Legal Procedure of Cicero's Time*. Oxford: Clarendon Press, 1901.
Groag, E. "Zu einem neuen Fragment der Fasti von Ostia." *JÖAI* 21 (1935): 177–204.
Gruen, Erich S. "The Trial of C. Antonius." *Latomus* 32 (1973): 301–10.
Guizzi, Francesco. "In tema di origini della 'cautio de rato.'" *Labeo* 7 (1961): 330–41.
Gulak, Asher. *Principles (Institutions) of Jewish Law III: Family Law*. Jerusalem: Dvir, 1922 (Hebrew).
Gulak, Asher. *Towards a Study of the History of Jewish Law in the Talmudic Period*. Jerusalem: Hasefer, 1929 (Hebrew).
Gurlitt, Ludwig. "De M. Tulli Ciceronis Epistulis Earumque Pristina Collectione." University of Göttingen Thesis, 1879.
Gurlitt, Ludwig. "Die Briefe Ciceros an M. Brutus." *Philologus Supplement* 4 (1884): 554–630.
Habicht, Christian. "New Evidence on the Province of Asia." *JRS* 65 (1975): 64–91.
Hackl, Ursula, Hanna Jenni, and Christoph Schneider. *Quellen zur Geschichte der Nabatäer*. Göttingen: Vandenhoeck & Ruprecht, 2003.
Hadas, Gideon. "Where was the Harbour of 'En-Gedi Situated?" *IEJ* 43 (1993): 45–49.
Haensch, Rudolf. *Capita Provinciarum*. Mainz am Rhein: von Zabern, 1997.
Haensch, Rudolf. "Zum Verständnis von P.Jericho 16 gr." *SCI* 20 (2001): 155–67.
Haensch, Rudolf. "Zur Konventsordnung in Aegyptus und den übrigen Provinzen des römischen Reiches." In *Akten des 21. Internationalen Papyrologenkongresses, Berlin, 13–19.8.1995*, edited by Barbara Kramer, Wolfgan Luppe, Herwig Maehler, and Gunter Poethke, Vol. I, 320–91. Stuttgart – Leipzig: Teubner, 1997.
Haensch, Rudolf, and Johannes Heinrichs, eds. *Herrschen und Verwalten: Der Alltag der römischen Administration in der Hohen Kaiserzeit*. Köln: Böhlau, 2007.
Hagedorn, Dieter. "Flurbereinigung in Theadelpheia?" *ZPE* 65 (1986): 93–100.
Halfmann, Helmut. *Itinera principum: Geschichte und Typologie der Kaiserreisen im römischen Reich*. Stuttgart: Steiner, 1986.

Halm, Carolus, ed. *Flori Epitomae de Tito Livio*. Lipsiae: Teubner, 1854.

Harmand, Louis. "Note sur une lettre de Cicéron (Ad Fam., XIII, 64)." *Latomus* 6 (1947): 23–29.

Harmon, Austin M. "Egyptian Property-Returns." In *Yale Classical Studies, Vol. IV*, edited by Austin M. Harmon, 135–234. New Haven: Yale University Press, 1934.

Harper, George McLean. *Village Administration in the Roman Province of Syria*. New Haven: Yale University Press, 1928.

Healey, John F. "Sources for the Study of Nabataean Law." *New Arabian Studies* 1 (1993): 203–14.

Healey, John F. *The Nabataean Tomb Inscriptions of Mada'in Salih*. Oxford: Oxford University Press, 1993.

Healey, John F. "The Writing on the Wall: Law in Aramaic Epigraphy." In *Writing and Ancient Near Eastern Society: Papers in Honour of Alan R. Millard*, edited by Piotr Bienkowski, Christopher Mee, and Elizabeth Slater, 128–41. New York: T&T Clark, 2005.

Heiman, A.M. *History of the Tannaim and Amoraim*. Vol. I. Jerusalem: Kirya Neemana, 1964 (Hebrew).

Helmbold, W.C., and E.N. O'Neil. "The Form and Purpose of Juvenal's Seventh 'Satire.'" *CPhil.* 54 (1959): 100–108.

Henderson, M.I. "Potestas Regia." *JRS* 57 (1957): 82–87.

Henzen, Wilhelm. *Acta Fratrum Arvalium*. Berlin: G. Reimeri, 1874.

Hezser, Catherine. *Jewish Literacy in Roman Palestine*. Tübingen: Mohr Siebeck, 2001.

Hezser, Catherine, ed. *Rabbinic Law in its Roman and Near Eastern Context*. Tübingen: Mohr Siebeck, 2003.

Hicks, E.L. "Inscriptions from Eastern Cilicia." *JHS* 11 (1890): 236–54.

Hirschfeld, Otto. *Die kaiserlichen Verwaltungsbeamten bis auf Diocletian*. Berlin: Weidmann, 1905.

Hirschfeld, Yizhar. "A Community of Hermits above Ein Gedi." *Cathedra* 96 (2000): 8–40 (Hebrew).

Hoftijzer, J., and K. Jongeling. *Dictionary of the North-West Semitic Inscriptions*. Leiden: Brill, 1995.

Hohlwein, Nicolas. "Palmiers et palmeraies dans l'Égypte romaine." *Études de Papyrologie* 5 (1939): 1–74.

Hombert, Marcel, and Claire Préaux. *Recherches sur le recensement dans l'Egypte romaine*. Leiden: Brill, 1952.

Honig, Richard M. *Humanitas und Rhetorik in spätrömischen Kaisergesetzen*. Göttingen: Schwartz, 1960.

Hopkins, Ian W. J. "The City Region in Roman Palestine." *PEQ* 112 (1980): 19–32.

Horovitz, H.S., and I.A. Rabin, eds. *Mekhilta d'R. Ishmael*. 2nd ed. Jerusalem: Wahrman, 1960 (Hebrew).

Hout, M.P.J. Van den, ed. *M. Cornelii Frontonis Epistulae*. Leiden: Brill, 1954.

Howard, G., and J.C. Shelton. "The Bar-Kokhba Letters and Palestinian Greek." *IEJ* 23 (1973): 101–102.

Hoyland, Robert G. "Language and Identity: The Twin Histories of Arabic and Aramaic (and: Why did Aramaic Succeed where Greek Failed?)." *SCI* 23 (2004): 183–99.

Ilan, Tal. "Julia Crispina, Daughter of Berenicianus, a Herodian Princess in the Babatha Archive: A Case Study in Historical Identification." *JQR* 82 (1992): 361–81.

Ilan, Tal. "On a Newly Published Divorce Bill from the Judaean Desert." *Harv. Theol. Rev.* 89 (1996): 195–202.

Ilan, Tal. "Premarital Cohabitation in Ancient Judea: The Evidence of the Babatha Archive and the Mishnah (Ketubbot 1.4)." *Harv. Theol. Rev.* 86 (1993): 247–64.
Ilan, Tal. "Witnesses in the Judaean Desert Documents: Prosopographical Observations." *SCI* 20 (2001): 169–78.
Ilan, Tal. "Yohana bar Makoutha and Other Pagans Bearing Jewish Names." In *These are the Names – Studies in Jewish Onomastics III*, edited by Aaron Demsky, 109–20. Ramat-Gan: Bar-Ilan University Press, 2002.
Ingholt, Harald. "Palmyrene Inscription from the Tomb of Malkû." *Mélanges de l'Université Saint-Joseph* 38 (1962): 101–19.
Isaac, Benjamin. "Tax Collection in Roman Arabia: A New Interpretation of the Evidence from the Babatha Archive." *Mediterranean Historical Review* 9 (1994): 256–66.
Isaac, Benjamin. "The Babatha Archive: A Review Article." *IEJ* 42 (1992): 62–75.
Isaac, Benjamin. "The Babatha Archive." In *The Near East under Roman Rule*, 159–181. Leiden: Brill, 1998.
Isaac, Benjamin. *The Limits of Empire: The Roman Army in the East.* Oxford: Clarendon Press, 1990.
Isaac, Benjamin. *The Limits of Empire: The Roman Army in the East.* 2nd ed. Oxford: Clarendon Press, 1992.
Isaac, Benjamin. *The Near East under Roman Rule: Selected Papers.* Leiden: Brill, 1997.
Isaac, Benjamin. "The Revolt of Bar Kokhba: Ideology and Modern Scholarship." In *The Near East under Roman Rule*, 220–256. Leiden: Brill, 1998.
Isaac, Benjamin, and Israel Roll. "Judaea in the Early Years of Hadrian's Reign." *Latomus* 38 (1979): 54–66.
Isaac, Benjamin, and Israel Roll. "Legio II Traiana in Judaea: A Reply." *ZPE* 47 (1982): 131–32.
Isaac, Benjamin, and Israel Roll. "Legio II Traiana in Judaea." *ZPE* 33 (1979): 149–56.
Jackson, Bernard S. "Marriage and Divorce: From Social Institution to Halakhic Norms." In *The Dead Sea Scrolls: Texts and Context*, edited by Charlotte Hempel, 339–64. Leiden: Brill, 2010.
Jal, Paul, ed. *Florus, Æuvres.* Collection Budé. Paris: Les Belles Lettres, 1967.
Jameson, Shelagh. "Cornutus Tertullus and the Plancii of Perge." *JRS* 55 (1965): 54–58.
Jastrow, Marcus. *A Dictionary of the Targumim, the Talmud Babli and Yerushalmi, and the Midrashic Literature.* London: Luzac, 1903.
Jastrow, Otto. *Die mesopotamisch-arabischen qəltu-Dialekte.* Vols. I–II. Wiesbaden: Steiner, 1978–81.
Johnson, J. de M., Victor Martin, and Arthur S. Hunt. *Catalogue of the Greek papyri in the John Rylands Library, Volume II: Documents of the Ptolemaic and Roman Periods.* Manchester: The University Press, 1915.
Jolowicz, H.F., and Barry Nicholas. *A Historical Introduction to the Study of Roman Law.* 3rd ed. Cambridge: Cambridge University Press, 1972.
Jones, A.H.M. "Imperial and Senatorial Jurisdiction in the Early Principate." In *Studies in Roman Government and Law*, 67–98. Oxford: Blackwell, 1960.
Jones, A.H.M. "Inscriptions from Jerash." *JRS* 18 (1928): 144–78.
Jones, A.H.M. *The Cities of the Eastern Roman Provinces.* Revised by Michael Avi-Yonah. 2nd ed. Oxford: Clarendon Press, 1971.
Jones, A.H.M. "The Imperium of Augustus." *JRS* 41 (1951): 112–19.
Jones, A.H.M. *The Later Roman Empire.* Oxford: Blackwell, 1964.

Jones, A.H.M. "The Urbanization of Palestine." *JRS* 21 (1931): 78–85.
Jones, Christopher P. "A New Commentary on the Letters of Pliny." *Phoenix* 22 (1968): 111–42.
Jones, Christopher P. "Sura and Senecio." *JRS* 60 (1970): 98–104.
Jones, Christopher P. "Towards a Chronology of Josephus." *SCI* 21 (2002): 113–21.
Juster, Jean. *Les Juifs dans l'Empire romain: leur condition juridique, economique et sociale.* Paris: Geuthner, 1914.
Kaizer, Ted. "The Near East in the Hellenistic and Roman Periods between Local, Regional and Supra-Regional Approaches." *SCI* 22 (2003): 283–95.
Kaser, Max. *Das römische Privatrecht.* 2nd ed. München: Beck, 1971.
Kaser, Max. *Das römische Zivilprozessrecht.* München: Beck, 1966.
Katzoff, Ranon. "Interpretation of P. Yadin 19: A Jewish Gift after Death." In *Proceedings of the 20th International Congress of Papyrologists, Copenhagen, 23–29 August, 1992*, edited by Adam Bülow-Jacobsen, 562–65. Copenhagen: Museum Tusculanum Press, 1994.
Katzoff, Ranon. "P. Yadin 19: A Gift after Death from the Judaean Desert." In *Proceedings of the World Congress of Jewish Studies* 10, Div. C, Vol. 1 (1989): 1–8 (Hebrew).
Katzoff, Ranon. "Papyrus Yadin 18 Again: A Rejoinder." *JQR* 82 (1991): 171–76.
Katzoff, Ranon. "Philo and Hillel on Violation of Betrothal in Alexandria." In *The Jews in the Hellenistic-Roman World: Studies in Memory of Menahem Stern*, edited by Isaiah M. Gafni, Aharon Oppenheimer, and Daniel R. Schwartz, 39–59. Jerusalem: Zalman Shazar Center, 1996.
Katzoff, Ranon. "Polygamy in P.Yadin?" *ZPE* 109 (1995): 128–32.
Katzoff, Ranon. "Review: Hannah M. Cotton and Ada Yardeni eds., Aramaic, Hebrew and Greek Documentary Texts from Nahal Hever and Other Sites." *SCI* 19 (2000): 316–27.
Katzoff, Ranon. "Sources of Law in Roman Egypt: The Role of the Prefect." In *Aufstieg und Niedergang der römischen Welt*, Vol. II.13, 807–46. Berlin: De Gruyter, 1980.
Katzoff, Ranon, and Bertram M. Schreiber. "Week and Sabbath in Judaean Desert Documents." *SCI* 17 (1998): 102–14.
Katzoff, Ranon, and Naphtali Lewis. "Understanding P.Ness. 18." *ZPE* 84 (1990): 211–13.
Kaygusuz, Ismail . "Eine neue Ehrung für Quintus Voconius Saxa Fidus in Perge." *Epigraphica Anatolica* 2 (1983): 37–39.
Keenan, James G. "Papyrology and Roman History: 1956–1980." *Classical World* 76 (1982): 23–31.
Kehoe, Dennis P. "Lease Regulations for Imperial Estates in North Africa. Part II." *ZPE* 59 (1985): 151–72.
Kehoe, Dennis P. *Management and Investment on Estates in Roman Egypt during the Early Empire.* Bonn: Habelt, 1992.
Kehoe, Dennis P. *The Economics of Agriculture on Roman Imperial Estates in North Africa.* Göttingen: Vandenhoeck & Ruprecht, 1988.
Kelly, John Maurice. *Roman Litigation.* Oxford: Clarendon Press, 1966.
Kelly, John Maurice. *Studies in the Civil Judicature of the Roman Republic.* Oxford: Clarendon Press, 1976.
Kennedy, David L. "Legio VI Ferrata: The Annexation and Early Garrison of Arabia." *Harv. Stud.* 84 (1980): 283–309.
Kenney, E.J. "The First Satire of Juvenal." *PCPS* 8 (1962): 29–40.
Keppie, Lawernce. "Legions in the East from Augustus to Trajan." In *The Defence of the Roman and Byzantine East: Proceedings of a Colloquium Held at the University of Sheffield in April 1986*, edited by Philip Freeman and David Kennedy, Vol. II, 411–29. Oxford: B.A.R., 1986.

Keppie, Lawernce. “The History and Disappearance of the Legion XXII Deiotariana.” In *Greece and Rome in Eretz Israel: Collected Essays*, edited by Aryeh Kasher, Uriel Rappaport, and Gideon Fuks, 54–61. Jerusalem: Yad Ben-Zvi Press, 1990.

Keppie, Lawernce. “The Legionary Garrison of Judaea under Hadrian.” *Latomus* 32 (1973): 859–64.

Khan, Geoffrey. “The Pre-Islamic Background of Muslim Legal Formularies.” *ARAM* 6 (1994): 193–224.

Kister, Menahem. “From Philotas to Hillel: ‘Betrothal’ Contracts and their Violation.” *SCI* 21 (2002): 57–60.

Kittel, Gerhard. *Theologisches Wörterbuch zum Neuen Testament*. Stuttgart: Kohlhammer, 1935.

Klebs, Elimar. *Die Erzählung von Apollonius aus Tyrus: Eine geschichtliche Untersuchung über ihre lateinische Urform und ihre späteren Bearbaitungen*. Berlin: G. Reimer, 1899.

Klein, Birgit E. “Die Stellung der Frau in Judentum: Rabbinische Initiative oder Legitimation? Demonstriert am Beispiel des jüdischen Vormundschaftsrechts.” Heidelberg, Hochschule für Jüdische Studien, Magisterarbeit, 1991.

Kloft, Hans. *Liberalitas Principis*. Köln: Böhlau, 1970.

Kloner, Amos, and Boaz Zissu. *The Necropolis of Jerusalem during the Hellenistic and Early Roman Periods*. Jerusalem: IES, 2003 (Hebrew).

Knauf, Ernst Axel. “Arabo-Aramaic and ‘Arabiyya: From Ancient Arabic to Early Standard Arabic, 200 CE – 600 CE.” In *The Quran in Context*, edited by Angelika Neuwirth, Nicolai Sinai, and Michael Marx, 197–254. Leiden – Boston: Brill, 2010.

Knauf, Ernst Axel. “Speaking and Writing in Galilee.” In *Zeichen aus Text und Stein. Studien auf dem Weg zu einer Archäologie des Neuen Testaments*, edited by Stefan Alkier and Jürgen Zangenberg, 336–50. Tübingen: A. Francke, 2003.

Knibbe, Dieter. “Neue Inschriften aus Ephesos II.” *JÖAI* 49, supp. (1968–71): 1–56.

Knibbe, Dieter, Helmut Engelmann, and Bülent Iplikçioglu. “Neue Inschriften aus Ephesos XII.” *JÖAI* 62 (1993): 113–50.

Koenen, Ludwig. “Preliminary Observations on Legal Matters in P.Petra 10.” In *Atti del XXII Congresso internazionale di papirologia, Firenze, 23–29 agosto 1998*, edited by Isabella Andorlini, Guido Bastianini, Manfredo Manfredi, and Giovanna Menci, 727–42. Florence: Istituto papirologico G. Vitelli, 2001.

Koffmahn, Elisabeth. *Die Doppelurkunden aus der Wüste Juda*. Leiden: Brill, 1968.

Köhler, Wilhelm. “Personifikationen abstrakter Begriffe auf römischen Münzen.” University of Königsberg Thesis, 1910.

Kokkinia, Christina. “Aphrodisias’ ‘Rights of Liberty’: Diplomatic Strategies and the Roman Governor,” in *Aphrodisias Papers 4: New Research on the City and Its Monuments*, edited by Ch. Ratté and R.R.R. Smith, 51–60. Portsmouth: Journal of Roman Archaeology, 2008.

Kraeling, Carl H., ed. *Gerasa: City of the Decapolis*. New Haven: American Schools of Oriental Research, 1938.

Kraemer, Casper J. *Excavations at Nessana III: Non-Literary Papyri*. Princeton: Princeton University Press, 1958.

Kramer, Bärbel, and Dieter Hagedorn. *Griechische Papyri der Staats- und Universitätsbibliothek Hamburg (P.Hamb.IV)*. Stuttgart – Leipzig: Teubner, 1998.

Kramer, Bärbel, and Dieter Hagedorn. “Zwei ptolemäische Texte aus der Hamburger Papyrus-sammlung.” *Archiv für Papyrusforschung* 33 (1987): 9–22.

Kreller, Hans. *Erbrechtliche Untersuchungen auf Grund der graeco-aegyptischen Papyrusurkunden*. Leipzig: Teubner, 1919.

Kroll, Wilhelm. *Die Kultur der ciceronischen Zeit*. Leipzig: Dieterich, 1933.
Kruse, Thomas. "Das jüdische politeuma von Herakleopolis und die Integration fremder Ethnien im Ptolemäerreich." In *Volk und Demokratie im Altertum*, edited by Vera Dement'eva and Tassilo Schmitt, 93–105. Göttingen: Edition Ruprecht, 2010.
Kühner, Raphael, and Carl Stegmann. *Ausführliche Grammatik der lateinischen Sprache*. Hannover: Hahn, 1976.
Kuhnke, Hans-Christian. "Οὐσιακὴ γῆ. Domänenland in den Papyri der Prinzipatszeit." Universität zu Köln Thesis, 1971.
Kunkel, Wolfgang. *Herkunft und soziale Stellung der römischen Juristen*. Graz: Böhlaus, 1967.
Kutscher, Eduard Yechezkel. *Hebrew and Aramaic Studies*. Jerusalem: Magnes Press, 1977 (Hebrew).
Kutscher, Eduard Yechezkel. "The Hebrew and Aramaic Letters of Bar Koseba and his Contemporaries: Part II: The Hebrew Letters." *Lĕšonénu* 26 (1961): 7–23 (Hebrew).
Kutscher, Edward Yechezkel. "Ugaritica Marginalia." *Lĕšonénu* 34 (1969): 5–19 (Hebrew).
Labahn, Michael, and Jürgen Zangenberg, eds. *Zwischen den Reichen: Neues Testament und römische Herrschaft. Vorträge auf der ersten Konferenz der European Association for Biblical Studies*. Tübingen: Francke Verlag, 2002.
Labbé, Gilbert. "Ponce Pilate et la munificence de Tibère. L'inscription de Césarée." *Revue des Études Anciennes* 93 (1991): 277–97.
Laffi, Umberto. "I limiti della competenza giurisdizionale dei magistrati locali." In *Estudios sobre la Tabula Siarensis*, edited by Julián González and Javier Arce, 141–56. Madrid: Centro de Estudios Históricos, 1988.
Lapin, Hayim. "Early Rabbinic Civil Law and the Literature of the Second Temple Period." *JSQ* 2 (1995): 149–83.
Lapin, Hayim. "Palm Fronds and Citrons: Notes on Two Letters from Bar Kosiba's Administration." *HUCA* 64 (1993): 111–35.
Last, Hugh. "Imperium Maius: A Note." *JRS* 37 (1947): 157–64.
Lehmann, Clayton Miles, and Kenneth G. Holum. *The Greek and Latin Inscriptions of Caesarea Maritima*. Boston: ACOR, 2000.
Lehmann, Manfred R. "Studies in the Murabbaʿat and Naḥal Ḥever Documents." *Revue de Qumran* 4 (1963): 53–81.
Lehnen, Joachim. *Adventus principis: Untersuchungen zu Sinngehalt und Zeremoniell der Kaiserankunft in den Städten des Imperium Romanum*. Frankfurt am Main: Peter Lang, 1997.
Leith, Mary Joan Winn. *Wadi Daliyah I: The Wadi Daliyeh Seal Impressions*. Oxford: Clarendon Press, 1997.
Lemosse, Maxime. "Le Procés de Babatha." *Irish Jurist* 3 (1968): 363–76.
Levin, Yigal. "Jesus, 'Son of God' and 'Son of David': The 'Adoption' of Jesus into the Davidic Line." *Journal for the Study of the New Testament* 28 (2006): 415–42.
Levine, Baruch A. "Comparative Perspectives on Jewish and Christian History." *JAOS* 99 (1979): 81–86.
Levine, Baruch A. "On the Origins of the Aramaic Legal Formulary of Elephantine." In *Christianity, Judaism, and Other Greco-Roman Cults: Studies for Morton Smith at Sixty*, edited by Jacob Neusner, Vol. III, 37–54. Leiden: Brill, 1975.
Levine, Baruch A. "The Various Workings of the Aramaic Legal Tradition: Jews and Nabateans in the Naḥal Ḥever Archive." In *The Dead Sea Scrolls: Fifty Years after their Discovery 1947–1997*, edited by Lawrence H. Schiffman, Emanuel Tov, and James C. Vanderkam, 836–51. Jerusalem: IES, 2000.

Levine, Lee I. *The Rabbinic Class of Roman Palestine in Late Antiquity*. Jerusalem – New York: Yad Ben-Zvi and Jewish Theological Seminary of America, 1989.
Lévy, Jean-Phillipe. "Cicéron et la preuve judiciaire." In *Droits de l'antiquité et sociologie juridique: mélanges Henri Lévy-Bruhl*, 187–97. Paris: Sirey, 1959.
Lévy, Jean-Phillipe. "Dignitas, Gravitas, Auctoritas Testium." In *Studi in onore di Biondo Biondi*, 27–94. Milano: Giuffrè, 1965.
Lévy, Jean-Phillipe. "La formation de la théorie romaine des preuves." In *Studi in onore di Siro Solazzi*. Naples: Jovene, 1948.
Lewald, Hans. "Conflits de lois dans le monde grec et romain." *'Αρχεῖον ἰδιωτικοῦ δικαίου* 13 (1946): 30–77.
Lewald, Hans. "Conflits de lois dans le monde grec et romain." *Labeo* 5 (1959): 334–69.
Lewald, Hans. "Conflits de lois dans le monde grec et romain." *Revue critique de droit international privé* 57 (1968): 419–40 and 615–39.
Lewis, Naphtali. "A Jewish Landowner from the Province of Arabia." *SCI* 8–9 (1985–88): 132–37.
Lewis, Naphtali. "'Greco-Roman Egypt': Fact or Fiction?" In *Proceedings of the Twelfth International Congress of Papyrology, Ann Arbor, Michigan, 12–17 August 1968*, edited by Deborah H. Samuel, 3–14. Toronto: Hakkert, 1970.
Lewis, Naphtali. "In the World of P.Yadin: Where did Judah's Wife Live?" *IEJ* 46 (1996): 256–57.
Lewis, Naphtali. "In the World of P.Yadin." *SCI* 18 (1999): 125–29.
Lewis, Naphtali. "Instructions for Appointing a Guardian." *BASP* 7 (1970): 116–18.
Lewis, Naphtali. "Judah's Bigamy." *ZPE* 116 (1997): 152.
Lewis, Naphtali. "Nouveau Texte sur la juridicion du préfet d'Égypte." *RHDFÉ* 50 (1972): 5–12.
Lewis, Naphtali. *On Government and Law in Roman Egypt: Collected Papers*. Atlanta: Scholars Press, 1995.
Lewis, Naphtali. "The Babatha Archive: A Response." *IEJ* 44 (1994): 243–46.
Lewis, Naphtali. *The Compulsory Public Services of Roman Egypt*. 2nd ed. Florence: Edizioni Gonnelli, 1997.
Lewis, Naphtali. "The Demise of the Aramaic Document in the Dead Sea Region." *SCI* 20 (2001): 178–81.
Lewis, Naphtali. "The Demise of the Demotic Document: When and Why." *JEA* 79 (1993): 276–81.
Lewis, Naphtali. *The Documents from the Bar Kokhba Period in the Cave of Letters. Greek Papyri*. Judean Desert Studies II. Jerusalem: IES, 1989.
Lewis, Naphtali. "The Romanity of Roman Egypt: A Growing Consensus." In *Atti del XVII Congresso internazionale di papirologia*, 1077–1084. Napoli: Centro internazionale per lo studio dei papiri ercolanesi, 1984.
Lewis, Naphtali. "The World of P.Yadin." *BASP* 28 (1991): 35–41.
Lewis, Naphtali. "Two Greek Documents from Provincia Arabia." *Illinois Classical Studies* 3 (1978): 100–114.
Lewis, Naphtali, Ranon Katzoff, and Jonas C. Greenfield. "Papyrus Yadin 18." *IEJ* 37 (1987): 229–50.
Lewis, Naphtali, and Meyer Reinhold, eds. *Roman Civilization: Selected Readings*. Vol. I. New York: Columbia University Press, 1951.
Lieberman, Saul. *Greek and Hellenism in Jewish Palestine*. Jerusalem: Mosad Bialik, 1984 (Hebrew).
Lieberman, Saul. "Roman Legal Institutions in Early Rabbinics and in the Acta Martyrum." *JQR* 35 (1944): 1–57.

Lieberman, Saul. "The Importance of the Bar-Kokhba Letters for Jewish History and Literature." In *Texts and Studies*, 208–9. New York: Ktav Pub. House, 1974.
Lieberman, Saul. *Tosefta Ki-fshutah. Part I: Order Zera'im ('Seeds')*. New York: Jewish Theological Seminary Press, 1955 (Hebrew).
Lieberman, Saul. *Tosefta Ki-fshutah. Part X: Order Nezikin*. New York: Jewish Theological Seminary Press, 1988.
Liebeschuetz, Wolf. "Did the Pelagian Movement Have Social Aims?" *Historia* 12 (1963): 227–41.
Lifshitz, Baruch. "Papyrus grecs du désert de Juda." *Aegyptus* 42 (1962): 240–56.
Lifshitz, Baruch. "The Greek Documents from Naḥal Ṣeelim and Naḥal Mishmar." *IEJ* 11 (1961): 53–62.
Lifshitz, Baruch. "The Greek Documents from the Cave of Horror." *IEJ* 12 (1962): 201–7.
Linder, Amnon. *The Jews in Roman Imperial Legislation*. Detroit: Wayne State University Press, 1987.
Lingenthal, K.E. Zachariae von. *Geschichte des griechisch-römischen Rechts*. Aalen in Wurttemberg: Scientia, 1955.
Lingenthal, K.E. Zachariae von. *Ius Graecoromanum*, 1931.
Lintott, Andrew W. *Imperium Romanum: Politics and Administration*. London: Routledge, 1993.
Lintott, Andrew W. "Provocatio. From the Struggle of the Orders to the Principate." In *Aufstieg und Niedergang der römischen Welt*, Vol. I.2, 226–67. Berlin: De Gruyter, 1972.
Lossmann, Friedrich. *Cicero und Caesar im Jahre 54: Studien zur Theorie und Praxis der römischen Freundschaft*. Wiesbaden: F. Steiner, 1962.
Lüddeckens, Erich. *Ägyptische Eheverträge*. Wiesbaden: Harrasowitz, 1960.
Lüddeckens, Erich. "Demotische und koptische Urkundenformeln." *Enchoria* 2 (1972): 21–31.
Luttwak, Edward N. *The Grand Strategy of the Roman Empire From the First Century CE to the Third*. Baltimore – London: Johns Hopkins University Press, 1976.
Luz, Ulrich. *Das Evangelium nach Matthäus, EKK I/1 (Mt 1–7)*. Düsseldorf: Benziger, 2002.
Luzzatto, Giuseppe Ignazio. *Epigrafia Giuridica Greca e Romana*. Milano: A. Giuffrè, 1942.
MacAdam, Henry Innes. *Studies in the History of the Roman Province of Arabia: The Northern Sector*. Oxford: B.A.R., 1986.
Macdonald, Michael C.A. "Languages, Scripts, and the Uses of Writing Among the Nabataeans." In *Petra Rediscovered: Lost City of the Nabataeans*, edited by Glenn Markoe, 37–56. New York: Harry N. Abrams, 2003.
Macdonald, Michael C.A. "Literacy in an Oral Environment." In *Writing and Ancient Near Eastern Society: Papers in Honour of Alan R. Millard*, edited by Piotr Bienkowski, Christopher Mee, and Elizabeth Slater, 49–118. New York: T&T Clark, 2005.
Macdonald, Michael C.A. "Personal Names in the Nabataean Realm: A Review Article." *JSS* 44 (1999): 251–89.
Macdonald, Michael C.A. "Reflections on the Linguistic Map of Pre-Islamic Arabia." *Arabian Archaeology and Epigraphy* 11 (2000): 28–79.
Macdonald, Michael C.A. "Some Reflections on Epigraphy and Ethnicity in the Roman Near East." *Mediterranean Archaeology* 11 (1998): 177–90.
Maier, Jean-Louis. *L'Episcopat de l'Afrique romaine, vandale et byzantine*. Neuchâtel: Institut suisse de Rome, 1973.
Malcovati, Henrica, ed. *L. Annaei flori quae extant*. Rome: Libreria dello Stato, 1938.
Marchetti Longhi, Giuseppe. "Scavi del Largo Argentina: il materiale archeologico. I. Le epigrafi." *Bull. Com. Arch.* 71 (1943–45): 57–95.

Marini, Gaetano. *I papyri diplomatici.* Rome, 1805.
Marshall, Anthony J. "Friends of the Roman People." *AJPhil.* 89 (1968): 39–55.
Marshall, Anthony J. "Governors on the Move." *Phoenix* 20 (1966): 231–46.
Marshall, Anthony J. "The Lex Pompeia de provinciis (52 BC) and Cicero's Imperium in 51–50 BC: Constitutional Aspects." In *Aufstieg und Niedergang der römischen Welt*, Vol. I.1, 887–921. Berlin: De Gruyter, 1972.
Marshall, Anthony J. "The Survival and Development of International Jurisdiction in the Greek World under Roman Rule." In *Aufstieg und Niedergang der römischen Welt*, Vol. II.13, 626–61. Berlin: De Gruyter, 1980.
Martino, Francesco De. *Storia della costituzione romana.* Vol. II. Napoli: E. Jovene, 1973.
Mason, Hugh J. *Greek Terms for Roman Institutions.* Toronto: Hakkert, 1974.
Matthews, Kenneth D., Jr. "Domitian: The Lost Divinity." *Expedition Magazine* 8 (1966): 30–36.
Mayerson, Philip. *Monks, Martyrs, Soldiers and Saracens. Papers on the Near East in Late Antiquity (1962–1993).* Jerusalem: IES, 1994.
Mayerson, Philip. "Nea Arabia (P.Oxy. 3574): An Addendum to ZPE 53." *ZPE* 64 (1986): 139–40.
Mayerson, Philip. "P.Oxy. 3574: 'Eleutheropolis of the New Arabia.'" *ZPE* 53 (1983): 251–58.
Mayerson, Philip. "'Palaestina' vs. 'Arabia' in the Byzantine Sources." *ZPE* 56 (1984): 223–30.
Mayor, John E.B., ed. *Thirteen Satires of Juvenal.* London: Macmillan, 1872–78.
Mazar, Benjamin, Trude Dothan, and Immanuel Dunayevsky. *En-Gedi: The First and Second Seasons of Excavations, 1961–1962.* Atiqot 5, 1966.
Mazar, Benjamin, and Immanuel Dunayevsky. "En-Gedi: Fourth and Fifth Seasons of Excavations: Preliminary Report." *IEJ* 17 (1967): 133–43.
Mazar, Benjamin, and Immanuel Dunayevsky. "En-Gedi: Third Season of Excavations: Preliminary Report." *IEJ* 14 (1964): 121–30.
Meerson, Michael. "Illegitimate Jesus: Family Matters with 'Toledot Yeshu.'" In *When West Met East. The Encounter of Greece and Rome with the Jews, Egyptians, and Others. Studies Presented to Ranon Katzoff in Honor of his 75th Birthday*, 91–114. Trieste: Edizioni Università di Trieste, 2016.
Melaerts, Henri, and Leon Mooren, eds. *Le rôle et le statut de la femme en Égypte hellénistique, romaine et byzantine: actes du colloque international, Bruxelles-Leuven 27–29 novembre 1997.* Leuven: Peeters, 2002.
Merlin, Alfred. *Inscriptions latines de la Tunisie.* Paris: Presses Universitaires de France, 1944.
Meyer, Elizabeth. "Diplomatics, Law and Romanisation in the Documents from the Judaean Desert." In *Beyond Dogmatics: Law and Society in the Roman World*, edited by John W. Cairns and Paul J. du Plessis, 53–82. Edinburgh: Edinburgh University Press, 2007.
Meyer, Elizabeth. *Legitimacy and Law in the Roman World.* Cambridge: Cambridge University Press, 2004.
Mildenberg, Leo. "A Bar Kokhba Didrachm." *INJ* 8 (1984–85): 33–36.
Mildenberg, Leo. "Bar Kochba in Jerusalem?" *Schweizer Münzblätter* 27 (1977): 1–6.
Milik, J.T. "Le travail d'édition des manuscrits du Désert de Juda." In *Volume du Congrès International pour l'étude de l'Ancien Testament, Strasbourg 1956*, 17–26. Leiden: Brill, 1957.
Millar, Fergus. *A Study of Cassius Dio.* Oxford: Clarendon Press, 1964.
Millar, Fergus. "Dura-Europos under Parthian Rule." In *Das Partherreich und seine Zeugnisse*, edited by Josef Wiesehöfer, 473–92. Stuttgart: F. Steiner, 1988.
Millar, Fergus. "Empire, Community and Culture in the Roman Near East: Greeks, Syrians, Jews and Arabs." *JJS* 38 (1987): 143–64.

Millar, Fergus. "Epigraphy." In *Sources for Ancient History*, edited by Michael Crawford, 80–136. Cambridge: Cambridge University Press, 1983.
Millar, Fergus. "Ethnic Identity in the Roman Near East, AD 325–450: Language, Religion and Culture." *Mediterranean Archaeology* 11 (1998): 159–76.
Millar, Fergus. "Introduction: Documentary Evidence, Social Realities and the History of Language." In *From Hellenism to Islam: Cultural and Linguistic Change in The Roman Near East*, edited by Hannah M. Cotton, Robert G. Hoyland, Jonathan J. Price, and David J. Wasserstein, 1–12. Cambridge: Cambridge University Press, 2009.
Millar, Fergus. "Last Year in Jerusalem: Monuments of the Jewish War in Rome." In *Flavius Josephus and Flavian Rome*, edited by Jonathan Edmondson, Steve Mason, and James Rives, 101–28. Oxford: Oxford University Press, 2005.
Millar, Fergus. "Latin in the Epigraphy of the Roman Near East." In *Acta Colloquii Epigraphici Latini*, edited by Heikki Solin, Olli Salomies, and Uta-Maria Liertz, 403–19. Helsinki: Societas Scientiarum Fennica, 1995.
Millar, Fergus. "Reflections on the Trial of Jesus." In *A Tribute to Geza Vermes: Essays on Jewish and Christian Literature and History*, edited by Philip R. Davies and Richard T. White, 355–81. Sheffield: JSOT Press, 1990.
Millar, Fergus. *Rome, the Greek World, and the East: Volume 1: The Roman Republic and the Augustan Revolution*. Edited by Hannah M. Cotton and Guy M. Rogers. Chapel Hill: University of North Carolina Press, 2002.
Millar, Fergus. *Rome, the Greek World, and the East: Volume 2: Government, Society, and Culture in the Roman Empire*. Edited by Hannah M. Cotton and Guy M. Rogers. Chapel Hill: University of North Carolina Press, 2004.
Millar, Fergus. *Rome, the Greek World, and the East: Volume 3: The Greek World, the Jews and the East*. Edited by Hannah M. Cotton and Guy M. Rogers. Chapel Hill: University of North Carolina Press, 2006.
Millar, Fergus. "'Senatorial' Provinces: An Institutionalized Ghost." *Ancient World* 20 (1989): 93–97.
Millar, Fergus. "State and Subject: the Impact of Monarchy." In *Caesar Augustus: Seven Aspects*, edited by Fergus Millar and Erich Segal, 37–60. Oxford: Clarendon Press, 1984.
Millar, Fergus. "The Emperor, the Senate and the Provinces." *JRS* 56 (1966): 156–66.
Millar, Fergus. *The Emperor in the Roman World*. London: Duckworth, 1977.
Millar, Fergus. "The Fiscus in the First Two Centuries." *JRS* 53 (1963): 29–42.
Millar, Fergus. "The Greek East and Roman Law: The Dossier of M. Cn. Licinius Rufinus." *JRS* 89 (1999): 90–108.
Millar, Fergus. "The Problem of Hellenistic Syria." In *Hellenism in the East*, edited by Amélie Kuhrt and Susan Sherwin-White, 110–33. London: Duckworth, 1987.
Millar, Fergus. "The Roman Coloniae of the Near East: A Study of Cultural Relations." In *Roman Eastern Policy and other Studies in Roman History*, edited by Heikki Solin and Mika Kajava, 7–58. Helsinki: Finnish Society of Sciences and Letters, 1990.
Millar, Fergus. *The Roman Near East, 31 BC-AD 337*. Cambridge, Mass.: Harvard University Press, 1993.
Miller, A.B. "Roman Etiquette of the Late Republic as Revealed by the Correspondence of Cicero." University of Pennsylvania Thesis, 1914.
Misgav, Haggai. "Jewish Courts of Law as Reflected in the Documents from the Dead Sea." *Cathedra* 82 (1996): 17–24 (Hebrew).

Misgav, Haggai. "Jewish Epigraphic Sources and the Traditions Reflected in Talmudic Literature." The Hebrew University of Jerusalem Thesis, 1999 (Hebrew).
Mitchell, Stephen. *Anatolia: Land, Men, and Gods in Asia Minor*. Vol. I. Oxford: Clarendon Press, 1993.
Mitchell, Stephen. "R.E.C.A.M. Notes and Studies No. 1: Inscriptions of Ancyra." *Anatolian Studies* 27 (1977): 63–103.
Mitchell, Stephen. "The Plancii in Asia Minor." *JRS* 64 (1974): 27–39.
Mitchell, Stephen. "The Treaty between Rome and Lycia of 46 BC." In *Papyri Graecae Schøyen (Papyrologica Florentina XXXV)*, edited by Rosario Pintaudi, 163–258. Florence: Edizioni Gonnelli, 2005.
Mittmann, Siegfried. "The Ascent of Luhith." *Studies in the History and Archaeology of Jordan* 1 (1982): 175–80.
Modrzejewski, Joseph. "La Règle de droit dans l'Egypte ptolémaïque." In *Essays in Honor of C. Bradford Welles*, 125–73. New Haven: American Society of Papyrologists, 1966.
Modrzejewski, Joseph. "La règle de droit dans l'Egypte romaine." In *Proceedings of the Twelfth International Congress of Papyrology, Ann Arbor, Michigan, 12–17 August 1968*, edited by Deborah H. Samuel, 317–77. Toronto: Hakkert, 1970.
Modrzejewski, Joseph. "Les juifs et le droit hellénistique: Divorce et égalité des époux (CP Jud. 144)." *Iura* 12 (1961): 162–93.
Modrzejewski, Joseph. "Note sur P. Strasb. 237." In *Symbolae Raphaeli Taubenschlag Dedicatae III*, 139–154. Vratislaviae-Varsaviae: Ossolineum, 1957.
Modrzejewski, Joseph. "Jewish Law and Hellenistic Legal Practice in the Light of Greek Papyri from Egypt." In *An Introduction to the History and Sources of Jewish Law*, edited by N.S. Hecht, B.S. Jackson, S.M. Passamaneck, Daniela Piattelli, and Alfredo Rabello, 75–99. Oxford: Clarendon Press, 1996.
Mommsen, Theodor. "Epigraphische Analekten: 18–28." *Ber. Sächs. Ges. Wiss.* 4 (1852): 188–282.
Mommsen, Theodor. *Gesammelte Schriften*. Vol. VIII. Berlin: Weidmann, 1913.
Mommsen, Theodor. *Römische Geschichte*. Vol. II. Leipzig: Weidmannsche Buchhandlung, 1855.
Mommsen, Theodor. *Römisches Staatsrecht*. Graz: Akademische Druck- u. Verlagsanstalt, 1952.
Mommsen, Theodor. *Römisches Strafrecht*. Leipzig: Duncker & Humblot, 1899.
Montevecchi, Orsolina. *La Papirologia*. Torino: Societe editrice internazionale, 1973.
Montevecchi, Orsolina. "Una donna 'prostatis' del figlio minorenne in un papiro del IIa." *Aegyptus* 61 (1981): 103–15.
Mor, Menachem. *The Bar-Kochba Revolt: Its Extent and Effect*. Jerusalem: Yad Ben-Zvi Press, 1991 (Hebrew).
Morris, J.H.C. *The Conflict of Laws*. 3rd ed. London: Stevens & Sons, 1984.
Muffs, Yochanan. *Studies in the Aramaic Legal Papyri from Elephantine*. Leiden: Brill, 1969.
Muhs, Brian. "The Grapheion and the Disappearance of Demotic Contracts in Early Roman Tebtynis and Soknopaiou Neso." In *Tebtynis und Soknopaiu Nesos. Leben im römerzeitlichen Fajum*, edited by Sandra Lippert and Maren Schentuleit, 93–104. Wiesbaden: Harrasowitz, 2005.
Musil, Alois. *Arabia Petraea I: Moab*. Wien: A. Hölder, 1907.
Mussies, Gerard. "Jewish Personal Names in Some Non-Literary Sources." In *Studies in Early Jewish Epigraphy*, edited by Pieter W. van der Horst and Jan Willem van Henten, 242–76. Leiden: Brill, 1994.

Nasti, Fara. "Un nuovo documento dalla Siria sulle competenze di governatori e procuratori provinciali in tema di interdetti." *Index* 21 (1993): 365–80.

Naveh, Joseph. *On Sherd and Papyrus*. Jerusalem: Magnes Press, 1992 (Hebrew).

Naveh, Joseph. *The History of Ein Gedi in light of the Archaeological Survey*. Ein Gedi: Ein Gedi Field School, 1966 (Hebrew).

Naveh, Joseph, and Jonas C. Greenfield. "Hebrew and Aramaic in the Persian Period." In *The Cambridge History of Judaism, Volume 1: Introduction: The Persian Period*, 115–29. Cambridge: Cambridge University Press, 1984.

Naveh, Joseph, and Shaul Shaked. *Aramaic Documents from Ancient Bactria*. London: The Khalili Family Trust, 2012.

Nebe, G. Wilhelm. "Die beiden griechischen Briefe des Jonatan Archivs in Engedi aus dem zweiten jüdischen Aufstand 132–135 nach Chr." *Revue de Qumran* 17 (1996): 275–89.

Neesen, Lutz. *Untersuchungen zu den direkten Staatsabgaben der römischen Kaiserzeit 27 v. Chr. bis 284 n. Chr.* Bonn: Habelt, 1980.

Negev, Avraham. *The Inscriptions of Wadi Haggag, Sinai*. Qedem Reports 6. Jerusalem: Institute of Archaeology, Hebrew University of Jerusalem, 1977.

Nehmé, Laïla, and Ahmad Al-Jallad, eds. *To the Madbar and Back Again: Studies in the Languages, Archaeology, and Cultures of Arabia Dedicated to Michael C.A. Macdonald*. Leiden: Brill, 2018.

Nelson Glueck. "Explorations in Eastern Palestine II." *Annual of the American Schools of Oriental Research* 15 (1934).

Nelson, H.L.W., and Ulrich Manthe. *Gai Institutiones III 88–181. Die Kontraktsobligationen: Text und Kommentar*. Berlin: Duncker & Humblot, 1999.

Nesselhauf, Herbert. "Zwei Bronzeurkunden aus Munigua." *Madrider Mitteilungen* 1 (1960): 148–54.

Netzer, Ehud. "The Rebels' Archives at Masada." *IEJ* 54 (2004): 218–29.

Newman, Hillel. "Old and New in the Documentary Papyri from the Bar Kokhba Period." *SCI* 23 (2004): 247–51.

Nicolet, Claude. "Control of the Human Sphere: the Census." In *Space, Geography, and Politics in the Early Roman Empire*, 123–47. Ann Arbor: University of Michigan Press, 1991.

Nicolet, Claude. *L'ordre équestre à l'époque républicaine (312–43 av. J.-C.)*. 2 Vols. Paris: E. De Boccard, 1966–74.

Nisbet, R.G.M., and Margaret Hubbard. *A Commentary on Horace: Odes, Book I*. Oxford: Clarendon Press, 1970.

Noam, Vered. "The Seventeenth of Elul in Megillat Ta'anit." *Zion* 59 (1994): 433–44 (Hebrew).

Norden, Eduard. *Agnostos Theos: Untersuchungen zur Formengeschichte religiöeser Rede*. Leipzig: Teubner, 1913.

Nörr, Dieter. "Prozessuales aus dem Babatha-Archiv." In *Mélanges de droit romain et d'histoire ancienne: hommage à la mémoire de André Magdelain*, edited by Michel Humbert and Yan Thomas, 317–41. Paris: Panthéon-Assas, 1998.

Nörr, Dieter. "Römisches Zivilprozeßrecht nach Max Kaser: Prozeßrecht und Prozeßpraxis in der Provinz Arabia." *ZSS* 115 (1998): 80–98.

Nörr, Dieter. "The Xenokritai in Babatha's Archive (Pap. Yadin 28–30)." *Israel Law Review* 29 (1995): 83–94.

Nörr, Dieter. "Zu den Xenokriten (Rekuperatoren) in der römischen Provinzialgerichtsbarkeit." In *Lokale Autonomie und römische Ordnungsmacht in den kaiserzeitlichen Provinzen vom 1. bis 3. Jahrhundert*, edited by Werner Eck, 257–301. München: Oldenbourg, 1999.

Nörr, Dieter. "Zur condemnatio cum taxatione im römischen Zivilprozeß." *ZSS* 112 (1995): 51–90.

North, Helen. *Sophrosyne: Self-Knowledge and Self-Restraint in Greek Literature*. Ithaca: Cornell University Press, 1966.

Obbink, Dirk. "Bilingual Literacy and Syrian Greek." *BASP* 28 (1991): 51–58.

Oertel, Friedrich. *Die Liturgie: Studien zur Ptolemäischen und Kaiserlichen Verwaltung Aegyptens*. Leipzig: Teubner, 1917.

Oliver, James H. *Greek Constitutions of Early Roman Emperors from Inscriptions and Papyri*. Philadelphia: American Philosophical Society, 1989.

Oliver, James H. "Text of the Tabula Banasitana, AD 177." *AJPhil.* 93 (1972): 336–40.

Oppenheimer, Aharon. "Jewish Penal Authority in Roman Judaea." In *Jews in a Greco-Roman World*, edited by Martin Goodman, 181–91. Oxford: Oxford University Press, 1998.

Oppenheimer, Aharon. "Urbanization and City Territories in Roman Palestine." In *The Jews in the Hellenistic-Roman World: Studies in Memory of Menahem Stern*, edited by Isaiah M. Gafni, Aharon Oppenheimer, and Daniel R. Schwartz, 209–26. Jerusalem: Zalman Shazar Center, 1996 (Hebrew).

Oudshoorn, Jacobine G. "Obtemperare legibus nostris Traianus conpulit imperator? The Relationship between Roman and Local Law in the Babatha and Salome Komaise Archives." University of Groningen Thesis, 2005.

Oudshoorn, Jacobine G. *The Relationship between Roman and Local Law in the Babatha and Salome Komaise Archives: General Analysis and Three Case Studies on Law of Succession, Guardianship and Marriage*. Leiden: Brill, 2007.

Palme, Bernhard. "Die ägyptische κατ' οἰκίαν ἀπογραφή und Lk 2,1–5." *Protokolle zur Bibel* 2 (1993): 1–24.

Palme, Bernhard. "Neues zum ägyptischen Provinzialzensus. Ein Nachtrag zum Artikel PzB 2 (1993) 1–24." *Protokolle zur Bibel* 3 (1994): 1–7.

Parássoglou, George M. *Imperial Estates in Roman Egypt*. Amsterdam: Hakkert, 1978.

Patrich, Joseph. "Agricultural Development in Antiquity: Improvements in the Cultivation and Production of the Balsam." In *Hikrei Eretz: Studies in the History of the Land of Israel Dedicated to Prof. Yehuda Felix*, edited by Ze'ev Safrai, Yvonne Friedman, and Joshua Schwartz, 139–48. Ramat-Gan: Bar-Ilan University Press, 1997 (Hebrew).

Patrich, Joseph, and David Amit, eds. *New studies in the Archaeology of Jerusalem and its Region*. Vol. I. Jerusalem: IAA, 2007.

Pestman, P.W. *Marriage and Matrimonial Property in Ancient Egypt*. Leiden: Brill, 1961.

Pflaum, Hans-Georg. *Le marbre de Thorigny*. Paris: H. Champion, 1948.

Pflaum, Hans-Georg. "Légats impériaux à l'intérieur des provinces sénatoriales." In *Hommages à Albert Grenier*, edited by Marcel Renard, 1232–42. Bruxelles: Peeters, 1962.

Pflaum, Hans-Georg. *Les carrières procuratoriennes équestres sous le haut-empire romain*. Paris: P. Geuthner, 1960.

Pflaum, Hans-Georg. "Remarques sur le changement de statut administratif de la province de Judée: À propos d'une inscription récémment découverte a Sidé de Pamphylie." *IEJ* 19 (1969): 225–33.

Pitt-Rivers, J.A. *The people of the Sierra*. London: Weidenfeld and Nicolson, 1954.

Plasberg, Otto. *Cicero in seinen Werken und Briefen*. Leipzig: Dieterich, 1926.

Polotsky, Hans Jakob. "The Greek Papyri from the Cave of Letters." *IEJ* 12 (1962): 258–62.

Polotsky, Hans Jakob. "Three Greek Documents from the Family Archive of Babatha." *Eretz Israel* 8 (1967): 46–51 (Hebrew).

Préaux, Claire. "Déclarations de propriété foncière dans l'Égypte romaine." *Chronique d'Egypte* 10 (1935): 393–96.
Préaux, Claire. "Le statut de la femme à l'époque hellenistique principalement en Égypte." *Recueils de la Société Jean Bodin* 11 (1959): 127–75.
Préaux, Claire. "Une source nouvelle sur l'annexion de l'Arabie par Trajan : les papyrus de Michigan 465 et 466." *Phoibos* 5 (1950): 123–39.
Preisigke, Friedrich. *Wörterbuch der griechischen Papyrusurkunden*. Berlin: Erben, 1925.
Premerstein, Anton von. "Die Offizierslaufbahn eines kleinasiatischen Ritters." *JÖAI* 13 (1910): 200–209.
Premerstein, Anton von. *Vom Werden und Wesen des Prinzipats*. München: Beck, 1937.
Price, Jonathan J. *Jerusalem under Siege: The Collapse of the Jewish State 66–70 CE*. Leiden: Brill, 1992.
Price, Jonathan J., and Shlomo Naeh. "On the Margins of Culture: The Practice of Transcription in the Ancient World." In *From Hellenism to Islam: Cultural and Linguistic Change in the Roman Near East*, edited by Hannah M. Cotton, Robert G. Hoyland, Jonathan J. Price, and David J. Wasserstein, 257–88. Cambridge: Cambridge University Press, 2009.
Priest, Nancy E. "A Loan of Money with Some Notes on the Ala Mauretana." *ZPE* 51 (1983): 65–70.
Pucci Ben Zeev, Miriam. *Jewish Rights in the Roman World*. Tübingen: Mohr Siebeck, 1998.
Puech, Émile. "Présence arabe dans les manuscrits de 'la grotte aux lettres' du Wadi Khabra." In *Présence arabe dans le croissant fertile avant l'Hégire. Actes de la Table ronde internationale organisée par l'Unité de recherche associée 1062 du CNRS, Études sémitiques au Collège de France, le 13 novembre 1993*, edited by Hélène Lozachmeur, 37–46. Paris: Éditions Recherche sur les Civilisations, 1995.
Pugliese, Giovanni. *Il processo civile romano*. Vol. II. Milano: Giuffre, 1963.
Pugliese, Giovanni. "La preuve dans le proces romain de l'epoque classique." In *La preuve. Première partie: Antiquité*, I:277–348. Brussels: Librairie encyclopédique, 1964.
Purpura, Gianfranco. "Gli editti dei prefetti d'Egitto, I sec. a.C. – I sec. d.C." *Annali del seminario giuridico del Università di Palermo* 42 (1992): 487–671.
Quarles, Charles. "Review: Jesus as Mamzer: A Response to Bruce Chilton's Reconstruction of the Circumstances Surrounding Jesus' Birth in Rabbi Jesus." *Bulletin for Biblical Research* 14 (2004): 243–55.
Rabel, Ernst, and Wilhelm Spiegelberg, eds. *Papyrusurkunden der Öffentlichen Bibliothek der Universität zu Basel*. Berlin, 1917.
Raggi, Andrea. "Senatus consultum de Asclepiade Clazomenio sociisque." *ZPE* 135 (2001): 73–116.
Rajak, Tessa. "Jewish Rights in the Greek Cities under Roman Rule: A New Approach." In *Approaches to Ancient Judaism, V: Studies in Judaism and Its Greco-Roman Context*, edited by W.S. Green, 19–36. Atlanta: Scholars Press, 1985.
Rajak, Tessa. "Was There a Roman Charter for the Jews?" *JRS* 74 (1984): 107–23.
Ramage, Edwin S. *Urbanitas: Ancient Sophistication and Refinement*. Norman, Oklahoma: University of Oklahoma Press, 1973.
Rathbone, Dominic. "Egypt, Augustus and Roman Taxation." *Cahiers du Centre Gustave Glotz* 4 (1993): 81–112.
Rathbone, Dominic. "PSI XI 1183: A Record of a Roman Census Declaration of AD 47/8." In *Essays and Texts in Honor of J. David Thomas*, edited by Traianos Gagos and Roger S. Bagnall, 99–113. Cincinnati: American Society of Papyrologists, 2001.

Rawson, Elizabeth. "Review: Shackleton Bailey Ad Fam." *CR* 29 (1979): 49–51.
Rawson, Elizabeth. "The Eastern Clientelae of Clodius and the Claudii." *Historia:* 22 (1973): 219–39.
Rea, J.R. "Masada and Pompeii: Another Link." *SCI* 18 (1999): 121–24.
Rea, J.R. "Ordinatus." *ZPE* 38 (1980): 217–19.
Rea, J.R. "The Legio II Traiana in Judaea?" *ZPE* 38 (1980): 220–21.
Rea, J.R. *The Oxyrhynchus Papyri.* Vol. 46. London: Egypt Exploration Society, 1978.
Rea, J.R. *The Oxyrhynchus Papyri.* Vol. 58. London: Egypt Exploration Society, 1991.
Reed, Stephen A., revised and edited by Marilyn J. Lundberg, with the collaboration of Michael B. Phelps. *The Dead Sea Scrolls Catalogue: Documents, Photographs, and Museum Inventory Numbers.* Atlanta: Scholars Press, 1994.
Reinitz, Y.K. "Appointment of a Woman as a Guardian." *Bar-Ilan Law Studies* 4 (1985): 167–203 (Hebrew).
Reinitz, Y.K. "Guardianship by Virtue of 'Orphans Boarding with the Householder.'" *Bar-Ilan Law Studies* 1 (1980): 219–50 (Hebrew).
Reinitz, Y.K. "The Guardian of Orphans in Jewish Law: His Responsibility, Methods of Supervision." Hebrew University of Jerusaelm Thesis, 1984 (Hebrew).
Rémy, Bernard. *Les carrières sénatoriales dans les provinces romaines d'Anatolie au Haut-Empire.* Istanbul – Paris: Institut Français d'Études Anatoliennes, 1989.
Restö, Jan. *The Arabs in Antiquity.* London: Routledge, 2003.
Reynolds, Joyce. *Aphrodisias and Rome.* London: Society for the Promotion of Roman Studies, 1982.
Riccobono, Salvatore, ed. *Fontes Iuris Romani AnteIustiniani.* Vol. I. Florence: Barbèra, 1941.
Richardson, J.S. "The Reception of Roman Law in the West: The Epigraphic Evidence." In *Pouvoir et Imperium,* edited by Ella Hermon, 65–75. Naples: Jovene, 1996.
Richardson, J.S. "The Tabula Contrebiensis: Roman Law in Spain in the Early First Century B.C." *JRS* 73 (1983): 33–41.
Richter, Tonio Sebastian. "Greek, Coptic and the 'Language of the Hijra': The Rise and Decline of the Coptic Language in Late Antique and Medieval Egypt." In *From Hellenism to Islam: Cultural and Linguistic Change in The Roman Near East,* edited by Hannah M. Cotton, Robert G. Hoyland, Jonathan J. Price, and David J. Wasserstein, 401–46. Cambridge: Cambridge University Press, 2009.
Richter, Tonio Sebastian. *Rechtsemantik und forensische Rhetorik.* 2nd Ed. Wiesbaden: Harrasowitz, 2008.
Richter, Tonio Sebastian. *Rechtssemantik und forensische Rhetorik.* Leipzig: Wodtke & Stegbauer, 2002.
Ritterling, Emil. "Legio." In *RE,* Vol. XII.1., 1186–1328, 1924.
Ritterling, Emil. "Legio." In *RE,* Vol. XII.2., 1329–1829, 1925.
Ritterling, Emil. "Zur Geschichte der leg. II Traiana unter Traian." *Rheinisches Museum für Philologie* 58 (1903): 476–80.
Robert, Jeanne, and Louis Robert. *Claros I: Décrets hellénistiques.* Paris: Éditions Recherche sur les Civilisations, 1989.
Robert, Louis. *Études anatoliennes.* Paris: de Boccard, 1937.
Robertson, Anne S. *Roman Imperial Coins in the Hunter Coin Cabinet, University of Glasgow, Vol. II: Trajan to Commodus.* London: Oxford University Press, 1971.
Rodger, Alan. "Jurisdictional Limits in the Lex Irnitana and the Lex de Gallia Cisalpina." *ZPE* 110 (1996): 189–206.

Rodger, Alan. "The Jurisdiction of Local Magistrates: Chapter 84 of the Lex Irnitana." *ZPE* 84 (1990): 147–61.
Roebuck, Derek. *Ancient Greek Arbitration*. Oxford: Holo Books, 2001.
Rosén, Haiim. "Die Sprachsituation im römischen Palästina." In *Die Sprachen im römischen Reich der Kaiserzeit*, edited by Günter Neumann and Jürgen Untermann, 215–39. Köln: Rheinland-Verlag, 1980.
Rosen, Klaus. "Jesu Geburtsdatum, der Census des Quirinius und eine jüdische Steuererklärung aus dem Jahr 127 nC." *Jahrbuch für Antike und Christentum* 38 (1995): 5–15.
Rosenberger, Meir. *The Coinage of Eastern Palestine and Legionary Countermarks, Bar-Kochba Overstrucks*. Jerusalem: M. Rosenberger, 1978.
Roth-Gerson, Leah. "The Civil and Religious Status of the Jews in Asia Minor from Alexander the Great to Constantine BC 336 – AD 337." Hebrew University of Jerusalem Thesis, 1972 (Hebrew).
Roth, Jonathan. "Review: Nachman Ben-Yehuda, The Masada Myth: Collective Memory and Mythmaking in Israel." *SCI* 17 (1998): 252–55.
Roth, Jonathan. "The Length of the Siege of Masada." *SCI* 14 (1995): 87–110.
Rowe, Gregory. "Trimalchio's World." *SCI* 20 (2001): 225–45.
Rowlandson, Jane. *Landowners and Tenants in Roman Egypt*. Oxford: Oxford University Press, 1996.
Roxan, Margaret M. *Roman Military Diplomas 1954 to 1977*. London: Routledge, 1978.
Rupprecht, Hans-Albert. "Ein Münchner Papyrus zum Provinzial-Zensus." In *Bayern und die Antike. 150 Jahre Maximilians-Gymnasium in München*, edited by Wolf-Arnim Frhr. V. Reitzenstein, 262–71. München: Beck, 1999.
Rupprecht, Hans-Albert. "Marriage Contract Regulations and Documentary Practice in the Greek Papyri." *SCI* 17 (1998): 60–76.
Rupprecht, Hans-Albert. *Studien zur Quittung im Recht der graeco-ägyptischen Papyri*. München: Beck, 1971.
Rupprecht, Hans-Albert. "Zur Frage der Frauentutel im römischen Ägypten." In *Festschrift für Arnold Kränzlein: Beiträge zur antiken Rechtsgeschichte*, edited by Gunter Wesener, 95–102. Graz: Leykam, 1986.
Russell, James. "A Roman Military Diploma from Rough Cilicia." *Bonner Jahrbücher* 195 (1995): 67–133.
Russi, Angelo. "Contributo al CIL, XVII: i miliari della via Traiana presso Aecae (Troia)." *Epigraphica* 43 (1981): 103–14.
Safrai, Ze'ev. *The Jewish Community in the Talmudic Period*. Jerusalem: Zalman Shazar Center, 1995 (Hebrew).
Safrai, Ze'ev. "The Village in the Time of the Mishnah and the Talmud." In *Nation and History: Studies in the History of the Jewish People*, edited by Menahem Stern, 173–95. Jerusalem: Zalman Shazar Center, 1983 (Hebrew).
Salway, Benet. "Fragment of Severan History: The Unusual Career of ...atus, Praetorian Prefect of Elagabalus." *Chiron* 27 (1997): 127–53.
Sanders, Henry Arthur. "Papyrus 1804 in the Michigan Collection." In *Classical Studies in Honor of John C. Rolfe*, edited by George Depue Hadzsits, 265–83. Philadelphia: University of Pennsylvania Press, 1931.
Sartre, Maurice. *Bostra: des origines à l'Islam*. Paris: Geuthner, 1985.
Sartre, Maurice. *Inscriptions de la Jordanie IV: Pétra et la Nabatène méridionale, du wadi al-Hasa au golfe de 'Aqaba*. IGLS XXI. Paris: P. Geuthner, 1993.

Sartre, Maurice. "Les Metrokomiai de Syrie du Sud." *Syria* 76 (1999): 197–222.
Sartre, Maurice. "Note sur la première légion stationnee en Arabie romaine." *ZPE* 13 (1974): 85–89.
Satlow, Michael. *Jewish Marriage in Antiquity*. Princeton: Princeton University Press, 2001.
Satlow, Michael. "Reconsidering the Jewish Ketubah Payment." In *The Jewish Family in Antiquity*, edited by Shaye J.D. Cohen, 133–52. Atlanta: Scholars Press, 1993.
Sauter, Franz. *Der römische Kaiserkult bei Martial und Statius*. Stuttgart – Berlin: Kohlhammer, 1934.
Savignac, Antoine-Raphael, and Jean Starcky. "Une inscription nabatéenne provenant du Djôf." *RB* 64 (1957): 196–215.
Schaberg, Jane. *The Illegitimacy of Jesus: A Feminist Theological Interpretation of the Infancy Narratives*. San Francisco: Harper & Row, 1987.
Schäfer, Jörg, ed. *Phaselis: Beiträge zur Topographie und Geschichte der Stadt und ihrer Häfen*. Tübingen: Wasmuth, 1981.
Schäfer, Peter. *Der Bar Kokhba-Aufstand*. Tübingen: Mohr Siebeck, 1981.
Schäfer, Peter. "Bar Kokhba and the Rabbis." In *The Bar Kokhba War Reconsidered*, edited by Peter Schäfer, 1–22. Tübingen: Mohr Siebeck, 2003.
Schäfer, Peter, ed. *The Bar Kokhba War Reconsidered*. Tübingen: Mohr Siebeck, 2003.
Schäfer, Peter, Michael Meerson, and Yaacov Deutsch, eds. *Toledot Yeshu ('The Life Story of Jesus') Revisited*. Tübingen: Mohr Siebeck, 2011.
Schäfer, Thomas. *Imperii insignia. Sella curulis und Fasces: zur Repräsentation römischer Magistrate*. Mainz: Philipp von Zabern, 1989.
Schalit, Abraham. "Alexander Yannai's Conquests in Moab." *Eretz Israel* 1 (1951): 104–21 (Hebrew).
Schalit, Abraham. "Die Eroberungen des Alexander Jannäus in Moab." *Theokratia: Jahrbuch des Institutum Judaicum Delitzschianum* 1 (1970): 3–50.
Schalit, Abraham. *King Herod: Portrait of a Ruler*. Jerusalem: Mosad Bialik, 1960 (Hebrew).
Schalit, Abraham. *The Roman Administration in Palestine*. Jerusalem: Mosad Bialik, 1937 (Hebrew).
Schiffman, Lawrence H., ed. *Semitic Papyrology in Context: A Climate of Creativity*. Leiden – Boston: Brill, 2003.
Schiffman, Lawrence H. "Witnesses and Signatures in the Hebrew and Aramaic documents from the Bar Kokhba Caves." In *Semitic Papyrology in Context: A Climate of Creativity*, edited by Lawrence H. Schiffman, 165–86. Leiden – Boston: Brill, 2003.
Schiffman, Lawrence H., and James Vanderkam, eds. *Encyclopedia of the Dead Sea Scrolls*. New York: Oxford University Press, 2000.
Schiller, Arthur A. "Coptic Documents: A Monograph on the Law of the Coptic Documents and a Survey of Coptic Legal Studies 1938–1956." *ZVglRWiss* 60 (1957): 190–211.
Schillinger-Häfele, Ute. "Der Urheber der Tafel von Banasa." *Chiron* 7 (1977): 323–31.
Schönbauer, Ernst. "Zur Entwicklung des 'ius publice respondendi.'" *Iura* 4 (1953): 224–27.
Schottroff, Willy. "Horonaim, Nimrim, Luhith und der Westrand des 'Landes Ataroth': Ein Beitrag zur historischen Topographie des Landes Moab." *ZDPV* 82 (1966): 163–208.
Schremer, Adiel. "Divorce in Papyrus Ṣe'elim 13 Once Again: A Reply to Tal Ilan." *Harv. Theol. Rev.* 91 (1998): 193–202.
Schremer, Adiel. "How much Jewish Polygyny in Roman Palestine?" *Proceedings of the American Academy for Jewish Research* 63 (1997–2001): 181–223.

Schultz, Fritz. *History of Roman Legal Science*. Oxford: Clarendon Press, 1946.

Schultz, Fritz. *Principles of Roman Law*. Oxford: Clarendon Press, 1936.

Schumacher, Leonhard, and Oliver Stoll, eds. *Sprache und Kultur in der kaiserzeitlichen Provinz Arabia: Althistorische Beiträgezur Erforschung von Akkulturationsphänomenen im römischen Nahen Osten*. St. Katharinen: Scripta Mercaturae Verlag, 2003.

Schürer, Emil. *The History of the Jewish People in the Age of Jesus Christ*. Edited by Fergus Millar and Géza Vermès. Vols. I–II. Edinburgh: Clark, 1973–79.

Schwartz, Daniel R. "Once Again: Who Captured Masada? On Doublets, Reading Against the Grain, and What Josephus Actually Wrote." *SCI* 24 (2005): 75–83.

Schwartz, Jacques. "Remarques sur des fragments grecs du Désert de Juda." *RB* 69 (1962): 61–63.

Schwartz, Seth. "Language, Power and Identity in Ancient Palestine." *Past & Present* 148 (1995): 3–47.

Schwartz, Seth. "The Composition and Publication of Josephus's Bellum Iudaicum Book 7." *Harv. Theol. Rev.* 78 (1986): 373–86.

Schweizer, Eduard. "Scheidungsrecht der jüdischen Frau?: Weibliche Jünger Jesu?" *Evangelische Theologie* 42 (1982): 294–300.

Seidl, Erwin. "Ein Papyrusfund zum klassischen Zivilprozessrecht." In *Studi in onore di Giuseppe Grosso*, Vol. II, 345–61. Torino: Giappichelli, 1968.

Seston, William, and Maurice Euzennat. "Un dossier de la chancellerie romaine, la Tabula Banasitana: étude de diplomatique." *CR Acad. Inscr.* 115 (1971): 468–90.

Shackleton Bailey, D.R., ed. *Cicero: Epistulae ad familiares*. Cambridge: Cambridge University Press, 1977.

Shackleton Bailey, D.R., ed. *Cicero's Letters to His Friends*. Harmondsworth: Penguin Books, 1978.

Shackleton Bailey, D.R. "Two Tribunes, 57 B. C." *CR* 12 (1962): 195–97.

Shahar, Yuval. "From Jerusalem to 'Orine' – Consequences of the First Revolt in the Vicinity of Jerusalem." In *New Studies on Jerusalem: Proceedings of the Sixth Conference*, edited by Avraham Faust and Eyal Baruch, 187–201. Ramat-Gan: Bar-Ilan University Press, 2000 (Hebrew).

Shahar, Yuval. "Har Hamelekh – A New Solution to an Old Puzzle." *Zion* 65 (2000): 275–306 (Hebrew).

Shahar, Yuval. "Josephus' Geography of Eretz Israel and its Relation to Talmudic Traditions and Hellenistic and Roman Literature." Tel-Aviv University Thesis, 1996 (Hebrew).

Shahar, Yuval. *Josephus Geographicus: The Classical Context of Geography in Josephus*. Tübingen: Mohr Siebeck, 2004.

Shaked, Shaul. *Le satrape de Bactriane et son gouverneur. Documents araméens du IVe s. avant notre ère provenant de Bactriane*. Paris: de Boccard, 2004.

Sharp, Michael. "Shearing Sheep: Rome and the Collection of Taxes in Egypt, 30 BC–AD 200." In *Lokale Autonomie und römische Ordnungsmacht in den kaiserzeitlichen Provinzen vom 1. bis 3. Jahrhundert*, edited by Werner Eck, 213–42. München: Oldenbourg, 1999.

Shatzman, Israel. "The Integration of Judaea into the Roman Empire." *SCI* 18 (1999): 49–84.

Shemesh, Aharon. "4Q271.3: A Key to Sectarian Matrimonial Law." *JJS* 49 (1998): 244–63.

Sherk, Robert K. *Roman Documents from the Greek East*. Baltimore: Johns Hopkins Press, 1969.

Sherwin-White, A.N. *The Letters of Pliny: A Historical and Social Commentary*. Oxford: Clarendon Press, 1966.

Sherwin-White, A.N. *The Roman Citizenship*. Oxford: Clarendon Press, 1973.

Sherwin-White, A.N. “The Tabula of Banasa and the Constitutio Antoniniana.” *JRS* 63 (1973): 86–98.
Shiffman, I.Sh. “To the Character of the Nabataean Private Law according to the Epigraphic Sources.” *Palestinski Sbornik* 11 (1964): 16–24 (Russian).
Sijpesteijn, P.J. “A note on P.Murabbaʿat 29.” *IEJ* 34 (1984): 49–50.
Sijpesteijn, P.J. *Penthemeros-Certificates in Graeco-Roman Egypt*. Leiden: Brill, 1964.
Sirat, Colette, P. Cauderlier, Michèle Dukan, and Mordechai Akiva Friedman. *La Ketouba de Cologne: Un contrat de mariage juif à Antinoopolis*. Opladen: Westdeutscher Verlag, 1986.
Smith, Morton. “Goodenough’s Jewish Symbols in Retrospect.” *Journal of Biblical Literature* 86 (1967): 53–68.
Sokoloff, Michael. *A Dictionary of Jewish Palestinian Aramaic of the Byzantine Period*. Ramat-Gan: Bar-Ilan University Press, 1990.
Sonnet, Paul. “Gaius Trebatius Testa.” University of Giessen Thesis, 1932.
Speidel, Michael Alexander. “Early Roman Rule in Commagene.” *SCI* 24 (2005): 85–100.
Speidel, Michael Alexander. “Ein unbekannter Patronus der Helvetier-Stadt Aventicum: Überlegungen zu CIL XIII 5089.” *MH* 47 (1990): 149–62.
Speidel, Michael P. “A Tile Stamp of Cohors I Thracum Milliaria from Hebron/Palestine.” *ZPE* 35 (1979): 170–72.
Speidel, Michael P. “The Roman Army in Arabia.” In *Aufstieg und Niedergang der römischen Welt*, Vol. II.8, 687–730. Berlin: De Gruyter, 1978.
Sperber, Daniel. *A Dictionary of Greek and Latin Legal Terms in Rabbinic Literature*. Ramat-Gan: Bar-Ilan University Press, 1984.
Starcky, Jean. “Un contrat nabatéen sur papyrus.” *RB* 61 (1954): 161–81.
Stein, Alla. “Studies in Greek and Latin Inscriptions on Palestinian Coinage under the Principate.” Tel-Aviv University Thesis, 1990.
Stein, Arthur. *Die Präfekten von Ägypten in der römischen Kaiserzeit*. Bern: Francke, 1950.
Stern, Menahem. *Greek and Latin Authors on Jews and Judaism*. Vol. I. Jerusalem: Israel Academy of Sciences and Humanities, 1976.
Stern, Menahem. “Josephus and the Roman Empire as Reflected in The Jewish War.” In *Josephus, Judaism, and Christianity*, edited by Louis H. Feldman and Gohei Hata, 71–80. Detroit: Wayne State University Press, 1987.
Stern, Menahem. *Studies in Jewish History. The Second Temple Period*. Edited by Yeshayahu Gafni, Moshe David Herr, and Moshe Amit. Jerusalem: Yad Ben-Zvi Press, 1991 (Hebrew).
Stern, Menahem. “The Description of Palestine by Pliny the Elder and the Administrative Division of Judea at the End of the Period of the Second Temple.” *Tarbiẓ* 37 (1978): 215–29 (Hebrew).
Stern, Menahem. “The Province of Judaea.” In *The Jewish People in the First Century, Volume 1*, edited by Shmuel Safrai and Menahem Stern, 308–376. Assen: Van Gorcum & Comp. B.V., 1974.
Strack, H.L., and Günter Stemberger. *Introduction to the Talmud and Midrash*. Edinburgh: T & T Clark, 1991.
Strack, Paul L. *Untersuchungen zur römischen Reichsprägung des zweiten Jahrhunderts, Vol. II: Die Reichsprägung zur Zeit des Hadrian*. Stuttgart: Kohlhammer, 1933.
Strassi, Silvia. *L’archivio di Claudius Tiberianus da Karanis*. Berlin – New York: De Gruyter, 2008.
Strobel, Karl. “Zu Fragen der frühen Geschichte der römischen Provinz Arabia und zu einigen Problemen der Legionsdislokation im Osten des Imperium Romanum zu Beginn des 2. Jh.n.Chr.” *ZPE* 71 (1988): 251–80.

Stroumsa, Rachel. "Greek and Arabic in Nessana." In *Documents and the History of the Early Islamic World*, edited by Petra Sijpesteijn and Alexander T. Schubert, 143–57. Leiden: Brill, 2015.

Stroumsa, Rachel. "People and Identities in Nessana." Duke University Thesis, 2008.

Suolahti, Jaakko. *The Junior Officers of the Roman Army in the Republican Period*. Helsinki: Suomalainen Tiedeakatemia, 1955.

Syme, Ronald. "C. Vibius Maximus, Prefect of Egypt." *Historia* 6 (1957): 480–87.

Syme, Ronald. "Consulates in Absence." *JRS* 48 (1958): 1–9.

Syme, Ronald. *Danubian Papers*. Bucharest: AIESEE, 1971.

Syme, Ronald. "Legates of Moesia." *Dacia* 12 (1968): 331–40.

Syme, Ronald. "Observations on the Province of Cilicia." In *Anatolian Studies Presented to William Hepburn Buckler*, edited by W.M. Calder and Josef Keil, 299–332. Manchester: Manchester University Press, 1939.

Syme, Ronald. "People in Pliny." *JRS* 58 (1968): 135–51.

Syme, Ronald. "Pliny's Less Successful Friends." *Historia* 9 (1960): 362–79.

Syme, Ronald. "Pliny and the Dacian Wars." *Latomus* 23 (1964): 750–59.

Syme, Ronald. *Roman Papers*. Vols. I & II. Oxford: Oxford University Press, 1979.

Syme, Ronald. *Tacitus*. 2 Vols. Oxford: Clarendon Press, 1958.

Syme, Ronald. "The Jurist Neratius Priscus." *Hermes* 85 (1957): 480–93.

Syme, Ronald. "The Lower Danube under Trajan." *JRS* 49 (1959): 26–33.

Syme, Ronald. *The Roman Revolution*. Oxford: Clarendon Press, 1939.

Tafel, G.L.F., C.N. Osiander, and Gustav Schwab, eds. *Griechische Prosaiker in neuen Uebersetzungen*. Stuttgart: Metzler, 1838.

Taubenschlag, Raphael. "La compétence du kurios dans le droit gréco-égyptien." In *Opera Minora*, Vol. II, 353–77. Warsaw: Panstwowe Wydawn Naukowe, 1959.

Taubenschlag, Raphael. *The Law of Greco-Roman Egypt in the light of the Papyri, 322 BC–640 AD*. Warsaw: Państwowe Wydawnictwo Naukowe, 1955.

Tcherikover, Victor A. *The Jews in Egypt in the Hellenistic-Roman Age in the Light of the Papyri*. Jerusalem: Magnes Press, 1963 (Hebrew).

Teixidor, Javier. "Deux documents syriaques du IIIe siècle ap. J.-C., provenant du Moyen Euphrate." *CR Acad. Inscr.* 134 (1990): 144–66.

Teixidor, Javier. "Un document syriaque de fermage de 242 ap. J.-C." *Semitica* 41 (1993): 195–208.

Teixidor, Javier, Denis Feissel, and Jean Gascou. "Documents d'archives romains inédits du Moyen Euphrate (IIIe s. après J-C): II. Les actes de vente- achat (P. Euphr. 6 À 10)." *Journal des Savants*, 1997, 3–57.

Thomas, John D. "Compulsory Public Service in Roman Egypt." In *Das römischbyzantinische Ägypten*, edited by Günter Grimm, Heinz Heinen, and Erich Winter, 35–40. Mainz: von Zabern, 1983.

Thomasson, B.E. "The One-Legion Provinces of the Roman Empire during the Principate." *Opuscula Romana* 9, no. 7 (1973): 61–66.

Thomasson, Bengt E. *Laterculi praesidum*. Göteborg: Radius, 1984.

Thompson, L.A. "Cicero's Succession-Problem in Cilicia." *AJPhil.* 86 (1965): 375–86.

Thompson, L.A. "The Relationship between Provincial Quaestors and Their Commanders-in-Chief." *Historia* 11 (1962): 339–55.

Thulin, Carl Olof, ed. *Corpus agrimensorum Romanorum I: Opuscula agrimensorum veterum*. Leipzig: Teubner, 1913.

Tjäder, Jan-Olof. *Die nichtliterarischen lateinischen Papyri Italiens aus der Zeit 445–700*. Lund: C.W.K. Gleerup, 1955.
Tomlin, R.S.O. "The Twentieth Legion at Wroxeter and Carlisle in the First Century: The Epigraphic Evidence." *Britannia* 23 (1992): 141–58.
Tóth, Endre. *Porolissum: Das Castellum in Moigrad. Ausgrabungen von a. Radnóti, 1943*. Budapest: Magyar Nemzeti Múzeum, 1978.
Tov, Emanuel, with the collaboration of Stephen J. Pfann. *Companion Volume to the Dead Sea Scrolls on Microfiche Edition*. Leiden: Brill, 1995.
Turner, E.G. "Tiberius Iulius Alexander." *JRS* 44 (1954): 54–64.
Turner, Eric Gardner. *The Hibeh Papyri, Part II*. London: Egypt Exploration Society, 1955.
Tyrrell, Robert Yelverton, and Louis Claude Purser, eds. *The Correspondance of M. Tullius Cicero*. Vol. IV. Dublin: Hodges, Figgis & Co., 1918.
Tzori, Nehemia. "An Inscription of the Legio VI Ferrata from the Northern Jordan Valley." *IEJ* 21 (1971): 53–54.
Urbach, Ephraim E. "The Laws of Idolatry in the Light of Historical and Archaeological Facts in the Third Century." *Eretz Israel* 5 (1958): 189–205 (Hebrew).
Urbach, Ephraim E. *The World of the Sages: Collected Studies*. Jerusalem: Magnes Press, 1988 (Hebrew).
Vaux, Roland de. "Fouille au Khirbet Qumrân." *RB* 60 (1953): 83–106.
Vessey, D.W.T.C. "Varia Statiana." *Classical Bulletin* 46 (1970): 49–55.
Veyne, Paul. "La Table des Ligures Baebiani et l'institution alimentaire de Trajan (2e article)." *MÉFRA* 70 (1958): 177–241.
Veyne, Paul. *Les "Alimenta" de Trajan*. Paris: CNRS, 1965.
Veyne, Paul. "Une hypothèse sur l'arc de Bénévent." *MÉFRA* 72 (1960): 191–219.
Villey, Michel. "L'idée du droit subjectif et les systèmes juridiques romains." *RHDFÉ* 24 (1946–47): 201–28.
Vismara, Novella. *Monetazione provinciale Romana, II: Collezione Winsemann Falghera, 4: Maximinus-Aemilianus*. Milano: Edizioni Ennerre, 1992.
Visscher, Fernand De. "La dualité des droits de cité et la 'Mutatio Civitatis.'" *Bulletin de la Classe des Lettres et des Sciences Morales et Politiques* 40 (1954): 49–67.
Visscher, Fernand De. "Le Statut juridique des nouveaux citoyens romains et l'inscription de Rhosos." *L'Antiquité Classique* 14 (1945): 29–59.
Vollmer, Friedrich, ed. *P. Papinii Statii Silvarum Libri*. Leipzig: Teubner, 1898.
Wacke, Andreas. "Gallisch, Punisch, Syrisch oder Griechisch statt Latein?" *ZSS* 110 (1993): 14–59.
Wageningen, Jacob van. *M. Tulli Ciceronis Oratio pro M. Caelio*. Groningen: Noordhoff, 1908.
Waldstein, Wolfgang. *Untersuchungen zum römischen Begnadigungsrecht: abolitio-indulgentia-venia*. Innsbruck: Universitätsverlag Wagner, 1964.
Wallace-Hadrill, Andrew. "Civilis Princeps: Between Citizen and King." *JRS* 72 (1982): 32–48.
Wallace, Sherman Leroy. *Taxation in Egypt from Augustus to Diocletian*. Princeton: Princeton University Press, 1938.
Wasserstein, Abraham. "A Marriage Contract from the Province of Arabia Nova: Notes on Papyrus Yadin 18." *JQR* 80 (1989): 93–130.
Wasserstein, Abraham. "Non-Hellenized Jews in the Semi-Hellenized East." *SCI* 14 (1995): 111–37.
Wasserstein, Abraham. "Review: Lewis, Yadin and Greenfield, 'Documents from the Cave of Letters.'" *JQR* 84 (1993): 373–77.

Wasserstein, David J. "Why did Arabic Succeed Where Greek Failed? Language Change in the Near East after Muhammad." *SCI* 22 (2003): 257–72.
Wasserstein Fassberg, Celia. "On Time and Place in Choice of Law for Property." *The International and Comparative Law Quarterly* 51 (2002): 385–400.
Watson, Alan. *The Law of Persons in the Later Roman Republic.* Oxford: Oxford University Press, 1967.
Weber, Max. "The Types of Legitimate Domination." In *Economy and Society.* Berkeley: University of California Press, 1978.
Weder, Hans. "Perspektive der Frauen?" *Evangelische Theologie* 43 (1983): 175–78.
Wegener, E.P. "Petition concerning the Dowry of a Widow (P. Berl. Inv. 16.277)." *Mnemosyne* 13 (1947): 302–16.
Welles, C.B., R.O. Fink, and J.F. Gilliam. *The Excavations at Dura-Europos Conducted by Yale University and the French Academy of Inscriptions and Letters, Final Report V, Part I: The Parchments and Papyri.* New Haven: Yale University Press, 1959.
Wenger, Leopold. "Neue Diskussionen zum Problem 'Reichsrecht und Volksrecht.'" In *Mélanges Fernand de Visscher (RIDA III)*, edited by Lucien Caes, Vol. II., 521–50. Bruxelles: Office international de librairie, 1949.
West, Allen Brown. "Latin Inscriptions, 1896–1926." *Corinth* 8 (1931).
White, Peter. "Vibius Maximus, the Friend of Statius." *Historia* 22 (1973): 295–301.
Whittaker, C.R. "Roman Africa: Augustus to Vespasian." In *The Cambridge Ancient History, Volume 10*, edited by Alan K. Bowman, Edward Champlin, and Andrew Lintott, 2nd ed., 586–618. Cambridge: Cambridge University Press, 1996.
Wiegels, Rainer. "'Solum Caesaris' – Zu einer Weihung im römischen Walheim." *Chiron* 19 (1979): 61–102.
Wilkes, J.J. "The Danubian and Balkan Provinces." In *The Cambridge Ancient History, Volume 10*, edited by Alan K. Bowman, Edward Champlin, and Andrew Lintott, 545–85. Cambridge: Cambridge University Press, 1996.
Williams, W. "Formal and Historical Aspects of Two New Documents of Marcus Aurelius." *ZPE* 17 (1975): 37–78.
Winkler, Gerhard. "Die Statthalter der römischen Provinz Raetia unter dem Prinzipat." *Bayerische Vorgeschichtsblätter* 36 (1971): 50–101.
Wirszubski, Chaim. *Libertas as a Political Idea at Rome during the Late Republic and Early Principate.* Cambridge: Cambridge University Press, 1950.
Wlassak, Moriz. *Der Judikationsbefehl der römischen Prozesse.* Wien: In Kommission bei A. Holder, 1921.
Wlassak, Moriz. *Römische Processgesetze.* Leipzig: Duncker & Humblot, 1891.
Wolff, H. "Raetia." In *The Cambridge Ancient History, Volume 10*, edited by Alan K. Bowman, Edward Champlin, and Andrew Lintott, 535–44. Cambridge: Cambridge University Press, 1996.
Wolff, Hans Julius. *Das Problem der Konkurrenz von Rechtsordnungen in der Antike.* Heidelberg: C. Winter, 1979.
Wolff, Hans Julius. *Das Recht der griechischen Papyri Ägyptens in der Zeit der Ptolemäer und des Prinzipats II: Organisation und Kontrolle des privaten Rechtsverkehrs.* München: Beck, 1978.
Wolff, Hans Julius. "Der byzantinische Urkundenstil Ägyptens im Lichte der Funde von Nessana und Dura." *RIDA* 8 (1961): 115–54.
Wolff, Hans Julius. "Le droit provincial dans la province romaine d'Arabie." *RIDA* 23 (1976): 271–90.

Wolff, Hans Julius. "Plurality of Laws in Ptolemaic Egypt'." *RIDA* 7 (1960): 191–223.
Wolff, Hans Julius. "Römisches Provinzialrecht in der Provinz Arabia (Rechtspolitik als Instrument der Beherrschung)." In *Aufstieg und Niedergang der römischen Welt*, Vol. II.13, 763–806. Berlin: De Gruyter, 1980.
Wolff, Hans Julius. "The Political Background of the Plurality of Laws in Ptolemaic Egypt." In *Proceedings of the Sixteenth International Congress of Papyrology*, edited by Roger S. Bagnall, Gerald M. Browne, Ann E. Hanson, and Ludwig Koenen, 313–18. Chico, California: Scholars Press, 1981.
Wolff, Hans Julius. *Written and Unwritten Marriages in Hellenistic and Post-Classical Roman Law*. Haverford: American Philological Association, 1939.
Wolff, Martin. *Private International Law*. 2nd ed. Oxford: Clarendon Press, 1950.
Wolter, Michael. "Erstmals unter Quirinius! Zum Verständnis von Lk 2,2." *Biblische Notizen* 102 (2000): 35–41.
Wörrle, Michael. *Stadt und Fest im kaiserzeitlichen Kleinasien*. München: Beck, 1988.
Wuthnow, Heinz. *Die semitischen Menschennamen in griechischen Inschriften und Papyri des vorderen Orients*. Leipzig: Dieterich, 1930.
Yadin, Yigael. *Bar-Kokhba: The Rediscovery of the Legendary Hero of the Second Jewish Revolt Against Rome*. London: Random House, 1971.
Yadin, Yigael. "Expedition D." *IEJ* 11 (1961): 36–52.
Yadin, Yigael. "Expedition D – The Cave of the Letters." *IEJ* 12 (1962): 227–57.
Yadin, Yigael. *The Finds from the Bar Kokhba Period in the Cave of Letters*. Judean Desert Studies I. Jerusalem: IES, 1963.
Yadin, Yigael. "The Nabataean Kingdom, Provincia Arabia, Petra and Ein-Geddi in the Documents from Naḥal Ḥever." *Ex Oriente Lux* 17 (1963): 227–41.
Yadin, Yigael, Jonas C. Greenfield, and Ada Yardeni. "A Deed of Gift in Aramaic Found in Naḥal Ḥever: Papyrus Yadin 7." *Eretz Israel* 25 (1996): 383–403 (Hebrew).
Yadin, Yigael, Jonas C. Greenfield, and Ada Yardeni. "Babatha's Ketubba." *IEJ* 44 (1994): 75–99.
Yadin, Yigael, Jonas C. Greenfield, Ada Yardeni, and Baruch A. Levine. *The Documents from the Bar Kokhba Period in the Cave of Letters: Hebrew, Aramaic and Nabatean-Aramaic Papyri*. Judean Desert Studies III. Jerusalem: IES, 2002.
Yadin, Yigael, and Joseph Naveh. *Masada I: The Aramaic and Hebrew Ostraca and Jar Inscriptions*. Jerusalem: IES, 1989.
Yardeni, Ada. "A Draft of a Deed on an Ostracon from Khirbet Qumrân." *IEJ* 47 (1997): 233–37.
Yardeni, Ada. *Naḥal Ṣe'elim Documents*. Beer-Sheva: Ben-Gurion University of the Negev Press, 1995 (Hebrew).
Yardeni, Ada. "Notes on Two Unpublished Nabataean Deeds from Naḥal Ḥever – P.Yadin 2 and 3." In *The Dead Sea Scrolls: Fifty Years after their Discovery 1947–1997*, edited by Lawrence H. Schiffman, Emanuel Tov, and James C. Vanderkam, 862–74. Jerusalem: IES, 2000.
Yardeni, Ada. *Textbook of Aramaic, Hebrew and Nabataean Documentary Texts from the Judaean Desert and Related Material*. 2 Vols. Jerusalem: The Hebrew University Press, 2000 (Hebrew & English).
Yardeni, Ada. "The Decipherment and Restoration of Legal Texts from the Judaean Desert: A Reexamination of Papyrus Stracky (P.Yadin 36)." *SCI* 20 (2001): 121–37.
Yardeni, Ada. "Two in one? A Deed of Sale from Wadi Murabba'at." *Eretz Israel* 26 (1999): 64–70 (Hebrew).
Yardeni, Ada, and Jonas C. Greenfield. "A Receipt for a Ketubba." In *The Jews in the Hellenistic-Roman World: Studies in Memory of Menahem Stern*, edited by Isaiah M. Gafni, Aharon

Oppenheimer, and Daniel R. Schwartz, 197–208. Jerusalem: Zalman Shazar Center, 1996 (Hebrew).
Yaron, Reuven. "CPJud. 144 et Alia." *Iura* 13 (1962): 170–75.
Yaron, Reuven. "The Mesadah Bill of Divorce." In *Studi in onore di Edoardo Volterra VI*, 433–55. Milano: Giuffrè, 1971.
Yavetz, Zvi. "Existimatio, Fama, and the Ides of March." *Harv. Stud.* 78 (1974): 35–65.
Yehuda, Felix. *Trees: Aromatic, Ornamental, and of the Forest in the Bible and Rabbinic Literature.* Jerusalem: Reuven Mass, 1997 (Hebrew).
Yiftach-Firanko, Uri. "Who killed the Double Document in Ptolemaic Egypt." *Arch. Pap.* 54 (2008): 203–18.
Youtie, Herbert C. "A Rhodian Auction Sale of a Slave." *ZPE* 15 (1974): 145–47.
Youtie, Herbert C. "Because They Do Not Know Letters." *ZPE* 19 (1975): 101–8.
Youtie, Herbert C. "Hypographeis and Witnesses of 2nd Century Tebtunis." *ZPE* 19 (1975): 191–201.
Youtie, Herbert C. "Notes on Subscriptions." *BASP* 13 (1976): 81–84.
Youtie, Herbert C. "Publicans and Sinners." *ZPE* 1 (1967): 1–20 (originally, 1937).
Youtie, Herbert C. "Review: Egyptian Property-Returns by Austin M. Harmon." *AJA* 40 (1936): 282–84.
Youtie, Herbert C. *Scriptiunculae.* Vol. II. Amsterdam: Hakkert, 1973.
Youtie, Herbert C. "ΑΓΡΑΜΜΑΤΟΣ: An Aspect of Greek Society in Egypt." *Harv. Stud.* 75 (1971): 161–76.
Youtie, Herbert C. "βραδέως γράφων: Between Literacy and Illiteracy." *GRBS* 12 (1974): 239–61.
Youtie, Herbert C. "ὑπογραφεύς: The Social Impact of Illiteracy in Graeco-Roman Egypt." *ZPE* 17 (1975): 201–21.
Zaas, Peter. "Matthew's Birth Story: An Early Milepost in the History of Jewish Marriage Law." *Biblical Theological Bulletin* 39 (2009): 125–128.
Zaas, Peter. "Spiritus Ex Machina: Jewish Legal Aspects of the Matthean Birth Narrative." *Jewish Law Association Studies* 16 (2005): 295–302.
Zissu, Boaz. "Rural Settlement in the Judaean Hills and Foothills from the Late Second Temple Period to The Bar Kokhba Revolt." Hebrew University of Jerusalem Thesis, 2002 (Hebrew).
Zwicky, Hans. "Zur Verwendung des Militärs in der Verwaltung des römischen Kaiserzeit." University of Zurich Thesis, 1944.

General Index

ab epistulis, 24 ff., 31
Achaea (province), 3, 19 f., 82, 108
M. Acilius Glabrio (governor of Sicily), 106, 109
actio tutelae, 226, 404, 424 ff., 428, 430, 483, 487
Aelia Capitolina, 142, 178 f., 192, 379, 384, 393 f.
L. Aemilius Rectus (prefect of Egypt), 315
Afghanistan, Aramaic documents from, 201, 243
Africa, 47 ff., 83
agoranomoi, 332, 382
Agrippa I, 318, 322, 388
Agrippa II, 318, 330, 381, 397 f.
Akiva, Rabbi, 527
Akrabatta, 143, 280, 329, 331, 381, 464
Alabanda (free city in Caria), 19, 72, 102, 109
Alföldy, Géza, 84, 96 f.
amicitia, 33, 58, 61, 64, 75, 78, 100
Amisus (city in Pontus), 48
Anablata (village near Jerusalem), 135
T. Aninius Sextius Florentinus (governor of Arabia), 115, 193, 374, 453
Antioch, 143, 494
Antoninus Pius, 47, 52, 85
C. Antonius Hibrida (consul), 15 f.
Apamea, 364, 367
Aquileia (city in Italy), 42, 51
Arabia, 115, 117, 127, 137 ff., 143 ff., 149, 158, 161, 199, 242, 309–316 *passim*, 339, 403, 410, 417, 426, 435, 458, 476, 481, 501, 503
– administration of, 334 f.
– annexation to Rome, 162, 192, 204, 238, 251, 260, 276, 280, 312 f., 373, 403, 420, 478, 479, 510
– census in, 369, 372 ff., 438, 453, 505
– era of, 135 f., 309–316 *passim*, 482
– *Nova Arabia*, 311 f.
– tax collection in, 304
Arabic, 128, 139, 163, 171, 206, 210, 212, 246
– in Nessana, 264
Aramaic, 124 f., 128 f., 130, 132, 136, 186, 201, 481
– language of legal contracts, 165, 197, 241, 259
– legal tradition, 170 f., 259
– Reichsaramäisch, 128, 165, 202, 243
– *Urtext*, 154, 169, 226, 454, 479
Arangio-Riuz, Vincenzo, 108
Archelaus (Herod's son), 313, 317 f., 351, 364
Aristoboulias (village of Zif), 143, 158, 280, 329, 331, 381, 435, 458, 461, 480, 502
Arjava, Antti, 250, 254
Arpinum (city in Italy), 28
Arval Brethren, acts of the, 57
Asia, 19 f., 63 f., 66, 81 f., 109, 202
Asisium (city in Italy), 47
assize, *see* conventus
Attic law, 432, 509
Atticus (Cicero's friend), 67, 72
auctoritas, 9, 39, 65, 68 f., 76 f.
Augustus, 29, 37, 49, 139, 219, 351, 364, 375, 391, 488
– edicts to Cyrene, 105, 218, 222
Aurelianus (emperor), 48
auxilium, 4, 10, 14 f.

Babatha, 106, 118 f., 122 f., 138, 180, 189, 253, 399 f., 403, 408, 410 f., 414, 420, 426 f., 439, 445 ff., 454 f., 506, 521
– archive of, 137, 139, 142, 157, 162 f., 199, 225, 251, 359, 403 f., 424, 432, 468, 475, 478, 482 f., 486, 503
– guardian of, 140, 159, 233
– guardianship of her son, 228, 420 f., 506
– identity of, 404
– illiteracy of, 437, 508
– land declaration of, 356, 369, 371, 373, 436, 453, 505, 508
– marriage contract of, 139, 461, 479, 525–532 *passim*
Bactria, *see* Afghanistan
Baetica, 37, 490
Balsam, 328, 350–361 *passim*, 474 ff.

Bar Kokhba, 117, 133, 141, 144, 149, 174, 470
- administration of, 175, 468, 473 f., 479, 504
- archive of, 175, 183, 188 f., 468, 478
- army of, 181, 376
- languages used by, 186 ff.
Bar Kokhba Revolt, 130–138 *passim*, 144, 161, 174, 178, 190, 197, 315, 323, 334, 338 f., 361, 375, 377, 379, 385, 389, 392, 439, 441, 457, 458, 480, 501, 510, 523, 535
- extension to Jerusalem, 131 f., 176, 472 f.
- Nabataean participation, 189, 192
- Roman army, 391
- spread to Arabia, 189, 191 f., 325, 361, 476
- use of Hebrew, 169, 208
Batharda (village of Gophna), 143, 280, 329, 331, 381, 458, 464, 480, 502
Beithar, 132, 473
Belgica, 86 ff., 91 f.
Benoit, Pierre, 177 f.
Bethbassi (village of Herodium), 143, 280, 329, 331, 381, 458, 480, 502
Bethlehem, 537
Beth Phoura (village in Syria), 348 f.
betrothal, viii ff., 516, 530, 533–544 *passim*
Biblical law, 144, 443, 462, 520, 522, 525, 533, 538
Bithynia, 43 f., 51, 56, 82, 91, 96 f., 110
Boissevain, Ursul Philip, 79, 93
Bostra, 192 f., 202, 211, 248, 335, 512
boulé, 48, 51, 109, 204, 405 ff., 415, 421, 423, 425, 510
bride-gift, *see* mohar

Caesarea Maritima, 191, 323, 339, 354, 389
Cairo Genizah, 242, 259, 525
Caparcotna, 337 ff.
Cappadocia, 313, 319
Cassius Dio, 79–97 *passim*,183, 189, 192, 338, 392, 394, 397
Cato the Younger, 67
Cave of Letters, 117, 134, 138, 157, 161, 175, 188, 369, 469, 478
census, 115, 183, 279, 305, 312 ff., 363–378 *passim*
- declarations of, 119, 122, 141, 154, 182, 281, 293, 305
Cerialis (Roman general), 398
Chajes, H.P., 495
Chapa, Juan, 531 f.
Cicero, 3–22 *passim*, 28 f., 33, 36, 53, 62 f., 105, 216 f., 222, 490
Cicero's letters of recommendation, 3, 5, 6, 9, 15 ff., 61–78 *passim*, 99–111 *passim*, 220
CIIP, 204, 392 f., 485
Cilicia, 3, 105, 216, 490
cities, free, 19, 48, 72, 110, 218
- courts of, 220
cities, Greek, 71, 101, 399, 476
citizen(s), Roman, 3 ff., 7, 11 ff., 19 f., 22, 105 ff., 144, 150, 217 f., 223, 245, 249, 366, 374, 410, 415, 481, 488
citizenship
- Alexandrian, 45
- double, 102, 107
- Roman, 12, 27, 35, 45 f., 50 f., 105, 108, 154, 219, 221
Claudius (emperor), 28, 37, 136, 315, 318, 322, 388
T. Claudius Nero (governor of Bithynia), 71, 101, 110
G. Claudius Severus (governor of Arabia), 204, 340
clementia, 36, 50, 54, 61, 68 f., 100
cohors prima Thracum milliaria, 142, 285, 354, 356, 448
Commagene, 387
Comum, inscription from, 97
conflict of laws, 103–111 *passim*, 213
Constantine, 48 f.
Constitutio Antoniniana (212 CE), 105, 149, 216, 222, 488
consul, 3–5, 10, 14–22 *passim*, 56, 59, 79, 177, 179
controversia, 8 f.
conubium, 154
conventus, 193, 224, 226, 427, 486, 494
Coptic, 210, 245 f.
A. Cornelius Palma (governor of Syria), 340
council, *see boulé*
CPJ, 415, 454, 498, 542
Cyprus, 19, 380

Dacia, 313, 323
Damascus, 337, 339
Danby, Herbert, 166
Daube, David, 13, 100
Dead Sea, 138, 161, 211, 227, 276, 353 f., 360, 403, 458, 468, 476, 480, 502 f.
decorum, 6 f., 9, 18, 66, 68, 73, 75, 101, 220
deed(s) of gift, 138, 152 f., 169, 173, 232, 239, 253 f., 278, 289, 290 ff., 300, 304, 315, 357, 374, 439–457 *passim*, 474, 483, 504 f., 507, 517, 520 f.
Demotic, 209, 241, 243, 245 f.
diaspora, Jewish, 543
– judicial autonomy in, 498
– revolts in, 390, 398
Diocletian, 371, 374
diplomatics, 147–160 *passim*, 206, 228, 240, 248, 311, 418, 431, 457, 478, 482 f.
divorce, ix f., 168, 534 f., 538, 542, 544
Domitian, 24, 26, 37 ff., 55
L. Domitius Ahenobarbus (consul), 29
Domitius Corbulo (Roman general), 45
double document(s), 130, 135 f., 142, 149 f., 152, 156, 169, 226, 240, 481, 487, 510
– Semitic tradition of, 151, 154, 171
dowry, ix, 144, 249, 250 f., 255 f., 261, 264 f., 438, 440 f., 445, 447, 460 ff., 505–522 *passim*, 528 ff.
duoviri, 332, 406, 430, 491
Dura Europos, 151, 158, 172, 201, 226, 248, 432

Ebraïsti, 187 f., 207
Eck, Werner, 99, 189 f., 388, 391
Egypt, 89, 145, 150, 159, 169, 182, 224, 226, 314, 403, 407, 481
– administration of, 331 f.
– census in, 363 f., 372, 377, 453, 537
– Jews in, 415 f., 498, 541 ff.
– land tenure in, 301 f., 368, 474
– marriage contracts from, ix, 460, 464, 512 ff., 527 f., 530
– papyri from, 116, 119, 123, 139, 144, 158, 202, 233, 248, 408 ff., 426
– taxes in, 300, 303 f.
Ein Gedi, 138, 142, 153, 161, 188, 190, 197, 252, 277, 279, 285–291 *passim*, 328, 331 f., 347–361 *passim*, 380, 382, 417, 448, 456, 458, 474 ff., 480, 502, 510, 519
– courtyard(s) in, 285–291 *passim*, 507
ekdosis, 512 f.
Elagabalus, 47, 90, 337
Eleazar Ben Yair, 397
epigraphic habit, 196, 203, 205, 429, 483
– *Memorialepigraphik*, 196
epitropos, *see* guardian(s)
Euphrates, documents from, 152, 202, 226, 248, 481, 502
Eusebius of Caesarea, 333
existimatio, 8, 19, 66 f., 70, 101, 109

Falerio (city in Picenum), 39
fasti, 179, 385, 395
Felix (governor of Judaea), 225, 399
First Revolt, 132 ff., 161, 176, 197, 322, 325, 328 f., 353, 359 f., 379, 381, 384, 388, 390, 392, 475 f., 489, 501
fiscus, 191, 301 f., 317, 352, 357 f., 474
Flavian dynasty, 200, 304, 366, 490
L. Flavius Silva (conqueror of Masada and governor of Judaea), 388, 395
Florus, 25
forma censualis, 369, 373, 375
Forum Clodii, 277
Forum Sempronii, 277
Fragmentum Atestinum, 14, 430
Friedman, Mordechai Akiva, 526
Fronto, 8, 32, 52, 76, 78
Q. Fufidius (Cicero's tribune), 28

Gaius (jurist), 214
Galatia, 49, 86, 87
Galen, 353
Galilee, 277, 317 f., 326, 339, 379, 389, 392, 477, 517, 534 f., 541, 543
Gallia, *see* Gaul
Gallienus (emperor), 47
Galoda (village of Akrabatta), 143, 280, 329, 331, 381, 458, 464, 480, 502
Galsterer, Hartmunt, 216, 224
Gardner, Jane F., 223, 420
Garnsey, Peter, 11 f., 14 f., 78
Gaul, 27 f., 83, 91 f., 375, 398 f.

Gavius Bassus (prefect of Pontic Coast), 44
Gerasa, 304, 393
– *cursus* inscription from, 340, 342 ff.
Ghor al-Safi, 282
gift forever, ix, 170, 301, 303, 455
Goodman, Martin, 393
Gophna, 143, 280, 329, 331, 381, 464
Great Revolt, *see* First Revolt
Greek
– *Koine*, 169, 457
– Language, 129, 142, 144, 149, 164, 396
– law, 158, 259, 411, 418, 503
– legal documents, 199, 201, 260
guardian(s), 119, 122 f., 149, 156, 158 f., 227, 332, 423, 482, 487, 508
– appointment of, 403–429 *passim*, 506
– in Egyptian papyri, 432 f., 509
– of a woman, 431–441 *passim*, 482
– removal of, 423 f., 506

Hadrian, 41, 49, 52, 54, 82, 85, 132, 178, 312 ff., 338 ff., 384, 393, 473
Halakha, 148, 249, 411, 416, 457, 464 f., 484, 518 f., 523
Hammat Ma'in (in Jordan), 190
Hardona (village near Jerusalem), 135, 480, 502
T. Haterius Nepos (governor of Arabia), 189, 191, 193, 427
Healey, John F., 237, 246
Hebrew, 128–136 *passim*, 186
– in legal documents, 198, 279
– legends on coins, 137
– symbol of Jewish nationalism, 176
Hebron, 136, 143, 158, 356, 380, 458, 480, 502
Hellenism/Hellenization, 128, 142, 164, 174, 203, 248, 259, 261, 263, 464, 479, 484, 523
– *Hellênikos nomos*, ix, 260–266 *passim*, 461, 463, 515, 522
– Hellenized Jews, 417, 429, 431, 454, 457, 479, 483, 502
Hellenistic law, 416, 542
Herakleoplis (in Egypt), documents from, 498, 541 f.
– Herculaneum,wax tablet from, 406
Herod the Great, 318, 328, 332, 351, 471
Herodium, 143, 280, 329, 331, 381, 458, 480, 502
Hezser, Catherine, 147
high priest, 145, 489
Hijaz, 162, 211
homologia, 435, 437 ff., 509

L. Iavolenus Priscus (jurist and governor of Syria), 32 f., 42, 51
Idios Logos, Gnomon of the, 223
Idumaea, 317, 328 f., 380
IGLS, 204
illiteracy, 120, 122 f., 159, 436, 453, 508
imperial legates, 23–27 *passim*
imperium, 5, 10, 16, 61, 96, 100
intercessio, 15, 27
interpretatio Hebraica, 260, 417, 463, 515
Irene (Byzantine empress), 120
Irni (city in Baetica), 221 f., 406, 430, 490, 493 f.
Italy, 14, 83, 85, 92, 110, 179 f., 221, 385
– census in, 366
Israel, freedom/redemption of, 131 ff., 176, 473
Iulia Crispina, 157, 253, 408 ff., 427, 438, 446, 455, 507, 510, 521
Iulius Severus (governor of Judaea), 191, 472
ius Quiritium, 45 f., 51
ius trium liberorum, 43, 50, 420

Jericho, 161, 197, 280, 328, 331, 339, 350 f., 353 f., 356, 380, 382, 471
Jerome, 352
Jerusalem, 130 ff., 135 f., 142 f., 145, 176 ff., 328 f., 379–385 *passim*, 392, 394 ff., 489, 502, 517
– siege of, 389–397 *passim*
Jesus Christ, 363
– languages in the days of, 183, 207
– conception of, ix f., 533–546 *passim*
– *Toledot Yeshu*, 539
Jesus (Babatha's first husband), 251
Jesus (Babatha's orphaned son), 371, 404, 411, 414, 425, 436, 449
– guardianship of, 405–429 *passim*

Jewish law, 144, 146, 198, 249, 258, 416 f., 419 f., 456, 461, 480, 484, 503, 518, 523
– arbitration, 146, 148, 494 f.
– development of, 457
– divorce, 517 ff., 538
– guardianship, 411, 414 f., 511
– litigation, 146
– marriage, 459, 461, 507, 512, 514, 516, 533 f.
– Roman toleration of, 146
– succession, 254, 258, 443–451 *passim*, 520 f.
Jewish region, 182, 224, 317, 325, 326–334 *passim*, 378 f., 383, 476 f., 493
Jewish script, 128, 188
Jewish sources, *see* rabbinic sources
Jezreel, valley of, 338 f., 389
Jones, A.H.M., 4, 10, 14 f., 18
Jordan, 163, 189, 260
– Safaitic inscription from, 189
Josephus, 145, 179, 186, 208, 318, 320, 327 f., 332 f., 354, 365, 380, 382 f., 388, 395 ff., 477, 485, 489, 493 f., 519
Judaea, 34, 82, 127 ff., 136, 143 ff., 149, 153, 161, 182, 280, 313, 317–335 *passim*, 339, 379, 417, 458, 474, 481, 485, 501, 517, 534
– administration of, 319, 476 f.
– Aramaic in, 168
– army in, 338, 387–399 *passim*
– census in, 320, 365, 375, 377
– change of name, 392
– Greek in, 141, 200, 489
– local organization of, 324–335 *passim*
– population of, 392
– provincialization of, 141, 317 f., 324, 365, 387, 389, 479 ff.
– territory of, 317 f.
– urbanization of, 333 f., 477 f.
Judaean Desert Documents, 103, 122, 125, 128, 132
– court(s) in, 146, 457
– Jewish society reflected in, 174, 458, 480, 483 f., 502 f., 523
– women and law in, 501–523 *passim*
Judah son of Ele'azar Khthousion (Babatha's second husband), 122 f., 139, 142, 146, 156 f., 159, 233, 252 f., 261, 285–291 *passim*, 328, 348, 354 f., 359 f., 408, 417, 432, 434, 436 ff., 444, 446, 448, 453, 455, 478 f., 505, 507, 512, 516, 520 f., 528 f., 531
judicial autonomy, 145, 150, 216 f., 220 f., 416, 486–499 *passim*
Julio-Claudian dynasty, 331, 539
Julius Africanus, 499
Julius Caesar, 27 ff., 33, 36, 39 f., 52, 100
Julius Julianus (governor of Arabia), 225, 339, 422, 426, 492, 506

Katzoff, Ranon, 155, 174, 260, 508
Kelly, John Maurice, 63 ff., 76, 78, 100, 102
Ketef Jericho, 127, 191, 502
ketubba, ix, 166, 258, 263, 441, 445, 447 f., 459 ff., 479, 505, 507, 512 ff., 516 ff., 522, 525–532 *passim*
Kfar Baru, 155, 190
Khisalon/Kesalon (village near Jerusalem), 135, 480, 502
Kutscher, Edward Yechezkel, 276 f.

Lactantius, 313
Lajjun, *see* Caparcotna
Lambaesis, 47 f., 86
land declaration(s), 115, 118 f., 122, 141, 474
land tenure, 293–308 *passim*, 474
Latin, language, 64, 87, 92, 100, 128, 179, 201, 203, 384, 407
– in the east, 202, 481
Latin status/community, 106, 221, 223, 366, 407, 491, 494
law of the papyri, 411, 420, 443, 520, 523
legio I Adiutrix, 86
legio II Traiana, 323, 339, 341 f.
legio III Augusta, 86
legio III Cyrenaica, 340 ff., 344
legio IV Scythica, 82
legio VI Ferrata, 83, 323, 337–346 *passim*
Legio X Fretensis, 128, 142, 153, 178, 322, 353, 384 f., 389, 471
legio X Gemina, 86
legio XXII Deiotariana, 341
leshon hakhamim, 165, 168
Levine, Baruch A., 171, 247
Lewald, Hans, 213

Lewis, Naphtali, 142, 157, 185, 234, 241, 263, 355
Lex Alimentorum, 40
Lex Irnitana, *see* Irni
Lex Iulia, 106
Lex Manciana, 302
Lex Municipii Salpensani, 406
Lex Rubria, 14
Lex Rupilia, 109, 217
liberalitas, 33, 36, 41, 50, 54, 61, 100
M. Gn. Licinius Rufinus (jurist), 397
Lifshitz, Baruch, 181
Lintott, Andrew W., 12 f.
Livia (Augustus' wife), 330, 381
Livias (city in the Peraea), 190, 262, 317 f. ,326, 330, 381 f., 462, 502
local law/custom, 104, 108, 110, 144, 216, 225, 228, 263, 265, 403, 410, 415, 420, 430, 453, 454, 490, 511, 526
– *see also Hellênikos nomos* under Hellenism/Hellenization
Sex. Lucilius Bassus (governor of Judaea), 389
Lucius Verus (emperor), 47
Lusius Quietus (Roman general), 341, 390
Luttwack, Edward N., 394 ff., 398

Machaerus, 190
Madaba, 199
– mosaic map of, 133, 360, 476
Mada'in Salih, 162, 170, 199, 238, 254
C. Maenius Gemellus (citizen of Patrae), 72, 102, 107, 108
Magonius Valens (centurion), 142, 285, 354 f., 448
Maḥoza/Maḥoz 'Aglatain, 118, 138 f., 156, 161, 170, 190, 192, 227, 253, 262, 276–283 *passim*, 300, 315, 334, 359, 403, 420, 435, 443, 445 f., 455, 458, 462, 464, 468, 470, 474 f., 480, 502 f., 505, 515, 519, 520 f.
Manyat Umm Hasan (in Jordan), 190
Marcus Aurelius, 47, 52, 85, 92
Marcus Brutus, 67 f.
marriage contracts, 146, 258, 262, 264 f., 457, 459, 462, 492, 511, 521, 544
– Aramaic, 135 f., 139, 146, 417, 460, 512, 530 f.
– Greek, viii f., 146, 261, 263 f., 417 f., 460, 462, 479, 512, 530
– in Christian sources, 531 f.
Masada, x, 129, 135, 328, 353, 380, 388, 471
– era of, 135
– papyri from, 127 f., 141 f., 471, 479, 488
– siege of, 394 ff.
Mazra'a, 359 f., 458, 480, 502
Meason (village in the Peraea), 191
L. Mescinius Rufus (Cicero's quaestor), 3 f., 10, 12 ff., 17 f., 20, 22, 71, 101
Mesopotamia, documents from, 152, 158, 432, 481, 502
metrocomia, 326 f.
Milik, J.T., 131, 135
Millar, Fergus, 79, 203, 223, 244, 259, 391
M. Mindius (knight), 3, 10, 18 f., 71, 101
C. Minucius Italus (prefect of Egypt), 31
Q. Minucius Thermus (proconsul in Asia), 69 f., 72, 101 f.
Mishnah, 165 f., 168, 198, 234, 242, 259, 411 f., 418, 432, 461, 465, 493 f., 503, 514, 522, 526
Mitteis, Ludwig, 213
Moab, 211, 276
mohar, 459 f., 513
Mommsen, Theodor, 4, 11, 15 f., 18, 25 ff., 33, 86, 93 f., 96, 217
Moschantic estate, 276, 297
Munigua (city in Baetica), 37, 45
Mylasa (free city in Caria), 19, 72

Nabataean(s)
– identity of, 164 f., 210, 212, 246
– kingdom, 127 f., 137 f., 149, 151, 161, 163, 199, 212, 260, 278, 293, 360, 374, 403, 468, 476, 485, 488, 503, 504
– language, 128, 138, 145, 162, 208, 210, 481
– law/legal tradition, 170 f., 237, 240, 244, 247, 249, 251, 411, 429
– legal documents, 170 f., 210, 239, 244
– money, 251 f., 307, 312, 373
– script, 136, 139, 187 f., 206, 209, 478
Nacolea (city in Phrygia), 49

Naḥal David (Wadi Sdeir), 161, 197, 468, 471, 502
Naḥal Ḥever, 117, 125, 127, 130, 134, 161, 188 f., 197, 469, 470, 502
– documents from, 144, 151, 172, 175, 199, 239, 247, 259, 347, 357, 468, 478, 503 f.
– flight of Jews to, 241, 259, 325
Naḥal Mishmar, 127, 161, 197, 470, 502
Naḥal Ṣe'elim, 127, 161, 181, 197, 375, 469, 470, 502
Nazareth, 537
Negev, 163, 211, 260, 481
Nero, 135 f., 330, 354, 381
Nerva, 35, 40, 43, 51, 56, 422
Nessana, 201, 211 f., 241, 247, 260,
– papyri from, 163, 200, 211, 226, 264
– languages in, 264
New Testament, ix f., 145, 169, 186, 208, 304, 320, 332, 363, 382, 409, 485, 489, 519, 535, 539, 543, 545

Old Testament, 169, 326, 540
one-legion province, 388, 390
Oppia (M. Mindius' widow), 18, 20 ff., 71, 101
Orcistus (city in Phrygia), 49 f.
Origen, 499, 539
Orine (toparchy), 178 ff., 329, 379–385 *passim*
ornamenta triumphalia, 189, 191, 391
Osrhoene, documents from, 242
Ossa (village in Syria), 515
Ostia, 49, 54

Palaestina Salutaris/Tertia, 163, 241, 247, 249, 260
Palmyra, 203
– funerary inscription from, 124
parangelia, 426
parnasim, 332, 358, 382, 473 ff.
pater patriae, 55 f.
Patrae (city in Greece), 72, 102, 107 f.
– citizenship of, 108
– local law of, 108
patrimony (*patrimonium*), 304, 349, 351, 356 f., 432, 509, 520
Paulus (jurist), 149
Pausanias (citizen of Aalabanda), 71, 101, 109
Pax Romana, 398
Peraea, 190 f., 262, 379, 381, 458, 464, 477, 480, 502, 515
peregrini, 12, 45, 105 f., 110, 215, 219, 366, 407, 425
– communities of, 221, 223, 491
– judicial autonomy of, 221, 224, 235, 491
– law of, 406
Petra, 163, 192 f., 204, 206, 211 f., 247, 249, 260, 335, 405, 407, 415, 421, 423, 425, 426 f., 438, 510
– tomb inscriptions from, 199
– papyri from, 163, 172, 200, 241
Philo of Alexandria, 145, 489
pietas, 53 f., 57 f.
Pliny the Elder, 72, 87, 179, 327 ff., 333, 350, 352, 354, 358, 380, 383 f., 474 ff., 477, 493
Pliny the Younger, 23, 25 ff., 30 ff., 35–59 *passim*, 82, 87, 96 f., 422
polis, 108, 145, 204, 325 f., 333 ff., 477, 488
– judicial autonomy of, 224, 493
– Hellenic pretensions of, 325
poll tax, 182, 368, 371 f., 377
Polotsky, Hans Jakob, 183, 227
polygamy, 144, 359, 462, 516 f., 522
Q. Pompeius Falco (governor of Judaea), 33 f., 323
Cn. Pompeius Magnus, 17, 36, 317
Pontius Pilatus, 388
Pontus, 44, 48, 82, 96 f.
power of patronage, 26 f., 29 f., 33
praetor, 4, 11, 15, 17, 20, 65, 71, 73 f., 75, 79 f., 83, 95, 97, 102, 423
Préaux, Claire, 501, 503
Principate, 5, 35 f.
private international law, 99–111 *passim*, 213, 235
provincial government/administration, 5, 16, 61, 64, 68 f., 100, 145, 182, 214, 403, 483, 499
– edict, 104 f., 158, 215 f., 314, 490
– governor, 4 ff., 16 ff., 28, 31 ff., 37, 63, 65–73 *passim*, 75, 79, 87, 92, 95 f., 100 f., 145, 180, 314

- *legati Augusti pro praetore*, 79 f., 82, 85, 87 f., 90 f., 93 ff., 322, 494
- lictors, 79 f., 92, 94 f.
- proconsul, 5, 10, 19, 79, 95
- tax collection, 367

provincialization, 139, 141, 144, 149, 163, 165, 317, 488

provincial jurisdiction, 5, 7, 63, 100, 104 f., 145, 149, 218
- administration of justice, 63, 70, 100, 430, 491
- governor's court, 145 f., 149, 154, 221, 226, 426, 439, 455 ff., 486, 491

Ptolemais, 339

publicani, 333

public archive(s), 145, 357, 419, 455, 456

public company, 62, 69, 101

Publicius Marcellus (governor of Syria), 82, 191

Puteoli, 39, 72

Quintilian (rhetorician), 75

Quintus (Cicero's brother), 9, 19, 27, 29, 62 ff., 66 ff.

Rabbath-Moab, 115, 315, 333, 427, 438, 453

rabbinic sources, 148, 165, 173, 332, 411, 432, 478, 481, 485, 503, 517, 523, 526
- contracts, 165 ff., 167, 456, 493
- courts, 146, 224, 457, 486, 495, 498
- criminal jurisdiction, 499
- gentile courts, 146, 419, 456
- judicial autonomy, 332, 486
- legal discussions, 198 f.
- public archives, 456
- Tannaitic, 411 f., 419, 456 f., 461, 526

Rabbis, 173, 416 f., 419, 432, 456, 458, 465, 480, 484, 495, 503, 526

Rab'el (Nabataean king), 296, 298, 429

Raetia, 83 f., 91 f.

Rathbone, Dominic, 182, 377

Ravenna, Latin papyri from, 116, 121 ff.

Rea, John, 409, 510

Republic, Roman 5, 11, 13, 15, 29, 63, 104 f., 216, 366

Ritterling, Emil, 337 f., 340

Roman custom (*ethos Rômaikon*), 265 f.

Romanization, 141, 200, 373, 404, 407, 410, 420, 435, 487, 511

Roman Near East, 128, 148 f., 155, 162, 164, 174, 192, 195, 197, 200, 202, 259, 378, 387, 396, 481, 488, 502, 514
- monuments of the Flavian period, 391

Roman law, 107, 149, 158, 247, 259, 265, 403, 408, 410, 412, 420, 428, 483, 490
- *actio*, 71, 102
- appeal before trial, 3, 11, 14
- arbitration, 8 f., 225, 498
- choice/change of courts, 4, 11 ff., 107, 110, 218, 222, 488
- court proceedings, 9, 70, 72, 101, 103
- equality before law, 63 f., 77 f., 215
- guardianship, 420, 434, 440, 482, 488, 509, 510
- *ius civile*, 64, 104 f., 215, 223, 245, 249
- *ius gentium*, 214
- litigation, 8 f., 17, 63, 75 f., 100 f., 507
- *provocatio*, 11
- *reiectio iudicii*, 11
- remittal of case to Rome, 4, 8, 10 ff., 18 ff., 71, 101
- *testatio*, 153, 159, 226, 232, 487
- women in, 159

Rome, 3 f., 8, 10, 11, 14, 16 f., 19 f., 31, 46, 55, 57, 65 f., 72, 75, 104, 108, 199, 221, 366, 391, 396, 423

Sabbath, 174, 498

Salamis (city in Cyprus), 67 ff.

Salome Komaïse, 120, 139 f., 155, 190, 262, 300, 418, 439, 440 f., 444 f., 454, 457, 463, 470, 479, 495, 497, 505, 515 f.
- archive of, 137, 139, 162, 199, 298, 374, 503, 514
- marriage contract of, 331, 381 f., 462, 464, 507

Samaria, 317, 326, 379, 458, 477, 480, 502

Sanhedrin, 145, 200, 489

Sardis, judicial autonomy of, 416, 498

Satlow, Michael, 534 f.

P. Scandilius (knight), 11 f.

SC de Asclepiade sociisque, 12, 218, 488

Schönbauer, Ernst, 108 f.

Schürer, Emil, 324, 476

scribe(s), 119, 122 f., 136, 140, 155 f., 316
- Jewish, 457
script and language, 188, 207 ff., 212
seal(s), 157
Second Revolt, *see* Bar Kokhba Revolt
Seiyâl Collection, 190, 258, 347, 469 f., 504
senate, 16, 48, 56, 65, 82
senatus consultum Tertullianum, 420
Seneca, 37, 55
Sepphoris, 339
P. Serviluis Isauricus (governor of Asia), 74
Severus Alexander (emperor), 47, 49, 89
sicarii, 135, 141, 328, 353 f., 360, 380, 394, 397, 471, 475, 479
Sicily, 19, 72, 102, 105 ff., 109, 216 f.
signature(s), *see* subscription(s)
Siirt (city in Turkey), 282
P. Silius Nerva (governor of Pontus-Bithynia), 69, 71, 101, 110
Sinai, 163, 210 f., 260, 481
soldiers(s), Roman, 143, 153, 178
Q. Sosius Senecio (governor of Upper Moesia), 32
speech acts, viii f.
Statius (poet), 24 ff., 38 ff., 43
stephanikon, 296, 303, 312, 373
stragetoi, 332, 407, 426, 494
Stroumsa, Rachel, 264
subscription(s), 149, 152, 164, 508
- Aramaic, 117, 119 f., 123, 130, 142, 211, 234, 434, 454, 479, 502, 509
- direction of writing, 152, 155, 232
- Greek, 117 ff., 123, 125, 437, 453
- Latin, 116 f., 119 f.
- Nabataean, 140, 211
- number of, 153, 156
- Semitic, 156
succession, 443–451 *passim*,
- daughter's right of, x, 448, 520 f.
Suetonius, 30 f., 33, 39, 43, 45, 50, 55
Sukkot, *see* Tabernacles
P. Sulpicius Quirinius (governor of Syria), 313, 321, 364
Ser. Sulpicius Rufus (governor of Achaea), 3, 6 ff., 15, 17 ff., 71, 74, 101, 108
Syria, 82, 182, 200, 313, 337, 481
- census in, 364, 377
Syria-Palaestina, 317–335 *passim*, 338, 481, 485
- army in, 387–399 *passim*
Syriac, 242, 481
Syrian-Roman law book, 263

Tabernacles, festival of, 185, 188 f.
Table of Banasa, 222
Table of the Ligures Baebiani, 41
Table of Veleia, 40
Tables of Albertini, 303
Tabula Banasitana, 27, 45
Tabula Heracleensis, 366
Tabula Irnitana, *see* Irni
Tacitus, 45, 54, 81, 313, 322, 398
Talmud, Babylonian, 332, 412 f.
Talmud, Palestinian (Jerusalem), 332, 412
Tel Shalem, 339 f.
Temple (in Jerusalem), 145, 200, 379, 391, 393, 395, 457, 459, 489
P. Terentius Hispo (representative of public company), 69, 71, 101
Tertullus (rhetorician), 225, 399, 400
Thebes, 139
Thorigny, marble inscription from, 88
Tiberius (emperor), 139
Tiberius Alexander (governor of Judaea), 399
Tifernum Tiberinum, 43, 50
Q. Tineius Rufus (governor of Judaea), 338 f.
Titus, 37, 40, 45, 389, 391, 395 f.
toparchy, 179, 182, 280, 327, 329–335 *passim*, 356, 377, 379, 383 f., 475, 477, 494
- list of, 328, 380
- Josephus' use of the term, 330, 381
Toseftah, 165, 168, 198, 242, 259, 412 f., 526
Trajan, 24, 30, 35 f., 38, 40, 42 ff., 48, 50 ff., 56, 59, 82, 97, 313, 338, 390, 422
C. Trebatius Testa (jurisconsult), 28, 33
M. Tullius Tiro (Cicero's freedman), 78
two-stage marriage, ix f., 534, 538 ff., 542 f.
tyche, 116, 435, 453 f.

Uchi Mauis (*colonia* in Africa), 49
Ulpian (jurist), 40, 369, 372, 375, 377
M. Ulpius Traianus (commander of *legio X Fretensis)*, 353

unwritten marriage, ix, 225, 262, 438, 445, 463 f., 514 f., 530
– *see also* written marriage
urbs Roma, 277

Valens (emperor), 48
Valentinian (emperor), 48
Valerian (emperor), 47
Verres (governor of Sicily), 11 ff.
Vespasian, 54, 352 ff., 388, 391, 395 f.
Via Annia, 47
Via Appia, 39
Via Domitiana, 39
B. Vibius Maximus (prefect of Egypt), 364
Vitellius (emperor), 45
Voconius Romanus (Pliny's friend), 43, 50
Q. Volusius (prefect), 19

Wadi Murabba'at, x, 127 f., 130, 133 ff., 157, 161, 178, 197, 502
– documents from, 135, 144, 175, 357, 375, 467 f., 504
– Hebrew documents from, 168, 176
– Roman army in, 180
Wasserstein, Abraham, 248, 260, 263, 464
witness(es), 149, 151, 153, 156, 481
Wolff, Hans Julius, 214, 222, 227, 248, 434 f., 509
written marriage, ix, 262, 438, 445, 462 ff., 515
– *see also* unwritten marriage

xenokritai, 226

Yadin, Yigael, 130, 157, 175, 183, 276, 360, 478
Yaqim (Yaqum), 143, 280, 329, 331, 381, 458, 480, 502
Yardeni, Ada, 125, 131 f., 134, 137, 151, 171, 240, 247, 282, 478

Zif (Zephine), 143, 264, 280, 329, 331, 380, 381
Zissu, Boaz, 392
Zo'ar, 276–283 *passim*, 334

Index of Sources

Biblical and Rabbinic

Bible
Cant. 1:13 352
Deut. 22:23–29 534, 538, 541
Deut. 24:1–4 ix, 519, 542
Ex. 21:1 419
Ex. 21:7–11 525
Gen. 6:1–4 540
Gen. 22:11–13 536
Isa. 7:14 543
Isa. 15:5 281
Isa. 50:1 542
Jer. 3:8 542
Jer. 48:5 281
Num. 27:8 254, 443, 520

Mishnah
mBB 8, 2 254, 443, 520
mBB 10, 2 167
mBK 8, 6 527
mBM 9, 3 167
mGitt. 1, 5 419, 456
mGitt. 2, 6–7 517
mGitt. 5, 4 414
mGitt. 9, 3 168, 518 f.
mGitt. 9, 8 419
mKet. 1, 5 534
mKet. 4, 6–12 263, 461
mKet. 4, 7 166
mKet. 4, 10–11 166
mKet. 4, 12 517
mKet. 9, 4–6 413
mKet. 13, 3 166
mYebam. 4, 10 534
mYebam. 16, 7 282

Tosefta
tBB 8.13 414
tBB 11.8 456
tGitt. 1.4 419
tKet. 3.1 416
tKet. 4:9 544
tKet. 9.6 413
tKet. 11.4 414
tKet. 12.1 459
tPeah 4.6 416
tTer. 1.11–12 413 f.

Talmud
bBB 131b 413
bBB 141a 413
bBK 89a 463, 516
bErub. 43b 281
bGitt. 11a 419
bGitt. 14a 413
bGitt. 52a 414 f.
bGitt. 52b 413
bGitt. 88b 419
bKet. 82b 459
bKet. 86b–88b 413
bKet. 102b 414
bShabb. 100b 281
yKet. 8.11 32b 459
yKet. 54a–55a 413
yMeg. 3.3 74a 495
yShevu. 93a 413

Other
Damas. Coven. 14:12–16 409
Mek. d'R. Ishmael, Nez. 1 419
Mek. d'R. Ishmael, Nez. 3 526

Inscriptions

Abbadi & Zayadine (1996) 189
Abbott & Johnson, no. 142 302
AE 1914, no. 281 345
AE 1917/18, no. 51 86
AE 1917/18, no. 68 47
AE 1917/18, nos. 74–5 24
AE 1920, no. 78 338

AE 1923, no. 4	81
AE 1930, no. 92	343
AE 1934, no. 61	346
AE 1934, no. 62	346
AE 1938, no. 178	345
AE 1941, no. 73	37, 39
AE 1941, no. 105	346
AE 1947, no. 127	345
AE 1947, no. 172	346
AE 1948, no. 91	37, 49
AE 1948, no. 145	337, 346
AE 1948, no. 146	346
AE 1949, nos. 136–7	88
AE 1949, no. 214	88
AE 1950, no. 66	338, 344 f.
AE 1950, no. 190	345
AE 1959, no. 95	88
AE 1961, no. 16	346
AE 1962, no. 269	345 f.
AE 1962, no. 288	37 f.
AE 1965, no. 320	345
AE 1966, nos. 593–4	47
AE 1967, no. 80	345
AE 1968, no. 104	319
AE 1969/70, no. 606	345
AE 1971, no. 573	44
AE 1973, no. 137	37
AE 1973, no. 551	343
AE 1974, no. 659	346
AE 1976, no. 265	345
AE 1977, no. 467	346
AE 1977, no. 810	57
AE 1979, no. 62	343
AE 1979, no. 492	54
AE 1979, no. 658	49
AE 1983, no. 825	338
AE 1984, no. 426	345
AE 1985, no. 829	346
AE 1987, no. 421	345
AE 1989, no. 681	303
AE 1992, no. 1687	346
AE 1993, nos. 1620–4	323
AE 1994, no. 1781	393
BE 1996, no. 486	393
CIIP I 712	389
CIIP II 1201	342
CIIP II 1202	341
CIIP II 1228	345
CIIP II 1276	339
CIIP II 1284	346
CIIP II 1351	345 f.
CIJ 741	416
CIJ 775–9	416
CIL II 3271	319, 388
CIL II 3865–6	32
CIL II 4616	319, 388
CIL II 4909	57
CIL III 42	341
CIL III 79	341
CIL III 797	54
CIL III 1378	54
CIL III 4020	57
CIL III 5745	57
CIL III 5998	57
CIL III 6814–6	338
CIL III 6900	57
CIL III 12117	323
CIL III 13587	341
CIL III 14120	47
CIL III 14147(6)	341
CIL V 875	42, 51
CIL V 1837	47, 52
CIL V 1838–9	320, 388
CIL V 4348	81
CIL V 5262	97
CIL V 5267	319
CIL V 7992	47
CIL VI 972	49, 54
CIL VI 1052	57
CIL VI 1065	57
CIL VI 1174	57
CIL VI 1492	41
CIL VI 1546	84
CIL VI 3492	338
CIL VI 8598–9	24
CIL VI 31320	52
CIL VI 31776	52
CIL VI 31863	345
CIL VI 41119	345
CIL VI 41134	84
CIL VI 41272	345
CIL VII 1044	26, 89
CIL VII 1045	89
CIL VIII 51	47

CIL VIII 1408	48
CIL VIII 2194	52
CIL VIII 2772	48
CIL VIII 4205	47
CIL VIII 6996	52
CIL VIII 7044	83
CIL VIII 7095	52
CIL VIII 10304	47
CIL VIII 10327	47
CIL VIII 12061–64	50
CIL VIII 15447	49
CIL VIII 18270	86
CIL VIII 18495	47
CIL VIII 20486	47
CIL VIII 20570	348
CIL VIII 23072	52
CIL VIII 25902	302
CIL VIII 25943	302
CIL IX 215	42
CIL IX 338	89
CIL IX 1455	41
CIL IX 3044	320, 388
CIL IX 5420	39
CIL IX 5825	41
CIL X 6310	41
CIL X 6321	323
CIL XI 556	48
CIL XI 826	48
CIL XI 1147	40
CIL XI 1552	97
CIL XI 3309	42, 46
CIL XI 5375	47
CIL XI 5395	41
CIL XI 5956	41
CIL XIII 3162	23, 26, 88
CIL XIII 5089	345
CIL XIV 95	49, 54
CIL XIV 2101	48
CIL XIV 2954	320
CIL XIV 3617	345
CIL XIV 5631	49, 52
CIL XVI 33	390
CIL XVI 48	30
CIL XVI 87	324, 338, 389
CIS II.1, no. 196	281
CIS II.1, no. 486	141
CIS II, no. 530	239
Cotton, Eck & Isaac (2003)	390
Crawford (1996), nos. 16, 28	491
Della Corte (1951)	406
Eck & Foerster (1999)	340
Eck & Weiß (2009)	390
FIRA I, no. 13	366
FIRA I, no. 19	14
FIRA I, no. 20	14, 430
FIRA I, no. 23	406
FIRA I, no. 67	430
FIRA I, no. 68	105, 218, 222
FIRA I, no. 75	39
FIRA III, no. 139	303
González (1986)	406, 430, 490, 494
Healey (1993), H 27	239, 254
Healey (1993), H 36	199, 238
IC IV 299	83
ICUR II 567	531
IGLS III 813	345
IGLS IV 1804	346
IGLS XIII 9063	343
IGLS XXI 26	309
IGLS XXI 37	204
IGLS XXI 51	193
IGRom. III 174	81
IGRom. III 175	81
IGRom. III 1119	326
IGRom. III 1152	187
IGRom. IV 1422	345
Ingholt (1962)	124, 508
ILS 282	41
ILS 286	50
ILS 298	50
ILS 313	50
ILS 432	49
ILS 471	47
ILS 539	48
ILS 613	50
ILS 703	50
ILS 1032	30
ILS 1035	323
ILS 1036	323
ILS 1163	83
ILS 1196	86
ILS 1349	320, 388

ILS 1374 42, 51
ILS 2288 338
ILS 2683 313, 321, 363
ILS 2684 320
ILS 2689 320, 388
ILS 2721 319
ILS 2722 34
ILS 2927 97
ILS 2933 52
ILS 3039 47
ILS 4393 341
ILS 5358 48
ILS 5589 47, 52
ILS 5685 50
ILS 5686 48
ILS 5687 48
ILS 5752 47
ILS 5777 47
ILS 5818–25 50
ILS 5860 47
ILS 5876 50
ILS 5874 47
ILS 5885 50
ILS 6106 41
ILS 6509 41
ILS 6620 41
ILS 6675 40
ILS 6948 319, 388
ILS 8826 81
ILS 8834[b] 83
ILS 9011 345
ILS 9471 24
ILS 10308 47
ILS 10328 47
ILS 22391 47
ILTG 341 88
IRT 545 338, 344 f.
Kraeling (1938), no. 58 393
Kraeling (1938), nos. 143–5 393
Kraeling (1938), no. 171 340, 342 ff.
Kraeling (1938), no. 173 343
LBW III.5 2496 187
LBW III.6 2506 187
Lehmann & Holum, no. 4 346
Lehmann & Holum, no. 46 342
Lehmann & Holum, no. 47 341
Lehmann & Holum, no. 146 345 f.
MAMA IV 305 49 f.
Negev (1977), no. 113 531
OGIS 595 406
OGIS 609 326
PPUAES IIIA 795[3] 187
RES 674 281
RIB 1280 26, 89
Roxan (1978), no. 4 354
Roxan (1978), no. 69 356
Savignac & Starcky (1957) 281
SEG 7, 1146 187
SEG 17, 584 338
SEG 31, 122 265
SEG 43, 77 85
SEG 44, 1361 393
Sherk (1969), no. 22 12, 218 f., 488
Sherk (1969), no. 43 20
Sherk (1969), no. 58 29, 219, 488
Syll. 684 20

Literary

Acts 24:2 225 f., 399, 422, 492
Aristid. *Or.* XXXVI, 82 353
Asc. *Corn.* 52 65
Asc. *Pro Scauro* 25 75
Caes. *BGall.* VII, 63 36
Cass. Dio 39, 14 183
Cass. Dio 53, 13 79, 95, 97
Cass. Dio 55, 23 338
Cass. Dio 57, 17 81, 93
Cass. Dio 69, 12 394
Cass. Dio 69, 13 189, 192
Cass. Dio 69, 14 82, 391
CGL III, 36 423

Cic. *Amic.* 33 f. 64
Cic. *Arch.* 7 106
Cic. *Att.* I, 13 220
Cic. *Att.* I, 16 13
Cic. *Att.* I, 19 72, 220
Cic. *Att.* I, 20 72, 220
Cic. *Att.* II, 1 220
Cic. *Att.* II, 13 220
Cic. *Att.* V, 3 67
Cic. *Att.* V, 9 67
Cic. *Att.* V, 20 74
Cic. *Att.* V, 21 19, 67 ff., 220
Cic. *Att.* VI, 1 67 ff., 73, 105, 216, 220, 490
Cic. *Att.* VI, 2 67, 74, 220
Cic. *Att.* VI, 3 67, 220
Cic. *Att.* IX, 7a 36
Cic. *Att.* IX, 9a 36
Cic. *Att.* XI, 1 72
Cic. *Balb.* 28 105, 222
Cic. *Caecin.* 73 64
Cic. *Cael.* 79 53
Cic. *Clu.* 70 77
Cic. *De imp. Cn. Pomp.* 41 74
Cic. *De or.* II, 100 77
Cic. *De or.* II, 168 53
Cic. *Fam.* II, 14 73
Cic. *Fam.* III, 8 69
Cic. *Fam.* III, 10 69
Cic. *Fam.* V, 5 15 f., 62, 72, 220
Cic. *Fam.* V, 19 3
Cic. *Fam.* V, 20 3
Cic. *Fam.* V, 21 3
Cic. *Fam.* VI, 8 18
Cic. *Fam.* VII, 5 28 f., 32, 61
Cic. *Fam.* VII, 8 28
Cic. *Fam.* VII, 23–7 73
Cic. *Fam.* VII, 30 17, 63
Cic. *Fam.* IX, 25 73
Cic. *Fam.* XII, 21 62
Cic. *Fam.* XII, 24 62
Cic. *Fam.* XII, 26 62
Cic. *Fam.* XII, 27 62
Cic. *Fam.* XII, 29 62
Cic. *Fam.* XIII, 1 6
Cic. *Fam.* XIII, 4 61
Cic. *Fam.* XIII, 5 78
Cic. *Fam.* XIII, 6 9, 61 f.
Cic. *Fam.* XIII, 9 62, 74
Cic. *Fam.* XIII, 11 28, 61
Cic. *Fam.* XIII, 12 28
Cic. *Fam.* XIII, 13 7
Cic. *Fam.* XIII, 14 8, 62, 67
Cic. *Fam.* XIII, 15 100
Cic. *Fam.* XIII, 16 6
Cic. *Fam.* XIII, 17 7, 62
Cic. *Fam.* XIII, 18 7, 62
Cic. *Fam.* XIII, 19 6, 61, 72, 74, 102, 107 f.
Cic. *Fam.* XIII, 20 7
Cic. *Fam.* XIII, 21 62, 74
Cic. *Fam.* XIII, 22 7, 8, 61, 67
Cic. *Fam.* XIII, 23 7, 62
Cic. *Fam.* XIII, 24 74
Cic. *Fam.* XIII, 25 7
Cic. *Fam.* XIII, 26 3–22 *passim*, 67, 74, 99, 101
Cic. *Fam.* XIII, 27 7, 62, 74
Cic. *Fam.* XIII, 28 3–22 *passim*, 61, 67, 71, 74
Cic. *Fam.* XIII, 30 72, 102, 106
Cic. *Fam.* XIII, 32 67
Cic. *Fam.* XIII, 35 61
Cic. *Fam.* XIII, 36 27
Cic. *Fam.* XIII, 37 109
Cic. *Fam.* XIII, 38 62
Cic. *Fam.* XIII, 41 17, 74
Cic. *Fam.* XIII, 42 9, 17, 74
Cic. *Fam.* XIII, 43 61, 74
Cic. *Fam.* XIII, 44 62, 74
Cic. *Fam.* XIII, 45 62
Cic. *Fam.* XIII, 47 62
Cic. *Fam.* XIII, 50 17
Cic. *Fam.* XIII, 53 62, 72, 102
Cic. *Fam.* XIII, 54 71, 101
Cic. *Fam.* XIII, 55 62, 67, 69, 71, 73 f.
Cic. *Fam.* XIII, 56 17, 19, 62, 72 f., 220
Cic. *Fam.* XIII, 57 62, 71, 74, 78, 101
Cic. *Fam.* XIII, 58 8, 73 ff.
Cic. *Fam.* XIII, 59 8, 73 ff.
Cic. *Fam.* XIII, 61 62, 73

Cic. *Fam.* XIII, 63 61 f., 67
Cic. *Fam.* XIII, 64 61, 71, 102, 110
Cic. *Fam.* XIII, 65 62, 69, 71, 101
Cic. *Fam.* XIII, 66 62
Cic. *Fam.* XIII, 67 7 f.
Cic. *Fam.* XIII, 69 62, 73
Cic. *Fam.* XIII, 70 6
Cic. *Fam.* XIII, 71 6
Cic. *Fam.* XIII, 72 20 f., 62, 74
Cic. *Fam.* XIII, 73 62, 66
Cic. *Fam.* XIII, 74 62
Cic. *Fam.* XIII, 75 74
Cic. *Fam.* XIII, 78 61, 74
Cic. *Fam.* XIII, 79 62
Cic. *Fam.* XV, 5 67
Cic. *Fam.* XV, 14 73
Cic. *Inv. rhet.* II, 160 77
Cic. *Off.* III, 43 64, 73
Cic. *Planc.* 36 13
Cic. *Prov. cons.* 6–7 72
Cic. *QFr.* I, 1 15, 19, 21, 62 f., 65 ff., 69, 74
Cic. *QFr.* I, 2 9, 64, 67
Cic. *QFr.* II, 14 29
Cic. *QFr.* III, 1 29
Cic. *Rep.* I, 43 77
Cic. *Rep.* I, 49 63
Cic. *Sull.* 92 13
Cic. *Top.* 73 77
Cic. *Vat.* 28 13
Cic. *Verr.* I 13
Cic. *Verr.* II, 1 35
Cic. *Verr.* II, 2 13, 15, 105, 109, 217
Cic. *Verr.* II, 3 11 f., 19
CJ 5, 31, 6–11 420
CJ 5, 34, 6 406
CJ 5, 50, 1 424
CJ 5, 50, 2 423
Cod. Theod. II, 6 54
Cod. Theod. II, 1 495
Cod. Theod. IX, 38 53
Dig. 1, 1, 10 77
Dig. 1, 3, 32 pr. 110
Dig. 1, 4, 3 42, 51, 52
Dig. 1, 16, 7, 2 4
Dig. 1, 17, 1 319
Dig. 4, 6, 32 31, 44
Dig. 4, 8 495
Dig. 6, 3 406
Dig. 24, 1, 4 31
Dig. 24, 1, 38 31
Dig. 26, 2, 26 420
Dig. 26, 5, 3 406
Dig. 26, 5, 19 pr. 406
Dig. 26, 5, 24 406
Dig. 26, 6, 2, 2 420
Dig. 26, 6, 4, 2 420
Dig. 26, 6, 4, 4 421
Dig. 26, 7, 5, 8 420
Dig. 26, 7, 12, 3 423
Dig. 26, 7, 13 pr. 423
Dig. 26, 7, 46, 6 406
Dig. 26, 10, 1, 3 424
Dig. 26, 10, 1, 7 421
Dig. 26, 10, 3, 14 424
Dig. 27, 1, 15, 6 415
Dig. 27, 1, 41, 2 32, 44
Dig. 27, 2, 1 423
Dig. 27, 3, 4 pr. 425
Dig. 27, 3, 9, 4 425
Dig. 27, 8 406 f.
Dig. 27, 10, 2 406
Dig. 29, 1, 1 40
Dig. 29, 1, 42 31
Dig. 33, 1, 7 pr. 424
Dig. 37, 13, 1, 2 31
Dig. 38, 17, 2, 23 406, 420
Dig. 41, 1, 65 pr. 18
Dig. 48, 2, 3, 2 122
Dig. 48, 5, 14 (13) 534
Dig. 50, 1, 28 494
Dig. 50, 4, 18, 7 409
Dig. 50, 12, 10 265
Dig. 50, 15, 3 pr. 182, 372
Dig. 50, 15, 4 pr. 369, 370
Ecloga legum 5.2 121
Eus. *Onom.* 86 353
Eus. *Onom.* 92, 15 333
Eus. *Onom.* 122, 28 281
Flor. *Ver. Poet.* 25 f.
Fronto, *Ep. ad am.* I, 1 8, 76
Fronto, *Ep. ad Ant.* II, 8 32
Fronto, *Ep. ad M. Caes.* V, 50 52

Gai. *Inst.* I, 1 214 f.
Gai. *Inst.* IV, 37 215
Gal. *De ant.* 1.4 350, 353
Hist. Apollonii regis Tyri 20 54
Hist. Aug. Alex. Sev. XXI 89
Hist. Aug. Claud. XIV 31
Hist. Aug. Hadr. VII 41
Hor. *Od.* I, 32 58
Hyg. Gramm. 306
Iambl. *VP* 161 116
Inst. Iust. I, 1 77
Inst. Iust. I, 26 421, 424
Jer. *Comm. in Hiez.* 352 f.
John 19:20 188
Joseph. *AJ* 9.7 350
Joseph. *AJ* 12.7 178, 384
Joseph. *AJ* 12.54 350
Joseph. *AJ* 14.117 416
Joseph. *AJ* 14.185–267 416, 498
Joseph. *AJ* 14.235 416, 498
Joseph. *AJ* 14.260 416
Joseph. *AJ* 15.95 350
Joseph. *AJ* 15.96 350 f.
Joseph. *AJ* 15.259 519
Joseph. *AJ* 16.203 332, 382
Joseph. *AJ* 17.227–314 389
Joseph. *AJ* 17.344 351
Joseph. *AJ* 17.355 318, 321, 365
Joseph. *AJ* 18.1 313, 321
Joseph. *AJ* 18.2 313, 318, 320 f., 365
Joseph. *AJ* 18.3–4 365
Joseph. *AJ* 18.31 330, 381
Joseph. *AJ* 19.365 389
Joseph. *AJ* 20.159 330, 381
Joseph. *AJ* 20.176 389
Joseph. *BJ* 1.138 350
Joseph. *BJ* 1.361–2 350 f.
Joseph. *BJ* 1.479 332, 382
Joseph. *BJ* 2.22–91 489
Joseph. *BJ* 2.111 351
Joseph. *BJ* 2.117 313, 318, 320
Joseph. *BJ* 2.252 330, 381
Joseph. *BJ* 2.345–404 397 f.
Joseph. *BJ* 2.385 366
Joseph. *BJ* 2.405 333
Joseph. *BJ* 2.408 389
Joseph. *BJ* 2.484–5 389
Joseph. *BJ* 2.509 330
Joseph. *BJ* 2.567 330
Joseph. *BJ* 3.12 389
Joseph. *BJ* 3.54 179, 380
Joseph. *BJ* 3.55 179, 327 f., 356, 379, 475
Joseph. *BJ* 3.56 179, 328
Joseph. *BJ* 3.66 389
Joseph. *BJ* 3.309 389
Joseph. *BJ* 3.361–91 397
Joseph. *BJ* 4.231–5 329, 380
Joseph. *BJ* 4.402–4 353, 360, 475
Joseph. *BJ* 4.450 353 f.
Joseph. *BJ* 4.451–90 354
Joseph. *BJ* 4.469 350
Joseph. *BJ* 4.491 354
Joseph. *BJ* 5.362–423 397
Joseph. *BJ* 6.238 322, 388
Joseph. *BJ* 6.354 416
Joseph. *BJ* 7.5 389
Joseph. *BJ* 7.180 133
Joseph. *BJ* 7.189 133
Joseph. *Vit.* 115 389
Joseph. *Vit.* 361–3 396
Juv. *Sat.* VII 26, 39
Juv. *Sat.* XIV 25
Lactant. *De mort. pers.* 313
Luke 1 540
Luke 1:25–35 537
Luke 2:5 537
Luke 20:22 304
Luke 21:1–3 363
Luke 23:2 304
Mark 6:3 536
Mark 10:11–12 519
Mark 12:14–17 304
Matt. 1:18–25 536, 537 f.
Matt. 1:16 541
Matt. 5:23 543
Matt. 13:55 536
Matt. 22:17–21 304
Nov. 27, 1–2 120, 121
Nov. 73, 8 122
Origen, *C. Cels.* 1.32 539
Origen, *Ep. ad Afr.* 499

Origen, *Hom. in Luc.* VI 539
Paulus, *Sent.* V, 25, 6 149
Plin. *Ep.* II, 13 23, 25, 32, 33, 43
Plin. *Ep.* III, 2 23
Plin. *Ep.* III, 8 23, 25, 30, 33
Plin. *Ep.* IV, 4 23, 25, 26, 32
Plin. *Ep.* IV, 8 51
Plin. *Ep.* IV, 19 87
Plin. *Ep.* VII, 22 23, 25, 33, 34
Plin. *Ep.* IX, 5 77
Plin. *Ep.* X, 2 43
Plin. *Ep.* X, 3a 43
Plin. *Ep.* X, 4 44, 50 f., 58
Plin. *Ep.* X, 5 45
Plin. *Ep.* X, 6 45, 51
Plin. *Ep.* X, 8 43, 50 f.
Plin. *Ep.* X, 10 45
Plin. *Ep.* X, 11 45, 50 f.
Plin. *Ep.* X, 12 44, 58, 422
Plin. *Ep.* X, 13 43, 51
Plin. *Ep.* X, 21 44, 51
Plin. *Ep.* X, 23 46
Plin. *Ep.* X, 24 46
Plin. *Ep.* X, 26 30, 44
Plin. *Ep.* X, 39 51
Plin. *Ep.* X, 51 44, 51
Plin. *Ep.* X, 58 40, 422
Plin. *Ep.* X, 70 46, 50 f.
Plin. *Ep.* X, 86b 44, 51
Plin. *Ep.* X, 87 44
Plin. *Ep.* X, 90 46
Plin. *Ep.* X, 92 48, 51
Plin. *Ep.* X, 93 48
Plin. *Ep.* X, 94 43, 50, 58
Plin. *Ep.* X, 98 50
Plin. *Ep.* X, 104 46, 51
Plin. *Ep.* X, 106 45
Plin. *Ep.* X, 112 48
Plin. *Ep.* X, 120 46
Plin. *NH* V, 70 179, 327, 328, 379 f., 384, 475
Plin. *NH* V, 73 328, 354, 380, 475
Plin. *NH* V, 108 19, 72, 109
Plin. *NH* VIII, 184 87
Plin. *NH* XII, 111 350, 352
Plin. *NH* XII, 112 360, 475
Plin. *NH* XII, 113 352
Plin. *NH* XII, 117 351
Plin. *NH* XII, 118 352
Plin. *NH* XII, 123 358, 474
Plin. *Pan.* II 56 f.
Plin. *Pan.* III 56
Plin. *Pan.* IV 56, 58
Plin. *Pan.* VI 56
Plin. *Pan.* VII 56
Plin. *Pan.* X 56 f.
Plin. *Pan.* XXI 55 f.
Plin. *Pan.* XXVI 56
Plin. *Pan.* XXXVI–XL 106, 223
Plin. *Pan.* XXXIX 45, 56
Plin. *Pan.* XLII 56 f.
Plin. *Pan.* LIII 56
Plin. *Pan.* LXI 45
Plin. *Pan.* LXII 56
Plin. *Pan.* LXIX 44
Plin. *Pan.* LXXIV 56
Plin. *Pan.* LXXXV 59
Plin. *Pan.* LXXXVII 56 f.
Plin. *Pan.* XC 44
Plin. *Pan.* XCIV 57
Ps.-Athan. *Quaest. ad Ant.* 116
Ps.-Quint., *Decl. min.* 77
Quint. *Inst.* III, 7 75
Sen. *Clem.* I, 14 55
Sen. *Cons. ad. Pol.* 37
Stat. *Silv.* I 38 ff., 43
Stat. *Silv.* IV 26
Stat. *Silv.* V, 1 24, 26
Stat. *Silv.* V, 2 38
Stat. *Theb.* I 25
Strab. 16, 2, 41 350 f.
Strab. 17, 1, 15 351
Suet. *Claud.* 25 28, 33
Suet. *Claud.* 29 88
Suet. *Dom.* 8–11 55
Suet. *Iul.* 69 39
Suet. *Tib.* 46 54
Suet. *Vit.* 5 45
Tac. *Agr.* 3 422
Tac. *Ann.* II, 42 313, 321
Tac. *Ann.* II, 47 81, 93
Tac. *Ann.* II, 56 313

Tac. *Ann.* III, 26–7 70
Tac. *Ann.* VI, 11 74
Tac. *Ann.* VI, 21 87
Tac. *Ann.* VI, 41 313
Tac. *Ann.* XI, 20 45
Tac. *Ann.* XII, 23 321 f.
Tac. *Ann.* XIV, 28 37
Tac. *Dial.* 9, 5 54
Tac. *Hist.* I, 1 422
Tac. *Hist.* I, 52 45
Tac. *Hist.* II, 58 322
Tac. *Hist.* II, 83 88
Tac. *Hist.* II, 94 45
Tac. *Hist.* IV, 74 398 f.
Tac. *Hist.* V, 9 322
Val. Max. VIII, 7, 6 15

Papyri and Parchment

4Q343 136
4Q348 136, 176
BGU 69 384
BGU 136 425
BGU 140 341
BGU 696 24
BGU 1050 529
BGU 1068 454
BGU 1210 223
BGU 1813 407
BGU 2558 203
CPJ I 128 542 f.
CPJ II 143 416
CPJ II 144 544
CPJ II 427 454
CPR I 25 529
CPR I 30 531
Doc. Mas. 725 352
Doc. Mas. 740 142, 479
Doc. Mas. 749 352
Fink (1971), no. 20 24
Fink (1971), no. 64 24
Fink (1971), no. 87 31
FIRA III, no. 30 409
Lewis (1985–88) *see P.Hever* 62
Mitteis, *Chr.*, no. 290 531
Naveh & Shaked (2012), A 4 202, 243
P.Bas. 2 116
P.Berol. 21652 190
P.Beit Israel 260, 535
P.Bostra 1 203, 335, 372, 448
P.Bostra 2 372, 512
P.Brem. 39 407
P.Cair.Isid. 2–3 374
P.Cair.Isid. 8 371
P.Dura 150, 158, 201, 226, 481
P.Dura 18 157
P.Dura 26 151, 157, 172, 240
P.Dura 28 151, 172, 240, 242, 433
P.Dura 29 151, 172, 240, 433
P.Dura 30 157, 433
P.Dura 31 433, 515
P.Dura 32 433
P.Dura 64 348
P.Enteux. 23 542 f.
P.Eleph. 1 527 f.
P.Euphr. 150, 152, 158, 201, 226, 242, 481, 502
P.Euphr. 1 110, 203, 225, 349, 494
P.Euphr. 2 203, 348 f.
P.Euphr. 5 203
P.Euphr. 6 433
P.Euphr. 7 433
P.Euphr.Syr. 151, 242
P.Giss. I 2 530 f.
P.Haun. I 14 209
P.Hever 1 *see P.Yadin* 36
P.Hever 2 137 f., 151, 162, 239, 275, 293, 441, 478 f., 504
P.Hever 3–6 240, 478
P.Hever 7 133, 239, 441, 473, 505
P.Hever 8 133, 136, 169, 190, 473
P.Hever 8a 133, 155, 190, 441, 505, 508
P.Hever 9 136, 329, 381
P.Hever 11 136, 441, 511, 525

P.Hever 12	139, 150, 281, 293, 298 f., 303, 306, 308, 311, 332, 383, 441, 474
P.Hever 13	x, 124, 133, 155, 168, 436, 441, 473, 496 f., 508, 510, 517 ff., 544
P.Hever 21–25	136
P.Hever 26	508
P.Hever 32	136
P.Hever 49	133, 473
P.Hever 50	136, 440, 505
P.Hever 60	139, 155, 163, 281, 293, 298, 304, 306, 308 f., 332, 383, 474
P.Hever 61	115–125 *passim*, 141, 159, 163, 203, 233, 369, 372 435 ff., 453 f., 474, 497
P.Hever 62	142, 151, 154, 163, 172, 240, 280 f., 289, 293, 297, 305 f., 308, 310 f., 314 f., 333, 335, 360, 369–373, 446, 474, 505
P.Hever 63	120, 157, 163, 300, 439 ff., 444, 463, 495–498, 508
P.Hever 64	viii, 140, 153–156, 163, 169, 232, 247, 279, 281, 288 f., 293, 297, 300 f., 304, 306, 308, 311, 315, 334, 374, 436, 439 f., 443–446, 454 f., 463, 474, 479, 504 f., 507 f., 520
P.Hever 65	ix, 163, 190, 248, 257 f., 261 f., 267 f., 280, 310, 311, 316, 330 f., 335, 356, 381, 410, 417 f., 438, 445, 447, 459, 461–464, 477, 507 ff., 511, 513 ff., 522, 530
P.Hever 66	139, 143, 163
P.Hever 67	329, 347, 380, 476
P.Hever 68	139, 163
P.Hever 69	ix, 143, 158, 258, 263, 276, 280, 311, 329, 331, 333 f., 380 ff., 417 ff., 435, 437, 459, 461, 477, 508, 511, 513 f., 521 f., 529
P.Hever 70–3	139, 163
P.Hib. II 198	409
P.IFAO III 34	203
P.Jericho 16	153, 226, 487
P.Lond. 904	314, 364
P.Lond. 1711	531
P.Lond. 1912	315
P.Masada	*see Doc. Mas.*
P.Med.Bar. 1	409
P.Mich. 164	24
P.Mich. 232	407
P.Mich. 468	99
P.Mich. 556–7	301
P.Mich. 607	120
P.Mich.Inv. 256	384
P.Mich.Inv. 2922	409
P.Mich.Inv. 4526	514
P.Mur 17	134
P.Mur 18	135, 153, 155, 436, 480
P.Mur 19	x, 135, 168, 441, 517 f., 544
P.Mur 20	135, 258, 418, 440 f., 447, 459 ff., 511 f., 517, 521 f., 525
P.Mur 21	135, 258, 418, 459 ff., 508, 511, 513, 517, 521 f., 525
P.Mur 22	132 f., 473
P.Mur 23	135

P.Mur 24 357 f., 473 f.
P.Mur 25 131, 135
P.Mur 26 136, 440, 505
P.Mur 29 130–133, 135, 157, 169, 176, 178, 441, 472 f., 492, 508
P.Mur 30 130–133, 135, 169, 176, 178, 441, 472 f., 492, 505
P.Mur 46 357, 474
P.Mur 50 508
P.Mur 89–107 375
P.Mur 113 143, 180, 241, 260
P.Mur 114 135, 141, 143, 150, 153, 177–180, 241, 260, 329, 381, 383–386, 489
P.Mur 115 143, 150, 180, 258, 263, 280, 329, 331, 334, 381 f., 417 f., 435, 440, 447, 459, 461, 464, 477, 511, 516, 522, 529
P.Mur 116 143, 144, 241, 258, 260, 263, 417 f., 459, 461 f., 511, 517, 521 f.
P.Nessana 200, 226, 247
P.Nessana 16 163, 241, 260
P.Nessana 18 249, 257, 264 f., 269 ff.
P.Nessana 19 426
P.Nessana 20 249, 257, 264 ff.
P.Nessana 60–67 212
P.Oslo III 78 314
P.Oxy. 237 110, 225
P.Oxy. 265 407
P.Oxy. 487 407
P.Oxy. 496–7 407, 414
P.Oxy. 706 110, 225
P.Oxy. 898 405, 407
P.Oxy. 907 448
P.Oxy. 1022 31
P.Oxy. 3285 409
P.Oxy. 3471 312
P.Oxy. 3574 312
P.Oxy. 3593 123, 125
P.Oxy. 3613 203
P.Oxy. 3921 410, 422, 510
P.Oxy. 3922 422
P.Petr. 3, 36 V(a) 409
P.Petra 172, 200, 247, 259, 372
P.Petra 1 163, 241, 249 ff., 254, 255 f., 260
P.Petra 2 256
P.Petra 18 256
P.Petra 19 256
P.Petra 39 256
P.Polit.Iud. 4 541 f., 544 ff.
P.Rev. 409
P.Ryl. 121 405, 407
P.Ryl. 614 52
P.Sdeir 2 133
P.Se'elim 4 181 ff., 375 f.
PSI 1026 52
PSI 1183 374
P.Starcky *see P.Yadin* 36
P.Teb. I 5 235
P.Teb. I 104 528
P.Teb. II 376 295
P.Teb. III.1 703 409
P.Würzb. 9 314
P.Yadin 1 138, 152, 162, 170, 239, 252, 429, 441, 478
P.Yadin 2 138, 152, 162, 170, 172, 239 f., 275, 278 f., 293–298, 302, 429, 441, 478, 504, 510
P.Yadin 3 138, 152, 156, 162, 170, 172, 239 f., 275, 278, 279, 281, 293–298, 302, 429, 441, 478, 504, 510
P.Yadin 4 138, 162, 170, 239, 293, 478
P.Yadin 5 139 f., 163, 251 f., 275, 277–280, 293, 309, 334, 429, 449 f.

P.Yadin 6 138, 150, 163, 170, 239, 275, 279, 309, 418, 478
P.Yadin 7 viii, 138, 150 ff., 163, 170 ff., 240, 275, 277 ff., 281 f., 289, 309, 374, 405, 418, 443, 446, 455, 504, 520
P.Yadin 8 138–141, 150, 163, 309, 418
P.Yadin 9 150, 163, 170, 239, 240, 309, 418, 478, 496 f.
P.Yadin 10 139, 146, 150 f., 163, 258, 277, 417 f., 434, 444, 447, 459 ff., 479, 511–514, 517, 521 f., 525–532 *passim*
P.Yadin 11 117, 142, 150, 152 f., 179, 285–291, 328, 347, 354, 356 f., 359, 380, 384, 417, 422, 448, 454, 476, 510
P.Yadin 12 140, 152, 187, 204, 206, 276 f., 279, 335, 404 f., 415, 525
P.Yadin 13 140, 203, 252, 405, 414, 421, 426, 525
P.Yadin 14 140, 153, 203, 276, 279 f., 309, 334, 405, 410, 414, 421, 426 ff., 437, 454, 508
P.Yadin 15 119, 122 f., 140, 153, 155, 159, 203, 225 f., 227–235 *passim*, 276, 279, 334, 359, 399, 405, 410, 414 f., 421, 424, 427, 434, 436 f., 454, 487, 492, 506, 508 f.
P.Yadin 16 115, 117 ff., 122, 140 f., 154, 203, 276–281, 289, 293, 295 ff., 305 f., 308, 310–315, 328, 331, 333 ff., 356, 360, 369–373, 380, 382, 410, 417, 429, 436 f., 446, 453, 474 f., 505, 507 f.
P.Yadin 17 140, 155, 279, 310, 334, 410, 432, 434, 438 f., 447, 454, 505, 508 f., 525
P.Yadin 18 125, 140, 146, 156, 248, 257 f., 260 ff., 266 f., 279, 310, 315, 334, 359, 410, 417 f., 445, 447, 454, 459, 461, 475, 479, 507, 511–514, 519, 522, 529 ff., 544
P.Yadin 19 117, 140 f., 153, 187, 190, 279, 285–291, 310, 315, 334, 355 ff., 359, 419, 439, 443 f., 448 f., 454 f., 475, 504, 507, 520
P.Yadin 20–7 140, 454
P.Yadin 20 140, 152 f., 155, 252 f., 279, 285–291, 310 f., 315, 334, 356 f., 359, 408, 410, 419, 433 f., 437 ff., 446, 448 ff., 456, 475, 508 ff., 521
P.Yadin 21 279, 290, 310 f., 315, 334, 359, 418, 439, 446 f., 449, 505, 508
P.Yadin 22 140, 152, 279, 290, 310 f., 315, 334, 359, 410, 418, 434,

436, 438 f., 446 f., 505, 508
P.Yadin 23 140, 153, 190, 193, 253, 311, 408, 427, 439, 444–447, 520 f.
P.Yadin 24 226, 253, 359, 373, 408, 439, 444–448, 487, 506, 520 f.
P.Yadin 25 157, 253, 279, 311, 334, 348, 359, 408, 427, 438 f., 444, 446, 506, 508, 510, 520 f.
P.Yadin 26 143, 154, 157, 180, 190, 279, 311, 334, 359, 417, 427, 439, 456, 475, 487, 516
P.Yadin 27 117, 139, 159, 162 f., 233, 241, 260, 279, 310 f., 316, 334, 361, 371 f., 410, 414, 421, 425, 428, 436, 438 f., 508, 535
P.Yadin 28–30 226, 404, 424 f., 430
P.Yadin 31 310 f.
P.Yadin 34 140, 516
P.Yadin 36 137 f., 151, 162, 171, 226, 239, 240, 275 f., 404, 418, 429, 478, 480, 489
P.Yadin 37 *see P.Hever* 65
P.Yadin 42 133, 169, 357, 473 f.
P.Yadin 43 133, 169, 357, 474
P.Yadin 44 133, 169, 357, 359, 473 ff.
P.Yadin 45 133, 357, 474
P.Yadin 46 133, 357, 474
P.Yadin 47 357
P.Yadin 47a 133
P.Yadin 47b 288
P.Yadin 49 357, 360, 474 f.
P.Yadin 50 357, 358, 474
P.Yadin 51 357, 474
P.Yadin 52 117, 141, 175, 183–193 *passim*, 207, 357, 360, 474 f., 479
P.Yadin 53 357, 474
P.Yadin 54 357, 474
P.Yadin 55 357, 474
P.Yadin 56 357, 474
P.Yadin 57 185, 188, 357, 474
P.Yadin 58 357, 474
P.Yadin 59 141, 188, 357, 474, 479
P.Yadin 60 357, 474
SB 4658 531
SB 6944 314
SB 7558 409
SB 7568 407
SB 9065 407
SB 9843 *see P.Yadin* 52
SB 9844 *see P.Yadin* 59
SB 10288 227
SB 13849 203
SB 15496 110
Sirat et al. (1986) 532
Stud. Pal. XX, 5 529
Tjäder (1995), no. 16 116, 122
Tjäder (1995), no. 20 116, 121 f.
Tjäder (1995), no. 27 116, 121 f.
XḤev/Se nab 1 *see P.Yadin* 36
XḤev/Se nab 2 *see P.Hever* 2

www.ingramcontent.com/pod-product-compliance
Lightning Source LLC
Chambersburg PA
CBHW031717230426
43669CB00007B/174
* 9 7 8 3 1 1 1 5 1 8 5 3 4 *